The Parliament Rolls of Medieval England 1275–1504

VOLUME SIX

RICHARD II · 1377–1384

General Editor Chris Given-Wilson

THE PARLIAMENT ROLLS OF MEDIEVAL ENGLAND

1275–1504

VI

RICHARD II · 1377–1384

EDITED BY GEOFFREY MARTIN & CHRIS GIVEN-WILSON

THE BOYDELL PRESS
LONDON: THE NATIONAL ARCHIVES

Research Assistants: Jill Hughes, Lisa Liddy, Elizabeth New, Rebecca Reader,
Shelagh Sneddon

Funding agencies: The Leverhulme Trust, The National Archives,
Cambridge University Press

the national archives
www.nationalarchives.gov.uk

Transcriptions of texts and translations © Crown Copyright. These transcripts and translations may be used for any non-commercial use without prior written consent as long as the source and document references are given.

Introductions and appendices © Paul Brand 2005. The text of these introductions may be used for any non-commercial use without prior written consent as long as the editor, source and document details are given. Publishers wishing to make commercial use of these should consult Paul Brand.

First published 2005
as volume VI of *The Parliament Rolls of Medieval England, 1275-1504*
The Boydell Press, Woodbridge
The National Archives, London
Reprinted and transferred to digital printing 2012

ISBN 978 1 84383 768 8

The Boydell Press is an imprint of Boydell & Brewer Ltd
PO Box 9, Woodbridge, Suffolk IP12 3DF, UK
and of Boydell & Brewer Inc,
668 Mt Hope Avenue, Rochester, NY 14620, USA
website: www.boydellandbrewer.com

A CIP catalogue record for this book is available
from the British Library

The publisher has no responsibility for the continued existence or accuracy of URLs for external or third-party internet websites referred to in this book, and does not guarantee that any content on such websites is, or will remain, accurate or appropriate.

This publication is printed on acid-free paper

Printed and bound in Great Britain

Contents

1377 October   **2**
  Text and Translation 6
  Appendix 65

1378 October   **67**
  Text and Translation 69
  Appendix 106

1379 April   **108**
  Text and Translation 110
  Appendix 139

1380 January   **142**
  Text and Translation 145
  Appendix 183

1380 November   **184**
  Text and Translation 187
  Appendix 208

1381 November   **209**
  Text and Translation 212
  Appendix 265

1382 May   **267**
  Text and Translation 269
  Appendix 276

1382 October   **277**
  Text and Translation 279
  Appendix 306

1383 February   **307**
  Text and Translation 309
  Appendix 319

1383 October   **320**
  Text and Translation 322
  Appendix 358

1384 April   **359**
  Text and Translation 362
  Appendix 381

1384 November   **382**
  Text and Translation 384
  Appendix 427

Richard II, 1377-1399

Twenty-four parliaments were held during the reign of Richard II, for twenty-three of which the rolls have survived, and even though that of the September 1388 parliament has been lost, fortunately the text of the common petition was preserved by a chronicler. For the parliaments of February 1388 (the 'Merciless Parliament') and September 1397 (the 'Revenge Parliament'), more than one roll has survived: the additional rolls were used to record the judicial proceedings against those accused of high crimes against the crown. The parliament of October 1399, which was initially summoned in Richard's name, did not meet until after his deposition on 30 September, and is thus included among the parliaments of Henry IV's reign.

1377 October

Westminster

13 October - 28 November

(C 65/32. *RP*, III.3-29. *SR*, II.1-5)

Richard II's first parliament met at Westminster on 13 October 1377, four months after his accession, at the age of ten, and three after his coronation. It ended formally six weeks later, on 28 November 1377, although the lords continued to sit well into December. Its proceedings are recorded on PRO C 65/32, a roll of 18 membranes, 340 mm (13 inches) wide, and sewn together in chancery style, head to tail. A membrane more than a foot wide is a skin of good quality: the clerks' supplies were not stinted. The script of the roll, in a number of chancery hands, covers only the recto, or face, of the membranes, leaving the dorse blank. That again, with the writing confined to the flesh side, the whiter face of the parchment, is a mark of comparative affluence. The roll appears to be complete, and includes an additional membrane which has been stitched to the face of m. 8 recto, a schedule of special requests by the commons, the text of which is in a hand different from though contemporary with that of m. 8. The roll is generally in good condition, though it is stained in places with gallic acid, especially on mm. 1, 12, 16, and 18. The dorse of m. 6 has been repaired with a piece of parchment bearing a fragment of text in a late medieval book-hand. It reads '... pi .. elassipi .. et melassipi. Qui cum essent uiginti annorum ... et cum aua sua Leonilla et Ionilla et Neone mater ... tihio coronati sunt.' The dorse of each membrane is inscribed 'Parliamentum anno primo Ricardi secundi pars unica'. The marginal headings on the face of the roll are of various dates, some original and others later. The arabic numerals on the face have all been added to facilitate reference since the roll was completed.

Writs of summons were sent on 4 August 1377 to the archbishops of Canterbury and York, the bishop of London, and nineteen other bishops, and to the abbot of St Augustine's, Canterbury, twenty-one other abbots, and the priors of the hospital of St John, Clerkenwell, and of St Mary's, Coventry. Summonses were addressed on the same day to John of Gaunt, titular king of Castile and Leon and duke of Lancaster, the king's younger uncles, Edmund earl of Cambridge and Thomas, earl of Buckingham, ten other earls, and forty-six tenants in chief, including James Audley of Helegh and Michael de la Pole, then admiral towards the north. Three of the peers were styled knight. John Cavendish, the lord chief justice, was summoned together with eleven other judges and clerks, of whom John Barnett and Nicholas Chaddesden were styled master.[1]

The opening of parliament was formally postponed for one day to allow more of the members to assemble. The inaugural address by archbishop Simon Sudbury was therefore delivered on Wednesday 14 October. Sudbury was not then, though he later became, chancellor, and he may have intruded himself into the proceedings, whether to mark an historic occasion or to promote political concord. The clerk noted that the discourse was divided into three parts as though it were a sermon. There are not many casual remarks in the record, and the observation may have been intended to register, if not actual disapproval, at least a sense of something exceptional in the event. Although Richard's assembled subjects were bidden by Sudbury to rejoice in the young king's advent, the occasion was fraught with apprehension. To the external crisis of an unsuccessful war, which had soured domestic politics in the last years of Edward III's reign, there were now added the uncertainties of a minority. The reversal of English successes in France, the old king's incapacity, the early death of Prince Edward, in 1376, and John of Gaunt's uncompromising defence of what he saw as the interests of the crown had made the mid-1370s a deeply troubled period. The fact of Richard's accession and his mother's tact in effecting or accepting a concordat with Gaunt had brought something of a respite. As the princess also contrived a reconciliation between Gaunt and the citizens of London there was even some outward show of harmony.[2] It was, however, a precarious peace. The Londoners were Gaunt's most vociferous but by no means his only enemies. Though the suspicion that he might subvert the succession was abated, there was still much discontent over the conduct of public affairs, and his own part in them, real or supposed. A minority put an exceptional strain on a system that depended upon the king's authority. From the very beginning of the reign the anxious adjustment of interests in what came to be called the continual council did nothing to promote decisive or particularly enlightened government. The most urgent political bargains had been struck in the summer, but there were still important adjustments to be made when parliament met. The effect of the manoeuvring had been to strengthen the

---

[1] *RDP*, IV.673-4; *CCR 1377-81*, 84-5.
[2] Saul, *Richard II*, 21-2.

numbers and influence of the deceased Black Prince's followers in Richard's household, and therefore at the heart of government.

Both the conduct of parliament and the form of its record on the parliament roll were well established by this time. The first business was a declaration of the purpose of the meeting, which almost invariably entailed taxation, whatever else might be at issue, then the arrangements to receive and consider petitions, and then the transaction of the fiscal, judicial, and administrative business of the session. The meetings brought a substantial number of people together from all parts of the kingdom for a wide variety of transactions, and they could only work effectively under a settled procedure. Nevertheless new categories of business, often the product of political crisis, such as the impeachments in the Good Parliament of 1376, might be introduced at any time and had to be assimilated. It was then the clerks' business to conceal, or rather not to reveal, the fact that anything unusual or untoward was going on. There was no serious eruption in 1377, but the circumstances were exceptional, and all were on their mettle. The first of the company who assembled at Westminster on 13 October had to wait through the morning until it proved, as it not infrequently did, that many of those summoned were still travelling. The term used of the commons was that not all the sheriffs had yet returned answers to their writs, but it seems as likely that there were knights and burgesses still on the road as that most were present but unrecognizable until they were formally enumerated. In any event the subsequent proceedings show that the commons were not an insignificant or inarticulate body. In the mean time the king's appearance and the opening ceremonies were postponed to the next day, when those present heard archbishop Sudbury enlarge upon Matthew xxi.5, 'Thy king has come unto thee'. He spoke in French, the language of business as of polite society, and translated the Latin of the Vulgate text explicitly for the benefit of the lords and the knights, but apparently not into English.[3]

The discourse was designed to served a double purpose, being in part an exhortation to loyalty, gratitude, and obedience to the king and partly a statement of the government's necessity and its urgent hopes of parliamentary subsidies. It may not have served either cause adequately; certainly the urgency of taxation had to be reiterated the next day, and eventually both king and primate met death at the hands of those who owed them obedience. In the meantime the archbishop observed that parliament had been postponed only to the harvest and to the pressing need to defend the coasts against incursions of enemies, referring thus to the kingdom's resources and to its besetting dangers. He urged the company to find the means to overcome the peril, and ended conventionally by announcing the names of those appointed to receive and to try or adjudicate petitions. There was nothing unusual about the total of eight receivers in two panels of four, recruited from amongst the chancellor's senior clerks, and headed at this time by William Burstall, the keeper of the rolls of chancery. On the other hand, twenty-nine triers of petitions from England, Wales, and Scotland and twenty-four for those from Gascony, other lordships in France, and the Channel Islands was well above the average provision for the reign. Those numbers were only closely matched in 1378 (twenty-five and twenty-three respectively), and were presumably a sign that the council expected a substantial volume of business. The customary provision that the triers should maintain a quorum of six lords and bishops, in consultation with the principal officers, would have allowed not only for necessary absence, but also for up to three or four committees in either group.

The proceedings continued the next day, Thursday 15 October, with an address by Richard le Scrope, an experienced Lancastrian captain and now the steward of the king's household, who enlarged upon the archbishop's warnings. The kingdom was threatened on all sides with enemies, and parliament was charged with weighing the dangers and proposing not merely remedies but the means of paying for them. As the commons were still not fully assembled in the morning, Scrope spoke yet again to them separately, later in the day, in their customary meeting-place, the chapter-house of the abbey. What followed had elements both of spontaneity and contrivance about it. The commons returned to say that the matters put before them were so weighty that they required the assistance of a group of thirteen peers and bishops, whom they named, beginning with the duke of Lancaster. Such appeals for counsel (or 'inter-communing') went back to 1373, but this was the first time that the panel was precisely defined. The request was readily granted, but Lancaster immediately rose and said that he could not discharge the commission unless the commons renounced the slanderous and disgraceful accusations that they had made against him. The peers were clamorous in his support, the commons said that their request showed their confidence in him, and congruity of a kind was restored.

That the commons had a programme of their own is shown in what followed. They came before the king again to present their speaker, Peter de la Mare, who had led the assault upon Edward III's ministers in 1376, and had incurred Gaunt's particular resentment. He now made what became the speaker's regular protestation that he spoke explicitly and impersonally for the commons as a whole, and went on to express two substantial complaints. The first was that knighthood, the traditional strength of the country, was slighted and the knightly virtues unrewarded, and the second that the kingdom's shipping was decayed, and its power at sea threatened. Those were conventionally the respective concerns of the knights of the shires on the one hand and the citizens and burgesses on the other. They were also matters of vital importance to the community at large. The reference to the neglect of knighthood is not merely a nostalgic invocation of former English victories in France, but a reflection of deep resentment of maladminstration in the shires, and a leitmotiv of the reign. The decay of the kingdom's naval power was manifest in the recent French and Castilian raids on the south coast, and a cause of general fear and resentment. The commons' hope was that those and other evils could be prevented by more competent government. They accordingly asked for the addition of eight suitably

---

[3]Cf. Parliament of 1394, Item 11.

qualified persons of diverse degrees to the continual council, the naming of officers and ministers in parliament, with the expenditure of the household carefully limited to its traditional income, and the due maintenance and enforcement of the law, in such wise that laws made in parliament should not be undone except by parliament. They were told that their requests would be considered, but an answer would be postponed for a week while the bishops and lords debated the matter and the commons discussed their own business.

The reference to the interval is interesting, as the rolls ordinarily indicate the initiation and conclusion of business but not its conduct and timing. When the commons returned on 22 October they were told in effect that their requests had been granted, with some reservations over the power of the great officers to discharge their duties without the interposition of the councillors, and the king's freedom to appoint and remove his own servants and officers. There were to be nine new members of the council, and Lord Latimer, who was unacceptable to the commons, was discreetly dropped.[4] There were also provisions to curb administrative abuses which went beyond the letter of the commons' proposals, which may at least have been gratifying to them in prospect. The third request, for the maintenance of the common law, was less surprisingly also approved. In return for those assurances the lords and commons together granted the king a substantial subsidy of two tenths and two fifteenths. The intervening week must therefore have been given in part to discussions between the two houses, as well as to consideration of their respective business. It may also be to this interval that the estimate of revenues which the commons 'demanded' from the 'realm of England' should be ascribed, although this was not included on or with the roll (Appendix, Item 1); as this makes clear, they were keen to ensure that every possible source of revenue was spent on the war, so it is not surprising that the announcement of the subsidy was accompanied by a further request, immediately granted, that the king would appoint special treasurers to ensure that the money was entirely and exclusively applied to the war. The readiness, or at least the celerity, with which the arrangements were made testify both to the general sense of urgency and also to the efficiency with which lords and commons, but especially the commons, had conducted their negotiations.

Parliament then proceeded with its ordinary business, in so far as any of its concerns can be described as ordinary. Two claims by tenants-in-chief, the earl of Salisbury and Sir John Cobham, were considered, the first being referred to the king's bench and the second, after a long review of the accumulated evidence, being determined in favour of the crown. Salisbury's suit, for the lordship of Denbigh and other estates in north Wales, was a matter of the greatest sensitivity, as it led back to the fall of Roger Mortimer, earl of March, at the beginning of Edward III's reign, and the subsequent distribution of his estates amongst the young king's closest associates. Other matters reviewed included a dispute in the city of London, the duke of Brittany's relations with the crown, the obduracy of Robert Hauley and John Shakell over a ransom, which later had a bloody outcome, trade and staples, and the condemnation of Sir John Gommegnies for the surrender of castles in the marches of Calais. That was a cause which revived the recriminations of the previous reign, as did the confirmation, after a long hearing, of the sentence of banishment on Alice Perrers, Edward III's predatory mistress. During these judicial proceedings the commons presented a further series of requests, written on the schedule which is stitched to the roll and is now numbered membrane 8. Both that fact, that the clerk chose to preserve the text rather than engross it, and the nature of the petition are highly interesting. The schedule is a prosaic document, but if it is not the parchment that the commons delivered to the clerk it is difficult to see why it should have been copied again. The requests are a refinement of the points which the commons had already made and which in a broad sense they had achieved. They refer to them as matters which ought to be determined, for the good both of the king and the kingdom, while the present parliament is sitting, and pray the aid of the lords to that end. They ask that all appointments should be made on the the grounds of personal qualities and fitness. They also ask that the nine additional lords of the council and the officers of state should receive their charge in the presence of the commons, that justices and others should be sworn in the same manner, and charged to do right and equity to all, that petitions made in the general interest, some of which may be declared orally, should be discussed in a constructive manner and determined in good faith and the light of reason, that the unauthorised surrender to foreign enemies of castles and towns should be condignly punished, that Alice Perrers should have her just deserts, and that monies intended for the defence of the realm should be honestly and effectively applied to that end and their receivers held accountable for their outlay. The implication is that the business of parliament was still in hand, and even that Gommegnies and Alice Perrers were yet to be heard, but that the commons were likely to take no further part in it. In answer to their requests it was announced that Alice Perrers would be summoned to answer the accusations against her (see the Appendix, Item 2), that some of their wishes had been met by the undertakings already given, and that others would be dealt with in the common petitions. That was an imprecise, if it was not an evasive answer, but at least the commons' concerns had not been brushed aside. The common petitions are enrolled immediately after the exchange, and we know that Alice Perrers did appear before the lords in December, when the sentence against her was upheld. It is not clear whether that was upon a first or a second summons, but it seems most likely that the schedule was delivered immediately before or early during Gommegnies' trial, and before Alice Perrers' cause began. It is also possible that the common petitions were not formally answered until after the commons had left or had begun to leave.

What is certain is that the commons dispersed, or began to disperse, while the lords were still sitting. The sixty-nine common petitions enrolled, with a further fourteen presented by the clergy and nine from the city of London, are exceptional in number. Together they issued in fifteen statutes. They begin conventionally by urging the maintenance

---

[4] Tout, *Chapters*, III.334.

of the peace and observance of the provisions of the great charter, and ask also, in the face of the uncertainties of a new reign, that the charters confirming the liberties of cities and boroughs should be renewed without charge. Those were uncontentious matters, but other petitions demonstrate a wide range of discontents, and include a number of themes that recur for the rest of the reign. Complaints of the misuse of powers by the purveyors of the royal household and the officials of the forest are amongst them. The formal confirmation of the charters, maintenance of the peace, and the regulation of purveyance became the subject of statutes, as did exception to actions concerning tithe in response to one of the clergy's petitions, but the loss of the sheriffs' income in the counties by the extenson of seignorial liberties and other processes remained a grievance to the end of the reign and beyond. A more unusual complaint was that tenants in bondage were seeking exemplifications of entries in Domesday Book in order to escape their obligations - a foretaste of the great revolt which would erupt less than four years later. It is also remarkable that the king's response was not that they should not be allowed to have such documents, but that they would not be allowed to argue from them that the conditions of their tenure should be changed. Those matters settled, the knights and burgesses were free to leave. Writs for expenses were issued on 6 December (more than a week after the formal dissolution) for the knights of thirty-six counties for periods varying between 70 and 54 days. Writs for the representatives of eleven cities and boroughs (Bath, Bedford, Devizes, Grimsby, Hereford, Newcastle upon Tyne, Northampton, Oxford, Shrewsbury, Wallingford and Worcester) were made out on the same day, for attendance varying from 70 to 58 days.[5] The parliament roll is a clerkly document, set out without unnecessary emphases, and without any notable provision to facilitate reference to its contents, beyond its adherence to a broadly established form. It may be, however, that the naming of Geoffrey Martin as clerk of the parliament, and of his colleague Edmund Brudenell as the clerk of the crown to whom the completed roll was delivered, were gestures to mark the beginning of a new reign. If there were some such consciousnes of change, it can hardly have extended to any apprehension of the storms that were to come.

---

[5] *CCR 1377-81*, 105-7.

Text and Translation

Text

Page iii-3, Membrane 1

ROTULUS PARLIAMENTI TENTI APUD WESTM', IN QUINDENA SANCTI MICHAELIS, ANNO REGNI REGIS RICARDI SECUNDI POST CONQUESTUM ANGLIE PRIMO.

Adjournement de pronunciacion.
1. A la quinszime de Saint Michel, qe fust le mardy le .xiij.ᵉ jour d'Octobre, l'an du regne nostre seignour le roi Richard, le secounde puis le conquest d'Engleterre, primer, et le primere jour de ce present parlement, s'assemblerent en la palays de Westm' en la chambre blanke, aucuns prelatz et seignours du roialme, q'avoient sommonce de venir a cest parlement, attendantz illoeqes longement la venue d'autres prelatz et seignours queux encores a celle temps estoient absentz. Et puis apres, bien entour l'eure de noune, pur tant qe fust tesmoigne qe plusours prelatz et seignours \n'estoient/ encores venuz a la ville, n'auxint aucuns des viscontz n'y avoient mye retournez lours briefs de parlement, nostre dit seignour le roy, luy quel estoit venuz a Westm' le lundy devant, et illoeqes estoit demurrez pur y attendre la venue des prelatz, seignours et autres, voloit et fist comander qe l'en sursist et lessast de faire la pronunciacion des causes del sommonce de ce present parlement tanqe al lendemain \proschein,/ Issint qe mesme le parlement feust continuez tanqe a mesme le lendemain. Et sur ce, les prelatz, seignours, et les communes qe y furent venuz, s'assemblerent en la chambre depeinte, et illoeqes l'ercevesqe de Canterbirs, reherceant \[les]/ causes dessusdites devant eulx touz, depar le roy adjornast mesme le parlement tanqe al dit lendemain; lour comandant q'ils y feusent touz le dit lendemain bien matin pur y oier les causes del sommonce de ce parlement. Et puis se ent departirent sanz pluis faire a celle jour.

Pronunciacion en parlement.
2. Au quiel lendemain, si venoient en parlement en la dite chambre depeinte sibien nostre seignour le roy mesmes come les deux arcevesqes de Canterbirs et d'Everwyk, monseignour d'Espaigne, duc de Lancastre, et a poy toutz les autres prelatz et seignours du roialme, et auxint justices, sergeantz, et autres qi poaient travailler, et q'avoient la dite sommonce; et auxint les chivalers des contees, citezeins des citees, et burgeys des burghes, et illoeqes, le dit ercevesqe de Canterbirs, par commandement nostre dit seignour le roi, si avoit les paroles de la dite pronunciacioun, et lour dist issint, Rex tuus venit tibi, et puis dist, Seignours et sires, ces paroles qe j'ay dist sont tant a dire en Franceys, Vostre roy vient a toy.⁶
3. Et sur ce le dit arcevesqe y dist plusours bones resons accordantz a sa theme, et devisa sa dite theme en trois parties par manere come \[ce fust]/ une predication, et dist en especial, et voirs est qe par reson chescun bon amy doit estre bien venuz a autre amy, qar si tielle venue \soit,/ q'est pur une des trois causes q'ensuent, c'est assavoir, ou ce est pur rejoier et solacer ensemble d'aucune grace et prosperitee y avenue, sicome nostre dame Sainte Marie et Elizabeth firent ensemble par \manere/ come l'escripture dit; Et exultavit infans in utero ejus, etc.; ou autrement, tielle venue est pur visiter et conforter son amy en adversitee et tribulacion pur \[lour]/ ent conseiller a mieltz q'il purra, come est

---
⁶Matthew 21:5.

Translation

THE ROLL OF THE PARLIAMENT HELD AT WESTMINSTER, ON THE QUINDENE OF MICHAELMAS, IN THE FIRST YEAR OF THE REIGN OF KING RICHARD, THE SECOND SINCE THE CONQUEST [13 October 1377].

The adjournment of the opening.
1. On the quindene of Michaelmas, which was Tuesday 13 October, in the first year of the reign of our lord King Richard, the second since the conquest of England [1377], and the first day of this present parliament, there assembled in the palace of Westminster in the white chamber certain prelates and lords of the kingdom, who had been summoned to attend the parliament, and who were long awaiting there the arrival of other prelates and lords who were still absent at that time. Subsequently, around noon, because it was reported that many lords and prelates had not yet arrived in town, and also that some of the sheriffs had still to return their writs to parliament, our said lord the king, who had arrived in Westminster on the previous Monday [12 October 1377], and was staying there to await the arrival of the prelates, lords, and others, willed and commanded that the announcement of the reasons for summoning this present parliament be delayed and prorogued until the next day, and hence that the same parliament should be adjourned until the same day. Whereupon, the prelates, lords, and the commons who had gathered there assembled in the painted chamber, and there the archbishop of Canterbury, recounting the aforesaid reasons before them all, adjourned the same parliament on behalf of the king until the next day, ordering that they should all be there early in the morning of that day to hear the reasons for summoning this parliament. Then they departed without attending to anything else on that day.

The opening of parliament.
2. The next day, our lord the king as well as the two archbishops of Canterbury and York, our lord of Spain, duke of Lancaster, and almost all the other prelates and lords of the kingdom, together with the justices, serjeants, and others who had business there, and who had received the said summons, and also the knights of the counties, citizens of the cities, and burgesses of the boroughs arrived in parliament in the said painted chamber and there the said archbishop of Canterbury, by command of our said lord the king, announced the said opening in the following words, 'Your king comes to you'; and then he said, 'Lords and sirs, those words which I have spoken are, in French, 'Vostre roy vient a toy''.
3. Whereupon, the said archbishop cited many examples according with his theme, and divided his said theme into three parts as though it were a sermon, and he said in particular (and it is true) that every good friend should rightly visit his friends, for if such a visit should come about, it would be for one of the three following reasons, namely, to rejoice and celebrate together any grace and prosperity which had arisen, as our lady St Mary and Elizabeth did together in the manner described in the scriptures; 'And the child leapt in her womb, et cetera.'; or else, such an appearance is for the purpose of visiting and comforting one's friend in adversity and tribulation and giving him advice as best one can, as

[Col. b] compris en le livre Job etc. Ou celle venue est pur assaier son amy en temps de necessitee, come l'escripture dit, In necessitate probabitur amicus.

4. Et ore est il einsi qe nostre seignour le roy cy present, qi Dieu salve, si est il ores venuz ycy en vostre presence come vostre droiturel seignour lige, et vostre bon et entier amy, nemye soulement pur une \des/ dites causes, einz pur toutes les dites trois causes ensemble. C'estassavoir, pur soy rejoier avec vous de la noble grace qe Dieu vous ad donez en sa persone, la quelle vous est naturel et droiturel seignour lige, come dit est, nemye par election ne par autre tielle collaterale voie, einz par droite succession de heritage: de quoy vous luy estez de nature moelt le pluis tenuz de luy amer perfitement, et humblement obbeir; et en oultre de regracier Dieu, de qi toute grace et bien procede, de ce par especial q'il vous ad donez tiel noble seignour a vostre roy et governour. Et veritablement ent deverez vous moelt le pluis rejoier \[en voz coers,]/ a cause qe toutdys depuis son coronement son perfit desir ad este de vous veer et parler, et se rejoier de vous, et de vous mercier de voz bons portz envers luy depuis q'il ad occupiez \aucun/ estat deinz le roialme apres la mort son noble pere le prince, qe Dieu assoille. Et en verite par celles causes eust il pluis tost fait somondre ceste son primer parlement, si ne fust q'il ne vous volloit destourber de voz affaires et grantz occupacions en cest derain augst, quant vous aviez euz grant occupacion en le roialme, sibien entour l'encres des fruitz de la terre, come autrement sur la coustee de meer pur faire resistence a les enemys qui s'afforcerent adonqes de faire grant damage et vilanie a tout le roialme.

5. Et auxint vous vint ore nostre dit seignour le roy pur vous visiter et conforter en voz grantz ennoys, perdes, et adversitees, quelles vous avez ja novellement soeffertz, sibien par la mort de noble roy Edward et de son eisnez fitz le prince pere nostre seignour le roi qe ore est, queux Deux assoille, come autrement par le grant triboille et damage q'ont este faitz en plusours costeres de meer deinz le dit roialme, par la venue de enemys avantditz. Et par tant soy mesmes vous profre il ores en socours et aide en tant come il poet, et est tenuz de faire, en lieu de ses ditz nobles aiel et pere, qi sont a Dieu comandez: et \[vous]/Voelt il et se profre de tenir, sibien a sainte esglise come a vous touz, seignours et pieres et commune de soun dit roialme, en toute voz bones franchises et libertees, et de vous faire garder et maintenir en bone paix, et vous governer par les bones loys et custumes de la terre, par manere come aucun de ses auncestres y ont mieltz fait devaunt luy, et de faire amender ce qe demande amendement entant come en luy est. Et par tant vous ent deverez auxint grantement rejoier et reconforter de si noble et gracious seignour. Et auxint vous vint il ore come vostre droit seignour et entier amy, pur se conseiller a vous de ce qe mieltz soit affaire pur resistence de la *[Page iii-4]*

[Col. a] grant malice et multitude de ses enemys et des vostres, qe vous sont tout entour environez a chescune part a jour de huy, et s'afforcent a destruire le roy, le roialme, et vous touz, qe Dieu ne veullie.

6. Et par tant si ad nostre dit seignour le roy grant busoigne de voz nobles conseilx et aides (qar pur cause qe la roialme si est ore en greindre peril qe n'estoit unqes devant) si l'en faut ore mettre greinours despenses en defens d'ycelle, qe l'en ne soloit unqes faire avant ceste heure; et nul roi Cristien purroit suffre n'endurer a sustenir tieux despenses mettre sanz l'aide de sa commune. Et pur ce en sa presente grante necessitee, qe ne touche soulement luy mesmes einz vous touz, serrez vous provez ses bons et vrais subgits et amys. Et par cestes trois causes semble chose resonable qe nostre seignour

[Col. b] in the book of Job, etc. Or this appearance is to turn to one's friend in time of need, as scripture says, 'In times of need the friend shall be proved'.

4. And so it is now that our lord the king here present, whom God preserve, comes before you as your rightful liege lord, and your good and whole-hearted friend, not merely for one of the said reasons, but for all the said three reasons together. Namely, to rejoice with you over the noble grace which God has granted you in the person who is your natural and rightful liege-lord, as has been said, not by election nor by other such a way, but solely by rightful succession to an inheritance: wherefore you are by nature the more fully obliged to love him completely, and obey him humbly; and also to thank God, from whom all grace and good proceeds, in particular because he has given you so noble a lord as your king and governor. And truly, you ought to rejoice the more fully in your hearts because ever since his coronation his earnest wish has been to see and speak to you, and rejoice with you, and thank you for your good bearing towards him since he occupied a special place in the realm after the death of his noble father the prince, whom God absolve. And it is truly for those reasons that he would the sooner have summoned this parliament, if it had not been that he did not wish to disturb you in your affairs and important occupations this last autumn, when you have had important business in the kingdom, as well in harvesting the fruits of the earth as in keeping the coasts of the sea against the enemies who then threatened to inflict great harm and villainy on all the realm.

5. And also, our said lord the king comes to visit and comfort you in the great troubles, losses, and adversities which you have recently suffered, both on account of the death of the noble King Edward [III] and of his only son the prince, father of our lord the present king, whom God absolve, and in the great disruption and damage which there has been on many coasts of the sea within the said kingdom, through the coming of the aforesaid enemies. And therefore, he now offers himself to you, to help and aid you as far as he is able and is obliged to do, in place of his noble grandfather and father, who are commended to God: and he wills and offers to keep you, holy church, as well as all the lords, peers, and commons of his said realm, in all your lawful franchises and liberties, and to protect and maintain you in a state of peace, and to govern you through the good laws and customs of the land, as well as any of his ancestors before him, and to amend anything which needs amendment as far as he is able. Wherefore ought you greatly to rejoice and seek comfort in so noble and gracious a lord. And moreover, he now comes before you as your rightful lord and whole-hearted friend, to be advised by you as to the best means of resisting the *[Page iii-4]*

[Col. a] great malice and multitude of his enemies and yours, by which you are, at present, encompassed on every side, and who threaten to destroy the king, the kingdom, and you, all together, yet may God not so wish it.

6. And because our said lord the king has so great a need for your noble counsel and aid, for that the kingdom is in greater peril than it has ever been before, so now it is necessary to make great investments in the defence of the same, such as have never been made in the past; and no Christian king can support or endure the levying of such expenses without the aid of his commons. Thus, in his present state of great need, which touches not only himself but you all, you shall prove his good and true subjects and friends. And for those three reasons it seems fitting that our lord the king

le roy vous doit estre moltz bien venuz, /et par sa dite venue doviez bien rejoier.\ Et depuis q'il est issint venuz a vous en tielle guyse, /si devez vous de pure reson remonstrer a luy perfitz\ \amour, naturesce, et vrai obeissance,/ en aide et socour de vous mesmes, sibien par voz conseilx come par voz corps et autres aides. Et par tant qe nostre seignour le roi ne voloit longement tenir cest son parlement en vein sanz fruit et profit, il vous prie moelt entierement qe vous vous veulliez conseiller ensemble coment et par quelle manere l'en purra mieltz resister la malice des enemys avantditz, et coment l'en purra mieltz avenir a les despenses qe l'en y faut mettre de pure necessitee, a meins desaise de poeple, et greindre honour et profit au roy et de son roialme avantdit. Et si tost come vous soiez accordez d'aucun certain purpos, le veulliez declarrer a nostre seignour le roy dessusdit et a son conseil, au fin q'il soit advisez. Et ces sont les causes de la somonce de ce present parlement. Et nostre seignour le roy desirant moelt la paix estre maintenuz en son roialme d'Engleterre, et les tortz y faitz estre redressez et amendez, et les malfaisours justicez, si ad il fait assigner certains clercz resceivours, et certains persones, prelatz, seignours, et autres, triours des peticions qe serront baillees en ce parlement, par la manere qe s'ensuit:

7. Resceivours des peticions d'Engleterre, Irlande, Gales, et Escoce:

Sire William de Burstall

Sire Richard de Ravensere

Sire Thomas de Newenham

Sire Johan de Freton'.

8. Resceivours des peticions de Gascoigne, et d'autres terres et paiis depar dela, et des Isles:
Meistre Wauter Skirlowe

Sire Michel de Ravendale

Sire Piers de Barton

Sire Johan Bouland.

Et ceux qi verront bailler lours petitions les baillent avant parentre cy et vendredy proschein venant, le dit jour accomptee. Et apres mesme le jour nul peticion soit aucunement resceuz.

9. Et sont assignez triours des petitions d'Engleterre, Gales, et Escoce:

Le roi de Castille et de Leon, duc de Lancastre

L'ercevesqe de Canterbirs

L'evesqe de Londres

L'evesqe de Wyncestr'

L'evesqe de Ely

L'evesqe de Bath

L'evesqe de Cardoill

L'evesqe de Roucestre

L'evesqe de Salesbirs

L'abbe de Westm'

L'abbe de Bury

Le conte de la Marche

Le conte d'Arondell

Le conte de Warr'

Le conte de Staff'

Le conte d'Angos

Le conte de Northumbr'

Le sire de Latymer

should be well received by you, and his coming much rejoiced. And since he has thus appeared before you in such a guise, so you ought, out of pure reason, to show him perfect love, kindness, and true obedience, in the aid and assistance which you give him, both through your counsels as well as in your bodies and in other ways. And because our lord the king does not wish vainly to prolong his parliament without fruit and profit, he desires you most earnestly to consult with one another as to how and in what manner the malice of the aforesaid enemies might be best resisted, and how it might be best to raise the money necessary for the purpose, with the least injury to the people, and to the great honour and profit of the king and his aforesaid kingdom. And as soon as you are agreed on a certain plan, that you inform our aforesaid lord the king and his counsel, so that he may seek advice. And those are the reasons for summoning the present parliament. Furthermore, our lord the king, greatly desiring that peace be preserved in his kingdom of England, and that wrongs done therein be redressed and amended, and malefactors brought to justice, has caused certain clerks to be appointed as receivers, and other persons, prelates, lords, and others, as triers of petitions which are to be submitted in this parliament, in the following manner:

7. Receivers of petitions from England, Ireland, Wales, and Scotland:

Sir William Burstall

Sir Richard Ravenser

Sir Thomas Newenham

Sir Johan Freton.

8. Receivers of petitions from Gascony, and other lands and countries overseas, and from the Channel Islands:
Master Walter Skirlawe

Sir Michael Ravendale

Sir Piers Barton

Sir John Bowland.

And those who wish to submit their petitions should deliver them between now and Friday next [16 October], the day allotted to them. And after that day no petition will be accepted for any reason.

9. The following are assigned to be triers of petitions from England, Wales, and Scotland:

The king of Castile and of Leon, duke of Lancaster

The archbishop of Canterbury

The bishop of London

The bishop of Winchester

The bishop of Ely

The bishop of Bath

The bishop of Carlisle

The bishop of Rochester

The bishop of Salisbury

The abbot of Westminster

The abbot of Bury

The earl of March

The earl of Arundel

The earl of Warwick

The earl of Stafford

The earl of Angus

The earl of Northumberland

Lord Latimer

Le sire de Nevill	Lord Neville
Le sire de Cobham	Lord Cobham
Le sire Fitz Wauter	Lord FitzWalter
Monsire Roger Beauchamp	Sir Roger Beauchamp
Monsire Johan Knyvet	Sir John Knyvet
Monsire Johan Cavendissh	Sir John Cavendish
Monsire Robert Bealknapp	Sir Robert Belknap
Monsire William Skipwith	Sir William Skipwith
Monsire William de Wychyngham	Sir William Wychyngham
Monsire Rouf' de Ferrers	Sir Ralph Ferrers
Monsire Hugh' de Segrave.	Sir Hugh Segrave.

- touz ensemble, ove .vi. des prelatz et seignours avantditz au meins; appellez a eux chanceller, tresorer, seneschal et chamberlein, quant il busoignera, et auxint les sergeantz le roy, quant il busoignera. Et tendront lour place en la chambre de chamberleyn, pres de la chambre depeinte.

10. Et sont assignez triours des peticions de Gascoigne, et d'autres terres et paiis de la la meer, et des Isles:

- to act all together, with at least six of the aforesaid lords and prelates; calling upon the chancellor, treasurer, steward, and chamberlain, as well as the king's serjeants, when necessary. And they shall hold their session in the chamberlain's room, by the painted chamber.

10. The following are assigned to be triers of petitions from Gascony, and from other lands and countries overseas, and from the Channel Islands:

L'ercevesque d'Everwyk	The archbishop of York
L'evesqe de Duresme	The bishop of Durham
L'evesqe de Nichole	The bishop of Lincoln
L'evesqe de Cicestre	The bishop of Chichester
L'evesqe de Norwiz	The bishop of Norwich
L'evesqe de Hereford	The bishop of Hereford
L'evesqe de Wircestre	The bishop of Worcester
L'evesqe de Seint Assaph	The bishop of St Asaph
L'evesqe de Bangor	The bishop of Bangor
L'abbe de Saint Austyn de Canterbirs	The abbot of St Augustine's, Canterbury
L'abbe de Waltham	The abbot of Waltham
Le conte de Cantebrugge	The earl of Cambridge
Le conte de Bukyngham	The earl of Buckingham
Le conte de Salesbirs	The earl of Salisbury
Le conte de Suff'	The earl of Suffolk
Le sire de Roos	Lord Roos
Le sire de Basset	Lord Basset
Le sire de Clifford	Lord Clifford
Le sire de Bardolf	Lord Bardolf
Monsire Richard de Stafford	Sir Richard Stafford
Monsire Thomas de Ingelby	Sir Thomas Ingleby
Monsire Roger de Kirketon	Sir Roger Kirkton
Monsire Roger de Fulthorp	Sir Roger Fulthorp
Monsire Johan Deverose.	Sir John Devereux.

- touz ensemble, ou six des ditz prelatz et seignours au meins; appellez a eux chanceller, tresorer, seneschal et chamberlein, sergeantz le roi, quant y busoignera. Et tendront lour place en la chambre marcolf.
Et puis apres le dit arcevesqe y dist depar le roy qe nostre seignour le roy voloit qe ce parlement feust *[Page iii-5]*

[Col. a] continuez de jour en autre tanqe les chargeantes busoignes du roialme feussent esploitez, et q'ils y eussent congie de luy a departir: enpriant a touz q'ils y preissent ceste lour charge tendrement a coer, et si avant come ils desiront la salvacion del roialme et de eulx mesmes; et q'ils retournassent lendemain par temps pur oier autre foitz lour charge.

- to act all together, or at least six of the said prelates and lords; calling upon the chancellor, treasurer, steward, chamberlain, and the king's serjeants, when necessary. And they shall hold their session in the Marcolf chamber.
And the said archbishop said, on behalf of the king, that our lord the king willed that this parliament should be *[Page iii-5]*

[Col. a] adjourned day by day until the important business of the kingdom was discharged, and they had his permission to depart: desiring of them that all hold their duties close to their heart, as they desired the security of the kingdom and with it their own; and to return early the next day to hear again their business.

Richard Scrope.

11. Also, the next day [15 October], which was a Thursday, the king himself, as well as the prelates and a large number of the commons, returned to the said parliament in the white chamber, and there in their presence and hearing Sir Richard le Scrope, steward of our said lord the king's household, by order of the king himself once again caused the charge given them the day before to be rehearsed; namely, to advise on how and in what manner the said enemies might best be resisted, and how, with the least injury to the people, and to the greater profit and honour of the kingdom, the money might be obtained and raised which would be needed for the defence and security of the aforesaid realm, and of them all. And later the same day, the matter was laid before all the said commons gathered in the place where they were assembled by order of the king, in the chapter-house of the abbey of Westminster, because the said commons as a whole had not yet assembled in the king's presence. Whereupon, the commons prayed of our lord the king that because of the arduous nature of their business, and the feebleness of their knowledge and abilities, it might please him to grant them the assistance and support of the prelates and lords named below, to consult with them in particular on their affairs, for the swifter and better despatch of the business with which they were charged.

The duke of Lancaster.

12. Namely, the king of Castile and of Leon, duke of Lancaster, the bishop of London, the bishop of Ely, the bishop of Rochester, the bishop of Carlisle, the earl of March, the earl of Arundel, the earl of Warwick, the earl of Angus, and Lord Neville, Sir Henry le Scrope, Sir Richard le Scrope, and Sir Richard Stafford; which was granted to them on behalf of the king in parliament.

13. However, the said duke immediately rose in parliament, and kneeling before our said lord the king, requested most humbly that he listen to him a while, concerning an important matter which touched the king himself and his own person. And he said that although the commons had thus elected him as one of the lords to consult with them over the said matters, he would not by any means so act, if it pleased the king, until he had been exonerated of that which the commons had wickedly said of him. For he said that although he was unworthy, he was a king's son, and one of the great lords of the realm after the king: and his person had been spoken of so malevolently, and accused of something which should rightfully be considered open treason, if it were true, which God forbid, that he had no desire to do anything until the truth was made publicly known. And further, he said that none of his ancestors, on either side, had ever been a traitor, but true and loyal. And a marvellous thing it would have been, if he were to have strayed from the tradition of his ancestors, as well by nature as for other reason; for he had more to lose than anyone else within the kingdom. Furthermore, he said that if any man, or whatever estate or condition, were so bold as to accuse him of treason, or other disloyalty, or any other deed prejudicial to the kingdom, he would be ready to defend himself by his body or otherwise, at the decision of the king and the lords, like the poorest gentleman of the kingdom.

The exoneration of the said duke.

14. Whereupon, all the prelates and lords stood and exonerated him with one voice, begging the said duke to refrain

[Col. b] des tielles paroles; qar ils pensoient qe nul vivant les vorroit dire. Et sur ce les communes y disrent qe apparisante chose feust et notoire q'ils avoient le dit duc excusez de toute blasme et diffame, quant ils luy avoient issint esluz d'estre lour principal aide, confortour, et conseillour en ce parlement; empriantz touz a une voice, de lour avoir touz pur excusez. Et puis le duc dit[7] qe coment qe tielles paroles avoient longement volez parmy le roialme fauxement, il se merveillast coment aucun homme purroit ou vorroit pur hounte et pur peril qe ent purroit sourdre \comencer ou/ continuer tiel fait. Qar celluy qi feust trovour de tielles paroles, par quelles l'en moeveroit legerement debat parentre les seignours du roialme, /si fust appert\ et verroi traitour, qar tieux debatz purroient tournir en destruccion de mesme le roialme a touz jours. Et y priast le dit duc qe bone ordinance et jouste punissement et redde feust ordenez sur tieux parlours \et trovours des mesonges/ en ce parlement, pur eschuir les meschiefs avantditz pur le temps a venir: mais de temps passez tout soit pardonez quant a sa propre persone.

Requeste des communes.
15. Et puis apres les communes y vindrent en parlement devant le roi, et illoeqes monsire Peres de la Mare, chivaler, q'avoit les paroles depar la commune, faisant sa protestacion, qe ce q'il y avoit a dire nel dirroit del soen propre moevement, einz del mocion, assent, et voluntee expres de toute la commune illoeqes esteante: et s'il avenist q'il y forveiast de rienz, ou par cas y deist chose qe ne fust del assent de ses compaignons, q'il ent fust par mesmes ses compaignons tantost amendez illoeqes, et devant q'il y partissent de la place.
16. Y dist, en compleignant qe tant come le noble chivalrie del roialme estoit bien nurriz, encherriz, honores, et noblement guerdonez pur lours grantz bienfaitz, si estoit celle chivalrie molt urgerouse, et ardantment desirouse afaire grantz emprises et grantz faitz d'armes, chescun devant \autre,/ paront le roialme fust grantement enrichez et pleintinouse de toute bien, et les habitantz en ycelle doutez de lours enemys, dont toutes nacions a poy en parlerent d'onour et de nobleye; et qe pluis est, lour fame de nobleye estoit espandue parmy le monde. Mais ore, depuis qe celle chivalrie ad este rebuquiz et tenuz en viletee, et qe pluis est, lours biens noblement gaignez de lours enemys de guerre lour tolluz sanz jouste cause, et auxint celle chivalrie et toute autre vertu mys a derire, et vice preisee, avancee, et honouree, et nullement puniz ou chasticee, si est mesme la chivalrie et les coers des bones et vertuouses persones grantement abeissez, paront nul homme ad talent al jour de huy, a ce qe semble par experience de fait, de bien faire: de qoy le roialme ad ore novellement suffert grantz /damages et outrage\ de lours ditz enemys des plusours partz, et est a douter qe pluis soeffrera, si Dieu n'y mette remede au gouvernaille d'ycelle.

17. Et auxint \d'autre part,/ quant les marchantz du roialme furent seignours et maistres, et avoient la disposicion et ordinance de lours propres niefs, si estoit la navye du roialme grande et pleintinouse, et estoit /graindre\ \nombre/ des bones niefs appurtenantes a une ville del roialme qe ore sont en tout le roialme avantdit. Et pur ce qe nostre seignour le roi, qi Dieu salve, si est a present innocent et de tendre age, la dite commune, pur amendement des meschiefs avauntditz \et autres,/ et pur salvacion du roialme qe maintenant est en grant peril, et pluis qe unqes n'estoit devant, priont \au

[Col. b] from such words, for they could not believe that any man living would utter them. Whereupon, the commons there said that it had been plain and apparent that they had exonerated the said duke of all blame and defamation, when they had thus elected him to be their chief aid, comforter, and counsellor in this parliament; all requesting in one voice that he might hold them all excused. Then the duke said that although such words had long been falsely circulated throughout the realm, he had personally marvelled that any man could or would utter or pass on such a rumour because of the shame and peril which would ensue. For whosoever was the originator of such words, which might easily have caused conflict between the lords of the kingdom, was himself the obvious and real traitor, for such conflict might have brought about the destruction of the same kingdom for ever. And the said duke prayed that an effective ordinance and just and rightful punishment be devised in this parliament for such rumour-mongers and promoters of lies, in order that the aforesaid troubles might be avoided in time to come: but in relation to things past everything should be pardoned with regard to himself.

The request of the commons.
15. Later, the commons came before the king in parliament, and there Sir Peter de la Mare, knight, who was to speak on the commons' behalf, made protestation that if there was anything to say he would say it not of his own accord, but by the will, consent, and express wish of all the commons there present: and if he should depart from their intent, or if he should say anything which had not been agreed by his companions, that he might be corrected by his same companions there as soon as possible, and before they had left that place.
16. He spoke there, in complaint that whereas the illustrious knighthood of the kingdom had long been well nurtured, cherished, honoured, and nobly rewarded for their many good deeds, so had their knighthood been most keen and ardently willing to undertake great enterprises and deeds of arms, every one competing with the other, whereby the kingdom had been greatly enriched and filled with all that was good, and the inhabitants of the same feared by their enemies, almost all nations speaking of their honour and nobility; and what is more, the fame of their nobility spread throughout the whole world. Now, however, since their knighthood had been rebutted and scorned, and furthermore, their goods, nobly won from their enemies in war, taken from them without just cause, and also their knighthood and all other virtue scorned, and vice prized, promoted, and honoured, and not punished or chastised at all, so had their same knighthood and the hearts of good and virtuous persons been greatly cast down, wherefore no man has any inclination these days, from what his past experience taught him, to do good: and so the kingdom has lately suffered great injuries and outrages from the said enemies from many parts, and it is to be feared that more will be suffered unless God provide remedy for the governance of the same.
17. And moreover, whereas once the merchants of the kingdom were lords and masters of the use and governance of their own ships, so was the kingdom's navy great and abundant, and as many good ships pertained to a single town as now there are in the aforesaid kingdom as a whole. And because our said lord the king, whom God preserve, is at present so innocent and tender in age, the said commons, for the ending of the aforesaid troubles as well as of others and for the security of the kingdom which is now in greater

---
[7] Original dit duc,

roi nostre seignour et/ as seignours du parlement des trois choses en especial:

18. Primerent, qe lour pleust ordeiner et lour nomer ore en ce present parlement oept suffisantz persones de diverses estatz, d'estre continuelment residentz *[Page iii-6]* *[Col. a]* du conseil sur les busoignes du roy et del roialme avec les officers du roi, des tieux persones qi mieltz scievent et pluis diligeaument vorront et purront travailler sur l'amendement des meschiefs avantditz, et le bone governement et salvacion del dit roialme; issint qe la commune purra estre clerement acertee des nouns d'yceux conseillers, qe serroient expendours et ordeinours de ce q'ils verront granter pur les guerres, et par tant avoir la greindre corage de faire a nostre seignour le roy ce q'ils ont de luy en charge, come dessus est dit.

19. Item, qe lour pleust ordener et nommer en ce parlement les persones qe serront delees la persone nostre seignour le roy mesmes, q'est issint de tendre age. Et qe celles persones fussent des pluis vertuouses, honestes, et suffisantz del roialme, issint qe mesme nostre seignour, q'est persone sacree et enoint, feust noblement et en bones vertuz governez et nurriz au plesance de Dieu, paront tout le roialme y purra estre salvez et amendez. Et qe feust auxint ordeine qe mesme nostre seignour le roy et sa maisoun fust governez a bone moderacion en despenses affaire, tantsoulement de les revenues du roialme et de les autres droitz de sa corone et seignouries. Et qe tout ce qe est ou serra grantez a nostre seignour le roi en maintenance de ses guerres, fust appliez et despenduz en les guerres et nulle part aillours, en aide et descharge de sa commune avantdite.

20. Item, qe la commune loy, et auxint les especialx loys, estatutz, et ordinances de la terre faitz \devant ces heures,/ pur commune profit et bone governance du roialme, lour feussent entierement tenuz, ratifiez, et confermez, et qe par ycelles ils fussent droiturelement governez: qar la commune soy ent ad sentuz moeltz grevez cea en ariere, qe ce ne lour ad my este fait toutes partz, einz qe par maistrie et singulertees d'aucuns entour le roy, qi Dieux assoille, ont este plusours de la dite commune malmesnez. Mais toutes voies la dite commune ny requert mye ore pur vengeance avoir de nully qi ait mesfait devant ceste heure, einz qe en temps avenir, quant plest au roy nostre seignour et son conseil, chastiement soit duement fait des tieux malfaisours: et qe y soit pris al oeps du roi ce q'il purra prendre par loy et reson, en donant bone ensample as autres de lour abstiner pur le temps avenir de semblablement malfaire. Requerante as seignours du parlement qe quanqe y feust ordenez en ce parlement ne fust repellez sanz parlement. Et qe aiantz due consideracion coment les jours sont courtz a present, et le temps se passe fortment, et l'en faut hastivement travailler entour l'ordinance du roialme et des guerres avantditz, ou autrement, qe Dieu ne veullie, le roialme est destruit, ils lour ent advisent, et sur ce lour donent hastive et bone responce. Salvant en toutes choses la regalie et dignitee nostre seignour le roi avauntdit; a la quelle les communes ne veullient qe par lours demandes chose prejudiciele y fust faite par aucune voie. Et sur ce fust responduz qe les prelatz et seignours y vorroit ent conseiller ensemble, comandant as communes de retournir a lour place, et treter de lours autres charges a eulx donez parentre cy et joefdy proschein: a quiel jour ils furent comandez a retournir en parlement pur oier la responce de lours requestes avant dites.

Membrane 3

danger than it has ever known before, pray of our said lord the king and the lords in parliament three things in particular:

18. First, that it please him to ordain and name for them in this present parliament eight worthy persons of divers estates, to be continually at hand *[Page iii-6]* *[Col. a]* to advise on matters concerning the king and kingdom with the king's officers, from amongst such persons who know best, and who wish and are able to work most diligently towards amending the aforesaid troubles, and the good governance and security of the said kingdom; so that the commons might be fully informed of the names of those councillors, who will spend and manage the money which is granted them for the wars, and therefore have greater heart to perform for our lord the king that with which he has charged them, as is said above.

19. Also, that it might please him to ordain and name in this parliament those who will accompany the person of our same lord the king, who is of so tender an age. And that those people might be the most virtuous, honest, and worthy of the kingdom, so that our same lord the king, who is a sacred and anointed person, might be nobly governed and imbued with all virtues to be pleasing to God, whereby the whole realm might be saved and preserved. And that it might also be ordained that our same lord the king and his house be governed with decent moderation, and especially its expenditure to be made solely from the revenues of the kingdom and from the other rights of his crown and lordships. And that everything which is or shall be granted to our lord the king for the maintenance of his wars, might be allocated to and spent on those wars and upon nothing else, to the support and relief of his aforesaid commons.

20. Also, that the common law, and also the particular laws, statutes, and ordinances of the land made in the past, for the general benefit and good governance of the kingdom, should be fully upheld, ratified, and confirmed, and that they should be lawfully governed by the same: for the commons had felt themselves much grieved in the past, because it had not applied to them in all instances, but by the tricks and singular conniving of some about the king, whom God absolve, many of the said commons had been misgoverned. Nevertheless, the said commons did not now request vengeance for any who had suffered wrong in the past, but only that in future, whensoever it pleased our lord the king and his counsel, punishment should be duly visited upon such malefactors: and that whatsoever could be taken by the king in accordance with law and reason, kept for the king's use, to set a good example to others, and encourage them to abstain in future from such misdeeds. They begged of the lords of parliament that whatsoever was ordained in this parliament should not be repealed without parliament, and that having due consideration for the shortness of the days at present, and the rapid passing of time, and the need to progress swiftly towards the ordinance of the aforesaid kingdom and the aforesaid wars, for otherwise, God forbid, the kingdom would be destroyed, they would consult hereon themselves, and subsequently give a speedy and considered response. Saving in all matters the regality and dignity of our aforesaid lord the king; to which the commons did not wish that through their demands anything prejudicial should be done in any maner. Whereupon, answer was made that the prelates and lords would consult there together, ordering the commons to return to their place, and deal with the other business which had been assigned them, between now and Thursday next [22 October]: on which day they were ordered to return to parliament to hear the reply to their aforesaid requests.

Conseillers et lour poair, etc..

21. /Quant a la primere requeste qe les dites communes monstrent a nostre seignour le roy et as seignours\ du parlement, \c'estassavoir,/ qe serroit honour al roi, et profit a toute le roialme - q'est maintenant grevez en diverse manere par plusours adversites, sibien par les guerres de France, d'Espaigne, d'Irlande, Guyenne, de Bretaigne, et tout plain d'autres parties par terre et par meer come autrement, paront le dit roialme est ores en greindre peril qe n'estoit unqes devant, et les officers del roialme ne suffisont mye sanz autre aide a si grande governaille, - qe

[Col. b] le conseille nostre dit seignour le roy fust enlargez par le nombre de oept suffisantz persones de diverses estatz et degrees, pur estre continuelment residentz du conseil avec les officers dessusditz sur les busoignes du roi et del roialme, meement tantcome nostre dit seignour soit issint de tendre age; par manere tielle qe nul grosse ou chargeante busoigne y passe ou soit deliverez sanz l'assent et advis de touz, et autres meindres busoignes par l'assent et advis de quatre au meins, selonc ce qe le cas requiert, issint qe quatre de ceux soient continuelment residentz du conseil le roy: empriantz humblement qe lour pleust ore en ce parlement mesmes les oept conseillers eslire de pluis suffisantz persones del roialme, et des tieux qi mieltz scievent, et pluis diligeaument purroient et vorroient travailler et mettre lours peines sur l'amendement des meschiefs et perils avantditz; et sur ce notifier lours nouns a mesme la commune en ce parlement, en grant confort de eux et de tout le roialme avauntdit. Et qe ceux conseillers ne soient desore purveuz, faitz, ou esluz forsqe en parlement, si ne soit qe aucun de eux moerge ou feust remuez par cause resonable entre parlement et parlement, en quiel cas le roy, par advis de son conseil, y face et ordeigne a sa plesance d'autres suffisantz en lours lieux.

Responce a la primere requeste.
22. Nostre seignour le roy entendant la dite requeste estre honurables et bien profitables, sibien a luy mesmes come a son roialme avantdit, l'ad ottroiez, purveuz toutes voies qe chanceller, tresorer, gardein du prive seal, justices del un bank et del autre, et touz les autres officers du roi, purront faire et esploiter les busoignes qe touchent lours offices sanz la presence de tieux conseillers. Et nostre seignour le roy, pur certains causes qe luy moevent a present, par l'advis des seignours de parlement y voet avoir ceste present anee tantsoulement neof persones ses tieux conseillers, et les ad fait eslire en dit parlement; c'estassavoir, les evesqes de Londres, de Kardoill' et de Salesbirs, les contes de la March' et de Staff', meseignours Richard de Stafford et Henry le Scrop, baneretz, et messires Johan Deverose, et Hugh Segrave, bachilers. Et est ordenez qe les ditz neof conseillers issint esluz, et auxint les oept conseillers qe pur le temps serront, ne demurront en dit office forsqe soulement un an entier. Et celle an fini ne deveront mye celles mesmes persones estre re-esluz a celle office par deux ans proschein ensuantz.

23. Et auxint est ordene qe nul doun d'eschete, de garde, mariage, rente, ne d'autre rienz appurteigne al roy, ne \se/ face a nully des ditz conseillers durant le terme del dit an, si ne soit par commune assent de touz les ditz conseillers, ou la greindre partie d'iceulx: ne q'ils preignent rienz de nulle partie par promesse, n'autrement, s'il ne soit mangier et boire de petite value, ou autre chose qe ne purra resonablement estre dit louer, pur nulle busoigne qe serra mesnee ou tretee devant eux, sur peyne de rendre a la partie le double de ce q'ils einsi prendront, avec les damages et despenses par

Counsellors and their powers, etc.

21. With regard to the first request which the said commons made of our lord the king and the lords in parliament, namely that it would be to the honour of the king and the profit of all the kingdom - which is now being injured in many ways by divers adversities, both by the wars of France, Spain, Ireland, Guyenne, Brittany, and in all other parts by land and sea and other means, wherefoe the kingdom is now in greater danger than ever before, and the officers of the kingdom can no longer manage without assistance in such burdensome governance - if

[Col. b] the council of our said lord the king were to be increased by eight worthy persons of divers estates and degrees, who would be continually at hand to consult with the aforementioned officers on matters concerning the king and kingdom, the more so because our said lord the king was of so tender an age; in such a way that no serious and important matter of business should pass or be discharged without the assent and advice of all, and other lesser matters by the assent and advice of at least four, as the case requires, so that four of them shall be continually resident in the king's council: humbly desiring that it might please him now in this parliament to elect the same eight councillors from amongst the most able persons of the kingdom, and from amongst those who knew best, and could and would most diligently work and apply themselves to remedying the aforesaid troubles and dangers; and thereupon to notify the same commons of their names in this parliament, to the great comfort of them and all the aforesaid kingdom. And that those councillors should not henceforth be provided, appointed, or elected except in parliament, unless one of them were to die or be removed for good reason between parliaments, when the king, with the advice of his council, would appoint and ordain someone at his pleasure from amongst others worthy in their place.

The reply to the first request.
22. Our lord the king, considering the said request to be honourable and wholly profitable, both for himself as well as his aforesaid kingdom, agreed, providing under all circumstances that the chancellor, treasurer, keeper of the privy seal, justices of either Bench, and all other officers of the king, might conduct and carry out the business pertaining to their offices without the presence of such councillors. And our lord the king, for certain considerations which moved him at the time, by the advice of the lords in parliament wished to have in this present year only nine persons as his counsellors, and he elected them in the said parliament; namely, the bishops of London, Carlisle, and Salisbury, the earls of March and Stafford, and lords Richard Stafford and Henry le Scrope, bannerets, and messires John Devereux and Sir Hugh Segrave, gentlemen. And it was ordained that the said nine counsellors thus elected and also the eight counsellors of the future would not remain in office longer than one whole year. And at the end of this year those same persons ought not to be re-elected to this office within the space of two years.

23. It is also ordained that no gift of escheat, wardship, marriage, rent, nor anything else pertaining to the king shall be made to any of the said counsellors during the course of the said year, unless it be by the common consent of all the said councillors, or the majority of them: nor shall they take anything from any party by promise, or otherwise, unless it be to eat and drink and of small value, or anything else which cannot reasonably be said to be a bribe, for any matter which shall be considered or decided before them, on pain of rendering to the party double that which they have thus

tant suffertz, et a nostre seignour le roi six foitz atant come ils y averont pris. Et auxint est ordenez qe nul tiel conseiller n'empreigne ou sustiene aucune querelle par maintenance en paiis, n'aillours, sur tielle grevouse payne qe serra ordenez par nostre seignour le roy, del advis des seignours du roialme; la conissance et jurisdiction des quelles choses serra au roi mesmes, et a ses uncles d'Espaigne, de Cantebrigge et de Bukyngham, pris a eux aucuns prelatz et seignours a la suite de partie donante, et nemye devant autres persones, ne en autre manere. Et si nully se pleigne de tieu conseiller, et ne purra prover sa entente, encourge la peine darreinerement ordene par estatut en temps le roi Edward aiel nostre seignour le roy q'ore est, des accusours qi font pleinte au roi mesmes.[8]

Page iii-7
24. Et auxint est ordenez qe les ditz conseillers qe ore sont ou qi pur le temps serront esluz, ordenez, et assignez, soient serementz en presence du roi mesmes, de garder ceste ordinance et bien et loialment conseiller le roy en toutes choses qe serront moevez ou tretez devant eux selonc lours sen et poairs: et qe toute chose qe y doit estre tenuz en secret sanz descovrir, \ne descovriront a aucun estrange,/ autrement qe nel doivent faire par reson.
25. Et fait a remembrer qe puis apres les neof prelatz, contes, et autres dessusditz, issint esluz en conseil pur cest an, si furent devant le roy mesmes \jurrez et sermentez a ce faire,/ en presence des plusours seignours du parlement, en la forme avantdite.

Responce a les autres deux requestes.
26. Et quant a la secounde requeste de la commune, c'estassavoir, de nommer ou assigner en certain les persones quelles serront entour la persone du roy nostre seignour, les seignours du parlement /y\ respoignent et diont qe ce lour semble estre trope chargeante et dure requeste de mettre aucune persone entour /lour seignour\ Le roi autre qe ne plust bien a luy par plusours causes, ou de remuer aucun son officer ou servant si ne fust par la volentee \du dit roi/ expresse, et encores pur notable defaute en tieux officers ou servantz trovez ou provez; paront les seignours ne vorroient volunters de ce entremettre. Mais lour sembloit chose bien resonable, necessarie, et profitable au roi et al roialme, qe les chivalers, esquiers, et toutz autres entour le roi, feussent defenduz sur griefs peines, qe tantcome nostre seignour le roy soit issint de tendre age, ils ne feissent nulles pursuites devers le roi pur eulx mesmes, ne pur autres, de chose qe feust aucunement chargeant au roy ou al roialme, n'autrement, sinoun soulement pur benefices, baillies, ou autres offices, les queux nul damage purra avenir au roi ou al roialme avantditz. Qar y fust dit qe bien fust qe des gardes, mariages, eschetes, et autres tieux profitz, les ditz conseillers et officers se medleroient al profit du roi et del roialme. Et quant a la moderacion de la meignee le roi, et ses despenses en sa maisoun, sur les revenues del roialme tantsoulement en descharge de la commune, estoit auxint responduz qe les seignours ent verroient communer a bone deliberacion avec les grantz officers du dit hostiel: et si par lour advis ce purroit estre fait, salvant \l'estat et/L'onour du roi, ceste lour \autre/ requeste serroit ensement perfourme. Et quant a la tierce requeste et darreine, sembloit resonable chose a touz les seignours quant au present qe ce lour soit ottroiez et grantez.

accepted, together with the damages and expenses incurred as a result, and to our lord the king six times as much as they have received. And it is also ordained that no such counsellor sustain any dispute by maintenance in the country or elsewhere, on pain of a grievous penalty which shall be ordained by our lord the king with the advice of the lords of the kingdom; the cognizance and jurisdiction over which matters shall belong to the king himself, and his uncles of Spain, Cambridge, and Buckingham, calling upon certain prelates and lords at the suit of the donor party, and not before others, nor in any other way. And if anyone should complain of such a counsellor, and is unable to prove his accusation, let him incur the penalty lately ordained by statute in the time of King Edward [III], grandfather of our lord the present king, concerning accusers who complain to the king himself.

24. It is ordained, furthermore, that the said counsellors now in office or those who shall be elected, ordained, and appointed in time to come, shall be sworn in the presence of the same king, to keep this ordinance and advise the king well and loyally in all matters which are raised or discussed before them in accordance with their knowledge and abilities: and that all which ought to be kept secret without disclosure, should be disclosed to no other person without good reason.
25. Moreover, be it remembered that later the aforementioned nine prelates, earls, and others thus elected to the counsel for this year were so sworn before the king himself, in the presence of many lords of parliament, in the aforesaid manner.

The reply to the other two requests.
26. And as for the second request of the commons, that is to name or appoint precisely the persons who would be about the person of the king our lord, the lords of parliament replied saying that it seemed to them too burdensome and difficult to place anyone about their lord the king who did not wholly please him for various reasons, or to remove any of his officers or servants unless it was by the express wish of the said king, or because some notable failing had been found or proven in such officers of servants; under which circumstances the lords would not willingly intervene therein. But it seemed to them wholly reasonable, necessary, and profitable to the king and kingdom that the knights, squires, and all about the king, should be restrained on pain of grievous penalties, inasmuch as our lord the king was at so tender an age, from seeking anything from the king on their own behalf, or on behalf of others, which could in any way be charged to the king or kingdom, nor otherwise, except only for benefices, bailiwicks, or other offices from which no injury could result to the aforesaid king or kingdom. For it was said that it was much to the profit of the king and kingdom that the said counsellors and officers should not concern themselves with wardships, marriages, escheats, and other such profits. And as for the moderation of the king's retinue, and the expenses of his household, in relation to the revenues of the realm so far as they were at the charge of the commons, it was also replied that the lords would discuss that in detail with the chief officers of the said household: and so, with their advice let that be done, saving the estate and honour of the king, and that their other request might be thus carried out. And with regard to the third and last request, it seemed reasonable to all the lords for the present that it should be agreed and granted.

---

[8] Stat.38 Edw.3 St.1 c.9.

La graunt fait par la commune de .xme et .xvme.

27. Item, les seignours et communes du roialme d'Engleterre apperceivantz clerement le grant peril du roialme, q'est en point d'estre perduz (si Dieu n'y mette remede le pluis en haste), parmy les grandes guerres queux y sont moevez a l'encontre, et assez overtz chescune part, sibien par terre come par meer, dont il y est ore pluis a douter q unqes n'estoit devant. Et partant en aide de les despenses qe l'en faut mettre entour la governance de la guerre /du roialme,\ en resistence de tantz des enemys, et en socour et rescous del roialme avantdit, al aide nostre seignour ils grantent ore de lour liberale volentee a mesme nostre seignour le roi deux quinszimes par dehors citees et burghs, et deux dismes deinz mesmes les citees et burghs, a lever de lour biens, sibien c'estassavoir des seignours des villes come des religious, pur leurs biens provenantz de lours terres et tenementz purchacez ou appropriez puis l'an vintisme le roi Edward filz le roi Henry, et d'autres seculers gentz quelconqes, nully esperniant en celle partie, parentre cy et la chandeleure proschein venant, par autielles sommes de deniers et nemye greignours ne meindres come ont este acustumez estre levez des villes parmy le roialme /quant\ tielles dismes et quinszismes \ont este/ grantez, a une foitz ou a diverses foitz pur deux ans.

[Col. b] Empriantz humblement a lour seignour lige, et les autres seignours du parlement, qe sibien de ceux deniers, come des deniers de les dismes ore a granters par la clergie d'Engleterre, et auxint de les deniers provenantes de les subsides de leynes, feussent certains persones suffisantz assignez depar le roi d'estre tresoriers ou gardeins, au tiel effect qe celles deniers feussent tout entierment appliez a les despenses de la guerre, et nemye autre part par aucune voie. Et fait a remembrer qe celle requeste lour estoit ottroiez par le roi, salvant au roi entierment la /due\ anciene custume de demi marc des denszeins, et /dis\ soldz des foreins, due de chescun saak de leyne a passer hors du roialme, etc.. Et sur ce nostre seignour le roi fist assigner William Walworth et Johan Philypot, marchantz de Londres, d'estre gardeins des dites sommes, al oeps avantdit, et de faire loial accompte de lours resceites et issues par manere come serroit ordene par nostre seignour le roy et son dit grant conseil en resonable manere.

Tresoriers pur la guerre. .xv. mille*li.* du roi.

/ Et sur ce, par comandement nostre dit seignour le roi, les ditz William et Johan, pristrent lour charge,\\ et a ce faire loialment furent ils/ sermentez et jurrez devant le roy mesmes en plein parlement. Sauvez toutes foitz au roi q'il soit repaiez primerement de la somme par luy chevee et paiee a ceste darreine viage sur la meer, q'amonte pluis qe \a/ .xv. mille livres d'esterlings, dont le \roi/ est encores dettour as creditours.

Touchant les contes de March' et de Sarum.

28. Item, William de Montagu, conte de Salesbirs, mist avant en parlement une sa peticion, en la forme qe s'ensuit: A nostre seignour le roi monstre son lige William de Montagu, conte de Salesbirs, come mon tresredoute seignour le roi, vostre aiel, qe Dieux assoille, dona et granta a mon piere William de Montagu, nadgaires conte de Salesbirs, et a ses heires de son corps issantz, ove clause de garrantie, le chastell, ville et honor /de Dynbeygh,\ et les cantredes de Roos, Roweynok' et Kaiemer, et la commot de Dymnael, ove les appurtenances, en Gales, salvant ent la revercion a luy et a ses heirs, come pluis pleinement piert par ses chartres a mon dit piere ent faitz;[9] les queux chastiel, ville, honor,

---
[9] PRO SC8/67/3330.

The grant of a tenth and fifteenth made by the commons.

27. Also, the lords and commons of the kingdom of England, clearly perceiving the great danger to the kingdom, which was on the point of being lost, unless God supplied a remedy with utmost haste, on account of the great wars which were being waged against it from all sides, both by land and sea, the likes of which it is doubted had ever been seen before. And therefore, in support of the expenses which shall need to be invested in the conduct of the war, in resisting such enemies, and for the succour and rescue of the aforesaid kingdom, and to help our lord, they grant now of their own free will to our same lord the king two fifteenths from outside the cities and boroughs, and two tenths from within the same cities and boroughs, to be levied on their goods, namely, from the lords of the land as well as from religious, for their goods arising from their lands and tenements purchased or appropriated since the twentieth year of King Edward [I], son of King Henry [III] [1291-2], and from other secular persons whatsoever, none being spared in the matter, between now and Candlemas next [2 February 1378], for such sums of money, neither more nor less, as have customarily been levied from towns throughout the kingdom when such tenths and fifteenths have been granted, at some one time or on occasion for two years.

[Col. b] They pray most humbly of their liege lord, and the other lords of parliament, that from that money, as well as from money arising out of the tenths now to be granted by the clergy of England, and also from the money raised from the subsidies on wool, certain worthy persons might be appointed on behalf of the king to be treasurers or wardens, to the end that such money might be wholly devoted to the costs of the war, and not put to any other use. And be it remembered that this request was granted them by the king, saving to the king entirely the ancient custom of half a mark from denizens, and ten shillings from aliens, due on each sack of wool to be exported from the kingdom, et cetera. Whereupon, our lord the king caused William Walworth and John Philpot, merchants of London, to be appointed as keepers of the said sums, to the use aforesaid, and to render faithful account of their receipts and issues in the manner which shall be ordained by our lord the king and his said great counsel in a reasonable way.

War treasurers. £15,000 for the king.

And thereupon, by order of our said lord the king, the said William and John accepted their charge and were sworn and took oath before the king in full parliament to perform it loyally. Saving at all times to the king, that he be repaid first of all for the sum procured and paid by him for that last expedition at sea, which amounted to more than fifteen thousand pounds sterling, for which the king is still a debtor to the creditors.

Concerning the earls of March and Salisbury.

28. Also, William Montagu, earl of Salisbury, laid a petition before parliament, in the following form: To our lord the king, his liege William Montagu, earl of Salisbury shows that whereas my most redoubtable lord, the king, your grandfather, whom God absolve, gave and granted to my father William Montagu, late earl of Salisbury, and to the heirs of his body, with a clause of warranty, the castle, town and honour of Denbigh, and the cantreds of Rhos, Rhyfiniog, and Chymeirch, and the commote of Dinmael with their appurtenances in Wales, saving the reversion thereof to him and his heirs, as appears more fully in his charters made thereon to my said father; which castle, town,

cantredes et commot, ove les appartenances, Roger de Mortimer, piere Esmon contee q'ore est, come cousin et heir Roger de Mortimer, nadgairs conte de la March', demanda devers moy, par noun de la terre de Dynbeygh ove les appurtenances en Gales, par brief de scire facias devant mon dit seignour le roi, vostre aiel, en sa courte en bank le roi, de ent avoir execucioun. En quele plee jeo pria aide de mon dit seignour le roi, vostre aiel, par la cause avantdite. Et apres brief de procedendo sur ce grante, le dit Roger, le piere Esmon, recoveri devers moy par juggement les ditz chastiel, vielle[10] honour, cantredes, et commot, ove les appurtenances, par noun de la terre de Dynbeigh ove les appurtenances en Gales, come en le record et proces sur ce faitz pleinement appiert. En quelles record et proces, et auxint en juggement sur ceo renduz, il y ad errour: et le quiel juggement estoit execut, et moi ouste de ma possession, l'an de son regne .xxxviij.^{me}, dont jeo n'avoie unqes rien en value, coment qe mon dit seignour le roy, vostre aiel, par sa chartre avoit grante a ceo faire, come dessus est dit. Puis quele perte j'ay suy de parlement en parlement par diverses peticions de ent avoir remedie, et entre autres au parlement tenuz a Westm' le .viij.^{me} jour de Novembrer l'an de son regne .xlvime, une ma peticion sur ceste matiere estoit endosse en ceux paroles, Le roi ne voet mye qe l'eir qi est deinz age, et en sa garde, ne pierde rienz pur le temps q'il est en sa garde; mais quant il vient a son pleine age, sue, et droit serra fait al une partie et a l'autre.[11] Et ore le dit heir, c'estassavoir Esmon de Mortimer ore conte de la Marche, filz et heir mesme celuy Roger le cousin, est avenuz a son plein age.

Qe plese a vostre tresgraciouse seignourie commander de faire venir le dit [Page iii-8]
[Col. a] record et proces devant vous et vostre tressage conseil en ceste present parlement, et appellez le dit Esmon, et ceux qe sont en celles parties et appellers, et vewes et examinez les ditz record et proces, de moi ordener ent remedie selonc droit et resoun. Et si errour y puisse estre trovez, qe le dit juggement soit reversez et adnulliz, et moi restitut a ma possession ove les issues d'icelle, come la loy demande.

29. Quele peticion lue en mesme le parlement et entendue, dist fust et comandez en cest parlement, par les prelatz et seignours pierres du /parlement\ Lors esteantz en mesme le parlement, a monsire Johan de Cavendisshe, chivaler, chief justice nostre seignour le roy, q'ad les record et proces dont la dite peticion fait mencion en garde, q'il ferroit venir mesmes les record et proces en cest parlement sanz delay.[12] Luy quiel monsire Johan apporta en dit parlement mesmes les record et proces \entre/ diverses autres recordz et proces comprises en certaines roulles tachez ou consutz ensemble. Et sur ce le dit conte de Salesbirs assigna en parlement par especial et par bouche diverses errours estre contenuz en ycelles record et proces, empriant qe par celles errours et par autres quelles en ycelles record et proces purront estre trovez, le juggement y renduz soit reversez, et qe le dit Esmon de Mortymer, filz et heir le dit Roger le cousin, ore conte de la March', y fust garniz par brief de scire facias d'estre a proschein parlement d'oier les ditz record et proces, et de faire et resceivre ce /q'adonqes\ en celle partie serra agardez. Et celle brief luy estoit grantez illoeqes, et comandez estre fait retournable en dit proschein parlement. Et puis apres sur le fin du dit parlement, le dit monsire Johan

---
[10] Original ville.
[11] PRO SC8/67/3330.
[12] PRO SC8/18/862.

honour, cantreds, and commote, with their appurtenances, Roger Mortimer, father of Edmund, the present earl, as cousin and heir of Roger Mortimer, late earl of March, demanded of me, in the name of the land of Denbigh with appurtenances in Wales, by writ of scire facias, before my said lord the king, your grandfather, in the court of the king's bench, to have execution thereof. In which plea I prayed aid of my said lord the king, your grandfather, in the aforesaid cause. And after a writ of procedendo upon the grant, the said Roger, father of Edmund, recovered from me by judgment the said castle, town, honour, cantreds, and commote, with appurtenances, by name of the land of Denbigh with appurtenances, in Wales, as appears more fully in the record and process thereon. In which record and process, and also in the judgment thereon rendered, there was error: which judgment was executed, and in the thirty-eighth year of his reign [1364] I was ousted from my title, of which I still have nothing of value, although my said lord the king, your grandfather, by his charter had granted as said above. Since which loss I have sued from parliament to parliament in various petitions to receive remedy therefor, and at the parliament held at Westminster on 8 November in the forty-sixth year of his reign [1372], amongst other petitions, my petition on this matter was endorsed with these words, 'The king does not wish the heir, who is under age and in his wardship, to lose anything for the time during which he is a ward; but when he comes of age let him sue and right shall be done to one party or the other'. And now the heir, namely Edmund Mortimer, now earl of March, son and heir of the same Roger the cousin, has come of age.

May it please your most gracious lordship to order the said [Page iii-8]
[Col. a] record and process to be brought before you and your most wise council in this present parliament, and having summoned the said Edmund, and those who are parties to be summoned in the matter, and having viewed and examined the said record and process, to ordain remedy for me therein in accordance with right and reason. And if error be found there, that the said judgment shall be reversed and annulled, and myself restored to possession with the issues of the same, as the law demands.

29. The which petition having been read in the same parliament and understood, the prelates and lords the peers then present in the parliament instructed and ordered Sir John Cavendish, knight, chief justice of our lord the king, who had in his keeping the record and process of which the said petition made mention, to bring the same record and process before this parliament without delay. The which Sir John brought to the said parliament the same record and process along with various other records and processes contained in certain rolls attached or sewn together. Whereupon the said earl of Salisbury spoke in parliament, and particularly of divers errors in the record and process, praying that on account of those errors and others which might be found in the record and process, the judgment thereon rendered should be reversed, and that the said Edmund Mortimer, son and heir of the said Roger the cousin, now earl of March, be warned by writ of scire facias to be at the next parliament to hear the said record and process, and to hear and receive whatsoever would then be decided in this matter. And the writ was issued to him there, and made returnable in the said next parliament. And at the end of the said parliament the said John Cavendish, by order of the prelates and lords of parliament,

de Cavendish, par comandement des prelatz et seignours du parlement ent a luy fait, portast mesmes les record et proces en le bank le roi pur y demurer come en garde tanqe au dit proschein parlement. Et est ordenez et accordez qe mesmes les record et proces soient en dit proschein parlement par la cause avant dite.[13]

Membrane 4

Touchant les terres monsire Johan de Cobham.

30. Item, monsire Johan de Cobham, fitz la contesse mareschal, chivaler, mist avant en parlement une sa peticion, en la fourme qe s'ensuit:

A nostre tresredote et tresexcellent seignour le roi et soun sage counseille supplie le soun lige Johan de Cobham, filtz la countesse mareschalle, qe Dieux assoille, qe en oevre de charitee lour plese \de/ prendre regard et consideracion, qe le dit Johan fist nostre seignour le roi son heir, qe Dieu assoille, ove entente qe soun dite heritage deust avoir demorez a nostre dit seignour, qe Dieu assoille, et a ses heirs a la corone, et le dit Johan aver le meuthe este maintenuz et le plus honurablement, et ses dites terres avoir rejoye a terme de sa vie. Dount le dit Johan prie a nostre dit seignour le roi et a soun counseille q'ils voleient en tiele manere ordeigner qe le purpos et la volente du dit Johan puisse estre acomplie, en descharge de l'alme nostre dit seignour, qe Dieu assoille, et la reversion de son dite heritage demorer a la corone, et q'il puisse rejoyer son dite heritage a terme de sa vie, come parlez feust. La declaracioun de quelle bille suisdite est qe le dit Johan de Cobham dona, par la seisine de un anel, a noble roi Edward qe darrayn morust, qe Dieux assoille, al Thorne pres Sandewiche, /sur\ La passage du dit roi as parties de Fraunce, la reversion des manoirs de Wedonhull, Padenore, Chelwoldesbury, Haukesherde, Holt, Wedon' in Yevale, Drayton Beauchamp, Messeworth, Saundresdon, Helpesthrop, Rolvesham en counte de Buk; Colston en le counte de Northff'; et le bon manoir de Ardyngton en le counte de Berk'; Rolleston en le counte de Leyc'; a avoir et tener au dit roi et a ses heirs les ditz manoirs, demurantz a la corone pur touz jours, en presence le count de la Marche, monsire Richard

[Col. b] de la Vache, mestre Johan Branketre, notorie, queux sont a Dieux comaundez; sire Johan de Bukyngham evesque de Nichol, monsire Gy Bryan, qe sont en playne vie.

31. Et fait a remembrer qe le dit mestre Johan Banktre fuist requis par les parties suisdites de faire sur le doun suisdit un instrument, et ensi fist, q'est demurant par devers la court. La quele peticion fust responduce et endosse en ces paroles, c'estassaver, le roi voet qe les ditz evesque de Nichole et monsire Gy de Bryan, et autres si aucuns y soient aiantz notice sur cest fait, soient diligeaument examinez, et auxint qe le dit monsire Johan de Cobham soit sermentiz, et chargez en peril de s'alme, a dire, c'estassavoir chescun de eulx la pleine verite sur la matere comprise en ceste peticion. Et sur ceo, le dit evesqe de Nichole, present en ceo parlement, examinez et apposez par le conseil nostre seignour le roi illeoqes, dist et confessast expressement qe voirs estoit q'il estoit un des secretz d'encoste le dit roi l'aiel, qi Dieux assoille, et present avec mesme le roi pres de Sandwiz, le dit roi lors esteant illeoqes sur soun passage vers France, et oiast illeoqes, coment le dit monsire Johan de Cobham y donast et grantast a mesme le roi les manoirs, terres, et tenementz comprisez en sa dite peticion, pur demurer au dit roi et a ses heirs rois d'Engleterre perpetuelment. Et sur ceo le dit monsire Johan, al entente qe soun dit doun ent fust effectuel, y donast a mesme le roi un anel d'or, en lieu de seisine et plenere

---

carried the same record and process to the king's bench so that it might be kept there until the said next parliament. And it was ordained and agreed that the same record and process should be brought to the next parliament for the aforesaid reason.

Concerning the lands of Sir John Cobham.

30. Also, Sir John Cobham, son of the countess marshal, knight, laid a petition before parliament in the following form:

To our most redoubtable and most excellent lord the king and his wise council, his liege John Cobham, son of the countess marshal, whom God absolve, prays that as a charitable deed it might please them to bear in mind and consider that the said John made our lord the king, whom God absolve, his heir, to the intent that his inheritance might remain with our said lord the king, whom God absolve, and with his heirs and the crown, and the said John might be the better and more honourably maintained, and have the enjoyment of his said lands for life. Whereupon, the said John prayed of our said lord the king and his counsel that they would ordain in such manner that the said John's purpose and wish might be accomplished, in discharge of the soul of our said lord, whom God absolve, and that the reversion of his said inheritance might remain with the crown, and that he might enjoy the said inheritance for the term of his life, as was said. The declaration of which aforesaid bill was that the said John Cobham gave, by sesin of a ring, to the noble King Edward [III] who lately died and whom God absolve, at Thorney near Sandwich, on the said king's departure to the parts of France, the reversion of the manors of Weedon Hill, Pednor, Cholesbury, Hawkeshead, Holt, Weedon-in-the-Vale, Drayton Beauchamp, Marsworth, Saunderton, Helsthorpe, Rowsham, in the county of Buckingham, Colston in Norfolk, and the rich manor of Ardington in Berkshire, Rolleston in the county of Leicester; the said manors to have and to hold to the said king and his heirs, and remain with the crown forever, in the presence of the earl of March, Sir Richard

[Col. b] de la Vache, Master John Braintree, notary, who are now commended to God, and Sir John Buckingham, bishop of Lincoln, and Sir Guy Bryan, still living.

31. And be it remembered that the said Master John Braintree was required by the aforesaid parties to draw up a document upon the aforesaid gift, and so it was made, and remains in the court. The which petition was answered and endorsed in these words, namely, 'The king wills that the said bishop of Lincoln and Sir Guy Bryan, and others if there be any who have any knowledge of the matter, shall be closely questioned, and also that the said Sir John Cobham be sworn and charged, on peril of his soul, to say, and indeed each of them shall say, the whole truth on the matter dealt with in this petition'. Whereupon the said bishop of Lincoln, present in parliament, being questioned and examined there by the counsel of our lord the king, said and openly confessed that it was true that he was one of the privy counsellors to the said king, the grandfather, whom God absolve, and had been present with the same king near Sandwich, the said king being on his way to France, and he heard there how the said Sir John Cobham had given and granted to the same king the manors, lands, and tenements mentioned in the said petition, to remain with the said king and his royal heirs of England in perpetuity. And thereupon, the said Sir John, with the intent that his said gift should be effectual, gave the same king a

---

[13] PRO SC8/18/882.

possessioun d'yceulx. Item, le dit monsire Guy de Bryan, present en parlement, et semblablement examinez de mesme la matire, y confessast et dist q'il estoit avec le dit roi l'aiel, qe Dieux assoille, a Thoern' pres de Sandewiz, quant le dit roi estoit en celles marches sur soun dit passage vers France, et illeoqes le dit roi luy monstrat un anel d'or, endisant a luy cestes paroles, Monsire Guy, ne conoissez vous mye cest anelle? Qi dist qe noun. Et adonqes le dit roi luy dist qe avec mesme le anelle le dit monsire Johan de Cobham avoit fait le dit roi soun heir des ditz manoirs, terres, et tenementz. Et enoutre le dit monsire Guy y dist q'il \ne/ savoit mye dire en certayn si le dit monsire Johan donast et grantast issint al dit roi les ditz manoirs, terres et tenementz au dit roi, pur demurer a la dite coroune, ou nemye. Mes s'il ent fust tant constraint qe luy covenist jurer en peril de s'arme, et sur sa conscience, l'un ou l'autre, pluis tost et pluis volenters jurreroit qe la volente et l'entente le dit monsire Johan estoit sur le dit doun par luy ent fait au dit roi, qe celles manoirs demurreient a la dite coroune qe autrement.

Item, Helmyn Leget, esquier, present en dit parlement, examinez sur ceste matire, dist q'il estoit avec le dit roi pres de Sandwiz, mesme le roi lors esteant sur son dit passage vers Fraunce, quant le dit monsire Johan de Cobham donast et grantast touz ses terres al dit roi, a aver a luy et a ses heirs a touz jours; et sur ceo, par un anel d'or quiel le dit monsire Johan y donast au dit roi en lieu de seisine, il suisrendi a mesme le roi celles terres pur touz jours. Et enoultre le dit Johan jura et afferma illeoqes qe toutes voies sa entente estoit qe celles terres demurassent au dit roi et a ses /heirs\ de la coroune perpetuelment, et nulle parte ailours. Item, sire Richard de Ravensere, archidiakne de Nichole, examinez illeoqes dist q'il estoit present en la sale de Westm', en la place de la chauncellerie le dit roi illeoqes, avec sire Davy de Wollore, lors clerk des roules de mesme la chauncellerie, seignour Wauter Power, clerk et autres, a un certain temps grantement passez, quant le dit monsire Johan y vint, et lour dist en appert q'il avoit fait le dit roi soun heir de touz ses terres, pur demurer perpetuelment a la coroune d'Engleterre.

Item, monsire William de Montagu, count de Salesbirs, present en dit parlement, examinez si scieust rienz de cest fait, y dist et confessast q'il feust avec le dit roi a Sandewiz en soun hostiel illeoqes, *[Page iii-9]*
[Col. a] al dit temps, ou estoient alors avec le dit roi, le dit monsire Johan de Cobham et monsire Rauff de Spigurnell'; et oiast coment le dit monsire Rauf y dist au roi ces paroles, c'estassaver, Sire, vous estez grantment tenuz a monsire Johan de Cobham cy present, a cause q'il vous ad fait soun heir. Et mesme le roi y respondist, et dist qe ensy fust il, et promist d'estre a dit monsire Johan bone heir et bone seignour. Mais le dit count dist q'il ne savoit deposer ou dire en certain si le doun se fist einsy a la coroune, ou autrement. Item, puis apres le dit monsire Johan de Cobham estoit chargez en peril de s'arme, et jurrez sur les saintz evangles, devant certaines persones a ce assignez en parlement, a dire et conter la plaine verite sur ceste matire. Le quiel dist expressement par le serement q'il y avoit fait qe voirs est q'il donast et grantast a mesme le roi al dit lieu de Thoern' les manoirs, terres, et tenementz issint comprisez en sa dite peticion, a avoir et tenir au dit roi, et a ses heirs rois d'Engleterre pur touz jours; et en lieu de chartre et seisyne sur le dit doun fait, il donast au dit roi un soun anel d'or. Et cest doun fist il, il dist, especialment pur cause de grant amour et bone affeccion q'il portoit et avoit devers monseignour le prince, qi Dieux assoille, lors filz eisnez du dit roi; qar le dit monsire Johan amoit le dit prince souverainement et sur toute rienz, a ce q'il

gold ring, by way of seisin and full possession of the same. Also, the said Sir Guy Bryan, present in parliament, and similarly examined upon the same matter, there confessed and stated that he was with the said king the grandfather, whom God absolve, at Thorney near Sandwich, when the said king was in those parts on his said journey to France, and there the said king showed him a gold ring, saying to him these words, 'Sir Guy, do you know what ring this is?' To which he replied that he did not. And then the said king told him that with that same ring the said Sir John Cobham had made the said king his heir to the said manors, lands, and tenements. And further, the said Sir Guy confessed that he could not say for certain whether the said Sir John had thus given and granted to the said king the manors, lands, and tenements to remain with the said crown or not. But that if he were forced to swear to one or the other on peril of his soul, and on his conscience, then he would swear most readily and most willingly that the wish and intent of the said Sir John upon the said gift which he made to the said king had been that those manors should remain with the said crown and not otherwise.

Also, Helmyn Leget, squire, present in the said parliament, examined on the matter, said that he was with the said king near Sandwich, the said king then being on his aforementioned journey to France, when the said Sir John Cobham gave and granted all his lands to the said king, to have to him and his heirs in perpetuity; whereupon, by a gold ring which the said John gave to the said king symbolizing seisin, he surrendered those lands to the same king for ever. Furthermore, the said John swore and affirmed there that his full intention was that those lands should remain with the said king and his heirs to the crown in perpetuity, and with no one else. Also, Sir Richard Ravenser, archdeacon of Lincoln, said there on questioning that he had been present in the hall at Westminster, in the chancery of the said king, with Sir David Wooler, then clerk of the rolls in the same chancery, Sir Walter Power, clerk, and others, at some time long past, when the said Sir John appeared there and publicly announced that he had made the said king heir to all his lands, to remain for ever with the crown of England.

Also, Sir William Montagu, earl of Salisbury, present in the said parliament, being asked whether he knew anything of the deed, stated and confessed there that he had been with the king at Sandwich in his household there, *[Page iii-9]*
[Col. a] at the said time, where the said Sir John Cobham and Sir Ralph Spigurnell were with the said king; and they heard how the said Sir Ralph had spoken these words to the king, namely, 'Sire, you are greatly beholden to Sir John Cobham here present, because he has made you his heir'. And the same king replied, saying that so he was, and he promised to be a good heir and lord to the said Sir John. But the said earl confessed that he could neither affirm nor say for certain whether the gift had thus been made to the crown or otherwise. Also, when the said Sir John Cobham was charged on peril of his soul, and sworn on the Holy Gospels, before certain persons thereto assigned in parliament, to tell and report the whole truth in this matter, he said clearly by oath that he had made that it was true that he had given and granted to the same king at the said place called Thorney the manors, lands, and tenements thus mentioned in the said petition, to have and to hold to the said king, and his royal heirs of England for ever; and in place of a charter and seisin made on the said act, he gave to the said king his gold ring. And he made this gift, he said, especially because of the great love and affection he felt and bore towards my lord the prince, whom God absolve, then the said king's oldest son; because the said Sir John loved the said prince in the highest degree

dist. Et auxint il le fist, pur ceo qe le dit roi et son dit filz luy aideroient d'autre part, et maintendroient le mieltz pur le temps lors avenir, sanz ceo q'il fist unqes bargaigne ou autre covenant avec le dit roi, ou nul des soens, par voie d'achat ou autrement, forsqe soulement d'encrestre par son dit doun pur les causes dessusdites la coroune d'Engleterre, dont le \dit/ prince lors estoit heir apparant. Et enoultre il dist par son dit serement qe lendemayn proschein apres le dit doun issint fait au dit roi - dont mesme le roi y /se\Loiast grantement, et promist par tant de aider le dit Johan et luy maintener en tout droit et bien - si donast mesme le roi au dit Johan touz les ditz manoirs, terres, et tenementz avec leurs appurtenaunces, a avoir et tenir au dit Johan pur terme de sa vie tantsoulement, salvant ent la reversion a dit roi et ses heirs rois d'Engleterre. Et sur ce le dit monsire Johan resceut le dit doun le roi, et se atturnast illeoqes tantost au dit roi des ditz manoirs par un florein d'or de vint deniers. Queux attornement et florein monsire Rauf Spigurnell, lors un des chivalers le roi, y resceut en noun del dit roi: et issint ent fust le dit roi seisiz de la reversion entour six ans, sanz autre fait ou escript entre eux ent fait. Et oultre il dist qe coment qe apres \il/ estoit constreint par aucunes lors privez entour le dit roi de ent faire sa chartre de feoffement au dit roi, a aver a luy et a ces heirs en fee simple (disantz a luy qe ce fust la volente du dit roi, et sur ceo mesme la chartre conoistre en place de record) toutes voies, il ent fist sa protestation qe en veritee ses purpos et voluntee estoient toutdys un, c'estassavoir, qe celles manoirs demurroient a la coroune d'Engleterre perpetuelment come sa dite peticion pleinement purporte. Et puis apres toutes cestes choses mises en escript par manere qe dessus est dit, et celle escripture, et les dites depositions oiez, veuez, et examinez par les justices, serjeantz le roi, et autres sages en dit parlement, si fust dit et recordez en parlement par mesmes les justices qe un susrendre de terre par un tiel anel, gaunt, corn, ou autre semblable chose donee a aucune persone, sanz autre fait ou escript, si fust assez valable et forcible en la ley: et moement quant tiel susrendre se fist a la persone du roi mesmes, de qi deinz le roialme toute temporaltee procede, et par mature toute chose legerement si retourne a sa droite mature dont il vint, et pluis tost qe autre part. Et enoultre y fust dit en parlement qe bone et diligente enquerre fust fait sur ceste matire et les dependences d'ycelles pur nostre seignour le roi en counte de Kent, ou le dit doun se fist, come dessus est dit, par bones et suffisantz gentz, et celle enqeste retourne

[Col. b] en la chauncellerie, et les parties appellez illeoqes, feust fait droit, si bien pur le roi, come pur mesmes les parties.

Membrane 5
Fitz Hugh et Chichestre.
32. Item, William filz Hugh, orfevre de Londres, mist avant en parlement une bille en la forme qe s'ensuit: a tresexcellent et tresnoble seignour le roy et a son treshonure et tressage conseil monstrent les poveres communes de la mistier d'orfeverye en la citee de Londres, coment Johan Chichestre, Johan Botesham, et plusours autres grantz et riches orefevres de mesme la mystier en mesme la citee, par lour compassement et sotile engyne, deceyvablement firont plusours gentz de les ditz communes enseller severalment diverses obligaciouns: et ceux qi refuserent de ce faire furent pris et emprisonez, et en peril de mort par grevouse manace des ditz grantz et riches orfevres, tanq'ils avoient ensellez severalment diverses obligaciouns come lours poveres compaignons avoient fait devant, a cause qe les ditz poveres

and above all else, as he said. Moreover he did it, because the said king and his said son would help him for their part, and support him well in time to come, without his having to make any other bargain or covenant with the king, or any of his men, by way of purchase or otherwise, except only to increase by his said gift and for the aforementioned reasons the crown of England, to which the said prince was then heir apparent. And further, he said on his oath that the day after the said gift was thus made to the king - with which the same king was greatly pleased, and promised on account of it to help the said John and well maintain him in all respects - so the king himself gave the said John all the said manors, lands, and tenements, with their appurtenances, for the said John to have and hold for the term of his life only, saving the reversion of them to the said king and his royal heirs of England. Whereupon, the said John recovered the said gift from the king, and himself attorned there to the said king for the said manors by one gold florin worth twenty pence. Which attornment and florin Sir Ralph Spigurnell, then one of the king's knights, received in the name of the said king: and thus the said king was seised of the reversion for about six years, without any other act or writing being made between them thereon. Furthermore, he said that although he was subsequently compelled by certain of the king's close advisers to make a charter of enfeoffment thereon to the said king, for him and his heirs to hold it in fee-simple, saying to him that this was the wish of the said king, and furthermore that the same charter would stand by way of a record, nevertheless, he made protestation thereon that his true purpose and wish had always been one, namely that these manors should fall to the crown of England in perpetuity as his said petition plainly shows. Then all these matters, having been written down in the aforesaid manner, and that writing and the said depositions having been heard, seen and examined by the justices, the king's serjeants, and other wise men of the said parliament, so it was declared and recorded in parliament by the same justices that a surrender of land by such a ring, glove, horn, or other such object being given to any one, without any other act or writing, was entirely valid and enforceable in law: and the more so when surrender is made to the person of the king himself, from whom all temporalities in the realm proceed, thus everything naturally returns in its own time to the origin from which it came, and the sooner to him. Moreover, it was said in parliament that a good and diligent inquest had been made into the matter and issues related to the same on behalf of our lord the king in Kent, where the said gift was made, as said above, by good and worthy men, and the inquest was returned

[Col. b] to the chancery, and the parties having been summoned there, right was done, both for the king and for the same parties.

Fitz Hugh and Chichester.
32. Also, William fitz Hugh, goldsmith of London, laid a bill before parliament in the following form: To the most excellent and most noble lord the king and to his most honoured and most wise counsel, the poor commons of the mistery of goldsmithery in the city of London that whereas John Chichester, John Botesham, and many other great and rich goldsmiths of the same mistery in the same city through their machinations and subtle ingenuity, deceitfully incited many of the said commons severally to seal divers bonds: and those who refused to do so were seized and imprisoned, and put in fear of their lives by the threats of the said rich and important goldsmiths, until they had severally sealed divers bonds as their poor companions had in the past, with the result that the said poor goldsmiths are unable to work, buy,

orefevres ne deussent overer, achater, ne vendre a nulle mercer, coteller, jualer, uphalder, ne a nul autre denszein ne forein, nul rienz de lour overeigne sinoun q'ils le vendissent a treble value; ne qe nul de eux deust porter vessell, ceynture, n'autre chose d'or ne d'argent, a nul seignour, dame, ne a nul autre, pur lour profit faire. Et s'ils firent, qe la payne compris deinz les obligacions encurreroit sur eux come devant le mair, viscontz, et aldermans de la dite citee, par la confessioun des ditz riches orfevres feust prove. Sur quel debat, non resonablement issint moeve, par bon mediacioun et advis de dit mair, et des plusours aldermans de la citee, les ditz riches et poveres orefevres soy mistrent en arbitrement des trois bones hommes, pur final acord des touz les debatz et querelle entre eux moevez. Les queux arbitrours assenterent sur certeins pointz rehercez a les parties susditz, et ordeignerent mesmes les pointz estre affermez et enrollez en la Guyhalle de Londres, pur final acord tenir sanz contredit as touz jours: et sur ce les parties susdites s'enterbaiserent. Mais ore a celle acord les ditz riches orefevres ne voillent assenter, ne suffrer qe les ditz pointz soient enrollez et tenuz come les ditz arbitrours ordeignerent. Et outre ce, par lour procurement plusours mesfeisours ont de jour en autre plusours de les ditz poveres communers en agait de tuer, qe Dieu defende; et auxi purchacer un novelle chartre, encountre le dit acord, et en defesance et annyntissement des ditz communers.

Plese a vostre tresgraciouse seignourie ordeigner et comander qe la dite acord pust estre afferme et tenuz finalment. Et qe chartre, ne nulle autre chose, soit grante a eux, en prejudice et annyntissement de les ditz poveres orfevres, pur Dieu, et en oevre de charitee.

33. Et sur ce les ditz Johan Chichestre et Johan Botesham, et plusours autres orfevres de Londres vindrent en parlement, et avoient oie de la dite bille. Et tantost estoit demandez en parlement del dit William filz Hugh, s'il vorroit maintenir la dite bille, et trover plegge de y faire et resceivre ce qe la loy demande. Qi dist qe si voloit il; et puis apres, pur ce q'il ne poait trover les plegges, einz guerpist outrement la dite bille, si fust le dit William filtz Hugh comandez a la tour, par agard des seignours du parlement.

Brest en Bretaigne.
34. Item, fait a remembrer qe un petit roulle, contenante .xiiii. articles faitz sur certains covenances taillez et parles parentre nostre seignour le roy et son trescher frere Johan duc de Bretaigne, touchant les chastiel et seignourie de Brest en Bretaigne, estoit lue en parlement devant les seignours. Et les seignours s'accorderent bien a toutes choses y comprises, excepte tantsoulement qe y fust dit qe l'en vorroit aviser del .xij.^{me} article, touchant les alliances, etc., et qe bon fust qe celles alliances feussent veues et examinez *[Page iii-10]*

[Col. a] devant le grant conseil a bone deliberation. La quelle roulle demoert en filace avec les petitions de parlement.

Hauleye et Shakell.
35. Item, fait a remembrer qe pur ce qe /Robert\ Hauleye et /Johan\ Shakell', esquiers, qi avoient en garde le fitz del conte de Dene, Espaignard, et prisoner pris a la bataille de Nazare (en quiel prisoner certains persones clayment envers eux droit et part, come plius au plein appiert par certains plees ent pendantz devant conestable et mareschalle, encores nient discusez) avoient fait esloigner mesme le prisoner pendantz celles plees, par tielle manere, qe le roy nostre seignour qi y ad grant interesse par plusours causes, n'auxint aucun autre aiant droit en dit prisoner, si juggement y passast

or sell to any mercer, cutler, jeweller, upholsterer, or any other denizen or foreigner any of their work unless they can sell it on at triple its value; nor dare any one of them take a vessel, belt, or other gold or silver object to any lord, lady, or anyone else to make a profit. And if they do so they incur the penalty contained in the bonds which are enforced by the rich goldsmiths as though they had been proved before the mayor, sheriffs, and aldermen. Upon which quarrel, unjustly moved, by the good intervention and advice of the said mayor and many aldermen of the said city, the said rich and poor goldsmiths submitted themselves to the arbitration of three good men, for the final settlement of all the disputes and contentions arising between them. Which arbitrators agreed on certain points set out by the aforesaid parties, and ordained that the same points be confirmed and enrolled in the Guildhall in London, as a final agreement to be preserved forever without contravention: upon which the aforesaid parties embraced each other. Yet to this agreement the said rich goldsmiths will not now assent, nor suffer the said points to be enrolled and upheld as the said arbitrators ordained. And beyond that, by their procurement, many malefactors have, from one day to the next, sought to kill many of the poor commons, which God forbid; and also to purchase a new charter, contradicting the said agreement, and to the destruction and ruin of the said commons.

May it please your most gracious lordship to ordain and command that the said agreement shall be conclusively confirmed and upheld. And that no charter, nor anything else, shall be granted to them, which is prejudicial or harmful to the said poor goldsmiths, for God and by way of charity.

33. Whereupon, the said John Chichester, and John Botesham, and many other goldsmiths of London came to parliament, and heard the said bill. And it was immediately asked in parliament of the said William fitz Hugh, whether he wished to maintain the said bill, and find a pledge to do and accept what law required. He said that he so wished; yet later, because he could not find the pledges, and entirely abandoned the said bill, the said William fitz Hugh was sent to the Tower, by the decision of the lords of parliament.

Brest in Brittany.
34. Also, be it remembered that a small roll, containing fourteen articles concerning certain covenants debated and discussed between our lord the king and his most beloved brother John, duke of Brittany, touching the castle and lordship of Brest in Brittany, was read in parliament before the lords. And the lords readily agreed to all items contained in it, except only that it was said that they wished to discuss the twelfth article, touching alliances, etc., and that it would be well that those alliances were reviewed and examined *[Page iii-10]*
[Col. a] before the great counsel and thoroughly discussed. Which roll remains in the file containing the petitions of parliament.

Hauley and Shakell.
35. Also, be it remembered that whereas Robert Hauley and John Shakell, esquires, who have in their keeping the son of the count of Denia, a Spaniard, and prisoner captured at the battle of Najera (to which prisoner certain persons lay claim to a right and share, as fully appears in certain pleas thereon pending before the constable and marshal, and not yet heard) have caused the same prisoner to be removed during those pleas, in such a way that neither the king our lord who has a great interest in the matter for many reasons, nor indeed any other having any right to the said prisoner, if judgment

encontre les ditz Hauleye et Shakell', purront savoir ou mesme le prisoner est devenuz, refusent en parlement a faire venir le dit prisoner a nostre seignour le roy, \de/L'avoir come en garde al oeps de celluy ou de ceux qi y ad le meillour droit a mesme le prisoner, sont comandez a le tour de Londres, etc..

Gascoigns.
36. Item, est assentuz et accordez qe touz marchantz, Gascoigns et Engleys, purront franchement faire et mesner hors du roialme en Gascoigne, et au Brest, as amys du roy nostre seignour illoeqes, lour furmage, et touz autres vivres et vitailles; et auxint /ceyntures, bonises\ et cappes de leyne, pointz, lanyers, sue, cornes, et toutz autres tielles menuez marchandises, pur ent y achater et amesner deinz le roialme, nientcontresteant aucune ordinance de l'estaple de Caleys fait a contraire. Purveuz toutes voies qe, sur payne de forfaiture d'ycelles marchandies, ils ne les facent amesner aillours hors del dit roialme vers le est ou le northe qe au dit estaple de Caleys, par aucune voie.

L'estaple de Quenesburgh'.
37. Item, est assentuz qe l'estaple des leynes, etc., q'estoit tenuz a Quenesburgh' soit tenuz a la ville de Sandewiz; et qe l'estaple avantdite soit de tout oustez et remuez de mesme la ville de Quenesburgh'.
Membrane 6[14]
Gomeniz, Weston'.
38. Item, par la ou supplie est par les communes qe touz ceux q'ont renduz et perduz chastelx ou villes par dela par verray defaute des capitains puissent estre a response a ceste parlement, et solonc lour desert fortement punis par agard des seignours et baronage, eschievant le malvoise ensample q'ils ount donez as autres qe sont gardeins des villes et chastelx; comande est a sire Alein de Buxhull', conestable del tour de Loundres, qe y face venir devant les seignours en parlement a Westm', le vendredy le .xxvij. jour de Novembre, l'an suisdit, Johan Sire de Gomenys et William de Weston', pris et detenuz en la dite tour a comandement nostre seignour le roi, par cause q'ils avoient perduz et renduz tielx chastelx et villes as enemys nostre seignour le roi, pur y respondre sur les articles qe lour serront surmys par la dite cause depart nostre seignour le roi. A quel jour de vendredy, les ditz Johan et William amesnes par le dit conestable devant les seignours avantditz, en plein parlement seantz en la blaunke chambre, ils sont severalment aresonez a comandement des ditz seignours par Sire Richard le Scrop', chivaler, seneschal del hostel nostre seignour le roi, en manere com s'ensuyt: William de Weston', vous empristez de lui trespuissant prince, qe Dieux assoille, sire Edward, jadys roi d'Engleterre, aiel nostre seignour le roi q'ore est, de sauvement garder a lui et a ses heirs rois d'Engleterre le chastel de Outhrewyk, sanz le susrendre a ascuny sinon au dit aiel ou a ses ditz heirs, ou par comandement de lui ou de ses ditz heirs; l'avez vous, William, q'estes homme liege nostre seignour le roi, en temps de mesme nostre seignour le roi q'ore est, verray heir au dit aiel, delivers et susrenduz as enemys nostre seignour le roi, sanz comandement de lui, en arrerisement de lui
[Col. b] et de sa corone, et del estat de soun roialme d'Engleterre, encontre vostre ligeance et emprise suisdiz: qe veullez a ceo dire?
39. Sur quoi le dit William disast q'il avoit mys ses responsez en escript, et myst avant une cedule contenauntz plusours

were to be passed against the said Hauley and Shakell, know where the same prisoner is kept; and refusing in parliament to bring the said prisoner to our lord the king, so that he might be kept under guard for the king's purpose or that of whomsoever had most right to the same prisoner, they were ordered to the Tower of London, etc.

Gascons.
36. Also, it was assented and agreed that all merchants, Gascon and English, might freely make and carry outside the kingdom to Gascony, and to Brest, to the friends of our lord the king there, their cheese, and all other provisions and victuals; as well as belts, bonnets and caps of wool, points, lanyards, towels, horn, and all other such small items of merchandise, to be bought there and carried into the kingdom, notwithstanding any ordinance concerning the staple of Calais made to the contrary. Provided at all times that, on pain of forfeiture of the same merchandise, they do not cause them to be carried anywhere else outside the said kingdom towards the east or north except to the said staple of Calais, by any means.

The staple of Queenborough.
37. Also, it was agreed that the staple of wools, etc., which was held at Queenborough should be held at the town of Sandwich; and that the aforesaid staple should be utterly ousted and removed from the same town of Queenborough.

Gommegnies, Weston.
38. Also, whereas it was requested by the commons that all those who had surrendered and lost castles or towns overseas through their failings as captains should be brought to answer in this parliament, and according to their desert be strictly punished by the decision of the lords and barons, to avoid the evil example they have set for others who are keepers of towns and castles; it was ordered of Sir Alan Buxhill, constable of the Tower of London, that he cause to be brought before the lords in parliament at Westminster, on Friday 27 November in the aforesaid year [1377], John, lord of Gommegnies, and William Weston, taken and detained in the said Tower at the command of our lord the king, because they had lost and surrendered such castles and towns to the enemies of our lord the king, there to answer to the articles which would be charged against them for that said reason on behalf of our lord the king. On which Friday, the said John and William, led by the said constable before the aforesaid lords in full parliament seated in the white chamber, were individually questioned on the orders of the said lords by Sir Richard le Scrope, knight, steward of the household of our lord the king, in the following manner: 'William Weston, you were appointed by the most high prince, whom God absolve, the lord Edward [III], lately king of England, grandfather of our lord the present king, safely to keep for him and his royal heirs of England the castle of Audruicq, and to yield it to none unless to the said grandfather or his said heirs, or by order of him or his said heirs; yet you, William, a liegeman of our lord the king, in the time of our same lord the present king, true heir of the said grandfather, delivered and surrendered it to the enemies of our lord the king, without his orders, to the injury of the king
[Col. b] and his crown, and of the estate of his kingdom of England, contrary to your allegiance and aforesaid undertaking: what have you to say thereto?'
39. To which the said William replied that he had submitted his answers in writing, and delivered a schedule containing

---
[14] The rest of membrane 5 has been left blank.

choses contenuz deinz ycelle. Et veuez et lieuz la dite cedule en plein parlement, surce lui fuist demande par le dit seneschal, si y myst avant ceste cedule pur final respons en cel partie, ou noun. Et sur ceo le dit William priast la dite cedule lui estre rebaille, et le mettroit einz sa respons finale: /quele\ cedule par la dite cause lui estoit reballe. Et puis apres le dit William myst avant la dite cedule, ove un addicion mys en ycelle, en plein parlement pur finale respons en celle partie; le tenour de quel cedule est tiel come s'ensuyt.

A tressage conseil nostre seignour le roi, et as autres nobles et communes du parlement, supplie et monstre William de Weston' qe com il soit accuse de ceo qe leu deust malvoisement aver rendu le chastel de Outhrewyk, le quel il avoit en gard du baille et assignement nostre seignour le roi, plese a vostre sage et just discrecion avoir de ceo le dit William excuse, pur les causes q'ensuent: primerement, vous plese remembrer qe com le dit William estoit nadgairs garni par un espye qe un grant poair des enemys vindroit sur lui pur le dit chastel asseger, ove tresgraundes et tresgrevouses ordinances; sur quoi le dit William maintenaunt par son attourne et par ses lettres requist au dit conseil q'il lour pluist de forcer le dit chastel du pluis des gentz pur la defense et la sauve garde d'ycelle, eiant regard qe la garnisoun du dit chastel q'adunqe estoit ne fuist my suffisant de la moyte pur la multitude de si grande force en si /large\ place resister, mays au finale nepurtant il n'en poiat du dit conseil ascun socour avoir. Et ensi le dit William, non pas en sa defaute, estoit lesse sanz suffisancz des gentz pur le dit chastel long temps garder et defendre: dont ils vous supplie qe prendre envuillez juste et benigne consideracion.

Item, plese vous savoir, coment par un lundy, houre de prime, viendront les enemys pur le dit chastel asseger, a la nombre entour .ii m. et .vi c. hommez d'armez, et .vii c. arblasters de Genevoys, ovesqe .v m. de la commune du pays eiantz .ix. grosses cannons, un grant engyn, et un trebuchet outre ascun mesure qe l'en avoit unqes veeu par devaunt en celles marches; et mesme l'oure maintenaunt grande partie des gentz d'armes et arblasters avauntditz vindront devaunt les portez pur le dit chastel assailler, et a ceo point estoit un chivaler de lour tuez, lui quel fuit cosyn au seignour de Clisson', a ce qe l'endisoit, et plousurs autres auci feuront adonqes qe tuez qe naufrez: et deins brief temps apres ils comenceront a traire et getter de lour canons et engyns, et ensi continueront de jour en autre lour assalt, c'esteassaver marsdy, meskerdy, jeody, et feuront adonqes les murs et les mesons du dit chastel routez et partusez en plousours lieux, et ils avoient auci par force trenche les fosses du dit chastel en troys lieux siqe l'eaue s'estoit del tout issue, et en cel nuyt vynt une grande partie d'eaux, et par force firont soier et abatre les barrers, si qe lendemain qe feuist vendredy ils vindront au point de jour ove tout lour effors pur le dit chastel assailler, mays ove l'aide de Dieu ils feurent encore hostez par force de lour assalt, et d'un part et d'autre y avoit des mortz et des blesces. Et mesme le jour le maresschal de Burgoyne parla au dit William et as autres del dit chastel rendre: sur qoi eantz consideracion a ceo qe le dit chastel ne se poiat tenir, qoi pur la petitesse des gentz, qoi pur ce qe les murs en plousours lieux feurent enfeblez par lour mervaillouses ordinances, trete fuist ovesqe les seignours au fyn qe le dit William ovesqe ses compaignons s'aviseroient contre lendimain, et ensi alours se departiront. Item, mesme celui nuyt les enemys firont attrere toutez lours ordinances des engins, trebuchett, et canons, et des fagotz et eschielx, *[Page iii-11]*

many things included therein. And the said schedule having been seen and read in full parliament, it was asked of him by the said steward, whether he had submitted that schedule as his final reply in the matter or not. Whereupon the said William asked that the said schedule be returned to him, that he might add to it his final reply: whereupon the schedule was returned to him. And later the said William submitted the said schedule to parliament with an addition inserted in the same, as his final reply in the matter; the tenor of which schedule is as follows:

'To the most wise council of our lord the king, and to the other lords and commons of parliament, William Weston prays and shows that whereas he is accused of having wickedly surrendered the castle of Audruicq, which he had in his keeping upon the authority and appointment of our lord the king, may it please your wise and just discretion to hold the said William excused for the following reasons: first, may it please you to remember that whereas the said William was lately warned by a spy that a great enemy force was descending on him to besiege the said castle, with great and formidable ordnance; on hearing which the said William immediately prayed the said council through his attorney and by letters that it should please them to reinforce the said castle with more men for the defence and safeguard of the same, bearing in mind that the garrison of the said castle then in place was not enough by half to resist the number of so great a force in so large a place, but ultimately, he was unable to gain any help from the said council. And so the said William, not through his own fault, was left without a sufficient number of men to guard and defend the said castle for any length of time: wherefore he prays you to take that into just and kindly consideration.

Also, may it please you to know that on a certain Monday, at the hour of prime, the enemies arrived to besiege the said castle, to the number of some 2,600 men-at-arms, and 700 Genoese crossbowmen, along with 5,000 of the commons of the country having nine great guns, a great siege-engine, and a trebuchet beyond anything which had been seen before in those parts; and at the same time a large number of the aforesaid men-at-arms and crossbowmen appeared before the gates to besiege the said castle, and at that point a knight of theirs was killed, who was said to be a cousin of the lord of Clisson, and many others were likewise killed or wounded: and shortly after they began to train and fire their guns, and so continued their attack from one day to the next, namely on Tuesday, Wednesday, and Thursday, and thereupon the walls and buildings of the said castle were broken and breached in many places, and they had also dug into the castle's ditches in three places so that all the water drained away, and that night a great party of them came, and forcefully hacked and battered the gates, and on the next day, which was a Friday they came at daybreak with their entire force to attack the said castle, but with God's aid they were again forcibly thwarted in their assault, and there were dead and wounded on all sides. On the same day the marshal of Burgundy called upon the said William and the others in the said castle to surrender: whereupon, considering that the said castle could not hold out, because of its small garrison, and because the walls had been weakened in many places by their wondrous artillery, an agreement was reached with the lords that the said William would discuss matters with his companions before the next day, and then they left. Also, on that same night the enemies caused all their siege-engines, trebuchets, and guns to be dragged, and their faggots and ladders *[Page iii-11]*

[Col. a] ove tout plain des autres, jusqes pres de fosse du chastel avauntdit, et lendemain, qe feust samady, ils se firont tout plainement ordiner d'assailler la place, et /lors\ primerement ils manderont un herald au dit William, pur savoir si le dit chastel lour serroit rendu ou noun.

Sur quoi le dit William, par l'avys des plussages de ses compaignons, eiant consideration coment la dit place estoit de lour ordinances destruyt et enfebli, et auci q'ils feuront poi de gent pur la defense, a ceo qe .xii. de lour compaignons feurent a celle temps qe mortz qe naufrez qe malades, siqe il ne remyst des toutz gentz de la garnisoun en saunte pur soi defendre forsqe soulement .xxxviij. et pur ceo, par commune assent le dit chastel, qe pluis ne se poet tenir, fuist par force renduz, pur les vies d'ommes et lours biens salver. Et qe toutez cestez choses avantditz sont verraiez le dit William se mettra a soun proeve solonc voz discretz ordinances. Item, fait a remembrer qe quant le dit chastel fuist ensi renduz, come par desuis est dit, certeins gentz de Franceys bargaineront ovesqe le dit William pur ses vitailles illoeqes acheter, ensemblement ovesqe certeignes prisoners queux le dit William tenoit deins le dit chastel emprisonez; pur queux choses il rescut de lour pur soun paiement .m. et cynk centz francs, des queux il paia a ses compaignons, pur partie de lour gages qe lour fuist a derere d'un quarter del an et demi, .vi.^{c} .lxxviij. francs. Item, puis fuist paie a Caloys pur vitailles du dit chastel avaunt ceo temps dues, .iiij.^{c} et .xlij. francs. Item, pur la passage du dit William et de ses compaignons tanq'en Engleterre auxi, et pur les despenses du dit William esteant a Caloys, .cxxxv. francs. Et pur ce supplie le dit William q'eiant regard de justice et benignite, coment par enviouse suggestion il ad estee contre toutz reisoun accuse, dont de soun estate et de soun noun par grant pecche des mesdisantz il est trope arieriz; eiant auci consideracion, coment de ses propres biens il ad pur greynour partie paie ses compaygnons pur lours feedz qe lour fuit due, come est desusdit; et auxi des grandes costages q'il ad eeu devaunt ceo temps pur le dit chastel vitailler, dont il ad baille ses obligacions en plusours lieux, et doit graundes sommes, si q'il est des toutz partz deffait si vostre juste benignitee ne lui socour. Vous plese, pur Dieu, et pur peti, d'ordeigner ensi pur lui, si q'il purra parmy vostre discrete noblesce recoverir soun estat et ses biens. Item, le dit William Weston' monstre, coment le primer jour quant les enemys vindront devaunt Arde, il s'en ala en haste a Caloys devers le capitaine, et lui pria de pluis de socour et aide des gentz pur meutz garder soun fort de Outhewyk, et deffendre si les enemys y venissent; et le capitaigne lui respondist brefment q'il ne lui deliverast ne baillerast socour ne aide a dit temps, pur ceo q'il soi doutoit mesmes qe les enemys venissent devaunt la ville de Caloys.

40. Et veuez et lieuz la dit cedule en plein parlement, meintenaunt apres estoit le dit Johan aresonez illoeqes par le dit seneschal en la manere qe s'ensuyt: Johan sire de Gomenys, vous empristes de lui trespuissant prince, qe Dieux assoille, sire Edward jadys roi d'Engleterre, aiel nostre seignour le roi q'ore est, de sauvement garder a lui et a ses heirs rois d'Engleterre, les ville et chastel de Arde, sanz les susrendre a ascuny sinoun au dit aiel, ou a ses ditz heirs, ou par comandement de lui ou de ses ditz heirs; les avetz vous, sire de Gomenys, en temps de nostre seignour le roi q'ore est, verray heir au dit aiel, delivers et susrenduz as enemys nostre seignour le roi, sanz comandement de lui, en arrerisement de lui et de sa corone et del estate de soun roialme d'Engleterre, encontre vostre emprise suisdit: qe veullez a ceo dire? Sur qoi disast le dit Johan qe les ditz ville et chastel de Arde estoisent si febles, q'il ne les poast bien garder contre si grant

[Col. a] with everything else, close to the ditch of the aforesaid castle, and the next day, which was a Saturday, they drew up everything to assault the place, but first they sent a herald to the said William, to see whether the said castle would be surrendered to them or not.

Whereupon, the said William, on the advice of his wisest companions, considering that the said place had been damaged and weakened by their machines, and also that there were very few to defend it, for twelve of their companions were at that time either dead, wounded, or sick, so that of all the men in the garrison he had only thirty-eight fit to defend it, by common consent decided that the said castle, which could no longer be held, should necessarily be surrendered, to save the lives of the men and their goods. And to prove that all these aforesaid matters were true the said William offered himself for trial as your discretion sees fit. Also, be it remembered that when the said castle was thus surrendered, as was said above, certain Frenchmen bargained with the said William to buy his victuals, together with certain prisoners which the said William had held imprisoned within the said castle; for which things he received a payment of 1,500 francs, from which he paid 678 francs to his companions as their wages which had fallen into arrears by a quarter of a year and a half. Also, he then paid 442 francs at Calais for the victuals of the said castle previously owed. Also, for the journey of the said William and his companions to England, and for the expenses incurred by the said William whilst remaining in Calais, 135 francs. Wherefore the said William pleaded that having due regard for justice and mercy, and that by jealous suggestion he had been accused against all reason, because of which he had been greatly injured in estate and name by the great fault of the slanderers; and considering that from his own goods he had for the most part paid his companions for the fees due to them, as said above; and also for the great costs he had borne in the past to provision the said castle, for which he has placed himself in debt in many places, and owes great sums, so that he will be entirely ruined if he is not aided by your gracious goodwill. May it please you, for love of God and for mercy, so to ordain for him, so that he might through your wise nobility, recover his estate and his goods. Also, the said William Weston explained that on the first day when the enemies arrived at Ardres, he hastened to Calais to find the captain, and prayed of him more aid and more men the better to keep his fort of Audruicq, and defend it if the enemy came there; and the captain replied briefly that he would neither lend nor send him aid or support at the said time, because he similarly feared that the enemies would head for Calais.'

40. The said schedule having been seen and read in full parliament, the said John was then addressed there by the said steward in the following manner: 'John, lord of Gommegnies, you undertook on behalf of the most mighty prince, whom God absolve, the lord Edward [III], lately king of England, grandfather of our lord the present king, safely to keep for him and his royal heirs of England the town and castle of Ardres, without yielding them to anyone except the said grandfather, or his said heirs, or by command of him or his said heirs; yet you, lord of Gommegnies, in the time of our lord the present king, true heir of the said grandfather, delivered and surrendered them to the enemies of our lord the king, without his orders, to the injury of him and his crown and the estate of his kingdom of England, contrary to your aforesaid undertaking: what have you to say thereto?' Whereupon, the said John replied that the said town and castle of Ardres had been in so weak a state that he had not been able effectively to keep them against so great an enemy

poiar des enemys q'estoit illoeqes prest d'assailler mesme les ville et chastel. Et pur ceo y fist [Col. b] assembler toutz les chivalers, esquiers, et autres esteantz en la dit ville, et lour disast les periles du dit ville, et la force des ditz enemys: et de commune conseil et assent des ditz chivalers, esquiers, et autres il s'en issa hors a les enemys pur traiter ovesqe eux, pur saver les lieges vostre seignour le roi esteantz deinz les ditz ville et chastel de Arde, sanz ceo q'il unqes riens prist pur la susrendre des ditz ville et chastel de Arde.

Sur quoi un Geffrey d'Argentein, chivaler, disast en plein parlement au dit Johan qe le dit Geffrey estoit a celle temps en la dit ville, en compaigne ove le dit Johan, et qe les ville et chastel de Arde ne feurent unqes delivers ne susrenduz par soun conseil ne assent; mes q'il estoit tutdys prest de morer et viver sur la sauve garde d'ycelles: et ceo offrit le dit Geffrey a prover qi qe le vodroit dedire. Et outre fuit demande au dit Johan, si y vodroit riens autre chose dire. Et il dist qe noun. Sur quoi le dit conestable estoit charge sur la sauve gard des ditz Johan et William tanqe a lendemeyn la samady proschyn ensuant, et de les sauvement remesner devant les ditz seignours en le dit parlement, as lieu et jour susditz. A quele jour de samady, c'esteassavoir le .xxviii. jour de Novembre, l'an susdit, estoient les ditz Johan et William remesnez en dit parlement al lieu susdit; et lour estoit monstre severalment par le dit seneschal a mesme le jour, a comandement des seignours avauntditz, coment sur les responsez qe les ditz Johan et William avoient donez en le dit parlement, come desus est dit, les seignours du dit parlement, c'esteassavoir le roi de Chastel et de Leon et duc de Lanc', Esmond counte de Cantebr', Esmond counte de la March, Richard counte d'Arundell', Thomas counte de Warr', Hugh' counte de Staff', William counte de Suff', William counte de Salesbris, Henry counte de Northumbr', Johan sire de Nevill', Roger sire de Clifford et plusours autres seignours, barons, et banerettes esteantz au dit parlement, s'avoient assemblez et avisez de temps qe les ditz responses feurent donez en parlement le vendredy, tanqe yce samady, al houre de tiercz, des choses touchantz les responses avauntditz: et veuez et examinez diligentement les ditz responses, et autres articles touchantz celles matirs, et eue sur ceo bone et meure deliberacion, et deue informacion des pluis vaillantz, et pluis discretz chivalers et autres esteantz en le dit parlement, estoit dit a deprimes en manere com s'ensuyt au dit William par le seneschal, recitant les chosez avauntditz touchantz le dit William: Y semble a les seignours avauntditz qe vous, William, qe avoistez empris de sauvement garder le chastel de Outhrewyk, com desus est dit, l'avetz vous, William, sanz nulle duresse, ou defaute de vitaillez, malement delivers et susrenduz as enemys nostre seignour le roi, par vostre defaute demesme, contre tout plain de droit ou de reisoun, et encontre voz liegeance et empris suisditz. Et eue par deue informacion en tieu cas qe par la ou nadgairs le baroun de Greystok, q'estoit seignour et un des piers du roialme, avoit empris de sauvement garder al avauntdit aiel la ville de Berewyk, le dit baron apparcevaunt apres, le dit aiel soi adresser a chivacher el roialme de France, le dit baroun sanz mandement du dit aiel remist la dit ville de Berewyk a un vaillant esquier Robert de Ogle, com lieu tenaunt au dit baroun, pur sauvement garder la dit ville de Berewyk au dit aiel, et le dit baroun s'en ala com chivaltrous homme as partiez de France au dit aiel, et illoeqes demura en sa compaignie; survient qe un assaut de guerre estoit fait a la dite ville de Berewyk par les Escotz, et le dit Robert com lieutenaunt du dit baron la defendi forciblement, et a darrain par tieux fortz assautz mesme ville estoit pris fur le dit Robert, et deux des filz le dit Robert illoeqes tuez sur

force as had been ready at that time to attack the same town and castle. And therefore he had [Col. b] assembled all the knights, squires, and others then in the said town, and told them of the dangers facing the said town, and the power of the said enemies: and with the common advice and consent of the said knights, squires, and others he went to meet the enemies to negotiate with them and save the lieges of your lord the king then in the said town and castle of Ardres, without wishing to accept anything for the surrender of the said town and castle of Ardres.

Whereupon, one Geoffrey Argentine, knight, said in full parliament to the said John that he the said Geoffrey had been at that time in the said town, in the company of the said John, and that the town and castle of Ardres had not at any stage been surrendered or handed over by his advice or consent; but that he had always been ready to live or die for the safe-keeping of the same: and this the said Geoffrey offered to prove against whomsoever wished to deny it. And the said John was asked if he had anything further to say. And he said that he had not. Whereupon the said constable was charged with the safe-keeping of the said John and William until the next day, a Saturday, and with bringing them safely back before the said lords in the said parliament, at the aforesaid time and place. On the which Saturday, that is to say, 28 November, in the aforesaid year [1377], the said John and William were brought back to the said parliament at the aforesaid place; and it was explained to them individually by the said steward on that day, by order of the aforesaid lords, that upon the answers which the said John and William had given in the said parliament, as is said above, the lords of the said parliament, namely the king of Castile and Leon and duke of Lancaster, Edmund, earl of Cambridge, Edmund, earl of March, Richard, earl of Arundel, Thomas, earl of Warwick, Hugh, earl of Stafford, William, earl of Suffolk, William, earl of Salisbury, Henry, earl of Northumberland, John, lord Neville, Roger, lord Clifford and many other lords, barons, and bannerets, present in the said parliament, had assembled and discussed, from the time when the said answers had been given in parliament on the Friday, until Saturday at the hour of tierce, the matters touching the aforesaid responses: and having seen and diligently examined the said responses, and other articles concerning these matters, and having held a full and thorough discussion thereof and had due testimony of the most worthy and most experienced knights and others present in the said parliament, the following was said, firstly to the said William by the steward, reciting the aforesaid things concerning the said William: 'It seems to the aforesaid lords that you, William, who had undertaken to keep safely the castle of Audruicq, as mentioned above, under no duress, and suffering no lack of victuals, wickedly delivered and surrendered to the enemies of our lord the king, by your own fault, contrary to all right and reason, and contrary to your aforesaid allegiance and undertaking. And having learnt through reliable testimony thereon that, in former times, the baron of Greystoke, who was a lord and one of the peers of the realm, undertook to keep safely for the aforesaid grandfather the town of Berwick, and the said baron learning later that the said grandfather was preparing to ride through the kingdom of France, without orders from the said grandfather delivered the said town of Berwick to a valiant squire Robert Ogle, as lieutenant of the said baron, to keep safely the said town of Berwick for the said grandfather, and the said baron, as a chivalrous man, left for France with the said king, and there remained in his company; it happened that a warlike attack was made on the said town of Berwick by the Scots, and the said Robert as the said baron's lieutenant strongly

la defense d'ycelle. Nientmains, a cause qe le dit baroun avoit mesmes empris de sauvement garder mesme la ville au dit aiel, et s'en deptist d'elleqes sanz mandement de mesme l'aiel, et la dite ville de Berewyk estoit perduz en absence du dit baroun, lui esteant en la companie *[Page iii-12]*

[Col. b] du dit aiel es partiez de France, come dit est, estoit ajugge par l'advis du dit aiel, le roi de chastel qe si est, les nobles duc, et countes, queux Dieux assoille, Henri jadys duc de Lancastre, les countes jadys de Northt' et Staff', et sire Wauter de Mauny, qe la dite ville estoit perduz en defaut du dit baroun; et par celle cause il averoit juggement de vie et de membre, et qe y deusse forfaire quant il avoit: et a celle juggement rendre avoit le dit seignour Wauter les paroles par comandement du dit aiel. Queux choses consideretz, et ceo auxint, qe vous, William, susrendistez le dit chastel de Outhrewyk as enemys nostre seignour le roi avauntditz, sanz nulle duresce, ou defaute des vitailes, contre voz liegeance et emprise suisditez, les seignours avauntnomez seantz cy en plein parlement vous ajuggent a la mort, et qe vous soiez trainez et penduz. Mes pur ceo qe nostre seignour le roi n'est unqore enforme del manere de ceste juggement, l'execution ent serra mys en respit tanqe le roi ent soit enforme. Sur quoi comande est a dit conestable, de sauvement garder le dit William, tanqe il eit autre mandement de nostre seignour le roi.

Et quant au dit Johan sire de Gomenys touchant ses responsez avauntditz, lui estoit monstre par le dit seneschal, coment les ditz seignours s'avoient assemblez et avisez des ditz responsez, come desus est dit. Et outre lui estoit monstre, coment qe au temps qe sire Rauf de Ferrers, chivaler, avoit la gard des ditz ville et chastel de Arde, la dite ville de Arde n'estoit si fort par la moyte q'ele n'estoit au temps qe le dit Johan la susrendist; et le dit Rauf avoit en mandement du dit aiel de les susrendre, pur la feblesse d'ycelle, avaunt ceo qe le dit Rauf soi mettroit a tresgrant peril pur la sauve gard d'ycelles: nientmains, le dit Rauf les tenoit et defendist forciblement contre un tresgrant et fort assaut de guerre. Et eue sur ceo et les chosez avauntditz et autres evidences touchant les responsez du dit Johan en celle partie, estoit dit en manere come s'ensuyt au dit Johan, esteant en parlement, par le dit seneschal, recitant toutz les chosez avaunt ditz touchantz le avauntdit Johan, et auxint l'avantdit juggement du dit baroun et la cause d'ycelle, en manere come desus: Y semble a les seignours avauntnomez, seantz cy en plein parlement, considerantz vous responses en celle partie, et les examinementz et enformacions sur ce euez, come desus; et eiant regard auxint a ce qe nadgairs, outre le nombre des gentz par queux aviestes autrefoithe empris de sauvement garder les ditz ville et chastel, .xx. hommez d'armes, et .xx. archers vous feurent envoiez as ditz ville et chastel de Arde, en afforcement d'ycelles, solonc vostre request ent fait as certeins seignours nadgairs esteantz en message a Caleys depar le dit aiel: et a ceo auxint qe au temps q'il estoit a vous dist par le roi de chastel, qe si est qe si vous ne les purroitz bien garder, vous ne les deussez en nulle manere prendre a garder, et un autre les averoit a garder, qe les vodroit emprendre de sauvement garder au dit aiel et a ses heirs avauntditz; et vous empristez de les sauvement garder sans les susrendre a nully sinoun par manere come desus est dit. Et ore vous, Johan, sanz nulle duresce, ou defaute de vitaillez ou de artillerie, ou d'autres choses necessaries pur la defense des ditz ville et chastel de Arde, sanz comandement nostre seignour le roi malement l'avetz delivers

defended it, and at length, because of those violent attacks the same town was captured from the said Robert, and two of Robert's sons were killed there defending the same. Nevertheless, because the said baron had himself undertaken to keep safely the same town for the said grandfather, and had left it without the permission of the same grandfather, and the said town of Berwick was lost in the absence of the said baron, the latter being in the company *[Page iii-12]*
[Col. b] of the said grandfather in the parts of France, as was said, it was adjudged by the advice of the said grandfather, as king of that castle, the noble duke and earls, whom God absolve, Henry, late duke of Lancaster, the former earls of Northampton and Stafford, and Sir Walter de Mauny, that the said town had been lost through the fault of the said baron; and for that reason he received judgment of life and limb, and forfeiture of whatsoever he owned: and judgment was pronounced by the said Sir Walter by order of the said grandfather. Which things considered, and this also that you, William, surrendered the said castle of Audruicq to the enemies of our aforesaid lord the king, when suffering no hardship or lack of victuals, contrary to your aforesaid allegiance and undertaking, the aforenamed lords seated here in full parliament adjudge you to death, and that you shall be hanged and drawn. But because our lord the king has not been informed of the nature of this judgment, execution thereof will be put in respite until the king has been informed.' Whereupon, the said constable was ordered to guard safely the said William, until he received some other order from our lord the king.
And as for the said John, lord Gommegnies, touching his aforesaid answer, it was explained to him by the said steward that the said lords had assembled and discussed the said answer, mentioned above. Furthermore, it was explained to him that, at the time when Sir Ralph Ferrers, knight, had had the guard of the said town and castle of Ardres, the said town of Ardres was not half as strong as it was when the said John surrendered it; and the said Ralph was ordered by the said grandfather to surrender them, because of the defenceless state of the same, before the said Ralph should put himself in very great danger in safeguarding the same: nevertheless, the said Ralph held and defended them vigorously against a great and violent warlike assault. And having considered that and the aforesaid matters and other evidence touching the responses of the said John in that matter, it was said to the aforementioned John, present in parliament, by the said steward, reciting all the aforesaid matters concerning the aforesaid John, and also the aforesaid judgment upon the said baron and the reason for the same, as mentioned above. 'It seems to the above-named lords, seated here in full parliament, considering your replies in this matter, and the examination made of them and evidence about them, as mentioned above; and bearing in mind also that formerly, in addition to the number of men with whom you once undertook safely to guard the said town and castle, twenty men-at-arms and twenty archers were sent to you at the said town and castle of Ardres, to reinforce the same, in response to the request made by you of certain lords then charged with business in Calais on behalf of the said grandfather: and bearing in mind also that at the time, you were told by the king of that castle that if you could not guard them well, you ought not to accept the keeping of them under any circumstances, and another person should have the guard, who wished to undertake their keeping for the said grandfather and his aforesaid heirs; yet you undertook to keep them safely without surrendering them to anyone unless under the circumstances described above. And now, you, John, suffering no hardship, nor lack of victuals or weaponry, or other things necessary

et susrenduz as enemys nostre seignour le roi, par vostre defaute demesme, contre tout plain de droit ou de reison, et encontre voz emprises suisditz. Par quoi les seignours avantditz, cy en plein parlement, vous ajuggent a la mort. Et pur ceo q'estes gentil homme et baneret, et avetz servy au dit aiel en ses guerres, et n'estes liege homme nostre seignour le roi, vous serrez decolle sanz autre juyse avoir. Et pur ceo auxint qe nostre seignour le roi n'est unqore enforme del manere de ceste juggement, l'execucion ent serra mys en respit tanqe nostre seignour le roi ent soit enforme. Sur quoi comandez est a l'avauntdit conestable de sauvement garder le

[Col. b] dit Johan tanqe il eit autre mandement de nostre seignour le roi.
Memorandum.

Et fait a remembrer qe Geffrey Martin, clerc de la coroune, fist mesmes ces record, et le delivrast issint escrit en ce present roulle par sa main propre.
Membrane 7
Perrers.
41. Item, le .xxii. jour de Decembre durant encore ce present parlement, Alice Perrers fuist fait venir en mesme le parlement, devant les prelates et seignours, pur y respondre sur certeins choses quelles pur lors serroient surmises \envers elle/ depar le roi. Et sur ceo, par comandement des prelatz /et\ seignours du dit parlement, monsire Richard le Scrop', chivaler, seneschal del hostel nostre seignour le roi, y rehercea en parlement, en presence de la dite Alice, une ordinance fait au parlement tenuz a Westm' le lundy prochein apres le feste de seint George, l'an du regne le roi Edward, aiel a nostre seignour le roi q'orest, cynquantisme, en cestes paroles: Pur ceo qe pleinte est fait au roi qe ascuns femmes ont pursuyz en les courtz du roi diverses bosoigns et quereles, par voie de meyntenance, et pur lower et part avoir; quele chose desplest au roi, et le roi defende qe desormes nulle femme le face, et par especial Alice Perres, sur peine de quanqe la dite Alice purra forfaire, et d'estre bannyz hors du roialme. Et celle reherceaille faite, le dit seneschal surmist a dite Alice qe sembloit as seignours du parlement q'ele avoit encurru la paine compris en la dite ordinance, et auxi forfait encontre la dite ordinance en certeinz pointz, et par especial en deux; c'estassavoir, qe par la ou monsire /Nicholas\ Dagworth, chivaler, fuist ordeinez par le conseil du dit aiel d'aler en Irland, pur certeins chargeantz bosoigns qe serroient profitables au dit aiel et a soun roialme, la dite Alice, puis la dite ordinance faite, come est dit, tant pursuast a dit aiel en sa court a Haveryng qe a sa singuler pursuyte et procurement le dit Nicholas fuist contermande, et son viage de tout lesse, a grant damage du dit aiel, et de son dit roialme. Item, qe par la ou Richard Lyons, pur certeins mesprisions desqueux il fuist convict al dit parlement tenuz le dit an cynquantisme, se submist en dit parlement en la grace du dit aiel, c'estassavoir son corps, toutz ses terres et tenementz, biens, et chateulx, et toutz ses autres possessions, par qoi le dit Richard fuist mys a prisone, et toutz ses terres et tenementz, biens, et chateux, et ses autres possessions avantditz, seisez en mayn du dit aiel; des queux terres et tenementz il dona ascuns al counte de Cantebrugge, et ascuns a monsire Thomas de Wodestok, ore counte de Bukyngham, a terme de lours vies. Le quiel aiel puis eiant pite du dit Richard, lui voillant par l'assent de son conseil faire grace, lui pardonast l'emprisonement de son corps, et lui fist restorer as certeins de ses terres et tenementz, biens, et chateulx avantditz: le quele pardon semblast a dit aiel et a son dit conseil estre grace assietz. Nyentmeyns,

[Col. b] said John until he should receive some other order from our lord the king.
Memorandum.

And be it remembered that Geoffrey Martin, clerk of the crown, made this same record, and submitted it as it is written in this present roll in his own hand.

Perrers.
41. Also, on 22 December during this present parliament, Alice Perrers was brought in to the same parliament, before the prelates and lords, to make answer there to certain matters which were to be alleged against her on behalf of the king. Whereupon, by order of the prelates and lords of the said parliament, Sir Richard le Scrope, knight, steward of the household of our lord the king, rehearsed in parliament, in the presence of the said Alice, an ordinance made at a parliament lately held at Westminster on the Monday following the feast of St George, in the fiftieth year of the reign of King Edward [III], grandfather of our lord the present king [28 April 1376], in these words: Inasmuch as plaint has been made to the king that certain women have pursued in the king's courts divers matters and disputes to gain their ends by way of maintenance and barratry, which displeases the king, the king prohibits any woman from so doing henceforth, and especially Alice Perrers, on pain of forfeiting whatsoever she is able to forfeit and being banished from the realm. And that recital made, the said steward told the said Alice that it seemed to the lords of parliament that she had incurred the penalty set out in the said ordinance, and the forfeit which it prescribed in various ways, and in two especially; namely, that whereas Sir Nicholas Dagworth, knight, had been appointed by the counsel of the said grandfather to go to Ireland, to deal with certain important matters of business which would benefit the said grandfather and his kingdom, the said Alice, after the said ordinance had been made, it was said, so importuned the said grandfather in his court at Havering, that by her singular pursuit and procurement the said Nicholas was countermanded, and his journey entirely abandoned, to the great damage of the said grandfather, and his said realm. Also, whereas Richard Lyons, for certain misprisions of which he was convicted at the said parliament held in the said fiftieth year [1376], submitted himself to the grace of the said grandfather in the said parliament, namely his person, all his lands, tenements, goods, and chattels, and all his other possessions, wherefore the said Richard was committed to prison, and all his lands, tenements, goods, and chattels, and his other aforesaid possessions were taken into the hands of the said grandfather; of which lands and tenements he gave some to the earl of Cambridge, and some to Sir Thomas Woodstock, now earl of Buckingham, for the terms of their lives. The said grandfather, then taking pity on the said Richard, and wishing, by the assent

la dite Alice pursuast tant a dit aiel, en sa court a Shene, qe par sa singuler pursuyte et procurement le dit aiel granta au dit Richard toutz ses terres et tenementz, biens, et chateux avantditz, ensemblement ove les ditz tenementz lesqueux le dit aiel avoit done as ditz countes a terme de lours vies, come desuz est dit: et outre ceo, pardona a dit Richard .ccc.*li.* de certeins arrerages dues par le dit Richard en l'escheqer, et auxi lui granta mille marcz de son tresor, a avoir de doun, la quele pursuyte et procurement feurent contre l'ordinance avantdite.

of his council to do him grace, revoked his imprisonment, and caused certain of his aforesaid lands, tenements, goods, and chattels to be restored to him: which pardon seemed to the said grandfather and his said council to be grace enough. Nevertheless, the said Alice so importuned the said grandfather, in his court at Sheen, that by her singular pursuit and procurement the said grandfather granted the said Richard all his aforesaid lands, tenements, goods, and chattels, together with the said tenements which the said grandfather had given to the said earls for the terms of their lives, as was mentioned above: and in addition, he pardoned the said Richard £300 of certain arrears owed by the said Richard in the exchequer, and he also granted him a thousand marks of his treasure, to have as a gift, which pursuit and procurement were contrary to the aforesaid ordinance.

42. Et le dit seneschal demanda la dite Alice, coment ele se voudroit de cestes articles escuser. La quele Alice respondist et dist qe de cestes articles ele n'est pas coupable, et ce ele est prest d'averer et prover par la tesmoignance de monsire Johan de Ipre, alors seneschal del hostel du dit aiel, et William Strete, *[Page iii-13]*

42. And the said steward asked of the said Alice, how she wished to defend herself against those accusations. Alice replied, saying that she was not guilty of those articles of accusation, and that she was ready to vouch for and prove this by the testimony of Sir John Ypres, then steward of the household of the said grandfather, and William Street, *[Page iii-13]*

[Col. a] adonqes counterollour du dit hostel, monsire Alein Buxhull', chivaler, et Nicholas Carreu adonqes gardein du prive seal du dit aiel, et d'autres qe feurrent entour le dit aiel et pres de lui al temps qe suppose est q'ele ensy deust avoir forfait, et qi mieltz y scievent \ent/La verite. Et sur ceo est jour done a dite Alice tanqe al mekerdy prochein enseuant; et en la mene temps par l'assent des prelates et des seignours du dit parlement ordeine fuist et assentuz qe cestes articles serroient triez par tesmoigns, ou par enqueste de ceux qe feurent del hostel du dit aiel, par queux la verite purroit estre conuz et enquis. Et sur ceo y feurent certeins persones jurrez et examinez devant le duc de Lanc', le counte de Cantebr', le counte de la March, le counte d'Arundell' et le counte de Warr'; c'estassavoir primerement monsire Roger Beauchamp, nadgaris chamberleyn du dit aiel, jurrez sur les seintz ewangiles, et diligealment examinez sur le article touchant le contremandement monsire Nicholas Dagworth, et sur le autre article touchant le pardoun et grace faitz a Richard Lyons, dist par son serement qe en presence de dame Alice Perrers une bille lui fuist baille a Haveryng pur bailler au \dit/ roi \et aiel,/ quele bille il prist, et puis quant il avoit entendu q'ele contenoit le revocation de monsire Nicholas Dagworth d'Irland, pur ceo q'il estoit enemy a monsire William de Wyndesore a ce qe la bille supposoit, il respondist q'il n'oosa ceo bailler au roi, pur ceo qe le conseil avoit ordeine la contrarie. Et la dite Alice lui requist, et dist qe hardiment le bailleroit au roi; et meyntenant le roi les demanda de quele chose ils parlerent. Et monsire Roger lui respondist, d'une bille qe contient tiel matiere. Et meyntenant quant le roi avoit entendu la bille, il respondist qe la peticion fuist resonable. Et quant monsire Roger repplia qe le conseil avoit ordeine ensy la contrarie, le roi respondist q'il mesmes fuist sovereyn juge, et lui sembloit qe la bille fuist resonable, et lui comanda q'il ferroit revener le dit monsire Nicholas, et ensi fuist fait: mais quiel jour ou mois ce fuist fait il ne soi recorde point. Et quant a la matiere de Richard Lyons le dit monsire Roger dist q'il ne fuist pas chamberleyn al heure, et pur ceo il n'ent sciet rienz sinoun par oy dire.

[Col. a] then controller of the said household, Sir Alan Buxhill, knight, and Nicholas Carew then keeper of the privy seal of the said grandfather, and others who had been in the said grandfather's entourage and with him at the time when she was supposed to have committed the offence, and who best knew the truth of the matter. After which, a day was set for the said Alice which was the following Wednesday; and in the mean time, by the assent of the prelates and lords of the said parliament it was ordained and agreed that the articles should be tested by witnesses, or by enquiry made of those who had belonged to the household of the said grandfather, whereby the truth might be sought and discovered. Whereupon, certain persons were sworn and questioned before the duke of Lancaster, the earl of Cambridge, the earl of March, the earl of Arundel, and the earl of Warwick; that is to say, firstly Sir Roger Beauchamp, late chamberlain of the said grandfather, having sworn on the Holy Gospels, and having been closely questioned on the article concerning the countermanding of Sir Nicholas Dagworth, and on the other article touching the pardon and grace granted to Richard Lyons, he said on oath that in the presence of Lady Alice Perrers a bill had been submitted to him at Havering to be delivered to the said king and grandfather, which bill he took, and then when he realised that it contained the recall of Sir Nicholas Dagworth from Ireland, because he was an enemy of Sir William Windsor or so the bill claimed, he replied that he dared not deliver it to the king, because the council had decreed the contrary. And the said Alice asked of him and said that he should boldly deliver it to the king; and then the king asked them of what they spoke. And Sir Roger replied that it was of a bill which contained such and such a matter. And when he heard the bill the king at once said that the petition was reasonable. And when Sir Roger replied that the council had ordained to the contrary, the king replied that he was the sovereign judge, and it seemed to him that the bill was reasonable. And he ordered him to cause the said Sir Nicholas to be recalled, and so it was done: but on which day or in which month it happened he had no record. And as for the matter of Richard Lyons the said Sir Roger said that he was not chamberlain at that time, and so he knew nothing except by hearsay.

Item, monsire de Lanc' diligealment examynez devant les ditz countes, dist q'il vient un jour a Haveryng, et trova dame Alice Perrers illoqes, et tantost monsire Roger Beauchamp

Also, my lord of Lancaster being diligently questioned before the said earls, stated that he arrived one day in Havering, and found Lady Alice Perrers there, and Sir Roger

lui monstra une bille contenante la matiere susdite; et bientost apres, quant il parla au roi, et la matire fuist touche, le roi dist qe ne lui sembla mye resoun q'un enemy deust estre juge d'autre. Et le duc respondist qe tiel enemistee parentre eulx ny estoit encores provez; mais voirs estoit qe le dit monsire Nicholas y estoit envoiez pur profit de la terre et de tout le roialme. Et sur ceo estoit ordeinez /devant\ Le roi qe les ditz monsire Nicholas et monsire William vendroient /devant\ Le conseil, et si le dit monsire William purroit prover ascune cause verroie de enemyte parentre eulx, q'adonqes le dit monsire Nicholas n'y irroit mye: et s'il ny purroit prover tiel enemistee, q'adonqes l'ordinance de conseil ent fait avant esterroit en sa force. A quele chose le roi s'assenty bien pur le heure. Mais tantost assailler de la chambre, la dite dame Alice vient au duc, et lui priast cherement q'il ne suffrist par aucune manere le dit monsire Nicholas aler illoeqes. Qi respondist q'il ne ferroit rienz autrement qe desuz n'estoit ordeinez devant le roi. Et quant ele y veoit q'autre grace ny purroit avoir de lui, se en passa. Et lendemain matin, quant le dit duc prist conge du roi en son lyt, mesme le roi lui comanda sur sa benison q'il ne suffrist en aucune manere qe le dit monsire Nicholas irroit vers Irland, l'ordinance ent fatte le jour devant au contrarie nient contresteant; et ensy fuist le dit monsire Nicholas contremandez. Et quant a l'article de Richard Lyons, il dist en sa consience qe la dite Alice si fuist principale promotrice du dit bosoigne; mais il ne fuist pas present quant ce estoit faite.

Item, monsire Phelip de la Vache jurrez come desuz, et diligialment examinez,
[Col. b] dist, quant al article de monsire Nicholas Dagworth, q'il n'oyast unqes la dite dame Alice parler au roi de meisme la matire; mais il oyast en l'ostel le roi la dite dame Alice faire grant murmur, et dire qe n'estoit pas reson ne ley qe le dit monsire Nicholas, q'estoit enemy al avant dit monsire William, deust aler en Irland pur enquere et faire justice encontre lui, et pluis ne sciet il parler de ceste matire. Mais quant al article de Richard Lyons, il dist q'il fuist un jour a Shene quant le dit Richard fuist amesnez devant le roi, et q'il fuist appellez a la chambre le roi, pur oyer ceo q'ent deust estre fait: et quant il entendoit la matire, il ne voudroit demurer, einz issist la chambre. Et outre il dist qe feurent alors dedeinz la chambre du roi la dite dame Alice, Nicholas Carreu, monsire Alein Buxhull', Waulter Walsshe et plusours autres: et dist outre qe comme parlance fuist en la court qe la dite dame Alice fuist grant aideur et amye en celle bosoigne.

Item, Nicholas Carreu jurrez come dessus, et diligealment examinez, dist q'il fuist comandez depar le roi de venir a Shene au roi, et la il trovast Richard Lyons; le quiel Richard et Nicholas feurent comandez /de venir\ devant le roi a soun lyt, ou ils troverent dame Alice Perrers seant al chief du lyt. Et la fuist monstree, et qe le roi vorroit pardoner a dit Richard .ccc.li.. en quelx il estoit encores tenuz au roi, come des arrerages de son acompte en l'escheker: et auxi qe le roi vorroit doner a dit Richard mille marcz de son tresor, et outre de faire pleine restitution de les tenementz queux il avoit done devant a ses filz de Cantebrugg, et Wodestok, /come dissus est dit. Et sur ceo le roi comanda\ le dit Nicholas de dire depar lui as ses ditz filz sa volunte. Mais il dist q'il ne se remembrast si ceste matire fuist monstre a celle heure devant le roi par relacion d'aucune autre persone, ou

Beauchamp at once showed him a bill setting out the aforesaid matter; and soon after, when he spoke with the king, and the matter was raised, the king said that it did not seem fair to him that an enemy should be the judge of another. And the duke replied that such enmity between them had still not been proven; but the truth was that the said Sir Nicholas had been sent there for the benefit of the land and all the kingdom. Whereupon, it was ordained before the king that the said Sir Nicholas and Sir William should appear before the council, and if the said Sir William were to prove any cause of real enmity between them, that then the said Sir Nicholas should go no further: and if he could not prove such enmity, then the ordinance of the council previously made thereon would remain in force. To which proposition the king wholly agreed at that time. But immediately upon his leaving the room, the said Lady Alice appeared before the duke, and earnestly besought him that he would not allow the said Sir Nicholas to go there in any way. He replied that he would do nothing other than that which had been previously ordained before the king. And when she realised that she would gain no other grace from him, she left. The next morning, when the said duke took leave of the king in his bed, the king himself ordered him, upon his blessing that he should by no means allow the said Sir Nicholas to go to Ireland, notwithstanding the ordinance to the contrary made the day before; and so the said Sir Nicholas was countermanded. And as for the article about Richard Lyons, he said that as far as he knew, the said Alice had been the principal instigator of the said matter; but that he had not been present when it was done.

Also, Sir Philip de la Vache, sworn as above and carefully examined,
[Col. b] said to the article concerning Sir Nicholas Dagworth, that he had never heard the said Lady Alice speak with the king himself on the matter; but that he had heard the said Lady Alice creating a great stir in the king's household, by saying that it was neither right nor reasonable that the said Sir Nicholas, who was an enemy of the aforesaid Sir William, should go to Ireland to enquire of and do justice upon him, and that he knew nothing more to tell in this matter. But as for the article concerning Richard Lyons, he said that he had been present at Sheen one day when the said Richard was brought before the king, and that he had been summoned to the king's chamber, to hear what was to be done thereon: and when he had heard the matter, he did not wish to remain, but left the chamber. Furthermore, he said that within the king's chamber at that time were the said Lady Alice, Nicholas Carew, Sir Alan Buxhill, Walter Walsh, and many others: and he also said that as word went in the court, the said Lady Alice had been the great abettor and instigator of the matter.

Also, Nicholas Carew, sworn as above and diligently examined, said that he had been ordered on behalf of the king to come to him at Sheen, and there he found Richard Lyons; the which Richard and Nicholas had been ordered to appear before the king at his bedside, where they found Lady Alice Perrers seated at the head of the bed. And it was explained to him that the king wished to pardon the said Richard £300 for which he was still bound to the king, as arrears on his account at the exchequer: and also that the king wished to give the said Richard a thousand marks of his treasure, and also to restore fully the tenements which he had previously granted to his sons of Cambridge and Woodstock, as said above. Whereupon, the king ordered the said Nicholas, on his behalf, to inform his said sons of his will. But he said that he could not remember whether the matter had been

par la bille du dit Richard illoeqes lieue, ou autrement par le dit Richard mesmes, ou par le dit Nicholas. Mais le dit Nicholas soy remembrast asse bien q'il requist au roi q'il vorroit faire venir dedeinz les curtyns monsire Alein de Buxhull', et autres chivalers, et esquiers qe feurent adonqes dehors, pur tesmoignir ceo qe le roi avoit dist a dit Nicholas en les ditz comandementz, et ensy fuist fait; et adonqes toutz les comandementz le roi feurent reherceez en presence de toutz yceulx. Et quant al matire de monsire Nicholas Dagworth, il dist q'il n'ent savoit rienz devant ceo qe monsire Roger Beauchamp lui envoia q'il deust faire contremander le dit monsire Nicholas.

Item, monsire Alein Buxhull', jurrez semblablement, et diligealment examinez, dist q'un jour, a Shene apres la darrein parlement, il fuist appellez au roi, ou il trovast dame Alice Perrers, Nicholas Carreu, et plousours autres chivalers et esquiers qe viendrent ovesqe lui, et illoeqes fuist rehercez par le dit Nicholas, coment le roi avoit fait grace a Richard Lyons de ses tenementz, queux estoient tenuz par le counte de Cantebrugg, et monsire Thomas de Wodestok, et lui avoit pardonez .ccc.li. de ses arrerages de son acompte en l'escheker, et lui avoit donez mille marcz de son tresor. Et quant ceo fuist fait, la dite dame Alice pria le dit monsire Alein q'il vorroit dire as ditz countes la volente du roi, et les charger sur la benison de lour piere de lour lesser et ouster des ditz tenementz. Et monsire Alein respondist qe ce ferroit il volenters si le roi lui comandast ceo faire. Et maintenant al instance de dite Alice le roi lui comanda d'ensy faire. Et quant al article de monsire Nicholas Dagworth, il dist q'il ne sciet rienz, sinoun q'il oiast la dite dame Alice dire plusours foitz qe n'est pas resoun ne ley qe le dit monsire Nicholas, qe fuist enemy a monsire William Wyndesore, deust estre envoie en Irland, pur faire inquisicion de lui, ou encontre lui.

Item, William Strete, nadgairs counterrollour del hostel du dit roi et aiel, jurrez en mesme la manere, et diligealment examinez, dist q'il estoit un jour a Haveryng quant William de York parlast au roi pur monsire William de Wyndesore, en presence de dame Alice Perrers, pur destorber la passage monsire *[Page iii-14]*
[Col. a] Nicholas Dagworth; et la dite Dame Alice disoit qe ne fuist pas resoun q'un enemy serroit juge d'autere. Et outre le dit William Strete dist en sa consience qe la dite Dame Alice fuist principale promotrice de la dite bosoigne, a ceo q'il creit. Et quant al article de Richard Lyons, il n'ent savoit rienz devant ceo qe tout fuist esploite.

Item, Johan Beverle jurrez en /mesme le manere,\ et diligealment examinez, dist q'il n'oiast unqes la dite dame Alice parler au roi del un article, ne del autre; qar ele soi gardast bien de lui q'ele ne parla rienz en sa presence. Mais il cryet en sa consience q'ele fuist promotrice en la dite bosoigne, qar il ne conoist nul autre qe purroit avoir pursuez celle matire: et pluis ne sciet il dire de ceste matire. Et nyentmeins feurent fait venir devant le dit duc, et les ditz countes, monsire Roger Beauchamp, monsire Alein Buxhull', monsire Johan de Burle, monsire Richard Stury, monsire Phelip de Vage, monsire Johan de Foxle, et monsire Thomas Garre, chivalers; Nicholas Carreu, Johan Beauchamp de Holt, Johan Beverle, George Felbrugge, Johan Salesbury, William Strete, Piers Cornewayle, Thomas Loveden, Helmyn Leget, esquiers, del hostel de dit aiel; les queux feurent jurrez et chargez a dire la plaine verite, sy la dite Alice fuist coupable de les articles avantditz, ou noun. Les queux diont sur lours serementz qe la dite Alice pur lower fuist principale promotrice a dit aiele en sa court a Haveryng, entour le feste

set out before the king at that time by someone else, or by the said Richard's bill having been read there, or else by the said Richard himself, or by the said Nicholas. But the said Nicholas remembered clearly that he had requested of the king that he call Sir Alan Buxhill inside the curtains, and other knights and squires who were then outside, to witness that which the king was about to say to the said Nicholas of the said orders, and so it was done; and then all the king's orders were repeated in the presence of them all. And regarding the matter of Sir Nicholas Dagworth, he said that he knew nothing beyond the fact that Sir Richard Beauchamp had sent him word that he must countermand the said Sir Nicholas.

Also, Sir Alan Buxhill, similarly sworn and diligently examined, said that one day, at Sheen, after the last parliament, he had been summoned to the king, where he found Lady Alice Perrers, Nicholas Carew, and many other knights and squires who had come with him, and there the said Nicholas described how the king had bestowed his grace upon Richard Lyons in his tenements, which had been held by the earl of Cambridge and Sir Thomas Woodstock, and had pardoned him £300 in arrears on his account at the exchequer, and had given him a thousand marks from his treasure. And when this had been done, the said Lady Alice requested of the said Sir Alan that he communicate the king's will to the said earls, and instruct them upon their father's blessing to leave and vacate the said tenements. And Sir Alan replied that he would willingly do so if the king so ordered him. And then at the instance of the said Alice the king ordered him to do it at once. And as for the article concerning Sir Nicholas Dagworth, he said that he knew nothing, except that he had heard the said Lady Alice say on many occasions that it was neither reasonable nor lawful that the said Sir Nicholas, who was an enemy of Sir William Windsor, should be sent to Ireland to inquire into his actions.

Also, William Street, late controller of the household of the said king and grandfather, having been similarly sworn and diligently examined, said that he was at Havering one day when William of York had spoken to the king on behalf of Sir William Windsor, in the presence of Lady Alice Perrers, to prevent the journey of Sir *[Page iii-14]*
[Col. a] Nicholas Dagworth; and the said Lady Alice said that it was unreasonable that one enemy should be the judge of another. Furthermore, the said William Street said that, according to his knowledge, the said Lady Alice had been the principal instigator of the said matter, or so he believed. And as for the article concerning Richard Lyons, he had nothing to say beyond what had been heard.

Also, John Beverley, sworn in the same way, and diligently examined, said that he had never heard the said Alice speak with the king concerning either matter; because she was wary of him, and never spoke of anything in his presence. Yet he believed in his own mind that she was the instigator of the said business, because he knew of no other who could have pursued it: and beyond that he had nothing to say. Nevertheless, Sir Roger Beauchamp, Sir Alan Buxhill, Sir John Burley, Sir Richard Stury, Sir Philip Vache, Sir John Foxle, and Sir Thomas Garre, knights; Nicholas Carew, John Beauchamp of Holt, John Beverley, George Felbridge, John Salisbury, William Street, Piers Cornwall, Thomas Loveden, and Helmyng Leget, squires, of the said grandfather's household, were brought before the said duke and the said earls; and were sworn and charged to tell the whole truth as to whether the said Alice was guilty on the aforesaid articles or not. And they said on their oaths that the said Alice was, for gain, the principal instigator about the said grandfather in his court at Havering, around the feast of All Saints, in

de Toutz Seintz, l'an du regne du dit aiel cynquantisme, del article touchant le revocacion du dit monsire Nicholas Dagworth, et pur \[ele]/ fait a lours escientz. Item, quant al article touchant Richard Lyons, ils sachent bien qe la dite Alice fuist bien voillante, et a lours escientz conseillante et eidante al dit bosoigne devers le dit aiel, a Shene, en le mois de May darrein passe.

43. Et pur ceo qe trove est q'ele est coupable des articles contenuz en mesme l'empechement, et les seignours du parlement, qe feurent au parlement quant la dite ordinance fuist faite, recordont qe lours entencion fuist qe mesme l'ordinance serroit estatut, et porteroit force du statut, et qe les generals paroles, Quanque la dite Alice purra forfaire, se tendroient sybien al forfaiture des terres et tenementz come biens et chateulx, et toutes autres possessions, considerez les damages et vilenyes par ele faitz au roi et au roialme, pur quele cause la dite ordinance ce fist en punycement de restrendre et punyr la dite Alice solement. Par qoi est agarde en ceste present parlement qe la dite ordinance tyne force et effect solonc l'entente avantdite, et q'ele soit bannyz hors du roialme, et ses terres et chateulx, tenementz, et ses possessions sybien en demeine come en reversion, soient forfaitz au roi, et seisez en sa mayn. Et est l'entencion du roi et des seignours, et ore ordeignez et assentuz en mesme le parlement qe toutz les terres des queux autres sont enfeffez, purchaces a son eups, et des queux ele prist les profites, ou fist la bargain a son profist demeine, soient forfaitz, a cause de la fraude et disseite qe poet estre presume, de ceo q'ele estoit pluis enbaude par celle cause des mesfaire, soient forfaitz au roi, et seisez come les autres. Et n'est pas l'entencion du roi, ne des seignours, qe ceste ordinance ne agarde faitz pur cy odiose chose en se cas especial, s'etendont a nulle autre persone, ne en nul autre cas soient pris en ensample. Item, ordeine est et assentuz qe nyentcontresteante la dite forfaiture, si ele purchasa ascuns terres ou possessions par force ou duresse, soit y par fyn, ou par fait, en pays, ou fait, enrollez ou autrement, qe ce purchase soit tenuz pur nulle; et eient les parties qe se sentent grevez lour recovrir par processe en la chauncellerie, et par avis des grandes du conseil soit droit fait as parties, et restitucion fait solonc ce qe la cas demande, issint qe les purchaces faitz en bone foy ne soient pas aniuntiz ou adnullez par aucune voie.

Memorandum.

Et istum rotulum sic factum et scriptum tradidit et liberavit Edmundus Brudenell, clericus de corona, etc., ad hoc in parliamento assignando, clerico parliamenti, etc..
Membrane 8
15

Cest cedule firent les communes bailler en parlement, empriantz as seignours de l'esploite et mettre en execucion.

Ceux sont les bosoignes nient unqore determinez, qe coviegnent estre terminez al honour du roi, et profit du poeple, deinz ceste parlement.

Primerement, qe les persones qe serront entour le corps de nostre dit seignour soient nomez de le plus sufficientz du roialme, sanz affeccioun, et devaunt le seignours et commune avoir lour charge pur governer nostre seignour suisdit sibien en vertue en manere come en honour; et qe son tynel et ceo q'appurtient a icelle soit mys en tiel ordeignaunce, qe les droites revenues de roialme purrent a ceo suffire, ou dedeinz si homme poet, en supportacioun du poeple.

the fiftieth year of the said grandfather's reign [1 November 1376], of the article touching the revocation of the said Sir Nicholas Dagworth, and to their knowledge she did it. Also, as for the article touching Richard Lyons, they knew well that the said Alice was wholly willing to advise and promote the said business before the said grandfather, at Sheen, in the month of May last past [1377].

43. And therefore it was found that she was guilty of the matters contained in the same impeachment, and the lords of parliament, who were present in parliament when the said ordinance was made, recorded that their intention was that the same ordinance should be a statute, and carry the force of a statute, and that the general words, 'whatsoever the said Alice can forfeit,' should apply both to the forfeiture of lands and tenements as well as goods and chattels, and all other possessions, considering the injuries and villainies committed by her against the king and kingdom, for which reason the said ordinance was made penal to restrain and punish the said Alice alone. On account of which it was decided in this present parliament that the said ordinance should accordingly keep its force and effect as aforesaid, and that she should be banished from the realm, and her lands, property, tenements and possessions, as well in demesne as in reversion, should be forfeit to the king, and taken into his hands. And it is the intention of the king and the lords, and has now been ordained and agreed in the same parliament that all the lands with which others are enfeoffed, purchased to her use, and from which she took the profits, or made the bargain for her own profit, shall be forfeit, because of the fraud and deceit which can be presumed, in which she was the more emboldened to act wrongfully, shall be forfeit to the king, and seized like the others. And it is neither the king's nor the lords' intention that this ordinance or decision made for so odious a crime in this particular case should apply to any other person, or be taken as an example in any other case. Also, it was ordained and agreed that, notwithstanding the said forfeiture, if she purchased any lands or possessions by force or duress, be it by fine, or by deed, at large, or made, enrolled, or otherwise, that that purchase shall be held at naught; and let the parties who feel aggrieved recover them by process in chancery, and by the advice of the great men of the counsel right shall be done to all parties, and restitution made as the cause demands, so that purchases made in good faith shall not be cancelled or annulled in any way.

Memorandum.

And Edmund Brudenell, clerk of the crown, etc., appointed to this parliament, compiled and wrote this roll, and delivered and gave it to the clerk of the parliament.

The commons caused this schedule to be submitted in parliament, requesting of the lords that they further it and put it into effect.

The following are the matters of business still to be completed, which call to be settled for the honour of the king, and the profit of the people in this parliament.

Firstly, those who are about the person of our said lord shall be chosen from amongst the most worthy of the kingdom, without partiality, and shall receive their charge before the lords and commons to guide our aforesaid lord as well in virtue in manner as in honour; and that his household and all that pertains to the same shall be so ordered that the normal revenues of the kingdom shall suffice, or more than suffice for it, if it be possible, to the relief of the people.

---

[15] The following, as far as 'et partie serra fait en les communes peticions' is written in a different hand on a loose-leaf of parchment stitched to m.8.

Secundement, qe les .ix. seignoures ore essuz du graunt conseil, ensemble ove les grauntz officers du roialme et de l'hostell, puissent avoir lour charge en audience des communes, et lour poair declareez devaunt la commune, ensy qe chescun persone de la ligeance puisse se affier d'avoir bone governaille, si bien deinz la roialme come pur la defence d'icelle a lour poair.

Item, coviegnent estre ordeigne par les seignours du parlement qe les justices, et autres qe governent et governeront les leyes, soient devaunt la commune chargez par serement, de governer le poeple en droit justice, solom les leyes et les bones usages du roialme, fesantz equitee sibien as poveres come as riches, sanz affeccioun de nulle part, sur certein peyne ent ordeigner a present, si ascun juge soit atteint de la contraire de ceo paramont escript, issint qe chescun lige qeconqe persone qe ceo soit puisse sentir qe droit et reson lui serra fait desore en apres, sibien en la commune leye come en especiale, sanz custages de achatier son droit juggement, come ad estee usez par avaunt.

Item, qe les petitions requiz par la commune pur bien et profit du roialme, des queux ascuns i covient desclarier par bouche, puissent estre devaunt les seignours et commune rehercez, et par amyable manere debatuz, et solom bone foi et reson q'ils puissent estre terminez, en honour du roi nostre seignour, et tranquillite du poeple.

Item, qe touz ceux qe ount perduz ou renduz sanz encheson chastelle, ville, ou forteresse a deshonour de nostre seignour, et damage du poeple, puissent estre a lour respounce devaunt les seignours et commune deinz ceste parlement, et qe chescun de eux atteint du coupe soit puny solonc lour dessert, sanz nul espernir, pur eschuer la malveys ensample q'ils ont donez as totes autres.

Item, qe droit execucion soit fait de Alice le Perrers solom sa dessert, sanz affeccion monstrer en la dite execution, considerant la graunt damage q'ele ad fait al roialme par diverses voies; et q'ele et touz autres puissent estre garnys des tielx extorsions faire et grevances, come ele ad fait, en temps avenir: et qe la forfaiture de ele puisse lieu tenir al supportacioun du poeple, a quele ele ad fait la outrage. ~~Cet qe celui ou ceux qe ount fait le~~ ~~la second parlement a contraire del~~ ....
~~des seigneurs et commune puisse estre conuz et puny pur la disserte pur ensaumple des autres et pur la meschief infinit qe pur tiel voie purroit avenir a toute la roialme.~~

Item, qe de les deniers graunteez pur la guerre, sibien de subside de priours aliens, come de les grotez, puisse estre fait verroie ...... soit malement despenduz par defaute de les ministres qe les deniers ministreront, et solom lour defaute q'ils puissent estre punys de lour biens, en eaise de la poeple, qe ount en defaute de bone garde del dit avoir pris toute la damage, qe au tan ad estee fait par les enemys.

Et pur tiel meschief q'est a venuz au roi et au roialme par tielx ministres nient covenables ne profitables, puisse ore estre ordeigne, par assent des seignours et commune, bones et loialx persones a garder les deniers qe ore serront graunteez pur la guerre, eiantz en charge par apart, qe des ditz deniers ensi ore graunteez rien en soit despenduz, meas soulement pur la defence du roialme: et qe de cele forme ils soient acomptables.

Cestes choses termynez en jouste manere, ove la bone eaide de Dieu, la grant qe enbosoigne pur la defence du roialme serra amyablement tretez par les seignours et commune, et en brief temps assentuz, al honour et plesance de Dieu, et profit du roi et toute la poeple.

Secondly, that the nine lords now appointed to the great council, together with the great officers of the kingdom and the household, shall receive their charge before the commons, and have their authority declared before the commons, so that every person of the allegiance might swear to effect good governance, both within the kingdom as well as for the defence of the same, to the best of his ability.

Also, they wish it to be ordained by the lords in parliament that the justices, and others who administer and will administer the law, shall be charged before the commons on oath to govern the people with true justice, in accordance with the laws and good usages of the kingdom, treating poor and rich equitably, without bias for any party on pain of a certain penalty to be ordained at this time, if any judge should be convicted of contravening that which is written above, so that every liege may henceforth feel that right and justice will be done to him, as well under common law as in special causes, without cost in securing his lawful judgment, as used to happen in the past.

Also, that the petitions submitted by the commons for the good and benefit of the kingdom, some of which they desire to declare there orally, might be recited before the lords and commons, and debated in an amicable manner, and in accordance with faith and reason that they may be determined to the honour of our lord the king, and for the tranquillity of the people.

Also, that all those who have lost or surrendered a castle, town, or fortress without reason, to the dishonour of our lord and the injury of the people, may be brought to answer before the lords and commons within this parliament, and that every one of them so convicted shall be punished as they deserve, without any being spared, to avoid the bad example they have set for all others.

Also, that lawful execution shall be done upon Alice Perrers as she deserves, without bias being shown in the said execution, considering the great harm she has inflicted on the realm in various ways; that she and all others may be warned against such extortion and injuries as she has done in the past: and that her forfeiture might be used to the relief of the people, upon whom she has visited that outrage. And that the person or persons who have done . the second parliament against .... lords and commons may be discovered and punished according to their deserts and as an example to others, and for the infinite harm which could in that manner be done to the kingdom.

Also, that of the money granted for the war, both from the subsidy from alien priors, as well as from the groats, it might indeed be ... . is ill spent through the fault of ministers who administered the money, and that according to their delict they might be punished by loss of their goods, for the ease of the people, who have, for want of adequate protection, sustained all the injury which has thus been inflicted by the enemies.

And because of the harm that has come to the king and the kingdom from such unsuitable and inefficient ministers, that there should now be appointed, by the assent of the lords and commons, good and loyal persons to keep the money now to be granted for the war, having their charge apart, that the said money thus now granted shall be spent on nothing but the defence of the kingdom: and that they shall be accountable therefor.

Those matters having been settled in a just manner, with God's good aid, the grant which is needed for the defence of the kingdom shall be amicably considered by the lords and commons, and agreed upon in a short time, to the honour and pleasure of God, and the benefit of the king and all the people.

Et fait a remembrer qe al clamour et instance des communes estoit ordeignez en parlement qe la dite Alice serroit envoiez, pur y ent respondre en parlement, et resceivre ce qe ent serroit ordeignez vers elle.

Et quant al remenant de cestes articles, responce est faite \en partie/ en lours autres requestes, et \partie/ serra fait en les communes peticions.

CY ENAPRES S'ENSUENT LES PETICIONS BAILLEES AVANT EN PARLEMENT PAR LES COMMUNES, AVEC LES RESPONCES Y ENT FAITES ET DONEES A YCELLES.

I.
44. Primes, al honour de Dieu et de seinte esglise soit requys qe toutes les franchises et libertees grantez a seinte esglise soient affermez si avant come ele les doit avoir.
Responsio.
Le roy le voet.[16]

II.
45. Item, qe la paix nostre seignour le roy soit fortment garde par tout le roialme, issint qe chescun puisse salvement aler et venir et demorer, selonc les loyes et l'usage del roialme; et qe bone justice, et owele droit soit fait en chescun person selonc les bones loyes et usages du roialme, en ease et tranquillitee de tout le poeple.

Responsio.
Le roy le voet.[17]

III.
Item, soit requys qe la graunte chartre soit conformez, et fortement tenuz en touz pointz; et qe touz les pointz de ycelles soient un jour luz en cest present parlement devant les prelats, seignours et toute la baronage, et commune; et si aucun point soit obscure, qe elle point eu pointz y purront estre declarrez, parentre cy et le parlement prochein, par ceux qi serront ordenez d'estre de le continuel conseil, ensemble ovesqe l'advys des toutz les justices et serjantz, et des autres tielx qe ceux de conseil veullient a eux appeller quant ils verront temps et heure deinz le terme avantdit: eiant regarde a la grante nobley et la sage descressioun q'estoit en le roialme quant la dite grande chartre estoit ordene et establiz. Et qe ceux pointz declarrez et amendez par le dit conseil, et des autres avant nommez, puissent estre monstrez as seignours et communes au prochein parlement, et adonqes estre encresceez et affermez pur estatut s'il semble a eux q'il soit affaire; eiant regarde coment le /roi est\ chargee a son coronement de tenir et garder la dite chartre en touz ses pointz.
Responsio.
La dite chartre \si/ ad este lue en ce parlement devant les seignours et communes, et le roi voet qe ce soit tenuz et fermement gardez.

IIII.
Item, qe la chartre du forest, et toutes les autres estatutz eyns ces heures faitz, et nient repelles, soient tenuz et fermement gardez, et duement executez.
Responsio.
Le roi le voet.[18]

I. [Confirmation of the liberties of the church.]
44. First, to the honour of God and holy church it is requested that all the franchises and liberties granted to holy church shall be confirmed, as they ought to be.
Answer.
The king wills it.

II. [Preservation of the peace.]
45. Also, that the peace of our lord the king shall be firmly preserved throughout the realm, so that every man may come and go and dwell in safety, in accordance with the laws and usage of the kingdom; and that good and impartial right and justice shall be done to all in accordance with the good laws and usages of the kingdom, to the ease and tranquillity of all the people.
Answer.
The king wills it.

III. [Magna carta.]
Also, be it required that the great charter be confirmed, and firmly upheld in all points; and that it shall be read in full on a particular day in this present parliament before the prelates, lords, and all the baronage and commons; and if any point be obscure, that such point or points be clarified, between now and the next parliament, by those who shall be ordained to be of the continual council, together with the advice of all the justices and serjeants, and others whom the council wishes to summon when they have time and occasion in the aforesaid term: having regard to the great nobility and wise discretion which was to be found in the kingdom when the said great charter was ordained and established. And that those points clarified and interpreted by the said council, and by the others aforenamed, be shown to the lords and commons at the next parliament, and then be enlarged and confirmed in a statute if it seems to them that that should be done; bearing in mind that the king was charged at his coronation with upholding and preserving the said charter in all its detail.
Answer.
The said charter was read in this parliament before the lords and commons, and the king wills that it be firmly kept and upheld.

IIII. [The charter of the forest and other statutes.]
Also, that the charter of the forest, and all other statutes made before this time, and not repealed, shall be upheld, carefully preserved, and duly executed.
Answer.
The king wills it.

---

[16] Stat. 1 Ric.2 c.1. The statutes of this parliament are printed in *SR* II.1-5.
[17] Stat. 1 Ric.2 c.2.
[18] Stat. 1 Ric.2 c.1.

V.

46. Item, qe les estatutz des purveiours en toutes choses soient confermez, et duement executez, et qe nul achatour des seignours ne dames del roialme riens ne preigne de nully encontre son gree et voluntee, sanz le verroy pris et prest paiement faire maintenant, avaunt q'il eit les biens et chateux queux il ad achate, sur mesme la payne ordeigne en le dit estatut de purveiours.

Responsio.

Le roi voet qe l'estatutz ent faitz soient tenuz et gardez.[19]

VI.

47. Item, soit requis, pur l'estat nostre seignour le roi relever, et le pluis honurablement son estat maintenir, qe nulle doune de terre, ne de rente, ne d'eschete, ne de garde, ne de mariage se face as nulles des conseillours durant lour terme ore ordeigne, ne a nulle autre sanz conseil et assent des ditz conseillers, ou de la greindre partie de eux; mes toutes les choses des queux profit purra sourdre, appurtenantz al roy en aucune manere, soient enprowez al profit du roy pur son vivre jesqes son estat soit avenantement relevez, et autre chose sur ce ordene, al honour et profit de luy, et alleggeance des prises, et autres grevances faitz avaunt ces heures al poeple; et qe semblables sont avenirs, si tieux profitz ne soient approwez et gardez pur nostre dit seignour. Et qe l'estat et poair des ditz conseillers puisse estre enrollez en le roulle de parlement, et les estatutz qe feuront faitz en le second parlement prochein passe sur conseillers puissent estre a ore confermez sur les conseillers q'ore sont de novelle ordenez si plusours enbusoigne. Et qe lour estat et poair ore confermez ne soit repellable si noun par parlement.

Responsio.

Le roi le voet bien a cause de son tendre age, salvant toutdys sa regalie en toutes choses.

Page iii-16

VII.

48. Item, ils prient, purceo qe la corone est moult abeisse et demembre par diverses douns donez en temps de nostre seignour, qe Dieux assoille, es queux douns il estoit malement deceux, et en plusours persones malement emploiez, come homme le poet declarrer, a grande damage de luy et de nostre seignour le roy q'ore est, sibien des chateux, villes, terres, tenementz, baillies, gardes, mariages, eschetes, et releves, auxibien en Gascoigne, l'Irlande, come en Engleterre.

Qe plese a nostre seignour le roi et son conseil faire examiner par les rolles de chancellerie du temps nostre seignour le roy, qi Dieux assoille, queux dounes, et as queux, et quele somme ils amountent, qe aviendront a trope haut somme sanz doute; et qe surceo ils soient sagement examinez as queux ils estoient donez notablement et profitablement pur le roy et le roialme, et es queux nostre dit seignour estoit deceux, et ses dounes malement emploiez, et queux touz ceux es queux nostre dit seignour estoit deceux, et qe sont malement emploiez, y puissent estre de tut repellez sanz estre redonez as mesmes ceux, ou a nulle autre, tanqe ses dettes soient acquitez, et l'estat de noz treshonures seignours les fitz de nostre seignour, qi Dieux assoille, qi sont povres a lour estat, y purra avenantment par ascuns des ditz douns estre relevez. Et soit le parnour q'ensy ad nostre dit seignour deceux puniz en cest present parlement, selonc son desert, par agarde de baronage, en supportacioun du charge qe le commune poeple y covient porter. Ratifiantz et confermantz

---

[19] Stat. 1 Ric.2 c.3.

V. [Purveyance]

46. Also, that the statutes of purveyors shall be confirmed in all respects, and duly executed, and that no purchaser for the lords and ladies of the kingdom shall take anything from anyone against their will and wish, without a fair price paid at once, before he receives the goods and chattels which he has bought, on pain of the same penalty ordained in the said statute of purveyors.

Answer.

The king wills that the statutes made thereon shall be kept and upheld.

VI. [Restraint on royal grants.]

47. Also, be it required, to relieve the state of our lord the king, and maintain his estate more honourably, that no gift of land, nor rent, nor escheat, nor wardship, nor marriage be made to any of the councillors during their term now ordained, nor to any other without the advice and assent of the said councillors, or the majority of them; but that all things from which profit might arise, pertaining to the king in any way, be used to benefit the king for his life until his condition has been appropriately relieved, and other ordinances made thereon, for his honour and profit, and the alleviation of the prises and other injuries inflicted in the past on the people, and such others as will come if such profits be not set aside and preserved for our said lord. And that the status and authority of the said councillors be enrolled in the roll of parliament, and the statutes made in the second parliament last past concerning councillors now be confirmed in respect of councillors who have been recently ordained, if it be necessary. And that their status and authority now confirmed shall not be repealed unless by parliament.

Answer.

The king earnestly wills it because of his tender age, saving always his regality in all respects.

VII. [Scrutiny of past grants.]

48. Also, they pray that whereas the crown has been much abased and dismembered by various gifts given in the time of our lord, whom God absolve, in which gifts he was wickedly deceived, and improperly used by many people, as one can tell from the great injury done to him and to our lord the present king, in goods and chattels, towns, lands, tenements, bailiwicks, wardships, marriages, escheats, and reliefs, as well in Gascony and Ireland as in England.

May it please our lord the king and his council to cause the chancery rolls to be examined from the time of our lord the king, whom God absolve, to see what the gifts then were, to whom they were made, and of what amounts - and they undoubtedly amount to a great deal - and furthermore, that they be well examined to determine which gifts were granted chiefly for the benefit of the king and kingdom, and which gifts were granted in deceit of our lord the king, his gifts being abused, and all those in which our said king was deceived, and which were improperly used, and let them be entirely repealed without being regranted to the same people, or to anyone else, until his debts have been met, and the estate of our most honoured lords the sons of our lord, whom God absolve, who are of poor standing, have been suitably relieved by some of the said gifts. And let the paramour who thus deceived our said lord the king be punished in this present parliament, as she deserves, by the decision of the baronage, to the relief of the charge which the common

as ceux qi ount deservi les dounes en manere come nostre dit seignour, qi Dieux assoille, lour avoit grauntez. Considerant a chescun soun longe service et son desert, et regardant, s'il pleast a nostre seignour, as touz ceux qe servierent a nostre dit seignour soun aiel, qe sont sanz rewarde pur lour service.

Responsio.

Les seignours de continuel conseil serront charges de veer et examiner les ditz douns, et les condicions, estatz et desertz des persones; et enoultre faire ce qe resoun demande.

VIII.
49. Item, les prient, pur ceo qe nostre seignour le roi, qe Dieux assoille, estoit giez et conseillez par ascuns conseillers nient covenables, qe touz les ditz tieux conseillers q'ont estez avaunt ces heures atteintz de reprove autentikement soient oustez et remuez de touz conseilles du roy, issint qe eux ne autres tieux ne soient mes pres de roy, n'en office ove le roy; et qe autres gentz covenables soient mys en lours lieux. Et q'en mesme le manere puisse estre fait des mesmes gentz et officers qe sont en l'ostiel du roy qe ne sont pas covenables, empriantz qe toutz les ditz officers sibien les grandes come les petitz el hostiel nostre seignour le roy puissent estre chargez, sibien les officers come les autres pres du roi, qe nully desormes face pursuite ne maintenance en courte n'en paiis, ne qe nulle de eux soy medle par colour de son office de nulle busoigne forsqe de ce qe a soun office appurtient: et ce sur peyne q'ent serra ordene par les seignours du parlement. Par quelle request, affermement et certeignement usez, aviendra grant honour a nostre seignour le roy, grande ease as touz ceux qi serront del grant conseil, et quiete et prosperitee de tout le roialme.

Responsio.

Quant a la primer requeste, le roi le voet bien. Et quant a la secounde requeste touchant maintenance, le roi defende estreitement qe nul conseiller, officer, ou servant, n'autre ovesque luy, n'aucune autre persone del roialme, de quiel estat ou condicion q'ils soient, n'empreignent ne susteignent aucune querelle par maintenance en paiis, n'aillours, sur grevouse peine: c'estassavoir, les ditz conseillours et grantz officers du /roy, \sur/ paine qe serra ordeigne par le roy de l'advys des seignours du roialme. Et les autres maindres officers et servantz\Le roi, sibien en l'escheqier et en toutes ses autres courtz, come de meisnee, sur payne de perdre lour offices et services, et d'estre emprisonez, et d'illoeqes estre reintz a la voluntee le roy, chescun de eux selonc
[Col. b] ses degree, estat et desert; et toutes autres persones parmy le roialme sur la dite payne d'emprisonement, et d'estre reintz come les autres dessusditz.

IX.
50. Item, ils prient, pur ceo qe moultz des malx et damages sont avenuz par tieux conseillers et tieux ministres avantnommez, sibien au roy come al roialme, qe plese ore a sa hautesse, par advys de touz les seignours du parlement, qe tanqe il soit au plein age a conustre les bons et les malx, granter qe touz les conseillers et officers apres escriptz puissent estre faitz et purveieuz par parlement; c'estassavoir, chanceller, haut tresorier, chief justices del un bank et del autre, et chief baron de l'escheqier, seneschal, et tresorier de son hostiel, chief chaumberlein, clerc de prive seal, un chief gardein de ses forestes decea Trent, et un autre dela. Et s'il aviegne par aucune aventure qe y covient a mettre aucuns

people have had to bear. Ratifying and confirming to those who have deserved them their gifts on the same terms as our lord the king, whom God absolve, granted them, and considering with every one his long service and his just deserts, and keeping in mind, if it please our lord, all those who served our said lord his grandfather, and who remain without reward for their service.

Answer.

The lords of the continual council will be charged to inspect and examine the said gifts, and the conditions, estates, and deserts of individuals; and further to do that which reason demands.

VIII. [Maintenance.]
49. Also, they pray that because our lord the king, whom God absolve, was guided and advised by certain unsuitable councillors, that all such said councillors who have been convicted in the past on good evidence shall be ousted and removed from all the king's councils, so that neither they nor other such persons shall remain about the king, or in office with the king; and that other suitable persons be put in their place. And in the same manner let it be done in respect of similarly unsuitable persons and officers in the king's household, praying that all the said officers of greater or lesser standing in the household of our lord the king be charged, as well the officers as others about the king, that henceforth, none shall bring a suit or maintenance in the king's court nor in the shires, and that none shall interfere by colour of his office in any matter of business except that which pertains to his office: and this on pain of the penalty which shall be ordained by the lords in parliament. Through which request, firmly and consistently imposed, great honour will accrue to our lord the king, and great comfort to all those who shall be of the great council, and peace and prosperity to all the kingdom.

Answer.

As for the first request, the king wholeheartedly wills it. And for the second request, touching maintenance, the king strictly forbids any councillor, officer, or servant, or any other with him, or anyone else in the kingdom, of whatsoever status or condition he be, to undertake or sustain any quarrel by maintenance in the king's court or in the shires, on pain of grievous penalty: namely, the said councillors and great officers of the king, on pain of a penalty which shall be ordained by the king with the advice of the lords of the kingdom. And other lesser officers and servants of the king, as well in the exchequer and in all his other courts, as in the household, on pain of losing their office and service, and being imprisoned, and held at the king's will, each in accordance
[Col. b] with his degree, status, and desert; and all other persons throughout the kingdom on the said pain of imprisonment, and being held like the others mentioned above.

IX. [Appointment of the chief officers]
50. Also, they pray that because many of the evils and injuries have been committed by such councillors and ministers aforenamed, as well against the king as the kingdom, that it might now please his highness, by the advice of all the lords of parliament, that until he reaches the age to distinguish good from evil, to grant that all the councillors and officers listed below might be appointed and provided by parliament; namely the chancellor, high treasurer, the chief justice of either Bench, and chief baron of the exchequer, steward, and treasurer of his household, chief chamberlain, clerk of the privy seal, a chief keeper of his forests on this side of Trent, and another beyond. And if it should happen

des ditz ministres parentre un parlement et autre, q'en tiel cas y plese au roy nostre dit seignour granter qe tiel ministre puisse estre mys par son grant conseil, tanqe le parlement proschein ensuant.
Responsio.

Quant a cest article, il est assentuz qe tantcome nostre seignour le roi soit issint de tendre age, qe les ditz conseillers, et aussint les chanceller, tresorier, seneschal de son hostiel et chaumberlein, soient esluz par les seignours en parlement: salvez toutdys l'estat et l'eritage du conte d'Oxenford del dit office de chaumberlein. Mais s'il avenist issint qe aucun de eux morust, ou feust par cause resonable remuez, entre parlement et parlement, adonqes le roi par l'advys des seignours de son continuel conseil les ferra en le moiene temps. Et quant as autres officers dessusnomez, le roy les ferra par l'assent des seignours du son dit conseil.

X.
51. Item, pur ce qe les terres de Gascoigne, d'Irlande, la seignourie en Artoys, et la marche d'Escoce sont en peril d'estre perduz par defaute des bons ministres, qe plese a nostre dit seignour par mesme le manere el proschein article, bons et suffisantz ministres y puissent estre mys, pur la governement faire en ses dites terres, en le plius hastyfe manere qe homme poet, pur le grant busoigne qe requirt. Et qe touz les chiefs gardeins des portz et chastelx sur la meer, come Dovre, et Baumburgh', Carlell', et autres marches, puissent estre mys en la forme susdit, et qe ceux gardeins des chastelx et cliefs del roialme soient suffisantz, qe poont forfaire lour heritages si meschief aviegne a cause de eux, come Dieux ne veullie. Et qe en touz les autres de voz chastelx soient mys autres suffisantz de voz lieges, qe poont forfaire en mesme le manere, pur salvacion del roialme.
Responsio.

Le roy le voet, et ent ferra ceo qe a luy appurtendra, par l'advis des seignours de son continuel conseil.

XI.
52. Item, supplient les dites communes au roy lour seignour qe toutes les franchises et libertees grantez par voz nobles progenitours as seignours du roialme, citeszeins des citees, burgeises de burghes, et autres de voz lieges.
Qe vous plese de vostre treshaute et trespuissante seignourie a eux ratefier, graunter, et confermer lours franchises et libertees susdites, issint qe par ycelle grante a present lours dites franchises et libertees ent viewes devant chescun de voz juges lour soient allouez. Et si aucun de eux y veullie pursuer qe lours dites franchises et libertees lour soient ratifiez et confermez et eseallez de vostre grante seal, q'ils les eient sanz fyn faire, ove le clause de licet, etc. Considerantz la grante discressioun et bountee de voz nobles progenitours et de lour sage conseil, qe ceo ont grantez pur grante encresce et profit du roialme. Et qe la citee de Londres puisse entierment et pesiblement rejoier toutes lours franchises et usages qe les nobles roys voz progenitours lour ont grantez devaunt ces heures. Et si aucune citee ou *[Page iii-17]*
[Col. a] autre ville du roialme eit aucune franchise grantee a eux plius qe le dite citee de Londres en ad enseallez, qe plese ore a nostre dit seignour a eux granter mesmes les franchises par nostre requeste qe les autres citees ou villes lours ont grantez par voz progenitours; considerant, coment la dite citee si est la principale du roialme, et toutdys ad este chargez plius qe nul autre cite ou ville du roialme: et semblable est q'ensi y sera en temps avenir.
Responsio.

that for any reason he would appoint any of the said ministers between parliaments, that in such a case it might please the king, our said lord, to grant that such minister might be appointed by his great council, until the next parliament.
Answer.

With regard to this article, it is agreed that as long as our lord the king is of so tender an age, the said councillors, and also the chancellor, treasurer, steward of his household, and chamberlain, shall be chosen by the lords in parliament: saving always the estate and inheritance of the earl of Oxford in the said office of chamberlain. But if it should so happen that one of them die, or be removed for a good reason between parliaments, then the king would appoint others in the meantime by the advice of the lords of his continual council. And with regard to the other aforementioned officers, the king will appoint them by the assent of lords of his said council.

X. [Officials and commanders overseas and in the marches.]
51. Also, because the lands of Gascony, Ireland, the lordship of Artois, and the marches of Scotland are in danger of being lost for want of good ministers, may it please our said lord the king, in the same fashion as the last article, to appoint with the utmost speed good and worthy ministers to govern in the said lands, because of the great need there is. And that all the chief keepers of ports and castles on the coast, such as Dover, Bamburgh, Carlisle, and other marches be appointed in the aforesaid manner, and that those keepers of the castles and keys of the realm shall be men of worth, who would forfeit their inheritance if trouble arises by their fault, which God forbid. And that in all your other castles worthy men from amongst your lieges shall be appointed, who might forfeit in the same way, for the security of the kingdom.

Answer.

The king wills it, and will do that which pertains to him, by the advice of the lords of his continual council.

XI. [Chartered franchises and liberties.]
52. Also, the commons pray their lord the king with regard to the franchises and liberties granted by your noble progenitors to the lords of the kingdom, citizens of the cities, burgesses of the boroughs, and other your lieges.
May it please your most high and most mighty lordship to ratify, grant, and confirm to them their aforesaid franchises and liberties, so that by such present grant their said franchises and liberties when viewed by your several judges may be allowed them. And if any wish to seek ratification and confirmation of their said franchises and liberties, and have them sealed by your great seal, that they shall receive them without paying a fine, with the clause 'de licet et cetera'; considering the great discretion and goodness of your noble progenitors and of their wise counsel, who granted that for the great benefit and profit of the kingdom. And that the city of London might fully and peacefully enjoy all the franchises and usages which your noble progenitors granted it in the past. And if any city or *[Page iii-17]*
[Col. a] other town of the kingdom have any franchise granted to it over and above those which the said city of London has sealed, that it may now please our said lord to grant the the same franchises at our request which the other cities and towns have been granted by your progenitors; considering that the said city is the capital of the kingdom, and has always been at greater charge than any other city or town of the kingdom: and is likely so to be in time to come.
Answer.

Quant a les confirmacions de libertees et franchises, le roi lour confermera les chartres a eux ent faitz par ses progenitours par manere come ses progenitours les ont confermez devant luy: et sur ce ils ent averont briefs et autres mandementz en la chancellarie, tantz et tieux come appurtint pur les faire duement estre allouez. Et quant a la citee de Londres, ils ent ont bailles de novel une lour autre bille continante ceste article et plusours autres, la quelle nostre seignour le roi ad fait examiner, et graciousement estre responduz. Et enoultre, le roi voet et grante qe les citees, burghes et autres villes quelles serront ore chargez de faire vesseux pur la guerre appellez balyngers en defens du roialme, aient par tant lours dites confirmacions quites de fyn ent paier en la dite chancellerie.

Membrane 9

XII.

53. Item, ils prient qe touz ceuz qe ont renduz et perduz chastelx ou villes pardela par verroie defaute des capitayns, puissent estre a cest parlement a responce, et selonc lour desert estre fortement puniz par agarde des seignours et baronage, eschievant les malvois ensample q'ils ont donez as autres qi sont gardeins de villes et chastelx, a grante vilanie et damage du roi nostre dit seignour, et de toute la lange; et qe pys n'aviegne, come Dieux ne le veuillie, par defaute de loure nounpunissement. Et ensement ils prient qe touz ceux qe ont euz la garde des chastelx, villes, et forteresces pardela en temps de triwe, en lour prosperitee, et a lour profit, et coustages du roy, q'ils soient a present constreintz par bone et suffisante seuretee pur aler mesmes illoeqes, et estoffer competentement mesmes les chastelx, villes, et forteresces esteant a present es mayns nostre dit seignour, de toutes estoffures busoignables, a lour coustages propres, outre ce qe devant costerent au roy. Ou autrement s'ils refusent d'ensy faire, q'ils soient constreintz a rebailler au profit du roy ceo q'ils ont pris d'avauntage en temps de prosperitee, outre ceo q'ils paieront a lour garnisons.

Responsio.

Quant a la primer requeste, le roi par l'advis des seignours, y ferra tieu punissement come mieltz luy semblera affaire pur son honour et profit du roialme. Et quant a la secounde requeste, les seignours de continuel conseil ent ordeineront due remede.

XIII.

54. Item, purceo qe les communes de vostre roialme d'Engleterre sont trope greefment enpoverez par les grevouses et outragiouses lowers des laborers, les queux sont trope sustenuz en lour mal fait; pur qoy supplient voz ditz communes, en grante relevacioun de eux, qe voz descretz justices qe sont ou serront assignez pur tiel cause, facent enquere deux foitz par an al meins de lour outrageousez prises: et quantqe serra trove en excesse, q'ils facent estretz endenteez, et livrer l'une partie as viscontz des countees, et l'autre partie endentee de les estreatez face deliverer a vostre escheqier, pur lever en aide de la guerre; et qe nulle fyn pur lour excesse ne soit pris par nul de voz justices. Et qe les conestables de chescune ville eient poair d'arester tielx laborers par lour corps tanqe ils aient trovez suffisante seuretee de lour excesse; et s'ils ne veullient ceo faire, q'ils respoignent come plegge du dit excesse. Et qe mesme le manere soit fait des artificers et vitaillers. Et si aucun laborer y soit qe soy escuse de servir pur cause d'un petit tenure q'il tient, ou par cause q'il voet estre artificer, q'ils ne soient soeffert a ce faire si aucun en paiis eit meister de

With regard to the confirmation of liberties and franchises, the king will confirm the charters issued to them by his progenitors just as his progenitors confirmed them before him: and further, they shall have as many and such writs and other mandates on them in the chancery as shall be necessary. And with regard to the city of London, they have recently submitted another bill containing that article and many others, which our lord the king has ordered to be examined and to which he has made gracious reply. And further, the king wills and grants that the cities, boroughs, and other towns which shall now be charged with making warships called balingers for the defence of the kingdom, shall through their said confirmations be quit of fines to be paid in the said chancery.

XII. [Castles and towns surrendered to the enemy.]

53. Also they pray that all those who have surrendered and lost castles or towns overseas by some real fault of the captains, shall be brought to answer in this parliament and be strictly punished in accordance with their desert by the decision of the lords and baronage, annulling the evil example they have set to others who are wardens of towns and castles, to the great harm and injury of the king our said lord, and all the people; that worse may not happen, which God forbid, by their escaping punishment. They further pray that all those who have had the keeping of castles, towns, and fortresses overseas in times of truce, enjoying prosperity and profit at the expense of the king, shall now be obliged by good and effective surety to repair to those places, and adequately garrison the same castles, towns, and fortresses, at present in the hands of our said lord, with all necessary things, at their own expense, even though this was previously charged to the king. Or else, if they refuse to do so that they be forced to repay for the king's benefit that of which they took advantage in times of prosperity, beyond what they pay their garrisons.

Answer.

With regard to the first request, the king, by the advice of the lords, shall inflict such punishment as shall seem best to him for his honour and the benefit of the kingdom. And with regard to the second request, the lords of the continual council shall ordain a due remedy.

XIII. [Labourers' wages.]

54. Also, whereas the commons of your kingdom of England have been most grievously impoverished by the large and outrageous wages of labourers, who are well supported in their wicked deeds; wherefore your said commons request, for their own great relief, that your learned justices who are or shall be appointed for such a cause, make enquiry at least twice a year into their outrageous demands: and when they find them to be excessive, that they issue indented estreats, and deliver one part to the sheriffs of the counties, and cause the other indented part of the estreats to be delivered to your exchequer, to be levied in support of the war; and that no fine for their excess shall be taken by any of your justices. And that the constables of every town have the power to detain such labourers by their bodies until they have found sufficient surety for their excess; and if they will not that they answer as pledge for the said excess. And that artificers and victuallers shall be dealt with in like wise. And if any labourer excuse himself from serving because of some tenure that he holds, or because he wishes to be an artificer, that he shall not be allowed to do so if anyone in the country has claim to

[Col. b] son labour; mes les conestables eux teignent en seps tanqe se veullie justifier, sur peyne q'est ordene en autre estatut. Et qe les justices qi serront assignez soient de pluis sages et pluis descretz des countes; et q'ils eient gages pur lour travailles, et d'estre paiez de voz viscontz, queux de ceo puissent avoir allouance en vostre escheqier. Et qe les mendivantz wakerantz qe sont suffisantz de corps de servir, et ne veullient ce faire, q'ils soient pris et mandez al proschein gaoele, illoeqes a demorer un quarter del an, sanz estre lesse a maynprise.

Responsio.

L'estatutz et ordinances avant ces heures en faites se tiegnent en touz pointz, et duement soient mises en execution par bones et suffisantz justices a ce assigners en chescune countee d'Engleterre.

XIIII.

55. Item, prient les communes qe nul mason, carpenter, ne nul autre artificer ne laborer, ne preigne nul lower pur les jours de festes quant ils n'averont point, mais q'ils preignent resonable lower pur les jours overables, et pur nulle autre; sur grevouse peyne sibien pur le donour come pur le receyvour.

Responsio.

Soit l'estatut autre foitz ent faitz tenuz et gardez.

XV.

56. Item, prient voz ditz lieges: qe la bone voluntee du roi vostre aiel, qi Dieux assoille, de peticions a luy monstre pur profit de son poeple al secound parlement ja passe, soit monstre as voz ditz communes, et qe ceo qe fust respoundu come a dire en parlement 'Le roi le voet,' soit afferme pur estatut: ce q'est dit as communes touchant partie des dites petitions qe ce ne fuist qe ordenenance et nemie estatut, qe ceo puisse estre viewe et rehercee as communes, et ceo qe resonable est qe y soit ordene pur estatut. Qar le subside des leynes pur trois ans par celle causes et pur la sustenance de la guerre fuist grantee. Et touz les jugementz et diffinicions faitz en mesme le parlement, q'ils soient pleinement demandez, et mys en execucion selonc lour force, si l'en ne puisse assigner cause pur quoi noun.

Responsio.

Il est fait en partie; et ce qe ent rement affaire, le roy par advys de son grande conseil ferra ce qe luy semble ent estre affaire de reson.

XVI.

57. Item, priont les communes: qe les tresoriers q'ont receux les subsides de leyns al secound parlement devant ore grauntez, et les profitz des terres alienez, et la taillage de grotes et autres revenues a cause de la guerre, puissent ore declarrer lour resceites et lours despenses d'ycelle as peres et baronage du roialme qy sont ore en parlement, issint qe droit et conissance de veritee puisse ent estre conceux as seignours et al poeple, pur la suspecioun q'ent ad este supposee devaunt ore, donant talent et voluntee as vos dites communes le pluis voluntierment estre eidantz a la necessite de voz guerres.

Responsio.

Certains prelatz et autres sont assignez de veer et examiner les resceites et issues des ditz subsides et taillages, et les faire traire hors des pealx de la resceite, et mettre en escrit, au fin qe celles soient monstrez as seignours du continuel conseil.

[Col. b] his labour; but the constables shall keep him in the stocks until he will justify himself, on pain of the penalty ordained in another statute. And that the justices who are assigned be selected from amongst the most wise and most discreet men of the counties; and that they shall receive payment for their labours, and be paid by your sheriffs, who shall have allowance therefor in your exchequer. And that the destitute vagabonds who are physically able to serve, and yet will not, be seized and sent to the nearest gaol, to remain there for a quarter of a year, without being released on bail.

Answer.

Let the statutes and ordinances made in the past be upheld in all respects, and duly put into execution by good and worthy justices assigned thereto in every county of England.

XIIII. [Payment for holy days.]

55. Also, the commons pray that no mason, carpenter, nor any other artificer nor labourer shall take any fee for feast days when they have no work but that they shall take a reasonable fee on working days, and on no other; on pain of a grievous penalty both for the giver as well as for the receiver.

Answer.

Let the statute made at another time be kept and upheld.

XV. [Acts of the Parliament of 1376]

56. Also, your said lieges pray that the good will of the king, your grandfather, whom God absolve, in respect of the petitions shown him for the benefit of his people at the second parliament last past, shall be shown to your said commons, and that that which was answered in parliament, 'The king wills it', be confirmed by statute: for it was said to the commons of some of the said petitions that they were neither ordinance nor statute, and that they should be shown and rehearsed to the commons, and that which was reasonable ordained as statute. For the subsidy on wool was granted for three years for those reasons and for the maintenance of the war. And that all the judgements and definitions made in the same parliament be fully addressed and put into effect according to their tenor, unless cause be shown why they should not be.

Answer.

It is done in part; and as regards that which remains to be done, the king shall do whatever seems reasonable to him by the advice of his great counsel.

XVI. [Accounts of subsidies paid.]

57. Also, the commons pray that the treasurers who received the wool subsidies granted before now at the second parliament, and the profits from aliens' lands, and the tallage of groats and other revenues for the war, now declare to the peers and baronage of the kingdom who are present in parliament their receipts and their expenses of the same, so that right and knowledge of the truth might be revealed to the lords and the people, because of the suspicion that has arisen before, giving your said commons the wish and desire the more willingly to come to your aid in your wars.

Answer.

Certain prelates and others have been assigned to inspect and examine the receipts and issues of the said subsidies and tallages, and cause them to be copied from the pells of the receipt, and put in writing so that they may be shown to the lords of the continual council.

XVII. [Aliens and goods of aliens.]

58. Also the commons pray that no alien shall be an innkeeper or keep a household of his own within the kingdom, the better to counter the influx of our enemies and their espionage. And that the goods of enemies arrested in England for theft and seizure of goods at sea during times of truce shall be delivered to those who have thus lost their goods, to each in accordance with the degree of his loss, until due reparation be made between the two kingdoms.

Answer.

With regard to the first request, the king wholeheartedly wills it, excepting his lieges. And for the second, the king also wills it, provided always that those who have such goods in their keeping by virtue of this grant shall find sufficient surety to answer to the king for their receipt of such goods, or else to the party which ought to receive restitution, if restitution or reparation in such case be ordained for one party or the other.

XVIII. [Swainmoots]

59. Also, the said commons pray that whereas it was ordained by a statute of the forest that the swainmoots ought to be held at certain times of the year, and in the said statute it is stated that no free man shall be distrained or summoned to appear at the said swainmoots, except foresters, verderers, regarders and agistors; yet notwithstanding that, people are summoned to appear there, and are fined for default. For which they seek remedy.

Answer.

The statutes made thereon shall be upheld in all respects. In addition, the king forbids that henceforth anyone shall be distrained by summons to appear at the said swainmoots, contrary to the form of the statutes and the assize of the forest.

XIX. [Vert and venison.]

60. Also, the said commons pray that no man shall be imprisoned or fined for vert or venison, nor for anything contrary to the assize of the forest, unless it be for something done contrary to one of the articles contained in the charter of the forest. And that if anything else be done, it shall be judged an error, and that every man may be able to hunt within the bounds of the forest without impeachment.

Answer.

Let the charter and the other statutes of the forest be upheld and strictly kept in all respects.

XX. [Bounds of the forest.]

61. Also, the said commons pray that the boundaries of all the forests of England determined, perambulated, and confirmed in the past by the charter of your progenitors, be not further enlarged, nor that any minister of the forests, outside the forest boundaries, interfere by colour of his office in anything done outside the forest; on pain of losing his office and compensating whomsoever complains if he prove to be telling the truth.

Answer.

The perambulations made before this time shall be strictly upheld. And the king forbids any forester or other minister of the forest to meddle outside the forest except when the assize of the forest requires it.

XXI. [(Forest officials]

62. Also, they pray that whereas it is has long been common knowledge, and often demonstrated that divers oppressions

---

[20] Charter of the forest 1225, c.8.

oppressions et moltz maneres des grevances qe gardeins, baillifs, ministres des forestes, et autres, ont faitz par colour de lours baillies et offices, des queux grevances le poeple qe tant est greve ne osent overtement compleindre, ne lour pleintz suir en la court tanqe come ils sont en lour office.

Qe plese a nostre dit seignour ordener qe des toutz gardeins, ballifs, ministres des forestes qe avant le temps du roy q'ore est soloient estre remuables, soient lours offices seisiz es mayns du roy, et bones gentz et loialx assignez justices, d'enquere sur lour grevances avauntditz, et d'oier et terminer touz qe devers tieux baillifs ou ministres suire vouldrent, pur le roi, ou pur eux mesmes, et de punisser les mesfesours solonc la ley et lour desert. Et ceux qi ont bien et loialment portez en lour office eient lours baillies reliverez, s'il plest a nostre dit seignour, et si aucun tiel ministre eit aucune baillie a terme de vie par fait du roy, qe un moys en l'an puisse estre assigne en quele il poet estre respondant al poeple, si aucun homme luy voet pleindre sur luy, eiant mesme l'issue come avant est dit de les autres.

Responsio.
Le roy ferra enquere du temps en temps, et quant il busoignera, des touz tieux gardeins, et les autres ministres de la forest; et ceux qe y serront trovez en defaute serront puniz selonc lours desertz. Et enoultre, si nully se vodra pleindre en especial d'aucun ministre de forest, il serra bien oiez, et enoultre droit serra fait.

XXII.
63. Item, supplient voz ditz communes: qe come diverses estatutz et observances ont este faitz, pur amender les leyes et les usages de l'escheqier, et nul estatut les poet amender mes endroit d'un article, qe par la ou releves

[Col. b] et autres dettez duez a nostre seignour le roi en l'escheqier sont paiez, et les tailles ent faites en la resceit, et reliverez a l'escheqier; et nientmains les clercs du dit escheqir mandont briefs et sommons a viscontz pur lever ce q'est paie, en destruccioun du poeple.

Qe plese ordener et affermer par estatut qe chescun remembrancer, clerc, ou autre ministre del escheqier qe maunde briefs ou sommons al viscont pur lever relief ou autre dette, la ou il est paie, q'il rende a celluy qi est greve par le dit brief dys foitz a tant, et ent avoir la suite par brief original a la chauncellerie, en manere come avera envers jurour qi prent pur dire son verdit.
Responsio.
Quant a le primer point, les estatutz et ordinances ent faitz soient tenuz et fermement gardez. Et quant a le seconde point de ceste article, le roi voet qe quant tieux dettes soient un foitz paiez, et les tailles ent faitz rejointz, et allouez en l'escheqier, qe celle dette ny courge jamais en demande. Et si aviegne einsi qe apres tielle allouance aucun clerc du dit escheqier face brief ou proces pur lever mesme le dette de novel, et ce provez; qe mesme le clerc perde soun office, et ait la prisone tanqe il avera fait gree a la partie par tant endamagee, par la discrecioun du tresorier et barons de l'escheqier nostre dit seignour le roy.[21]

XXIII.
64. Item, supplient les dites communes: qe nulle officer en l'escheqier le roi ne maintiegne querele en paiis, sur peine

---
[21] Stat. 1 Ric.2 c.5.

and a great many injuries have been inflicted by wardens, bailiffs, ministers of the forest, and others, by colour of their offices and positions, of which grievances the people, being so greatly disturbed, dare not openly complain or pursue their complaints through the courts while they remain in office.

May it please our said lord the king to ordain that all the wardens, bailiffs, and ministers of the forests who used to be removable before the time of the present king have their offices taken into the king's hands, and that good and loyal people shall be appointed as justices, to enquire into their aforesaid grievances, and hear and determine the cases of all those who wish to sue such bailiffs or ministers, on behalf of the king or for themselves, and to punish the malefactors according to the law and their deserts. And those who have performed their office well and loyally shall receive their offices again, if it please our said lord the king, and if such a minister has an office for the term of life by grant of the king, that one month in the year shall be set aside in which he answers the people, if anyone wishes to complain of him, to the same effect as is said above of the others.
Answer.
The king will make enquiries from time to time, whenever necessary, concerning all such wardens and the other ministers of the forest; and those who are found to be at fault shall be punished as they deserve. Furthermore, if anyone wishes to complain of any particular minister of the forest, he shall be given a good hearing, and further, right shall be done.

XXII. [No process upon debts cleared in the exchequer.]
63. Also, your said commons pray that whereas various statutes and decrees have been made to amend the laws and usages of the exchequer, yet no statute has been able to amend them with respect to one particular article of accusation, that although reliefs

[Col. b] and other debts owed to our lord the king in the exchequer are paid, and the tallies made on them in the office of receipt, and returned to the exchequer; yet, nevertheless the clerks of the said exchequer send writs and summonses to the sheriffs to levy that which has been paid, to the injury of the people.

May it please you to ordain and confirm by statute that any remembrancer, clerk, or other minister of the exchequer who sends writs or summons to the sheriff to levy relief or another debt, when it has been paid, shall pay to whoever has been grieved by the said writ ten times as much, and have the suit thereon by original writ at the chancery, as with the juror who accepts anything for giving his verdict.
Answer.
With regard to the first point, the statutes and ordinances made thereon shall be upheld and strictly kept. And with regard to the second point of this article, the king wills that when such debts have been once paid, and the tallies made thereon rejoined, and allowed in the exchequer, that that debt shall never be demanded again. And if it should happen that after such an allowance a clerk of the said exchequer issues a writ or process to levy the same debt again, and that is proved; that the same clerk shall lose his office, and be imprisoned until he has compensated the injured party, at the discretion of the treasurer and barons of the exchequer of our said lord the king.

XXIII. [Personal suits by exchequer officers.]
64. Also, the said commons pray that no officer of the king's exchequer shall maintain a suit in the shires, on pain of

de perdre son office a touz jours, et de gree faire a treble a celluy qe soy sente greve par tielle cause; qar les ditz viscontz n'osent faire encontre eux. Et mesme la payne soit ordene sur toutes les autres officers le roy, sibien de son hostiel come des autres. Et pur cause qe aucuns marchantz, et autres plusours du poeple, sont receux de pledeer al escheqier plees de dettes et trespas, a cause q'ils sont avowez par les ministres de la place plus avant qe estre ne deveroient, a grande grevance du poeple.

Qe plese a cest present parlement qe ceo puisse estre declarrez par bone deliberacioun, en queu cas les ditz ministres averont tiele privilege, en queu cas ou noun.

Responsio.

Quant al maintenance faire, il y a ordinance faite paramont. Et quant a la declaracioun affaire, il y a este usez en dit escheqier qe des actions personeles les officers et ministres du dit escheqier, et lours servantz demurantz ovesqe eux en courte ou l'escheqier est, y deurent pleder et estre pledez, et nemy aillours.

XXIIII.

65. Item, supplient les dites communes: qe la court de marchalsie soit ordene pluis resonable, et lour jurisdiccion pluis mys en certein, et les errours et abusions faites en la courte soient de tout adnullez; entendantz qe les estatutz qe furent faites del hostiel du roi sont voides et nient affermez en parlement. Qar, d'auncien temps lour jurisdiccion ne fust autre, ne ne deust estre, mes de felonie, trespas fait deinz la verge, et puis lour venue, et de contract, covenant, et dette due, ou fait outre le menee le roy, et ceux qe pursuyent la court. Et qe seignours et autres q'ont franchises puissent avoir lour franchises allouez, sibien deinz la verge come dehors, queux eux, lours auncestres, et ceux queux estat ils ont euz et use de temps dount memorie ne court, par adurement sibien devaunt eux de la marchalsie, come devaunt autres juges. Et qe nulle court d'ancien demesne ne soit /destourbe\ par cause de dit marchalsie, depuis q'ils sont courtz²² q'ont conissance sibien de plee de terre come d'autres plees.

Responsio.

Eit la marchalsie tielle jurisdiccion come devant ces heures y ad este resonablement usee. Et si aucun se vorra pleindre en especial, se pleigne a seneschal del hostiel le roy, et droit luy ent serra fait.

Membrane 10

XXV.

66. Item, priount les communes: qe come le collectour de nostre seint piere le pape fait lever de toutes les provisours *[Page iii-19]*
[Col. a] voz lieges, de grace especial a eux fait par nostre seint piere q'orest, les primers frutz de touz les benefices par voz ditz /lieges\ acceptez, par vertue de lour dite grace, soit le benefice plus soit il meyns, come due a la chaumbre nostre dit seint piere par celle cause; des queux voz lieges plusours pur doute de censure luy ount paiez grandes sommes, et plusours se ount obligez appaier; quele chose n'ad mye estee viewe ne use en vostre dit roialme avant ces heures, eins est novel charge de voz ditz lieges, en tresgraund damage, et enpovrissement de vostre dit roialme par le temps avenir, si remedie ne soit mys; et auxi encontre la purpot de la /tretee\ a piece purparle parentre nostre seignour le roi, qe Dieux pardoint, et nostre dit seint piere.

losing his office forever and paying treble compensation to whomsoever feels himself aggrieved in the matter; because the said sheriffs dare not act against them. And the same penalty shall be ordained for all the king's officers, both of his household as well as others. And because certain merchants, and many other people, are received to plead pleas of debts and trespass at the exchequer, as a result of which they are called by the ministers of that place sooner than they ought to be, to the great injury of the people.

May it please this present parliament, to announce, after thorough deliberation, the causes in which the said ministers have such a privilege, and those in which they do not.

Answer.

With regard to maintenance, there is an ordinance made above. And regarding the declaration to be made, it has been the custom in the said exchequer that the personal actions of officers and ministers of the said exchequer, and their servants accompanying them in the court where the exchequer is, ought and are to be pleaded there and nowhere else.

XXIIII. [The court of the marshalsea.]

65. Also, the said commons pray that the court of the marshalsea shall be the subject of a more reasonable ordinance, and its jurisdiction placed on a more certain footing, and that the errors and abuses which occur in the court shall be entirely abolished; bearing in mind that the statutes which were made on the king's household are void and have not been confirmed in parliament. Since, from ancient times their jurisdiction has not been and never ought to be over anything other than felony, trespass committed within the verge, and then their venue, and contract, covenant, and debts owed, or made beyond the king's household, and by those who follow the court. And that lords and others who have franchises shall have them allowed, as well within the verge as without, which they and their predecessors have had and used from time immemorial, by long use as well before those of the marshalsea as before other judges. And that no court of ancient demesne shall be harmed by the said marshalsea, since they are courts which have cognizance both of pleas of land as well as others.

Answer.

Let the marshalsea have such jurisdiction as it has had and reasonably exercised in the past. And if anyone wishes to make a particular complaint, let him complain to the steward of the king's household, and right shall be done him.

XXV. [First fruits from provisions.]

66. Also, the commons pray that whereas the collector of our holy father the pope levied from all the provisors *[Page iii-19]* *[Col. a]* your lieges, for the special grace shown them by our present holy father, the first fruits of all the benefices accepted by your said lieges, by virtue of their said grace, be the benefice large or small, as a payment owed to the chamber of our said holy father therefor; and many of your lieges have paid him great sums through fear of censure, and many have bound themselves to pay; something neither seen nor practised in your said kingdom in the past, and a new burden upon your said lieges, to the very great injury and impoverishment of your said kingdom in time to come, unless remedy be provided; and also contrary to the purport of the treaty negotiated between our lord the king, whom God pardon, and our said holy father.

---

²²*Original* coutz

Qe vous plese sur ceo purvoire de remedie covenable, al honour de vous, et profit de vostre dit roialme, et comander al dit collectour, qe de tielx novelleries ja par luy comencez il ceesse d'ore enavant, sibien devers ceux qe ceo sount ensy obligez a luy pur les ditz primers frutz, come d'autres: et auxint comaunder a voz lieges en tieux guyses esploitez qe nulle ne luy paie riens pur la cause susdit, sur quanqe ils purront forfaire devers vostre treshaute seignourie.

XXVI.

67. Item, suppliont les dites communes: qe come nostre tresseint piere le pape doune benefices vacantz deins vostre dit roialme par voie de reservacioun, auxi bien dignetees et provendes come autres benefices, encontre la purport de la tretee susdit, et encontre la ley escript: et par consequence si ceste chose soit supporte il purra donir touz les benefices de vostre dit roialme par reservacioun, pur les queux il voet auxi avoir le primer frut, a tresgraunde damage et destruccion du roialme.

Qe vous plese a cest parlement ordeigner par bone /deliberation,\ qe nulle liege ne pursuye ne receyve nulles benefices deins la roialme du doune ne provisioun de l'apostoile, sur peyne de perdre sa liegeance, et d'estre hors la proteccion le roi.

XXVII.

68. Item, suppliont les ditz communes: qe come alienes soient graundement beneficez en vostre dit roialme, et se taillent du temps en temps y estre plus avancez, tant par voie de reservacions come autrement; les queux alienes pur la plus graunde partie sont aliez a la partie de voz adversairs du Fraunce, et ount amys et lynage entre eux, queux ils refreshent et eident a mayntenir la guerre encontre vous, enpaiantz lour raunsons s'ils soient pris entre voz lieges, et en les remountantz et arayantz a la dite guerre: et par consequence susteignent tresgraunde partie a voz ditz adversairs encontre vous ovesqe lour benefices q'ils ount en vostre dit roialme, q'amountent a dys mille livres par an, ou plus.

Qe vous plese sur ceo purvoire de remedie, et comaunder as touz voz lieges qe nulle ne soit si hardys de tenir a ferme les benefices des ditz alienes, ne eux servir sur quanqe q'ils poont forfaire devers vostre treshaute seignourie et corps et biens. Et qe les peticions liverez par les communes a les deux darreins parlementz touchantz cestes matiers soient viewes et lieuz a ore, et covenable remedie ordeigne.

Responsio.

Les seignours du grant conseil ordeigneront due remede sur la matire comprise en cestes trois billes proschein precedentz.[23]

XXVIII.

69. Item, pur ceo qe les religiouses purchacent terre, et fount autres de ceo estre enfeffez, et les ditz religiouses pernantz les profitz; et auxi terre lour est done et autres persones enfeffez d'icelles, et les ditz religiouses de ce pernont les profites: q'en celle cas, et en touz autres qe purront estre ymagynez, q'ils puissent estre ajugez en cas d'estatutz de religiouse ent faitz, et qe le roi et autres seignours eient l'avantage en celle cas, come est ordeigne en le dit estatut.[24]

Responsio.

Les seignours ne sont mye advisez de chaunger la ley devant usee.

XXVI. [Papal reservations.]

67. Also, the said commons pray that whereas our most holy father the pope grants vacant benefices within your said kingdom by way of reservation, as well dignities and prebends as other benefices, contrary to the tenor of the aforesaid treaty, and contrary to written law: and in consequence, if that be allowed, he will be able to grant all the benefices of your said kingdom by reservation, from which he will also wish to have first fruits, to the great injury and ruin of the kingdom.

May it please you, in this present parliament, to ordain after thorough deliberation that no liege shall pursue or receive any benefices within the kingdom by papal gift or provision, on pain of forfeiting his allegiance and the king's protection.

XXVII. [Benefices held by aliens.]

68. Also, the said commons pray that whereas aliens are widely beneficed in your said kingdom, and strive from time to time to be advanced even further, both by way of reservation and otherwise; those aliens for the most part are allied to the party of your French enemies, and share with them friends and kin, whom they relieve and aid to support the war against you, paying their ransoms if they are captured by your lieges, and re-establishing them and equipping them for the said war: and in consequence, they support a very large number of your said adversaries against you with the benefices which they have in your realm, amounting to £10,000 a year or more.

May it please you to provide remedy for this, and order all your lieges that none be so bold as to hold the said benefices of the said aliens at farm or serve them, on pain of forfeiting whatsoever they have in their persons and their goods to your most high lordship. And that the petitions delivered by the commons at the last two parliaments touching those matters be seen and read now, and a suitable remedy ordained.

Answer.

The lords of the great council will ordain a fitting remedy for the matter dealt with in the preceding three bills.

XXVIII. [Feoffments to use by religious.]

69. Also, whereas the religious buy land, and cause others to be enfeoffed with it, with the said religious taking the profits; and also land is given to them and other persons enfeoffed with the same, and the said religious take the profits: in that and all other foreseeable instances, let them be judged by the statutes of the religious made thereon, and the king and other lords shall have the advantage thereof, as is ordained in the statute.

Answer.

The lords have not considered it necessary to amend the law followed in the past.

---

[23] Stat. 3 Ric.2 c.3.
[24] Stat. 3 Ric.2 c.3.

XXIX.

70. Item, supplient les ditz communes: qe les seignours qe ount letees et viewe de frank plegge q'ils facent due punissement as taverners de vyns, si avant come des autres vitailles, et q'ils ne soient destourbez pur cause qe lour leetes sont aucunz foiz dedeinz la verge de la marchalsie, depuis qe tieux leetes et viwes de frank plegge sont courtes realx, et ne poient estre delaiez s'il ne soit a graunde damage sibien du roi come de soun people.

Responsio.
Il n'est mye article de veue de frank plegge, mais ent soit usee come ad estee fait resonablement devant ces heures.

XXX.

71. /Item, supplient sibien les communes de la terre come ses lieges mair, aldermans, et communes de la citee de Loundres: par cause qe plusours pistours, et autres vitaillers, et faux overours, communes mesfesours, et felons qe eschieuent les punissementz de la citee, soy retreiont et tapisont en la ville de Suthwerk, ou les ministres de la citee nules poont arester ne punir, nomement pur la court de la marchalsie qe sovent est illoeqes, queux ne soeffrent qe les ditz ministres de la citee facent ascuns executions ne punissementz illoeqes, taunt come lour boundes soy extendent a ycelle ville; nient contreesteant qe voz progenitours par lour chartre eient donez la dite ville\ a voz citezeins de Loundres, paiantz annuelment pur ycelle certein ferme a vostre escheker; dount avient sovent trope graunde meschief sibien as repeirantz de la /dite citee,\ come a eux mesmes.

Qe plese a vostre treshaute /et\ trespuissante seignourie, pur Dieu, et pur meyntenance de vostre pees, et pur destruyre graunde multitude de facines, de faire renoveler mesme celle chartre, ajustant a ycelle par expresses paroles, qe les ministres de la citee puissent faire dues execucions et punissementz sur les mesfesours deins cest ville, solonc les leyes et usages de la citee, si avaunt come ils fount deins la citee et les suburbes d'iceles. Et qe nulle ministre de marchalsie, ne autre vostre ministre quecunqe de queu condicioun q'il soit, fors voz ministres de la citee, facent en la dite ville, c'estassaver en celle partie q'est apelle gildable, ascuns atachementz oue autres execucions qecunqes, mes qe celle partie de la ville demoerge perpetuelment annexe al jurisdiccioun de la citee, en manere come sont autres suburbes de mesme la citee. Savant a touz autres seignours lour dites franchises en mesme la ville.

Responsio.
Il est prejudiciel a roi, et a les esglises de Canterbirs et de Wync', et d'autres seignours. Mais les seignours y serront chargez q'ils y facent garder l'assise par due punissement deins lour franchises.

XXXI.

72. Item, supplient les dites communes, maire, et aldermans, et commune de la citee de Loundres, au roi lour seignour: qe pur diverses meschiefs qe aviegnent en la dite citee, par cause qe le coroner n'est pas justisable par maire, aldermans, ne par autres ministres d'icels; q'ils puissent eslire coroner de eux mesmes, et remoever quaunt lour plest, come plusours citees et villes deins la terre respoignent au roi, en manere come appent a celle office.

Responsio.
Le roy n'y voet mye departir de soun ancien droit.

XXXII.

73. Item, suppliont les dites communes au roy lour seignour, pur les communes des countees d'Essex et de Hertford: qe

XXIX. [Courts leet and the marshalsea]

70. Also, the said commons pray that the lords who have leets and view of frankpledge may duly punish tavern-keepers for wines, as for other victuals as in the past, and they shall not be hindered because their leets are sometimes within the verge of the marshalsea, since such leets and views of frankpledge are royal courts, and cannot be delayed without causing great injury to the king as to his people.

Answer.
There is no further article on view of frankpledge, but let it be performed as has been reasonably done in time past.

XXX. [Southwark.]

71. Also, as well the commons of the land as his lieges, the mayor, aldermen, and commons of the city of London, do pray that whereas many bakers and other victuallers, and dishonest workers, common criminals and felons who escape the punishments of the city, withdraw to and hide in the town of Southwark, where the ministers of the city cannot arrest or punish them, particularly because the court of the marshalsea is often there, and does not suffer the said ministers of the city to carry out executions or punishments there, although their boundaries extend over that same town; notwithstanding that your progenitors, by their charter, gave the said town to your citizens of London, they paying annually for the same a certain farm to your exchequer; wherefore great trouble often arises both for those who come to the said city as well as for themselves.

May it please your most high and exalted lordship, for the love of God and the keeping of your peace, and to end a multitude of frauds, to renew the same charter, expressly adding to the same that the ministers of the city might carry out due executions and punishments of the malefactors within that town, in accordance with the laws and usages of the city, as they have done in the past in the city and suburbs of the same. And that no minister of the marshalsea, nor any other minister, of whatsoever status he may be, except your ministers of the city, shall make in the said town, namely in that part which is termed the geldable, any attachments or other executions whatsoever, but that that part of the town shall remain perpetually annexed to the jurisdiction of the city, like the other suburbs of the same. Saving to all the lords their said franchises in the same town.

Answer.
It is prejudicial to the king, and to the churches of Canterbury and Winchester, and to other lords. But the lords there shall be charged with causing the assize to be kept by due punishment within their franchises.

XXXI. [The coroner's jurisdiction in London.]

72. Also, the said commons, mayor, aldermen, and commons of the city of London pray of the king their lord that because of various troubles which arise in the said city, because the coroner is not subject to the mayor, aldermen, nor any other ministers of the same; that they may elect the coroner from amongst themselves, and remove him from office when it pleases them, since many cities and towns within the land answer to the king, in such manner as pertains to this office.

Answer.
The king does not wish to relinquish his ancient right.

XXXII. [The farms of Essex and Hertfordshire.]

73. Also, the said commons pray the king, their lord, on behalf of the commons of the counties of Essex and

come le viscount des dites countees soit charge annuelment de lever .cclvij.*li.* .xvij. *s.* de fermes de serjanties, et de menues fermes des dites countees, come piert en la pipe del escheker, dount chescun viscount perdy devant la darrein pestilence .c.*li.* par an; et ore par cause del darrein pestilence est la perde plus grande, pur ceo qe les ditz profitz des ditz countees ne puissent en nulle manere estre levez: et coment qe nostre seignour le roy qe mort est, qe Dieux assoille, lour pardona ascun foiz .c. marcz par an, voz ditz ministres sont anientiz et destruytz.

Par qoy vous plese, en honour de charite, et pur les almes des voz progenitours, mettre la dite pardoun a certein, a durer perpetuelment, ou d'abregger la somme des dites fermes de taunt ou voz ditz viscontz soient approuwours, et de ceo repoignantz al escheker; et illoeqes soient chargez de ce sur lour acompt de quantque q'ils ount de ceo resceu, par lour serement, et de nient plus; nient contreesteant ascun cource de l'escheker en ceo cas eyns ces heures autrement usez.
Responsio.

Le roi s'advisera par son graunt conseil, et y ferra sa grace quaunt luy plerra.

XXXIII.

74. Item, les viscontz de Bed' et Buk', Northumbr', et plusours autres viscontz del roialme, sont \[en]/ tieux meschiefs; de queux prient remedie.
Responsio.

Le roi s'advisera par semblable manere.

XXXIIII.

75. Item, supplient les dites communes: qe la ou le roy qe mort est, qe Dieux assoille, et ses progenitours, ount grauntez par lour chartres, et confermez qe diverses citees et burghes tenuz du roi a fee ferme eient celles fraunchises par expresses paroles, Qe nulle seneschalle, mareschalle, ne clerc de market soy entremettent de nulles choses faites dedeins les fraunchises susdites; et nient contreesteant tieux franchises, les avaunditz officers soy entremellent des choses faites dedeins les dites citees et burghes, encountre la tenure de lour ditz chartres, par cause qe n'est pas expressement parlee en les chartres: tam in presencia nostra quam alibi. Pur qoy ils priount q'il soit ordeigne et comaunde en cest present parlement, sur grevouse peyne ordeigne par avys de tressage conseil nostre tresredoute seignour le roi, qe les avaunditz officers, ne nulle de tieux, ne soy desoreenavaunt plus entremellent encontre la dite tenure de lour chartres avantditz, ou autrement ils ne poont paier lour ferme.
Responsio.

Soient tielles chartres allowes come devant ceste heure ount estez; et si nulle y se vorra pleindre en especial, il serra oie, et droit luy serra fait.[25]

XXXV.

76. Item, supplient les communes de citees et burghes d'Engleterre: qe come les dites citees et burghes, quelles d'ancien temps estoient afforcez ove mures, fosses, et autres choses defensables, bosoignent tresgraundes reparacions et hastiefs, en cest present necessitee de guerre, sibien pur la salvacioun de eux come de tout le roialme; queux reparacions volont demaunder si graundes costages et hastiefs, queles les ditz communes ne purront susteiner sanz eide de ceux q'ount tenementz, possessions, ou rentes en les ditz

---
[25] PRO SC8/101/5044.

Hertford that whereas the sheriff of the said counties is charged annually to levy £257 17s. from the farms of serjeanties, and from the petty farms of the said counties, as can be seen in the pipe roll of the exchequer, of which each sheriff lost before the last pestilence £100 a year; and now, because of the last pestilence the loss is even greater, because the said profits of the said counties can by no means be levied: and although our lord the king who is dead, whom God absolve, once pardoned them £100 a year, your said ministers are now injured and ruined.

Wherefore may it please you, in honour and charity, and for the souls of your progenitors, to put the said pardon on a firmer footing, that it may last forever, or reduce the sum of the said farms by an amount of which your said sheriffs be approvers, answering therefor at the exchequer; and let them be charged thereon in their account for so much as they have received, on their oaths, and for no more; notwithstanding any other course of the exchequer customary in the past.
Answer.

The king will discuss this further with his great council, and bestow his grace when it pleases him.

XXXIII. [The farms of the shires of Bedford, Buckingham, Northumberland, and others.]

74. Also, the sheriffs of Bedfordshire, Buckinghamshire, Northumberland, and many other sheriffs of the realm suffer great losses; for which they pray a remedy.
Answer.

The king will consider that in a similar manner.

XXXIIII. [Officers of the household and borough franchises.]

75. Also the said commons pray that whereas the king now dead, whom God absolve, and his progenitors granted by their charters and confirmed that various cities and boroughs held of the king at fee-farm might have these franchises by expressed words, 'That no steward, marshal, nor clerk of the market, shall meddle in anything done within the aforesaid franchises'; and, notwithstanding such franchises, the aforesaid officers do meddle in the things done within the said cities and boroughs, contrary to the tenor of their said charters, because it is not clearly stated in the charters, 'as well in our presence as elsewhere', wherefore they pray that it might be ordained and ordered in this present parliament, on pain of a grievous penalty determined by the advice of the most wise council of our most redoubtable lord the king, that neither the aforesaid officers, nor any of them, shall henceforth meddle contrary to the tenor of the aforesaid charters, for otherwise they will not be able to pay their farm.
Answer.

Let such charters be allowed their force as they have been in the past; and if any wish to make a particular complaint, he shall be heard, and right shall be done by him.

XXXV. [Murage]

76. Also, the commons of the cities and boroughs of England request that whereas the said cities and boroughs, which were fortified long ago with walls, ditches, and other defensive structures, are in urgent need of repair, in this present time of war, as well for their own safety as for that of all the kingdom; the which repairs require so great and immediate expenditure that the said commons cannot undertake them without the aid of those who have tenements, possessions, or rents in the said cities and boroughs, both religious and

citees et burghes, sibien de religiouses come d'autres, qe avaunt ces heures n'ount porte nulle charge pur la sustenance susdit.

Qe plese a cest present parlement graunter qe touz les ditz possessioners, sibien come les autres q'ount possessioun en les ditz citees et burghes, soient resonablement agistez pur lour tenementz et rentz ove les marchantz de les ditz citees et burghes de toutes lour marchandises, pur la forcement et defense susdit.

Responsio.

Le roi voet qe touz yceulx q'ount terres, tenementz, oue rentes deins tieux citees et burghes soient constreintz de faire contribucioun a tielles charges, solonc l'afferant de lour tenure, come y ad estee usee devant cest heure; salvant a chescun son privilege.

XXXVI.

77. Item, supplient ses lieges et subgitz q'entre les autres pointz touchez en la tretee parentre nostre /seint\ piere le pape et nostre seignour le roi l'aiel, qe Dieux assoille, sur touz benefices touchant sa regalie, acorde fuist depar nostre dit seint piere, et sur espoire de bon pees final sur toutes choses tretez par les ambassatours d'un part et d'autre part en Flaundres, le seint piere ottroia et graunta, de soy abstiner de toutes maneres

[Col. b] provisions par voie de reservacion des benefices en Engleterre, et specialment des dignetees electives, issint qe le roi feisse ensy durant la dite tretee en droit des benefices touchantz sa regalite par antiqe voidance; les queux pointz entre les autres si estoient les ditz ambassatours le roi l'aiel chargez a pursuier diligentement a tout lour poair. Et come bien qe nostre dit seignour l'aiel avoit escript a l'apostoille pur ascunes eleccions confermer des benefices electivez, q'estoient faitz depuis le dit graunto, cessant la reservacion susdit come graunte fuist, ascuns des ditz messagers du roy noun eiantz regard de lour dit charge, ne de la priere du roi, ount depuis impetrez en la court de Rome auxi bien dignetees electives, pur queles l'aiel avoit issint escript, come plusours autres benefices, contre l'effect du dit tretee, et la graunt et l'acorde susditz, en graunde prejudice nostre dit seignour le roi, et de ses subgitz avauntditz. Par qoy supplient a nostre dit seignour le roi et a son treshonurable conseil de remedie.

Membrane 11

Responsio.

Le chaunceller, appellez a luy des tieux qe luy plerra, et veue l'accord fait, ent ferra et ordeignera ce qe luy mieltz semblera affaire de resoun, sibien pur le roi come pur la partie, si nulle se vorra pleindre en especial.

XXXVII.

78. Item, suppliont les dites communes: qe come ordeigne est en estatut de Westm' secund, 'Qe cirographers ne lour clerkes preignent pur lour fees pur fyns engrosser mes .iiij. *s.* pur chescun fyn'; la quele ordeignance fuist assetz covenable: les queux cirographers et lour clerkes ne voillent celle estatut tenir, et plus graunde somme parnount, a graunde damage del poeple.

Par qoy plese au roi d'ordeignir qe si lour ditz cirographers ou clerkes plus y preignent q'ils facent gree al partie qe se vouldra pleindre de dys foiz atant, en le manere come est en l'estatut de jurours.

Responsio.

Il y /ad\ estatut ent fait, lequel soit tenuz et gardez.[26]

---

[26] Stat.13 Edw.1 St.1 c.44.

XXXVI. [Provisors]

77. Also, his lieges and subjects request that amongst other matters touched upon in the treaty between our holy father the pope and our lord king, the grandfather, whom God absolve, concerning all benefices connected with his regality, and in the expectation of ultimate peace with regard to all matters considered by the ambassadors on either side in Flanders, the holy father agreed and granted that he would abstain from all manner of

[Col. b] provisions by means of reservation of benefices in England, and especially of elective dignities, so that the king was able during the said treaty to procure his right to the said benefices touching his regality by ancient voidance; which matters amongst others the said ambassadors of the king, the grandfather, were charged diligently to pursue to the best of their power. And although our said lord the grandfather wrote to the pope to confirm certain elections to elective benefices, which were made since the said grant, ending the aforesaid reservation as if it had been granted, some of the said king's messengers not having any regard for their said instruction or the king's wishes, later themselves obtained elective dignities in the court of Rome, for which the grandfather had also written, as well as many other benefices, contrary to the effect of the said treaty, and the aforesaid grant and agreement, greatly prejudicing our said lord the king and his aforesaid subjects. In consequence of which they request remedy of our said lord the king and his most honourable council.

Answer.

The chancellor, having summoned whomsoever he will, and having inspected the said agreement, shall do and ordain on this matter whatsoever seem best and most reasonable to him, both on behalf of the king and on behalf of the party concerned, if any wish to raise a complaint.

XXXVII. [Chirographers' fees.]

78. Also, the said commons pray that whereas it was ordained in the second statute of Westminster, 'That neither chirographers nor their clerks shall take as their fee for engrossing, more than 4*s.* for each fine'; which ordinance was reasonable enough: yet the chirographers and their clerks will not abide by the statute, and take a larger sum, to the great harm of the people.

Wherefore may it please the king to ordain that if the said chirographers or clerks take more, they shall compensate the party who wishes to complain for ten times as much, as in the statute of jurors.

Answer.

There is a statute made thereon which shall be kept and upheld.

XXXVIII.
79. Item, pur diverses causes eyns ces heures estatut fuist fait qe les parentz as heirs esteantz deinz age en la garde du roi, a qi la heritage ne purra descendre, deussent avoir les terres des ditz heirs a ferme durant le nounage, devaunt nulle autre; quel estatut n'est pas tenuz.
Par qoy vous plese affermer q'il soit tenuz, et si ascuns autres y soient q'ount maners ou terres d'ascun des ditz heirs, et les parentz ceo voillent avoir ferme, et tant donir pur ycelle come autres y voillent, q'ils les eient tanqe al age du dit heir; nient contreestant ascun patent fait ou affaire as ascuns autres q'as ditz parentz.

Responsio.
Le roi voet qe mesme l'estatut soit fermement tenuz et gardez.[27]

XXXIX.
80. Item, supplie la commune qe les assises qe sont purchaces el temps le roi l'aiel puissent estre en lour force, et qe brief soit graunte as justices d'assises de les prendre: qar autrement plusours gentz serroient desheritez par alienacion fait puis les dites assises purchacez, qe serroit graunde meschief as plusours.
Responsio.
Il y a remedie ordeigne devaunt ceste heure.

XL.
81. Item, qe chescun manere brief soit auxi bien mayntenable en hamel ou maynauntie qe porte certein noun, par quel le lieu est bien conue, come en ville.
Responsio.
Courge la ley devant usee.

XLI.
82. Item, qe brief de particione facienda, de faire purpartie des terres et tenementz, soit auxi bien meyntenable parentre estranges purchaceours, come entre parceners, et privez de sank.
Responsio.
Ent courge l'auncien ley usee.
Page iii-21

XLII.
83. Item, supplont les dites communes: qe la ou plusours gentz del roialme, sibien graundes gentz come menues gentz, q'ount accions verroies as terres et tenementz come autres accions personels, qe les defendantz en ycelle accions par meyntenance avoir donont les terres et tenementz en debate, et auxint lour biens et chateux as seignours et as graundes gentz, pur estre sustenuz et mayntenuz en lour tort; les queux issint feffez maundont a les ditz actours, barectours, et autres gentz qe sont debatuz, et les manacent par lour seignours et mestres, et diont qe s'ils soient si hardys de riens pursuier encontre les gentz de lour seignours, q'ils serront batuz ou occys s'ils ne voillent lesser lour actions et cleymes: issint qe par cause de tieux manaces plusours gentz n'osont lour droit pursuier, pur doute d'estre maymez ou occyz.
Par qoy suppliont qe tieux douns /desore\ soient defenduz, et qe bon et hastief remedie sur cest meschief soit ordeigne, pur salvacion de la leye de la terre, quele le roi est tenuz de sustiner et mayntenir. Qar autrement deins brief temps le roialme d'Engleterre serra sanz ley, qe serroit deshonour au roi, et cause de destruccion de son roialme.

---
[27] Stat.14 Edw.3 St.1 c.13.

XXXVIII. [Farms of minors' lands.]
79. Also, for divers reasons a statute was made in the past that the kinsmen of heirs under age, being wards of the king, to whom the inheritance could not pass, might have the lands of the said heirs at farm during the minority, before anyone else; which statute is not observed.
Wherefore, may it please you to affirm that it shall be observed, and if there be any others who hold manors or lands of any such heirs, and the kinsmen wish to hold them at farm, and will pay as much for the same as others would, that they shall have them until the said heir comes of age; notwithstanding any letters patent made or to be made to persons other than the said kinsmen.
Answer.
The king wills that the same statute be firmly kept and upheld.

XXXIX. [Assizes.]
80. Also, the commons request that the assizes which were negotiated in the time of the king the grandfather shall remain in force, and that a writ be granted to justices of assizes to take them: since otherwise many people will be disinherited by alienations made since the said assizes were purchased, which would bring great trouble to many.
Answer.
A remedy was ordained before this time.

XL. [Place-names.]
81. Also, that every writ have force in a hamlet or a places with a certain name by which it is well known, as in towns.
Answer.
Let the law continue in its established course.

XLI. [Writs of purparty.]
82. Also, that the writ of purparty, to make a division of lands and tenements, shall be as maintainable between other purchasers as between parceners and blood relations.

Answer.
Let the ancient law continue in its established course.

XLII. [Enfeoffments for maintenance.]
83. Also,the said commons pray that whereas many of the kingdom, both greater and lesser, who have real actions on lands and tenements as well as other, personal actions, the defendants in such actions have by maintenance granted the lands and tenements in contention, and also their goods and chattels, to lords and great men, to be aided and maintained in their wrongdoing; and they, thus enfeoffed, tell the said plaintiffs, advocates, and others that they are defeated, and threaten them for their lords and masters, and say that if they are so bold as to pursue any claim against their lords' followers, that they will be beaten and slain if they do not cease their actions and claims: so that because of such threats many do not dare to pursue their right, through fear being maimed or killed.
Wherefore they pray that such gifts shall henceforth be forbidden, and that a swift and effective remedy shall be ordained for this trouble, to preserve the law of the land, which the king is obliged to uphold and maintain. For otherwise, within a short time the kingdom of England will be without law, which would be dishonourable to the king, and cause the destruction of his kingdom.

Responsio.
Le roi le voet; et en outre, pur ce qe pleinte est faite al roi qe plusours disseisont meintesfoitz autres de lour tenementz, et maintenant apres la disseisine faite font diverses alienacions et feffementz aucun foitz as seignours et grauntz du roialme pur maintenance, et aucun foitz as plusours diverses persones, des queux les disseisiz ne poent avoir conissance de lour nouns, au fyn d'aloigner les ditz disseisez et lour heirs par tielx fraudes de lour recoverir, ordene est et establiz qe desore tieux alienacions par fraudes ne soient faitz; et si aucuns soient faitz, soient tenuz pur nulles. Et qe les ditz disseisez eient lour recoverir vers les primeres disseisours, sibien des ditz terres et tenementz come des double damages, sanz avoir regarde de tieux alienacions, par issint qe les ditz disseisiz comencent lour suites deins l'an prochein apres la disseisine faite. Et est ordeignez qe mesme l'estatut tiegne auxi bien en chescun autre accion de terre, ou tieux feffementz sont faitz par fraude, d'avoir lour recoverir vers le primer occupiour, ent parnant le profit.[28]

Answer.
The king wills it; and further, because complaint is made to the king that many often disseise others of their tenements, and immediately after the disseisin, make various alienations and enfeoffments, sometimes to lords and great men of the kingdom for maintenance, and sometimes to many other people, of whose names the disseised have no knowledge, with the intention of denying by such frauds the said disseised and their heirs their recovery, it is ordained and established that henceforth there shall be no such fraudulent alienations; and if any are made, they shall be deemed null. And that the said disseised shall have their recovery from the principal disseisors, both of the said lands and tenements as well as double damages, without regard to such alienations, provided that the said disseised begin their suits within a year of the disseisin made. And it is ordained that the same statute should apply as well in every other action of land, where such enfeoffments are made by fraud, for the disseised to recover from the principal occupant, taking the profit from it.

XLIII.
84. Item, supplient qe y puisse estre declaree en cest present parlement, si la charge de le denier seint piere, appelle Rome-peny, serra leve des dites communes, et paie al collectour nostre seint piere le pape, ou noun.
Responsio.
Soit fait come devant ad este usee.

XLIII. [Peter's pence.]
84. Also, they pray that it be announced in this parliament whether the burden of Peter's Pence, called Rome-penny, is to be levied from the said commons, and paid to the collector of our holy father the pope, or not.
Answer.
Let it be done as has reasonably been done in the past.

XLIIII.
85. Item, supplient les dites communes: qe justices assignez en paiis de prendre assises, poient prendre nisi prius des mises et issues prises entre le roi et autres persones de l'escheker, come ils poont des issues en le bank du roi, et commune bank.
Responsio.
En soit fait come devaunt ad este resonablement usee.

XLIIII. [Nisi prius.]
85. Also, the said commons pray that the justices appointed in the counties to hold assizes, take nisi prius for expenses and issues taken between the king and other persons from the exchequer, as they are able to do from issues in the king's bench and common bench.
Answer.
Let it be done as has reasonably been done in the past.

XLV.
86. Item, supplient les dites communes: qe come les viscountz en lour tournes ont pris plusours enditementz du mort de homme, par cause des queux les ditz enditez sount pris et enprisonez, et mys as graundes raunsons, et ne purront avoir nulle deliverance devant justices assignez as gaoles deliverer, a cause qe aucuns des justices teignent en lour opinions qe les ditz viscountz en lour dites tournes n'ount mye poair de prendre tielx enditementz.
Qe plese a nostre dit seignour le roy et a son bon conseil ent ordeigner remedie, pur Dieux, et en eovre de charite.
Responsio.
Es countees de Northumbr', Cumbr' et Westmerl' soit fait come devant ent y ad este usez;[29] et es autres parties del roialme, se /tiegnent\ Les anciennes leyes.

XLV. [Mort d'homme.]
86. Also, the said commons pray that whereas the sheriffs on their tourns have received many indictments of mort de homme, whereupon those indicted are taken and imprisoned, and held for great ransoms, and can have no deliverance before the justices assigned to gaol-delivery, because some of the justices hold the opinion that the said sheriffs on their said tourns have no authority to accept such indictments.
May it please our said lord the king and his good council to provide remedy therefor, for God and by way of charity.
Answer.
In the counties of Northumberland, Cumberland, and Westmorland let it be done as has been done in the past; and let the ancient laws be kept in other parts of the kingdom.

XLVI.
87. Item, qe querele entre parties ne soit atttemptez terminez devant seignours ne officers du
[Col. b] conseil, mes qe la commune ley courge sanz estre tarie par eux es lieux ou y soloient d'ancien temps estre terminez, s'il ne soit tiele querele, et encontre si graunde persone, qe homme ne suppose aillours d'avoir droit.

Responsio.
Le roy le voet.

XLVI. [Actions before the officers or councillors.]
87. Also, that no attempt should be made to settle a dispute between parties before lords or officers of the
[Col. b] council, but that the common law should take its course without being delayed by them in places where it used to be determined, unless the suit is of such a nature, and against so great a person, that one might not expect to have justice elsewhere.
Answer.
The king wills it.

---

[28] Stat.1 Ric.2 c.9
[29] PRO SC8/46/2260.

XLVII.

88. A nostre seignour le roi et a consail du parlement monstrent la commune du roialme, q'en plusours parties de roialme d'Engleterre les villeyns, et terre-tenauntz en villenage, qi deivont services et custumes as seignours par quelconqe cause deins diverses seignouries, sibien de seint esglise come des laies seignouries, ount par conseil, procurement, meyntenance, et abettement de certeines persones pur profit pris des villeyns et terre-tenauntz sus ditz, purchacent en court le roi exemplificacions de le livre de Domesday, des manoirs et villes deins queux les ditz villeyns et terre-tenauntz sont demourantz; par colour des queux exemplificacions, par mal entendement de ycels, et par mavoise interpretacioun faites par les ditz consaillers, procurours, maintenours, et abettours ils ount retret et retreount lour custumes et services dues a lours seignours, entendauntz q'ils sont quitement deschargeez de toute manere servage due sibien de lour corps come de lour tenures susditz: et ount denoie as ministres des ditz seignours de les destreindre pur les custumes et services susditz, et sont confedres et entrealies de countrestere lour ditz seignours et lour ministres a fortmayn: et qe chescun serra aidant a autre a quele heure q'ils soient destreinez par celle cause; et manacent les ministres lour ditz seignours de les tuer si les destreinount pur les custumes et services susditz, issint qe les seignours et lour ministres ne les destreinent pas pur lour custumes et services, pur doute de mort de homme qe de leger purroit avener par lour rebellion et recistence. Et issint les ditz seignours perdount et ount perdu graunt profit de lour seignories, a tresgraunde dishereticion et anientisement de lour estat, et les blees des plusours parties du roialme demurount nient scies, et sont peris pur touz jours a la cause susdit, a graunt damage de toute la comune; issint qe l'ein doute, qe si hastive remedie ne soit mis, qe de leger /gere\ purroit sourder deins mesme le roialme a cause de lour rebellion susdit, ou q'ils soy aherderont as enemys de delaa pur soy venger de lours seignours, si sodeyne venue des ditz enemys y fuist. Et pur sustenaunce des queux errours et rebellions y ount coilles entre eux grauntz sumez de deniers, pur mettre costages et despences. Et sont venuz si a court ore a present plusours d'eux, pur avoir counfort de lour purpos susdit.

Par qoy plese a nostre dit seignour le roi et au conseil, de ent ordeigner due et hastive remedie, auxi bien devers les ditz conseillers, procurours, meyntenours, et abettours come devers les /ditz\ Villeins et terre-tenauntz, et nomement devers eux qi sont venuz a present, come dit est, issint qe les demourantz al hostel puissent avoir conissance de lour chastmement et pur eschuere tiel peril come nadgairs sourdy en la roialme de Fraunce par tiel rebellioun et entre alliaunce des villeins encontre lour seignours.

Responsio.

Quant as exemplifications grauntez et faites en la chauncellerie, est declaree en parlement qe celles ne lour poent ou doivent valer ou lieu tenir quant a la fraunchise de lour corps, ne a chaunger la condicion de lour tenure et custumes ancienement dues, ne faire prejudice as seignours, d'avoir lour services et custumes come ils soloient d'ancien temps: et ent aient les seignours patentes sonz le graunt seal faites sur /ceste declaration,\ s'ils /les\ Verront avoir. Et quant al remenant del dit article, eient les seignours qe se sentent grevez commissions especialx souz le graunt seal as justices de la paiis, ou a autres persones suffisantz, d'enquerre de touz tieles rebelx, et de lour conseillours, procurours, meyntenours, et abettours: et de ceux qi ent serront enditez *[Page iii-22]*

XLVII. [Exemplifications of Domesday Book.]

88. To our lord the king and to the council of parliament the commons of the realm show: that in many parts of the kingdom of England the villeins and those holding lands in villeinage, who owe services and customary dues to lords for whatever reason within various lordships, as well of holy church as of lay lordships, have by counsel, procurement, maintenance and manipulation of certain persons, for money received from the aforesaid villeins and tenants, purchased in the king's court exemplifications from Domesday Book, concerning the manors and lands in which the said villeins and tenants reside; by colour of which copies, through the evil intention of the same, and through wicked interpretations provided by the said counsellors, procurers, maintainers, and abettors, they have withdrawn and do withdraw the customs and services they owe from their lords, claiming that they are entirely released from all manner of service as well of their bodies as for their aforesaid holdings: and have prevented the ministers of the said lords from distraining them to perform the aforesaid customs and services, and have formed leagues and confederacies forcibly to oppose their said lords and ministers: and each is supported by the others when they are distrained for that reason; and they threaten to kill the ministers of their said lords if they distrain them for the aforesaid customs and services, so that the lords and their ministers do not distrain them for their customs and services, through fear of death which might arise from their rebellion and resistance. And therefore the said lords lose and have lost large profits from their lordships, bringing about their disinheritance and injury to their estate, and the crops of many in the realm remain unreaped, and have perished forever for that reason, to the great injury of all the community; so it is feared, if remedy be not swiftly provided, that war might arise within the same kingdom because of their aforesaid rebellion, or that they might ally themselves to the enemies from overseas to seek vengeance on their lords, if the said enemies make some inroad. And for the support of such misdeeds they have collected amongst themselves large sums of money, to meet costs and expenses. And many of them have now come to court to gain support for their aforesaid purpose.

Wherefore may it please our said lord the king and the council to ordain a swift and fitting remedy for this, against the said counsellors, procurers, maintainers, and abettors, as well as against the said villeins and tenants, and especially against those who have appeared here now, as has been said, in order that those staying in the household might have knowledge of their punishment and to avert the kind of peril which has previously arisen in the kingdom of France through such rebellions and alliances of villeins against their lords.

Answer.

As for the copies granted and made in the chancery, it was declared in parliament that these could not nor should not have value or force in respect of the franchise of their persons, nor change the condition of their tenure and customs due of old, nor work to the prejudice of the lords enjoying their services and customs as they used to long ago: and let the lords have letters patent made under the great seal on this declaration, if they wish to have them. And as for the rest of the article, let the lords who feel aggrieved have special commissions under the great seal to the justices in the counties, or to other worthy persons, to enquire about all such rebels, and their counsellors, procurers, maintainers, and abettors: and those who shall be indicted *[Page iii-22]*

[Col. a] devaunt eux, sibien pur le temps passez come avenir, emprisoner, sanz estre deliverez hors de prisoun par maynprise, bail, n'autrement, sanz assent de lour seignours, tanqe ils soient atteintez ou acquitez. Et s'ils soient de ceo atteintz, ne soient aucunement deliverez les ditz tenantz rebelx, tanqe ils aient fait fyn au roi, et aient l'assent de lour ditz seignours: sauvant tutdys quant as ditz fyns les fraunchises et libertees des seignours q'ount fyns et amerciamentz de lour tenauntz. Et quant as conseillours, procurours, meyntenours et abettours, soit au tiel proces, et semblablement fait, et q'ils ne soient nullement deliverez tanqe ils eient fait fyn au roi et gree as seignours ensi grevez solonc lour estatz, et la quantite de lour trespas, si mesmes les seignours veullent suire envers eux par brief ou par bille. Sauvant les fraunchises et libertees des seignours, come desus est dit.

XLVIII.
89. Item, supplient sibien voz povres bachilers et esquiers de vostre roialme queux ceo sont travaillez en voz diverses guerres, et auxint ceux qe sount a travaillers, come voz autres lieges qe soient passez l'age de cessant anz, qe vous plese de vostre bone grace a eux graunter q'ils ne soient mis en office de viscont, eschetour, coroner, couillour; ne mis en jures, n'en nulles autres offices portantz chargez ou travailles, encountre lour gree: et qe si nulle qe soit passe l'age susdit soit greve par amercimentes, issues, fyns, ou peynes, absent ou present, contre la tenure de vostre dite graunte, q'ils de ceo soient en toutes voz courtes deschargez, siqe partie de lour vie puissent Dieux et eux mesmes servir.
Responsio.
Le roy, par advis de son conseil, ferra desporter tielles persones travaillez en la guerre la ou /luy\ semble qe soit affaire. Et quant a ceux qi sont issint enveillez et impotentz, il y a estatut en le cas quel le roi voet qe soit fermement tenuz et gardez en touz pointz.[30]
Membrane 12

XLIX.
90. Item, supplient les dites communes qe excepcion de bigamye ne soit allowe devaunt nulle de voz justices en cas de felonie, mes q'il eit privilege de sa clergie, nient contreesteaunt la bigamye.
Responsio.
Courgee la leye devant usee.

L.
91. Item, supplient les dites communes: qe come diverses profites sourdantz de la terre mesme, a graunde somme par an, sont resceuz par les mayns des enemys en la terre, sibien en sustenaunce de eux qe sont deins le roialme demurantz, come en sustenaunce et confort des enemys par dehors, a graunde damage du roi nostre seignour par moult des voies, come l'en purra declarer, et en la soeffrance graunde simplesse.
Qe plese ore ordeigner qe touz maners des aliens enemys, sibien religiouses come autres, puissent estre voidez hors de le roialme parentre cy et la chaundeleure, pur touz jours durant la guerre: et qe touz les profitz prises ore par eux purront entierment estre approwez en eide de la guerre, en supportacion du people, parensi qe les seignours qe sont lour fundours et patrones purrent avoir touz lour possessions en lour ordeignaunce, paiantz au roi a tant come aucun autre durant la guerre; ordeignantz en chescun lieu divine service estre

[Col. a] before them, both in time past as well as time to come, let them be imprisoned and not released without the assent of their lords by mainprise, bail, or any other means, until they be attainted or acquitted. And if they be attainted thereof, the said rebellious tenants shall not be freed in any way until they have paid the king a fine, and have the assent of their said lords: saving always with regard to the said fines the franchises and liberties of the lords who have the fines and amercements of their tenants. And as for the counsellors, procurers, maintainers, and abettors let there again be such a process, similarly carried out, and they shall never be freed until they have paid the king a fine and compensated the lords thus aggrieved in accordance with their estates, and the degree of their wrongdoing, if the same lords wish to proceed against them by writ or by bill. Saving the franchises and liberties of the lords, as said above.

XLVIII. [Exemptions from office.]
89. Also, the poor gentlemen and squires of your kingdom, both those who have served in your various wars, as well as those who are to serve, and your other lieges who are aged sixty or over, request that it might please you in your good grace to grant them that they shall not be appointed to the office of sheriff, escheator, coroner, collector nor placed on a jury, nor in any other burdensome or costly offices, contrary to their will: and if anyone who has passed the aforesaid age, absent or present, be injured by amercements, issues, fines or penalties, absent or present, contrary to the tenor of your said grant, that they be released from your courts, so that they may be free to serve God and themselves.
Answer.
The king, by the advice of his council, will deploy such persons serving in the wars wheresoever it seems to him that they are needed. And with regard to those who are old and weak, there is a statute on the matter which the king wishes to be firmly kept and upheld in all detail.

XLIX. [Bigamy.]
90. Also, the said commons pray that exception of bigamy should not be allowed before any of your justices in a case of felony, but that he may have privilege of clergy, notwithstanding the bigamy.
Answer.
Let the law take its established course.

L. [Expulsion of aliens.]
91. Also, the said commons pray that whereas various profits arising from the land, amounting to a great sum each year, are received into the hands of the enemy in the land, both in supporting those who live within the kingdom, as well as provisioning and supporting enemies without, greatly injuring the king in divers ways, which could be revealed, and which it would be foolish to tolerate.

May it please you now to ordain that all manner of alien enemies, both religious and others, be banished from the realm between now and Candlemas [2 February 1378], for the duration of the war: and that all the profits now received by them be spent entirely on the said war, in support of the people, so that the lords who are founders and patrons may have all their possessions under their sway, paying to the king as much as any other for the duration of the war; ordaining divine service to be performed in every place by a suitable

---
[30] Stat.14 Edw.3 St.1 cc. 6,7.

fait, de resonable nombre des Engleis la ou les ditz enemys a ore fount colour pur lour demure par divine service. En quele chose fesant une graunde somme ent serra approwez a la guerre par mye le roialme, et moult des choses de noz ordinaunces nient conuz a noz enemys, q'ore sont descovertez et espies par les persones avaunt nomez, en graunde arerissement et desceit de chescun bon purpos. Considerantz ovesqe ceo qe nulle de nostre lange, de quel condicion q'il soit, ne poet estre soeffert, ne graunde temps ad estee, deins la terre de noz enemys, pur nulle rien de mounde, sur peril de sa vie.[31]

Responsio.
Quant a ceo q'ils prient qe touz maneres des aliens des nacions enemys, sibien religieux come autres,
[Col. b] soient fait voider hors du roiaume parentre cy et la chaundeleure proschein, sanz revenir durantes les guerres, le roi le voet, horspris les priours conventuelle, et autres persones q'ount title a terme de vie en lour benefices ou offices, et conuz pur bones persones et loiaulx, et nyent suspectes d'espiaille ne d'autre prejudice au roi ne au roialme. Et horspris auxi les seculers, queux sont mariez, ou enheritez, ou autrement demurez avec les seignours dedeins le roialme, et sont conuz bons et loiaulx a nostre dit seignour le roi et a son roialme, et nient suspectez, et poent trover suffisaunte seourtee de lour loiaultee et bon port devers nostre dit seignour le roi et son dit roiaume. Et voet nostre dit seignour le roi qe ceux priours conventuelle, et autres persones exceptez, come dit est, demoergent continuelment pardecea, sanz passer ne envoier hors du roialme, ne recevoir lettre ne message de dela, durantes les guerres ou trewes parentre nostre seignour le roi et ses enemys, si celles lettres et messages ne soient primerement monstrez au roi ou a son conseil, sur peyne de forfaiture de quanqe ils purront \[forfaire a nostre]/ dit seignour le roi en corps et /en biens.\

Et sur ce soit fait proclamacion en touz les lieux notables en chescun countee qe touz les autres aliens enemys nient \[exceptez par desus,]/ sibien freres mendinantz come autres persones religieux et seculers qeconqes, voident le roialme dedeins le dit jour de la chaundeleure, sur la peine avantdite, \[et q'ils]/ passent touz au port de Dovorre par brief du roi, et nemye aillours, et d'illoqes au port de Caleys. Et qe illoqes soient deputes certeins suffisantz serchours \[pur les sercher]/ q'ils n'apportent or, n'argent, /en plate ne en vesselle, n'autre chose, forsqe les deniers\ pur lour despenses necessaires. Et qe par nulle paiement, ne par eschaunge, en or, argent, plate, vesselle, ne marchandise qeconqes, riens pluis ne soit tret, apportes, n'envoiez hors du roialme desore en avant par nulle de touz les aliens dessus ditz, ne a lour profit auxi poy par ceux qe demurrerent pardecea come dit est, come par les autres qeconqes, sur peyne de quanqe purra estre forfait a nostre dit seignour le roi, sibien par les eschangeours come par les ditz aliens mesmes. Et ceux qi serront trovez deins le roialme apres le dit jour encontre ceste ordinaunce, soient pris et raunsonez, et ceux qe les prendront averont la tierce partie de lour raunson, et le roi le remanant. Et a quele heure qe les dites priories conventuelle et autres benefices et offices issint eues par le title qe dessuz est dit voident par le ces ou deces des ditz priours et autres occupiours, qe ore sont . .   autre manere durantes les guerres, qe honestes persones Engleys y soient mys en lieux de eux, pur acomplir le divine service, et nul des enemys susditz. Et \[au]/ fyn qe le divin service soit sustenuz en les ditz priores aliens, est ordenez qe chescun esvesqe en sa diocise, a la presentacion des patrones fundours de mesmes

---
[31] PRO SC8/102/5052.

number of Englishmen; for the said enemies at present excuse their stay by maintaining divine service. And thereby a large sum can be set aside for the war throughout the kingdom, and many things in our ordinances concealed from our enemies, which have now been discovered and spied upon by the aforenamed persons, to the great injury and frustration of every good purpose; also considering that no one of our mother tongue, of whatever condition he be, would be allowed to so spend any length of time in the land of our enemies, for any purpose whatsoever, on danger of his life.

Answer.
As for what they request, that all kinds of aliens from enemy nations, both religious as well as others,
[Col. b] should be banished from the kingdom between now and next Candlemas [2 February 1378], without returning during the wars, the king wills it, except for conventual priors and others who hold a title for life in their benefices or offices, and who are known by good and loyal people, and are not suspected of espionage or any other injury against the king or kingdom. And excepting also lay people, who are married, or heirs, or otherwise dwell with the lords in the realm, and are known to be good and loyal to our said lord the king and his kingdom, and are not suspected, and can find sufficient surety for their loyalty and good bearing towards our said lord the king and his said kingdom. And our said lord the king wills that those conventual priors, and the other people excepted, as has been said, shall dwell continually on this side of the sea, without leaving or sending anyone outside the kingdom, or receiving letters or messages from overseas, during the wars or truces between our lord the king and his enemies, unless such letters and messages have been first shown to the king or his council, on pain of forfeiting whatsoever they have to forfeit to our said lord the king in their persons and goods.

Whereupon, let proclamation be made in all the chief places in each county that all other alien enemies not excepted as above, as well mendicant friars as other religious and lay persons of any kind, are to leave the realm before the said day of Candlemas [2 February 1378], on pain of the aforesaid penalty, and that they shall all journey to the port of Dover by the king's writ, and nowhere else, and from there to the port of Calais. And that there certain worthy searchers shall be appointed to search them to ensure that they are not carrying gold nor silver, in plate nor in vessel, nor anything else, except money for their necessary expenses. And that by no payment, nor exchange, in gold, silver, plate, vessel, nor merchandise of any sort, should anything else be taken, carried, or sent outside the kingdom henceforth by any of the aforesaid aliens, nor by those remaining here as was said, for their own profit, nor by any others, on pain of the said exchangers as well as the said aliens themselves forfeiting whatever they have to forfeit to our said lord the king. And those who shall be found within the kingdom after the said day contrary to this ordinance, shall be taken and held to ransom, and those who take them shall have a third of their ransom, and the king the remainder. And when the said conventual priories, and other benefices and offices thus held by the title mentioned above, fall vacant by the resignation or death of the said priors and other occupants, now in office . . . . in other manner during the wars, that honest Englishmen shall be appointed in their place, to perform divine service, and none of the aforesaid enemies. And so that divine service may be maintained in the said alien priories, it is ordained that each bishop in his

les priories, ferra accepter et mettre en ycelles autres honestes persones religieux mesons Engloys, ou bons et honestes chapellains seculers, pur demurrer et avoir covenable sustenaunce en les dites priories, affaire le divin service en ycelles durantes les guerres, jusqes a nombre q'est a present en chescun des dites priories. /Et qe de ce qe purra estre levez des profites\ des dites priories outre les charges susditz le roi soit responduz, en eide de soun estat, en descharge pur tant de son people. Et si aucunes priories y soient qe sont droitement funduz de spiritualtee, ou autrement esglises parochieles appropriez as tieux maisons aliens, et les priours, ou autres possessours de ycelles qi demurront deins le roialme par cest accord ne vorront ou ne purront les prendre a resonable ferme de nostre seignour le roi, adonqes soient celles priories et esglises durant la guerre lessez a ferme as autres suffisantz gentz de seint esglise, troefsantz seurtee suffisante d'y sustenir le divin service acustume, et sustenir et garder les priories, esglises, maisons, boys, et autres appurtenir sanz gast, exil, ou destruccion, et a les ditz priours ou autres tielx possessours, et lour moignes ou chapeleins, lour sustenaunces [Page iii-23]

[Col. a] et vesture covenablement. Et quant as baillies, et autres lour possessions qi sont de temporaltee, soit proclamacion faite parmye les contees qe quelconqe persone suffisant les vorra prendre a ferme de nostre seignour le roi a pluis haut pris, il les avera durant la guerre, troefsant suertee suffisante de les salver de tout gast et exil, et de trover les divins services, almoigns, es manoirs et baillies issint de lay fee; salvaunt au roi qe par l'advis en son graunt conseil puisse despenser avec eulx qe lui semblera mieltz affaire.

LI.
92. Item, supplient la commune: pur ceo q'en plusours lieux du roialme est usee qe diverses gentz de petitz garisons de terre ou de rent facent graunde mayntenance de quereles, et retenues des gentz sibien des esquiers come des autres, donant a eux lour \[liverees,]/ et pernantz la value d'icelle, ou la double, pur eux mayntenir en quereles, et auxi par alliaunce et affinitees faites par tieux gentz pur eux vestier sont entreseureez chescun a maintener autre querel resonable, et noun resonable, a graunde meschief du people: si priont qe sufficient remedie par bone chasticement du corps et de biens en ceo cas soit ordeigne.
Responsio.
Il y a estatutz et ordeinaunces en le cas, et auxint la commune loye y seit, les queux le roi voet qe soient mys en execucion. Et oultre ce soit crie faite parmie le roialme qe nulle liveree de chaperons, n'autrement, soit desormes donee, pur maintenance des quereles, n'autre confederacie, sur peyne d'emprisonement et grevouse forfaiture. Et enquergent les justices des assises en lour sessions diligeaument de touz ceux qi se coillent ensemble en fraternitee par tiele liveree affaire maintenance, et ceux qi serront trovez coupables soient duement puniz chescun solonc la quantitee de sa desert.[32]

LII.
93. Item, priont la comune: qe si ascun robbour ou tuour des gentz soit atteint et convicte a prisoun de evesqe, defamez pur commune tuour ou commune robbour, qe plese as evesqes meux estre avisez de lour purgacion qe devant

diocese, at the presentation of the patron founders of the same priories, shall cause to be accepted and appointed there other honest religious persons from English houses, or good and honest secular chaplains, to remain and receive suitable sustenance in the said priories, to perform divine service in the same during the wars, up to the number now in each of the said priories. And as for that which can be levied from the profits of the said priories in addition to the aforesaid charges, the king will answer, aiding his estate and relieving his people. And if there be any priories which have been duly founded by a spirituality, or parochial churches appropriated to such alien houses, and the priors, or other owners of the same who dwell within the kingdom under this agreement do not wish or are unable to take them at a reasonable farm from our lord the king, then those priories and churches shall, during the war, be leased at farm to other worthy persons of holy church, upon their giving an adequate guarantee of their ability to maintain the customary divine service, and support and protect the priories, churches, houses, woods, and other things pertaining to them without waste, ruin or destruction, and supplying the said priors and other such owners, and their monks or chaplains, with fitting sustenance [Page iii-23]

[Col. a] and clothing. And as for bailiwicks and other their temporal possessions, proclamation shall be made throughout the counties that whatsoever worthy person wishes to take them at farm from our lord the king at the highest price, shall have them for the duration of the war, on giving adequate reassurance of being able to save them from all waste and ruin, and of providing divine service and alms in the manors and bailliwicks of lay fee; saving to the king that by the advice of his great council he might except any who seem useful to him.

LI. [Maintenance and livery.]
92. Also, the commons pray that whereas in many places in the kingdom it is customary for many people with small holdings of land or rent to perform great maintenance in lawsuits, and keep retinues of men, as well of squires as of others, giving them liveries, and taking the value of the same or double, to support them in disputes, and also because by alliances and affinities made by such people to give their livery, they are there bound to support both reasonable and unreasonable suits, to the great injury of the people: therefore they pray that adequate remedy be ordained in the matter to punish them in their persons and their possessions.
Answer.
There are statutes and ordinances thereon, and there is also the common law, which the king wills to be enforced. Furthermore, let it be proclaimed throughout the kingdom that no livery of hoods, nor any other, shall henceforth be given for the maintenance of lawsuits, or any other confederacy, on pain of imprisonment and heavy forfeiture. And let the justices of the assizes make thorough enquiries in their sessions concerning all those who have banded themselves together in such fraternities through such livery to effect maintenance, and those who are found guilty shall be duly punished, according to their deserts.

LII. [Purgation of notorious criminals.]
93. Also, the commons pray that if any robber or murderer be attainted and convicted to the bishop's prison, defamed as a common murderer or robber, that it shall please the

---
[32] Stat. 1 Ric.2 c.7.

ces heures n'ad este usee, en eschieuant graunde damage del people.
Responsio.

Le roi ad chargez les prelatz q'ils se abstiennent mieltz de faire tielles \[purgacions, et especialment des communes]/ et notoirs felons; et s'ils ne le facent, le roi ent ordeignera par advis des seignours d'autre remedie covenable.

LIII.
94. Item, prient la commune: qe nulle eschetour face seisir terres ne tenementz de frank homme pur ascune \[enqueste de office]/ trove pur le roi tanqe brief de scire facias hors del chauncellerie soit issis al terre-tenaunt; et qe par due processe il soit adjugge et descusse qe le dite \[terre ou tenement soit de]/ droit appartenant a nostre dit seignour par voie d'eschete.
Responsio.

Ent soit usez come devant y ad este faite.

LIIII.
95. Item, pur ce qe mayntz gentz sont delaiez en la court du roi de lour demandes, partaunt qe ascun foitz la partie allegge qe les demaundantz ne doyvent estre responduz sanz le roi, et ascun foitz la partie pleintif allegge en mesme la manere, et auxint \[moult des gentz grevez]/ par les ministres du roi, encountre droiture: des queux grevances homme ne purra avoir recoverir sanz commune parlement.
Qe plese a nostre dit seignour de tenir \[parlement]/un foitz par an au meynz, et ceo en lieu covenable: et q'en mesmes les parlementz soient les plees qe en la dite forme delaiez, et les plees la ou les justices \[sont en diverses]/ opinions recordez et terminez: et q'en mesme la manere purrent les billes estre terminez qe serront \[liverez]/ en parlement si avaunt come raison et ley demaunde.
Responsio.

Quant a ceo qe parlement serroit tenuz chescun an, soient les estatutz ent faitz tenuz et gardez; mais \[quant]/
[Col. b] al lieu ou \[le]/ parlement se tendra, le roi ent ferra sa volentee. Et quant as plees des quelles les justices serroient en diverses opinions, il y a estatutz ent faitz, queux le roi voet qe soient tardez et fermement tenuz.

LV.
96. Item, purceo qe /la ley de la terre et commune droit ont estez\ sovent delaiez par lettres issues sibien desouz prive seal le roi come de secret signet, a graunde grevaunce du people.
Qe plese a nostre seignour qe desoremes la ley de la terre ne commune droit ne soient delaiez ne destourbez par lettres des ditz sealx; et si rien soit fait en nulle place de la court nostre seignour le roi, ou aillours, par tielx lettres issues desouthe les ditz sealx encountre droiture et ley de la terre, rien ne vaille, et \[pur]/ nient soit tenuz.
Responsio.

Se tiegnent les estatutz ent faitz en touz pointz.[33]

LVI.
97. Item, pur ceo qe moult des gentz sont delaiez de lour suyte en courtees par proteccions grauntez as gentz qe soy feignent d'aler en service du roy, et ne sont mye, mes qe pur delaier la suyte le pleintiff auxi bien en plee de terre, come des dettes, ou trespas. Et pur tiel malice restreindre y plese

---
[33] Stat.2 Edw.3 c.8; Stat.14 Edw.3 St.1 c.14.

bishops to be better advised upon their purgation than they have lately been, to avoid great injury to the people.
Answer.

The king has charged the prelates that they should rather abstain from making such purgations, and especially in respect of common and notorious criminals; and if they do not, the king will ordain some remedy by the advice of the lords.

LIII. [Escheators.]
94. Also, the commons pray that no escheator shall cause the lands or tenements of a free man to be seized for any ex officio inquest held for the king until a writ of scire facias has been issued from the chancery to the tenant; and that it shall be adjudged and discussed by due process whether the said land or tenement rightfully pertains to our said lord the king by way of escheat.
Answer.

Let it be done as is accustomed.

LIIII. [Pleas referred to parliament.]
95. Also, whereas the pleas of many are delayed in the king's court, sometimes because the other party alleges that the claimants ought not to be answered without the king, and sometimes the plaintiffs allege the same, and also many are oppressed by the king's ministers, contrary to right: which grievances cannot be redressed without common parliament.

May it please our said lord the king to hold a parliament at least once a year, and that in a convenient place: and that in the same parliaments the pleas which are delayed in the said manner, and the pleas in which the justices differ in their opinions shall be recorded and determined: and that in a similar manner bills shall be settled which are submitted in parliament as aforesaid, as reason and law require.
Answer.

In respect of the request that parliament be held once a year, let the statutes made thereon be kept and upheld; but as
[Col. b] to the place where parliament shall be held, the king will act as he chooses. And with regard to pleas in which the justices are of differing opinions, there are statutes made thereon, which the king wishes to remain in force and be firmly upheld.

LV. [Pleas delayed by privy seal and signet letters.]
96. Also, whereas the law of the land and common right have often been delayed by letters issued both under the privy seal of the king as well as the secret signet, to the great injury of the people.
May it please our lord that henceforth neither the law of the land nor common right shall be delayed or disrupted by letters under the said seals; and if anything is done in any part of the court of our said lord the king, or elsewhere, by such letters issued under the said seals, contrary to right and the law of the land, it shall be invalid and held at naught.
Answer.

Let the statutes concerning this remain in force in all respects.

LVI. [Misuse of protections.]
97. Also, whereas many are delayed in their suits in courts by protections granted to persons who pretend to be in the service of the king when they are not, merely to delay the plaintiff's suit, as well in pleas of land as in debt and trespass, to curb such wrongdoing may it please our said lord

a nostre dit seignour qe si le tenaunt en plee de terre use la proteccioun nostre seignour le roi apres apparance, et le demaundant puisse /averrer\ qe le tenaunt ne fuist mie en service le roi le jour qe la plee demurra saunz jour par la proteccion, soit l'absence du tenaunt journee defaute. Et si le tenaunt use proteccion avant apparance, qe bien list al demaundant, s'il entent son profit affaire, de prendre brief en chauncellerie sur le tenaunt d'averrer q'il ne fuist mie en service du roi le jour qe la suite fuist delaie par la proteccion. Et si le tenaunt de ceo soit atteint, soient agardez al demandant ses damages par descressioun des justices, eiant regard a son purchas, costages, mises et perdes; et soit le tenant jugge a prisoun.

Responsio.

Adverement ne gist mye en le cas. Et quant al remenant de la peticion la commune ley y sert assez bien. Et si aucun ait proteccioun, et la courte le roi soit acertee de cause resonable pur qoy ce doit estre repellee, en tieu cas serra la proteccion repellee. Et est assentuz qe nulle proteccion soit alloue devant aucune juge pur vitailes achatez ou prises sur le viage ou service dont la proteccion fait mencion, ne auxint pur trespas ou contract faitz \[puis]/La date de mesme la proteccion fait.[34]

Membrane 13

LVII.

98. Item, priont les communes, pur le bien du roi, des seignours, et toute le roialme: qe la ou les leynes et autres marchaundises del roialme repeiront al estaple, puisse a present estre ordeigne par bone descrecion meillour et plus seure garde qe n'ad estee fait devaunt la guerre: considerant sibien q'en les ditz leynes et marchaundises illoeqes repeirables la substance de toute la tresore du roialme si est contenuz, come pur le desir du dit richesse les enemys lour enforcent pur ceo atteindre, come Dieux defende. Et si tiel cas aviegne parentre un parlement et un autre, qe la poiar des enemys fuisse si graunde en la course des marchantz sur la meer, ou environ la ville ou l'estaple est, qe les marchantz sibien vendours come achatours ne purront ne n'oseront illoeqes repoier, sibien pur doute de lour vies come de lour biens.

Qe ore plese a nostre seignour, et les seignours du parlement d'ordeigner pur tiel cas, ou pur semblable, ou et en quel lieu les marchaundises susditz purront mieux au profit du roialme repeirir, issint qe le roi, seignours, ne poeple ne soient endamagez par cause de deliverance ne issue des marchaundises avantdites. Et durant la guerre, qe les marchantz entre eux par lour commune assent puissent fraunchement lever de lour biens ceo qe lour bosoigne pur sauf-conduyt de lour biens, sibien par meer come par terre, entre Gravenyng et Caleis: et ce a tant et tant de foitz come bosoigne lour requirt, saunz offense du roi ou de ley. Purveux qe les deniers entre *[Page iii-24]*

[Col. a] eux levez pur la dite cause ne soient despenduz n'enprowez a nulle autre bosoigne du roi nostre seignour, ne a l'avantage de nulle singler persone ne persones des ditz marchantz, mes soulement a commune bosoigne de salvacioun de lour ditz biens en commune, par la manere come entre eux mesmes serra assentuz.

Responsio.

Quant al lieu ou l'estaple de leynes serroit tenuz, si tiel cas avenoit, le roi voet qe endementiers mesme l'estaple soit tenuz deins le roialme d'Engleterre, es portz esluz ou ce fust tenuz quant estoit darreinement tenuz deins la roialme. Et quant as dites imposisions, si le cas aviegne q'ils eient

---

that if the tenant in a plea of land produce the protection of our lord the king after appearing in court, and the claimant is able to prove that the tenant was not indeed in the king's service on the day when the plea was delayed sine die by the protection, let the absence of the tenant count as default. And if the tenant claim protection before appearing, then it shall be lawful for the claimant, if he choose to take advantage of it, to take a writ in the chancery averring that the tenant was not in the king's service on the day when the suit was delayed by the protection. And if the tenant be thus attainted, let the claimant be awarded damages at the discretion of the justices, with due regard given for his purchase, expenses, outlay, and losses; and let the tenant be adjudged to prison.

Answer.

Averment does not lie in such an action. And for the rest of the petition the common law will serve well enough. And if anyone has protection, and the king's court has sufficient grounds for believing that it should be repealed, then let the protection be repealed. And it is agreed that no protection shall be allowed before any judge merely for victuals bought or taken in the course of the journey or service of which the protection makes mention, or for trespass or contracts made since the date when the said protection was granted.

LVII. [The staple.]

98. Also, the commons, for the good of the king, the lords and all the kingdom pray that whereas wool and other merchandise of the kingdom goes to the staple, there might now be ordained, with wise discretion, a better and greater safeguard than that in place before the war: considering that the substance of all the kingdom's treasure lies in the said wool and merchandise returnable there, and that out of lust for the said riches the enemies would attack them to secure it, which God forbid. And so it has come about, between one parliament and the next, that the power of the enemy is so great in the routes of the merchants on the sea, or about the town where the staple is, that the merchants, as well sellers as buyers, cannot and dare not repair there, for fear both of their lives and their goods.

May it now please our lord, and the lords of parliament, to ordain for such a cause or for the like, where and in what place the aforesaid merchandise might be taken for the benefit of the kingdom, so that neither the king, lords, nor people shall be injured by the deliverance or issue of the aforesaid merchandise. And for the duration of the war, that the merchants amongst themselves by their common assent might freely levy from their goods that which they need for the safe-conduct of their goods, both by sea and by land, between Gravelines and Calais: and this as much and so often as need be, without offence to the king or to the law. It being understood that the money *[Page iii-24]*

[Col. a] raised amongst themselves for the said cause should be not spent or devoted to any other need of our lord the king, nor for the advantage of any individual of individuals from amongst the said merchants, but only for the general need to protect their said goods as a whole, in a manner which shall be decided amongst themselves.

Answer.

As for the place where the staple of wool shall be held, if need be, the king wills that the same staple shall, for the present, be held in the kingdom of England, in the designated ports where it was held when it was last in the kingdom. And as for the said impositions, if it should happen that they

---

[34] Stat.1 Ric.2 c.8.

busoigne de sauf-conduit pur mesmes les leynes sur le meer, et par tant lour covendra despender de lour avoir, le facent assavoir a graunt conseil, et reson lour ent serra fait.

LVIII.
99. Item, supplient les communes en cest present parlement assembles: qe come en le parlement tenuz a Westm' en la quinzeine de Seint Hiller darrein passe, general grace, pardoun, et remission estoit graunte par vostre aiel a touz ses subgitz et liges de son roialme d'Engleterre, de chescun manere de gree, estat, et condicion come piert en les roules de dit parlement; en la quele generale grace, pardoun, et remission le dit evesqe estoit except et forpris: et puis de vostre roiale magestee grauntastes au dit evesqe q'il averoit et enjoiereit plenement et entierment en touz pointz mesmes les graces, pardouns, et remissions faites as autres ses liges en le dit parlement par vostre dit aiel, nient contreestantz la exception et forsprise susdites. Et outre ce lui pardonastes plusours diverses articles et empeschementz a lui surmises en temps de vostre dit aiel, et autres diverses graces, pardouns, et remissions lui feistes, et des toutes les articles, empeschementz, et choses avantdites lui grauntastes et feistes faire voz graciouses /chartres\ assetz pleneres, come plus plenement piert en ycelles.

Qe plese a vostre noble hautesse, de l'avys et commune assent des prelatz, duc, countes, barons et autres grauntz et communes, affermer, approver, ratifier, et conferrer en cest present parlement voz dites chartres, ove touz les articles, pardons, graces, remissions, et cercumstances qecunqes en ycelles comprises, al honour de Dieu, et pur la salvacioun et seuretee de l'estat du dit evesqe, et de sa esglise de Wyncestre.

Responsio.

Le roi en sa propre persone de sa bouche demesne de commune assent et avys des prelatz, duc, countes, barons, et autres grauntz en plein parlement assemblez, ad graunte ceste peticion pleinement et en touz pointz, et quanqe en ycelle est compris. Et voet et graunte del commune assent et advis avantditz qe les chartres ou lettres des queles ceste peticion fait mencion, et les quelles feurent par bone deliberacion veues, luez, et pleinement entenduz en dit parlement, et soient ore affermez, approvez, ratifiez, et confirmez souz son grant seal, solonc le purport de mesme la peticion, et l'effect, tenour, et fourme de chartres ou lettres avantdites.[35]

Membrane 14

LIX.
100. Item, qe come les progenitours nostre seignour le roy ont grantez as diverses seignours, citeins, et burgeises, connyssance de touz maneres des plees de terre; et purce qe par plees d'assises de no' dis' et mort d'auncestre expresse mencion n'est pas fait en les chartres les ditz progenitours, les ditz seignours, citeins, et burgeoys n'ont eut conissance de tieux assises.

Qe plese a nostre seignour le roy q'ils qe ont tiels chartres de touz maneres plees du terre, q'ils purront par tiel parole general avoir conissance d'assises de novel disseisin, et mort d'ancestre.

Responsio.

Eient or allouance selonc la forme de leur ancienes chartres, et les allouances ent faitz devant ces heures.

LVIII. [The bishop of Winchester.]
99. Also, the commons assembled in this present parliament pray that whereas in the parliament held at Westminster at the quindene of St Hilary last [27 January 1377], general grace, pardon, and remission were granted by your grandfather to all his subjects and lieges of his kingdom of England, of every degree, estate and standing, as appears in the rolls of the said parliament; from which general grace, pardon, and remission the said bishop was excepted and excluded: and subsequently your royal majesty granted to the said bishop that he might have and fully and completely enjoy in all respects the same graces, pardons, and remissions granted to his other lieges in the said parliament by your said grandfather, notwithstanding the aforesaid exception and exclusion. And further, you pardoned him on many different articles and impeachments levelled against him in the time of your said grandfather, and you granted him various other graces, pardons, and remissions, and for all those articles, accusations, and aforesaid things you granted and caused to be issued your gracious charters, as appears more fully therein.

May it please your noble highness, with the advice and common assent of the prelates, dukes, earls, barons, and other great men and commons, to affirm, approve, ratify, and confirm in the present parliament your said charters, with all the articles, pardons, graces, remissions, and circumstances contained in the same, to the honour of God, and for the salvation and security of the estate of the said bishop, and of his church at Winchester.

Answer.

The king in person, by his own voice and with the common assent and advice of prelates, dukes, earls, barons, and other great men assembled in full parliament, has granted this petition in its entirety and in all detail, and whatsoever is contained in the same. And he wills and grants with the aforesaid common assent and advice that the charters or letters of which this petition makes mention, and which were, with thorough deliberation viewed, read, and plainly heard in the said parliament, shall now be affirmed, approved, ratified, and confirmed under his great seal, in accordance with the purport of the same petition, and the effect, tenor, and form of the aforesaid charters or letters.

LIX. [Possessory asssizes in franchise courts.].]
100. Also, whereas the progenitors of our lord the king have granted to various lords, citizens and burgesses cognizance of all manner of pleas of land; and because express mention is not made of pleas of assizes of novel disseisin and mort d'ancestor in the charters of the said progenitors, the said lords, citizens and burgesses have not had cognizance of such assizes.

May it please our said lord the king that those who have charters for all manner of pleas of land, might through such general words have cognizance of assizes of novel disseisin and mort d'ancestor.

Answer.

Let them now have such an allowance in accordance with the form of their ancient charters, and the allowances made thereon in the past.

---
[35] PRO C49/9/2; Stat.1 Ric.2 c.10

LX.
101. Item, ils prient qe nul manere de eyre, ne traillebastoun, courge el royaume durant la guerre, ou par l'espace de vynt anz.
Responsio.
Le roy soi avisera.

102. Item, supplie la dicte commune: qe par la ou aucune taillage ou subside est grantez a nostre dit seignour le roy, en eide de lui et de son royaume, as queux subsides et taillages chescun de ses liges serra charge selonc leur possessions et lour avoir, et les grantz seignours du roiaume, aussi bien religiouses come autres, ont plusours terres et tenementz en leur mayns, aucuns par purchace, aucuns par voidance et par eschete, queux terres et tenementz furent contributoires a les taillages et subsides et subsides avantditz: et les seignours qe ore les tiegnent et ont nulles contribucions faire ou paier ne voillent pur eux, a grande pitee et charge de voz liges avantditz.
Par quoi plese a nostre dit seignour le roy et a son bon conseil, de remede ordener pur ses liges de les grevances et charges avantditz, en eovre de charite.
Responsio.
Paient les gentz de seinte eglise leur afferant entre les lays gentz pur touz leur possessions qe sont devenuz a lour mayns, ou queles ils ont purchacez puis l'an .xx.ᵉ Le roy Edward filz le roy Henry.

LXI.
103. Item, purce qe le bon roy vostre ael, qi Dieu assoille, en eide de s'alme, et de la bone voillance q'il avoit a son poeple, au darein parlement, qe fust son an jubile, fist grace et pardon a son poeple, supposant en sa dite grace qe sa entente de ce en toutes choses lour deveroit valoir, ne qe subtilitee de cource de l'escheqer, ne juggement de eux ne d'autre, deveroit defaire sa dite grace en nul point qe purra estre ymagine au contraire, en especial, ne en generale. Et ore, voz ditz liges se sentent grandement greve de subtilite et ymaginacions faites au contraire l'entente de sa dite grace par ministres et juges de l'escheqer, disantz expressement au poeple qe les pointz especialx nient declarez deveront estre parcelles de son pardon, q'est vrayment le contraire de l'entente de la grace nostre bon roy, qe Dieux assoille, en especial nient expressement declarez purra valoir a vostre poeple, et l'entente de sa bone grace si avant come il eust estee declaree de point en point, et nemye estre defait par ymaginacion et subtilite de tieux ministres et juges.

Responsio.
Eient touz gentz comprises en dite pardoun allouance de toutes choses comprises deinz meisme la pardoun, si bien c'estassavoir des niefs, vitailles, artillerie, et nient expressez especialment en ycelle, come de toutz dettes et acontes en generaltee expressez en la pardoun avantdite.

LXII.
104. Item, qe celui q'ad estee visconte du contee un an, ou eschetour du roy, ne soit deinz trois anz apres fait visconte ne eschetour, si autre en dit contee soit suffisant de possession de biens et chateux a respondre au roy et al poeple.

Responsio.
Le roy le voet des viscontes tantsoulement.[36]

---
[36] Stat.1 Ric.2 c.11.

LX. [Eyres and trailbaston.]
101. Also, they pray that no manner of eyre or trailbaston shall run in the kingdom during the war, or for a period of twenty years.
Answer.
The king will consider it further.

[Lords and prelates to contribute to subsidies.]
102. Also, the said commons pray that when a tallage or subsidy is granted to our said lord the king, in support of him and his kingdom, to which subsidies and tallages everyone of his lieges would be obliged to contribute in accordance with their possessions and property, the great lords of the kingdom, as well the religious as others, have many lands and tenements in their hands, some by purchase, some by voidance and by escheat, which lands and tenements were liable to contribute towards the aforesaid tallages and subsidies: and the lords who hold them now have not made or paid any contributions for them and will not do so, to the great sorrow and oppression of your aforesaid lieges.
Wherefore may it please our said lord the king and his good council to ordain remedy for his lieges upon the aforesaid grievances and burdens, by way of charity.
Answer.
Let those of holy church pay their share along with the laity for all the possessions which have fallen into their hands, or which they have purchased since the twentieth year of King Edward [I], son of King Henry [III] [1291-2].

LXI. [Edward III's general pardon]
103. Also, whereas the good king, your grandfather, whom God absolve, for the salvation of his soul, and for the good will he bore towards his people, at the last parliament, which was in his jubilee year, bestowed grace and pardon on his people, in the belief that his good intent in all things would give it value, and not that cunning in the workings of the exchequer, nor their judgements nor those of others, would annul his said grace in any way which could be devised to the contrary, in particular or in general. Yet now your said lieges feel themselves greatly oppressed by the plots and devices carried out contrary to the intentions of his said grace by ministers and judges of the exchequer, who plainly inform the people that particular matters not specified ought not to be covered by his pardon, which is truly contrary to the intention of the grace of our good king, whom God absolve, and in particular, what is expressly declared might be of great value to your people, and the intention of his good grace was as though it were specified point by point, and not to be undone by the plotting and scheming of such ministers and judges.
Answer.
Let all those included in the said pardon have allowance for all things mentioned in the same pardon, namely for ships, victuals, and artillery not given particular mention in the same, as well as all debts and accounts generally included in the aforesaid pardon.

LXII. [Sheriffs and escheators.]
104. Also, that anyone who has been sheriff of a county for a year, or the king's escheator, shall not be appointed sheriff or escheator within the next three years, if there be any in the said county sufficient in goods and chattels to answer to the king and people.
Answer.
The king wills it with regard to sheriffs only.

LXIII.
105. Item, qe errour fait en l'escheqer puisse estre adresse en bank le roy, ou en parlement.
Responsio.
Il \[y]/ ad un estatut fait en le cas, quel le roy voet qe soit tenuz.[37]

LXIIII.
106. Item, monstrent les communes et liges du royaume q'ils sont grandement anientiz, et pluseurs de eux destruitz, par cause qe leur niefs et bateux ont estees sovent foiz devant ces heures forfaites au roy et as autres seignours de franchises, quant homme, femme, ou garceon par infortune ou mesaventure fust mort, ou par eschier des niefs, bateux, ou autre vesseux encontre la volunte de eux as queux les dites niefs, bateux, ou autres vesseux furent; et par cause de quele forfaiture les dites liges ne ont talent des niefs faire, ne leur avoir sur fesure ou reparacion d'ycelle mettre, come soleient faire en temps passe, au grande anientisement de lour *[Page iii-25]*

[Col. a] navie, et damage de la terre.
Dont ils prient qe plese a nostre tresredoute seignour le roy et son conseil ordener par estatut qe nulle nief ne bateu, ne nulles autres vesseux, ne soit de ore en avant forfait par cause de mort d'aucune persone en la forme sus dite, pur Dieux, et equite, et en eovre de charite, et encrese de la navye, confort de ses communes et liges, et grant profit de toute la terre en temps avenir.
Responsio.
Le roy y ferra en eise manere a touz ceux queux ent vorront pleindre \en/ especial, sauvant toutdys sa regalye.

LXV.
107. Item, supplient les povres communes de la terre qe come plusours gentz a la suite des parties sont ajugez a la prisone de Flete par plee de dette en le commune bank nostre seignour le roy, et ailours, pur avoir leur recoverir, et ils sont ajugez a la prisone de Flete, le gardeyn de la dite prisone de Flete suffre plusours de les persones aler a large, et faire leur marchandisez, et vendent et achatent en paiis, en villes, et en citees, et sont les jours et les nuytz hors de prisoun a leur volunte; et par tiel colour et suffrance homme ne poet avoir lour recoverir devers eux, a grant tort et meschief et anientisment des plusours gentz.

Par quoi plese a nostre tresredoute seignour le roy et son bon conseil, en eovre de charire, ordener remede, et outre ce comander, charger et defende qe nulle gardeyn de Flete desore ne soeffre nul prisoner, apres ce q'il soit ajugge a la prisone, aler hors du prisone, par maynprise, ne par baille, ne par bastoun, sanz gree faire as parties pleintiefs qe ont par juggement recoveriz lour dettes, s'il ne soit par briefs nostre seignur le roy, sur forfaiture de perdre son office et la garde du dite persone: et outre qe les ditz pleintiefs eient lour dettes issint ajuggez du dite gardeyn ou gardeyns du prison par briefe du roy, selonc la matire d'estatut marchant, en qi mains qe lour terres et tenementz ove leur appurtenances deviegnent, en cas qe ce poet estre prove par bones gentz, pur Dieu, et en eovre de charite, et en avantage et profit du dit povre commune.

Responsio.
Il plest au roy, adjoustant a ycelle qe si nullui a suite de partie adjuggez a autre prisone pur dette, trespas, ou autre querele se voile conistre en l'escheqer voluntrivement, et par feynte cause dettour au roy, et par tant estre ajuggez a Flete pur

---
[37] Stat. 14 Edw. 3 St. 1 c.5.

LXIII. [Error in the exchequer.]
105. Also, that error made in the exchequer might be amended in the king's bench, or in parliament.
Answer.
There is a statute made on the matter, which the king wills shall be upheld.

LXIIII. [Ships as deodands.]
106. Also, the commons and lieges of the kingdom show that they have been greatly injured, and many of them ruined, because their ships and boats have many times in the past been forfeited to the king and to other lords of franchises, whensoever a man, woman, or boy has been killed by accident, or misadventure, or when escaping from ships, boats or other vessels against the wish of those to whom the said ships, boats, or other vessels belong; and because of that forfeiture the said lieges have no means to keep ships, or invest their money in the making or repair of the same, as they did in the past, to the great reduction of their *[Page iii-25]*

[Col. a] fleet and harm to the land.
Wherefore they pray that it might please our most redoubtable lord the king and his council to ordain by statute that no ship or boat, nor any other vessels, shall henceforth be forfeit for the death of anyone in the aforesaid way, for the love of God, and in equity, and by way of charity, and to strengthen the fleet to the comfort of his commons and lieges, and the great benefit of all the land in time to come.
Answer.
The king will readily do that for all who wish to plead thereon in particular, saving always his regality.

LXV. [Debtors.]
107. Also, the poor commons of the land pray that whereas many at the suit of parties in the common bench of our lord the king, or elsewhere, are adjudged to the prison of Fleet by plea of debt to secure recovery, the warden of the said prison of Fleet allows many such persons to wander at large, and deal in merchandise, and sell and buy in the country, in the towns, and in the cities, and they spend their days and nights outside the prison as they choose; by which colour and tolerance their creditors cannot recover against them, to the great wrong, trouble, and injury of many.

Wherefore, may it please our most redoubtable lord the king and his good council, by way of charity, to ordain remedy, and in addition to order, charge, and forbid any warden of the Fleet henceforth to allow any prisoner, after he has been adjudged to prison, to leave prison by mainprise, bail, or pledge, without compensating the plaintiffs who by judgment have recovery of their debts, unless it be by writ of our lord the king; on pain of forfeiting their office and the keeping of the said person: and moreover, that the said plaintiffs shall have their debts thus adjudged, by the king's writ, in accordance with the provisions of the statute merchant, from the said keeper or keepers of the prison, into whose hands their lands and tenements with appurtenances have fallen, where that can be proven by good people, for God and by way of charity, and to the advantage and profit of the said poor commons.
Answer.
It pleases the king, adding thereto that if anyone at the suit of a party for debt, trespass, or other plea be adjudged to another prison, and wilfully and on false grounds has resort to the exchequer as a debtor of the king, and for that reason

greindre suite y avoir de prisone qe aillours, et issint delaier la partie de son recoverir, soit celle reconissance resceuz illoeqes; et s'il ne soit autre part dettour au roy de record, soit son corps tantost remandez a la prisone ou il estoit devant, a y demurrer tanqe il avera fait gree a la dite partie. Et tiel gree fait, soit immediat remandez a Flete, pur y demurrer tanqe il avera fait gree au roy de sa reconissance avantdite.[38]

is sentenced to the Fleet as having a greater suit there than elsewhere, thus to delay the plaintiffs in their recovery, let the recognizance be received there; and if there be no such debtor to the king on record elsewhere, his person shall be immediately remanded to the prison where he was before, there to remain until he has satisfied the said party. And such compensation having been made, he shall at once be remanded to the Fleet, to remain there until he has satisfied the king for his aforesaid recognizance.

LXVI.
108. Item, ils prient, en honour de Dieu, et profit del poeple, qe desore nul dean, official, archideaken,
[Col. b] ne autres /curatours\ de seinte eglise, preignent del poeple pur coreccion de pesche sommes pecuniels plus ne meyns, mes doigne a chescun en coreccion penance espirituel, qe plus assez sera plesante a Dieu, et profit al alme du peccheour, pur eschuiant les grandes ransons prises del petit poeple par les coreccions des peyns pecuniels: entendantz, treshonures seignours qe pur syngulir avantage des ditz curatours il y ad des pluseurs cures lessez a ferme par encrese d'an en an, come sont terres et tenementz de lay fee, a grande esclandre de seinte eglise, et grande districcion del povre poeple.
Responsio.
Le roy chargera les prelatz, et autres ordinairs d'ent faire due punissement selonc les loys de seinte eglise, et nemye autrement.

LXVI. [Mulcts levied in penance.]
108. Also, they pray, in honour of God, and for the benefit of the people, that henceforth no dean, official, archdeacon,
[Col. b] nor other curate of holy church, shall take from the people for the punishment of sins pecuniary sums large or small, but shall give to each as a punishment a spiritual penance, which will be more than pleasing to God, and of benefit to the soul of the sinner, that great sums of money be not taken in pecuniary penalties from lesser people for such corrections: bearing in mind, most honoured lords, that for the singular advantage of the said curates, many cures are leased at farm increasing from year to year, as though they were lands and tenements of the lay fee, to the great slander of holy church, and great injury of the poor people.
Answer.
The king will instruct the prelates and other ordinaries to administer due correction in accordance with the laws of holy church, and not otherwise.

LXVII.
109. Item, qe y puisse estre declare en cest parlement de certein, combien les curatours prendront pur proeve de chescun testament, et pur l'acquitance d'ycels: car ils preignent au present tresgrantz fyns et extorcions pur ycels, a grant damage du poeple.
Responsio.
Le roy chargera les prelatz et autres ordenairs q'ils ne preignent pur tieux proeves des testamentz et acquitances, si noun qe resonablement, et en eisee manere.

LXVII. [Probate fees.]
109. Also, that it be declared in this parliament for certain how much curates should take for proving a testament, and for the acquittance of the same: because at present they take very great fines and extortionate sums for the same, to the great injury of the people.
Answer.
The king will charge the prelates and other ordinaries to take only reasonable sums in a fair manner for proof and acquittance of wills.

LXVIII.
110. Item, prient la commune: qe come la grande meschief est avenuz a toute la navye del royaume par diverses causes; qe plese a present faire examiner ceux qe sont sachantz de la dite matire, par queles causes la dite meschief est avenuz, et par quele manere remede ent poet estre ordeigne.
Responsio.
Le roy ent ferra par l'avys de son grant conseil ce qe mieulz lui semblera affaire.
Membrane 15

LXVIII. [The navy.]
110. Also, the commons pray: whereas great trouble has befallen the entire fleet of the kingdom for various reasons; may it please you now to question those who have knowledge of the matter, as to the manner in which the said trouble has arisen, and how remedy might be ordained.
Answer.
The king will act with the advice of his great council in the way which seems best to him.

LXIX.
111. Item, ils prient: qe nulle persone travaillez vers cest parlement pur leur contee, burghe, ou citee soit constreynt d'estre coillour de la grant ore grantez pur la guerre, etc.; et leur gages, custumables de ancien temps, puisse estre levez de chescune manere de persone, dedeinz franchise et dehors, eiante lay fee dedeinz le contee: et qe nullui, de quele condicion q'il soit, eiant de lay fee en le contee soit espernyz; mes selonc l'afferant de sa tenure q'il soit contributoire as ditz gages, et aussi au taxe ore grantez, issint qe les poveres gentz du poeple puissent ore estre supportez par les seignours et autres qe unqes ne paierent as taxes avant ces heures.

LXIX. [Members of the commons.]
111. Also they pray that no one who has laboured in this parliament on behalf of his county, borough, or city shall be compelled to be a collector of the grant lately made for the war, et cetera.; and their wages, which are customary dues from ancient times, shall be levied from all manner of persons, within franchise and without, having a lay fee within the county: and that no one, of whatsoever condition he be, having a lay fee in the county shall be spared; but according to the worth of his tenure he shall contribute to the said wages, and also to the tax now granted, so that the poorest amongst the people may be supported by the lords and others who have never paid taxes before this time.

---

[38] Stat.1 Ric.2 c.12.

Responsio.

Quant a la primere demande, le roy le voet bien. Et quant a la secunde, les seignours du royaume ne vorront mye departir de leur anciene libertee et franchise.

S'ENSUONT LES PETICIONS DE LA CLERGIE.
Peticions pur le clergie.
A nostre tresexcellent seignour le roy supplient humblement ses devoutes oratours, les prelatz et la clergie de la province de Canterbirs et d'Evewyk, qe plese a vostre reale hautesse benignement et graciousement oyer et escuter les grevouses pleintes des diverses injuries et grevances faites a Dieu, seinte eglise, et a les avantditz prelatz, clergie, lour justes peticions,
[Col. b] a la reverence de Dieu et de seinte eglise, gracieusement et effectuelement granter. La forme des queles peticions ensuit es cestes paroles:

I.
112. Primerement supplient les avantditz prelatz et clergie qe plese a nostre dit seignour le roy prendre et retenir a sa presence, ses conseils, et ses services *[Page te-iii-26]*
[Col. a] prodes hommes, voillantz, sachantz, esprovez, et nient covettous; et si sagement et resonablement modifier sibien le nombre de ses familiers, come les despenses cotidiens de son houstel, qe par tant l'eglise d'Engleterre, mesme nostre seignour le roy, ses liges, et tout son royaume soient par meyndres subsidies et autres charges extraordinaries des ses liges le plus justement, seintement, profitablement, et a greindre eise de lui et de son poeple, reulez et governez; et qe par tant lour estat soit en Dieu et en felicite le mieultz gardez et encreuez.

II.
113. Item, qe plese a nostre dit seignour le roy gracieusement et sufficeaument ratifier et conferrer, pur lui et pur ses heirs, touz les privileges, libertes, et droitures avant ces heures grantez et confermez par les nobles progenitours nostre dit seignour le roy /a\ les avantditz prelatz et clergie, et a lour precessours predecessours, esglises, benefices de seinte eglise, et lour universitees. Et qe sur ce lui plese granter ses lettres patentes tantes et tieles come leur busoignera, gracieusement et sanz fyn.
Responsio.
Le roy chargera son chanceller d'y faire aussi gracieusement come il purra bonement.[39]

III.
114. Item, se pleinent les avantditz prelatz et clergie qe coment qe les hommes de seinte eglise soient artez en vertue d'obedience, et de droit tenuz, d'obeier a les mandementz de leur ordenaires et sovereignes es choses congeables par la ley de seinte eglise, nient meyns les issint obeiantz et fesantz execucions de tieux mandementz sont enditez, et en molt des maneres torcenousement et ledement tretez par lays gentz, a cause de tieles execucions.
Responsio.
Le roy voet bien qe les execucions de mandementz de gentz de seinte eglise soient desore duement faites, sanz empeschement ou destourbance de nullui; issint qe riens n'y soit fait en prejudice du roy, de sa corone, ne de la ley du terre.

Answer.

As for the first demand, the king wills it. And for the second, the lords of the kingdom do not wish to depart from their ancient liberty and franchise.

THERE FOLLOW THE PETITIONS OF THE CLERGY.
Petitions on behalf of the clergy.
To our most excellent lord the king his devout bedesmen, the prelates and clergy of the provinces of Canterbury and of York humbly pray that it might please your royal highness kindly and graciously to hear and listen to the grievous complaints of divers injuries and wrongs committed against God and holy church, and the aforesaid prelates and clergy, and graciously and effectively grant their just petitions,
[Col. b] to the reverence of God and holy church. The form of which petitions follows in these words:

I. [Retrenchment of expenditure.]
112. Firstly, the aforesaid prelates and clergy request that it might please our said lord the king to take and retain in his presence, his council and his service *[Page tr-iii-26]*
[Col. a] worthy men, willing, knowledgeable, proven, and not covetous; and so wisely and reasonably moderate both the number of his household, and the daily expenses thereof, that the church of England, our same lord the king, his lieges, and all his kingdom shall be the more justly, reverently, and profitably ruled and governed, with smaller subsidies and other extraordinary expenses from his lieges, for the greater comfort of himself and his people; in order that their estate shall be the better protected and enriched in God and in felicity.

II. [Confirmation of liberties.]
113. Also, that it might please our said lord the king graciously and fittingly to ratify and confirm, on behalf of himself and his heirs, all the privileges, liberties, and rights granted and confirmed before this time by the noble progenitors of our said lord the king to the aforesaid prelates and clergy, and to their predecessors, churches, benefices of holy church, and their corporations. And thereupon, that it might please him to grant as many and such letters patent as they may need, graciously and without fine.
Answer.
The king will charge his chancellor so to do as graciously as it can be done.

III. [Ecclesiastical mandates.]
114. Also, the aforesaid prelates and clergy protest that although the men of holy church are obliged by virtue of their obedience, and bound by right, to obey the mandates of their ordinaries and superiors in matters ruled by the law of holy church, nevertheless the executions thus obeyed and performed upon such orders are indicted, and treated wrongfully and wickedly in many ways by lay people, on account of such executions.
Answer.
The king earnestly wills that henceforth the executions of mandates by those of holy church shall be duly performed without accusation or disruption from anyone; so that nothing be done to prejudice the king, his crown or the law of the land.

---

[39] PRO E175/3/2.

IIII.

115. Item, qe les hommes de seinte eglise a la simple suggestion de qeconqe, coment qe la suggestion soit ja si fause, sont pris /par les ministres de la mareschalcie\ del houstel nostre dit seignour le roy, toutes les foiz qe aucune tiele suggestion soit faite, et a chescun foiz q'ils soient ensi pris ils sont compuls de paier demy marc en noun de fee, la ou les leys gentz ne paient en tiel cas fors tantsoulement un gros: et qe les fesantz tieles suggestions sont suffert a lesser franchement lour dites suggestions, et mesmes les suggestions issint lessez repeter et recomencer tantz de foiz come ils voudront sanz peyne.

Responsio.

Celui qi se sente grevez en especial face sa pleinte au seneschalle del houstel nostre seignour le roy, et il ent avera bone et due remede.

V.

116. Item, qe les purveours, ministres, et achatours deputez pur l'oustel nostre dit seignour le roy, des autres nobles et seignours du royaume, entrent et occupient benefices et lieux de seinte eglise, encontre la volunte sibien de ceux as queux les ditz benefices et lieux appurtenent, come de lour lieu-tenantz, et les enhabitantz en yceux deboutent et enchacent, et les biens qeconqes illoeqes trovez parnont, degastent, enportont, et amesnont, et cariages et autres biens des ditz hommes de seinte eglise trovez en chemyn ou aillours parnont aussint, et amesnont, a lour grande damage, et prejudice de la franchise de seinte eglise.

Responsio.

Soient les estatutz et ordenances avant ces heures ent faitz tenuz et fermement gardez en touz pointz; adjoustant a ycelles qe pur ce qe clercs ne poent ent faire lour suites envers nullui par voie de cryme, come l'estatut des purveours demande, q'ils y poent avoir leur accions envers toutz tieux purveiours par voie de

[Col. b] trespas, et recoverir vers eux leur damages a treble, par manere come le dit estatut des purveiours en partie fait mencions.

VI.

117. Item, qe les viscontes et eschetours nostre dit seignour le roy venantz ove lour femmes et autre excessif nombre de gentz, sibien a chival come a pee, as abbeys, priories, et autres mesons de religion, tout soient /els\ foundez en pure et perpetuele asmoigne par les roys et les autres nobles du royaume, trop chargent et grevent les avantdites abbeys et priories en despenses et autrement, et jadumeyns demandent et afforcent grandes sommes des deniers a eux non-duement estre paiez.

Responsio.

Les estatutz ent faitz soient tenuz et gardez fermement en touz pointz.[40]

VII.

118. Item, qe hommes de seinte eglise, et autres pursuantz duement causes des dismes et autres causes de seinte eglise en court Cristien, a la quele tieles causes appurtignont, deyvont, et soloient appurtiner, et les juges de seinte eglise conissantz en tieles causes, et autres soi ent entremetrantz selonc la ley, sont maliciousement et noun-duement par celle cause enditez, enprisonez, et par seculer poair /horriblement\ oppressez, et aussint afforcez ove violence

IIII. [The marshalsea]

115. Also, that the men of holy church, at the mere assertion of anyone, even if the assertion is false, are taken by the ministers of the marshalsea of the household of our said lord the king, whensoever such an assertion is made, and each time they are thus seized they are compelled to pay half a mark in the name of a fee, whereas laymen in like case pay no more than a groat: and the instigators of such rumours are allowed freely to circulate their accusations, and to repeat and reiterate the same as often as they will without penalty.

Answer.

Let whosoever feels himself particularly aggrieved bring his complaint before the steward of the household of our lord the king, and he shall have a proper and effective remedy.

V. [Purveyors.]

116. Also, that the purveyors, ministers, and buyers appointed by the household of our said lord the king and of other nobles and lords of the kingdom enter upon and occupy benefices and property of holy church, contrary to the will of those to whom the said benefices and properties pertain, as well as of their tenants, and drive out and expel the inhabitants of the same, and whatsoever goods they find there they appropriate, waste, carry off, and lead away, and they also seize and take away carriages with other goods belonging to the said men of holy church, found on the road or elsewhere, to the great injury and prejudice of the franchise of holy church.

Answer.

Let the statutes and ordinances already made thereon in the past be upheld and strictly enforced in all respects; adding to the same that because the clerks are unable to bring suits hereon against anyone by criminal process, as the statute of purveyors requires, they may have their actions against all such purveyors by way of

[Col. b] trespass, and recover from them triple damages, as the said statute of purveyors in part prescribes.

VI. [Exactions by sheriffs and escheators.]

117. Also, that the sheriffs and escheators of our said lord the king coming with their wives and excessive numbers of other people, as well on horse as on foot, to abbeys, priories, and other religious houses which were all founded in pure and perpetual alms by the kings and other nobles of the kingdom, overburden and trouble the aforesaid abbeys and priories with expenses and other charges, and even demand and extort from them payment of great sums of money which are not owed.

Answer.

Let the statutes made thereon be kept and firmly enforced in all respects.

VII. [Malicious indictments of churchmen.]

118. Also, that men of holy church and others, duly pursuing causes of tithes and other concerns of holy church in the court Christian, to which such matters do, should, and customarily pertain, and the judges of holy church possessing knowledge of such matters and others intervening in accordance with the law, are maliciously and improperly indicted for that reason, imprisoned, and horribly oppressed by the secular power, and also are compelled by violence to take

---

[40] Stat.20 Edw.3 c.6; Stat.31 Edw.3 St.1 c.15; Stat.36 Edw.3 St.1 c.13.

par serementz et grevouses obligacions, et molt d'autres maneres, noun-duement compuls a desister et cesser outrement es choses susdites.

Responsio.

Il est assentuz /qe tieles obligations\ et autres liens faites ou affaire par duretee et violence ne soient d'aucune value. Et quant a ceux qi procuront par malice tieux enditementz et d'estre mesmes des enditours, apres ce qe les enditez en soient acquitez, eient et encourgent tieux procurours et enditours mesme la peine q'est contenue en l'estatut de Westm' secund, de ceux qi procurent faus appels estre faitz. Et enquergent les justices des assises, ou autres justices devant queux tieux enditez seront acquitez, poair des tieux procurours et editours, et de les punir duement chescun selonc son desert.[41]

VIII.

119. Item, suppliont les avantditz prelatz et clergie: qe la ou plee est mew devant juge de seinte eglise de pension due d'une eglise ou benefice de seinte eglise a autre eglise ou benefice, qe en tieu cas nulle prohibicion roiale soit grantez; et si aucune prohibicion passe, par plenere consultacion en ce cas soit franchement grantez. Et qe la conissance et decision de celle cause soit a juge de seinte eglise, et nemye a seculer, nomement come ensi deuez de droit, et d'ancien temps soleit estre fait.

Responsio.

Le roy chargera ses justices de ent faire sercher les anciens recordz, et come y ad este usee d'ancientee soit usee pur le temps avenir.

IX.

120. Item, qe come juges de seinte eglise et parties soient sovent foiz dampnablement destourbez par prohibicions roiales, es causes et busoignes regardantz sibien de droit come de custume a la conissance de seinte eglise et la court Cristien, qe desore nulle prohibicion roiale soit grantez au juge, partie, ne a nul autre a destourber la conissance ou pursuite en tieu cas, sanz ce qe libel citatorie ou autre muniment sealees, signees, ou autrement provez, soit avantmayn vew et discusse en la chancellerie du roy, par quel appierge sufficeantment, qe la conissance de tiele cause deuez appurtenir a la court seculer, et nemye a la court Cristien, nomement come issint deveroit et soleit in effect estre fait en temps passez.

Responsio.

Nulle prohibicion issera dehors forsqe en manere q'ad este usee devant cest temps. Et en outre, quanqe ent *[Page iii-27] [Col. a]* feust ordenez ou grantez en darein parlement estoise en sa force.

Membrane 16

X.

121. Item, supplient qe a toutes les foiz a quele heure aucun soit tret en plee de dismes devant juge seculer, souz le noun des biens et chateux de celui ensi tret face excepcion, ou allegge, qe la matire, substance, et sourse de la busoigne soit soulement sur dismes duz de droit et possession a sa eglise, et nemye autrement des biens et chateux; qe tiel juge seculer soit tenuz a receivre tiele excepcion allegeance, et la receive en fait, et q'il ne procede dampnablement en la busoigne, a injurie de Dieu, de seinte eglise, et de la partie, la dite excepcion et allegeance nient discusse, mes ent soit la discussion

---
[41] Stat.1 Ric.2 c.13.

oaths and enter into damaging obligations, and in many other ways are improperly compelled entirely to cease and desist from the aforesaid actions.

Answer.

It is agreed that such obligations and other bonds made or to be made by extortion or violence must be invalid. And as for those who procure such indictments by malice and act as indictors, after the indicted have been acquitted, those procurers and indictors shall suffer and incur the penalty contained in the second statute of Westminster concerning those who cause false appeals to be made. And let the justices of the assizes, or other justices before whom those indicted are acquitted, enquire into the authority of those procurers and indictors, and punish them duly, each according to his just deserts.

VIII. [Prohibitions in ecclesiastical causes.]

119. Also, the aforesaid prelates and clergy pray that when a plea is moved before a judge of holy church concerning rent due from a church, or a benefice of holy church in another church or benefice, that in such a case no royal prohibition should be granted; and if any prohibition be made, let it be granted freely after full consultation on the matter. And that the cognizance and decision in the matter shall lie with the judge of holy church, and not with a secular person, especially since it ought by right and has been customary since ancient times.

Answer.

The king will order his justices to search the ancient records, and whatsoever has been practised of old shall continue thus in future.

IX. [Cognizance of ecclesiastical courts.]

120. Also, whereas judges of holy church and litigants have often been seriously impeded by royal prohibitions in matters and concerns relating as well by right as by custom to the cognizance of holy church and the court Christian, that henceforth no royal prohibition shall be made to the judge, party, nor any other, hindering the cognizance or pursuit of such an action, without a citatory bill or other muniment sealed, signed, or otherwise authenticated being shown and discussed in advance in the king's chancery, by which it is sufficiently clear that the cognizance of such a case ought to pertain to the secular court, and not to the court Christian, especially as that was customarily done in the past.

Answer.

No prohibition shall be issued except where that has been done in the past. And in addition, whatsoever *[Page iii-27] [Col. a]* was ordained or granted in connection herewith in the last parliament shall remain in force.

X. [Pleas of tithe.]

121. Also, they pray that so often as anyone is brought before a secular judge in a plea of tithes, in the name of goods and chattels of him thus treated, and makes exception, or claims that the matter, substance, and origin of the business is solely concerned with the tithes due by right and possession to his church, and not with his goods and chattels; that such a secular judge shall be obliged to receive such an exception offered, and accept it, and shall not proceed harmfully in the matter, to the injury of God, holy church, and the party himself, the said exception and allegiance not being

remys a juge de seinte eglise, sicome en busoigne de bastardie et autres cas semblables est acustumez.

Responsio.
General adverrement ne soit pris en tieu cas, sanz monstrer matire especiale coment ce feust lay chatelle.[42]

XI.
122. Item, qe si en aucune cause pendante devant juge de seinte eglise, en quele la prohibicion du roy soit mys avant, et aussint consultacion du roy sur certeine manere, forme, et condicion ove tiele clause Ita tamen, ou Dum tamen, ou autre clause semblable soit sur ce grantez; qe bien lice sanz empeschement au juge et as parties proceder outre franchement en la cause. Et si tiel juge troeve par proeves legales ministres judicielment tiel manere, forme, ou condicion estre acompliz, il puisse franchement mesme la cause discuter, et a fyn droiturel terminer.
Responsio.
Soit fait come ad este fait devant ces heures.

XII.
123. Item, qe toute manere disme de boys appellez silva cedua, due a Dieu et seinte eglise, soit loialment paiez. Et en cas qe prohibition du roy soit mys avant au juge ou a partie en cause de tiele disme, qe pleine et plenere consultacion, sanz aucune novelle ou noun-due restitucion celle partie soit hastivement grantez: et qe les juges procedantz, et les parties pursuantz,
[Col. b] et autres qeconqes fesant lour devoir celle partie, ne soient par celle cause par enditementz, enpresonementz, condempnementz, ou en autre manere qeconqe enpeschez ne grevez.
Responsio.
Soit fait en ce cas come ent ad este usee devant ces heures.

XIII.
124. Item, qe la imunite de seinte eglise, tant endroit des persones fuantz as esglises ou lieux a Dieu dediez, come endroit de tielx lieux a queux ils fuent, soit en toutes choses conservez et gardez. Nomement, qe dedeinz les lieux de tiele imunite nulle garde soit mys par ley poair, qe tieux futifs ne soient en nulle manere non-duement constreintz dedeinz les bondes et termes de tieles franchises et immunite: et qe les violantz tieles franchises soient selonc les censures de seinte eglise reddement puniz.

Responsio.
Ceux qi sont chargeables de tieles gardes les gardent bien et salvement, mes ent facent leur garde hors del saintewaire, et nemye dedeinz en aucune manere.

XIIII.
125. Item, se pleinont qe gentz de seinte eglise, benefices et autres, sont arestuz et horstrez des eglises cathedrales, et d'autres eglises, et de lour simiters tant come y sont aucune foiz entendantz a divine service, et aussint en autres lieux tant soient ils portantz le corps nostre seignours as malades meement, par colour d'une cry appelle outhees fait sur eux par malice de lour accusours; et issint forstrez et arestuz sont liez, mesnez a prison, encontre la franchise de seinte eglise.

Responsio.
Le roy voet qe si nullui face arester aucune tiele persone de seinte eglise par tiele manere, et ent soit duement convict,

---
[42] Stat.1 Ric.2 c.14.

discussed, but the discussion thereof shall be assigned to the judges of holy church, as is customary in cases of bastardy and other similar matters.
Answer.
General averment ought not to lie in such a case, without special proof being given that these are lay chattels.

XI. [Abatement of prohibitions.]
122. Also, that if any case pending before a judge of holy church, in which the king's prohibition has been submitted in advance, and also consultation with the king in a certain manner, form, and condition with the clause 'Ita tamen', or 'Dum tamen', or some similar clause has been granted thereon; it shall be fully lawful for the judge and parties without hindrance to proceed freely in the cause. And if such a judge finds by worthy testimony offered that such manner, form, and condition have been judicially effected, he may freely discuss the same case, and lawfully determine it.
Answer.
Let it be done as it has previously been done in the past.

XII. [Tithes of coppice woods.]
123. Also, that all manner of tithes on woodland called coppice woods, owed to God and holy church, shall be faithfully paid. And when a prohibition of the king is submitted to a judge or party over such a tithe, then full and thorough consultation, without any novel or improper restitution, shall be swiftly granted to the party: and that the judges proceeding and the parties pursuing,
[Col. b] and any others doing their duty in the matter, should not for that reason be hindered or harmed by indictments, imprisonment, condemnation, or in any other way.
Answer.
Let it be done in such cases as has been done in the past.

XIII. [Sanctuary.]
124. Also, that the immunity of holy church, with respect to persons fleeing to churches or places dedicated to God, as also to the places to which they flee, shall be entirely preserved and respected. And in particular, that within the places covered by such an immunity no guard shall be mounted by the lay power, and that such fugitives shall in no way be improperly restrained within the boundaries and limits of such franchises and immunity: and the violators of such franchises shall be severely punished in accordance with the censures of holy church.
Answer.
Let those who are responsible for such custody keep them securely and well, but let them keep guard outside the sanctuary and not within it in any way.

XIIII. [Arrests made on clerics.]
125. Also, they complain that whereas men of holy church, both beneficed and others, are arrested and dragged from cathedral churches, and other churches, and from their churchyards, sometimes as they are hearing divine service, and sometimes in other places, even as they carry the body of our Lord to the sick, by colour of a cry called 'Outhees' raised against them by malicious accusers; and having been thus dragged out and arrested are bound and led to prison, contrary to the franchise of holy church.
Answer.
The king wills that if anyone arrests any person of holy church in such a way, and is duly convicted of it, he shall

soit emprisonez, et ent reint a la volunte de roy, et face gree a partie issint arestuz.[43]

Sur queux peintes et peticions et chescun d'eux supplient devoutement les prelatz et clergie susditz, qe droiture et favour lour soient faitz, et gracieusement.

LES PETICIONS PUR LA CITEE DE LONDRES.
Pur la citee de Londres.
Plese a nostre seignour le roy de sa grace ore en cest present parlement granter a ses citeins de Londres les peticions desouz escrites:

I.
En primes, ils demandent qe les chartres et confirmacions a eux faites de leur franchises par nostre seignour le roy Edward vostre ael, et voz autres progenitours, soient as ditz citeins par vous et vostre conseil du parlement confermes, ovesqe la clause Licet, et nient contreesteantz aucuns estatuz, privileges, chartres, ou juggementz faitz ou affaire au contraire.
Responsio.
Quant a la confirmacion ove clause de licet, soit fait. Et quant a ce q'ils demandent, non obstant estatutz, privileges, chartres, ou juggementz, soient les estatutz, privileges, chartres, et juggementz faitz au contraire veuez et examinez devant le conseil, et sur ce le roy en ferra ce q'il purra bonement.

II.
127. Item, demandent les ditz citeins qe come d'ancien temps encea ils eient usez quatre franches custumes dedeinz escrites, tanqe poi des anz passez ils furent restreintz meyns justement d'ycelles, sicome evidentement purra apparoir, c'estassavoir, qe nul estrange de la franchise de la dite citee vende ou achate d'autre estrange aucunes marchandises deinz la franchise de meisme la citee, sur forfaiture d'ycelles: nientmains, les ditz citeins demandent, a les controversies ent desore apesez et tollir, qe ce leur soit expressez par chartre nostre seignour le roy.
Responsio.
Le roy le voet parentre marchant et marchant tantsoulement; sauvant toudys les privileges des liges nostre seignour le roy d'Aquitaigne.
Page iii-28

III.
128. Item, come les ditz citeins tienent sanz moien de nostre seignour le roy, et d'ancienete n'estoient tenuz ne ne soleient estre entendantz as comandementz ou mandementz d'aucun seignour, ne conestable, seneschal, ne d'aucun mareschal, admiral, clerc du marchee, ne d'autre officer ou ministre du roy, et ses progenitours qeconqe, sinon tantsoulement a les mandementz et comandemantz du roy et ses progenitours, sealez de leur sealx publik ou prive de leur nouns et titles, forspris les mandementz des justices selonc la forme de leur chartres sur eux a assigner; demandent nientmains les ditz citeins, a controversies ent desore apeser et tollir, qe ce leur soit expressez par chartre nostre seignour le roy.

Responsio.
Soit use come ad este d'ancien temps.

---
[43] Stat.1 Ric.2 c.15.

be imprisoned and placed at the king's mercy, and shall compensate the party thus arrested.

Concerning each of which complaints and petitions the aforesaid prelates and clergy devoutly pray that right and favour be graciously shown them.

THE PETITIONS FOR THE CITY OF LONDON.
For the city of London.
May it please our lord the king by his grace to grant now in the present parliament to the citizens of London the petitions written below:

I. [Confirmation of liberties.]
First, they ask that the charters and confirmations of their franchises granted to them by our lord the king Edward [III] your grandfather and your other progenitors, be confirmed to the said citizens by you and your council in parliament, with the clause 'Licet', and notwithstanding any statutes, privileges, charters, or judgements made or to be made to the contrary.
Answer.
With regard to the confirmation containing the clause 'Licet', let it be done. And with regard to that which they ask notwithstanding statutes, privileges, charters or judgements, let the statutes, privileges, charters, and judgements made to the contrary be reviewed and examined before the council, and thereupon the king will do what he is well able to do.

II. [Merchant strangers.]
127. Also, the said citizens pray that whereas from ancient times until now they have enjoyed the four free customs written herein, some years since they were unjustly hindered in the same, as is plainly apparent, namely that no stranger to the franchise of the said city should sell or buy from another stranger any merchandise within the franchise of the same city, on pain of forfeiting the same: nevertheless, the said citizens ask, to settle and lay aside controversy henceforth, that it be set out for them in a charter of our lord the king.

Answer.
The king wills it as between merchant and merchant alone; saving always the privileges of the lieges of our lord the king from Aquitaine.

III. [Exemptions from jurisdiction.]
128. Also, whereas the said citizens hold immediately of our lord the king without a mesne lord, and since ancient times have not been obliged nor accustomed to obey the commands or mandates of any lord, nor constable, steward, nor of any marshal, admiral, clerk of the market, nor any other officer or minister of the king, nor of any of his progenitors, except and only at the command and order of the king and his progenitors sealed with the public or privy seals of their names and titles, excepting the mandates of justices in accordance with the form of their charters thereto assigned; nevertheless the said citizens request, to settle and lay aside controversy henceforth, that it should be set out for them in a charter of our lord the king.
Answer.
Let it be done as it was done in ancient times.

IIII.

129. Item, come de tresanciene franche custume de la dite citee deust et soleit estre enquis par les ditz citeins, et non pas par autres, de toutes custumes, consuetudines, imposicions, marches, et bondous de la franchise de meisme la citee; et aussi de purprestures et autres choses qeconqes avenantz deinz la franchise de la citee avantdite, ou regardantz a la cominaltee de meisme la citee, ou a aucun office d'ycelle; demandent nientmains les ditz citeins, a controversies ent desore apeser et tollr, qe ce leur soit expressez par chartre nostre seignour le roy, nient contreesteantz aucuns estatutz ou juggementz faitz au contraire.

Responsio.

Quant a lour custumes, imposicions, consuetudines, et purprestures avenantz deinz la franchise de la dite citee, soit enquys par eux mesmes. Et quant as boundes et marches, soient declarez en especial, si aucun doute \y/ soit.

V.

130. Item, come de tresanciene franche custume de la dite citee, les gardes des orfanyns de meisme la citee deinz la citee avantdite, et aussi de leur \[terres, tenementz, et]/ chateux deinz la franchise de meisme la citee esteantz, deivent de droit appurtenir a les maire et chamberlein qi pur le temps serroient de la dite citee, et non \[pas aucun]/ autre: rendant as ditz orphanyns come ils vendroient a leur age resonable aconte des profitz et issues de meismes les terres et tenementz et de leur chateux, \[solonc]/L'anciene custume de la dite citee; demandent nientmains les ditz citeins, a controversies ent desore apeser et tollr, qe ce leur soit expressez par chartre nostre seignour \[le roy,]/ nonobstantz aucuns estatutz ou juggementz qeconqes renduz au contraire, ou proces novellement comencez.

Responsio.

Des toutes choses queux tieux orfanyns des citeins illoeqes ont deinz meisme la citee, eient ils la garde: sauvant au roy et a touz autres seignours lour droit de ceux qi tiegnent de eux aillours pardehors la franchise de meisme la citee.

VI.

131. Item, demandent les ditz citeins de la grace especiale nostre seignour le roy, en eslargissement de la franchise de la dite citee, qe si aucun article es chartres par nostre seignour le roy ou par ses progenitours faites, ou par lui ou par ses heirs affaire, as ditz citeins soit tant difficultuous ou doutous q'il puisse estre pris a diverses ententes, adonqes l'entente quel les ditz citeins clameront pur eux, leur soit allouez, et qe ce leur soit expressez par chartre nostre seignour le roy.

Responsio.

L'ynterpretacions des chartres des roys appurtiegnent au roy. Et si nul doute y sourde, le roy par l'avys de son conseil ent ferra tiel interpretacion come serra plus acordante a reson et bone foy.

VII.

132. Item, demandent les ditz citeins qe si aucune citee ou burghe en Engleterre eit aucunes franchises

[Col. b] du grant nostre seignur le roy ou de ses progenitours, les queles ne sont eues es chartres des citeins avantditz, nientmains la citee de Londres joyse \et/ use desore de meismes les franchises si aucunes y soient, si avant come si es chartres de meismes les citeins se ferroit de mesmes les franchises mencion especiale.

IIII. [Inquests.]

129. Also, whereas in accordance with the most ancient free custom of the said city inquests ought and are accustomed to be made by the said citizens, and not by others, into all the customs, usages, impositions, marches, and bounds of the franchise of the same city; and also into purprestures and any other matters arising within the franchise of the aforesaid city, or relating to the community of the same, or to any office of the same; nevertheless the said citizens request, to settle and end controversy thereon henceforth, that it be set out for them in a charter of our lord the king, notwithstanding any statutes or judgements made to the contrary.

Answer.

With regard to their customs, impositions, usages, and purprestures arising within the franchise of the said city, let inquest be made by themselves. And as for the boundaries and limits, they should be declared in detail, if there be any doubt.

V. [Care of orphans.]

130. Also, whereas in accordance with the most ancient free custom of the said city, the wardship of orphans of the same city within the aforesaid city, and also of their lands, tenements, and chattels being within the franchise of the same city, ought by right to pertain to the mayor and chamberlain for the time being in the said city, and to no one else: rendering to the said orphans when they come of age reasonable account of the profits and issues of the same land and tenements and from their chattels, in accordance with the ancient custom of the said city; nevertheless the said citizens ask, to settle and lay aside controversy henceforth, that it be set out for them by charter of our lord the king, notwithstanding any statutes or judgements rendered to the contrary, or process recently commenced.

Answer.

Let them have the keeping of all things which such orphans amongst the citizens have in the same city: saving to the king and to all other lords their right over those who hold from them elsewhere outside the franchise of the same city.

VI. [Interpretation of charters.]

131. Also, the said citizens ask of the special grace of our lord the king, to the augmentation of the franchise of the said city, that if any article in the charters issued by our lord the king or by his progenitors, or to be issued by him or his heirs, to the said citizens be so complex or uncertain that it might be interpreted in various ways, then the interpretation which the said citizens choose to place on it for themselves shall be allowed them, and that that shall be set out for them in a charter of our lord the king.

Answer.

Interpretation of the king's charters pertains to the king. And if any doubt arise, the king by the advice of his council shall make such interpretation as seems to him best in accordance with reason and good faith.

VII. [Liberties by emulation.]

132. Also, the said citizens ask that if any city or borough in England has any franchises

[Col. b] by grant of our lord the king or his progenitors which are not included in the charters of the aforesaid citizens, the city of London shall nevertheless henceforth enjoy and practise the same franchises if any there be, as though those same franchises had been expressly mentioned in the charters of the same citizens.

Responsio.
Declarent ce qe le roy purra bonement faire par l'avys de son conseil il y ferra.
Membrane 17

VIII.
133. Item, come en la grande chartre des franchises d'Engleterre soit contenuz qe nostre seignour le roy ne vendra, ne deniera, ne delaiera a nullui droit ou justice, demandent les ditz citeins qe proteccions roiales donees a doner a qeconqes persones, ne soient desore allouees devant les justices du roy qeconqes, en plee de dette, aconte, ou trespas, la ou la partie pleintif sera franche homme de la dite citee.[44]

Responsio.
Quant as proteccions, le roy voet qe pur vitailles achatez sur le viage ou service dont la proteccion faite mencion, qe la proteccion n'y tiegne pas lieu; n'auxint pur trespas ou contracts fait apres la date de tiele proteccion purchace.[45]

IX.
134. Item, qe les emprisonez en la gaole nostre seignour le roy de Neugate ou aillours deinz la franchise de la dite citee pur dettes ou damages adjuggez as ditz citeins, en aucunes accions ne soient desore remuez de celle prisone a la prisone du roy de Flete, ne aillours, pur dettes du roy, ou par colour de officers ovesqes aucun de l'escheqer du roy, avant qe gree soit fait as ditz citeins pleintifs de leur justes demandes pleinement; si non qe as ditz citeins puisse vrayement apparoir, qe avant qe tieux furent emprisonez a leur suyte ils feurent a nostre seignur le roy vrais et non pas feintz dettours.

Responsio.
Le roy chargera ses barons et ses ministres de l'escheqer qe nul brief issera de faire venir le corps qe est ycy condempnez a respondre en l'escheqer pur nul dette due a roy ou a autre ministre du dit escheqer, s'ils ne troeffent par examinement qe le dette soit verraie et nemye dette feynt, et due avant qe l'enprisone fust condempne.[46]

135. \[Fait]/ a remembrer qe en outre nostre seignour le roy ad grantez as ditz citeins en son parlement q'il ne voet my, ne n'est pas sa entencion, qe par vertu d'aucuns .... response par lui face en son parlement a lour petitions come desus est dit, mesmes les citeins, ou leur successours, soient aucunement .... aucuns leur libertees ou ancienes custumes approvez de mesme la citee.
Membrane 18

Requeste des communes.
136. Item, al darrein jour de ce parlement, les dites communes firent lour autres requestes par bouche par la manere qe s'ensuent:
Primerement, ils priont as seignours du parlement q'ils preignent tendrement au coer de veer qe nostre seignour le roi puisse avoir en aide de sa sustenance les terres purchacez par son dit aielle, en descharge par tant de sa commune avantdite.
Item, q'ils preignent aussint garde qe mesme nostre seignour le roy ne soit oustez par subtiletee n'autrement de ce qe a luy appurtient d'avoir des biens et joiaulx qe furent *[Page iii-29]*

Answer.
Let them explain what the king should by right do by the advice of his council, and it will be done.

VIII. [Protections.]
133. Also, whereas in the great charter of liberties of England it states that our lord the king will not sell, deny, nor delay right nor justice to anyone, the said citizens ask that royal protections given or to be given to any shall not henceforth be allowed before any of the king's justices in pleas of debt, account, or trespass, where the plaintiff is a free man of the said city.

Answer.
With regard to protections, the king wills that for victuals bought for the journey or the service of which the protection makes mention, that the protection shall not be valid; nor yet for trespass nor contracts made after the date when such protection was bought.

IX. [Debtors.]
134. Also, that those imprisoned in the gaol of our lord the king at Newgate or elsewhere within the franchise of the said city for debts or injuries adjudged to the said citizens, in no actions shall be removed henceforth from that prison to the king's prison at Fleet, or elsewhere, for debts to the king, or on the authority of any in the king's exchequer, before full compensation has been made to the said plaintiff citizens for their just demands; unless it is truly apparent to the said citizens that before such people were imprisoned at their suit they were truly and not feigned debtors to our lord the king.

Answer.
The king will instruct the barons and ministers of his exchequer that no writ is to be issued which causes a person thus condemned to be brought to answer in the exchequer for any debt owed to the king or a minister of the said exchequer, if they do not find upon examination that the debt is genuine and not a false debt, and owed before the prisoner was condemned.

135. Be it remembered that, further, our lord the king has granted to the citizens in his parliament that it is not his will, and neither is it his intention that by virtue of any response made by him in his parliament to their petitions as set out above, the same citizens or their successors should in any way   any of their liberties or ancient customs approved for the same city.

The commons' requests.
136. Also, on the last day of this parliament, the said commons made their other requests by word of mouth, the tenor of which follows:
First, they pray to the lords of parliament that they take it to heart to ensure that our lord the king has the lands purchased by his said grandfather for his support to himself, thus relieving to that extent his aforesaid commons.

Also that they also take care that our same lord the king is not deprived by cunning or any other means of those things which pertain to him in terms of goods and jewels which belonged *[Page iii-29]*

---

[44] Magna carta 1227 c. 29.
[45] Stat.1 Ric.2 c.8.
[46] Stat.1 Ric.2 c.12.

[Col. a] to his said grandfather, bearing in mind that which has been done in like case in time past during the reigns of former kings; yet no certain answer has been given, written, or made in the aforesaid parliament, only that the lords have said that they wish that to be done, both for the sake of the present king, as well as of the king dead, whom God absolve.

The end of parliament.

137. And be it remembered that this parliament continued from day to day, from the said first day of parliament which was 13 October in the present year until 28 November in the same [Col. b] year [1377]; that is to say, for forty-seven days, including the said first and last days. On which 28 November [1377] the said petitions with the said answers given and written were read before our lord the king in full parliament. And thereupon, other requests having been made by the commons and answers given as above, our lord the king heartily thanked the prelates, lords, and commons for their great and good endeavours in discharging the said needs and requests made there for the common good, and for the handsome and generous sum granted to himself for the defence of the entire kingdom; ordering the knights of the counties, citizens of the cities and burgesses of the boroughs to make their suit for writs to have their parliamentary wages in the customary manner, and he gave them permission to leave. And so ended this present parliament.

Appendix

13 October 1377

Westminster

1. *Estimate of Revenues put forward by the Commons (Text and Translation)*

Ceux sont les sommes qe les communes demandount del re' du roialme d'Engleterre.

Primes, de la subside des leynes, pealx, quirs, plumbe, e esteyne pur le roialme d'Engleterre mountent par an .liij. m. li.

Item, des terres renti des priours aliens, .viij. m. li.

Item, des benefices de aliens, .x. m. li.

Item, del collectour du pape, .x. m. li.

Item, de ceo qe remeynt unqore rien compte des subsides e des grotes.

Item, de remanent des grotes qe ne sount unquore levez.

Item, des gardes des terres e mariages duez a roy qui Dieux assoille.

Item, del dette duez pur les ercevesqes de Rauen e de Roian.

Item, d'argent duez pur les enfants de Bretaigne.

Item, de raunceon counte Seynt Paule e de ceo qe apartient a roy del counte de Deane, si nul y soit.

Item, de ceo qe homme avera de Alice Perrys.

Item, qe toutez chosez adquises de guere qe appartient a roy, soient despenduz por la sustenance de la defense del dit roialme d'Engleterre.

Item, qe tout qe poet estre appowe qe ne soit parcelle de la corone soit assigne por la sustenance de la dite defense.

These are the sums for which the commons asked from the [?receipt of the exchequer] of the kingdom of England.

First, from the subsidies on wool, woolfells, hides, lead, and tin for the kingdom of England, there amounts £53,000 a year.

Also, from lands rented to alien priors, £8,000.

Also, from the benefices of aliens, £10,000.

Also, from the papal collector, £10,000.

Also, from that which still remains unaccounted for from the subsidies and the groats.

Also, from the arrears of the groats which have still not been levied.

Also, from the wardships of lands and marriages owed to the king, whom God absolve.

Also, from the debt due for the archbishops of Ravenna and Rouen.

Also, from the silver due for the children of Brittany.

Also, from the ransom of the count of St Pol and from that to which the king is entitled from the count of Denia, if anything.

Also, from that which is to be had from Alice Perrers.

Also, that all gains made from war which pertain to the king shall be spent on maintaining the defence of the said realm of England.

Item, that everything which can be shown not to be part of the crown's patrimony shall be assigned for maintaining the said defence.

Source: Durham, Dean and Chapter Muniments, Locellus 20, no.7; previously published in Michael Prestwich, 'An estimate by the commons of royal revenue in England under Richard II', *Parliamentary History*, 3 (1984), 147-55.

2. Order to the mayor and sheriffs of London to make proclamation that all those who wish to sue Alice Perrers for offences against the king and people shall present their petitions to the council before next Saturday [21 November]. By king and council. Dated 19 November 1377.

Source: *CCR 1377-81*, 112.

3. Grant to Isabella, the king's aunt, daughter of Edward III, following her petition in parliament, of the profits from various lands in order to maintain her estate, following the defection of her husband, Ingelram de Coucy, former earl of Bedford, to the French allegiance; provided that she does not leave the realm or make these revenues available to her husband. Dated 27 November 1377.

Source: *CPR 1377-81*, 174.

4. Grant to the shoemakers or cordwainers of London that they may choose four good men of their trade to regulate their trade within the suburbs of the city until the next parliament. By petition of parliament. Dated 3 February 1378.

Source: *CPR 1377-81*, 132.

5. Grant to the abbot and convent of Shrewsbury of the wood called 'Lythewode' in Shropshire, following their petition in parliament that it be restored to them. Dated 2 June 1378.

Source: *CPR 1377-81*, 224-5.

6. Order to the collectors of customs in the port of Hull to pay 400 marks a year to Michael de la Pole, with arrears. By petition in parliament. Dated 17 October 1377.

Source: *CCR 1377-81*, 25.

7. Order to the mayor and bailiffs of Lincoln to pay to the dean and chapter of Lincoln cathedral sixty pounds a year from the farm of the city, formerly granted to them, with the king's licence, by Bartholomew de Burghersh. By petition of parliament. Dated 26 October 1377.

Source: *CCR 1377-81*, 32.

8. Order to the mayor and bailiffs of various towns to arrange for balingers to be made and delivered to the admiral for the defence of the seas, as ordained by the king and council in the last parliament. Dated 30 November 1377.

Source: *CCR 1377-81*, 32-3.

9. Order to all whom it may concern, by petition of the 'commons of England', not to allow Master John Sheppey to take possession of the deanery of Lincoln, to which he has craftily gained papal provision despite the wishes of parliament concerning such provisions. By petition of parliament. Dated 8 December 1377.
Source: *CCR 1377-81*, 35.

10. Order to Henry Percy, earl of Northumberland, to do justice to William de Wele of Grimsby, who has submitted a petition requesting redress for the capture of his crayer, plundered by men of Scotland. By the council in parliament. Dated 24 November 1377.
Source: *CCR 1377-81*, 39.

11. Order to the king's justices to proceed to execution of a judgment in favour of Maud, daughter of Thomas Charnels, who has petitioned in this parliament for restitution of two manors in Leicestershire and Warwickshire which were seized into the king's hand following the death of the Prince of Wales. By petition in parliament. Dated 6 November 1377.
Source: *CCR 1377-81*, 40.

12. Order to the sheriff of Cornwall, following a petition in the last parliament from the collectors of tenths and fifteenths in Cornwall, to assess the taxable capacity of the borough of Truro, the inhabitants of which are pleading poverty. Dated 4 March 1378.
Source: *CCR 1377-81*, 54-5.

13. Order to John king of Castile and Leon and duke of Lancaster to stop the officials of his exchequer from distressing Henry de Chatherton of Lancashire, who submitted a petition to the last parliament in relation to a charge of harbouring the killers of Richard de Molyneux. Since the duke has been granted all forfeitures in Lancashire, his minister are demanding one hundred pounds from Chatherton. Dated 4 March 1378.
Source: *CCR 1377-81*, 125.

14. Petition to the king from the counties of Cumberland, Northumberland and Westmorland to provide for their effective defence against the king's enemies of Scotland, and for the repair of Carlisle, Newcastle, Roxburgh and Berwick.
Endorsed: The present ordinance on this subject is to be enforced.
Source: Printed in full in *RP*, III.30.

15. Petition to the king and the noble lords of parliament from Margaret Marshal, countess of Norfolk, that the tenants of the towns of Emerton and Fen Stanton, which she holds, should not be distrained by the king's ministers to contribute to the repair of the bridge at Huntingdon, from which they have in the past been exempted.
Endorsed: This bill is to be sent into the chancery, where right will be done to the countess; in the meantime the process of distraint will cease.
Source: Printed in full in *RP*, III.30.

16. Petition to the king and the noble lords of parliament from Joan, countess of Hereford, that the tenants of the manor of Kinbanton and one third of the manor of Worsley, which she holds, should not be distrained by the king's ministers to contribute to the repair of the bridge at Huntingdon, from which they have in the past been exempted.
Endorsed: This bill is to be sent into the chancery, where right will be done to the countess; in the meantime the process of distraint will cease.
Source: Printed in full in *RP*, III.30.

17. Petition to the king and council from the constable and marshal of England complaining that they have been prevented from exercising their offices by the mayor and sheriffs of London, and asking the king to summon the mayor, sheriffs and other officers of the city into his presence to explain their behaviour.
No endorsement.
Source: Printed in full in *RP*, III.30.

18. Petition to the king and council in parliament from William de Burstall, keeper of the rolls of chancery and guardian of the House of Converts in London, that the king might confirm the grant of his predecessor, Edward III, to the effect that, in return for Burstall paying for the repair of the chapel and other buildings of the House of Converts, it would remain for ever in the custody of successive keepers of the rolls of chancery.
Endorsed: the king wills and grants it.
Source: Printed in full in *RP*, III.31.

1378 October

Gloucester

20 October - 16 November

(C 65/33. *RP*, III.32-49. *SR*, II.6-11)

Richard II's second parliament was summoned to meet at Gloucester on 20 October 1378. The city was probably chosen as being as far from Westminster as was practicable, because the varied and weighty business of the assembly had to include issues arising from a scandalous affray in Westminster abbey in the previous August, the so-called Hawley-Shakell affair.[1] The parliament lasted for four weeks, ending in mid-November. Its proceedings are recorded on PRO C 65/33, a roll of eight membranes, 350 mm (14 inches) wide, sewn chancery-style and numbered in a later hand. The text, written by a number of chancery clerks, occupies only the recto, or face, of the membranes, the dorse being blank apart from a later heading, 'Rotulus parliamenti de anno 2 R. secundi pars prima', and similar notes at the joins of the membranes: 'Parl. 2 R. Glouc.' and 'Parl anno 2 R. 2 die mercurii apud Gloucester'. The last two membranes, being the outside of the roll, are much stained and torn, and the dorse of membrane 1 has been repaired at some period, probably in the sixteenth century, with pieces of musical manuscripts of late fourteenth-century date. There are both contemporaneous and later marginal headings to the text, but the arabic numerals are all of a later date. The text of the roll appears to be complete.

Writs of summons had been addressed on 3 September 1378 to the two archbishops, the bishop of London and eighteen other diocesans, and the abbots of St Augustine's, Canterbury and St Albans, with twenty-one other abbots and the priors of Coventry and the hospital of St John, Clerkenwell. The temporal peers summoned were John of Gaunt, duke of Lancaster, and Edmund earl of Cambridge, eleven other earls, and forty-seven tenants in chief. Fifteen judges and serjeants were called, but the writ for Thomas Ingleby was not sealed, perhaps because he died before the writs were sent.[2] A substantial number of towns are known to have been represented in this parliament, in contrast to the tally of the previous session. Returns survive for a total of ninety-three, including London, which customarily sent four citizens, and the Cinque Ports. The uncertainties of the record make close comparisons unprofitable, but it seems likely that on this occasion at least the numbers bear some relation to the political excitements of the day. The cities and boroughs were summoned through the sheriffs, so their numbers could and sometimes did vary even from year to year. The mere survival of the writs *de expensis*, or rather of their enrolments, is more remarkable than the fact that there are gaps in the records.

The parliament met on 20 October 1378 in the Benedictine abbey of St Peter's, Gloucester, where the members first gathered in a room appointed for the use of the royal counsellors. The parliament rolls often, though only incidentally, refer to meeting places, but the Gloucester parliament is particularly interesting not only for such local and domestic details, but also because a chronicler who was present noted and deplored the disruption of conventual life and its amenities which attended the session - most particularly the disturbing presence of professional entertainers of various kinds and the abrasive effect of ball games on the abbey's lawns.[3] The formal opening of the parliament had to be postponed for two days, for the customary reason that not all the members had arrived on time, and was eventually enacted in the great hall of the abbey. When the members went about their business the commons were directed to the chapter-house, a setting familiar to them from Westminster, and the triers of petitions were accommodated in the Lady chapel and the chapel of St Andrew. In the meantime, however, there was the chancellor's charge (Items 2-10). Bishop Houghton, whose words are recorded in direct speech throughout, began with the customary references to the king's concern to preserve the liberties of the church and the good laws and usages of the realm, and continued with a statement that an ancient ordinance prescribed a meeting of parliament every year, with the unblushing implication that the present session was a matter of routine. The burden of his address was the need for unity, which was evidently likely to be strained by an equally urgent need for money. To the dangers posed by enemies without the bishop added the ingratitude of those who slandered and traduced the magnates and the king's officers. He was evidently under pressure, and his resignation of the great seal on 29 October seems to have been prompted by the pertinacious requests of the commons to be informed of the names of the king's principal ministers.

---

[1] Saul, *Richard II*, 36-8.
[2] J. Sainty, *The Judges of England, 1272-1990*, (London 1993), 25.
[3] *Chronique de la Traison et Mort de Richart Deux Roy Dengleterre*, ed. B. Williams, xlviii.

By that time the detailed exposition of the crown's needs and the task of arguing with the commons, who were deeply dissatisfied with the conduct of affairs, had already fallen to William le Scrope, as steward of the household (Item 15). Scrope now succeeded Houghton, and continued in office as chancellor until the beginning of 1380, when he gave place to the ill-fated Archbishop Sudbury. Scrope's exchanges with the commons' speaker, Sir James Pickering, had been robust. Pickering reviewed the chancellor's charge in detail, and in answer to the crown's continuing pleas for money declared simply that the commons thought that there was still and ought to be a great plenty available to the king, including the resources of the alien priories, the mere existence of which was a constant irritation (Item 18). The commons were reluctant to believe that the previous year's subsidies had been fully and honestly spent, and suspected that John of Gaunt had had access to them. The crown's answer was that the subsidies had been entirely in the hands of the treasurers for war, the commons' own colleagues William Walworth and John Philpot, Londoners, of whom Philpot in particular was a long-standing opponent of the duke (Item 19). The commons persisted in their disbelief, asking to have the accounts presented in detail, and the names of ministers certified to them (Item 20). In the course of his reply Scrope took occasion to remind them that the longer they protracted the business of parliament, the greater would be the charges which their long-suffering constituents had to meet.

There were, as Tout observed, many cross-currents in the debates.[4] The commons were and remained baffled by the government's steady consumption of revenues which produced no improvement in the state of the kingdom's affairs. The ministers were apprehensive of the popular mood. They wished to preserve the king's prerogative and their own privileges, but they urgently needed money. Their own agenda included parrying the indignation of the clergy over the violation of sanctuary at Westminster. In that they might count on some anti-clerical feeling among the commons, which in turn might be offset by the involvement of Lancastrian retainers in the outrage. The abbot of Westminster seems to have made some impression on the commons, and the ministers imported John Wyclif, the most formidable disputant of his day, to rebut the abbot's arguments and to denounce both the principle of sanctuary and the fraudulent protection of debtors which it permitted (Items 27-8). In the event the lords rallied to the ministerial and commercial cause, while seeking also to protect the young king's interests during his minority. The prelates were thus deprived of restitution and a public endorsement of clerical privileges, and yet the fact that parliament declared firmly for the Roman Pope Urban VI, and against the Avignonese papacy, and that the outcome for the church was no worse than it was, allowed clerical commentators to rejoice that the enemies of righteousness had been thwarted.[5] Amid those and other distractions Scrope so far prevailed as to extract a subsidy from the commons, though not the tax on moveable goods for which he had hoped (Items 29-30).

Some judicial business was conducted during the session, including the continuation of the earl of Salisbury's suit against the earl of March (Item 31), and a concession of error in the proceedings against the former king Edward III's mistress, Alice Perrers (Item 37). As a result of the review, Alice was pardoned her offences 'with the assent of the magnates of the realm' a few weeks later.[6] The business of the parliament was brought to an abrupt and early end by an unexplained crisis which caused the ministers to remove to London. The cause may have lain in the complex diplomatic negotiations in which they were involved with Aragon and Navarre, in their attempts to contain and offset the destructive hostility of Castile.[7] One consequence was that although the chancellor was constrained, despite his earlier refusal, to agree to inform the commons of the names of the king's new counsellors, he was able to do so piecemeal, and before the new ministry was complete. The carefully constructed panel of the previous year had now passed the end of its commission, but the ministers were spared the necessity and the implications of remodelling the king's government in the sight of parliament. On the other hand the exigencies of the political and military situation that developed during the winter compelled them to further gestures and some concessions when they faced the commons again in the following spring.

The commons submitted thirty-six common petitions at Gloucester, of which eight issued in statutes. That was a substantial volume of public business, though smaller than the previous year's. Among several persistent themes the grievance over demands for tithe from woodland had a long run ahead of it, and it is notable that the confirmation of corporate liberties was raised again, despite a reassuring response to a similar petition in 1377. The processing of petitions and the business of framing the first statute of the year was probably completed at Westminster. Writs *de expensis* were sealed on 16 November, and it seems that on this occasion the departure of the commons marked the end of the session both formally and literally.[8] The feelings of those departing were probably mixed, but the ministers must have had some cause for relief, at least temporarily, and the chancery, although inured to travelling, would have been glad to return to Westminster, whatever Gloucester had to offer. The busking, footballing and other distractions of which the chronicler complained may have impressed only the country members, but they evidently left a longer-lasting mark on the monastic community.

---

[4] Tout, *Chapters*, III.340.
[5] Saul, *Richard II*, 37-8.
[6] *CPR 1377-81*, 412.
[7] Saul, *Richard II*, 38-42.
[8] *CCR 1377-81*, 220-22.

Text and Translation

Text

Page iii-32, Membrane 8

ROTULUS PARLIAMENTI TENTI APUD GLOUCESTRE, DIE MERCURII PROXIMO POST FESTUM SANCTI LUCE EWANGELISTE, ANNO REGNI REGIS RICARDI SECUNDI POST CONQUESTUM ANGLIE SECUNDO.

Pars I.

Continuance de parlement.

1. Le mesqardy proschein apres la fest de Saint Luk l'Ewangelist, qe fust le .xxme jour d'Octobre, l'an du regne nostre seignour le roi Richard secounde, et qe fust le primer jour de ce parlement, aucuns des prelatz et seignours, et les grantz officers du roi, s'assemblerent en une chambre ordeinez pur le conseil nostre seignour le roi en l'abbeye de Saint Pere de Gloucestre, et longement y attendirent la venue des autres prelatz, et seignours, et de la commune; et sur ce apres pur ce q'estoit tesmoignez qe plusours des prelatz et seignours n'estoient unqores venuz a la ville, n'auxint les viscontz des plusours contees n'avoient fait retourner lours briefs de parlement, mesme le parlement par comandement nostre dit seignour le roi feust adjornez tanqe al lendemain lors proschein ensuant. Et sur ce comandez estoit as seignours et prelatz, et cry fait a la commune dehors en apart, q'ils s'en departirent a lours hosteux pur lour aiser, et qe touz y retournassent le dit lendemain bien matin pur oier la pronunciacioun des causes pur quelles nostre dit seignour le roi issint ad fait somondre ce present parlement.

Pronunciacion de parlement, etc.

2. A quel lendemain, qe fust le joesdy lors proschein venant, et le .xxi. jour d'Octobre, nostre dit seignour le roi mesmes avec ses trois uncles d'Espaigne, de Cantebrugge, et de Bukyngham, et les deux erchevesqes de Canterbirs et d'Everwyk, le conte de la Marche, et bien a poy touz les evesqes et contes d'Engleterre qi poient travailler, et plusours abbes, priours, barons et banerettz, justices et sergeantz q'avoient la dite somonce s'assemblerent en la grant sale deinz mesme l'abbeye, q'estoit ordeinez, apparaillez et aornez, pur y tenir mesme le parlement. Et appellez la einz les chivalers des contees, barons de cynk portz, citezeins des citees et burgeys des burghes, q'alors estoient bien pres touz venuz, l'evesqe de Saint Davy, chanceller d'Engleterre,[9] y avoit les paroles de la pronunciacion des causes de la somonce de \ce/ parlement, par comandement nostre dit seignour le roi mesmes, par la manere qe s'ensuit, et dist, seignours et sires, nostre seignour le roi cy present, qe Dieu salve, m'ad comandez de vous dire et exposer sa volentee, et les causes de la somonce de ce present \parlement/; qe sont tielles:

3. Primerement, a l'honour et reverence de Dieu, et de sainte esglise, et pur profit et quiete de son poeple, il desire souvrainement qe les libertees et franchises de sainte esglise, et les bones loys et custumes de son roialme d'Engleterre soient entierment gardez et salvez sanz emblemissement aucun, et si avant come celles ont este gardez et salvez en aucun temps passez

[Col. b] par nul de ses progenitours rois d'Engleterre, et qe les trespassours a l'encontre soient duement chastisez: et si nully se vorra pleindre qe mesprision, grief ou damage a luy soit fait encontre les libertees, franchises, loys et custumes avantdites, nostre seignour le roi de sa bone et liberale

Translation

THE ROLL OF THE PARLIAMENT HELD AT GLOUCESTER, ON THE WEDNESDAY AFTER THE FEAST OF ST LUKE THE EVANGELIST IN THE SECOND YEAR OF THE REIGN OF KING RICHARD, THE SECOND SINCE THE CONQUEST.

First part.

The adjournment of parliament.

1. On the Wednesday next after the feast of St Luke the Evangelist, which was 20 October, in the second year of the reign of our lord King Richard, which was the first day of parliament, some of the prelates and lords, and the great officers of the king, assembled in a chamber assigned for the council of our lord the king in the abbey of St Peter of Gloucester, and there they long awaited the arrival of the other prelates and lords and the commons; whereupon, because it was reported that many of the prelates and lords had still not arrived in the town, nor yet had the sheriffs of many counties returned their writs to parliament, that same parliament, by order of our said lord the king, was adjourned until the next day. And thereupon, orders were given to the lords and prelates, and a public announcement made to the commons outside that they should depart to their lodgings and take their rest, and that all should return early in the morning of the next day to hear declared the reasons for which our said lord the king had thus caused this present parliament to be summoned.

The opening of parliament, etc.

2. The next day, which was the Thursday next following, and 21 October, our said lord the king himself with his three uncles of Spain, Cambridge, and Buckingham, and the two archbishops, of Canterbury and York, and the earl of March, and almost all the bishops and earls of England who had able to travel there, and many of the abbots, priors, barons and bannerets, justices and serjeants who had received the said summons, assembled in the great hall within the same abbey, which had been chosen, furnished and bedecked for the holding of the same parliament. And the knights of the counties, barons of the Cinque Ports, citizens of the cities and burgesses of the boroughs, who had nearly all arrived, having first of all been called within, it fell to the bishop of St David's, chancellor of England, to present the reasons for the summons of this parliament, upon the king's own orders, in the following manner, who said, lords and sirs, our lord the king here present, whom God preserve, has ordered me declare and expound his will, and the reasons for the summoning of this present parliament, which are these:

3. First, in honour and reverence of God, and of holy church, and for the benefit and tranquillity of his people, he desires above all that the liberties and the franchises of holy church, and the good laws and customs of his kingdom of England be fully protected and preserved without suffering detriment of any sort, just as they have been protected and preserved ever in the past

[Col. b] by any of his progenitors, the kings of England, and that those acting to the contrary shall be duly punished: and if anyone wishes to complain that crime, harm or injury has been done him contrary to the aforesaid liberties, franchises, laws and customs, our lord the king, of his own good and

---

[9] Adam Houghton, bishop of St David's 1362-89, was chancellor from 11 Jan. 1377 and resigned during this parliament, 29 Oct. 1378.

volentee soi offre d'y faire a chescuny, sibien as povres come as riches, plein droit et justice entant q'a lui appartient, et est tenuz del faire par le serement fait a son corounement.

4. Secoundement, pur ce qe autre foitz a la priere des seignours et communes estoit ordeignez et assentuz qe parlement serroit tenuz chescun an, mesme nostre seignour le roi veulliant toutdys faire tenir toute bone covenant et mettre en execucion chescun ordinance faite en ses parlementz, si ad il par tant fait somondre ce parlement.

5. Item, la terce cause y a, c'estassavoir, pur ce qe mesme nostre seignour le roi desire moelt entierment de vous veer et parler, et meement en si bele et honurable congregacion, ou chescun de vous se purra bien et ad grant cause de se solacer autre, et rejoier en Dieu, et moelt le pluis par encheson qe celle congregacion q'est seinte esglise, ou l'escripture dit, 'Congregatio justorum est ecclesia Dei'; et si est celle congregacion droitement fait et foundu en cest noble abbeye, q'est founduz et dediez en l'onour de Dieu, et de Saint Pere prince de touz les apostles, sur qi nostre seignour Jehsu Crist founda sa sainte esglise nostre mere espiritele, en disant, 'Tu es Petrus et super hanc petram edificabo ecclesiam mea'; la quele congregacion issint faite en si saint lieu, dont l'escripture dist 'Terribilis est locus iste'; si est fait, si Dieu plest, en le noun de Dieu \et/ de la grace del Sainte Espirit, dont l'Evangile dit, 'Quod ubi sunt duo vel tres congregati in nomine meo, in medio eorum sum, dicit Dominus'. Et par tant si aucun descort ou male volentee par l'instigacion du deable y feust moevez ou conceuz parentre aucunes persones cy presentz, qe Dieu ne veulle, le perre du corner de seinte esglise, qe droitement signifie Dieu par l'escripture, qe dit, 'Lapis angularis Christus est'; les fra mettre et trera a unitee et concorde. Qar sicome le pere du corner tret ensemble et fortment lie et joint ensemble les deux mures de pareies del esglise par forte syment q'est perfit charitee, ensi nostre salvour Jehsu Crist q'est le pere du corner come dit est, entrelie et tret a soi \[par forte]/ charitee touz ceux qe \se/ sont departiz par hayne, ire, envye ou autre rancoure, si nul y soit aucune part *[Page iii-33]*

[Col. a] consceuz, come l'escripture dit, 'Hic lapis angularis facit utraque unum';

6. Item, une autre grante cause y a de la dite somonce, et vous le devez bien entendre, coment nostre seignour le roi estoit lessez au temps q'il feust corounez en plousours grandes et fortes guerres de toutes partz, et les mises et coustages qe l'en y faut mettre entour le defens de vous touz, et salvacion du roialme, nul roi Cristien purroit endurer sanz l'aide de sa commune.

7. Et ore il est ensi, qe apres la vilenie et damage q'estoit nadgairs fait a Roxburgh' par les Escotz, et qe sur ce une treve ou soeffrance de guerre estoit pris tanqe a la Saint Martyn proschein venant, mesmes les Escotz se sont en le moien temps alliez a noz enemys de France, de lour aider encontre touz gentz, et par especial envers le roi nostre seignour, et touz les \[soens]/ sitost come les grandes treves soient finiz, qe ne durent oultre quatre ans. Et si par aucune ymaginacion ou cause /colourable\ ils purroient departir de celles grandes treves, q'ils nous ferront overte et forte guerre. Et de verite clerement purra apparoir chescun jour, sibien par l'entente et les subtiles paroles de lours lettres et messages q'ils envoient par decea, \come autrement,/ q'ils s'afforcent en toutes maneres a departir de celles grandes treves ore a cest proschein jour de March' qe serra tenuz a la Saint Martin. Dont est moelt a doter d'avoir une guerre si pres de

free will, shall offer to do to poor men as well as rich, full right and justice, as far as he is able, and as he is obliged to grant them because of the oath he took at his coronation.

4. Second, because on another occasion at the request of the lords and commons it was ordained and assented that parliament would be held each year, our same lord the king, always wishing to uphold every good covenant and put into practice each ordinance made in his parliaments, has caused this parliament to be summoned, for that very reason.

5. Also, the third reason is this, namely that because our same lord the king desires most earnestly to see and speak with you, especially amidst so pleasing and honourable a congregation, in which you all may well take comfort amongst yourselves, and with good cause, and rejoice in God, and most of all for the reason that this congregation resembles holy church, since the scriptures say, 'The congregation of the righteous is the church of God'; and so it is right that this congregation is assembled and situated in this noble abbey, which was founded and dedicated in honour of God and St Peter, prince of all the apostles, upon whom our Lord Jesus Christ founded his holy church our spiritual, saying 'Thou art Peter and on this rock shall I build my church'; and which congregation is thus assembled in so holy a place, of which the scriptures say 'Terribilis est locus iste, 'Terrible is this place'; so it be done, if God pleases, in the name of God and with the grace of the Holy Spirit, concerning which the Gospel says, 'Wherever two or three are gathered in my name, I am amongst them, sayeth the Lord'. And because of this, if any discord or ill will should arise or be conceived amongst any persons here present, which God forbid, the cornerstone of holy church, which rightly signifies God, for as the holy scriptures say, 'Christ is the cornerstone', shall reconcile them and draw them together in unity and concord. Because just as the cornerstone draws together and strongly binds the two walls of holy church with strong cement which is perfect charity, thus our saviour Jesus Christ who is the cornerstone, as said above, joins and draws to himself with strong charity those who have abandoned him in hate, anger, envy or any other kind of rancour, if these have in any way been *[Page iii-33]*

[Col. a] conceived, for as the scriptures say 'This cornerstone brings two together in one'.

6. Also, there is another important reason for the said summons, which you ought to take fully into account, namely that our lord the king, at the time when he was crowned, had suffered in many great and vigorous wars in all parts, and the costs and expenses which were necessarily incurred in the defence of you all, and the salvation of the realm, no Christian king could endure without the aid of his commons.

7. And now it happens that after the villainy and injuries which were recently perpetrated by the Scots at Roxburgh, whereupon a truce or suspension of hostilities was agreed until the following Martinmas, the same Scots, in the meantime, allied themselves with our enemies of France, offering to help them against all others, and especially against the king our lord and all his people as soon as the great truces are ended, and these last no longer than four years. And if through ruse or for some other dubious reason they contrive to break these great truces, they will wage open and fierce war against us. And indeed, this could happen at any time, since it is clear from the tenor and careful wording of their letters and messages which they send overseas, and in other ways, that they strive in all ways to break these great truces now at the coming March Day which should be held at Martinmas. Since a war so imminent is greatly to be feared,

nous, avec le remenant qe nous avons affaire avec autres terres et paiis, paront nostre seignour le roi vous prie touz moelt entierment qe vous, prelatz, seignours et peres de son roialme par vous mesmes, et vous ses communes par vous mesmes assemblez, veulliez conseiller, et profoundement vous aviser, coment l'en purra resister a la malice des tantz des enemys a meillour salvacion de vous touz, et de l'estat de nostre seignour le roi et de tout son roialme, et greindre ennoy et grevance a ses enemys avantditz, et coment a meindre grevance du poeple l'en purra avenir et atteindre a les grandes despenses qe l'en y faut mettre au fyne force. Et vostre advis ent pris a plus en haste qe \bonement/ purrez vous le vorrez monstrer a mesme nostre seignour le roi et son conseil, aiantz toudiz devant voz oilx due consideracion a la grande necessitee apparante.

8. Et seignours et sires, d'autre part, quant a les meschiefs deinz le roialme ore currantz qe demandent amendement, j'ai en memoire une grante meschief pur vous monstrer. C'estassavoir, de ce qe les loys de la terre et les loys d'armes doivent estre come relatives, l'une loy toutdys aidant a l'autre en tous cas busoignables. Qar en chescun cas ou la loy de la terre ne purroit justicer un malfait, la loy et poair des armes la doit aider et maintenir. Et semblablement arieremain en chescun cas ou le loy des armes ne sauroit ou ne purroit faire ce qe a lui appartiendroit affaire, la loy de la terre y doit socourer et aider, issint qe l'une loy sanz l'autre ne purroit longement esteer, n'endurer. Et en cest roialme sont eles a poy departiz, dont est a doler, qar plusours gentz nient aiant consideracion a la loy de la terre, ne a droit ne a bone justice, s'enterlient, et se coillent ensemble a grant multitude et force des gentz armes, et voluntrifment et sanz juste cause disseisent autres, et les botent hors de lours maisons et tenementz, sanz ce q'ils veullent attendre aucune reson ou diffinicion de la loy de la terre. Et d'autre part, a tielle force armee ravisent virges et veves, et les enmesnent et detiegnent a lour volentee sanz autre parlance ou tretee de mariage faire. Et a la foitz batent et tuent moelt dispitousement les bones et innocens gentz en paiis.

9. Item, il y a un autre grant meschief deinz le roialme a ce qe semble qe faut estre amendez, de ce qe en plusours parties de roialme les malvoys gentz moelt communement s'afforcent a dire et controver et conter fauxes, horribles et perilouses mensonges des seignours et autres grantz officers et bones gentz del roialme, et les font privement notefier et semer entre les communes et autres, et ne les poent ne ne veullent avouer en appart: dont est a merveille et bien grantement a doter qe descort et ryot ent purroit sourdre deinz le roialme, si due remedie n'y soit mys le pluis en haste. Les queux \controvours/ et contours, qi sont appellez bacbyters, sont auxi come chiens qi mangeont les chars crues. Qar auxint font les ditz fauxes bacbyters par lours malx paroles, ils mangent les bons et loialx gentz tout cruez a deriere eulx, qi n'osent rienz latrer ne faire contenance de mal par devant les bones gentz avantdites. De quoy, seignours et sires, si vous plest entre autres y faut prier a nostre seignour le roi de bone ordinance et due amendement.[10]

10. Et de celles meschiefs, et de touz autres si nuls y soient, mette avant voz peticions as certains clercs de la chancellarie assignez de resceivre les peticions en ce parlement, dont les nouns vous y serront tantost rehercez. Pur le triement des quelles peticions nostre seignour le roi ad fait assigner certains prelatz, seignours, justices et autres dessouz escritz; et voet et comande qe bone ordinance et due remede ent soit

together with all else that we have to do in other lands and countries, our lord the king most earnestly prays of you all that you, the prelates, lords and peers of his realm amongst yourselves, and with his commons assembled by you yourselves, might consult and thoroughly consider how we might best resist the malice of such enemies for the greater safety of you all, and of the estate of our lord the king and all his realm, and greatly vexing and grieving his aforesaid enemies, and how, with least injury to the people, we might secure and obtain the considerable revenue which must be invested through sheer necessity. And when your decision has been reached that you might inform our same lord the king and his council of it as swiftly as you possibly can, keeping always in sight the fact that due consideration should to be given to a state of obvious need.

8. And for another thing, lords and sirs, with regard to the troubles currently afoot within the kingdom which require a solution, I have in mind one considerable trouble which I wish to bring to your attention. Namely, that the laws of the land and the laws of arms should bear a relation to each other, the one law always assisting the other wherever necessary. So that in each case where the law of the land is unable to punish a crime, the law and authority of arms should support and complement it. And likewise conversely, in each case where the law of arms is ill-suited or unable to perform that which pertains to it, the law of the land should be a help and support, so that the one law cannot exist or endure for long without the other. Yet in this kingdom they have almost completely diverged, which is to be lamented, since many people, having no thought for the law of the land, or for right or impartial justice, ally with each other, and congregate in great multitudes and forces of armed men, and deliberately and without good reason disseise others, and expel them from their houses and tenements, paying no attention to right or the word of the law. And besides, armed with such force they ravish virgins and widows, and carry them off and keep them at their will without any word or agreement of marriage. And sometimes they beat and kill most mercilessly the good and innocent people of the country.

9. Also, there is another great trouble within the kingdom which it seems must be remedied, namely, that in many parts of the kingdom evil people strive openly to tell, fabricate and recount false, terrible and dangerous lies about the lords and other great officers and the good people of the kingdom, and they cause them secretly to be made known and disseminated amongst the commons and others, and they cannot and do not wish to confess this openly: in view whereof, it is to be greatly and overwhelmingly feared that discord and riot will arise within the kingdom, unless a proper remedy is supplied as soon as possible. These liars and gossips, who are called back-biters, resemble dogs who chew raw meat. For the said false back-biters thus do this when, with their evil words, they devour raw good and loyal people, who do not dare to protest at anything or adopt an angry countenance before the aforesaid good people. Whereupon, lords and sirs, if it please you, a request must be made of our lord the king amongst other things, for some good ordinance and due remedy.

10. And concerning these troubles, and such others as there may be, you shall submit your petitions to certain clerks of the chancery designated to receive the petitions in this parliament, whose names shall be given to you forthwith. For the examination of these petitions our lord the king has caused certain prelates, lords, justices and others listed below to be appointed; and he wishes and orders that a good ordinance

---

[10] 2 Ric.2 stat.1 c.5; The statutes of this parliament are printed in *SR*, II.6-11.

fait et purveuz de les peticions avantdites. Et nostre seignour le roi comande a vous touz, de retourner ycy lendemain proschein, entour le .viij.^{me} heure del clok, pur oier greindre declaracion de les necessitees en defens du roialme; et a vous les communes est assignez la maison appellez le chapitre deinz le grante cloystre de ceste abbeye, pur y faire voz congregations, \parlances,/ et affaires, par manere acustume.

11. Resceivours des peticions d'Engleterre, Irlande, Gales et Escoce:
Sire William de Burstall'
Sire Richard de Ravenser
Sire Thomas de Newenham
Sire Johan de Freton'.

12. Resceivours des peticions de Gascoigne, et d'autres terres et paiis depar dela, et des Isles:
Sire Henry de Codyngton'
Sire Piers de Barton'
Sire Johan Bouland
Sire Thomas Thelwall.

Et ceux qi vorront bailler lours peticions les baillent avant, parentre cy et mesqardy proschein venant, le dit jour accomptee; et apres mesme le jour nul peticion soit aucunement resceuz.

Page iii-34

13. Et sont assignez triours des peticions d'Engleterre, Irlande, Gales et Escoce:
Le roi de Castille et de Leon, Duc de Lancastre
L'ercevesqe de Canterbirs
L'evesqe de Londres
L'evesqe de Wyncestre
L'evesqe de Ely
L'evesqe de Norwiz
L'evesqe de Salesbirs
L'evesqe de Cardoill'
L'abbe de Glastyngbirs
L'abbe de Gloucestre
Le conte de la Marche
Le conte d'Arondell'
Le conte de Warr'
Le conte de Stafford
Le conte de Northumbr'
Le seignour de Latymer
Le seignour de Cobham
Monsieur Henry le Scrop'
Monsieur Roger Beauchamp'
Monsieur Richard de Stafford
Monsieur Johan Knyvet
Monsieur Johan Cavendissh'
Monsieur Robert Bealknap'
Monsieur William Skipwyth'
Monsieur Hugh Segrave.

- touz ensemble, ove .vi. des prelatz et seignours avantditz au meins; appellez a eux chanceller, tresorer, seneschal et chamberlein et auxint le sergeantz nostre seignour le roi quant il busoignera. Et tendront lour place en la grante chapelle nostre dame deinz ceste abbeye.

and due remedy shall be provided and carried out for the said petitions. And our lord the king commands you all to return here tomorrow, at around eight o'clock, to hear an important announcement touching matters related to the defence of the realm; and to you the commons is assigned the building called the chapter-house within the great cloister of this abbey, to hold your meetings and debates, and to perform your business, in the customary manner.

11. The receivers of petitions from England, Ireland, Wales and Scotland:
Sir William Burstall
Sir Richard Ravenser
Sir Thomas Newenham
Sir John Freton.

12. The receivers of petitions from Gascony, and from other lands and countries overseas, and from the Channel Islands:
Sir Henry Codington
Sir Peter Barton
Sire John Bowland
Sire Thomas Thelwall.

And those who wish to submit their petitions should hand them in between now and next Wednesday, the day appointed for this; and after that day no petitions should be received for any reason.

13. The following are assigned to be triers of petitions from England, Ireland, Wales and Scotland:
The king of Castile and of Leon, the duke of Lancaster
The archbishop of Canterbury
The bishop of London
The bishop of Winchester
The bishop of Ely
The bishop of Norwich
The bishop of Salisbury
The bishop of Carlisle
The abbot of Glastonbury
The abbot of Gloucester
The earl of March
The earl of Arundel
The earl of Warwick
The earl of Stafford
The earl of Northumberland
Lord Latimer
Lord Cobham
Sir Henry le Scrope
Sir Roger Beauchamp
Sir Richard Stafford
Sir John Knyvet
Sir John Cavendish
Sir Robert Bealknap
Sir William Skipwith
Sir Hugh Segrave.

- to act all together, or at least six of the aforesaid prelates and lords; consulting with the chancellor, treasurer, steward and chamberlain, and also the serjeants of our lord the king, when necessary. And they shall hold their session in the great chapel of Our Lady within this abbey.

14. The following are assigned to be triers of petitions from Gascony, and from other lands and countries overseas, and from the Channel Islands:

The archbishop of York

The bishop of Durham

The bishop of Lincoln

The bishop of Bath and Wells

The bishop of Hereford

The bishop of Rochester

The bishop of Worcester

The bishop of St Asaph

The bishop of Bangor

The abbot of Westminster

The prior of St John of Jerusalem in England

The earl of Canterbury

The earl of Buckingham, constable of England

The earl of Salisbury

The earl of Suffolk

Lord Lestrange of Knockin

Lord FitzWalter

Sir John Montagu

Sir John Arundel, marshal of England

Sir Robert Tresilian

Sir Roger Fulthorp

Sir Henry Asty

Sir John Devereux.

- to act all together, or at least six of the aforesaid prelates and lords; consulting with the chancellor, treasurer, steward, chamberlain and the aforesaid serjeants when necessary. And they shall hold their session in the chapel of St Andrew, near the great chapel of Our Lady within this abbey.

The announcement of the opening of parliament.

15. Also, on the following Friday, which was 22 October, the prelates, lords and commons assembled in the said great hall, and there Sir Richard le Scrope, steward of the household of our lord the king, to whom it fell to speak, said that he was neither learned nor worthy enough for such matters in so exalted and noble a place; nevertheless [Col. b] our lord the king ordered him to say what he had to say. And he said that it was clear and apparent to everyone that the king our lord, his kingdom of England, and his other lands, countries, and lordships were beset and surrounded by our enemies, who were multiplying daily both in parts of Scotland as well as elsewhere, in the ways in which our lord the chancellor fully explained yesterday much better than I can tell: and that we have opened many fine and noble entries and ports with which to grieve our enemies, which have not long been in the hands of the English; namely, Cherbourg and Brest, not to mention Calais, Bordeaux and Bayonne, which require no small amount of money to protect, and indeed, a very great sum must be devoted to safeguarding the same. On account of which the king our lord spends each year at Calais, and in the surrounding marches, more than £24,000, and at Brest a full £12,000 marks, and at Cherbourg it is now necessary to spend huge sums; and at Bordeaux, and Bayonne, for the safety of the same; and in the lands and lordships of our lord the king in Guyenne and elsewhere overseas; and also in Ireland, for the safe-keeping and

d'ycelles; sanz ce qe l'en faut faire de necessite et au fine force entour la salve garde et de les costes du meer, qe demandent moelt grant somme. Mais par cas aucuns de vous y vorroient \[penser]/ et merveiller en queux places, et par quelle manere les deux quinszimes de lays gentz, et les deux dismes de la clergie, grantez en defens du roialme, et pur maintenance de la guerre, al derrain parlement, avec la subside des leynes, feussent ore \en/ si brief terme devenuz ou despenduz. A quoy, seignours et sires, je vous die pur verite, et vouche record al haut tresorier, et a touz les seignours qi cy sont, qe celles deux dismes et quinszimes, avec le dit subside, si sont entierment despenduz entour les dites guerres, et nulle part aillours, par les mains de Johan Philipot et William Walworth', tresorers assignez pur la dite guerre come bien savez, sanz ce qe ent vint unqes un soul denier es mains du roi nostre seignour, ou nul de ses officers, a /son\ oeps propre. Et bien devez savoir qe decy enavant nostre seignour le roi ne suffist mye, ne ne purroit nul roi Cristien suffire, a tiele charge porter sanz l'aide de son poeple. Et par tant nostre seignour le roi vous prie moelt entierment, mes seignours, prelatz et autres peres de son roialme, qe vous vous ent verrez aviser par vous mesmes /ensemble; et vous auxint, mes sires les chivalers, citeins et burgeys de son dit roialme,\ par vous mesmes, coment a greinour salvacion del honeir nostre seignour le roi et de son dit roialme, et de vous touz queux la dite defens touche auxi avant come nul autre, et \a/ greinour ennoy, damage, et grevance de ses enemys avantdites, l'en purra resister a lour malice et fauxes ymaginations; et dont, au meindre grevance de son loial poeple, les despenses qe l'en y faut mettre, come dessus est dit, doivent sourdre, et estre levez. Et sitost come aucun certain purpos ent aurez pris, le veulliez demain, ou le seconde jour, monstrer a nostre seignour le roi, ou a son conseil. Et qe vous vous y veulliez haster de bien faire, a fin qe ce parlement en aise du roi nostre seignour, et de vous touz, puisse prendre bon et hastive effect, et esploit prospre, Dieu pur sa mercy la grante. Et nostre seignour le roi voet et comande qe ce present parlement soit continuez de jour en autre tanqe les chargeantz busoignes feussent esploitz, et qe le roi nostre seignour ent eust donez \a vous/ sa congie pur departir.'

Rehercealle faite par la commune de lour charge donee et lour response.
16. Et puis apres les communes y revindrent devant le roi, les prelatz et seignours en parlement, et illoeqes monsire James de Pekeryng, chivaler, q'avoit les paroles depar la commune, faisant sa protestacion sibien pur lui mesmes come pur toute la commune d'Engleterre illoeqes assemble: et primerement pur la dite commune, qe si par cas il y deist chose qe purroit soner en prejudice, damage, esclaundre ou vilanie de nostre seignour le roi ou de sa coroune, ou en amenusement *[Page iii-35]*
[Col. a] del honour et l'estat des grantz seignours \du roialme,/ qe ce ne feust acceptez par le roi et les seignours, einz tenuz pur nul, et come rienz n'ent eust este dit: desicome la commune n'est en autre volentee, mais souverainement desirent l'oneur et l'estat de nostre seignour le roi et les dreitures de sa coroune estre maintenuz et gardez en touz pointz, et la reverence d'autres seignours estre duement gardez toutz partz. Et pur sa propre persone demesne, faisant sa protestacion, qe si pur meins bone discrecion, ou en autre manere, il y deist chose qe ne fust del commune assent de ses compaignons, ou par cas forvoiast de rienz en ses paroles, q'il feust par eulx supportez et amendez, ore devant lour departir, ou en apres quant lour pleust.

effective protection of the same; not forgetting that it is necessary to maintain a great force for the safeguard of the coasts, which requires a very large sum of money. But perhaps some of you will be considering and wondering how and on what the two fifteenths from the laity, and the two tenths from the clergy, granted for the defence of the realm and for the maintaining of the war at the last parliament, together with the subsidy on wool, have now, in so short a time been used and spent. To which, lords and sirs, I tell you truly, and call the high treasurer, and all the lords here present, to affirm that these two tenths and fifteenths, together with the said subsidy, have been devoted solely to the said wars, and to nothing else, being in the hands of John Philpot and William Walworth, the treasurers appointed for the said war as you well know, without a single penny from them coming into the hands of our lord the king, or any of his officers, for his own use. And you ought fully to appreciate that from now on our lord the king cannot endure, nor could any Christian king endure, the burden of such a responsibility without the help of his people. On account of which our lord the king most earnestly prays of you, my lords, prelates and other peers of his kingdom, that you consult amongst yourselves; and that you also, my lords the knights, citizens and burgesses of his said kingdom, consult with each other as to the best means of preserving the honour of our lord the king and his said kingdom, and you all whom the said defence concerns as well as any other, and how, to the greatest annoyance, injury and harassment of the aforesaid enemies, one might resist their malice and fraudulent schemes; and how, with the least harm being done to his loyal people, the necessary sums, as said above, might be raised and levied. And as soon as a definite conclusion has been reached, that you explain it to our lord the king and his council, either tomorrow or on the second day. And that you may act well and swiftly, so that this parliament, for the comfort of the king our lord, and of you all, might be brought to a speedy and effective conclusion, and its business prosper, may God in his mercy grant it. And our lord the king wishes and commands that this present parliament be adjourned until another day until the important matters have been discharged, and the king our lord has given you permission to depart.'

The account given by the commons of the duties assigned to them and their reply.
16. And then the commons reappeared before the king, the prelates and lords in parliament, and there Sir James Pickering, knight, who was to speak on behalf of the commons, made his protestation on behalf of himself and also on behalf of all the commons of England there assembled: and primarily for the said commons, that if it should happen that he should say anything which smacked of prejudice, malice, slander or evil intent against our lord the king or his crown, or lessened *[Page iii-35]*
[Col. a] the honour and estate of the great lords of the kingdom, that this should not be lent credence by the king and the lords, but held at naught, and considered unsaid: just as if the commons desired nothing else than that the honour and status of our lord the king and the rights of his crown be maintained and protected in every respect, and that reverence for other lords be duly preserved in all ways. And on behalf of himself, he protested that if through a lack of discretion, or in any other way, he should say anything which had not been given the common consent of his companions, or in case he should wander from the point, that he might be supported and corrected by them, immediately before their departure or afterwards as suited them.

17. Il reherceast en courtes paroles les articles et les charges a eux donez depar nostre dit seignour le roi sur la pronunciacion de ce parlement. Et quant as primers deux articles, touchantz ce qe nostre seignour le roi al honour de Dieu et reverence de sainte esglise voloit qe toutes les libertees et franchises de sainte esglise, et les bones loys et custumes de son roialme d'Engleterre, fuissent entierement gardez et savez sanz emblemissement quelconqe, et si avant come eles aient este gardez et salvez en temps de nully de ses progenitours rois d'Engleterre, et les trespassours contre ycelles duement chastisez et puniz, et qe touz ses liges feussent tretez et amesnez par ses dites bones loys et custumes, et nemye autrement, sa dite commune rendent a lour dit seignour lige graces et mercys humblement et de tout lour coer, les genulx a terre, et prient pur Dieu qe ce soit fait et mys a due et bone execucion, pur honour nostre dit seignour le roi, et commune profit de tout le roialme.

18. Et quant a ce qe nostre seignour le roi demande aide de sa commune, a les despenses qe l'en faut mettre entour la defens et salvacion du roialme, et entour la salve garde de ses seignouries, terres, villes et fortz depar dela, et entour l'esploit de ses guerres, la commune dit, qe a drain parlement mesme la matire lour feust autre foitz monstrez assez clerement depar le roi. A quel temps la commune respondist et dist qe lour sembloit et apparisante chose estoit, qe nostre seignour le roi n'auroit mye si grant busoigne come l'en lour disoit, desicome il avoit en ses mains touz les priories aliens, les subsides des leynes, les revenues del roialme, et des terres et seignouries son noble pere le prince, qi Dieux assoille, et des plusours autres grantz seignours du roialme par le noun-age de lours heirs, dont grantz revenues sourdent annuelment, et ent deust avoir este en la tresorie, a ce qe lour sembloit, bien grante plente de monoie.

A quoy estoit pur lors responduz par le conseil nostre seignour le roi, qe coment qe fuist voirs qe celles seignouries avoit le roi en ses mains, /son corounement\ ja novellement fait luy cousta grandement, et toutes voies les deniers ne feurent adonqes, ne ne poaient par long temps \lors/ a vener, ent estre levez si tost come enbusoignast pur un viage faire, en /celle\ proschein seisoun. Mais y fust dit oultre a mesme la commune qe si nostre seignour le roi feust aidez adonqes d'une bone et grande somme, dont il purroit faire une grant voiage et forte guerre en destruction de ses enemys en le dit proschein seisoun, qe serroit son comencement en le primer an de son regne, q'adonqes l'en avoit esperance en Dieu q'il auroit apres es mains de temps en temps bien suffisaument de monoie pur maintenir la guerre, et defendre son roialme avauntdit. Et par tant dit ore la commune d'Engleterre qe souz esperance de celle promesse, c'estassavoir d'estre deschargez des tallages pur un grant temps apres, la commune lui grantast a celle temps la greindre somme q'onqes feust donez a nul roi en dit roialme, a lever de eux en si brief /terme,\ lour preignant pur lors si pres, qe celluy qi /n'avoit\ dont paier ent fist chevance d'autres, a grant perde et meschief de eulx;

[Col. b] et ce souz l'esperance avantdite, et de la bone gouvernance qe lour estoit promis d'estre fait deslors sibien deinz le roialme come dehors sur la gouvernance de les guerres. Et pur rienz q'est encores fait semble a la commune, \[qe depuis qe]/ celle grant somme fust grantez et levez de eulx, qe partie de celle grande somme, oultre ce q'ent deust avoir este despenduz sur /le\ drain viage fait sur la

17. He briefly recited the articles and duties assigned to them on behalf of our said lord the king on the opening of this parliament. And with regard to the first two articles, concerning the fact that our lord the king, in honour of God and out of reverence for holy church, wished that all the liberties and franchises of holy church, and the good laws and customs of his kingdom of England, be completely protected and preserved without suffering any detriment, just as they were protected and preserved in the time of any of his progenitors, the kings of England, and contravenors of the same being duly chastised and punished, and that all his lieges might be treated and dealt with in accordance with his said good laws and customs, and not in any other way, his said commons gave their liege lord their humble thanks and wholehearted gratitude on bended knee, and they prayed that this should be done for love of God and put into proper and good effect, in honour of our said lord the king, and for the common good of all the realm.

18. And in connection with the our lord the king demanding the help of his commons, with the money which it would be necessary to invest in the defence and salvation of the kingdom, and in the safeguard of his lordships, lands, towns and forts overseas, and in the waging of his wars, the commons said that on another occasion, at the last parliament, the matter had been put to them quite clearly on behalf of the king. At which time the commons had replied and said that it seemed to them and was clearly the case that our lord the king was not in so great a need as he would have them believe, inasmuch as he had in his hands all the alien priories, the wool subsidies, the revenues of the kingdom, and the lands and lordships of his noble father the prince, whom God absolve, and those of many other great lords of the kingdom because of the minority of their heirs, out of which great revenues arose each year, and so there should have been a plentiful supply of money in the treasury, as it seemed to them.

To that the council of our lord the king replied that although it was true that the king held these lordships in his hands, his coronation, recently performed, had cost him greatly, and thereafter the money had not been available, and could not for a long time be levied, soon enough to enable an expedition to be made in the next season. But the same commons were also informed that if our lord the king were to be helped out at that time with a large and considerable sum, with which he might make a long journey and wage fierce war for the destruction of his enemies in the said next season, which would be his starting point in the first year of his reign, that then one might have hope in God that he would subsequently have in his possession from time to time a plentiful amount of money with which to maintain the war, and defend his aforesaid kingdom. And to this the commons of England now replied that in hope of that promise being fulfilled, namely of them being relieved of tallages for a long time after, the commons granted to him on that occasion a great sum of money which had never previously been granted to any king in the said kingdom, to be levied from them in so short a time, and at such short notice, that whoever had no means of paying had to borrow from others, at their great loss and inconvenience;

[Col. b] and in that aforesaid hope, and for the good governance which they had been promised would be done henceforth both within the realm as well as outside it in the governance of the wars. And concerning the matter still in hand it seemed to the commons that after this great sum had been granted and levied by them, that part of this great sum, over and above that which ought to have been spent on the last

meer, et auxint partie des autres subsides grantez, et des autres revenues et profitz avauntditz serroit en la tresorie nostre seignour le roi, paront mesme nostre seignour le roi n'auroit ore busoigne de recharger sa commune avauntdite, q'est ore pluis povres qe unqes en nul temps estoit devant, sibien par le dit paiement fait a nostre seignour le roi ja novellement, come dit est, et par morine de lours bestes, et arsures des enemys sur les coustes de la meer; come pur ce qe lours bledz et autres chateux sont ore de si petite value, qe nul homme ent poet a poy lever aucune monoie al jour del huy. Et par tant ils prient a nostre seignour le roi, qe luy pleust, pur Dieu, lour avoir et tenir pur excusez a ceste foitz: qar, pur verite dire, mes qe le roi nostre seignour eusse de fait grant busoigne de lour aide, ils ne purroient ore porter aucune charge pur pure poverte.

Responce donee depar le roi.
19. A quoy monsire Richard le Scrope, adonqes seneschal del hostiel nostre seignour le roi, y faisant protestacion, q'il ne conoist nulle tielle promesse fait en dit derrain parlement, y dist par comandement nostre dit seignour le roi, qe salve l'onour et la reverence de nostre seignour le roi et des seignours illoeqes esteantz, le dit de la commune en celle partie ne contient mye verite de ce, c'estassavoir, qe del derrain subside grantez grant partie serroit encores en /le\ tresorie; qar notoire chose est qe chescun denier provenant de mesme le subside, c'estassavoir de les deux .xv.^{mes} et deux dismes darrein grantez, et auxint des subsides des leynes puis le dit parlement, si ad este resceuz par les mains de William Walworth et Johan Philipot, citezeins de Londres, tresoriers assignez et jurez en dit darrein parlement a ce garder pur la guerre de vostre assent, et enoultre a ce qe les William et Johan diont, ils ent ont paiez et despenduz chescun denier sur les guerres et nul part aillours, sanz ce qe aucun denier ent sourdant devint unqes a les mains del haut tresorier d'Engleterre, ou de nul autre al oeps nostre dit seignour le roi. Et ce vouche il a tesmoignez et \a/ record les ditz William et Johan, horspris soulement les revenues del roialme, qe sont de trespetit value al jour de huy; oultre les annuytes et autres charges ent donez et grantez par les nobles aielle et pere, qe Dieu assoille, et salvez ce q'al roi et a son coroune d'Engleterre appartint du saak de layne, et des priours aliens d'ancien temps, dont il faut necessairement a maintenir son honour et estat de roi, come bien le doivez savoir. Paront quant a celle pleinte vous faut par reson cesser, si vous plest.

Requeste de la commune.
20. Et sur ce la commune, eue un poy de deliberacion, requiste autre foitz a nostre seignour le roi qe pleust a luy de faire monstrer a sa dite commune, coment et en quiel manere les dites grantz sommes issint donez et ordenez pur la dite guerre feurent despenduz, et \qe/ due ordinance y feusse faite qe si einsi avenoit, qe aucun seignour ou nul autre persone retenuz al derrain viage, ou nul part aillours, eust meindre nombre des gentz a sa monstre q'il n'estoit retenuz d'avoir avec luy, et eust resceuz gages et les deniers le roi, qe celle surpluis de monoie oultre les gages des gentz monstrez feust repaiez a nostre dit seignour le roi, pur estre appliez a la guerre, en descharge par tant de la commune avauntdite. Et auxint ils requirgent qe pleust a nostre seignour le roi granter qe la commune feust \[acertez]/ des nouns qi serroient les grantz officers del roialme, et qi serroient conseillers a nostre

voyage made by sea, and also part of the other subsidies granted, and the other aforesaid revenues and profits, should be in the treasury of our lord the king, so that our same lord the king would not now have the need to further burden his aforesaid commons, who are now poorer than they have ever been before, because of the said payment recently made to our lord the king, as was said, and because of disease amongst their cattle, and the burning inflicted by the enemies on the coasts of the sea; as well as because their corn and other chattels are now of so small a value, that no one is able to raise any money at all these days. And so they pray of our lord the king that it might please him, for love of God, to excuse them on this occasion: since, to tell the truth, even though the king our lord might have great need of their help, they would not now be able to shoulder any further burden through simple poverty.

The answer given on behalf of the king.
19. To which Sir Richard le Scrope, then steward of the household of our lord the king, making protestation that he knew of no such promise having been made in the said last parliament, said by order of our said lord the king, that saving the honour and reverence of our lord the king and the lords there present, the said commons were not possessed of the truth in this matter, namely, that a great part of the last subsidy granted should still be in the treasury; since it was well-known that every penny arising out of the said subsidy, namely from the two fifteenths and two tenths previously granted, and also from the subsidies on wool since the said parliament, had been received by William Walworth and John Philpot, citizens of London, the treasurers appointed and sworn in the said last parliament to keep that for the war with your consent, and in addition that William and John say that they have paid and spent every penny on the wars and on nothing else, without any penny which had been levied from this falling into the hands of the high treasurer of England or any other person for the use of our said lord the king. And he vouched for this on the basis of the testimonies and record of the said William and John, excepting only the revenues of the kingdom, which are of very small value these days; in addition to the annuities and other charges given and granted by the noble grandfather and father, whom God absolve, and saving that which pertains to the king and his crown of England from the sacks of wool, and from the alien priories since long ago, which are necessary to maintain the honour and estate of the king, as should be well known. On account of which, you should desist from pursuing this plea out of good sense, if it please you.

The request of the commons.
20. And thereupon, the commons, after a brief discussion, again requested of our lord the king, that it might please him to explain to his said commons how and in what manner the said great sums, thus given and ordained for the said war, had been spent, and assure them that it had been duly ordained that if it should happen that any lord or other person retained on the last expedition, or anywhere else, had a smaller number of people in his muster than he was contracted to have, and had received wages and money from the king, that the surplus of money in addition to the wages of the people mustered should be repaid to our said lord the king, to be spent on the war, thus relieving the aforesaid commons. They also requested that it might please our lord the king to grant that the commons be informed of the names of those who were to be great officers of the kingdom, and who were to be

seignour le roi, et governours de sa persone, tantcome il soit issint de tendre *[Page iii-36]*
[Col. a] age, pur l'an ensuant, par manere come autre foitz estoit ordeignez en parlement.

Responce donee de par le roi.
21. A quoi feust responduz par le dit monsire Richard del dit comandement qe coment qe n'estoit unqes veuz, qe de subside ou autre grant fait au roi en parlement ou hors du parlement par la commune, ent feust accomptee apres renduz a la commune, ou a aucun autre forsqe a roi et ses officers, nientmeins nostre dit seignour le roi voet et comande, en plesance de sa commune, del son propre moevement, sanz ce q'il \le/ fait de droit, ou par coartacion parmy la dite requeste ore a luy faite qe le dit William Walworth cy present, ensemble avec certaines autres persones del conseil nostre seignour le roi a ce a assigners depar le roi, vous monstrent en escrit clerement les receites et despenses ent faites, par tielle covenante qe ce ne soit desore trete en ensaumple ne consequentie qe ce feust autrement fait, forsqe soulement des propres moevement et comandement nostre dit seignour le roi, come dit est. Et quant a ce qe remaint des gages resceuz oultre les gentz monstrez, vous doivez entendre, qe ce appartint a nostre dit seignour le roi mesmes, et a ses ministres de l'escheqier, et nulle part aillours; et ceux de l'escheqier ne vorront ne ne soloient mettre en ubblie tieux choses, mes qe ce feust le greinour seignour d'Engleterre. Et quant as ditz officers et conseillers, nostre dit seignour le roi par advis des seignours ad fait eslire les ditz officers, et ferra ses conseillers de tieux come luy plerra, sitost come il purra a ce attendre; de qi nouns vous serrez bien acertes, si plest au roi. Et nostre seignour le roi vous comande et charge en priant, et einsi vous priont touz les seignours cy presentz, qe aiantz due consideracion a les grantz perils apparantz toutes partes; et auxint a ce qe la maintenance de la guerre par dehors est assez clerement devant ceste heure provez de pure reson le necessarie et meillour defens de tout le roialme avantdit: quiel defens ne touche soulement nostre dit seignour le roi, einz vous touz, et chescun de vous, et en celle defens vous ne purrez ne ne devrez departir l'un de l'autre par aucune voie, ne en despenses faire, ni autrement. Vous vous vorrez adviser

Membrane 6 coment et de quoy les dites guerre et defens serront faitz et maintenuz, et ent doner voz bones responces a pluis en haste qe vous purrez, au fin qe ce parlement feust finiz et bien esploitz, en aise du roi, des seignours, et de vous touz, et pur profit del roialme, et en descharge de la dite povre commune, qi paient chescun jour pur voz despenses durant cest parlement: et ce fust un et le principal de voz charges vous donez al dit primer jour. Une autre charge vous y avoistes qe si defaute feust trovez nul part deinz le roialme, ou del governance en les loys du roialme, ou en autre manere, qe de ce vous meissez avant voz supplicacions, et due remede vous ent serroit ordeignez. A quoy la dite commune priast d'avoir le jour limitez al dit primer jour de parlement, a deliverer lours communes billes, proloignez oultre tanqe al jour de almes proschein venant, tout cel jour accomptez; et ce lour estoit ottroiez.

Requeste de la commune.
22. Et auxi la commune y priast autre foitz a nostre dit seignour le roi, pur avoir la copie de l'enroullement del dit

councillors of our lord the king, and governors of his person, whilst he remained at so tender *[Page iii-36]*
[Col. a] an age, for the following year, in the manner which had been ordained on another occasion in parliament.

The answer given on behalf of the king.
21. To which the said Sir Richard, on the said orders, replied that although it had never happened before that a subsidy or other great grant made to the king in parliament or outside parliament by the commons had been accounted for to the commons after it had been rendered, or to anyone else except the king and his officers, nevertheless our said lord the king willed and ordered, to please his commons, and of his own accord, and not because he rightfully should, or had been forced to by the said request recently made of him, that the said William Walworth here present, together with certain other persons in the council of our lord the king assigned thereto on behalf of the king, should clearly set out in writing for you the receipts and expenses involved, on the understanding that this should not henceforth be treated as an example or precedent for what should otherwise be done, it being solely on the orders and personal initiative of our said lord the king, as aforesaid. And with regard to that which remains of wages received in excess of the persons mustered, you should understand that that pertains to our same said lord the king, and his ministers of the exchequer, and to none other; and those of the exchequer will not and are not accustomed to forgetting such matters, even for the greatest lord of England. And with regard to the said officers and councillors, our said lord the king by the advice of the lords had caused the said officers to be elected, and would select such councillors as pleased him, as soon as he could attend to that; of whose names you will be fully notified, if it please the king. And our lord the king orders and charges, and all the lords here present similarly request of you, that you lend due consideration to the great perils emerging in all parts; and also to the fact that the maintenance of the war abroad has been clearly proven in the past on grounds of pure reason to be the necessary and best defence of all the aforesaid kingdom: which defence concerns not merely our said lord the king, but all, and every one of you, and from this defence you should and ought not to waver at all, neither in investing money, nor in anything else. You may wish to consult amongst yourselves as to

Membrane 6 how and by what means the said wars and defence are to be carried out and sustained, and to present your worthy conclusions as soon as you are able, in order that this parliament might be conducted efficiently and drawn to a close, for the comfort of the king, the lords, and you all, and for the benefit of the kingdom, and to relieve the said poor commons, who are having to pay your daily expenses during this parliament: and that was the first and foremost of the obligations assigned to you on the said first day. Another duty you have is that if fault should be found in any part of the kingdom, or in governance through the laws of the kingdom, or in any other area, that you should submit petitions concerning that, and due remedy shall be provided for you. To which the said commons prayed that the day fixed for delivering their common petitions, the said first day of parliament, might be postponed until the following feast of All Souls [2 November], all being reckoned on that day; and that was granted to them.

The request of the commons.
22. And further, the commons prayed of our said lord the king that they might have a copy of the enrolment of the

derrain subside de les deux .xv.^mes et deux dismes issint grantez au roi par sa commune, par manere come ce est enroulle en le roulle del dit parlement, pur lour ent adviser: et ce lour estoit ottroiez, come de la volente nostre seignour le roi, et nemye a lour requeste.

23. Item, ils prierent qe cynk ou .vi. des prelatz et seignours venissent a la commune, pur treter et communer avec eux sur lours dites charges. Et a celle requeste les seignours responderent, en disantz qe ce ne devroient ne ne vorroient faire: qar tielle affaire et manere n'estoit unqes veuz en nul parlement, sinon en les trois

[Col. b] derrains parlementz proschein passez. Mais ils diont et confessont q'ad este bien acustumez qe les seignours elisoient de eux mesmes un certaine petite nombre de /.vi.\ ou .x., \et les/ communes \une autre tielle petite nombre de eux mesmes,/ et yceux seignours et communes issint esluz deussent entrecomuner en aisee manere, sanz murmur, crye et noise. Et issint /serroient\ ils tost a /aucun\ certain bon purpos par mocions entre eux affaire, et /celle\ purpos serroit oultre reportez a lours compaignons de l'une et l'autre partie: et a tielle guyse vorront les seignours ore faire et en nulle autre manere: qar ils diont qe si la commune se vorra tenir entiere sanz eux departir par autielle manere, diont les seignours q'ils vorront faire sanz lour departir. Et sur ce la commune assenti bien de eslire certains seignours et communes en petite et resonable nombre, par manere come ent ad este usez d'ancienetee.

24. Item, apres qe les ditz communes avoient veu et examinez le dit enroullement, \et/ les receites et les despenses faitz de les deniers provenantz del dit subside par les mains des ditz tresoriers de la guerre, ils revindrent autre foitz en parlement, reherceantz mesme la matire q'ils avoient fait devant; et enoultre reherceantz, coment lour pleust bien les despenses faitz sur le derrain viage, come chose honurablement fait, pur profit del roialme avantdit, et l'onour le roi nostre seignour et de son dit roialme. Mais il diont qe les ditz tresoriers de la guerre ont despenduz par lour accompte entour .xlvi. mille*li.* d'esterlings sur la salve garde de certains paiis, lieux et forteresces qe n'appartiegnent mye a la charge de la commune. C'estassavoir, partie en la marche de Calays, et partie a Brest, Chirburgh', Gascoigne et Irlande; et auxint partie sur certains messangers en Flaundres, Lumbardie, Navarre et Escoce; et entour l'apport del raunceon d'Escoce; de quiel raunceon les ditz tresoriers ne lour ont mye chargez en lour receite; mais yceux tresoriers y sont bien mention /en\ lour accompte des coustages qe un Thomas Durant fist entour /l'apport\ de mesme la raunceon, les quex coustages ils ont paiez al dit Thomas. Et oultre dit la commune, celles charges ne sont mye appartenir a eulx ne al defens du roialme, einz sont touz par dehors: et par tant lour semble qe celles charges foreins ne doivent ils \porter ne sustenir,/ mesqe issint fust q'ils purroient porter aucun charge.

Responce done a la commune depar le roi.
25. A quoy lour estoit responduz qe Gascoigne, et les autres fortz qe nostre seignour le roi ad pardela sont et doivent estre come barbicans al roialme d'Engleterre, et si les barbicans soient bien gardez, avec la salve garde de meer, le roialme serra en assez bone paix; et autrement n'averons jammais quiete ne paix avec noz enemys: qar adonqes ils nous ferroient chaude guerre a les heuz de noz maisons, qe Dieu defende; et auxi par yceux barbicans si ad nostre dit seignour le roi bones portz et bone entree a ses adversaires de lour

said last subsidy of the two fifteenths and two tenths thus granted to the king by his commons, found in the roll of the said parliament, to discuss amongst themselves: and it was granted to them, because it was the wish of the king and not because they had made the request.

23. Also, they pray that five or six of the prelates and lords might join the commons to consider and discuss with them their said duties. To which request the lords replied saying that they ought not and would not wish to do so: since such a thing done in such a manner had never been witnessed before in any parliament, except in the last three.

[Col. b] But they stated and admitted that it had been fully customary for the lords to choose from amongst themselves a certain small number of between six and ten, and the commons a similarly small number from amongst themselves, and those lords and commons thus elected would consult with one another in an informal manner, without trouble, clamour or disturbance. And so they would soon reach an effective conclusion by motions passed between them, and that conclusion would then be reported to their companions on both sides: and the lords now wished to act under such a guise and in no other way: since they said that if the commons wished to act as a whole without separating in any way, then the lords would wish to act without separating themselves. Whereupon, the commons wholeheartedly agreed that a small and reasonable number of lords and commons should be elected, as had been anciently accustomed.

24. Also, after the said commons had seen and examined the said enrolment, and the receipts and expenditure resulting from the money raised by the said subsidy which was in the hands of the said treasurers of war, they reappeared once more in parliament, and returned to the matter they had touched on before; and restated that they were fully satisfied with the expenditure incurred on the last expedition, as a venture honourably made, for the benefit of the aforesaid kingdom, and the honour of the king our lord and his said kingdom. But they said that the said treasurers of war had spent, by their reckoning, around £46,000 sterling on the safeguard of certain countries, places and fortresses, which were not the responsibility of the commons. Part of it, namely, in the march of Calais, and part in Brest, Cherbourg, Gascony and Ireland; and also part on certain envoys in Flanders, Lombardy, Navarre and Scotland; and towards the payment of the ransom of Scotland; with which ransom the said treasurers had not charged themselves in their receipt; but those same treasurers referred to it in their account of the costs which one Thomas Durant incurred in connection with the payment of the same ransom, which costs they paid to the said Thomas. Moreover, said the commons, these charges certainly did not pertain to them nor to the defence of the kingdom, but were quite distinct: and for that reason it seemed to them that they should not have to shoulder or fulfil the extraneous charges even if they were able to.

The reply given to the commons on behalf of the king.
25. To which it was answered that Gascony and the other strong places which our lord the king had overseas are and ought to be like barbicans to the kingdom of England, and if the barbicans are well guarded, and the sea safeguarded, the kingdom shall find itself well enough secure; otherwise we shall never have tranquillity or peace from our enemies: because they will then wage fierce war with us on the thresholds of our houses, which God forbid; and also in those barbicans our said lord the king has good ports and

grever quant il serra en aise, et purra travailler. Et pur ce quant a cestes paroles, doivez cesser par bone reson: et quant al raunceon d'Escoce, dit fuist qe coment qe le dit Thomas alast pur mesme le raunceon, toutes voies par subtiles excusacions de les Escotz il n'ent portast rienz, et par tant ny poaient les ditz tresoriers lour ent charger en lour dite accompte. Et auxint autrefoitz la commune dit qe lour sembloit qe le roi serroit bien riches des biens de son nobles aiel, qi Dieux assoille, les queux furent touz en ses mains.

Autre responce donee /a la commune.\
26. A quoy feust auxi responduz qe apres qe les ditz biens devindrent en ses mains, mesmes les biens furent joustement preisez, et baillez a la pris fait a ceulx as queux le dit noble aiel estoit dettour, horspris certains necessaires pur l'oustiel nostre seignour le roi, les queux il avoit devers luy, et pur queux il avoit paiez en partie, et pur le remenant luy faut paier et satisfaction *[Page iii-37]*
[Col. a] faire as creditours le dit aielle, qe serra fait le pluis en haste q'il purra: et issint, quant a ce n'avoit il rienz forsqe pur ses deniers appaiers, come un estrange persone purroit avoir, ne ne peuse avoir. Et pur ce nostre seignour le roy vous comande, et les prelatz et seignours vous priont come devant, de vous adviser de vos ditz charges, et ent doner bone et effectuelle responce a pluis en haste qe vouz purrez, pur commune profit del roialme, et pur aise des seignours et de vous touz.

Requeste des prelatz touchant l'abbe de Westm'.

27. Et sur ceo l'ercevesqe de Canterbirs y priast a nostre seignour le roi et as seignours du parlement qe lour pleust a lui un poy doner ascoult et audience, en ce q'il y avoit a dire pur la clergie. Et dist qe toutes les prelatz et le remenant de la clergie illoeqes esteantz rendent graces et mercies a nostre seignour le roi, et as seignours du roialme, et auxint a toute la commune illoeqes esteant, de tout lours coers, de ce, c'estassavoir, qe pleust au roi et as seignours de granter si noblement lours libertees et franchises, et qe la commune vorroit si humblement prier pur l'esglise et pur la salvacion de la libertee d'ycelle. Et oultre il y dit qe voirs estoit, et chose notoire parmy le roialme, coment l'esglise d'Engleterre soi sentoit grantement grevez, et sa libertee grantement enblemiz, parmy ce qe l'esglise ou monster de Saint Pere de Westm', q'est un lour membre, avoit nadgairs suffert si grant vilenie et damage, par la violence y faite au temps quant Robert de Haulay, esquier, et un autre persone qe estoit propre famuler et servant de mesme l'esglise, si feurent moelt dispitousement et horriblement tuez en mesme l'esglise a grant multitude des gentz armez, al heure quant le prestre y estoit chantant la haute messe al haute hautier deinz mesme l'esglise, en despit de Dieu et de seinte esglise: quel vilenie ne touchast soulement l'abbe del dit monster, \et/ le dit arcevesqe qi y est metropolitan coment q'il ne soit dignes, et son frere l'evesqe de Londres, en qi diocese .... la dite abbeie est foundue, coment qe celle abbeie soit exempt de toute jurisdiction d'evesqe, et subject immediat a la seinte see de Rome; einz touchast nostre seint pere le pape, a qi mesme la maison est peculierement subject, come dessus est dit, et a toute la clergie. Dont le dit ercevesqe et touz les autres prelatz y prierent a touz les seignours avant ditz moelt entierment q'ils voussissent lour estre en aide par lours bones mediacions envers nostre seignour le roi, q'est joefne, innocent, et sanz coulpe, si Dieux plest, de tout mal, qe due satisfaction et amendes ent feussent faites a Dieu et a seinte

esglise de si horrible mesfait, et a la partie endamagez. Qar il sciet bien, a ce q'il dist qe si nostre dit seignour le roi y soit bien conseillez, et saintement governez en sa jovente, si ne serra trovez en luy sibien noun ne en ce cas ne en nulle autre.

Responce.

28. Et tantost aucun des seignours prierent arieremain de lour part au tielle requeste come les prelatz y firent; c'estassavoir, qe pur salvacioun de la regalie nostre seignour le roi, et des droitures de sa coroune, et des anciencs loyes de sa terre, qe mesme nostre seignour le roi soit conseillez et governez en sa dite juvente a tiel guise, qe rienz n'ent soit tolluz n'acrochez par la dite clergie. Et si rienz y soit mesfait ou meinz joustement usez par les clercz, encontre les loys de la terre, et contre bone foi, qe ce soit tout repellez, et mise en tiel plit come d'anciente soloit et devroit estre de reson. Et oultre ce, y distrent les ditz seignours, et vouchent a record les justices et autres gentz de loy de la terre, qe scievent bien, qe en l'esglise d'Engleterre ne soloit ne ne doit nully avoir immunite pur dette, trespas, ne pur autre cause quelconqe, sinoun pur cryme tantsoulement. Et auxint, coment qe certains doctours en theologie de canoun et de civil aient este sur ce examinez et jurez devant le roi mesmes a dire la plaine veritee de ce qe lour ent sembloit de resoun, et ent aient dit et determinez, \eue/ sur ce meure

[Col. b] et bone deliberacion qe en cas de dette, d'acompte, ne pur trespas fait, si homme n'y doit perdre vie ou membre, nully doit en sainte esglise avoir immunite. Et oultre diont qe Dieux, salvez sa perfectioun, ne le pape, salve sa saintitee, ne nul roi ou prince, purroit granter tiel privilege. Et mesqe aucun prince vorroit tiel privilege granter, l'esglise, q'est et doit estre founz et noricement de touz vertuz, ne doit celle privilege accepter, dont pecche ou occasion de pecche purroit sourdre; qar pecche est, et occacion de pecche, pur delaier une homme voluntrifment de son dette, et jouste recoverir del soen. Meintineins, diont les ditz seignours qe nientcontresteant tout ce, ceulx del dit abbeie claimantz avoir tiel privilege del grant des progenitours nostre seignour le roi, resceivent plusours et diverses persones deinz lour franchise, sibien avec lours biens propres come avec autry biens a grant value, et illoeqes demurront les ditz gentz avec autry biens si longement come lour plest, sanz gree faire a lours creditours, encontre toute loy, bone foy et resoun. Dont ils priont pur commune profit, et pur salvation de la regalie nostre seignour le roi, qe lour dite franchise, si nule eient /tielle,\ soit veue et examinee, et sur ce due remede fait, pur aise et profit de tout le roialme. Et sur ce vindrent en parlement les ditz doctours en theologie canoun et civil, et les autres clercz depar le roi, et illoeqes devaunt nostre seignour le roi mesmes, /illoeqes\ presentz les prelatz, seignours, et toute la commune, firent lours argumentz et proeves encontre les prelatz sur la matire avantdite par plusours collourables et fortes resons. Mais les prelatz ne lour y firent responce a celle jour en effect, einz prierent jour d'avisement, pur ent doner lour responce; et ce lour estoit ottroiez.

La grant des subsides des leynes.

29. Item, fair assavoir, coment les seignours et communes d'Engleterre granterent a seignour Edward nadgairs roi d'Engleterre, aielle nostre seignour le roi q'ore est, en salvacion et defens del roialme d'Engleterre, a son parlement tenuz a Westm' le lundy proschein apres la feste de Saint George, l'an du regne le dit aielle cynquantisme, certains subsides des leynes, quirs et peaulx lanutz, passantz hors del

for so horrible a crime, and to the injured party. Since he well knew, as he said that if our said lord the king were to be well advised, and correctly governed in his youth, so no evil would be found in him in this matter or any other.

Answer.

28. And on the other hand, some of the lords, for their part, prayed against the prelates request that for the salvation of the regality of our lord the king, and the rights of his crown, and the ancient laws of his land, our same lord the king might be counselled and governed in his said youth in such a way that nothing should be arrogated or accroached by the said clergy. And if anything should be done by clerks which was wrongful or less than just, contrary to the laws of the land, and contrary to good faith, that that should be entirely resisted, and impleaded as was customary in the past and as it ought to be in reason. Furthermore, the said lords said, and called the justices and other men of law as witness that they well knew, that in the English church no one should or ought to have immunity for debt, trespass or in any other cause whatsoever, still less for crime. And also, that certain doctors of theology, learned in canon and civil law, had been questioned thereon and had sworn before the king himself to speak the whole truth according to what seemed reasonable to them, and they said and concluded, having thoroughly and [Col. b] fully discussed the matter before the king himself, that in cases of debt, account or trespass, as no one should lose life or limb, so no one ought to have immunity in holy church. They also said that neither God, saving his perfection, nor the pope, saving his sanctity, nor any king or prince, could grant such a privilege. And even if any prince wished to grant such a privilege, the church, which is and ought to be founded and nourished on all virtues, should not accept such privilege, from which sin or the occasion for sin might arise; since it is a sin and the occasion of sin to keep a man deliberately from his due and just recovery of his own. Now, said the said lords, notwithstanding all that, those of the said abbey claiming to have such a privilege by the grant of the progenitors of our lord the king, received many and various people within their franchise, both with their own goods as well as with other goods which are of great value, and there the said people stay with the other goods as long as they please, without paying their creditors, contrary to all law, good faith and reason. In view of which they pray for the common good, and for the salvation of the regality of our lord the king, that their said franchise, if they have such a thing, should be inspected and examined, and a remedy provided for this, for the comfort and benefit of all the kingdom. Whereupon the said doctors of theology learned in canon and civil law and the other clerks representing the king appeared in parliament, and there before our same lord the king, the attendant prelates, lords and all the commons, they presented their arguments and evidence against the prelates in the aforesaid case on strong and convincing grounds. But the prelates did not actually reply to them on this day, but prayed for a day of consultation, before giving their response; which was granted them.

The grant of the subsidies on wool.

29. Also, be it known, whereas the lords and commons of England granted to Lord Edward, late king of England, grandfather of our lord the present king, for the security and defence of the kingdom of England, at his parliament held at Westminster on the Monday following the feast of St George, in the fiftieth year of the reign of the said grandfather [28 April 1376], certain subsidies on wool, hides

roialme d'Engleterre par denszeins et foreins, par la forme et manere qe s'ensuit; c'estassavoir de denszeins, pur et de chescun saak de leyne .xliij. s., .iiij. d.; de touz les deux centz et quarante peaulx lanutz, le cent accompte par cynk vintz, .xliij. s., .iiij. d.; et de chescun lait des quirs quatre livres six soldz .viij. d. des leynes, quirs et peaulx lanutz qi passeront hors del dit roialme par les denszeins ou en lours nouns, oultre l'anciene custume ent due: quelle anciene custume amonte .vi. s., .viij. d. de chescun saak et .vi. s., .viij. d. de deux centz et quarante peaulx lanutz, et .xiij. s., .iiij. d. del last des quirs. Et des aliens, de chescun saak de layne, .xliij. s., .iiij. d.; de touz les deux centz et quarante peaulx lanutz, .xliij. s., .iiij. d.; et de chescun last des quirs quatre livres sis soldz oept deniers, des leynes, quirs et peaulx lanutz qi passeront hors del dit roialme par les ditz aliens ou en lours nouns, oultre l'anciene custume ent due par mesmes les aliens: la quelle anciene custume \amonte/ de chescun saak de leyne .x. s.; de les deux centz et quarante peaulx lanutz .x. s.; et del last des quirs .xx. s.; a avoir, prendre et rescevre mesmes les subsides par tout le roialme d'Engleterre, de la feste de Saint Michel adonqes procheinement ensuant continuelment tanqe au fyn de trois ans deslors proschein avenirs, et pleinement accompliz, come plainement appiert en les roulles de mesme le parlement. Et les prelatz, seignours et communes du dit roialme apparceivantz ore clerement les grantz perils et doutes en queux mesme le roialme si est environez toutes partz, si ont mesmes les prelatz, seignours et communes, de lour liberale voluntee, et par commune assent en ce parlement, grantez a nostre seignour le roi, en aide de les grandes et outrageouses despenses qe l'en faut mettre au *[Page iii-38]*
[Col. a] fyn force, en resistence de tantz des enemys, et en salvacion et defens de mesme le roialme d'Engleterre; au tielles mesmes les subsides a prendre et /rescevoir\ de chescun saak de leyne, des deux centz et quarante \peaulx lanutz, et del last des/ quirs, passantz hors del dit roialme, par denszeins et par foreins, de la feste de Seint Michel proschein avenir, a quel feste de Seint Michel les ditz subsides grantes le dit an cynquantisme deivent cesser et faillier, tanqe al feste de Pasqe deslors proschein ensuant.

De la novel encrees de subside.
Et oultre ce, mesmes les prelatz, seignours et communes ont ore grantez de novel encrees a nostre dit seignour le roi, en defens et salvacion de mesme le roialme .xiij. s. .iiij. d. de chescun saak de leyne; .xiij. s. .iiij. d. de touz les deux centz et .xl. peaulx lanutz; et .xxvi. s. .viij. d. de chescun last des quirs passantz hors del dit roialme, par manere come dessus est dit; a prendre, avoir et rescevoir le dit novel encrees, sibien c'estassavoir des foreins come de denszeins quelconqes, oultre les autres subsides et anciens custumes avantdites, de la feste de Pasqe proschein avenir par un an entier et pleinement accompliz.

De .vi. d. a libre.
30. Item, ils ont grante a mesme nostre seignour le roi, en defens et salvacion avantdites .vi. d. del livre de chescune manere de marchandie passant hors del dit roialme d'Engleterre, ou venant deinz mesme le roialme, leynes, quirs, peaulx lanutz et vins tantsolement horspris; a prendre et resceivoir sibien de denszeins come \de foreins,/ del .xvime jour de Novembre l'an present, tanqe a la .xv.^e de Saint Michel proschein avenir.
Et prient humblement mesmes les seignours et communes a nostre seignour le roi dessusdit qe les deniers provenantz

and woolfells, exported from the kingdom of England by denizens and foreigners, on the following terms; namely from denizens, for and on each sack of wool 43s. 4d.; from every 240 woolfells, a hundred counting as five score, 43s. 4d.; and from each last of hides four pounds, six shillings and 8d. from wool, hides, and woolfells which are exported from the said kingdom by the denizens or in their name, in addition to the ancient custom due on them: which ancient custom amounts to 6s. 8d. on each sack and 6s. 8d. on every two hundred and forty woolfells, and 13s. 4d. on every last of hides. And from aliens, on every sack of wool, 43s. 4d.; from every two hundred and forty woolfells, 43s. 4d.; and from every last of hides four pounds, six shillings and eight pence, from wool, hides and woolfells which are exported from the said realm by the said aliens or in their names, over and above the ancient custom owed thereon by the same aliens: which ancient custom amounts to 10s. on every sack of wool; 10s. on every two hundred and forty woolfells; and on each last of hides 20s.; to have, take and receive the same subsidies throughout the whole kingdom of England, from the next Michaelmas [29 September 1376] continuing for three years to come; which was fully performed, as plainly appears in the rolls of the same parliament. And the prelates, lords and commons of the said kingdom, clearly perceiving at this time the great perils and dangers with which the same kingdom was surrounded on all sides, granted to our lord the king, of their own free will and by common consent in this parliament, as a contribution towards the great and outrageous expense which must by incurred out of *[Page iii-38]*

[Col. a] sheer necessity, in resisting such enemies, and for the security and defence of the same kingdom of England, similar subsidies to be had and received from every sack of wool, two hundred and forty woolfells, and each last of hides exported from the said kingdom, by denizens and foreigners, from Michaelmas to come [29 September 1379], on which Michaelmas the said subsidies granted in the said fiftieth year should come to an end and cease, until Easter next.

Concerning the novel increase of the subsidy.
Beyond which, the same prelates, lords and commons recently granted a new increment to our said lord the king, for the defence and security of the same kingdom, of 13s. 4d. on every sack of wool; 13s. 4d. on every 240 woolfells; and 26s. 8d. on every last of hides exported from the said realm in the aforesaid manner; the said novel increment to be taken, had and received from foreigners as well as denizens of any sort, in addition to the other aforesaid subsidies and ancient customs, from Easter next for one whole year fully passed.

Concerning 6d. in the pound.
30. Also, they have granted to our same lord the king, for the aforesaid defence and security 6d. in the pound on every kind of merchandise exported from the said kingdom of England, or coming into the same kingdom, excepting only wool, hides, woolfells and wine; to be taken and received from denizens as well as foreigners, from 16 November in the present year [1378], until fifteen days after Michaelmas next [13 October 1379].
And the same lords and commons humbly pray of our lord the aforesaid king that the money arising from the said

des ditz subsides, ensemble avec les autres profitz ordenez estre despenduz sur les dites defens et salvacion, soient appliez a celle oeps et a nul autre; et qe certaines suffisantz persones soient assignez pur estre tresoriers d'ycelles, par manere come autre foitz estoit ordeignez en parlement. Et auxint priont au roi nostre seignour qe lui plese, pur Dieu, lour tenir et avoir quant a present pur excusez de ce q'ils ne luy grantent greinour aide. Qar ils dient qe la commune est ore tant enfebliz et empovriz, qoi par pestilences et par les guerres qe lour grevent fortement, qoi par moryne de leurs bestes, et les bledz et autres fruitz de la terre en partie faillez; et encores celles fruitz q'ils /ont si ne\ soi extendent en effect a nul pris, paront la commune quant a present ne poet autrement granter, mais de bone et perfit voluntee ce diont ils, q'ils ferrent greinour aide si tost come ils purront et ent soient requiz, a tout lour poair sibien par lours corps come autrement.

Membrane 5

Pur le conte de Salesbirs.

31. Item, fait a remembrer qe sur la demande qe William de Montagu conte de Salesbirs fait, d'avoir les terres de Dynbegh en Gales, il y a un enroullement entrez es les roulles de parlement tenuz a Westm' a la .xv.^{e} de Saint Michel, l'an du regne nostre seignour le roi q'or est primer, en la forme qe s'ensuit:[11]

Item, William de Montagu, conte de Salesbirs, mist avant en parlement une sa peticion en la forme qe s'ensuit: a nostre seignour le roi monstre son lige William de Montagu, conte de Salesbirs, come mon tresredoute seignour le roi, vostre aielle, qi Dieux assoille, dona et granta a mon pere William de Montagu, nadgairs conte de Salesbirs, et \a/ ses heirs de son corps issantz, ove clause de garantie, le chastiel, ville et honour de Dynbeygh', et les cantredes de Roos, Roweynok et Kaiemer, et la commot de Dynmael, ove les appurtenantz en Gales, salvant ent la reversion a lui et a ses heirs, come pluis pleinement piert par ses chartres a mon dit pere ent faites. Les queux chastel, ville et honour, cantredes, et commot, ove

[Col. b] les appurtenantz, Roger de Mortymer, pere Esmon conte q'or est, come cousin et heir Roger de Mortimer, nadgairs conte de la Marche, demanda devers moi; et par noun de la terre de Dynbeigh' ove les appurtenances en Gales, par brief de scire facias devant mon dit seignour le roi vostre aiel, en sa courte en bank le roi, de ent avoir execucion. En quiel plee je pria aide de mon dit seignour le roi vostre aielle par la cause avantdite. Et apres brief de procedendo sur ce grantez, le dit Roger, \le/ pere Esmon, recoveri devers moi par juggement les ditz chastiel, ville, honour, cantredes, et commot, ove les appurtenances, par noun de la terre de Dynbeigh' ove les appurtenances en Gales; come en le record et proces sur ce faitz pleinement appiert. En quelles record et proces, et auxint en juggement sur ce renduz, il y ad errour, et le quiel juggement estoit execut, et moi ouste de ma possessioun, l'an de son regne .xxviij.^{me} dont je n'avoie unqes rien en value, coment qe mon dit seignour le roi vostre aiel par sa chartre avoit grante a ce faire, come dessus est dit. Puis quel perte, j'ai sui de parlement en parlement par diverses peticions de ent avoir remedie, et entre autres au parlement tenuz a Westm' le .viij.^{me} jour de Novembre, l'an de son regne .xlvime, une ma peticion sur ceste matire estoit endosse en ceux paroles, Le roi ne voet mie qe l'eir q'est deinz age et en sa garde ne perde rienz pur le temps q'il est en sa garde; mais quant il vient a son pleine age, sue, et droit serra fait al une partie et al autre; et ore le dit heir, c'estassavoir Esmon de Mortimer, ore conte de la

---

[11] PRO SC8/18/882.

subsidies, together with the other profits ordained to be spent on the said defence and security, shall be put to that use and no other; and that certain worthy people shall be appointed to be treasurers of the same, as ordained at other times in parliament. And they pray of our lord the king that it might please him, for the love of God, to excuse them at the present time for not granting him greater help. Since they say that the commons are now so enfeebled and impoverished, what with pestilence and wars which have greatly injured them, and the loss of their beasts, and the failure of their corn and other fruits of the land; and even that produce which they do have does not fetch any real price, because of which the commons at present are unable, as they say, to grant anything more, but of their earnest and wholehearted will they say this, that they will provide a greater degree of aid as soon as they can and are required to do so, to the best of their power and capabilities.

For the earl of Salisbury.

31. Also, be it remembered that on the claim which William Montagu earl of Salisbury made, to have the lands of Denbigh in Wales, there is an enrolment entered in the rolls of parliament held at Westminster under the fifteenth day after Michaelmas, in the first year of the reign of our lord the present king [13 October 1377], which reads as follows:

Item, William Montagu, earl of Salisbury, submitted to parliament a petition worded as follows: to our lord the king shows his liege William Montagu, earl of Salisbury, that whereas my most redoubtable lord the king, your grandfather, whom God absolve, gave and granted, with a clause of warranty, to my father William Montagu, late earl of Salisbury, and to the heirs issuing from his body, with a clause of warranty, the castle, town and honour of Denbigh, and the cantreds of Rhos, Rhufiniog and Cymeirch, and the commote of Dinmael, with appurtenances in Wales, saving the reversion of them to him and his heirs, as can clearly be seen from the charters issued thereon to my said father. This castle, honour and town, and these cantreds and commote with

[Col. b] appurtenances, Roger Mortimer, father of Edmund the present earl, as cousin and heir of Roger Mortimer, late earl of March, demanded from me; and particularly the land of Denbigh with its appurtenances in Wales, by writ of scire facias before my said lord the king your grandfather, in his court in the King's Bench, to have execution of it. In which plea I prayed for the help of my said lord the king your grandfather for the aforesaid reason. And after the writ of procedendo thereon granted, the said Roger, father of Edmund, recovered from me by a judgment the said castle, town, honour, cantreds and commote, with appurtenances, and by the name of the land of Denbigh with its appurtenances in Wales; as fully appears from the record and process made thereon. With which record and process, and also in the judgment rendered thereon, there is error, and following execution of that judgment I was ousted from my possession in the twenty-eighth year of his reign [1355], and was left with nothing of any value, even though my said lord the king your grandfather by his charter had made grant to me, as said above. Since which loss, I have sued from parliament to parliament through various petitions to gain a remedy for this, and amongst others at the parliament held at Westminster on 8 November, in the forty-sixth year of his reign [1372], one of my petitions on the matter was endorsed with the following words, The king does not indeed wish that the heir who is under-age and in his wardship shall lose anything for the time during which he is in his keep; but that

Marche, fitz et heir mesme celuy Roger le cousin, est avenuz a son pleine age.

Qe plese a vostre tresgraciouse seignourie comander, de faire venir le dit record et proces devant vous et vostre tres-sage conseil en ceste present parlement; et appellez le dit Esmon et ceux qi sont en celles parties a appellers, et veuez et examinez les ditz record et proces, de moi ordener ent remedie, selonc droit et reson. Et si errour y puisse estre trovez, qe le dit juggement soit reversez et adnulliz, et moi restitut a ma possession ove les issues d'icelle, come la loy demande. Quele peticion lue en mesme le parlement et entendue, dit feust et comandez en cest parlement, par les prelatz et seignours pierres du parlement lors esteantz en mesme le parlement, a monsire Johan Cavendissh, \chivaler,/ chief justice nostre seignour le roi, q'ad les record et proces dont la dite peticion fait mencion en garde, q'il ferroit venir mesmes les record et proces en cest parlement sanz delai. Lui quiel monsire Johan apporta en dit parlement mesmes les record et proces entre diverses autres recordz et proces comprises en certains roulles tachez ou consutz ensemble. Et sur ce le dit conte de Salesbirs assigna en parlement par especial et par bouche diverses errours estre contenuz en ycelle record et proces, empriant qe par celles errours, et par autres quelles en ycelle record et proces purront estre trovez, le juggement y renduz soit reversez; et qe le dit Esmon de Mortymer, filz et heir le dit Roger le cousin, ore conte de la Marche, y fuist garniz par brief de scire facias d'estre a proschein parlement d'oier les ditz record et proces, et de faire et resceivre ce q'adonqes en celle partie serra agardez. Et cel brief lui estoit grantez illoeqes, et commandez estre fait retornable en dit proschein parlement. Et puis apres sur le fin du dit parlement, le dit monsire Johan de Cavendissh', par comandement des prelatz et seignours du parlement ent a lui fait, portast mesmes les record et proces en le bank le roi, pur y demurer come en garde tanqe au dit proschein parlement. \Et/ est ordenez et accordez qe mesmes les record et proces soient en dit proschein parlement par la cause avauntdite. A quiel proschein parlement, c'estassavoir en cest present parlement tenuz a Gloucestr' le mesqardy proschein apres la feste de Saint Luk l'Ewangelist, vient le dit conte de Salesbirs en sa persone devant nostre seignour le roi, en presence des prelatz, pierres et autres seignours du parlement, le dit monsire Johan de Cavendissh' q'ad mesmes les record et proces dont la *[Page iii-39]*

[Col. a] dite peticion fait mencion en garde illoeqes present, et monsire Brian de Cornewaille, viscont de Shropshire, retorna en cest parlement le dit brief de scire facias issint fait et grante a darrain parlement; dont sibien del dit brief come del retorn ent fait par le \dit viscont,/ le tenour s'ensuit de mot en mot:

32. 'Ricardus, Dei gratia, rex Anglie et Francie, et dominus Hibernie, vicecomiti Salop', salutem. Cum Rogerus de Mortuo Mari, filius Edmundi de Mortuo Mari, nuper comes Marchie, ut consanguineus et heres Rogeri de Mortuo Mari nuper comitis Marchie, avi sui, in curia domini Edwardi nuper regis Anglie avi nostri, coram eodem avo nostro, termino Trinitatis, anno regni sui Anglie vicesimo octavo, par breve ipsius avi nostri, ac consideracionem ejusdem curia, recuperaverit versus Willelmum de Monte Acuto, comitem Sar', terram de Dynbegh' cum pertinentiis in Wallie; idemque comes Sar' per peticionem suam nobis in presenti parliamento nostro exhibitam nobis supplicaverit, ut cum diversi errores in recordo et processu ac reddicione judicii loquele

when he comes of age he shall sue, and right shall be done to the one party and the other; and now the said heir, namely Edmund Mortimer, now earl of March, son and heir of the same Roger the cousin, has come of age.

May it please your most gracious lordship to command that the said record and process be brought before you and your most wise council in this present parliament; and having summoned the said Edmund and those who are to be summoned in the matter, and having inspected and examined the said record and process, to ordain a remedy for me, in accordance with right and reason. And if error should be found, that the said judgment shall be reversed and annulled, and my seisin restored to me with the issues from the same, as the law requires. Which petition having been read and heard in the same parliament, the prelates and lords, peers of parliament, told and instructed Sir John Cavendish, knight, chief justice of our lord the king, who had the record and process of which the said petition made mention in his keeping, to cause the same record and process to be brought to that parliament without delay. This Sir John brought to the said parliament the same record and process amongst various other records and processes contained in certain rolls attached or sewn together. Whereupon, the said earl of Salisbury drew particular attention to various errors contained in the same record and process, requesting that because of those errors, and because of others which might be found in the record and process, the judgment there rendered should be reversed; and that the said Edmund Mortimer, son and heir of the said Roger the cousin, now earl of March, should be instructed by writ of scire facias to be at the next parliament to hear the said record and process, and to do and receive that which would then be decided in this matter. And the writ was issued to him there, and ordered to be made returnable in the said next parliament. Subsequently, at the end of the said parliament, the said Sir John Cavendish, by command of the prelates and lords of parliament, brought the same record and process to the King's Bench, for it to be kept there until the said next parliament. And it was ordained and agreed that the same record and process should be brought to the said next parliament for the aforesaid reason. At which next parliament, namely in this present parliament held at Gloucester on the Wednesday following the feast of St Luke the Evangelist [20 October], the said earl of Salisbury appearing in person before our lord the king, in the presence of the prelates, peers and other lords of parliament, the said Sir John Cavendish who had the same record and process of which the *[Page iii-39]*

[Col. a] said petition made mention in his possession at that time, and Sir Brian Cornwall, sheriff of Shropshire, returned in this parliament the said writ of scire facias thus issued and granted at the last parliament; the texts of which writ and the return issued by the said sheriff, follow word for word:

32. 'Richard, by the grace of God, king of England and France and lord of Ireland, to the sheriff of Shropshire, greeting. Whereas Roger Mortimer, son of Edmund Mortimer, late earl of March, and the kinsman and heir of Roger Mortimer, late earl of March, his grandfather, in the court of the lord Edward, late king of England and our grandfather, in the presence of our same grandfather, in Trinity term, in the twenty-eighth year of his reign over England, by our grandfather's writ, and with the consideration of the same court, recovered from William Montagu, earl of Salisbury, the land of Denbigh with appurtenances in Wales; and the same earl of Salisbury through his petition presented to us in our present parliament requested that as various errors had

predicte intervenissent, ad grave dampnum ipsius comitis Sarum, vellemus recordum et processum inde habita coram nobis et consilio nostro in dicto parliamento nostro venire, eademqe recordum et processum \ibidem/ examinari, ac errores inde repertos corrigi jubere: nos supplicacioni predicti comitis Sar' in hac parte annuentes, recordum et processum predicta coram nobis ac prelatis et magnatibus in dicto parliamento ea de causa venire fecimus, ac insuper errores illos, si qui fuerint, modo debito corrigi: et ulterius inde fieri volentes quod est justum, tibi precipimus quod per probos et legales homines de comitatu tuo scire facias Edmundo de Mortuo Mari, nunc comiti Marchie, filius et heredi prefati Rogeri filius Edmundi, quod sit coram nobis in proximo parliamento nostro ubicumqe tunc fuerit, auditurus recordum et processum predicta, si sibi viderit expedire, ulteriusqe facturus et recepturus quod considerari contigerit tunc ibidem. Et habeas ibi nomina illorum per quos ei scire feceris, et hoc breve. Teste meipso apud Westm' primo die Decembris, anno regni nostri primo.

found their way into the record and process and rendering of the judgment in the aforesaid case, to the grave injury of this earl of Salisbury, we might order the record and process to be brought before us and our council in the said parliament, the same record and process to be examined in the same place, and the errors found therein to be corrected: we, agreeing to the aforesaid request of the earl of Salisbury, caused the aforesaid record and process to be brought before us and the prelates and magnates in the said parliament for that reason, and also its errors, if there were any, to be corrected in an appropriate manner: and also wishing to do that which is just, we order you that through honest and law-worthy men of your county you instruct Edmund Mortimer, now earl of March, son and heir of the aforesaid Roger son of Edmund, that he appear before us in our next parliament, wheresoever that shall be, to hear the aforesaid record and process, if it shall be to him expedient, and also to do and accept whatever is decided there at that time. And you shall have there the names of those through whom you caused him to be notified, and this writ. Witnessed myself at Westminster 1 December, in the first year of our reign [1377].

33. Responcio Briani de Cornewaille vicecomes: Edmundus de Mortuo Mari nunc comes Marchie, filius et heres Rogeri de Mortuo Mari filius Edmundi de Mortuo Mari nuper comitis Marchie, non est inventus in balliva mea postquam istud breve michi liberatum fuit, nec aliqua habet terras seu tenementa in eadem ubi premuniri potest.

Et sur ce le dit conte de Salesbirs en ce parlement pria a nostre seignour le roy qe luy pleust a luy granter un autre brief de scire facias, pur garnir le dit Esmon, ore conte de la March, filz et heir le dit Roger filz Esmon a la dite terre de Dynbeigh', d'estre devant nostre seignour le roi en son proschein parlement, d'oier, faire et resceivre ce qe la loy demande, come dessus est dit. Quiel brief par nostre dit seignour le roi, par l'advis des seignours et autres sages de parlement luy ad grantez, et commandez estre fait retornable en dit proschein parlement. Et enoultre est accordez en ce parlement, /qe les ditz record et proces par la dite cause soient en dit proschein parlement.\

33. The response of Brian Cornwall, sheriff: Edmund Mortimer now earl of March, son and heir of Roger Mortimer son of Edmund Mortimer, late earl of March, was not to be found in my bailiwick after this writ was delivered to me, nor does he have any lands or tenements in the same whereby he could be attached.

And thereupon, the said earl of Salisbury in this parliament prayed of our lord the king that it might please him to grant him another writ of scire facias, to warn the said Edmund, now earl of March, son and heir of the said Roger son of Edmund for the said land of Denbigh, to appear before our lord the king in his next parliament, to hear, do and receive that which the law demanded, as said above. Which writ was granted him by our said lord the king, by the advice of the lords and other wise men of parliament, and it was ordered returnable in the said next parliament. Moreover, it was agreed in this parliament that the said record and process for their said cause should be available in the said next parliament.

12

Membrane 4
Pur monsire Robert Howard.
34. Item, la dame de Neville d'Essex mist avant en parlement une sa bille en forme qe s'ensuit: a nostre seignour le roi et son conseille de ceste present parlement supplie Aleise de Neville qe come nadgairs Johan Brewes et autres mesfesours debruserent l'ostiel la dite Aleise en Londres, et une Margerie, file a Johan de Nerford fitz la dite Aleise, illoeqes trove forciblement pristrent, et amesnerent par ewe en Thamise tanqe a l'ostiel l'esvesqe de Norwiz; en quel lieu monsire Robert Howard les encontrant resceut la dite Margerie, et d'illoeqes la mesna par eawe tanqe a Chelchehith, et puis la esloignant de countee enautre, et la deteignant en places secreez, a l'entente pur resister un apel pendant en la court

[Col. b] l'apostoille, sur un processe d'adnullacioun d'un contract du matrimoine atame a la suite du dit Margerie par devers le dit Johan; quel Robert, sur certaine matiere trove par examinement devaunt le conseil nostre seignour le roi, par consideracion ewe, qe chescune persone pursuyant queconqe processe ou par loy de sainte esglise ou de la terre, doit de droit estre a larges de pursuir son dit processe sanz impediment quecunqe, tanqe mesme le processe soit pleinement termine, il feust agarde al tour de Londres, a y

For Sir Robert Howard.
34. Also, Lady Neville of Essex submitted to parliament a petition in the following form: to our lord the king and his council of this present parliament, the plaint of Alice Neville: whereas formerly John Brewes and other malefactors broke into the house of the said Alice in London, and having found there one Marjory, daughter of John Nerford son of the said Alice, they forcibly seized her, and took her on the Thames to the house of the bishop of Norwich; in which place Sir Robert Howard, meeting them, received the said Marjory and from there led her by water as far as Chelsea Hythe, and then carried her off from one county to another, keeping her in secret places, with the intention of resisting an appeal pending in the papal court

[Col. b] concerning a process over the annulment of a matrimonial contract begun at the suit of the said Marjory and involving the said John; which Robert, after a conclusion reached through an examination before the council of our lord the king, and thorough consideration that every person pursuing a process of any kind whether by the law of holy church or the law of the land, should by right be free to pursue his said process without any impediment, until the same process has been fully settled, was sent to the Tower of

---
[12] The rest of m.5 has been left blank.

demurer tanqe la dite Margerie feusse amesne devant mesme le conseil. Quel Robert apres a sa grant pursuite fust lesse aler a ses larges par acord du dit conseil, sur tiele condicion, q'il metteroit sa loial peine et diligence pur amesner la dite Margerie a Londres devant mesme la conseil, a la quinszeine de Saint Michel darrein passe, en cas qe le dit conseil feusse alors a Londres, et autrement de deliverer la dite Margerie a madame de Bedeford, ou de re-entrer son corps al dit tour a la dite quinszeine, sur peine du paier a nostre dit seignour le roi mille livres. Et de ce faire il plevy sa foy, et le promist come il fust loial chivaler, come plus a plein piert par record de ce ent fait en la chancellerie. Quele chose en rienz parfourny depar le dit seignour Robert, il unqore esteant a ses larges a contraire de la dit agard et acord, q'il plese comander le dit seignour Robert al dit tour, a y demurer selonc l'effect du dit agard, et de faire execucion de les dites mille livres pur le profist nostre seignour le roi. Quelle bille lieue en parlement, un certain record touchant le dit monsire Robert fait et entrez es roulles de la chancellarie quelles al instance la dite dame estoient fait venir en mesme le parlement, et y fust auxint lieue sibien en la presence de dite dame come le dit monsire Robert, en la forme qe s'ensuit: endroit de monsire Robert Howard, q'estoit nadgairs comandez a la tour de Londres pur certains mesprisions des queux il feust accusez et empeschez, le second jour d'Aust, le dit monsire Robert fist foy, et promist sur sa loialte, come loial chivaler, devaunt le conseil, q'il mettroit sa loial peine et diligence a tout son poair le plustost q'il purroit bonement, sanz fraude, pur avoir a luy le corps de Margerie de Nerford: et qe si en haste q'il la purroit avoir il la amesneroit devant le conseil, si le conseil feusse lors a Londres; et sinoun q'il deliveroit mesme celle Margerie a ma dame de Bedford, pur demurrer en sa compaignie en sauve garde, tanqe a la quinszeine de Seint Michel proschein venant. Et sur ce comande feust de faire brief hors de la chancellarie a conestable de la dite tour, de deliverer le dit monsire Robert hors d'icelle, sur tielle condicion qe en cas q'il ne purroit avenir a le corps la dite Margerie, q'adonqes le dit monsire Robert re-entreroit son corps /en\ la dite tour en prisone, a la .xv.^{ine} avauntdite a plus tard, sanz aucun defaut, sur la peine de paier au roi mille livres d'esterlings. Et par habundant, monsire le conte de \la/ Marche devint plegge, et emprist alors pur le dit monsire Robert, de re-entrer son corps s'il soit en vie, sanz jouste impediment, en la dite tour, a la dite .xv.^{ine} en cas susdit. Et oultre /ceo\ fist loy auxi, et emprist le dit monsire Robert devaunt le dit conseil, et pur le temps qe la dite Margerie serroit en sa compaignie, il ne la ferroit ne ne suffreroit estre fait duretee, oppression, artacioun, ne villenie par qecunqe persone; ne la indueroit, arteroit, ne exciteroit, ne ne soefferoit estre induee, artee, ne excitee par /queconqes,\ de faire assentir, ne dire aucune chose contre sa \propre/ volente. Et auxi acorde feust qe autres qe sont arestez par la dite cause, \horspris Richard Cok q'est en la mareschalcie, et enditez par celle cause et autres,/ soient deliverez hors de prisone tanqe a la dite .xv.^{ine}, pur ce qe le dit monsire Robert ad empris pur chescun de eux sur peine de .c.*li.* q'ils serront a lui aidantz a faire les dites choses, et q'ils /se\ rendront semblablement a prisone a la dite .xv.^{ine} en le cas avantdit. Item, promist devaunt le conseil le dit monsire Robert, sur peine de mille*li.* au paier au roi, q'il, ne nul de soen, ne ferroient ne ne procuroient estre fait a la   dame de Neville, ne a nul de soen, damage, *[Page iii-40]*

London, to remain there until the said Marjory was brought before the same council. Which Robert, following his persistent suit, was set free by the agreement of the said council, on condition that he invest his loyal efforts and diligence in bringing the said Marjory to London to appear before the same council, on the quinzaine of Michaelmas last, if the said council were then at London, and otherwise to deliver the said Marjory to Lady Bedford, or he would be reimprisoned in the said Tower on the said quinzaine and suffer the penalty of paying £1000 to our said lord the king. And he pledged his faith to do this, and promised it since he was a loyal knight, as is apparent from the record made thereof in the chancery. Which is as yet unperformed by the said Sir Robert, and he is still at large contrary to the said award and settlement, and so may it please the king to order the said lord Robert to the said Tower, to remain there in accordance with the tenor of the said award, and to enforce the payment of the said thousand pounds for the benefit of our lord the king. Which bill having been read in parliament, a certain record touching the said Sir Robert was made and entered in the rolls of the chancery which, at the instance of the said lady, were brought to the same parliament, and they were also read, in the presence of the said lady as well as the said Sir Robert, and they were worded in the following way: 'Regarding Sir Robert Howard, who was recently sent to the Tower of London for certain misdeeds of which he had been accused and impeached: on 2 August, the said Sir Robert pledged his faith, and promised on his loyalty, as a loyal knight, before the council, that he would apply all his loyal efforts and energies as far as he was able to securing the person of Marjory Nerford, as soon as he possibly could, without fraud: and that as soon as he had secured her he would bring her before the council, if the council were then in London; and if not, that he would deliver this same Marjory to Lady Bedford, to be kept safely in her company, until the quinzaine of Michaelmas next. Whereupon, orders were given for the writ to be taken from the chancery to the constable of the said Tower, instructing him to free the said Sir Robert from the same, on condition that if he failed to acquire the person of the said Marjory, that then the said Sir Robert would render his body to prison once more in the said Tower, on the aforesaid quinzaine at the latest, without fail, and suffer the penalty of paying a thousand pounds sterling to the king. In addition, my lord the earl of March offered a pledge, and undertook for the said Sir Robert, to render his body to prison if he were still alive, without delay, in the said Tower, on the said quinzaine in the aforesaid case. And moreover he pledged himself to bring the said Sir Robert before the said council, and during the time when the said Marjory was to be in his company, he would not inflict on her or allow anyone to inflict hardship, oppression, restraint, or villainy; nor would he induce, compel, or urge her, or allow her to be induced, compelled or urged by anyone, to agree to, or say anything against her will. It was also agreed that others who are arrested for the said reason, except Richard Cook who is in the marshalsea, and indicted for this reason and others, shall be freed from prison until the said quinzaine, because the said Sir Robert undertook on behalf of each of them, on pain of a penalty of £100, that they would help him carry out the same things, and that they would present themselves at the prison on the said quinzaine for the aforesaid matter. Also, the said Sir Robert promised before the council, on pain of 1000 marks to be paid to the king, that neither he, nor any of his followers, would inflict or cause to be inflicted injury, duress or harm on Lady Neville, or any of her affinity, *[Page iii-40]*

[Col. a] /violence,\ duretee, ne grevance contre la paix. Item, promist devant le conseil le dit monsire Robert, sur peine de mille marcz, q'il, ne nul de soens, ne ferroient ne ne procureroient estre fait, a monsire Johan L'Estrange, ne au nul de soens, damage, violence, duretee, ne grevance contre la paix. Item, semblablement ad promis le dit monsire Johan, sur peine de mille marcz a paier au roi, q'il, ne nul de soens, ne /ferront,\ ne /ne\ /procureront\ estre fait, au dit monsire Robert, damage, violence, duretee, ne grevance contre la paix. Et sur ce ordene feust et acordez qe le chanceller ferroit entrer de record es roules de la chancellarie, sibien toute la matire susdite, come les seuretes \faites/ en sa presence par celles enchesons. Item, ordene feust qe touz autres qe sont empeschables et nemye arestuz a cause des dites mesprisions, soient a large sanz arest tanqe a la .xv.^{ine} avauntdite. Et sur ce, apres aucuns paroles et resons ditz de l'une et l'autre part, finalment estoit recordez en parlement qe voirs est qe parmy ceste seurtee faite et enroulle come dit est, le dit monsire Robert et les autres furent lessez aler a large hors du prisone. Et coment le dit monsire Robert n'avoit mye restitut son corps al dite tour, ne fist amesner la persone de dite Margerie, ne perfourniz la remenant /de\ sa emprise par manere come il estoit tenuz par le dit promesse a mesme la quinszeine, ne riens est trove es roulles de record q'il ent avoit jour oultre, paront l'en lui purroit surmetter q'il avoit encurruz la dite peine: nientmeins, pur ce q'il est tesmoignes pur voir en parlement par aucuns prelatz et seignours esteantz de grant conseil nostre seignour le roi, qe le dit monsire Robert vient a Londres a la dite .xv.^{ine} devaunt le dite conseil, \et/ y dist qe coment q'il avoit fait ses loial peine et diligence par luy et les soens pur sercher et prendre la dite Margerie, nientmeins il ne l'avoit peu trover encores en aucun manere, le dit conseil a sa priere enlargist et fist proroger oultre son dit terme de re-entrer la prisone, tanqe au fin du trois semaignes apres la dite .xv.^{ine} proschein ensuantz durantz. Et salvez en le moen temps toutes les suretes, peines, condicions et emprises avauntdites entierment en lour force et vertu.

35. Et puis apres les ditz trois semaignes, le dit monsire Robert vient a Glouc' devant le conseil nostre seignour le roi en parlement, et se fist autre foitz excuser q'il ne poaist unqore trover n'avoir la dite Margerie, coment q'il avoit mis grantz travailx, paines et diligences. Et pria par tant jour oultre, ou d'estre deschargez et deliverez del emprise avauntdite, come celui q'alors n'ent savoit plus faire. Et sur ce, par cause qe en dit record appart clerement qe le dit monsire Robert estoit tenuz d'amesner la dite Margerie, ou de re-entrer son corps a la dite prisone, et nel ad mie amesnez, il est agarde a la dite tour, et liverez en parlement a monsire Alein de Buxhull', conestable de la tour avauntdit, pur salvement garder tanqe il ent avera autre mandement. Et enoultre est assentuz qe pur ce qe le dit monsire Robert est issint comandez a la dite prisone, toutes les peines et seuretees comprises en dit record soient retretz, dampnez, et cancellez, et de tout perdent lour force et vertu. Purveuz toutz foitz qe pur tant qe les dites seurtees de la paix sont par ceste agarde retretz et adnullez, come dit est, et si les ditz dame de Neville, monsire Johan L'Estrange, ou nul autre, vorra avoir de novelle seurtee de paix del dit monsire Robert, ent facent lour pursuite devers mesme le conseil devant la finale deliverance de prisone; et y aient de lui seurtee suffisante selonc la loy de la terre. Et sur ce estoit commissioun ottroiez d'estre fait as certaines

[Col. a] contrary to the peace. Also, the said Sir Robert promised before the council, on pain of a thousand marks, that neither he, nor any of his followers, would inflict or cause to be inflicted, on Sir John L'Estrange, or on any of his affinity, injury, violence, duress or harm contrary to the peace. Also, the said Sir John similarly promised, on pain of £1000 to be paid to the king, that neither he, nor any one of his followers would inflict or cause to be inflicted on the said Sir Robert, injury, violence, duress or harm contrary to the peace. Whereupon, it was ordained and agreed that the chancellor would cause to be entered on record in the rolls of the chancery, both the entire matter aforesaid, as well as the pledges made in his presence to that end. It was also ordained that all others who were impeachable and not arrested because of the said misdeeds, should remain free from arrest until the aforesaid quinzaine. And then, after a number of submissions and arguments had been uttered on both sides, it was finally recorded in parliament, and it is the truth that as a result of this pledge made and enrolled as was said, the said Robert and the others had been released from prison. And that the said Sir Robert had not been sent back to the said Tower, and he had neither caused the person of the said Marjory to be brought forward, nor carried out the remainder of his undertaking as he had been obliged to do by the said promise on the same quinzaine, nor is anything to be found on record in the rolls to indicate that he had another day therefor, by reason of which one might surmise that he had incurred the said penalty: nevertheless, because certain prelates and lords being in the great council of our lord the king had testified in parliament that it was true that the said Sir Robert had come to London on the said quinzaine and appeared before the said council, and said that although he had tried and endeavoured loyally and diligently, both himself and through his men, to find and get hold of the said Margaret, he had still not managed to find her, the said council at his request delayed and caused to be further extended his said date for re-entering prison, until three weeks after the said quinzaine then approaching. And in the meantime preserving in their entirety all the aforesaid pledges, penalties, conditions and undertakings in their force and validity.

35. After the said three weeks, the said Sir Robert came to Gloucester and appeared before the council of our lord the king in parliament, and again asked to be excused for still failing to find and obtain the said Marjory, although he had been to great effort, lengths and pains. And for this reason he requested another day, or to be discharged and released from the aforesaid undertaking, as one who no longer knew what to do. Whereupon, because it was clearly apparent from the said record that the said Sir Robert had been bound to bring forward the said Marjory, or re-enter the said prison, never again be released, he was sentenced to the said Tower, and delivered in parliament to Sir Alan Buxhill, constable of the aforesaid Tower, to be closely guarded until he should receive further instructions concerning this. Furthermore, it was agreed that because the said Sir Robert had been sent to the said prison, all the penalties and pledges contained in the said record should be withdrawn, invalidated and cancelled, and all should completely lose their force and validity. Provided always that because the said guarantees of the peace were withdrawn and annulled by that decision, as was said, if the said Lady Neville, Sir John L'Estrange, and any other, wish to have a new guarantee of peace from the said Sir Robert, let them pursue their cause to the same council before the final release from prison; and they shall have from

autres persones, de prendre la dite Margerie en quelconqe place elle purra estre trovez, deins franchise et dehors, et la salvement amesner sanz vilenie devant le dit conseil, a toute le haste qe l'en purra bonement.

Pur monsire William de Wyndesore.
36. Item, /fait a remember qe monsire William de Wyndesore mist\ avant en parlement une /bille en la\ fourme qe s'ensuit: 'A tresredoute seignour nostre seignour le roi supplient William de Wyndesore et Alice sa femme qe come en le record, proces et jugement renduz vers la dit Alice, par noun Alice Perriers, en le derrein parlement tenuz a Westm', sont diverses errours, come pleinement piert en le dit record. Qe plese a dit tresredoute seignour le roi de faire venir devant vous le dit record, et d'oier les ditz William et Alice, de assigner les errours comprisez deinz le dit record, et sur ce lour faire droit et resoun, selonc ce qe la loy de la terre demande.' Quelle bille lue en parlement et entendue, les record et proces des queux ceste peticion fait mencion, fuerent fait venir en parlement, /et ycelles\ luez et entenduz, le dit monsire William esteant en sa persone en dit parlement, par son conseil allegeast certeins errours estre contenuz en les record et proces avantditz. Et puis apres celles errours /par luy\ mises en escrit et baillez avant en parlement, il priast sibien pur lui mesmes come pur sa dite femme qe par celles errours ore alleggez, et par autres quelles en apres y purront estre trovez, le juggement y renduz envers sa dite femme feust reversez, et enoultre droit et resoun plenerement fait a eulx, selonc les loys de la terre. A quoy illoeqes estoit replie par les sergeantz le roi, en disantz qe voirs est qe la dite Alice par juggement /en\ parlement estoit nadgairs banniz hors du roialme, de quiel banissement nul pardon ou restitucion a la loy est montrez ore en parlement; ne l'en ne sache si elle soit hors du roialme ou deinz mesme le roialme; et si elle soit dehors, elle n'y /purra\ re-entrer sanz la grace le roi; et mes qe elle feust dedeinz sanz le congie /de\ roi, si feust elle adonqes en le greindre peril par la loy; et coment qe soit /en l'une manere ou en l'autre, ils n'entendent mye qe par la loy elle\ serra resceuz a dire ceste plee ne nulle autre; mesqe elle y feusse present, come de verite \elle/ est absente, ne par attourne en s'absence \ne purra elle faire ceste suite/ tanqe elle ent ait la grace du roi mesmes, par quelle grace elle feust fait hables de faire la suite; et priont juggement, etc. Sur quoy feust dit en parlement au dit monsire William q'il pursuast a la grace du roi en celle partie.

37. Par quoi le dit monsire William /fist pursuir une\ ..... supplicacioun a nostre seignour le /roi en la\ forme qe s'ensuit: a tresredoute seignour le roi supplient humblement voz /humbles\ liges William de Wyndesore et Alice sa femme qe come en le record, processe et juggement renduz vers la dite Alice, par noun Alice Perriers, en le derrain parlement tenuz a Westmonster, sont diverses errours, come pleinement piert en mesme le record.
Qe plese a vostre hautesse granter licence as ditz William et Alice, de pursuir par la ley /de la terre en\ parlement de reverser le dit juggement, nient contreestant qe la dite Alice estoit banneez par juggement, et qe les ditz William et Alice purroient pursuer le dit plee par Esmond del Clay et Robert Brom de Warrewyk, lour attournes jointement et severalment

him adequate surety according to the law of the land. After which it was agreed that a commission be directed to certain other people, to take the said Marjory in whatsoever place she might be found, within or outside franchise, and bring her safely without injury before the said council, with all the haste that could be made.

On behalf of Sir William Windsor.
36. Also, be it remembered that Sir William Windsor laid before parliament a petition in the following form: to the most redoubtable lord our lord the king plead William Windsor, and Alice his wife, that whereas in the record, process and judgment passed against the said Alice, by the name of Alice Perrers, in the last parliament held at Westminster, various errors are to be found, as plainly appear in the said record.
May it please the said most redoubtable lord the king to cause the said record to be brought before you, and to hear the said William and Alice, to identify the errors contained in the said record, and thereupon to do for them what is right and reasonable, as the law requires. Which bill having been read and heard in parliament, the record and process of which the bill made mention were brought before parliament, and were themselves read and heard, and the said Sir William, being present in person in the said parliament, claimed that according to his counsel certain errors were contained in the aforesaid record and process. And then after these same errors had been set out in writing by him and submitted to parliament, he prayed on behalf of himself as well as his said wife that because of these errors now alleged, and because of others which might subsequently be found therein, the judgment passed against his said wife might be reversed, and furthermore that full right and justice might be done her, in accordance with the laws of the land. To which reply was given there by the king's serjeants, who said that it was true that the said Alice, by a judgment in parliament, had been recently banished from the realm, for which banishment no pardon or restitution according to law would now be carried out in parliament; nor was it known whether she was outside the kingdom or within the same kingdom; and if she was outside it, she would not be able to re-enter it without the king's grace; and even if she were within the kingdom without the king's permission, she would then be in great danger according to the law; and howsoever it might be, they certainly did not intend that by the law she should be allowed to make this plea or any other; whether she were to be present or indeed absent, and neither by attorney in her absence could she bring this suit until she had the grace of the king himself, with which grace she would be able to bring the suit; and they prayed that the judgment, etc. Whereupon, the said Sir William was advised in parliament that he should seek the king's grace in this matter.
37. Whereupon, the said Sir William petitioned our lord the king in the following way: to the most redoubtable lord the king, your humble lieges William Windsor, and Alice his wife numbly beg that whereas in the record, process and judgment rendered against the said Alice, under the name of Alice Perrers, in the last parliament held at Westminster, various errors are to be found, as are plainly apparent in the same record.
May it please your highness to grant the said William and Alice permission to pursue by the law of the land in parliament a reversal of the said judgment, notwithstanding that the said Alice was banished by the judgment, and that the said William and Alice might pursue the said plea through Edmund del Clay and Robert Broom of Warwick, their

en la cause suisdite, pur Dieux, et en oevre de charitee. Et fait a remembrer qe ceste derrain bille, issint baillee a nostre dit seignour le roi depar les ditz monsire William et Alice, estoit par mesme nostre seignour le roi envoiez a son grant conseil en parlement, as queux le roi avoit comis la discussion de mesme la bille, et feust issint escrit sur mesme la bille, c'estassavoir, Symond de Burleye, le roi ad commis ceste bille au conseil, come pleinement appert par l'original de la dite derrain bille q'est en fillace ensemble avec autres billes de cest parlement; et laquelle derrain bille estoit puis apres par mesme le grant conseil en parlement, par la dite auctoritee a eux done par le roi, come dit est, estoit respondue, endossee et liveree /avant en\ parlement en la [Page iii-41]

[Col. a] forme qe s'ensuit: Il semble as seignours du conseil nostre seignour le roi qe le roi le poet faire de sa grace. Par quoi il est assentuz qe les suppliantz soient resceuz a pursuir la loy par leur attournes deinz escritz, selonc l'effect de ceste supplicacioun, de la grace du roi come desus.

38. A nostre seignour le roi et son tressage conseil en cest present parlement suppliont touz les soens humbles liges, les cetezeins de Norwiz, qe come ils soloient d'auncien temps avoir tielle libertee, et continuelment l'ont usez tanqe ore tard, c'estassavoir, qe nul estrange de lour fraunchise averoit poair de vendre ne d'achater nulles maneres de marchandises a retaille deinz lour franchise, sur paine de forfaiture d'ycelles. Et mesqe ils ent ont ore tard pursuez devant vostre dit conseil, et sur ceo les seignours du dit conseil ent furent bien assentuz de lour renoveller et granter celle article par point de chartre, nientmeins lour feust finalment responduz qe la grante ne fuist valable pur certaine cause sanz parlement.

Qe vous plese lour granter le dit article par point de chartre, pur Dieu, et en oevre de charitee. Item, coment qe d'auncien temps ils ont tanqe en cea usez tielle custume, c'estassavoir, sur noveulx defautes et meschief, si nulles y fuissent ou sourdassent par manere tielle, qe lour aunciens usages ne purroient aider, de les remedier par novelles ordinances affaires entre eux mesmes et deinz leur ville /avantdite, et de\ tielles remedies come mieltz lour sembloit acordant a bone foy et resoun, pur commune profit de lour ville et des cetezeins et d'autres venantz ou conversantz illoeqes: nientmeyns, pur ceo qe plusours de la commune de lour dite ville ont este ore tard moelt grantemont contrarious, et unqore par aventure vorront sinoun qe les meillours remedes et ordinances pur le bone governaille n'y fuissent faitz. Et purceo ils priont qe vous pleise granter a eux et a lours successours, par point de chartre, pur greindre et plus forcible auctoritee y ent avoir envers les ditz citezeins, et auxint pur le meillour governement du ville et des vitailles y avoir, qe les quatre baillifs et .xxiiij. cetezeins esluz chescun an pur la commune de la dite ville, ou la greindre partie de ceux, aient poiar de faire et establier deinz la dite citee tieux ordinances et remedes, pur le bone governement de la dite ville et de cetezeins et del poeple illoeqes venantz ou conversantz, queux lours semblont mieltz acordant a bone foy et resoun, et profitable pur le roi nostre seignour et pur son poeple: et qe ycelles remedes et ordinances ils purront desore amender et corriger de temps en temps, quant embusoignera, et bon lour semblera, pur le commune profit del poeple. Et qe cestes deux articles purront estre adjoustez a vostre autre gracious grant fait a eux en vostre primer parlement, pur Dieu, et en oevre de charitee, sanz fyn ent paier en vostre chancellerie, a cause q'ils firent un balynger. Et qe sur ce commande soit al gardein de prive seal depar vous, qe sibien de ceste

attorneys jointly and individually in the aforesaid cause, for God and by way of charity. And be it remembered that this recent bill, thus submitted to our said lord the king on behalf of the said Sir William and Alice, was sent by our same lord the king to his great council in parliament, to whom the king had committed discussion of the same bill, and so it was written on the same bill thus, 'Simon Burley, the king has committed this bill to council', as can clearly be seen on the original of the said last bill which is filed together with other bills of this parliament; which recent bill was subsequently answered by the same great council, by the said authority given them by the king, as aforesaid, and it was endorsed and delivered to parliament in the [Page iii-41]

[Col. a] following form: 'it appears to the lords of the council of our lord the king that the king is able to grant his grace. Because of which it is agreed that the supplicants shall be allowed to pursue the law through their attorneys named herein, in accordance with the tenor of the request, by the king's grace as mentioned above'.

38. To our lord the king and his most wise council in this present parliament, all his humble lieges, the citizens of Norwich request: whereas they have been accustomed since ancient times to enjoy a certain liberty, and they have continually exercised it until of late, namely, that none outside their franchise should have the power to sell or buy any kinds of merchandise at retail within their franchise, on pain of forfeiting the same. And even though they recently brought a suit before your said council, the result of which was that the lords of the said council wholly consented to renew and grant to them that article by way of charter, nevertheless they were ultimately informed that the grant was not valid for a certain reason without parliament's consent.

May it please you to grant the said article by way of charter, for God and by way of charity. Also, although from ancient times until now they have exercised such a custom, new troubles and negligences have arisen in such a way that their ancient usages do not help; may it please you to remedy them with new ordinances to be made amongst themselves and within the aforesaid town, and to apply such remedies as seem to them to accord best with good faith and reason, for the common benefit of their town and of the citizens and others entering or doing business there: nevertheless, many of the commons of their said town have been extremely troublesome of late, and will perhaps continue to be unless better remedies and ordinances for good governance are made. And so they pray that it might please you to grant to them and their successors, by way of charter, greater and stronger authority amongst the said citizens, and also for the better government of the said town and its victualling, and that the four bailiffs and twenty-four citizens chosen each year by the commons of the said town, or the majority of the same, shall have the power to instigate and establish within the said city such ordinances and remedies, for the good government of the said town and of the citizens and the people entering or doing business there, as shall seem to them to accord most with good faith and reason, and to be beneficial for our lord the king and his people: and they shall henceforth be able to amend and correct such remedies and ordinances from time to time, whensoever it shall seem good and necessary to them, for the common benefit of the people. And that these two articles might be added to the other gracious grant you made to them in your first parliament, for God and by way of charity, without fine paid to your chancery, in exchange for which they shall build a balinger. And that thereupon orders be given to the keeper of the privy seal on

vostre grace devant faite as ditz suppliantz l'ont face suffisant garant a chaunceller de vostre prive seal dessusdit.[13]

39. Quant au primer article, il y a estatut ent fait en ce parlement, et selonc la forme de mesme l'estatut soit ce a eux grante. Et quant al second article, assentuz est auxint en parlement qe si lours custumes et usages devant ceste heure euez et usez illoeqes soient aucunement difficulteuses ou defectives en partie ou en tout, ou pur aucunes causes de novel sourdantz *[Page iii-42]*

[Col. a] illoeqes, pur quelles due remede n'estoit devant purveuz, aient busoigne d'amendement, q'adonqes les baillifs et .xxiiij. citezeins de mesme la citee issint a eslire illoeqes chescun an, et ou la greindre partie d'yceux, aient desore poair d'ordeigner et purvoier de temps en temps des tielles remedes qe mieltz soient acordantz au bone foy et resoun, et pluis profitables al bon et bon et peisible governement de la ville, et d'autres estranges illoeqes venantz,
[Col. b] \si/ sovent /come\ lour mieltz semblera a faire pur commune profit, parissint qe ycelles lours ordinances soient profitables pur nostre seignour le roi et son poeple, et acordantez a bone foy et reson, come dessuis est dit. Et ent aient lour chartre sanz fyn paier pur ycelle pur tant q'ils ont fait un balynger, ensemble avec les autres articles a eux devant ceste heure grantez.
Membrane 3

CY EN APRES S'ENSUENT LES PETICIONS BAILLEEZ PAR LA COMMUNE EN PARLEMENT, AVEC LES RESPONCES Y FAITES ET DONEZ EN MESME LE PARLEMENT.

[Liberties of the church.]
40. En primes, prient les communes, desicome la volentee le roi est qe seinte esglise eit ses fraunchises et droitures en touz pointz - sauve au roi sa regaltee et la commune loy de la terre, - tenuz come ils ad este en temps de ses progenitours. Qe plese qe les dites fraunchises et loyes, ensemblement ove la grande chartre et la chartre de la foreste, soient tenuz et gardez en touz pointz.

[Responsio.]/
Le roi le voet.

[Duchy of Cornwall.]
41. Item, supplient voz communes de duche de Cornewaill' qe come ils sont trope malement grevez et mys a grantz meschiefs par la guerre de les enemys depar dela de an en an; et lours mariners qe sont une grante partie de lour force a defendre leurs terres encontre lours enemys, sont amesnez hors du paiis en diverses viages par force de les commissions nostre seignour le roi, en grante damage et arerissement du communealtee du dite duche; et ore a ceste an present vendrent les galeyes d'Espaigne, et arderent tutz les niefs, batelx et villes queux sont sur les portz et cousties de la meer, et les ditz enemys ont mys une grante partie du dite duche a grevouse raunceon, pur defaute de poair et force de contrester les enemys suisditz. Et les ditz enemys manacent q'ils veullent venir ore en ceste proschein seson en la dite duche ove pluis grant force, et prendre et enheriter la dite terre, et mettre les ditz communes a meschief as touz jours. Dont les ditz communes supplient a nostre seignour le roi et son sage conseil q'ils veullent doner conseil, comfort, et remedie as ditz communes, en avauntage nostre dit seignour le roi et

---
[13] PRO SC8/18/892.

your behalf that hereby the grace you previously granted to the said supplicants shall be sufficient warrant to the keeper of your aforesaid privy seal.

39. With regard to the first article, a statute was made in this parliament, and in accordance with the tenor of the same statute let that be granted to them. And with regard to the second article, it was also agreed in parliament that if the customs and usages which they have had and exercised there before this time are in any way flawed or defective, in whole or in part, or because of any matters newly arising *[Page iii-42]*

[Col. a] there, for which due remedy has not previously been provided, they shall require amendment, and the bailiffs and twenty-four citizens of the same city to be elected there each year, or the majority of the same, shall henceforth have power to ordain and provide from time to time such remedies as shall seem to them to accord best with good faith and reason, and be most beneficial for the good and peaceable government of the town, and of strangers resorting there,
[Col. b] as often as shall seem best to them for the common good, so that these their ordinances shall benefit our lord the king and his people, and accord with good faith and reason, as said above. And let them have their charter thereon without paying fine for the same because in exchange for this they have built a balinger, together with the other articles granted to them in the past.

HEREAFTER FOLLOW THE PETITIONS SUBMITTED BY THE COMMONS IN PARLIAMENT, WITH THE ANSWERS MADE AND GIVEN IN THE SAME PARLIAMENT.

[Liberties of the church.]
40. First, the commons pray, inasmuch as it is the king's will that the franchises and rights of holy church be maintained in every respect, saving to the king his regality and the common law of the land, and upheld as they were in the time of his progenitors, may it please him to ordain that the said franchises and laws, together with the Great Charter and the Charter of the Forest, shall be upheld and preserved in all points.
Answer.
The king wills it.

[Duchy of Cornwall.]
41. Item, your commons of the duchy of Cornwall request: whereas they are greatly harrassed and beladen with great troubles on account of the war with the enemies overseas on all sides and from year to year; and their mariners, who constitute a large part of their power to defend their lands against their enemies, have been taken abroad on various expeditions by force of the commissions of our lord the king, to the great damage and injury of the community of the said duchy; and now, in this present year, come galleys from Spain, burning all the ships, boats and towns which are in the ports and along the coasts of the sea, and the said enemies have put to grievous ransom a great part of the said duchy, for want of strength and power to resist the aforesaid enemies. And the said enemies threaten to return next season to the said duchy with an even greater force, and seize and claim the said land as their own, and trouble the said commons forever. Because of this the said commons request of our lord the king and his wise council that they might give counsel, comfort and remedy to the said commons, to the advantage

roialme, sibien come as communes du dite duche. Et mesme la peticion priont toutz les marches de la mier parmy tout le roialme.

\[Responsio.]/

Nostre seignour le roi par l'advis de son counseil y ferra purvoier et ordener de remede.

[County of Cumberland.]

42. Item, supplient les communes, et nomement del countee de Cumbrelande qe come la marche du dit countee adjoinant as parties d'Escoce issint est destruit et degaste par les enemys Escotes q'il n'ad nulle Engleis ville parentre la citee de Cardoille et la dite terre d'Escoce, et ovesqe ceo, par la ou la chastelle et la citee de Cardoill' serroient le souverein refuit et governaille de tout le countee; les queux chastelle et citee sont tout oultrement sanz seure et sauve garde, pur defaute des reparacions et gardeins et poair des gentz q'illoeqes soloient et covient demurrer.

Qe plese a nostre tresexcellent seignour le roi et son consel issint ordener pur les ditz meschiefs qe ses povres communes de le dit countee purront estre sauvement gardez et defenduz; considerantz les

[Col. b] grantz meschiefs et perils queux sont en point en haste d'avenir, en defaute de reparacions et bone governaille des chastel et citee suisditz.

\[Responsio.]/

Le roi y ferra ordinance par advis de son conseil, sibien pur le governaille du paiis come pur la reparacion du chastiel.

[Actions of assize abainst disseisors.]

43. Item, supplient les communes qe come diverses gentz soient disseisiz de lours frank tenementz, et les disseisours apres font feoffement as diverses gentz a cause d'avoir maintenance, en lour tort, et auxint de mettre le pleintif en delay pur defaute q'ils n'eient toutz les nouns en certein qe sont issint enfeoffez; \[et issint sont mys en delay/ pur tout lours vies.

Qe plese a nostre seignour le roy granter qe l'action del assise soit tutdys maintenable devers le principal disseisour, et ascuns de eux qe viegnont en aide de lui, nietcontreesteant les feoffementz avantditz.

\[Responsio.]/

Il y a estatut fait en les cas au derrain parlement, quiel le roi voet qe soit tenuz et gardez.[14]

[Malefactors of Cheshire and Lancashire.]

44. Item, supplient les communes qe come diverses gentz malfaisours des countes de Cestre et Lancastre, et autres lieux franchises, alont vagans de jour en autre pur vous gentz liges tuer, raunsoner, et grosses sommes, et auscuns qe ne veullient \[raunsoner a eux ils lour]/ colleront les coliousez, et les files de vous liges ravissont, \[et eux amesnont]/ et resceivont en les franchises avauntdites, \[renvoiantz as peres et mieres,]/ eux comandant de faire departisone de lours biens en trois s'il aient de femme, \[et la purpartie de fille a]/ eux envoier sur peril de perder lours \[vies. Et quant]/ les biens sont degastez \[et despenduz renvoiant]/ as pieres des ditz filles, eux comandant sur peril susdit q'ils resceivent lour filles arere, et qe a eux ne facent mal ne molest par celle encheson. Et les ditz gentz de franchises avauntdites viegnent ove grant force ove gentz armez as feires et marchees, \[en affrai]/ de voz communes, et a grant perde des seignours

of our lord the king and kingdom, as well as the commons of the said duchy. And in the same petition they prayed for all the marches of the sea throughout the kingdom.

Answer.

Our lord the king by the advice of his council shall provide and ordain a remedy.

[County of Cumberland.]

42. Item, the commons, and especially the county of Cumberland request: whereas the march of the said county adjoining the parts of Scotland has been so destroyed and wasted by the Scottish enemies that there is no English settlement left between the city of Carlisle and the said land of Scotland, and so, because the castle and the city of Carlisle should be the chief refuge and seat of government of the whole county; which castle and city are altogether lacking sure and safe protection, for want of repairs and keepers and the weakness of the people who are accustomed to dwell and come together there.

May it please our most excellent lord the king and his council to so ordain in connection with the said troubles that his poor commons of the said county might be safely guarded and protected; considering the

[Col. b] great troubles and perils which will soon arise through a lack of repairs and good governance of the aforesaid castle and city.

Answer.

The king shall make an ordinance by the advice of his council, both for the governance of the country as well as for the repair of the castle.

[Actions of assize against disseisors.]

43. Item, the commons request: whereas, all manner of people have been dispossessed of their free tenements, and the disseisors later wrongfully enfeoff various persons to secure maintenance, and also to hinder the plaintiffs who do not know for certain all the names of those who are thus enfeoffed; and so they are put to delay for their whole lives.

May it please our lord the king to grant that the action of assize shall ever lie against the principal disseisor, and any who assist him, notwithstanding the aforesaid enfeoffments.

Answer.

A statute was made thereon at the last parliament, which the king wishes upheld and preserved.

[Malefactors of Cheshire and Lancashire.]

44. Item, the commons request: whereas various malefactors of Cheshire and Lancashire, and other franchises, wander about from day to day with the intention of killing and ransoming your liege people, forcibly extorting from them vast sums of money, and they behead those who will not pay them ransoms, and ravish the daughters of your lieges, and carry them off and keep them in the aforesaid franchises, sending orders back to their fathers and mothers that they should part with three times the value of their goods if they want to recover the woman, and should send them their daughter's portion on pain of losing their lives. And when the goods are wasted and spent they send messages to the fathers of the said daughters, informing them that on pain of the aforesaid peril they shall agree to take their daughter back, and that they shall neither harm nor injure them on that account. And the said people of the aforesaid franchises come with a

---

[14] Stat. 1 Ric.2 c.9.

des ditz feires, et enpovrisement des communes des paiis. Dont ils prient remedie.

[Malefactors practising extortion.]
Item, prie la commune qe come diverses malfaisours en diverses countees de roialme, par confederacies et faux alliances entre eux mesmes font si grantz malveis extorsions as povres gentz en paiis, et preignont lour biens, lour avoir, encontre lours grees, et lour oustont torcenousement de lours terres et tenementz, et eux manacent de lour vies, issint q'ils ne se osont de eux pleindre, a grant arerisement de plusours communes de roailme.
Qe pleise en cest present parlement en ordener remedie qe
[Page iii-43]
[Col. a] nulles tielles compaignies ne confederacies ne soient desormes soeffrez, en ease et quiete de touz les bones communes du roialme.
Pur ce qe nostre seignour le roi ad entenduz sibien par cestes pleintes et plusours autres ent a luy faites, come par la notoritee de la chose, qe sibien plusours des liges nostre seignour le roi en diverses parties del roialme, come auxint les gentz de Gales en le countee de Hereford, et les gentz del countee de Cestr' en les countees joinantz a Cestreshire, aucuns de eux claimantz avoir droit as diverses terres, tenementz et autres possessions, et aucuns espiantz dames et damoisels nient mariez, et aucuns desirantz a faire maintenance en lour marchees, se coillent ensemble a grant nombre des gentz armez et archiers a fier de guerre, et soi entrelient par serement et par autre confederacie, nient aiantz consideracion a Dieu, ne as loies de seinte esglise ne de la terre, ne a droit ne a justice, einz refusantz a entrelessantz tout proces de loy, chivachent en grant routes en plusours parties d'Engleterre, et preignent possession et se mettent en diverses manoirs, terres et autres possessions de lour propre auctoritee, et les tiegnent longement a tiel force, y faisantz mondes maners d'apparailementz de guerre, et en aucuns lieux ravissent dames et damoisels, et les enmesnent en estrange pays ou lour plest, et en aucuns lieux en tieux routes gisent en agait, et batont, mahaiment, mordrent et tuont les /gentz,\ pur lour femmes et biens avoir, et celles femmes et biens retiegnent a lour propre oeps, et a la foitz preignent a force les liges le roi en lours propres maisons, et les enmesnent et detiegnent come prisoners, et a drain les mettent au fin et raunceon, come ce fuist en terre de guerre, et a la foitz viegnent devant les justices en lours cessions a tielle guise ove grant force, paront les justices sont moelt esbaiez, on ne sont hardiz de faire la loie. Et plusours autres riotes et horribles malfaitz y font, paront le roialme en diverses parties est mys en grant troboille, a grant meschiefe et anientissement de povre poeple, et lesion de la roiale majestee, et encontre la coroune nostre seignour le roi: et nostre seignour le roi desirant souveraignement la paix et la quiete de son roialme, et ses bones loys et custumes d'icelle et les droitures de sa dite coroune estre maintenuz \[et gardez en touz pointz, et]/ les trespassours duement chastisez et puniz, come il est serementez a son corounement; del assent de touz les seignours et pieres esteantz en ce parlement est \[defenduz sur le perill q'appent, qe]/ nully soit desore si hardiz de faire riens qe soit en affrai du poeple, ou contre la paix. Et enoultre est ordenez et establiz qe l'estatut de Norht' fait tieu cas, en temps le dit aielle, soit tenuz et gardez en touz pointz. Et auxint est assentuz qe certains suffisantz et vaillantz persons, seignours ou autres, soient assignez par commission nostre seignour le roi en chescun countee parmy le roialme, ou il busoigne et mestier serra, qe aient poair par lour commissioun, qe si

great force of armed men to fairs and markets, to the alarm of your commons, and to the great loss of the lords of the said fairs, and the impoverishment of the commons of the country. For this they seek a remedy.

[Malefactors practising extortion.]
Item, the commons pray: whereas various malefactors in diverse counties of the kingdom, through confederacies and fraudulent alliances amongst themselves, visit such great and evil extortions upon the poor people in the country, and take their goods and possessions against their will, and wrongfully oust them from their lands and tenements, and threaten their lives, so that they dare not complain of them, to the great injury of many of the commons of the realm.
May it please you in this present parliament to ordain a remedy, so that *[Page iii-43]*
[Col. a] no such companies or confederacies be allowed henceforth, for the ease and tranquillity of all the good commons of the kingdom.
Whereas our lord the king has learnt through these complaints and many others made to him, as well as from the general notoriety of the matter, that many of the lieges of our lord the king in various parts of the realm, as well as the people of Wales in the county of Hereford, and the people of Cheshire in the counties adjoining Cheshire, claiming a right to various lands, tenements and other possessions, and marking down unmarried ladies and damsels, or desiring to promote maintenance in the marches, gather together in great numbers of men-at-arms and archers in a warlike manner, and are bound together by oaths and in confederacies, unmindful of God or the laws of holy church, or right or justice, but rejecting all legal process they ride in great bands throughout various parts of England, and take possession of and install themselves in various manors, lands and other possessions on their own authority, and hold them for a long while by such force, making there kinds of warlike apparatus; and in some places they ravish women and damsels, and take them to whatever other place thus pleases them, and in some places they lay in wait in such bands, and assault, maim, murder and kill the people to take their wives and possessions, and those wives and possessions they keep for their own use, and sometimes forcibly seize the king's lieges in their own houses, and lead them away and detain them like prisoners, and at last put them to fine and ransom them, as if this were a land at war, and sometimes they appear before the justices in their sessions in such threatening guise that the justices are so intimidated that they dare not enforce the law. And they perpetrate many other riots and misdeeds, as a result of which the kingdom in various parts is thrown into great trouble, to the great injury and ruin of poor people and the derogation of royal majesty, and against the crown of our lord the king: and our lord the king desiring above all the peace and tranquillity of his realm, that his good laws and customs of the same and the rights of his said crown be upheld and preserved in all ways, and wrongdoers duly chastised and punished, as he was sworn to do at his coronation; with the assent of all the lords and peers present in this parliament it is forbidden on pain of the penalty appended, that none henceforth be so bold as to do anything which shall disturb the people, or which is contrary to the peace. Furthermore, it is ordained and established that the statute of Northampton concerning such matters, made in the time of the said grandfather, shall be kept and upheld in all its points. And it is also agreed that certain sufficient and worthy persons, lords or others, be assigned by commission of our lord the king to each county throughout the kingdom, wheresoever there be need or occasion, who shall have

tost come ils scievent, ou qe lour soit creablement certifiez, d'ascuns assemblez, routes ou chivachez, des malfaisours, barettours ou autres tieux riotours, en lours marchees, en affray de poeple, et contre la paix, de lour arester tantost, sanz attendre enditement ou autres proces de loy, par lours corps, et meement les chieftens et dustres d'ycelle routes, et les envoier au proschein gaiole, ensemble avec la cause de lour arest clerement et distinctement mys en escrit, illoeqes a demurrer en prisone, en sure et bone garde, tanqe a la venue des justices en pays, sanz ent estre delivrez en le moien temps par mainprise, baille ou en autre manere. Et les seignours trestouz esteantz en parlement sont chargez depar le roi, et ont ils auxint de lour bone gree et liberale volentee promis loiaument, d'estre en aide a lour poair as ditz commissioners, si mestier ent est et soient requis, et de garder et faire garder par eux et les leurs ceste ordinance en quanqe a eux touche, sanz avoir regard a persone quelconqe pur amistee, alliance, ne autrement.

[Col. b] Et nostre seignour le roi voet et comande a touz ses justices, aiantz poair a lour deliverance faire, qe redde punissement et justice soit faite sur toutes les persones qe serront attentiz de tieux riotes et malfaitz, a chescun selonc ce qe le cas requiert, et par manere tiele qe cel punissement soit ensample as autres.

[Nihil accounts at the exchequer.]
45. Item, supplient les communes qe come plusours soient grantement travaillez et damagez de ce q'ils sont faitz d'avenir et accompter en l'escheqier des vins douces et del argent d'Escoce, et quant ils viegnent a lour accompte il est trove nichil: et ce nientcontreesteant, ils sont mys as grantz costages travaille, et perde. Dont ils prient remedie, pur Dieu, et en oevre de charitee.
\[Responsio.]/
Nostre seignour le roi ferra veer par ses officers les accomptes dont la peticion fait mention, et celles accomptes dont le poeple est issint grevez et le roi nient profitez, serront de tout adnullez.[15]

[Fees for probate of wills.]
46. Item, supplient les communes qe come diverses officialx parmy le roialme, et lours deans et autres ministres, facent de jour en autre grantez duresces et extorsions as ditz communes, de ce qe par la ou ils deussent prendre une certaine somme, c'estassavoir .viij. d. pur la proeve d'un testament, ore ils preignent tresgrant somme, pluis qe unqes ne soloit estre paie, disant qe ce est pur certein lour fee. Et si les ditz communes ne veullent voluntiers paier les sommes as queux ils sont mys par les ditz officialx et les autres ministres, mesmes les officialx et ministres adjoinantz as foreins /lieuez,\ et travaillent les ditz povres communes torcenousement, a grant desease, et preignent de eux tielx grantz sommes par tiele faux extorsioun, et auxint les ditz somnours facent lour sommons as diverses gentz par malice, come ils sont en alantz a lour charuetz en les champes, et aillours, et les surmettont diverses crimes torcenouses, et la facent les povres gentz de faire fin, q'ils appellont 'The Bisshope Almois': ou autrement le dit somnour les face somons de .xx. ou .xl. leukes de la, einz et aucun foitz en deux lieux a un jour, a grant desease, empovreisment, et oppression des ditz povres communes. Dont vous plese considerer le grant meschief, et ent ordener due remedie, pur Dieu, et en oevre de charitee.

power by their commission, as soon as they know, or are credibly informed of any assemblies, bands or raids of malefactors, troublemakers or other such rioters in their districts causing disturbance to the people, and contrary to the peace, at once to place them under bodily arrest, without awaiting indictment or other process of law, and especially the chieftains and leaders of the same bands, and to send them to the nearest jail, together with the reason for their arrest clearly and distinctly set out in writing, there to remain in prison in good and safe-keeping, until the coming of the justices to the county, without allowing them to be released in the meantime by mainprise, on bail or in any other way. And all the lords being in parliament are charged on behalf of the king, and they have also loyally promised of their own good grace and free will to assist the said commissioners as far as they are able, if there be need and they are required, and to keep and cause to be kept this ordinance by themselves and their affinity in as far as it shall touch them, without showing favour to anyone at all by way of friendship, alliance or any other cause.

[Col. b] And our lord the king wills and commands all his justices, having the power to carry out their deliverance, that severe punishment and justice be done to all persons convicted of such riots and crimes, each person being dealt with as the case requires, and in such a fashion that the punishment shall be an example to others.

[Nihil accounts at the exchequer.]
45. Item, the commons request: whereas many people are greatly distressed and injured because they are made to appear in the exchequer and account for sweet wines and silver from Scotland, and when they come to their account it is found to be nothing; and yet nevertheless they have been burdened with great loss and expense. For which they seek a remedy, for God and by way of charity.
Answer.
Our lord the king shall cause the accounts of which the petition makes mention to be inspected by his officers, and those accounts through which the people are thus grieved and which do not profit the king shall be altogether annulled.

[Fees for probate of wills.]
46. Item, the commons request: whereas various officials throughout the kingdom, and their deputies and other ministers, do daily inflict great duress and extortion upon the said commons, inasmuch as when they ought to take a certain sum, namely 8d. for the proving of a will, now they take a greater sum, more than has ever been customarily paid, saying that that is assuredly their fee. And if the said commons will not pay the sums which are levied on this by the said officials and the other ministers, the same officials and ministers, and others from elsewhere, wrongfully harass the said poor commons, greatly harming them, and take from them these great sums by fraudulent extortion, and also, the said summoners execute their summons on various people through malice, as they are making for their ploughs in the fields, and elsewhere, and inflict on them various wicked wrongs, and make the poor people pay a fine, which they call 'The bishop's alms': or otherwise the said summoner summons them to a place twenty or forty miles distant, and sometimes to two places on one day, to the great injury, impoverishment and oppression of the said poor commons. On account of which, may it please you to consider this great trouble, and ordain a proper remedy for it, for God and by way of charity.

---
[15] See stat. 5 Ric.2 c.14.

\[Responsio.]/
Les anciens loys et auxint les estatutz faitz en le cas doivent suffire; mais s'il a aucun especial cas ou les dites loys et estatutz ne poent suffire, soit le cas monstree, et remede ent serra ordenez.

[Tithes from great wood.]
47. Item, prie le commune qe come nadgaires en l'estatut fait darrein a Wyncestr'[16] estoit ordene qe homme averoit prohibicion si dismes estoient demandes en court Cristiene de gros bois outre l'age de .xx. ans: et jademains persones del esglises demandent dismes de tiel bois, et compellent par cessures de seinte esglise lour parocheins de les paier nient contreesteant le dit estatut, ne considerant de quel age tiel bois soit.

Qe plese a nostre dit seignour le roy et a son conseil, de faire declaracion en presence de prelatz coment les dismes de dit bois serroit donez en temps avenir, pur quiete du dit roialme.

\[Responsio.]/
Soit usez come ad este fait devant ces heures.

[Forest bounds.]
48. Item, supplient les communes q'ils puissent avoir lour /porales\ come y soloit avant ces heures, selonc le purport del grande chartre, sanz destourbance de nul forester ou autre ministre le roi qecunqe et qe perambulacion ent soit faite, come il fuist en temps du roy Henry.

\[Responsio.]/
Le roi pense qe les dites perambulacions soient duement faites; et si aucun se vorra pleindre en especial qe grief lui soit fait encontre ycelles, ou le tenour de la chartre de la forest, monstre sa pleinte, et due remedie ent serra fait.

Page iii-44

[Writs and letters from chancery concerning free tenements.]
49. Item, supplient les communes qe nul brief isse hors de la chancellarie, lettre de prive seal ne secret, direct a nully pur luy faire venir devant le conseil du roi, ou d'autre, a respondre a son frank tenement, ou choses appartenantz a ycelle, come ordene estoit avant ces heures; mais soit la commune loy de la terre maintenu d'avoir son droit cours.
\[Responsio.]/
Il ne semble mye resonable qe le roi nostre seignour feusse restreint q'il ne purroit pur resonable cause envoier pur ses liges, mais ceux qe serront envoiez devant le conseil, a lour venue ne serront mye compellez a y respondre finalment de lour frank tenement, einz serront d'illoeqes convoiez as places ou la loy le demande, et le cas requiert, et mis en le droit cours. Purveuz toutes voies qe a suite de partie, ou le roi et son conseil serront creablement enformez qe pur maintenances, oppressions, et autres outrages \[d'aucuns]/ en paiis le commune loy ne purra avoir duement son cours, qe en tieu cas le conseil purra envoier pur la persone de qi la pleinte est faite, pur lui mettre a respons de sa mesprission: et enoultre, par lour bone discrecion de lui compeller a faire seurtee par serement, et en autre manere, sicome semblera mieltz affaire, de son bone port, et q'il ne ferra par lui ne par autre maintenance, n'autre riens, qe purra destourber le cours de commune loy, en oppression du poeple.

---
[16]Stat. Winchester 13 Edw. 1 1285.

[Commissions of the peace.]

50. Item, prie la commune, purce qe commissions du garde la paix en chescun countee sont directes a les seignours du paiis, queux ne puissent entendre a lour cessions, \[assignez et]/ associez a eux plus povres et nient suffisantz q'occupient l'office en lour absence, queux reteignent envers eux les enditementz prises de malfaisours sanz mandement de leur \[precepts as]/ visconts pur tielx endites prendre, parensi qe les mesfesours du paiis sont plus abaudez de mesfaire, queux chivachent en grantz \[routes]/ sibien par jour come \[par noet, affraiantz ferres et]/ marchees, \[pernantz]/ gentz en lours maisons ou ailleurs, et batent et naufrent, et a la foitz tount et mahaiment les povres communes de la terre.

Qe plese qe tielx povres et nient suffisantz soient oustez, et les plus suffisantz et mieltz vaniz du paiis soient assignez en lour lieux, queux puissent et veullent justifier et faire redresser les mesfaitz des \[tieux]/ mesfaisours, lours maintenours, coadjutours, fautours, rescettours et abettours, en maintenance de commune loy de la terre, et salvacion de commune poeple suisdit.
\[Responsio.]/
Les chanceller, tresorier et autres du conseil le roi ferront ordener de pluis suffisantz gentz de chescun paiis, d'estre commissioners en tieux cas.

[Justices to enforce the law.]

51. Item, supplient les communes qe depuis la volentee le roi est qe les meschiefs du roialme et de commune loy de la terre soient amendez ou defaut y est, et qe la loy de la terre soit fermement tenuz, et ordene est par estatut devant ces heures qe nul justice du roi lesse de faire son office pur lettre du prive seal ne de grant seal, le quel estatut n'est pas pleinement tenuz au present.

Qe plese qe le dit estatut soit afferme, adjoustant a ycel qe pur nulle lettre d'autre seignour du roialme ne lesse de faire son office, en manere come est dit en l'autre estatut suisdit.

\[Responsio.]/
Le roi ne voet mye qe pur brief, ou lettre de grant ou prive seal, ou del secret seal, ou autre mandement quelconqe issant contre la loy, ou les estatutz avant ces heures faitz, les justices ne surseent de faire la loy, ne pur priere de nully.

[Charters to towns.]

52. Item, prie le commune qe les chartres de franchise grantez as citees, et autres villes, par ses nobles progenitours, soient confermez, selonc ce q'il graunta a son darrein parlement, sanz fin faire; nomement as touz yceux q'ont fait balingers pur ses guerres.
\[Responsio.]/
Ceux qi vorront avoir tieles confirmacions monstrent leurs chartres en la chancellarie, et illoeqes ent aient lours confirmacions, c'estassavoir ceux q'ont fait balyngers, sanz fin, selonc ce q'estoit ordeinez en darrein parlement, et les autres pur resonable fins.

[Letters patent of farms.]

53. Item, supplient voz ditz communes qe toutes les patentes des farmes, auxibien des denzeins come des aliens, soient fermez et establiz sanz les repeller, selonc le tenure des lettres patentes ent faites.
\[Responsio.]/

[Commissions of the peace.]

50. Item, the commons pray: whereas commissions for the keeping of the peace in each county are addressed to the lords of the country, who are not able to attend at their sessions, and who appoint and associate with themselves poor and unworthy people who occupy the office in their absence, and who keep to themselves the indictments made of the malefactors without sending instructions to the sheriffs to take such indictments, so that the malefactors of the county are more inclined to wrongdoing, and ride in large bands by day as well as night, disrupting fairs and markets, seizing people in their houses or elsewhere, beating, wounding, and sometimes killing and maiming the poor commons of the land.

If it please you, may such poor and unworthy people be removed, and more worthy and respected people of the country be appointed in their place, who are able and wish to set right and redress the wrongdoing of such malefactors, their maintainers, collaborators, supporters, harbourers and abettors, for the upholding of the common law of the land, and salvation of the aforesaid commons.
Answer.
The chancellor, treasurer and others of the king's council shall cause it to be ordained that the most worthy people of each county are to be commissioners in such causes.

[Justices to enforce the law.]

51. Item, the commons request, and it has long been the wish of the king, that the troubles afflicting the kingdom and the common law of the land shall be amended wherever fault is to be found, and that the law of the land shall be firmly upheld, and it was ordained by statute before this time, that no king's justice should cease from performing his duties through a letter of privy seal or great seal, which statute is not fully observed at present.

As it please you, may the said statute be confirmed, with the adjunct that through no letter of another lord of the realm should he cease from performing his duties, in the manner outlined in the aforesaid statute.
Answer.
The king certainly does not wish that through writ, or letter of great or privy seal, or of secret seal, or any other mandate issued contrary to the law, or the statutes made in the past, the justices should cease from carrying out the law, or at the request of anyone.

[Charters to towns.]

52. Item, the commons pray that charters of franchise granted to cities and other towns, by his noble progenitors, shall be confirmed, according to the grant in his last parliament, without payment of a fine; especially to all those who have built balingers for the wars.
Answer.
Let those who wish to receive such confirmations show their charters in the chancery, and there they shall have their confirmations, namely, those who have built balingers, without paying a fine, in accordance with what was ordained in the last parliament, and the others for a reasonable fine.

[Letters patent of farms.]

53. Item, your said commons request that all the letters patent of farms shall be confirmed and ratified to denizens as well as aliens, in accordance with the letters patent made on them, without being recalled.
Answer.

Le roi le voet, sinon q'il soit ensi qe pur extentes mains vraiement faitz et retournez, ou pur autre cause resonable, le roi eit cause de les repeller.

Membrane 2

[Staple at Calais.]
54. Item, supplient les communes qe come ordene fust et grante a vostre darrein parlement a Westm' qe toutes les petites marchandies serroient amesnez a vostre estaple de Caleys, et nul part ailleurs, selonc le purport et tenure de la chartre de vostre tresgracious aiel ent faite, par vous conferme, a grant profit a vous, et en relevacion et encres de vostre dite ville de Caleys.
Qe plese a vostre tresgraciouse seignourie leur granter qe les dites ordinances et grante puissent esteer en lour force en manere come il fuist ordeine et grantee, forspris et sauve toutes foitz les draps appellez worstedes, q'ils puissent passer \[par aillour pur]/ leur profit faire, selonc l'avis et ordinance du conseil.
\[*Responsio.*]/
Le roi le voet, horspris qe bien lise as Gascoignes qe amesnent vins deinz le roialme, ent purront re-amesner avec eux en leur paiis, furmage, bure et autres vitailles qelconqes, draps et capps de leine, ceintures, laniers et autres tielx manner marchandises, sanz empeschement; et horspris qe les ditz worstedes purront aler a large come nadgairs feust \[grante en parlement.]/

[Nisi prius.]
55. Item, prie la commune qe come gentz \[empanelez]/ en \[bank]/ nostre seignour le roi en cas del corone, sovent sont mys as grantz issues, et a cause qe le pays est loinz du dit bank forfaitent leur issues, et les prisones qi \[n'ont]/ dont \[carier]/ les enquestes si loinz, pur \[defaute]/ de panel moergent en prisone devant q'ils poent avoir lour deliverance; q'en tiel cas, les justices de mesme \[la place eient]/ poair desormes \[grantier]/ nisi prius sanz lettre du prive seal ou brief hors del chancellarie nostre seignour le roi.
\[*Responsio.*]/
Soit use come ent ad este devant ces heures.

[Terms of office of sheriffs, etc.]
56. Item, supplient les communes, \[qe come par estatut]/ soit establi, \[qe nul viscount, n'eschetour, ne demoerge en]/ son office outre un an, \[et puis par un autre estatut]/ soit ordeine qe nul south-viscount, ne clerc de viscount, ne demoerge en son office \[outre un an, si plese a vostre hautesse]/ ordeiner en cest present \[parlement qe meme]/ l'ordinance se tiegne de south-eschetours pur \[tresgrant]/ profit et du roialme et du poeple.
\[*Responsio.*]/
Quant as viscountz et southviscountz, soit l'estatut tenuz, si soit ensi q'il y a des autres qe soient covenables et scievent et purront faire la charge de l'office de southviscount: et quant a les \[eschetours et southeschetours, pur ce]/ qe nostre seignour le roi est enformez qe serroit damage a luy de les remuer chescun an, est assentuz q'ils demurront en lours office oultre trois ans.

[Expenses of members of parliament.]
57. Item, prie la commune, \[qe par la ou lour]/ despenses sont ordenez par brief nostre seignour le roi, assignez as viscontz des chescuns countees, a lever selonc \[le purport]/ du dit brief a eux direct, al oeps des chivalers du \[parlement

The king wills it, unless it happens that because of assessments dishonestly calculated and returned, or for any other valid reason, he has cause to recall them.

[Staple at Calais.]
54. Item, the commons request: whereas it was ordained and granted at your last parliament at Westminster that all petty merchandise should be taken to your staple at Calais and nowhere else, in accordance with the purport and tenor of the charter of your most gracious grandfather made thereon and confirmed by you, to your great profit, and to relieve and benefit your said town of Calais.
May it please your most gracious lordship to grant that the said ordinances and grant might remain in force in the form in which they were ordained and granted, excepting and saving at all times cloths called worsteds, so that they may be taken elsewhere for the making of profit, in accordance with the advice and ordinance of the council.
Answer.
The king wills it, except that it is fully permitted to Gascons who bring wine into the kingdom to take back with them to their countries cheese, butter and other kinds of victuals whatsoever, cloth and woollen capes, belts, lace, and other such merchandise, without hindrance; and except that the said worsteds may be freely taken abroad as was previously granted in parliament.

[Nisi prius.]
55. Item, the commons pray: whereas people empanelled in the Bench of our lord the king in pleas of the crown are often put to great expense, and because their county is far from the said Bench they forfeit their issues, and because prisoners cannot seek inquests held far away, for want of a jury, they die in prison before they can be freed; that in such case, the justices of that place may henceforth have the power to grant nisi prius without a letter of privy seal or a writ issued by the chancery of our lord the king.
Answer.
Let it be done as it was done in the past.

[Terms of office of sheriffs, etc.]
56. Item, the commons request: whereas it was decreed by statute that no sheriff, or escheator, should remain in office for longer than one year, and that later, another statute ordained that no deputy sheriff or sheriff's clerk should remain in his office for longer than one year, may it please your highness to ordain in this present parliament that the same ordinance shall also apply to deputy escheators, to the great benefit of the kingdom and the people.
Answer.
As for sheriffs and deputy sheriffs, let the statute be upheld, if it be that there are others who are suitable and who know and are able to perform the duties of the office of deputy sheriff: and as for escheators and deputy escheators, because our lord the king is informed that it would be to his prejudice to change them each year, it is agreed that they shall remain in office for three years.

[Expenses of members of parliament.]
57. Item, the commons pray: whereas their expenses are ordained by writ of our lord the king, sent to the sheriffs of each county, to be levied in accordance with the purport of the said writ addressed to them, for the use of the knights

nostre]/ seignour le roi illoeqes esteantz, la sont lour ditz despenses assis sur chescune ville des ditz countees selonc \[l'afferant, par la ou le uns villes sont]/ tenuz du roi, et riens ne veullent paier coment qe lour tenure ne soit d'ancien demesne nostre seignour le roi; et les unes villes \[deinz franchise, et des pieres du roialme qi tiegnent par]/ baronie, *[Page iii-45]*
[Col. a] qi \[rienz ne veullent]/ paier a cause qe lour seignours sont au parlement pur eux et lours hommes en propre persone, et preignent si largement \[cest parol leur homes,]/ ....
\[coment]/ .... \[ad en un ville qe quatre ou cynk]/ bondes et centz ou deux centz qi tiegnent franchement ou par roulle des \[courtes et sont franks du corps unqore ne]/ veullent .... \[dites despenses, issint qe]/ toute la \[somme]/ par celle \[cause abregge et]/ nient leve si est recoupe en paiement \[des dispenses des ditz chivalers a grant damage]/ . \[a eux: dont ils prient]/ remede.
\[*Responsio.*]/
\[Ent soit fait come ad este use]/ devant ces heures .

[Accounts of sheriffs.]
58. Item, prient les communes qe come diverses franchises et libertees sont ore tard grantez as diverses seignours as certains lieux et seignouries, les queux sont exemptz des jurisdictions des viscontz des touz countees et diverses profitz et comodites a certaine some, les queux les viscontz soloient prendre illoeqes devant les dites franchises grantez, come ce q'appertient en eide de lour ferme. Et a cause des dites franchises et libertees ensi grantez, les viscontz ne puissent nul profit des dites franchises ..... ne leur ferme a l'escheqier ....
nostre dit seignour le roi et seignours, piers du parlement, ordeiner pur les viscontz de celles countees qi serront pur le temps avenir q'ils puissent avoir allouance sur leur accompt en l'escheqier, selonc la quantitee de la somme q'ils soloient prendre illoeqes devaunt les fraunchises grantez.
\[*Responsio.*]/
Les seignours ne sont mye avisez \[d'assenter]/ a chose qe purroit \[tourner]/ en descrees de les anciens fermes del roialme, ou en damage de la coroune a perpetuitee, tant come le roi soit issint deinz tendre age. Mais les officers du roi serront chargez de leur enformer veritablement des causes comprises en ceste peticion; et sur ce, par l'advis du conseil le roi, ent ferra de meillour remede q'il bonement purra.

[Sheriff of Essex and Hertford.]
59. Item, prie la commune des countees d'Essex et Hertf' qe come le viscont des countees suisditz soit chargez \[d'an]/ en an des graundes sommes lever en les ditz countees, a la somme de .c.li. et plus plus[17] q'il ne purra jammays resonablement lever des ditz countees: et ce est pur anciens custumes on temps qe le paiis estoit enhabite et maynovre, et les hundredz as greindres sommes lessez q'ore ne poent; de quel paiis plusours villages, terres et tenementz sont depuis par plusours voies anientiz et destruitz; come par plusours pestilences; par cretyn de meer et de Thamise; et par certeins hundredz depuis \[enfranchises,]/ dont le viscont susdit est charge, et \[ne prent]/ avauntages; et par autres plusours voies, paront chescun an est un de plus suffisantz des ditz countees par tiele voie destruit et anienti, come verraiement appiert.

Qe plese a vostre tresgraciouse seignourie, en oevre de charite, ordeiner descharge del somme suisdit au dit

---
[17] plus *repeated*

attending the parliament of our lord the king, whereas the said expenses are assessed on each town of the said counties proportionately, even though some towns are held of the king, and wish to pay nothing because their tenure is not from the ancient demesne of our lord the king; and some towns within franchises, and of peers of the realm who hold by barony, *[Page iii-45]*
[Col. a] wish to pay nothing because their lords attend parliament in person on behalf of them and their men, and their men interpret those words so broadly that .. in one town that four or five bondsmen and a hundred or two hundred who hold freely or by copy of court and are personally free do not wish the said expenses, so that the entire sum for this reason is reduced and remains unlevied and so the expenses paid to the said knights fall short, to their great loss: for which they seek a remedy.
Answer.
Let it be done as it was done in the past ....

[Accounts of sheriffs.]
58. Item, the commons pray: whereas divers franchises and liberties have of late been granted to various lords of certain places and lordships, which are now exempt from the jurisdictions of the sheriffs of all counties, as are various profits and commodities amounting to a certain sum, which the sheriffs were accustomed to take before the said franchises were granted, since they contributed towards their farm. And because of the said franchises and liberties thus granted, the sheriffs can take no profit from the said franchises .... nor pay their farm at the exchequer, ... our said lord the king and the lords, peers of parliament, to ordain for the sheriffs of these counties that in future they may have allowance made in their account in the exchequer, accounting for the size of the sum they were accustomed to collect before the franchises granted.
Answer.
The lords are not willing to agree to a thing which might prejudice the ancient farms of the kingdom, or injure the crown in perpetuity, given that the king is of so tender an age. But the king's officers shall be charged truthfully with informing them of the matters contained in this petition; and thereupon, by the advice of the king's council, the best possible remedy will be provided.

[Sheriff of Essex and Hertford.]
59. Item, the commons of the counties of Essex and Hertford pray: whereas the sheriff of the aforesaid counties is yearly charged with levying great sums in the said counties, amounting to £100 and more, which he can never reasonably levy from the said counties: which are from ancient customs dating from a time when the land was inhabited and cultivated, and the hundreds leased for great sums which are inconceivable now; many of which villages, lands and tenements of those counties have since been ruined and destroyed by various means; by numerous pestilences, for example; by the flooding of the sea and of the Thames; and because of certain hundreds since enfranchised, with which the aforesaid sheriff is charged, and from which he receives no profits; and in numerous other ways, on account of which each year one of the more worthy men of the said counties is destroyed and ruined, as is painfully evident.
May it please your most gracious lordship, as a work of charity, to ordain the release of the said sheriff from paying

viscont, desicome il ne poet estre leve par nulle voie resonable, come est suisdit; eiantz consideracion qe chescun an les plus suffisantz des ditz countees se retreont et aloignent de lour demoere en le dit paiis, pur doute des meschiefs suisditz; a grant anientisement du dit paiis et de tout le roialme si cas aviegne d'arrivail des enemys, ou cretyn de eawe, \[qe casuel]/ est de jour en autre, desicome le paiis d'Essex est de la mier environe.
\[Responsio.]/
Le roi \[par advis]/ de soun conseil en ce parlement lour ent ad grante pardoun de cent marcz par an; c'estassavoir, cent marcz pur l'an ore passe, \[et cent marcz par]/ an durantz les trois \[ans]/ proschein avenirs tantsoulement de sa grace especiale.

[Fugitive labourers.]
60. Item, \[prie la commune qe come]/ diverses laborers et servantz, quant ils deussent estre chastisez de leur mesfaitz en un countee s'enfuent et \[s'alloignent en autre]/
[Col. b] countee, la \[ou lour seignours et mestres ne poont]/ \[notice de lour]/ demoer; par quoy lours ditz seignours et mestres sont a grant diseas et perde, et les ditz servantz nient puniz pur lour \[trespas. Par quoy ils sont le]/ plus baudes, \[et s'alloignent par manere]/ suisdite.

Si plese ordener qe certains gentz en chescun countee des plus loialx soient assignez d'arester touz tielz futifs, \[sibien dedeinz]/ franchise come dehors, \[s'ils n'eient]/ .... enseale de ceux issint assignez en countee dont les ditz servantz departirent pur servir. Quel seal soit mande par le conseil nostre seignour le roi a ceux issint \[assignez en chescun countee,]/ issint qe nostre seignour le roi soit responduz de un certein de chescune bille.
\[Responsio.]/
L'estatutz et ordinances ent faitz, et par especial l'ordinance qe comence, Quia magna pars populi, soient fermement tenuz pur estatut, et mys en execucion.[18]

[Merchants on the Welsh March.]
61. Item, prient voz liges citezeins et burgeys de Bristowe, Shrouesbury, \Hereford,/ Gloucestr', Worcestre et les autres villes marchees qe come ils soloient travailler en les parties de Gales pur vitailler les dites citees, villes et marchandire pur lour sustinance gaigner, sont empressez par destresses pris la ou ils ne sont detours, plegges ne trespassours, et issint les dettes a force recoverez q'ils n'osent travailler en les dites parties de Gales pur vitailler les dites citees et burghes, ne marchandier pur lour sustinance gayner.

Qe plese ordener tiel remede en cest present parlement qe nul de eux soit distreint s'il ne soit dettour, plegge ou trespassour, q'ils puissent en pees vivre, en eovre de charitee, et en relevacion de voz villes et citees suisdites.
\[Responsio.]/
Le roi, par assent de son conseil et des seignours marchiz, ent ferra ordener de remede.

[Justices of labourers.]
62. Item, prient les communes qe come pur commune profit du roialme avant ces heures est ordeine, et par estatutz en diverses parlementz afferme qe certains justices de la pees et pur justisier laborers, vitaillers et artificiers serront assignez en touz countees; et leur sessions faire tant des foitz qe mestier serroit, en punissement des malfaisours, laborers,

the aforesaid sum, since he cannot levy it by any reasonable means, as aforesaid; bearing in mind that each year the more worthy men of the said counties remove and distance themselves from their dwelling in the said region, through fear of the aforesaid troubles, to the great injury of the said region and of all the kingdom should it happen that enemies appear, or the waters rise, which is a daily occurrence, since the land of Essex is by the sea.
Answer.
The king, by the advice of his council in this parliament, has granted them pardon of the hundred marks a year; namely, a hundred marks for the year past, and a hundred marks a year for the next three years to come, by his special grace alone.

[Fugitive labourers.]
60. Item, the commons pray: whereas numerous labourers and servants, when they ought to be punished for their crimes in one county flee and escape to another
[Col. b] county, whereby their lords and masters are unable to .... knowledge of their location; whereby their said lords and masters suffer great injury and loss, and the said servants remain unpunished for their offences. In consequence, they are the more emboldened ..... and remove themselves in the aforesaid manner.
May it please you to ordain that certain people in each county from amongst the most loyal shall be appointed to arrest all such fugitives, both within franchises as well as without, if they shall not have .. sealed by those thus appointed in the county in which the said servants ceased to serve. Which seal shall be sent by the council of our lord the king to those thus appointed in each county, so that our lord the king shall be answered by one in respect of each return.
Answer.
The statutes and ordinances made thereon, and in particular the ordinance which begins, 'Since most people', shall be upheld firmly as a statute, and put into practice.

[Merchants on the Welsh March.]
61. Item, your liege citizens and burgesses of Bristol, Shrewsbury, Hereford, Gloucester, Worcester and the other marcher towns pray: whereas they have been accustomed to travelling in parts of Wales to provision the said cities and towns and to traffic for their livelihood, they are burdened with distress levied on them although they are not debtors, pledges or offenders; and the debts are thus recovered by force, so that they dare not travel in the said parts of Wales to provision the said cities and boroughs, or trade for their livelihood.
May it please you to ordain such remedy in this present parliament that none shall be distrained unless he be a debtor, pledge or offender, so that they might live in peace, as a work of charity and to the relief of your aforesaid towns and cities.
Answer.
The king, by the assent of his council and the lords of the march, shall ordain a remedy for this.

[Justices of labourers.]
62. Item, the commons pray: whereas for the common benefit of the kingdom it was ordained in the past, and confirmed by statutes in several parliaments, that certain justices of the peace and justices of labourers, victuallers and artificers would be appointed in every county; and their sessions would be held as often as necessary to punish

---
[18] See 2 Ric.2 stat.1 c.6; and 12 Ric.2 c.3.

vitaillers et artificers, queux justices rienz ne font en plusours paiis, par tant qe gages as tielx justices sont retretz, a damage du roi, come des fins et amerciementz. Paront malfesours sont despuniz, laborers outrajous en lour prise, vitaillers plus chiers en vente des vitailles, et artificers en lour degree.

Sur quoi plese qe touz les estatutz avantnomez puissent estre duement executz, en chastisement des ditz malfesours, laborers, vitaillers et artificers. Et outre, qe gages soient assignez as ditz justices pur lour sessions, et qe suffisantz justices et sages soient assignez en chescun countee pur l'execucion suisdit parfournir, a tant des foitz come mestier serra.

\[Responsio.]/
Aient deux ou trois des justices qi ent tiegnent lour sessions pur profit du roi et son poeple, la sisme part des profitz provenantz de lours estretz, pur un an tantsoulement.

[Delays in making judgments.]
63. Item, prient la commune qe la ou juggement est pendant en bank le roi, ou en commune bank, ou aillours devant justices le roi, et le juggement est souvent tariez et targez, a cause qe aucuns des justices de la place ne sont pas presentz a doner juggement; et auxint aucuns des justices sont en \[diverses opinions]/ de la loy, issint qe la partie demandant ne poet venir par action a son \[recoverir]/ par la loy.
Qe plese qe l'accion et jugement issint pendantz soit veu et redres en parlement \[proschein,]/ et execucion faite come la loy demande.
\[Responsio.]/
Il plest au roi qe l'estatut ent fait l'an .xiiij.^{me} seignour Edward nadgairs roi d'Engleterre soit fermement tenuz et gardez.

[Commons of Kent.]
64. Item, prient les communes en countee de Kent qe coment ils ont grant paiis et large a defendre et garder encontre les enemys de France, et \[nomement]/ .... y sourdont souvent plus q'en autres paiis: et le plus de cel countee est en mayns des grantz seignours. Item et come les nostre seignour le roi qe \[mort est, et autres countees et]/ . \[du roialme qi rienz font al]/ defens du dit countee pur lour grandes possessions. \[Et auxi]/ les seignours de seinte esglise qi tiegnent le plus del remenant ..... par quoi les .... et autres communes du paiis ne sont mye a la value, ne de poair de defendre lour paiis sans plus aide et poair avoir des seignours avauntditz. Dont ils \[prient remedie.]/ Et auxi monstrent les dites \[communes,]/ coment y ad grant meschief des chastelx et forceletz du paiis avantdit, qe sont parnables en defaut de reparaille, des gentz, et de vivre suffisantz as ditz \[lieuz garder,]/ a tresgrant meschief du paiis. \[Qar si]/ les enemys viegnent sodeynement aryver ove bone gyde, ils puissent bien avoir un ou deux chastelx en un noet, tant sont \[desgarniz et mal gardez, a]/ grant destruction du dit countee, et a damage et deshonur de tout le roialme. Dont vous plese ordener remede, pur Dieu, et en eovre de charitee.

\[Responsio.]/
Le roi, par advis de son conseil, ent ordenera due remede.

[Weirs, etc. on the Severn.]
65. Item, prient les communes qe come une commune grevance soit en les countees de Gloucestre, Bristoll, Wircestr',

offenders, labourers, victuallers, and artificers; those justices do nothing in many counties, because their wages have been withdrawn, to the detriment of the king, as well as of fines and amercements. In consequence of which, offenders go unpunished, labourers charge outrageous prices, victuallers sell their victuals at a more expensive rate, and artificers in like manner.
On account of which, may it please you to ordain that all the aforesaid statutes shall be duly enforced, for the punishment of the said offenders, labourers, victuallers and artificers. Furthermore, that wages shall be allotted to the said justices for their sessions, and that worthy and learned justices be appointed in each county to put the aforesaid into effect, as often as is necessary.
Answer.
Let every two or three of the justices who hold their sessions for the benefit of the king and his people have a sixth of the profits arising from their estreats, for one year only.

[Delays in making judgments.]
63. Item, the commons pray: whereas when judgment is pending in the King's Bench, or in the Common Pleas Bench, or elsewhere before the king's justices, the judgment is often delayed and postponed, because some of the justices of that place are not present to pass judgment; and also some of the justices have other views of the law, so that the plaintiff party cannot make his recovery by action at law.
May it please you for the action and judgment thus pending to be inspected and redressed in the next parliament, and execution made as the law demands.
Answer.
It pleases the king that the statute made thereon in the fourteenth year of the lord Edward, late king of England, shall be strictly kept and upheld.

[Commons of Kent.]
64. Item, the commons of Kent pray: whereas they have a great and wide county to defend and protect against the enemies of France, and especially .... arise there more often than in other counties: and most of this county is in the hands of great lords. Also, as the ..... our lord the king now dead, and other counties and .... of the kingdom who do nothing towards the defence of the said county for their great possessions. And also, the lords of holy church who hold most of the remaining   as a result of which the .... and other commons of the county cannot afford, and do not have the power to defend their county without more aid and support from the aforesaid lords. For which they seek remedy. The said commons also show that considerable trouble has arisen in the castles and fortalices of the said region, which are liable to capture for want of repair, and of people and provision necessary for the keeping of the said places, to the very great injury of the county. Because of this, if the enemies happen to arrive suddenly with good intelligence, they might well capture one or two castles overnight, so defenceless and poorly guarded are they, to the great ruin of the said county, and to the injury and dishonour of all the kingdom. And so may it please you to ordain remedy, for God and by way of charity.
Answer.
The king, by the advice of his council, will ordain due remedy.

[Weirs, etc. on the Severn.]
65. Item, the commons pray: whereas the counties of Gloucester, Bristol, Worcester, Hereford and Shropshire

Hereford' et Shrouesbury, de ce qe diverses gorces et kidelx sont assis sur l'eawe de Severne, si longement et fortement faitz qe grant damage et perisement des femmes et enfantz viegnent de jour en autre es ditz countees.

Plese au dit seignour le roi et son conseil grantir qe les estatutz \[avant ces]/ heures faitz touchant la matire avauntdit puissent tenir lour force, et qe due execucion ent soit faite, pur Dieu, et en eovre de charitee. Item, prient qe mesme l'ordinance soit faite par tout le roialme.
\[Responsio.]/
Il plest au roi.

[False patents to procure lands.]
66. Item, prient les communes qe come plusours gentz font diverses suggestions nient veritables en vostre courte, qe plusours terres sont es voz mayns, la ou ils ne sont mye, et purchacent sur ce patentes a eux d'avoir les dites terres, en oustantz les gentz de lour frank tenement par tiele cause, sanz respons, et encontre la fourme de grande chartre, et grant damage et disheriteson de eux.
Qe plese ordeiner et comander qe nul tiel patent soit fait desormes, en oustant issint les dites gentz de leur frank tenement par tieles suggestions, si ne soit trove par enquest pur le roi, ou par evidence en vostre dite courte de record: et qe tielx patentes ensi faites soient tout oultrement repellez.

\[Responsio.]/
Le roi le voet.

[Impressment of ships.]
67. Item, prient les communes qe come en temps passe la terre d'Engleterre fust bien repleny de navie auxibien des niefs groses come petitz; par quel navie la dite terre estoit a celle heure grandement enrichez, et des toutes terres enviroun grandement doutes; et puis la comencement du guerre entre Engleterre et France la dite navie ad este si sovvent arestuz pur diverses viages vers France et aillours - pur queux arestes et viages les possessioners du dit navie ont suffertz si outrages perdes et coustages, come en perdicion des niefs, batelx, et en empeirance et gastance des mastes, tresnes, ankres, cables et toutz autres attilmentz, sanz aucun regard avoir du roi ou de roialme - qe plusours de eux sont oultrement destruitz, et la dit navie bien pres gaste par toutes les parties d'Engleterre, a grant damage du roi et du roialme, et plein anientissement des possessours des niefs, et grant abaudicement as touz les enemys d'Engleterre.
Qe plese a nostre seignour le roi ent ordeiner remede [Col. b] en cest present parlement; issi qe les possessours des niefs ne soient mys as tielx perdes et coustages en temps a venir come ils ont suffert en temps passe.
\[Responsio.]/
Le roi, par l'advis de son conseil, ent ferra tiele ordinance come il purra bonement.

[Ships of Normandy.]
68. Item, prie \[la commune,]/ qe come les barges et balyngers de Normandie sont gisantz sur les costes del north del ryver de Thamise tanqal eawe .... vitailler, pessoner, n'autre queconqe, n'oserent a peyne passer par mier ne revenir pur profit du roialme, des queux ont pris sur les ditz costes puis le   et grantz, ove grand some des biens et d'avoir des gentz du dit paiis, et leur mariners, vitaillers, pessoners et autres gentz du roialme illoeqes, ...   furent

have common grievance in so far as numerous gorces and kiddles have been placed in the waters of the Severn for so long, and are so strongly made that they greatly injure and bring about the death of women and children coming to the said counties day by day.
May it please the said lord the king and his council to grant that the statutes made before this time touching the aforesaid matter shall take effect, and be duly carried out, for God and by way of charity. Also, they pray that the same ordinance shall apply throughout the kingdom.
Answer.
It is pleasing to the king.

[False patents to procure lands.]
66. Item, the commons pray: whereas many people falsely suggest in your court that numerous lands are in your hands, when they are not at all, and thereupon they purchase letters patent for themselves to receive the said lands, ousting people from their freehold on such grounds, without the latter having right of reply, and contrary to the form of the Great Charter, to their great loss and disherison.
May it please you to ordain and command that no such letter patent shall henceforth be granted, which results in the ousting of the said people from their freehold by such representations, unless they are found to be true by king's inquest or through evidence in your said court of record: and that such letters patent thus issued shall be completely repealed.
Answer.
The king wills it.

[Impressment of ships.]
67. Item, the commons pray: whereas in the past the land of England had a resplendent navy abounding in ships great as well as small; by which navy the said land was then greatly enriched, and much feared by all surrounding lands; yet since the war began between England and France the said fleet has been so often impressed for various expeditions to France and elsewhere - through which arrests and expeditions the owners of the said ships have suffered exorbitant losses and expenses, as a result of the loss of ships and boats as well as damage and wrecking of masts, spars, anchors, cables and all other types of equipment, without any thought being given to the king or the kingdom - that many of them are utterly ruined, and the said fleet almost completely devastated in all parts of England, to the great loss of the king and kingdom and the ruin of the owners of ships, and to the great emboldening of all of England's enemies.
May it please our lord the king to ordain a remedy for this [Col. b] in this present parliament; so that the owners of ships do not incur in future the losses and expenses they have suffered in the past.
Answer.
The king, by the advice of his council, shall provide the best ordinance he effectively can.

[Ships of Normandy.]
68. Item, the commons pray: whereas the barges and balingers of Normandy lie on the coasts to the north of the River Thames as far as the water .... to provision, fish, nor for anything else, neither dare they cross the sea or return for the benefit of the kingdom, from whom are taken on the said coasts after the .... and great, with a large quantity of goods and to have from the people of the said region, and their mariners, victuallers, fishermen and other people of the kingdom there, ...

had been ordained there, greatly harming and disrupting the whole of the northern country, and to the relief and great comfort to your said enemies.

May it please your most gracious .... to consider that all the said commons there have in every way born their charge for the defence of the kingdom with others, and to ordain for the said enemies there that they .... expelled, in honour of the entire realm, and for the salvation of the whole country.

Answer.

The king, by the advice of his council, shall ordain a remedy for this.

[Servants and labourers.]

69. Item, the commons pray: whereas in several parliaments held in the time of the most excellent king, King Edward III, your grandfather, whom God absolve, by the advice and assent of other prelates and lords present at the said parliaments, at the request of the commons of his said kingdom of England, there were shown various troubles and complaints which were rife in the kingdom in connection with the misdeeds of servants and labourers, and many statutes and ordinances providing remedy for the aforesaid misdeeds were enacted; nevertheless, a large number of the said servants and labourers, learning that a good and just remedy in the said statutes had been made in response to complaints of their said misdeeds, committing them to live in peace and avoiding the punishments thus ordained, refuse now to work, serve, or labour, and take themselves off to the towns, boroughs and cities, both old and young, some of whom become artificers, and others mariners, or clerks, so that husbandry cannot be maintained, nor the lands of the realm cultivated, to the great injury of the kingdom; as will be the ruin of it in time to come, unless a remedy is swiftly supplied.

Answer.

The king, by the advice of his council, will provide the best remedy he reasonably can.

[Benefices held by aliens.]

70. Item, the commons pray: whereas, the kingdom is greatly injured and impoverished because many of the great benefices of the kingdom, both parochial churches as well as deaneries, archdeaconries and prebends, are occupied by people from foreign countries, more now than ever before; and the number will increase daily unless remedy be provided: and also they take from the said kingdom all the profits of the said benefices, which amount to a very considerable sum each year, and they let all the houses of the same benefices fall to ruin, and they offer no hospitality, maintain no divine services, and fulfil none of the other charges and duties pertaining to the same benefices, which they ought to do in accordance with God's will and the intention of the founders.

May it please our said lord the king, by the advice of all lords and councillors who are in this present parliament, to provide a good and proper remedy, for the salvation of the estate of the said kingdom.

Answer.

71. It is ordained and agreed that all the benefices of cardinals and others rebelling against the present pope Urban *[Page iii-47]*

[Col. a] shall be taken into the hands of .... in his hands for this reason.

[Commons of the Isle of Wight.]
72. Item, prient \[les]/ ....
\[de]/ l'Isle de Wyght qe pur les grantz damages et duresces q'ils ont resceuz par les \[enemys,]/ sibien par arsyn et roberie   q'ils ont portez par la flote q'ad este entour eux cest proschein seson sur la mier, et auxint pur les grantz paiementz   ils ont .   qe la greindre partie des dites communes ...   aloignez ove lour biens hors de l'isle avauntdite, ...
soit faite pur salvacion d'ycelle.
Qe plese a vostre tresgraciouse seignourie d'avoir regard al povertee et meschiefs du dite isle et sur ce ordeiner .... de nostre dit seignour le roi, et en salvation de tout le roialme.
\[Responsio.]/
Le roi, del advis de son conseil, ent ordeignera a mieltz q'il purra.
Membrane 1

[Purveyors.]
73. Item, prient les communes qe touz les estatutz faitz en temps l'aielle de purveiours puissent estre tenuz en touz pointz; et qe les penances comprises deinz les ditz estatutz soient executz devers   qi sont trovez faisantz le contraire.

\[Responsio.]/
Le roy le voet.

[Foreign merchants.]
74. A nostre tresredoute seignour le roi prie la commune qe touz maneres des gentz, sibien estraungers come denzeins, amys a nostre seignour le roi, puissent savement venir et demurrer deinz le roialme, et parmy le roialme passer a lour voluntee, pur achater des leynes et autres marchandises quelconqes, et auxint leurs marchandises vendre as gentz du dit roialme communement, sanz contredit de nully, nonobstante nulle chartre faite a contraire avant ces heures.

De marchantz estraunges, etc.
Nostre seignour le roi considerant clerement la venue des marchantz estranges deinz le roialme estre bien profitable par moelt des causes a tout le roialme avantdit, del assent des prelatz, ducs, contes, barons et de la commune de son roialme, ad ordenez et establiz qe touz marchantz aliens, de quelconqes roialmes, paiis, ou seignouries q'ils viegnent, qi soient del amistee nostre seignour le roi et de son roialme, puissent desore salvement et surement venir deinz le roialme d'Engleterre, et en quelconqes citees, burghs, portz de meer, feires, marchees ou autres lieux deinz mesme le roialme, deinz franchise et dehors, demurrer avec lour biens et marchandises quelconqes, souz le salve garde et proteccion nostre seignour le roi, tant et si longement come lour plerra, sanz destourbance ou contredit de persone quelconqe. Et qe sibien yceux marchantz, aliens come denzeins quelconqes, et chescun de eux qi achater ou vendre voillent bledz, char, pessons et toutes maneres d'autres vivres et vitailles, et auxint toutes maneres d'espiceries, de fruit, de pellure, et des menues ou petitz merceries, come soie, fil d'or et d'argent, ...   et autres tieux \[petitz]/ merceries, les puissent desore \[franchement]/ et sanz contredit ou destourbance qelconqe, sibien en la citee de Londres come en touz ....
meer, feires, marchees et autres lieux \[deinz]/ le roialme vendre et achater en groos et par parcelles, a qi et de qi qe lour plest, ...   horspris, qe toutes maneres de vins, sibien douces come autres, ... par les ditz estraungers en groos par les

[Commons of the Isle of Wight.]
72. Item, the .... of the Isle of Wight pray that by reason of the great injuries and hardships they have suffered at the hands of enemies, including arson and robbery ...... which they have visited upon the fleet which surrounds them this year on the sea, and also for the great payments .... they have ....
that the greater part of the said commons ...   fled with their possessions from the aforesaid island, ...
be done for the salvation of the same.
May it please your most gracious lordship to bear in mind the poverty and troubles of the said island and thereupon to ordain ...   of our said lord the king, and for the salvation of the entire kingdom.
Answer.
The king, with the advice of his council, shall ordain on this as best he can.

[Purveyors.]
73. Item, the commons pray that all the statutes made in the time of the grandfather concerning purveyors shall be preserved in all points; and that the penalties contained in the said statutes be exercised against   who are found to be acting to the contrary.
Answer.
The king wills it.

[Foreign merchants.]
74. To our most redoubtable lord the king the commons pray that all kinds of people, both foreigners as well as denizens, friends of our lord the king, may safely enter and remain within the kingdom, and travel throughout the kingdom at their will, to buy wool and other merchandise whatsoever, and also sell commonly their merchandise to people of the said realm, without being hindered by anyone, notwithstanding any charter made to the contrary before this time.

Concerning foreign merchants, etc.
Our lord the king, considering well the coming of foreign merchants to the kingdom to be nothing but profitable to all the aforesaid kingdom for many reasons, with the assent of the prelates, dukes, earls, barons and commons of his kingdom, has ordained and decreed that all alien merchants, from whichever kingdoms, countries or lordships they may come, who are bound by friendship to our lord the king and his kingdom, may henceforth safely and securely enter the said kingdom of England, and whatsoever cities, boroughs, seaports, fairs, markets or other places within the same kingdom, within franchise or without, and remain there with their goods and merchandise of any kind, under the safeguard and protection of our lord the king, under whatsoever circumstances and for as long as it please them, without being disturbed or hindered by anyone. And that such merchants, aliens as well as denizens of any kind, and every one of them, who wish to buy or sell corn, meat, fish, and all other kinds of provisions and victuals, and also all sorts of spices, fruit, fur, and small or petty wares, such as silk, gold or silver thread, ...   and other such small wares, may henceforth freely and without impediment or disturbance of any kind, buy and sell them in gross or parcel both within the city of London as well as in all ....   seaports, fairs, markets, and other places within the kingdom, to whomsoever and from whomsoever they please, ... except that all kinds of wine, both sweet and others, ...

101

of napery, linen, kinds of canvas and of other such large wares; and also all types of large merchandise not specified, whatsoever they be, may henceforth, both aliens as well as denizens, in the said city of London as well as in other cities, boroughs, ports, towns, fairs, markets and elsewhere throughout the aforesaid realm, within franchise or without, to whomsoever may wish to buy them, be they foreigner or denizen; except enemies of the king and his kingdom; freely and without any impediment sell only in gross, as by bale of cloth, or by the whole piece as they please, but not by retail, on pain of forfeiting the same merchandise; except only the citizens and burgesses in their own cities and boroughs and other good towns enfranchised, to whom and to no other foreign merchant of their franchise may they without hindrance break, cut and divide, in those their own cities and boroughs, the gross wares, and other gross merchandise aforesaid: and to sell there as well wines and other merchandise whatsoever, in gross, and by retail, as they wish, paying in all cases the customs and subsidies owed; notwithstanding statutes, ordinances, charters, judgments, allowances, customs and usages made or allowed to the contrary; which charters and franchises, if there be any, are entirely repealed and annulled, as things done, practised or granted contrary to the common good, bringing oppression to the people. Saving always to the prelates and lords of the realm their liberties and franchises in their entirety, so that they might make their purveyance and purchase of victuals and other necessities, as they have been accustomed to do of old. And saving that the ordinances made before this time concerning the staple of Calais shall remain valid and in force. And it is indeed not the intention of our lord the king that foreign or denizen merchants who wish to buy or sell wool, woolfells, mercery, drapery and other merchandise in the fairs and markets of the land, should be restrained or prevented by this statute from selling and buying freely, in gross or .... retail, as they have been accustomed since ancient times. And if it should happen in the future that an obstacle is placed in the way of any merchant or denizen or other, in selling such things in city, borough, town, seaport, or any other place which has a franchise, contrary to the form of this ordinance, and the mayor, bailiffs or others who have the keeping of the said franchise, having been asked for remedy by the said merchants, or anyone else on their behalf, fail to provide it, and are so convicted, then the franchise shall be taken into the king's hands. And nevertheless, those who have caused such disturbance contrary to this statute shall be obliged to render and restore to the plaintiff twice the damages he has thus incurred. And if such a disruption should be caused to such merchants or others, in towns or places which have no franchise, and the lord if he is present, or his bailiff, constable or other keeper of the said towns and places in the absence of the said lord, being required to act, do not so, and are so convicted, let them render double damages to the plaintiff, as is said above. And the disrupters in both instances, within franchise and without, if they be convicted, shall be imprisoned for one year, and shall be released at the king's will. It is also ordained and decreed that the chancellor, treasurer and justices appointed to hold the king's pleas shall enquire into such disturbances and grievances in the places they visit, and shall mete out punishment in accordance with what is ordained above. And

face assigner par commission certeins gentz ....
luy pleira d'enquere de tielles destourbances et grevances, et de faire punissement des trespassours en celle partie, come dessus est dit.

Page iii-48

\[De forstallerie.]/

75. Item, est ordene et establi qe l'estatut fait en temps le dit le roi le aiel, l'an de son regne d'Engleterre \[.xxv.[20] des forstallours de]/ ... a les bones villes deinz le roialme, par terre ou par eawe, \[soit tenuz et fermement gardez en touz]/ pointz, et mys en due execucion.[21]

\[Pur Geneweys, Veneciens et autres.]/

76. Item, ordene est et assentuz qe touz marchantz de Je ... et d'autres roialmes et terres et paiis vers le west .... amesner a \[Hampton,]/ ou aillours deinz le roialme, ... galeye ou autre vesselx chargez ou deschargez et puissent . plest par manere ..... illoeqes ..... recharger lour dit vesselx des leyns quirs, pealx lanutz, plumb, esteyn et d'autres marchandises .... amesner en ... le west, paiantz en ce portz ou . toutes maneres de custumes, subsides et autres devoirs de Caleys, auxi .... come .... les marchandes a l'estaple de Caleys, parissint q'ils troeffent seurtee suffisant q'ils les amesneront issint devers le west ...... aillours devers le est .. qe a l'estaple de Caleys, .. par .. ils y vorroiont aler, sur la paine ent ordeigne devant ces heures.[22]

Ordinance de mariners.

77. Item, pur ceo qe plusours mariners, apres ce q'ils sont arestuz et retenuz pur service du roi sur la meer, en defense du roialme, et en ount resceu lour gages appurtenantz, \[s'enfuent]/ hors du dit service sanz congie des admiralx ou de lour lieutenantz, a grand damage du roi nostre seignour et du roiaume, et arrerissement de ses viages avauntdites; ordene est et establi qe touz ceux mariners queux desore ferront en tiel manere, et cela trovez et provez veritablement devant l'admiralle ou son lieutenant, soient tenuz de restorer a nostre seignour le /roi\ le double de ceo q'ils averont pris pur lour gages, et mentineins eient la prisone d'un an, sanz ent estre delivrez par mainprise, baille ou autre voie. Et le roi voet, et commande as touz viscontz, mairs et baillifs, deinz franchise et dehors, qe a la certificacioun des ditz admiralx, ou lour lieutenantz, par lour lettres ent affaires, tesmoignantes la dite \[prove,]/ facent tantost, sanz attendre autre mandement du roi nostre seignour, prendre et attache touz ceux mariners futifs par lour corps, deinz leurs baillies, deinz franchise et dehors, et les mettre en prisone, illoeqes a demurrer en bone et sure garde tanqe il averont fait gree au roi, come dessus est dit; et ent aient especial mandement du roi nostre seignour de lour deliverance.[23]

Sergeantz d'armes.[24]

Et autiel punissement soit fait des sergeantz d'armes, meistres des niefs et touz autres, qe serront atteintz q'ils aient rienz pris des ditz mariners pur lour soeffrer aler a lour large hors del service avauntdit apres ce q'ils aient este arestuz pur mesme le service.

nevertheless, that the king shall cause certain people to be appointed by commission .... shall please him to enquire into such disturbances and grievances, and punish contravenors thereof, as said above.

Concerning forestalling.

75. Item, it is ordained and established that the statute made in the time of the said king the grandfather, in the twenty-fifth year of his reign over England, concerning forestallers of .. to the good towns within the kingdom, by land or by water, shall be upheld and strictly kept in all detail, and duly enforced.

For the Genoese, Venetians, and others.

76. Item, it is ordained and assented that all merchants of Genoa .. and of other kingdoms, lands and regions towards the west to bring to Southampton, or elsewhere within the kingdom, ... galley or other vessels laden or unladen and might .... ply by way there reload their said vessels with wool, hides, woolfells, lead, tin and other merchandise .... brought to . the west, paying in such ports or . all kinds of customs, subsidies and other duties of Calais, as well .... as .... the merchants at the staple of Calais, so that they give adequate guarantee that they will take them to the west .... elsewhere towards the east ... other than at the staple of Calais, by they wish to go there, on pain of the penalty ordained for this in the past.

Ordinance concerning mariners.

77. Item, whereas many mariners, after they have been taken and retained for the king's service at sea, in defence of the kingdom, and have received the appropriate wages, flee from the said service without the permission of the admirals or their lieutenants, to the great injury of the king our lord and of the kingdom, and to the detriment of his aforesaid expeditions; it is ordained and decreed that all those mariners who shall henceforth act in such a manner, when this is found and proven to be the truth before the admiral or his lieutenant, shall be obliged to restore to our lord the king double that which they took as their wages, and they shall thereupon be imprisoned for one year, without being freed by mainprise, bail, or by any other means. And the king wills and orders all sheriffs, mayors and bailiffs, within franchises and without, that upon written notification from the said admirals or their lieutenants in letters testifying to the matter, they shall act forthwith, without awaiting any other mandate from the king our lord, to take and attach the bodies of such fugitive mariners within their bailiwicks, within franchise or without, and commit them to prison, to remain there in good and safe-keeping until they have compensated the king, as mentioned above; and let them have a special mandate from the king our lord for their release.

Serjeants-of-arms.

And so shall be punished serjeants-of-arms, masters of ships and all others, who shall be convicted of having taken anything from the said mariners for allowing them to leave the aforesaid service after they have been pressed for the same service.

---

[20] 25 Edw.3 stat.4 c.3.
[21] 2 Ric.2 stat.1 c.2.
[22] 2 Ric.2 Stat.1 c.3.
[23] 2 Ric.2 Stat.1 c.4.
[24] This note is contemporary and marginal.

[Recognition of Pope Urban.]

78. Item, whereas our lord the king has heard, both through certain letters patent which have recently arrived from certain cardinals rebelling against our holy father Urban now pope, as well as through common report, that there is division and discord between our said holy father and the said cardinals, who strive with all their power to depose our said holy father from his position as pope, and attempt with their false allegations to turn and influence the kings, princes and Christian people against him, to the great peril of their souls, and most evil example; our said lord the king caused the said letters to be shown to the prelates, lords, and other great and wise men of his kingdom present at the said parliament; and the aforesaid letters having been seen and heard,

[Col. b] and after thorough discussion of the matter, it was by the said prelates .... and made known for many great and noteworthy reasons there explained in full parliament, both through the matter found in the said letters and otherwise, that the said Urban had been duly elected pope, and that he is and ought to be the true pope, and the ..... pope and head of holy church ought to be accepted and obeyed; and thus it was agreed by all the prelates, lords and commons in the aforesaid parliament. Furthermore, it was agreed that all the benefices and other possessions which the said rebel cardinals, and all their other collaborators, supporters, adherents, and all other enemies of our said lord the king and his kingdom .... of our same lord the king. And that our lord the king should be informed of the fruits and profits of the same benefices and possessions, just as .... ordained that if the king's liege, or other within his power, purchase a provision, benefice .... any other in the name of the pope, person as the pope, shall be put out of the protection of our lord the king, and .... and ....

On behalf of the lords, prelates, clergy, justices and serjeants of the law.

79. To our lord the king and his council, his humble prelates and clergy of the kingdom of England pray: whereas two tenths were granted to our said lord the king by the said prelates and clergy from their benefices of holy church in the said kingdom, to be levied by the prelates, or their deputies. And also to our said lord the king were granted by the commons of the said kingdom, at the last parliament, two fifteenths from their goods and chattels, to be levied from them by commission of our said lord the king. Subsequently, the collectors and deputy collectors of the said fifteenths in the city of London, and elsewhere within the said kingdom, under the authority of the said commission, levied great sums of money, and took distraints from many of the aforesaid clergy contrary to their will, and contrary to the franchise of holy church and the form of the aforesaid grant and commission, as had never previously been done. Therefore the said prelates and clergy pray that a swift and adequate remedy be ordained for them in this present parliament, as a work of charity, and for the salvation of the liberties and franchises of the aforesaid holy church.

Answer.

Whereas the clerics are obliged and accustomed to paying tithes on their benefices, and on all their other spiritual possessions, to their prelates, or to collectors appointed for this by their prelates, in places where they hold their said benefices and spiritual possessions, and not by any means to laymen, nor are they so accustomed, nor ought any of the said clerics, or the lords of the realm, or the justices, serjeants of the law, or other laity who are not continually

continuelment resceantz en Londres, et es autres villes, si-noun come survenantz illoeqes, rienz paier pur lour hostielx, n'auxint pur lours livres, vessellementz, chivaux, n'autres lours biens et necessaires pur lour demoere esteantz en yceux lours hostielx. Ordenez est et assentuz en ce parlement qe tiele exaction ou demande ne soit desore fait des ditz clercs, ne des seignours ou autres laies gentz, par ceux de Londres, n'aillours parmy le roialme; et si rienz y soit pris par tiele action des clercs, seignours ou autres laies gentz avantditz, \[ent soit due et pleniere]/ restitution \[fait]/ a ceux dont les biens furent issint pris, ou a lour attournes, sanz nule difficultee. Et sur ceste ordinance, s'il busoigne, eient les empleignantz en especial, et autres, briefs et autres mandementz tantz et tieux come apartient, et embusoignera, nient-contreesteant aucune commission, ou autre garant, si nul y soit fait en contraire.
Page iii-49

Pur Jernemuth.
80. Item, prie la commune qe come grant clamour ad este \[de cheerte de harang a Jernemuth]/ en plusours parlementz devant ces heures; et a derrain parlement acorde feust par les seignours du parlement qe due inquisition serroit fait sur le dit clamour, coment le dit \[meschief purroit estre amende]/ pur commune profit de tout le roialme; par vertue de quelle commission pleine inquisition est faite.
Qe plese a nostre seignour le roi, vewe la dite inquisition, de faire \[due amendement pur profit]/ de tut le roialme.[25]

\[*Responsio.*]/
Est assentuz q'ils aient lours anciens franchises confirmez,

[Col. b] avec la franchise \[de]/ leur feire de harang deinz lour ville, et \[avec]/ la rode de Kirkeleye, par la manere et . . . . l'aiel les lour granta darrainement par sa chartre, ove la clause 'de licet,' \[sans fin ent]/ paier. \[Par issint,]/ toutes voies qe toutes maneres des gentz, sibien denizeins \[come aliens,]/ peussent franchement vendre et achatre harang deinz la dite ville durante leur feire, sanz empeschement queconqe. Et auxi franchement come . . . . illoeqes, nientcontreesteant le repelle nadgairs ent fait en parlement.

resident in London and in other towns, unless as visitors there, pay anything for their households, or their books, vessels, horses, or other possessions and necessities for their dwelling in those their households. It is ordained and agreed in this parliament that no such exaction or demand shall henceforth be made from the said clerics, or from the lords or other lay people, by those of London or elsewhere throughout the kingdom; and if anything be taken by such an action from the clerics, lords or other aforesaid lay people, full and proper restitution shall be made to those whose goods were thus taken, or to their attorneys, without any hindrance. And with regard to this ordinance, if it be necessary, let individual plaintiffs and others have writs and other mandates, as many and such as are appropriate and necessary, notwithstanding any commission or other warrant, if there be any, made to the contrary.

For Yarmouth.
80. Item, the commons pray: whereas, great complaint has been made in several parliaments in the past concerning the dearness of herrings at Yarmouth; and at the last parliament it was agreed by the lords of parliament that a proper inquest should be made on the said matter, as to how the said trouble might be amended for the common benefit of all the kingdom; by virtue of which commission a full inquest was held. May it please our lord the king, in the light of the results of the said inquest, to rectify the matter for the benefit of all the kingdom.
Answer.

It is agreed that they shall have their ancient franchises confirmed,

[Col. b] together with the franchise of their herring fair in their town, and with the roadstead of Kirkley [Roads], in the manner and   the grandfather previously granted them by his charter, with the clause 'de licet', without fine being paid. So that, in every way, all kinds of people, both denizens as well as aliens, might freely sell and buy herrings within the said town during their fair, without any impediment. And as freely as . . . . . there, notwithstanding the repeal thereof formerly made in parliament.

---
[25] See PRO SC8/264/13188.

The Parliament Rolls of Medieval England 1378 October

Appendix

20 October 1378

Gloucester

1. There survives in the National Archives (formerly the Public Record Office), an account of payments made to various royal messengers for delivering the writs of summons to this parliament. A total of twelve messengers were employed to deliver the writs. The same messengers were usually employed both to summon the lords and to deliver the writs to the sheriffs ordering them to hold elections for the parliament, although the final membrane of the document (m. 4) gives a separate list of messengers employed to take letters of privy seal to the sheriffs 'to return representatives for the aforesaid parliament of the king'. It is not clear why the sheriffs needed to receive two separate writs
    Source: PRO E 175/11/26.

2. Grant to John of Gaunt, duke of Lancaster, of the right to have for life an exchequer in his county palatine of Lancaster, with the same customs and usages as the king's exchequer, and the power to appoint justices of the forest and others, except in pleas where the crown is a party. By petition of the said duke in parliament. Dated 10 November 1378.
    Source: *CPR 1377-81*, 284.

3. Order to the proctors of the University of Oxford, following a petition from the regent master of the friars preachers in the university, to stop impeding the friars from being admitted to degrees in the university, etc. Dated 22 May 1379.
    Source: *CCR 1377-81*, 189.

4. Order to the king's justices to proceed in a suit between Richard de Weston, goldsmith of London, and Roese his wife, and Thomas de Farndon [or Farringdon], concerning seven shops and a garden in the suburb of the city, following a petition to this parliament from Richard and Roese. Dated 18 January 1379.
    Source: *CCR 1377-81*, 177.

5. Petition to the king and lords of parliament from Robert Hawley and John Shakell for compensation for the ransoms of two Flemish prisoners to the value of 1100 marks, of which they have been deprived by the king's officers; and petition from Robert Hawley for payment of 20 marks a year granted to him by Edward III for the capture of the castle of Hammes and other services performed by him in the march of Calais.
    Endorsed: The council considers that they should have a reasonable reward, when this can be done.
    Source: Printed in full in *RP*, III.50.
    [N. B. Since Hawley was killed in Westminster abbey in August 1378, this and the next petition must have been drawn up before the parliament and presumably submitted to it by Shakell alone.]

6. Petition to the king and lords of parliament from Robert Hawley and John Shakell that right be done to them concerning the son of the Count of Denia, hostage for his father's ransom, for which cause they have been imprisoned in the Tower of London.
    No endorsement
    Source: Printed in full in *RP*, III.50.

7. Petition to the knights, citizens, burgesses and commons from the abbot and convent of Westminster, following the killing in the abbey of Robert Hawley and a sergeant of the church while they sought sanctuary there, for a suitable remedy for this invasion of their liberties.

8. Petition to the king and council to clarify the terms of the privilege of sanctuary at Westminster abbey, to avoid misunderstandings of the sort that have occurred in the past.
    Endorsed: The privilege of sanctuary at Westminster has been much abused in the past. The king therefore asked various masters of theology and doctors of laws to examine it, and he now declares that it covers only cases of felony, although of his special grace he will also respect the privilege of sanctuary there in certain cases of debt.
    Source: Printed in full in *RP*, III.50-51.

9. Petition to the king and council from William Knyth, praying restitution in the case of a grant in mortmain of twenty-six shops and other lands in London to three chaplains in the churches of St John Zachary in London and St Andrew in Holborn.
    Endorsed: This bill is to be sent into chancery, where right will be done to the plaintiff.
    Source: Printed in full in *RP*, III.51-2.

10. Petition to the king and council in parliament from the merchants of the German Hansa for restoration and confirmation of the trading privileges granted to them by the charters of previous kings, so that harassment of them by the king's ministers might cease.
    Endorsed: It is agreed in parliament that their charter be confirmed, on condition that similar privileges are allowed to English merchants trading in Prussia, Denmark, Norway, etc.
    Source: Printed in full in *RP*, III.52.

11. Petition to the king and council from the prelates and clergy of England [As in Item 79 on the roll, with the same endorsement].
    Source: Printed in full in *RP*, III.52.

12. Petition to the king and council from the abbot and convent of Cockersand (Lancashire) for confirmation of charters relating to their endowment.
    Endorsed: Let the king be spoken to.
    Source: Printed in full in *RP*, III.52.

13. Petition to the king and council in parliament from Ralph de Arundel for restitution of the third part of the hundred of Penwith (Cornwall), which is currently in the king's hands.
    Endorsed: This bill is to be sent into the chancery, where right will be done to the plaintiff.
    Source: Printed in full in *RP*, III.52-3.

14. Petition to the king and peers of parliament that the wages of knights of the shire for Kent be paid in future by the commons of the county rather than from the knights' fees in the county.
    Endorsed: Let this be done as it has been done in the past.
    Source: Printed in full in *RP*, III.53.

15. Petition to the king from the bailiffs and citizens of Canterbury to be allowed to raise murage and other levies for a period of five years in order to repair the walls of the city.
    Endorsed: They can raise these sums for five years in aid of murage.
    Source: Printed in full in *RP*, III.53.

16. Petition to the king and lords of parliament from John Lord Nevill for compensation for hostages worth 4500 marks which he was obliged to deliver to the French because of the failure of the duke of Brittany to come to his aid during the time that he was keeper of the castle of 'Drist' [?Brest] by order of King Edward III.
    Endorsed: The agreement between the king and the duke of Brittany is to be inspected, and right will be done to the parties.
    Source: Printed in full in *RP*, III.53.

17. Petition to the king and council from John Blaunchard asking that a writ be sent to the clerk of the privy seal ordering him to proceed in determining Blaunchard's claims to a bailiwick in Groveley forest and lands in Bereford St Martin, for which he has already petitioned the king in the previous parliament.
    Endorsed: Let him have a letter of privy seal de procedendo, on condition that they do not proceed to judgment without consulting the king.
    [Schedule attached]
    Source: Printed in full in *RP*, III.53-4.

18. Petition to the council in this parliament from John Charnels for the recovery of three manors in Leicestershire and Warwickshire which are in the king's hands.
    Endorsed: Response has been made to the bill of the opponent's party, already submitted to parliament.
    Source: Printed in full in *RP*, III.54.

19. Petition to the king and council in parliament from Paul Odbek, merchant of Bruges, for compensation for his cargo of wine, shipwrecked and scattered by a storm on a voyage from Spain and Portugal to Bristol.
    Endorsed: This bill is to be sent into chancery, where right will be done to the plaintiff.
    Source: Printed in full in *RP*, III.54.

20. Power granted to the chancellor of the University of Cambridge, until the next parliament, to punish offenders against the assizes of bread, wine, ale and other victuals in the town, if the mayor and bailiffs are negligent in this matter. By petition in parliament. Dated 6 November 1378.
    Source: *CPR 1377-81*, 289.

1379 April

Westminster

24 April - 27 May

(C 65/34. *RP*, III.55-68. *SR*, II.12)

Richard II's third parliament was convened at Westminster in April 1379. Its business is recorded on C 65/34, a roll of eight membranes stitched together in chancery style, head to tail, and numbered in a later hand. The text, written by a number of chancery clerks, occupies only the recto, or face, of the membranes. The upper half of membrane 7 has been left blank. The dorse of the roll is blank except for some later notes written at the joins of membranes: 'Parl.2 R.2 apud Westm.', and on the dorse of membrane 1 (the last in the sequence of the text) 'Parliamentum de anno 2 R. secundi pars secunda'. There is a contemporaneous schedule stitched to the margin of membrane 4 which is in a hand different from that of the text on that membrane. Of the marginal headings some are original and others of later date; the arabic numerals are all later. The roll, which appears to be complete, is generally in good condition, though membrane 6 is stained with gallic acid.

Writs of summons were issued on 16 February 1379 to the archbishops of Canterbury and York, the bishop of London, and eighteen other diocesans.[1] The heads of houses summoned were the abbots of St Augustine's, Canterbury, and of St Albans, with twenty-one other abbots and the priors of Coventry and the hospital of St John. The peers summoned were the duke of Lancaster, the royal earls Edmund of Cambridge and Thomas of Buckingham, who was named as constable of England, and twelve other earls of whom John de Montfort, earl of Richmond, was also the duke of Brittany, and whose return to his duchy the ministers were urgently seeking to contrive. There were also forty-six other temporal lords, including three described as knights. The chief justice, John Cavendish, was summoned with eleven other justices and serjeants. At the end of the session writs *de expensis* were issued for, besides knights of the shire from every county, the representatives of eighteen boroughs, to whom can be added two members for the city and county of Bristol and four citizens of London.

The parliament began to assemble at Westminster on 25 April, but was twice adjourned to allow late-comers, one of whom was the king himself, to appear. The first session then began in the painted chamber of the palace on Wednesday 27 April. The chancellor Richard le Scrope's address on the purposes of the assembly, reported on the roll in direct speech, was eloquent of the government's embarrassments (Items 3-7). Scrope explained that after the sudden end of the parliament at Gloucester the numbers of the continual council had been made up in London. They were sworn in, and immediately set to work to resolve the problems that had defeated their predecessors. With the slender resources offered by the subsidy granted at Gloucester they found themselves unable to sustain the operations that were already in hand, and still less to propose any scheme for the defence of the realm. They accordingly decided to convene a great council after Christmas, which the prelates, tenants in chief, and professional advisers summoned declined to attend on the grounds that their late exertions at Gloucester had left them with pressing business of their own. The result was a more sharply worded order which brought the company together at the beginning of February. It was plain, however, when the ministers presented their agenda, that the needs were real, that there was nothing in the treasury, that effective funds could only be raised by a communal levy, and that the commons could only be taxed by a parliament. That was a remarkable admission, in an unusually frank and detailed account of the administrative process, born of desperation.

In the meantime, loans were raised from the peers themselves, from London, and from other towns, and secured by the king's jewels. The king's credit and the safety of the kingdom were both at stake, and the commons were left with no option but to come to their rescue. The roll bears no evidence of any serious demur by the commons, though there must have been at least some discussion, and even debate, before a graduated poll tax, ranging from ten marks for a duke to four pence for the generality, was agreed and the session concluded on 27 May. The king consented to waive the rest of the subsidy granted at Gloucester (Item 18), but a more powerful incentive was the concession of a searching review of the collection and disposal of the revenue and expenses of the household by a panel of bishops and peers appointed at the request of the commons, and enrolled with some emphasis (Item 12).

The judicial business of the session was confined to the earl of Salisbury's plea against the earl of March, which was once again postponed, and further consideration of the deepening dispute over the enfeoffment of lands for the

---

[1] *CCR 1377-81*, 235-6.

performance of Edward III's will.[2] The commons presented thirty petitions, among the more noteworthy of which were one which requested that all petitions in parliament should be granted the courtesy of a response before the dissolution (Item 28); another which obliged the justices of the peace to hold their sessions quarterly and gave them the power to force all able-bodied vagrants in their counties either to work or to face imprisonment (Item 48); and a third which ordered all goldsmiths henceforward to identify their work with individual hallmarks (Item 56). A further six petitions were submitted by the burgesses of Calais, while the final petition on the roll was from the chancellor and scholars of Cambridge; it appears to be something of an afterthought, and it is not clear whether it was adopted as a part of the 'common petition'.

The parliament was dissolved on 27 May,[3] and the collection of what one chronicler called 'a subsidy so extraordinary that its like had never been seen nor heard of before'[4] - that is, the second poll tax, began almost immediately. It provided only minimal relief from the government's financial embarrassment, however, and just over four months later, at the beginning of September, writs had to be issued for yet another parliament to meet in January 1380.

---

[2] C. Given-Wilson, 'Richard II and his Grandfather's Will', *EHR*, 93 (1978).
[3] *CCR 1377-81*, 252-3.
[4] *Anonimalle Chronicle 1333-1381*, 127.

Text and Translation

Text

Page iii-55

ROTULUS PARLIAMENTI TENTI APUD WESTM' IN .XV. PASCHE, ANNO REGNI REGIS RICARDI SECUNDI POST CONQUESTUM ANGLIE SECUNDO.

Pars II.

1. En la quinszeine de Pasqe, qe fuist le .xxv. jour du moys d'Avrille l'an dessuisdit, \et/ qe fuist le primer jour de cest parlement, s'assemblerent en /le\ palays du roi a Westm' monseignour d'Espaigne et aucuns des prelats et seignours du roialme, et illoeqes attenderent longement la venue de nostre seignour le roi et d'autres seignours, qi pur lors n'y estoient encores venuz. Et au darrein, en mesme le jour, pur ce qe aucuns des viscontz n'avoient encores retornez lour brief du parlement, et auxint, pur ce qe plusours prelats et autres grantz du roialme q'avoient \[la]/ sommonz du parlement, n'estoient unqores venuz, si estoit assentuz et comandez depar le roi qe mesme le parlement feust continuez tanqe al lendemain proschein venant, et \[ainsi]/ fuist fait; et de ce crie fust fait solempnement en la sale de Westm', donant en mandement a toux as queux il appartint q'ils retornassent le dit lendemain bien matin, pur y oier en presence de nostre seignour le roi la pronunciacion des causes de la somonce de ce present parlement.

2. Item, le maresdy proschein, pur ce qe les chivalers des countees, citezeins des citees, burgeis de burghes, q'avoient la dite somonce, appellez par le retourn ent fait par les viscontz, et grant partie de eux nient comparante, a cause qe encores n'estoient \ils/ venuz a la ville, a ce q'estoit tesmoignez illoeqes, et auxint partie de prelatz et seignours si fuist encores absent, si fuist mesme le parlement autrefoitz adjornez del comandement nostre seignour le roi tanqe al lendemain proschein par la dite cause. Et sur ce autre foitz fuist crie fait en appert qe touz retournassent par temps le dit lendemain, pur y oier la dite pronunciacioun en presence de nostre dit seignour le roi.

3. Au quiel lendemain, qe fuist le mesqardy, et le .xxvij. jour d'Avrille, vint en parlement mesme nostre seignour le roi, et bien pres touz les grantz, prelatz et seignours du roialme; et illoeqes en la chambre depeinte, appellez la einz les ditz chivalers, citezeins et burgeis, et autres qe avoient la dite somonce, monsire Richard le Scrope, chivaler, chancellor d'Engleterre, del comandement mesme nostre seignour le roi, y avoit les paroles, et dist:

4. Seigneurs et sires, nostre seignour le roi cy present, qi Dieu salve, moy ad comandez de vous dire et exposer le causes de la somonce de cest son parlement, qe sont tielles, c'estassavoir; primerement et principalement, al reverence de Dieu, nostre seignour le roi voet qe les libertees de seinte esglise, et les bones loys et custumes de son roialme soient entierment salvez et

[Col. b] gardez. Et si nully se vorra pleindre qe grief luy soit fait a l'encontre, dont remede ne purra estre purveuz sanz parlement, qe ce soit touchez en ce parlement, et due remede ent serra purveuz.

5. Et d'autre parte, notoire chose est, et conuz a la greindre partie de vous touz, coment sur le fyn et departement del darrein parlement tenuz a Gloucestr', nostre seignour le roi fist assigner aucuns prelatz et seignours pur estre de son continuel conseil pur l'an ensuant, selonc ce q'autrefoitz estoit assentuz. Mais pur le sodein departement d'ycelle parlement il n'y purroit assigner le nombre entier de ses dites continuelx conseillers, si fist il apres assigner le remenant des ditz

Translation

THE ROLL OF THE PARLIAMENT HELD AT WESTMINSTER ON THE QUINZAINE OF EASTER, IN THE SECOND YEAR OF THE REIGN OF KING RICHARD, THE SECOND SINCE THE CONQUEST OF ENGLAND.

Second part.

1. On the quinzaine of Easter, which was 25 April in the aforesaid year [1379] and the first day of the parliament, messire of Spain and some of the prelates and lords of the kingdom assembled in the king's palace at Westminster, and there they long awaited the arrival of our lord the king and other lords, who had not as yet arrived. And at last, on the same day, because some of the sheriffs had still not returned their writs of parliament, and also because many prelates and other great men of the kingdom who had received summons to parliament had still not arrived, it was agreed and ordered on behalf of the king that the parliament be adjourned until the next day, and so it was done; and a solemn announcement thereof was made in the hall of Westminster, in which orders were given to all concerned that they return early in the morning of the next day, there to hear in the presence of our lord the king the declaration of the reasons for summoning this present parliament.

2. Also, the following Tuesday [26 April], because a great number of the knights of the shires, citizens of the cities, and burgesses of the boroughs, who had received the said summons, being named in the return made by the said sheriffs, had not appeared, as they had not yet arrived in town, as it was reported, and also some of the prelates and lords still being absent, so the same parliament was for that reason again adjourned at the command of our lord the king until the following day. And thereupon, a further public announcement was made that everyone should return early the following day, to hear there the said declaration in the presence of our said lord the king.

3. The following day, which was Wednesday 27 April, there appeared in parliament our same lord the king, and almost all the great men, prelates and lords of the kingdom; and there in the Painted Chamber, the said knights, citizens and burgesses and others who had received the said summons having been called within first, it fell to Sir Richard le Scrope, knight, chancellor of England, to speak, by order of our same lord the king, and he said:

4. Lords and sirs, our lord the king here present, whom God preserve, has ordered me to speak and explain the reasons for the summoning of this his parliament, which are these, namely; first and foremost, out of reverence for love of God, our lord the king wishes that the liberties of holy church and the good laws and customs of his kingdom shall be wholly preserved and

[Col. b] kept. And if anyone wishes to complain that injury has been done him in contravention thereof, for which remedy cannot be provided without parliament, that it shall be dealt with in this parliament, and a proper remedy provided.

5. And for the other part, it is well known, and familiar to the great majority of you all, how at the end and dissolving of the last parliament held at Gloucester [20 October-16 November 1378], our lord the king caused certain prelates and lords to be appointed to his continual council for the following year, in accordance with what had been agreed. But because of the sudden dissolution of that same parliament it was not possible to appoint the full quota of the said

conseillers a Londres, et lour fist jurer de faire loialment lours /aides\ et diligences sur le bon governement des busoignes del roialme. Les queux conseillers tretantz des ditz busoignes, et eiantz devant lours oilx les grantz meschiefs et perils apparantz par les enemys qi nous sont environez toutz partz, et le temps et seisone de estee hastir, pur quelle seisone nulle ordinance estoit purveuz en dit parlement en salvacioun du roialme et resistence de tantz des enemys, n'oserent emprendre, a ce q'ils distrent, sur eux soul l'ordinance de si perilous et haut fait. Mais lour fuist advis pur le mieltz qe si tost come le feste de Nowelle feust passez, qe lors estoit tresprocheinement venant, si feust pur mesme la cause assemblez un grant conseil de touz les \[grantz]/ seignours du roialme, prelatz et autres, et par tant furent envoiez les ditz prelatz et seignours pur venir a Westm' a les oetaves de Seint Hiller lors proschein venant. A quiel temps, les prelatz et \[seignours soi]/ excuserent de lour venue; aucuns d'eulx disantz qe pur grandes et necessaires occupacions q'ils avoient affaire autre part, sibien c'estassavoir des busoignes du roialme come de lours propres busoignes, paront ils ne poient venir ne travailler al dit conseil, et meement si fresshement apres lour autre long travaille et long demoeure q'ils avoient fait al dit parlement de Gloucestre. Par quoy avoient \en/ comandement \autrefoitz/ de venir, toute excusacion cessante, le lundy proschein apres le Chandeleure proschein passe. Au quiel temps vindrent bien pres touz les prelatz, sibien abbes, come autres, ducs, contes, barons, banerettes et autres sages du roialme; et illoeqes exposez les grantz perils et meschiefs du roialme parmy les grandes guerres apparantz par terre et par meer, dont nulle ordinance estoit purveuz encontre la dite proschein seisone de estee; et enoultre declarre devant eulx touz par les officers et ministres du roi, et les tresoriers de la guerre, l'estat du roi et de roialme; et trovez par examinacion qe rienz en effect estoit \[remys]/ en la dite tresorie pur la guerre, estoit dit en mesme *[Page iii-56]*

[Col. a] le conseil pur conclusion final, q'ils ne poaient celle meschief remedier sanz charger la commune du roialme. Quelle charge ne poait estre fait ne grantez sanz parlement. Et par tant par assent de eulx touz, dont la greindre partie sont ycy ore presentz, estoit cest parlement sommonez, et par eulx assentuz qe en le moien temps fuist une suffisante armee ordenez a la meer, en defense et salvacion du dit roialme et de la navie et des costiers du meer, par manere come ce est ore apparaille. A quelles coustages touz les seignours illoeqes esteantz appresterent, voluntrifment a nostre seignour le roi diverses grandes sommes de deniers; et einsi firent les bones /gentz de Londres, et plousours\ autres villes et severals persones du roialme, as queux nostre seignour le roi par assent fait en dit grant conseil avoit envoiez par celle cause, et s'est par tant obligez a eux pur le repaiement d'ycelles sommes par seuretees, et ses fortz obligacions; et ses grantz joialx ad fait mettre en gage, pur chevance faire a la dite armee. Et issint est nostre seignour le roi grantement endettez.

6. Et par tant nostre seignour le roi vous prie, mes seignours les prelatz, et autres grantz seignours du roialme, qe vous par vous mesmes, et vous, mes seignours de sa bone commune, par vous mesmes, duement considerez les choses dessusdites, et nient merveillantz par tant qe cest parlement est si hastivement sommonez apres l'autre parlement si novellement tenuz a Glouc', veullez vous adviser diligeaument, coment, al meindre grevance, desaise et charge, de vous touz et de son bon poeple, l'oneur de nostre seignour le roi, les droitures de sa coroune et de son dit roialme et de ses autres

continual councillors, and so he caused the rest of the said councillors to be appointed in London, and made them swear loyally to perform their tasks and duties in managing the affairs of the realm. The councillors dealing with the said matters, and having before their eyes the great troubles and perils arising from the enemies who surrounded us on all sides, and considering the fast approaching time and season of summer, for which season no ordinance had been made in the said parliament for the security of the realm and for resisting such enemies, dared not, as they confessed, take upon themselves alone the ordinance of so perilous and important a matter. But they were advised for the best that as soon as Christmas had passed, which was then close upon them, a great council of all the great lords of the realm, prelates and others would be assembled for the same reason, and therefore the said prelates and lords were instructed to come to Westminster on the octave of St Hilary next following [21 January 1379]. At which time, the prelates and lords excused themselves from attending; some of them saying that because of important and urgent matters which they had to attend to elsewhere, namely both the business of the kingdom as well as their own affairs, they were not able to come to nor stay at the said council, and especially so soon after the long labour they they had undertaken at the said parliament of Gloucester. On account of which they were ordered to attend on another occasion, with no excuses accepted, on the Monday following the next Candlemas [7 February 1379]. On which date almost all the prelates, abbots as well as others, dukes, earls, barons, bannerets and other wise men of the kingdom appeared; and there they recounted the great perils and troubles of the kingdom arising from the great and manifest wars by land and by sea, for which no provision had been made in preparation for the said season of summer soon approaching; and further, there was laid before them by the king's officers and ministers, and the treasurers of the war, an account of the state of the king and kingdom; and after it was found upon examination that, in effect, nothing had been paid into the said treasury for the war, it was *[Page iii-56]* [Col. a] finally concluded by the same council that they could not remedy the situation without further burdening the commons of the kingdom. Which charge could not be made or granted without parliament. And for that reason, by the assent of them all, the majority of whom are here present at this time, this parliament was summoned, and it was agreed by them that in the meantime an adequate force would be ordained for the sea, for the defence and security of the said realm, the fleet and the sea coasts, in the manner which is now evident. Towards the costs of which all the lords there present voluntarily lent our lord the king various great sums of money; as did the good people of London, and many other towns and several persons of the realm, to whom our lord the king, with the consent of his great council had written for this reason, and he is for this reason obliged to repay them the same sums through sureties and firm bonds; and his great jewels have been placed in pledge to obtain money on loan for the said armed expedition. And so our lord the king is deeply in debt.

6. And therefore our lord the king asks of you, my lords the prelates and other great lords of the realm, that you, amongst yourselves, and you, my lords of his good commons, amongst yourselves, duly consider the aforesaid matters, and rather than marvelling that this parliament has been summoned with such haste so soon after the other parliament recently held at Gloucester, that you diligently discuss how, with the least harm, injury and burden being inflicted on you and his good people, the honour of our lord the king, the rights of his crown, of his said kingdom and of his other

inheritances, and of you all, may best be saved, and the said realm and you defended, to the great trouble and confusion of his enemies and yours; and how and by what means the said expeditions made, and other essential costs incurred and to be incurred daily in the said defence and security of the kingdom, and the other lands and lordships of our lord the king, and of you all, might with the greatest ease be funded.

7. And that you may be fully informed of the true extent of these said necessary expenses incurred and to be incurred, the treasurers of the said war shall be ready and equipped, whensoever you please, to show you clearly set out in writing their receipts and expenses since the said last parliament, and the sums due, together with the other necessary expenditure mentioned above to be assigned to the marches of Calais, as well as to Cherbourg, Brest, the marches of Scotland, Ireland and elsewhere. And our lord the king wills it that if anyone feels aggrieved by anything done him which is improper and contrary to the law, and which cannot be remedied without parliament, that he shall bring forward a petition thereon in parliament. And to receive, try and examine such bills, our said lord the king has caused certain prelates, lords, justices and clerks to be appointed, in the following form and manner; and he wills and commands that full justice be done and ordained in this parliament to all, both lesser and greater; and that this present parliament shall continue from one day to the next until the king our lord has given you his permission and licence to depart.

8. Receivers of petitions from England, Ireland, Wales and Scotland:

Sir William Borstal

Sir Richard Ravenser

Sir Thomas Newenham

Sir John Freton.

9. Receivers of petitions from Gascony, and other lands and countries overseas, and from the Channel Islands:

Master Walter Skirlawe

Sir Henry Codington

Sir Piers Barton

Sir John Bowland

Sir Thomas Thelwall.

And let those who wish to submit petitions, hand them in within the next eight days [5 May 1379].

10. The following are assigned to be triers of petitions from England, Ireland, Wales, and Scotland:

The king of Castile and Leon, duke of Lancaster

The archbishop of Canterbury

The bishop of London

The bishop of Winchester

The bishop of Ely

The bishop of Lincoln

The bishop of Salisbury

The abbot of Glastonbury

The abbot of St Augustine's, Canterbury

The earl of Cambridge

The earl of March

The earl of Arundel

The earl of Warwick

Le conte de Northumbr'	The earl of Northumberland
Le seignour de Latymer	Lord Latimer
Monsire Johan d'Arondell', mareschalle d'Engleterre	Sir John Arundel, marshal of England
Le seignour de Cobham	Lord Cobham
Monsire Roger Beauchamp	Sir Roger Beauchamp
Monsire Richard de Staff'	Sir Richard Stafford
Monsire Johan Knyvet	Sir John Knyvet
Monsire Johan Cavendissh'	Sir John Cavendish
Monsire Robert Bealknapp'	Sir Robert Bealknap
Monsire William Skipwyth'	Sir William Skipwith

- touz ensemble, ove .vi. des prelatz et seignours avantditz au meins: appellez a eux chanceller, tresorier, seneschal et chamberlein, et auxint les sergeantz nostre seigneur le roi quant il busoignera. Et tendront lour place en la chambre du chamberlein, pres de la chambre depeinte.

- to act all together, with at least six of the aforesaid prelates and lords: consulting with the chancellor, treasurer, steward and chamberlain, and also the serjeants of our lord the king when necessary. And they shall hold their session in the chamberlain's room, near the Painted Chamber.

Page iii-57

11. Et sont assignez triours des peticions de Gascoigne, et d'autres terres et paiis de dela la mier, et des Isles:

11. The following are assigned to be triers of petitions from Gascony, and other lands and countries overseas, and from the Channel Islands:

L'ercevesqe d'Everwyk	The archbishop of York
L'evesqe de Duresme	The bishop of Durham
L'evesqe de Nichole	The bishop of Lincoln
L'evesqe de Bathe et de Welles	The bishop of Bath and Wells
L'evesqe de Cicestre	The bishop of Chichester
L'evesqe de Hereford'	The bishop of Hereford
L'evesqe de Roucestre	The bishop of Rochester
L'evesqe de Seint Assaph'	The bishop of St Asaph
L'abbe de Westm'	The abbot of Westminster
L'abbe de Waltham	The abbot of Waltham
Le conte de Buk', conestable d'Engleterre	The earl of Buckingham, constable of England
Le duc de Bretaigne, conte de Richemond	The duke of Brittany, earl of Richmond
Le priour de Seint Johan Jerusalem en Engleterre	The prior of St John of Jerusalem in England
Le conte de Staff'	The earl of Stafford
Le conte de Suff'	The earl of Suffolk
Le seignour Lestrange de Knokyn	Lord Lestrange of Knockin
Le seignour de Bardolf	Lord Bardolf
Monsire Johan Montagu	Sir John Montagu
Monsire Robert Tresilian	Sir Robert Tresilian
Monsire Roger de Fulthorp'	Sir Roger of Fulthorp
Monsire Henry Asty	Sir Henry Asty

- touz ensemble, ou .vi. des prelatz et seignours avauntditz; appellez a eux chanceller, tresorier, seneschal, chamberlein et les sergeantz le roi quant il busoignera. Et tendront lour place en la chambre marcolf.

- to act all together, or at least six of the aforesaid prelates and lords; consulting with the chancellor, treasurer, steward, chamberlain and the king's serjeants when necessary. And they shall hold their session in the Marcolf Chamber.

Membrane 7[5]

Item, pur certaines enchesons des queux nostre seigneur le roi estoit moevez, il comandoit qe certaines cedules a lui baillez en parlement, contenantes diverses articles, feussent enroullez es roulles de /cest\ parlement, des queux cedules la tenour s'ensuit de mot a mot:

Also, for certain reasons which influenced our lord the king, he ordered that certain schedules submitted to him in parliament, containing various articles, should be enrolled in the rolls of this parliament, the texts of which schedules are given verbatim below:

12. Ces sont les nouns des prelatz et seignours assignez pur examiner l'estat du roi, a la requeste des communes; c'estassavoir, l'ercevesqe de Canterbirs, l'evesqe de Londres, l'evesqe de Roucestre, le conte de la Marche, le conte \de/ Warr', le conte de Staff', le seignour de Latymer,

12. These are the names of the prelates and lords appointed to examine the estate of the king, at the request of the commons; namely, the archbishop of Canterbury, the bishop of London, the bishop of Rochester, the earl of March, the earl of Warwick, the earl of Stafford, Lord Latimer, Sir Guy de

---
[5] The upper half of membrane 7 has been left blank.

monsire Guy de Brien, ou monsire Johan de Cobham et monsire Roger de Beauchamp'. Primerement, d'examiner les revenues provenantz del subside des leynes rescuz puis la feste de Seint Michel \darrein,/ et qe vraisemblablement ent sont a resceivre, tanqe al feste de Seint Michel proschein. Item, de veoir sibien touz les revenues du roialme resceuz depuis le dit temps, come les revenues des priours aliens, et del auncien maltolt des leynes, des voidances des evesqes, abbeis et des autres profitz quelconqes, et queux vraisemblablement ent purront estre resceuz et levez tanqe al dit feste de Seint Michel, sibien par les mains des tresorers de la guerre come en le resceite, et del hanaper de la chauncellerie, et es autres places nostre seignour le roi qeconqes. Item, d'examiner queles maneres de fees ou gaiges les grantz et petites officers du roi soloient prendre en le primer temps le roi Edward l'aiel nostre seignour qi ore est. Item, d'examiner queux annuites grantez par \nostre seignour/ le roi le dit aiel, et par monsire le prince, queux Dieux assoille, sont paiez. Item, de surveer les moebles del roi l'aiel, c'estassavoir ou elles soient devenuz, et en queux mains; et queux persones sont paiez en descharge de l'alme le dit aiel; et quelle parcelle ent demoert al oeps nostre seignour le roi; et ou le remenant est devenuz. Et qe ceux qi ent ont distribucioun soient tenuz de les monstrer as ditz seignours, et s'ils sont venuz al profit du roi en descharge de son poeple, ou noun. Item, de veer et examiner la somme de les expenses del hostiel nostre seignour le roi, appellantz devant eux les officers

[Col. b] del avantdit hostiel, pur mieltz estre aformez. Item, des gardes, mariages, forfaitures et eschetes. Item, des revenues de Caleys et des autres chastelx et forcelettes, et autres revenues de la guerre par meer et par terre. Item, des revenues de Burdeux, c'estassavoir de vin et del billion et des autres tieux profitz. Item, del subside des draps, c'estassavoir le drape ove le seal .xviij. d. Item, des profitz des possessions des cardinalx rebealx. Item, de veer qe ceux q'ont pris gaiges pur la guerre soient fait d'acompter et respondre de ce qe remeint en lours mains. Item, de les deniers appellez Rome-penies, q'amont a grande somme, et de les arrerages des plusours ans. Et fait a remembrer qe les ditz seignours assignez ont comaundement du roi mesmes en parlement, d'entrer, c'est assavoir touz ensemble, ou trois de eux al meins, des queux serront de chescun degree un, es lieux et places le roi necessaires a ceste affaire, avec les officers ou gardeins d'ycelles, et de y sercher ensemble avec les ditz officers les roulles, accomptes, et autres choses quelconqes qe touchent ceste matire, et de faire et accomplir quanqe dessus est dit, et de reporter distinctement a nostre dit seignour le roi et a son conseil quanqe ils \ent/ averont fait ou trovez, avec lour bone advis en celle partie. Et nostre seignour le roi voet et comande as touz ses officers et ministres des dites places q'ils monstrent as ditz seignours assignez, ou trois de eux, les roulles, accomptes, tailles et autres evidences quelconqes touchantz ceste matire, et lour ent soient entendantz en la fourme avantdite, tant et si sovent q'ils soient requiz par les ditz seignours ou nul de eux.

13. Item, les seignours et communes du roialme \d'Engleterre/ esteantz a ceste parlement granterent pur eux et pur tout la commune d'Engleterre le subside des leynes, quirs et peaux lanutz; et un autre subside a prendre des biens des certaines persones parmy le roialme, souz certeines fourme et manere comprisez en une cedule ent faite et baillee avant en parlement, dont le tenour s'ensuit de mot a mot:

Brienne or Sir John Cobham, and Sir Roger Beauchamp. Firstly, to examine the revenues arising from the subsidy on wool received since Michaelmas last [29 September 1378], and those which are likely to be received, up to Michaelmas next [29 September 1379]. Also, to inspect all the revenues of the kingdom received since the said time, as well as the revenues of alien priors, and from the ancient levy on wool, from vacancies of bishoprics, abbacies and other profits whatsoever, and which will probably be received and levied from them until the said Michaelmas, both by the treasurers of war as well as in the office of receipt, and the chancellor's coffers, and in any other places of our lord the king whatsoever. Also, to examine what manner of fees or wages the great and petty officers of the king were accustomed to take in the time of King Edward, grandfather of our lord the present king. Also, to examine what annuities granted by our lord the king the said grandfather, and by our lord the prince, whom God absolve, have been paid. Also, to make an inventory of the chattels of the king the grandfather, namely where they are to be found, and in whose hands; and which persons were paid for the relief of the said grandfather's soul; and what part of them remains for the use of our lord the king; and where that remainder is to be found. And that those who have the disbursement of them shall be obliged to show them to the said lords, and whether they have resulted in profit to the king in relief of his people, or not. Also, to inspect and examine the whole expenses of the household of our lord the king, having the officers

[Col. b] of the aforesaid household called to appear before them, to be the better informed. Also, of wardships, marriages, forfeitures and escheats. Also, of the revenues of Calais, and of other castles and strong places, and other revenues of the war by land and sea. Also, of the revenues of Bordeaux, namely of wine and of bullion and other such profits. Also, of the subsidy on cloth, namely the cloth with the 18*d.* seal. Also, of the profits from the possessions of the rebel cardinals. Also, to see that those who have taken wages for the war shall make account and answer for what remains in their hands. Also, of the payment called Rome-pennies, which amounts to a great sum, and the arrears of many years. And be it remembered that the said lords appointed have been ordered by the king himself in parliament to enter, all together - or at least three of them, of whom there shall be one of each degree - into the places or properties of the king required for their purpose, with the officers or wardens of the same, to search there together with the said officers for the rolls, accounts and any other things which touch thereon, and to carry out and accomplish it as mentioned above, and to make a clear report to our said lord the king and his council on whatsoever they have done or found, and give their considered advice on the matter. And our lord the king wills and commands all his officers and ministers of the said places that they shall show the said appointed lords, or three of them, the rolls, accounts, tallies and any other relevant pieces of evidence, and they shall attend to this in such a way and as often as they shall be required by the said lords or any of them.

13. Also, the lords and commons of the kingdom of England present at this parliament grant on behalf of themselves and on behalf of all the commons of England the subsidy on wool, hides and woolfells; and another subsidy to be taken from the goods of certain persons throughout the kingdom, under certain conditions set out in a schedule made thereon and submitted in parliament, the text of which follows verbatim:

Les seignours et communes du roialme d'Engleterre considerantz les grandes necessitees du dit roialme, et la malice des enemys de France et aillours, entendantz grant recoverer au dit roialme, et destruccioun des ditz enemys, qe poent avenir par la grace de Dieu, si suffisantie des gentz d'armes et des archiers en brief soit envoie outre la meer sur les ditz enemys, pur eux grever et lour malice aresteer, selonc la sage discrecion nostre tresredoute seignour le roi et les seignours esteantz a cest present parlement, en lieu ou leur semblera pluis necessaire et profitable, en esploit de nostre seignour le roi et de son dit roialme, grantent qe si la marke du saak des leynes, et les sys deniers de la livre, qe furent grantez au darrein parlement tenuz a Gloucestre, soient pardonez et adnullez a present, la subside des leynes a durer par un an entier apres la feste de Seint Michel proschein avenir, c'estassavoir, \de/ chescun saak tant come estoit grantez devant le dit parlement de Gloucestre et une somme d'argent a lever des diverses persones du roialme, en manere come ensuit, sibien dedeinz franchises realx come dehors; c'estassavoir,

The lords and commons of the kingdom of England - considering the great needs of the said kingdom, and the malice of the enemies of France and elsewhere, and seeking full recovery of the said kingdom and the destruction of the said enemies, which could come about by God's grace, if sufficient numbers of men-at-arms and archers were swiftly sent overseas to oppose the said enemies to grieve them and end their malice, in accordance with the wise discretion of our most redoubtable lord the king and the lords attending this present parliament, wheresoever shall seem to them most necessary and profitable, to discharge the business of our lord the king and his said kingdom - do grant that if the mark on the sack of wool, and the six pence in the pound, which were granted at the first parliament held at Gloucester, are pardoned and annulled for the moment, the subsidy on wool shall last for one whole year after Michaelmas next [29 September 1379], namely, there being paid on each sack as much as was granted before the said parliament of Gloucester, and also a sum of silver shall be levied from various persons of the kingdom, in the manner which follows, both within royal franchises as well as outside them; namely:

Membrane 6

14. Le duc de Lancastre et le duc de Bretaigne, chescun a	.x. marcz
Item, chescun conte d'Engleterre	.iiij.li.
Item, chescun des countesses veoves en Engleterre, atant come les conts	.iiij.li.
Item, chescun baron et baneret, ou chivaler qi poet atant despendre	.xl. s.
Item, chescun baronesse veove paiera come le baron, et banresse come le baneret	.xl. s.
Item, chescun \bacheler,/ et chescun esquier /qi\ par l'estatut devroit estre chivaler	.xx. s.
Item, chescune veove dame, femme de bachiler ou esquier, al afferant	.xx. s.
Item, chescun esquier de meindre estat	.vi. s. .viij. d.
Item, chescune femme veove de tiel esquier ou marchant suffisant	.vi. s. .viij. d.
Item, chescun esquier nient possessionez des terres, rent ne chateux, q'est en service ou ad este armez	.iij. s. .iiij. d.
Item, le chief priour del hospital de Seint Johan, come un baron	.xl. s.
Item, chescun comandour de cel ordre d'Engleterre, come un bachiler	.xx. s.
Item, chescun autre frere chivaler du dit ordre	.xiij. s. .iiij. d.
Item, des touz les autres freres du dit ordre, chescun come esquier nient possessione	.iij. s. .iiij. d.
15. Item, chescun justice, sibien de l'un bank come de l'autre, et ceux q'ont este justices de mesmes les bankes, et le chief baroun de l'escheqier, chescun	.c.s.
Item, chescun sergeant et grant apprentice du loy	.xl. s.
Item, autres apprentices qi pursuent la loy, /chescun\	.xx. s.
Item, touz les autres apprentices de meindre estat et attournez, chescun	.vi. s. .viij. d.

14. The duke of Lancaster, and the duke of Brittany, each at	10 marks
Also, every earl of England	£4
Also, every widowed countess in England, as much as the earls	£4
Also, every baron and banneret, or knight who is able to spend so much	40s.
Also, every widowed baroness, as much as a baron, and a banneress as much as a banneret	40s.
Also, every gentleman, and every squire who ought, by statute, to be a knight	20s.
Also, every widowed lady, wife of a gentleman or a squire, by assessment	20s.
Also, every squire of lesser estate	6s. 8d.
Also, every widowed wife of such a squire or of a sufficient merchant	6s. 8d.
Also, every squire not in possession of lands, rents or chattels, who is in service or has borne arms	3s. 4d.
Also, the chief prior of the Hospital of St John, as much as a baron	40s.
Also, every commander of the order in England, the same as a bachelor	20s.
Also, every other brother knight of the said order	13s. 4d.
Also, from all the other brothers of the said order, each as much as a squire without possessions	3s. 4d.
15. Also, every justice of either bench, and those who have been justices of the same benches, and the chief baron of the exchequer, each	100s.
Also, every serjeant and great apprentice of the law	40s.
Also, other apprentices who practise the law, each	20s.
Also, all other apprentices of lesser estate and attorneys, each	6s. 8d.

16. Item, le meir de Londres paie come un conte	.iiij.li.
Item, les aldermen de Londres, chescun come un baroun	.xl. s.
Item, touz les meirs de les grandes villes d'Engleterre, chescun come un baroun	.xl. s.
Item, les autres meirs des autres petites villes, selonc l'afferant de lour estat	.xx. s., .x. s. ou demi marc
Et touz les jurates des bones villes et grantz marchantz du roialme, paient come bachilers	.xx. s.
Item, autres marchantz suffisantz	.xiij. s. .iiij. d.
Item, touz les meindres marchantz et artificers q'ont la gaigne de la terre, selonc l'afferant de lour estat	.vi. s. .viij. d., .iij. s. .iiij. d. ij s. .xij. d., ou .vi.
Item, chescun sergeant et frankelein du paiis, selonc lour estat	.vi. s. .viij. d. ou .xl. d.
Item, les fermers des manoirs, parsonages et granges, marchantz des bestes et d'autre mesnue marchandie, selonc lour estat	demi marc, .xl. d., .ij. s. ou .xij. d.
17. Item, touz les advocatz, notairs et procuratours mariez, paient come sergeantz de loy; apprentices du loy et attournez, chescun selonc son estat	.xl. s. .xx. s. ou demi marc
Item, pardoners et sommoners mariez, chescun selonc son estat,	.iij. s. .iiij. d., .ij. s. ou .xij. d.
Item, touz les ostilers qi ne sont mye al estat de marchant, chescun selonc son estat	.xl. d., .ij. s. ou .xij. d.
Item, chescun homme mariee, pur lui et sa femme qi ne sont mye des estatz suisnomez, outre l'age de .xvi. ans, forspris verroies mendinantz	.iiij. d.
Et chescun homme et femme soles de tiel estat et oultre l'age suisdite	.iiij. d.

16. Also, the mayor of London is to pay as much as an earl	£4
Also, the aldermen of London, each as much as a baron	40s.
Also, all the mayors of the great towns of England, each as much as a baron	40s.
Also, the other mayors of the remaining small towns, according to the extent of their estate	20s., 10s. or half a mark
And all the jurats of large towns, and the great merchants of the kingdom, are to pay as much as gentlemen	20s.
Also, other sufficient merchants,	13s. 4d.
Also, all lesser merchants and artificers who have profit from the land, according to the extent of their estate	6s. 8d., 3s. 4d., 2s. 12d., or 6
Also, every serjeant and franklin of the country, according to their estate	6s. 8d. or 40d.
Also, the farmers of manors, parsonages and granges, merchants dealing in livestock, and other lesser merchandise, according to their estate,	half a mark, 40d. 2s. or 12d.
17. Also, all advocates, notaries and proctors who are married are to pay as much as serjeants at law, apprentices of the law and attorneys, each according to his estate,	40s. 20s. or half a mark
Also, pardoners and summoners who are married, each according to his estate	3s. 4d., 2s. or 12d.
Also, all innkeepers who do not belong to the estate of merchants, each according to his estate	40d. 2s. or 12d.
Also, every married man, for himself and his wife, if they do not belong to the estates named above and are over the age of 16, except genuine beggars	4d.
And every single man and woman of such estate and over the said age	4d.

Item, chescun marchant estrange, de quelle condicion q'il soit, paie a son afferant come autres denzeins.
Et qe toutes les paiementz suisnomez ne soient levez de nule persone mais en lieu ou il est demurrant, et nul part ailleurs.

Et fait a remembrer qe les sommes suisnomez queux ne sont pas mises en certain, soient assis par la discrecion des assessours et contoullours a ce ordenez.
Et qe les coillours de le subside suisdit eiont jours de lour paiement, a la feste de Seint Johan Baptistre proschein avenir, et la feste de Seint Pere ad Vincula delors proschein ensuant.
18. Et est assavoir qe nostre seignour le roi esteant mesmes en parlement le .xxvij. jour de Maii, l'an present, del assent des prelatz, ducs, conts, barons et autres grantz de son roialme, a la priere de sa dite commune fist relesser mesme le jour, sibien les .vi. d. grantez en dit parlement de Gloucestre, a prendre des marchandises a passers pardehors, et a amesners deinz le roialme d'Engleterre, come le novel subside de .xiij. s. .iiij. d. grante en mesme le parlement de Gloucestre, a prendre de chescun saak de leyne, et de .xiij. s. .iiij. d. de touz les .ccxl. peaux lanutz, et .ij. marcz de chescun last de quirs a passers hors de mesme le roialme: veulliant et grantant qe del dit .xxvij. jour de May, la demande et paiement des ditz subsides cessent, et de tout soient oustez.
Purveuz toutes voies qe les subsides et custumes des ditz

Also, every foreign merchant, of whatsoever status he be, to pay according to their estate like denizens.
And that all the aforenamed payments shall be levied from people only in the place where they are resident, and nowhere else.
And be it remembered that those of the sums named above which are not fixed shall be assessed at the discretion of the assessors and controllers thereto appointed.
And that the collectors of the aforesaid subsidy shall have days for their payment at the feast of St John the Baptist next to come [24 June 1379], and at the feast of St Peter ad vincula then next following [1 August 1379].
18. And be it known that our lord the king, being himself in parliament on 27 May in the present year, with the assent of the prelates, dukes, earls, barons and other great men of his kingdom, at the prayer of his said commons caused to be remitted on the same day, both the 6d. granted in the said parliament of Gloucester, to be taken from merchandise exported and imported into the kingdom of England, as well as the new subsidy of 13s. 4d. granted in the same parliament of Gloucester, to be levied on each sack of wool, and 13s. 4d. on every 240 woolfells, and 2 marks on every last of hides to be exported from the same kingdom: willing and granting that on the said 27 May the demand and payment of the said subsidies should cease, and be entirely set aside.
Provided always that the subsidies and customs on the said

leynes, quirs et peaux lanutz grantez et duez a nostre seignour le roi devant le dit parlement de Glouc', estoisent en lour force, et soient coillez et levez par fourme des commissions sur ce faitz devaunt mesme le parlement as custumers nostre seignour le roi parmy le roialme.

/Pro comite Sar'.\
19. Item, est assavoir q'il y a un certa in enroullement enroullez es roulles du darrein parlement tenuz a Gloucestre, en la fourme qe s'ensuit:
Page iii-59
Item, fait a remembrer qe sur la demande qe William de Montagu, cont de Salesbirs, fait d'avoir les terres de Dynbegh' en Gales, il y a un enroullement entrez es les roulles du parlement tenuz a Westm' a la .xv.^{e} de Seint Michel, l'an du regne nostre seignour le roi q'orest primer, en la fourme qe s'ensuit:^{6} Item, William de Montagu, conte de Salesbirs, mist avant en parlement une sa petition, en la forme qe s'ensuit;

A nostre seignour le roi monstre son lige William de Montagu, conte de Salesbirs, come mon tresredoute seignour le roi vostre aiel, qi Dieu assoille, dona et granta a mon pier William de Montagu, nadgaires conte de Salesbirs, et a ses heirs de son corps issantz, ove clause de garantie, le chastiel, ville et honeur de Dynbeygh', et les cantredes de Roos, Roweynok et Kaiemer, et la commot de Dynmael, ove les appurtenantz en Gales, salvant ent la reversion a lui et a ses heirs, come pluis pleinement piert par ses chartres a mon dit pier ent faites. Les queux chastiel, ville et honour, cantredes et commot, ove les appurtenantz, Roger de Mortimer, pere Esmon conte q'orest, come cousin et heir Roger de Mortymer, nadgairs conte de la Marche, demanda devers moi, par noun de la terre de Dynbeygh' ove les appurtenantz en Gales, par brief de scire facias devant mon dit seignour le roi vostre aiel, en sa courte en bank le roi, de ent avoir execucioun. En quiel plee je pria aide de mon dit seignour le roi, vostre aielle, par la cause avauntdite. Et apres brief de procedendo sur ce grantez, le dit Roger, le pere Esmon, recoveri devers moi par juggement les ditz chastiel, ville, honeur, cantredes et commot, ove les appurtenances, par noun de la terre de Dynbeigh' ove les appurtenances en Gales; come en le record et proces sur ce faitz pleinement appiert. En quelles record et proces, et auxint en juggement sur ce renduz, il y ad errour; et le quelle jugement estoit execut, et moi ouste de ma possession, l'an de son regne .xxviij.^{me}, dont je n'avoie unqes rien en value, coment qe mon dit seignour le roi vostre aiel par sa chartre avoit grante a ce faire, come dessuis est dit. Puis quiel perte, j'ai sui de parlement en parlement par diverses peticions de ent avoir remedie, et entre autres au parlement tenuz a Westm' le .viij.^{me} jour de Novembre, l'an de son regne .xlvime une ma peticion sur ceste matire estoit endosse en ceux paroles,^{7} Le roi ne voet mie qe l'eir q'est deinz age et en sa garde ne perde rienz pur le temps q'il est en sa garde; mais quant il vient a son pleine age, sue, et droit serra faite al une partie et al autre; et ore le dit heir, c'estassavoir Esmon de Mortymer ore conte de la Marche, fitz et heir mesme celui Roger le cousin, est avenuz a son pleine age.

Qe plese a vostre tresgraciouse seignourie comander, de faire venir le dit record et proces devant vous et vostre tressage conseil en ceste present parlement; et appellez le dit Esmon et ceux qi sont en celles parties a appellers, et veuez et examinez les dites record et proces, de moi ordeiner ent

---
^{6}See PRO C49/9/6-7.
^{7}PRO SC8/267/13330.

wool, hides and woolfells granted and owed to our lord the king before the said parliament of Gloucester shall remain in force, and be collected and levied by means of commissions directed before the same parliament to customs officers of our lord the king throughout the kingdom.

On behalf of the earl of Salisbury.
19. Also, be it known that a certain enrolment, enrolled in the rolls of the last parliament held at Gloucester [1378], reads as follows:

Also, be it remembered that upon the request made by William Montagu, earl of Salisbury, that he receive the lands of Denbigh in Wales, an enrolment was made in the rolls of the parliament held at Westminster on the quinzaine of Michaelmas, in the first year of the reign of our lord the present king, in the following form: Item, William Montagu, earl of Salisbury, submitted in parliament a petition in the following form:

To our lord the king, his liege William Montagu shows that whereas our most redoubtable lord king, your grandfather, whom God absolve, gave and granted to my father William Montagu, late earl of Salisbury, and to the heirs of his body, with a clause of warranty, the castle, town and honour of Denbigh, and the cantreds of Rhos, Rhufiniog and Cymeirch, and the commote of Dinmael, with their appurtenances in Wales, saving the reversion of them to him and his heirs, as appears fully in the charters thereon granted to my said father. Which castle, town and honour, cantreds and commote, with their appurtenances, Roger Mortimer, father of Edmund the present earl, as cousin and heir of Roger Mortimer, late earl of March, demanded from me, by the name of the land of Denbigh with its appurtenances in Wales, by writ of scire facias before my said lord king your grandfather, in his court of King's Bench, thereof to have execution. In which plea I sought the aid of my said lord the king, your grandfather, in the aforesaid matter. And after a writ of procedendo had been granted thereon, the said Roger, the father of Edmund, recovered from me by judgment the said castle, town, honour, cantreds and commote, with their appurtenances, by the name of the land of Denbigh with its appurtenances in Wales; as appears fully in the record and process made thereon. In which record and process, and also in the judgment rendered thereon, there is error; and the judgment was executed, and I ousted from my possession, in the twenty-eighth year of his reign, of which I have nothing left of value, even though my said lord the king your grandfather by his charter granted to do so, as said above. Since which loss, I have sued from parliament to parliament by various petitions to obtain a remedy, and amongst other petitions at the parliament held at Westminster on 8 November, in the forty-sixth year of his reign [1372] one of my petitions hereon was endorsed with these words, The king does indeed not wish that the heir who is under age and under his protection should lose anything for the time when he is in his wardship; but when he comes of age, let him sue and right shall be done to either party; and now the said heir, namely Edmund Mortimer who is now earl of March, son and heir of the same Roger the cousin, has come of age.

May it please your most gracious lordship to order that the said record and process be brought before you and your most wise council in this present parliament; and having called the said Edmund and those who ought to be called as parties to the suit, and having inspected and examined the said record

remedie, selonc droit et resoun. Et si errour y puisse estre trovez qe le dit jugement soit reversez et adnulliz, et moi restitut a ma possession ove les issues d'ycelle, come la loy demande.

Quelle peticion lue en mesme le parlement et entendue, dit feust et comandez en cest parlement, par les prelatz et seignours pierres du /parlement\ lors esteantz en mesme le parlement, a monsire Johan Cavendissh', chivaler, chief justice nostre seignour le roi, q'ad les record et proces dont la dite peticion fait mencion en garde, q'il ferroit venir mesmes les record et proces en cest parlement sanz delaie. Luiquiel monsire Johan apporta en dit parlement mesmes les record et proces, entre diverses autres recordz et proces comprises en certains roulles tachez ou consutz ensemble. Et sur ce, le dit conte de Salesbirs assigna en parlement par especial et par bouche diverses errours estre contenuz en ycelle record et proces, empriant qe par celles errours, et par autres quelles en ycelle record et proces purront estre trovez, le jugement y renduz soit reversez; et qe le dit

[Col. b] Esmon de Mortymer, filz et heir le dit Roger \le/ cousin, ore conte de la Marche, y fuist \[garniz]/ par brief de scire facias d'estre a proschein parlement d'oier les ditz record et proces, et de faire et resceivre ce q'adonqes en celle partie serra agardez. Et cel brief lui estoit grantez illoeqes, et comandez estre fait retornable en dit proschein parlement. Et puis apres sur le fin du dit parlement, le dit monsire Johan Cavendissh', par comandement des prelatz et seignours du parlement ent a lui fait, portast mesmes les record et proces en le bank le roi, pur y demurrer come en garde tanqe au dit proschein parlement. Et est ordeinez et acordez qe mesmes les record et proces soient en dit proschein parlement par la cause avauntdite. A quele proschein parlement, c'estassavoir en cest present parlement tenuz a Gloucestre le mesqardy proschein apres la feste de Seint Luk l'Ewangelist, vient le dit \[conte]/ de Salesbirs en sa persone devaunt nostre seignour le roi, en presence des prelatz, pierres et autres seignours du parlement, le dit monsire Johan de Cavendissh q'ad mesmes les record et proces dont la dite peticion fait mencion en garde illoeqes present, et monsire Brian de Cornewaille, viscont de Shropshire, retourna en cest parlement le dit brief de scire facias issint fait et grante au darrein parlement; dont sibien del dit brief come del retourn ent fait par le dit viscont, le tenour s'ensuit de mot en mot:

Ricardus, Dei gratia, rex Anglie, et Francie, et dominus Hibernie, vicecomiti Salop', salutem. Cum Rogerus de Mortuo Mari, filius Edmundi de Mortuo Mari nuper comes Marchie, ut consanguineus et heres Rogeri de Mortuo Mari nuper comitis Marchie, avi sui, in curia domini Edwardi nuper regis Anglie, avi nostri, coram eodem avo nostro, termino Trinitatis, anno regni sui Anglie vicesimo octavo, per breve ipsius avi /nostri,\ ac consideracionem ejusdem curie, recuperaverit versus Willielmum de Monte Acuto, comitem Sarum, terram de Dynbeigh' cum pertinentiis in Wallie; idemque comes Sarum per peticionem suam nobis in presenti parliamento nostro exhibitam nobis supplicaverit. Ut cum diversi errores in recordo et processu ac reddicione judicii loquele predicte intervenissent, ad grave dampnum ipsius comitis Sarum, vellemus recordum et processum inde habita coram nobis et consilio nostro in dicto parliamento nostro venire, eademque recordum et processum ibidem examinari, ac errores inde repertos corrigi jubere: nos supplicacioni predicti comitis Sarum in hac parte annuentes, recordum et processum predicta coram nobis ac prelatis et magnatibus in dicto parliamento ea de causa venire fecimus, ac insuper errores illos, si qui fuerint, modo debito corrigi, et

and process, to ordain remedy for me, according to right and reason. And if error be found therein, that the said judgment shall be reversed and annulled, and myself restored to my possession along with the issues from the same, as the law demands.

Which petition having been read and heard in the same parliament, the prelates and lord peers attending the same parliament ordered Sir John Cavendish, knight, chief justice of our lord the king, who had the record and process of which the said petition made mention in his keeping, to cause the same record and process to be brought before this parliament without delay. Which Sir John brought the same record and process to the said parliament, along with various other records and processes contained in certain rolls attached or stitched together. And thereupon, the said earl of Salisbury spoke in parliament of particular errors contained in the same record and process, praying that on account of those errors, and because of others which might be found in the same record and process, the judgment passed be reversed; and that the said

[Col. b] Edmund Mortimer, son and heir of the said Roger the cousin, now earl of March, be summoned by writ of scire facias to be at the next parliament to hear the said record and process, and to do and receive whatsoever would then be decided on the matter. And the writ was thereupon granted to him there, and was deemed returnable in the said next parliament. And later, at the close of the said parliament, the said Sir John Cavendish, at the command of the prelates and lords of parliament, brought the same record and process to the King's Bench, for it to remain there in safe-keeping until the said next parliament. And it was ordained and agreed that the same record and process should be available in the said next parliament for the aforesaid reason. At which parliament, namely in this present parliament held at Gloucester on the Wednesday next after the feast of St Luke the Evangelist [20 October 1378], the said earl of Salisbury appeared in person before our lord the king, in the presence of the prelates, peers and other lords of parliament, and the said Sir John Cavendish who had the same record and process of which the said petition made mention in his keep, and Sir Brian Cornwall, sheriff of Shropshire, returned in this parliament the said writ of scire facias thus issued and granted at the last parliament; the texts of which writ and return thereof uttered by the said sheriff, are given verbatim here:

Richard, by the grace of God, king of England and France, and lord of Ireland, to the sheriff of Shropshire, greeting. Whereas Roger Mortimer, son of Edmund Mortimer late earl of March, as cousin and heir of Roger Mortimer late earl of March, his grandfather, in the court of the lord Edward late king of England, our grandfather, in the presence of our same grandfather, in Trinity term in the twenty-eighth year of his reign over England [1354], by a writ of our same grandfather, and judgment of the same court, recovered from William Montagu, earl of Salisbury, the land of Denbigh with appurtenances in Wales; and the same earl of Salisbury petitioned us through a petition shown to us in our present parliament that since various errors were to be found in the record and process and in the judgment passed in this case, to the grave injury of the earl of Salisbury, we might order the said record and process to be brought before us and our council in our said parliament, and the same record and process to be examined there, and order the errors found in it to be corrected: we, granting the request of the aforesaid earl of Salisbury in the matter, caused the aforesaid record and process of the cause to be brought before us and the prelates and magnates in the said parliament, and errors subsequently

ulterius inde fieri volentes quod est justum, tibi precipimus quod per probos et legales homines de comitatu tuo scire facias Edmundo de Mortuo Mari, nunc comiti Marchie, filio et heredi prefati Rogeri filii Edmundi, quod sit coram nobis in proximo parliamento nostro ubicumque tunc fuerit, auditurus recordum et processum predicta, si sibi viderit expedire, ulteriusqe facturus et recepturus quod considerari contigerit tunc ibidem. Et habeas ibi nomina illorum per quos ei scire feceris, et hoc breve. Teste meipso apud Westm' primo die Decembris, anno regni nostri primo.[8]

Responcio Briani de Cornewaille/vicecomiti:\ Edmundus de Mortuo Mari nunc comes Marchie, filius et heres Rogeri de Mortuo Mari filius Edmundi de Mortuo Mari nuper comitis Marchie, non est inventus in balliva mea postquam istud breve michi liberatum fuit, nec aliqua habet terras seu tenementa in eadem ubi premuniri potest.

Et sur ce le dit cont de Salesbirs en ce parlement pria nostre seignour le roi qe luy pleust a luy granter un autre brief de scire facias, pur garnir le dit Esmon ore conte de la Marche, filz et heir le dit Roger filz Esmon, a la dite terre de Dynbeigh', d'estre devaunt nostre seignour le roi en son proschein parlement, d'oier, faire et resceivre ce qe la loye demande, come dessuis est dit. Quiel brief *[Page iii-60]*

[Col. a] par nostre dit seignour le roi, par l'advis des seignours et autres sages du parlement lui ad grantez, et comandez estre fait retornable en dit proschein parlement. Et enoultre est acordez en ce parlement qe les ditz record et proces par la dite cause soient en dit proschein parlement. Au quiel proschein parlement, c'estassavoir en cest present parlement tenuz a Westm' a la .xv.ᵉ de Pasqe, monsire Johan de Lodelowe, viscont de Salop', retornast le dit brief de scire facias grante au dit parlement de Glouc', de quiel brief, ovesqe l'endossement et retourn ent faitz par le dit viscount, le tenour s'ensuit de mot a mot:

20. Ricardus, Dei gratia, rex Anglie et Francie, et dominus Hibernie, vicecomiti Salop', salutem. Cum Rogerus de Mortuo Mari, filius Edmundi de Mortuo Mari, nuper comes Marchie, et consanguineus et heres Rogeri de Mortuo Mari nuper comitis Marchie, avi sui, in curia domini Edwardi nuper regis Anglie, avi nostri, coram eodem avo nostro, termino Trinitatis, anno regni sui Anglie vicesimo octavo, per breve ipsius avi nostri, ac consideracionem ejusdem curie, recuperaverit versus Willelmum de Monte Acuto, comitem Sarum, terram de Dynbegh' cum pertinentiis in Wallie; idemque comes Sar', per peticionem suam nobis in parliamento nostro apud Westm', in quindena Sancti Michaelis anno regni nostri Anglie primo tento, exhibitam, nobis supplicaverit, ut cum diversi errores in recordo et processu, ac reddicione judicii loquele predicte intervenissent, ad grave dampnum ipsius comitis Sar', vellemus recordum et processum inde habita /coram\ nobis et consilio nostro in dicto parliamento nostro venire, eademque recordum et processum ibidem examinari, ac errores inde repertos corrigi jubere; et nos supplicacioni predicti comitis Sar' in hac parte tunc annuentes, recordum et processum predicta coram nobis ac prelatis et magnatibus in parliamento nostro predicto ea de causa venire fecimus; ac insuper errores illos, si qui forent, modo debito corrigi, ulteriusque inde fieri volentes quod esset justum, per breve nostrum tibi preceperimus quod scire faceres Edmundo de Mortuo Mari, nunc comiti March', filio et heredi prefati Rogeri filii Edmundi,

---
[8] This appears to be an error for 1378.

found in them, if any, to be corrected by the proper means, and further wishing to do what is just, we order you that through worthy and lawful men of your county you make known to Edmund Mortimer, now earl of March, son and heir of the aforementioned Roger son of Edmund, that he should appear before us in our next parliament wheresoever that may be held, to hear the aforesaid record and process, if that should seem expedient, and also to perform and accept whatever shall happen to be decided there. And you shall have with you the names of those through whom you caused him to be notified, together with this writ. Witnessed by me at Westminster on 1 December, in the first year of our reign [1377].

The answer of Brian Cornwall, sheriff: Edmund Mortimer, now earl of March, son and heir of Roger Mortimer son of Edmund Mortimer, late earl of March, was not to be found in my bailiwick after this writ had been delivered to me, nor does he have any lands or tenements in the same wherein he might be summoned.

Whereupon, the said earl of Salisbury in this parliament prayed of our lord the king that it might please him to grant him another writ of scire facias, instructing the said Edmund, now earl of March, son of the said Roger son of Edmund, and heir in the said land of Denbigh, to appear before our lord the king in his next parliament, to hear, perform and receive whatever the law demands, as said above. Which writ *[Page iii-60]*

[Col. a] was granted to him by our said lord the king, by the advice of the lords and other learned men of parliament, and it was deemed returnable at the said next parliament. And furthermore it was agreed in the parliament that the said record and process of the said cause should be available in the said next parliament. At which parliament, namely in this present parliament held at Westminster on the quinzaine of Easter, Sir John Ludlow, sheriff of Shropshire, returned the said writ of scire facias issued at the said parliament of Gloucester, which writ, together with the endorsement and the return made by the said sheriff, runs as follows:

20. Richard, by the grace of God king of England and France, and lord of Ireland, to the sheriff of Shropshire, greeting. Whereas Roger Mortimer, son of Edmund Mortimer, late earl of March, and cousin and heir of Roger Mortimer, late earl of March, his grandfather, in the court of the lord Edward, late king of England, our grandfather, in the presence of our same grandfather, in Trinity term, in the twenty-eighth year of his reign over England [1354], by a writ of our grandfather, and the judgment of the same court, recovered from William Montagu, earl of Salisbury, the land of Denbigh together with appurtenances in Wales; in consequence of which the earl of Salisbury petitioned us through his petition presented to us in our parliament held at Westminster, on the quinzaine of Michaelmas, in the first year of our reign over England [1377], that since various errors were to be found in the record and process, and the judgment rendered in the aforesaid case, to the grave injury of the earl of Salisbury, we should order the said record and process made thereon to be brought before us and our council in our said parliament, and the same record and process to be examined there, and the errors found therein corrected; and we, granting the petition of the aforesaid earl of Salisbury, caused the aforesaid record and process of the cause to be brought before us and the prelates and magnates attending our aforesaid parliament; and errors subsequently detected, if any, were to be duly corrected; and wishing further to do in this whatever was just, by our writ we ordered you to instruct

quod esset coram nobis in parliamento nostro extunc proximo tenendo ubicumque tunc foret, auditurus recordum et processum predicta, si sibi videret expedire, ulteriusque facturus et recepturus quod considerari contingeret tunc ibidem; ac tu in dicto proximo parliamento, videlicet in presenti parliamento nostro apud Glouc', die Mercurii proximo post festum Sancti Luce Ewangeliste tento, retornaveris quod prefatus Edmundus de Mortuo Mari, comes Marchie, filius et heres Rogeri de Mortuo Mari, filii Edmundi de Mortuo Mari nuper comitis Marchie, non fuit inventus in balliva tua postquam dictum breve tibi liberatum fuit, nec aliqua \habuit/ terras seu tenementa in eadem ubi ipse premuniri potuit. Tibi precipimus quod per probos et legales homines de comitatu scire facias prefato Edmundo de Mortuo Mari, comiti Marchie, filio et heredi prefati Rogeri filii Edmundi, apud predictam terram de Dynbegh', quod sit coram /nobis\ in proximo parliamento nostro ubicumque tunc fuerit, auditurus recordum et processum predicta, si sibi viderit expedire, ulteriusque facturus et recepturus quod considerari contigerit tunc ibidem. Et habeas ibi nomina eorum per quos ei scire feceris, et hoc breve. Teste me ipso apud Westm' .xij. die Decembris, anno regni nostri secundo.

21. Responcio Johannis de Lodelowe, vicecomitis: Virtute istius brevis scire feci Edmundo de Mortuo Mari, comiti Marchie, filio et heredi Rogeri de Mortuo Mari filii Edmundi de Mortuo Mari nuper comitis Marchie, per Johannem \de/ Hodenet, Thomam de Ledebury, Johannem filium Radulfi de Hodenet et Walterum de Suggedon, probos et legales homines de balliva mea apud terram de Dynbegh' infra nominatos, vicesimo quarto die Martii, anno regni domini regis nunc secundo, quod sit coram domino rege in proximo parliamento suo ubicumque tunc fuerit, auditurus,

[Col. b] facturus et recepturus, quod considerari contigerit tunc in eodem parliamento de omnibus et singulis in isto brevi contentis, secundum formam, vim et effectum ejusdem brevis, et prout per idem breve precipitur.

22. Sur quoi vint en ce present parlement sibien le dit conte de Salesbirs par monsire Johan de Montagu, chivaler, un de ses generalx attournes fait par patente nostre dit seignour le roi, dont la date est a Westm' le .xij. jour d'Averill l'an present, mesme le conte de Salesbirs esteant es parties de dela en la service nostre seignour le roi, come le dit conte de la March' en sa persone, et illoeqes oiez et entenduz le ditz brief et retourn, et les recordz et proces dont mesme le brief fait mencion, esteantz en parlement le dit

Membrane 5 conte de Salesbirs par son dit attourne, se profri d'assigner illoeqes les errours quieles il dit estre comprises en les record et proces avauntdites.

23. Et le conte de la March' adonqes present en parlement, dist qe le dit brief n'est pas servi sicome mesme le brief demande: qar il dit qe en le dit brief est contenuz qe le viscont ferroit garnir Esmon de Mortimer, conte de la Marche, filz et heir Roger de Mortymer nadgaires conte de la March fitz Esmon de Mortymer. Et par le retourn de mesme le brief expressement apiert qe le viscont ad garni Esmon de Mortymer conte de la March, filz et heir Roger de Mortimer filz Esmon de Mortymer nadgairs conte de la March, par quel retourn einsi fait doit estre entendu par la /loy\ autre persone estre garni qe en le dit brief est contenuz; qar le dit Esmon le pier Roger n'estoit unqes conte; et n'entende mye le dit Esmon ore conte de la March' qe par tiel retourn del dit brief la court voille oultre proceder en dite busoigne.

the aforementioned Edmund Mortimer, now earl of March, son and heir of the aforementioned Roger son of Edmund, to appear before us in our next parliament to be held, wheresoever that may be, to hear the aforesaid record and process, if it seemed expedient, and also to perform and receive whatever was then decided; and you in the said following parliament, namely in our present parliament held at Gloucester [1378], on the Wednesday next after the feast of St Luke the Evangelist, returned that the aforementioned Edmund Mortimer, earl of March, son and heir of Roger Mortimer, son of Edmund Mortimer, late earl of March, had not been found in your bailiwick after the said writ had been delivered to you, and neither did he have any lands or tenements in the same in which he might be summoned. We order you that through worthy and lawful men of the county you instruct the aforementioned Edmund Mortimer, earl of March, son of the aforementioned Roger son of Edmund, and heir to the aforesaid land of Denbigh, to appear before us in our next parliament wheresoever that may be, to hear the aforesaid record and process, if it seems expedient, and further to perform and receive whatsoever may be decided there. And you shall have the names of those through whom you caused him to be notified, together with this writ. Witnessed by myself at Westminster on 12 December, in the second year of our reign [1378].

21. The answer of John Ludlow, sheriff: By virtue of this writ I notified Edmund Mortimer, earl of March, son and heir of Roger Mortimer son of Edmund Mortimer late earl of March, through John Hodenet, Thomas Ledbury, John son of Ralph Hodenet, and Walter Sugden, worthy and lawful men of my bailiwick on the said land of Denbigh, on 24 March, in the second year of the reign of the lord king, that he should appear before the lord king in his next parliament, wheresoever that might be, to hear,

[Col. b] perform and accept whatsoever may be decided in the same parliament concerning each and every item mentioned in the writ, in accordance with the form, force and effect of the same writ, and as is ordered therein.

22. Whereupon there appeared in this present parliament, as well the said earl of Salisbury, by one Sir John Montagu, knight, one of his general attorneys appointed by a letter patent of our said lord the king dated at Westminster on 12 April in the present year [1379] - the same earl of Salisbury being in foreign parts in the service of our lord the king - as the said earl of March, who appeared in person; and there, the said writ and return having been heard and understood, as well as the record and process of which the writ made mention, the earl of Salisbury being represented in parliament *Membrane 5* by his said attorney, offered to point out there the errors which he claimed were to be found in the aforesaid record and process.

23. And the earl of March, then present in parliament, said that the said writ had not been served as the same writ had demanded: since he said that in the said writ it was stated that the sheriff should notify Edmund Mortimer, earl of March, son and heir of Roger Mortimer late earl of March, son of Edmund Mortimer. And from the return of the same writ it plainly appeared that the sheriff had notified Edmund Mortimer earl of March, son and heir of Roger Mortimer son of Edmund Mortimer late earl of March, with respect to which return thus issued the law would understand another person to have been notified rather him named in the said writ; since the said Edmund father of Roger has never been earl; and the said Edmund, now earl of March, certainly did not believe that through such a return of the said writ the court should proceed further in the said matter.

24. A quoi le dit conte de Salesbirs dist qe le dit Esmon ore conte de la March' est suffisantement garni, par quiel garnissement il apparust et feust present, empriant a nostre seignour le roi et as seignours du parlement, q'il poet estre resceuz d'assigner les errours comprises en le record et proces avauntditz, qe sur ce les ditz record et proces duement examinez en parlement, plese a nostre seignour le roi et as seignours du parlement, pur les errours comprises en ycelles record et proces, repeller et de tout adnuller le juggement erroinement y renduz envers lui. Et enoultre, a mesme le conte de Salesbirs faire plein restitucion de la terre susdite, avec ses appertenantz qelconqes, et avec les issues en le moien temps prisez et resceuz.

25. Et est assavoir qe pur ce qe cest parlement si estoit bien pres au fyn quant cest busoigne feust issint touchez et parlez; et par tant, et pur autres chargeantz busoignes touchantz /l'estat\ nostre seignour le roi, et la salvation du roialme, dont les seignours du parlement d'autre part estoient alors moelt grandement occupiez; mesmes les seignours qi alors ne furent suffisantement avisez sur si haute et chargeante matire, ne poaient a ceste busoigne pluis attendre. Mais, par assent du parlement, jour ent est donez as ditz contes en le proschein parlement, toutes /choses\ esteantz en mesme l'estat q'ore sont, et sauvez as parties lours resons et chalanges qelconqes. Et enoultre est accordez qe les record et proces avauntditz soient en dit proschein parlement, /par la\ cause avantdite.

Pur les executours le roi Edward.
Item, les executours de seignour Edward nadgairs roi d'Engleterre, \aiel, etc./ mistrent avant en parlement nadgairs tenuz a Gloucestre une certaine lour bille dessouzescrite. Et apres qe mesme la bille fuist lue en dit parlement, une certeine question y estoit demandez des *[Page iii-61]*
[Col. a] justices, sergeantz et les autres gentz du loy lors presentz, par les seignours en dit parlement; a la quelle question les ditz justices, et les autres dessuisditz, parmy le charge a eux donez illoeqes, si firent devaunt les seignours lour responce en escrit, et le baillerent au clerc du parlement.

26. Et ore les dites bille, question et responce de novel rehercez devant les prelatz \et/ seignours en ce present parlement, al instance des ditz executours, en presence de monsire Johan de Cavendissh', monsire Robert Bealknapp', monsire William de Skipwyth', monsire Roger de Fulthorp', monsire Henry Percy, monsire Robert Tresilian, \justices; et/ monsire Henry Asty, \chief baron de l'escheqier; et/ Johan Holt, Davy Hanmere, Wauter Clopton et Johan de Middelton, sergeantz le roi, \et plusours autres,/ mesmes les executours prieront qe celles question et responce fuist enroullez en roulle de parlement de record, et sur ce mesme la responce q'estoit fait a Gloucestr' en partie corrigez par les seignours et justices en cest parlement, fuist acordez et assentuz qe les dites bille, question et responce feussent entrez et enroullez en roulle de parlement, en la fourme qe s'ensuit:[9]

A nostre seignour le roi et as seignours en cest present parlement, monstrent les executours nostre seignour le roi Edward qi Dieux assoille, l'aiel nostre seignour le roi q'or est; qe come ils furent enfeoffez en certains manoirs, terres et tenementz par le dit aiel, a eux et lours heirs, queux le dit aiel avoit de son purchas; et les ditz feoffez firent lour rescevour des issues et profitz provenantz des ditz manoirs, terres et tenementz: la le dit rescevour est defenduz et comandez par

---
[9] PRO C49/9/4.

24. To which the said earl of Salisbury replied that the said Edmund now earl of March had been adequately summoned, and as a result of which summons he had appeared and was present, praying of our lord the king and lords of parliament that he might be allowed to indicate the errors contained in the aforesaid record and process, and that thereupon, the said record and process having been duly examined in the parliament, it might please our lord the king and the lords of parliament, on account of the errors contained in the same record and process, to repeal and altogether annul the judgment erroneously passed against him. And furthermore, that the aforesaid land might be fully restored to the same earl of Salisbury, together with its appurtenances whatsoever, and with the issues taken and received in the meantime.

25. And be it known that because this parliament was so close to ending when the matter was raised and discussed; and for this reason as well as other burdensome matters concerning the estate of our lord the king and the security of the kingdom, with which the lords of parliament were also then greatly preoccupied; the same lords, who were then inadequately informed upon so important and burdensome a matter, could not attend any further to this matter. But, by the assent of parliament, a day for this was fixed for the said earls in the next parliament, all things remaining equal, and saving to the parties their explanations and arguments of any kind. And further, it was agreed that the aforesaid record and process of the cause should be available at the said next parliament.

On behalf of King Edward's executors.
Also, the executors of Lord Edward, late king of England, grandfather, etc., submitted in the parliament lately held at Gloucester a certain bill of theirs written out below. And after the same bill had been read in the said parliament, a certain question had been asked of the *[Page iii-61]*
[Col. a] judges, serjeants and other men of the law then present, by the lords in the said parliament; to which question the said judges and the others aforesaid, fulfilling the charge laid upon them there, caused their written answers to be presented to the lords, and delivered them to the clerk of parliament.

26. And now the said bill, question and response being rehearsed anew before the prelates and lords in this present parliament, at the instance of the said executors, in the presence of Sir John Cavendish, Sir Robert Bealknap, Sir William Skipwith, Sir Roger Fulthorp, Sir Henry Percy, Sir Robert Tresilian, justices; and Sir Henry Asty, chief baron of the exchequer; and John Holt, Davy Hanmer, Walter Clopton and John Middleton, king's serjeants, and many others, the same executors prayed that the question and response might be enrolled on the roll of parliament as of record, and thereupon that answer which was made at Gloucester, having been corrected in part by the lords and justices in this parliament, it was agreed and assented that the said bill, question and answer be entered and enrolled on the roll of parliament, in the following form:

To our lord the king and the lords in this present parliament, the executors of our lord the king Edward, whom God absolve, the grandfather of our lord the present king, show: whereas they and their heirs were enfeoffed with certain manors, lands and tenements by the said grandfather, which the said grandfather had by purchase; and the said enfeoffed persons appointed a receiver for the issues and profits arising from the said manors, lands and tenements: and the said

aucuns du conseil nostre seignour le roi q'orest, de riens paier pur mandement des ditz feoffes, sanz especial mandement du roi. Par quoy prient les ditz feoffez qe comande soit a le dit resceivour, \de/ faire son office es ditz manoirs, terres et tenementz, come il avoit en charge par les ditz feoffes, non obstantz les ditz mandement et defense faitz au contraire. Et qe les ditz feoffez purront rejoier leur possessioun des ditz manoirs, terres et tenementz, en manere come ils furent enfeoffez par nostre

[Col. b] dit seignour le roi, l'aiel.
Et est assavoir qe \monsire d'Espaigne,/ duc de Lancastre et les seignours du parlement, et monsire Richard le Scrope, chaunceller d'Engleterre, chargerent justices et les sergeantz le roi, en parlement, par le serement q'ils avoient fait au roi, et sur lour ligeaunce, et en peril de \lours/ almes, et einsi come ils veullent respondre devant le roi en temps avenir, q'ils deussent veritablement dire la veritee des articles ensuantz, sur la loy de la terre. C'estassavoir, qe par la ou seignour Edward jadys roi d'Engleterre, aiel nostre seignour le roi q'orest, autrefoitz enfeoffa le dit duc, et autres seignours, des certains manoirs et terres qe furent del purchas le dit aielle, en fee simplement, sanz aucun condicioun, par sa chartre souz son grant seal, quelle lour estoit alors monstree, /de la\ \date del quinte jour d'Octobre, l'an du regne le dit aielle cynquantisme; et qe mesme l'aielle/ les fist liverer sur ceo plenere seisine, auxint sanz aucun condition en escrit ou par parole. Et puis long temps apres, le dit roi l'aiel pria les feoffes susditz par sa bouche q'ils deussent ordener pur la susteignance des freres de Langle et des nonaignes de Dertford, et de faire un obit perpetuel pur l'alme la countesse de Huntyngdon', et un autre pur l'alme la countesse mareschal, \et certaines autres charges;/ si celle charge fait a les ditz enfeoffez en tiel manere puis le doun suisdit serroit par la loy de la terre ajugeable condicioun, issint qe par tant le dit doun serroit ajugge condicional, ou noun? A la quelle question les ditz justices disoient qe si le doun suisdit fuist simple, come dit est, sanz parlaunce devant le doun, ou sur le doun, ou sur la liveree d'aucun charge ou fesaunce qe les enfeoffez deussent faire; qe par nulle priere faite a eux apres ceo q'ils furent en possessioun, nomement par la chartre de roi q'est de record, le dit doun precedent quel fuist adonqes simple ne poet estre fait condicionel. Et enoultre diont qe si le roi q'orest ait droit as ditz manoirs et terres, par autre title, come il poet avoir par plusours voies, par quelconqe cause resonable de quelle ils ne sont a ore /enfourmez\ ne chargez, il lour semble qe son droit lui ent est, et doit toutdis estre, salvez.

CY APRES S'ENSUENT LES PETITIONS BAILLEES A NOSTRE SEIGNEUR LE ROI PAR LA COMMUNE D'ENGLETERRE, AVEC LES RESPONCES FAITES ET DONEES EN PARLEMENT.
A trespuissant et tresredoute seignour le roi et a son conseil, prelatz et autres seignours de cest parlement, tenuz a Westm' le lundy en la quinzisme jour de Pasqe, l'an de vostre regne second, supplient voz humbles communes pur les peticions dessouz escritz, en aide et profit du roialme:

Membrane 4
I. [Liberties and Charters.]
27. En primes, supplient les communes, desicome la volentee le roi est, qe seinte esglise eit ses franchises et droitures en touz pointz, sauve au roi sa regalie et la commune loye de la terre, tenuz come il ad este en temps de ses progenitours.

receiver was challenged and forbidden by certain of the council of our lord the present king to pay anything on the orders of the said feoffees, without special mandate from the king. On account of which the said feoffees pray that the said receiver be ordered to perform his office in the said manors, lands and tenements, as he was charged by the said feoffees, notwithstanding the said mandate and prohibition made to the contrary. And that the said feoffees may again enjoy their possession of the said manors, lands and tenements, as they were enfeoffed by our

[Col. b] said lord the king, the grandfather.
And be it known that messire of Spain, duke of Lancaster, and the lords of parliament, and Sir Richard le Scrope, chancellor of England, charged the judges and the king's serjeants in parliament, by their oath which they made to the king, and on their allegiance, and on peril of their souls, as they would answer to the king in time to come, that they accurately recount the truth about the following articles, according to the law of the land. Namely, that whereas the lord Edward, once king of England, grandfather of our lord the present king, sometime enfeoffed the said duke and other lords with certain manors and lands which had been acquired by the said grandfather, in fee simple, without conditions, by his charter under his great seal, dated 5 October, in the fiftieth year of the reign of the said grandfather [1376], which was then shown to them; and the said grandfather thereupon granted them seisin, without any conditions, spoken or in writing. And long after, the said king the grandfather requested of the said enfeoffed persons, by his own mouth, that they might ordain for the maintenance of the friars of Langley and the nuns of Dartford, to celebrate a perpetual obit for the soul of the countess of Huntingdon, and another for the soul of the countess marshal, with certain other charges; if that charge laid upon the said feoffees in such manner after the aforesaid grant should be judged a condition by the law of the land, and would the said grant then be judged conditional, or not? To which question the said justices replied that if the aforesaid gift was simple, as said, without discussion before the grant, at the time of the grant itself, or the delivery of any charge or action which the feoffees ought to undertake; that by no request made of them after they had been granted possession, especially by the charter of the king which bears record, could the said preceding gift which had then been simple be made conditional. And they said further that if the present king had a right to the said manors and lands by another title, which he could have in various ways, for whatsoever just cause of which they were not at present informed or charged, it seemed to them that his right is and ought always to be preserved for him.

HERE FOLLOW THE PETITIONS SUBMITTED TO OUR LORD THE KING BY THE COMMONS OF ENGLAND, TOGETHER WITH THE ANSWERS MADE AND GIVEN IN PARLIAMENT.
To the most exalted and redoubtable lord the king and his council, prelates and other lords of this parliament held at Westminster on Monday on the quinzaine of Easter, in the second year of your reign, your humble commons request support for the petitions written below, to the aid and benefit of the realm:

I. [Liberties and Charters.]
27. First, the commons request, as is the king's wish, that holy church shall have its franchises and liberties in all points, saving to the king his regality and the common law of the land, upheld as it was in the time of his progenitors.

Qe plese qe les dites franchises et loyes, ensemblement ove la grant chartre et la chartre de la foreste, soient tenuz et gardez en touz pointz, pur Dieu, et en oevre de charitee, nientcontreestant aucun estatut fait a contraire.
Responsio.

Il plest au roi qe seint esglise eit sa franchise et libertees en touz pointz, salve au roi sa regalie, et qe la grant chartre et la chartre de la foreste et les loyes de la terre, soient fermement tenuz et gardez.[10]

II. [Petitions to receive answers.]
28. Item, supplient les communes, purce qe peticions et billes mises en parlement par diverses persones des communes ne purront d'ycelles devant ces heures nul responce avoir, qe de lour peticions et billes mises ore en cest present parlement, et des tous autres queux serront mises en parlementz en temps avenir, qe bone et gracious respons et remede lour ent soit ordeine devant lour departir de chescun parlement; et surce due estatut soit fait en ce present parlement, et enseale a demurrer en tout temps avenir, s'il vous plest.
Page iii-62
Responsio.

Il plest au roi qe des tielles peticions baillez en parlement des choses qe aillours ne purront estre terminez, bone et resonable responce soit fait et donez devaunt departir de parlement.

III. [Forest bounds.]
29. Item, supplient les communes qe come grantee estoit au parlement tenuz a Westm', l'an primer du tresnoble aiel a nostre seignour le roi q'orest, qi Dieux assoille, qe les purales qe chivachez estoient en temps le roi Edward son aiel se tendroient en manere come ils estoient alors chivachez; et qe par la ou ils n'estoient pas chivachez q'ils serroient chivachez, et qe sur ce chartres serroient faites as touz les countees d'Engleterre: quelles choses estoient faites et confermez en touz les parlementz puis encea. Et jalemeyns les gardeins et ministres des forestes font lour attachementz hors de boundes ensi chivachez, et font enditer les gentz des choses faites hors de mesmes les boundes de jour en autre, a grant damage du poeple, et au contraire des dites grantz[11] et confermentz.
Par quoi supplient les dites communes, qe les dites communes qe les dites boundes soient chivachez de novel, en manere come ils sont boundez par les dites chartres, parentre cy et la feste de Seint Michel proschein avenir. Et q'en touz enditementz faitz de vert ou de venisoun, les lieux ou les trespasses sont faites soient specifez en mesmes les enditementz; et si autrement, q'ils soient voides et tenuz pur nul, et qe peyne soit ordene sur les ditz gardeins et ministres qi font lour attachementz, ou grevent les gentz pur choses faites hors des dites boundes. Et qe les compleynantz puissent recoverir lour damages a tresble vers les ditz gardeins et ministres, s'ils soient atteintz a leur suite.
Responsio.

Il plest au roi qe la chartre et les autres estatutz de la foreste soient tenuz et gardez, et meintenuz en touz lour pointz. Et si les ministres de la foreste trespassent, en grevance del poeple, encontre la loye et l'assise de foreste, q'ils soient puniz selonc ce qe la loy demande: et si aucun soi vorra ent

If it please, may the said franchises and laws, together with the Great Charter, and the Charter of the Forest, be upheld and kept in all respects, for God and by way of charity, notwithstanding any statute made to the contrary.
Answer.

It is pleasing to the king that holy church should have its franchise and liberties in all points, saving to the king his regality, and that the Great Charter, and the Charter of the Forest, and the laws of the land shall be strictly kept and upheld.

II. [Petitions to receive answers.]
28. Item, the commons request that because petitions and bills submitted in parliament by various members of the commons have received no answer in the past, a good and gracious response and remedy shall be ordained before their departure from each parliament for the petitions and bills now submitted in this present parliament, and all others which shall be submitted in parliaments in time to come; and that a proper statute shall be made thereon in this present parliament, and sealed so as to remain in force in all time to come, if it please you.

Answer.

It is pleasing to the king that to such petitions submitted in parliament on matters which cannot be settled elsewhere, a good and reasonable answer should be given and granted before the end of parliament.

III. [Forest bounds.]
29. Item, the commons request: whereas it was granted in the parliament held at Westminster, in the first year of the most noble grandfather of our lord the present king [1327], whom God absolve, that the bounds of the forest which were ridden in the time of King Edward his grandfather should remain as they were when ridden; and that where they had not been ridden they would be ridden, and that charters would be made thereupon for all the counties of England: which things were done and confirmed in all the parliaments since this. Yet nevertheless, the wardens and ministers of the forests make attachments outside the bounds thus ridden, and cause people to be indicted from day to day for things done outside the same bounds, to the great injury of the people, and contrary to the said grants and confirmations.
In consequence of which the said commons request that the said bounds be ridden again, in the way in which they were defined by the said charters, between now and Michaelmas next. And that in all indictments of vert or venison, the places where the offences were committed shall be specified in the same indictments; and if they are not, they shall be invalid and held at naught, and a penalty be ordained for the said wardens and ministers who make their attachments or grieve the people for things done outside the said bounds. And that plaintiffs shall recover triple damages from the said wardens and ministers if they are convicted at their suit.

Answer.

It pleases the king that the charter and the other charters of the forest shall be kept and upheld and fully maintained. And if the ministers of the forest, to the harm of the people, trespass against the law and the assize of the forest, that they shall be punished in accordance with the law's demand: and

---

[10] 2 Ric.2 stat.2 c.1; the statutes of this parliament are printed in *SR*, II.12.
[11] *Original* gentz

pleindre en especial, pursue devers le conseil nostre seignour le roi, et droit luy ent serra fait.

IV. [Raising of loans.]
30. Item, monstrent les communes, coment ore tarde, puis la darrein conseil tenuz a Westm', furent mandez diverses lettres de credence dessouz le prive seal, par certains chivalers et esquiers de la courte le roi, es diverses parties du roialme, pur faire chevance d'argent al oeps le roi; queles lettres avoient les cowes blankes, et les ditz credensours de lour auctoritee demesne escriverent les nouns des plusours gentz sur les cowes des lettres suis dites, et baillerent a eux les lettres, affermantz qe le roi les maunda a eux, et demanderent de eux grandes sommes tielles come lour pleust, et ceux qi se excuserent de les paier tielles sommes les manacerent fortement depar le roi, et les comanderent depar le roi d'estre devant le conseil le roi, et assignerent a eux jours a leur volentee; a grande damage et affraye des ditz povres communes, et ensclandre du roi, et encontre la loye de la terre.

Par quoy supplient les dites communes q'ordene soit qe coment q'il plese au roi d'envoier lettres pur apprompter argent en temps avenir, et celui a qi la lettre vient excuse resonablement du dit appromt, q'il soit a ce \[receu,]/ sanz lui mettre au travail, ou lui grever par sommons, ou par autre manere.

Responsio.
Il plest au roi.

V. [Replacement of customs collectors.]
31. Item, monstrent les communes, coment ordeine soit en parlement qe touz les viscontz d'Engleterre chescun an seront changez et grande partie del profit du roialme pertienant a nostre dit seignour le roi est en le subside des leynes; qe vous plese qe touz les custumers et les countreroullours d'Engleterre soient en mesme le
[Col. b] manere remuez, pur profit nostre dit seignour le roi, et commune profit du roialme.
Responsio.
Le roi, par l'advis de son conseil, ent ordenera de tieux officers come luy semblera.

VI. [Malefactors from Cheshire.]
32. Item, monstrent les communes qe come gentz del countee de Cestre q'est conte palays, et autres q'ont tielle franchises, viegnent de jour en autre as force et armes ove grantz routes des gentz es diverses countees parmy tout le roialme, et nomement gentz del countee de Cestre, et font diverses felonies, roberies et arcines, ravisementz des femmes, dames et damoisels, et pluseurs horribles trespasses y font; et puis repaierent al dit countee de Cestre, et es autres lieux queux sont ensi enfranchisez, et mes q'ils soient enditez et utlagez pur tiel manere des trespas et felonie, nulle execucion est fait es ditz countees, queux sont ensi enfranchisez.

Par quoy prient les ditz communes q'execucion soit faite des forfaitures des terres et tenementz, biens et chateux, et punissement de corps, sibien en le countee de Cestre et es autres countees q'ont tielles franchises, come en autres countees qi ne sont mye enfranchisez, pur grant profit nostre seignour le roi, et autres seignours de la terre.
Responsio.
Il plest au roi qe les trespassours soient duement puniz, et la manere coment ils serront puniz le roi par l'advis de son conseil ent ferra ordener de melliour remedie q'il purra; sauvant au roi et a chescun autre son lige ses droitures.

if anyone wishes to make particular complaint, let him sue to the council of our lord the king, and right shall be done him.

IV. [Raising of loans.]
30. Item, the commons show that of late, since the last council held at Westminster, various letters of credence under the privy seal were sent to various parts of the realm by certain knights and squires of the king's court, to request loans of silver for the king's use; which letters had blank seal-strips, and the said creditors of their own authority wrote the names of many persons on the seal-strips of the aforesaid letters, and delivered the letters to them, affirming that the king had sent them to them, and they demanded from them sums as great as they wished, and those who excused themselves from paying such sums they fiercely threatened on behalf of the king, and ordered them on the king's behalf to appear before the king's council, and assigned them days at will; to the great injury and consternation of the said poor commons, and the slander of the king, and contrary to the law of the land.

Because of which the said commons request that it be ordained that whenever it pleases the king to send letters to borrow silver in the future, if anyone whom the letter reaches excuses himself on reasonable grounds from the said loan, that it be allowed, without him being put to any trouble, or being grieved by summons, or in any other way.
Answer.
It pleases the king.

V. [Replacement of customs collectors.]
31. Item, the commons showed that whereas it was ordained in parliament that all the sheriffs of England should be replaced annually, and a great part of the profit of the kingdom pertaining to our said lord the king is in the subsidy on wool; that it may please you that all the customs officers and controllers of England shall be removed in the same
[Col. b] way, to the benefit of our said lord the king, and the common profit of the realm.
Answer.
The king, by the advice of his council, will ordain such officers as he chooses.

VI. [Malefactors from Cheshire.]
32. Item, the commons show: whereas the people of Cheshire, which is a county palatine, and others who have such franchises, by force and arms with great bands of people daily enter various counties throughout the kingdom, and especially men of Cheshire; and they commit various felonies, thefts and arsons, ravishing wives, ladies and damsels, and commit many, horrible offences there; and then return to the said county of Cheshire, and to other places which are thus enfranchised, and even if they are indicted and outlawed for such offence and felony, no execution is made in the said counties, which are thus enfranchised.

On account of which the said commons pray that execution shall be made of forfeitures of lands and tenements, goods and chattels, and corporal punishment, both in Cheshire and in other counties which have such franchises, as well as in other counties which are not enfranchised at all, for the great benefit of our lord the king and other lords of the land.
Answer.
It pleases the king that the offenders be duly punished, and the king by the advice of his council will ordain the manner in which they are to be punished in order to provide the best remedy he can; saving to the king and all his other lieges their rights.

VII. [Scottish prisoners.]

33. Item, monstrent les communes qe toutesfoitz puis les trues prises parentre les roialmes d'Engleterre et d'Escoce, toutes les persones d'Escoce qi furent prises chivachantz a fere de guerre, et autrement trespassantz en Engleterre, et ailleurs deinz la seignourie nostre seignour le roi, ont este liverez quitz de raunson par vertu des trues avantdites; et ore, diverses persones Engleises tarde prises par d'Escotz sont aucuns raunsonez, et aucuns detenuz en prisone, par cause q'ils ne veullent assentir a raunseon faire.

Sur quoy plese a nostre dit seignour le roi, pur son honour demesne, et aide et socour des ditz liges et subsigtz, ent ordener remede et comander as gardeins de la marche, et les seignours assignez de tenir jour de marche, q'ils ne soeffrent tielle injurie estre faite au roi et ses liges. Mais qe les ditz liges nostre seignour le roi queux sont ou serront issint prises par Escotz, soient \[liverez]/ de auxi bon condicion come l'Escotz prises par les Engleys ont este devant ces heures, sanz aucun raunseon faire.

Responsio.

Il y a un jour prise sur mesme la matire en les marches, parentre les gardeins d'ambes partz, le darrein jour de Juyn proschein venant; au quiel jour, si Dieu plest, resonable remede ent serra ordenez.

VIII. [Sheriffs' farms.]

34. Item, supplient les communes qe come nostre seignour le roi ait grantez par ses lettres patentes as diverses gentz grandes sommes, a prendre del corps des diverses countees; et les viscontz des dites countees sont chargez de tout le profit del entir corps sur lour acompt, et ne purront lever les dites sommes, a cause des lettres patentes suisdites as diverses gentz grantez, issint qe plusours viscontz des countees sont destruitz et anientiz.

Qe plese a nostre dit seignour le roi et a son bon conseil ordeiner qe les viscontz des countees purront avoir allouance en l'escheqier sur lour acompt, de les deniers des corps des countees as diverses gentz issi grantez, come dessuis est dit.

Responsio

Le roi s'advisera par son conseil.

IX. [Robbers.]

35. Item, supplient les communes qe come diverses larons, robbours et autres felons, soient prises et emprisonez; les unes, avaunt aucune deliverance soit faite de eux, debrusent la prisone et eschapent; les unes aparnent clergie par quoi ils sont sauvez; et les unes par brocage et maintenance faites en le mesne temps sont deliverez, en grant confort et abaundissement des tielx malfeisours *[Page iii-63]*

[Col. a] et routours et destourbance de la pees et quiete del commune poeple.

Qe pleise a nostre dit seignour le roi et son conseil avoir regarde quelles roberies sont ore es diverses parties d'Engleterre par grandes routes et compaignies overtement faitz, et ent ordeiner, qe deux ou trois des meillours et pluis vaux et loialx de chescun countee soient assignez d'enquere des tieux mesfesours, et d'aler maintenant a leur deliverance apres ce q'ils soient prises; horspris en cas de mort de homme, dont soit fait come ad este devant ces heures: quelle ordinance serra grant comfort et quiete al povre poeple, et grant destructioun des dites mesfeisours. Et qe viscontz certifient a ceux qi serront issint assignez en lours countees des nouns de ceux qi serront issint prises, et en lour garde, dedeinz un moys apres qe tielx mesfeisours soient prises,

VII. [Scottish prisoners.]

33. Item, the commons show that ever since the truces made between the realms of England and Scotland, all the Scots who had been captured whilst riding to war and otherwise committing offences in England and elsewhere within the lordship of our lord the king have been freed without payment of a ransom by virtue of the aforesaid truces; yet now, of various Englishmen lately captured by the Scots, some have been ransomed and some detained in prison because they will not to agree to pay a ransom.

In view of which may it please our said lord the king, for his own honour, and to help and support his said lieges and subjects, to ordain a remedy, and order the wardens of the march, and the lords appointed to hold Marchdays, that they shall allow no such injury to be inflicted on the king and his lieges. But that the said lieges of our lord the king who are or shall be captured by the Scots shall be freed in as good condition as the Scots taken in the past by the English, without any ransom paid.

Answer.

A day has been fixed for discussion of the matter in the marches, between the wardens of both parts, on the last day of June next [1379]; on which day, if it pleases God, a reasonable remedy shall be ordained.

VIII. [Sheriffs' farms.]

34. Item, the commons request: whereas our lord the king has granted great sums by his letters patent to various men, to be taken from the body of the people of various counties; and the sheriffs of the said counties are charged with all the profit from the entire body of people on their account, and they are unable to levy the said sums, because of the aforesaid letters patent granted to various people, so that many sheriffs of the counties are destroyed and ruined.

May it please our said lord the king and his good council to ordain that the sheriffs of the counties shall have allowance in the exchequer on their account, for the money from the body of the county thus granted to various persons, as is said above.

Answer.

The king will consider this further with his council.

IX. [Robbers.]

35. Item, the commons request: whereas various thieves, robbers and other felons are captured and imprisoned; some of whom, before any deliverance has been made upon them, break out of prison and escape; some by plea of clergy by which they are saved; and some are freed by brokage and maintenance, to the comfort and emboldenment of such malefactors *[Page iii-63]*

[Col. a] and rioters and disturbers of the peace and tranquillity of the common people.

May it please our said lord the king and his council to consider the robberies which are at present flagrantly committed in various parts of England by great bands and companies, and to ordain that two or three of the best and most respected and loyal people of each county be appointed to inquire into such malefactors, and to proceed immediately to their trial after they have been captured; except in a case of homicide, where it shall be done as it has been in the past: which ordinance will bring great comfort and tranquillity to the poor people, and the great ruin of the said malefactors. And that sheriffs shall notify those thus appointed in their counties of the names of those who are thus taken, and in their keep, within a month of such malefactors being taken, on pain of

sur peine de paier au roi pur chescun q'ils concelerent par manere susdit .x.*li.*

Responsio.

Il a diverses estatutz faitz en ce cas, queux le roi voet qe soient veuez par les seignours et autres de son conseil; et ceux qi serront profitables pur son poeple le roi voet qe soient mises en execution. Et enoultre, le roi chargera ses justices de faire les deliverances si sovent come embusoignera.

X. [Wool of northern couties.]

36. Item, supplient les communes qe come a cause d'entre commune parentre les roialmes d'Engleterre et Escoce la greindre partie des leynes d'Everwyk, Duresme, Westmerl', Cumbr' et Northumbr', forspris une petite somme q'est eskippe a Berewyk sur Twede, paiant a custume et subside .ij. marcz pur le saak, \sont/ emmesnez en Escoce sanz riens paier a nostre seignour le roi pur subside ou custume; issint qe la ou nostre seignour le roi soloit prendre une grande somme pur custume et subside de les leynes suisdites en le port de Noef-Chastel sur Tyne, annuelment, il ne prist riens par yces deux ans darrein passez, come poet estre trovez par acompt des custumers de mesme le port. Qe vous plese ent ordeiner remede.

Responsio.

\[Le]/ roi le voet qe due remede ent soit ordeinez, par l'advis de son consel.

XI. [Scarborough: Defence of the coast.]

37. Item, supplient les communes qe come les enemys de France ove grandes armes et pluseurs vessealx de guerre ont estee continuelment, et unqores sont, en les parties de North; et nomement devers le couste de Scardeburgh', la quelle ville est perillousement assis sur la meer overtement as assautes des ditz enemys; et les gentz du dite ville, par prise et raunceons des dites enemys q'amonte a .m.*li.*, q'ont este paiez deinz ces deux ans darrein passez, ensi destruitz et amesnusez; et plusours des dites gentz en Boloigne et autres lieux depar dela unqores en prisone esteantz; qe la dite ville est \en/ point d'estre ars et destruite et tout le couste environ; et ce en brief temps sinoun qe hastive remede soit ent ordeine.

Qe plese a nostre dit seignour le roi et a son tressage conseil, considerantz les grantz damages et perils qe au dit ville et la couste environ sont avenuz, et unqores apparantz d'avenir, ordener et assigner certeins vessealx de guerre sur les dites coustiers, de les garder encontre la malice et poair des ditz enemys, et ce durant les guerres, en salvation du dite ville, et la chastel nostre seignour le roi illoeqes assis, et de tout la paiis environ.

Responsio.

Ceste matire est en partie touchez as marchantz des dites costieres qi sont a cest parlement, et par lour advis, et d'autres q'ont appassers lours marchandies en celles marches par la meer, remede ent est ordeinez, par manere come le conte de Northumbr', et le mair de Londres, qi furent assignez en parlement de treter sur ceste busoigne, le sachent pluis au plein declarrer.

[12]

Ceste l'ordinance et grante par l'advis des marchaundz de Londres, et des autres marchaundz vers la northe, par assent de touz les communes de parlement, pardevant le comte de Northumbr' et le meair de

[Col. b] Londres; pur la garde et tuicion du mier, et costerz del admiralte de northe, ove deux niefs, deux bargis et deux

paying a penalty of £10 to the king for each person they conceal in the aforesaid manner.

Answer.

There are various statutes made in this case, which the king wishes to be reviewed by the lords and others of his council; and those which shall be found profitable for his people the king wishes to put into effect. Furthermore, the king entrusts the justices with carrying out the trials as often as needs be.

X. [Wool of northern counties.]

36. Item, the commons request: whereas because of the common boundary between the kingdoms of England and Scotland the greater part of wool from York, Durham, Westmorland, Cumberland and Northumberland, except for a small amount which is shipped to Berwick upon Tweed, paying a custom and subsidy of two marks per sack, is taken into Scotland without anything being paid to our lord the king for subsidy or custom; so that, whereas our lord the king used to receive a large sum from the aforesaid custom and subsidy on wool in the port of Newcastle upon Tyne each year, he has received nothing for the past two years, as may be discerned from the account of the customs officers of the same port. May it please you to ordain a remedy for this.

Answer.

The king wills that due remedy shall be ordained by the advice of his council.

XI. [Scarborough: Defence of the coast]

37. Item, the commons request: whereas the French enemies with considerable arms and numerous ships of war have continually been and are still in northern parts; and particularly about the coast of Scarborough, which town is perilously situated on the sea and open to the attacks of the said enemies; and the people of the said town, through the exactions and ransoms of the said enemies which amount to £1000, and have been paid within the last two years, are thus crushed and ruined; and many of the said people are still imprisoned in Boulogne and in other places overseas; so that the said town is on the point of being burnt and destroyed and all the surrounding coast with it; and that within a short time unless remedy be swiftly ordained.

May it please our said lord the king and his most wise council, considering the great damage and perils which have come upon the said town and surrounding coast, and are still likely to arise in future, to ordain and assign certain ships of war to the said coasts, to guard them from the malice and power of the said enemies, and that during the wars, for the security of the said town and the castle of our lord the king situated there, and of all the surrounding countryside.

Answer.

This matter partly concerns the merchants of the said coasts who are present at this parliament, and by their advice and that of others who have conveyed their merchandise to those marches by sea, remedy is ordained for this, of which the earl of Northumberland and the mayor of London, who were appointed in parliament to deal with the matter, know and will explain the matter.

This is the ordinance and grant made by the advice of the merchants of London, and others, merchants towards the north, and with the assent of all of the commons of parliament, before the earl of Northumberland and the mayor of

[Col. b] London; for the protection and keeping of the sea, and the coasts of the admiralty of the north, with two ships,

---

[12] The following as far as 'Novel-Chastiel sur Tyne' is written in a different, contemporary hand on a loose leaf of parchment stitched to m.4.

balengers, armez et arraiez pur la guerre sur les coustages qe s'ensuient:

Primerement, pur prendre de chescun nief et craier, de quele portage q'il soit, qe passe par la mier dedeinz le dite admiralte alant et retournant, pur le voiage de chescun tonne-tight, .vi. *d*.; horspris niefs chargez ove vins, et niefs chargez ove marchandises en Flaundres qe serront frettez et deschargez a Londres; et niefs chargez ove leynes et peues a Londres, ou ailleurs dedeinz la dite admiralte, qe serront deschargez a Caleis: les queux niefs les gardeins de la dite mier ne serront tenuz de les \[conduire]/ sanz estre allouez. Item, de prendre de chescun vesseau pessoner, qe pessent sur la mier du dit admiralte entour harang, de quele portage q'il soit, en un simaigne de chescun tonne-tight, .vi. *d*. Item, de prendre des autres niefs et vesseaux pessoners, qe pessent entour autres pessons sur la mier dedeinz la dite admiralte, de quele portage q'il soit, en troiz simaignes de chescun tonne-thight, .vi. *d*. Item, de prendre de touz autres niefs et vesseaux passanz par mier dedeinz la dite admiralte, chargez ove charbons au Novel-Chastiel seur Tyne, de quele portage q'il soit, en le quarter de un an, de chescun tonne-tight, .vi. *d*. Item, de prendre de touz autres niefs, craiers et vesseaux, passanz par mier dedeinz la dite admiralte, chargez ove biens des marchanz qeconqes en Espreux, ou en Northwhay, ou en Scone, ou en ascune lieu en mesme les parties depardela, pur le voiage alant et retournant, de chescun last quir[13] viz lastas graves, .vi. *d*.

Item, d'avoir de nostre seignour le roy commissions a monsire Thomas Percy, admiral del northe, Thomas Rust, John Hesildene, John de Scharbourgh' et Robert Rust de Blakenay, gardeins du dite mier, pur lever et parner le dite grante et subside, sibien par terre come par mier, par tout la dite admiralte, et pouer de faire deputez a lever et receivre les diz grante et subsides en les portes par tout la dite admiralte ou les diz gardeins sembliront mestier, issint qe les diz commissioners, et coilleurs, ove leur deputez, soient acomptables a les surveiours et controllours des bones citees et villes desouz escripz, et a nule autres; /et qe leurs commissions soient faites\ jointement et devisement a durer tanqe a la feste de Seinte Katerine prochein venant.

Item, ordeine est, par l'advis des avandiz marchanz, qe ceux desouz escriz soient surveiours et controllours des avandiz gardeins et coillours, et q'ils averont commissions de ensi fere, et de lever et parner la dite subside en leurs portz, \et entierement deliverer as gardeins susditz/ sanz estre acomptable devers le roy.

Seurviours et controllours.

Wauter Sibile, Johan Horn, de Londres

Geffrey Dawe, de Colchestre

Robert Whaleis, de Zipiswich'

William Oxnay, Johan de Marchham, de Jernemouth'

Johan Dokkinge, Johan Kepe, de Lynne

William Thymbilby, de Botston'

Johan Barden, de Everwik.

Wauter Frost, de Hull'.

William Schropham, William Sage, de Scardebourgh'

William Bischopdale, Robert Oliver, de Novel-Chastiel sur Tyne.

two barges and two balingers, armed and equipped for war upon the costs which follow:

First, taking from each ship and boat, of whatsoever tonnage it be, which sails the sea within the said admiralty going and returning, for the voyage of each ton weight, 6*d*.; except ships laden with wine, and ships laden with merchandise in Flanders to be shipped to and unloaded at London; and ships laden with wool and hides at London, or elsewhere within the said admiralty, which will be unloaded at Calais: which ships the wardens of the said sea shall not be obliged to escort without an allowance made. Also, taking from each fishing vessel which fishes for herring in the sea of the said admiralty, of whatsoever tonnage it be, in one week for each ton weight, 6*d*. Also, taking from other ships and fishing vessels which fish for other fish in the sea within the said admiralty, of whatsoever tonnage they be, in three weeks for each ton weight, 6*d*. Also, taking from all other ships and vessels passing by sea within the said admiralty laden with coal of Newcastle upon Tyne, of whatsoever tonnage they be, in a quarter of a year, for every ton, 6*d*. Also, taking from all other ships, boats and vessels, passing by sea within the said admiralty, laden with the goods of merchants of any kind to Esbjerg, or to Norway, or to Skane, or to any place in those parts overseas, for the outward and inward journey, from each last of hides, namely heavy lasts, 6*d*.

Item, to have from our lord the king commissions for Sir Thomas Percy, admiral of the north, Thomas Rust, John Hesildene, John Scarborough, and Robert Rust of Blakeney, wardens of the said sea, to levy and take the said grant and subsidy, both by land as well as sea, throughout the said admiralty, and to have power to appoint deputies to levy and receive the said grant and subsidies in ports throughout the said admiralty wheresoever the said wardens deem it necessary, so that the said commissioners and collectors, together with their deputies, be accountable to the surveyors and controllers of the good cities and towns named below, and to no others; and that their commissions shall be made jointly and severally to last until the feast of St Katherine next coming [25 November 1379].

Item, it is ordained by the advice of the aforesaid merchants that those named below shall be the surveyors and controllers of the aforesaid wardens and collectors, and that they shall have commissions so to act, and to levy and take the said subsidy in their ports, and deliver it in its entirety to the aforesaid wardens, without being accountable to the king.

Surveyors and controllers.

Walter Sibile, John Horn, of London

Geoffrey Dawe, of Colchester

Robert Wales, of Ipswich

William Oxnay, John Marchham of Yarmouth

John Docking, John Keep, of Lynne

William Thimbleby, of Boston

John Barden, of York

Walter Frost, of Hull

William Schropham, William Sage, of Scarborough

William Bishopdale, Robert Oliver, of Newcastle upon Tyne.

---

[13] *Original* quar,

XII. [County of Cumberland.]

Item, monstrent les communes, et nomement les povres communes del countee de Cumbr', come souvent as diverses parlementz ont monstrez, qe come la marche du dit countee adjoynant as parties d'Escoce issint est *[Page iii-64]* *[Col. a]* destruite et degaste par les enemys Escotz, qe n'y ad nully q'ose demurrer parentre la citee de Cardiol et la dite terre d'Escoce, et ovesqe ce, par la ou le chastel et la citee de Cardoil serroient le sovereyn resuit et governayl de tout le countee, les queux chastel et citee sont outrement sanz sure et sauve garde pur defaut de reparacion, et q'ils sont sanz gardein.

Sur quoy plese a nostre dit seignour le roi et son sage conseil considerer les grantz perils queux sont en point d'avenir de jour en autre, et les grantz povert et noun poair de ses communes suisditz, et issint ordeiner qe les ditz chastel et citee soient suffisantment reparaillez, et q'ils aient un puissant gardein illoeqes demurrant as coustages du roi.

Responsio.

Quant a la reparacion de la citee, il n'appartint mye au roi, mais ent soit mandement fait de compeller ceux a la reparacion faire qi sont tenuz de faire. Et quant au dit chastel, il est en reparant, et covenablement serra reparez. Et quant as gardeins de la marche y faire, le roi voet, par l'advis de son conseil, ordeiner le mieltz qe lui semblera affaire.

XIII. [Bullion.]

39. Item, supplient les communes qe come ils soient enformez par les officers sur la monoie de la toure de Londres, coment, pur defaute de bone ordinance, nul or, n'argent, n'en vient en Engleterre, mais de ce q'est en Engleterre grande partie ad este, et de jour en autre est, emporte \hors/ de la terre: et ce qe demoert en Engleterre par les clippers et par autre voie est devenuz trop feble, et de jour en autre tiele damage encresce.

Par quoy vous plese sur ce prendre bon conseil et remede, autrement les ditz officers ont garniz, come devant vous veullent estre excusez, qe si vous n'y mettez brief remede en poy de temps avenir, la ou vous purrez avoir .v. *s.* vous n'averez pas .iiij. *s.* Et oultre, l'entente des ditz officers est qe la monoie ne soit chaunge en aucun poynt, mais qe tielle ordinance soit prise, par laquel l'or et l'argent q'est pardela viegne en Engleterre, et qe ce q'est en Engleterre y demoert, auxi avant qe homme purra. Et qe ce qe demoert en Engleterre soit tenuz bone et fort, et en sa nature come reson est; au profit du roi et de tout son roialme; et au profit des marchantz d'Engleterre, qi vendent lours leynes a Caleys; et au profit des marchantz d'Engleterre, q'achatent leur marchandises en Flandres pur amesner en Engleterre; et au profit de touz ceux qi despendent les dites marchandises.[14]

Membrane 3

Le roi ent voet estre advisez par les officers de la monoie et les marchantz et autres de pluis sages sur ceste matire; et sur ce faire ordeiner le meillour remede qe ce purra faire.

XIV. [Alien religious.]

40. Item, supplient les communes, purceo q'en parlement darrein tenuz a Westm' estoit ordeine qe toutes maneres religiouses .... deussent avoir este voidez hors du roialme devant la Chaundeleure adonqes proschein

XII. [County of Cumberland.]

38. Item, the commons show, and especially the poor commons of the county of Cumberland, as they have often shown to various parliaments: whereas the march of the said county adjoining parts of Scotland is so *[Page iii-64]* *[Col. a]* destroyed and wasted by the Scottish enemies that no one dare dwell between the city of Carlisle and the said land of Scotland, and what is more, although the castle and city of Carlisle ought to be the chief resort and seat of government of the entire county, that castle and city are entirely without a sure safeguard through lack of repair, and they have no keeper.

In view of which may it please our said lord the king and his wise council to consider the great perils which are on the point of arising every day, and the great poverty and weakness of the aforesaid commons, and to ordain that the said castle and city shall be adequately repaired, and that they shall have a powerful warden dwelling there at the king's expense.

Answer.

As for the repair of the city, that is certainly not the duty of the king, but a mandate shall be issued to compel those whose obligation it is to carry out the repairs. And as for the said castle, it is being repaired and shall be fittingly repaired. And as for the wardens of the march to be appointed there, the king will, by the advice of his council, ordain as seems best to him.

XIII. [Bullion.]

39. Item, the commons request: whereas they have been informed by the officers of the mint of the Tower of London, that, because of a lack of good ordinance, neither gold nor silver arrives in England, but that most of what is in England has been, and still is withdrawn daily from the land: and what remains in England is weakened by clipping and by other means, and such damage increases from day to day.

On account of which may it please you to take good counsel and remedy, otherwise the said officers have warned us, as they wish to be excused before you, that if you do not provide a swift remedy within a short space of time, where you once could have had 5*s.* you will not have even 4*s.* And further, the opinion of the said officers is that the money should not be changed in any way, but that such an ordinance should be made by which the gold and silver which are overseas should be brought into England as quickly as possible, and the money which is in England should remain there. And that that which remains in England should be kept good and strong and of sound quality; for the profit of the king and all his realm, and for the profit of the merchants of England who sell their wool at Calais; and for the profit of the merchants of England who buy their merchandise in Flanders to be brought to England; and for the profit of all those who distribute the said merchandise.

The king will be advised in the matter by the officers of the mint and the merchants and others from amongst the most experienced, and thereupon cause the best possible remedy to be ordained.

XIV. [Alien religious.]

40. Item, the commons request: whereas in the last parliament held at Westminster it was ordained that all manner of religious .... ought to have been expelled from the realm before Candlemas then

---

[14] See PRO SC8/19/932; SC8/271/13512.

ensuant, pur certains grosses causes alors illoeqes assignez; et unqore nientmeins sont plusours des tielx religiouses deinz le roialme, a grant peril du poeple nostre seignour le roi; et nomement de ceux quex sont des /coustees\ de la meer, qar en aucuns places les enemys purront legerment et sodeynement par covyne et assent dex tielx religiouses entrer les dites places, et aler a chival ou a pee mille persones ensemble hors de mesmes les /places\ en la terre foreine du roialme, et ce deux foitz as marrees par noeet et par jour a chescun recrest de la meer, come apertement poet estre prove en l'Isle de Haillyng en Hamptshire, et ailleurs. Et auxint ils poent en un noet d'illoeqes envoier en Normandie, et certifier les enemys de novelx de roialme. Pur queux meschiefs et autres eschiure, prient les communes qe touz tielx religiouses datives soient de tout oustez hors du roialme, pur greindre asseurance d'icelle, selonc l'ordinance et l'effect del parlement avantdit.

Le roi ent ad fait faire ce q'ent estoit ordeinez pur la greindre partie; et si aucun se vorra pleindre en especial d'autre persone demurrante, due remede ent serra fait. Et le priour de Hayllyng ent ad trovez suffisante seuretee, selonc la forme del dite ordinance.

XV. [Sheriffs not to be justices of the peace.]
41. Item, monstrent les communes qe la ou plusours viscontz de les countees sont diverses foitz assignez par comissioun nostre seignour le roi d'estre justices de la pees en mesmes les countees dont ils sont viscontz, souvent foitz font lours sessions de la pees a cause d'enditer pluseurs gentz des felonies et des autres trespasses, a tiel purpos de prendre de les endites outrageouses mainprises et fynes, en grant arriresment et oppression du people.

Sur quoi plese a nostre tresgracious seignour le roi et son conseil, issint ordener qe nul homme pur le temps q'il serra viscont ne soit mye ordeine justice de la pees en mesme le countee dont il est viscont, en amendement des meschiefs suisditz.
Responsio.
Le roi le voet.

XVI. [Loans to Edward III.]
42. Item, supplient les communes qe come en temps de vostre noble aiel, qe Dieux assoille, l'an de son regne quarrant et tierce, pluseurs gentz de son roialme, sibien citezeins et burgeis des citees et burghes come autres, appresterent a vostre dit aiel plusours grandes sommes des deniers en aide de sa guerre, des quelles summes les unes sont en partie repaiez, et pleusours nient unqore de riens paiez, a grant anientisement de voz ditz povres communes, les queux ont sovent en diverses parlementz et conseilx tenuz devant ces heures pursuez, sanz due responce, remede ou paiement ent avoir; a lour grant destructioun et damage, et tresmale ensample d'autresfoitz appresĕer.

Qe plese a vostre tresgraciouse seignourie, pur Dieu, et en oevre de charitee, et en descharge del alme de vostre dit aiel, comander graciousement qe gree et plenere satisfaccion lour ent soit faite ore au present de les biens queux furent a vostre dit aiel.
Responsio.
Le roi lour ent ferra paiement si tost come il purra bonement.

XVII. [Expenses of members of parliament.]
43. Item, supplient les communes qe par la ou lours despenses sont ordeinez en brief nostre seignour le roi, assignez as viscontz de chescun countee a lever selonc le purport du dit brief a eux direct, al oeps des chivalers du parlement nostre seignour le roi illoeqes esteantz; la sont lour

approaching [2 February 1378], for certain important reasons then given there; yet nevertheless there are still many such religious within the kingdom, to the great peril of the people of our lord the king; and especially of those who dwell on the coasts of the sea, for in some places the enemies can easily and suddenly with the co-operation and assent of such religious enter the said places, and send out by horse or by foot a thousand men together from those same places into remote parts of the kingdom, and this twice with the tides by night and by day on each rising of the sea, as can clearly be proven on Hayling Island in Hampshire and elsewhere. Moreover, they can send from there to Normandy within the night, and inform the enemies of the state of the kingdom. To avoid which troubles and others the commons pray that all such endowed religious be entirely driven from the said kingdom, for the greater security thereof, in accordance with the ordinance and intention of the aforesaid parliament

The king has caused most of what was ordained to be done; and if anyone wishes to make a particular complaint about someone remaining, due remedy shall be provided. And the prior of Hayling has found sufficient guarantee thereon, in accordance with the form of the said ordinance.

XV. [Sheriffs not to be justices of the peace.]
41. Item, the commons show: whereas many sheriffs of counties have on several occasions been appointed by commission of our lord the king to be justices of the peace in the same counties in which they are sheriffs, they often hold their sessions of the peace to indict many people of felonies and other trespasses, with the intention of exacting from those indicted outrageous mainprises and fines, to the great injury and oppression of the people.

In consequence of which may it please our most gracious lord the king and his council to ordain that no man during the time when he is sheriff shall be appointed a justice of the peace in the same county of which he is sheriff, to correct the aforesaid abuses.
Answer.
The king wills it..

XVI. [Loans to Edward III.]
42. Item, the commons request: whereas in the time of your noble grandfather, whom God absolve, in the forty-third year of his reign [1369-70], many people of his kingdom, both the citizens and burgesses of the cities and boroughs as well as others, lent to your said grandfather numerous large sums of money in support of his war, of which sums some were repaid in part, yet some have not yet been paid at all, to the great injury of your said commons, who have often sued in various parliaments and councils held in the past without due answer, remedy or payment; to their great ruin and harm, and setting a very bad example for future occasions.

May it please your most gracious lordship, for God and by way of charity, and in relief of your said grandfather's soul, graciously to command that compensation and full satisfaction now be granted them from the goods which were your said grandfather's.
Answer.
The king will pay them as soon as he well can.

XVII. [Expenses of members of parliament.]
43. Item, the commons request: whereas their expenses are ordained by a writ of our lord the king instructing the sheriffs of each county to levy them in accordance with the purport of the said writ addressed to them, for the use of the knights of the parliament of our lord the king there present;

dites despenses assises sur chescune ville des ditz countees, selonc l'afferant, par la ou les unes villes sont tenuz du roi qe riens ne veullent paier, coment qe lour tenure ne soit d'auncien demesne nostre seignour le roi; et les unes villes des piers du roialme, qi tiegnent par baronie, qi riens ne veullent paier, a cause qe lours seignours sont au parlement pur eux \et/ lours hommes en propres persones, et preignent si largement cel parol 'lour hommes', qe coment q'il ne ad en une ville qe quatre ou cynk bondes, et cent ou deux centz qi tiegnent franchement, ou par rolle de courte et sont frankes du corps, unqore ne veullent riens paier as dites despenses; issint qe toute la somme par celle cause abregge et nient leve, si est recoupe en paiement des despenses des ditz chivalers, a grant damage et coustages de eux; dont ils prient remede.

Responsio.
Soit use come ent ad este devant ces heures.

XVIII. [Halfpennies and farthings.]
44. Item, monstrent les communes qe come il est ordeine par estatut, certaines poises de payn, et de cervoise certeines mesures; c'estassavoir, galon, potel et quart; et les ditz communes n'ont petit monoye pur paier pur les petites mesures, a grant damage des dites communes.
Qe plese a nostre dit seignour le roi et a son sage conseil, de faire ordeiner mayles et ferthinges, pur paier pur les petites mesures, et autres petites marchandies, pur Dieu, et en eovre de charitee; et qe les vitaillers parmy *[Page iii-65]* *[Col. a]* le roialme soient chargez de vendre lour vitailles selonc la quantitee du monoye.
Responsio.
Si tost come le roi nostre seignour purra estre purveuz de boilloun, il voet qe ce soit fait, pur commune profit du roialme.

XIX. [Tithes from woodland.]
45. Item, monstrent les communes, de ce qe grant meschief est par les persones de seinte esglise, qi demandent dismes de tout manere de boys, par colour de silva cedua, et les font travailler torcenousement par sommons grevouses devant /juges\ de seinte esglise es plusours lieux du roialme; issint qe par tiels sommons et grevances paient dismes de grosses arbres, et auxint pur maeresme q'ils abatent pur amender leur maisons, et pur foail, la ou ils ne soloient ne deussent paier du droit. Mais les dites communes, pur noun poair, et pur grant favour qe les dites persones de seinte esglise ont devant les juges, et purce qe les juges sont parties en ce cas, ils grantent lour volentee a tort, pur greindre meschief avenir eschuir, q'ad este fait as plusours des communes avant ces heures molt sovent: dont ils prient remede qe silva cedua soit declarre en autre manere qe les clercs avant ces heures le ont declarrez pur lour profit, sanz assent des seignours; et par estatut soit ordeine de subboys, ou de certeyne age dedeinz dys: qar devant le primer pestilence nulles dismes de nul manere de bois ne furent donez, grantez ne demandez. Et sur ce qe chescun homme poet avoir prohibicion sur son cas: qar ceux de la chauncellerie entendent qe de quele age qe le bois soit, s'il voet requere qe prohibicion sur ce ne gist mye.

Responsio.
Soit use come resonablement ad este devant ceste heure.

XX. [False accusations and imprisonment.]
46. Item, supplient les communes qe come au darrein parlement tenuz a Gloucestre feust ordeine qe certeines

whereas their said expenses are assessed proportionately on each town in the said counties, there are some towns held of our lord the king which will not pay anything, even though their tenure is not of the ancient demesne of our lord the king; and some towns of the peers of the realm, who hold by barony, who will not pay anything, because their lords are attending parliament in person on behalf of them and their men, and they interpret the phrase 'their men' so broadly, that although there are only four or five bondsmen, and a hundred or two hundred people who hold freely, or by roll of court and are personally free, still they will not pay anything towards the said expenses; so that the total sum for that reason is reduced and remains unlevied, and so it is deducted from the payment of the expenses of the said knights, to their great injury and cost; for which they seek remedy.
Answer.
Let it be done as it has been done before this time.

XVIII. [Halfpennies and farthings.]
44. Item, the commons show: whereas certain weights of bread and certain measures of beer were ordained by statute; namely, gallon, pottle and quart; yet the said commons do not have small coinage with which to pay for small measures, to the great injury of the said commons.
May it please our said lord the king and his wise council to order halfpennies and farthings to pay for the small measures and other small items of merchandise, for God and by way of charity; and that victuallers throughout *[Page iii-65]* *[Col. a]* the kingdom shall be charged to sell their victuals in accordance with the availability of the coinage.
Answer.
As soon as the king our lord is provided with bullion, he wills that this shall be done, for the general benefit of the kingdom.

XIX. [Tithes from woodland.]
45. Item, the commons show: that great trouble which is caused by persons of holy church, who demand tithes from all kinds of woodland by colour of silva cedua, and wickedly cause them to appear on grievous summons before judges of holy church in many places in the kingdom; so that on account of such summons and grievances they pay tithes on great trees, and also on timber which they cut to repair their houses, and for fuel, even though they are neither accustomed nor ought to pay that by right. But the said commons, through their weakness, and because of the great favour which the said persons of holy church are shown by the judges, and because the judges are party to the deed, acquiesce in the wrong, to avoid greater trouble in the future, which has been inflicted on many of the commons very often in the past: for which they seek remedy, that silva cedua shall be defined in a way other than that in which the clerics have defined it in the past to their advantage without the assent of the lords; and a statute shall be made for brushwood, or woodland of a certain age below ten years: since before the first pestilence no tithes on any kind of woodland were given, granted nor demanded. And thereupon, that each man may have prohibition on his case, since those of the chancery pay no heed to the age of the wood if a man wishes to claim that prohibition thereon.
Answer.
Let it be done as was reasonably done before this time.

XX. [False accusations and imprisonment.]
46. Item, the commons request: whereas at the last parliament held at Gloucester [1378] it was ordained that

persones, seignours et autres, serroient assignez par commission en chescun countee parmy le roialme, q'aient poair par lour commission, qe si tost come ils sachent, ou q'ils soient creablement certifiez, des aucuns routes, assemblees des mesfesours, barettours, ou autres tielx riotours, en lour marchees, en affraie du poeple, et contre la paix, de les arester tantost par lour corps, sanz attendre enditement ou autre proces de loy, et les envoier au procheine gaole ovesqe la cause de l'arest mys en escript, illoeqes a demurrer sanz estre deliverez par mainprise, baille ou en autre manere, tanq'al venue des justices de deliverance en paiis. Quelle ordinance semble a les dites communes treshorrible et perillouse pur les bones gentz et loialx parmy le roialme, les queux par celle ordinance serront pluis communement arestuz et emprisonez par manere susdit, sanz aucune cause qe les mesfeisours, come par male volentee des aucuns des ditz commissioners, et malveises informacions et fauxes acusementz de lour enemys, maintenours et mesfeisours, en paiis endossez as aucuns des justices, surmettantz q'ils sont malfeisours, q'unqes ne trespasserent. Issint qe chescun frank homme du roialme serroit en servage as ditz seignours et commissioners, et a leur retenues. La quelle ordinance est overtement encontre la grande chartre, et diverses estatutz ent faitz en temps des progenitours nostre dit seignour le roi, qe nul frank homme ne soit pris, n'emprisone, sanz due proces du loy.

Par quoy pleise a nostre dit seignour lige, et a les tresnobles seignours du parlement, qe ceste horrible et grevouse ordinance soit repelle au present; et ordeiner bone et redde punissement des toutz tielx mesfeisours, issint qe les bones gentz purront vivre en quiete, sanz estre arestuz ou emprisonez, s'il ne soit par enditement, ou autre cause resonable, come l'aunciene loy le voet.

Responsio.

Soit mesme l'estatut fait a Gloucestre de tut repellez; esteisant toutes voies l'estatut de Norht' en sa force et vertu; et ceux qi sont pris et emprisonez par vertu d'aucuns

[Col. b] parols contenuz en le dit estatut de Glouc' sanz autre enditement, soient outrement deliverez.

XXI. [Pleas of the constable and marshal.]

47. Item, supplient les communes, purce qe nous veons novelx faitz moevez devant le conestable et mareschalle, de ce qe certaines persones des liges le roi sont appellez par bille devant les ditz conestable et mareschall, des tresons et felonies supposes estre faitz deinz le roialme d'Engleterre, et illoeqes demesnez et emprisonez, contre la loy du roialme, et contre la forme del grande chartre, qe voet qe nul homme serra n'emprisone, n'en autre manere destrint, sinoun par loial jugement des ses piers, et la loy de la terre. Quelle chose s'il soit suffert serroit tresmal ensample, et anientisement de la loy de roialme.

Par quoi vous pleise ent ordeiner remede qe les dites conestable et mareschalle cessent des tielx plees tenir; et touz tieux plees des choses supposez estre faite deinz le roialme d'Engleterre soient triez et terminez devaunt justice, par commune loy du roialme, et la forme del grande chartre susdite; eantz regard qe touz les gentz du roialme, de quel estat ou condicioun q'ils soient, purront estre issint empeschez et destruitz par fauxe compassement de lour enemys.

Responsio.

Pur ce qe les heirs qi cleiment l'office de conestable sont de tendre age, et en la garde nostre seignour le roi, et la chose demande grant deliberation, et tuche si haute matire,

certain persons, lords and others, would be appointed by commission in each county throughout the kingdom, and would have authority by their commission, as soon as they knew, or were credibly informed of any bands, assemblies of malefactors, troublemakers, or other such rioters in their marches, disturbing the people, contrary to the peace, to place them immediately under bodily arrest, without waiting for indictment or any other process of law, and send them to the nearest prison with the reason for their arrest set out in writing, there to remain without being freed by mainprise, bail or any other means until the arrival of justices of delivery in the county. Which ordinance seems to the said commons most terrible and perilous for good and loyal people throughout the kingdom, who, as a result of this ordinance, shall be more commonly arrested and imprisoned in the aforesaid manner, for no other reason than that the malefactors, as well as through the ill-will of some of the said commissioners, and the wicked rumours and false accusations of their enemies, maintainers and malefactors, endorsed in the region by some of the justices, allege that they are malefactors, when they have never offended. So that every free man of the realm shall be in servitude to the said lords and commissioners and their retinues. Which ordinance is blatantly contrary to the Great Charter and various statutes made thereon in the time of the progenitors of our lord the king, that no free man should be seized or imprisoned without due process of law.

On account of which may it please our said liege lord, and the most noble lords of parliament, at once to repeal this terrible and grievous ordinance; and ordain for a good and strict punishment of all such malefactors, so that good people may live in tranquillity, without being arrested and imprisoned, if there has been no indictment or other reasonable cause, as the ancient law wills it.

Answer.

Let the statute made at Gloucester be wholly repealed; whilst the statute of Northampton shall in all ways retain its force and validity; and those who have been seized and imprisoned by virtue of any

[Col. b] words contained in the said statute of Gloucester without any other indictment shall all be freed..

XXI. [Pleas of the constable and marshal.]

47. Item, the commons request: whereas we are witnessing new actions made before the constable and marshal, in the sense that certain of the king's lieges are summoned by bill before the said constable and marshal for treasons and felonies supposedly committed within the kingdom of England, and there they are demeaned and imprisoned, contrary to the law of the realm, and contrary to the form of the Great Charter, which states that no man be imprisoned, nor distrained in any way, unless by the loyal judgment of his peers, and the law of the land. Which action, if it continues to be allowed shall set a very bad example and be destructive to the law of the land.

In consequence of which, may it please you to ordain remedy, so that the said constable and marshal shall cease to hold such pleas; and all such pleas upon things supposed to have been done within the kingdom of England shall be tried and determined before a judge, by the common law of the land and the form of the aforesaid Great Charter; bearing in mind that all the people of the kingdom, of whatever status or condition they may be, may be thus impeached and ruined by the fraudulent machinations of their enemies.

Answer.

Because the heirs who claim the office of constable are of tender age, and in the ward of our lord the king, and because the matter requires lengthy deliberation, and concerns so

et l'estat de la corone nostre seignour le roi, et le parlement est pres a fyn, les seignours du parlement ne poent, ne ne oesent, ent faire finale discution quant au present. Mais quant a la querele q'est novelement attame devaunt les ditz conestable et mareschalle, tuchant un appell de treson faite en Cornewaill', a ce q'est dit; nostre seignour le roi prendra la dite querele en sa main, et en outre ferra assigner des tieux commissioners come luy plerra, pur oier et terminer la dite querele, selonc les loys et usages de la terre, sauvant chescuny droit.

XXII. [Justices of the peace and labourers.]
48. Item, supplient les communes qe en chescun countee d'Engleterre soient ordeinez .vi. ou .vij. justices de la paix, dont les deux soient aprisez de la loy, et q'ils soient fermement chargez par nostre seignour le roi et son conseil, de faire lour sessions quatre foitz par an au meins, selonc l'estatut, et qe touz les servantz, vitaillers, laborers et artificers queux serront atteintz devant eux d'exces, et queux ferront fyn pur leur trespas, qe lour fyn ne soit meyns qe lour exces, mais pluis s'il busoigne, par discretion des justices issint a punir et par toutes les autres voies qe les estatutz de eux ent faitz purportent. Et qe chescun des ditz justices, pur le temps q'ils soient present en aucuns des sessions, aient gages de nostre seignour le roi pur chescun jour un certein, pur lour sessions, a paier par les maynes des viscontz ou ils serront justices, des issues de lour baillie. Et qe les justices aient franchement brief pur lour fee de seal hors del chauncellerie as viscontz, pur paier lour gages avauntdites. Et qe les viscontz aient auxint brief hors del chauncellerie as barons del escheqier, de lour allouer tielx paiementz sur leur acompt; et qe nul soit associe du coste par brief de la chauncellerie, n'en autre manere, as justices avantditz. Et qe les ditz justices, viscontz, seignours des villes, conestables, et bailliffs, en chescune countee aient poair d'attacher et arester toutz les puissantz de corps, wagarantz en leur baillies, de servir et laborer selonc l'estatut; et s'ils refusent de servir, q'ils soient mandez al proschein gaole, a demurrer en prisone tanq'ils se veullent justifier, selonc l'estatut ent ordeine. Et q'un estatut soit fait en ce present parlement de ceste matire, perpetuelment a durer de la feste de Seinte Michel proschein avenir: et q'en le mesne temps soit crie fait par les viscontz en chescune ville marchee par tout le roialme de la force de cest estatut, siqe les ditz servantz, vitaillers, artificers et laborers, se purroient retrere de lours outrageouses prises s'ils veullent, ou autrement les ditz *[Page iii-66]*

[Col. a] communes serront en brief temps destruitz et anientiz as touz jours. Et qe les dites justices soient esluz par l'advis des seignours et communes de parlement de les pluis vanis et sages de chescun countee, q'a celle office puissent et veullent continuelment entendre.

Responsio.
Le roi, par l'avis de son conseil, ferra ordeiner de resonable nombre des bones et suffisantz justices en chescun countee d'Engleterre, aiant consideracioun a la quantitee des countees; et voet q'ils ne soient remuez, n'autres a eux associez, sanz l'assent du conseil. Et quant a les peynes ent a ordener, il a des suffisantz paines ordeinez par estatut devaunt ceste heure, les queux peines et estatutz le roi voet qe soient mises en due execucion. Et quant as gages des justices, aient trois ou deux des ditz justices qi tendront les sessions, pur profit

important a matter as well as the estate of the crown of our lord the king, and because the parliament is near to its end, the lords of parliament are unable to, and dare not, conclude the matter at present. But as for the action which has recently begun before the said constable and marshal touching an appeal of treason made in Cornwall, as it is said, our lord the king shall take the said case into his own hands, and furthermore he will cause to be appointed such commissioners as he chooses to hear and settle the said case, in accordance with the laws and usages of the land, saving to everyone his right.

XXII. [Justices of the peace and labourers.]
48. Item, the commons request: that in every county of England there shall be ordained six or seven justices of the peace, of whom two shall be learned in law, and that they shall be strictly charged by our lord the king and his council to hold their sessions at least four times a year, in accordance with the statute, and that all servants, victuallers, labourers and artificers who shall be convicted before them of excess and who shall pay a fine for their offence shall not pay a fine which is less than their excess, but more if need be, at the discretion of the justices inflicting the punishment, and shall be punished by all the other ways provided in the statute made thereon. And that each of the said justices, for the time during which they attend any of the sessions, shall have wages from our lord the king, consisting of a fixed amount for each day of their sessions, to be paid by the sheriffs of the counties where they are justices from the issues of their bailiwick. And that the justices shall freely receive a writ for their fee sealed in chancery and instructing the sheriffs to pay their aforesaid wages. And that the sheriffs shall also have a writ from the chancery addressed to the barons of the exchequer instructing them to allow such payments on their account; and that no one shall be associated with the aforesaid justices by writ of the chancery or in any other way. And that the said justices, sheriffs, lords of the towns, constables, and bailiffs in each county shall have the power to attach and arrest all the able-bodied, wandering about their bailiwicks, to serve and labour in accordance with the statute; and if they refuse to serve, that they shall be sent to the nearest gaol, to remain in prison until they will justify themselves in accordance with the statute ordained thereon. And that a statute shall be made in this present parliament hereon, to endure forever from Michaelmas next: and that in the meantime proclamation shall be made by the sheriffs in each market town throughout the realm of the substance of this statute, so that the said servants, victuallers, artificers and labourers may withdraw their outrageous demands if they will, for otherwise the said *[Page iii-66]*

[Col. a] commons will be forever ruined and destroyed within a short space of time. And that the said justices shall be elected upon the advice of the lords and commons of parliament from amongst the most respected and experienced men of each county, who are able to and will attend continually to this duty.

Answer.
The king, upon the advice of his council, will cause a reasonable number of good and sufficient justices to be ordained in each county of England, bearing in mind the size of the counties; and he wills that they shall not be removed, or others associated with them, without the assent of the council. And as for the penalties to be ordained hereon, he has ordained adequate penalties by statute before this time, which penalties and statutes the king wills shall be duly put into practice. And as for the wages of the justices, let two or

du roi et de son poeple, la sisme partie des profitz provenantz de lours estretz, tanqe au proschein parlement.

XXIII. [Writs not to be delayed.]
49. Item, prient les communes qe come par estatut soit ordeine qe la ou tenementz sont demandez devers le roi, et evidences sont serchez en tresorie par brief, soit celui qi suit pur le roi mys a respondre apres quatre briefs retournez, chescun brief eant l'espace de .xl. jours devant le retourne, et qe cel estatut ne soit mys en delaye par mandement de petit ou de grant seal le roi. Mais, purce qe nul remede est ordene devers les gardeins du dite tresorie s'ils ne retornent les ditz briefs, si sont pluseurs du roialme delaiez de lour droit, aucun foitz a terme des ans, aucun foitz a terme de vie. Qe plese a vostre tresexcellent seignourie, en celle partie ordeiner bone et gracious remede.

Responsio.
Soit mesme l'estatut gardez et mys en execucion.

XXIV. [Shipowners and mariners.]
50. Item, prie la commune, purce qe en temps passe la terre d'Engleterre estoit bien repleine de navie, auxibien des niefs grosses come des petites, par quiel navie la dite terre estoit a celle heure grandement enrichez, et des toutes terres environ grandement redoutez. Et puis la comencement de la guerre les ditz niefs ont este si sovent arestuz pur diverses viages sur la meer, paront les possessours du dit navie /ont\ suffertz si grant damage et perde, sibien des niefs et batelx come des autres attilementz a ce appurtenantz, sanz avoir aucun regard du roi ou de roialme; et auxint leurs mariners, les unes armez, et les autres archiers, ne preignent qe .iiij. *d.* le jour; quelle prise leur semble si petite qe grande partie des mariners sont retretz des ditz offices, issint par une voie et par autre les possessours des niefs, et la navie est bien pres gaste et destruit.
Sur quoy pleise ordeiner, par advys du conseil, qe les possessours des niefs aient regard pur lour niefs, et les marineres lours gages oweles as autres archiers, comenceant les dites gages a lour moustre: quelles amendement ferront si grant esploit en temps avenir, q'il tournera a grant profit du roi et du roialme.

Responsio.
Soit usez come devant ent ad este usez.

XXV. [Knights and burgesses.]
51. Item, prient les chivalers, citezeins et burgeis, queux sont travaillez a ce present parlement pur lour countees, citees et burghes, q'ils ne soient coillours, assessours, ne contrerollours de ceste summe grante a nostre seigneur le roi au present.

Responsio.
Il plest au roi, parissint q'ils deliverent au conseil en escrit devant lour departir les nouns de pluis suffisantz et discretes persones en chescune countee, citee et burghe, sibien pur l'assession, come pur coiller le dit subside.

XXVI. [Royal pardons.]
52. Item, prie la commune qe nostre seigneur le roi de sa grace especial lour face pardoun de toutes maneres pointz d'eir tanqe a cest present feste de Pentecost, et de toutz les

three of the said justices who hold their sessions, for the benefit of the king and his people, have a sixth of the profits arising from their estreats, until the next parliament.

XXIII. [Writs not to be delayed.]
49. Item, the commons pray: whereas it is ordained by statute that where tenements are demanded from the king, and documentary evidence is searched for in the treasury by writ, whosoever sues for the king shall be brought to answer after four writs returned, each writ having the space of forty days before the return, that this statute shall not be delayed by mandate of the king's petty or great seal; but because no remedy is ordained against the keepers of the said treasury if they do not return the said writs, many people of the kingdom are delayed from obtaining their due, sometimes for years, sometimes for life. May it please your most excellent lordship, to ordain a good and gracious remedy for this matter.
Answer.
Let the same statute be kept and put into practice.

XXIV. [Shipowners and mariners.]
50. Item, the commons pray: whereas in the past the land of England was well provided with a resplendent navy, comprising large ships as well as small, by which navy the said land was greatly enriched at that time, and greatly feared by all neighbouring lands. Yet since the beginning of the war the said ships have been seized too often for various expeditions on the sea, as a result of which the owners of the said fleet have suffered very great damage and loss, both of ships and boats as well as equipment pertaining to them, without any regard given to the king or the kingdom; and in addition, their mariners, some armed and some archers, only receive 4*d.* a day; which payment seems so small to them that a large number of the mariners have abandoned their said duties, so that by one means or another the shipowners and the fleet are almost wholly wasted and destroyed.
Whereupon, may it please you to ordain, by the advice of the council, that the owners of ships shall receive consideration for their ships, and that the mariners shall receive wages equal to other archers, beginning the said wages at their muster: which amendment shall encourage such effort in time to come that it will turn to the great advantage of the king and the kingdom.
Answer.
Let it be done as it has been done in the past.

XXV. [Knights and burgesses.]
51. Item, the knights, citizens and burgesses who have travelled to this present parliament to represent their counties, cities and boroughs, pray that they be not made collectors, assessors or controllers of the great sum now granted to our lord the king.
Answer.
It is pleasing to the king, provided that they submit to the council in writing before their departure the names of the most worthy and discreet people in each county, city and borough, both for the assessment as well as for the collection of the said subsidy.

XXVI. [Royal pardons.]
52. Item, the commons pray: that our lord the king of his special grace shall grant them pardon of all manner of eyre until this present feast of Whitsun, and from all the

[Col. b] desperate debts pending in the exchequer from the time of his progenitors; and also from all points of eyre of the forest until the aforesaid feast. And thereupon to grant charters from the chancery in each county to those who will sue, for the price of sealing.

Answer.

The king will consider it.

XXVII. [Treasurers of war.]

53. Item, the commons pray: that the treasurers of war shall be discharged from their offices, and that the treasurer of the king of England shall be appointed to receive all the silver, and all the grants which shall be made henceforth for the wars, in the way which it has been done in the past.

Answer.

It is pleasing to the king that the said treasurers of the war shall henceforth be discharged from performance of their duties, and that the treasurer of England and the chamberlain of the exchequer shall continue in office, as has customarily been done in the past.

XXVIII. [Merchants and bullion.]

54. Item, the commons pray: that no man shall bring into England cloth of gold or of silk, kerchiefs, precious stones, or any kind of jewels, nor fur; nor take any wool out of England from this day onwards unless he brings 2*s.* sterling in bullion for each pound, to increase the gold and silver within the kingdom; to last until the next parliament.

Answer.

It is ordained in parliament that for each pound's worth of gold and silk cloth, of kerchiefs, precious stones and all kinds of jewels, and fur, to be brought into the kingdom after the feast of St John next [24 June 1379]; and also for each pound by number arising from the last sale in England to be made, the wool, woolfells and hides which shall be taken out of the kingdom after the said feast, the merchants shall be obliged to bring bullion of gold or silver to a value of twelve silver pennies to the Tower of London. That is to say, for the said cloth, kerchiefs, precious stones, jewels, and fur, within half a year of the arrival of the same within the kingdom of England; and for the said wool, hides, and skins, within a year of the passage of the same out of the said kingdom. And the merchants shall give surety before the customs officers in the ports where the said items are being imported or exported, that they shall perform it well and loyally; namely, the said merchants entering the said kingdom with the said cloth, kerchiefs, precious stones, jewels and fur, on their arrival; and the merchants of wool, woolfells and hides, on their passage out of the said kingdom. And this ordinance shall take effect from the said feast of St John next, and shall remain in force until the next parliament, so that in the meantime it can be gauged whether it is beneficial for the king and his kingdom or not. And if our said lord the king wills it, that the said pledges thus made in the aforementioned manner shall be sent by the said customs officers to the exchequer at the end of the said year.

XXIX. [Sumptuary law.]

55. Item, that no man or woman within the said kingdom, except knights and ladies, shall wear any kind of fur, cloth of gold, or ribbon of gold, or cloth of silk, if they cannot spend £40 a year, on pain of forfeiting whatever they wear if they contravene this.

Responsio.

Le roi s'advisera tanqe a proschein parlement.

XXX. [Goldsmiths' hallmarks.]

56. Item, pur ce qe l'or et l'argent q'est oevere par orfevres en Engleterre est plusours foitz trove meyns fyn q'il doit estre, par cause qe les orfevres sont lours juges mesmes; soit ordeine decy enavant, qe chescune orfevre eit son merche propre sur son oevereigne, et l'assaie de touche soit as mairs et governours des citees et burghes, ovesqe l'eide de meistre del monoye, s'il mestre soit; portant le merche del citee ou burghe ou il est assaie.

Page iii-67

Item, est ordenez qe chescun orfevre d'Engleterre eit desore son propre merche par soi mesmes; et si aucun vesselle q'est affaire soit trovez deinz le roialme apres la nativite Seint Johan proschein venant nient merchez del merche del orfevre qe le fist, ou soit de /pir\ alay qe l'esterling; qe mesme l'orfevre soit tenuz de paier a la partie pleignante le double value de mesme le vesselle, et jademeins eit la prisone, et face fyn selonc la quantitee et qualitee de trespas. Et enoutre nostre seignour le roi ferra assigner des tieux come luy plerra, de faire la dite assaie sibien a Londres come aillours, as touz les foitz come embusoignera; et apres l'assaie faite, de mercher le dit oeveraigne de une autre merche a ce assigner par nostre dit seignour le roi. Et est assentuz qe ceste ordinance comencera de tenir lieu a la dite feste de Seint Johan, et durera tanqe a proschein parlement, pur assaier en le moien temps si ce soit profitable, ou nemye.

SEQUNTUR QUEDAM SUPPLICATIONES PRO VILLA DE CALES'.

[Staple at Calais.]

57. A nostre treshaut et trespuissant seignour le roi et son tresnoble et tressage conseil monstrent voz simples burgeis de Caleis qe come les estoit grantez en parlement par chartre du nostre tresredoute seignour le roi Edward qi Dieux assoille; la quelle chartre est conferme en parlement par nostre dit seignour le roi q'orest; qe l'estaple des leynes, quirs, peaux lanutz, plounc, esteym, furmage, \[buir,]/ plumes, gaule, felparie et su qe deveroient estre amesnez hors d'Engleterre, Irlande et Gales, et la ville de Berewyk sur Twede, serroient amesnez a la ville de Caleys, et nul autre part aillours, pur profit du roi. Des quelles marchandises, leynes et peaux lanutz, de Jernemuth' et d'icelle paiis, et grant partie de furmage, et de buyr, de plounc et d'esteyn, et marchandises d'Irland et de Gales, ont este retraitez par long temps, et sont amesnez en Flandres et aillours; a grant damage du roi, come \de/ prendre sa custume des dites marchandises a la ville de Caleys, sibien al entre come al issue. Et auxi oue les dites marchandises sont amesnez, ils ne sont mye serchez pur le roi s'ils soient loialment custumez en Engleterre, ou noun.

Plese a vostre tresnoble hautesse et seignourie ordeiner qe toutes marchandises susdites soient constreintz d'estre amesnez a l'estaple de Caleys, come est contenu en leur dite chartre, et confirmacion, a grant profit du roi, et amendement de la dite ville.

\[*Responsio.*]/

Quant a cest primer article, le roi voet qe la chartre estoise en sa force en touz pointz, forspris des choses q'ont congie en parlement, puis la date de mesme la chartre, de passer aillours.

Answer.

The king will consider it further before the next parliament.

XXX. [Goldsmiths' hallmarks.]

56. Item, whereas gold and silver which is worked by goldsmiths in England is on many occasions found to be less pure than it ought to be, because the goldsmiths are their own judges; be it ordained from now on that each goldsmith shall place his own stamp upon his work, and the assay of touch shall fall to the mayors and governors of the cities and boroughs, assisted by the master of the mint if need be; bearing the stamp of the city or borough where it was assayed.

Item, it is ordained that every goldsmith of England shall henceforth have his own personal stamp; and if any vessel to be made is found within the kingdom after the nativity of St John next [24 June 1379] without the stamp of the goldsmith who made it, or is made of base alloy rather than sterling silver; that the same goldsmith shall be obliged to pay to the plaintiff party twice the value of the same vessel, and even then he shall be sent to prison, and pay a fine in accordance with the degree and nature of his offence. Furthermore, our lord the king shall appoint whomsoever he chooses to carry out the said assay at London as well as elsewhere, as often as need be; and after the assay is done, to stamp the said work with another mark assigned for the purpose by our said lord the king. And it is agreed that this ordinance shall begin to take effect on the said feast of St John, and last until the next parliament, so as to see in the meantime whether it be profitable or not.

HERE FOLLOW CERTAIN REQUESTS MADE ON BEHALF OF THE TOWN OF CALAIS.

[Staple at Calais.]

57. To our most high and exalted lord the king and his most noble and wise council, your simple burgesses of Calais show: whereas it was granted them in parliament by a charter of our most redoubtable lord the king Edward, whom God absolve - which charter was confirmed in parliament by our said lord the present king - that the staple of wool, hides, woolfells, lead, tin, cheese, butter, feathers, gall, frippery, and fat which ought to be taken out of England, Ireland and Wales and the town of Berwick upon Tweed, should be taken to the town of Calais, and nowhere else, for the profit of the king. Of which merchandise, wool and woolfells from Yarmouth and the lands there, and a large amount of cheese, butter, lead, tin, and merchandise of Ireland and Wales, have long been withdrawn, and are taken to Flanders and elsewhere, to the great injury of the king in taking his custom from the said merchandise at the town of Calais, both on entry and exit. Moreover, where the said customs are taken, they are not searched on behalf of the king to see whether they have had customs faithfully paid on them in England or not.

May it please your most noble highness and lordship to ordain that it shall be compulsory to take all the aforesaid merchandise to the staple of Calais, as is contained in their said charter and confirmation, to the great profit of the king and amendment of the said town.

Answer.

As for the first article, the king wills that the charter shall remain in force in all points, except for things which have been permitted in parliament, since the date of the same charter, to pass elsewhere.

[Evasion of Calais staple.]

Item, d'enquere pur profit du roi, de diverses marchandises qe duissent estre amesnez a l'estaple en la ville de Caleis, et sont amesnez en Flandres et aillours, a grant prejudice et damage du roi.

Pleise a conseil nostre seignour le roi, faire venir un foitz en l'an toutes les cokettes de les custumers de toutz les portz d'Engleterre, Irlande et Gales, et auxint toutes les cokettes del sercheour de Caleis, pur examiner l'un cokett encountre l'autre, et issint purra homme savoir queux marchantz ont amesnez lour marchandises aillours qe a Caleys, encontre l'ordinance del parlement, et la chartre de Caleis, et par ycele voie le roi poet avoir grant profit des forfaitures de ceux q'ont fait encontre l'ordinance avauntdite. Et soient les custumers chargez qe nul alien face eskipper nulles marchandises a nul port d'Engleterre forsqe en niefs ovesqe les biens d'autres marchantz Engleis, et qe les dites aliens troevent suffisante seuretee par meinprise d'Engleis, devaunt lour departir hors del port, de les amesner a Caleys, et nul part aillours, sur peine de forfaiture

[Col. b] de lours dites biens issint amesnez, et lours persones d'estre emprisonez a la volente le roi.

\[Responsio.]/

Le roi ad grantez ceste article en touz pointz des choses en Engleterre tantsoulement; et voet qe per fourme de mesme l'article bone ordinance ent soit faite, et proclame en touz les portz d'Engleterre, et sur ce soient briefs et mandementz faitz, sibien as tresorer et sercheour de Caleys come a les custumers des ditz portz; lours chargeantz estroitement q'ils facent venir et porter d'an en an, a les oeptaves de Seint Michel a pluis tard, a l'escheqier nostre seignour le roi, touz les ditz cokettes, ensemble ovesqe toutes les suretees issint faites as ditz portz d'Engleterre, par obligations ou en autre manere, aufyn qe les tresorer et barons del dit escheqier y purront loialment estre acertez de la pleine veritee; et par tant purront ordiner oultre, pur le profit nostre seignour le roi en celle partie, come mieltz lour semblera.

[Great hall at Calais.]

Item, come grante estoit par la dite chartre as ditz burgeys, en sustentacion des plusours chargez q'ils deveront faire et supporter deinz la dite ville, l'assise du pain, vin et de cervoise, et le stallage des des[15] drapers, et de bochiers, et autres marchantz illoeqes: ore vient le tresorer de Caleys, et les voet ouster d'un partie de la grant sale en la quele les bochiers tienent lour bocherie, par vertu et maundement d'une lettre du prive seal, par suggestioun nient resonable; la quele sale le dit tresorer les delivera par vertu d'un brief du roi a la primer grante de lour dite chartre, et ont toutdis depuis, et plusours ans a devant, este en possessioun.

Pleise a vostre tresnoble hautesse, et tresgraciouse seignourie, granter as dites burgeys q'ils puissent rejoier la dite sale, ovesqe la stallage des drapers et de bochiers avauntnomez, selonc la tenure des chartre et confirmacioun, et usage avauntdites; qar si la dite sale lour soit detenu, ils n'averont lieu ou a tenir la draperie ne la bocherie, ne les loys de la ville suisdite.

[Bequests of chattels at Calais.]

Item, come lour estoit grante en la dite chartre q'ils puissent deviser en testament lour terres et tenementz auxi franchement come les citezeins de Londres; supplient les ditz

[Evasion of Calais Staple.]

Item, to inquire for the king's benefit, into various goods which ought to be brought to the staple in the town of Calais, and yet are taken to Flanders and elsewhere, to the great detriment and injury of the king.

May it please the council of our lord the king, to assemble once a year all the cockets of the customs officers of all the ports of England, Ireland and Wales, and also all the cockets of the searcher of Calais, to compare one cocket with another, for thus it would be possible to know which merchants had taken their merchandise to places other than Calais, contrary to the ordinance of parliament and the charter of Calais; and by that means the king could make a large profit from the forfeitures of those who have acted against the aforesaid ordinance. And let the customs officers be charged to ensure that no alien cause any merchandise to be shipped from any English port except in ships also carrying the goods of other English merchants, and that the said aliens shall provide adequate surety by mainprise of an Englishman before their departure from the port to take them to Calais and nowhere else, on pain of forfeiting

[Col. b] their said goods thus taken elsewhere, and being imprisoned at the king's will.

Answer.

The king has granted this article in its entirety so far as it touches England; and he wills that by way of the same article a good ordinance may be made thereon, and proclaimed in all the ports of England, and writs and mandates on this issued, both to the treasurer and searcher of Calais as well as to the customs officers of the said ports; strictly charging them that they appear each year by the octaves of Michaelmas at the latest, and bring with them to the exchequer of our lord the king all the said cockets, together with all the sureties thus made at the said ports of England by bonds or in other manner, that the treasurer and barons of the said exchequer may be faithfully assured of the whole truth; that they may ordain further for the profit of our lord the king in the matter, as shall seem best to them.

[Great hall at Calais.]

Item, whereas the assize of bread, wine, and beer, and the stallage of drapers and butchers and other merchants there was granted by the said charter to the said burgesses, in support of the many charges they are obliged to bear and fulfill within the said town: yet now the treasurer of Calais comes, and wishes to oust them from one part of the great hall in which the butchers hold their market, by virtue and mandate of a letter of privy seal, on unreasonable grounds; which hall the said treasurer assigned them by virtue of a writ of the king on the occasion of the first grant of their said charter, and they have had it ever since in their possession, and for many years preceding this.

May it please your most noble highness, and most gracious lordship, to grant to the said burgesses that they may again enjoy use of the said hall, together with the stallage of the aforenamed drapers and butchers, in accordance with the tenor of the aforesaid charter and confirmation, and previous usage; for if they are deprived of the said hall, they will have nowhere to hold their drapers' or butchers' markets, nor the business laws of the aforesaid town.

[Bequests of chattels at Calais.]

Item, whereas it was granted them in the said charter that they might bequeath their lands and tenements by testament as freely as the citizens of London; the said burgesses

---

[15] des *repeated*

burgeys q'ils puissent deviser en testament lours moebles auxi franchement come lours terres et tenementz desuisditz; nonobstante aucuns articles, usages, ou custumes usees en les dites parties selonc les aunciens loys: purceo qe par ycelles loys le baroun ne poet rien deviser a sa femme, ne la femme a son baroun.

\[*Responsio.*]/

Estoisent lours aunciens loys et custumes.

[Exemption from customs at Calais.]

Item, supplient les dites burgeys q'ils puissent estre frankes de custume et de tollonu des draps lanuz et liengez q'ils amesnent a la dite ville pur la sustenance d'ycelle, sibien al entre come al issu, come lour estoit graunte par chartre nostre seignour le roi, qi Dieux assoille, q'ils deveroient estre auxi frankes come les burgeys estoient illoeqes en auncien temps; pur les queux le tresorer de Caleys ad eue plusours mandementz de certifier al conseil nostre seignour le roi q'orest, par quoi ils ne deveroient mye estre quitz des dites custumes; la quele certificacioun il n'ad mye fait.

\[*Responsio.*]/

Quant as vitailles necessaires pur lours despenses, il plest au roi.

[Plea of debt at Calais.]

Item, monstrent les meir et aldermen de la dite ville qe come ils avoient renduz un jugement, selonc les lois et usages auncienement en la dite ville, come lour chartre fait mencion, parentre William de Montagu, conte de Salesbury, procuratour et attorne de Johan de Biterleigh', et Alice sa femme, executrice du testament William Tenturer le puisne, nadgaires citezein de Novel Salesbury, et autres executours du dite Alice del testament desuisdit, demandant, et William Gilbert *[Page iii-68]*

[Col. a] de Salesbury, defendant, en un plee de dette. Le quiel jugement l'avauntdit William Gilbert fist appeller envers le conseil nostre dit seignour le roi. Et pur le quiel jugement corriger certains commissairs estoient assignez par commissioun nostre seignour le roi suisdit, a la denominacion le dit William Gilbert: les queux comissairs ont affermez le dit jugement selonc les loys avauntdites; supplient les avauntdites meir et aldermen qe si le dit jugement serra autre foitz corrige, il purra estre corige par tielles gentz qi scievent les loys du dit paiis: qar la loy d'Engleterre est expressement encontre lour chartre, s'il ne soit des terres et tenementz: considere qe depuis le conquest n'estoit unqes jugement qe fuist rendu en la dite ville par les loys et custumes d'ycele, corige, ne reverse, par les loys d'Engleterre.

\[*Responsio.*]/

Soit la dite chartre et les franchises de Caleys monstrez en la chauncellarie, et illoeqes appellez les parties, les justices et les sergeantz le roi, si par inspeccion de mesmes les chartre et libertees purra apparoir, qe la chose appartint a la discussion de la courte le roi en Engleterre, adonqes illoeqes soit la querele determine; et si noun, soit remandez a Caleys pur y estre terminez, selonc les loys et usages du paiis.

Membrane 1

[University and town of Cambridge.]

58. A nostre tresredoute seignour le roi et son tressage conseil supplient voz humbles chappelleins et oratours le chaunceller et escolers de vostre universite de Cantebrigg' qe come, al derrain parlement tenuz a Gloucestre, vous lours

request that they may bequeath by testament their chattels as freely as their aforesaid lands and tenements; notwithstanding certain articles, usages, or customs practised in those parts by ancient laws: because by those laws the husband cannot leave anything to his wife, nor the wife anything to her husband.

Answer.

Let their ancient laws and customs remain in force.

[Exemption from customs at Calais.]

Item, the said burgesses request: that they may be spared custom and tax on woollen and linen cloth which they take to the said town for the sustenance of the same, both on entry as well as on exit, as was granted to them by a charter of our lord the king, whom God absolve, and that they ought to be as free as the burgesses dwelling there in ancient times; on behalf of whom the treasurer of Calais had received many mandates ordering him to inform the council of our lord the present king as to the reasons why they should not indeed be quit of the said customs; yet he has not provided that information.

Answer.

With regard to the victuals necessary for their expenses, it pleases the king.

[Plea of debt at Calais.]

Item, the mayor and aldermen of the said town show: whereas they have made a judgment in accordance with the ancient laws and usages of the said town, as their charter makes mention, in the case between William Montagu, earl of Salisbury, proctor and attorney of John Bitterley, Alice his wife, executrix of the will of William Dyer the younger, lately a citizen of New Salisbury, and other executors of the said Alice of the aforesaid will, plaintiff, and William Gilbert *[Page iii-68]*

[Col. a] of Salisbury defendant, in a plea of debt. Which judgment the aforesaid William Gilbert caused to be taken before the council of our said lord the king. And for the correction of the judgment certain commissioners were appointed by commission of our aforesaid lord the king, at the nomination of the said William Gilbert, which commissioners affirmed the said judgment in accordance with the aforesaid laws; the aforesaid mayor and aldermen request that if the said judgment is corrected on another occasion, it may be corrected by persons as know the laws of the land, since the law of England expressly runs contrary to their charter, if it be not of lands and tenements: considering that since the conquest there never was a judgment rendered in the said town by the laws and customs of the same, which has been corrected or reversed by the laws of England.

Answer.

Let the said charter and the franchises of Calais be shown in the chancery and let there be called the parties, the justices and the king's serjeants, so that if is appears on inspection of the same charters and liberties that the matter ought to be discussed by the court of the king in England, then the case shall be determined there; and if not, it shall be sent back to Calais to be determined there, in accordance with the laws and usages of the country.

[University and town of Cambridge.]

58. To our most redoubtable lord the king and his most wise council, your humble chaplains and orators the chancellor and scholars of your university of Cambridge request: whereas, at the last parliament held at Gloucester,

grantastes par voz graciouses lettres patentes les punissementz de vendours de touz maneres vitailles, et fauxes mesures et poiis faitz et

[Col. b] usez en la dite ville, en defaute del mair illoeqes; c'estassavoir, s'il n'ent fist due punishment, ou feust necligent et remys en celle partie; quelle vostre grant et l'execucioun d'ycelle, coment qe celle feust faite pur ease et commune profit del dite universitee, et qe plusours notables defautes y soient sovent trovez en defaute del dit mair et ses ministres, mesme le mair et baillifs, et autres gentz du dite ville par covyne entre eux faite, lour destourbent en quanqe ils puissent de mettre vostre dit grant en execucion, a grante chiertee des vitales, et descrees de vostre dite universitee, et encountre commune profit.

Qe plese a vostre roial majeste, pur l'amour de Dieu, et pur encrees et quiete de vostre dite universitee, et pur commune profit, graciousement confermer as ditz suppliantz et a lours successours le dit vostre grant: adjustant oultre a ycelle, si vous plest, q'ils aient poair de punir les ditz mair et baillifs et lours officers, s'ils soient vitaillers tantcome ils soient en lour offices, et lours fauxes mesures sibien come autres; et s'il busoigne d'enquere des ditz officers vitaillers, pur Dieu, et en oevre de /charitee.\ Et auxint, qe le dit chanceller, ses deputes et commissairs, aient poiar de veer et examiner les proces[16] par eux comenciez par vertu des dites lettres en celle partie, et mesmes les proces comenciez duement oier et terminer selonc les loys de la terre, pur commune profit d'ycelle.

\[*Responsio.*]/

Si plest au roi, semble as seignours de parlement qe ce lour est a granter pur cynk \ans/ proschein avenirs.[17]

you granted them by your gracious letters patent the punishments for sellers of all kinds of victuals and false measures and weights made and

[Col. b] used in the said town, in default of the mayor there; namely, that if he did not inflict due punishment, or was negligent or remiss in the matter; which grant by you and its execution were made for the ease and general benefit of the said university; and many noteworthy faults are often found in the actions of the mayor and his ministers, for the same mayor and bailiffs, and other men of the said town, by a plot conceived amongst them, disturb them whenever they are about to put your said grant into practice, causing a great dearth of victuals, and the injury of your said university, and contrary to the common good.

May it please your royal majesty, for the love of God and for the advancement and tranquillity of your said university, and for the common good, graciously to confirm your said grant for the said supplicants and their successors: adding to the same, if it please you, that they shall have the authority to punish the said mayor and bailiffs and their officers if they are victuallers while they remain in office, and their false measures as well as other things; and if necessary, to make inquiries about the said officer victuallers, for God and by way of charity. Furthermore, that the said chancellor, his deputies and commissioners shall have the power to inspect and examine the process begun by them by virtue of the said letters in this matter, and that the same process once begun shall be duly heard and determined in accordance with the laws of the land, for the common benefit thereof.

Answer.

If it please the king, it seems to the lords of parliament that this is to be granted to them for five years to come.

---

[16] *Original* parties
[17] PRO SC8/19/913.

Appendix

Westminster

24 April 1379

1. Grant to the chancellor of the University of Cambridge of a five-year extension to his right to punish offenders against the assizes of bread, wine, ale and other victuals in the town, if the mayor and bailiffs are negligent in this matter. By king and petition of parliament. Dated 24 April 1379.
   Source: *CPR 1377-81*, 349. (Cf. Parliament of 1378, Appendix, and no. 18 below).

2. Order to the sheriffs to proclaim an ordinance made in this parliament that every goldsmith shall have his particular mark to mark vessels of silver made by him. By king in parliament. Dated 6 June 1379.
   Source: *CCR 1377-81*, 255.

3. Order to the justices to proceed to judgment in a suit between the king and Thomas bishop of Exeter concerning the patronage of Plympton priory (Devon), following a petition by the bishop to parliament. Dated 13 November 1379.
   Source: *CCR 1377-81*, 274.

4. Appointment of Thomas de Percy, admiral of the north, and others to defend Scarborough and the surrounding coast, and to collect a subsidy for their expenses; simultaneous appointment of various persons to survey and control them. By petition of the commonalty in parliament. Dated 16 June 1379.
   Source: *CPR 1377-81*, 355.

5. Petition to the king and council from the master and scholars of the college called 'Mokel University Hall' at Oxford, said to have been founded by King Alfred and at which Bede among others is said to have been a scholar, for the recovery of certain lands of which they claim to have been unjustly deprived by Edmund Franceys, citizen of London. *No endorsement*
   Source: Printed in full in *RP*, III.69.

6. Petition to the king and council from Alexander, archbishop of York, claiming the right to confirm the provost of a college called 'Otuenhall' in Oxford, which right has recently been denied to him due to dissensions with in the college.
   Endorsed: A commission of bishops and royal clerks is to be appointed in parliament to decided this matter.
   Source: Printed in full in *RP*, III.69.

7. Petition to the council and lords of parliament from the people of Northumberland for relief from the depredations of the Scots and their consequent poverty.
   Endorsed: Let the supplicants, by the advice of the wardens of the March, state clearly how the situation might best be remedied, and discuss this with the lords.
   Source: Printed in full in *RP*, III.69.

8. Petition to the king and his council of parliament from Reginald Lord Grey of Ruthin complaining of a process which has been brought to his prejudice before John de la Pole, justice of Chester, concerning his lands in North Wales.
   Endorsed: A letter of privy seal is to be sent to de la Pole to appear before the council concerning this matter.
   Source: Printed in full in *RP*, III.70.

9. Petition to the king and council from the people of the town of Rye (Sussex), which has been taken several times by the king's enemies, asking that they be granted the fines paid by labourers and artificers to the justices of the peace in Sussex to enable them to repair their walls. *No endorsement*
   Source: Printed in full in *RP*, III.70.

10. Petition to the council from the mayor and burgesses of [King's] Lynn (Norfolk) asking that men of the town should not be arrayed for service by outsiders since they are needed for the defence of the town. *No endorsement*
   Source: Printed in full in *RP*, III.70.

11. Petition to the king from the mayor and commonalty of the town of Melcombe (Dorset) complaining that the town has recently been devastated by the king's enemies and asking for various financial privileges such as are enjoyed by other towns. *No endorsement*
   Source: Printed in full in *RP*, III.70.

12. Petition to the king, nobles and commons in parliament from the mariners of England complaining that they are only paid 'threepence per day, and sixpence per week', and asking to be paid higher wages.
   Endorsed: The king will take the advice of the great council.
   Source: Printed in full in *RP*, III.253. (See Item 50 on the roll).

13. Petition to the king, nobles and commons in parliament from the masters of ships and barges of the realm asking for rewards and compensation for the use of their vessels in the crown's service.
   Endorsed: The king wishes to reward those who deserve it.
   Source: Printed in full in *RP*, III.253.

14. Petition to the lords of parliament requesting that the agreement that masters of ships be permitted to claim three shillings and fourpence per tuntight for each quarter that they serve, in order to pay for their equipment, be adhered to. *No Endorsement*
   Source: Printed in full in *RP*, III.253.

15. Petition to the lords of parliament from the merchants of the German Hansa who are accustomed to coming to England, requesting confirmation of the franchises granted to them by the charters of former kings, which have not been respected in recent times, as a result of which they have been obliged to pay additional dues and some of them have had their goods arrested or been imprisoned, on the pretext that similar wrongs were being committed by the lords of Prussia against English merchants.

Endorsed: It is agreed in parliament that goods and merchandise should be returned to the petitioners in return for pledges, or divided up between them, and that a letter of privy seal be sent to the Master of Prussia asking him to make similar redress to English merchants there.
Source: Printed in full in *RP*, III.253-4.

16. Petition to the king and council from the merchants of England complaining that the recent ordinance of parliament to the effect that 'no cloth shall be offered for sale before it has been sealed with the appropriate seal' has been misinterpreted, and asking that the wording of the ordinance be clarified.
Endorsed: It should be explained how this has damaged people.
Source: Printed in full in *RP*, III.254.

17. Petition to the king and council from the burgesses of Dunwich (Suffolk) asking that the inhabitants of neighbouring towns and religious houses be prohibited from holding their fairs and markets within the haven of Dunwich, as this is affecting their profits from customs and subsidies, which contribute to their annual fee-farm payable to the king. *No Endorsement*
Source: Printed in full in *RP*, III.254.

18. Petition to the king and council from the chancellor and scholars of the University of Cambridge requesting confirmation of certain privileges granted to them formerly concerning the sale of wine and victuals within the town and the execution of justice upon persons who transgress against the university authorities. *No Endorsement*
Source: Printed in full in *RP*, III.254. (See no. 1 above).

19. Petition to the king and council from the inhabitants of the town of Salisbury complaining that the king's officers in Clarendon Park choose certain persons in the town each year and compel them to sell the underwood from the park, to the great damage of the latter.
Endorsed: The officers and ministers of the forest and park have no authority to act outside the bounds of the forest without the king's licence.
Source: Printed in full in *RP*, III.254-5.

20. Petition to the king from the people of the city of Salisbury informing him that they have begun to enclose the city with great ditches for its protection from the king's enemies, and asking that all those who hold tenements or rents within the city be obliged to contribute to the cost of this.
Endorsed: Let the mayor and bailiffs have the power to compel those who are recalcitrant to do this.
Source: Printed in full in *RP*, III.255.

21. Petition to the king from the community of the borough of Wareham (Dorset), who are tenants of the earl of March, who is in the king's wardship, asking that their two port-reeves should not be called to account at the exchequer as they have been for the past twenty-four years, for they are obliged to account only to the earl of March and his ministers. *No Endorsement*
Source: Printed in full in *RP*, III.255.

22. (a) Petition to the king from the inhabitants of the county of Sussex asking him to appoint a sufficient guard for the castle of Bramber, which is dilapidated and, being on the coast, open to attack by the king's enemies. (b) Petition to the king and council from the inhabitants of the county of Sussex complaining that they have suffered greatly at the hands of the king's enemies and asking them to ordain a remedy for this. *Endorsement*: These two bills are to be sent before the lords.
Source: Printed in full in *RP*, III.255.

23. Petition to the king and council from the commons of various cities and boroughs requesting repayment of loans which they made to Edward III in support of his wars.
Endorsed: Let them ask the executors or administrators of the goods of the former king.
Source: Printed in full in *RP*, III.255. (See Item 42 on the roll)

24. Petition to the king and lords of parliament from William Heron of Ford (Northumberland) complaining that the Scots have committed damage to the value of £100 to his tenants, lands and beasts, in return for which his men rode against the Scots and seized a pound, for which the earl of Northumberland obliged him to hand over 320 cattle, 1600 sheep and £100 to the Scots, promising him restitution in due course, which he has not received. The earl also imprisoned him at Newcastle, and various of the earl's men assaulted his castle of Ford; for all of which he prays remedy.
Endorsed: Certain lords are appointed to arbitrate between the two parties.
Source: Printed in full in *RP*, III.255-6.

25. Petition to the king and council from Joan, wife of Sir Thomas Felton, who is being held as a prisoner of war in Aquitaine, asking that the Count of St-Pol, a French prisoner of war in England, should not be released until Sir Thomas has also been released.
Endorsed: The king by advice of his council will do what seems best to him.
Source: Printed in full in *RP*, III.256.

26. Petition to the king and his council from Maud, wife of Sir John de Bourchier, who has spent a long time in prison in Brittany and has been put to ransom for 12,000 francs but has been let down as a result of various agreements not being fulfilled by others; his wife now asks the king and council to help in securing his release, in part by not releasin Roger Belfort, a French prisoner, until the said agreements have been performed.
Endorsed: The king will do what seems best to him.
Source: Printed in full in *RP*, III.256.

27. Petition to the king from his lieges of the county of Kent complaining that they are amerced and constrained by the ministers of Dover castle, especially those called catchpoles, to respond to writs, pleas and so forth, and asking him to restrict the power of his ministers at the castle to what it used by custom to be, as it was agreed to do in the parliament of 1376.
Endorsed: This bill is to be sent to the chancery, where on the advice of the justices right will be done to the parties.
Source: Printed in full in *RP*, III.256.

28. Petition to the king, prelates and lords in parliament from the prior of Blyth (Nottinghamshire), complaining that although he is a perpetual, instituted by the archbishop of York, and not removable, one Master John de Middleton, a secular, has ousted him from his priory by colour of a letter patent purchased from the king, and has sold and wasted his goods. The prior asks that this letter patent be cancelled and that he be restored to his priory. He also attaches a copy of the letter from Pope Lucius II (1144-45) forbidding anyone to remove the priors of Byth. *No Endorsement*

Source: Printed in full in *RP*, III.256.

29. Petition to the king and council from the lords and commons of England that it be ordained in this parliament that all the 'special bills' submitted to this parliament to which no response or endorsement has been made before the end of the parliament should be endorsed or responded to within a short time afterwards by certain lords assigned to do this, and that they should subsequently be regarded as just as valid and enforceable as other bills of parliament, just as if this had been done in full parliament; and that the same should be the case in all parliaments in the future. *No Endorsement*

Source: Printed in full in *RP*, III.256. (See Item 28 on the roll).

30. Petition to the king and lords of parliament from Edmund, earl of March, that his tenants in the towns of Great Gransden and Wells (Huntingdonshire) should not be distrained to contribute to the repair of the bridge at Huntingdon, since they are by right exempted from this and other similar impositions.

Endorsed: This bill is to be sent into the chancery, where right will be done, and in the meantime the process against the said tenants is to be halted.

Source: Printed in full in *RP*, III.177-8.

1380 January

Westminster

16 January - 3 March

(C 65/35. *RP*, III.71-87. *SR*, II.13-15)

C 65/35 is a roll of nine membranes, each approximately 360mm in width, sewn together in chancery style and numbered in a later hand. The text, written in the official chancery scripts of several scribes, occupies the rectos of the membranes only. The dorses are blank apart from later notes, 'Parl. 3 R. 2 pars prima', where the membranes are joined, and a later heading on the dorse of the last membrane (membrane 1) reads 'Parliamentum de anno 3 R. 2^{di}'. The roll is in good condition and is legible throughout, although membranes 9 and 1 are slightly stained with gallic acid. After item 14 about half of membrane 7 has been left blank, and this membrane is blank again after item 18. The marginal headings are both contemporary and of a later date. The Arabic numerals are of later date. Membrane 2 has been stitched to the left-hand side of membrane 3 and its text is written in a contemporary hand which differs from that of membrane 3. The roll appears to be complete.

By January 1380, despite the expenditure of more than a quarter of a million pounds on the war since the beginning of Richard II's reign, there was little to show for it, and when a naval expedition intended for Brittany and led by Sir John Arundel was shipwrecked off the Irish coast in early December 1379 - largely, according to contemporary rumours, because its commander had allowed it to degenerate into a drunken orgy - patience with the government began to run dangerously thin. By this time, a new parliament had already been summoned, writs having been issued on 20 October calling the lords and commons to Westminster for 16 January 1380. As so often, it was financial necessity which was uppermost in the royal councillors' minds: the graduated poll tax granted by the commons in the parliament of April 1379 had brought in only about £22,000, whereas it had been expected to yield at least double that amount, and funds were urgently needed to send another English army to help Duke John of Brittany, who had returned to his duchy in August 1379 after seven years of enforced exile in England. The duke was, as a result, the only temporal lord missing from those who had been summoned in April 1379, while from the spiritual peers, the only name missing by comparison with the 1379 list was the abbot of Shrewsbury. The only newcomers to the lords were the new abbot of Bury (whose election, which was disputed, would be a matter for discussion during this session) and Sir Thomas Morley, whose father William had died while the previous parliament was in session.[1]

Torrential rain apparently made it difficult for several of the members to reach Westminster on time, but when parliament did get under way on Tuesday 17 January, it was once again Richard le Scrope, lord of Bolton and chancellor of England, who delivered the opening speech on behalf of the government. His theme was a familiar one: England was hard-pressed militarily on all sides, and the government urgently needed more money (Items 1-5). The commons were in an angry mood, however, and their speaker, Sir John Gildesborough of Essex, responded by accusing the government of financial mismanagement and asking for the dismissal of the 'continual councillors' who had been chosen to govern the realm at the previous parliament. The king, Gildesborough went on, was now almost exactly the same age as his grandfather (Edward III) had been at the time of his coronation, and should be advised primarily by his five chief ministers: the chancellor, treasurer, keeper of the privy seal, chamberlain and steward. These five should be appointed in parliament and should remain in office until the subsequent parliament (Items 11-12). The councillors were duly dismissed, as was Richard le Scrope, who was replaced as chancellor by Simon Sudbury, archbishop of Canterbury. All this was probably accomplished during the first two weeks of the session, for Sudbury became chancellor on 30 January.[2] The dismissal of the councillors marked the end of the system of minority government by Continual Council which had been in operation since Richard II's first parliament in October 1377.

In the parliament of April 1379, in addition to the appointment of the third Continual Council of the reign, a commission had been appointed to review the state of the royal finances and household. Despite (or, perhaps, because of) the fact that this seems never to have met, the commons now once again demanded that a similar commission be appointed, and its members were nominated, and their powers defined, by royal letters dated 2 March, the penultimate day of the session (Items 13-15).[3] According to the St Albans chronicler Thomas Walsingham, the commons also asked

---

[1] For general accounts of the events leading up to and during the parliament of January 1380, see Tuck, *Richard II and the English Nobility*, 44-8, and Saul, *Richard II*, 44-52. The writs of summons are in *CCR 1377-81*, 333-4.

[2] *HBC*, 86.

[3] Cf. *CPR 1377-81*, 459.

that one of the lords, a man of discernment and experience, should be appointed 'to reside permanently with the king', and the choice fell upon the earl of Warwick.[4] This was not a novel expedient: between June 1379 and February 1380, Sir John Cobham, another experienced and widely-respected lord of parliament, had been paid to 'remain in the [royal] household for the safeguard of the king's person'; on the other hand, there is no evidence that Warwick ever took up his post, and Walsingham may be wrong in stating that the commons made such a request in January 1380.[5] Nevertheless, the commons evidently believed that they had done enough in this parliament to ensure more effective government for the foreseeable future, and were eventually - albeit reluctantly - persuaded to make the far from ungenerous grant of one and a half fifteenths and tenths, although they were careful to stipulate that the extra half lay subsidy was only a 'loan' to the king. They also stated that the taxes should be used for one purpose only - the financing of an expedition to Brittany - that they should be received and disbursed by specially-appointed treasurers of war rather than being collected by the exchequer, and that no parliament which 'further burdens the poor commons' should be held for at least another eighteen months - a condition which, as Walsingham pointed out, was not adhered to.[6] The wool subsidy was also extended to September 1381, presumably with the same thought in mind (Items 16-17).

Speaker Gildesborough's insistence that the lay subsidy be spent solely on the planned Breton expedition may not have been entirely disinterested, for he was a tenant and retainer of the king's uncle Thomas of Woodstock, earl of Buckingham, and Buckingham had been chosen to lead the English army to Brittany. Indeed, it may also be that the choice as speaker of Gildesborough (who, unusually, was sitting in his first parliament) should be seen as a sign of the growing influence of Buckingham, who would certainly leave his mark on English politics over the next few years. Yet dissatisfaction with the government's performance, and especially with its perceived financial incompetence, was clearly not restricted to a few malcontents. Among the issues discussed in the parliament were a complaint that extensive loans to the exchequer had not been repaid, and a petition from the commons demanding compensation for merchant ships impressed for use in the royal navy. The king apologised for his failure to satisfy his creditors and promised to do so as speedily as possible (Items 33, 47).

Among other matters dealt with in this parliament, perhaps the most noteworthy was the discussion of the role of Justices of the Peace, which eventually resulted in a wide-ranging ordinance defining their powers issued following a meeting of the council on 26 May 1380 (Items 39-41). Also worth noting is the ordinance concerning the behaviour of troops waiting at English ports for shipping overseas, which may well have been prompted by the allegedly unruly and predatory behaviour of Sir John Arundel's troops before departing on their ill-fated expedition just a few weeks earlier (Appendix, Item 1). Matters relating to Ireland also demanded attention: regulations were passed to try to alleviate the shortage of bullion there, and to encourage Irish-Portuguese trade; more urgently, the gradual erosion of English authority in Ireland also led to an order that all holders of lands and benefices in the English lordship there must, before 24 June, either go to Ireland in person or make proper arrangements for the defence of their possessions (Items 42-44). One who certainly did so was Edmund Mortimer, earl of March, who had been appointed as the king's lieutenant in Ireland in October 1379, and departed to take up his post in the following May; when the earl of Salisbury made an attempt in this parliament to recover from him the lordship of Denbigh, which had been granted (wrongly, in his opinion) to the Mortimer family in 1354, his case failed on the grounds that March's appointment in Ireland placed him under royal protection (Items 19-21).

Various ecclesiastical matters, some of which are noted only in the chronicles, were also discussed. One of the petitions from the commons complained about the number of aliens being provided by the pope to English benefices (Item 37). According to Walsingham, envoys from the Roman Curia arrived at the parliament to try to sort out the disputed election to the abbacy of Bury St Edmunds (which was a major scandal at the time, and to which the chronicler devotes considerable space); a long-running dispute between the monks of Westminster abbey and their neighbours, the dean and college of St Stephen's chapel within the royal palace of Westminster, was also discussed in this parliament.[7]

The last two items on the roll are also worth noting. One was a complaint from the residents of Holborn and Smithfield against the butchers of London, suggesting that the slaughtering of animals ought to be carried out at Knightsbridge (outside the city) rather than within or close to the city walls, because of the filth, stench and danger of disease which resulted (Item 49).[8] The other was the confirmation by the king of the promise made by Edward III on the renewal of the war in 1369 that those who fought in France could expect to enjoy rights of possession over any lands which they seized in the king's name (Item 50).[9] How practical this was is difficult to know, but its aim was clearly to encourage men to serve in France, and in this it may have had some effect, for when Buckingham eventually crossed the Channel in July 1380, he took more than 5000 men with him. Even by this time, however, the government must have known that the taxes granted by the commons would not be sufficient to keep his army in the field, for only a month later, notwithstanding the promise made to the January 1380 parliament, writs were issued summoning yet another parliament, the fifth in three years. In the slightly longer term, however, the most important consequences of this parliament lay in the political rather than the financial sphere.[10] The abolition of the last of the Continual Councils - which had, on

---

[4] *St Albans Chronicle 1376-1394*, 342-4.
[5] Tuck, *Richard II and the English Nobility*, 44.
[6] *St Albans Chronicle 1376-1394*, 48.
[7] *St Albans Chronicle 1376-1394*, 344-8; *Westminster Chronicle*, 38.
[8] For the subsequent royal ordinance, dated 8 March, see *CCR 1377-81*, 363-4.
[9] Parliament of 1369, Item 25.
[10] Saul, *Richard II*, 52.

the whole, done a reasonable job in difficult circumstances - left something of a power vacuum at the heart of government. As Richard II grew up and increasingly began to make his own decisions about whom to consult, that vacuum increasingly came to be filled by members of the royal household; government became less transparent, and jealousy and hostility spread among the magnates, eventually to erupt in the political crisis of 1386-88.

Text and Translation

Text

Page iii-71, Membrane 9

ROTULUS PARLIAMENTI TENTI APUD WESTM', DIE LUNE PROXIMO POST FESTUM SANCTI HILLARII, ANNO REGNI REGIS RICARDI SECUNDI POST CONQUESTUM TERTIO.

Adjournement de parlement.

1. Fait a remembrer qe le lundy proschein apres la feste de Seint Hiller, l'an du regne nostre seignour le roi Richard second apres le conquest d'Engleterre tierce, qe fuist le .xvime jour de Janver, et primer jour de ce parlement, si vint a Westm' \[sibien nostre]/ seignour le roi en sa persone, come une partie des prelatz, seignours et communes; mais par tant qe ascuns des viscontes d'Engleterre n'y avoient encores retournez lours briefs de parlement, n'auxint [grande partie] des prelatz et seignours qi avoient la somonce de ce parlement n'estoient encores venuz, a cause de grant pluvie et autre male temps q'avoit este les trois ou quatre jours devant, [nostre seignour] le roi voloit et comanda qe la pronunciacioun de la cause del somonce de cest parlement feust adjournez tanqe al lendemein lors proschein venant. Et ensi estoit mesme l'adjournement fait et crie overtement en la chaumbre depeintte, del comandement avantdit; donant en mandement par mesme le crie a toute la commune q'ils y retornassent le dit lendemein bien matin, pur y oier en presence de nostre seignour le roi la cause del somonce avauntdite.

Pronunciation des causes de la somonce de parlement.

2. Item, le mardy proschein venant, si vindrent en parlement sibien nostre seignour le roi, come les prelats, seignours et autres, qi avoient la dite somonce, et les procuratours d'aucuns evesques, abbes, chapitres, esglise cathedraux. Et yceux assemblez en la dite chaumbre depeinte et appellez laeinz par lours nouns les chivalers des contees, citezeins des citees, burgeys de burghs et ceux de les cynk ports, selonc ce q'ils estoient retournez par briefs de parlement, monsire Richard le Scrop', chivaler, et chanceller d'Engleterre, avoit les paroles de la dite pronunciation, del comandement nostre dit seignour le roi ent a lui fait; et dist, Vous, mes seignours, les prelats, ducs, contes et barons, et vous mes seignours de la commune d'Engleterre, nostre seignour le roi qi cy est, et qi Dieux salve, m'ad comandez de vous exposer et monstrer depar luy la cause del somonce de cest present parlement, q'est tielle:

3. Primerement, nostre dit seignour le roi disirant souvrainement l'estat et les libertees de seinte esglise, et la bone paix, estre salvez /et maintenuz deinz le roialme d'Engleterre, et fermement\ gardez en touz pointz par manere come celles ont este mieltz salvez en temps de ses nobles progenitours, rois d'Engleterre; et qe les bones loys et custumes y faitz et usez devaunt ceste heure pur le bone governement deinz le roialme avauntdit soient fermement tenuz et gardez, et myses en dieu execucioun, au quiete de son poeple, sibien les greindres come les meindres, et qe les ryottes qe ja sont comencez en plusours parties del roialme, a ce q'est dit, soient oustez de tout, et appeisez, et due remede sur ce purveuz envers les trespassours en celle partie.

4. Item, pur tant qe la regalie nostre seignour le roi ad este novellement enblemiz en diverse manere sibien par ceux de la courte de Rome come autrement-dont y a de remede purveuz en partie, mes n'est assez suffisant, ne encore ad este celle remede duement execut avant ceste heure, come

Translation

THE ROLL OF THE PARLIAMENT HELD AT WESTMINSTER ON THE MONDAY AFTER THE FEAST OF ST HILARY, IN THE THIRD YEAR OF THE REIGN OF RICHARD THE SECOND SINCE THE CONQUEST.

The adjournment of parliament.

1. Be it remembered that on the Monday after the feast of St Hilary, in the third year of the reign of our lord King Richard, the second since the conquest [1380], the day being 16 January and the first day of parliament, the king came in person to Westminster, together with some of the prelates, lords and commons; but because some of the sheriffs of England had still not returned their writs of parliament, and a large number of the prelates and lords who had received summons to this parliament had still not arrived, on account of torrential rain, and other bad weather over the previous three or four days, our lord the king willed and ordered that the announcement of the reasons for summoning the parliament be adjourned until the following day. And so the same adjournment was made, and publicly announced in the Painted Chamber, at the aforesaid command; and orders were given in the same announcement that all the commons should return early the next day, there to hear, in the presence of our lord the king, the reasons for the aforesaid summons.

The announcement of the reasons for the summoning of parliament.

2. Also, on the following Tuesday [17 January], our lord the king came to parliament with the prelates, lords and others who had received the said summons, and the proctors of certain bishoprics, abbeys, chapters and cathedral churches. And when they had assembled in the said Painted Chamber, and the knights of the shires, citizens of the cities, burgesses of the boroughs, and those of the Cinque Ports had been called within by name, in accordance with their return by writ to parliament, Sir Richard le Scrope, knight and chancellor of England, made the said announcement, by command of our said lord the king, and said, You, my lords, the prelates, dukes, earls and barons, and you my lords of the commons of England, our lord the king here present, whom God absolve, has ordered me to divulge and explain to you the reason for summoning the present parliament, which is this:

3. First, our said lord the king chiefly desires that the estate and liberties of holy church and good peace shall be preserved and maintained within the kingdom of England, and strictly guarded on all counts in the way in which they have been best preserved in the time of his noble progenitors, the kings of England; and that the good laws and customs made and used before this time for good government within the aforesaid kingdom are firmly kept and upheld, and put into proper practice, for the tranquillity of the people, both greater and lesser, and that the riots which have commenced in many parts of the kingdom, according to reports, shall be completely crushed and pacified, and due remedy provided for the offenders in this matter.

4. Also, because the regality of our lord the king has been recently impaired in various ways as well by those from the court of Rome as in other ways - for which remedy was provided, yet proved inadequate, that remedy not being duly

pluis au plein en apres serra declarrez en especial-feusse ore duement remediez par assent de vouz toutz.

5. Item, pur ce qe *[conue]* chose est a vous touz, coment si-bien les enemys nostre seignour le roi de France, d'Espaigne, d'Escoce et des autres terres et paiis, avec lours alliez adherantz, come auxint les gentz propres de mesme nostre seignour le roi en ses seignouries de Irlande et de Guyenne, par lours malveys et faux rebellioun si font moelt forte guerre a lui, sibien par terre come par meer, et de jour en autre pluis et pluis; et pur la restence de lour malice y faut avoir bone ordenance et force, et grantement de quoi dont si hautes chargeantz choses serront remediez, dont rienz en effect est encores purveuz pur l'an avenir, les quelles, avec la salve-garde des ville et les autres fortz en la marche de Caleys, le chastiel et ville de Brest et le chastiel et ville de Chirburgh', et avec autres necessaires despenses qe l'en faut mettre a fin force en plusours maneres, demandent si grant avoir qe ce ne poet estre portez sanz le vostre aide, sicome vous le savez, et s'il enbusoigne vous serra pluis a plein declarrez en lieu et temps covenables. Et devrez savoir qe nostre seignour le roi voet qe ses grantz officers del roialme, avec les prelats et autres seignours, q'ont este l'an passe de son continuel conseil, vous facent clerement monstrer les sommes resceuz; sibien, c'estassaver des sommes sourdantz del grant fait au derrain parlement, come des subsides des leins, quirs et peaulx lanutz; coment, et en quelle manere celles summes sont depuis despenduz, a quelle heure qe embusoigne, et le voirez demander. Et pur cestes choses, et pur autres matires quelles vous serront declarrez pluis avant en especial, si est ore cest present parlement somonez; et nostre seignour le roi vous comande qe vous retournez au parlement dismain assez matin, et issint de jour en autre, tanqe vous ent avez de luy congie a departir. Et enoultre lour dist le dit chanceller, si aucune persone del roialme d'Engleterre, ou des terres, seignouries et paiis nostre seignour le roi depar dela, se vorra pleindre a nostre seignour le roi en cest son parlement de greef ou tort a luy fait, dont remede n'ad este encores purveuz, ne ne poet estre sanz parlement, nostre dit seignour le roi veulliant ce duement remedier, voet q'ils ent baillent avaunt lours peticions en parlement, pur quelles il ad fait assigner certains clercz pur resceivre, et certains prelatz, seignours et justices pur oier, discuter et terminer, mesmes les billes ou peticions qelconqes, par manere et selonc la fourme qe s'ensuit:

Page iii-72

6. Resceivours de peticions d'Engleterre, Irlande, Gales et Escoce:

Sire William de Burstall'

Sire Richard de Ravenser

Sire Thomas de Newenham

Sire Johan de Freton'.

7. Resceivours de peticions de Gascoigne, et d'autres terres et paiis depar dela, et des Isles:

Meister Wauter Skirlowe

Sire Henry Codyngton'

Sire Piers de Barton'

Sire Johan Boulande

Sire Thomas de Thelwall'.

Et ceux qi vorront bailler lour peticions les baillent avant devaunt dymenge proschein venant; et apres mesme le dymenge ne soit aucune peticion resceuz.

8. Et sont assignez triours des peticions d'Engleterre, Irlande, Gales, et Escoce:

applied in the past, as will be explained more fully later on - that it may now be duly corrected by the assent of you all.

5. Also, it is well known to you all how the enemies of our lord the king from France, Spain and Scotland, and other lands and countries, together with their allies, as well as such men of our same lord the king in the lordships of Ireland and Guyenne, who through their wicked and fraudulent rebellion wage fierce war on him, both by land as well as sea, with increasing intensity from one day to the next; and to resist their malice a good ordinance and armed might are needed, strong enough to meet such important and burdensome matters, since nothing has yet been provided for the year to come; which, together with the safeguard of the town and the strong places in the march of Calais, the castle and town of Brest, and the castle and town of Cherbourg, and with other necessary sums which must be laid out, require so large an amount of money that it cannot be borne without your aid, as you well know, and if necessary it will be more fully and clearly explained to you at a suitable time and place. And you ought to know that our lord the king wills that the great officers of the kingdom, together with the prelates and other lords who have belonged to his continual council for the last year, shall clearly show you the sums received; namely from the sums arising out of the grant made at the last parliament, as well as the subsidies on wool, hides and woolfells; how, and in what way those sums have since been spent, at whatever time is necessary, and you wish to ask it. And for those things, as well as for other reasons of which you shall later be especially informed, so has this parliament now been summoned; and our lord the king orders you that you return to parliament early tomorrow, and so from day to day, until he gives you permission to depart. Furthermore, the said chancellor told them that if any person of the kingdom of England, or lands, lordships and countries overseas, wished to complain to our lord the king in this his parliament of any harm or injury done him, for which remedy had still not been provided and could not be so without parliament, our said lord the king, desiring duly to correct it, willed that they hand their petitions in to parliament; and he had appointed certain clerks to receive them, and certain prelates, lords and justices to hear, discuss and settle the same bills or petitions of any sort, as they are listed below:

6. Receivers of petitions from England, Ireland, Wales and Scotland:

Sir William Burstall

Sir Richard Ravenser

Sir Thomas Newenham

Sir John Freton.

7. Receivers of petitions from Gascony, and from other lands and countries overseas, and from the Channel Islands:

Master Walter Skirlawe

Sir Henry Codington

Sir Piers Barton

Sir John Bowland

Sir Thomas Thelwall.

And those who wish to submit their petitions should hand them in before next Sunday [22 January]; and no petition will be accepted after the same Sunday.

8. The following are assigned to be triers of petitions from England, Ireland, Wales and Scotland:

Le roi de Castille et de Leon, duc de Lancastre	The king of Castile and of Leon, duke of Lancaster
L'ercevesque de Canterbirs	The archbishop of Canterbury
L'evesque de Londres	The bishop of London
L'evesque de Wyncestre	The bishop of Winchester
L'evesque de Ely	The bishop of Ely
L'evesque de Nichole	The bishop of Lincoln
L'evesque de Salesbirs	The bishop of Salisbury
L'abbe de Glastynbirs	The abbot of Glastonbury
L'abbe de Westm'	The abbot of Westminster
Le conte de Cantebrugge	The earl of Cambridge
Le conte d'Arundell	The earl of Arundel
Le conte de Warr'	The earl of Warwick
Le conte de Northumbr'	The earl of Northumberland
Le seignour de Latymer	Lord Latimer
Le seignour de Cobham	Lord Cobham
Monsire Richard Staff'	Sir Richard Stafford
Monsire Johan Knyvet	Sir John Knyvet
Monsire Johan Cavendissh'	Sir John Cavendish
Monsire Robert Bealknap'	Sir Robert Bealknap
Monsire William Skipwyth	Sir William Skipwith

- touz ensemble, ou .vi. des prelatz et seignours avauntditz au meins; appellez a eux chanceller, tresorier, seneschal et chamberlein, et auxin les sergeantz nostre seignour le roi quant il busoignera. Et tendront lour place en la chambre de chamberlein, pres de la chambre depeintee.

9. Et sont assignez triours de peticions de Gascoigne, et d'autres terres et paiis de dela la meer, et des Isles:

- to act all together, or at least six of the aforesaid prelates and lords; consulting with the chancellor, treasurer, steward and chamberlain, and also the serjeants of our lord the king when necessary. And they shall hold their session in the chamberlain's room, near the Painted Chamber.

9. The following are assigned to be triers of petitions from Gascony, and from other lands and countries overseas, and from the Channel Islands:

L'ercevesque d'Everwyk	The archbishop of York
L'evesque de Duresme	The bishop of Durham
L'evesque de Bathe et Welles	The bishop of Bath and Wells
L'evesque de Cicestre	The bishop of Chichester
L'evesque de Hereford	The bishop of Hereford
L'evesque de Roucestre	The bishop of Rochester
L'abbe de Seint Austyn de Canterbirs	The abbot of St Augustine's, Canterbury
L'abbe de Gloucestr'	The abbot of Gloucester
L'abbe de Waltham	The abbot of Waltham
Le conte de Buk', conestable d'Engleterre	The earl of Buckingham, constable of England
Le priour de Seint \Johan/ Jerusalem en Engleterre	The prior of St John of Jerusalem in England
Le conte de Staff'	The earl of Stafford
Le conte de Suff'	The earl of Suffolk
Le seignour Lestrange de Knokyn'	Lord Lestrange of Knokyn
Le seignour de Bardolf	Lord Bardolf
Monsire Johan Montagu	Sir John Montagu
Monsire Robert Tresilian	Sir Robert Tresilian
Monsire Henry Asty	Sir Henry Asty

- touz ensemble, ou .vi.des prelats et seignours avauntditz; appellez a eux chanceller, tresorer, seneschal, chamberlein et les sergeantz le roi quant il busoignera. Et tendront lour place en la chambre marcolf.

10. Item, puis apres les seignours et communes autrefoitz assemblez en parlement, en presence de nostre seignour le roi mesme, le dit monsire Richard le Scrop', chanceller d'Engleterre, faisant greindre declaracioun de la cause del somonce de ce present parlement, lour dit, del comandement nostre seignour le roi, qe voirs est, et conuz chose doit

- to act all together, or at least six of the aforesaid prelates and lords; consulting with the chancellor, treasurer, steward, chamberlain, and the king's serjeants when necessary. And they shall hold their session in the Marcolf Chamber.

10. Also, after the lords and commons had again assembled in parliament, in the presence of our lord the king himself, the said Sir Richard le Scrope, chancellor of England, made an important announcement of the reasons for summoning the present parliament, and told them, by order of our said lord the king, that it was true and ought to be well-known to

estre a eux *[trestouz,]* coment, a parlement nadgairs tenuz a Gloucestre, si estoit grantez a nostre dit seignour le roi, en aide a les tresgrevouses despenses queux luy *[faudroit pur lors,]* et encores luy convient continuelment faire faire[11], sibien entour le defens de son roialme et ses autres terres et seignouries depar dela, come autrement par meer \[et par terre]/ en diverse manere durant tielle forte guerre come est de present moevez envers lui de chescun part, une certeine encrees del subside des leynes, quirs et peaulx lanutz, a prendre et resceivre, nemye tantost apres le dit parlement finiz, einz apres la Pasqe deslors proschein ensuant; ensemble avec .vi.*d.* au livre, queux luy estoient auxint grantez en dit parlement, al oeps avauntdit. Et coment qe tut apres le dit parlement de Glouc' finiz, les prelatz et autres seignours lors assignez par parlement d'estre du continuel conseil, avec les grantz officers du roialme s'assembleront a Londres, et tretantz des busoignes del roialme, et veiantz qe n'estoit rienz en la tresorie du roi, ne rienz serroit par long terme levez en effect des dites subsides grantez, et[12] la seisone d'estee estoit bien pres, au quiele seisone l'en faudroit faire aucune ordinance sur la meer, ou en autre manere, en defens del roialme, si firent une grant chevance, pur quiele ils engaigerent les joialx le roi, avec autres fortes obligacions faitz desouz le grant seal le roi pur seurtee du /paiement\ faire au certein jour, long temps a passe, souz espoir d'avoir un autre parlement en haste apres la Pasqe lors proschein venant, par lequiel remede ent purroit estre purveuz, et en nul autre manere. Et issint par tielle chevance fust une grant armee tenuz sur la meer mesme la seisone, et un novel parlement derechief sommonez a la .xv.[e] de Pasqe lors proschein ensuant, pur la cause dessusdite, del assent de greignour partie des seignours du roialme. A quiel second parlement estoit monstrez la grante necessitee du roi, et la dite chevance q'amontoit pluis qe .xx. mille marcz, et coment touz les deniers resceuz parmy les dites grantz issint faitz a Glouc' n'amonteroient en tut .vi. mille marcz. Et par tant lors fuist priez *[Page iii-73]*

[Col. a] depar le roi sibien as seignours come as communes en dit derrain parlement, d'estre sur ce advisez, et aider lour seignour lige en celle partie, sibien pur paier les ditz deniers chevez, come pur ordeiner de paiement a les gaiges rewardz de guerre acustumez pur .ij. mille hommes d'armes, et .ij. mille archiers, qe serroient ordeinez d'aler en Bretaigne avec le duc de Bretaigne: qi lors fuist graciousement accordez avec la greindre partie de son paiis, dont l'en espoir qe grant bien a nous et meschief et confusioun a touz noz enemys ent purront avenir. Et coment qe apres longe demure et grante tretee en dit parlement y feust grantez un certain subside, aprendre par un novel manere de chescune singuler persone parmy le roialme - donant a entendre as officers de roi, et l'affermantz par serementz qe celle subside suffiseroit assez sibien pur la dite nombre des gentz vers Bretaigne, come pur la dite chevance paier, et autres necessaires charges porter, avec les subsides des leynes - nientmeins, quant mesme le subside estoit levez et coillez parmy le roialme, avec un semblable subside lors grantez au roi par le clergie de son roialme, quanqe estoit issint levez n'amonteroit en tout .xxij. mille*li.* Et les dites gaiges pur la dite nombre des gentz /pur un demy an si amonteroient\ au meins .l. mille*li.* Et les ditz seignours du dit continuel conseil, avec les /autres\ grantz officers du roi, apparceivantz cel meschief, abreggeront la nombre des dites gentz vers Bretaigne, et a grante peine les envoierent vers Bretaigne.

them all how, at the parliament formerly held at Gloucester, there had been granted to our said lord the king, to help towards the most grievous costs he was then required to meet, as they still wished to do continually for him, both for the defence of his kingdom and his other lands and lordships overseas, as well as by sea and land in various ways during such a fierce war as is presently being waged on him from all sides, a certain increment in the subsidy on wool, hides and woolfells, to be taken and received, not immediately after the said parliament had finished, but after the following Easter [10 April 1379]; together with 6*d.* in the pound, which was also granted to him in the said parliament for the aforesaid purpose. Subsequently, however, after the said parliament of Gloucester had ended, the prelates and other lords then appointed by parliament to be of the continual council, together with the the great officers of the realm assembled in London, dealing with the business of the kingdom, and seeing that there was nothing in the king's treasury, and that nothing would effectively be levied for a long time from the said subsidies granted, and that the season of summer was fast approaching, in which season some ordinance would have to be made to keep the sea, or in some other manner for the defence of the kingdom, they raised a large loan, for which they pledged the king's jewels, together with other strict bonds issued under the great seal of the king to guarantee repayment by a certain day, now long past, in the hope of having another parliament soon after the Easter next following [10 April 1379], in which remedy could be provided, and in no other way. And so with this loan a great force was kept on the sea during the same season, and a new parliament again summoned on the quinzaine of the following Easter, for the aforesaid reason, with the assent of the majority of the lords of the kingdom. At which second parliament the great need of the king was explained, inasmuch as the said loan amounted to more than twenty thousand marks, whereas all the money received from the said grants made at Gloucester did not amount even to six thousand marks in total. And so it was asked *[Page iii-73]*

[Col. a] on behalf of the king, both of the lords as well as the commons in the said last parliament, that they discuss this and aid their liege lord in this matter, to pay off the said loans, as well as to ordain for the payment of the customary wages of war for two thousand men-at-arms and two thousand archers, who would be ordered to go to Brittany with the duke of Brittany: the latter having then come to a gracious agreement with a great part of his land, from which there was hope that great good would come to us and and that trouble and confusion might result for all our enemies. And although, after dealing with the matter at great length in the said parliament a certain subsidy was granted, to be levied in a new way from each individual throughout the realm - giving the king's officers to understand, and affirming on oath that this subsidy would be quite adequate for the said number of people sent to Brittany, as well as to pay the said loan, and to bear other necessary charges, together with the subsidies on wool - nevertheless, when the said subsidy was levied and collected throughout the kingdom, together with a similar subsidy then granted to the king by the clergy of his kingdom, it did not amount to £22,000. Yet the said wages for the said number of people for half a year come to at least £50,000. And the said lords of the continual council, together with the other great officers of the king, perceiving the problem, reduced the number of the said men going to Brittany, and sent them there with great difficulty.

---

[11] faire *repeated*
[12] *Original* a

/Des queux, et d'autres gentz\ envoiez en Gascoigne pur salvacioun du paiis del roi illoeqes, les dites gaiges, avec les rewards de guerre, amonteront avec lour eskippesoun bien pres .xxij. mille*li*. ou pluis. Et issint nient remaint rienz pur paier la dite primere chevance faite, ne de paier les gaiges de Caleys et d'autres chasteulx et fortz del roi, sibien en Pykardye, Bretaigne, et Normandie, come autrement pur la salvacioun d'Irlande, et de la marche d'Escoce, queux demandent tresgrandes sommes qe doivent estre hastivement estre paiez, ou les places serront en point d'estre perduz, qe Dieu ne veulle. Qar del subside des leines rienz n'ad este pris par longe terme, a cause qe Flemmynges aient este en debat entre eux mesmes, paront ils n'achaterent my des leines rienz. Et issint nostre seignour le roi n'ad ore rienz en tresorie, mais est grantement endettez par les causes dessusdites; ne rien est purveuz encontre le proscheine seisone. Dont le roi vous prie et requiert moelt especialment qe vous vous veullez adviser coment, et par quiel manere a *[meinz desaise]* de vous il purra estre relevez, noun pas soulement en aide de luy mesmes, einz pur la salvacioun de vous touz, et del roialme avant dite.

Membrane 8

11. Item, les communes, apres q'ils furent advisez de lour dite charge, retournerent en parlement en presence de nostre seignour le roi: et monsire Johan de Gildesburgh', chivaler, q'estoit eslit par la commune d'avoir pur eulx les paroles, faisant sa protestacioun qe s'il y deist rienz qe purroit tourner ou sonnir en desplesance ou deshonur de nostre seignour le roi, ou des autres seignours illoeqes presentz, qe ce ne feust arettez a la commune come chose dite illoeqes de lour voluntee, einz en defaute, et par le noun-sachance ou negligence del dit monsire Johan, et qe ce feust tenuz pur rienz dit; et auxint s'il dit pluis ou meins qe n'estoit assentuz par ses compaignons, q'il ent feust amendez a quelle heure qe leur pleust:

12. Dist qe lour sembloit a la dite commune qe si lour seignour lige eust este bien et resonablement governez en ses despenses par dedeinz le roialme et autrement, il n'eust ore busoigne de lour aide par chargeant sa dite commune q'ore est trop povres, et pluis q'unqes devaunt ne fuist, a ce q'ils entendent. Empriantz qe les prelatz et autres seignours du continuel conseil, q'ont longement travaillez en dit affaire, feussent oultreement deschargez,

[Col. b] a lour grant aise, et en descharge de roi de lour coustages; et qe nuls tielx conseillers soient pluis retenuz devers le roi; aiant regard qe nostre seignour le roi si est ore de bone discrecioun et de bele stature; aiant regard de son age q'est ore bien pres accordant al age de son noble aiel, qi Dieux assoille, al temps de son coronement; luy quiel n'avoit autres conseillers el comencement de soun regne sinoun les cynk principalx officers de son roialme acustumez. Empriantz oultre qe en ce parlement soient esluz et choises les cynk principalx officers, des pluis suffisantz deinz le roialme, qi soient tretables, et qi mieltz scievent et purront faire lours offices: cestassavoir, chanceller, tresorer, gardein du prive seal, chief chamberlein et seneschal del hostiel le roi. Et qe ceux issint achoisers - des queux la commune vorroit estre acertez de lours persones et nouns durant cest parlement, lour tresgrant confort et aide a l'esploit faire as busoygnes de roi, declarrez a mesme la commune - ne feussent remuz devant le proschein parlement, si ne feust pur cause de mort, maladie, ou autre tielle cause necessaire.

13. Et auxint empriantz, pur remeder le defaute del dit governail, si nul y soit en celle partie, qe une suffisante commissioun et general feusse fait, a mieltz qe l'on le sauroit deviser, a certains prelatz, seignours et autres des pluis

Of whom, and of the others sent to Gascony for the security of the king's territory there, the said wages, together with the rewards of war, amounted with their transport to close on £22,000 or more. And so nothing was left with which to pay off the said first loan, or pay the wages at Calais and the other castles and forts of the king in Picardy, Brittany and Normandy, nor for the security of Ireland or the march of Scotland, which require very great sums, which ought to be paid swiftly or the places will be on the point of being lost, which God forbid. For nothing has been received from the subsidy on wool for a long time, because the Flemings have been in conflict amongst themselves, and therefore have not bought any wool. And thus our lord the king has nothing in the treasury, but is deeply in debt for the aforesaid reasons; nor has anything been provided for the season to come. And so the king prays and requests of you most particularly that you consult amongst yourselves as to how and in what way with the least pain to yourselves he may be relieved, not only for his own sake, but for the security of you all and the aforesaid kingdom.

11. Also, the commons, after they had been advised of their said charge, returned to parliament in the presence of our lord the king: and Sir John Gildesburgh, knight, who had been elected by the commons to speak on their behalf, protested that if he should say anything which might result in displeasure or sound dishonourable to our lord the king or other lords there present, that it would not be ascribed to the commons as a thing uttered with their consent, but that it would be considered the fault through ignorance or negligence of the said Sir John, and treated as if nothing had been said; furthermore if he should say any more or less which had not been given the agreement of his companions, that he would be corrected whenever they chose:

12. He said that it seemed to the said commons that if their lord liege had been well and reasonably governed in his expenses throughout the kingdom and elsewhere, he would not now have felt the need for their help by burdening his said commons, who were very poor, to a greater extent than ever before, as they understood. They requested that the prelates and other lords of the continual council, who had long dealt with the said affair, might be fully discharged,

[Col. b] for their greater ease, and to relieve the king of their costs; and that no such councillors should be retained any longer around the king; bearing in mind that our lord the king was now of great discretion and handsome stature; and bearing in mind his age, which was very nearly that of his noble grandfather, whom God absolve, at the time of his coronation; and who, at the beginning of his reign, had no other councillors than the customary five principal officers of his kingdom. They also requested that in this parliament the five principal officers should be elected and chosen from the most worthy of the kingdom, men who should be knowledgable and well able to perform their duties: namely, the chancellor, treasurer, keeper of the privy seal, chief chamberlain and steward of the king's household; and those to be thus chosen - of whose identities and names the commons would wish to be informed during this parliament, and for their greater ease and convenience in carrying out of the king's business, announced to the commons - should not be changed before the next parliament, unless by death, illness, or for any other serious reason.

13. They prayed also that to remedy the faults of the said government, if there were any in this matter, that a general, worthy commission might be set up and devised in the best possible way, consisting of certain prelates, lords and others

suffisantz, loialx et sages del roialme d'Engleterre, de surveer diligeaument, et examiner en toutes les courtes et places du roi, sibien en son hostiel mesmes come aillours, l'estat del dit hostiel, et les despenses et resceites quelconqes faitz par quelconqe ses ministres en quelconqes offices del roialme et des autres ses seignouries et terres par meer, et sibien decea come dela la meer depuis le corounement nostre dit seignour le roi tanqe en cea; issint qe si nul defaute y soit par le dit examinement trovez en ascune manere, par negligence des officers, ou en autre manere, les dites commissioners le certifient a nostre seignour le roi pur l'aumender et corriger, aufin qe le roi nostre seignour puisse estre honurablement governez deinz son roialme, come appartient au roi d'estre gouvernez; et en partie de soen propre supporter le charge des despenses a mettre entour le dit defens del roialme, et des autres despenses dessusdites.

14. Et puis apres nostre seignour le roi, par l'advis des seignours de son parlement, volont bien et grantent la dite commissioun estre faite as persones compris en mesme la commissioun, qi furent a ce esluz en parlement, et la dite commission faite par lour advis a mieltz q'ils la sacheroient deviser estoit rehercez en plein parlement, et assentuz illoeqes: et enoultre accordez qe si les ditz commissioners y vorroient en apres avoir novelles articles en ycelle commissioun adjoustez en novel, et pluis plein poair, qe ce feust amendez de temps en temps a mieltz q'ils le sauroient deviser, salvant toutdys l'estat et regalie nostre dit seignour le roi en toutes choses. De quelle commissioun privement enseallez et monstrez en parlement le tenour s'ensuit de mot a mot: [13]

Commissio ad scrutinium faciendum in hospicio et curia regis.

[14]15. Rex venerabilibus in Christo patribus Willelmo Wynton', Johanni Hereforden' et Thome Roffen', episcopis; ac dilectis et fidelibus suis Ricardo Arundell', Thome de Bello Campo, Warr', et Hugoni Staff', comitibus; Willelmo de Latymer, Guydoni \de/ Briene et Johanni de Monte-Acuto, banerettis; Radulpho de Hastyngs, Johanni de Gildesburgh' et Edwardo Dalyngrugge, militibus; Willelmo de Walleworth' et Johanni Philipot, civibus London', et Thome Graa, civi Ebor', salutem. Reducentes corditer ad memoriam, qualiter tempore suscepti regni nostri regiminis eramus et jam sumus undique guerris gravibus involuti, ac inimicis quampluribus qui nos et *[Page iii-74]*
[Col. a] regnum nostrum Anglie destruere, quod absit, hactenus laborarunt, et indies pro viribus elaborant, circumdati miro modo, necdum inde credenda est finis. Et licet eo pretextu nos oportuit, ac oportet in presenti, nostrorum subsidium subditorum pro nostri et illorum defensione multipliciter invocare, ipsi tamen subditi nobis in presenti parliamento nostro graviter querelando monstrarunt, qualiter communitates regni nostri per multiplices soluciones decimarum, quintarumdecimarum et aliorum subsidiorum diversorum, tam domino Edwardo nuper regi Anglie avo nostro quam nobis pro defensione regni sepius concessorum, ac aliis de causis quampluribus, in tantam inopiam sunt collapse, quod ipsi onera hujusmodi que sibi, nisi dictis guerris celerius detur finis, seu de alio remedio succurratur, eisdem omnino importabilia existunt, nec ea poterunt aliqualiter sustinere: et nobis humiliter supplicarunt, ut ad honorem nostrum pariter et commodum, ac pro dictorum fidelium ligeorum nostrorum in hac parte relevacione, vellemus nos

from amongst the most worthy, loyal and wise of the kingdom of England, diligently to survey and examine in all the courts and places of the king, both in his household as well as elsewhere, the state of the said household, and the expenses and receipts whatsoever incurred by any of his ministers occupying any offices of the kingdom and of his other lordships and lands overseas, on this side of the sea as well as overseas, from the coronation of our said lord the king until now; so that if any fault should be found there in any way through the said examination through the negligence of officers, or any other fault, the said commissioners would notify our lord the king that it might be amended and corrected, with the intention that our lord the king might be the more honourably governed within his kingdom, as it befits a king to be governed; and that he might from his own resources support the burden of expenses met in the defence of the realm, and the other aforementioned expenses.

14. Later, our lord the king, by the advice of the lords of his parliament, wholeheartedly wished and granted that the said commission be directed to the persons mentioned in the same commission who had been elected thereto in parliament, and that the said commission, set up with the best advice they could provide, might be rehearsed in full parliament and given assent there: and it was also agreed that if the said commissioners later wished to have new articles added to the same commission, and fuller authority, that amendments would be made from time to time as best they knew how, saving always the estate and regality of our said lord the king in all respects. Which commission, privately sealed and displayed in parliament, reads as follows:

Commission to make an inspection of the household and court of the king.

15. The king to the venerable fathers in Christ William of Winchester, John of Hereford, and Thomas of Rochester, bishops; and his beloved and faithful men Richard of Arundel, Thomas Beauchamp of Warwick and Hugh Stafford, earls; William Latimer, Guy Bryan, and John Montagu, bannerets; Ralph Hastings, John Gildesburgh, and Edward Dallingridge, knights; William Walworth and John Philpot, citizens of London, and Thomas Gray, citizen of York, greeting. Earnestly recalling to mind, how in time past the kingdom under our government has been and is yet harrassed on all sides by the burdens of war, and by numerous enemies who have *[Page iii-74]*
[Col. a] hitherto striven to destroy our kingdom of England, which God forbid, and with its strength daily slipping away, it is surrounded in an amazing fashion, and neither should the process be believed to have ended. And although on that account we have had and ought yet to call many times for a subsidy from our subjects for our defence and theirs, these our subjects have made serious complaint to us in our present parliament, explaining that the commons of our kingdom, through numerous payments of tenths, fifteenths and various other subsidies, to both the lord Edward, late king of England, our grandfather, as well as to us frequently granted for the defence of the kingdom, and for many other reasons, have fallen into so great a state of need that burdens of this kind are utterly unsustainable by them, unless the said war be swiftly ended or some other remedy found, nor yet can they shoulder them in any other way: and they request of us humbly, for our honour as well as benefit, and to relieve our said faithful lieges therein, that we might allow ourselves

---
[13] About a third of membrane 7 has been left blank here.
[14] A change of hand occurs at this point.

et statum nostrum sub tam decenti et conformi regimine gubernari, ac gestum officiariorum et ministrorum nostrorum per quorum inadventanciam et negligenciam, et ob defectum boni regiminis possessionum et rerum nostrarum, ac propter excessivum et insolitum modum expensarum in officiis predictis dampna quamplurima et incommoda, tam nobis quam regno nostro predicto, ut asserunt, multipliciter evenerunt, necnon emolumenta et proventus terrarum et dominiorum nostrorum ac recepciones quorumcumque denariorum tam pro guerris quam ad opus et expensas nostra deputatorum, sic inspici et diligenter examinari jubere, ut nos prout regie convenit magestati decenter vivere, et partem nostram aliorum onerum predictorum in relevacionem et auxilium dictorum nostrorum subditorum, salvis in omnibus nostris regalitate et honore, poterimus supportare. Nos ad quietem et relevamen omnium fidelium subditorum nostrorum ubique prospicere volentes, ut tenemur, advertentesque dampna quam maxima, ac incommoda tam nobis quam toti regno nostro, ob defectum et incuriam officiariorum et ministrorum nostrorum, si fortassis negligentes vel remissi fuerint, de facili posse evenire; cupientesque ea de causa omnem inmoderanciam quatenus honeste debuerimus, honore nostro in omnibus salvo, penitus extirpare: ac de industria, fidelitate et circumspeccione vestris plenius confidentes, assignavimus vos quatuordecim, tresdecim, duodecim, undecim, decem, novem, octo, septem, sex et quinque vestrum, quorum de quolibet gradu et statu vestrum unum ad minus interesse volumus, ad omnia loca, curias et placeas nostra, tam videlicet /in\ receptam scaccarii nostri quam alia loca nostra, una cum custodibus et officiariis eorundem, intrandi et ibidem una cum ministris et officiariis predictis rotulos, compota et quecumque alia memoranda, recepciones reddituum et proventuum, ac soluciones denariorum nostrorum concernentia diligenter inspiciendi, examinandi et scrutandi; specialiterque supervidendi et examinandi revensiones et emolumenta quecumque tam regni nostri predicti, ac terrarum, dominiorum, civitatum, villarum, castrorum, fortaliciorum et aliarum possessionum nostrorum quorumcumque, tam cismarinis quam transmarinis partibus ..... existencium, proficuumque et emolumentum omnium monetarum nostrarum et billionum ibidem. Necnon prioratuum et domorum alienigenarum, vacationumque archiepiscopatuum, episcopatuum, abbaciarum, \et/ prioratuum, ac de wardis, maritagiis, escaetis et forisfacturis universis ad nos pertinentibus; et de capcione prisonariorum, villarum, locorum, navium et bonorum de guerra, ubicumque tam per terram quam per mare captorum, et de beneficiis et aliis possessionibus omnibus cardinalium rebellium et aliorum inimicorum nostrorum, et emolumenta omnia tam de antiquis custumis quam novis subsidiis lanarum, coriorum, pellium lanutarum et de pannis, vinis et aliis rebus et mercimoniis quibuscumque infra regnum et dominia nostra predicta ductis et ducendis, et ab eisdem eductis et educendis, ac eciam recepta et proficua hanaperii cancellarie, et aliorum curiarum, placearum et locorum nostrorum quorumcumque, tam per manus thesaurarii nostrorum pro guerra nuper deputatorum, et in recepta scaccarii nostri quam in hanaperio et aliis locis et placeis nostris

[Col. b] predictis qualitercumque recepta, a tempore coronacionis \nostre/ hucusque. Examinandi insuper et diligenter inspiciendi qualia vadia et feoda officiarii majores et minores domini Edwardi nuper regis Anglie avi nostri in principio regni sui ab eodem percipere solebant et habere; ac quibus personis de annuitatibus tam per dominum Edwardum nuper principem patrem nostrum quam avum nostrum predictum per multiplices literas /suas\ patentes concessis, in feodo vel ad terminum vite, satisfactum fuerit sive

and our estate to be suitably and fittingly governed, and that we might order inspections and diligent examination of the deeds of our officers and ministers, by whose inadvertency and negligence, and a lack of efficient management of our items and possessions, and by excessive and exceptional expenditure in the aforesaid offices, much harm, they claim, is inflicted on us and our aforesaid realm, as well as on the emoluments and profits from our lands and lordships and various receipts of money both for wars as well as for the use and expenses of our lieutenants, so that we may live worthily as befits royal majesty, and so that we may support some of our other aforesaid burdens to relieve and assist our aforesaid subjects, saving always our regality and honour. For the tranquillity and relief of all our faithful subjects wherever they are, we earnestly wish, as we are bound, to avoid such great injuries and inconvenience to ourselves and to all our kingdom, which might easily arise through the faults and negligence of our officers and ministers, if they should happen to be negligent or remiss, as they might; and desiring for those reasons that all excess be throughly rooted out, as in honesty we should, saving our honour in all things: and fully trusting in your industry, fidelity and circumspection, we appointed fourteen, thirteen, twelve, eleven, ten, nine, eight, seven, six, and five of you, desiring that at least one of you of each grade and condition be included, at all our sites, courts and residences, and also at the receipt of our treasury as in our other places, and that you enter along with the custodians and officials of the same, and there, together with the ministers and officials, that you diligently inspect, examine and scrutinize the aforesaid rolls, accounts and all other sorts of memoranda, receipts of rents and proceeds, and things relating to payments of our money; and especially to survey and investigate revenues and emoluments whatsoever of our aforesaid kingdom, and lands, lordships, cities, towns, castles, fortresses, and all our other possessions of any kind, located on this side of the sea and overseas, and the profits and emoluments from all our revenues and bullion there. And also from all alien priories and houses, and vacancies of archbishoprics, bishoprics, abbacies, and priories, and from all wards, marriages, escheats and forfeitures belonging to us; and from prisoners, towns, places, ships and goods in war, wheresoever taken by land or by sea, and from the benefices and other possessions of all rebel cardinals and our other enemies, and all emoluments from ancient customs as well as from new subsidies on wool, hides and woolfells, and from bread, wine and other items and merchandise of any sort brought or to be brought within our aforesaid kingdom and dominions, and taken or to be taken out of it; and moreover, the receipts and profits of the hanaper of the chancery, and our other courts, residences and locations of any kind, received through the hands of our treasurers recently appointed for the war, and at the receipt of our exchequer as well as in the hanaper and our other aforesaid places and locations

[Col. b] whatsoever, from the time of our coronation until now. Examining in the meantime and diligently investigating what kind of pledges and fees of officials, greater and lesser, the lord Edward late king of England our grandfather was accustomed to take and receive from the same at the beginning of his reign; and which persons, for annuities conceded both by the lord Edward, late prince, our father, as well by our aforesaid grandfather by their many letters patent, in fee or for the term of life, have been

solutum; ac de quanto, qualiter et quo modo. Inquirendi[15] eciam, ac alias vos informandi viis et modis quibus melius poteritis, de omnibus et singulis defectibus sive mesprisionibus in quibuscumque officiis majoribus sive minoribus medio tempore emergentibus, per quos nostra seu regni nostri utilitas impedita fuerit sive retardata, ac per quos, vel per quem, quando, qualiter et quo modo. Ac insuper de bonis et rebus omnibus que fuerunt predicti avi nostri tempore mortis sue, ac qualia, cujusque precii vel valoris bona illa fuerunt, et in cujus vel quorum manibus jam existunt; ac specialiter que et cujusmode parcelle inde ad opus nostrum devenerunt, sive in eisdem nostris manibus remanent in presenti; que eciam parcelle inde abstracte sive elongate fuerint, et ad cujus, vel quorum manus devenerunt, et que summe denariorum creditoribus dicti avi nostri inde solute fuerint, quando, qualiter et quo modo. Examinandi insuper et supervidendi quascumque summas et modum expensarum ac statum hospicii nostri, quascumque eciam soluciones circa salvacionem et defensionem regni et dominiorum nostrorum predictorum tam hominibus ad arma armatis et sagittariis quam marinariis; et alio modo, tam videlicet per dictos thesaurarios guerre quam alias per thesaurarium nostrum Anglie medio tempore qualitercumque factas. Supervidendi eciam quod omnes soldarii nostri qui vadia seu rewarda nostra receperunt, et servicium suum in hac parte nondum perfecerunt, sint inde computabiles, et fideliter respondeant ad scaccarium nostrum. Vos insuper, tam per examinacionem officiariorum et ministrorum nostrorum quorumcumque, quam aliis viis et modis quibus melius et celerius expedire videritis informandi de veritate omnium et singulorum premissorum, ac omnia alia faciendi et exequendi que in hac parte fore videritis necessaria, sive oportuna. Ac defectus, si quos in hac parte reperitis, nobis et consilio nostro fideliter reportandi, nosque de toto facto vestro in ea parte distincte et aperte certificandi. Vobis insuper tenore presencium plenam committimus potestatem, ut quoscumque ligeos nostros, per \[quos]/ vestro judicio de alicujus premissorum veritate plenius informari poteritis, coram vobis evocare, ipsos que ad corporale juramentum de veritate super hiis dicendis coram vobis prestandis, majoribus officiariis regni nostri dumtaxat exceptis, quotiens opus fuerit, et vobis videbitur expedire, compellere et districte artare possitis. Et ideo, vobis in fide et ligeancea quibus nobis tenemini firmiter injungendo[16] mandamus quod circa premissa omnia et singula cum continuacione temporis et dierum si expediens et necesse fuerit, cum ea tamen celeritate qua fieri poterit diligenter intendatis, et ea facere et exequamini in forma predicta. Damus autem universis et singulis custodibus sive administratoribus bonorum ejusdem avi nostri, ac officiariis et ministris nostris tam hospicii nostri predicti quam aliis quibuscumque tenore presencium firmiter in mandatis, quatinus vobis quatuordecim, tresdecim, duodecim, undecim, decem, novem, octo, septem, sex et quinque vestrum, quorum de quolibet gradu et statu vestrum unum interesse volumus, ut predictum est, in premissis omnibus et singulis faciendis et exequendis ad mandatum vestrum intendentes sint, respondentes, et auxiliantes. Ac insuper dicta libros, rotulos, compota et alia memoranda premissa qualitercumque concernencia, vobis clare monstrari facere et aperte, sine difficultate quacumque, quociens ipsi vel eorum aliquis per vos vel aliquem vestrum super hoc fuerint vel fuerit requisiti ex parte nostra. In cujus, etc. Teste rege apud Westm', secundo die Marcii.

satisfied or paid; and for how much, of what kind and by what means. Also inquiring into and informing yourselves by the best ways and means available to you in the meantime of each and every deficiency and misdeed which emerges in whatsoever offices, greater and lesser, through which we or the profit of our kingdoms shall have been impeded or hampered, and by whom, when, how, and by what means. And further, inquiring into all goods and possessions which belonged to our aforesaid grandfather at the time of his death, and of what sort, and the price or value which these items had, and in whose hands they are now to be found; and especially, the size and nature of the portion which has fallen to our use, or remains at present in our same hands; and moreover, what portion has been abstracted or removed, and into whose hands it has come, and what sums of money have been thus paid to the creditors of our said grandfather, when, in what form and by what means. Examining also and surveying sums, methods of expenditure, and the state of our household, and also payments for the security and defence of our aforesaid kingdom and lordships, to men-at-arms and archers as well as sailors; and otherwise, namely through the said treasurers of war as well as others appointed in the meantime by our treasurer of England. Ensuring moreover that all our soldiers who have received our pledges or rewards, and have not yet performed their service in return, account for this and faithfully answer at our exchequer. Furthermore, by examining our officers and ministers of any kind, as well as by other ways and means which shall seem to you the best and the most expeditious to perform, you inform yourselves of the truth of each and every one of the aforesaid, and perform and carry out all other things which shall seem necessary or appropriate to you in this instance. And if you find fault therein, you shall faithfully report it to us and our council, also notifying us clearly and distinctly or all your actions in the said matter. In addition, we give you full authority by the tenor of these presents to summon before you any of our lieges through whom in your opinion you might be better informed of the truth in any of the aforesaid matters, and you shall be able to strictly oblige and compel them to take a corporal oath in your presence of the truth of the words to be spoken therein, excepting however, the greater officers of our kingdom, as often as is necessary and shall seem expedient to you. And therefore we order you, on the faith and allegiance with which you are firmly bound to us, that you deal with each and every one of the aforesaid matters, for as long a time and as many days as may be necessary and expedient, but that you nevertheless diligently seek to discharge them as swiftly as you can, and execute and accomplish them in the aforesaid manner. Moreover, according to the tenor of these presents we strictly order each and every custodian or administrator of the goods of our same grandfather, and the officers and ministers both of our aforesaid household and of any other, to be attendant upon, answer to and assist you, the fourteen, thirteen, twelve, eleven, ten, nine, eight, seven, six or five of you; amongst whom we will one of each grade and condition to take part, as is said, in the execution and accomplishment of all the aforesaid things at your mandate. And also that they cause the said books, rolls, accounts and other aforesaid memoranda relevant in any way, to be shown to you freely and openly, without diffulties of any sort, as often as they or any one of them shall be made or required to do this by you or any one of you on our behalf. In testimony of which, etc. Witnessed by the king at Westminster 2 March.

---

[15] A change of hand occurs at this point.

[16] There is a change of hand at this point. The hand resembles that which opened item 15.

Per ipsum regem et consilium in pleno parliamento.
Page iii-75, Membrane 7

Concessio .xme et .xvme et demy.
16. Item, les seignours et communes du roialme d'Engleterre assemblez en ce present parlement apparceivantz coment nostre seignour le roi et son dit roialme sont come envyrounez et assis chescune part de lour enemys, les queux a grant multitude s'afforcent a toutes lours poairs sibien par terre come par meer a destruire mesme nostre seignour et son roialme avauntdit, qe Dieu ne voille, et qe pluis est, s'ils purroient d'ouster oultreement la lange Engleise; et par tant, en aide a les despenses qe l'en faut ore en cest proschein seisone mettre au fin force, sibien entour le defens et salvacioun de mesme le roialme come sur le viage ordeine vers Bretaigne, quelle, si Deux plest, tournera a bone remede en ce cas, et a grant socour et salvacion de mesme le roialme, et destruccioun des enemys avauntdites; mesmes les seignours et communes de lour liberale vountee et bone gree, coment qe ce soit ore grevouse charge pur eux d'endurer ou porter, grantent, pur eux et pur toute la commune d'Engleterre, a nostre dit seignour le roi une quinszisme et demy par dehors citees et burghs, et une disme et demy par dedeinz mesmes les citees et burghs, a avoir, c'estassavoir les dites quinzisme et disme de lour doun, et la dite moitee de quinszisme et disme par voie d'apprest tanqe al proschein parlement: a lever la dite disme et demy, et quinszisme et demy, de lours chateux et biens, et des biens de chescun de eux, et auxint des biens provenantz des terres et tenementz appropriez as religiouses depuis l'an vintisme le roi Edward filz le roi Henry, parentre cy et la feste de Seint George le Martir proschein venant, par mesme la fourme et manere qe les deux quinszismes et deux dismes furent derrainement grantez, coillez et levez al oeps nostre dit seignour le roi deinz son roialme avantdit, empriantz humblement a nostre dit seignour le roi qe les deniers provenantz sibien de cest lour grant come del grant q'est ore a faire par le clergie de mesme le roialme, ensemble avec les sommes de deniers q'encore remainent es mains des certains persones coillours, sibien des derraines subsides grantez al darrein parlement aprendre de chescun singulere persone del roialme, come del autre subside de quatre deniers grantez par les lays gentz en temps le roi Edward aiel nostre dit seignour le roi aprendre de chescune persone del roialme; et auxint del subside lors grantez par le clergie, dont y a /grandes summes es\ \mains/ des ditz coillours a ce q'est dit; soient entierment appliez al dit viage de Bretaigne, ... et nulle part aillours: et qe une suffisante persone soit assigne par commissioun nostre dit seignour le roi d'avoir la garde et administracioun des deniers provenantz des grantz et subsides dessuisdites, issint qe celles deniers ne soient medlez avec autres deniers le roi, n'autrement expenduz qe dessuis n'est dit par garant de prive seal ne de grant seal, n'autre mandement quelconqe, si par cas aucune y feusse fait au contraire par quelconqe voie.

Concessio subsidii lanarum, etc.
17. Item, mesmes les seignours et communes semblablement apperceivantz coment les subsides des leynes, quirs et peaux lanutz, \grantez/ a nostre dit seignour le roi a son parlement tenuz a Westm' a la .xv.^{e} de Pasqe darrein passe, doivent pur la forme et vertu de mesme le grant cesser de tout a la feste de Seint Michel proschein avenir - par quoi, si ce ne feust remediez, nostre seignour le roy ne purroit deslors endurer les grantz charges quelles luy convient au fyn force porter, come en paiant les gages de guerre en la marche de Caleys, Brest, Chirburgh', Gascoigne, Irlande, la

By the king himself and council in full parliament.

The concession of a tenth and a fifteenth and a half.
16. Also, the lords and commons of the kingdom of England assembled in this present parliament, perceiving that our lord the king and his said kingdom are surrounded and hemmed in on every side by their enemies, who in great numbers strive with all their might both by land and sea to destroy our lord and his aforesaid kingdom, which God forbid, and what is more, entirely to oust the English tongue if they can; because of this, to support the costs which shall have to be met in the coming season out of sheer necessity, for the defence and security of the same kingdom as well as in the planned expedition to Brittanny, which, if God pleases, shall result in an effective end to the problem, and to assist in the support and security of the same kingdom, and the destruction of the aforesaid enemies; the same lords and commons of their own free will and good grace, though now this be a grievous charge for them to bear and endure, grant to our said lord the king, on their own behalf as well as of all the commons of England, one fifteenth and a half from outside the cities and boroughs, and one tenth and a half from within the same cities and boroughs, for him to have, namely the said fifteenths and tenth as their gift, and the said half-fifteenth and tenth by way of a loan until the next parliament: the said tenth and a half and the said fifteenth and a half to be levied on their chattels and goods, and the goods of each one of them, and also from the goods arising from lands and tenements appropriated to the religious since the twentieth year of king Edward [I] son of king Henry [1291-2], between now and the feast of St George the Martyr next [23 April 1380], in the same form and manner in which the two fifteenths and two tenths were recently granted, collected and levied for the use of our said lord the king within his aforesaid kingdom; praying humbly of our said lord the king that the money ensuing from this their grant, as well as from the grant which is now to be made by the clergy of the same kingdom, together with the sums of money which still remain in the hands of certain collectors from the recent subsidies granted at the last parliament to be taken from each person in the kingdom, as well as from the other subsidy of four pence granted by the laity in the time of King Edward [III] the grandfather of our said lord the king to be taken from each person in the kingdom; and also from the subsidy then granted by the clergy, of which large sums are in the hands of the said collectors, as it is said; shall be devoted entirely to the said expedition to Brittany, and nowhere else: and that a worthy person be appointed by commission of our said lord the king to have the keeping and administration of the money arising from the aforesaid grants and subsidies, so that that money shall not be mingled with the rest of the king's money, nor spent in a way other than that mentioned above either by warrant of privy or great seal, or by any other mandate, if any has been issued to the contrary of the above by any means.

The grant of the subsidies on wool, etc.
17. Also, the same lords and commons, perceiving likewise that the subsidies on wool, hides and woolfells granted to our said lord the king at his parliament held at Westminster on the quinzaine of Easter last [25 April 1379], ought by the form and virtue of the same grant to cease entirely on the feast of Michaelmas next coming [29 September 1380] - on account of which, unless it be remedied, our lord the king would be unable thereafter to endure the great burdens which he has to bear out of sheer necessity, such as paying the wages of war in the march of Calais, Brest, Cherbourg,

marche d'Escoce, /et\ plusours autres charges, si la guerre dure - ont proloignez le terme d'avoir et resceivre mesmes les subsides; c'estassavoir, del dit feste \de/ Seint Michel proschein avenir, a quiel terme celles doivent cesser, come dit est, tanqe al feste de Seint Michel deslors proschein ensuant. Veullantz et grantantz a nostre dit seignour le roi q'il ait et preigne en le moien temps del dites leynes, quirs et peaux lanutz, et autielles custumes et subsides en toutes choses come il ent prent de present, par vertu del autre grant [Col. b] a luy fait en dit parlement, come dessuis est dit.[17] Enpriantz a nostre seignour le roi qe nul parlement soit tenuz deinz le dit railme pur pluis charger sa poevre commune parentre cy et le dit feste de Saint Michel proschein venant en un an.

Declaracion prodicionis.
18. Item, par la ou en l'estatut nadgairs fait a Westm', en l'an du regne du noble roy aielle nostre seignour le roi q'orest .xxv.,[18] sur declaracioun de tresoun, estoient declarrez certeins cas limitez en mesme l'estatut, et feust assentu illoeqes qe si autres cas suppose tresoun qe n'estoit especifiez en la declaracioun du dit estatut aviendroit de novel devant aucun justice, demurroit le justice sanz aler a juggement de tresoun, tanqe pardevant le roi et son parlement serroit le cas monstre et declare, le quiele ce doit estre ajugge tresoun ou autre felonie. Et ore en ceste present parlement soit monstre, coment qe nostre dit seignour le roi, de l'advis de soun conseil, nadgairs par ses lettres patentes desouz son grant seal, portantz date du .vime jour de Marz l'an de son regne primer, adurers par deux ans proscheins ensuantz, avoit pris en son sauf conduit et en ses proteccioun et defens especialx un Jane imperial Janevois, patroun d'une carice appelle le Seinte Marie de Jene, c'estassavoir, pur le dit patroun avenir et demurrer en Engleterre, \et/ sauvement retourner en ses propres parties. Sur espoir et tuicioun des queux lettres du conduit, proteccioun, et defens, le dit Jane vint en Engleterre a la citee de Londres, et illoeqes demurra sur une trete d'alliance a faire parentre nostre seignour le roi et le duc et la comminaltee de Jene, sicome il avoit en mandement par lettres depar les ditz duc et comminaltee desouz lour sealx, monstre devant nostre dit seignour le roi et son conseil: quele trete monstre devant nostre dit seignour le roi et son dit conseil, lour sembloit honurable et profitable a nostre dit seignour le roi et son roialme, come pleinement estoit recorde en le dit parlement par le chaunceller et le conseil nostre dit seignour le roi alors esteant, nientmains, le dit Jane ensi esteant /souz les\ sauf conduit et proteccioun nostre dit seignour le roi par la manere come dessuis est dit, estoit felenousement occis et murdrez par aucuns liges nostre dit seignour le roi en la citee de Londres, a ce q'est dit, et come pluis pleinement purra apparer par l'enditement pris sur la veue de corps mesme celuy Jane, durantz la force de mesmes les lettres du sauf conduit, proteccioun, et defens nostre dit seignour le roi. Quel cas examine et despute entre les seignours et communes, et puis monstre au roi en plein parlement, estoit illoeqes devaunt nostre dit seignour le roi declarez, determinez et assentuz qe tielle fait et coupe est treson, et crime du roiale magestee blemye, en quel cas y ne doit allouer a nully d'enjoier privilege de clergie.

[19]Et fait a remembrer qe cest darrein acte issint faite, si fust fait par les justices en presence du roi nostre seignour, et les

Gascony, Ireland and the march of Scotland, and many other charges, if the war last - have extended the term for taking and receiving the same subsidies; namely, from the said feast of Michaelmas next, at which time they ought to have ceased, as was said, until the feast of Michaelmas following thereupon. Willing and granting to our said lord the king that he shall have and take in the meantime from the said wool, hides and woolfells all such customs and subsidies as he takes at present, by virtue of the other grant [Col. b] made to him in the said parliament, as is said above; requesting of our lord the king that no parliament shall be held within the kingdom which further burdens his poor commons between now and the said feast of Michaelmas in a year's time [29 September 1381].

Declaration of treason.
18. Also, whereas in a statute formerly made at Westminster, in the twenty-fifth year of the reign of the noble king, grandfather of our present lord the king [1351], upon the declaration of treason, only a limited number of causes were mentioned, and it was agreed there that if other instances of alleged treason which had not been specified in the declaration of the said statute should arise anew before any justice, the justice should stay without proceeding to a judgment of treason, until the cause should be explained and declared before the king and his council, who would judge whether this should be adjudged a treason or another felony. Yet now, in this present parliament, it has been shown that whereas our said lord the king, with the advice of his council, recently, by his letters patent under his great seal, carrying the date 6 March in the first year of his reign [1378], to last for the following two years, took under his safeconduct and into his special protection and defence, one Gian of the Genoese empire, owner of a carrack called the St Mary of Genoa, that is to say, for the said owner to come and dwell in England and safely return to his own parts. Under the hope and protection of these letters of safeconduct, protection and defence, the said Gian came to England and arrived in the city of London, and there remained under a treaty of alliance to be made between our lord the king and the doge and community of Genoa, the mandate for which he possessed in letters from the said doge and community under their seals, shown before our said lord the king and his council: which treaty having been laid before our said lord the king and his said council, seemed to them honourable and profitable to our said lord the king and his kingdom, as was fully recorded in the said parliament by the chancellor and the council of our said lord the king then present; nevertheless, the said Gian being under the safeconduct and protection of our said lord the king in the said manner, was basely killed and murdered by some of the lieges of our said lord the king in the city of London, as it is said, and as is more fully apparent from the indictment made upon the inspection of the corpse of the same Gian, while the same letters of safeconduct, protection and defence issued by our said lord the king were still in force. Which cause having been examined and discussed between the lords and commons, and then laid before the king in full parliament, it was there declared, determined and agreed before our said lord the king that such a deed carried the guilt of treason, and the crime of lese majesty, in which no one should enjoy privilege of clergy.
And be it remembered that this last act was performed by the justices in the presence of the king our lord and the lords

---

[17] The following sentence is written in a different, contemporary hand. This untidy hand is to be found elsewhere in the roll.
[18] 25 Edw.3 c.2.
[19] This paragraph is written in the untidy hand found on a previous occasion in this roll.

seignours temporelx en ce parlement, et puis baillez en escrit pur enrouller es roulles de cest parlement de record depar le roi au clerc de parlement, par les mains Geffrey Martin un des clercz de la coroune nostre dit seignour le roi, lui quiel escrit la note originale, etc. [20]

Membrane 6

Salesbirs marche.

19. Et est assavoir qe es roulles du darrein parlement tenuz a Westm' il y a un certain roullement enroullez en la fourme qe s'ensuit:

Item, est assavoir q'il y a un certain enroullement enrollez es roulles du darrein parlement tenuz a Gloucestr', en la fourme qe s'ensuit:[21]

Item, fait a remembrer qe sur la demande qe William de Montagu, conte de Salesbirs, fait d'avoir les terres de Dynbeygh' en Gales, il y a un enroullement entres en les roulles du parlement tenuz a Westm', a la .xv.^{e} de Seint Michel, l'an du regne nostre seignour le roi q'orest primer, en la fourme qe s'ensuit: Item, William de Montagu, conte de Salesbirs, mist avant en parlement *[Page iii-76]*

[Col. a] une sa peticion, en la fourme qe s'ensuit: A nostre seignour le roi monstre son lige William de Montagu, conte de Salesbirs, come mon tresredoute seignour le roi vostre aiel, qi Dieux assoille, dona et granta a mon pier William de Montagu, nadgairs conte de Salesbirs, et as ses heirs de son corps issantz, ove clause de garantie, le chastiel, ville et honour de Dynbeygh', et les cantredes de Roos, Rowynok' et Kaiemer, et la commot de Dynmael, ove \les/ appurtenauntz en Gales, salvant ent la reversion a lui et a ses heirs, come pluis pleinement piert par ses chartres a mon dit pier ent faites. Les queux chastiel, ville et honour, cantredes et commot, ove les appurtenantz, Roger de Mortymer, pier Esmon conte q'orest, come cousin et heir Roger de Mortymer, nadgairs conte de la Marche, demanda devers moy, par noun de la terre de Dynbeygh' ove les appurtenantes en Gales, par brief de scire facias, devant mon dit seignour le roi vostre aiel, en sa courte en bank le roi, de ent avoir execucioun. En quiel plee jeo pria aide de mon dit seignour le roi, vostre aiel, par la cause avauntdite. Et apres brief de procedendo sur ce grantez, le dit Roger, le pere Esmon, recoveri devers moi par juggement les ditz chastiel, ville, honour, cantredes et commot, ove les appurtenantz, par noun de la terre de Dynbeygh' ove les appurtenantes en Gales, come en le record et proces sur ce faitz pleinement appiert. En quelles record et proces, et auxint en jugement sur ce /renduz,\ il y ad errour; et le quel jugement estoit /execut,\ et moy ouste de \ma/ possession, l'an de son regne .xxviij.^{me}, dont je n'avoie unqes rien en value, coment qe mon dit seignour le roi vostre aiel par sa chartre avoit grante a ce faire, come dessuis est dit. Puis quiel perte, j'ai sui de parlement en parlement par diverses peticions de ent avoir remedie, et oultre autres au parlement tenuz a Westm' le .viij.^{me} jour de Novembre, l'an de son regne .xlvime une ma peticion sur ceste matire estoit endosse en ceux paroles, Le roi ne voet mie qe l'eir qe est deinz age et en sa garde ne perde riens pur le temps q'il est en sa garde; mais quant il vient a son plein age, sue, et droit serra faite al une partie et al autre. Et ore le dit heir, c'estassavoir Esmon de Mortymer ore conte de la Marche, fitz et heir mesme celui Roger le cousin, est avenuz a son plein age. Qe plese a vostre tresgraciouse seignourie commander, de faire venir les ditz record et proces devant vous et vostre tressage conseil en cest present parlement, et appellez le dit Esmon et ceux qi sont en celles parties a appellers, et

---

[20] The rest of membrane 7 has been left blank.
[21] PRO SC8/18/882.

veuez et examinez les dites record et proces de moi ordeiner ent remedie selonc droit et resoun. Et si errour y puisse estre trovez, qe le dit jugement soit reversez et adnullez, et moy restitut a ma possession ove les issues d'ycelle come la loy demande. Quelle peticion lue en mesme le parlement et entendue, dit feust et commandez en cest parlement, par les prelatz et seignours, peres du parlement lors esteantz en mesme le parlement, a monsire Johan Cavendissh', chivaler, chief justice nostre seignour le roi, q'ad les record et proces dont la dite peticion fait mencioun en garde, q'il ferroit venir mesmes les record et proces en cest parlement sanz delaie. Lui quiel Monsire Johan apporta en dit parlement mesmes les record et proces, entre diverses autres recordz et proces comprises en certains roulles tachez ou consutz ensemble. Et sur ce, le dit conte de Salesbirs assigna en parlement par especial et par bouche diverses errours estre contenuz en ycelle record et proces, empriant qe par celle errours, et par autres quelles en ycelles record et proces purront estre trovez, le jugement y renduz soit reversez; et qe le dit Esmon de Mortymer, filz et heir le dit Roger le cousin, ore conte de la Marche, y fuist garniz par brief de scire facias d'estre au proschein parlement d'oier les dites record et proces, et de faire et resceivre ce q'adonqes en celle partie serra agardez. Et cel brief lui estoit grantez illoeqes, et commandez estre fait retournable en dit proschein parlement. Et puis apres sur le fin du dit parlement,

[Col. b] le dit monsire \Johan/ Cavendissh, par commandement des prelats et seignours du parlement ent a lui fait, portast mesmes les record et proces en le bank le roi, pur y demurrer come en garde tanqe au dit proschein parlement. Et est ordeinez et acordez qe mesmes les record et proces soient en dit proschein parlement par la cause avantdite. A quiel proschein parlement, c'estassavoir en cest present parlement tenuz a Gloucestre le mesqardy proschein apres la feste de Seint Luk l'Ewangelist, vient le dit conte de Salesbirs en sa persone devaunt nostre seignour le roi, en presence des prelats, peres et autres seignours du parlement, le dit monsire Johan Cavendissh' q'ad mesmes les record et proces dont la dite peticioun fait mention en garde illoeqes present, et monsire Brian de Cornewaill', viscont de Shropshire, retourna en cest parlement le dit brief de scire facias issint fait et grante au darrein parlement; dont sibien del dit brief come del retourne ent fait par le dit viscont, le tenour s'ensuit de mot en mot:

Ricardus, Dei gratia, rex Anglie et Francie, et dominus Hibernie, vicecomiti Salop', salutem. Cum Rogerus de Mortuo Mari, filius Edmundi de Mortuo Mari nuper comes Marchie, ut consanguineus et heres Rogeri de Mortuo Mari nuper comitis Marchie, avi sui, in curia domini Edwardi nuper regis Anglie, avi nostri, coram eodem avo nostro, termino trinitatis, anno regni sui Anglie vicesimo octavo, per breve ipsius avi nostri, ac consideracionem ejusdem curie, recuperaverit versus Willielmum de Monte Acuto comitem Sar', terram de Dynbeigh' cum pertinentiis in Wallie; idemque comes Sar' per peticionem suam nobis in presenti parliamento nostro exhibitam nobis supplicaverit, ut cum diversi errores in recordo et processu ac reddicione judicii loquele predicte intervenissent, ad grave dampnum ipsius comitis Sar', vellemus recordum et processum inde habita coram nobis et consilio nostro in dicto parliamento nostro venire,

and process be brought before you and your most wise council in this present parliament, and having summoned the said Edmund and those who ought to be summoned in this matter, and having inspected and examined the said record and process, to ordain remedy for me in accordance with right and reason. And if error be discovered that the said judgment shall be reversed and annulled, and I restored to my possession together with the issues from the same as the law demands. Which petition having been read and heard in the same parliament, the prelates and lords, peers of parliament attending this same parliament, instructed and ordered Sir John Cavendish, knight, chief justice of our lord the king, who had in his keeping the record and process of which the said petition made mention, to cause the same record and process to be brought to this parliament without delay. Which Sir John brought the same record and process to parliament, along with various other records and processes contained in certain rolls attached or stitched together. Whereupon, the said earl of Salisbury, speaking for himself in parliament, drew particular attention to various errors contained in the same record and process, requesting that because of those errors and because of others which might be found in the same record and process, the judgment rendered thereon should be reversed; and that the said Edmund Mortimer, son and heir of the said Roger the cousin, now earl of March, should be instructed by writ of scire facias to attend the next parliament to hear the said record and process, and to do and accept whatever would then be decided in that matter. And that writ was granted to him there, and was deemed returnable in the said next parliament. And then, after the end of the said parliament,

[Col. b] the said Sir John Cavendish, by order of the prelates and lords of parliament made to him, brought the same record and process into the King's Bench, for them to be kept there until the said next parliament. And it was ordained and agreed that the same record and process should be available at the next parliament for the aforesaid reason. At which next parliament, namely in this present parliament held at Gloucester on the Tuesday next after the feast of St Luke the Evangelist [20 October 1378], the said earl of Salisbury came in person before our lord the king, in the presence of the prelates, peers and other lords of parliament, and the said Sir John Cavendish who had in his keeping the same record and process of which the said petition made mention; and Sir Brian Cornwall, sheriff of Shropshire, returned to this parliament the said writ of scire facias thus made and granted at the last parliament; the verbatim texts of which said writ as well as the return made thereon by the said sheriff, are as follows:

Richard, by the grace of God, king of England and France, and lord of Ireland, to the sheriff of Shropshire, greeting. Whereas Roger Mortimer, son of Edmund Mortimer late earl of March, as cousin and heir of Roger Mortimer late earl of March, his grandfather, in the court of Lord Edward late king of England, our grandfather, in the presence of our same grandfather, in Trinity term, in the twenty-eighth year of his reign over England, by writ of this our grandfather, and with the consent of the same court, recovered from William Montagu, earl of Salisbury, the land of Denbigh with appurtenances in Wales; and the same earl of Salisbury requested of us through his petition shown to us in our present parliament that since various errors were to be found in the record and process and judgment rendered on the aforesaid case, which gravely injured this earl of Salisbury, we might will the record and process made thereon to be brought before us

eademque recordum et processum ibidem examinari, ac errores inde repertos corrigi jubere: nos supplicacioni predicti comitis Sar' in hac parte annuentes, recordum et processum predicta coram nobis ac prelatis et magnatibus in dicto parliamento ea de causa venire fecimus, ac insuper errores illos, si qui fuerint, modo debito corrigi, et ulterius inde fieri volentes quod est justum, tibi precipimus quod per probos et legales homines de comitatu tuo scire facias Edmundo de Mortuo Mari nunc comiti Marchie, filio et heredi prefati Rogeri filii Edmundi quod sit coram nobis in proximo parliamento nostro ubicumque tunc fuerit, auditurus recordum et processum predicta, si sibi viderit expedire, ulteriusque facturus et recepturus quod considerari contigerit tunc ibidem. Et habeas ibi nomina illorum per quos ei scire feceris, et hoc breve. Teste me ipso apud Westm' primo die Decembris, anno regni nostri primo.

Responcio Briani de Cornewaille, vicecomiti: Edmundus de Mortuo Mari nunc comes Marchie, filius et heres Rogeri de Mortuo Mari filii Edmundi de Mortuo Mari nuper comitis Marchie, non est inventus in balliva mea postquam istud breve michi liberatum fuit, nec aliqua habet terras seu tenementa in eadem ubi premuniri potest.

Et sur ce le dit conte de Salesbirs en ce parlement pria a nostre seignour le roi qe luy pleust a lui granter un autre brief de scire facias, pur garnir le dit Esmon ore conte de la March', filz et heir le dit Roger filz Esmon, a la dicte terre de Dynbeigh', d'estre devaunt nostre seignour le roi en son proschein parlement, d'oier, faire et resceivre ce qe la loye demande, come dessuis est dit. Quiel brief par nostre dit seignour le roi, par l'advis des seignours et autres sages du parlement lui ad grantez, et comandez estre fait retournable en dit proschein parlement. Et enoultre est acordez en ce parlement qe les dites record et proces par la dite cause soient en dit proschein parlement. *[Page iii-77]*

[Col. a] A quiel proschein parlement, c'estassavoir en cest present parlement tenuz a Westm' a la .xv.^{e} de Pasqe, monsire Johan de Lodelowe, viscont de Salop, retornast le dit brief de scire facias grante au dit parlement de Glouc', de quiel brief, ovesqe l'endossement et retourn ent faitz par le dit viscont, le tenour s'ensuit de mot a mot:

Ricardus, Dei gratia, rex Anglie et Francie, et dominus Hibernie, vicecomiti Salop', salutem. Cum Rogerus de Mortuo Mari, filius Edmundi di Mortuo Mari, nuper comes Marchie, et consanguineus et heres Rogeri de Mortuo Mari nuper comitis Marchie, avi sui, in curia domini Edwardi nuper regis Anglie, avi nostri, coram eodem avo nostro, termino Trinitatis, anno regni sui Anglie vicesimo octavo, per breve ipsius avi nostri, ac consideracionem ejusdem curie, recuperaverit versus Willelmum de Monte Acuto, comitem Sarum, terram de Dynbeigh' cum pertinentiis in Wallie; idemque comes Sar' per peticionem suam nobis in parliamento nostro apud Westm', in quindena Sancti Michaelis anno regni nostri Anglie primo tento, exhibitam, nobis supplicaverit, ut cum diversi errores in recordo et processus ac reddicione judicii loquele predicte intervenissent, ad grave dampnum ipsius comitis Sar', vellemus recordum et processum inde habita coram nobis et consilio nostro in dicto parliamento nostro venire, eademque recordum et processum ibidem examinari, ac errores inde repertos corrigi jubere: et nos supplicacioni predicti comitis Sar' in hac parte tunc annuentes, recordum et processum predicta coram nobis ac prelatis et magnatibus in parliamento nostro predicto ea de causa venire fecimus; ac insuper errores illos, si qui forent, modo debito corrigi, ulteriusque inde fieri volentes quod justum, per breve

and our council in our said parliament, and the same record and process to be there examined, and order the errors found therein to be corrected: we, agreeing with the request of the aforesaid earl of Salisbury in this matter, caused the aforesaid record and process, for that reason, to be brought before us and the prelates and magnates in the said parliament, and furthermore, those errors, if any there were, to be corrected in due manner, and finally, wishing to act justly therein, we order you that through worthy and lawful men from your county you cause Edmund Mortimer now earl of March, son and heir of the aforesaid Roger son of Edmund, to appear before us in our next parliament, wheresover that may be, to hear the aforesaid record and process, if it seem expedient to him, and also to do and accept whatever shall happen to be decided there. And you shall have there the names of those through whom you caused him to be notified, together with this writ. Witnessed by myself at Westminster 1 December, in the first year of our reign [1377].

The response of Brian Cornwall, sheriff: Edmund Mortimer now earl of March, son and heir of Roger Mortimer son of Edmund Mortimer late earl of March, was not to be found in my bailiwick after this writ was delivered to me, nor does he have any lands or tenements in the same where he might be attached.

Whereupon, the said earl of Salisbury in this parliament prayed of our lord the king that it might please him to grant another writ of scire facias instructing the said Edmund earl of March, son and heir of the said Roger son of Edmund, at the said land of Denbigh, to appear before our lord the king in his next parliament, to hear, perform and receive what the law demanded, as said above. Which writ our said lord the king, by the advice of the lords and other wise men of parliament, granted him, and it was deemed returnable in the said next parliament. Furthermore, it was agreed in this parliament that the said record and process for the said reason should be available in the said next parliament. *[Page iii-77]*

[Col. a] At which next parliament, namely in this present parliament held at Westminster on the quinzaine of Easter [24 April 1379], Sir John Ludlow, sheriff of Shropshire, returned the said writ of scire facias granted at the said parliament of Gloucester, the verbatim text of which writ, together with the endorsement and return on it made by the said sheriff, here follow:

Richard, by the grace of God, king of England and France, and lord of Ireland, to the sheriff of Shropshire, greeting. Whereas Roger Mortimer, son of Edmund Mortimer, late earl of March, and cousin and heir of Roger Mortimer late earl of March, his grandfather, in the court of the lord Edward late king of England, our grandfather, in the presence of our same grandfather, in Trinity term, in the twenty-eighth year of his reign over England [1354], by writ of our same grandfather, and by the judgment of the same court, recovered from William Montagu, earl of Salisbury, the land of Denbigh with its appurtenances in Wales; and the same earl of Salisbury by his petition shown to us in our parliament at Westminster, on the quinzaine of Michaelmas in the first year of our reign over England [13 October 1377], prayed of us that since various errors were to be found in the record and process and rendering of the judgment in the aforesaid case, to the great injury of the earl of Salisbury, that we might cause the record and process made thereon to be brought before us and our council in the said parliament, and the same record and process to be examined there, and the errors found therein to be corrected: and we, agreeing to the request of the aforesaid earl of Salisbury in the matter, caused the aforesaid record and process of the cause to be brought before us and the prelates and magnates in our

nostrum tibi preceperimus quod scire faceres Edmundo de Mortuo Mari, nunc comiti Marchie, filio et heredi prefati Rogeri filii Edmundi quod esset coram nobis in parliamento nostro extunc proximo tenendo ubicumque tunc foret, auditurus recordum et processum predicta, si sibi viderit expedire, ulteriusque facturus et recepturus quod considerari contingeret tunc ibidem; ac tu in dicto proximo parliamento, videlicet in presenti parliamento nostro apud Glouc', die Mercurii proximo post festum Sancti Luce Ewangeliste tento, retornaveris quod prefatus Edmundus de Mortuo Mari comes Marchie, filius et heres Rogeri de Mortuo Mari, filii Edmundi de Mortuo Mari nuper comitis Marchie, non fuit inventus in balliva tua postquam dictum breve tibi liberatum fuit, nec aliqua habuit terras seu tenementa in eadem ubi /ipse premuniri\ potuit. Tibi precipimus quod per probos et legales homines de comitatu tuo scire facias prefato Edmundo de Mortuo Mari, comiti Marchie, filio et heredi prefati Rogeri filii Edmundi, apud predictam terram de Dynbeigh', quod sit coram nobis, in proximo parliamento nostro ubicumque tunc fuerit, auditurus recordum et processum predicta, si sibi viderit expedire, ulteriusque facturus et recepturus quod considerari contigerit tunc ibidem. Et habeas ibi nomina eorum per quos ei scire feceris, et hoc breve. Teste me ipso apud Westm' .xij. die Decembris, anno regni nostri secundo.

Responcio Johannis de Lodelowe, vicecomiti: Virtute istius brevis scire feci Edmundo de Mortuo Mari, comiti Marchie, filio et heredi Rogeri de Mortuo Mari nuper comitis Marchie, per Johannem de Hodenet, et Thomam de Ludebury, Johannem filium Radulphi de Hodenet, et Walterum de Suggedon', probos et legales homines de balliva mea, apud terram de Dynbeygh' infra nominatam, vicesimo quarto die Martii, anno regni domini regis nunc secundo, quod sit coram domino rege in proximo parliamento suo ubicumque tunc fuerit, auditurus, facturus et recepturus quod considerari contigerit tunc in eodem parliamento de omnibus et singulis in isto brevi contentis, secundum formam, vim et effectum ejusdem brevis, et prout per idem breve precipitur.

Sur quoi vint en ce present parlement sibien le conte de Salesbirs par monsire Johan de Montagu, chivaler,

[Col. b] un de ses generalx attournes fait par patente nostre dit seignour le roi, dont la date est a Westm' le .xij. jour d'Averill' l'an present, mesme le conte de Salesbirs esteant es parties de dela en la service nostre seignour le roi, come le dit conte de la Marche en sa persone, et illoeqes oiez et entenduz le ditz brief et retourn, et les record et proces dont mesme le brief fait mencion, esteantz en parlement le dit conte de Salesbirs par son dit attourne, se profri d'assigner illoeqes les errours quieles il dit estre comprises en les record et proces avauntdites. Et si le conte de la Marche adonqes present en parlement, dist qe le dit brief n'est pas servi sicome mesme le brief demande: qar il dit qe en le dit brief est contenuz qe le viscont ferroit garnir Esmon de Mortymer, conte de la Marche, filz et heir Roger de Mortymer nadgaires conte de la March filz Esmon de Mortimer. Et par le retourn de mesme le brief expressement apiert qe le viscont ad garni Esmon de Mortymer conte de la Marche, filz et heir Roger de Mortymer filz Esmon de Mortymer nadgairs conte de la Marche. Par quiel retourn ensi fait doit estre entenduz par la loy autre persone estre garni qe en le dit brief est contenuz; qar le dit Esmon le pere Roger n'estoit unqes conte, et n'entende mye le dit Esmon ore conte de la Marche qe par tiel retourn del dit brief la courte voille oultre proceder en

aforesaid parliament; and order those errors, if any there were, to be corrected in due manner, and further wishing to do therein what was just, we ordered you by our writ that you instruct Edmund Mortimer, now earl of March, son and heir of the aforesaid Roger son of Edmund to appear before us in our next parliament to be held, wheresover that might be, to hear the aforesaid record and process, if it suited him, and further to do and receive whatever would happen to be decided then and there; and you, in the said next parliament, namely in our present parliament at Gloucester, held on the Wednesday next following the feast of St Luke the Evangelist [20 October 1378], returned that the aforementioned Edmund Mortimer, earl of March, son and heir of Roger Mortimer, son of Edmund Mortimer late earl of March, had not been found in your bailliwick after the said writ had been delivered to you, and neither did he have lands or tenements by which he might be attached. We order you that through worthy and lawful men of your county you instruct the aforementioned Edmund Mortimer, earl of March, son and heir of the aforesaid Roger son of Edmund, in the aforesaid land of Denbigh, to appear before us, in our next parliament wheresover that might be held, to hear the aforesaid record and process, if it seem expedient to him, and further to do and accept whatever happened to be then decided there. And you shall have there the names of those through whom you caused him to be notified, together with this writ. Witnessed by myself at Westminster 12 December, in the second year of our reign [1378].

The answer of John Ludlow, sheriff: By virtue of this writ I made known to Edmund Mortimer, earl of March, son and heir of Roger Mortimer late earl of March, by John Hodnet, and Thomas Ludbury, John son of Ralph Hodnet, and Walter Sugden, worthy and lawful men of my bailliwick, in the land of Denbigh mentioned above, on 24 March, in the second year of the reign of the present lord king, that he should be before the lord king in his next parliament wheresoever that might be, to hear, perform and receive whatsoever might then be decided in the same parliament concerning each and every item contained in this writ, in accordance with the form, force and effect of this same writ, and as I was instructed by this writ.

Whereupon, there appeared in this present parliament both the earl of Salisbury as represented by Sir John Montagu, knight,

[Col. b] one of his general attorneys appointed by letter patent of our said lord the king, dated Westminster 12 April in the present year [1379] - the same earl of Salisbury being overseas in the service of our lord the king - and the said earl of March in person, and there having heard and understood the said writ and return, and the record and process of which the same writ made mention, the said earl of Salisbury, being in parliament by his said attorney, offered to indicate there the errors which he said were contained in the aforesaid record and process. And so the earl of March, then present in parliament, said that the said writ had not been served as the same writ required: for he said that in the said writ it was stated that the sheriffs should instruct Edmund Mortimer, earl of March, son and heir of Roger Mortimer late earl of March, son of Edmund Mortimer. Yet from the return of the same writ it appeared that the sheriff had warned Edmund Mortimer, earl of March, son and heir of Roger Mortimer son of Edmund Mortimer late earl of March. From which return thus made it was to be understood that in the eyes of the law the person who had been notified was different from the person mentioned in the said writ; since the said Edmund the father of Roger had never been earl, and the said Edmund now earl of March certainly

dit busoigne. A quoi le dit conte de Salesbirs dist qe le dit Esmon ore conte de la Marche est suffisamentdite garni: par quiel garnissement il apparust et feust present, empriant a nostre seignour le roi et as seignours du parlement q'il poet estre resceuz d'assigner les errours comprises en le record et proces avauntditz, et qe sur ce les ditz record et proces duement examinez en parlement, plese a nostre seignour le roi, et as seignours du parlement, pur les errours comprises en ycelles record et proces, repeller et de tout adnuller le juggement erroinement y renduz envers lui. Et enoultre, a mesme le conte de Salesbirs faire plein restitucion de la terre suisdite, avec ses appurtenants qelconqes, et avec les issues en le moien temps prises et resceuz. Et est assavoir qe pur ce qe cest parlement si estoit bien pres au fyn quant cest busoigne feust issint touchez et parlez: et par tant, et pur autres chargeants busoignes touchant l'estat nostre seignour le roi, et la salvacion du roialme, dont les seignours du parlement d'autre part estoient alors moelt grandement occupiez; mesmes les seignours, qi alors ne furent suffisantement advisez sur si haute et chargeante matire, ne poaient a ceste busoigne pluis attendre. Mais par assent du parlement, jour ent est donez as ditz contes en le proschein parlement, toutes choses esteantz en mesme l'estat qe ore sont, et sauvez as parties lours resons et chalanges quelconqes. Et enoultre est acordez qe les record et proces avauntdites soient en dit proschein parlement, par la cause avantdite.

Au quiel proschein parlement, c'estassavoir a cest parlement tenuz a Westm' le lundy proschein apres le feste[22] de Seint Hiller, l'an du regne nostre seignour le roi Richard tierce, vint le dit conte de Salesbirs en sa persone, empriant a nostre seignour le roi et as seignours du parlement, qe aiantz consideracioun coment a derrain parlement jour lui estoit donez en cest parlement, et entenduz sa longe pursuite q'il ad fait devant ceste heure de parlement en parlement sanz rienz en effect esploiter pur les dites terre et seignourie de Dynbegh' avec ses appurtenants, dont il estoit nadgairs torcenousement oustez par juggement envers lui renduz, moelt erroinement come dit est, a ce qe lui semble, pleust a mesme nostre seignour le roi, et as autres seignours avauntdites comander a monsire Johan de Cavendissh', chivaler, cy present, q'ad les ditz recordz et proces en garde, del assent de parlement faire lire mesmes les recordz et proces en cest parlement, et sur ce doner ascoult et audience au dit conte de Salesbirs, d'assigner les errours y comprises. Et enoultre si par examinement de mesmes les record et proces, ou en autre due *[Page iii-78]*

[Col. a] manere, purra apparoir errour y estre comprises, q'adonqes le juggement y renduz soit reversez, et le dit conte de Salesbirs restitut a ses terre et seignourie dessusdites; ensemblement avec les issues resceuz en le moien temps, selonc les loys de la terre, bone foy et reson.

20. Et sur ce seignour Johan de Bishopeston', clerc et familier del dit conte de la Marche, mesme le conte de la March' lors absent, et esteant en Gales, a ce qe fuist dit, sur son passage vers Irlande, illoeqes a demurrer en le service nostre seignour le roi, et mist avaunt en parlement une proteccioun, avec clause 'de volumus', faite et ensealee desouz le

---

[22] *Original* steste

did not realise that on the basis of such a return made on the said writ the court would wish to proceed any further in the said matter. To which the said earl of Salisbury replied that the said Edmund now earl of March had been given adequate warning: as a result of which warning he had appeared and was now present, requesting of our lord the king and the lords of parliament that he might be allowed to point out the errors contained in the aforesaid record and process, and that upon the said record and process having been duly examined in parliament, it might please our lord the king, and the lords of parliament, on account of the errors contained in the same record and process, to repeal and entirely annul the judgment erroneously passed against him. And further to make to the same earl of Salisbury full restitution of his aforesaid land, together with its appurtenances whatsoever, and with the issues taken and received in the meantime. And be it known that because this parliament had been so close to ending when this matter was thus raised and spoken of: and for this reason as well as because of other important matters concerning the estate of our lord the king and the security of the kingdom, with which the lords of parliament had also been greatly preoccupied; the same lords, who were at that stage insufficiently informed on so serious and important a matter, could not attend any further to this business. But by the assent of parliament, a day was given to the said earls in the next parliament, all things remaining equal, and saving to the parties their arguments and challenges of any sort. Furthermore, it was agreed that the aforesaid record and process should be made available at the next parliament, for the aforesaid reason.

At which next parliament, namely at this parliament held at Westminster on the Monday following the feast of St Hilary in the third year of the reign of our lord the king Richard [16 January 1380], the said earl of Salisbury appeared in person, requesting of our lord the king and the lords of parliament that - bearing in mind that at the last parliament a day had been given him in this present parliament, and taking into account the lengthy suit which he had made before this time from parliament to parliament without effectively achieving anything for the said land and lordship of Denbigh with its appurtenances, from which he had previously been wrongfully ousted by the judgment rendered against him, most erroneously as was said and as it seemed to him - it might please our same lord the king, and the other aforesaid lords to order Sir John Cavendish, knight, here present, who had the said record and process in his keeping, by the assent of parliament to cause the same record and process to be read in this parliament, and thereupon to afford hearing and audience to the said earl of Salisbury, who would point out the errors contained in it. Moreover, if by examination of the same record and process, or by other proper *[Page iii-78]*
[Col. a] means, it were to become apparent that error lay therein, that then the judgment there rendered might be reversed, and the said earl of Salisbury restored to his aforesaid land and lordship, together with the issues received in the meantime, in accordance with the laws of the land, good faith and reason.

20. Whereupon, Sir John Bishopston, clerk and councillor of the said earl of March - the same earl of March then being absent in Wales, as it was said, on his way to Ireland, to remain there in the service of our lord the king - laid before parliament a protection, with the clause de volumus,

grant seal nostre dit seignour le roi pur mesme le conte de la Marche, en la fourme qe s'ensuit:[23]

21. Ricardus, Dei gratia, rex Anglie et Francie, et dominus Hibernie, omnibus ballivis, et fidelibus suis ad quos presentes litere pervenerint, salutem. Sciatis quod suscepimus in proteccionem et defencionem nostram dilectum consanguineum et /fidelem\ nostrum Edmundum de Mortuo Mari, comitem Marchie, filium et heredem Rogeri de Mortuo Mari, nuper comitis Marchie, filii Edmundi de Mortuo Mari, et consanguinei et heredis Rogeri de Mortuo Mari, nuper comitis Marchie, qui in obsequium nostrum ad partes Hibernie profecturus est, ibidem in obsequio nostro locumtenens noster terre nostre Hibernie moraturus, homines, terras, res, redditus et omnes possessiones suas. Et ideo vobis mandamus, quod ipsum comitem, homines, terras, res, redditus et omnes /possessiones\ suas manuteneatis, protegatis et defendatis, non inferentes eis vel inferri permittentes injuriam, molestiam, dampnum, aut gravamen. Et si quid eis forisfactum fuerit id eis sine dilacione faciatis emendari. In cujus rei testimonium has literas nostras fieri fecimus patentes per unum annum duraturum. Volumus eciam quod idem comes interim sit quietus de omnibus placitis et querelis, exceptis placitis de dote, unde nichil habet, et quare impedit, et assisis nove disseisine, et ultime presentacionis, et attinctis; et exceptis loquelis quas coram justiciariis nostris itinerantibus in itinerantibus suis summoneri contigerit. Presentibus minime valituris si contingat ipsum comitem iter illud non aripere, vel postquam citra terminum illum in Anglie redierit a partibus supradictis. Teste me ipso apud Westm', primo die Decembris, anno regni nostri tertio.
Per billam de privato sigillo.
Quelle protection lue en parlement, et entendue, et diligeaument examinee et allouee, agarde fuist en mesme le parlement qe le dit conte de la March' ent aille sanz jour.

Membrane 5
Pur Phelip Darcy.
22. Phelip Darcy, chivaler, mist avant en ce present parlement une sa bille en la forme qe s'ensuit: A nostre tresgracious seignour le roi et son sage conseil supplie Philipp' Darcy, chivaler, qe come le priour del hospital de Seint Johan de Jerusalem en Engleterre ad suy un scire facias en bank nostre dit seignour le roi vers le dit Philipp', de manoirs de Templehirst et Templeneusom', sur l'ordinance et l'agard nadgairs faitz en le parlement vostre tresgracious besaiel, l'an de son regne .xvij., de les terres et tenementz queux feuront jadis as Templers; a quiel brief le dit Philipp' ad alege et plede qe le roi Edward aiel nostre seignour le roi q'orest, dona et granta mesmes les manoirs a Marie de Seint Poul, a terme de la vie la dite Marie, et puis par /sa\ patente granta la reversioun des mesmes les manoirs a Johan Darcy, chivaler, et a les heirs males de son corps issantz, et pur defaute d'issue male sauvant la reversion au dit roi, et a ses heirs; et qe le dit Phelip' est cousin et heir au dit Johan Darcy, c'estassavoir, filz Johan, fitz au dit Johan Darcy, et tient les ditz manoirs en la fourme avantdite, et ent ad prie en aide nostre \dit/ seignour le roi, quiel aide

[Col. b] est grante. Sur quoi le dit prior ad pursui en la chancellarie nostre dit seignour le roi d'avoir un brief de procedendo avaunt en le dit plee. Et sur ce en la dite chancellarie le dit Philipp' ad monstre qe apres pleines livere et execucioun faitz a Thomas le archier, adonqes priour, sur l'ordinance

---
[23] Cf. *CPR 1377-81*, 459.

issued and sealed under the great seal of our said lord the king on behalf of the same earl of March, worded as follows:
21. Richard, by the grace of God, king of England and France, and lord of Ireland, to all his bailiffs and faithful subjects whom these present letters shall reach, greeting. Know that we have taken under our protection and defence our beloved cousin and faithful subject Edmund Mortimer, earl of March, son and heir of Roger Mortimer, late earl of March, son of Edmund Mortimer, and cousin and heir of Roger Mortimer, late earl of March, who is to journey to the parts of Ireland in our service, to there remain in our service as our lieutenant of our land of Ireland, his men, lands, chattels, rents and all his possessions. And therefore we order you that you support, protect and defend this earl, his men, lands, chattels, rents and other possessions, not entering upon them or allowing any injury, molestation, damage or harm to be inflicted on them. And if any injury befall them, that you cause it to be amended without delay. In testimony of which we have caused these our letters patent to be made, to last for one year. Willing, moreover, that the same earl shall in the meantime be quit of all pleas and actions, except for pleas of dowry, unde nichil habet, and quare impedit, and assizes of novel disseisin, and darrein presentment, and attaints; and except for cases which may happen to come before our itinerant justices. The present requests shall become invalid, if it shall happen that the earl does not make this journey, or subsequently returns to England from the aforesaid parts before the end of the said term. Witnessed myself at Westminster, 1 December, in the third year of our reign [1379].
Through a bill of privy seal.
Which protection, having been read and understood in parliament, and diligently examined and allowed, it was decided in the same parliament that the said earl of March should go without day assigned.

On behalf of Philip Darcy.
22. Philip Darcy, knight, submitted in this present parliament a bill in the following form: To our most gracious lord the king and his wise council Philip Darcy, knight, requests that whereas the prior of the hospital of St John of Jerusalem in England has sued a writ of scire facias in the Bench of our said lord the king against the said Philip concerning the manors of Temple Hurst and Temple Newsom, on the basis of the ordinance and decision previously made in the parliament of your most gracious great-grandfather, in the seventeenth year of his reign [1323-4], concerning lands and tenements which were once the Templars'; to which writ the said Philip has claimed and pleaded that the king Edward, grandfather of our lord the present king, gave and granted the same manors to Mary de Pol, for the term of the life of the said Mary, and then by her letters patent she granted the reversion of the same manors to John Darcy, knight, and to the male heirs issuing from his body, and in the absence of male issue saving the reversion to the said king and to his heirs; and that the said Philip was the cousin and and heir of the said John Darcy, namely, son of John, son of the said John Darcy, and he holds the aforesaid manors in the aforesaid form, and has prayed in aid our said lord the king, which aid

[Col. b] has been granted. Whereupon the said prior sued in the chancery of our said lord the king to receive a writ of procedendo in the said cause. And thereupon in the said chancery the said Philip showed that after full delivery and execution was made to Thomas Archer, then prior,

et l'agard avauntditz, mesme celui priour, predecessour cest priour, ove l'assent ses confrers, si dona et granta a vostre dit besaiel et ses heirs a touz jours, par une chartre mis avant par le dit Philipp', ore demurrant en vostre dite chancellarie, mesmes les manoirs de Templehirst et Templeneusom', ensemblement ove les manoirs de Deneye, Strode, et Flaxflete, quiel manoir de Flaxflete demoert unqore en la main nostre dit seigneur le roi; et par vertue du quelle chartre vostre dit besaiel commanda par certeins briefs de seisir les ditz manoirs en sa main; queux briefs sont de record en la \dite/ chancellarie; et tout son temps respounduz des issues de mesmes les manoirs, come piert par plusours recordz.

Qe plese a nostre dit seigneur le roi et son conseil comander son chanceller qe nul brief de procedendo soit grante a dit priour countre la chartre et la matire avantdite, en desheritesoun de nostre dit seigneur le roi, et de dit Philipp', mais commande soit par brief as justices de bank nostre dit seigneur le roi, de sursere oultrement en le dit plee, tanqe les matires comprises en ceste peticioun, ove touz les circumstances d'icelle, soient pleinement declarez en parlement, par advis de les seignours du parlement et autres sages de la loy, en salvacion de droit nostre seigneur le roi, en qi droit le dit Philipp' tient les manoirs /suisditz.\ Et mesme la bille lue et entendue illoeqes, le dit Phelipp' mist auxi avant en parlement une chartre, enseale, a ce q'il dist, desouz le commune seal del dit hospital Seint Johan, tesmoignante le doun et grant estre faitz au dit besaiel nostre seigneur le roi, come sa dite bille pluis pleinement purporte: dont le dit Phelipp auxint dist q'il y a certains briefs et mandementz faitz et enroullez en la chancellarie du dit besaiel de record, directz as certains eschetours, reherceantz les doun et grant avantdites, pur seisir les ditz manoirs es mains du dit besaiel. Empriant a nostre seigneur le roi qe veuez la chartre et recordz avauntdites, et entenduz coment nostre seigneur le roi est au present en possession del dit manoir de Flaxflete par vertu del doun et grant avauntditz; et coment la reversion des ditz manoirs de Templehirst et Templeneusom' appartient a nostre seigneur le roi, il voille tielment ordeiner qe le droit nostre dit seigneur le roi et le dit Philipp' soit entierment sauve en celle partie, et q'il, ne le dit Phelipp', n'ent soient a tort disheritez. De quielle chartre le tenour s'ensuit de mot a mot:

Sciant presentes et futuri quod nos frater Thomas l'Archier, sancte domus hospitalis Sancti Johannis Jerusalem[24] prior humilis in Anglie, et ejusdem domus fratres, unanimi consilio et voluntate dedimus, concessimus et presenti carta confirmavimus, nobili principi ac domino nostro reverendo domino Edwardo, Dei gratia, regi Anglie illustri, domino Hibernie, et duci Acquietanie, maneria nostra de Templehirst, Templeneusom', Flaxflete, Deneye, et de Strode juxta Raucestre, cum pertinentiis, que quondam fuerunt Templariorum, una cum feodis militum, advocacionibus ecclesiarum, hundredis, visibus franciplegii, mercatis, feriis, chaceis, warennis, parcis, boscis, alnetis, pratis, planis, pascuis, pasturis, stagnis, vivariis, fossatis, aquis, viis, semitis, marleris, piscariis, domibus, edificiis, gardinis, molendinis, terris, tenementis, redditibus, homagiis et serviciis tam liberorum tenencium quam villanorum, et eorum catallis et sequelis, necnon libertatibus et consuetudinibus ad dicta maneria pertinentibus; salvis semper nobis et successoribus nostris ecclesiis infra limites dictorum maneriorum seu pertinenciis eorundem dictis Templariis appropriatis. Habendo et tenendo dicto domino nostro regi, heredibus et assignatis

following the aforesaid ordinance and award, the same prior, predecessor of this prior, with the assent of his brethren, gave and granted to your said great-grandfather and his heirs forever, by a charter submitted by the said Philip, and now lying in your said chancery, the same manors of Temple Hurst and Temple Newsom, together with the manors of Deneye, Strood, and Flaxflete, which manor of Flaxflete still remains in the hands of our said lord the king; and by virtue of which charter your said great-grandfather through certain writs ordered the said manors to be taken into his hands; which writs are on record in the said chancery; and throughout his time he answered for the issues from the same manors, as appears in many records.

May it please our said lord the king and his council to instruct his chancellor that no writ of procedendo shall be granted to the said prior contrary to the aforesaid charter and matter, to the disinheritance of our said lord the king and the said Philip, but that the justices of the Bench of our said lord the king shall be ordered to cease proceedings on the said plea until the matters dealt with in this petition, together with all the circumstances of the same, have been fully explained in parliament, by the advice of the lords of parliament and other wise men of the law, for the preservation of the right of our lord the king, in whose right the said Philip holds the aforesaid manors. And the same bill having been read and heard there, the said Philip laid before parliament a charter, sealed he said, under the common seal of the said hospital of St John, and witnessing the gift and grant to have been made to the said great-grandfather of our lord the king, as the said bill plainly shows: of which the said Philip also said that there were certain writs and orders issued and enrolled in the chancery of the said great-grandfather on record, addressed to certain escheators, rehearsing the aforesaid gift and grant, for them to take the said manors into the hands of the said great-grandfather. Praying of our lord the king that having inspected the aforesaid charter and record, and having understood that our lord the king is at present in possession of the said manor of Flaxflete by virtue of the aforesaid gift and grant; and that the reversion of the said manors of Temple Hurst and Temple Newsom pertain to our lord the king, he might wish to ordain in such a way that the right of our said lord the king and the said Philip be wholly preserved in this matter, and that the said Philip shall not be wrongfully disinherited. The verbatim text of which charter is as follows:

Be it known to those present and future that we, brother Thomas Archer, humble prior of the holy house of the hospital of St John of Jerusalem in England, and the brethren of this same house, with unanimous consent and wish, have given, conceded, and by this present charter confirmed to our noble prince and revered lord Edward, by grace of God, illustrious king of England, lord of Ireland, and duke of Aquitaine, our manors of Temple Hurst, Temple Newsom, Flaxflete, Deneye, and Strood near Rochester, with appurtenances, which once were the Templars', together with knights' fees, advowsons of churches, hundreds, views of frankpledge, markets, fairs, chases, warrens, parks, woods, groves, meadows, plains, pastures, ponds, fishponds, ditches, waterways, roads, paths, marl-pits, fisheries, houses, buildings, gardens, mills, lands, tenements, rents, homages and services as well of free tenants as of villeins, and their chattels and effects, and also the liberties and customs pertaining to the said manors; saving always to us and our successors the churches within the boundaries of the said manors or their appurtenances appropriated by the said Templars. To have and to hold of our said lord the king and his

---

[24] *Original* Jerusalimit'

suis, omnia et singula prenotata, exceptis ecclesiis ut premittitur appropriatis, per servicia inde debita et consueta, imperpetuum; et faciendo omnimoda *[Page iii-79]*

[Col. a] onera in quibus dicta maneria erga quoscumque et /in\ quibuscumque onerantur, seu debeant onerari. Et nos prior et fratres predicti, ac successores nostri, dicta maneria cum omnibus suis pertinentiis prenotatis prefato domino regi, heredibus et assignatis suis, contra omnes gentes warantizabimus in forma supradicta, dum terras et tenementa que fuerunt dictorum Templariorum in Anglia ad valorem dictorum maneriorum cum pertinentiis in manibus nostris habuerimus. In cujus rei testimonium sigillum nostrum commune huic carte apposuimus. Hiis testibus, venerabilibus patribus Stephano London', Waltero Exon' et Henrico Lincoln', episcopis; dominis Edmundo comite Arundell', Willelmo de Roos de Hamelak, Henrico de Percy, et aliis. Data London' decimo nono die Augusti, anno regni regis Edwardi filii regis Edwardi decimo octavo.

23. Et celle chartre lue ensement en cest parlement, fuist demande du dit Philip' par les sergeantz du roi, coment celle chartre, quele par resoun deust estre en la tresorie nostre seignour le roi et nemye es mains du dit Philip', devient as mains mesme celui Philip' hors de la tresorie avauntdite. Et pur tant qe le dit Philip' n'y dona aucun responce effectuel in celle partie, est agarde qe mesme la chartre demoerge vers la courte, come chose q'appartient a nostre seignour le roi d'avoir par resoun. Et puis apres mesme la chartre estoit liveree en parlement depar le roi a l'onurable pere en Dieu l'evesqe d'Excestre, tresorier d'Engleterre, et as chamberleins de l'escheqer, pur sauvement garder en la dite tresorie tanqe ils ent averont autre mandement. Et coment qe le dit priour ait ore mys avant en parlement une sa supplicacioun, par la quelle semble q'il s'afforce a denier la dite chartre estre le fait de sa dite maison - empriant oultre par mesme sa peticion d'avoir brief de procedendo en dit plee - nientmeins, pur certains enchesons, et par especial pur tant qe la matire touche si pres a nostre seignour le roi; et auxint, pur tant qe n'est mye unqore ne ne poet \par cas/ estre legerement serchez en la dite tresorie, et es autres places du roi, coment, et par quiel manere la dite chartre devient as mains du dit Phelip' hors de mesme la tresorie, ne les autres recordz, evidences et munimentz touchantz ceste matire, sibien pur le roi nostre seignour come pur les dites parties, n'y sont encores serchez, est advis a les seignours de parlement, et \par eux/ assentuz qe nul tiel brief de procedendo ent soit fait ou grantez, parentre cy et la quinszeine de Seint Michel proschein venant; issint qe en le moien temps l'en purra avoir resonables espace et terme de faire le dit serche, sibien pur le roi nostre seignour come . . . . pur les parties avauntdites. Et le roi voet qe le dit Philip' eit le tenour de mesme la chartre exemplifie souz son grant seal s'il le vorra demander.

Pembr', Zouch', Roos.

24. Item, memorandum quod quedam peticio liberata fuit in presenti parliamento ex parte Johannis comitis Pembr', in custodia domini regis existenta, et Willelmi la Zouch' de Haryngworth', in hec verba:[25]

A lour tresredoute seignour le roi et as seignours du parlement monstront Johan conte de Pembr' et William la Zouche de Haryngworth qe come le dit conte en la garde le roi, et le dit William, soient empledez en la chancellarie nostre seignour le roi de certeins terres et tenementz en le

heirs and assignees each and every one abovementioned, excepting the aforementioned appropriated churches, for due and customary service in perpetuity; and discharging all the *[Page iii-79]*

[Col. a] obligations with which these said manors are charged or ought to be charged, whatever and towards whomsoever. And we, the prior and aforesaid brethren, and our successors, will warrant the said manors with all their aforementioned appurtenances to the aforesaid lord king and his heirs and assignees, in the aforesaid manner and against all persons, while we have in our hands lands and tenements which belonged to the said Templars in England equalling the said manors and their appurtenances in value. In testimony of which we have affixed our common seal to this charter. Witnessed by the venerable fathers Stephen of London, Walter of Exeter, and Henry of Lincoln, bishops; the lords Edmund, earl of Arundel, William Roos of Hamelak, Henry Percy, and others. Given at London 19 August, in the eighteenth year of the reign of King Edward, son of King Edward [1324].

23. And this charter having been read in this parliament, the king's serjeants asked of the said Philip how this charter, which ought by rights to have been in the treasury of our lord the king and not in the hands of the said Philip, had come into the hands of the same Philip outside the aforesaid treasury. And because the said Philip gave no effective reply to this, it was decided that the same charter should remain with the court, as something which the king ought by rights to have. Subsequently, the same charter was delivered to parliament on behalf of the king to the honourable father in God the bishop of Exeter, treasurer of England, and to the chamberlains of the exchequer, to be kept safely in the said treasury until they received further orders. Yet although the said prior has laid a petition before parliament, in which it seems he tries to deny that the said charter is the deed of his said house - requesting also in the same petition that he have a writ of procedendo in the said plea - nevertheless, for certain reasons, and especially because the matter so closely concerns our lord the king; and also because it is still not certain and cannot easily, in the circumstances, be ascertained in the said treasury, and in other places of the king, how, and in what manner the said charter fell into the hands of the said Philip outside the same treasury, neither have the other records, documents and muniments touching this matter yet been searched, both on behalf of the king our lord as well as for the said parties; the lords of parliament are advised and agree that no such writ of precedendo thereon shall be made or granted, between now and the quinzaine of Michaelmas next [14 October 1380]; so that in the meantime there should be time and room enough to make the said search, for the king our lord as well as for the aforesaid parties. And the king wills that the said Philip shall have the tenor of the same charter copied under his great seal if he will demand it.

Pembroke, Zouche, Roos.

24. Also, be it remembered that a certain petition was delivered to this present parliament on behalf of John, earl of Pembroke, being in the wardship of the lord king, and William la Zouche of Haringworth, in these words:

To their most redoubtable lord the king and to the lords of parliament, John earl of Pembroke and William la Zouche of Haringworth show: whereas the said earl, who is in the king's wardship, and the said William are impleaded in the chancery of our lord the king of certain lands and

---

[25] PRO SC8/183/9127.

countee d'everwyk, queux nadgairs furent a monsire William de Cauntelow, qi cosyns et heirs les ditz conte et William la Zouche sont, par Thomas fitz monsire Robert de Roos, de Ingmanthorp'; de queles terres et tenementz le dit William de Cauntelow, long temps devant son moreiant, quant il fuist en alant de la la mier, feist feffement a monsire Marmaduc Conestable, William de Aldeburgh', chivalers, et as autres, sur certeines condicions, come par endentures ent faitz pleinement apiert: et sur quoi les ditz feffes ont estez examinez devaunt ces heures devaunt le chanceller nostre seignour le roi,

[Col. b] seignours, et autres du conseille nostre seignour le roi adonqes presentz. Et auxint un Robert de Clecham, qe fuist seneschal au dit monsire William de Cauntelowe, et prive de son conseil, fuist examinez: et puis a la suite et requeste du dit monsire Robert qe sueist pur son dit fitz, fesant suggestioun qe le dit examinement ne la scripture d'icelle ne contine pas verite, comissioun issist a sire Richard Ravensere, clerc, et as autres, d'examiner le dit monsire William de Aldeburgh' de novelle; par force de quele comissioun il fuist de novelle examinez, quel examinement fuist escrit de sa main demene. Et par queles examinementz est trove, le dit feffement fait sur condicions, et autres circumstances, queles oeveront en avauntage de savacioun del droit les dites conte, et William la Zouche, et queles examinementz sont de record en la \dite/ chauncellarie. Et le dit Robert weyvant le juggement par la loy en celle partie, desirant touz jours d'estre al issue du pays, trop suspeciousement ad tenduz d'averrer en noun de son dit fitz, qe le dit feffement fuist fait simple sanz condicioun, et autres choses encontre bone foi, concience, et verite, come y semble.

Sur quoi suppliont les ditz cont et William la Zouche qe les dites endentures et examinementz, et tute la matire, puissent estre monstre en cest present parlement par les serjantz nostre dit seignour le roi, q'ont pleigne conisance de la dite matire; et qe la dit busoigne soit issint menez qe les droitz les ditz counte, et William la Zouche, puissent estre savez; et q'ils par tiel malveys compassement et procurement en pays ne soient desheritez.

25. Et super hoc, visa et audita et intellecta dicta peticione in parliamento predicto, preceptum fuit et injunctum ibidem Johanni Knyvet, Johanni Cavendissh' \capitalibus justiciariis,/ et Roberto Bealknap' capitali justiciario de banco, quod habitis coram eis partibus predictis die martis proximo ante festum Sancti Petri in Cathedra, anno supradicto, apud mansionem fratrum predicatorum London', examinarent materiam in dicta billa contentam, et quid inde et omnibus aliis circumstanciis billam tangentis invenerint in dictum parliamentum certificarent. Ad quos diem et locum, partibus predictis coram dictis Johanne, Johanne et Roberto Bealknap, comparentibus, presentibus Guidon' de Briene, chivaler; Henr' Asty, capitali baroni de scaccario, chivaler; Ricardo de Waldegrave, chivaler; Johanne de Freton', clerico, et servientibus domini regis ad placita; Willelmo de Burgh', et aliis; Johannes Bygot, chivaler, examinatus ibidem super materia predicta, dicit quod tempore quo fuit escaetor domini regis in comitatu Ebor', et cepit inquisicionem virtute cujusdam brevis domini regis \ei/ directi post mortem Willelmi de Cantilupo, de terris et tenementis predictis, in presencia dicti Roberti de Roos qui sequebatur pro dicto Thoma, et pro se ipso, domini de Roos, et aliorum pluriorum, prolata fuit per Thomam de Beverle, ex parte dicti Thome de Roos, coram eo apud Malton in Rydale, indentura, sigillis predictorum feoffatorum sigillata, continens dictum feoffamentum sub certis condicionibus fore factum, et quod ipse tunc vidit indenturam predictam in manibus dicti Thome de Beverle.

Et insuper Willemus Halden' de comitatu predicto examinatus, dixit quod tempore capcionis inquisicionis predicte vidit indenturam predictam in manibus dicti Thome de Beverle, et per ipsum Thomam lectam, et feoffamentum predictum sub condicionibus subscriptis fore factum testificatum, videlicet, quod feoffamentum predictum factum fuit tam per indenturam predictam quam per factum feoffamenti predicti. Et quod postquam idem Willelmus de Cantilupo redierit de ultra mare, et ipsi feoffati per ipsum requisiti fuerint ipsum refeoffare de tenementis predictis, quod ipsum de eisdem refeoffarent: et si non redierit quod ipsi feoffarent dictum Thomam filium Roberti de Roos de tenementis predictis; tenendis sibi et heredibus de corpore suo exeuntibus. Et si dictus Thomas obisset sine herede de corpore suo exeunte quod tenementa predicta remanerent rectis heredibus predicti Willelmi de Cantilupo. *[Page iii-80]*

[Col. a] Et si predicti feoffati recusaverint ipsum Thomam feoffare modo supradicto quod bene liceret dicto Thome et heredibus suis predictis dicta tenementa intrare, et tenere sibi et heredibus suis modo supradicto. Item, Johannes Tyndale examinatus, dixit quod vidit indenturam predictam sigillis dictorum feoffatorum signatum, et illam legit in manibus dicti Roberti, in presencia Gilberti Culwen', nuper escaetor domini regis, apud Helmesley, in comitatu predicto, dictas condiciones specificantem. Et super hoc predictus Robertus de Roos examinatus, si habuerit dictam partem indenture predicte, qui dixit quod quondam habuit dictam partem indenture predicte, et omnia alia facta et munimenta, dicta terras et tenementa tangentia. Et dixit quod tempore quo dictus Willelmus de Cantilupo iturus erat ultra mare in comitiva ducis Lancastr', venit ad predictum Robertum ad castrum Ebor', tempore quo idem Robertus fuit vicecomes ibidem; et dixit tunc eidem Roberto quod vellet facere certa feoffamenta de terris suis sub certis condicionibus predictis, quia Radulphus de Hastyngs, chivaler, qui similiter tunc iturus erat ultra mare, feoffamentum fecerat de aliquibus terris suis. Et super hoc predictus Robertus requisivit quendam Thomam Nessefeld quod ipse faceret facta et feoffamentum et indenturas de condicionibus predictis. Et pro eo quod idem Wilelmus de Cantilupo non habuit tempus commorandi, quia in crastino iturus erat, et dictus Thomas Nessefeld dixit quod non habuit spacium in tam brevi

[Col. b] tempore faciendi feoffamentum, et omnes indenturas conditionum predictarum dicti Willelmus de Cantilupo, et Robertus, eidem Thome \Nesfeld/ sic responderunt quod ipse inciperet, et faceret medio tempore hoc quod posset facere. Qui quidam Thomas Nessefeld factum de feoffamento tunc fecit; et dictus Willelmus de Cantilupo sigillum suum apposuit: et supplicavit predicto Roberto quod ipse vellet accipere sigillum suum penes se, et alteram partem indenturarum predictarum cum facte fuerint sigillare. Qui quidem Robertus sigillum illud penes se habere recusavit; dicens quod idem Willelmus partem suam indenturarum predictarum cum redierit poterit sigillare. Et ulterius dixit idem Robertus quod predictus Thomas Nessefeld dictas indenturas condiciones predictas continentes postea fecit. Et idem Robertus alteram partem indenturarum predictarum dictis feoffatis ad sigillandum detulit, qui sigilla sua eidem parti apposuerunt. Et postea idem Robertus indenturam predictam, et omnia alia facta et munimenta predicta predicto Willelmo de Cantilupo, post reventum suum in Angliam, liberavit.

the said Thomas Beverley. Furthermore, William Halden of the aforesaid county, being questioned, said that at the time of the aforesaid inquest, he saw the aforesaid indenture in the hands of the said Thomas Beverley, and saw it read by Thomas, and saw the aforesaid enfeoffment (to be made under the abovementioned conditions) witnessed, namely, that the aforesaid enfeoffment had been made both by the aforesaid indenture as well as by the act of the aforesaid persons enfeoffed. And that after the same William Cantilupe had returned from overseas, the feoffees would be asked to re-enfeoff him with the aforesaid tenements: and if he did not return that they should enfeoff the said Thomas son of Robert Roos with the aforesaid tenements; to be held by him and the heirs of his body. And if the said Thomas were to die without an heir of his body that the aforesaid tenements should fall to the true heirs of the aforesaid William Cantilupe. *[Page iii-80]*

[Col. a] And if the aforesaid enfeoffed persons refused to enfeoff this Thomas in the aforesaid manner, then it would be fully lawful for the said Thomas and his aforesaid heirs to enter the said tenements and hold them in the aforesaid manner. Also John Tyndale, being questioned, said that he saw the aforesaid indenture sealed with the seals of the said enfeoffed persons, and read it in the hands of the said Robert, in the presence of Gilbert Culwen, late escheator of the lord king, at Helmsley in the aforesaid county, the said conditions being specified. And thereupon the aforesaid Robert Roos, being questioned as to whether he had the said part of the aforesaid indenture, replied that he had once had the said part of the aforesaid indenture and all other deeds and muniments touching the said lands and tenements. And he said that at the time when the said William Cantilupe was to go overseas in the company of the duke of Lancaster, he visited the aforesaid Robert at the castle of York, at the time when the same Robert was sheriff there; and on that occasion he said to the same Robert that he wished to make certain enfeoffments of his lands on the aforesaid specified conditions, because Ralph Hastings, knight, who was similarly to journey overseas at that time, had made feoffments of some of his lands. Whereupon, the aforesaid Robert asked one Thomas Nessfield to make deeds, feoffments and indentures on the aforesaid conditions. And because the same William Cantilupe did not have time to spare, since he was to set off the next day, and the said Thomas Nessfield said that he could not in so short

[Col. b] a time make the feoffments and all the indentures on the aforesaid conditions for the said William Cantilupe, Robert replied to the same Thomas Nessfield that he should begin and do what he could in the meantime. And so Thomas Nessfield then made the deed of feoffment; and the said William Cantilupe affixed his seal: and he asked of the aforesaid Robert that he might agree to keep his seal on him and seal the other part of the aforesaid indentures when they had been made. Which Robert declined to keep the seal, saying that the same William could seal his part of the aforesaid indentures when he returned. The same Robert also said that the aforesaid Thomas Nessfield later completed the said indentures containing the aforesaid conditions. And Robert took the other part of the aforesaid indentures to the said feoffees to seal, and they affixed their seals to that part. And afterwards the same Robert delivered the aforesaid indenture, and all the other aforesaid deeds and muniments to the aforesaid William Cantilupe after his return to England.

[26] Et memorandum quod Robertus Bealknap predictus istud memorandum, et examinationem scriptam et factam in forma hic inmediate recitata de verbo ad verbum, nichil inde postea mutatum, tradidit manu propria clerico parliamenti ex parte domini regis in rotulis istius parliamenti irrotulandis.

[27] SEQUNTUR PETICIONES TRADITE DOMINO NOSTRO REGI ET CONSILIO SUO IN PRESENTI PARLIAMENTO PRO PARTE COMMUNITATIS REGNI ANGLIE, UNA \CUM/ RESPONSIONIBUS EARUNDEM IN EODEM PARLIAMENTO FACTIS.

Membrane 4
A lour trespuissant et tresredoute seignour le roi, et a son conseil, prelats, et autres seignours, en ce present parlement tenuz a Westm' lundy proschein apres la feste de Seint Hiller, l'an du regne nostre dit seignour le roi tierce, supplient voz humbles communes, pur les pecicions dessouz escritz, en aide et profit du roialme:

I. [Liberties and Charters.]
26. En primes supplient les communes, desicome la volunte le roi est, qe   seinte esglise ait ses fraunchises, libertees, \et droitures/ en toutz pointz, sauve au roi sa regalie; et qe la commune loy de la terre soit tenuz come el ad este usee en temps de ses progenitours, qe plese qe les dites fraunchises, droitures et loies, emsemblement ove la grande chartre et la chartre de la foreste, et les autres bones estatutz ordinances faitz devant ces heures, soient tenuz et gardez, et duement executz, pur Dieu, et en oevre de charitee.
Responsio.
Il plest au roi.[28]

II. [Destruction by the king's soldiers.]
27. Item, prient les communes et les bones gentz enhabitantz pres de les costes du meer, c'estadire, de Norff', Suff', \Kent,/Suss'[29] Hamptshire, Dorset, Devenshire et Cornewaille qe come ils et lour chateux ount este sovent foitz robbez, et sont destruitz et degastez par gentz d'armes, archiers et autres venantz et passantz par les dites parties vers le service nostre seignour le roy de guerre, et par lour long demoer; et nomement les gentz de Hamptshire a derrain viage qi feust taille et ordene, qar par la demoere et destruccioun faitz par gentz ordenez au dit /viage,\ les chateux et biens des
[Col. b] bones gentz des parties de Hamptshire sont destruitz, degastez et anientiz, a tresgrant abassement et destruccioun des toutes les communes illoeqes, sibien gentz de seinte esglise come autres, et soi logeront de lour auctoritee demesne, nient eantz regarde al herbegage par nostre seignour le \[roi]/ a eux assigne, en anientisement del commune poeple, s'il ne soit le plustost remedez.
/Qe plese a nostre seignour le roi et as touz les bones seignours, de lour tressage\ descrecion, ordeiner et establir pur touz jours en ce present parlement qe les chiefteins des gentz passantz et demurrantz parmy les dites parties soient resonables, et effectuelment chargez pur touz les damages qe serront faitz as aucuns des gentz des dites parties, et soient constreintz d'ent faire due et resonable restitution, par pleintes faites as chiefteins de ceux qi se sentent grevez: et

And let it be remembered that the aforesaid Robert Bealknap gave with his own hands the memorandum and the examination written out and made in the form recited here, word for word, nothing therein having been altered, to the clerk of the parliament on behalf of the lord king, to be enrolled in the rolls of this parliament.

HERE FOLLOW THE PETITIONS PRESENTED TO THE LORD OUR KING AND HIS COUNCIL IN THE PRESENT PARLIAMENT ON BEHALF OF THE COMMUNITY OF THE KINGDOM OF ENGLAND, TOGETHER WITH THE ANSWERS GIVEN TO THEM IN THIS SAME PARLIAMENT.

To their most potent and redoubtable lord the king and his council, the bishops and other lords in this present parliament held at Westminster on the Monday next following the feast of St Hilary, in the third year of the reign of our said lord the king, your humble commons request the granting of the petitions written below, for the aid and benefit of the kingdom:

I. [Liberties and Charters.]
26. First, the commons request that as it is the wish of the king that holy church have its franchises, liberties and rights in all respects, saving to the king his regality; and that the common law of the land be upheld as it was in the time of his progenitors, that it may may please him that the said franchises, rights and laws, together with the Great Charter, and the Charter of the Forest, and the other good statutes and ordinances made in the past, be kept and upheld, and duly executed, for God and by way of charity.
Answer.
It pleases the king.

II. [Destruction by the king's soldiers.]
27. Item, the commons and the good people living near the coasts of the sea, that is to say, of Norfolk, Suffolk, Kent, Sussex, Hampshire, Dorset, Devonshire and Cornwall, pray: whereas they and their chattels have often been robbed, and they are ruined and wasted by men-at-arms, archers and others coming and going through the said parts in the service of our lord the king in war, and by their lengthy stays; and especially the people of Hampshire at the last expedition which was arranged and ordained, since as a result of the sojourn made and destruction carried out by the people recruited for the said expedition, the chattels and goods of the
[Col. b] good people of the parts of Hampshire have been ruined, wasted and destroyed, to the great crushing and destruction of all the commons there, both those of holy church and others, and they make encampments of their own free will, lending no thought to the encampments assigned them by our lord the king, risking the ruin of the common people unless remedy be swiftly provided.
May it please our lord the king and all the good lords, at their most wise discretion, to ordain and decree in perpetuity in this present parliament that the leaders of the people coming and going throughout the said parts shall act reasonably, and be effectively charged for all the damage which is inflicted on any of the people of the said parts, and shall be obliged to make due and reasonable restitution for it, by plaints made to the leaders by those who feel themselves aggrieved: and

---
[26] The following sentence is written in the untidy hand which appears sporadically throughout the roll.
[27] The beginning of the common petitions is accompanied by a change of hand.
[28] 3 Ric.2 c.1. The statutes of this parliament are printed in *SR*, II.13-15.
[29] *Original* Surr',

qe nully soit fait dustour s'il n'eyt dont a respondre au roy et poeple pur luy et pur ses gentz.

Responsio.
Il plest au roi, parissint qe ceux qe se sentent grevez de tiel damage a eux fait par nul des tielx gentz d'armes, archiers et les autres dessuisditz, ils ent facent lours pleintes as chiefteins des dites gentz devant lour passage hors du roialme.

III. [Scottish march.]
28. Item, prient les communes et nomement ses povres liges des countees de Northumbr', Cumbr' et Westmerl' qe plese considerere les tresgrantz meschiefs et damages queux ils des dites countees ont soeffertz, et soeffront de jour en autre, sibien par pestilence, come par continuele destruccion des enemys d'Escoce, come contenuz est en une bille livere en parlement, et ordeiner suffisantz gardeinz a demurrer en les countees avauntdites, *[Page iii-81]*
[Col. a] come y ad este usee devant ses heures, ove suffisantz gardeins et garnisons en les villes et chastelx de Berewyk, Rokesburgh et Cardoill'. Et qe touz les seignours des chastelx, forcelettes, seignouries et terres en les countees avauntdites, soient chargez sur leur ligeance a demurrer continuelment sur lours ditz chastelx, forcelettes, seignouries et terres, en salvacioun du roialme. Et outre, qe mesme l'ordeinance se tiegne par toutes les costees du meer des chasteux et villes du roi, sicome le chastel de Dovorr' et autres tielx chastelx du roi, et forcelettes.

Responsio.
Quant as dites gardeins et garnisons de la marche d'Escoce, nostre seignour le roi ent ferra faire ordeinance par l'advis des seignours de son conseil. Et quant al remenant de cest article, le roi le voet; et comande qe due execution ent soit faite. Et qe semblablement soit fait en chescune marche et costere du meer parmy le roialme, selonc ce qe le cas requiert, et la necessite demande. Et enoultre soient les commissions nadgaires faites d'arraier les gentz parmy le roialme, renovellez, et suffisantz et diligentz arraiours assignez.

IIII. [Welsh march.]
29. Item, monstrent les ditz communes qe come sur le conquest de Gales, le roi Edward filz le roi Henry establist et ordeina plusours villes en Gales d'estre enhabitez ove hommes Engleis, et qe nul homme ne femme qe feust Galeies ne enhabiteroit \ne purchaceroit/ deinz les dites villes nule terre, ne tenement, ne rent, n'autre chose, en fee, terme de vie, ou terme de ans, sur peine de forfaiture et d'enprisonement; quel establisement est unqore en sa force. Et ore de jour en autre plusours de ceux queux sont Galeies, \et/ lours auncestres ont este merement Galeies, purchasont diverses terres et tenementz en les countees de Hereford, Gloucestre, Wyrcestre, Salop' et Stafford, quelle countees sont ajoinantz inmediate a Gales; et plusours foitz lours parentes et amys viegnont ascun foithe par cenx, et ascun foithe par deux cenx, et ascun foithe par trois cenx, ou plius, ove force et armes, et en manere de guerre deinz les ditz countees, et tuent diverses gentz, robbent et raunsenont, et preignent bestes, biens, et /chateux,\ et les amesnent hors des dites countees en diverses seignouries en Gales, deinz quelle seignouries les viscountz des dites countees, n'autres officers nostre seignour le roi, ne osent nulle jurisdiccioun exenger, issint qe les dites countees sont degastez et destruz, et deinz brief temps par tielx malfaitz purront estre anientiz.

that no one should be made a leader if he be not willing to answer to the king and the people on behalf of himself and his men.

Answer.
It pleases the king, so that those who feel themselves harmed by such injury inflicted on them by such men-at-arms, archers and others mentioned above shall lay their plaints before the leaders of the said men before their passage out of the kingdom.

III. [Scottish march.]
28. Item, the commons, and especially his poor lieges of the counties of Northumberland, Cumbria and Westmorland pray that it please him to consider the most serious troubles and injuries which they the said commons have suffered, and suffer from day to day, both through pestilence, and through the continual attacks of the enemies of Scotland, as is contained in a bill delivered in parliament, and to ordain capable wardens to remain in the aforesaid counties, *[Page iii-81]*
[Col. a] as there were in times past, together with competent keepers and garrisons in the towns and castles of Berwick, Roxburgh and Carlisle. And that all the lords of the castles, fortresses, lordships and lands in the aforesaid counties, shall be charged on their allegiance to dwell continually in their said castles, fortresses, lordships and lands, for the security of the kingdom. Furthermore, that the same ordinance shall apply to all castles and towns of the king on the coasts of the sea, such as the castle at Dover and other such royal castles and fortresses.

Answer.
As for the said wardens and garrisons of the march of Scotland, our lord the king will cause an ordinance to be made thereon by the advice of the lords of his council. And as for the rest of the article, the king wills it; and orders that due execution of it be carried out. And it shall be done likewise in each march and coast of the sea throughout the kingdom, as the situation requires, and need be. Moreover, let the commissions recently issued to array the people throughout the kingdom be renewed, and diligent and capable arrayers appointed.

IIII. [Welsh march.]
29. Item, the said commons show: whereas on the conquest of Wales, King Edward [I] son of King Henry established and ordained many towns in Wales to be populated with Englishmen, and that no man or woman who was Welsh should live nor purchase within the said towns any land, tenement, rent nor anything else in fee, for the term of life, or for a term of years, on pain of forfeiture and imprisonment; which decree is still in force. Yet now, from one day to the next many of those who are Welsh, and whose ancestors were all Welsh, purchase various lands and tenements in the counties of Hereford, Gloucester, Worcester, Shropshire and Staffordshire, which counties immediately adjoin Wales; and on many occasions their kinsmen and friends come sometimes by the hundred, sometimes in two hundreds and sometimes in three hundreds, or more, by force and arms, and in a warlike manner into the said counties, and kill, rob and kidnap many, and take beasts, goods and chattels, and lead them out of the said counties to various lordships in Wales, within which lordships neither the sheriffs of the said counties, nor the other officers of our lord the king, dare exercise any jurisdiction, so that the said counties are wasted and destroyed, and could be ruined within a short space of time through such misdeeds.

Sur qi pri ont les communes pur les countes de Hereford, Glouc', Wircestr', Salop et Stafford, avauntdites, de ce remedie, et oultre ce, q'il soit defendu desore qe nul homme de Gales (dont il et ses auncestres ont este et sont purement Galeies, forspris ceux qe sont a present ou serront demurrant ou retenuz \[ovesqe]/ nostre seignour le roi, ou les autres seignours d'Engleterre) ne facent en apres nul purchace d'ascuns franks tenementz, ne soient resceantz deinz les dites countees, deinz franchises ne dehors, parentre la ryvere de Sevarne et Gales. Et si ascun autre Galeies purchace ascuns terres, rentes, ou autre frank tenement, en fee, terme de vie, ou terme des ans, deinz les dites boundes, qe le tenement issint purchace en fee, q'est tenuz de roi soit forfait a roi, et q'est tenuz d'autre seignour soit forfait au seignour de qi le tenement est tenuz, et ce q'est purchace soulement a terme de vie, ou terme des ans, qe le roi ait totes les profitz pur celle temps, sauve qe toutes maneres des servantz et laborers pussent demurrer en les countes avantditz, nientcontreesteant ceste ordinance.

Responsio.
Le roi le voet quant as purchas affere desore par gentz merement Galeies dedeinz les dites countees dela Sevarne, s'ils ne purront trover suffisante seurtee de la paix de lour bone port. Et quant a les routes et assembles venantz issint hors de Gales par assent et covyne des ditz autres gentz Galeys enhabitantz es dites contees, encourgent ceux de tiele covyne, et aient au tiele
[Col. b] peine, et mesme le juggement qe les ditz trespassours mesmes ent auroient, s'ils ent feussent atteintz.

V. [Malefactors from Cheshire.]
30. Item, monstrent les communes des countees de Staff', Salop', Warr', Derby, Hereford' et Everwik qe les gentz del countee de Cestre viegnent de jour en autre, et sibien par noetz come par jours, ove grande nombre et multitude de poeple, sibien gentz utlaiez come autres, deinz les dites countes, affere de guerre armez, et chivachent deinz les dites countees, et font roberies, arcines, felonies et ravissent dames et damoisels, et sodeinement batent et maheyment diverses gentz des ditz countees, et aucuns mettent au fyn et raunceoun, et repeirent arere . en leur dit countee de Cestre, /sanz\ estre arestuz par cause de lour sodeigne venue, a grant meschief et arrerisement des ditz countees. Et par cause qe le dit counte de Cestre est counte paloys, et riens ne forfacent pur tielx oppressions faitez hors de lour countee, ils ne doutent riens de mesfaire; dont moltz diverses gentz des ditz countees par tiele venue des tielx gentz sont destruitz et anientiz, et la greindre partie des dites communes queux sont demurrantz environ le dit countee n'osent demurrer en lour paiis en leur ditz maisons, s'ils n'aient diverses gentz gisantz sibien par nuyt come par jour en agait de eux, pur doute de mort a cause de lour sodeigne venue. Les ditz communes ont monstrez les grevances avantdites de parlement en autre, et nul remede de ce en est ordene, a grant damage de vostre dit poeple. Par quoi supplient les ditz communes qe en cest present parlement les ditz mesfesours, et les routeleders, soient restreintz de lour grante malice, et de ce ordeiner covenable remede selonc vos bones discrecions, ou autrement ensuera en temps avenir grant discensioun et meschief en celles parties des choses susditz; entendant qe si covenable remede ne soit fait en ce present parlement, y covient as ditz gentz demurrantz environ le dit countee de fuir lour paiis, pur les damages et grevances q'ils soeffrent de jour en autre.
Responsio.

In view of which, the commons of the aforesaid counties of Herefordshire, Gloucestershire, Worcestershire, Shropshire and Staffordshire pray for a remedy, and also that it shall be henceforth forbidden that any Welshman (he himself and his ancestors having been and being purely Welsh, except those who are at present or shall be residing with and retained by our lord the king or the other lords of England) shall henceforth make a purchase of any free tenements, nor reside in the said counties, within franchises or without, between the River Severn and Wales. And if any other Welshman purchase any lands, rents, or other free tenement in fee, for the term of life, or for a term of years within the said boundaries, that the tenement thus purchased in fee which is held of the king shall be forfeited to the king, and if held of another lord shall be forfeited to the lord of whom the tenement is held, and of that which is purchased only for the term of a life or for a term of years, the king shall have all the profits for that time; saving that all kinds of servants and labourers may remain in the aforesaid counties, notwithstanding this ordinance.

Answer.
The king wills it with regard to purchases made henceforth by those who are purely Welsh within the said counties beyond the Severn, if they cannot find adequate guarantee for their good behaviour. And as for the bands and armies issuing from Wales with the assent and co-operation of the other Welsh people living in the said counties, let those conspirators incur and suffer such
[Col. b] penalty and the same judgment that the said offenders themselves have, if they are so convicted.

V. [Malefactors from Cheshire.]
30. Item, the commons of the counties of Stafford, Shropshire, Warwick, Derby, Hereford and York show that the people of Cheshire daily come, both by day and night, with a great number and multitude of people, both outlaws and others, in the said counties, to wage armed war, and they ride through the said counties, committing robberies, arsons, felonies and ravishment of ladies and damsels, and without warning they beat and maim various people of the said counties, and some they hold to fine or ransom, and return to their said county of Cheshire without being arrested because of the sudden nature of their arrival, to the great injury and ruin of the said counties. And because the said county of Cheshire is a county palatine, and they forfeit nothing for such oppressions committed outside their county, they are not at all afraid of offending; as a result of which many people of the said counties are destroyed and ruined by the coming of those people, and the greater part of the said commons who live near the said county dare not remain in their said houses in that country unless they have people on guard by night as well as day to keep watch for them, since they fear death on their sudden coming. The said commons have presented their said grievances from one parliament to the next, and no remedy has been ordained for them, to the great injury of your said people. In consequence of which, the said commons request that in this present parliament the said malefactors and the gangleaders be curbed in their great malice, and that a suitable remedy be ordained at your good discretions, or else there will be great trouble and dissension over the aforesaid matters in these parts; bearing in mind that if a suitable remedy be not provided in this present parliament, the said people dwelling near the said county will find it necessary to flee from their country, because of the harm and injuries which they daily endure.
Answer.

Nostre seignour le roi, par l'advis et assent des seignours marchez a le dit contee, ent ordeinera de due remede.

VI. [Escheators' inquests.]
31. Item, monstrent les communes qe sovent foitz avient qe par favorables enquestes procurez et prises par eschetours, voz gentz sont sovent foitz fauxement disheritez, et sodeignement oustez de lours terres et tenementz, et les dites terres et tenementz donez par patente du roi, paront ils sont delaiez de leur droit, aucuns par maistrie, aucuns par proteccioun, aucuns par aide et priere, et aucuns par autres sotils delaies, a grant meschief et empoverissement de eux.

Par quoy ils vous supplient q'en cel cas nul patente ne soit fait ou grantee a nully, tanqe le droit soit discusse entre /vous\ et les tenantz, et q'en le mesne temps ils puissent tenir leur terres et tenementz en pees, trovantz suffisante seurete de respondre a vous des issues si vostre droit soit trovez. Et si aucunes patentes en tiel cas desormes soient faites, q'ils soient tenuz pur nulles.

Responsio.
Ils y a estatut fait en le cas, lequel soit fermement tenuz et gardez, et mis en due execucioun.

VII. [Assize of cloth.]
32. Item, prient les communes qe coment q'il soit ordeine par estatut qe chescun drape contiegne l'assise selonc l'effect du dit estatut, sibien en longure come en laeure, sur peine de forfaiture d'icel, et nientconstenant cel estatut, aucuns gentz font diverses drapes a vendre, queux ne tiegnent celle assise en longeure n'en laeure, et auxi font draps rumpuz tachez ensemble ovesqe [fil] pur faire le poeple quider qe les draps sont de longure et sanz autre defaute, procurent l'alneour nostre dit /seignour\ le roi de mettre le seal ordeine pur l'alnage sur les ditz draps, en desceite du poeple, et tresgrant esclaundre nostre dit seignour le roi, nomement es parties dela la meer.

Par quoi plese en ce present parlement ordeiner qe si l'alneour mette le dit seal sur aucun drap s'il ne contiegne l'assise en longure et laeure donez par le dit estatut, q'il puisse forfaire la value du drap issint enseale.

Responsio.
Le roi voet qe l'estatutz faitz devant ces heures des dites draps soient tenuz et gardez, et mys en due execucion; adjoustant oultre a ycelles qe si aucun des dites auneours, ou des coillours del subside des ditz draps avera desore mis aucun seal a nul tiel drape issint consuite, soit mesme le drape, ou q'il soit trovez, forfait a nostre seignour le roi, et forface l'auneour, ou coillour, \de ce trovez coupable/ son dit office, et s'il ait mys mesme le seal a nul autre drap qe ne soit de l'assise ordeine .... par estatut avantdit qe le dit auneour ou coillour forface devers nostre dit seignour le roi la value de mesme le drape issint ensealez en desceite du poeple, ensemble avec mesme son office; et jademeinz ait mesme l'auneour ou coillour la prisone, et ent soit reint a la volunte le roi. Et comencera ceste ordinance a tenir lieu a la Nativitee Seint Johan proschein venant, et nemye devant.[30]

VIII. [Loans to the king.]
33. Item, prient les communes qe come nadgairs diverses lettres du prive seal isserent as diverses citees et burghs, et as autres gentz du roialme, de faire chevance au roi nostre seignour des certeines sommes d'argent; par vertue des queux, chevance fuist faite, et promys y feust a cel temps de

Our lord the king, by the advice and assent of the marcher lords of the said county, shall ordain a proper remedy for it.

VI. [Escheators' inquests.]
31. Item, the commons show that it has often happened that through biased inquests procured and taken by escheators, your people have been disinherited frequently and fraudulently, and suddenly ousted from their lands and tenements, and from the said lands and tenements given by the king's letters patent, as a result of which they are kept waiting for their rights, some by cunning, some by protections, some by aid and prayer, and some by crafty delays, to their great injury and impoverishment.

As a result of which they ask of you that in such cases no letters patent be made nor granted to anyone until the right has been discussed between you and the tenants, and that in the meantime they may hold their lands and tenements in peace, finding sufficient surety to answer to you for the issues if right be yours. And if any letters patent are issued henceforth, that they be held at naught.

Answer.
A statute has been made on this matter, which shall be strictly upheld, kept and duly executed.

VII. [Assize of cloth.]
32. Item, the commons pray: whereas it is ordained by statute that each cloth should conform to the assize according to the said statute, as well in length as in width, on pain of forfeiture of the same, yet notwithstanding the statute, people make various cloths to sell which do not conform to the assize in length or width, and also they stitch torn cloths together with yarn to make people believe that the cloths are of the proper length and without any fault, and they persuade our said lord the king's alnager to apply the seal ordained for the alnage to the said cloths, to the deceit of the people, and the great shame of our said lord the king, especially in parts beyond the sea.

And therefore may it please you to ordain in this present parliament that if the alnager applies the said seal to any cloth which is not of the true size in terms of length and width prescribed in the said statute, he shall forfeit the value of the cloth thus sealed.

Answer.
The king wills that the statutes made in the past concerning the said cloths be kept and upheld, and duly executed; adding further that if any of the said alnagers, or the collectors of the subsidy of the said cloths henceforth place any seal on any such cloth thus stitched, the same cloth, wheresoever it be found, shall be forfeit to our lord the king, and the alnager or collector then found guilty shall forfeit his said office, and if he has placed the same seal on any other cloth which is not of the size ordained in the aforesaid statute that the said alnager or collector shall forfeit to our said lord the king the value of the same cloth thus sealed in deceit of the people, together with his own office; and further, let the same alnager or collector be imprisoned, and kept there at the king's will. And this ordinance shall take effect from the Nativity of St John next [24 June 1380], and not before.

VIII. [Loans to the king.]
33. Item, the commons pray: whereas various letters of privy seal are issued to various cities and boroughs, and to other people of the kingdom, to make loans to the king our lord of certain sums of silver; by virtue of which loans have been made, and it was promised at the time that they would be

---
[30] 3 Ric.2 c.2.

leur avoir repaiez al feste de Seint Martyn alors proschein ensuant; des queux summes riens ne leur fuist paiez a cel temps, ne unqore est. Qe plese faire repaiement as ditz creditours de les sommes par eux ensi creancez.[31]

Responsio.

Le roi nostre seignour lour mercie entierement de ce q'ils lui ont tant attenduz et suffertz, et voet qe gree lour ent soit fait a pluis en haste qe purra estre fait.

IX. [Five principal officers.]

34. Item, prient les communes qe les cynk principalx officers ore establiz en cest parlement puissent demurrer en lours offices, sans estre remuez parentre cy et le proschein parlement, si defaut especial n'y soit trovez en aucun de eux en le mesne temps, come l'en suppose qe ne serra my, si Dieux plest.

Responsio.

Il y a une ordeinance ent faite en parlement, l'an nostre seignour le roi primer, quele le roi voet qe soit tenuz et gardez selonc le purport d'ycelle.[32]

X. [Compensation for goods taken by Scots.]

35. Item, prient les communes, de grantir as marchantz d'Engleterre, qe gree lour soit fait des biens d'Escoce esteantz en Engleterre, pur lour biens et chateux queux sont prises en la terre d'Escoce, sur la meer par les gentz d'Escoce, et ailleurs.

Responsio.

Le roi ent ferra de temps en temps ce qe ent purra estre fait resonablement, par l'advis de son conseil et des gardeins de la marche d'Escoce.

XI. [Corpse presents of arms and armour.]

36. Item, come par l'estatut de Wyncestre et autres estatutz, soit ordeinez qe chescun homme soit armez et arraiez selonc lours estates en defense du roialme, par force des queux estatutz chescun homme est arme selonc son estat, et auxi plusours soy arment plus avant qe lour estat demande, et plusours soi arment a greindre value qe le remenant de touz lours biens, come gentz demurrantz sur les costes du meer, sur les marches d'Escoce et autres marches, la leur parsones et vikers apres la mort des tielx demandent lours armures en noun des mortuaires et corps presantz; c'estassavoir plates, haubergeons, bacinettes, aventailes, gauntz de plates, actons, palettes, jackes defensibles, et autres armures, et impledont lours executours des choses suisditz en courte Cristiene, la ou ils sont juges mesmes. Si prient les communes q'en cest parlement soit ordenez par estatut qe les ditz parsones et vikers n'aient

[Col. b] nul tiel corps presant ne mortuaire d'armure, einz qe les armuers demoergent a les heirs ou executours, en defens du roialme.

Responsio.

Ent soit use come duement ad este devant ceste heure.

Membrane 3

XII. [Papal provisions.]

37. Item, monstrent voz liges comunes de vostre roialme presentment assemblez en cest parlement qe come verite et notoire chose soit qe les esglises cathedralx, collegialx, abbeies, priories et autres benefices de vostre dit roialme

---

[31] A line and a half of text have been erased at this point.
[32] Parliament of 1377, item 50.

---

repaid on the following Martinmas [11 November]; yet not a penny of those sums has been paid to them and nothing has yet been received. May it please you to repay the said creditors the sums they thus lent.

Answer.

The king wholeheartedly thanks them for what they have undertaken and suffered for him, and wills that they shall be compensated as swiftly as possible.

IX. [Five principal officers.]

34. Item, the commons pray that the five principal officers now appointed in this present parliament may remain in their offices, and not be replaced between now and the next parliament, unless a particular fault is found with any one of them in the meantime, which it is assumed will not happen, if it please God.

Answer.

An ordinance was made thereon in parliament, in the first year of our lord the king, which the king wills shall be kept and upheld in accordance with its purport.

X. [Compensation for goods taken by Scots.]

35. Item, the commons pray that it shall be granted to the merchants of England that they shall receive compensation from Scottish goods in England, for their goods and chattels seized in the land of Scotland and taken on the sea by the men of Scotland, and elsewhere.

Answer.

The king shall do from time to time what can reasonably be done, by the advice of his council and the wardens of the march of Scotland.

XI. [Corpse presents of arms and armour.]

36. Item, whereas by the statute of Winchester, and other statutes, it was ordained that every man should be armed and arrayed according to his estate for the defence of the realm, by force of which statute each man is armed in accordance with his condition, and what is more, many have armed themselves over and above the demands of their status, and many have armed themselves at a greater cost than the remainder of all their possessions, such as those people dwelling on the coasts of the sea, in the marches of Scotland, and other marches, but their parsons and vicars after the deaths of those people demand their weaponry in the name of mortuaries and corpse presents; that is to say, plate-armour, haubergeons, bassinets, visors, plated gauntlets, haketons, helmets, jackets, and other armour, and they bring actions against their executors for the aforesaid items in the court Christian, where they themselves are the judges. Therefore the commons pray that in this parliament it be ordained by statute that the said parsons and vicars shall not have *[Col. b]* any corpse presents or mortuary of armour, but that the pieces of armour shall descend to the heirs or executors for the defence of the kingdom.

Answer.

Let it be done as it has duly been done in the past.

XII. [Papal provisions.]

37. Item, the common lieges of your kingdom presently assembled in this parliament show: whereas it is true and well known that the cathedral and collegiate churches, the abbeys, priories, and other benefices of your said kingdom were

furent jadys foundez et richement dowez par voz nobles progenitours, en lesqueles diverses dignitees, offices, parsonies, chanoignyes, prebendes et autres benefices estoient solempnement ordenez et establiz pur Dieux servir et honurer plus devoutement, et auxi pur hospitalitee tenir, et pur enformer et enseigner le poeple, et faire les autres choses appurtenantz a cure des almes selonc l'estat et la qualite des dites benefices, la collacioun des queux pur la greindre partie voz ditz nobles progenitours granterent hors de leur possessioun as arcevesqes, evesqes, abbees, priours et autres ordinaires et pastours des ditz lieux, a l'entente et purpos qe par mesmes les ordinaires et pastours les dites benefices serroient done as persones honestes et covenables du dit roiaume; et ensi fesoient ils par grant temps tanqe ore tard, et especialment tanqe au temps du Pape Clement le quint. Depuis quiel temps les ditz ordinaires et pastours ont este ensi destourbez et enpeschez de leur dites collacions, par provisions, expectations, \et reservations/ de la courte de Rome, q'ils n'ont peu d'aucun benefice purvoir franchement, selonc l'entencioun de vos ditz progenitours: einz toutes les dites dignites et autres benefices ont este depuis comunement donez en la dite courte de Rome, as gentz d'estrange lange, et sovent as enemys, les queux ne fesoient unqes residence en ycelles, ne ne scievent, ne poeient, ne volont, nullement porter ne perfaire les charges des dites benefices, come en oier confessions, prescher, ne enseigner le poeple, hospitalitee tenir, ne en plusours autres choses necessaire a governement de mesmes les benefices, mes soeffrent les nobles edifices auncienement faitz quant ils estoient occupiez par Engleis, de tout cheoir a ruyne, come gentz qi querent soulement les temporels profitz et emolumentz, noun aiant regard a la cure espirituel, ne as autres charges a mesmes les benefices incumbentz; paront le dyvyn service est tresgrandement diminuez, la cure des almes negligee et lesse, et la /clergie\ enfibles, le tresor du roialme emportez as mains aliens, et tout l'estat de seinte esglise mesnez a meindre reverence. As queux meschiefs et grevances vostre noble aiel, /le roi\ qi Dieux assoille, et les seignours du dit roialme estoient par diverses foitz en purpos a remedier. Et tut soit il qe entre le Gregoire qe derrain morust et vostre dit aiel estoit acordez qe les dites grevances deussent estre retretez, et modifiez en tiel manere qe le roi ne le dit roiaume ne s'en sentiroient deslors grevez, et auxi qe nul benefice en vostre dit roiaume ne serroit donez a aucun de voz enemys ou rebelles. Unqore, ce nient contreesteant le pape Urban [VI] q'orest ad done a un cardinal alien la priorie de Derherst, ce qe unqes n'estoit soeffert en ce paiis: et ad grante au cardinal de Cisteron', neez du paiis de Limosin, q'est a present a vous rebelle, une expectacion par toute la province de Cantirbirs, ove la clause de anteferri, a la taxe de .iiij. mille florens: quel manere de provision est de novelle trovez, mais nul autre roiaume ne l'ad voluz, ne le voet, accepter ne soeffrir, et auxi il ad done ore tard au dit cardinal l'ercedeaknee de Bathe, encontre l'acorde susdit. Et auxi ad donez, et doune, et est entour de doner, de jour en autre, tant par voie de reservacioun come par voie de provisioun, a plusours autres persones aliens les benefices du dit roiaume: et ce par informacioun d'ascuns de voz Engleis liges esteantz en la dite courte de Rome; les queux, pur avoir avauntage des fermes des ditz benefices, et autres favours en la *[Page iii-83]*

[Col. a] dite courte, n'ont consideracioun au bien comun de vous et de vostre dit roialme, mes a lour singuler profit, ensi qe le dit roialme ne feust unqes tant chargez de persones aliens avancez en ycelle, come il serra deinz brief temps, en grant damage et enpoverissement du dit roialme, si bone remede n'y soit en ce present parlement ordenez.

once founded and richly endowed by your noble progenitors, in which various dignities, offices, parsonages, canonries, prebends and other benefices were solemnly ordained and established most devoutly to serve and honour God, and also to offer hospitality, and to inform and instruct the people, and perform the other duties pertaining to the care of souls in accordance with the condition and nature of the said benefices, the collation of which for the most part your said noble progenitors granted out of their possession to archbishops, bishops, abbots, priors and other ordinaries and pastors of the said places, to the intent and purpose that by those same ordinaries and pastors the said benefices might be conferred on honest and suitable people of the said kingdom; which they did for a long time, until of late, and more particularly until the time of Pope Clement V [1305-14]. Since which time the said ordinaries and pastors have been so disturbed and impeded in their said collations, by provisions, expectations, and reservations from the court of Rome, that they have not been able to bestow any benefice freely, in accordance with the intention of your said progenitors: but all the said dignities and other benefices have since been commonly given in the said court of Rome, to persons of a foreign tongue, and often to enemies, who never take up residence in the same, and do not know, are unable and do not wish to bear in any way or fulfil the charges of the said benefices, as in hearing confessions, preaching, instructing the people, offering hospitality, or any other duties inherent in the enjoyment of the same benefices, but they allow the noble edifices built of old when they were occupied by Englishmen to fall into ruin, like people who seek only the temporal profits and emoluments, having no regard for spiritual care, nor any of the other charges incumbent on the same benefices; because of which divine service is greatly diminished, the cure of souls neglected and impaired, and the clergy weakened, the treasure of the realm taken away in alien hands, and the entire estate of holy church degraded to a lesser reverence. For which mischiefs and grievances your noble grandfather the king, whom God absolve, and the lords of the said realm intended on various occasions to provide remedy. And in particular, between Gregory [XI] who died of late [1378] and your said grandfather it was agreed that the said grievances should be addressed and rectified in such a way that neither the king nor the said realm should feel themselves aggrieved from now on, and also that no benefice in your said realm should be given to any of your enemies or rebels. Yet, nevertheless, the present pope Urban [VI] gave to an alien cardinal the priory of Deerhurst, never before allowed in that country: and he granted to the cardinal of Cisteron, born in the region of Limousin, which is at present in rebellion against you, an expectation throughout the province of Canterbury, with the clause de anteferri, worth four thousand florins: which is a manner of provision newly instituted, and which no other kingdom wishes to accept or suffer. Furthermore, he has recently given to the said cardinal the archdeaconry of Bath, contrary to the aforesaid agreement, and he has also given, and gives, from one day to the next, both by way of reservation and by way of provision, the benefices of the said kingdom to many other aliens: and this on the information of some of your English lieges attending the said court of Rome, who, to gain advantage from the farms of the said benefices, and other favours in the *[Page iii-83]*
[Col. a] said court, do not consider the common good of you and your said kingdom, but only their individual benefit, so that the said kingdom will never have been so burdened with aliens as it will be within a brief space of time, to the great injury and impoverishment of the said realm, unless remedy be ordained in this present parliament.

Par quoy supplient a vostre roiale mageste les dites communes qe considerez tendrement les grevances et inconvenientz avantdites, il vous en plese ordener en ce present parlement due remede, et s'il plest a vostre hautesse d'ent savoir l'avis de voz ditz comunes, ils le declareront quant il vous plerra.

Responsio.

Le roi nostre seignour, par l'advis de toutz les seignours temporels esteantz en ce parlement, pur remedier et eschuir les grandes damages et enpoverissementz queux le roialme ad sustenuz [et susteint] parmy les causes dessusdites, et assez d'autres, est acordez, a la requeste de les dites communes, d'escrire a nostre seint pere le pape par lettres, affaires sibien souz le seal nostre dit seignour le roi come souz les sealx des autres grandez seignours temporels du roialme, le pluis effectuelment qe par le bone et sage advis des ditz seignours purra estre fait, sur la dite matire, aufin qe nostre dit seint pere se voille oultrement abstiner de doner desore aucun benefice dedeinz le dit roialme a aucune persone alien. Et pur mettre greindre remede en celle partie, ordene est et establi par l'advis et assent des seignours avauntditz qe nul des liges le roi, n'autre persone quelconqe, de quiel estat ou condicioun q'il soit, ne preigne ne resceive deinz le roialme d'Engleterre procuracie, lettre d'attourne, ne ferme, n'autre administracioun, par endenture, ne en autre manere quelconqe de nule persone du mounde, d'ascun benefice deinz le dit roialme, forsqe tant soulement des liges de nostre seignour le roi de mesme le roialme, sanz especial et expres congie de nostre dit seignour le roi, par l'advis de son conseil. Et si ascuns devaunt ceste heure aient acceptez d'aucuns aliens tielx procuracies, fermes ou administracioun, q'il les lessent oultrement deinz .xl. jours apres la publicacioun de ceste ordeinance. Et qe nul des ditz liges, n'autre qe purra estre trovez en dit roialme, ne envoie par vertue de tiele procuracie, ferme ou administracioun, or, argent, n'autre tresor, ne comodite, hors du dit roialme, par lettre d'eschange, par marchandie, n'en autre manere quelconqe, au profit des ditz aliens, sanz semblable congie du roi, par l'advis de son dit conseil. Et si aucun face le contraire en aucun point contenuz en ceste ordenance, encourge la peine et punissement contenuz en l'estatut des provisours, fait en temps le roi Edward aiel nostre seignour le roi q'orest, l'an de son regne .xxvij.^{me},[33] par mesme le proces compris en dit estatut, et par garnissement a faire a eux en lours benefices, ou autres lours possessions deinz le roialme: et s'ils soient hors del roialme, et n'aient benefices et possessions deinz mesme le roialme ou ils purront estre garniz, adonqes soit brief fait en la chancellarie, foundez sur ceste ordeinance, as viscontz de Londres, ou al viscont del conte en quiel ils furent ou serront neez, a la suite le roi, retournable en l'un bank ou en l'autre; par quiel brief soit commande proclamacioun estre faite overtement, q'ils soient devaunt les justices en le bank ou le brief est retournable, a certein jour compris en mesme le brief, contenant l'espace de demy an, pur respondre sur les matires compris en le dit brief. Et cel brief retornez, deslors procedent les justices envers eux, selonc la fourme dessuis ordeine. Et qe nul evesqe, n'autre persone de seinte esglise parmy le roialme, ne se medle, par voie de sequestracioun, n'en autre manere, des fruitz de tielx benefices donez ou a doners as ditz aliens, au profit de mesmes les aliens, sur le peril q'appent.

On account of which the said commons beg of your royal majesty that having tenderly considered the aforesaid grievances and inconveniences, it please you to ordain due remedy in this present parliament; and if it please your highness to receive the advice of your said commons in this, they will offer it whenever it please you.

Answer.

The king our lord, by the advice of all the lords temporal present in this parliament, to remedy and avert the great injuries and impoverishment which the kingdom has sustained and sustains for the aforesaid reasons, and others enough, has agreed, at the request of the said commons, to send letters to our holy father the pope, under the seal of our said lord the king as well as under the seals of the other great lords temporal of the kingdom, and couched in the most effective way possible by the good and wise advice of the said lords, on the said matter, with the intent that our said holy father should entirely abstain henceforth from granting any benefice within the said kingdom to any alien person. And to effect a greater remedy, it is ordained and established by the advice and assent of the aforesaid lords that no liege of the king, nor any other person whatsoever, of whatever status or condition they may be, shall take or receive, without the particular and express permission of our said lord the king, by the advice of his council, within the kingdom of England, the office of procurator, letter of attorney, farm nor other administration by indenture, or in any other manner from anyone in the world, of any benefice within the said kingdom, except only from the lieges of our lord the king of the same kingdom. And if any have in the past accepted from such aliens such procuracies, farms or administration, that they shall entirely relinquish them within forty days of the publication of this ordinance, and that none of the said lieges, nor any other who may be found in the said realm, shall send by virtue of such procuracy, farm or administration, gold, silver, or any other commodity out of the said kingdom, by letter of exchange, or by way of merchandise, or in any other manner, for the profit of the said aliens, without similar permission from the king, by the advice of his said council. And if anyone contravenes a particular provision in this ordinance, let him incur the penalty and punishment contained in the statute of provisors, made in the time of King Edward, grandfather of our lord the present king, in the twenty-seventh year of his reign [1353], by the same process contained in the said statute, and with notification being given to them in their benefices or their other possessions within the kingdom: and if they are outside the kingdom, and have no benefices nor possessions within the same kingdom in which they can be notified, then a writ shall be made in the chancery, based on this ordinance and addressed to the sheriffs of London, or to the sheriff of the county in which they were or shall be born, at the suit of the king, returnable in either Bench; in which writ order shall be given for a public proclamation to be made, instructing them to appear before the justices of the Bench in which the writ is returnable, on a certain day specified in the same writ, within the space of six months, to answer the matter set out in the said writ. And the writ having been returned, the justices shall then proceed against them, in accordance with the form ordained above. And that no bishop, or any other person of holy church throughout the kingdom, shall interfere, by way of sequestration, or in any other manner, with the fruits of such benefices given or to be given to the said aliens, to profit the same aliens, on pain of the appended penalty.

---

[33] 23 Edw.3 stat.4.

XIII. [Justices of the peace.]

38. Item, let the following points be added to the commission of the justices of the peace: first, that they shall have the power to inquire into and execute the statute of purveyors. Also, that they shall have the power to inquire into and determine extortions, confederacies and maintainers of pleas, and to determine notorious larcenies and murders and people killed with malicious intent, without awaiting the coming of the justices of assize, and that the statute formerly ordained concerning those who give hoods and liveries to do maintenance shall be duly executed in accordance with the tenor of the same. Also, to inquire and determine of all those who ride the highway in disturbance of the peace, similarly of all who lie in wait to kill, rob or maim, and similarly all who shall be indicted of any such offences, and convicted thereof, so that they shall forfeit their goods and chattels to the king and be imprisoned for a year and a day; and if they have no chattels that they shall be imprisoned for two years, without being released by mainprise, bail nor in any other way whatsoever, without the special mandate of the king. And that, on their release, they shall provide an adequate security for their good bearing towards the king and the people on pain of a certain penalty.

Answer.

The king wills and commands, by the assent of the lords temporal, that they shall have such power as they had through the last commission, adding further to the said commission that they shall have the power to hear and determine in cases of murder and extortion; and of those who ride armed, or in force, and in bands, breaking the peace and to the terror of the people; and those who lie in wait to kill or maim; and those who wear hoods and other livery by way of confederacy, and to do maintenance, contrary to the prohibition and the form of the statutes and ordinances made thereon in the past. Provided always that in difficult cases of extortion one of the king's justices from one Bench or the other, or at least the justices appointed for the taking of assizes, shall be present before they proceed to judgment in the matter. And as for forfeiture and the other penalties requested above, the king will consider them further: but he wills that the laws previously prescribed in such cases shall be duly executed. And be it remembered that the prelates and the clergy made their protestation in this parliament expressly in connection with this new grant, to hear and determine cases of extortion, that their will and assent should and ought never to be bypassed, to the infringement of the liberty of holy church, if perchance it should be sought by virtue of the same word, extortion, to proceed more widely against the ordinaries and other men of holy church, nor would they give their assent, unless those things were dealt with in the future as they had been in the past. To which answer was made on behalf of our lord the king that the king would not, neither on account of their said protestation nor their other words in the matter, fail to appoint his justices in this case, or in all others as he had been accustomed to do in times past and was obliged to do by virtue of the oath he swore at his coronation.

XIIII. [Justices of the peace.]

39. Item, that the justices appointed to keep the peace should hold their sessions in accordance with the statute; and that all justices should receive wages of half a mark for each day on which they hold their sessions, and their clerk, 2*s*. from fines, issues and amercements, both within franchise and without, arising in their sessions. And that the justices for the aforesaid articles be elected by the lords and knights of the counties in this present parliament; namely eight persons at the most, from amongst the most reputable knights

deux soient apprises de la loy, sanz nul associacioun faire de couste en apres par nule voie. Et qe mesmes les justices, a chescun quartier de l'an, facent liverer as viscontz de lour countees leur extretes des fyns, issues et amerciementz suisnommez, par endenture. Et qe les ditz viscontz aient garrant par brief de paier as dites justices lours gages susditz de session en sessioun, parnant ent acquitances devers les ditz viscontz dessouz les sealx les ditz justices, pur les quelles due allouance soit faite as ditz visconts *[Page iii-84]*

[Col. a] en l'escheqier sur lour acompte: et qe l'autre partie del dite endenture enseallee desouz le seal les ditz justices et viscont soit envoiez en l'escheqier, pur y charger le viscont de lever ce qe serra aderere oultre les gages susdites, al oeps nostre seignour le roi. Et qe proclamacioun soit faite de les estatutz et ordeinances suisdites deux foitz par an, al venue des justices d'assises en paiis. Et en cas qe la venue des \dites/ justices ne se face, ou soit tarie siqe les assises ne se tiegnent, q'adonqes proclamacioun se face de mesmes les estatutz et ordeinances a pluis plein countee qi serra tenuz, et es villes, feires, marchees, come y semblera mieltz as ditz justices.

Responsio.

Quant as gages des ditz justices, est assentuz qe chivaler prendra .iiij. s., esquier .ij. s. et lour clerc .xij. d. pur chescun jour q'ils tendront leurs sessions tantsoulement des issues de lours ditz extretes, en la fourme q'est demande. Et tendront mesmes les justices lours sessions quatre foitz l'an en chescun countee, et chescun foitz deux ou trois jours ensemble, selonc ce qe le countee est grant ou petit, et selonc ce qe les ditz justices averont affaire devant eux; issint qe celles leurs quatre sessions soient tenuz chescun an parmy et par tut chescun countee, mais nemye pluis sovent qe n'est dit dessuis, si n'y \a/ cause necessaire qe demande pluis hastive remede. Et .... le roi nostre seignour voet qe les viscontz de chescun countee soient tenuz de faire la dite proclamacioun en plein countee, al mandement de mesmes les justices, un foiz ou deux foitz l'an. Et quant a les endentures et le manere du paiement des gages avauntdites, il plest au roi qe soit fait par manere q'est demande. Et endroit de nombre et des nouns des ditz justices baillez avant en parlement en escrit, le roi nostre seignour s'advisera. Et pur tant qe mesmes justices averont le dit poair d'oier et terminer mort d'omme, et les autres choses dessuisdites, soient ils jurrez de faire a chescuny droit, par manere come les autres justices le roi sont de lour part jurrez et serementez.

Membrane 2 [34]

Declaration faite sur le poair donez as justices de la paix, dont il y a une certaine acte enroullez en roulle de parlement anno tercio.

40. Et fait a remembrer qe en terme de Pasqe proschein apres le fyn de cest parlement, les seignours temporelx assemblez a Westm' a un grant conseil illoeqes tenuz, si firent autrefoitz lire devant eulx l'enroullement del ordinance faite en cest parlement touchant la poair des justices de la paix, en presence de monseignour d'Espaigne, chanceller, tresorier et de touz les justices, et illoeqes mesmes les seignours temporelx firent declaracioun de poair des justices de la paix avantditz. Qar ils y disoient qe lour entente estoit en dit parlement coment ce n'estoit clerement enroullez a celle foitz, qe entre autres articles et pointz, mesmes les justices de la paix auroient poair d'oier et terminer toutes maneres d'extorsions

and squires in each county, of whom two shall be learned in the law, without making any association later by any means. And that the same justices, at each quarter, shall deliver to the sheriffs of their counties the estreats of the aforesaid fines, issues and amercements by indenture. And that the said sheriffs shall have a warrant by writ to pay the said justices their aforesaid wages from session to session, receiving acquittances of the said sheriffs under the seals of the said justices, for which due allowance shall be made to the said sheriffs *[Page iii-84]*

[Col. a] in the exchequer on their account: and that the other part of the said indenture sealed under the seals of the said justices and sheriff shall be sent to the exchequer, for the sheriff to be charged there to levy what is in arrears over and above the aforesaid wages, for the use of our lord the king. And that proclamation be made of the aforesaid statutes and ordinances twice a year, on the arrival of the justices of the assizes in the country. And where the arrival of the said justices does not come about, or it is delayed so that the assizes are not held, that then proclamation shall be made of the same statutes and ordinances at the fullest meeting of the county court to be held, and in the towns, fairs and markets, as shall seem best to the said justices.

Answer.

As for the wages of the said justices, it is agreed that a knight shall take 4s., a squire 2s. and their clerk 12d. for each day on which they hold their sessions, from the issues of their said estreats only, in the required form. And the same justices shall hold their sessions four times a year in each county, and on each occasion for two or three days together, according to whether the county be great or small, and to what the said justices have before them to complete; so that these their four sessions shall be held each year throughout and everywhere within each county, but not more often than has been stated above, if there be no urgent matter requiring swift remedy. And the king our lord wills that the sheriffs of every county shall be obliged to make the said proclamation in the full county court, on the order of the same justices, once or twice a year. And as for the indentures and the manner of paying the aforesaid wages, it pleases the king that it be done in the manner requested. And as for the number and the names of the said justices being submitted in parliament in writing, the king our lord will consider it further. And because the same justices will have the right to hear and determine cases of homicide and other matters aforesaid, let them be sworn to do right by all, as the other king's justices are for their part sworn and bound by oath to do.

The declaration made on the power given to the justices of the peace, of which there is a certain act enrolled on the roll of parliament for the third year.

40. And be it remembered that in Easter term next after the end of this parliament [11 April-7 May 1380]), the lords temporal assembled at Westminster at a great council held there again caused to be read before them the enrolment of the ordinance made in this parliament touching the power of the justices of the peace, in the presence of messire of Spain, the chancellor, treasurer and all the justices, and there the same lords temporal made a declaration of the power of the aforesaid justices of the peace. And they said there that their intention in the said parliament, although it was not clearly enrolled at that time, was that amongst other articles and points the same justices of the peace should have the power

---

[34] The following text as far as the end of item 41 is written in a different contemporary hand on a loose leaf of parchment (numbered '2') stitched to membrane 3.

sibien a la suite le roi, come de partie, \et/ de certaines autres articles comprises en dit poair. Ils y firent auxint declaracion, et sur ce estoit une certaine note faite de la commission, par l'advis de touz les justices nostre seignour le roy sibien de l'un bank come de l'autre lors presentz illoeqes: et celle note lue en dit conseil devant eulx touz, assentirent a ycelle note, et lour pleust bien qe ce passast le seal le roy souz celle forme. Et issint furent les commissions faites, enseales et envoiez a chescun countee d'Engleterre, ensemble avec un brief direct al viscont de \chescun/ countee, del prendre les seremenz des commissioners de bien et loialment user lour commission, et droit faire a chescune persone, sibien as povres come as riches, selonc la forme d'une cedule enclose en chescun des ditz briefs. Des queux brief et cedule, qe furent auxint faites par l'advis du conseil le roi, et de la note de la commission avantdite, les tenours ou copies s'ensuent de mot a mot:

Rex dilectis et fidelibus suis A. B. C. D., etc., salutem. Sciatis quod assignavimus vos conjunctim et divisim ad pacem nostram, necnon statuta apud Wynton', Norht', et Westm', pro conservacione pacis ejusdem

[Col. b] edita, in omnibus et singulis suis articulis in comitatu H. tam infra libertates quam extra, custodiendam et custodiri faciendam: et ad omnes illos quos contra formam statutorum predictorum delinquentes inveneritis castigandum et puniendum prout secundum formam statutorum eorundem fuerit faciendum, et ad omnes illos qui /aliquibus de populo\ nostro de corporibus suis vel de incendio domorum suarum minas fecerint, ad sufficientem securitatem de pace et bono gestu suo erga nos et populum nostrum inveniendam coram vobis venire, et si hujusmodi securitatem invenire recusaverint, tunc eos in prisonis nostris quousque hujusmodi securitatem invenerint salvo custodiri faciendos. Assignavimus eciam vos quinque, quatuor tres, et duos vestrum, justiciarios nostros ad inquirendum per sacrum proborum et legalium hominum in comitatu predicto, tam infra libertates quam extra, per quos rei veritas melius sciri poterit, de quibuscumque latrociniis notorie vel aperte, ac mahemiis, et /hominum\ interfectionibus per insidias vel maliciam precogitatam, ac murdris, et aliis feloniis, transgressionibus, forstallariis, regratariis et extorsionibus in comitatu predicto per quoscumque et qualitercumque factis sive perpetratis, et que exnunc ibidem fieri contingat. Et eciam de omnibus illis qui in conventiculis contra pacem nostram et in perturbacionem populi nostri seu vi armata ierint vel equitaverint, seu exnunc ire vel equitare presumpserint. Ac eciam de hiis qui in insidiis ad gentem nostram mahemiandam vel interficiendam jacuerint, et exnunc jacere presumpserint. Et eciam de hiis qui capiciis, et alia liberata de unica secta, per confederacionem et pro manutenencia, contra defensionem ad formam ordinacionum et statutorum inde ante hec tempora factorum, usi fuerint, ac aliis hujusmodi liberata imposterum utentibus. Ac eciam de hostelariis, et aliis qui in abusu mensurarum et ponderum ac in vendicione victualium; et eciam de quibuscumque operariis, artificibus et servitoribus, et aliis qui contra formam ordinacionum et statutorum pro omni utilitate regni nostri Anglie de hujusmodi operariis, artificibus, servitoribus, hostellariis et aliis inde \factorum delinquerint, vel attemptaverint,/ in comitatu predicto, vel exnunc delinquere vel attemptare presumpserint. Et ad processus versus omnes quos de feloniis hujusmodi contigerit indictari quousque capiantur, reddantur, vel utlagentur, faciendos. Et ad latrocinia, mahemia, interfectiones et murdra predicta, ac ea omnia et singula que per hujusmodi conventicula contra pacem nostram, et in

to hear and determine all kinds of extortion, both at the suit of the king as well as of an individual, and of certain other articles comprised by the said authority. They also made a declaration there, and thereon a certain note was made of the commission, by the advice of all the justices of our lord the king of either Bench, then present there: and that note having been read in the said council before them all, they gave their assent to it, and it pleased them well that it should receive the king's seal in that form. And so the commissions were made, sealed and sent to every county of England, together with a writ addressed to the sheriff of each county, to receive the oaths of the commissioners for the loyal and effective discharge of their commission, and to do right to all, both the rich and poor, according to the form of a schedule enclosed with each of the said writs. The tenor or text of which writ and schedule, which were also made by the advice of the king's council, and the abstract of the aforesaid commission here follow verbatim:

The king to his beloved and faithful A. B. C. D., etc., greeting. Know that we have appointed you jointly and severally to keep and cause to be kept our peace, and also the statutes issued at Winchester, Northampton, and Westminster, for the preservation of the same peace,

[Col. b] in each and every one of their articles, in the county of H., within liberties and without: and to castigate and punish all those whom you find to contravene the principle of the aforesaid statutes, according to the form of the same statutes, and to cause to be brought before you all those who threaten our people with physical injury or the burning of their houses, to provide adequate pledges of peace and good behaviour towards us and our people; and if they refuse to give this pledge, you shall cause them to be kept securely in our prison until they find such a pledge. Moreover, we have appointed five, four, three and two of you to be our justices to inquire through the oath of worthy and lawful men in the aforesaid county, both within liberties and without, through whom the truth of the matter may more easily be known, into all manner of notorious or manifest thefts, maimings, and homicides resulting from ambushes or evil intent, and murders, and other felonies, trespasses, forestallings, regratings and extortions in the aforesaid county howsoever and by whomsoever they have been committed or perpetrated, and which henceforth happen to be perpetrated in that place. And also, to inquire into all those who journey or ride in bands or as an armed force contrary to our peace and disturbing our people, or who shall presume to journey or ride henceforth. And moreover to inquire into those who lie in wait to maim or kill our people, and who shall henceforth presume so to lie in wait. And also to inquire into those who wear hoods and other liveries of a particular style, as part of a confederation and for maintenance, contrary to the prohibition and form of the ordinances and statutes made thereon in the past, and the wearing of all other kinds of liveries in the future. And also to inquire of inn-keepers and others who are guilty of abuse of measures and weights and in the sale of victuals; and moreover, of all kinds of labourers, artificers and servants, and others in the aforesaid county who act or seek to act contrary to the form of the ordinances and statutes made for the benefit of our kingdom of England concerning such workers, artificers, servants, inn-keepers and others in the aforesaid county, or who henceforth act wrongly or attempt to do so. And to pursue all those indicted of such felonies until they are captured, bailed or outlawed. And against the aforesaid thefts, maimings, slayings and murders, and each and every one of those who through such conventicles attempt or shall attempt to act against our peace and to the disturbance of our people; and also those who attempt or

perturbacionem populi nostri; et eciam ea que per hujusmodi insidias ad gentem nostram mahemiandam vel interficiendam: et ea eciam per usum hujusmodi capiciorum et aliarum liberatarum per confederacionem et pro manutenentia, sicut predictum est, attemptata fuerint, et attemptari contigerit, ac transgressiones et forstallarias predictas ad sectam nostram terminandas. Ac extorsiones, et regratarias predictas, et omnia alia que per hujusmodi hostellarios et alios in abusu mensurarum et ponderum, ac in vendicione victualium, et omnia alia que per hujusmodi operarios, artifices, et servitores, contra formam ordinacionum et statutorum predictorum, seu in enervacionem eorundem, in aliquo presumpta vel attemptata fuerint, tam ad sectam nostram quam aliorum quorumcumque, coram vobis pro nobis vel pro seipsis conqueri vel prosequi volencium, audienda et terminanda; et ad eosdem operarios, artifices et servitores, per fines, redempciones et amerciamenta, et alio modo, pro delictis suis, prout ante ordinacionem de punicione corporali hujusmodi operariis, artificibus et servitoribus pro delictis suis exhibendam factam fieri consuevit, castiganda et punienda, secundum legem et consuetudinem regni nostri Anglie, ac formam ordinationum et statutorum predictorum. Proviso semper, quod si casus difficultatis super determinacione extorsionum hujusmodi coram vobis evenire contigerit quod ad judicium inde nisi in presencia unius justiciariorum nostrorum de uno vel de altero banco, aut justiciariorum nostrorum ad assisas in comitatu predicto capiendas assignatorum, coram vobis minime procedatur. Assignavimus eciam vos quinque, quatuor et tres et duos vestrum, quorum alterum vestrum vos prefati A. et B. unum esse volumus, justiciarios nostros ad felonias *[Page iii-85]*

[Col. a] predictas, quarum determinacio superius declarata non existit, ac omnia processus et indictamenta, felonias et transgressiones, forstallarias, regratarias et alia predicta tangencia, coram vobis prefate A. et sociis vestris nuper custodibus pacis nostre, et justiciariis nostris ad hujusmodi felonias et transgressiones in comitatu predicto audiendas et terminandas assignatis, facta, que nondum terminata existunt, inspicienda et debito fine terminanda, secundum legem et consuetudinem predictas ac formam ordinacionum et statutorum predictorum. Et ideo vobis et cuilibet vestrum mandamus quod circa custodiam pacis et statutorum predictorum diligenter intendatis, et ad certos dies et loca, quos vos quinque, quatuor, tres, vel duo vestrum ad hoc provideritis, inquisiciones super premissis faciatis, et premissa omnia et singula audiatis et terminetis, ac modo debito et effectualiter expleatis, in forma supradicta: facturi inde quod ad justiciam pertinet, secundum legem et consuetudinem regni nostri Anglie, salvis nobis amerciamentis et aliis ad nos inde spectantibus. Mandavimus enim vicecomiti nostro comitatu predicti quod ad certos dies et loca, quos vos quinque, etc., vel duo vestrum ei scire facias, venire faciatis coram vobis quinque, etc., et duobus vestrum, tot et tales probos et legales homines de balliva sua, tam infra libertates quam extra, per quos rei veritas in premissis melius sciri poterit et inquiri. Et insuper vobis et cuiuslibet vestrum super salva custodia pacis et statutorum predictorum pareat et intendat, quando et prout per vos vel aliquem vestrum fuerit super hoc ex parte nostra racionabiliter premunitus. Et vos prefate A. ad certos dies et loca per vos et dictos socios vestros super hoc prefigendum, processus et indictamenta predicta coram vobis et

shall attempt to maim of kill people through such ambushes: and also those who shall wear or seek to wear henceforth these kinds of hoods and other liveries by way of confederacy and maintenance, as was said above, and also the aforesaid transgressions and forestallings at our suit. And the aforesaid extortions and regratings, and all other things attempted or presumed by such inn-keepers and others in terms of abuse of weights and measures and in the sale of victuals, and all other things done by such labourers, artificers and servants, contrary to the form of the aforesaid ordinances and statutes, or weakening the same, both at our suit as well as at those of others, to hear and determine before you for us or for those wishing to complain or prosecute; and to castigate and punish those same labourers, artificers and servants through fines, redemptions and amercements, and by other means, for their offences, as was customarily done before the ordinance for the corporal punishment of such workers, artificers and servants for their offences made in accordance with the law and custom of our kingdom of England and the form of the aforesaid ordinances and statutes. Provided always that if a difficult case of extortion happens to come before you, you do not proceed to judgment in the matter unless one of our justices of either Bench, or at least our justices appointed for the holding of assizes in the aforesaid county, be present. Moreover, we have appointed five, four, three, and two of you, amongst whom we wish the aforesaid A and B to be included, as our justices to *[Page iii-85]*

[Col. a] investigate and bring to a proper conclusion the aforesaid felonies, the determining of which is not declared above, and all processes and indictments, felonies and transgressions, waylayings, regratings and all the other relevant aforesaid offences committed, before you the aforesaid A. and your friends recently appointed custodians of our peace, and our justices for the hearing and determining of those such felonies and transgressions in the aforesaid county, which have not yet been settled, in accordance with the aforesaid law and custom and the form of the aforesaid ordinances and statutes. And therefore we order each and every one of you that you diligently attend to the keeping of the peace and the aforesaid statutes, and that at certain times and places you shall make available five, four, three, or two of yourselves for that purpose, holding inquests on the aforesaid matters, and that you hear and determine each and every one of the aforesaid, and conclude matters in the aforesaid form by due and effective means: to do herein whatever is just, in accordance with the law and custom of our kingdom of England, saving to us amercements and all other things pertaining to us in this matter. For we have ordered our sheriff of the aforesaid county that at certain times and places, you five, etc., or two of you shall notify him, to cause to be brought before you five, etc., and two of you, so many and such worthy and lawful men from his bailliwick as are within liberties and without, through whom the truth of the aforesaid matters may be more easily known and established. In the meantime, that each and every one of you should attend to and ensure the safe-keeping of the peace and the aforesaid statutes, whensoever and howsoever, through you or one of

dictis sociis vestris venire faciatis et ea inspiciatis, et debito fine terminetis, sicut predictum est. In cujus, etc. Teste rege apud Westm' .xxvi. die Maii [1380].

Per ipsum regem et consilium.
Rex vicecomiti, etc., salutem. Quasdam literas nostras patentes, per quas certos ligeos nostros ad pacem nostram in comitatu tuo conservandam, et ad quedam alia in eisdem litteris contenta facienda et explenda assignavimus, tibi mittimus per presencium portitorem: mandantes districcius quo poterimus injungendo quod statim visis presentibus, quibuscumque dilacione et excusacione postpositis, tot personas de eodem sic per nos assignatos quot inde infra ballivam tuam invenire poteris, ad certos diem et locum eis per te ad hoc in proxime statuendum et prefigendum coram te sine dilacione venire faciatis, et capto sacramento eorundem juxta formam cujusdam cedule presentibus intercluse, eisdem sic juratis literas nostras predictas liberari faciatis indilate; dicens et injungens eisdem ex parte nostra quod ipsi non permittant, sicut nec est intencionis nostre, nec omnino volumus quod aliquis dictorum sic assignatorum se inde in aliquo intromittat, seu auctoritatem in hac parte virtute literarum predictarum habeat aliqualem, nec vadia ad hoc ordinata recipiat, seu ei ut justiciario nostro tu vel aliquis alius intendens sis aut sit quovis modo, nisi prius ad hoc juratus fuerit in forma predicta. Et qualiter presens mandatum nostrum fueris executus, ac de nominibus coram te sic juratorum, nos in cancellaria nostra cum ea celeritate qua fieri poterit sub sigillo tuo distincte et aperte certificando: ita quod pro capcione sacrarum aliorum sic assignatorum, si qui remanserint non jurati, debite prout convenit ordinare poterimus. Et hoc sicut gravem indignacionem nostram evitare volueris nullatenus omittas. Teste rege apud Westm' .xxvij. die Maii [1380].
41. Vous jurrez qe bien et loialment servirez le roy en l'office de gardein de la paix, et de justicierie des artificers, laborers, pois et mesures, et d'oier et terminer les tortz et grevances faitz au roi et a son poeple, et des autres choses quelconqes comprises pluis pleinement en la commissioun a vous et autres voz compaignons ent fait; selonc voz seu et poair ent ferrez

[Col. b] avoir plein droit as touz, sibien as povres come as riches, siqe pur hayour, favour, amistee, ou estat de nulluy persone, ne pur bienfait, doun, ou promesse qe vous soit ou serra fait en temps avenir, n'autrement par art ou engyn quelconqe, droiture nient respiterez ne delaierez a nulluy, contre reson, ne contre les loies, estatutz, ordinances et custumes del roialme. Mes sanz regard avoir de persone qelconqe, loialment ent frez droit a touz, selonc les lois, estatutz, ordinances et custumes avantdites. Et conseil le roi touchant ceux qi serront enditez devant vous, celerez, et auxint compellerez les jurrez en enquestes de le celer de lour part loialment, et touz les recordz et proces qe serront faitz devant vous ferrez mettre en bone et seure garde, et les extretes des fins et amerciementz, et d'autres profitz ent au roi appurtenantz, ferrez entierment mettre en escript endentee, de temps en temps, dont l'une partie ferrez deliverer a viscount del countee, et l'autre partie ent ferrez envoier seurement en l'escheqier le roi, pur y charger le viscount sur son accompt. Et touz les briefs /qe\ vous vendront souz le grant seal le roi loialment servirez, et ferrez executer sanz delaie. Et qe vous ne prendrez ne resceiverez nul clerc devers vous pur faire

you, you shall be reasonably forewarned on our behalf. And you the aforesaid A., at certain times and places through you and your said colleagues appointed hereto, shall cause the aforesaid process and indictments to be brought before you and your said friends and investigated and duly determined, as is said above. In testimony of which, etc. Witnessed by the king at Westminster 26 May [1380].
By the king himself and the council.
The king to the sheriff, etc., greeting. Certain of our letters patent, in which we appointed certain of our lieges for the keeping of the peace in your county and for certain other matters mentioned in the same letters, we are sending to you by the bearer of these presents: ordering as strictly as we can that as soon as you have seen the present documents, setting aside any delay or excuse, you cause to be summoned before you at once all those mentioned in the same and appointed by us whom you are able to find within your bailliwick, on a certain day and at a certain place appointed and set aside for this by you, and having taken their oaths in accordance with the form of the schedule enclosed herein, you cause our aforesaid letters to be delivered without delay to those then sworn; saying and ordering them on our behalf that they should not allow, just as it is not our intention and certainly not our wish, that any of the aforesaid thus appointed should concern himself with anything, nor have any authority in the matter by virtue of the aforesaid letters, nor receive any pledges hereon ordained, or that you or anyone else should take him as our justice in any way, unless he has previously sworn in the aforesaid manner. And you shall notify us in our chancery as soon as possible, and distinctly and openly under your seal, of how you have executed our present mandate, and of the names of those thus sworn before you: so that we can order the taking of oaths from the others thus appointed, if any remain unsworn. And do not by any means fail to do this if you wish to avoid our grave displeasure. Witnessed by the king at Westminster 27 May [1380].
41. You swear that you shall serve the king loyally and well in the office of keeper of the peace and of justice of artificers, labourers, weights and measures, and in hearing and determining the wrongs and injustices committed against the king and his people, and in all other things set out more fully in the commission directed to you and others of your colleagues; to the best of your knowledge and ability you will do

[Col. b] right by all, rich and poor, so that neither for hatred, favour, friendship nor the status of any one, nor for a benefit, gift or promise which may be offered to you in the future, nor by any other device or scheme, shall right be impeded or delayed for any one contrary to reason and the laws, statutes, ordinances and customs of the kingdom. But without bias against anyone in particular, you shall faithfully do right by all in accordance with the aforesaid laws, statutes, ordinances and customs. And you shall not reveal the advice of the king touching those indicted before you, and shall also compel the juries in inquests faithfully not to divulge it for their part, and all the records and processes which shall be made before you, you shall cause to be safely and securely kept, and the estreats of fines and amercements, and of other profits from these pertaining to the king, you shall set out fully in indented documents from time to time, one part of which you shall cause to be delivered to the sheriff of the county, and the other part you shall safely send to the king's exchequer, there to be charged to the sheriff's account. And you shall loyally serve all the writs under the great seal of the king which you receive, and cause them to be executed

escrire ou garder les recordes et proces avantdites, s'il ne soit primerement jurez devant vous de celer le conseil le roi, et de faire et perfournir bien et loialment de sa part qant qe a son office et degree apent en celle partie, si Dieu vous aide, et ses seintz.

Membrane 3
PRO HIBERNIA SEQUNTUR PETICIONES LIBERATE IN PRESENTI PARLIAMENTO, UNA CUM RESPONSIONIBUS EISDEM IBIDEM FACTIS. [35]

[Absentee landlords in Ireland.]
42. Endroit des terres et benefices en Irlande de ceux qe ne sount demurrantz illoeqes, sibien prelatz, seignours et dames come autres; en cas q'il semble dure d'ordeinere touz les profitz des dites terres et benefices pur le governement des guerres illoeqes, come estoit ordeinez avant ces heures, et come l'endenture de lour message demande; soit ordeine qe tieux benefices et terres respoignantz a les guerres, trovantz gentz d'armes et hobelours, pur lour afferant, fesant auxint en touz autres pointz come autres de lour degree demurrantz en la dite terre ferrount: nomement, q'ils soient constreintz reparaler lours chastelx et forcelettes el dite terre; en defaute des queux q'ils sont si ruinouses, la terre est grandement feblez, et les marchees degastez.[36]
Responsio.

Purce\ qe nostre seignour le roi ad entenduz par la certificacion de ses foialx liges de la terre d'Irlande, prelatz, nobles et communes, qe la dite terre a este et est moelt endamagez et empovriz, parmy ce qe plusours des liges nostre dit seignour le roi eiantz terres, rents, benefices, offices et autres possessions en la dite terre, ne sont pas resceantz ne demurrantz illoeqes, einz se absentent, et sont hors de la dite terre, preignantz et treiantz devers eux hors de mesme la terre les profitz et revenues des dites terres, rentz, possessions, benefices et offices, et les uns lessantz les chasteux et forteresces a eulx appertenantz en les dites parties aler a ruine, et esteer sanz garde, ordinance et governement, a grant peril de la dite terre, et des dites liges. Par les quelles causes les rebealx Irrois en la dite terre sont encruz, et encrecent et conquerent de jour en autre, et les ditz foialx le plus annintiz d'avoir et de puissance a resister a lour malice, siqe la dite terre est en point d'estre perduz, en deseretisoun nostre dit seignour le roy et de sa coroune d'Engleterre, si sur ceo ne soit ordeigne de hastive remede; ordeigne est par nostre dit seignour le roy, del advis et assent des seignours et nobles de son roialme esteantz en ce parlement qe toutes maners de gentz, de quel estat *[Page iii-86]*

[Col. a] ou condicion q'ils soient, aiantz illoeqes terres, rentes, benefices et offices, et autres possessions quelconqes, se treent devers la dite terre d'Irlande, parentre cy et la Nativite de Seint Johan proschein venant, et deslors soient reseantz et demurrantz illoeqes, en aide et afforcement des dites foialx lieges, a garder et defendre la dite terre encontre les ditz Irroys rebelx: et qe touz ceux qi ount chastelx et forteresses en mesme la terre, les facent reparer, et tener en estat covenable, et y mettent bone et seure garde pur la salvacioun de mesmes les chastelx et forteresses, sur le peril q'appent. Et en cas qe ascun de ceulx q'ont terres, offices, rentes, benefices ou autres possessions en la dite terre, soient pur resonable cause absentz hors de mesme la terre apres la dite feste, adonqes pur le temps de lour absence soient

without delay. And that you shall not take nor receive any clerk for yourself to write or protect the aforesaid records and processes, unless he shall first be sworn before you to keep the counsel of the king, and to well and loyally perform for his part whatsoever pertains to his office and degree in that respect, with the help of God and his saints.

FOR IRELAND, HERE FOLLOW THE PETITIONS SUBMITTED IN THIS PRESENT PARLIAMENT, TOGETHER WITH THE ANSWERS MADE THERE TO THEM.

[Absentee landlords in Ireland.]
42. In respect of the lands and benefices in Ireland of those who do not dwell there, both prelates, lords and ladies, and others; where it seems harsh to ordain all the profits of the said lands and benefices for the administration of the wars there, as was ordained in the past, and as the indenture of their messuage demands; be it ordained that such benefices and lands which should contribute to the wars, finding men-at-arms and hobelars, in accordance with their means, doing also in all other things as much as others of their degree do who are resident in the said land: namely that they shall be constrained to repair their castles and fortresses in the said land; for want of which repair they are so ruinous that the land is greatly weakened, and the marches wasted.
Answer.

Whereas our lord the king has heard by the testimony of his faithful lieges of the land of Ireland, prelates, nobles and commons that the said land has been and is greatly endangered and impoverished, because many of the lieges of our said lord the king possessing lands, rents, benefices, offices and other possessions in the said land are not resident or dwelling there, but are absent and outside the said country, taking and withdrawing to themselves from the said country the profits and revenues of the said lands, rents, possessions, benefices and offices, and some of them leaving the castles and fortresses pertaining to them in the said parts to fall into ruin, and to remain without guard, direction or administration, to the great peril of the said land and the said lieges. As a result of this the rebel Irish in the said land have increased and are increasing and prevailing from one day to the next, and the said faithful lieges are too far weakened to be able to resist their malice, so that the said land is on the point of being lost, to the disinheritance of our said lord the king and his crown of England, unless a swift remedy be provided; so it is ordained by our said lord the king, with the advice and assent of the lords and nobles of his kingdom present in this parliament, that all manner of men, of whatsoever status *[Page iii-86]*

[Col. a] or condition they be, having there lands, rents, benefices, offices and other possessions whatsoever, shall take themselves to the said land of Ireland between now and the Nativity of St John next [24 June 1380], and henceforth shall reside and dwell there, to aid and strengthen the said faithful lieges in guarding and defending the said land against the said Irish rebels: and all those who have castles and fortresses in the same land shall cause them to be repaired and maintained in a fitting condition, and they shall install in them a good and sure garrison for the safekeeping of the same castles and fortresses, on pain of the appended penalty. And if any of those who have lands, offices, rent, benefices or other possessions in the said lands be absent from the said land on reasonable grounds after the said feast,

---

[35]The following is to be found in the main body of the roll, halfway down membrane 3.
[36]PRO E175/3/4.

tenuz d'envoier et de trover illoeqes gentz defensables en lour lieux, en defens de mesme la terre, selonc ce qe la /necessitee requerra;\ eiant regard a la quantitee et a la value de mesmes les terres, rentes, offices et autres possessions. Et s'ils nel facent, soient les deux partz des profitz de lours ... terres, rentes, offices et possessions avantdites levez, et convertiz a la garde et defens de mesme la terre, par l'advis des justices et governours de mesme la terre qi pur le temps serront: horspris toutz foitz, qe les benefices de ceux qi sont en le service du roi, ou estudiantz en universitees, ou hors de mesme la terre pur resonable cause, de la licence du roi dessouz son grant seal en Engleterre, ne serra pris n'appliez a les ditz garde et defens, forsqe tantsoulement la tierce partie de la value d'icelles apres les ordinairs et necessaires charges rebatuz, selonc la certificacioun de lours ordinairs.

[Bullion in Ireland.]
43. Item, a cause qe marchantz pur singuler profit apportent hors de la terre or et argent pur faire lour marchandises, siqe poy ou riens \[remaint]/en la dite terre, paront les dites liges sount grandement empoveriz, qe plese a nostre seignour le roi ordener et grantier en la dite terre myne et coigne; c'estassavoir, myne de tout manere de metail, et coigne de or et argent. Et qe chescun seignour de la terre dedeinz la seignourie eit myne, fesant, plate, pece pur apporter a bullioun, ou de faire vesseulx et autres lours necessaires, sanz mander ou carier come marchandise hors de la terre. Et sur ceo de maunder mynours et overours de mettre ceste ordinance en execucioun.

Membrane 1
\[Responsio.]/

Il plest au roi qe chescun puisse myner et fouer deinz son propre soil en la dite terre or, argent et toutz autres metalx, par .vi. ans proschein avenirs; rendant au roi la neofisme part: et q'ils facent plate, ou pede, del or et argent q'ensy foueront, et l'apportent a coignage du roi deinz la citee de Dyvelyn, repreignant illoeqes monoie du roi a la value, sauvant la seignourage du roi, et les fees acustumes pur le dit coignage, sanz ce qe le dit plate, pece, ou autre billion, soit envoiez ou cariez par voie de marchandie n'en autre manere hors de la dite terre, sanz especial congie du roi par ses lettres; except en Engleterre; sur peine de forfaiture d'ycelle s'il soit trovez, ou de la value a paier par celluy qi ent serra atteint.

[Trade between Portugal and Ireland.]
44. Item, qe les marchantz de Portyngale et de Lusshebon puissent sauvement venir en Irlande ove vins et autres marchaundises qeconqes, et illoeqes demurrer et retourner franchement, et auxint qe les marchantz d'Irlande puissent fraunchement et sanz empeschement aler ove lours marchandises as ditz parties de Portingale et de Lusshebon': et qe sur ce proclamacioun soit fait a Bristuit et aillours en Engleterre, et en Irlande, ou mestier serra. Et qe patentes et briefs nostre seignour le roi ent soient faitz tantz et tieux come busoignera; et ce pur profit le roi, et grant relevacion de sa terre d'Irlande.
Responsio.

Le roi nostre seignour, par l'advis de conseil, ent ordeignera de remede.

[Papal concordat.]
45. A nostre tresredoute seignour le roi supplient humblement ses devoutz oratours le clergie de vostre roialme d'Engleterre qe attendu qe l'accord et composition faitz

then they shall be obliged to send and place other fencible men there in their place to defend the same land, as needs be; having regard to the size and value of the same lands, rents, offices and other possessions. And if they do not do that, let two parts of the profits from their aforesaid lands, rents, offices and possessions be levied and spent upon the guarding and defence of the same land, by the advice of the justices and governors of the same land then in office: excepting always that the benefices of those who are in the service of the king, or studying in universities, or are out of the country for any good reason, with the permission of the king under his great seal of England, shall not be be taken or assigned for the said guard and defence, except only a third of the value of the same after the deduction of ordinary and necessary charges, according to the certification of their ordinaries.

[Bullion in Ireland.]
43. Item, because merchants, for their personal benefit, take gold and silver out of the country to finance their trade, so that little or nothing remains in the said land, whereby the said lieges are greatly impoverished, may it please our lord the king to ordain and grant in the said land, mining and coinage; that is to say, mining of all kinds of metal, and coinage of gold and silver. And that each lord of the land within the lordship may have a mine, making plate or pieces or metal for conversion into bullion, or to make vessels or their other essentials, without sending or carrying it as merchandise out of the country. And thereupon to order miners and craftsmen to put this ordinance into practice.

Answer.

It pleases the king that anyone may mine and excavate from their own soil in the said land gold, silver and all other metals, for six years to come; rendering a ninth to the king: and that they may make plate or pieces from the gold and silver which they have thus dug out, and convert it to the king's coinage in the city of Dublin, receiving the king's money of an equal value, saving the lordship of the king, and the customary fees for the said coinage, and without the said plate, piece or other bullion being sent or carried by way of merchandise or in any other way out of the said land, save by the special permission of the king in his letters, except to England; on pain of forfeiture of the same if it be found, or payment of the value of the same by whomsoever shall be thus convicted.

[Trade between Portugal and Ireland.]
44. Item, that the merchants of Portugal and Lisbon may safely come to Ireland with wines and other merchandise whatsoever, and freely remain and return from there, and also that the merchants of Ireland may freely and without hindrance go with their merchandise to the said parts of Portugal and Lisbon: and that proclamation thereof shall be made at Bristol and elsewhere in England, and in Ireland, wherever there be need. And that letters patent and writs of our lord the king made thereon shall be issued as often and in such form as need requires; and this for the benefit of the king, and to the great relief of his land of Ireland.
Answer.

The king our lord, by the advice of the council, shall ordain a remedy.

[Papal concordat.]
45. To our most redoubtable lord the king, his devout orators, the clergy of your kingdom of England humbly request: whereas the agreement and composition made between the

parentre le pape Gregoire [XI, 1370-8] qi derrain morust, et vostre noble aielle, qi Dieux assoille, l'an de son regne cynquantisme, furent faitz a grant aise et quiete del dite clergie, et de l'esglise d'Engleterre, touchant sibien la revocacioun faite par le dit pape de toutes maneres de reservacions faites par lui et touz ses predecessours avaunt le dit accord, come la grace et remission faite par vostre dit aiel par ses lettres au dite clergie de ses titles de collacioun ou presentacioun as benefices de sainte esglise a cause des temporalitees de seinte esglise en temps de voidance devant mesme l'accord.

Il plese a vostre hautesse, par l'advis des seignours et autres grantz en ce present parlement, pur commune profit et quiete du dit roialme, affermer les ditz accord et composicioun; et ordeiner q'ils soient fermement tenuz, et qe nul de voz liges, n'autre, face, n'attempte rienz au contraire, sur certaine peine par vous a mettre par l'advis des seignours et autres sages de vostre parlement avauntdit.

Responsio.

Le roi le voet et l'ad grantez, parissint qe la pape le tiegne semblables de sa part.

\Pur clerez, justices, sergeantz etc/

46. Plese a nostre seignour le roi comander qe l'ordeinance nadgaires faite en le derrain parlement tenuz a Gloucestre, touchantz les hostelx, livres, vesselmentz, biens et chateux des clercs, et gentz de loy q'ont hostelx en Londres et aillours en le roialme, la quiele ordeinance semble as prelatz et seignours bone et resonable, soit mys en estatut, en affirmance /d'icelle.\

\[*Responsio.*]/

[37] Soit mesme l'ordeinance faite a Gloucestre tenuz et gardez pur estatut, issint qe tielle noun- resonable exaccion \ne/ soit jammais demandez, ne rienz levez a tiel guise de nulle tielle persone, s'il ne soit franke homme des citees ou burghes ou la chose est demande. Et est assentuz en parlement qe quanqe ad este pris contre ceste ordinance soit pleinement restitut, sanz delai ou difficultee aucune.

\Pur seignours des niefs reward./

47. Item, monstre la commune qe come la force de la navie d'Engleterre qe soleit estre si noble qe toutes roialmes dotoient le pluis d'avoir moever guerre devers mesme le roialme, est ore si enfebliz et degastez par plusours et longes arestz ent faitz sanz nul reward avoir du roi, q'a peyne quant l'en en ait busoigne pur aucun viage suffisantie ne poet estre trovez, a grant arrerisement, deshonour et damage de tut le roialme, si remede n'y soit sagement et hastifment ordeinez, par faisant as seignours des niefs et d'autres vesselx ascun reward pur le gast et appairement de lour attil de mesmes les vesselx en temps d'arest avantdit, et del longe service fait a nostre dit seignour le roi paront mesme la navie ad este devant ceste heure principalment destruit et annyntiz.

\[*Responsio.*]/

Quant as seignours des niefs et d'autres vesseulx q'ensi seront arestuz pur le service du roi; nostre seignour le roi voet q'ils aient a lour reward pur chescun tunnetight' d'yceulx lours vesseulx pur chescun quarter del an q'ils demurront en la service nostre seignour le roi .iiij. s., .iiij. d. comenceant lour primer quarter le jour q'ils serront venuz al havene, ou autre lieu qe lour serra assignez: et si meins ou plus q'un

late Pope Gregory [XI, 1370-8], and your noble grandfather, whom God absolve, in the fiftieth year of his reign, were made for the greater ease and tranquillity of the said clergy, and the church of England, touching both the revocation made by the said pope of all kinds of reservations made by him and all his predecessors before that agreement, as well as the grace and remission made by your said grandfather in his letters to the said clergy of his titles of collation or presentation before the same agreement, to the benefices of holy church, being temporalities of holy church in times of vacancy.

May it please your highness, by the advice of the lords and other great men in this present parliament, for the general benefit and tranquillity of the said kingdom, to confirm the said agreement and composition; and ordain that they be strictly upheld, and that none of your lieges, nor any other, shall do or attempt anything to the contrary, on pain of a certain penalty to be set by you with the advice of the lords and other wise men of your aforesaid parliament.

Answer.

The king wills it, and has granted it provided that the pope similarly upholds it for his part.

On behalf of clerics, justices, serjeants, etc.

46. May it please our lord the king to order that the ordinance lately made in the last parliament held at Gloucester, touching the households, books, vessels, goods and chattels of clerics and men of law who have households in London and elsewhere in the kingdom, which ordinance seemed good and reasonable to the prelates and lords, shall be made into a statute, as confirmation of the same.

Answer.

Let the same ordinance made at Gloucester be kept and upheld as a statute, so that such unreasonable exactions shall never be made, and nothing levied under such a guise from such a person if he be not a free man of the cities or boroughs, or when the situation does not demand it. And it is agreed in parliament that whatever has been taken contrary to the ordinance shall be fully restored, without any delay or difficulty.

Payment for the owners of ships.

47. Item, the commons show that the might of the English navy, which used to be so noble that other kingdoms feared all the more to wage war against the same kingdom, is now so enfeebled and wasted on account of numerous and lengthy seizures having been made without any payment received from the king, that whenever there may be future need of a voyage, sufficient means will not be found, bringing great injury, dishonour and harm to the entire realm, unless a wise remedy be swiftly ordained, such as offering the owners of ships and other vessels a payment for the ruin and impairment of the equipment of the same ships during the time of the aforesaid seizure, and the lengthy service done for our said lord the king, as a chief result of which the same fleet has been destroyed and ruined in the past.

Answer.

As for owners of ships and other vessels which shall thus be taken into the king's service, our lord the king wills it, and they shall receive a payment of 3*s*., 4*d*. for every ton weight of those their vessels, for each quarter in which they remain in the service of our lord the king, beginning their first quarter on the day on which they reach harbour or any other place assigned to them: and so for less or more than a

---

[37] The following paragraph, as far as 'difficulteee aucune' has been added later in the untidy hand to be found at work elsewhere in this manuscript.

quarter, selonc l'afferant. Et durera ceste ordinance tanqe a proschein parlement, pur assaier en le moien temps quiel profit et bien ent purra avenir a l'encrees de mesme la navie, ou en autre manere.

Page iii-87
SEQUITUR BILLA PRO VILLA CALES'.

Caleys.
48. A nostre tresredoute et tresexcellent seignour le roi supplient voz poveres liges burgeys de la ville de Caleys qe come vostre gracious aielle, qi Dieux assoille, par sa chartre, quele vous, tresredoute seignour, avez conferme, lour granta conisance /de\ toutes maneres des causes et quereles, sibien des terres et tenementz come des trespasses, dettes, acomptes et autres contractz queconqes; c'estassavoir, des terres et tenementz selonc la loy d'Engleterre, et des trespasses, dettes, acomptes et touz autres contractz, selonc la loy \et usage/ illoeqes auncienement acustumez: et qe nulle des dites burgeys, ne lours heirs, soit amesne en plee hors de fraunchise de dite ville par voz briefs, n'en nulle autre manere sinoun par voie d'errour, ou qe la cause touche vous mesmes ou voz heirs; come es dites chartre et confirmacioun pluis pleinement appiert.

Qe plese a vostre tresexcellent seignourie granter a voz dites burgeis par vostre graciouse chartre qe si aveigne qe auscun appelle ou pleint vous soit fait en temps avenir des ascuns errours compris en lours juggementz donez selonc lours loys et usages avauntdites, qe bones et sages gentz q'ont conissance des mesmes les lois et usages, purrent estre assignez voz comissairs a trier et justifier mesmes les errours si ascuns y soient en mesmes les parties, par avys et conseil des sages gentz du mesme la paiis qe des tielx loies et usages moeltz en ount conissance, et nul part aillours. Et qe voz liges illoeqes ne soient my chacez de venir par decea la meer \[a]/ chescune suggestioun, pur peril qe poet avenir, sibien a vostre dite ville par lour absence, come as voz ditz liges de lour vies en tieux venuz sibien del aventure de meer come de lour enemys. Eiant auxi regarde, tresdoute seignour, qe voz /ditz\ burgeys jamais devaunt ces heures furent compellez de venir hors /de lours\ dites fraunchises nulle part aillours, pur tielle cause.

Item, prient voz ditz burgeys qe come devaunt ces heures ils avoient un de voz maisons appellez la grande /sale\ en Caleys, pur le stallage de lour bocherie, le quiels ils ont long temps ewe en possession, est ore pris en voz mains par vostre tresorer a vostre /oeps.\

/Qe plese a vostre\ tresexcellent seignourie granter a voz ditz burgeis et lours heirs, un voide place q'est joignant sur mesme la sale vers le south, qe est de nule value ne profit a vous ne a nul autre, pur edifier et ordeiner pur le stallage avauntdit, sanz fee paier pur la chartre ent affaire, pur Dieux, et en oevre de charitee.

Responsio.
Quant a la correccioun et redresce de tieux errours, si nulles soient desore comprises es juggementz a rendre par les ditz mair et jures selonc lours ditz usages et custumes, de dettes, trespasses, acomptes, covenantes, et d'autres contractz et accions personeles quelconqes, escheiantz deinz lour dite ville et la jurisdiccion d'icelle, sinoun qe la chose touche nostre seignour le roi ou ses heirs mesmes, nostre seignour le roi ce lour ad grantez, et lour ottroie q'il ferra assigner par ses commissions de temps en temps quant embusoigne, et il soit sur ce requis, des suffisantz gentz qi mieltz scievent des dites custumes et usages, et de tieux autres come lui plerra, as coustages de partie. Et le roi voet qe les dites suppliantz,

quarter proportionately. And this ordinance shall remain in force until the next parliament, so that in the meantime it can be gauged whether there are any benefits which result in the improvement of the same fleet, or otherwise.

HERE FOLLOWS A BILL FOR THE TOWN OF CALAIS.

Calais.
48. To our most redoubtable lord and most excellent lord the king, your poor lieges the burgesses of the town of Calais request: whereas your most gracious grandfather, whom God absolve, by his charter, which you, most redoubtable lord, have confirmed, granted them cognizance of all kinds of causes and pleas, as well of lands and tenements as of trespasses, debts, accounts and other contracts of various kinds; namely, of lands and tenements according to the law of England, and of trespasses, debts, accounts and other contracts, according to the law and usage customarily practised there of old: and that none of the said burgesses or their heirs shall be called to account outside the franchise of the said town by your writs, or in any other manner unless by way of error, or because the case touches you or your heirs; as appears more fully apparent in the said charter and confirmation.

May it please your most excellent lordship to grant to your said burgesses by your gracious charter that if it should happen that any appeal or complaint be made to you in the future of any errors contained in their judgments made in accordance with the aforesaid laws and usages, that good and wise people who have knowledge of the same laws and usages be appointed as your commissioners to try and determine the same errors, if there be any in the same matters, by the advice and counsel of the wise men of that country who best know such laws and usages, and of nowhere else. And that your lieges there shall no longer be driven to travel overseas on such occasion, for the dangers that may arise for your said town through their absence, and for your said lieges' lives during such journeys, given the risks of the sea as well as the danger of the enemy. Also bearing in mind, most redoubtable lord, that your said burgesses have never in the past been compelled to travel outside their said franchises to any other places for such a reason.

Item, your said burgesses pray: whereas in the past they had one of your houses called the great hall in Calais for the stallage of their butchery, which they have long had in their possession, yet it has now been taken into your hands by your treasurer for your use.

May it please your most excellent lordship the king to grant to your said burgesses and their heirs an empty place which adjoins the same hall towards the south, and which is of no value or benefit to you or any other, to be built upon and appointed for the aforesaid stallage, without fee being paid for the charter to be made for this, for God and by way of charity.

Answer.
As regards the correction and redress of such errors, if any are henceforth to be found in the judgments rendered by the said mayor and juries in accordance with their said usages and customs, concerning debts, trespasses, accounts, covenants and other contracts and personal actions of any kind falling within their said town and the jurisdiction thereof, unless the matter touch our lord the king or his heirs themselves - our lord the king has granted that to them, and agrees to appoint by his commissions from time to time whensoever necessary, and whensoever he may be asked to do so, suitable persons who well know the said customs and usages, and any other such persons as he pleases, at the

ne lours successours, ne soient constreintz desore de venir pardecea pur nul tiel errour, excepte soulement pur errour fait es quereles ou le roi est partie,

[Col. b] et es plees des terres et tenementz. Et quant al second article, ent soit diligeaument enquis par brief de ad quod dampnum: et celle enqueste retourne en la chancellarie d'Engleterre, si trove soit qe ne purra tourner a damage ou prejudice de nostre seignour le roi, ne a disease de nule autre persone, soit mesme la place grantez a eux et a lours successours, a tenir du roi par le service de .vi. s., .viij. d. annuelment, pur edifier covenablement, al oeps avauntdit, sanz damage faire al grant sale du roi illoeqes, ou a aucune singulere persone en mesme la ville en aucun manere. Et soient cestes deux graces, ou grantz, \du roi/ adjoustez a lour chartre, s'ils les veullent demander, sanz fin ent paier.

Encontre les bochers de Londres.
49. A nostre seignour le roi et son bon conseil monstrent ses subgitz les gentz de courte, et les repairantz et inhabitantz les rues de Smethfeld et de Holbourne, coment parmy les grantz et horribles puours et abhominacions morteles qe de jour en autre aviegnent illoeqes, du sank corrupt, et de les entrailles de boefs, barbiz et des porcs, tuez en la bocherie pres de l'esglise de Seint Nicholas dedeinz Neugate, et jettez en diverses fossees dedeinz deux gardyns pres de Holbournbrigge, les ditz gentz de la courte, repairantz et enhabitantz, par l'enfection del eire, les abhominacions et puours susditz, et auxint par plusours malx qe notoirement ensuent, preignent diverses maladies, et sont tropegrevousement mys a disease.
Par quoy prient humblement les ditz subgitz qe tant pur lour eese et quiete, come pur l'onestee de la citee, qe remedie en soit fait par ordeinance penale, qe les ditz bochers tuent lours bestes a Knyghtebrigg, ou aillours qe ne soit a la nusance de mesmes voz subgitz, sicome autrefoitz estoit ordeine en parlement; c'estassavoir, sur peine de forfaire la chare de toutes les bestes tuez en la dite bocherie, et d'avoir la prisone d'un an. Et sur ce prient mesmes voz subgiz, qe briefs ent soient grantez en vostre chancellarie, directz as mairs et aldermans de vostre dite citee, a la pursuite de ceux qi y voudront compleindre, a toutes les foitz qe mestier serra de faire due execucioun de la dite ordeinance.

Responsio.
Il y a ordinance faite sur ceste matire devaunt ceste heure, come pleinement appiert par briefs sur ce faitz, et enroullez en la chancellarie le roi Edward aielle nostre seignour le roi q'ore est, es ans de son regne d'Engleterre trent quint, et quarrant quarte, la quele ordeinance nostre seignour le roi voet qe soit tenue et garde, et mys en due execucioun, et briefs sur ce faitz de novel tantz et tieux come enbusoignera, si nul se vorra ent pleindre.[38]

Conquest de France.
50. Item, est ordenez et assentuz en ce parlement qe l'ordinance qe nadgairs feust fait en parlement tenuz a Westm' en temps le roi Edward aielle nostre seignour le roi q'orest, l'an de son regne .xliij., touchant la conquest des chasteulx, forteresces et autres terres et possessions deslors affaire sur ses enemys en le roialme de France, soit affermez

expense of the party concerned. And the king wills that neither the said supplicants nor their successors shall be forced from now on to journey overseas on account of such error, except only for error made in suits to which the king is a party,
[Col. b] and in pleas of lands and tenements. And as for the second article, let diligent inquiry be made by writ 'ad quod damnum': and the inquest returned to the chancery of England, and if it be found that it would not injure or prejudice the interests of our lord the king, nor harm any other person, let the same place be granted to them and to their successors, to be held of the king by the service of 6s., 8d. annually, for it to be suitably equipped for the aforesaid purpose, without damage done to the king's great hall there, or to any individual in the same town in any way. And those two graces or grants of the king shall be added to their charter, if they so wish, without fine paid.

Against the butchers of London.
49. To our lord the king and his good council, his subjects, the men of the courts, and the frequenters and inhabitants of the streets of Smithfield and Holborn pray: whereas because of the great and horrible stenches and deadly abominations which daily arise there from stale blood and from the entrails of oxen, sheep and pigs slaughtered in the butchery near the church of St Nicholas in Newgate, and thrown into various ditches in two gardens near Holborn bridge, the said people of the courts, frequenting and dwelling there, contract numerous illnesses and fall victim to serious diseases because of the infection of the air and the aforesaid abominations and stenches, and all manner of evils which ensue.

On account of which the said subjects humbly pray, as much for their own ease and tranquillity as for the honourable state of the city, that remedy be supplied in the shape of a penal ordinance, decreeing that the said butchers kill their cattle at Knightsbridge or somewhere else which does not inconvenience your subjects, as was ordained on another occasion in parliament; namely, on pain of forfeiting the meat of all their cattle killed in the said butchery, and being imprisoned for one year. And thereupon, your same subjects pray that writs be granted in your chancery addressed to the mayor and aldermen of your said city, at the suit of those who wish to complain there, instructing them duly to perform the said ordinance as often as needs be.
Answer.
An ordinance was made on this matter in the past, as can plainly be seen from writs issued thereon and enrolled in the chancery of the king Edward [III], grandfather of our lord the present king, in the thirty-fifth [1361] and forty-fourth [1370] years of his reign over England, which ordinance our lord the king wills to be kept and upheld and put into proper practice, and writs issued thereon, such and so many as may be necessary, if anyone wishes to lodge a complaint.

The conquest of France.
50. Item, it is ordained and agreed in this parliament that the ordinance which was formerly made in the parliament held at Westminster in the time of the king Edward [III], grandfather of our lord the present king, in the forty-third year of his reign [1369], touching the conquest of the castles, fortresses and other lands and possessions henceforth from his enemies in the kingdom of France, shall be confirmed and considered

---
[38] PRO SC8/19/927.

et tenuz pur estatut. Et le roi /voet qe sur\ ceste ordinance chescun eit patente en especial s'il le vorroit demander.[39]

a statute. And the king wills that upon that ordinance everyone shall receive an individual letter patent if he wishes to ask for one.

---

[39] PRO SC8/110/5471.

Appendix

16 January 1380

Westminster

1. Reminder to the sheriff of Kent of an ordinance made in the last parliament at the complaint of the commons that captains of retinues shall answer for the behaviour of their men-at-arms and archers while they are waiting at ports or elsewhere for shipping to carry them overseas, especially in respect of goods seized for them or their horses. Dated 1 June 1380.
   Source: *CCR 1377-81*, 385.

2. Order to John Cavendish, king's justice, following a petition in parliament from Thomas, bishop of Exeter, by assent of parliament to proceed to judgment in a plea between the bishop and the king concerning the patronage of Plympton priory (Devon). By petition of parliament. Dated 1 February 1380.
   Source: *CCR 1377-81*, 282.

3. Order to the farmer of the bailiwick of Rye to pay eighteen pounds a year for two years to the barons of Rye, following a petition from them in this parliament for aid towards the rebuilding of their town walls, recently destroyed by enemy action; this sum has been granted to them with the assent of the prelates and lords in parliament. Dated 13 February 1380.
   Source: *CCR 1377-81*, 288 (See also *CPR 1377-81*, 434).

4. Order to the burgesses of Southampton to restore to the masters of a Portuguese ship called 'le Johan Crist' *(sic)* their ship and gear, seized by the former admiral Sir Thomas Percy, and to allow them to leave the port unmolested, with the assent of the council in the last parliament. Dated 10 June 1380.
   Source: *CCR 1377-81*, 317.

5. Grant to the burgesses of Shrewsbury of murage for five years. By petition in parliament. Dated 18 February 1380.
   Source: *CPR 1377-81*, 436.

6. Remission to the scholars of Oxford University, with the assent of parliament, of their share of the subsidy granted to the king in the last parliament by the clergy and province of Canterbury. By petition of parliament. Dated 6 February 1380.
   Source: *CPR 1377-81*, 426.

7. Remission to the burgesses of Southampton of their yearly farm for three years, on condition that it is used to repair the town's fortifications. By bill of parliament. Dated 4 March 1380.
   Source: *CPR 1377-81*, 448.

8. Confirmation to the fishermen of Blakeney (Norfolk) and the surrounding area, following their submission of a petition to this parliament, of their exemption from having their boats seized by the king's commissioners, since this deprives them of their only means of livelihood.. Dated 23 February 1380.
   Source: *CPR 1377-81*, 443.

9. Order to William Latimer and others to investigate the petition submitted to parliament by Hugh de Dacre, knight, concerning the bailiwick of chief forester of Inglewood forest, Cumberland, which has been in the king's hands since the reign of Edward I, but for which Dacre has offered ten pounds annually. Dated 22 March 1380.
   Source: *CPR 1377-81*, 470.

10. Order to the exchequer, following a petition presented in this parliament by the abbot of Tintern, to cease their demands from him for the arrears of clerical tenths recently granted to the king by the province of Canterbury. By petition in parliament. Dated 28 February 1380.
    Source: *CCR 1377-81*, 297.

11. Order to the escheator in Berkshire, following a petition submitted to the last parliament by Elizabeth, widow of Gilbert de Ellesfeld, to restore to her the manor of Drayton (Berkshire), seized into the king's hands as a result of the forfeiture of the lands of Alice Perrers, to whom the manor had been demised for life by Edmund Rose, in accordance with the judgment of the council. Dated 10 May 1380.
    Source: *CCR 1377-81*, 315 (See also *CPR 1377-81*, 468).

1380 November

Northampton

5 November - 6 December

(C 65/36. *RP*, III.88-97. *SR*, II.16)

C 65/36 is a roll of five membranes, each approximately 330mm in width, sewn together in chancery style and numbered in a later hand. The text, written in the official chancery scripts of several scribes, occupies the rectos of the membranes only. The dorses are blank apart from later notes, 'Parl. 4 R. 2 apud Northt' pars prima', or 'Parliamentum 4 R.2 apud North'ton die lune', where the membranes are joined, and a later heading on the dorse of the last membrane (membrane 1) reads 'Parliamentum de anno 4 R. 2^{di}'. The roll is in very good condition. The marginal headings are both contemporary and of a later date. The Arabic numerals are of later date, while the Roman numerals alongside the common petitions are contemporary. The roll appears to be complete.

If for no other reason, the parliament summoned to meet at Northampton in November 1380 will always be remembered for its decision to grant the third poll tax, the attempts to collect which would, six months later, provide the spark for the most celebrated popular uprising in medieval English history, the so-called Peasants' Revolt of June 1381. Had the government kept faith with the commons, all this might have been avoided, for one of the conditions under which they had been persuaded to grant one and a half fifteenths and tenths in the January 1380 parliament was that no parliament should be asked to increase further the burden of taxation for at least another eighteen months.[1] Within less than six months of the dissolution of this parliament, however, the funds required to pay for the earl of Buckingham's expedition - which had crossed to France in July - had effectively run dry, and with Ireland, the Scottish border, the defence of the sea, and the garrisoning of Calais and the other English-held 'barbicans' on the French coast all needing injections of men and money, Richard II and his advisers bowed to the inevitable and, on 26 August, issued writs of summons for an assembly to meet on 5 November.[2]

The lists of those summoned differed significantly from the January parliament: the lords spiritual included the abbots of Battle, Winchcombe and Eynsham, none of whom had been summoned to any of the first four parliaments of the reign, while the lords temporal included Richard Seymour (or Saint Maur) and 'John' Deyncourt (whose name was actually William), both of whose ancestors had previously been summoned.[3] More noteworthy than the new summonses, however, is the fact that seventeen of the lords temporal who had been summoned in January 1380 were now omitted from the list. One or two of these had died, such as Guichard d'Angle, earl of Huntingdon, but the majority of them were omitted because they were abroad on military service, mostly with the earl of Buckingham. Since several others were accompanying John of Gaunt, duke of Lancaster, on his journey north to treat with the Scots, the number of lords temporal that actually gathered at Northampton at the beginning of November was, as the clerk who compiled the roll noted, only a 'very small number'. Also worth noting is the fact that he referred to them as the 'lords temporal' (seigneurs temporeles) - the first time that this phrase had been used to designate the lay peers (Item 2).[4]

Thomas Walsingham, the St Albans chronicler, criticised the choice of Northampton as the venue for the assembly, saying that it was against the wishes of both the citizens of London and most of the magnates, and that there were neither sufficient provisions nor lodgings for such a large gathering. His feelings on the subject may well have been influenced by the fact that St Albans was one of six towns in Hertfordshire and Northamptonshire to receive a writ from the king in late September ordering them to collect provisions to be sent to Northampton ahead of the parliament.[5] Yet the real reason for the choice of Northampton, Walsingham declared, was because some of the king's councillors had determined that John Kirkeby, a London mercer, should be condemned to die for the murder of a Genoese merchant, Janus Imperialis, and they feared the reaction of the Londoners to a sentence of death on him. In fact, Janus Imperialis was not simply a merchant. At the time of his murder, he had been visiting England, under safe-conduct from the king, as the ambassador of the doge of Genoa, and his murder had specifically been declared in the previous parliament of January 1380 to have been an act of treason. It was, then, as Walsingham pointed out, 'not surprising that they had

---

[1] Parliament of January 1380, Introduction.
[2] *CCR 1377-81*, 477-8.
[3] *CP*, IV.123.
[4] Powell and Wallis, *House of Lords*, 387.
[5] *CCR 1377-81*, 406.

Kirkeby drawn and hanged, while the people of London looked on at all that went on', although it cannot have been until the last day or two of the parliament that the sentence was carried out, for it was only on 29 November - following the arrival at Northampton of John of Gaunt, who was believed by some to be the prime mover in the decision to execute him - that an order was sent out to bring Kirkeby before the king and council in parliament.[6]

The early stages of the assembly were, by contrast, given over largely to the financial question. As in January, storms and floods prevented several members from reaching Northampton on the appointed day, so that it was not until Thursday 8 November that the session eventually got under way. The parliament was held in the priory of St Andrew, with the 'new dormitory' assigned to the commons as their meeting-place, a separate chamber set aside for the king's council, and another (unspecified) 'place ordained and furnished for the parliament', perhaps the refectory of the priory. It was presumably in this 'place' that the chancellor, Simon Sudbury, archbishop of Canterbury, delivered the opening speech. He only had one real point to make: the government's financial commitments were overwhelming, while its revenues - partly due to a decline in wool exports, a consequence of the civil war then raging in Flanders - were hopelessly inadequate to the task (Items 1-4). The commons were sent away to ponder this for the night, and told to re-assemble in the dormitory on the following day.

When they next came before the king and lords (the day-by-day chronology of the parliament is unfortunately rather vague), the commons had once again, as in January, chosen as their Speaker Sir John Gildesborough, knight of the shire for Essex and a retainer of the earl of Buckingham. Gildesborough began by asking how much was needed to cover present needs. The king's councillors were clearly prepared for this, and promptly produced a 'schedule' which they had drawn up, the implication of which was that the sum required immediately was one hundred and sixty thousand pounds. This, said Gildesborough, was 'quite outrageous'; how, he asked the lords, did they think that such a sum might be raised? After some consideration, the lords replied that as far as they could see there were three options: a poll tax, a sales tax, or the traditional fifteenths and tenths; they preferred the first option, and suggested a poll tax of 'four or five groats per person' - that is, sixteen or twenty pence per person, a groat being worth four pence (Items 10-13).

It is reasonably clear, then, that it was from the lords rather than the commons that the idea came to levy the third poll tax in four years. On the other hand, it was of course the commons who granted it, although they were at least successful in modifying the government's demands. One hundred thousand pounds, they declared, was the maximum that could be raised, of which they agreed to grant two thirds, on condition that the clergy would grant one third. The clergy, as was to be expected, complained of this constraint on their freedom to grant or refuse taxation, but the government accepted the commons' offer regardless. The laity's two thirds of the money was to be raised by a poll tax of three groats (twelve pence) from each person, male or female, over the age of fifteen, genuine indigents excepted. The elaborate sliding scale for the assessment of the second poll tax, granted in April 1379, was discarded in favour of the more flexible idea that the rich ought to help the poor, although it was said that no individual should pay more than one pound (sixty groats) or less than four pence for himself and his wife. The proceeds of the tax were to be applied solely to the financing of the earl of Buckingham's expedition and the defence of the seas. The wool subsidy was also renewed until Christmas 1381. The final request of the commons was that none of them should be appointed as a collector or controller of the tax which they had just granted (Items 13-16).

Apart from the common petitions, the only other item mentioned on the roll was the investigation into allegations of treason which had been made against Sir Ralph Ferrers. Ferrers was both an important and a controversial character. He had been a member of the first Continual Council, which had been entrusted with the government of the country during the latter half of 1377, but had subsequently earned notoriety as one of the two royal knights who had violated the sanctuary of Westminster abbey during the infamous Hawley-Shakell affair in August 1378 - an incident which culminated in the murder, right by the shrine of Edward the Confessor in the abbey, of the esquire Robert Hawley and a sacristan. Thomas Walsingham, who clearly disliked Ferrers, told the story of the allegations against him in some detail.[7] What happened was that a casket containing five letters of a treasonable nature had been discovered by a beggar near London and handed in to the mayor of the city (the letters themselves are reproduced on the parliamentary roll, Items 17-26). The letters were signed by Ferrers, and apparently sealed with impressions of his seal - a 'fact' which was subsequently verified when Ferrers, who at the time was accompanying John of Gaunt in the north, was asked to produce his seal for comparative purposes. He was arrested, brought into parliament, told that he stood suspected of high treason, and asked what he had to say. Naturally, he denied everything: he had never seen the letters before, and had certainly never committed treason; how, indeed, could anyone with his record of service to the crown even be suspected of treason? Fortunately for him, the lords and royal justices chose to believe him: more detailed comparison of the seals suggested that there were discrepancies, they declared, and what is more all the letters, some of which were addressed to Ferrers and others from him, were written in the same hand and bore the same date. The letters had been forged, they concluded, in an attempt to incriminate him - a not implausible hypothesis, since he was certainly a man with enemies. Ferrers was duly bailed and released, while the beggar, who was now suspected of having been involved in a plot to incriminate him, was imprisoned. What became of him is not recorded.

---

[6]*St Albans Chronicle 1376-1394*, 400; Parliament of January 1380, Item 18; Goodman, *John of Gaunt*, 77; *Vita Ricardi Secundi*, 179; *CCR 1377-81*, 412.
[7]*St Albans Chronicle 1376-1394*, 394-8.

Since Ferrers had been accompanying Gaunt in the north at the time of his arrest, he presumably arrived at Northampton at the same time as the duke, that is, probably during the last week in November.[8] A further item of information which can only have reached the parliament during its last few days was the news of the recent riots at York, for, as was pointed out in the petition from the commons asking the king to intervene there, these riots had only occurred on 26 November, just ten days before the parliament came to an end. The king responded by appointing a commission under the earl of Northumberland to investigate the disturbances, and a number of 'malefactors' were subsequently arrested, though later released on oath (Item 50).[9] Two further petitions which were not enrolled concerned similar recent disturbances at Shrewsbury; these seem to have been submitted by opposing factions.[10].

Of the remaining common petitions, perhaps the most noteworthy are a series of complaints which served to reinforce the commons' concern about the government's financial incompetence: they asked that the commission to review income and expenditure which had been appointed in the previous parliament should now meet (Item 28); that Edward III's debts be paid off (Item 45); that taxes be spent on nothing but the war (Item 30); and that there were too many wars ('pluralitee des guerres'), the costs of which were unsustainable (Item 29). To this last point, Richard replied that he would willingly find a remedy, saving his honour, and to judge by the policies developed by him and his advisers over the next few years, he may well have meant what he said. For the moment, however, there was little that the king could do, and collection of the third poll tax began as soon as the parliament ended on 6 December,[11] in the hope that most of the money could be brought into the exchequer by mid-January. As it turned out, only about two thirds of the expected sum had been raised by mid-March. Evasion, it was clear, had been widespread, and from 16 March onwards commissioners were appointed to re-assess and enforce the tax in a number of counties. It was the actions of these commissioners which provoked the first outbreaks of violent resistance in Essex at the end of May, which within two weeks would have engulfed the south-eastern counties of England in an orgy of murder and destruction. There were, of course, much deeper and more diverse reasons for the Peasants' Revolt than what one chronicler called 'the taxes lightly granted at the parliament of Northampton',[12] but there is no doubt that they provided the spark that ignited the conflagration.

---

[8] Goodman, *John of Gaunt*, 77, 85.
[9] *CPR 1377-81*, 580; *CCR 1377-81*, 421, 486-7.
[10] Appendix, Items 1 and 2.
[11] *CCR 1377-81*, 496-8.
[12] *Anonimalle Chronicle 1333-1381*, 134.

Text and Translation

Page iii-88, Membrane 5

ROTULUS PARLIAMENTI TENTI APUD NORHAMPTON', DIE LUNE PROXIMO POST FESTUM OMNIUM SANCTORUM, ANNO REGNI DOMINI NOSTRI REGIS RICARDI SECUNDI ETC. QUARTO.

Adjournement fait del pronunciacion de parlement.
Le lundy proschein apres la feste de tousseintz, qe fuist le quint jour de Novembre, l'an du regne nostre seignour le roi Richard, qi Dieux salve, quarte, et qe fuist le primer jour de ce present parlement, aucuns des prelatz et seignours de roialme qi furent lors venuz a la ville de Norhampton', avec les grantz officers du dit nostre seignour le roi, s'assemblerent en une chambre ordenez pur le conseil nostre seignour le roy deinz la priorie de Seint Andreu, et illoeqes, /en audience\ de toutz, l'arcevesqe de Canterbirs, adonqes chaunceller d'Engleterre, fist faire lire la grante chartre de libertatibus Anglie. Et apres quant ce fuist fait, et oultre ils y avoient longement attenduz la venue des autres prelatz, seignours et de la commune du roialme, les queux pur les perilouses chemyns qe lors estoient en plusours parties del roialme, parmy le outrageous cretyn de eawe q'estoit sourdez des grantz et continueles pluuyes et tempestes, come conue chose estoit a eulx touz, n'estoient unqores venuz a la ville; et pur tant auxint, et qe les viscontz n'avoient mye adonqes fait retourner les briefs de parlement, et mesme le parlement, par comandement nostre seignour le roy qi adonqes estoit venuz en sa persone a grant peine al manoir de Multon bien pres de Norhampton', estoit adjournez tanqe al joefdy lors proschein ensuant. Et sur ce comandez estoit illoeqes as seignours et prelatz, et cry fait a la commune pardehors en apert, q'ils s'en departirent par tant a lours hostielx pur lour aisir; et qe touz y retournassent le dit joefdy bien matin, pur oier la pronunciation des causes pur quelles nostre dit seignour le roi ad fait somondre cest son parlement.

Pronunciacion de parlement.
2. A quel joefdy, qe fuist le oeptisme jour del dit moys de Novembre, nostre seignour le roi mesmes vint en parlement en place a ce ordenez et aournez deinz mesme la priorie, avec les prelatz, chancellor, tresorier et aucuns des prelatz et seignours temporeles queux y furent venuz. Mais des ditz seignours temporeles y avoit adonqes moelt petite nombre, a cause qe monseignour d'Espaigne, avec grant partie des contes et barons del roialme, estoit devant assignez par nostre dit seignour le roy pur certaines causes d'estre sur la marche d'Escoce, dont ils ne estoient encores departiz: et appellez la einz les justices et sergeantz le roi, et autres del conseil le roi, procuratours des prelatz absentz, chivalers des countees, barons del cynk portz, citezeins des citees et burgeys des burghs, q'avoient la somonce de ce parlement, le chanceller avauntdit, qi avoit les paroles depar le roy et de son comandement, y fist sur l'yntroduction de sa matire q'il y avoit a dire depar le roi une bone collation.
3. Et puis reherceant, coment le roy estoit souvrainement desirant qe les libertees de seinte esglise, et le paix de son roialme estoient entierement gardez et maintenuz en touz pointz, et les trespassours chastiez, descendi a la matire dont il estoit chargez depar le
[Col. b] roy, et dist en especial, Sires, il n'est ne doit my estre chose desconue a vous, coment le nobles sire

| Translation |

THE ROLL OF THE PARLIAMENT HELD AT NORTHAMPTON, ON THE MONDAY NEXT AFTER THE FEAST OF ALL SAINTS, IN THE FOURTH YEAR OF THE REIGN OF OUR LORD THE KING RICHARD THE SECOND.

Adjournment made of the opening of parliament.
On the Monday next after the feast of All Saints, which was 5 November, in the fourth year of the reign of our lord the King Richard [1380], whom God preserve, and the first day of this present parliament, some of the prelates and lords of the realm who had then arrived in the town of Northampton assembled together with the great officers of our said lord the king in a chamber set aside in St Andrew's priory by the council of our lord the king, and there, in the hearing of all, the archbishop of Canterbury, then chancellor of England, caused the great charter of the liberties of England to be read aloud. Afterwards, when that had been done, and when they had waited a long time for the arrival of the other prelates, lords and commons of the realm who had not yet reached the town because of perilous roads in many parts of the kingdom, with the extraordinary floods following heavy and continual rains and storms, as was known to them all, and also because the sheriffs had not yet returned their writs of parliament, the same parliament was adjourned until the following Thursday [8 November] by order of our lord the king, who had with great difficulty reached the manor of Moulton near Northampton. Accordingly, orders were given there to the lords and prelates and a public announcement was made to the commons outside that they should, for this reason, retire to their lodgings to rest; and all should return early in the morning of the said Thursday, to hear the declaration of the reasons for which our said lord the king had summoned this parliament.

The opening of parliament.
2. On the which Thursday, 8 November, our lord the king himself arrived in parliament at the place assigned and furnished for its meeting in the same priory, along with the prelates, chancellor, treasurer, and some of the prelates and lords temporal who had arrived. But the number of lords temporal there was small because our lord of Spain, with a large number of the earls and barons of the realm, had, for particular reasons, been sent by our said lord the king to the march of Scotland, where they still were: and the king's justices and serjeants, and others of the king's council, proctors of absent bishops, knights of the shires, barons of the Cinque Ports, citizens of the cities and burgesses of the boroughs who had been summoned to this parliament having been called in, the aforesaid chancellor, speaking on behalf of and at the command of the king, introduced the matters on which he was to speak on the king's behalf with a fitting address.
3. Thus, rehearsing how the king desired above all else that the liberties of holy church and the peace of his realm should be thoroughly preserved and maintained in every point, and offenders punished, he turned to the matter with which he had been entrusted by the
[Col. b] king, and said in particular, Sirs, it neither is nor ought to be unknown to you that the noble messire, the earl

monseignour le cont de Bukyngham, avec grant nombre des autres grantz seignours, chivalers, esquiers, archiers et autres bones gentz del roialme, queux Dieux salve pur sa mercy, si sont ore en le service de nostre seignour le roi et de son roialme es parties de France; sur quiel viage le roy ad despenduz quanqe vous luy avoistz donez al derrain parlement, et oultre ce grantement del son propre. Et qe pluis est, pur chevance q'il fait, sibien pur celle viage vers Escoce, come pur le defens et socour des liges nostre seignour le roy en Guyenne', et pur les deniers duez al cont de March' pur la terre de Irlande, et en autre manere, il ad mys en gaige la greindre partie de ses grantz joialx, queux sont en point d'estre perduz.

4. Et voirs est qe del subside des leynes, a cause de cest present riot en Flandres, rienz en effect n'est resceuz: et par tant les gaiges des soudeours de la marche de Caleys, Brest, et Chirburgh', sont a deriere pluis qe un quarter et demy; par quoy les chasteulx et forteresces del roi si sont en grant peril, a cause qe les ditz soldeours si sont en point pur defaute a departir. Et bien savez qe le roi nostre seignour, ne nul autre roi Cristien, purroit endurer tielles charges sanz l'aide de sa commune. Et pur ce, aiantz consideracion a ce qe le roi est issint outrageousement endettez, et ses joialx en point d'estre perduz, come dit est; et a ce qe le roi est tenuz par covenant et par endentures faites de faire paiement al cont de Bukyngham et les autres en sa compaignie, pur l'autre demy an q'est ore proscheinement avenir: et auxint de leur refrescher des gentz et chivals, qe amontera a molt grant somme. Et auxint, a ce qe l'en faut mettre outrageouses despenses pur la salve garde des costees de la meer pur les Galeys ceste proscheine seisone, aufin qe les enemys soient mieltz resistez de leur malice et malfait q'ils n'y furent la seisone passee (a quiel temps, sicome vous savez, ils firent grant damage et vilenie en le roialme avauntdit), veuilliez conseiller nostre dit seignour le roi, et faire monstrer a mieltz qe vous purrez, coment et de quoi vous semble qe cestes charges purront estre mieltz et a meindre desaise de vous et de la commune de la terre estre portez, et le roialme mieltz defenduz envers touz les enemys sibien par terre come par meer. Et qe sur ce vous plese de prendre advisement a si brief terme qe vous purrez, a l'entente qe de ce feust fait /bon et effectuel esploit si hastivement come vous\ bonement purrez, en aise del dit nostre seignour, des seignours, et de vous touz. Et le roi voet et comande qe si aucun se sente grevez de chose qe ne purra estre remediez sanz parlement, q'il ent baille sa supplicacion avaunt en parlement as certains clercz de la chancellerie cy dessouz escritz, queux il ad assignez de resceiver mesmes les peticions. Et auxint il ad fait assigner certains prelatz, seignours et autres, pur oier et trier mesmes les supplicacions, dont les nouns y apres s'ensuent:

Page iii-89

5. Resceivours des peticions d'Engleterre, Irlande, Gales et Escoce:

Sire William de Burstall'

Sire Richard de Ravensere

Sire Thomas de Newenham

Sire Johan de Freton'.

6. Resceivours des peticions de Gascoigne, et d'autres terres et paiis depar dela, et des /Isles\:

Meister Wauter Skirlawe

Sire Henry Codyngton'

Sire Piers de Barton'

Sire Johan Boulande,

Sire Thomas de Thelwall'.

---

of Buckingham, together with a large number of other great lords, knights, squires, archers and other good men of the kingdom, whom God preserve in his mercy, are now in the service of our lord the king and his kingdom in the parts of France; on which expedition the king has spent what you granted him at the last parliament, and beyond that much of his own money. What is more, because of debts he has incurred for the expedition to Scotland and the defence and aid of the lieges of our lord the king in Guyenne, the money due to the earl of March for the land of Ireland, and for other things, he has pledged most of his great jewels, and they are now in danger of being lost.

4. And it is indeed true that nothing has actually been received from the subsidy on wool because of the present rising in Flanders: and as a result, the wages of the soldiers of the march of Calais, and of Brest and Cherbourg, are by more than nine months in arrears; wherefore the castles and fortresses of the king are in great danger because the said soldiers are on the point of deserting because of their arrears. Let it be well understood that neither the king our lord nor any other Christian king can endure such burdens without the help of his commons. Therefore, bearing in mind that the king is thus deeply in debt, and his jewels on the point of being lost, as has been said; and that the king is obliged by covenant and indentures to pay the earl of Buckingham and other members of his company for the half-year to come: and also to reinforce them with men and horses, which will amount to a very large sum, and also that vast sums must be invested in the safeguard of the sea coasts against galleys this coming season, so that the enemy's malice and misdeeds can be better resisted than they were last season, when, as you know, they inflicted great harm and villainy on the aforesaid kingdom, that you may advise our said lord the king and show him, as best you can, how and by what means you think these expenses may be best met with the least discomfort to youselves and the commons of the realm, and the kingdom better defended against all its enemies both by land and by sea. And thereupon, let it please you to conclude your counsel in as short a time as you can, so that the matter can be dealt with well and effectively, and as quickly as possible, for the ease of our the said lord, the lords, and of you all. And the king wills and commands that if anyone feels himself aggrieved over anything which cannot be remedied without parliament, that he shall submit his request beforehand in parliament to certain clerks of the chancery listed below whom he has appointed to receive the same petitions. Moreover, he has caused certain prelates, lords and others to be appointed to hear and try the same requests, whose names are as follows:

5. Receivers of petitions from England, Ireland, Wales and Scotland:

Sir William Burstall

Sir Richard Ravenser

Sir Thomas Newenham

Sir John Freton.

6. Receivers of petitions from Gascony and other lands and countries overseas, and from the Channel Islands:

Master Walter Skirlawe

Sir Henry Codington

Sir Piers Barton

Sir John Bowland

Sir Thomas Thelwall.

Et ceux qi vorront bailler lour peticions les baillent avant devaunt lundy proschein venant.

7. Et sont assignez triours des peticions d'Engleterre, Irlande, Gales, et Escoce:

Le roi de Castill' et de Leon, duc de Lancastre,[13]

L'evesque de Londres

L'evesqe de Wyncestre

L'evesqe de Ely

L'evesqe de Nichole

L'abbe de Saint Austyn de Canterbirs

Le cont de Cantebrugg

Le cont d'Arundell'

Le cont de Warr'

Le cont de Northumbr'

Le seignour de la Zouche

Le seignour de Bardolf

Monsire Johan Knyvet

Monsire Johan Cavendissh'

Monsire Robert Bealknapp.

- touz ensemble, ou .vi. des prelatz et seignours avauntditz au meinz; appellez a eux chanceller, tresorer, seneschal et chamberlein et auxint les sergeantz nostre seignour le roi quant il busoignera. Et tendront lour place en la chapele joust la chambre assignee pur le conseil.

8. Et sont assignez triours des peticions de Gascoigne, et d'autres terres et paiis dela la meer, et des Isles:

L'ercevesqe d'Everwyk

L'evesqe de Duresme

L'evesqe de Cardoill'

L'evesqe de Roucestre

L'evesqe de Hereford

L'evesqe de Salesbirs

L'evesqe de Seint Assaph'

L'abbe de Gloucestre

Le cont de Staff'

Le cont de Salesbirs

Le seignour Lestrange de Knokyn

Le seignour de Scales

Monsire Guy de Bryen

Monsire Johan Montagu

Monsire William de Skipwith'

Monsire Robert Tressilian.

- touz ensemble, ou .vi. des prelatz et seignours avauntditz; appellez a eux chanceller, tresorer, seneschal, chamberlein et les sergeantz le roi quant il busoignera. Et tendront lour place en la petite chambre juxte la chambre assignez pur le conseil.

9. Et puis apres le dit chanceller y dist a les communes depar le roi q'ils se departissent a lours hostielx pur lour aiser pur celle jour, et q'ils retournassent lendemain par temps. Et firent lour assemble en la novelle dortour deinz mesme /la\ priorie, assignez pur lour commune assemble: et qe pur Dieux ils lessassent toutes foreines matires dont rancour ou brige purront sourdre, et effectuelment tretassent de ceste lour charge, et d'autres matires necessaires et

And those who wish to submit their petitions should hand them in before Monday next [12 November 1380].

7. The following are assigned to be triers of petitions from England, Ireland, Wales and Scotland:

The king of Castile and Leon, duke of Lancaster

The bishop of London

The bishop of Winchester

The bishop of Ely

The bishop of Lincoln

The abbot of St Augustine's, Canterbury

The earl of Cambridge

The earl of Arundel

The earl of Warwick

The earl of Northumberland

Lord de la Zouche

Lord Bardolf

Sir John Knyvet

Sir John Cavendish

Sir Robert Bealknap.

- to act all together, or at least six of the aforesaid prelates and lords; consulting with the chancellor, treasurer, steward and chamberlain, and also the serjeants of our lord the king when necessary. And they shall hold their sessions in the chapel near the chamber assigned to the council.

8. The following are assigned to be triers of petitions from Gascony and from other lands and countries overseas, and from the Channel Islands:

The archbishop of York

The bishop of Durham

The bishop of Carlisle

The bishop of Rochester

The bishop of Hereford

The bishop of Salisbury

The bishop of St Asaph

The abbot of Gloucester

The earl of Stafford

The earl of Salisbury

Lord Lestrange of Knokyn

Lord Scales

Sir Guy de Brienne

Sir John Montagu

Sir William Skipwith

Sir Robert Tresilian.

- to act all together, or at least six of the aforesaid prelates and lords; consulting with the chancellor, treasurer, steward, chamberlain and the king's serjeants when necessary. And they shall hold their sessions in the small chamber next to the chamber assigned for the council.

9. And afterwards, the said chancellor instructed the said commons on behalf of the king to depart for their lodgings to rest for the day, and return early the next day. And that they were to gather in the new dormitory within the same priory, set aside for their common assembly: and that for love of God they were to avoid all extraneous topics which might provoke rancour or conflict, and deal effectively with this their charge, and other matters necessary and beneficial

---

[13] This entry has been added to this list at a later date but still in a contemporary hand.

profitables au roi et a son roialme avauntdit.[14] Et oultre ce, le dit chanceller illoeqes comandast a touz les prelatz, seignours et communes illoeqes esteantz depar le roi, qe ce parlement feust continuez de jour en autre tanqe les busoignes del roy fuissent esploitez: et defendoit qe nully q'ad somonce de ce parlement se departist tanqe le parlement feust finiz, et ils ent auroient licence a departir.

Demande des communes.

10. Et apres, quant les dites communes avoient entrecommunes et /tretez\ un jour de lour dit charge, ils retournerent en parlement en presence nostre seignour le roy, des prelatz et seignours, et illoeqes monsire Johan Gildesburgh', chivaler, q'avoit les paroles pur la commune, demandast depar la commune illoeqes, d'avoir pluis clere declaracion de leur dites, et par especial de la somme totale quelle l'en leur vorroit ore demander pur les ditz charges supporter; empriantz qe celle somme feust tiellement modifiez, qe pluis n'y feust demandez qe ne covendroit necessairement, et a fyne force. Qar il soivent qe la commune soit ore moelt povre et de feble estat de porter charge aucune pluis oultre; toutes voies nientmeins, le bone esperance q'ils ont ore au bon esploit de la guerre, et d'ent avoir profitable et honurable fin pur nostre seignour le roi et son roialme, parmy l'aide de Dieux, et del bon governement de nostre ost esteant au present es parties de France; et meillour esploit y averont, si Dieux plest, si mesme l'ost soit refreschez par temps de monoye et des gentz. Dont ils priont a Nostre Seignour qe pur sa mercy il hast le terme lour fait, de grant coer et confort de faire ore et granter moelt grantement.

11. Et sur ce une cedule q'estoit fait devant par les grantz officers et le conseil le roi, contenante diverses sommes necessaires en celle partie, a ce q'estoit dit; quelles sommes s'extendoient a cent et sessante mille livres d'esterlings. Et celle cedule leur estoit liveree pur ent adviser et doner lour bone responce a le hast q'ils purroient.

12. Et sur ce mesme la commune retournast autre foitz en parlement, empriant illoeqes a nostre seignour le roi et as seignours du parlement, qe pur ce qe lour semble qe la somme de eulx ore demandez si est moelt outrageouse, et oultrement importable a eux, ... qe leur plerroit faire tielle moderacion de mesme la somme, au fin qe rienz ne y feust demandez forsqe ce qe feust portable a la commune, et necessaire d'avoir ore pur les causes dessus limitez. Et enoultre ils prierent qe les prelatz et seignours par eux mesmes vorroient communer de la matire par eux mesmes, et touchassent les voies par quelles lour semblast qe aucune tielle somme portable purroit a meindre desaise del poeple purroit estre levez et coillez.

13. Et puis apres, quant les prelatz et seignours lour ent furent advisez, et avoient tretez longement de la matire, ils firent la commune venir autre foitz devant eulx, et leur monstrerent lour advis, coment lour sembloit q'ils purroient ore faire. Primerement, lour advis est q'ils grantassent une certaine somme des grotes de chescune persone masle et femmale parmy le roialme, le fort aidant al feable; ou si ce ne lour pleust, adonqes lours advis est, d'avoir pur un terme une certaine imposicion currante parmy le roialme, et aprendre del livree de chescune manere de marchandises achatez et venduz en dit roialme, atantz des foitz q'ils furent venduz par les mains des vendours. Et tiercement lour *[Page iii-90]* [Col. a] advis est, d'avoir une somme par .x.^{mes} et .xv.^{mes}. Mais pur tant qe les dismes et quinszimes si sont moelt grevouses par plusours maneres a la povre commune, et qe

to the king and his aforesaid kingdom. Furthermore, the said chancellor informed all the prelates, lords and commons there present on behalf of the king that this parliament would continue from day to day until the king's business had been concluded: and he forbade anyone summoned to this parliament to leave until the parliament had ended, and they had been given licence to depart.

The request of the commons.

10. And later, when the said commons had consulted amongst themselves for a day and discussed their said charge, they returned to parliament, in the presence of our lord the king, the prelates and lords, and there Sir John Gildesburgh, knight, speaking for the commons, asked on their behalf to have a clearer statement of their business and in particular the total sum which would be asked of them to support the said charges; requesting that the sum be modified in such a way that no more was demanded than was strictly necessary. For they knew that the commons were now too poor and in too weak a state to shoulder any greater burden; although they harboured the earnest hope that the war would be effectively conducted, and brought to a profitable and honourable end for our lord the king and his kingdom, with the aid of God, and through the good management of our armies now at present in the parts of France; and a better outcome would be secured, should it please God, if the same host were to be reinforced soon with money and men. On account of which they pray of Our Lord that in his mercy he shorten the term of their trial, to give greater heart and comfort now, and to grant it ever more generously.

11. Accordingly, a schedule was drawn up by the great officers of the king's council, setting out the various sums needed in this instance, as they claimed; which amounted to £160,000 sterling. And the schedule was delivered to the commons that they might discuss it and give their reply as soon as they could.

12. After which, the commons once more returned to parliament, begging of our lord the king and the lords of parliament, because it seemed to them that the sum now asked of them was quite outrageous, and altogether beyond them, that it would please them so to reduce the said sum that nothing was demanded from the commons except what they were able to bear, and which was necessary for the reasons described above. They further prayed that the prelates and lords would discuss the matter amongst themselves and consider the means by which it seemed to them that a tolerable sum could be levied and collected from the people with the least distress.

13. And later, when the prelates and lords had consulted with each other and had discussed the matter at length, they called the commons to appear before them once more, and informed them of their decision as to how it seemed to them they might now proceed. Their first suggestion was that the commons should grant a certain sum in groats from every male and female person throughout the kingdom, the strong helping the weak; or if that did not please them, then their advice was to levy, on a single occasion, a certain tax applicable throughout the kingdom, and to take a certain amount on the pound for every kind of merchandise bought and sold in the said kingdom, as often as they were sold by the vendors. And thirdly, their *[Page iii-90]* [Col. a] advice was to levy a sum from tenths and fifteenths. But because the tenths and fifteenths are greatly burdensome to the poor commons in various ways, and because such

---

[14] A change of hand occurs at this point.

tielles imposicions ne aient este encores assaiez, issint qe chescun ne poet savoir a quele somme extendroit, et qe long terme serroit qe aucune notable somme ent feust levez; si semble as seignours qe si l'en vorront granter quatre ou cynk grotes de chescune persone, /ce serroit une bone et notable somme,\ par quelle le roi purroit bien estre aidez, et chescune persone del roialme le purroit bien supporter, parissint qe les fortz feussent constreintz d'aider les feobles. Et issint semble as seignours qe celle manere levee des grotes serroit le meillour, et le pluis aisee, come dit est.

Item, quant les communes s'avoient autre foitz avisez, et longement tretez de le manere del dit levee, ils vindrent en parlement, faisantz lour protestacion q'ils ne vindrent illoeqes quant a cel jour pur rienz grantir; mais ils pensoient bien a ce q'ils disoient qe si la clergie vousist supporter le tierce denier de la charge, ils vorroient granter .c. mille*li*. a lever une certaine quantitee des grotes de chescune singulere persone masle et femmele parmy le roialme, issint qe les /lays\ feussent mys a .c. mille marz, et le clergie qe occupie la tierce partie del roialme feust mys a cynquante mille marz: empriantz a nostre seignour le roi et as seignours temporelx, q'ils vousissent prier le clergie q'ils vousissent hastier le terme de lour conseil et assemble, \et/ emprendre sur eux la dite charge de .l. mille marz a cest foitz. A quoy feust reppliez par le clergie qe lour grant ne feust unqes fait en parlement, ne ne doit estre, ne les laies gentz devroient ne ne purroient constreindre le clergie, ne ne poet ne doit en celle partie constreindre les layes gentz; mais leur semble qe si aucun deust estre frank ce serroit pluis tost la clergie qe les lays gentz.

14. Empriant a nostre seignour le roi qe la libertee de seinte esglise leur feust salvez entierement, come ent ad este devant ceste heure; et qe la commune feust chargez de faire ce q'ils doivent faire de lour part, qar pur certain auxint voet le clergie de lour part si avant come ils \le/ doivent et sont tenuz del faire, aiant consideracion de ce present grant necessitee, et come ils ont fait devaunt ceste heure. Et sur ce au drain, quant le commune leur avoient longement advisez sur ceste matire en presence des seignours temporelx, si vindrent en parlement en presence de nostre seignour le roy, et illoeqes firent leur grant a nostre dit seignour le roy, et le baillerent avaunt en escrit /en une cedule, en la fourme\ q'ensuit:

Le grant del subside.
La declaracion a nostre seignour le roi et a son conseil par la commune d'Engleterre des matires dont les communes si sont chargez en ce present parlement, pur diverses necessitees queux lour sont monstrez sibien pur salvacion du roialme come pur \le/ salve-garde de meer.

Membrane 4
15. En primes, les seignours et communes si sont assentuz qe y serra donez pur les necessitees suisdites, /de\ chescune laie persone du roialme deinz franchise et dehors, sibien des madles come des females, de quiel estat ou condicion . . . . q'ils soient, qi sont passez l'age de .xv. ans, trois grotes, forspris les verrois mendinantz qi ne serront de riens chargez. Sauvant toutesfoitz qe la levee se face en ordeinance et en forme, qe chescune laye persone soit chargez owelment selonc son afferant, et en manere q'ensuyt: c'estassavoir, qe a la somme totale acomptez en chescune ville les suffisantz selonc lour afferant eident les meindres; issint qe les pluis suffisantz ne paient oultre la somme de .lx. grotes pur lui et pur sa femme, et nule persone meins q'un grot pur lui et pur sa femme: et qe nule persone soit chargez de paier

taxes have not yet been assessed to know what sum they will raise, and that it would be a long time before they produced any notable amount, it seems to the lords that if they would grant four or five groats from each person, then that would amount to a good and substantial sum, which would considerably help the king, and every person in the kingdom would be well able to sustain it, provided that the strong were compelled to aid the weak. And so it seems to the lords that this kind of levy of groats would be the best and the easiest course, as they said.

And when the commons had again discussed it, and considered the said levy at length, they came to parliament, protesting that they had come on this occasion to make a grant; but that they had thought carefully about what they were now saying - that if the clergy were to support a third part of the charge, they would grant £100,000 to be levied from a certain number of groats drawn from every individual male and female throughout the kingdom; so that the laity would be liable for 100,000 marks, and the clergy who occupy a third of the kingdom would be liable for 50,000 marks: requesting of our lord the king and the lords temporal that they would ask the clergy to bring forward the term of their council and assembly, and impose on them the said charge of 50,000 marks at this time. To which the clergy replied that they never made their grant within parliament, nor ought they to do so, and neither ought the laity to be able to constrain the clergy, and neither should the laity be constrained in this way; but it seemed to them that if any one ought to be free, it should be rather the clergy that the laity.

14. Praying of our lord the king that the entire liberty of holy church be preserved, as it has been in the past; and that the commons be charged to do what they ought to do, for the clergy also wish for their part to do what they ought and are obliged to do, as they have in the past, bearing in mind the present great necessity. Whereupon, when the commons had at last discussed the matter at length in the presence of the lords temporal, they appeared in parliament before our lord the king, and there made their grant to our said lord the king, and submitted it to him in a written schedule in the form which follows:

The grant of the subsidy.
The declaration to our lord the king and his council by the commons of England on matters with which the commons have been charged in this present parliament, regarding the various necessities which have been explained to them both for the security of the kingdom and for keeping the sea.

15. First, the lords and commons are agreed that there shall be given, to meet the aforesaid needs, three groats from every lay person whether within or without franchises, from males as well as females, of whatsoever status or condition they be, who are over fifteen years of age, except for genuine beggars who will be charged nothing. Provided at all times that the levy shall be made by such means and in such a way that each lay person will be charged in accordance with his means, and in the following manner: namely, that for the total sum assessed on every place, those of adequate means shall help those of lesser means as far as they are able; provided that he who is most affluent shall pay no more than 60 groats for himself and his wife, and none shall pay less than one groat for himself and his wife: and that none shall be charged to pay

[Col. b] forsqe par la ou la demoere de lui et de fa femme et ses enfantz en sont, ou en lieu ou il demoert en service. Et qe touz artificers, laborers, servantz et autres laies, sibien des servantz demurrantz ove prelatz et seignours temporelx qeconqes, abbees, priours collegieles, clercz de la chancellerie et en le commune bank, bank le roi, escheqier, receite et ove touz autres officers, chivalers, esquiers, marchantz, citeins, burgeis et ove toutes autres persones, qe chescun de eux soit assis et taillez selonc l'afferant de son estat, et en la fourme suisdite. Et qe commissions soient faites as suffisantz persones, sibien es countees come es citees et burghes, d'estre collectours et countrollours de la somme avantdite: et q'ils soient serementez de faire bien et loialment lours offices. Et n'est pas l'entencion de la dite commune de faire ce presente grant sinoun tant soulement pur la sustenance de counte de Bukyngham, et les autres seignours et gentz esteantz en sa compaignie es parties de Bretaigne, et pur la defense du roialme, et salve-garde de mier. Et qe ceste presente grant ne soit mis ne pris en forme, n'ensample, de nule levee des grotes avant ces heures, mais soulement chargiez de les persones q'ore sont en vie; /issint qe les deux parties du dit paiement se facent a la quinszeine Seint Hiller proschein avenir, et la tierce partie al\ feste de Penticost adonqes proschein ensuant: issint toutes voies qe nul des chivalers, citeins, et burgeis venuz a ce present parlement, ne soit fait collectour ne controllour de les sommes avauntdites. Et qe plese a nostre seignour le roi et son conseil d'ordeigner pur la dite levee, sibien des meynalx en l'oustel nostre seignour le roi come des autres seignours parmy le roialme, q'ils purront estre owelment chargez, selonc le purport de ceste grant.

Et prient les communes qe durante la guerre justice d'eire ne trailbastoun courge entre mesmes les povres communes, mais qe les justices de la pees tiegnent lour cours selonc le tenure de lour commissioun.

[15]Et grantent les communes a nostre seignour le roi le subside des leynes, a durer tanqe al feste de Seint Martyn proschein avenir.

16. Et fait a remembrer qe cest grant des subsides avauntdites si estoit fait le .vime jour de Decembre l'an present. Et apres mesme le jour, quant la dite cedule estoit lue en parlement, le dit monsire Johan de Gildesburgh, de l'assent de toute la commune avauntdite, dist a nostre seignour le roi en parlement avantdit qe les seignours et communes de son roialme, pur les causes dessus touchez, granterent a mesme nostre seignour le roi le dit subside des leynes, quirs et peaux lanutz, a avoir del feste de Seint Martyn adonqes proschein venant - a quele feste le dit subside par la fourme de mesme le grant devroit cesser et faillir - tanqe a feste de la Nativitee Nostre Seignour proschein ensuant, par la fourme et manere en touz pointz come ce fust darreinement grante a nostre seignour le roi avantdit, a son parlement tenuz a Westm' le lundy proschein apres la feste de Seint Hiller, l'an de son regne tierz.

/Proces fait en cest parlement encontre monsire Rauf de Ferriers.\
17. Fait a remembrer qe monsire Rauf de Ferriers, chivaler, lui quiel par suspicioun /de treson a luy surmise, de ce\ q'il serroit /aherdant\ as Frauncois enemys du roi nostre seignour, et de lours \conseil/ et covyne, estoit arestez el marche d'Escoce par monsire de Lancastre et les autres seignours temporelx lors esteantz el dite marche, sur la

[Col. b] elsewhere than in the place where he, his wife, and his children dwell, or where he lives in service. And that all artificers, labourers, servants and other laymen, both servants dwelling with prelates and lords temporal whatsoever, abbots, collegiate priors, clerks of the chancery and of the common and king's bench, of the exchequer, of the office of receipt, and those living with all other officers, knights, squires, merchants, citizens, burgesses, and all other persons, shall each of them be assessed and taxed according to the amount of their estate, in the form described above. And that commissions shall be directed to suitable persons, in the counties as well as in the cities and boroughs, appointing them collectors and controllers of the aforesaid sum: and that they shall be sworn to perform their duties loyally and well. It is not the intention of the said commons to make this present grant for anything other than the support of the earl of Buckingham and the other lords and men in his company in the parts of Brittany, and for the defence of the realm, and for keeping the sea. And they do not intend that this present grant should be taken in the manner or form in which any previous levy of groats was taken, but that it should be charged only on persons who are now living; so that two-thirds of the said payment should be made on the quindene of the feast of St Hilary next [28 January 1381], and the remaining third by Whitsun following [2 June 1381]: and the knights, citizens, and burgesses who have come to this present parliament are by no means to be made collectors or controllers of the aforesaid sums. And may it please our lord the king and his council to ordain for the said levy, as regards servants in the household of our lord the king as well as other lords throughout the kingdom, that they shall be equally charged, according to the intention of this grant.
And the commons pray that for the duration of the war neither judgment of eyre nor of trailbaston should be imposed upon the poor commons, but that the justices of peace should continue their activities according to the terms of their commission.
And the commons grant to our lord the king the subsidy on wool, to last until Martinmas next [11 November 1381].

16. And be it remembered that this grant of the aforesaid subsidies was made on 6 December in the present year [1380]. And after that day, when the said schedule had been read in parliament, the said Sir John Gildesburgh, with the assent of all the aforesaid commons, informed our lord the king in the aforesaid parliament that the lords and commons of his kingdom, for the reasons touched on above, granted to our same lord the king the said subsidy on wool, hides and woolfells, to be received from the said next Martinmas [11 November 1381] - on which feast the said subsidy ought to have come to an end and cease according to the terms of the same charter - until the feast of Christmas next following [25 December 1381], in the manner and form in which it had been last granted to our lord the aforesaid king at his parliament held at Westminster on the Monday next after the feast of St Hilary in the third year of his reign [16 January 1380].

The process made in this parliament against Sir Ralph Ferrers.
17. Be it remembered that Sir Ralph Ferrers, knight, who on suspicion of treason alleged of him, namely his adhering to the French enemies of the king our lord, and advising and plotting with them, was arrested in the march of Scotland by messire of Lancaster and the other lords temporal then present in the said march for the treaty with the Scots,

---
[15] A change of hand occurs at this point.

traitee avec les Escotz, et amesnez souz le dit arest par commandement des ditz seignours, a respondre en ce parlement, de ce qe l'en luy vorroit surmettre, et par especial de certaines lettres qe furent novellement trovez es champs pres de Londres, et portez al mair illoeqes; lui quiel mair les ad depuis envoiez au roi nostre seignour et a son conseil, et /quelles furent monstrez en cest parlement:\ dont aucunes sont directz *[Page iii-91]*

[Col. a] as certains persones en le roialme de France, enemys a nostre dit seignour, souz le ...... seal des armes le dit monsire Rauf, et aucunes directes al dit monsire Rauf, /depar \ .... les ditz enemys, /a ce qe semble,\ ..... contenantes matires appertement sonantz, /qe le dit monsire Rauf serroit aherdant as ditz enemys\\ et de lour covine, come dessus est dit,/ come par mesmes les lettres purra pluis au plain apparoir. Des quielles les tenours s'ensuent de mot a mot:

A mon treshonure seignour B. de la River.
18. Honures et reverence, treshonure seignour, je ay bien entendu vostre lettre, come vous me sachetz gree pur le novelles qe je vous envoia par mon derren lettres, et qe mes lettres furont le primers de autres. Et ce ma plest, treshonure seignour, plese a remembrer come vous et mes autres seignours me donatz pleine poair par voz lettres a treter de l'alliance entre vous et les Escotz, et a grant payne je fitz l'acorde parentre vous autres, grant argent meins qe vous me mandatz a oferer. Et ore me semble qe ils ont fait bone comencement come le portor de cestes vous dirra par bouche. Treshonure seignour, vous pris entierment qe vostre jour de proschein payement soit tenuz, ou autrement le ore q'est paie est perdu, et si serra je en grant disese, si ne est le tresgracious eide de vous et mes autres seignours. Treshonure seignour, vous face assavoir qe le count de Bukyngham et autres seignours erunt en Bretaigne a trois mille hommes d'armes et trois mille archiers, ensi le dieux chastelx qe vous bien savez sont prestz si je sui garne resonablement devant le jour qe vous savez. Et ensi je ay envoye un lettre a le cont, et a Clysson', par les enfantz de Bloys. Treshonure seignour, vous face assavoir qe le[16] canoun est ale de messages, et pur ce soit avise et tenez bone credence a le portour de cestes, kar il vous dirra pluis pleinement par bouche. A Dieu, me treshonure seignour, qe sa garde de vous, et encres vostres honures.

Done le .xx. jour de May.
Le vostre R. de F.

A moun treshonurez et tresreverentz seignour le cont de Longeville, ou a seignour de Clysson'.
Honures et reverence, mes treshonures seignours, je ay bien entendu vostre lettres endroit de les deux fitz de Bloys. Plese assavoir, je ay fait vostre maundement a grant paine a deliverer. Je sui destourbe pur cause de la mort R. nepurquant je sui seor de lour deliverance si vous me avoys de oer en le manere come le portour de cestes vous dirra par bouche. Mes treshonurez seignours, tenez credence a lui, kar il dirra pluis pleinement de ce, et de autres novelles qe je poit escrier. Mes treshonurez seignours, soiez avisez kar il est grant mister. A Dieu, mes treshonurez seignours, qe se garde de vous, et encres voz honures.
Done le .xx. jour de May.
Le vostre R. de F.

and was brought under the said arrest by order of the said lords to answer in this parliament for that which would be alleged against him, and especially with regard to certain letters which had recently been found in a field near London and were carried to the mayor there; which mayor then sent them to the king our lord and his council, and they were displayed in this parliament: of which some were addressed *[Page iii-91]*

[Col. a] to certain persons in the kingdom of France, enemies of our said lord, under the seal of arms of the said Sir Ralph, and some addressed to the said Sir Ralph by the said enemies, as it seemed, containing material clearly implying that the said Sir Ralph supported the said enemies and their plots, as is said above, and as more fully appears in the same letters. The tenor of which is as follows:

To my most honoured lord B. de la Riviere.
18. Honours and reverence, most honoured lord, I gladly received your letter in which you thanked me for the news I sent you in my last letters and for the fact that my letters were the first of others. And it would please me, most honoured lord, if you were to remember how you and my other lords gave me full authority by your letters to arrange the alliance between you and the Scots, and with great difficulty I arranged the agreement between you for a good deal less silver than you permitted me to offer. And now it seems to me that they have made a good beginning, as the bearer of this will tell you. Most honoured lord, I pray of you earnestly that you keep to your next day of payment, or otherwise the gold which has been paid will be lost, and so I shall be in great trouble unless I receive the most gracious aid of you and my other lords. Most honoured lord, may you know that the earl of Buckingham and other lords will enter Brittany with three thousand men-at-arms and three thousand archers, and so the two castles which you well know will be ready if I have reasonable notice before the agreed day. And so I have sent a letter to the count and to Clisson, via the children of the count of Blois. Most honoured lord, may you know that the canon has left with messages, and therefore you would be well advised to lend credence to the bearer of these, since he will explain matters more fully to you by word of mouth. My most honoured lord, may God protect you and increase your honours.
Given on 20 May.
Yours, Ralph Ferrers.

To my most honoured and most reverend lord the count of Longueville, or to the lord of Clisson.
Honours and reverence, my most honoured lords, I have well understood your letters about the two sons of Blois. May it please you to know that I have caused your mandate to be delivered at great cost. I am disturbed by the death of R., nevertheless I am confident of their delivery if you lend an ear to the matters of which the bearer will speak to you. My most honoured lords, lend him credence, since he will speak of this, and of other news more fully than I am able to write. My most honoured lords, follow this advice since it is most necessary. My most honoured lords, may God protect you and increase your honours.
Given on 20 May.
Yours, Ralph Ferrers.

---

[16] *Original* lu

A treshonure seignour C. de B.

Treshonure seignour, et bien ame, vous prie cherement, si vous plese, envoier cestes lettres, et le messanger qi porte a vostre seignour et le min, le plus tost qe vous purrez bonement, /fetez\ lui avoir un bon gide a lui mesner surement, qar cestes lettres ont este depar dela trois foitz, et le messanger n'ose passer pluis avaunt, come il vous dirra la cause. Endroit de noz gentz qe sont passez, il ne estoint pas tiele somme come je ay autre foit escrit; en le vant-garde sont .vij.c. gentz de armes, et .vij.c. archiers; en le mi-garde mille gentz d'armes et mille archiers; en le rere-garde atant come devant. Hugh' de Calvelle et Robert Conellus sont deus illus pur le mi-garde. Enoutre plese assavoir qe l'Escotz \ont/ bien comence a tenir lour covenant qe ils ont fait avec vous. Et pur ce priez nostre seignour qe le primer jour de lour paiement soit bien tenuz, ou autrement le or qe est paie soit perduz, et toute vostre covenant failiz; et si serra-je en grant poure, et en grant desese, si il ne est le gracious eide de vostre seignour et le min. Endroit de les chastelx de D . . et burghe la roine, mon conseil est, caunt le amerail ad tout fet soun journe, lesse lui tourner arere a enstable

[Col. b] les deux chastelx, et cel serra vostre recoverir a mon avis. Endroit de la ville de Thomas, il n'est pas fort a tenir, autrement fetez vostre profit, et je vous trovera deux chastelx qe serront bone bastes. Pur la ville de Londres, treshonurez seignour, plese a certifier vostre seignour, come Bernard et Robert et Simond sont ale de message; et le canoun et Johan Firando ne sont pas venuz, mes ordinez pur eux, par il ne est /nul meistre\ pur vous. Treshonure seignour, vous \pri/ cherement qe vous soiez mon attorne a resceivre mon anute qi est a derer, et me enbont par le portour de cestes a prendre vostre part come ad fet devant ses heures: ensi vous prie me excusez devers mon seignour de longe demurrance de la lettre, qar messager fuit devers l'Escotz, et il vous emportera bones novelles de set parti. Ensi je fu bien enforme qe autres ont envoie devers vous, et caunt mon clerc est venuz devers vous a kere, mille francus ordenez pur lui, come le portour de cestes vous dirra par bouche, et tenez credence a lui pur ce il vous dirra plus pleinement qe je escrire[17] et me tenez pur /excuse,\ qar je ne autre clerc si ne est frere W. pur ce me ordenez un autre tiel qe nous pussum afier, et qe set escrire[18] Pur serten je ai pour qe vous n'entendez pas set lettre le frer escrit si malement, et si vous ne savit mie lire, mostrit a le portour de setus, et il vous lira bien. A Dieu, mon treshonure seignour, qe soit garde de vous, et encresse vostre honures.

Done le tierce jour d'Aust.
R. de F.

A mon treshonure et tresreverent seignour le Amerayll'.
19. Treshonure et tresreverent seignour, plese assavoir qe le portour de cestes vous ad seriche touz les costes de le mire de Cornewaille d'Ex' a Winchulce, et il ad este pres de vous, et il ne ose vous prochir pur vostre gentz; et pur ce je ay envoie devers vous frere W. a demurrer de equus le hile dox vostre venuz a vous certifier toutes les novelles par desa. Et endroit de la navee, le pluis grant partie ne poet escapir si vous veulliez. Ensi je ay bien entenduz vostre lettre come vous \est/ bien ordene de bones gides a vous mesner l'entre de Thamisse. De ce je vous conseil qe cest purpos soit tarie

---
[17] Original crire,
[18] Original crire.

To the most honoured lord C. de B.

Most honoured lord and well beloved friend, I earnestly pray of you, if you please, to send these letters and the messenger who bears them to your lord and mine, as soon as you well can, providing him with a good guide to lead him there safely, since these letters have been overseas three times, and the messenger dares not travel again, the reason for which he will tell you. As for our people who have crossed, they do not number as many as I previously estimated; in the vanguard there are 700 men-at-arms and 700 archers; in the main body a thousand men-at-arms and a thousand archers; in the rearguard, as many as at the front. Hugh Calverley and Robert Knolles are two of those in the middle guard. Furthermore, may it please you to know that the Scots have already begun to honour the covenant they made with you. And therefore ask of our lord that the first day of their payment be honoured, or otherwise the gold which has been paid will be lost, and your covenant completely broken; and so I shall fall into great poverty and trouble, if no gracious aid is forthcoming from your lord and mine. With regard to the castles of D . . and Queenborough, my advice is that whenever the admiral has completely finished his journey, let him turn back to weaken

[Col. b] the two castles, and they will be yours to retrieve in my opinion. As regard to Canterbury, it is not strong enough for holding, and you shall gain your advantage elsewhere when I find you two castles which are well built. For the town of London, most honoured lord, may it please you to inform your lord that Bernard, Robert and Simon have gone with messages; and the canon and John Firando have not arrived, but give orders for them, for it is not important for you. Most honoured lord, I pray earnestly of you that you be my attorney to receive my annuity which is in arrears, and that you vouch me by the bearer of these to take your share as has been done in the past: and I pray that you excuse me before my lord for the long delay in this letter, since the messenger was towards Scotland, and he will bring you good news from these parts. Thus I am well informed that others have sent to you, and when my clerk has reached you to collect the thousand francs ordained for him, as the bearer of these will tell you by word of mouth, and believe him because he will explain matters to you more fully than I dare write, and excuse me, since I have used another clerk who is not brother W. because you ordained for me another such person whom we could strongly trust and who would write this. Yet I truly fear that you will not understand this letter of the friar which has been written so badly, and if you are unable to read it, show it to the bearer of this, and he will duly read it to you. My most honoured lord, may God protect you and increase your honours.
Given on 3 August.
Ralph Ferrers.

To my most honoured and most revered Lord Admiral.
19. Most honoured and most revered lord, may it please you to know that the bearer of these sought you along all the Channel coast from Exeter to Winchelsea, and he had been near you, yet he dared not approach you on account of your people; and because of this I have sent to you brother W. to wait at Horsehill(?) until your arrival to inform you of all the news on this side of the sea. And as for the fleet, the greater part of it will not be able to escape if you so desire. Also, I fully understand from your letter that you have been well provided with good guides to lead you to the mouth of

auxi pres le jour de Seint Michel come vous purrez bonement; qar le pluis grant partie de noz gentz serront hors du paiis devers vous, et devers l'Escotz, donqes je sceai bien qe les orglous vileins de Londres veullent ordeiner une armee encountre vous la. Si vous serrez bien avisez vous averez bele journe, et feris bone larder, si Dieu plest. Outre, si vous plese, je ay envoie le capitain de Boloine toutes mes lettres et le credence avec ce, a certifier mon seignour et vous de toutes les novelles par desa. Endroit de mestre qe je sceai faire, le enchantment avoit li a Brigus, et je envoiera pur lui, et il demurra avec moy; et s'il sceit faire bien le busoigne je lui monstra touz les rolles a bone leiser; et s'il est bon mestre il ferra bon journee a brief temps. Treshonure seignour, vous prie parlez a mon treshonure seignour, si lour plese me ordenez un clerc qe poet escire[19] lettre parentre nous; qar mon clerc fust en purpos a moi descoverir de nostre conseil, la ou je fu bien lez a faire soun gree, et li ay done grauntz douns, et je luy ai promis grant argent plus qe je ne pense a doner, pur a tenir conseil de nostre fet; et je sui en grant disese avec lui, pur ce je ai \lui/ envoie qe il vendra devers vous a Boloine a kere mille frankes, et je lui ai promis le dit mille pur aler a courte de Rome. De ce je vous prie cherement, quant il est venuz devers vous, ordenez pur lui qe nous serrons seure de lui pur toutz jours, en tiel manere qe nostre conseille ne soit pas descovere. Ceste chose tenez a coer, come je m'affie grantement en vous. Et, treshonure seignour, si plesir vous soit, me excusez devers mon seignour qe mes lettres sont si malement escrit, je ne ay point autre clerc se il ne est frere W. qe vous come bien, et si le portour de cestes vendra devers vous tenez credence a lui, et si non le capta noun ...... tut son credence. A Dieu, *[Page iii-92]*

[Col. a] mon treshonure seignour, qe soit garde de vous, et encresse[20] vostre honures.
Done le tierce jour d'Aust.
R. de F.

A mon treshonure mestre R. de F.
20. Treshonure seignour et mestre, plese assavoir qe je ai este dedeynus[21] le ille ou vous me envoiastz, et je trove la un vessel de Bretaigne, le quiel me ad amesne droit a Areflut, et la je trova le chamberlein et l'ameral et tout le prive conseil de roi, et le captan de Bolloyn; et le captan me fist delivere mes lettres a le conseille, et puis je su amesne deinz un prive chambre devant le chamberlein et l'ameral, et le captan de . Boloyn, et un clerc sanz pluis, et la je counta mon credence, et le clerc metta tout en escrit. En le moien temps venoit une lettre hors de Flandres a le captan /de\ Boloyn, come vostre messager fut malade a Brugus, et qe il dusse avoir un certein homme a quere les dites lettres. Et puis ils pristront lour conseil, et pur peril qe peut avenir ils ont ordeinez qe je alasse deveir Brugus, et un clerc avec moy pur acrire son credence, et le merci Dieu nostre credence fust tout un. Et puis il bailla vostre messager .c. franks, et mandast vostre messager qe il dusse aler a l'oustel arere quant il fuist garri, et q'il dusse arder la lettre de monsire Bertram pur ce q'il fuist mort; et les autres trois lettres pur ce qe les autres lettres furont de mesme fourme, et il ne voet pas arder pur chose qe nous purrons fere. Il dit puis les autres noun volont pas reserver il vous enportera arere, et quant je veie sel je ai asele les deux lettres arere avec moun seal. Endroit \de/ les Escots, avons une lettre a eux de credence [22] qe il vous porta, et surement

---
[19] *Original* crire
[20] *Original* en
[21] *Original* de eynus
[22] A change of hand occurs at this point.

the Thames. With regard to this I suggest that the plan be delayed until as close to Michaelmas [29 September] as possible; since most of our people will be out of the country in your parts and in Scotland, since I know well that the proud villains of London wish to mount an army against you there. If you are well advised you will have a successful journey and obtain great booty, if it please God. Furthermore, if it please you, I have sent the captain of Boulogne all my letters and the credence with this, to notify my lord and you of all the news on this side of the sea. As for the master whom I informed, he has been detained by infirmity at Bruges, and I shall send for him and he shall remain with me; and if he knows well how to carry out the business I will show him all the rolls at leisure; and if he knows his business he will make a good journey in a short while. Most honoured lord, I ask you to request of my most honoured lord that it may please him to ordain for me a clerk who can write a letter between us, since my clerk intended to disclose our counsel, even though I thanked him well and gave him great gifts, and promised him much silver, more than I thought I could give, to keep our deeds secret; and I have been greatly perturbed by him, and have told him to come to you at Boulogne to collect a thousand francs, and I promised him the said thousand to go to the court of Rome. And so I earnestly pray you, when he reaches you, to deal with him so that we shall be sure of him forever, in such a way that our counsel shall not be discovered. Keep this matter close to your heart since I trust greatly in you. And, most honoured lord, if you please, excuse me to my lord for that my letters are so badly written, since I have another clerk who is not brother W. whom you well know, and so lend credence to the bearer of these coming to you, unless you do not trust him. *[Page iii-92]*
[Col. a] My most honoured lord, may God protect you, and increase your honours.
Given on 3 August.
Ralph Ferrers.

To my most honoured lord Master Ralph Ferrers.
20. Most honoured lord and master, may it please you to know that I have been upon the isle to which you sent me, and I found there a vessel from Brittany which took me straight to Harfleur, and there I found the chamberlain and the admiral and all the king's privy council, and the captain of Boulogne; and the captain caused me to deliver my letters to the council, and then I was led into a private chamber before the chamberlain and the admiral and the captain of Boulogne and one clerk and no more, and there I delivered my message, and the clerk put it all in writing. In the meantime a letter came from Flanders for the captain of Boulogne, saying that your messenger was ill in Bruges, and that he needed someone to collect the said letters. And then they discussed the matter, and on account of the peril which might arise they appointed me to go to Bruges, and a clerk with me to vouch for me, and by God's mercy we were believed. And then he gave your messenger a hundred francs and instructed him to go to the lodgings later when he had recovered, and burn Sir Bertram's letter because he was dead, and the other three letters because the rest were of the same nature, and he does not wish to burn them as we can use them. He then said that he did not wish to keep the others but would send them back to you, and when I realised that I sealed the two letters shut with my seal. As for the Scots, we have a

il serra tenuz. Et endroit \de/ les deux fitz de Bloys a gardez, qe vous serrez seur de lour deliverance, et je enportera lour finance avec moy a mon venu, et vostre anute avec, si come il ont me promis. Et endroit de vostre clerc lesse lui venir, il ont bien ordenez pur lui, ensi me covient demurrir avec eux pur aporter certeins novelle de toutes choses, pur ce qe le roi est bien malade ensi le seignours sont en poy de sensum, pur ce qe noz gentz font si grant male et nul voile faire remede. En le meen temps je voille assaier si je puisse gayner vostre paiement. Endroit de vostre messager, ne corse vous point avec lui, qar par moun foi il ad este bien malade, et tenez bone credence a lui ce qe vouz dirra par bouche. A Dieu, mon treshonure mestre, qe soit garde de vous, et encresse voz honures.

Escrit a Brugus, le jour de Seint Croys.

Par le vostre servant frere W.

Treshonure seignour, purce qe je ay entenduz qe voz busoignes serront persez a cause'

A mon treshonure seignour, veulliez savoir qe je vous euse escriptz devant ces heures autres novelle; mes pur ce qe je ne m'affia bien en mon clerc, etc., mais jeo me tiegne bien contenz qe mes lettres sont les primers. A Dieu, etc.

Par R. de F.

Membrane 3

21. Et le dit monsire Rauf amesnez en ce parlement souz la garde du mareschale d'Engleterre, et illoeqes aresonez depar le roi de les dites lettres, et de la matire y comprise, priast au roi et as seignours, d'avoir conseille en le cas. A quoi lui feust dit qe en toutes choses en quelles conseil lui deust par la loy de la terre estre grantez, le roy nostre seignour luy vorroit bien ottroier conseil, et autrement nemye. Et feust dit oultre a dit monsire Rauf qe pur tant qe ceste matire sonast si hautement en treisoun, qe par la loy il n'y doit avoir conseil en ce cas de nulle terriene persone forsqe de Dieux et de lui mesmes;............ comande feust a lui qe il \y/ feist sa responce a son peril. Et adonqes monsire Rauf avauntdit y dist qe par ensample evident, et experience de fait, toutes gentz par resoun lui deussent tenir et

[*Col. b*] ent avoir pur innocent oultrement. Et reherceant, coment il avoit este longement \come/ de sa juvente travaillez en diverses guerres le roi, en presence des plusours nobles seignours du roiaume, dont aucuns sont mortz, \et/ aucuns en pleine vie, et coment il fuist auxint capitain de Caleys et d'autres forteresces depar dela, ou il poaist avoir resceuz moelt grant tresor s'il vousist ent avoir trahi son /seignour\ lige, qe Dieux defende, et /nel fist\ unqes, Dieux mercis. Einz notoire chose est qe apres ce qe autres capitains des chastelx et forteresces nostre dit seignour avoient renduz lours chastelx et fortz en pontif as adversairs de France pur doute de lour manace, il tint longement \apres/ son fort, et nel rendist mye as Franceys pur manace, ne pur assaut, ne pur siege fait entour lui; combien q'il avoit plusours lettres du noble roi Edward aiel nostre seignour le roi q'orest, qi Dieux assoille, del avoir fait rendre as Franceys avauntdites. issint par bone experience doit apparoir a toutes gentz, qe si je deusse avoir este desloial a monseignour lige, qe Dieux ne veullie, je l'eusse avoir fait pur lors, quant je purroie avoir resceuz pluis de profit qe maintenant ne purroie, come vrai semblable chose est a tout homme resonable. A quoy feust reppliez depar le roy, et dit au dit monsire Rauf qe par cas l'en y feist dissimulacioun pur un temps, et ce encores par moelt grant seu del adversaire de France et de son conseil. Qar chescun homme doit savoir par fine reson, qe pluis profiteroit et plerroit al dit adversaire et a son conseil d'avoir une tielle persone come vous estes, de lour covyne et assent en le conseil de nostre seignour le roi d'Engleterre, pur lour

letter of credence from them which he will bring to you, and he will be kept safe. And as for the two sons of Blois to be guarded, that you may be sure of their delivery, and I shall bear their money with me on my arrival, together with your annuity, as they promised me. And as for your clerk, let him come, he has been well provided for, and also it suits me to stay with them to bring certain news of everything, since the king is truly ill and thus the lords are besides themselves, because our people carry out such great evils and no one wishes to provide a remedy. In the meantime, I will try and obtain your payment if I can. As for your messenger, do not be hard on him, since by my faith he truly has been ill, and believe what he tells you. My most honoured lord, may God protect you and increase your honours.

Written at Bruges, on the day of Holy Cross [14 September].

By your servant, brother W.

Most honoured lord, because I have heard that your business will be urgent.

To my most honoured lord, please know that I have written to you already with other news, because I do not wholly trust in my clerk, etc., but I am well content that my letters are the first. To God, etc.

By Ralph Ferrers.

21. And the said Sir Ralph, having been conducted to this parliament under the guard of the marshal of England, and there questioned on behalf of the king concerning the said letters, and the matter contained in them, prayed of the king and the lords that he might seek advice in this case. To which he was told that in all matters on which counsel ought to be granted him by the law of the land, the king our lord would wholeheartedly grant him counsel, but not in other matters. And the said Sir Ralph was also told that because this matter smacked so strongly of treason, by law he was not entitled to counsel in this case from any earthly person but only from God and from himself; he was ordered to make his answer there, at his peril. And then the aforesaid Sir Ralph said there that by clear example, and from his past record, everyone ought with good reason to believe and

[*Col. b*] consider him altogether innocent in the matter. And he described how for a long time, ever since his youth, he had laboured in various of the king's wars, in the presence of many noble lords of the realm, of whom some are dead, and some alive, and how he had also been captain of Calais and other fortresses overseas, where he could have received plentiful treasure if he had wished to use it to betray his lord liege, which God forbid, and yet he still did not do this, God be thanked. Yet it was well known that after other captains of the castles and fortresses of our said lord the king had surrendered their castles and forts straight away to the French adversaries through fear of their threats, he long retained his fort, and certainly did not surrender it to the French because of threats, or assault, or siege carried out against him; and he had many letters from the noble king Edward grandfather of our lord the present king, whom God absolve, to surrender it to the aforesaid French. And so by worthy conduct it ought to be apparent to everyone that if I had meant to be disloyal to my lord liege, which God forbid, I would have done it then, when I might have received more advantage than I am able to receive now, as a matter convincing to all reasonable men. To which reply was given on behalf of the king, and the said Sir Ralph was told that perhaps he had pretended for a time, and was now on the side of the enemy of France and in his counsel. For every man should know through pure reason that it would be more beneficial and pleasing to the said adversary and his council to have a person such as yourself of their mind and opinion in the council of our lord the king

conforter et acerter de privitees, purpos et affaires en nostre conseil, qe d'avoir la ville de Caleys, ou autre forteresce du roi nostre seignour a lour volentee. Et par tant y feust dit al dit monsire Rauf qe il ent feist sa responce final as dites lettres a son peril; c'estassavoir, qe il deist expressement si les dites lettres furent les soens lettres ou nemye; preignant garde a ce q'il ent avoit dit devaunt sur le primer arest a lui fait par la dite cause. A quiel temps il avoit dit, quant les lettres furent a lui monstrez qe celles mesmes lettres sembloient par lours sealx estre les soenes lettres, seales de son seal de ses armes.

22. A quoi le dit monsire Rauf respondist \ore,/ et dit expressement qe \il ne se remembroit mye q'il avoit conuz unqes qe celles lettres furent les soens; et/ si nul homme en especial vorroit susmettre a lui, qe celles lettres furent faites par lui ou de sa science par voie quelconqe, il se vorroit defendre par son corps come chivaler doit faire. A quoy autre foitz feust reppliez depar le roi qe a ce ne vendroit il mye, qar y ne feust nul homme qe en fait rienz a lui surmist en celle partie, mesqe soulement la contenue des dites lettres, sealez souz son noun et le seal de ses armes, a ce qe sembloit, purportoit grant traisoun fait par lui: et par especial q'il serroit adherdant as enemys du roy nostre seignour et de son roialme avauntdit; et partant autre foitz estoit comandez a lui de doner sa responce a son peril. A quoy le dit monsire Rauf finalment respondist, et dist qe les dites lettres ne furent unqes faites ne sealees de sa science ou volentee, ne unqes en prive n'en appert a ce feust il assentant, par lui ne par autre, ne unqes vist il les dites lettres, n'aucune d'icelles, tanqe celles a lui furent monstrez \en la dite marche/ depar les /ditz seignours:\ et ceo est il prest de prover par qeconqe resonable voie qe la ley de la terre vorra adjugger.

23. Et /celle\ responce /donee,\ le dit monsire Rauf fuist commandez de retourner a la prisone, aufin qe en le mesne temps homme s'avisast de la matire. Et sur ceo sibien un seignour Thomas, parsone de l'esglise de Brington' en countee de Northt', et certeins autres familiers le dit monsire Rauf, et un certein poevere homme mendivant, qi primerement trovast les ditz lettres, \queux furent/ prys et emprisonez a Loundres pur la dit cause, *[Page iii-93]*

[Col. a] come John de Haddeleye, lors mair de Loundres, a qi les ditz lettres primerement par le dit mendivant feurent bailliez, furent par celle cause faitz venir en parlement; et illoeqes examinez diligeaument et singulerement de la matire, et de les circumstances d'icelles par les justices nostre seignour le roy et autres sagez a ceo assignez, et chargez sur peril de lour armes d'examiner la verite de la matire, et \les dites lettres,/ le prente des sealx bien regardez, et advisez avec certeins autres verroies lettres del propre seal le dit monsire Rauf ensealeez, sembloit as ditz justices par moultz des resons qe celles lettres issint trovez, et les sealx d'icelles, si furent fauxement contrefaites par aucunes malveis gentz, pur destruire le dit monsire Rauf. Et /lour\ reson et cause fuist tielle, c'estassavoir, purtant qe par le dit examination apparust qe toutes les dites lettres quelles furent trovez toutz closes et ensealees et nemye freintes, dont aucunes furont directes au dit monsire Rauf depar les ditz seignours depar dela, et aucunes directes as ditz seignours depar dela /par le\ dit monsire Rauf, portantes toutes bien pres une mesme date, et escrites come ce feust d'une main; si furent trovez toutes ensemble en une boiste par le dit mendivant, paront apparust qe celles lettres furent forgiez et contrefaites, come dit est.

24. Et par une autre grant cause sembloit auxint qe celles lettres furent contrefaites; \qar/ le seal des dites lettres si fuist auxint contrefait, qar le seal de mesmes les lettres si est

of England, to support them and inform them of the private matters, plans and affairs of our council, than to have the town of Calais, or another fortress of our lord the king in their hands. And therefore the said Sir Ralph was told that he should make his final reply to the said letters at his peril; namely, that he ought to state expressly whether the said letters were his or not; taking care to consider what he had previously said on his first arrest for the said matter. On which occasion he had said, when the letters had been shown to him, that these letters appeared from their seals to be his letters, sealed with the seal of his arms.

22. To which the said Sir Ralph now replied and expressly stated that he could not indeed recall that he had ever recognized these letters as his; and if anyone in particular wished to allege that these letters had been issued by him or with his knowledge by any means whatsoever, he would defend himself bodily as a knight ought to do. Once again, reply was given on behalf of the king that it would certainly not come to that, since no one had accused him of anything in the matter, except that the content of the said letters, sealed under his name and the seal of his arms, or so it appeared, implied that he had committed high treason: and in particular that he adhered to the enemies of the king our lord and his aforesaid kingdom; and because of this he was ordered once more to make answer at his peril. To which the said Sir Ralph finally replied and said that the said letters had never been written or sealed with his knowledge or consent, and that neither private nor public consent had been given to them by him or by another, and neither had he ever seen the said letters, not a single one of them, until they had been shown to him in the said march by the said lords: and he was ready to prove this by any means judged reasonable by the law of the land.

23. This reply having been made, the said Sir Ralph was ordered to return to prison, so that in the meantime the matter could be discussed. Thereupon one Sir Thomas, parson of the church of Brington in the county of Northampton, and certain other familiars of the said Sir Ralph, and a certain poor beggar man, who had been the first to discover the said letters, and who had been seized and imprisoned at London for the said reason, *[Page iii-93]*

[Col. a] as well as John Hadley, then mayor of London, to whom these letters had first been submitted by the said beggar, were summoned to parliament for that reason; and the matter and its circumstances having been closely and diligently examined there by the justices of our lord the king and other wise men assigned thereto, who had been charged on peril of their souls to investigate the truth of the matter and of the said letters, and the imprint of the seals having been closely scrutinized and compared with certain other genuine letters sealed with the personal seal of the said Ralph, it seemed to the said justices for many reasons that these letters thus found, and the seals on the same, had been fraudulently counterfeited by certain evil people in order to ruin the said Sir Ralph. And their reason and justification were such, namely that as a result of the said examination it appeared that all the said letters which had been found were tightly closed and sealed and not broken, some of them having been sent to the said Sir Ralph by the lords overseas, and some sent to the said lords overseas by the said Ralph, and bearing very nearly the same date, and seeming to be written in one hand; and so they had been found all together in a box by the said beggar, from which it appeared that these letters had been forged and counterfeited, as has been said.

24. Moreover, it seemed for another particular reason that these letters had been forged; since the seal of the said letters was also counterfeit, in as far as it was larger in size, and the

pluis large in quantitee, et le prente d'icelle moelt grantement et appertement variant au dit verroi seal. Par quoy, et par autres causes resonables, semblast as seignours du parlement qe le dit monsire Rauf estoit innocent de ce qe a lui estoit issint surmis illoeqes; et partant, et auxint a la requeste des seignours en ce parlement, le dit monsire Rauf estoit deliverez as contes de

[Col. b] Warr', Staff', Salesbirs et Northumberland, et a Reynald de Grey de Ruthyn, et /al\ priour de Saint Johan Jerusalem en Engleterre .... : les queux contes et seignours en dit parlement deviendrent plegges a nostre seignour le roi pur le dit monsire Rauf, c'estassavoir corps pur corps, de lui avoir devaunt le roi et son conseil, ou, et quant, et si sovent, come plerra a nostre dit seignour le roi d'assigner, parentre cy et le proschein parlement a tenir en Engleterre, sur resonablement garnissement ent as ditz mainparnours affaire depar le roi, pur y faire et resceivre en ce cas ce qe la loy demande, en cas qe nostre dit seignour, ou nulle autre persone vorra pluis avaunt ent parler vers le dit monsire Rauf.

25. Et issint estoit le dit monsire Rauf lessez/aler\\a//large,\ et les dites lettres, avec le verroi seal le dit monsire Rauf q'estoit d'argent, illoeqes furent baillez en parlement a monsire Johan de Cavendissh', chief justice le roy, come en garde, si par cas aucun homme vorroit ent dire pluis avant al dit monsire Rauf: et puis furent ycelles lettres et seal liverez en banc le roi, etc.

26. Et sur ce le dit mendivant, pur suspicioun qe /l'en\ avoit de lui q'il feust assentant a ceste fauxetee, et aucunement conissant d'icelle, estoit comandez a la prisone. Mais le dit parsone de Brington, et autres servantz le dit monsire Rauf, qi furent prises et emprisonez par la dite cause, apres ce q'ils furent examinez en ce parlement de la matire avantdite, et rienz trovez par le dit examinement /en\ eulx de mal en celle partie, si furent deliverez par meinprise /d'esteer\ a lour responce a quelle heure qe ils furent demandez par celle cause.

Membrane 2

A NOSTRE TRES REDOUTE ET TRESGRACIOUS SEIGNOUR NOSTRE SEIGNOUR LE ROI, ET A SON SAGE CONSEIL, SUPPLIENT VOZ POVRES LIGES COMMUNES DE VOSTRE ROIALME D'ENGLETERRE PUR LES ARTICLES Q'ENSUENT:

I. [Charters and Statutes.]
27. Adeprimes, qe la grande chartre, la chartre de la foreste, et les estatutz queux sont ordeignez pur la pees, et les estatutz des laborers et artificers, et des purveours, et l'estatut des fauxes acusours, et touz les autres estatutz et bones loies, faitz sibien en temps nostre seignour le roi q'orest, come en temps de ses nobles progenitours, soient bien tenuz et gardez en touz pointz, et duement executz.
Responsio.
Il plest au roy.

II. [Commission on revenues.]
28. Item, prie la dite commune qe la commission enseale a derrain parlement a leur request as certaines seignours et autres de la terre, pur ent surveoir les despenses del hostiel nostre seignour le roi, et les revenues de la terre coment ils furent despenduz, qe celles commissioun soit mys en due execucion au present, a comencer la serche du dit commission a les oetaves Seint Hiller proschein, pur honur et profit nostre seignour le \roi/ et de son roialme. Et qe les ditz commissioners puissent avoir dues gages de nostre seignour le roi pur lour despenses, pur le temps q'ils serront occupiez sur les busoignes avauntditz. Et qe les seignours, et autres

imprint varied greatly and obviously from the said true seal. On account of which, and on other reasonable grounds, it seemed to the lords of parliament that the said Sir Ralph was innocent of that which had been alleged against him there; and for this reason, and also at the request of the lords in this parliament, the said Sir Ralph was delivered to the earls of

[Col. b] Warwick, Stafford, Salisbury and Northumberland, and to Reginald Grey of Ruthin, and to the prior of St John of Jerusalem in England: which earls and lords in the said parliament became pledges of our lord the king on behalf of the said Ralph, namely body for body, to summon him before the king and his council wheresoever and when and as often as it pleased our said lord the king to decide, between now and the next parliament to be held in England, on reasonable notice of this being given by our lord the king to the said mainpernors, to act and receive there in this matter as the law demanded, in case our said lord the king or any other person wishes beforehand to speak about the said Sir Ralph.

25. And so the said Sir Ralph was set free, and the said letters, with the true seal of the said Sir Ralph which was made of silver, were delivered in parliament to Sir John Cavendish, chief justice of the king, for safe-keeping, in case anyone wished from now on to speak about the said Sir Ralph: and then the letters and seal were delivered to the King's Bench, etc.

26. And thereupon the said beggar was sent to prison upon the suspicion that he had been implicated in this fraud, or had otherwise known of it. But the said parson of Brington and the other servants of the said Ralph who had been seized and imprisoned for the said reason, after they had been questioned in parliament upon the aforesaid matter and nothing had been found during the said interrogation to implicate them in this matter, were released on bail to be available to give their answer in this matter whenever they were asked.

TO OUR MOST FEARED AND MOST GRACIOUS LORD, OUR LORD THE KING AND HIS WISE COUNCIL, YOUR POOR LIEGE COMMONS OF YOUR KINGDOM OF ENGLAND PRAY FOR THE ARTICLES WHICH FOLLOW:

I. [Charters and Statutes.]
27. First, that the Great Charter, the Charter of the Forest, and the statutes which are ordained for the peace, and the statutes of labourers, artificers and purveyors, and the statute on false accusers, and all the other statutes and good laws made in the time of our lord the present king, as well as in the time of his noble progenitors, shall be fully kept and upheld in all points, and duly executed.
Answer.
It pleases the king.

II. [Commission on revenues.]
28. Item, the said commons pray that the commission sealed at the last parliament following their request, and given to certain lords and others of the land, to survey the expenses of the household of our lord the king and assess how the revenues of the land were being spent, shall now be put duly into effect, to begin the review from the octave of St Hilary next [21 January 1381], for the honour and benefit of our lord the king and his kingdom. And that the said commissioners shall receive the wages due from our lord the king for their expenses during the period in which they shall be occupied with the aforesaid business. And that the lords and other

nomez en la dite commission, a ore esteantz en ce present parlement, soient *[Col. b]* chargez d'estre sur la dite serche a les oetaves suisditz.

Responsio.

Il plest au roy.

III. [Burden of wars.]

29. Item, prie la dite commune: qe come ils se sentent de jour en autre outrageousement estre grevez par pluralitee des guerres, as coustages importables, qe plese a nostre seignour le roy et son sage conseil ordeiner ent remede; qar tieux chargez outre porter la commune ne purra en nul manere sustenir.

Responsio.

Le roi le fra volenters, ses honeur et estat toutdiz salvez.

IIII. [Appropriation of subsidy.]

30. Item, prie la dite commune: qe la taillage grante a nostre seignour le roy ore en ce present parlement soit despenduz en defense du roialme, et nul part ailleurs: c'estassavoir, en refresement le counte de Bukyngham et les autres seignours et gentz esteantz en sa compaignie es parties de Bretaigne; auxibien en deniers et gentz d'armes et archiers come sur la sauve-garde du mier, en manere come il estoit declarrez par les seignours as communes en parlement. Et prient les ditz communes qe les covenantz *[Page iii-94]* *[Col. a]* taillez parentre nostre seignour le roy et le dit conte lui soient perfourniz, selonc le tenure des endentures entre eux ent faites.

Responsio.

Il plest au roi qe ce soit despenduz a mieltz qe faire se purra, en salvation et defens del roialme, par l'advis des grantz de son roialme et de son conseil.[23]

V. [Cheshire, Durham, the Cinque Ports.]

31. Item, prie la dite commune: come ils ont priez devant ces heures qe le countee de Cestre, l'eveschie de Duresme, les cynk portz, et touz autres semblables dedeinz le roialme, qi ne sont pas comprises deinz les communes taxes, puissent entre eux mesmes estre chargez selonc lour avoir, en aide pur la defense de eux et de nous, come reson demande.

Responsio.

Quant as cynk portz, il plest au roi. Et quant a la countee de Cestre et l'eveschee de Duresme, le roi en ferra ce q'il purra; sauvant lour franchise.

VI. [Halfpennies and farthings.]

32. Item, prie la dite commune: qe la ou ils soloient avoir mayl de paier pur une maylee de payn ou de cervoise, et ferthyng de paier selonc l'afferant, tiele monoye leur defaute par toute Engleterre, a grant damage de eux.

Qe plese ordeiner qe mayl et ferthyng soient ore faitz et usez communement a desparpler entre les communes, a grant relevacion de mesmes les communes. Et q'il soit de mesmes la alaye et poys come y soleit estre avant ces heures, et qe de chescune livre soient faitz .iij. s. .iiij. d. en mayl et ferthing.

Responsio.

Le ferra qe certaine quantite serra faite des mailles et ferthynges, en aise du poeple, par l'advis de son conseil.

---

[23] See also PRO SC8/19/928.

named in the said commission, being present in parliament, shall be *[Col. b]* charged to undertake the said investigation on the aforesaid octave.

Answer.

It pleases the king.

III. [Burden of wars.]

29. Item, the said commons pray: whereas they feel greatly aggrieved from one day to the next by the multitude of wars resulting in unsustainable costs, that it may please our lord the king and his wise council to ordain remedy for this; since the commons are unable to sustain further such burdens.

Answer.

The king will willingly do so, saving always his honour and estate.

IIII. [Appropriation of subsidy.]

30. Item, the said commons pray: that the tallage now granted to our lord the king in this present parliament shall be spent on the defence of the realm, and on nothing else: that is to say, to send reinforcements to the earl of Buckingham and the other lords and men in his company in the parts of Brittany; as well for money for men-at-arms and archers as for the safeguard of the sea, in the manner announced by the lords to the commons in parliament. And the said commons pray that the covenants *[Page iii-94]* *[Col. a]* drawn up between our lord the king and the said earl shall be performed in accordance with the tenor of the indentures made between them.

Answer.

It is pleasing to the king that it shall be spent in the best way possible for the security and defence of the kingdom, by the advice of the great men of his kingdom and his council.

V. [Cheshire, Durham, the Cinque Ports.]

31. Item, the said commons pray, as they have prayed before this time: that Cheshire, the bishopric of Durham, the Cinque Ports, and other similar places within the kingdom which are not liable for the common taxes, may be charged amongst themselves according to their means, to assist the defence both of them and of us, as reason demands.

Answer.

With regard to the Cinque Ports, it pleases the king. And with regard to Cheshire and the bishopric of Durham, the king will do what he can; saving their franchise.

VI. [Halfpennies and farthings.]

32. Item, the said commons pray: whereas they have been accustomed to pay a halfpenny for a halfpenny-worth of bread or beer, and a farthing for a proportionately smaller amount, yet such coinage has become rare throughout the whole of England, to their great loss.

May it please you to ordain that the halfpenny and farthing shall now be issued and generally distributed amongst the commons, to the great relief of the same commons. And that they shall be of the same alloy and weight as they were in the past, and that of each pound shall be made 3*s*. 4*d*. in halfpennies and farthings.

Answer.

He will ensure that a certain number of halfpennies and farthings are issued, for the benefit of the people, by the advice of his council.

VII. [Forfeiture of ships.]

33. Item, the commons pray: whereas much trouble and harm has resulted for our said lord the king and his kingdom for want of a fleet, which has been a problem and remains so at this point in time, in as far as no lord, citizen, burgess, or other member of the community of the realm has the will to maintain the present fleet, nor dares to equip it or build it anew, for the problems which ensue: namely, that if someone has caused a ship to be built at his own expense of £500, more or less, and his said vessel arrives or anchors within any English port, or anywhere else within the kingdom, if any man on the same vessel foolishly falls overboard, so that he dies by misfortune, the said ship is forfeited, to the great injury of the parties who built the ship, and ruin of the same, and destruction of the kingdom.

In view of which the said commons pray that it may be ordained that henceforth no ship, barge, boat or other vessel within the said realm shall be forfeited for such a reason, to the relief of the said fleet.

Answer.

The king will consider further how this has reasonably been dealt with in the past in matters pertaining to him; and if anyone complains of another person claiming the right to such a forfeiture in particular, let him sue at common law, and right shall be done him.

VIII. [Ships from Normandy.]

34. Item, the commons pray: whereas they are greatly injured by barges and balingers from Normandy, and other enemies on the sea, through a lack of adequate keeping of the same.

May it please our said lord the king to ordain that an effective guard shall be placed on the sea, both in northern as well as southern parts, for the security of the same in time to come.

Answer.

The king, by the advice of the great men of his kingdom, will provide for this as best he can.

IX. [Writs of oyer and terminer.]

35. Item, the commons show: whereas the people are and have often in the past been greatly harmed and injured because of writs of oyer et terminer, which are too commonly granted at the suit of a party for petty trespass.

Because of this, may it please our said lord the king to [Col. b] uphold the statute made thereon in the past, and ordain that plaintiffs in such a case shall prove on their oath, and the oath of three men of good repute, that their allegation is true on all counts, before any writ of oyer et terminer is granted.

Answer.

The statutes made thereon in the past suffice, and the king wills that they be kept and upheld.

X. [Writs of outlawry.]

36. Item, the commons pray: whereas many people bear the same name or surname, and by suits brought against others similarly named they are placed in great danger of their lives and loss of their lands and goods, because of a sentence of outlawry passed against another.

May it please our lord the king to ordain by statute in this present parliament that no writ, indictment nor accusation for which outlawry could be pronounced shall be issued henceforth unless the town or the place where the accused

soit adjoustez al noun del defendant. Et si autrement soit fait, et addicion ne soit mis al noun del defendant, qe les ditz brief, enditement et acusement, et utlagaries sur ycelles pronunciez, soient voides et tenuz pur nul.

Responsio.
La commune loie, avec l'estatut ent fait, sont assetz suffisantz.

XI. [Escheators' inquests.]
37. Item, monstre la commune: qe sovent foitz avient, qe par favorables enquestes procurez et prisez par eschetours, voz gentz sont sovent foitz fauxement disheritez, et sodeynement oustez de lours terres et tenementz donez par patente du roy, paront ils sont delaiez de lour droit, aucuns par mestrie, aucuns par protection, aucuns par eide priere, et aucuns par autres sotiles delaies, a grant meschief et empoverissement de eux.

Par quoy ils vous supplient, come sovent en diverses parlementz ont suppliez q'en cest cas nule patente ne soit fait ne grante a nully tanqe le droit soit discus entre vous et les tenantz: et q'en le mesne temps ils puissent tenir lours terres et tenementz en pees, trovantz suffisante seuretee de respondre a vous des issues si vostre droit soit trove; et si aucunes patentes en tiel cas desormes soient faitz, soient tenuz pur nulles; et qe chescun eschetour face plein retourne deinz un moys apres tieles enquestes prises, sur peyne de .xl.*li.* a paiers a nostre seignour le roy l'un moitee, et l'autre moitee au partie qi le vorra suir devers tiel eschetour.

Responsio.
Les estatutz ent faitz devant ces heures suffisent, les queux le roi voet qe soient gardez.

XII. [Sheriffs of Essex and Hertford.]
38. Item, monstrent voz communes des countees d'Essex et Hertf': qe come les viscontz des ditz countees avant ces heures ont paiez ou roi annuelment certeine ferme a grande summe, quele a ore ne poet estre levee par .cxl.*li.* et pluis, par cause des diverses pestilences, et auxi par cause qe .viij. hundredes et demi en les ditz countees sont es maynes du roy et autres seignours, deinz queux hundredes le viscont, ne nul de ses ministres n'entre, ne rien ne medle; et auxint par cause qe la mier q'enviroune grande partie del countee d'Essex suronde plusours terres, a grant damage et perde des toutz les costeantz, issint chescun an un homme destruyt q'ad la charge du dit office.

Sur qoy plese a nostre dit seignour le roy de sa grace ordeigner de ce remede.

Responsio.
Le roi voet qe apres le fin des ans par queux il lour fist derrain pardon de .c. marz par an, ils aient autiele remission et pardoun de .c. marz par an durantz autres trois ans tantsoulement.

XIII. [Yarmouth and Kirkley Roads.]
39. Item, supplient les communes de Suff' et Norff' et touz autres countees d'Engleterre: qe come avant ces heures estoit ordenez par estatut qe chescun lige du roialme purra achatre et vendre sanz empeschement en citee, burghe, port du mier, et aillours par tout le roialme; et si chartres ou patentes fuissent grantez a *[Page iii-95]*
[Col. a] contraire soient tenuz pur nul; quel estatut feust conferme au derrain parlement tenuz a Gloucestre: et nient-contreestant le dit estatut, une chartre en mesme le parlement feust grante as gentz de Jernemuth' qe nul homme

is resident is added beside the name of the defendant. And if that be not done, and the addition is not made alongside the name of the defendant, that the said writ, indictment, accusations and outlawry pronounced on the same shall be invalid and held at naught.

Answer.
The common law, together with the statute made thereon, are effective enough.

XI. [Escheators' inquests.]
37. Item, the commons show: whereas it often happens that by biased inquests procured and held by escheators, your people are frequently and fraudulently disinherited, and suddenly ousted from their lands and tenements granted by letters patent of the king, whereby they are delayed in obtaining their due, sometimes by cunning, sometimes by protection and sometimes by prayer in aid, and sometimes by other crafty delays, to their great injury and impoverishment.

Accordingly, they request of you, as they have often requested in various parliaments, that in such cause no letters patent shall be issued or granted to anyone until the right in the matter has been discussed between you and the tenants: and that in the meantime they may hold their lands and tenements in peace, giving sufficient surety to answer to you for the issues if right be found to be on your side; and if any letters patent shall henceforth be granted in such causes, they shall be held at naught; and that each escheator shall make a full return within a month of such inquests having been held, on pain of paying £40, half to our lord the king, and the other half to the party who wishes to sue such an escheator.

Answer.
The statutes made thereon in the past suffice, and the king wills that they shall be kept.

XII. [Sheriffs of Essex and Hertford.]
38. Item, your commons of the counties of Essex and Hertford show: whereas the sheriffs of the said counties in the past have paid the king annually a certain farm amounting to a great sum, which can no longer be levied, falling short by £140 or more, because of various pestilences, and also because eight and a half hundreds in the said counties are in the hands of the king and other lords, into which hundreds neither the sheriff nor any of his ministers may enter nor meddle in anything; and also because the sea which encircles a large part of Essex floods much land, to the great injury and loss of all inhabitants of the coast, so that each year the man who has charge of the same office is ruined.

May it please our said lord the king of his grace to ordain remedy for this.

Answer.
The king wills that after the end of the number of years for which he decreed their last pardon of 100 marks a year, they shall have another such remission and pardon of 100 marks a year for three years only.

XIII. [Yarmouth and Kirkley Roads.]
39. Item, the commons of Suffolk and Norfolk, and all other counties of England request: whereas in the past it was ordained by statute that every liege of the kingdom could buy and sell without hindrance in any city, borough, seaport and elsewhere throughout the realm; and if charters or letters patent had been granted to the *[Page iii-95]*
[Col. a] contrary they would be held at naught; which statute was confirmed at the last parliament held at Gloucester: yet notwithstanding the said statute, a charter was granted in the same parliament to the people of Yarmouth that no man

achateroit ne venderoit entour la dite ville par sept leukes, et q'un lieu appelle Kirkelerode en le dit countee de Suff' q'est sys leukes de Jernemuth' serra annexe a mesme la ville q'est en le dit countee de Norff', et une chartre estoit repelle en temps l'aiel en plein parlement, pur ce q'il feust damageouse et grevouse as communes d'Engleterre, et acontraire des estatutz faitz en avantage ditz communes, pur ce qe les niefs en le dit rode ancorez quant le vent est encontre eux ne poont en nul manere le havene de Jernemuth' entrer, mais les covient lour harang gettre en la mier. A cause de quiel grante les gentz de Jernemuth' ne soeffrent les ditz communes en nul temps del an nulles maneres des vitailles, ne des marchandises, en la dite rode achatre ne vendre.

Qe plese a nostre dit seignour le roy et a son conseil, pur profit des communes, repeller la dite chartre issint grante as gentz de Jernemuth', et qe desormes nule chartre leur soit grantee a contraire.
Responsio.
Il plest au roy qe l'inquisicion nadgairs certifiez en la chancellerie par le conte de Suff', et autres qi furent deputez d'enquerre des certaines circumstances touchant la franchise grantee a la ville de Jernemuth' en celle partie, par consideracioun de quele inquisicion entre autres causes la dite chartre leur ent feust renovellez, soit veue par son conseil, appellez a eux ceux qe bon lour semblera. Et si la dite inquisicion ou certificacioun ne leur semble suffisante, soit faite novelle commissioun as persones suffisantz et indifferentz, sibien de veoir les lieux en lours propres persones, come d'enquerre de novel en due forme, et par gentz loialx et indifferentz, de toutes choses touchant la dite busoigne, et les circumstances d'icelle, au fin qe sur ce nostre seignour le roy puisse faire /ce\ qe mieltz lui semblera, par l'advis de son conseil avantdit. Et en le moien temps, soit mandez as baillifs et bones gentz de la dite ville de Jernemuth' par briefs souz le grand seal, sur grief peine, de user la dite franchise si duement, et d'ent faire tiele ordeinance et governement entre eux qe nul n'ait cause resonable d'ent pleindre desore enavant.

XIIII. [Staple at Calais.]
40. Item, prie la commune: qe come grande partie de lour sustenance est du profit de bestail, c'estassavoir, de buyre et furmage, et la deliverance de ce soleit estre faite as esterlynges et Flemmynges, et ore de ce sont ils restreintz qi ne deyvent ailleurs celle marchandise vendre forsqe a Caleys, paront ils sont grandement empoveriz.

Par quoy ils supplient q'ils les puissent vendre et carier, et leur profit ent faire a leur volentee, forspris a voz enemys.
Responsio.
Le roi le voet, et l'ad grantez pur un an proschein venant, au fin qe en le moien temps l'en purra assaier si ce soit profitable ou noun.

XV. [Holland and Kesteven in Lincolnshire.]
41. Item, prie la commune: qe come les metes et boundes qe font devise entre les parties de Holand et Kesteven en le counte de Nicol, c'estassavoir, en le marreis qi s'extende parentre l'eawe de Weland et de Wythum, sont si suroundez et estopes de wreke de eawe douce, qe les gentz d'un paiis et de l'autre n'ont pas verraie conissance d'icelles, dont pluseurs altercations et debates sourdent plusours foitz parentre les gentz d'une coustee et de l'autre, par cause q'en le dit paiis severales commissions pur garder la pees, et severalx coroners, ont este de tout temps, et nul se medle ov autre, issint

could buy or sell within a radius of seven miles from the town, and that a place named Kirkley Roads in the said Suffolk which is six miles from Yarmouth should be annexed to the same town, which is in the said county of Norfolk,, and a charter was repealed in the time of the grandfather in full parliament, because it was damaging and grievous to the commons of England and contrary to the statutes made which benefited the said commons, since the ships anchored in the said roadstead, when the wind was against them, could by no means enter the harbour of Yarmouth, but they agreed then to throw their herring into the sea. Because of which grant the people of Yarmouth do not allow the said commons at any time to buy or sell any type of victuals or merchandise in the said roadstead.

May it please our said lord the king and his council, for the benefit of the commons, to repeal the said charter thus granted to the people of Yarmouth, and to decree that henceforth no charter shall be granted to them contrary to this.
Answer.
It pleases the king that the inquest formerly certified in the chancery by the earl of Suffolk and others who were sent to inquire into the particular circumstances touching the franchise granted to the town of Yarmouth in this matter, through consideration of which inquest amongst other things the said charter was renewed for them, shall be inspected by his council, after they have summoned those whom it seems to them good to consult. And if the said inquest or certification does not appear adequate to them, let a new commission be directed to worthy and unbiased persons, both to inspect the places in person and to make fresh inquiries in an appropriate manner, and, through loyal and unbiased persons, into all matters touching the said business, and the circumstances of the same, so that our lord the king may be able to do that which seems best to him by the advice of his aforesaid council. And in the meantime, writs under the great seal shall be sent to the bailiffs and good people of the said town of Yarmouth, on pain of a grievous penalty, to exercise the said franchise duly, and carry out such ordinance and government amongst them that no one shall henceforth have reasonable cause for complaint.

XIIII. [Staple at Calais.]
40. Item, the commons pray: whereas a large part of their substance derives from profits from cattle, namely, from butter and cheese, and these are customarily exported to the Easterlings and the Flemish, yet now they are deprived of it because they are not allowed to sell their merchandise anywhere other than Calais, and as a result they are greatly impoverished.

Therefore they request that they may sell, transport and make profit as they please, except for dealing with your enemies.
Answer.
The king wills it, and has granted it for the year coming, with the intention that it may be assessed in the meantime to see whether it is beneficial or not.

XV. [Holland and Kesteven in Lincolnshire.]
41. Item, the commons pray: whereas the limits and bounds which were fixed between the parts of Holland and Kesteven in the county of Lincoln, that is to say on the marsh which stretches between the waters of Welland and Witham, have been so flooded and obscured by the damage caused by fresh water that the people of the one county and the other no longer have an accurate knowledge of them, because of which many altercations and debates arise between the people of the one side and the other, for in the said region there have always been several commissions for the keeping of

qe pluseurs presentementz, sibien devant les justices de la pees come devant les ditz coroners, aucuns ne sont pas executz, ou aucuns nient duement executz, a grant damage et prejudice sibien a nostre seignour le roy come a les

[Col. b] gentz *[veisins]* de les parties avauntdites.
Par quoi plese grauntir commissioun de vostre chancellerie, directe as gentz suffisantz de l'un paiis et de l'autre, d'enquere de les aunciens metes et boundes, et les surveoir et renoveller: et eux issint surveues et renovelles signer et mercher sibien par pales, fossees, et croices du pere, come en autre manere, par queles les gentz des ditz paiis purront le mieltz conoistre les metes et boundes de les paiis avauntdites.
Responsio.
Il plest au roy q'il soit fait, si homme ne monstre resonable cause pur quoy la chose ne se devera faire.

XVI. [Assizes in Derbyshire.]
42. Item, prient les communes du countee de Derby: qe come les assises et deliverances du dit countee ont este sovent foitz tenuz a Sallowe, q'est une povre et foreine ville, et nul herbergage ne vital y poet estre trove pur la dite communalte, a grant disease et oppression de mesme la commune.
Qe plese ordener qe les dites assises et deliverances soient tenuz a Derby, q'est la mellioure ville du dite countee, pur tout temps avenir, en ease du dite commune, et profit et relevacion du dite ville, q'est tenuz de nostre seignour le roi par fee ferme.
Responsio.
Le roi chargera ses justices de tenir les assises et deliverances en place le dit countee pluis covenable et aisee pur le poeple.

Membrane 1

XVII. [Rape of Arundel.]
43. Item, prient les communes des countees de Surr' et Sussex': qe come le roy Edward, aiel nostre seignour le roi q'orest, graunta au counte d'Arundell' qi derrain morust, et a ses heirs, pur touz jours, le rope d'Arundell', en quele rope sont contenuz pluseurs hundredes, rendant ent par an a l'escheqier .xv.*li.* les queux .xv.*li.* deussent estre paiez as viscontz des ditz countees, en eide del ferme des mesmes les countees; et nepurquant qe le dit conte paie les dites .xv.*li.* a l'escheqier, les ditz viscontz sont chargez de mesme la sume de an en an en le dit escheqier.
Qe plese ordeiner qe le counte d'Arundell' q'orest puisse paier les dites .xv.*li.* as ditz viscontz de an en an, ou autrement descharger les ditz viscontz del summe avauntdite.
Responsio.
Soit ce qe le counte d'Arundell' paie en l'escheqier allowez al viscont, si ce estoit parcel de la ferme del countee de Sussex' avaunt le grant ent fait au conte d'Arundell' qi mort est, et sur ce ait brief, etc..

XVIII. [Papal collector.]
44. Item, monstre la commune: qe come par le collectour nostre tresseint pere le pape devant ces heures pleusers grandes summes de monoie ont este sustretes du roialme, des benefices de seinte esglise, sibien del patronage et fundacion nostre seignour le roi come des autres seignours du roialme, clamant et demandant les primers fruitz apres les voidances d'icelles: et le collectour nostre dit tresseint pere le pape q'orest ad de novel acrochez al oeps de mesme

the peace and several coroners, and neither meddles with the other, so that of many presentments, both before justices of the peace as well as before the said coroners, some are not executed, or not duly executed, to the great injury and prejudice of our lord the king as well as the
[Col. b] neighbours of the aforesaid parties.
And so may it please you to grant a commission of your chancery directing worthy people of either county to inquire into the ancient limits and bounds, and survey and re-instate them: and having thus surveyed and re-instated them, to indicate and mark them with stakes, ditches and crosses of stone, as well as in other ways, whereby the people of the said region may the more easily recognise the limits and bounds of the said parts.
Answer.
It pleases the king that this shall be done, unless anyone presents a good reason as to why it ought not to be.

XVI. [Assizes in Derbyshire.]
42. Item, the commons of the county of Derby pray: whereas the assizes and gaol deliveries of the said county have often been held at Sawley, which is a poor and remote town, and no lodgings or victuals can be found for the said commons, to the great detriment and oppression of the same.

May it please you to ordain that in future the said assizes and deliveries shall be held at Derby, which is the best town of the said county, to the ease of the said commons, and the benefit and relief of the said town, which is held of our lord the king by fee-farm.
Answer.
The king will charge his justices to hold the assizes and deliveries in a place in the said county more suitable and convenient for the people.

XVII. [Rape of Arundel.]
43. Item, the commons of the counties of Surrey and Sussex pray: whereas the king Edward, grandfather of our lord the present king, granted to the earl of Arundel who died of late, and to his heirs, for all time, the rape of Arundel, in which rape there are many hundreds, rendering annually to the exchequer £15 which ought to be paid to the sheriffs of the said counties to assist the farm of the same counties; and even though the said earl pays the said £15 to the exchequer, the said sheriffs are charged with the same sum each year in the said exchequer.
May it please you to ordain that the present earl of Arundel shall pay the said £15 to the said sheriffs each year, or otherwise discharge the said sheriffs of the aforesaid sum.

Answer.
Let the sum which the earl of Arundel pays to the exchequer be allowed to the sheriff, if it was part of the farm of the county of Sussex before it was granted to the earl of Arundel who is dead, and let him have a writ thereon, etc.

XVIII. [Papal collector.]
44. Item, the commons show: whereas through the collector of our most holy father the pope many large sums of money have in the past been withdrawn from the kingdom from benefices of holy church of the patronage and foundation of our lord the king as well as of other lords of the kingdom, claiming and demanding the first fruits after the vacancies of the same: and the collector of our said most holy father the present pope [Urban VI] has again accroached for the use

of our same holy father the fruits of dignities and prebends vacant in cathedral and collegiate churches; which fruits the deans and chapters of the same have in times past received for their own use; and those fruits have been most of their sustenance during the aforesaid periods of vacancy: and they have caused them to be levied by sequestration, summonses and various other censures, to the great impoverishment of the said kingdom.

May it please our most redoubtable lord the king, and the most wise lords of parliament, to ordain a good and suitable remedy, for the relief and security of the said kingdom in time to come.

Answer.
Let him have a secure prohibition and another such remedy as shall be adequate in this instance, as well as in all causes where the same collector practises or attempts any novelties or usurpations which have not been customarily used within the same kingdom.[25]

XIX. [Debts of Edward III.]

45. Item, the commons pray: whereas at various previous parliaments they have requested that payment should be made of the debts of the late King Edward, whom God absolve, from the goods of the same king; and they have been told that this would be done, yet it still remains to be done, as they understand.

May it please our lord the king and his good council to ordain that the said debts shall be paid from the said goods, in return for the victuals and other items taken in this time, and in particular for the sums of money taken as prests in various places throughout his realm, that by setting a good example to the lieges of our lord the king they shall be the more ready to lend to our said lord the present king, to assist him and all his kingdom in any urgent need.

Answer.
It has been done for the most part; and with regard to the remainder, it pleases the king that this shall be done according to the purport of the petition.

XX. [Alien priors.]

46. Item, the commons pray: that all the alien priors throughout the land shall be removed from their houses and altogether expelled from the land, without returning, and other Englishmen put in their place, being liable for the same farm and charge which the alien priors have borne until now, to the great benefit of our lord the king and his commons.

Answer.
The king will consider this further.

XXI. [Office of sheriff.]

47. Item, the commons pray: that because of the great harm and loss which various people have endured whilst occupying the office of sheriff in the past, no one who has been a sheriff in the past shall be made a sheriff in the future as long as there is another worthy person in the same county who has not been a sheriff.

Answer.
It seems that the statutes made thereon in the past are sufficient, and so they shall be kept and upheld.

XXII. [Five principal officers.]

48. Item, the commons pray: that the present five chief officers shall remain in their offices without being replaced

---
[25] The section from 'accrochementz' to 'le roialme' has been written in later in a contemporary hand.

remuez parentre cy et le proschein parlement, si defaut especial ne soit trovez en aucun de eux en le moien temps, come l'en espoire qe ne serra mye, si Dieux plest.

Responsio.

Le roi ent ferra, par l'advis de son conseil, selonc ce qe mieulz lui semblera qe soit affaire, pur le profit de lui et de son roialme.

XXIII. [Royal pardons.]

49. Item, prie la commune: qe la ou nostre seignour le roi, aiel nostre seignour le roy q'orest, qi Dieux assoille, en les ans de son regne .xxxvime et cynquantisme, si fist pardoun et relees a son poeple de touz eschapes des felons, sibien des prisones des ordinaires come des autres, et chateux des felons et des futifs, trespasses, negligences et mesprisions, et des pleuseurs autres articles comprises deinz la dite pardon.[26]

Qe plese a nostre dit seignour le roy, pur les almes de ses nobles progenitours aiel et piere, leur faire au tiele pardon au present come dessuis est dit, forspris toutes maneres des felonies del dit an cynquantisme tanqe al primer jour de ce present parlement; et de ce grauntir lettres patentes a touz qi les voudra suire.

Responsio.

Quant as eschaps eschuz tanqe al comencement de cest parlement, sibien des clercz convictz hors de la prisone ordinairs, come d'autres prisons \felons/ quelconqes, le roi ad grante de sa grace, \horspris des eschaps adjuggiez./ Et purveuz toutes voies qe si celles eschaps se firent fraudeleusement, par covyne ou de l'assent des ordinairs, viscontz, ou d'autres gardeins des dites prisones, qe ceste grace ne extende as yceulx eschaps par nule voie. Et quant al remenant, semble qe ce ne serroit mie profitable pur le bone governement del roialme; qar il durroit greindre baudour as mesfesours de mesprendre. Et n'est mye l'entencion du

[Col. b] roi qe aucun enjoise la grace de pardone avauntdite s'il ne pursuie en nostre chancellerie pur sa chartre en especial, parentre cy et la Nativitee de Seint [27] proschein venant.

XXIV. [Disturbances at York.]

50. Item, prie la commune au roi lour seignour: qe come il ad un grant et notoire rumour en ceste present parlement d'un horrible chose ore tard faite par diverses malefesours de les communes de la citee d'Everwyk, acrochant a eux roiale poair, par fauxe confederacie et alliance entre eux faite; qe la ou, par les franchise et custumes de la dite citee lour mair serra eslieuz lendemayne de la Purificacion par un an a durrer. Par force de quele ils avoient esliu, lendemayne de la Purification derrain passe, Johan de Gysburgh', d'estre lour mair par cest an entier, par force de quele eleccion il avoit occupie le dit office peisiblement tanqe le lundy proschein apres la feste de Seinte Katerine darrein passe, qe les ditz malefesours leverunt forciblement, et enchaceront lour dit mair hors de la citee. Et sur ce freskement debruserunt par haches et autres armes les hostes et fenestres de lour gyldhalle, et entrerunt, et fesoient un Simon de Quixlay jurrer d'estre lour mair, encontre son gree et les bones gentz de la dite citee, et fesoient toutes les bones gentz adonqes esteantz en la dite citee encontre lour gree pur doute de mort jurrer a lour novelle mair. Et fesoient un novelle ordeinance qe a quele heure qe les cloches sur le pount fuissent sonez aukeward, sibien de jour come de nuyt, qe touz les communes de la dite citee leverent touz ensemble, et fesoient proclamer

between now and the next parliament, unless a particular fault is found in any one of them in the meantime, which it is hoped shall not be the case, God willing.

Answer.

By the advice of his council the king will do whatsoever he thinks best, for the benefit of himself and his kingdom.

XXIII. [Royal pardons.]

49. Item, the commons pray: whereas our lord the king, grandfather of our lord the present king, whom God absolve, in the thirty-sixth and fiftieth years of his reign, pardoned and released his people from all fines for the escape of felons, both from prisons of ordinaries and others, and the chattels of felons and fugitives, trespasses, negligences and misprisions, and many other articles contained in the said pardon.

May it please our said lord the king, for the souls of his noble progenitors, his grandfather and father, to issue them another such pardon at this time as outlined above, excepting all kinds of felonies from the said fiftieth year until the first day of this present parliament; and to grant letters patent thereon to all those who wish to sue.

Answer.

As for fines for escapes effected before the beginning of this parliament, both of clerks convicted outside the ordinary's prison, as well as other felons imprisoned, the king has granted his grace, excepting fine for escapes which have been adjudged. And provided always that if such escapes are made by fraud, with the co-operation or assent of the ordinaries, sheriffs or other keepers of the said prison, that this grace shall not extend to those escapes by any means. And as for the remainder, it seems that it would certainly not be profitable for the good government of the kingdom; since it might mistakenly encourage greater boldness in criminals. And it is certainly not the intention of the

[Col. b] king that anyone shall enjoy the grace of the aforesaid pardon unless he sues in our chancery for his individual charter, between now and the nativity of St ... next.

XXIV. [Disturbances at York.]

50. Item, the commons pray of our lord king: whereas a prevalent and disturbing rumour has circulated in this present parliament of a terrible deed recently performed by various malefactors amongst the commons of the city of York, accroaching to themselves by fraudulent confederacy and alliance made amongst them; and whereas, according to the liberties and customs of the said city their mayor should be elected on the morrow of the feast of the Purification [3 February], to serve for one year. Accordingly, they elected, on the morrow of the last feast of the Purification last past [3 February 1380], John Guisborough to be their mayor for the whole year, by virtue of which election he occupied the said office peacefully until the Monday after the feast of St Katherine last [26 November 1380] when the said malefactors rose in force and drove their said mayor out of the city. Thereupon they promptly broke the doors and windows of their guildhall with axes and other weapons, and on entering it made one Simon Quixley swear to be their mayor, against his will and that of the good men of the said city, and they forced all the good men then in the said city to swear loyalty to their new mayor, against their will and for fear of death. And they made a new ordinance declaring that whenever the bells on the bridge rang backwards, whether by day

---

[26] Stat. 26 Edw.3 c.2.

[27] The name of the saint has been omitted but no gap has been left in the manuscript.

plusours ordeinances faites par eux de novelle a contraire de la loie et les bones custumes de la dite citee devant faitz. Et issint continuantz, et aboundantz es leur ditz malveistes et plusours autres horribles faitz de jour en autre, en anientissement del dite citee, et grant peril a toute le roialme, si hastive et freske chastisement ent ne soit ordeine au present.

Qe plese, par les bones avises des seignours et autres sages du roialme en cest present parlement ordeiner tiel remedie qe touz autres malefesours du roialme purront estre chasties par punissement de eux.

Responsio.

Le roi voet, de l'assent des seignours et communes en parlement, primerement, qe commission soit faite en haste al counte de Northumbr' et as autres seignours, chivalers et esquiers de paiis, pur enquerre de les ditz malefeisours, sibien par bones gentz vaillantz bien pres enviroun la citee, come autrement viis et modis, et en toute autre manere qe mieultz lour semble; et pur ent avenir a la droite verite, et les nouns de ceux qe serront trovez en coupe certifier au conseil le roy sanz delaie, pur faire tiel punissement de eux qe soit ensample a toutz autres riotours et malefaisours en temps avenir. Et qe briefs soient faitz et envoiez a Everwyk par deux sergeantz d'armes, pur faire venir devant le roy et son conseil sanz delaie vint et quatre persones de les pluis notoires conseillours et assemblours des ditz riotours et malefaisours; des queux .xxiiij. persones les nouns sont baillez au chancellor d'Engleterre. Et a plustost q'ils serront venuz, soient ils comandez en salve garde, sanz estre deliverez au mainprise, tanqe le dit counte et ses compaignons justices en la dite commission eient certifiez ce q'ils averont trovez de eux en celle partie.

Item, auxint qe brief soit fait a Simon de Quixlay, q'est jure maire des ditz confederatours, q'il ne se medle desore de celle office de maire, acrochant a luy roiale poair encountre la corone le roi; lui comandant oultre par le dit brief q'il soit devant le roy et son conseil certein jour, pur respondre de son fait, etc.

Item, qe autre brief soit fait a Johan de Gysbourn', mair de la dite citee, qe feust esluz mair par fraunche *[Page iii-97]*

[Col. a] et commune election, lui comandant par mesme le brief q'il occupie et ministre en son office du mairalte tanqe lendemayn de la Purificacioun Nostre Dame proschein venant, come les franchises et custumes de la dite citee voillent.

Item, qe autre brief soit fait as baillifs, bones gentz, et toute la communaltee de la /dite\ citee, q'ils soient entendantz au dit Johan lour mair, come a celuy qe represent l'estat nostre seignour le roy en le dite citee, sur peine forfaiture de lours biens et chateux, et quanqe ils purront forfaire devers le roi. Et le roi voet qe proclamacioun soit fait parmye la citee, au fin de nulluy soi ent purra excuser de ignorance, etc.

XXV. [Imported wines.]

51. Item, prie la commune: qe come plusours vyns de diverses maneres sont sovent amesnez deinz la terre, queux passont sovent sanz gaugie, par cause qe l'estatut sur ycel fait touche trop briefment la matire, a grant damage des seignours et communes, qe sont sovent desceuz en lours achatz, a cause q'ils ne poent sanz gaugie avoir conisance comebien les vesseulx contienent.

and night, all the commons of the said city should rise together and have proclaimed various ordinances newly composed by them, contrary to the law and good customs of the said city previously made. And so they continue to perform their evil and terrible deeds from one day to the next, to the destruction of the said city and great danger to all the kingdom, unless a swift and forceful punishment is now decreed. May it please you, by the good advice of the lords and other wise men of the kingdom in this present parliament, to ordain such remedy that all other malefactors of the kingdom shall be thereby chastened.

Answer.

The king wills, with the assent of the lords and commons in parliament, first, that a commission should be directed in haste to the earl of Northumberland and to other lords, knights and squires of the country to enquire about the said malefactors, by means of good and worthy men who live near the city, or by other such means as seem best to them; thereby to reach the truth of the matter, and to inform the king's council without delay of the names of those found guilty, so that they can be punished as an example to all other rioters and malefactors in time to come. And let writs also be made and sent to York by two serjeants-at-arms, to summon before the king and his council without delay twenty-four of the most notorious leaders and abettors of the said rioters and malefactors; the names of whom are to be sent to the chancellor of England. And as soon as they arrive, let them be committed into custody without bail until the said earl and the justices accompanying him on the said commission have certified what they have discovered about them.

Item, that a writ should be sent to Simon Quixley, sworn mayor of the said conspirators, ordering him to abandon that office which he holds to the detriment of royal power and against the crown; commanding him also by the same writ to come before the king and his council on an appointed day to account for his action, etc.

Item, that another writ should be issued to John Guisborough, mayor of the said city, who was elected by a free *[Page iii-97]*

[Col. a] and common election, ordering him by the same writ, to occupy and serve in his office of mayor until the day after the next feast of the Purification of Our Lady [3 February 1381], as the franchises and customs of the said city have it.

Item, let another writ be sent to the bailiffs, good men and the whole commonalty of the said city ordering them to be obedient to the said John, their mayor, as the person who represents the state of our lord the king in the said city, on pain of forfeiting their goods and chattels and whatsoever else they are capable of forfeiting to the king. And the king wills that a proclamation to that effect should be made within the city, so that none can excuse himself on the grounds of ignorance, etc.

XXV. [Imported wines.]

51. Item, the commons pray: whereas many wines of various sorts are imported into the land which often pass through without being measured, because the statute made thereon touches too briefly on the matter, to the great injury of the lords and commons, who are often deceived in their purchases, because they cannot tell without gauge how much the vessels contain.

Qe plese, pur profit du roy et du roialme, pluis overtement declarrer mesme l'estatut, fesant pluis exprese mencioun en general de toutes maneres vins, de quelconque paiis q'ils soient, sibien vins doulces et renys, come touz autres, ovesqe vynegre, oyle, meel et touz autres licours qe sont deinz vesselx, qe poent estre gaugiez.

Responsio.

Le roi[28] voet et commande qe les estatutz ent faitz \soient/ veuz et enlargez, selonc ce q'est demandez.[29]

May it please you, for the benefit of the king and the kingdom, to proclaim the same statute more widely, making express mention of all the types of wine, of whatsoever region they come, as well of sweet and Rhenish wines as of all others, together with vinegar, oil, honey, and all other liquids which are to be found in vessels and which can be measured.

Answer.

The king wills and commands that the statutes made thereon shall be inspected and amplified to take account of these requests.

---

[28] *Original* le
[29] Stat. 4 Ric.2 c.1; *SR*, II.16

Appendix

5 November 1380

Northampton

1. Commissioners appointed following a complaint from the 'mayor and good men' of Shrewsbury that certain 'men of lesser sufficiency' of the town banded together and chose two bailiffs for the town in advance of the appointed time, who have since removed money from the town coffers and 'risen against their betters and assaulted and imprisoned one of them, Reginald Scryveyn, refusing to obey the king's writ for his release, so that his three sons died of grief'. By petition in parliament. Dated 24 November 1380
    Source: *CPR 1377-81*, 579 (see also Item 2)

2. Commissioners appointed following a complaint by William Biriton (or Bureton), bailiff of Shrewsbury, that Reginald Scryveyn rescued an outlaw indicted for murder and assaulted the former bailiff of Shrewsbury, who had arrested the outlaw. By petition in parliament. Dated 24 November 1380.
    Source: *CPR 1377-81*, 579 (see also Item 1, and *CCR 1377-81*, 486)

3. Order to David Cradock, justice of North and South Wales, to appear before the king and council at Westminster in January 1381 to answer to 'divers petitions presented to the king in the parliament at Northampton by certain lieges of those parts' complaining of wrongs committed by him against the people of Caernarvonshire and Anglesey. Dated 16 December 1380.
    Source: *CCR 1377-81*, 486.

4. Order to the sheriffs of London to have it proclaimed that at the request of the commons in this parliament the king has granted licence for one year to both native and alien merchants to export butter and cheese not just to Calais but to other foreign parts as well, 'that it may be seen whether this be to the advantage of the realm or no'. Dated 4 *(sic)* November 1380.
    Source: *CCR 1377-81*, 501.

5. Grant to the chancellor and scholars of the university of Cambridge of a seven-year extension of their present five-year grant of right of jurisdiction over breaches of the assizes of bread, wine, ale and other victuals in Cambridge, in default of the mayor. By petition of parliament. Dated 4 December 1380.
    Source: *CPR 1377-81*, 582.

6. Order to the admiral, following discussion of a petition in parliament from James Moy and his fellow merchants and seamen of Flanders, to release them and their ships and goods and allow them to leave, since they were wrongly arrested. Dated 4 December 1380.
    Source: *CCR 1377-81*, 424.

7. Order to the treasurer and barons of the exchequer to cancel a recognisance for six hundred marks made to the king in March 1380 by Hugh Fastolf of Great Yarmouth and his brother John concerning a ship called 'la Cristofre' of Barcelona, since it was shown at the parliament at Northampton that the goods and men in the ship belonged to the allegiance of the king of Aragon. By petition of parliament. Dated 24 January 1381.
    Source: *CCR 1377-81*, 492-3.

1381 November

Westminster

3 November - 13 December 1381 (prorogued)

24 January - 25 February 1382

(C 65/37. *RP*, III.98-121. *SR*, II.17-23)

C 65/37 is a roll of thirteen membranes, each approximately 350mm in width, sewn together in chancery style and numbered in a later hand. The text, written in the official chancery scripts of several scribes, occupies the rectos of the membranes only. The dorses are blank apart from a later heading on membrane 1, 'Rotulus parliamenti de anno V^{ti}R. 2^{di}'. An earlier, outer membrane displays a further later heading which reads 'Rotulus parliamenti de anno regni regis Ricardi secundi quinto. Pars prima'. An accompanying note states that 'This roll is much perished'. The roll is not in good condition, with tears and staining on several of its membranes, especially membranes 3, 2 and 1, parts of which are illegible. The marginal headings are both contemporary and of a later date. The Arabic numerals are of a later date, while the Roman numerals alongside the common petitions are contemporary. The list of those exempted from the king's grace in this parliament spans membranes 6 and 5, which together form a separate piece stitched to the foot of membrane 7, and this overlaps membrane 5 of the main body of the roll. The roll appears to be complete.

The event which should have dominated discussion in the parliament of November 1381 was, of course, the Peasants' Revolt of June-July that year, the aftershocks of which were still reverberating through the realm; and, if we had nothing but the roll to go on, that might indeed seem to have been the case. The chroniclers, however, showed considerably more interest in a different matter, the bitter quarrel which had broken out in the summer between John of Gaunt, duke of Lancaster, and Henry Percy, earl of Northumberland, which, according to the Westminster chronicler, threatened to 'destroy the whole of England'.[1] The origin of this dispute lay in Percy's refusal to offer hospitality to Gaunt while the latter was in Northumberland (and in fear of his life from the mob, so he believed) in June 1381 - although it may well be that behind this lay something deeper, namely, Percy's resentment at the increasingly active role that Gaunt was playing in the politics of the Anglo-Scottish border, which Percy regarded as his sphere of influence. Be that as it may, the dispute flared to the point where it began seriously to threaten the stability of the kingdom, and on three occasions (4 August, 15 August and 9 October) meetings of the royal council were held in an attempt to patch it up. Unfortunately they seem only to have exacerbated matters, and by the time parliament was due to meet in early November, both magnates had arrived at Westminster with substantial armed retinues, and a violent confrontation seemed a real possibility.[2]

The clerk who compiled the roll of parliament said as little as he decently could about the quarrel, merely noting that because of the king's desire to settle it, parliament was adjourned until Saturday 9 November (Item 1). The *Anonimalle*, Westminster and St Albans chroniclers all provided much more detail: on Wednesday 6 November, Gaunt formally set out his grievances against Percy in the presence of the king and lords, while Percy listened in silence; on the following day it was Percy's turn, while Gaunt listened in silence, and on the Friday it was Gaunt's turn once again to reply to Percy's complaints. It was, in the end, Gaunt who prevailed, for on the Saturday Percy was obliged, in order to recover the king's grace, to make a formal and humiliating apology in full parliament to Gaunt, following which the duke agreed to forgive him and the two men publicly kissed. The Londoners, most of whom hated Gaunt and had openly sided with Percy, were similarly reconciled with the duke on the following Monday and, with the dispute settled (ostensibly, at any rate), the real business for which parliament had been summoned could begin.

Writs summoning the lords and commons had originally been issued on 16 July (at the height of the suppression of the revolt) for a parliament to meet on 16 September, but on 22 August the assembly was prorogued to 3 November.[3] The significant change among the list of lords spiritual summoned arose from the fact that Simon Sudbury, the former archbishop of Canterbury and chancellor, had been beheaded by the mob on Tower Hill on 14 June, so that his archiepiscopal see was vacant (in fact, William Courtenay was the new archbishop-elect, and had also replaced

---

[1] *Westminster Chronicle*, 20-22; *St Albans Chronicle 1376-1394*, 566-78; *Anonimalle Chronicle 1333-1381*, 154-6.
[2] For a recent account of the quarrel see K.Towson, 'Hearts warped by passion: The Percy-Gaunt dispute of 1381', *Fourteenth Century England III*, ed. W. M. Ormrod (Woodbridge, 2004), 143-53.
[3] *CCR 1381-5*, 79-82.

Sudbury as chancellor, but he was still summoned as bishop of London). Also missing from the lords spiritual was the prior of St John of Jerusalem - the former prior, the treasurer Robert Hales, having shared Sudbury's fate. Among the lords temporal, there were several newcomers, including Thomas Holand, the king's half-brother and the new earl of Kent; William de Windsor, husband of Edward III's former mistress Alice Perrers; William Thorp; John Bourchier; John Lovell of Tichmarsh; and John de Montacute. Among those missing since the previous parliament was Edmund, earl of Cambridge, the king's uncle, who was leading an ill-fated expedition to Portugal - a point which would give rise to some controversy during the second session of this parliament.

On Saturday 9 November, the day on which Gaunt and Percy were reconciled, chancellor William Courtenay had made a brief address to the lords and commons, and triers and receivers of petitions were appointed, but the substantive opening speech was delivered by the treasurer, Sir Hugh Segrave, in the white chamber of Westminster palace on Wednesday 13 November.[4] The government, he explained, wished to hear the views of the assembly as to why the revolt had taken place. The king also wished to know whether the lords and commons agreed that he had done the right thing in unilaterally repealing the charters of manumission which he had been forced, under duress, to concede to the rebels at the time of the rising - for, Segrave declared, he had heard it said that some of the members did not agree with what the king had done (Item 8). How widespread such feelings were is difficult to know, but it is rather interesting that at least some of the lords and/or commons believed that the promises of freedom made by the king to the villeins ought to be upheld, even if (as seems likely) their main reason for thinking so was fear that repeal of the charters might provoke a fresh revolt. The eventual - and probably predictable - decision of the commons, delivered through the mouth of their speaker Sir Richard Waldegrave, was that the king had done well, and that the repeal of the charters ought to be confirmed; nevertheless, it is clear that the issue had generated a genuine debate among the members (Items 9-12).

With this point settled, Waldegrave now turned to the first of Segrave's questions, and once again his reply was largely predictable. In effect, the commons used the opportunity to comment on the reasons for the revolt as an excuse to launch a wide-ranging attack on the government incorporating most of their traditional causes for complaint: the king's household was over-staffed and extravagant, the royal purveyors were abusing their office, and the officers of the chancery, exchequer and law courts were either corrupt or incompetent; if suitable remedies were not soon put into place, it was difficult to see how further disasters could not be averted. The government, on the defensive, not only agreed to the appointment of a commission of reform (as it had before, to no effect), but actually allowed it to start sitting almost immediately, while the parliament was still in session: the king's confessor, the unpopular Dominican Thomas Rushook, was expelled from the household (although he was allowed to attend on the four principal feasts of the year), and a series of petitions for reform was drawn up. In early December, Richard le Scrope was appointed chancellor in place of Courtenay. Most telling perhaps, was the commons' plea for the king to bring to an end the numerous wars in which England was embroiled, which were bleeding the country dry and imperilling its citizens with no apparent benefit (Items 17-27).

There was also, inevitably, the question of money. Whether the government asked the commons for a tenth and fifteenth is not clear, but it certainly made some sort of request for financial aid, which the commons did their best to evade, replying that they dared not grant a 'tallage' because of the 'ill will' of the people (Item 36). There were, however, things which the commons wanted which the king might be obliged to withhold in the absence of a grant of taxation, such as a general amnesty to cover crimes committed during the revolt (including its suppression). Eventually the commons agreed to renew the wool subsidy, although only until 2 February 1382 (which by now was less than two months away). What is more, they insisted that no subsidy should be paid for the week between Christmas and 1 January, a symbolic gesture to demonstrate that the government should not come to think of it as a permanent tax (Item 40). In return for the wool subsidy, the king granted the pardons and general amnesty requested by the commons, although many scores of named 'malefactors' were excluded from it, as was the town of Bury St Edmunds, where the rising had been especially violent (Items, 41, 63, 95). The last few days of the first session also witnessed prolonged investigation in parliament concerning the culpability or otherwise of certain civic officials and others accused of having taken part in the revolts at Bridgwater (Somerset) and Cambridge. On 13 December, however, since Christmas was approaching and Richard II's bride-to-be, the daughter of the former Holy Roman Emperor Charles IV, had arrived in England to be crowned and married, it was decided that the parliament should be adjourned until 24 January 1382 (Item 64).

Richard married Anne of Bohemia on 20 January 1382, and two days later she was crowned at Westminster. Not until 27 January, therefore, was parliament reconvened for a second session which lasted for a little less than a month. As far as the wool subsidy was concerned, the commons now proved much more accommodating, agreeing to renew it for no less than four and a half years, until 24 June 1386. This was the longest extension to the wool subsidy granted by parliament since 1356, and may have gone some way - in the commons' eyes, at any rate - towards compensating for the lack of a direct subsidy. Moreover, they left it up to the king and the lords to determine how it might best be spent, provided that it was spent on the defence of the realm (Item 67). One way in which it might be used, as they explicitly recognised, was to finance a campaign to Iberia led by John of Gaunt, although they were careful not to be seen to be advocating this, since it was, as they knew only too well, a controversial topic. Gaunt had proposed such an expedition right at the beginning of the second session: his 'offer' was to lead an army of 2000 men-at-arms and 2000 archers

---

[4]For general accounts of this parliament, see Tuck, *Richard II and the English Nobility*, 54-6; Saul, *Richard II*, 79-82.

to Portugal and Spain, in return for which he asked for a 'loan' of sixty thousand pounds from 'the realm'. Not only would this army go to the aid of his brother Edmund of Langley, whose expedition to Portugal had run into trouble, and vindicate Gaunt's own claim to the throne of Castile; it would also - as he was careful to point out - contribute to making the seas safer for English shipping and to the security of the English realm (Item 66). Not surprisingly, there was considerable scepticism on this latter point, and there followed 'great disputation and altercation in parliament' on Gaunt's proposal. For the moment, nothing was decided. John of Gaunt was a determined character, however, and 'the way of Spain' was an issue which would continue to dominate the parliamentary agenda over the next few years.

Many of the commons' petitions were concerned with questions arising from the revolt, while others recommended new procedures in the exchequer in order to improve efficiency (Items 97-105; these may have been drawn up by the commission of reform set up during the first session). There was also much discussion of the dire financial situation in which the government found itself, coupled with suggestions as to appropriate remedies: a shortage of bullion and restrictive mercantile practices were both identified as matters that needed to be dealt with, but the root of the problem was that England was engaged in hostilities on too many fronts, and once again the commons took the opportunity to pray the king to bring the wars to an end, 'so that the poor commons can live in peace and quiet' (Item 70). This was, however, inevitably easier said than done. Shackled with commitments they could not meet and embroiled in wars from which they could not just slip free, it must have been with something approaching despair that the king and his ministers dissolved the parliament on 25 February. Precisely four weeks later, they issued writs for another one to meet.

Text and Translation

Text

Page iii-98, Membrane 13

ROTULUS PARLIAMENTI TENTI APUD WESTM', IN CRASTINO ANIMARUM, ANNO REGNI REGIS RICARDI, SECUNDI POST CONQUESTUM ANGLIE QUINTO [3 November 1381].

Adjournement de parlement.
1. Fait a remembrer qe la comemoracion des almes escheust l'an present en le jour de samady [2 November], et pur le dymenge proschein venant si ne fuist mye cest parlement comencez tanqe le lundy proschein venant, qe fuist le quart jour de Novembre [1381]. A quel lundy si vindrent sibien nostre seignour le roi come grant partie des prelatz et seignours del roialme: mais pur tant qe aucuns des viscountz n'avoient mye fait retourner lours briefs de parlement, et auxint, purce qe grant parte des prelatz et seignours del roailme q'avoient la somonce de parlement si ne furent encores venuz, si fist nostre seignour le roi adjorner cest parlement tanqe al lendemain proschein venant. A quiel lendemain, c'estassavoir le mardy [5 November 1381], si vindrent nostre seignour le roi et les seignours et prelats qi furent venuz a Westm' deinz la chambre depeintee, et illoeqes al dit mardy les chivalers, citezeins, et burgeys appellez, furent par lours nouns appellez la einz, dont plusours y firent defaute, et pur tant si fuist autrefoitz mesme le parlement adjournez depar le roi et de son comandement tanqe al mesqardy lors proschein venant. A quiel mesqardy [6 November 1381], pur tant qe un grant debat q'estoit sourde parentre messeignours le duc de Lancastre et le cont de Northumbr', dont pleint estoit fait au roi, et grant rumour sourdez en le poeple, parmy le grant force des gentz d'armes et d'archers arraiez au fier de guerre venuz a parlement de l'une et de l'autre partie, et dont nostre seignour le roi avec son conseil, et les seignours du roialme furent moelt grantement occupiez de lour appeiser en bone et aisee manere, si fist nostre dit seignour le roi autre foiz adjourner mesme le parlement tanqe al samedy lors proschein venant, et einsi feust fait. Et outre y estoit commandez a touz q'avoient la somonce de ce parlement depar le roi q'ils retournassent en dit lieu par temps le dit samedy, pur y \[oier les causes]/ pur queles nostre seignour le roi avoit fait somondre cest parlement, au fin qe en le moien temps l'en purroit oier les ditz duc et cont, et mettre fin, al aide nostre Seignour, sur le debat avauntdit.

Exposicion de la cause de la somonce de parlement.
2. Item, le samedy proschein [9 November 1381] nostre seignour le roi esteant en parlement, et les communes laeinz trestouz appellez par lours nouns, lui reverent pier en Dieu William de Courteney, nadgaires evesqe de Londres, elyt de Canterbirs \[confermez chancellier d'Engleterre,]/ del comandement nostre seignour le roi dist, 'Seignours et sires, nostre seignour le roi cy present, qi Dieux salve, m'ad commandez de vous exposer en partie les causes de la somonce \[de ce parlement: et dist pur son theme 'Rex]/ convenire fecit consilium, Actuum .xv.º'. Des queux paroles prises pur theme il fist une bone collacioun en Engleys, dont il appliast toute sa matire \[al bone et vertuouse governement]/ de roi et del regne, affermant par ycelle collacioun,

[Col. b] qe regne ne poet longement esteer, n'endurer par aucune voie, si les enhabitantz soient viciouses. Et quant il avoit fait fin de sa dite collacion, il dist, 'Et, seignours, nostre seignour le roi desirant toutdys le bone governement de son

Translation

THE ROLL OF THE PARLIAMENT HELD AT WESTMINSTER ON THE MORROW OF ALL SOULS, IN THE FIFTH YEAR OF THE REIGN OF KING RICHARD, THE SECOND SINCE THE CONQUEST [3 November 1381].

The adjournment of parliament.
1. Be it remembered that as All Souls [2 November] this year fell on a Saturday, and as the next day was a Sunday, this parliament did not begin until the Monday next following, which was 4 November [1381]. On which Monday our lord the king arrived as well as a large number of the prelates and lords of the realm: but because some of the sheriffs had not yet returned their writs of parliament, and also because a great number of the prelates and lords of the realm who had received summons to parliament had not yet arrived, our said lord the king had this parliament adjourned until the following day. On which day, namely Tuesday [5 November 1381], our lord the king and those lords and prelates who had come to Westminster entered the Painted Chamber, and there on the said Tuesday, the knights, citizens and burgesses who had been summoned were called in by their names, and as many of them were absent, the same parliament was again adjourned on the king's orders until the following Wednesday [6 November 1381]. On which Wednesday, because a great dispute had broken out between my lords the duke of Lancaster and the earl of Northumberland, which had caused complaint to be made to the king and alarming rumours to circulate amongst the people, because of the great force of men-at-arms and archers, arrayed in warlike manner, who had come to parliament for one or other of the parties. And as our lord the king, his council, and the lords of the realm had been fully occupied in arranging a peaceable and effective settlement, our said lord the king caused the same parliament to be adjourned once more until the following Saturday [9 November 1381], which was done. Furthermore, orders were given to all those who had been summoned to this parliament by the king that they should return to the said place early on the said Saturday, to hear the reasons why our lord the king had caused the parliament to be summoned, so that in the meantime he could hear the said duke and earl and, with the help of our Lord, put an end to their dispute.

An account of the reasons for summoning parliament.
2. Also, on the following Saturday [9 November 1381], when our lord the king was in parliament and the commons had been called by name, the reverend father in God, William Courtenay, lately bishop of London, archbishop-elect of Canterbury and the confirmed chancellor of England, at the command of our said lord the king, said, 'Lords and sirs, our lord the king here present, whom God protect, has ordered me to expound before you some of the reasons for summoning this parliament, and he took as his theme, 'The king caused his council to be convened' [John 11:47]. And having taken these words as his theme he delivered a sound sermon in English, in which he devoted his whole matter to the good and virtuous government of the king and kingdom, affirming in that address

[Col. b] that a kingdom could not long endure or survive at all if its inhabitants were wicked. And when he had ended his said address he said, 'And, lords, our lord the king desiring altogether the good government of his kingdom, and

roailme, par especial qe amendement soit fait toutes partz ou defautes notables sont trovez en dit governement: dont, si nully se sente ore grevez qe rienz lui soit fait qe ne purra estre remediez a la commune loy, mette avaunt sa bille en parlement, et certeins clercs de la chancellerie sont assignez de les resceivre, et certains prelatz, seignours et justices de les veer, oier, trier et terminer, des queux les nouns vous serront luez par le clerc du parlement en manere acustumee.' Et einsi fuist apres fait, et les ditz nouns lues en parlement par manere qe s'ensuit:

3. Resceivours des peticions d'Engleterre, Irlande, Gales, et Escoce:

Sire Johan de Waltham,

Sire Richard Ravenser,

Sire Thomas de Newenham,

Sire Johan de Freton.

4. Resceivours des peticions de Gascoigne, et d'autres terres et paiis depar dela, et des Isles:

Sire Michel de Ravendale,

Sire Piers de Barton',

Sire Johan Bouland,

Sire Thomas Thelwall'.

Et ceux qi veullent bailler lours billes les baillent avant parentre cy et mesqardy proschein venant [13 November 1381]; et apres le dit meskardy ne soit nulle bille parcial [resceuz.] *Page iii-99*

5. Et sont assignez triours de peticions d'Engleterre, Irlande, Gales, et Escoce:

Le roi de Castelle et de Leon, duc de Lancastre,

L'evesqe de Wyncestre,

L'evesqe de Ely,

L'evesqe de Nichol,

L'evesqe de Salesbirs,

L'abbe de Glastyngbirs,

L'abbe de Westm',

L'abbe de Waltham,

Le cont de Kent, mareschal d'Engleterre,

Le cont d'Arondell',

Le cont de Warr',

Le cont de Salesbirs,

Monsire Johan Cobham,

Monsire Richard le Scrope,

Monsire Guy de Bryen,

Monsire Robert Tresilian,

Monsire Robert Bealknapp',

Monsire William Skipwith',

–touz ensemble, ou .vi. des prelats et seignours avauntditz au meins; appellez a eux chanceller, tresorer, seneschal et chamberlein; et auxint les sergeantz nostre seignour le roi quant il busoignera. Et tendront leur place en la chambre de chamberlein, pres de la chambre depeinte.

6. Et sont assignez triours des peticions de Gascoigne, et d'autres terres et paiis dela la meer, et des Isles:

L'ercevesqe d'Everwyk,

L'evesqe de Norwiz,

L'evesqe de Salesbirs,

L'evesqe de Hereford,

especially that there should be correction wheresoever faults are found in the said government: wherefore, if there be any one who now feels injured by something which cannot be remedied by the common law, let him submit his bill to parliament, where certain clerks of the chancery have been appointed to receive them, and certain prelates, lords, and justices to inspect, hear, try, and determine them, whose names shall be read to you by the clerk of parliament in the accustomed manner.' And thereupon that was done, and the said names were read in parliament in the following manner:

3. Receivers of petitions from England, Ireland, Wales, and Scotland:

Sir John Waltham,

Sir Richard Ravenser,

Sir Thomas Newenham,

Sir John Freton.

4. Receivers of petitions from Gascony, and from other lands and countries overseas, and from the Channel Islands:

Sir Michael Ravendale,

Sir Piers Barton,

Sir John Bowland,

Sir Thomas Thelwall.

And those who wish to submit bills should hand them in between now and next Wednesday [13 November 1381]; and after the said Wednesday no individual bill will be received.

5. The following are assigned to be triers of petitions from England, Ireland, Wales, and Scotland:

The king of Castile and Leon, duke of Lancaster,

The bishop of Winchester,

The bishop of Ely,

The bishop of Lincoln,

The bishop of Salisbury,

The abbot of Glastonbury,

The abbot of Westminster,

The abbot of Waltham,

The earl of Kent, marshal of England,

The earl of Arundel,

The earl of Warwick,

The earl of Salisbury,

Sir John Cobham,

Sir Richard le Scrope,

Sir Guy Bryan,

Sir Robert Tresilian,

Sir Robert Bealknap,

Sir William Skipwith,

- to act all together, or at least six of the aforesaid prelates and lords; consulting with the chancellor, treasurer, steward, and chamberlain, and also the serjeants of our lord the king when necessary. And they shall hold their sessions in the chamberlain's room, near the Painted Chamber.

6. The following are assigned to be triers of petitions from Gascony, and from other lands and countries overseas, and from the Channel Islands:

The archbishop of York,

The bishop of Norwich,

The bishop of Salisbury,

The bishop of Hereford,

L'evesqe d'Excestre,	The bishop of Exeter,
L'abbe de Seynt Austyn de Canterbirs,	The abbot of St Augustine's, Canterbury,
L'abbe de Rameseye,	The abbot of Ramsey,
L'abbe de Evesham,	The abbot of Evesham,
Le cont de Bukyngham, conestable d'Engleterre,	The earl of Buckingham, constable of England,
Le cont de Staff',	The earl of Stafford,
Le cont de Suff',	The earl of Suffolk,
Le seignour la Souch,	Lord de la Zouche,
Le seignour Fitz-Wautier,	Lord FitzWalter,
Monsire Henry le Scrope,	Sir Henry le Scrope,
Le seignour de Wilughby,	Lord Willoughby,
Monsire Roger de Fulthorp,	Sir Roger Fulthorp,
Monsire Henry de Asty,	Sir Henry Asty,

–touz ensemble, ou quatre des prelats et seignours avauntditz; appellez a eux chanceller, tresorer, seneschal, chamberlein et les sergeantz le roi quant il busoignera. Et tendront lour place en la chambre marcolf.

7. Et quant les nouns des resceivours et triours des peticions estoient lues en parlement, le dit chanceller leur dit depar le roi qe lundy proschein venant [11 November 1381] lour serroient les causes de la somonce de ce parlement exposez depar le roy en pluis especiale manere. Comandant a touz illoeqes esteantz q'ils y fuissent par temps le dit lundy, et einsi de jour en autre tanqe ils eussent licence del roi en especial a departir.

Declaration des causes de la somonce de ce parlement.

8. Item, le mesqardy lors proschein ensuant [13 November 1381], les communes furent autrefoiz appellez par leurs nouns deinz la chambre blanc, et illoeqes, en presence nostre seignour le roi, monsire Hugh' Segrave, tresorer d'Engleterre, q'avoit les paroles depar le roy, leur dist, 'Seignours et sires, vous savez coment ore tarde luy honurable pere en Dieux, seignour William, elit de Canterbirs confermez

[Col. b] chanceller d'Engleterre, depar le roi nostre seignour vous fist exposer en partie les causes de la somonce de ce parlement en general, vous disant a celle foitz entre autres choses qe mesmes les causes vous serroient en apres declarez plus overtement en especial. Et pur ce nostre seignour le roy cy present, qi Dieux salve, m'ad comandez de vous dire la dite declaration q'est tielle; primerement, nostre seignour le roi dessuisdit desirant soverainement la libertee de seinte esglise estre entierement salvez sanz emblemissement; et l'estat, paix, et bone gouvernement de son dit roialme estre maintenuz et salvez come mieultz en temps de nul de ses nobles progenitours jadys rois d'Engleterre, voillant qi si defaute y soit trovez en aucune partie qe ce puisse ore estre amendez par l'advis des prelats et seignours en ce parlement; et meement de faire et purvoier ore de bone ordinance; pur mettre le roi et son roialme en paix et quiete sur le grant truboille et rumour q'estoient nadgaires moevez en certeins parties del dit roialme, parmy la levee et insurreccioun de certeins menues communes et autres, et sur lour horrible et dispitouse maufait encontre Dieux, la paix de la terre, le regalie, l'estat, dignitee, et la coroune nostre seignour le roi; combien qe mesme les communes colurerent lours ditz malfaitz en autre manere, en disantz q'ils veulloient avoir nul roi sinoun nostre seignour le roi Richard, si par cas, qe Dieux defende, autrefoiz vorroient faire en semblable manere; et de sercher et toucher les voies par quelles

7. And when the names of the receivers and triers of petitions had been read in parliament, the said chancellor informed them on behalf of the king that on the following Monday [11 November 1381] the reasons for summoning this parliament would be explained to them in detail on the king's behalf. And orders were given to all present to appear there early on the said Monday, and to continue from one day to the next until they were given explicit permission by the king to depart.

The declaration of the reasons for summoning this parliament.

8. Also, on the following Wednesday [13 November 1381], the commons were once again called by their names into the White Chamber, and there in the presence of our lord the king, Sir Hugh Segrave, treasurer of England, speaking on the king's behalf, said to them, 'Lords and sirs, you know that the honourable father in God, the lord William, archbishop-elect of Canterbury, and

[Col. b] chancellor of England, on behalf of the king our lord, lately explained to you in general the reasons for the summoning of this parliament, telling you on that occasion amongst other things, that those causes would later be revealed to you more explicitly and in greater detail. Accordingly, our lord the king here present, whom God preserve, has ordered me to make the following announcement to you which is this; first, our aforesaid lord the king, desiring above all that the liberty of holy church be preserved entirely without blemish; and the stability, peace, and good government of his said realm be maintained and preserved as well as ever in the time of any of his noble progenitors, once kings of England, willing that if fault can be found anywhere, it be rectified by the advice of the prelates and lords in this parliament; and likewise he wishes to make a good ordinance at this time, to bestow peace and tranquillity upon the king and his kingdom in the wake of the great turmoil and tumult which occurred recently in various parts of the said kingdom by the uprising and insurrection of certain of the merest commons and others, and their terrible and dispiteous offences against God, the peace of the land, and the regality, estate, dignity, and the crown of our lord the king; even though the said commons portrayed their said misdeeds in another light by saying that they wished to have no king except King Richard. The king wishing to prevent another such uprising happening, which God forbid, and to seek and

les dites malfaisours purroient estre chastisez, et le dit rumour de tut oustez et cessez, et d'enquere et sercher les causes, mocions, et principalx enchesons de les rumour et insurreccions avauntditz, afin qe celles enchesons trovez et scieues, et puis de tout oustez, homme purra le plus surement s'affier en le remede sur ce a ordener, si les communes autrefoitz vorroient ou se tailleroient par malice de malfaire par semblable manere. Item, n'est mye chose a vous disconue, coment nostre seignour le roi, durant le dit rumour, fuist constreint de faire et granter ses lettres desouz son grant seal a les neifs de son roialme et autres, de libertee, franchise, et manumissions, sachant /bien\ adonqes qe ce ne poait il faire de bone foy et la loy de sa terre, mais ce fist il pur le mieultz, pur estopper et cesser lour clamour et malice, come celluy qe n'estoit alors en son droit poair /de\ roi. Mais tantost come Dieux de sa grace lui avoit restitut a son poair et primer estat de roi, paront la dite meschief estoit en partie cessez, mesme nostre seignour le roi, par l'advis de son conseil lors esteant pres de lui, fist revoquer et repeller les ditz grantz, come celles qe par compulsion, encontre resoun, loy et bone foy, furent faitz et grantez, en desheritance des prelatz et seignours de son roialme avauntdit. Et partant le roi vorroit ore savoir les volentes de vous messeignours, prelatz, seignours, et communes cy presentz, si vous semble qe par celle repelle ad il bien fait et a vostre plesir, ou noun. Qar il dit, si vous desirez d'enfranchiser et manumettre les ditz neifs de vostre commune assent, come ce luy ad este reportez qe aucuns de vous le desiront, le roi assentera ovesqe vous a vostre priere.' Et sur ce le dit tresorer dit a mesme les communes en lour priant depar le roi q'ils se retraierent vers lour place deinz l'abbe de Westm', et q'ils se advisassent bien et diligeaument de cestes matires, et des remedes qe lour sembloit sur celles a ordener. Et si tost come ils furent assentuz d'aucun certein purpos en \celle/ partie q'ils le fussent assavoir a nostre seignour le roi et as seignours de parlement. Lour faisant oultre assavoir qe le roi si fust grantement endettez, sibien pur le maintenance de son estat et de son hostiel, come par les guerres et en autre diverse manere: paront il lour dist qe les officers del roi lour serroient envoiez pur lour enfourmer, et monstrer outre la grant necessitee \du roi,/ a quele heure q'ils furent requiz, et tielle ent fuist la voluntee du roi.

Page iii-100, Membrane 12 [5]

Responce de la commune.

9. Item, le lundy proschein ensuant la tierce semaigne de parlement, qe fu le .xviij. jour de Novembre, les communes revindrent en parlement, et illoeqes monsire Richard de Waldegrave, chivaler, q'avoit les paroles depar la commune, s'afforceast de lui avoir excusez de cel office de vantparlour, mais le roi lui chargeast del faire par sa ligeance, depuis q'il estoit a ce esluz par ses compaignons.

10. Et adonqes le dit monsire Richard faisant sa protestacion qe s'il y dist rienz autrement, ou plus ou meins qe ne fuist devant assentuz et acordez par ses compaignons qe il le poaist amender par l'advis de mesmes ses compaignons, dist:

11. 'Monseignour lige, mes compaignons cy presentz et moy aions entreparlez de noz charges ore tard a nous donez depar vostre roiale magestee, mais nous sumes en partie de variance entre nous touchant mesme la charge. Et par tant s'il vous pleust vorroions rehercer ycy devaunt vous mesme la charge, ou qe pleust a vostre roiale magestee del faire rehercer autrefoitz devant nous qe nous le purrons clerement

discover the means by which the said malefactors might be punished, and the said uprising thoroughly quashed and ended, and to investigate and search for the causes, motives, and principal reasons for the aforesaid uprising and insurrections, so that having discovered and learnt them, and having entirely rooted them out, people will place the greater trust in the remedy to be ordained, should the commons ever again wish or wickedly propose to perpetrate evil in such a manner. Also, it is not unknown to you indeed that our lord the king, during the said troubles, was constrained to make and grant letters of franchise and manumission under his great seal to the villeins of his kingdom and others, knowing full well that he should not do so in good faith and according to the law of the land, but that he did for the best, to stop and put an end to their clamour and malice, for he did not then enjoy his rightful power as king. But as soon as God, by his grace, had restored him to his authority and former state as king, and when the trouble had partly ceased, our same lord the king, by the advice of his council then about him, had the said grants revoked and repealed, for they had been made and granted under compulsion, contrary to reason, law, and good faith, to the disinheritance of the prelates and lords of his aforesaid realm. And now the king wishes to know the will of you, my lords, prelates, lords and commons here present, and whether it seems to you that he acted well in that repeal and pleased you, or not. For he says that if you wish to enfranchise and make free the said villeins by your common agreement, as he has been informed some of you wish to do, he will assent to your request.' And thereupon the said treasurer spoke to the same commons, praying them upon the king's behalf to withdraw to their place in the abbey of Westminster, and to discuss those matters fully and diligently amongst themselves, and the remedies which they thought should be ordained. And as soon as they were agreed on a certain purpose in the matter, they were to notify our lord the king, and the lords of parliament. He also informed them that the king was in considerable debt through the upkeep of his estate and household and maintenance of the wars, and in various other ways: wherefore he told them that the king's officers would be sent to inform them thereof and explain the king's great need, whensoever they were required to do so, and that such was the king's will.

The reply of the commons.

9. Also, on the following Monday in the third week of parliament, which was 18 November, the commons returned to parliament, and there Sir Richard Waldegrave, knight, who was to speak on behalf of the commons, sought to excuse himself the office of speaker, but the king charged him to perform it on the strength of his allegiance, because he had been elected to that office by his companions.

10. Then, the said Sir Richard making his protestation that if he should say anything other or more or less than had been previously assented and agreed to by his colleagues, he might amend it by the advice of his colleagues, said:

11. 'My liege lord, my companions here present and I have discussed the charge recently laid upon us by your royal majesty, but we differ amongst ourselves over the same. Wherefore, if it please you, we wish to have the same charge rehearsed before you here, or, if it please your royal majesty, may you have it rehearsed another time before us, so that we

---

[5] The first half of this membrane has been left blank.

entendre, et depuis par tant estre entre nous quant a ce d'un acord.'

12. Et le roi comandast a monsire Richard le Scrope, chivaler, lors novellement crees en chanceller d'Engleterre, de rehercer illoeqes mesme lour charge touchant les pointz suisditz. Et einsi fist il clerement, et en especial quant al repelle issint fait del grant de la franchise et manumissioun des neifs et villeins de la terre. Estoit autrefoitz effectuelment demandez de toutz esteantz illoeqes en plein parlement depar le roi, si celle repelle lour pleust, ou nemye.

Reppel des manumissions et franchise grantiz el rumour.

13. A quoy, sibien prelatz et seignours temporels come les chivalers, citeins et burgeys, respondirent a une voice qe celle repelle fuist bien faite, adjoustant qe tiele manumission ou franchise des neifs ne ne poast estre fait sanz lour assent q'ont le greindre interesse: a quoy ils n'assenterent unqes de lour bone gree, n'autrement, ne jamais ne ferroient pur vivre /et\ murrir touz en un jour. Enpriantz humblement a nostre seignour le roi, sibien c'estassavoir les prelatz et seignours come les dites communes, qe celles manumissions et franchises issint faitz et grantez par cohercioun, en desheritance de eux et destruccion del roialme, feussent annientiz et adnullez par auctoritee de ce parlement, et le dit repelle affermez, come celle qe bien et joustement estoit fait. Et ce estoit grantez et assentuz illoeqes de touz a une voice. Et puis les communes prierent au roi nostre seignour d'avoir certains prelatz et seignours pur communer avec eux de leurs ditz charges, a cause qe les matires touchent moelt hautement l'estat du roialme, et par tant busoignent grantement de ent lour advis. A quoi lour feust dit q'ils meissent en escrit les nouns de ceulx queux ils vorront avoir, et les bailleroient au roi, et le roi s'adviseroit.

Seignours assignez pur entrecommuner.
14. /Et sur ce bailleront en escrit les nouns de prelatz et seignours dessouz escritz\ en une cedule, c'estassavoir:
L'evesqe de Wyncestre,
L'evesque du Norwiz,
L'evesqe d'Excestre,
Johan roi de Castille et de Leon, duc de Lancastr',
Le cont de Buk',
Le cont de Warr',
Le cont d'Arondell',
Le cont de Suff',
Le cont de Northumbr',
Le seignour de Nevill',
Le seignour de Clifford,
Le seignour Fitz-Wauter,
Le seignour la Zouche de Haryngworth',
Le seignour de Wilughby,
Johan de Cobham,
Richard le Scrop',
Guy de Bryan, banerettz.

Et celles mesmes seignours le roi lour grantast al effect q'ils furent demandez.
15. Item, puis apres quant la commune soi avoit communez avec les ditz seignours, ils retournerent autrefoitz en
[Col. b] parlement, en disant qe bon fust qe nostre seignour le roi fist sa grace a ceulx q'ont trespassez en cest rumour,

may well understand it, and later come to some agreement about it.'

12. And the king ordered Sir Richard le Scrope, knight, recently created chancellor of England, to rehearse the same charge, touching on the points mentioned. And he did so clearly, with reference to the recent repeal made of the grant of the franchise and manumission of the bondsmen and villeins of the land in particular. Those present in full parliament were then directly asked once again, on the king's behalf, whether that repeal would please them or not.

The repeal of the manumissions and franchise granted during the uprising.

13. To which, both the prelates and lords temporal as well as the knights, citizens, and burgesses answered with one voice, that the repeal was well made, adding that such a manumission or enfranchisement of the villeins could not be made without the assent of those who had the chief interest in the matter: and they had never agreed to it, either voluntarily or otherwise, nor would they ever do so, even if it were their dying day. And the prelates and lords and the said commons humbly prayed our lord the king that as those letters of manumission and enfranchisement had been made and granted by coercion, to the disinheritance of themselves and the ruin of the kingdom, they might be quashed and annulled by authority of this parliament, and the said repeal confirmed, because it had been well and justly done. And everyone there agreed and assented thereto with one voice. And then the commons prayed of the king our lord that certain prelates and lords might discuss their said charges with them, because those matters bore weightily upon the estate of the realm, and therefore they were in great need of their advice. To which it was said that they should write down the names of those they wished to have, and submit them to the king who would consider it further.

The lords appointed for the discussions.
14. Whereupon, they submitted in a written schedule the names of the prelates and lords listed below, namely:
The bishop of Winchester,
The bishop of Norwich,
The bishop of Exeter,
John king of Castile and of Leon, duke of Lancaster,
The earl of Buckingham,
The earl of Warwick,
The earl of Arundel,
The earl of Suffolk,
The earl of Northumberland,
Lord Neville,
Lord Clifford,
Lord FitzWalter,
Lord de la Zouche of Haringworth,
Lord Willoughby,
John Cobham,
Richard le Scrope,
Guy Bryan, bannerets.

And the king granted them those lords to the end for which they had been requested.
15. Also, when the commons had consulted with the said lords, they again returned to
[Col. b] parliament, saying that it was good that our lord the king had granted his grace to those who had participated

aufin de mettre par tant le meillour repos et quiete en /le\ roialme.

Requeste de la commune.
16. Et priast outre la dite commune qe les prelatz par eux mesmes, les grantz seignours temporelx par eux mesmes, les chivalers par eux, les justices par eux, et touz autres estatz singulerement fussent chargez de treter et communer sur ceste lour charge, et qe lour advis fust reportez a la commune, afyn qe bon remede fust ordenez. A quoy fust dit et responduz qe le roi ad fait charger les seignours et autres sages de communer et treter diligeaument sur les dites matires, mais l'anciene custume et forme de parlement a este toutdys, qe la commune reporteroit leur advis sur \les/ matires a eux donez au roi nostre seignour, et as seignours du parlement primerement, et noun pas econtra. Et ce fait, adonqes l'advis de seignours sur ce lour serroit monstrez, et purce le roi voet qe les anciennes et bones custumes et forme de parlement soient tenuz et bien gardez.

[6]*Membrane 11*

Requestes faites par la commune.
17. Item, les communes avauntdites retournerent autrefoitz en parlement, faisantz lour protestacioun come devant, en disantz qe sur les charges a eux donez ils avoient diligeaument communez avec les prelats et seignours a eux sur ce donez, et lour sembloit purvoir qe si la governance du roailme ne soit en brief temps amendez, mesme le roailme serra oultrement perduz et destruit pur toutz jours, et par consequens nostre seignour le roi, et touz les seignours et communes, qe Dieux ne voille pur sa mercy. Qar voirs est qe y a tielles defautes en dit governaille, quoi entour la persone le roi, et en son hostelle, et pur outrageouses nombre des familiers esteantz en dit hostiel; et quoy en ses courtes, sibien c'estassavoir en la chancellerie, bank le roi, commune bank, et l'escheqier; et par grevouses oppressions en paiis par la outrageouse multitude braceours des querelles, et maintenours, qi sont come rois en paiis, qe droit ne loye est a poy fait a nully, et la povre commune est de temps en temps a tiel guyse pilez et destruitz, quoy par les purveiours del dit hostiel le roi, et d'autres qi rienz ne paient a mesme la commune pur lour vitailles et cariage de eux pris, quoy par les subsides et taillages qui souent de eux levez a grantz destresses, et autrement par grevouses et outrageous oppressions a eux faitz par diverses ministres du roi et des autres seignours del roialme, et especialment par les ditz maintenours, qe mesme le commune est mys a grant cheitivetee et mesaise, et plus qe unqes ne fuist devant. Et sanz cella encores, combien qe grant tresor en continuelment grantez et levez de eux pur le defens du roialme, nientmeins ils n'ent sont le plus defenduz ne socourez encontre les enemys du roialme a leur escient, einz de an en an sont ars, robbez, et pilez, par terre et par meer par les ditz enemys, et par lours barges et galeys et autres vesseulx, de quoy nulle remede lour ad este, ne encores est, purveuz. Quelles meschiefs la dite povre commune, qe soleit ore tard vivre en toute honure et prosperitee, ne poet plus outre endurer par aucune voie. Et pur dire droit veritee, les dites outrages et autres q'aient este ore tard fait a la povre commune pluis communement qe unqes devant, dont ils soi sentirent si grantement grevtz qe celles \firent/ les dites menues communes lour moever, et faire le meschief q'ils firent en dit riot; et encores est a douter de greindre meschiefs, si de bone et due remedie ne

in this uprising, for the greater repose and tranquillity of the kingdom.

The request of the commons.
16. The said commons further prayed that the prelates themselves, the great lords temporal themselves, the knights themselves, the justices themselves, and all other estates be severally charged to discuss and consider their charge, and that their advice might be reported to the commons, so that an effective remedy could be ordained. To which it was said and replied that the king had instructed his lords and other wise men to discuss thoroughly and consider the said matters, but the ancient custom and form of parliament had always been that the commons reported their conclusions on the matters assigned them to the king our lord, and to the lords of parliament in the first instance, and not the other way round. And that said, the advice of the lords thereon would be revealed to them, for the king willed that the good and ancient customs and form of parliament be observed and fully protected.

The requests made by the commons.
17. Also, the aforesaid commons returned once more to parliament, making their protestation as before, and saying that they had diligently consulted on the matter with the prelates and lords assigned to them for the purpose, and it seemed to them that if the governance of the kingdom were not improved within a short space of time, the very kingdom itself would be utterly ruined and lost forever, as would our lord the king and all the lords and commons as a consequence, which God in his mercy forbid. For it is true that there are many faults in the said governance about the king's person, and in his household, and because of the outrageous number of servants in the said household; as well as in the king's courts, namely in the chancery, king's bench, common bench, and the exchequer; and there are grievous oppressions throughout the country from the excessive number of embracers of quarrels and maintainers, who act so much like kings in their shires that right and justice are scarcely administered to anyone, and the poor commons are periodically robbed and destroyed in such ways by the purveyors of the said king's household, and by others who pay them nothing for the victuals and carriage taken from them, and by the subsidies and tallages which are often forcibly levied from them, and by other grievous and outrageous oppressions inflicted on them by the ministers of the king and of the other lords of the realm, and especially by the said maintainers. Wherefore the said commons have lapsed into greater poverty and hardship than ever before. Moreover, although great sums are continually granted and levied from the commons for the defence of the realm, they are still no better defended or secured against the enemies of the kingdom, as far as they know, but are burned, robbed, and pillaged every year by the said enemies, by land and by sea, with their barges, galleys, and other vessels, against which no defence has ever been, nor is yet, provided. Which troubles the said poor commons, who were once accustomed to live in great honour and prosperity, can by no means endure any longer. And to tell the whole truth, the said outrages and others, recently committed against the poor commons more generally than ever before, made them feel so greatly oppressed that the lesser commons rose up and wrought havoc in the said tumult; and greater turmoil is still to be feared, unless good

---

[6]The rest of m.12 has been left blank.

soit par temps purveuz sur les outrageouses oppressions et meschiefs de dessusditz.

Qe plese a nostre seignour le roy, et as nobles seignours du roialme ore assemblez en ce parlement, pur la mercy Jhesu Crist, y mettre tiel remede et amendement sur le dit governaille toutz partes, qe l'estat et dignitee nostre dit seignour le roi principalement, et les nobles estatz des seignours du roialme soient entierment salvez, come l'entente de la commune est, et toutdys l'ont desirez; et mesme la commune puisse estre *[Page iii-101]* [Col. a] mys en quiete et paix, oustantz de tout si avaunt come homme les purra conustre, les malx officers et conseillers, et y mettantz en lour lieux des meillours, pluis vertuouses, et plus suffisantz, et oustantz touz les malx enchesons q'ont issint este motion del derrain rumour, et des autres meschiefs eschuz deinz le roialme, come dessus est dit, ou autrement ne pense mye homme qe ceste roialme puisse longement esser sanz greinour meschief qe unqes devaunt n'avenist a ycelle, qe Dieux defende. Et pur Dieux ne soit mis en ublie qe en toutes maneres soient mys entour la persone du roi pur et de son conseil, des plus suffisantz et discretz seignours et bachilers qe homme purra avoir ou trover deinz le roailme.

Grant fait par nostre seignour le roi.

18. Et est assavoir qe puis apres quant le roi nostre seignour avec les seignours du roialme et son conseil s'avoit fait adviser sur cestes requestes a lui faites pur le mieulx de lui et de son dit roialme, a ce qe veritablement lui appareust, il voloit et grantast qe certains prelats, seignours, et autres, furent assignez pur survere et examiner en prive conseil sibien l'estat et governaille de la persone nostre dit seignour, come de son dit hostiel, et de lour adviser des remedes suffisantz s'il embusoigneroit, \et ent faire lour report a roi dessusdit./ Et y fust dit par les seignours en parlement qe lour sembloit qe si amendement de governement serroit fait parmy le roialme l'en coviendroit commencer au principal membre q'est le roi mesmes, et puis de persone a persone, sibien de seinte esglise come autres, et de place en place, de pluis haut degre a pluis baas; nule persone, degree, ne place esparniant.

Les seignours esluz et assignez de entrecommuner avec la commune.

Et furent esluz a ce faire en dit hostiel, les seignours dessouz escritz, c'estassavoir:

Le duc de Lancastre,

Le eslit de Canterbirs,

L'ercevesqe d'Everwyk,

Les evesqes de Wyncestr', Ely, Excestre et Roucestre,

Le conts d'Arondell, Warr', Staff', Suff' et Salesbirs,

Le seignour de la Zouch',

Le seignour de Nevill'

Le seignour de Grey de Ruthin,

Le seignour Fitz Wauter,

\Monsire Richard le Scrop,/

Monsire Guy de Brian, et autres.

Et sur celle charge seierent en prive conseil plusours jours, sanz rienz faire de autre chose en parlement.

Confessour du roi. Et fait a remembrer qe le confessour nostre dit seignour le roi fust chargez en presence du roi et des seignours q'il soi abstiegnast de venir ou demurer en l'ostiel

and due remedy is soon provided for the abovesaid outrageous oppressions and mischiefs.

May it please our lord the king and the noble lords of the realm now assembled in this parliament, for the mercy of Jesus Christ, to apply such remedy and amendment to every part of the said governance, that the estate and dignity of our said lord the king in particular, and the noble estates of the lords of the realm be entirely preserved, as the commons intend, and have always desired; and that the commons themselves may *[Page iii-101]* [Col. a] live in peace and tranquillity, ousting evil officers and counsellors as soon as they can be identified, and placing others worthier and more virtuous in their stead, as well as uprooting the evils which led to the last uprising, and the other troubles which befell the said kingdom, as is said above, or else it cannot be believed that the kingdom will not, before long, experience greater trouble than has ever come upon it before, which God forbid. And for love of God, it should not be forgotten that the person of the king and his council should be surrounded with the most worthy and discreet lords and bachelors to be found and had within the kingdom.

The grant made by our lord the king.

18. Be it known that later, when the king our lord together with the lords of the realm and his council had considered those requests made of him, and what could best be done for himself and his said kingdom, as it truly seemed to him, he willed and granted that certain prelates, lords, and others might be appointed to investigate and examine the estate and governance of the person of our said lord, as well as his said counsel, in privy counsel, and to advise them of such suitable remedies as may be needed, and to report thereon to the aforesaid king. And the lords in parliament said that it seemed to them that if improvements in government were to be made throughout the realm it would be desirable to begin with its principal member, the king himself, progressing from person to person, both of holy church and others, and from place to place, from the highest degree to the lowest; no person, degree, or place being spared.

The lords elected and appointed to consult with the commons.

And the following lords were chosen to examine the said household:

The duke of Lancaster,

The elect of Canterbury,

The archbishop of York,

The bishops of Winchester, Ely, Exeter and Rochester,

The earls of Arundel, Warwick, Stafford, Suffolk and Salisbury,

Lord de la Zouche,

Lord Neville,

Lord Grey of Ruthin,

Lord FitzWalter,

Sir Richard le Scrope,

Sir Guy Bryan, and others.

And they were to deliberate on the charge in private for several days, without dealing with any other matter in parliament.

The king's confessor. And be it remembered that the confessor of our said lord the king was charged in the presence of the king and the lords, to abstain from visiting or staying in

du roi, sinoun tantseulement a les quatre principalx festes del an; et ce estoit fait par l'assent des seignours, a la requeste de la commune, q'avoit priez au roi d'avoir le dit confessour oultreement remuez del roi et de son office.

[7]Et puis autrefoitz, quant la dite commune estoit acertes qe les ditz seignours estoient issint assignez de faire le dit charge, mesme la commune revient en parlement, et y firent certeins lours requestes mises en escrit, et liverez avant en parlement, en certeins articles en la fourme qe s'ensuit:

PETICIONS DES COMMUNES.
19. [Reform of the king's household] Prient les communes a mon treshonure[8] seignour de Lancastre, et a touz noz autres seignours ov lui esluz par nostre tresredoute seignour le roi, pur ordener l'estat nostre dit seignour honurablement et honestement, sibien des bones gentz et dignes entour sa persone come bones et vaillantz officers pur son hostiel, sibien de ceux qe ore sont ove nostre dit seignour, come des autres la ou les pluis suffisantz y soient, pensantz tendrement, s'il vous plest, sur les principales persones qe serront entour sa persone, et les principals officers qe serront de son hostiel, q'ils soient de les pluis discretz et pluis vaillantz de roialme et de nulle autres, oustant les mals, si aucuns soient, sibien pur conseiller les grandes officers par dehors l'ostelle quant busoigne serra, come pur governaille du persone nostre dit seignour et de son hostelle, en honour et profit de lui et de son roialme:

[Col. b] pensant auxi, s'il vous plest, de la grande repaire des gentz sibien a chival come a pee qi sont repairantz au dit hostelle, faisant tiel nombre et tiel gent en le dit hostielle qe nostre dit seignour puisse vivre honestement de son propre desore enavant, sanz charger son poeple come ad este fait pardevant. Considerantz, pur Dieux, les greves et pleintes qe le povre poeple ont fait sovent pur mal governaille et outrageouses despenses, et ne scievent ne ne poent qe pleindre et clamer pur remedie.

Chancellerie.
20. [The chancellor and chancery] Item, ils prient qe l'ordenance faite pur le corps nostre dit seignour et pur son hostelle, vous plese, par avis de nostre tresredoute seignour suisdit ordeiner un sage, un discret, et le plus suffisant qe l'en poet trover de la roialme, soit il espirituel ou temporel, pur chanceller d'Engleterre: considerantz la necessitee qe le roi nostre dit seignour et sa roialme ont au present du dit office avoir le plus sage et le plus vaillant, sibien pur busoignes par dehors la roialme, come dedeins. Et quant il eslu, adonqes par vous noz seignours, et par luy, en plesance de Dieux, et honour et profit al roialme, qe l'estat du chancellerie soit bien examinez, et triez hors les bons a demurrer, et les malveises a remoever si pres come homme lour poet conustre, sanz hayne ou affection. Entenduz, s'il vous plest qe grant rumour en la roialme par tout ad estee, et est q'ils sont pur le plus graunde partie trope graas sibien en corps come en burse, et trop bien furrez, et lours benefices mal giez, par grevouses oppressions faitz et par eux usez vers le poeple, par colour de lour office: et nientmeins a grantz coustages nostre dit seignour sanz busoigne, et grande desplesance et offense a Dieux, et a deshoneur de seinte esglise, come l'en poet bien le declarrer, si mistier soit.

the king's household, except on the four principal feasts of the year; which was done with the assent of the lords, at the request of the commons, who had prayed of the king that the said confessor be altogether removed from the king's company and his office.

Subsequently, when the said commons learnt that the said lords had been thus appointed to carry out the said charge, the same commons returned to parliament, and there they put certain of their requests in writing, and submitted them to parliament in the form of certain articles, as follows:

THE PETITIONS OF THE COMMONS.
19.[Reform of the king's household]. The commons pray of my most honoured lord of Lancaster, and of all our other lords elected with him by our most redoubtable lord the king, to order the estate of our said lord honourably and honestly, as well to have good and worthy people about his person as good and worthy officers for his household, as well those who are now with our said lord, as others who be the most worthy, carefully considering, if it please you, the chief persons who shall be about his person, and the principal officers who shall be in his household, that they may be the most discreet and worthy of the kingdom and no others, ousting the evil ones if there are any, and both to advise the great officers outside the household whenever necessary, and to govern the person of our said lord and his household, for the honour and profit of himself and his kingdom:

[Col. b] considering also, if it please you, that the great company of people on horse and foot who come to the said household, be reduced to such a number and comprise such persons that our said lord may live honestly within his own means from now on, without charging his people as has been done before. Considering also, for the love of God, the grievances and complaints that the poor people have often made about bad governance and outrageous expense, and that they do not know how, and are unable, to secure a remedy.

Chancery.
20.[The chancellor and chancery]. Also, they pray that the ordinance made for the person of our said lord and for his household, if it please you, with the advice of our aforesaid most redoubtable lord shall ordain a wise and discreet man, the best qualified to be found in the kingdom, be he spiritual or temporal, to be chancellor of England: considering the present need of the king our said lord and his kingdom that the said office be occupied by the most wise and the most enterprising, both for business outside the kingdom and within it. And when he has been appointed, then let the estate of the chancery be thoroughly investigated and examined by you our lords, and by him, for the sake of God, and the honour and profit of the realm, so that the good are retained and the bad replaced as soon as they are known, without hatred or favour. Understanding, if you please, that there was and is a great murmuring thoughout the realm that they are for the most part too fat in body and in purse, and too well provided, and their benefices ill managed, through the grievous oppressions done and practised by them against the people, by colour of their office: and yet they are a great and unnecessary expense to our said lord, a cause of great displeasure and offence to God, and dishonour to holy church, as can be fully explained if need be.

---

[7] A change of hand occurs here.
[8] *Original* treshone

Escheqier.

21. [The treasurer and the exchequer] Item, ils prient a nostre dit seignour et a noz autres seignours qe en mesme le manere puisse estre ordene du tresorer d'Engleterre, et des barons et toutz autres officers en l'escheqier, et l'estat d'icelle bien taster et roigner en plesance de Dieux, et profit a tout le roialme; considerantz, s'il vous plest qe certes par le place suisdit bien et loialment governez, et en due manere, aviendra grant profit a nostre dit seignour, et tranquilitee a tout le poeple, qe sovent paravant ses heures ont este en la dite place malement amesnez, sanz nul profit vers le roi, mes soul pur lour mesmes de la dite place. Dont remedie pur Dieux.

Justices. La loy de la terre.

22. [Judges and the law] Item, ils prient qe en mesme le manere puisse estre ordene de les justices de l'un bank et del autre, et de lour deux places. Et pur Dieux, seignours, et pur paix seurement sustiner dedeinz le roialme, qe les loies soient desore enapres duement et egalment amesnez et executez, sibien entre povres et riches come entre touz autres. Et qe les delaies et destourbes encountre droit usez pardevaunt ces heures puissent par bone ordenance ore apres estre redressez par les justices, et autres vaillantz et loialx apris en la loye, pur appeiser et nurrir le poeple en quiete, sibien en les deux places susdites come dehors en assises, et en toutz autres lieux ou les loies serront usez. Et qe au present, par serement des deux justices, deux serjantz, et quatre loialx apprentices vous plese estre enfourmez de les meschiefs qe le poeple ont soeffert par termes /en\ la loie, et par delaies et destourbes, et par queux ils ont amenuz qi ont grevez le poeple: et par lour dit serement a vous declarrer le mal et le bien q'ils scievent, et en quelle manere desore enapres les loies et gentz du loie en chescun paiis puissent mieultz et plus peisiblement en droiture estre governez. Et par celle manere, treshonurez seignours, avendretz en ceste matire a grant esploit et bon effect; par quiel article bien ordenez et bien [Page iii-102]

[Col. a] purveue pur les loies droitement governer, et par brief cours, aviendra grant establissement pur paix et quiete du poeple, sanz nul doute.

23. [Notification to the commons of appointments proposed] Item, treshonurez seignours, prient les communes qe quant vous avez appointez par avis nostre tresredoute seignour le roi les officers et l'estat des toutes les dites places, en manere come vous veez pur l'onour et bien de /nostre\ dit seignour, et profit du roialme, q'il plese a nostre dit seignour, et a vous, qe vostre dite commune ent puissent savoir les persones et manere del dite ordenance, devant q'ils soient engrossez et affermez, pur le plus seurement estre enfourmez de ce qe bosoigne requert, s'il vous plest.

24. [Preservation of the peace] Item, ils prient qe quant les dites articles et remedies soient appointez qe vous veulliez penser outre et ordeiner pur establisement de la roialme a pees, \et/ a seurete du roi nostre seignour et son loial poeple, considerant les larons et robbours sibien a chival come au pee en diverses paiis, a grant destruccion de les bones gentz de la terre; et par tiel manere ordener qe le poeple et gentz busoignouses del roialme laborent de lour mayn, sanz paresce et sanz robber et peril de poeple. Et auxi ordener qe si ascun poeple vorroit assembler pur rumour faire en manere come tard avenist qe Dieux ne veulle, en tiel cas quoy fuisse a faire sibien pur le roi come pur la paiis, et pur lour appeiser et destourber de lour malice, qe tiel damage et peril n'aviegne apres come ad este pardevant.

The exchequer.

21. [The treasurer and the exchequer]. Also, they pray of our said lord and our other lords that the treasurer of England, and the barons and all other officers in the exchequer be governed in the same manner, and the state thereof thoroughly examined and investigated, for the sake of God, and the profit of all the kingdom; considering if it please you, that if the aforesaid place were to be well, loyally and appropriately governed, great profit would ensue for our said lord, and tranquillity for all the people, profit which has too often been abused in the said place, without any profit to the king, but only to those of the said place. For which remedy is sought, for the love of God.

Justices. The law of the land.

22. [Justices and the law]. Also, they pray that justices of the one bench or the other, and of both places, be ordained in the same manner. And for love of God, lords, and for the sure maintenance of the peace within the kingdom, that the laws henceforth be duly and impartially enforced and executed, between the rich and the poor, and between all others. And that the delays and obstruction of right practised in the past may be avoided from now on by the judges under good ordinance, and by other worthy and loyal men learned in the law, to pacify the people and nurture tranquillity, as well in the two aforementioned places as beyond them in the assizes, and in all other places where the law is practised. And that now, on the oath of the two judges, two serjeants, and four faithful apprentices it may please you to be informed of the troubles which the people have suffered under the law, and through delays and obstructions by which those who have grieved others prosper: and on their said oath to inform you of the good and bad of which they know, and advise you as to how in the future the laws and men of the law in every part may be better and more peacably governed in accordance with right. And in the same way, most honoured lords, that this matter may be duly concluded and put to good effect; by which article it is well ordained and [Page iii-102]

[Col. a] provided that the laws be honestly administered, and the peace and tranquillity of the people no doubt will shortly follow.

23. [Notification to the commons of appointments proposed]. Also, most honoured lords, the commons pray that when, by the advice of our most redoubtable lord the king, you have appointed the officers and estate of all the said places, as you see fit for the honour and good of our said lord, and the profit of the kingdom, that it may please our said lord, and you, that your said commons hence be informed of the persons appointed and the nature of the said ordinance, before they are entered and sworn, so that they be better informed of what their business requires, if it please you.

24. [Preservation of the peace]. Also, they pray that when the said articles and remedies have been agreed upon, you will further consider and provide for the establishment of peace within the realm and the security of the king our lord and his loyal people, considering the thieves and robbers on horse as well as on foot in various parts, destroying the good people of the land; and to ordain in such a way that the needy people and folk of the kingdom labour for themselves without idleness, and without robbing and endangering the people. And also to ordain that if any seek to gather forces to stage such an uprising as happened of late, which God forbid, then action may be taken for the king as well as for the country, to pacify them and obstruct their malice, so that the injury and peril which arose in the past shall not arise again.

25. [Defence of the realm] Item, ils prient q'ore entre vous noz seignours qe soiez ordenez pur les dites matiers remedier, veulliez auxi penser de les guerres, sagement et distinctement les amenuser, si ce poet estre, en descharge du roi et du roialme, lours perdez des biens par meer et par terre perduz considerer, et ent purvoier amendement, sibien en encrees de nostre poeple come pur eschuer l'encrees et richesse de noz enemys, qi susteignent leur guerre en grant partie par noz biens robbez et raunsonez, a grande esclaundre de la governaille de nous et de la roialme, et tout oultrement en destruccioun de tut le roialme par povert sensible, si avaunt qe sanz doute il est importable au roi et a roialme pur susteiner plus avant les coustages et biens degastez sur les dites guerres, et auxi de susteiner autres perdes et damages portez par le roialme, si remedie ne soit purveu au present, de quele matire la busoigne est si grant par toute la terre, qe lour covient de force ent compleindre, et avoir et savoir le remedie devant lour departir.

26. [The realm impoverished] Item, supplient les ditz communes a nostre tresredoute seignour le roi, et a noz autres seignours esluz qe lour plese devant lour departir avoir bone consideracioun al grant povertee dedeins le roialme au present, q'est tout voide de tresor et de tout autre bien a regarde de ce q'ad este en la dite roialme pardevant, et q'est avenuz par moultz enchesons; c'estassavoir, par la monoie d'or et d'argent apportez et trehez hors le roialme; et ce q'est demurrez est roignez pur la plus grant parte, a perde deinz une libre de pois d'or .xiij. s., .iiij. d. et pluis; auxi par les outrageouses guerres sustenuz par le roialme a nul esploit, et par les perdes du meer et terre pur les dites guerres perduz, et les costes du meer nient gardez ne defenduz. Et nientmeins voz comoditees du roialme, come leines, estein, et plum, nient a value come out este devaunt ces heures, a grant empoverissement de tout le roialme. Et jademeyns les coustages de chescun estat plus outrageouses par tout le roialme qe unqes ne ount este pardevaunt, toutdis enclynant a povertee sanz encrees, et si ad le roialme este en declyn a poverte cestes .xvi. ans et pluis sanz remedie purveuz.

Sur queux matiers, treshonurez seignours, pur Dieux, pur honour et profit de vous, et

[Col. b] pur relevere les povres du roialme, veulliez tendrement penser par vous et par autres sages par queux vous veez qe soient pur appeller a vous, remedie ent puisse duement au present estre ordenez, et seurement les remedies pur les ditz perils tenuz, ou autrement, treshonurez seignours, il n'est pas a crere bien ne prosperitee endurer parentre les gentz de la terre, pur la povertee q'est semblable avenir.

27. Et quant Dieux ad pleu ottroier par vous, nostre seignour lige, et par noz autres seignours par vous esluz, bones ordenances et remedies pur les greves et perils avauntditz, plese a vostre nobleye, en plesance de Dieux, et en perfaite esploit de bone governaille, overtement devant tut vostre present parlement priere a voz peres, et as touz autres seignours de vostre terre ycy assemblez q'ils veullient, et chescun soy veulle prometre, en lui, et pur lui, a tenir fermement ce q'orest purveu pur remedie de tout le poeple, nient contrevenaunt pur nule puissance q'ils ont en lours grantz estatz, et sur les officers ore esluz, et sur les justices, et sur touz autres commissioners qi averont affaire entre le poeple, tiele peine ordeiner, et lour peyne en pleyn parlement faire declarrer qe due execucioun se purra estre fait de toutes les remedies ore appointez entre /toutes\ persones, et en toutes temps; et en acomplissement de bon et gracious conseille en ceste parlement tiele grace et pardoun ottroier as touz les liges ore esteantz en awere de lours vies, come par une peticioun ent

25. [Defence of the realm]. Also, they pray that now amongst yourselves, our lords, you make ordinance to remedy the said matters, and that you consider the wars, wisely and considerably to reduce them if it can be done, for the relief of the king and the kingdom, and that you consider the goods that have been lost by land and sea, and provide some remedy, both for the benefit of our people and to annul the gains and enrichment of our enemies, who sustain their war largely by stealing and ransoming our goods, to the great slander of our governance and of the kingdom, and to the entire destruction of the kingdom by poverty, so that without doubt the king and kingdom can no longer support the charges and the goods wasted by the said wars, and the other losses and injuries which the kingdom bears, if remedy be not now provided, the need of which is so great throughout the land that the commons must complain of sheer necessity, and wish to receive and learn of the remedy before their departure.

26. [The realm impoverished]. Also, the said commons request of our most redoubtable lord the king, and our other lords chosen that it may please them, before their departure, fully to consider the great poverty in the kingdom at present, which is empty of riches and of all other wealth because of what has already occurred and arisen in the said kingdom for many reasons; namely, the removal and withdrawal of gold and silver money from the kingdom; and that what remains has been clipped for the most part, to the loss in a pound's weight of gold, of 13s., 4d. or more; also, as a result of the outrageous number of wars sustained by the kingdom to no effect, and the losses by land and sea sustained as a result of the said wars, and the coasts of the sea not being guarded or defended. And yet your commodities of the kingdom, like wool, tin, and lead, are not worth what they were in the past, to the great impoverishment of the whole realm. And yet, the expenses of each estate are more exorbitant throughout the realm than they have ever been before, leading always to poverty without gain, so that this kingdom has declined into misery these past fifteen years or more without a remedy being supplied.

Most honoured lords, for love of God, for your honour and benefit, and

[Col. b] to relieve the poor of the kingdom, may you carefully consider these matters, consulting with such other wise men as you see fit to call upon, so that remedy for this may be duly and now ordained, and the remedies for the said perils securely established, for otherwise, most honoured lords, it is inconceivable that good or prosperity will abound amongst the people of the land, because of the poverty which is bound to arise.

27. And when it has pleased God to grant through you, our liege lord, and through our other lords chosen by you, good ordinances and remedies for the aforesaid perils and grievances, may it please your nobility, to the pleasure of God, and for the perfect execution of good governance, before all your present parliament to pray openly of your peers, and all the other lords of your land here assembled, that each and every one of them will promise firmly to uphold that which is now provided by way of remedy for all the people, and not undo it by any power which they have in their great estates, and upon the officers now elected, and upon the justices, and all other commissioners, who have to act amongst the people, to ordain such penalties, and to cause them to be declared in full parliament on certain pain, that all the remedies which have now been decided shall be duly performed amongst everyone and for all time; and by good and gracious counsel in this parliament, to grant grace and pardon to all the lieges who now fear for their lives, as is set

faite et declarrez est compris. Et si en avera nostre dit seignour, et toutes noz autres seignours et communes, grande gree de Dieux et de gentz. Dieux le veulle, amen.

Ottroi fait par le roi as ditz articles.
28. Et fait a remembrer quant mesmes les articles estoient lues en dit parlement si fuist assentuz qe sibien les clercs de la chancellerie de les deux principalx degrees, et les justices, et sergeantz, barons et grantz officers de l'escheqier trestouz, et auxint certaines persones des mellious apprentices de la loi, serront chargez par lour ligeances et serementz, chescune degree par soy, de lour adviser diligealment de les abusions, tortz et defautes qe furent faites et usez en lours places, et en les courtes du roi, et auxint en les courtes d'autres seignours parmy le roialme; et par especial des ditz maintenours et extorcioners en paiis, et de lours malfaitz, d'amender le dit governaille, come devant ad este requis. Et auxint estoit advis qe les marchantz serroient de lour part semblablement chargez de lour adviser sur les meschiefs qe sont deinz le roialme, de ce qe les commoditees cresceantz deinz le roialme sont ore de pluis petit pris qe unqes devant ne soleient; et les marchandises qe viegnent depar dela si sont de plus grant pris qe ne soloient; et la navie du roialme a poy destruit; et la monoie tundue, et autrement appeirez, et emportez hors du roialme, en tiele manere qe riens n'est a poy remys \ne/ de bien ne de bountee quant as dites choses deinz le roialme avauntdit. Et qe sur lour advis ent pris chescun des dites degrees et places par soi mettroit en escrit les meschiefs usez en le governaille q'a luy appartient, et avec ce leur avis des remedies a purvoier pur amendement, au fin qe les seignours et communes apris del purpos de ceulx qi mieulz ent sont conissantz, par reson purront le plus

Membrane 10 discretement aler avant a bone conclusion d'amender ce q'est a amender en dit governaill, come devant est demandez. Et einsi furent chargez de faire singulerement.

Chancellerie et l'escheqier.
29. Et puis apres quant ils s'avoient advis de lours charges et appointes, les meschiefs et remedies, les ditz degres singulerement firent report devant les seignours et communes a diverses journees, aucuns en escrit, et aucuns par bouche, de ce qe lour ent sembloit par leur charge a remedier, dont en partie remede est purveuz en *[Page iii-103]*
[Col. a] cest parlement, sibien c'estassavoir de ceulx de l'escheqier, come de les marchandies. Et de la chancellerie, si defaute y serra trovez en lour governaille, le chanceller ad dit q'il le fra amender a tout son poair, et sanz delay.

Requeste de la commune pur grace et pardoun avoir, etc.
30. Item, autrefoitz reviendrent les communes en parlement, monstrantz une cedule contenant en trois articles le manere de trois maneres de graces et pardoun affaire, si plest a nostre seignour le roi, /ore a sa commune\ de son dit roialme. La primere grace, pur les seignours, gentils, et autres qe en resistence des ryotours et treitours firent occire certains persones sanz due proces de /loy.\ La secounde, pur appaiser les malx gentz qe ensi leverent en dit rumour, pur treson et felonie fait en dit rumour; et la tierce, d'autre grace affaire as bones gentz qi se tindrent en paix, et ne leverent mye, empriantz qe \sur/ celles graces vousissent aviser de faire graciouse responce, pur la quiete et commune profit de roialme, purveuz toutes voies qe certeins persones qe furent principalx excitours et comenceours del dit rumour, dont les nouns ore sont et en apres serront liverez en parlement, n'aient aucune part de la dite grace par quelconqe voie. Et sur ce le

out in a petition made and announced thereon. And for this, our said lord, and all our other lords and commons shall have great thanks of God and of men, God willing, Amen.

Agreement given by the king to the said articles.
28. And be it remembered that when the same articles had been read in the said parliament it was agreed that the clerks of the chancery of the two first degrees, and all the justices, serjeants, barons, and great officers of the exchequer, as well as certain of the greater apprentices of the law, should be charged on oath and on the strength of their allegiance, in their several degrees, diligently to inform themselves of abuses, wrongs, and faults committed and practised in their offices, and in the king's courts, and also in the courts of other lords throughout the kingdom; and especially of the said maintainers and extortioners in the county, and of their misdeeds, to improve the said governance, as had been requested in the past. And it was also recommended that the merchants should for their part similarly be charged to advise themselves of the troubles occurring within the kingdom, in so far as commodities produced in the kingdom are now worth less than ever before; and the merchandise which comes from overseas is of a higher price than it was; and the kingdom's fleet almost destroyed; and the coinage clipped and otherwise defaced, and carried out of the kingdom, to such an extent that scarcely anything of worth or quality is left of the said resources within the aforesaid kingdom. And that on their advice, the said degrees and estates should take it upon themselves severally to write down the faults found in governance, together with advice on the corrective remedies to be applied, so that the lords and commons, having learnt the opinions of those who are most knowledgeable therein, may with reason
Membrane 10 the better proceed to an effective decision to amend that which is to be amended in the said governance, as has previously been requested. And that they were severally charged to do so.

The chancery and the exchequer.
29. Later, when they had discussed their charges and decisions, and the troubles and remedies, the said degrees individually and on various days, some in writing and some by word of mouth, reported on that which seemed to them in need of remedy, which remedy was provided in part in *[Page iii-103]*
[Col. a] this parliament, namely for those in the exchequer, as in matters of commerce. As for the chancery, if fault be found in its governance, the chancellor has said that he will rectify it to the best of his power, and without delay.

The request of the commons to have graces and pardons, etc..
30. Also, the commons returned again to parliament, displaying a schedule containing in three articles the three kinds of grace and pardon now to be made, if it pleased our lord the king, to the commons of his said realm. The first grace was for the lords, gentles, and others who in resisting the rioters and traitors, had killed certain persons without due process of law. The second was to pardon the evil doers who had taken part in the said rebellion, of the treason and felony they had committed in the said uprising; and the third was the grace to be awarded to good men who remained in peace and did not rebel, requesting that they might wait for the king's gracious reply concerning these graces, for the tranquillity and common profit of the kingdom, provided in all cases that certain persons who were the principal instigators and initiators of the said uprising, whose names are known and shall later be delivered in parliament, should have not

roi nostre seignour, par l'advis des seignours, justices, et autres de son conseil, si \fist/ appointer le manere et fourme des dites pardouns, en la forme qe s'ensuit:

La forme grantez des chartres de pardoun de la grace le roi. Grace pur les seignours et gentils, etc.
31. Ce est la fourme accordez en parlement sur la grace et pardoun qe le roi ferroit ore a sa commune par les causes suisdites: primerement, touchant les seignours, gentils, et autres, queux en les rumour et insurreccioun de villeins et d'autres malfaisours, q'ore tard se leverent \traiterousement/ par assemblees en outrageouse multitude en diverses parties du roialme, contre Dieux, bone foi et resoun, et contre la dignitee nostre seignour le roi et sa corone, et les loies de sa terre, firent diverses punissementz sur les ditz villeyns et autres issint levantz, sanz due proces de loy, et en autre manere qe la loy et usage de la terre demandent, combien qe ce firent ils noun pas de malice purpensez, einz soulement pur contresteer la malice comencez, et pur cesser et appeiser le dit meschief; nostre seignour le roi considerant les grantz diligences et loialtee des seignours et gentilx en celle partie, et qe a celle foitz pur la meschief apparant homme ne poast sur les ditz punissementz avoir attendu de faire proces de loy; et aiant regarde a ce qe les ditz seignours et gentilx faisantz les ditz punissementz selonc lours propres avis et discretions, et a bone entente, ne furent touz apris de loy; et voillant par tant a eux faire grace sicome moelt bien \[l'ont deserviz,]/ lour ad pardone et relessez, de l'assent des seignours et communes en ce parlement, quanqe a lui ent appartient, ou a lui et ses heirs purra appartenir; issint qe en temps avenir pur chose issint faite par eux ou nul de eux sur les ditz punissementz et resistence quelconqe ce soit, ils ne soient jammais empeschez ne grevez en quelconqe manere, en corps, n'en biens, ne en lours heritages et possessions quelconqes, par nostre seignour le roi, ses heirs, et ministres, n'autres quelconqes, en aucun temps avenir: mais tout oultrement ent soient quitz a touz jours par cest estatut, sanz autre chartre en avoir en especial, ou pursuir.

Grace pur les rebelx.
32. Item, nostre seignour le roi, considerant coment ses liges et subgitz de son dit roialme tutdys depuis sa coronement tanqe as dites insurreccions et levees faitz se sont bien portez et peisiblement lour governez, et lour ad trovez propices et bone voluntee devers lui en toutz ses affaires et necessitees; et par tant combien qe plusours de eux en dites insurreccions aient commys tiel traisoun et felonie envers lui et sa coroune et les loyes de sa terre q'ils ont forfait envers lui lours corps, terres, et biens; nientmeins, al reverence de Dieux, et de sa doulce mere Seinte Marie, et al especiale requeste de noblee dame, dame Anne, file a noble Prince Charles nadgaires emperour
[Col. b] de Rome, roigne d'Engleterre, si Dieux plest, proscheinement avenir; et auxint au fin qe mesme les subgitz eient la greindre corage a demurrer en lour foialtee et ligeance pur temps avenir, sicome ils firent devant la /dite\ levee; de /sa\ grace especiale ad pardonez a sa dite commune, et a chescune singulere persone d'ycelle qe ne soit ou sont mye des villes de Canterbirs, Bury Seint Esmon, Beverleye, Scardeburgh', Bruggewater, et Cantebrugg', horspris par especial /les\ persones des queux les nouns en apres sont escritz, queux nouns sont mis avant en parlement, come ceux qi sont arettez et /accusez\ pur chiefteins, dustres, excitours, et principalx des dites insurreccions et malfaitz, par la

the least part in the said graces. And thereupon, the king our lord, by the advice of the lords, justices, and others of his council, had the manner and form of the said pardons set out in the following way:

The form given to the charters of pardon of the king's grace. Grace for the lords and gentry, et cetera.
31. This is the form agreed in parliament for the grace and pardon which the king will now grant to his commons for the aforesaid reasons: firstly, touching the lords, gentles, and others who during the uprising and insurrection of the villeins and other malefactors, who lately rebelled treacherously by assembling in great multitudes in various parts of the kingdom, and against God, good faith, and reason, and against the dignity of our lord the king and his crown, and the laws of his land, inflicted various punishments on the said villeins and others so rebelling, without due process of the law, and contrary to the requirements of the law and usages of the land, although they did this so not with malice aforethought, but solely to resist the evil begun, and to quell and end the said mischief; our lord the king, considering the great diligence and loyalty of the lords and noblemen in that regard, and that at that time, there was no time for legal procedure to be followed in the said punishments; and bearing in mind that the said lords and noblemen inflicting the said punishments at their own judgment and discretion, and with good intent, were not all learned in law; and wishing for that reason to grant them the grace which they have fully deserved, has pardoned and released them, with the assent of the lords and commons in this parliament, as far as it pertains to him to do so, or may pertain to him and his heirs; so that in time to come, for anything done by them or one of them in respect of the said punishments and resistance, whatsoever it may be, they shall never be prosecuted or punished in any way, in body, nor in goods, nor in their inheritances or possessions whatsoever, by our lord the king, his heirs, and ministers, nor any others, at any time in the future: but that they shall be quit entirely and forever by this statute, without receiving any other special charter, or bringing suit. Grace for the lords and gentry, et cetera.

Grace for the rebels.
32. Also, our lord the king considering that the lieges and subjects of his said realm, from the time of his coronation until the said insurrections and uprisings, had conducted themselves well, governed themselves peaceably, and shown him favour and good will in all his needs and affairs; and although some of them during the said insurrections had committed such treason and felony towards him, his crown, and the laws of the land that they had forfeited their bodies, lands, and goods to him; nevertheless, out of reverence for God and His sweet mother St Mary, and at the special request of the noble lady, the Lady Anne, daughter of the noble prince Charles, late emperor
[Col. b] of Rome, soon, if it please God, to be queen of England; and also to the end that the same subjects should be the more strongly inclined to remain faithful and loyal in future, as they were before the said uprising; of his special grace he has pardoned the said commons, and each and every member of them not of the towns of Canterbury, Bury St Edmunds, Beverley, Scarborough, Bridgwater, and Cambridge, excepting in particular the persons whose names are listed below, their names being put forward in parliament as those who are the arrested and accused by the commons of their country in this parliament, as the heads, leaders, instigators, and principals of the said insurrections and misdeeds

commune de lour paiis en ce parlement; et horspris touz provours et appellez des dites traisons et felonies, et horspris ceux qi tuerent Symon l'ercevesqe de Canterbirs nadgairs chanceller, le priour de Seint Johan adonqes tresorer, et Johan de Cavendissh' chief justice nostre dit seignour, et horspris ceux qi se sont eschapez ou departiz de prisone, et ne se sont encores renduz ne retournez a ycelle. Les queux persones le roi ne voet mie, quant au present, q'ils aient part de sa dite grace toutes maneres des tresons et felonies par eux es dites insurreccions parentre le primer jour de Maii derrain passez [1381] et la feste de Tousseintz lors proschein ensuant [1 November 1381] faitz ou perpetrez, dont ils sont enditez, rettes, ou enchesonez, et auxint les utlagaries, etc. Et n'est mye l'entencioun le roi qe les parties endamagez es dites insurreccions soient forclos parmye ceste grace, q'ils ne purront pur le recoverir de lours damages et perdes euz et soeffertz es dites insurrections pursuir par quelconqes accions, par quelles homme ne purra \[proceder a]/ juggement de vie. Et est assentuz qe cellui qi vorra enjoier ceste grace, ent pursue d'avoir sa chartre en especial parentre cy et la fest de Pentecost proschein avenir [25 May 1382].

\[Grace pur la bone et loiale commune, etc.]/
33. Item, nostre seignour le roi, considerant \[coment plusours]/ gentilx, et autres bones \[communes, sibien es countees et paiis ou le dit rumour et]/ insurrection se firent, \[come]/ en autres \[paiis et countees ou les dites insurrections ore se]/ firent mye, al temps du dit rumour, se avoient et governoient en bone paiis et quiete, sanz faire ou consentir au chose aucune qe purroit soner en perturbacion de la paix, combien qe grant excitacion avoient a contraire, aucuns par manaces de malfaisours survenantz, et aucuns en diverse autre manere - dont ils \[ont]/ deserviz grant reward et \[guerdon -]/ et par tant pur \[eschancier]/la corage de touz \[ceux qi]/ ont bien fait en celle partie de lour continuer bien pur temps avenir, et pur ensample doner as autres de bien faire, al reverence de Dieux, et al instance et especiale requeste del dite dame, nostre dit seignour le roy de sa grace especiale ad pardonez a sa commune, et a chescune persone de mesme le roialme qi ne se leverent mye, etc., en dite insurrection .... toutes maneres de felonies faitez ou perpetrez devant le .xiiij.^{me} jour de Decembre, l'an present, dont ils sont enditez, etc., ou enchesonez; exceptz traisones, murdres, et ravissementz des femmes, et auxint les utlagaries, si nules, etc. Horspris ceux qi sont enditez pur communes larons, ou communes homicides, et ceux qi sont communes larons, et communes homicides: et exceptz toutes provours et appellez; et ceux qi sont eschapez ou issiz hors de prisone et ne se sont depuis renduz a ycelle; et ceux auxint horspris qe furent detenuz en prisone pur felonie le dit .xiiij.^{me} jour de Decembre [1381]. Et auxint, pur greindre reward faire as dites bones communes, le roi lour ad pardonez et relessez quanqe a lui appartient, pur toutes maneres de trespas et mesprisions par eux faitz, ou nul de eux, devant mesme le xiiij jour de Decembre, qe cherroient en fin ou raunceon devers le roi ou ses heirs; horspris les dettes le roy, et horspris reconisances et obligacions faites au roi ou a ses progenitours pur toutes maneres de seuretees de paix, et en autre manere. Et ordenez est qe ceux qi vorront enjoier ceste pardon, ent pursuent lours chartres en especial entre cy et la feste de Pentecost suisdite [25 May 1382].
Page iii-104
34. Item, le venderdy qe fuist le .xiij. jour de Decembre, revindrent en presence les dites communes, et illoeqes nostre seignour le roi lors present, firent reherceal et recapitulacioun de leurs requestes devaunt faitz, et prierent a nostre seignour le roi, et as seignours du parlement, d'avoir veue

committed; also excluding all approvers and those appealed of the said treasons and felonies, as well as those who killed Simon, archbishop of Canterbury, lately chancellor, the prior of St John, then treasurer, and John Cavendish, chief justice of our said lord; and excluding those who have escaped or fled from prison, and have not yet returned or been returned there. For the king assuredly does not wish that those people shall, for the present, have any part in the said grace in respect of all manner of treasons and felonies committed and perpetrated by them in the said insurrections between 1 May last and the following feast of All Saints [1 November 1381], for which they have been indicted, charged, or accused, and also outlawries, etc.. And it is indeed not the intention of the king that parties injured in the said insurrections shall be prevented by this grace from recovering, by various legal actions which stop short of a judgment of death, their damages and losses suffered in the said insurrections. And it is agreed that he who wishes to enjoy this grace shall seek his individual charter between now and the feast of Whitsun next. [25 May 1382]

Grace for the good and loyal commons, etc..
33. Also, our lord the king, considering that many gentlemen and other good commons, as well in the counties and parts where the said uprising and insurrection took place, as in other parts and counties where the said insurrections have since occurred, conducted and governed themselves in peace and tranquillity, without doing or agreeing to anything which might result in a disturbance of the peace, even though they were greatly urged to do so, some by the threats of malefactors coming upon them, and some in various other ways - for which they deserve considerable reward and recompense - and also to encourage thereby those who acted well in that matter to continue to do so in future, and as an inspiration to others, out of reverence for God, and at the instance and special request of the said lady, our said lord the king, by his special grace, has pardoned his commons, and any of the same kingdom who did not rebel, et cetera, in the said insurrections, of all manner of felonies committed and perpetrated before 14 December in the present year, of which they have been indicted, etc., or accused; except treasons, murders, and ravishment of women, and also outlawries, if any, et cetera.. And except those who are indicted of common theft, or common homicide, and those who were common thieves or common murderers: and except all those approvers and appealers; and those who have escaped or fled prison and have not since returned to the same; and those also who were imprisoned for felony on 14 December aforesaid. And further to reward the said good commons, the king has pardoned and released them, as far at pertains to him to do, from all kinds of trespasses and misprisions committed by them, or any one of them, before the same 14 December, for which a fine or ransom was owed to the king or his heirs; except the king's debts, and except recognizances and bonds made to the king or his progenitors for all manner of guarantees of peace, or in other ways. And it is ordained that those who wish to enjoy this pardon, shall sue for individual charters between now and the aforesaid feast of Whitsun [25 May 1382].

34. Also, on Friday 13 December, the said commons returned, and in the presence of our lord the king rehearsed and reiterated the requests they had previously made, and prayed of our lord the king and the lords of parliament that they might hear the decisions reached on the grace to be granted

de l'appointement de les graces ore affaires en aide et comfort de sa commune, et de les autres choses par eux devant requises touchant le governement de la persone le roi nostre seignour, et de son hostiel, et del ordenance affaire et purvoier encontre les malurez communes, s'ils, qe defende, \[s'afforceassent autrefoitz de lever]/ ou malx congregations faire.

De la monoie.
Et auxint sur l'amendement des meschiefs de la monoie, qi est si oultrageousement \[appeirez et]/ [emportez hors] du roialme, et auxint de l'ordenance affaire contre la malice des jurrours, embraceours des quereles, et maintenours en paiis, vers queux par enquestes ou enquerrees par un duszein, solonc ce q'ad este usez devant, sanz autre remede purvoier, homme n'avera jammais recoverir, ne leur purra de riens atteindre, a cause q'ils sont confederez et entreliez trestouz ensemble, qe chescun de eux meintendra autre, soit en tort ou en droit. Et par especial prient la commune qe l'estatut des purveiours soit ore afermez qe mys en due execucion, sanz pardon faire a les trespassours a l'encontre par aucune voie: qar la commune dit qe les purveiours rienz ne paient pur vitailles ne cariages par eux purveuz ou prises, einz sont en paiis pluis des tortz, d'oppressions, et d'outrages a la povre commune, qe unqes ne firent devaunt en nul temps.
35. A quoi fust reppliez pur le roi qe voirs est qe le roi ad grantement despenduz sur le paisement de cest derrain rumour, et en autre diverse manere, paront il est moelt grandement endettez, sicome ad este reportez et declarez a vous sa dite commune par les officers le roi devant ceste heure. Et grantement lui convient a despendre, \sibien/ sur la venue de madame la roigne, et \sur/ les mariage et coronement d'ele, qe proscheinement serront faitz, si Dieux plest, come sur la salve garde de paiis et foreresces le roi depar dela, et sur le defens du roialme: pur queux dettes ne despenses rienz est ordenez de paier, ne rienz est demurrez devers le roi en tresor, terres, ne possessions, en effect dont sustenir la disme partie de la charge qe lui faudroit a fine force supporter; ne les subsides des leynes, n'autre rienz. Et par tant lour convient ordener auxi \[avant]/ pur salvation del estat le roi, come pur la commune avauntdite, et d'ordener dont paier tielx charges, qar avec la commune ne poet mye bien estre, sinoun qe bien ne soit avec lour roi et seignour.

36. A quoy la commune respondi, \[qe aiant]/ consideracioun al mal coer qe la commune porte encores en rancour par tout le roialme, ils n'osent ne ne veullent en aucune manere granter taillage, n'autre chose quele curroit entre la dite commune, et en lour \charge./ Et adonqes fuist demandez de la commune, de granter prorogacion del subside des leynes, quirs, peulx lanutz, pur un temps, au fin qe le roi ent purroit paier les gaiges de Caleys; quiel subside deust ore \[cesser]/ a Nowelle proschein venant [25 December 1381].
37. Et la commune respondi qe de ce ne furent encores advisez. Et oultre ils disoient a nostre seignour le roi qe depuis q'ils avoient longement \[demurrez, et]/ la feste de Nowelle si fust bien pres, et les plus chargeantz et necessaires matires touchez en cest parlement si ne furent mye encores terminez, ne remediez les meschiefs \[apparantz pur l'arduite d'icelles,]/ lour sembloit ore pur le mieultz qe cest parlement fuist adjourne tanqe apres Nowelle, issint qe en le moien temps chescun de eux purroit soi adviser
[Col. b] de sa part de bone remede. Et \[pensoient qe devant lour]/ retourn ils einsi ferront devers lour communes, et \[les indueront]/ tiellement chescun en son paiis qe mesme la commune serra de milliour volentee d'aider et doner a lour

to the aid and comfort of his commons, and the other matters previously raised by them, touching the government of our lord the king's person, and his household, and the ordinance to be devised and provided against the unhappy commons, should they ever try again to rise or organize evil assemblies, which God forbid.

Concerning money.
And also, respecting some solution for the problems with money, which is excessively clipped and withdrawn from the kingdom, and also the ordinance to be made against the malice of jurors, embracers of suits, and maintainers in the shires, from whom by inquests and inquiries by the dozen, in accordance with past practice, without other remedy being provided, one cannot ever recover or obtain anything, because they are all in league and bound to one another, each supporting the other, be it for wrong or for right. And the commons pray in particular that the statute of purveyors should now be confirmed and duly executed, without pardon being given to contravenors in any way: for the commons say that the purveyors pay nothing for victuals nor carriage purveyed or taken from themselves, and that many wrongs, oppressions, and outrages are happening in the country at the expense of the poor commons, as have never happened before.
35. To which it was replied on the king's behalf that it was true that the king had spent large amounts on the pacification of that late uprising, and in various other ways, wherefore he was greatly in debt, as was reported and announced to the said commons by the king's officers heretofore. Moreover it would be most necessary for him to spend upon the coming of our lady the queen, and her marriage and coronation which would happen soon, if it please God, as well as on the safeguarding of the king's lands and fortresses overseas, and on the defence of the realm: for which debts or expenses nothing had been set aside, and there remained to the king wealth, lands, and possessions which would provide no more than a tenth of the amount he would have to find out of sheer necessity; nor yet the subsidies on wool, nor anything else. And for this reason it would fall to them to ordain for the security of the estate of the king as well as for the aforesaid commons, and to order that such expenses might be met, for prosperity will never befall the commons if it be not enjoyed by their king the lord.
36. To which the commons replied that bearing in mind the ill will which the common people still express in rancour throughout the kingdom, they did not dare nor wish to grant tallage in any way, or anything else for which the said commons would be liable or responsible. Then the commons were asked whether they would grant a prorogation of the subsidy on wool, hides, and woolfells, for a time, so that the king might pay the wages of Calais; which subsidy ought to end at Christmas next coming [25 December 1381].
37. And the commons replied that they could not even agree to that. Moreover, they told our lord the king that since they had remained in parliament a long while, and the feast of Christmas was fast approaching, and the most weighty and urgent matters touched on in this parliament had not yet been settled, nor the problems resulting from the difficulties of the same resolved, it now seemed to them for the best that this parliament should be adjourned until after Christmas, so that in the meantime they might each consider
[Col. b] for his part some good remedy. And they thought that before their return they should go back to their own communities, and that each in his own country should make such explanation that the same commons would be more willing

to aid and grant money to our lord the king than they were at present. And it was answered on the king's behalf that it was wholly pleasing to the king to adjourn the same parliament for the said reason; and also it needed to be done, because our said lady the queen had now arrived in the kingdom, and the said lords were to meet her and pay their respects, as reason demanded.

38. And it was reported to the commons on the king's behalf that the earl of Arundel and Sir Michael de la Pole had been elected, ordained, and sworn to accompany the person of the king, and belong to his household, to advise and govern his person, et cetera. Then the commons prayed that they might see the decision reached over the said graces to be granted, so that having reported them in their counties, the commons might be the more reassured.

39. To which it was replied on the king's behalf that it had not been customary in parliaments in the past for a general pardon and such grace to be had from the king, when the commons wished to grant the king nothing; moreover, even if he should now grant to the commons what they demanded, that had never been known before, namely that the king should make a grant to the commons unless the same commons had first submitted their request in writing, to which request it was usual for the king to make his response in writing on the last day of parliament, and not by word of mouth. To which the commons again replied that they would further discuss and consult on their grant to be made of the subsidy on wool, and it was then said on the king's behalf that the king would consider his said grace until the commons had done for their part that which pertained to them.

Grant of the subsidy on wool.

40. Also, when the same commons had briefly discussed the matter, they returned before the aforesaid lords, saying that they heard of the excessive burdens which our said lord the king bore and sustained in various ways, both on this side of the sea and beyond: and that the subsidies on wool, woolfells and hides, from which the king derived the most profit, enabling him to pay for the said burdens, were due to cease and come to an end this Christmas next [1381] under the terms of the grant last made thereon at the parliament held at Northampton; and so they earnestly wished to aid our lord the king in supporting the said charge to the best of their feeble means. Yet, on the other hand, they thought that if the said subsidy were to remain in the hands of our said lord the king without interruption for a while, the receipt of the said subsidies might easily be claimed as a right and custom for and in the name of the king, even though the king got nothing from the said subsidies except by their grant. Which, in the process of time, would disinherit and continually burden all the commons of England forever, which God forbid; and for that reason, and to avoid that problem, the prelates, lords, and aforesaid commons grant to our lord the king, on behalf of themselves and all the commons of England, such subsidies on wool, woolfells, and hides, in all detail as he had or received before, by the aforesaid last grant; to have and receive from the feast of the Circumcision of Our Lord next [1 January 1382], until the following feast of Candlemas only [2 February 1382]: so that the period between Christmas [25 December 1381] and the said Circumcision [1 January 1382] shall be completely free thereof, to ensure such interruption. Whereupon, in this parliament, in the hearing of the commons were read aloud the form and nature of the graces and pardon mentioned above, which the king had made to the commons. *[Page iii-105]*

[Col. a] dessuis est escrit. Dont la commune fist grande joie, et ent mercierent par tant moelt humblement et entierement nostre seignour le roi dessusdit.

Declaration de la grace le roi fait a la commune.
41. Item, les seignours et autres de conseil le roi firent faire et ordener une note de les commissions qe serroient faitz en chescun countee et paiis d'Engleterre as seignours et autres des plus /vanez\ gentz /del\ lieu, pur contresteer et punir les rebeulx si nul par cas, qe Dieux ne voille, s'afforceast ou vousist autrefoitz rumour comencer ou ryot deinz le roialme, en la forme qe s'ensuit:

La fourme des commissions affaire parmy le roialme pur riotours et rebelx.
Ricardus, etc., dilectis et fidelibus suis A. B. C., salutem. Sciatis quod cum plures malefactores in diversis congregacionibus et conventiculis in diversis partibus regni nostri Anglie, contra fidem et ligeanciam suam nobis debitas, proditorie et quasi hostiliter nuper insurgentes, diversa prodiciones, homicida, incendia, et alia mala intollerabilia et inaudita, tam nobis quam fidelibus subditis nostris horribiliter fecerint et perpetraverint, nos, de avisamento et consensu procerum et magnatum in ultimo parliamento nobis assistencium, volentes pro quiete populi nostri stabiliendo et firmando, ac pro consimilibus insurreccionibus, dampnis, et prejudiciis evitando, ut tenemur, salubriter providere; et de fidelitate, industria, et circumspeccione vestris plenius confidentes,
Membrane 9 assignaverimus vos conjunctim et divisim ad pacem nostram in comitatu B. et singulis partibus ejusdem, tam infra libertates quam extra, integram et illesam viis et modis quibus convenit custodiendam et custodiri faciendam, et ad omnes et singulos si quos in hujusmodi conventiculis seu congregacionibus contra dictam pacem nostram in futuro levare seu se congregare contigerit, ac omnes alios quos vobis vel alicui vestrum legitime constare poterit populum nostrum exnunc verbo, facto, arte, vel ingenio aut colore quocumque, ad levandum et insurgendum in hujusmodi conventiculis et congregacionibus movere, excitare, vel procurare, arestandos, et arestari, ac in prisonis nostris sub arta custodia quousque pro eorum punicione duxerimus ordinando detineri faciendos, et si vobis rebelles vel resistentes fuerint, juxta discreciones vestras puniendos seu destruendos, et ad hujusmodi conventicula et congregaciones illicita quibuscumque viis et modis quibus poteritis, eciam per vim et potenciam armatam si necesse fuerit, deprimenda, repellenda, et resistenda. Et ad omnia et singula que pro evitacione hujusmodi rebellionis, ac stabilitate et firmacione pacis nostre, ac resistencia, castigacione, et punicione omnium illorum qui exnunc contra pacem nostram et eorum ligeanciam taliter insurgere, vel in aliquo numero illicito convenire, seu alios ad hoc excitare, movere, vel procurare, aut verbo, actu, vel gestu, erga quemcumque ligeum nostrum, per quod occasio sive suspitio hujusmodi insurreccionis sive levacionis oriri poterit, indebite se habere presumpserint, necessaria fuerint vel oportuna, tam per incarceracionem corporum et arestacionem bonorum et catallorum suorum, quam alio modo quocumque, ordinanda et disponenda, et ad hujusmodi ordinaciones et disposiciones a quibuscumque personis tam per sacramenta et alias securitates, quam aliis quibuscumque viis rigidis sive modestis quibus in hoc casu magis expedire videritis, observari faciendis. Et cum citius informari poteritis hujusmodi conventicula et congregaciones suspecta fieri in excessivo numero, se tenere ad posse comitatus predicti tam militum et armigerorum quam aliorum quotiens, ubi, et prout,

[Col. a] Whereupon the commons expressed great joy, and most humbly and earnestly thanked our aforesaid lord the king therefor.

The declaration of the king's grace made to the commons.
41. Also, the lords and others of the king's council caused there to be made and ordained in the following form, a note of the commissions which would be granted in each county and region of England to the lords and others from amongst the most respected people of the place, to oppose and punish rebels if any by chance strove or sought to promote another rising or riot within the kingdom, which God forbid.

The form of the commissions to be established throughout the kingdom against rioters and rebels.
Richard, etc., to his beloved and faithful A. B. C., greeting. Know that since malefactors in divers assemblies and conventicles in divers parts of our kingdom of England, contrary to the loyalty and allegiance they owed us, lately rebelling in a treacherous and hostile manner, horribly committed and perpetrated various treasons, murders, arsons, and other intolerable and unheard of evils against us and our faithful subjects, we, with the advice and assent of the nobles and magnates attending our last parliament, wishing to establish and ensure the peace of our people, and securely to provide for the future avoidance of such insurrections, injuries, and harm, as we are bound to do; and trusting fully in your loyalty, industry, and circumspection
Membrane 9 have appointed you jointly and severally to keep the peace intact and unimpaired and cause it to be kept so in the county of B. and every part of it, both within liberties and without, by any appropriate methods and means, and to arrest and caused to be arrested each and every person who may in future arrange or participate in such conventicles or gatherings contrary to our said peace, and all others whom you or any one of you know for certain to be persuading, encouraging, and inciting our people, whether by word, deed, act, cunning, or any other art, to rise up and rebel in such conventicles and gatherings, and cause them to be detained in our prisons in strict custody until we have determined and ordained their punishment, and punish and destroy them at your discretion if they rebel against you or resist you, and to crush, extinguish, and oppose all such illicit conventicles and gatherings by any methods or means within your power, even by force and armed might if necessary. And to do each and every one of such things, for the avoidance of such rebellion, and the stability and affirmation of our peace, and for the repression, castigation, and punishment of all those who shall henceforth unnaturally presume to rebel in such fashion against our peace and contrary to their allegiance, or gather together in any illicit number, or incite, persuade, or encourage others to do so, whether by word, act, or deed against any of our lieges, from which small beginnings or origins such insurrection or uprising might spring, as shall be necessary or appropriate, as well by imprisonment of their bodies and seizure of their goods and chattels, as in other ways, to ordain and make regulations, and cause such ordinations and regulations to be observed by all persons both upon oath and with other guarantees, as well as by other means whether strict or moderate and as shall seem most suitable to you. And as soon as you shall be informed that such conventicles and congregations are multiplying, you shall gather with all haste, and in accordance with the means of the aforesaid county, so many knights and men-at-arms, wheresoever and howsoever it shall seem expedient to do, and lead and cause them to be led against those rebels to oppose, punish, and

expediens fuerit, cum omni festinacione congregandum, et contra hujusmodi rebelles pro eorum resistencia, castigacione, et destruccione ducendum, et ducere[9] faciendum, et ad omnes hujusmodi proditores et malefactores quos vos vel aliquem vestrum consimilia prodiciones, homicidia, felonias, vel incendia de facto perpetrare, aut roberias vel latrocinia actualiter facere cum manuopere contigerit invenire, capiendos et execucionem justicie de eis absque dilacione faciendam, et fieri [Col. b] demandandam, etc. Et ad premissa ac alia omnia et singula que in premissis fore videritis necessaria, prout casus exigit et requirit, juxta maturas discreciones vestras facienda, ordinanda, excercenda, et exequenda. Dantes vobis et cuilibet vestrum tenore presencium potestatem et mandatum speciale, ad premissa omnia et singula et dependencia ab eisdem que conservacionem pacis nostre concernere poterunt, quociens et prout vobis et cuilibet vestrum melius pro pace nostra conservanda in hac parte expedire videbitur, ut predictum est, facienda, exequenda, et excercenda. Et ideo vobis et cuilibet vestrum mandamus districtius pro possimus, et eciam sub forisfactura omnium que nobis forisfacere poteritis injungentes quod circa premissa diligenter intendatis, et ea faciatis et exequamini in forma predicta. Damus autem universis et singulis militibus, armigeris, vicecomitibus, majoribus, ballivis, ministris, ac aliis ligeis, subditis, et fidelibus nostris quibuscumque, in fide et ligeantia quibus nobis tenentur, tenore presencium in mandatis quod vobis et cuilibet vestrum nomine nostro in premissis faciendis et exequendis, sicut predictum est, intendentes sint, consulentes, et auxiliantes, prout decet. Volentes quod si qui fuerint qui ad premissa per vos vel aliquem vestrum in forma predicta facienda et exequenda nomine nostro requisiti fuerint, et vobis in premissis parere, consulere, et auxiliare noluerint, vel recusaverint quod idem sic recusantes per vos vel aliquem vestrum arestentur, /imprisonentur, et\ quibuscumque viis et modis ad arbitrium vestrum castigentur et puniantur. Mandavimus enim, etc. In cujus, etc. Teste rege apud Westm' .viij. die Martii.

destroy them, and to seize and take and execute justice on all such traitors and malefactors as shall truly perpetrate against you or any one of you similar treasons, murders, felonies, or arsons, or who be found in the act of committing thefts and robbery,

[Col. b] etc.. And to do, ordain, exercise, and execute each and every one of the premises as shall seem necessary to you, and as the situation demands and requires, at your mature discretion, giving to you and each and every one of you by the tenor of these presents a special power and mandate to do, exercise, and execute each and every one of the aforesaid and other things relevant to them which concern the preservation of our peace, as often and in whatsoever way shall seem best to you or any one of you for the preservation of our peace, as said above. And so we order you and every one of you as strictly as we are able that, on pain of forfeiting everything you can to us, you diligently attend to all the aforesaid matters, and perform and execute them in the aforesaid manner. We also give, by the tenor of these presents, orders that all knights, men-at-arms, sheriffs, mayors, bailiffs, ministers, and other lieges, subjects, and faithful men, on the faith and allegiance by which they are bound to us, should attend, advise, and assist you and every one of you on our behalf as they ought, in doing and executing the aforesaid things, as mentioned above. Willing that if any persons be requested, in our name, by you or any one of you to do and carry out the aforesaid in the aforesaid manner, and they refuse or will not obey you in the aforesaid, that such recusants shall be arrested by you or any one of you, imprisoned, castigated, and punished by whatsoever means and methods you may decide. For we have ordered, etc.. In witness whereof, etc.. Witnessed by the king at Westminster 8 March [1382].

Pur les meinpernours monsire Rauf de Ferriers.
42. Item, les contes de Warr', Staff', Salesbirs et Northumbr', et le seignour de Grey de Ruthin, prierent a nostre seignour le roi qe desicome ils, avec le priour de Seint Johan Jerusalem en Engleterre, qi Dieux assoille, s'estoient nadgaires en parlement tenuz a Norhampton', obligez a nostre seignour le roi, sur grief peine, et par especial corps pur corps, d'avoir monsire Rauf de Ferriers, chivaler, devant le roi et son conseil, a quele heure q'ils ent furent resonablement garniz, devant le proschein parlement deslors a tenir deinz le roialme d'Engleterre, pur respondre a nostre dit seignour le roy sur certaines chargeantes matires comprises en certeines lettres quelles furent devant trovez pres de Londres, et depuis baillez a nostre seignour le roi; par quelles matires, si celles lettres eussent este les propres lettres du dit monsire Rauf, et faites de son science, come celles ne furent, einz furent fauxement contrefaites pur destruire le dit monsire Rauf, come plus pleinement /apparust\ en dit parlement de Norhampton', quant le dit monsire Rauf y ent fust \a/resonez, et mys a sa responce; \mais par ycelles lettres/ sembloit qe le dit monsire Rauf deust avoir este adherdant as enemys nostre seignour le roi, qe Dieux defende, et depuis qe le dit monsire Rauf ad este toutdys encea, et encores est ycy present en parlement, a respondre a quelconqe qe lui vorra rienz susmettre en celle partie autre qe bien, qe yceux mainpernours y soient deschargez de leur dite

For the mainpernors of Sir Ralph Ferrers.
42. Also, the earls of Warwick, Stafford, Salisbury, and Northumberland, and Lord Grey of Ruthin, pray of our lord the king that whereas they, with the prior of Saint John of Jerusalem in England, whom God absolve, in the parliament recently held at Northampton, were bound by our lord the king, on pain of a grievous penalty, and in particular body for body, to bring Sir Ralph Ferrers, knight, before the king and his council, whensoever they were given adequate warning, before the next parliament to be held in the realm of England, to answer to our said lord the king on certain serious matters contained in letters which had been found near London, and later delivered to our lord the king; whether those letters were the genuine letters of the said Sir Ralph, and written with his knowledge, which they were not, but instead fraudulent counterfeits to destroy the said Sir Ralph, as more fully appeared in the said parliament of Northampton, when the said Sir Ralph was arrested and brought to answer; but from the same letters it seemed that the said Ralph must have been adherent to the enemies of our lord the king, which God forbid, and since the said Sir Ralph has until now been and is still present here in this parliament, to answer anyone who wishes to allege anything other than good against him in the matter, that these mainpernors shall be there discharged from their said mainprise, as reason demands; because they were only to be his mainpernors until the said next

---

[9] Original duci

mainprise, come resoun vorra; a cause qe tanqe al dit proschein parlement qe ce est ils devindrent tantsoulement ses mainpernours, et nemye plus oultre. A quoy fust responduz depar le roi, et nostre seignour le roi lour avoit et tenoit deschargez de leur mainprise avantdite. Et auxint le dit monsire Rauf alors en dit parlement esteant, nostre seignour le roi avoit et tenoit son foial lige, et pur excusez de les dites lettres, et les matires comprises en ycelles.

Clyvedon', Cogan'.
43. Item, Richard de Clyvedon', esquier, mist avaunt en parlement une bille en la fourme qe s'ensuit: 'A tressovereyn et tresgracious seignour nostre seignour le roi monstre Richard Clyvedon' qe come une debate estoit entre les communes de la ville de Bruggewater et le meistre del hospital de Seint Johan de mesme la ville, par cause de une vicarie en mesme la ville; de quele debate, qe par *[Page iii-106]*
[Col. a] ley, qe par autre manere, furent accordez. Et auroient[10] depuis qe grant rumour estoit en Londres, a grant damage a roi et al roialme; et la foitz fuist un Nicholas Frompton', chapellein et provisour du dite vicarie, et autres de la dite ville, queux departiront tost de Londres apres le rumour fait. Et a lour venu a Bruggewater pristeront lour conseille, et firont mander William Cogan, chivaler, et il venoit, et ove lour conseilloit. Et apres, le dit William ove autres gentz de mesme la ville aloit al avauntdit hospital, demandant en noun del dite commune qe le meistre et ses freres les engreent et amendent choses devaunt faites, sur paine qe purroit avenir. En qe dona jour au dit meistre lendemayn a dyys en le clokke a respondre, et departist. Apres aloyt a l'ostel a Honespull', et lendemayn tournea arere as ditz communes, a acomplere le jour q'il avoit pris ove le meistre. Et quant ils avoient eu parler il aloit al dit hospital, et la commune lui sueront ove le baner levee, et einsi treta ove le dit meistre q'il finast .cc.*li.* d'esterlings, et delivera une obligacioun de .c.*li.* de dit meistre, et autres munimentz, a saver lour vie, et lours biens. Et si le dit William contredit ceste bille, le dit Richard provera ove son corps devaunt nostre tresredoute seignour le roi, et son tressage conseille, en la manere come la loy d'armes demande, faisant protestatioun ceste bille de encrecer come jeo trove matire et conseile. Le quelle bille lue en parlement, le dit Richard de sa bouche illoeqes se profri de prover par son corps par la loy d'armes, et autre manere come la courte lui vorroit comander; sinoun par verdit des jurrours. Qar il dit, le dit monsire William estoit riche homme, et il povre; paront enqueste ne ferroit il ent passer encontre le dit monsire Wiliam, coment qe la cause feust auxi verroi come ce est qe Dieu est en ciel.

44. A quoy le dit monsire William illoeqes present, affermant q'il estoit lays homme, ne ne fuist apris de loy, n'autrement, de respondre en si haute place; et pur tant priast d'avoir conseille, au fyn qe par son conseille il ent poaist respondre selonc la loy. A quoy luy feust dit par les sergeantz le roy qe le matire de la dite bille touchast traison, en quel cas il deust par la loy de la terre faire sa responce en sa persone, et nemye par son conseil. Et adonqes le dit monsire William soy conseillast un poy avec ses amys et allies; et puis en sa persone faisant . . . .
protestacioun d'amender et corriger en temps avenir si, etc. Et dist qe de quanqe est surmys envers lui par le dit Richard, et par la dite bille, il n'est de rienz coupable, et de ce il soi mette a bien et a mal sur le verdit du paiis. Et sur ce, al fin

parliament which was this one, and for no longer. To which it was answered, on behalf of the king, that our lord the king held and considered them discharged from their aforesaid mainprise. Furthermore, our lord the king held and considered the said Sir Ralph, being then present in the said parliament, to be his faithful liege, and exonerated of the business of the said letters and the matters contained therein.

Clyvedon, Cogan.
43. Also, Richard Clyvedon, esquire, laid before parliament a bill in the following form: 'To the most sovereign and most gracious lord our lord the king, Richard Clyvedon shows that whereas there was a dispute between the commons of the town of Bridgwater and the master of the hospital of St John in the same town on account of a vicarage in the same place; which dispute was composed either by *[Page iii-106]*
[Col. a] legal process or by other means. Afterwards they heard that there was a great disturbance in London, to the great harm of the king and the kingdom; and there were then one Nicholas Frompton, chaplain and provisor of the said vicarage, and others of the said town, who immediately left London after the uprising was over. And on their arrival in Bridgwater, they took counsel, and caused one William Cogan, knight, to be sent for, and he came and discussed matters with them. Then, the said William, in the company of others from the same town went to the aforesaid hospital, demanding in the name of the said commons that the master and the brothers submit to them and alter things previously done, under threat of a future penalty if they did not. He gave the master until ten o'clock on the next day to reply, and then left. He then went to his lodgings at Huntspill, and on the next day he returned to the said commons to complete the business he had undertaken with the master. And when they had spoken he went to the said hospital, followed by the commons with banner raised, and it was decided that the said master should pay a fine of £200 sterling, and deliver a bond of £100 and other muniments to save the brethren's lives and goods. And if the said William denies this bill, the said Richard will prove it with his body before our redoubtable lord the king, and his most wise council, in accordance with the law of arms, making protestation to improve this bill as I find material and counsel. The which bill having been read in parliament, the said Richard by word of mouth offered to prove it by his body according to the law of arms, or in any other way that the court might order of him; but not by the verdict of jurors. For he said that the said Sir William was a rich man, and he poor; and therefore he would not be able to prevail by inquest against the said Sir William, even though his cause was as true as there is God in heaven above.
44. To this the said Sir William, there present, affirmed that he was a layman, and not sufficiently learned in the law or other matters to reply in so high a place; and for this reason he asked to have counsel, that by his counsel he might reply in accordance with the law. Whereupon he was told by the king's serjeants that the contents of the said bill raised the question of treason, in which case, by the law of the land, he had to make his reply in person, and not by counsel. And then the said Sir William deliberated a little with his friends and allies; and later in person he made protestation that in time to come he would amend and correct, et cetera. And he said that he was not guilty of anything alleged against him by the said Richard in the said bill, and he was willing to put himself for good or ill upon the verdict of the country. Whereupon, at the end of this parliament the case between

---

[10] *Original* avoient

de ce parlement furent les dites parties adjournez devant les justices a la commune loy, de quanqe \y/ appartient a la loy.

Cantebrugge.[11]

45. Fait a remembrer qe grantz pleintes et clamour estoient faitz en ceste parlement des mair, baillifs, et la comminaltee de la ville de Canterbrugge, de ce qe en temps del rumour et levee de malurez gentz, ils, avec plusours autres malfaisours de lours assent et covine, en oultrageouses multitudes qi estoient venuz a lour envoie a la dite ville de Cantebrugge; les queux entre autres leurs malfaites debriserent le tresorie de l'universitee illoeqes, et les privileges et chartres des rois, bulles del pape, et autres munimentz del dite universite arderent. Et qe plus est, compellerent les chanceller et escolers del dite universitee de relesser par lettres sealees de lours sealx as ditz mair et burgeys toutes maneres d'actions realx et personeles quelles ils avoient envers eux, ou avoir purroient par quelconque cause. Et encores sanz ce leur compellerent de leur faire une autre lettre desouz lours sealx, par quelle ils se obligerent en certaines grandes sommes de deniers a paiers as ditz burgeis deinz un certein brief [Col. b] terme, et celles deux lettres detiegnent devers eux encores, issint qe pur brief n'autre mandement ou requeste qe lour ent ad este fait par nostre seignour le roi ou les ditz escolers ne les ont voluz encores deliverer, einz par dilacions et fryvoles excusacions s'afforcent de retenir les dites lettres, en destruccioun de la dite universitee pur touz jours, si remede suffisant n'y soit mys. Paront estoit agardez en parlement qe deux mandementz serroient faitz, l'un as mair, baillifs, et comminaltee qe ore sont en la dite ville, et l'autre as mair et baillifs qi furent en temps del dit rumour, en la forme qe s'ensuit:

46. 'Ricardus, etc., dilectis sibi Ricardo Maisterman, majori; ac Simoni Glovere, Johanni Upwere, Johanni Calne, et Willelmo Listere, ballivis; ac communitati ville Cantebr', salutem. Quia ex populari conquestione nobis in presenti parliamento nostro est intimatum quod Edmundus Lystere, nuper major, ac Johannes Herries, Hugo Candesby, Willelmus Cote, et Robertus Bloutesham, nuper ballivi ville Cantebr', aggregata sibi magna potestate de communitate ejusdem ville ad loca et mansiones cancellarii, magistrorum, et scolarium universitatis Cantebr' vi et armis accesserunt, et clause et domos sua ibidem et alibi in villa predicta fregerunt, et cartas per quas progenitores nostri quondam reges Anglie diversa libertates, quietantias, et privilegia cancellario, magistris, et scolaribus universitatis predicte et successoribus suis concesserunt imperpetuum optinendas, combusserunt; et ipsos cancellarium, magistros, et scolares, diversa scripta obligatoria, non modicas summas continentia, quod ipsi libertates, quietantias, et privilegia hujusmodi in villa predicta extunc non excercerent, nec clamarent, seu ipsos nuper majorem et ballivos vel communitatem ex hac causa non impetirent, molestarent, seu gravarent, facere compulerunt, et eadem scripta penes se habent, ut dicitur: et nos unicuique ligeorum nostrorum in hac parte fieri volentes quod est justum, vobis precipimus quod vos prefati major et ballivi in propriis personis vestris, et prefata communitas per tres vel quatuor vestrum, sufficientem potestatem sub communi sigillo vestro habentes, sitis coram nobis et dicto consilio nostro, hac instanti die mercurii proximo futuro, ad informandum nos et ipsum consilium nostrum de veritate premissorum; et insuper prefatos nuper majorem et ballivos, ac tres vel quatuor de communitate predicta, hujusmodi potestatem a dicta communitate in hac parte habentes, et de premissis plenarie informatos, coram nobis in dicto parliamento

the said parties was adjourned before the justices of the common law, so far as it pertained to the law.

Cambridge.

45. Be it remembered that great complaints and appeals were made in this parliament of the mayor, bailiffs, and community of the town of Cambridge, because during the time of the rebellion and uprising of the unhappy people, they, together with many other malefactors of their cause and conspiracy, who had come in great multitudes at their behest to the said town of Cambridge, amongst other misdeeds, broke into the treasury of the university there, and burned the privileges and charters of the king, papal bulls, and other muniments of the said university. And what is more, they forced the chancellor and scholars of the said university to release by letters sealed with their seals to the said mayor and burgesses all manner of real and personal actions which they had against them, or could have for any reason. And further, they compelled them to issue another letter under their seals, by which they bound themselves in certain large sums of money to pay the said burgesses within a short [Col. b] time, and they still keep those two letters with them, so that neither by writ or any other mandate or request which has been made of them by our lord the king or the said scholars, will they deliver them up, but by delays and frivolous excuses they strive to retain the said letters, to the eternal ruin of the university, unless an adequate remedy be provided. Wherefore it was decided in parliament that two orders would be made, one to the mayor, bailiffs, and community who were now in the said town, and the other to the mayor and bailiffs who were there at the said uprising, in the following form:

46. 'Richard, etc., to his beloved Richard Masterman, mayor; and Simon Glover, John Upwere, John Calne and William Lister, bailiffs, and the community of the town of Cambridge, greeting. Whereas by popular compaint in our present parliament it has been intimated to us that Edmund Lister, late mayor, and John Herries, Hugo Candesby, William Cote, and Robert Bloutesham, late bailiffs of the town of Cambridge, having gathered a great force from the community of the same town, went with force and arms to the places and dwellings of the chancellor, masters and scholars of the university of Cambridge, and broke into their closes and houses there and elsewhere in the aforesaid town, and having obtained the charters by which our progenitors, formerly kings of England, granted divers liberties, acquittances, and privileges to the chancellor, masters, and scholars of the aforesaid university and their successors in perpetuity, they burned them; and forced the chancellor, masters, and scholars to make various written bonds, for immoderate sums, and promising that they would not henceforth exercise or claim such liberties, acquittances, and privileges in the aforesaid town, nor attack, harass, nor grieve the former mayor, bailiffs, and community for that reason, and they have these writings still, as it is said: and we, wishing to do what is just in this matter for every one of our lieges, order that you the aforementioned mayor and bailiffs and three or four of the aforesaid community, having sufficient authority under your common seal, do appear in person before us and our said council on Wednesday next [11 December 1381], to inform us and this our council of the truth of the aforesaid matters; and in the meantime the aforesaid former mayor and bailiffs and three or four of the aforesaid community, having such authority from the said community, and being fully informed of the aforesaid matter, shall appear before

---

[11] A small, contemporary note in the margin reads 'nondum examinatur'.

tunc ex causa predicta venire, et ipsos eadem scripta obligatoria ibidem tunc habere faceatis, ut nos, hiis visis, et super premissis plenius informati, ulterius inde fieri jubere valeamus quod justum fuerit et racionis. Et habeatis ibi hoc breve. Et hoc sub pena mille librarum nullatenus omittatis. Teste rege apud Westm' .vi. die Decembris.'

Per ipsum regem et consilium in parliamento.

47. 'Ricardus, etc., dilectis sibi Edmundo Lystere, nuper majori, ac Johanni Herries, Hugoni Candesby, Willelmo Cote, Roberto Bloutesham, nuper ballivis ville Cantebr', et eorum cuilibet, salutem. Quia ex populari conquestione nobis in presenti parliamento nostro est intimatum quod vos cum magna potestate de communitate ejusdem ville ad loca et mansiones cancellarii, magistrorum, et scolarium universitatis Cantebr', apud Cantebr', vi et armis accessistis, et clausa et domos sua ibidem et alibi in villa predicta fregistis, et cartas per quas progenitores nostri quondam reges Anglie diversa libertates, quietancias, et privilegia cancellario, magistris, et scolaribus universitatis predicte et successoribus suis concesserunt imperpetuum optinendas, \[cremari]/ fecistis, et ipsos cancellarium, magistros, et scolares, diversa scripta obligatoria, non modicas summas continencia, quod ipsi libertates, quietancias, et privilegia hujusmodi in villa predicta extunc excercerent nec clamarent, /seu\ vos vel communitatem ejusdem ville ex hac causa

[Page iii-107]

[Col. a] non impetirent, molestarent, seu gravarent, facere compulistis, et eadem scripta penes vos habetis, ut dicitur: et nos unicuique ligeorum nostrorum in hac parte fieri volentes quod est justum, vobis et cuilibet vestrum districte precipimus quod sitis in propris personis vestris coram nobis et consilio nostro in dicto parliamento nostro hac instanti die mercurii proximo futuro [11 December 1381], ad informandum nos et ipsum consilium nostrum super plena veritate premissorum. Et habeatis ibi hoc breve. Et hoc sub pena mille librarum nullatenus omittatis. Teste /rege\ apud Westm' .vi. die Decembris [1381].

Per ipsum regem et consilium in parliamento.

48. A quel mesqardy [11 December 1381], sibien les ditz ore mair et baillifs en lour persones, et la dite communaltee par William Berdefeld, Robert Coxford, et Robert Martyn lours comburgeys, esluz pur la dite commune de Cantebrugge, come les ditz Esmon Lystere, nadgairs mair, et les ditz Johan Herries, Hugh Candesby, William Cote, et Robert Bloutesham, adonqes baillifs, par vertu des ditz mandementz vindrent en parlement, et les ditz William Berdefeld, Robert Coxford, et Robert Martyn, examinez s'ils avoient auctoritee souz le commune seal de lour ville, ou autre mandement depar le commune en ce cas, ou nemye. Les queux respondirent qe la dite ville n'avoit commune seal, mais confesserent illoeqes qe par vertu del dit mandement direct a leur ville, ils furent esluz en l'assemble de lour commune \fait par ceste cause,/ de venir a ce parlement depar la commune, et pur y respondre pur mesme la commune, et resceivre ce qe la loy voet, selonc ce qe le mandement a eux direct volloit et demandoit.

Membrane 8 Et adonqes, sibien les mair et baillifs, et les autres trois esluz pur la commune, come les autres mair et baillifs qi furent le derrain an, examinez sur les ditz deux faitz issint faitz, c'estassaver, s'ils les eussent illoeqes avec eux en parlement selonc ce q'ils avoient en mandement, ou nemye. A quoy le dit mair q'ore est respondist pur sa persone soulement, et dist q'il n'estoit unqes assentant ne parcener en prive ne appart a la matire dont les ditz mandementz a eux faitz font mencion; einz quanqe ent fuist fait

us in the said parliament for the aforesaid reason, and shall bring with them the same written bonds, so that we, having seen them, and having been fully informed of the aforesaid matters, may further order to be done whatsoever is just and proper. And have this writ there with you. And upon pain of £1000 do not omit to do so. Witnessed by the king at Westminster 6 December.

By the king himself and counsel in parliament.

47. 'Richard, etc., to his beloved Edmund Lister, late mayor, and John Herries, Hugh Candesby, William Cote, Robert Bloutesham, late bailiffs of the town of Cambridge, and each one of them, greeting. Whereas by popular complaint it has been intimated to us in our present parliament that you, with a great force of the community of the same town, went to the places and houses of the chancellor, masters, and scholars of the university of Cambridge, in Cambridge, by force and arms, and broke into their closes and houses there and elsewhere in the aforesaid town, and having taken charters by which our progenitors, once kings of England granted in perpetuity various liberties, acquittances, and privileges to the chancellor, masters, and scholars of the aforesaid university and their successors, caused them to be burned, and you compelled the chancellor, masters, and scholars to make various written bonds for sums of no small value, promising that they would not henceforth exercise or claim those liberties, acquittances, and privileges in the aforesaid town, nor for that reason *[Page iii-107]*

[Col. a] sue, harass, nor aggrieve you nor the community of the same town, and you have this writing in your possession, as it is said: and we, wishing to act in the matter in a way which is just to every one of our lieges, order you and each one of you strictly, that you appear in person before us and our council in our said parliament upon the matter on Wednesday next [11 December 1381], to inform us and this our council of the full truth of the matter. And have this writ there with you. And on pain of £1000 do not omit to do so. Witnessed by the king at Westminster, 6 December.

By the king himself and counsel in parliament.

48. On the which Wednesday [11 December 1381], as well the present mayor and bailiffs in person, and the said community represented by William Birdfield, Robert Coxford, and Robert Martin, their fellow burgesses elected by the said commons of Cambridge, as the said Edmund Lister, late mayor, and the said Johan Herries, Hugh Candesby, William Cote, and Robert Bloutesham, then bailiffs, by virtue of the said mandates came into parliament, and the said William Berdefeld, Robert Coxford, and Robert Martyn were asked whether they had authority under the common seal of their town, or otherwise on behalf of the commons in this case, or not. They answered that the said town had no common seal, but they intimated there that by virtue of the said mandate addressed to their town, they had been chosen in the assembly of their commons held for the purpose, to come to parliament on behalf of the community, and answer there on behalf of the same community, and accept whatever the law wills, as the mandate addressed to them willed and demanded.

Membrane 8 And then, as well the mayor and bailiffs and the other three elected to represent the commons, as the mayor and bailiffs of the previous year, were questioned upon the said two deeds thus made, namely, whether they had them with them in parliament as ordered, or not. To which the present mayor replied on his own behalf only, that he had never been assentient nor accomplice in private nor in public in the matters contained in the said mandates sent to them; but that whatsoever had been done therein, had been done

si estoit fait encontre sa volentee et bone gree. Et pluis il dist qe le dit Esmon, nadgaires mair, son proschein predecessour illoeqes, avoit profriz a lui les ditz deux faitz plusours foitz al temps q'il estoit a Cantebrugg, et par especial al temps quant le dit ore mair estoit en alant sur son chemyn a cest parlement, come un burgeys sommonez a parlement pur leur ville; et encores depuis sa venue a Londres furent portez a lui a Londres par un Henry Brasyer burgeys de Cantebrugge depar mesme son predecessour, pur les avoir fait liverer as parties, ou autre part ou celles devroient estre deliverez: mais il dist q'il les refusast toutdys de resceivre, ne autrement ne les vist, ne se entremist unqes d'ycelles.

49. Et adonqes le dit Esmon, nadgairs mair illoeqes present respondist, et dist q'il ne fust unqes assentant, aidant, ne conseillant, au dit malfait ne rumour, ne rienz unqes y fist ne deist qe y purroit eschere en damage ou deshoneur de la dite universitee, sinoun soulement par cohercion et oultrageous compulsioun d'autres, si rienz y fist. Et oultre il dit pur sa responce qe voirs est qe celles deux faitz furent portez en sa chambre a Cantebrugge, et illoeqes privement lessez, mais par qi, ou par queux, il ne savoit, ne unqes puis le poait savoir. Mais tantost come il les avoit apparceuz en dite chambre, il les prist et prostra a son dit successour ore mair de Cantebrugge, et al drain les envoiast a lui a Londres, come le dit mair ad conuz: et par tant mesme le mair ne les voloit resceivre a nul temps, si furent lessez a Londres par le portour d'icelles, pur y estre prestz quant celles furent demandez. A quoi fust repliez par les sergeantz le roi qe ce ne poait mye estre: qar ils disoient qe voirs est qe plusours requestes ont este faitz depar les ditz escolers as burgeis de Cantebrugge devaunt

[Col. b] ceste heure pur la restitucioun faire d'iceulx faitz, et aucuns d'iceulx burgeys par tant ont este en la chancellerie le roi mesnez en responce, et unqes ne voloient faire la dite deliverance ne restitucion, ne encores les detiegnent devers eux, come par lour propre confessioun appiert pleinement. A quoy ils respondirent qe les ditz faitz sont ore prestz a restituer et a rebailler la ou ceste noble courte vorroit agarder. Affermantz avec ce qe unqes ne furent ils, ne nule autre persone de value de leur ville, assentantz a celle ryot: einz ce qe fust fait estoit fait par force des gentz d'estranges paiis survenantz avec aucuns riotours de lour dite ville, dont ils avoient depuis fait justice et punissement tiel qe touz ceulx queux ils ent purroient prendre sont mortz. Paront de reson l'en ne doit vers eux susmettre blame ou defaute aucune en ce cas. A quoy feust autrefoitz repliez depar le roi qe longe detenue d'icelles faitz en les mains des ditz burgeys, encontre la volentee des ditz escolers, et encontre les requestes avauntdites, provent clerement les ditz burgeys estre en defaute. Et coment q'ils soi excusent, voirs est qe le mair qe fuist le derrain an, estoit toutdys present sur la fesance et ensealement des ditz deux faitz.

50. /Et sur ce les ditz burgeys\ de Cantebrigge delivrerent les deux faitz ensealez souz les sealx avauntditz en cest parlement, des queux deux faitz les tenures s'ensuent de mot a mot:

Relees et obligacion.

51. 'Omnibus Christi fidelibus ad quos presentes litere pervenerint, cancellarius universitatis Cantebrigg singulique magistri et custodes collegiorum, ac scolares dicte universitatis, salutem in Domino sempiternam. Noveritis, nos unanimi consensu et assensu tocius universitatis Cantebr', renunciasse, pro nobis et successoribus nostris imperpetuum,

against his will and good grace. He also said that the said Edmund, late mayor, his immediate predecessor there, had offered him the said two deeds on many occasions when he had been in Cambridge, and in particular at the time when the said present mayor was on his way to this parliament, as a burgess summoned to parliament for their town; and yet again, after his arrival they were brought to him in London by one Henry Brasyer, burgess of Cambridge, on behalf of his same predecessor, to cause them to be delivered to the parties, or anywhere else they ought to be delivered: but he said that he always refused to accept them, or even see them, or ever to meddle with them.

49. Then the said Edmund, the former mayor, there present, answered and said that he had never been an assentient, aider, nor adviser in the said offence nor uprising, nor had he nor would he ever do anything which might result in harm and dishonour to the said university, unless it was by the coercion and outrageous force of others, if any there were. Furthermore, he said that it was true that the two deeds had been brought to his chamber in Cambridge, and secretly left there, but by whom he did not know, nor was he ever likely to know. But as soon as he had realised that they were in the said chamber, he had taken them and offered them to his said successor now mayor of Cambridge, and at last had sent them to him in London, as the said mayor had admitted: and because the same mayor would not receive them on any occasion, they had been left in London by their bearer, so that they would be close at hand when they were asked for. It was answered by the king's serjeants that that could not be: since they said that it was certain that many requests had been made on behalf of the said scholars to the burgesses of Cambridge heretofore

[Col. b] for the deeds to be returned to them, and some of those burgesses for that reason had been brought to answer in the king's chancery, and would never make the said deliverance or restitution, nor yet keep them themselves, as plainly appears from their own confession. To which they replied that the said deeds were now ready to be restored and returned to whersoever this noble court would decide. Asserting also that neither they nor any other person of worth in their town had ever been assentient to the riot: but that what had been done had been done by the violence of men of other parts gathering in their region with certain rioters from their said town, upon whom they had subsequently inflicted such justice and punishment, that all those whom they had been able to capture were dead. And so no blame or fault ought to be attributed to them in the matter. To which reply was again made on the king's behalf that the long time during which the deeds had remained in the hands of the said burgesses, contrary to the wish of the said scholars, and contrary to the aforesaid requests, clearly proved that the said burgesses were at fault. And even though they had made their excuses, it was clear that the mayor of the previous year had been present all through the making and sealing of the said two deeds.

50. Whereupon, the said burgesses of Cambridge delivered the two deeds sealed under the aforesaid seals in this parliament, the texts of which two deeds follow verbatim:

Release and obligation.

51. 'To all the faithful of Christ whom these present letters shall come, the chancellor of the university of Cambridge and all the masters and wardens of the colleges, and the scholars of the said university, greeting in the Lord eternal. Know that we, by the unanimous assent and consent of the whole university of Cambridge, have renounced, for us

quibuscumque privilegiis nobis qualitercumque concessis a quibuscumque regibus Anglie a principio mundi usque in diem confeccionis presencium; submittentes nos ac singulos nostrum pro perpetuo regulis ac consuetudinibus hactenus usitatis, secundum legem Anglie et antiquam consuetudinem burgi Cantebr'. Volentes eciam et promittentes sub pena trium millium librarum per dictam universitatem dictis burgensibus in festo Natali domini proximo futuro post datum presentium [25 December 1381] solvendarum, exonerare sumptibus nostris propriis et expensis burgenses quoscumque et alios de communitate dicte ville, tam versus dominum regem quam quoscumque alios, de quibuscumque recognicionibus et obligacionibus factis pretextu quarumcumque contensionum et litium dudum ortarum inter universitatem nostram predictam et collegium quodlibet ac communitatem dicte ville; de quibus recognitionibus in rotulis cancellarie domini regis plenius continetur. Promittentes eciam sub eadem pena quod procurabimus et faciemus, sumptibus nostris, istam composicionem sigillari sigillo patenti cancellarii excellentissimi principis domini nostri Ricardi secundi regis Anglie. In cujus rei testimonium sigillum commune dicte universitatis nostre, una cum sigillo cujuslibet collegii ejusdem universitatis, presentibus est appensum. Data Cantebrigg' in festo apostolorum Philippi et Jacobi, anno regni regis Ricardi secundi post conquestum quarto [1 May 1381].

52. 'Omnibus Christi fidelibus ad quos presentes pervenerint, cancellarius et universitas Cantebr', singulique magistris et custodes ac scolares cujuslibet collegii dicte universitatis, salutem in Domino. Noveritis, nos unanimi assensu et consensu nostro, tractatu inter nos prehabito diligenti, remisse, relaxasse et omnino pro nobis et successoribus nostris imperpetuum quietum clamasse, majori ville Cantebr', ballivis, burgensibus, et communitatibus, singulisque personis dicte communitatis ejusdem ville Cantebr', heredibus et assignatis suis, omnimodas acciones tam reales quam personales, quas *[Page iii-108]*

[Col. a] erga eos, vel eorum aliquem habuimus, habemus, et quovis modo habere poterimus, occasione cujuscumque recognicionis, obligacionis, transgressionis, delicti, scripti, indenture, seu alterius contractus cujuscumque, a principio mundi usque in diem confeccionis presencium. In cujus rei testimonium, nos cancellarius, et universitas predicta sigillum nostrum commune, ac nos magistri et custodes collegiorum predictorum, et scolares eorundem, singuli videlicet sigilla nostra communi presentibus apposuimus. Data Cantebr', die lune proximo ante festum apostolorum Philippi et Jacobi, anno regni regis Ricardi secundi post conquestum Anglie quarto [29 April 1381].

Bille.
53. Et fait a remembrer qe celles deux lettres issint restitutes lues en parlement, si furent elles par agard de parlement illoeqes cancellez, et de tout cassez et adnullez, par les causes dessuis allegiez; les quelles literes issint cancellez demuront en filace entre les billes de cest parlement. Et ce fait tantost apres si estoit une bille contiegnant certains articles mis avaunt en parlement encontre les mair et burgeis avauntditz, en la forme qe s'ensuit:
54. 'Fait a remembrer qe le samady proschein apres la feste de corps Crist, l'an du regne le roi q'orest quart [15 June 1381], les baillifs et comminaltee des burgeys de la ville de Cantebr', par l'advis et commune assent de eux et de lour mair, coillerent eux ensemble, et chivacherent al hospital de Shengey, et a la maisoun Thomas Haselden q'est /hors\ du dite ville de Cantebr' .vi. leukes et plus, et la encontreront

and our successors in perpetuity, any privileges whatsoever granted to us by any kings of England from the beginning of the world until the making of these presents; submitting ourselves and each one of us forever to the rules and customs used until now, in accordance with the law of England and the ancient custom of the borough of Cambridge. Willing moreover and promising, on pain of £3,000 to be paid by the said university to the said burgesses on the feast of Christmas following the date of the present document [25 December 1381], to exonerate from our charges and expenses any burgesses and others whomsoever of the community of the said town, both toward the lord king as well as toward any others, from any recognizances and bonds made on the pretext of any recent contention or dispute between our aforesaid university and any college and the community of the said town; of which recognizances more is contained in the rolls of the chancery of the lord king. Promising moreover, on pain of the same penalty that at our own expense, we shall procure and cause this composition to be sealed with the seal patent of the chancery of the most excellent prince our lord Richard II king of England. In testimony whereof the common seal of our said university, together with the seal of every college of the same, is affixed to these presents. Given at Cambridge on the feast of the apostles Philip and James, in the fourth year of the reign of Richard, the second since the conquest [1 May 1381].

52. 'To all the faithful of Christ to whom these presents shall come, the chancellor and university of Cambridge, and all the masters, wardens, and scholars of each of the colleges of the said university, greeting in the Lord. Know that we, by our unanimous assent and consent, having diligently considered the matter amongst us, have remitted, released, and entirely quit-claimed for ourselves and our successors in perpetuity, to the mayor of the town of Cambridge, the bailifs, burgesses, and commons and every person of the said community of the same town of Cambridge, and their heirs and assigns, all actions, both real as well as personal, which *[Page iii-108]*

[Col. a] we have brought, are bringing, and should in anyway be able to bring against them, or any one of them, by reason of such recognizances, bonds, trespasses, delicts, writings, indentures, or any other contract whatsoever, from the beginning of the world until the making of these presents. In testimony whereof, we the aforesaid chancellor and university, and we the masters and wardens of the aforesaid colleges, and the scholars of the same, have each affixed our common seals to these presents. Given at Cambridge, on the Monday before the feast of the apostles Philip and James, in the fourth year of the reign of king Richard, the second since the conquest of England.[29 April 1381]

A bill.
53. And be it remembered that the two letters thus returned, having been read in parliament, were cancelled there by judgment of parliament, and entirely quashed and annulled, for the reasons given above; the which letters thus cancelled remain in a file amongst the bills of this parliament. And immediately after that was done a bill was submitted in parliament containing certain articles against the aforesaid mayor and burgesses in the following form:
54. 'Be it remembered that on the Saturday next after the feast of Corpus Christi, in the fourth year of the reign of the present king [15 June 1381], the bailiffs and commonalty of burgesses of the town of Cambridge, by their common advice and consent and that of their mayor, assembled together, and rode to the hospital of Shingay, and to the house of Thomas Haselden which lies six miles or more outside the

plusours traitours et enemys du roi, de ceux queux leveront encontre nostre seignour le roi et sa coroune, en la countee de Cantebr', et illoeqes conspireront ensemble les damages desouz escritz.

Item, mesme le jour a lour revenu a l'ostiel, les mair, baillifs, burgeys, et comminaltee du dite ville firent une /solempne\ proclamacioun et cry, et de un assent alerent jeske a tolbothe du dite ville, et illoeqes eslirent Jakes de Grancestre a lour capitein, et lui firent par manace du mort jurrer d'estre lour loial capitain et governour.

Item, maintenant apres, le mair, baillifs, burgeys, et comminaltee du dite ville, d'un acord et un assent firent le dit Jakes, et Thomas son frere, frankes burgeis du dite ville de Cantebr'.

Item, les mair, baillifs, burgeys, et comminaltee du dite ville, entour .x. de la clokke le noet ensuant [15 June 1381], eux assemblerent al tolbothe, et illoeqes pristerent lour conseil, et adonqes firent un proclamacioun qe chescun homme se alerent al maison William Bedell' de mesme la ville, et la maison du dit William deussent debruser et destrure: et si aucun purroit encounter ou trover le dit William dusse couper sa teste. Et surce les ditz mair, baillifs, burgeys et comminaltee alerent al maisoun le dit William, et sa dite maisoun illoeqes debruseront et destrueront, et ses biens et chateux a grant value illoeqes trovez embleront et emporteront.

Item, les mair, baillifs, burgeis, et /la\ comminalte avauntditz alerent al collage de corps Crist q'est del fundacion de nostre tresexcellent seignour de Lancastre, et illoeqes les clos, maisons des scolers du dit college debruserunt, et lours chartres, escritz, liveres et autres munimentz, et autres biens et chateux, a grant value, la trovez pristrent et emporteront.

Item, la dymenge proschein ensuant [16 June 1381], les ditz burgeys et comminaltee ensemblerent en grantz routes, et chivacherent hors du dite ville a les traitours et enemys du roi du dit countee, et eux amesnerent au dite ville, la ou ils ne furent hardiz aprocher la dite

[Col. b] ville s'il ne fust par assent des burgeis et comminaltee du dite ville.

Item, mesme le jour les mair, baillifs, burgeys, et comminaltee du dite ville, compellerent les maistres et scolers du dite universitee, sur peyne de mort et destruccion de lours maisons, de renuncier toutes maneres des franchises et privileges a eux grantez par quelconqes rois d'Engleterre a comencement del mounde tanqe a celle jour, et firent les ditz maistres et escolers eux oultrement submettre souz les reules et governances des ditz burgeys a touz jours.

Item, les ditz mair, baillifs, burgeis, et comminaltee compellerent par manace de mort les avauntditz maistres et escolers, de faire obligacions de grantz summes, de paier as avauntditz burgeys, pur descharger chescun burgeis du dit ville sibien devers le roi come devers qeconqe autre persone, de qeconqe recognicioun ou obligacion faite a cause d'aucun contension ou debat en aucun temps en avaunt sourdez entre les ditz maistres et escolers et les burgeys du dite ville; et a eux firent par tiel duresce les ditz maistres et escolers faire une general acquitance de touz maneres d'accions reales et personeles; la quele acquitance ency faite, ensemble ove les obligacions susdites, furent baillez as mair, baillifs et comminaltee suisdites, et furent mises en lour tresorie en sauf garde d'ycelles.

Item, les mair, baillifs, burgeis, et comminaltee suisditz compelleront par manace de mort les avauntditz maistres et escolers pur deliverer et bailler a eux lours chartres et privileges, et autres patentes enseallez souz le seal le roi q'orest,

said town of Cambridge, and there they met many traitors and enemies of the king who had risen against our lord the king and his crown in the county of Cambridge, and there they plotted the mischiefs mentioned below.

Also, on the same day and after their return to the town hall, the mayor, bailiffs, and commonalty of the said town made a solemn announcement and proclamation, and with one assent went up to the tolbooth of the said town, and elected Jack of Grantchester as their leader, making him swear, under threat of death, to be their loyal leader and governor.

Also, immediately thereafter, the mayor, bailiffs, burgesses, and commonalty of the said town with one accord and assent made the said Jack and Thomas his brother free burgesses of the said town of Cambridge.

Also, the mayor, bailiffs, burgesses, and commonalty of the said town assembled at the tolbooth around 10 o'clock the following night [15 June 1381], and held discussions there, and then they made a proclamation that everyone should go and break into and destroy the house of William Bedell of the same town: and if anyone were to find the said William they should cut off his head. Accordingly, the said mayor, bailiffs, burgesses, and commonalty went to, broke into, and destroyed the house of the said William, and stole and carried off his goods and chattels of great value found there.

Also, the mayor, bailiffs, burgesses and aforesaid commonalty went to Corpus Christi College, of the foundation of our most excellent lord of Lancaster, and there they broke into the close of the college and the dwellings of its scholars, and seized and carried off their charters, writings, books, and other muniments, as well as other goods and chattels of great value which they found there.

Also, on the following Sunday [16 June 1381], the said burgesses and commonalty assembled in great bands, and rode out of the said town to meet the traitors and enemies of the king in the same county, and they led them into the said town, which the said rebels would not have dared approach [Col. b] without the assent of the burgesses and commonalty of the said town.

Also, on the same day the mayor, bailiffs, burgesses and commonalty of the said town compelled the masters and scholars of the said university, on pain of death and destruction of their houses, to renounce all kinds of franchises and privileges which had been granted to them by the kings of England from the beginning of the world until the present day, and further they made the said masters and scholars submit to the rules and governance of the said burgesses for all time.

Also, the said mayor, bailiffs, burgesses, and commonalty forced the aforesaid masters and scholars on threat of death, to make bonds for large sums to be paid to the aforesaid burgesses to release every burgess of the said town, as well before the king as anyone else, from any recognizance or bond arising from any previous dispute or strife between the said masters and scholars and the burgesses of the said town; and the said masters and scholars were compelled by them under similar duress to make a general acquittance from all kinds of actions, real and personal; which acquittance thus made, together with the aforesaid bonds, were delivered to the aforesaid mayor, bailiffs, and commonalty, and placed in their treasury for safe-keeping.

Also, the mayor, bailiffs, burgesses, and aforesaid commonalty forced the aforesaid ministers and scholars on threat of death to deliver and hand to them their charters and privileges and the letters patent sealed under the seal of the

grantez au dite universitee; les chartres, privileges, et lettres patentes les ditz mair, baillifs, burgeis, et comminaltee forsablement arderont en la fore du dite ville; et ove cutelles, bastouns, et autres wepens, les sealx des chartres et patentes suisdites dispitousement deraserent, en despit de nostre seignour le roi.

Item, apres qe les lettres patentes de nostre seignour le roi furent envoiez au dite ville de Cantebr', et illoeqes proclamez qe chescun homme, sur la peine de forfaiture de vie et de membre, et toutes autres choses q'ils purront forfaire, se tiendrent en pees sanz ascuns congregacions ou conventicules, ou autres affraies faire en aucune manere, les avauntditz mair, baillifs, burgeys, et comminaltes acoillez a eux grant noumbre d'autres traitours et enemys du roi, firent une grant proclamacioun en un pree q'est appelle Grenecroft qe est pres du dite ville de Cantebr'; et apres ce d'un acord et un assent s'en alerent a la priorie de Bernewell', et la le clos du dit priorie illoeqes a fier de guerre debruserent, et grantz noumbers des arbres cressantz illoeqes couperont et emporteront, et autres grantz affraies illoeqes firent.

Item, les ditz mair, baillifs, burgeys, et comminaltee, apres la proclamacioun faitz des dites lettres patentes du roi, come suisdit est, les estatutz, ordinances, et plusours autres evidences du dite universitee forceablement arderont, en contempt du roi, et encontre les lettres patentes avauntdites.'

55. Quelle bille lue en parlement en presence des ditz mair et burgeys dit[12] demandez estoit de eux depar le roi, s'ils savoient rienz dire ou alleggier pur eux, pur quoy par les ~~les~~ causes comprises en la dite bille et autres causes a declarer si meister est, la franchise de leur ville, quele ils avoient del doun et grant des rois d'Engleterre, et de la confirmacioun nostre seignour le roi q'orest, ne dusse estre pris en la main nostre dit seignour come forfait. Et les ditz mair et /burgeys\ prierent *[Page iii-109]*

[Col. a] illoeqes, pur Dieu, d'avoir copie d'icelle bille, et conseil et temps d'avisement pur respondre devant tielx seignours en si haute place.

56. Et quant a la copie, leur estoit dit par la courte qe depuis q'ils avoient oiez la bille, ce leur devroit suffire, qar par la loy copie n'ent deussent avoir. Et quant a conseil avoir, ce lour estoit grantez es articles en quelles conseil leur estoit grantable tantsoulement, si tiel article y feust, et autrement nemye. Mais la dite courte leur garnist qe quant a present ils ne serroient mys a responce de chose qe touche cryme, ne d'autre chose quant au present, forsqe soulement de leur dite franchise, come dit est.

57. Et sur ce les ditz mair et burgeys respondirent par lour conseill, et plederent qe ceste courte n'ent doit avoir conissance ne jurisdiccioun, par certains lour resons alleggiez. Mais a drain lour estoit comandez de dire q'ils vorroient, ou autrement l'en ferroit juggement envers eux, come ceux qi rienz ne savoient dire. Et ils firent rehercer certains matires de la bille, et faisantz lours protestacion q'ils ne conurent qe la bille contenoit aucune veritee; ils respondirent qe les mair, baillifs, n'autres bones gentz de leur ville, ne firent unqes rienz de les choses qe sont comprises en mesme la bille, ne ne procurerent estre fait par aucune voie, n'assenteront a ycelles, mais y firent la resistence q'ils purroient adonqes. Et disoient oultre qe quanqe y estoit fait si fust fait par les traitours et malfaisours de les contees de Essex, Hertford', et Kent, qi vindrent a leur ville en moelt oultrageouse multitude, et avec eulx une certaine petite noumbre des malfaisours et riotours de lour ville, les queux depuis par tant

---

[12] dit *superfluous*

present king, and granted to the said university; which charters, privileges, and letters patent the said mayor, burgesses, and community burnt with a show of force in the market-place of the said town; and with knives, sticks, and other weapons they shamelessly defaced the seals of the aforesaid charters and letters patent, to the despite of our lord the king.

Also, after letters patent of our lord the king had been sent to the said town of Cambridge and it was there proclaimed that everyone, on pain of losing life and limb, and everything else they could forfeit, should remain in peace without holding assemblies or conventicles, or other affray of any kind, the aforesaid mayor, bailiffs, burgesses, and commonalty, having gathered a large number of other traitors and enemies of the king, made a great proclamation in a meadow called Greencroft, near the said town of Cambridge; and afterwards, with one accord and assent, they went to the priory of Barnwell, and broke into the cloister of the said priory in a warlike manner, and cut down and carried off a large number of trees growing there, and caused other great disturbances.

Also, the said mayor, bailiffs, burgesses and commonalty, after the proclamation made in the said letters patent of the king, as mentioned above, burned the statutes, ordinances, and many other documents of the said university in a show of force, in contempt of the king, and contrary to the said letters patent.'

55. The which bill having been read in parliament in the presence of the said mayor and burgesses, it was asked of them on the king's behalf, if they had anything to say or claim in their defence as to why, for the reasons given in the said bill and for other reasons to be related if necessary, the franchise of their town, which they had by gift and grant of the kings of England, and by the confirmation of our lord the present king, should not be taken into the hands of our said lord the king as forfeit. And the said mayor and burgesses prayed *[Page iii-109]*

[Col. a] there, for love of God, that they might have a copy of this bill, and counsel and time for consideration before answering before such lords in so exalted a place.

56. As to the copy, they were informed by the court that since they had heard the bill that ought to suffice, for they were not entitled to a copy by law. And as to the holding of counsel, that had been granted to them in the articles in which counsel was grantable to them if such an article there was, and not otherwise. But the said court informed them that for the moment they would not be made to answer for anything which touched crime, or anything else at present, except only their said franchise, as was said.

57. Whereupon the said mayor and burgesses replied by their counsel, and pleaded that the court ought not herein to have cognizance or jurisdiction, for certain reasons which they gave. But at the last they were ordered to say what they would or else judgment would be passed against them, as persons who had nothing to say. And they rehearsed certain aspects of the bill, and protested that they did not believe the bill to contain any truth; replying that neither the mayor, bailiffs, nor any other good people of their town had ever done any of the things mentioned in the same bill, nor procured them in any way, nor agreed to them, but had resisted as best they could. And they also said that whatsoever had been done, had been done by traitors and malefactors from the counties from Essex, Hertford, and Kent who had flocked to their town in overwhelming numbers, together with a small number of malefactors and rioters from their own town, of whom they had subsequently taken and put to

sont pris et mortz trestouz q'ils ont peu prendre, et les autres sont fuiz le paiis. Et issint ils distrent qe les mair, baillifs, et les autres bones gentz de Cantebrigg' y sont quant a ce qe lour est surmis innocentz, et n'y doivent reporter blasme ne defame. A quoy fuist repliez depar le roi qe voirs est qe illoeqes ad este grantez qe le dit Esmon nadgairs mair avoit les ditz deux lettres en garde, et voirs est qe celles ont este longement et voluntrivement detenuz par les ditz burgeys, a tiele guyse, qe pur requeste, mandement, n'autre rienz qe leur ent ad este fait, ne les ont voluz deliverer tanqe ore q'ils furent a ce compellez, come dessuis est dit. Paront et pur tant auxint qe le dit nadgairs mair et baillifs si furent toutdys presentz avec les ditz malfaisours sur lours ditz malfaitz aggreantz, et ratifiantz quanqe les ditz malurez gentz einsi firent; semble clerement q'ils ne se purront excuser en veritee, et par tant dit fuist expressement as ditz burgeis q'ils elisoient a leur peril s'ils vorront ester sur lour dite responce finalment, ou q'ils se vorront mettre en la grace le roi, ou pleder autre plee en lour dit excusacion. Et surce les ditz mair et burgeis quant a lour dite franchise tantsoulement, ils se submetterent haut et baas en la graciouse ordinance de nostre seignour le roi, a faire de celle franchise qe lui plest. Toutes voies, salvez as ditz mair et burgeys leur responce quant a toutes autres matires, si pluis avant ils serront aresonez.

58. Par vertu de quele submission nostre seignour le roi, del assent des prelats et seignours en cest parlement, fist seisir la dite franchise en sa main, come forfait par les dites causes. Et puis, pur tant qe la dite ville ne demurroit sanz governaille le roi nostre seignour le roi fist mettre la dite franchise entierment as mair et burgeys, a tenir pur un temps tanqe le roi ent eust autrement purveuz.

59. Et al drain, par l'advis des ditz prelats et seignours en ce parlement, et pur tant qe sembloit qe reson fuist qe
[Col. b] yceulx burgeys avoient en celle partie si malement fait, q'ils furent dignes de reporter par tant un damage \et/ reproche perpetuel: et pensoient de l'autre part qe la ville de Cantebr' si est une de les aunciens villes del roialme, et principale ville del countee de Cantebrigg'; et pur tant nostre dit seignour le roi, del assent avauntdit, fist doner et comittre as chanceller et escolers de la dite universitee la garde de l'assise de payn, vin, et cervoise, et la conissance et punissementz d'icelles; et auxint la garde del assise et \del/ assaie et la surveue des mesures et poys en la dite ville, et les suburbes d'icelles; et auxint plein poair d'enquere et conustre de toutes forstallaries et regrateries, et des chars et pessons, sibien corrumpuz, viciouses, et incompetens, qe autres; et de faire sur ce due punissement: et auxint le governaille, correccioun et punissement, des ditz choses, et d'autres vitailles quelconqes, avec les fins, forfaitures, et amerciementz provenantz d'icelles, par manere come le chanceller et escolers de l'universitee d'Oxenford les ont en leur ville et suburbes avauntditz: a tenir del roi nostre seignour et de ses heirs pur touz jours; rendant ent a nostre seignour le roi .x.*li.* par an a son escheqier.

60. Et le remenant de toute la franchise de la dite ville commist et donast as ditz mair et baillifs, a tenir del dit roi et de ses heirs a touz jours; rendant ent al dit escheqer par an cent et une marz, quelles ils rendirent pardevaunt ceste forfaiture; et oultre de novele encrees, quatre marz a touz jours.

Membrane 7

death all those they could find for this reason, the others having fled the county. And so they maintained that the mayor, bailiffs, and other good people of Cambridge were innocent of that which was alleged against them, and ought not to be blamed or defamed therefor. To which it was answered for the king that in truth it had been admitted there that the said Edmund, lately mayor, had had the said two letters in his keeping, and that they had been long and deliberately retained by the said burgesses, in such a way that on request, order, or other representation made to them, they would not relinquish them until now when they have been compelled to do so, as mentioned above. Wherefore, and also because the said former mayor and bailiffs were in the company of the said malefactors at all times, agreeing to their misdeeds, and ratifying whatsoever the said evil persons thus did; it seemed clear that they could not honestly be excused, and for that reason the said burgesses were expressly informed that they should choose at their peril whether they wished to make a final reply, or whether they would put themselves in the king's grace, or plead some other plea in their said excuse. Whereupon, the said mayor and burgesses, in respect of their said franchise alone, wholly submitted themselves to the gracious ordinance of our lord the king, to do with the franchise whatsoever he chose. Saving always to the said mayor and burgesses their response in respect of all other matters, if they should be further charged.

58. By virtue of which submission our lord the king, with the assent of the prelates and lords in this parliament, caused the said franchise to be taken into his hands, as forfeit for the said reasons. And then, because the said town ought not to remain without governance the king our lord caused the said franchise in its entirety to be rendered to the mayor and burgesses, to be held for a certain time until the king should have made other arrangements for it.

59. And at length, with the advice of the said prelates and lords in this parliament, and because it seemed that
[Col. b] the burgesses had behaved so ill in this matter that they deserved to bear an eternal punishment and reproach: and yet on the other hand the town of Cambridge was one of the ancient towns of the kingdom, and the principal town of the county of Cambridge; therefore our said lord the king, with the aforesaid assent, caused the custody of the assize of bread, wine, and ale to be granted and committed to the chancellor and scholars of the said university, together with the cognizance and punishment of the same; and also the custody of the assize and the assay and inspection of measures and weights in the said town, and the suburbs of the same; and also full authority to inquire into and take account of all forestallings and regratings, and of meat and fish, corrupt, defective, and incompetent, and other matters; and to inflict due punishment therefor: and also the governance, correction, and punishment of the said matters, and of any other victuals, together with fines, forfeitures, and amercements arising from the same, as the chancellor and scholars of the university of Oxford receive them in their aforesaid town and suburbs: to be held of the king our lord and his heirs forever; rendering our lord the king therefor £10 a year at his exchequer.

60. And the rest of all the franchise of the said town he committed and gave to the said mayor and bailiffs, to be held of the said king and his heirs forever; paying to the said exchequer one hundred and one marks therefor, which they paid before this forfeiture; and in addition, a further increment of four marks for ever.

Burcestre, Hongerford.

61. Item, fait a remembrer qe monsire William de Burcestre, chivaler, \[et]/ Margarete sa femme, mistrent avant en parlement une leur bille, en la forme qe s'ensuit: 'A tresexcellent seignour le roy et son tressage conseil monstront William \[Burcestre, chivaler, et Margarete]/ sa femme, qe come Thomas de Hungreford, chivaler, estoit del conseil monsire Bertheu de \[Burghersh]/ qe darrein morust, et pur estre de soun conseil .... \[terre]/ a la value de quarrant marcz par an pur terme de sa vie; et le dit Thomas fuist charge par le dit monsire Bertheu q'il, ovesqe autres duissent estre enfeffez par le dit \[monsire Bertheu de les]/ manoirs de Heghtresbury, Steorte, et Colerne en le counte de Wiltes', et d'autres terres et tenementz en Gales: et qe le dit Thomas et ses jointfeffez duissent \[faire reffment a]/ l'avantdit monsire Bertheu, et la dite Margarete adonqe sa femme, a avoir et tenir a eux et a les heires le dit monsire Bertheu: quel Thomas enprist \[sur luy pur]/ les ditz feffement et refeffement duissent bien estre faitz et perfourniz, acordant a la ley. Queux feffement et refeffement furent bien et duement faitz par l'avis et conseil de dit Thomas par chartres, et par licence le tresnoble roy l'aiel nostre seignour le roy q'ore est. Et sur ce, apres la mort le dite monsire Bertheu le dit Thomas promyst, et soi chargea \[au dite]/ Margarete, d'estre de soun consail bone et loial, et a luy estre aidant come il \[avoit estee au dit]/ monsire Bertheu. Sur quoy par l'avis et conseil le dit Thomas, un diem clausit extremum fuist suy en le noun la dite Margarete, directe a l'eschetour de dit countee, \[par quele]/ fuist trove par serement de dusze bones et loialx gentz qe les ditz feffement et refeffement furent bien et duement faitz, issint qe la dite Margarete avoit jointestat ovesqe le dit monsire Bertheu a terme de sa vie, et ce par licence de roy. Par quoy la dite Margarete avoit livere de ditz manoirs hors de main le roy par due processe, et avoit bref \[direct]/au dit Thomas de resceivere la feaute la dite Margarete \[au noun]/ de roy quel il receult, come pleinement appiert par record en la chauncellerie. Quel \[Thomas longement]/ apres avoit l'estat la dite Margarete de les ditz manoirs, rendant ent par an a luy .cc. marcz par fait endente de ce entre eux faite, \[consaillant]/ la dite Margarete de discharger Thomas Dru, Nicholas Bonham, Warneford et Steorton, *[Page iii-110]*

[Col. a] qi furent retenuz ove la dite Margarete; \[disant q'a luy appartient la defense des ditz manoirs,]/ et a nulle autre, si mester soit, a cause \[de son estat]/ avantdit. Nient mains, le dit Thomas ad enfourme \[la dame le Despenser file et heir le dit monsire Bertheu,]/ qe sont dit piere morust soul seisi, et qe \[livere]/ de seisine ne fuist pas fait au dit Thomas et ses compaignons, \[ne q'ils firent livere de seisine as ditz monsire]/ Berthu et Margarete, come desus est dit. \[Issint qe par]/ le procurement, covine, et malice le dit Thomas la dite dame \[entra sur le dit Thomas, pur defaire son estat]/ demesne en la terre et defesance de l'estat les ditz William et Margarete en la rente susdite. Sur quoi le dit Thomas ad \[bargaine le manoir de Heightersburie avantdit,]/ a avoir et tenir a luy et ses heires a toutz jours, de doun et feffement la dite dame. Par quoy les dites William et Margarete ne poent avoir droit et resoun touchant ceste matiere, a cause de grant maintenance de dit Thomas en le dit countee. Et outre ce, la ou le dit Thomas est assigne par commission justice de la paix en mesme le countee, le dit Thomas a diverses sessions, quant les gentz de pais enviroun furent presentez et \[venuz par]/ comandement du dit Thomas et ses compaignons, \[encontre]/ le gree de ses ditz compaignons n'ad rien ou poy enquyz pur nostre seignour le roy, n'autre chose faite en effect touchant les ditz sessions,

Burchester, Hungerford.

61. Also, be it remembered that Sir William Burchester, knight, and Margaret his wife, submitted a bill to parliament, in the following form: 'To the most excellent lord the king and his most wise council, William Burchester, knight, and Margaret his wife show that whereas Thomas Hungerford, knight, was of the council of the late Sir Bartholomew Burghersh, and to be of his council.....land to the value of forty marks a year for the term of his life; and the said Thomas was charged by the said Sir Bartholomew that he, along with others, should be enfeoffed by the said Sir Bartholomew with the manors of Heytesbury, Stert, and Colerne, in Wiltshire, and with other lands and tenements in Wales: and that the said Thomas and those jointly enfeoffed with him should re-enfeoff the aforesaid Sir Bartholomew, and the said Margaret, then his wife, to have and hold to them and the heirs of the said Sir Bartholomew: and Thomas undertook to see that the said enfeoffment and re-enfeoffment were duly made and performed, according to the law. Which enfeoffment and re-enfeoffment were well and duly performed by the advice and counsel of the said Thomas by charters, and by licence of the most noble king, the grandfather of our lord the present king. Whereupon, after the death of the said Sir Bartholomew the said Thomas promised and undertook to the said Margaret, to be of her good and loyal counsel and assist her as he had the said Sir Bartholomew. Whereupon, by the advice and counsel of the said Thomas, a diem clausit extremum was sued in the name of the said Margaret, addressed to the escheator of the said county, by which it was found on the oath of twelve good and loyal men that the said enfeoffments and re-enfeoffments had been well and duly performed, so that the said Margaret had joint estate with the said Sir Bartholomew for the term of her life, and that by licence of the king. Wherefore the said Margaret had delivery of the said manors out of the king's hands by due process, and had a writ sent to the said Thomas to receive the fealty of the said Margaret in the king's name, which he received, as clearly appears on record in the chancery. The which Thomas for long after had the estate of the said Margaret in the said manors, paying her two hundred marks a year therefor by an indenture drawn up between them, advising the said Margaret to discharge Thomas Drew, Nicholas Bonham, Warneford, and Steorton, *[Page iii-110]*

[Col. a] who were retained by the said Margaret; saying that the defence of the said manors pertained to him and no one else, if need arose, by reason of his aforesaid estate. Nevertheless, the said Thomas informed the Lady Despenser, daughter and heir of the said Sir Bartholomew, that her said father had died seised, and that livery of seisin had not been made to the said Thomas and his colleagues, and neither had they delivered the seisin to the said Sir Bartholomew and Margaret, as mentioned above. So that by the procurement, plotting, and malice of the said Thomas, the said lady entered on the said Thomas, to annul his demesne estate in the land, and to the defeasance of the estate of the said William and Margaret in the aforesaid rent. Whereupon, the said Thomas bargained for the aforesaid manor of Heytesbury, to have and to hold to him and his heirs forever, by the gift and enfeoffment of the said lady. In consequence whereof the said William and Margaret could have no right or reason in the matter, because of the great maintenance of the said Thomas in the said county. Furthermore, although the said Thomas was appointed by commission a justice of the peace in the same county, at various sessions, when the men of the county were present on the orders of the said Thomas and his colleagues, there was nothing into which our lord the king could inquire, contrary to the will of his said

mes ad \[enforme]/ les dites gentz de paiis qe la dit dame ad droit a les manoirs avauntditz, et qe l'entre la dite dame fait \[sur le dit Thomas]/ est bon et congeable.

Plese a vostre noble seignourie ordeiner qe les ditz William et Margarete ne soient subduytz /n'oustez\ de leur droit par la graunt maintenance de dit Thomas et \[autres de son affynyte: et oultre]/ ordeiner tiele remedie pur tiel maintenaunce qe les meintenours soient \[tant chastiez]/ q'il n'osent pur doute faire tiel maintenance de ce enavant: eiantz regard qe tiel maintenance fait grand murmour en le poeple.'

Et celle bille lue en parlement, en presence nostre seignour le roy, \[dit]/ fust qe le dit monsire Thomas Hungreford fuist garniz a respondre a la bille avauntdit. Luy quiel monsire Thomas vint en parlement, et en sa persone \ faisant primerement sa protestacion de adjouster, corriger, et amender si embusoigneroit,/ y fist sa responce, et le mist avaunt en parlement en escript, en la fourme qe s'ensuit:

La responce de Hungerford.
62. La responce Thomas Hungreford, chivaler, a la bille et les pleintz comprisez en ycelle a la sute William de Burcestre, chivaler, et Margarete sa femme. En droit del primer point q'ils ont surmis le dit Thomas q'il dusse avoir certeins terres d'estre du conseil .... monsire Berthu de Burgherssh' a la value de quarrant marcz par an a terme de sa vie; le dit monsire Berthu dona au dit Thomas certeins terres a la value de vint livers par an a cause susdite; et ce par quatre ans avant les esposails le dit monsire Berthu et le dit Margarete: et issint le dit Thomas n'est pas respongnable au dite Margarete pur le dit doun. Quant a secunde point qe le dit monsire Berthu dusse avoir cheargge le dit Thomas et autres d'estre enfeffez en les manoirs de Heightredebury, Stoerte, et Colerne, ove autres terres en Gales, et qe le dit Thomas et les jointfeffez dussent faire reffeffementz as ditz monsire Berthu et Margarete, et a les heirs le dit monsire Berthu accordant a la ley par licence nostre seignour le roi, a cause qe les ditz manoirs sont tenuz de roy, lequele cheargge le dit Thomas dusse avoir empris: la responce du dit Thomas est tiel q'il ne emprist nulle tiel charge, einz tansoulement qe le dit monsire Berthu cheargea le dit Thomas et autres de soun conseil en comune, d'ordeiner qe tieulx \chartres/ furent faitz de feffementz, et pus apres de reffeffementz, accordantz a la licence nostre seignour le roy, \[ove]/ lettres \[d'attornes]/ des persones nomez par l'avis et acord le dit monsire Berthu; les queux chartres et faitz furent deliverez a sire William Stele, clerc au dit monsire Berthu, et general seutour de ses bosoignes, a

[Col. b] mander a les ditz attournes. Et plus outre de lour faitz le dit Thomas n'est tenuz a respondre, qar le dit \Thomas/ estoit hors du paiis au dit temps en les bosoignes l'evesqe de Wyncestre, qe Dieu assoille, en les parties de Hamps', et aillours, et adonqes seneschal de ses terres. En droit del tierce point qe le dit Thomas dusse prometre au dit Margarete d'estre de soun conseil: la responce est tiel q'apres la mort le dit monsire Berthu, monsire John de Gildesburgh estoit priez par la dite Margarete de parler au dit Thomas de luy retenir d'estre de soun conseil, et luy profrist du part la Margarete .c. s. par an, pur terme de la vie la dite Margarete. Luy quel Thomas outrement le refusast, et ce ne voleit granter, mais disoit a dit monsire Johan, s'il

companions, and nothing could be done in the said sessions, but he informed the said people of the region that the said lady had a right to the aforesaid manors, and that the entry which the said lady made on the said Thomas was good and lawful.

May it please your noble lordship to ordain that the said William and Margaret shall not be undone or ousted from their right by the great maintenance of the said Thomas and others of his affinity: and also ordain such remedy for the maintenance that the maintainers shall be so chastised that they will not dare, through fear, make such maintenance in the future: bearing in mind the great trouble amongst the people which such maintenance causes.'

And the bill having been read in parliament, in the presence of our lord the king, it was said that the said Sir Thomas Hungerford had been warned to reply to the aforesaid bill. Which Sir Thomas came to parliament in person, protesting first of all that he might make adjustment, correction, and emendation if they should be needed, and there he gave his reply, and laid it in writing before parliament, in the following form:

The response of Hungerford.
62. The response of Thomas Hungerford, knight, to the bill and the complaints contained in the same at the suit of William Burchester, knight, and Margaret his wife. As to the first point they had alleged against the said Thomas that he should have had certain lands to the value of forty marks a year for the term of his life to be of the council of Sir Bartholomew Burghersh; the said Sir Bartholomew gave the said Thomas certain lands to the value of twenty pounds a year for the aforesaid reason; and that was done four years before the marriage of the said Bartholomew and the said Margaret: and so the said Thomas was not answerable to the said Margaret for the said gift. As to the second point that the said Sir Bartholomew ought to have charged the said Thomas and others to be enfeoffed with the manors of Heytesbury, Stert, and Colerne, and with other lands in Wales, and that the said Thomas and those enfeoffed with him were meant to have re-enfeoffed the said Sir Bartholomew and Margaret and the heirs of the said Sir Bartholomew in accordance with the law and by the licence of our lord the king, because the said manors were held of the king, which charge the said Thomas was meant to have undertaken: the response of the said Thomas was this, that he undertook no such charge, but only that the said Sir Bartholomew charged the said Thomas and others of his counsel in common, to ordain that such charters were made of enfeoffments, and subsequently of re-enfeoffments, according to the licence of our lord the king, with letters of attorney of persons named on the advice and with the agreement of the said Sir Bartholomew; which charters and deeds had been delivered to Sir William Steel, clerk to the said Sir Bartholomew, and the chief agent of his affairs, to

[Col. b] send to the said attorneys. And the said Thomas is not obliged to answer any further concerning their deeds, since the said Thomas was out of the county at the said time on business for the bishop of Winchester, whom God absolve, in the parts of Hampshire, and elsewhere, and was then steward of his lands. To the third point, that the said Thomas should have promised the said Margaret that he would be of her council: the answer is this, that after the death of the said Sir Bartholomew, Sir John Gildesburgh was asked by the said Margaret to speak to the said Thomas and retain him for her council and he offered him on behalf of the said Margaret 100*s.* a year, for the term of the life of the said Margaret. Which Thomas entirely refused, and did not

feisse aucun chose qe le purroit tenir lieu, la dite Margarete luy purroit guerdonir. Et a ce il si vouche en tesmoignance le dit monsire Johan, et qe a nulle temps lui fuist plus parlee de celle matire, n'autrement obligez, et sur ce la dite Margarete prist autre conseil. Endroit del quart point qe le dit Thomas dusse avoir pursuy diem clausit extremum, apres la mort le dit monsire Berthu, pur la dite Margarete, direct a l'eschetour de Wiltes'; et qe par enqueste /prise\ devant le dit eschetour par serement de dusze loialx gentz fuist retournez en la chancellarie, et certifiez qe la dite Margarete estoit jointfeffez ove le dit monsire Barthu en les manoirs susditz, et sur ceo qe le dit Thomas dusse avoir brief de prendre la feaute la dite Margerete, en noun nostre seignour le roy, et retournez en la chancellarie q'il avoit resceuz sa feaute: la responce du dit Thomas est tiele qe la dite Margarete et le dit monsire Johan prierent qe le dit /Thomas voleit\ envoier ses lettres ove le bref au dit eschetour et autres amys pur avoir le greindre et le plus hastive esploit de la bosoigne, sanz ce qe nulle autre /seute\ fuist faite par luy. Et quant au brief pur avoir resceu sa feaute, le dit Thomas ne soivent point qe nulle tiel brief luy vient. Quant a quint point qe le dit Thomas avoit pris estat du dite Margarete longement apres des ditz manoirs, rendant pur iceulx .cc. marcz par an, par fait endentez, conseillant la dite Margarete a discharger Thomas Dru, Nicholas Bonham, Warneford, et Stourton qe furent retenuz ove la dite Margarete, disant \[q'a luy]/ appartient le defens de la dite terre et a nulle autre, a cause de soun estat \[avantdit]/: la responce du dit Thomas est tiel qe par mediacion le dit monsire Johan, seignoure William Stele, et autres des amys /la\ dite Margarete, et a sa requeste, le dit Thomas \[achatea,]/ come piert par endenture, \[l'estor et]/ chatelx \[esteantz sur]/ les ditz manoirs, et apres a grant instance d'eaux prist les ditz manoirs a ferme \pluis chier/ q'ils ne sont de valu, et selonc la promesse la dite Margarete qe si le dit \[Thomas]/ fusse perdant, par soun tesmoignance demesne, q'adonqes la dite Margarete luy voloit relesser de la dit ferme solonc \[la bon foy le]/ dit Thomas de ce q'il voleit \[dire de son perde.]/ Et a temps de la prise de la dite ferme, ne par oet ou dys ans apres, y n'y avoit nulle debat ne plee mewe des ditz manoirs; einz qe le dit Thomas \[entendy]/ qe les faitz susditz ussent este bien executez. Et de ce q'il deveroit conseiller la dite Margarete de discharger Thomas Dru, Nicholas Bonham, /Warneford, et Stourton,/ qe furent retenuz ove la dite Margarete de conseil, le dit Thomas ce mette en tesmoignance des ditz persones q'ils ne furent unqes retenuz ove la dite Margarete, einz tantsoulement le dit Thomas Dru; et ce apres qe plee et debat se meust parentre la dame Despenser et la dite Margarete et soun dit baroun. Endroit de sisme point qe le dit Thomas dusse avoir enfourme la dame Despenser, file et heir le dit monsire Berthu qe soun dit piere \[morust soul seysy]/ des ditz manoirs, et qe liveree de seysine ne fuist pas fait d'icelx de feffement ne de refeffement, issint qe par covyne, malice, et procurement le dit Thomas, la dite dame Despenser entrast les ditz manoirs: la responce du dit Thomas est tiele q'apres qe William de Burcestre \[avoit esposez]/ la dite Margarete, la dame Despenser demandea du dit *[Page iii-111]*

[Col. a] \Thomas,/ quel estat le dit monsire Berthu son piere en avoit en les ditz manoirs \[a temps de son moriant.]/ Et le dit Thomas luy respondy q'il ne savoit mye de certein coment y fust de dite matire, ne quel estat le dit monsire Berthu avoit \[au dit temps, mais qe bon]/ serroit q'ele

wish to accept, but said to the said John that if he did something else which would serve instead, the said Margaret could reward him. And he called the said Sir John to witness that nothing more was ever said to him on this matter, nor was he otherwise obliged, and that thereupon the said Margaret had taken other counsel. As for the fourth point, that the said Thomas should have sued a diem clausit extremum, after the death of the said Sir Bartholomew, for the said Margaret, addressed to the escheator of Wiltshire; and that by inquest taken before the said escheator on the oath of a dozen loyal men it was returned to the chancery and certified that the said Margaret had been jointly enfeoffed with the said Sir Bartholomew with the aforesaid manors, and thereupon that the said Thomas was to have received a writ to take the fealty of the said Margaret, in the name of our lord the king, and that it was returned to the chancery that he had received her fealty: the said Thomas's answer was that the said Margaret and the said Sir John asked the said Thomas to send their letters with the writ to the said escheator and other friends to obtain a more speedy and effective dispatch of the business, without any other suit made by him. And as for the writ for receiving her fealty, the said Thomas had no knowledge of any such writ having reached him. To the fifth point, that the said Thomas had for a long time after taken the estate of the said Margaret in the said manors, paying for the same two hundred marks a year, by indentured deed, advising the said Margaret to discharge Thomas Drew, Nicholas Bonham, Warneford, and Stourton, who had been retained with the said Margaret, and saying that the defence of the said land pertained to himself and to no one else, because of his aforesaid title: the answer of the said Thomas was that through the mediation of the said Sir John, Sir William Steel, and other friends of the said Margaret, and at her request, the said Thomas bought, as appears in the indenture, the livestock and castles in the said manors, and later, at their great insistence, he took the said manors at farm, for a price which was more than they were worth, and in return for the said Margaret's promise that if the said Thomas were to suffer losses, by his own testimony, then the said Margaret would release him from the said farm, trusting in Thomas's good faith in reckoning his loss. And when the said farm was valued, not more than eight or nine years later, there was no dispute or plea concerning the said manors; but the said Thomas had understood that the aforesaid matters had been well performed. And as for the claim that he advised the said Margaret to discharge Thomas Drew, Nicholas Bonham, Warneford, and Stourton, who were retained by the said Margaret for counsel, the said Thomas called those said persons to witness that they had never been retained by the said Margaret, except only the said Thomas Drew; and that after the plea and dispute had begun between the lady Despenser and the said Margaret and her said husband. On the sixth point, that the said Thomas informed Lady Despenser, daughter and heir of the said Sir Bartholomew, that her said father had died seised of the said manors, and that the delivery of the seisin of the same had never been made for feoffment or re-enfeoffment, so that by the plotting, malice, and procurement of the said Thomas, the said Lady Despenser had entered the said manors: the answer of the said Thomas was that after William Burchester had married the said Margaret, Lady Despenser asked of the said *[Page iii-111]* *[Col. a]* Thomas what title the said Sir Bartholomew his lord had had in the said manors at the time of his death. And the said Thomas told her that he did not know for certain how the said matter lay, nor what title the said Sir Bartholomew had at the said time, but that it would be well if she were to

mandasse son conseil as ditz manoirs, d'estre enfourmez de les gentz de les villes ou les ditz manoirs en sont de savoir la verite \[de quel]/ estat il morust seisy, saunz ce qe le dit Thomas conseilla la dite dame a nulle temps d'entrier en les ditz manoirs, et ce prent il la dite dame Despenser en record et son conseil. Endroit de septisme point, de ce qe le dit Thomas Hungreford deveroit avoir bargaynez le manoir de Heightredebury, a tenir a luy et a ses heirs, de feffement la dite dame Despenser, par quoy les ditz William et Margerete ne pont avoir droit ne resoun touchant ceste matere, par maintenance du dit Thomas: le dit Thomas soi mette en Dieu et tout soun paiis q'il n'est nulle meintenour, n'embraceour de querelles, et q'il n'avoit unqes feffement n'estat en le dit manoir en demesne ne par fait en reversioun: et ce prent il la dite dame et son conseil en record. Endroit del oetisme point qe par la ou le dit Thomas si est nome justice de la pees en la counte de Wiltes' par la ou il dust devant les gentz venuz et assemblez pur lour sessions encontre le gree de ses compaignons nient enquis pur nostre dit seignour le roy en effect touchant les dites sessions, mais ad enfourme les ditz gentz du pays qe la dame Despenser ad droit a les ditz manoirs, et qe l'entre la dite dame est bone et congeable: la responce du dit Thomas est tiele qe a sessions dont est surmys au dit Thomas avoir fait tiel demonstrance, le dit Thomas et ses compaignons chargerent enquestes pur nostre seignour le roy des materes q'apartient estre enquiz en icelx, et autres choses fist ce q'apartient de duetee; et ce prent il en record toutz les bones gentz du pays, et les rolles des ditz sessions. Et la declaracioun q'il fist pur la dame Despenser encontre les ditz William et Margerete sa femme, si fuist en excusacioun de luy mesmes de les malveises et grevouses paroles des ditz materes par le dit William et les soens publiez en plein countee a Wilton, proschein devaunt les ditz sessions, en desclandre et en defesance de l'estat le dit Thomas. Et se prent il en record toutz les bones gentz q'a dit countee \[estoient.]/

Membrane 6
Nomina excepta de gracia in parliamento. [13]
63. Memorandum quod nomina subscripta sunt nomina quorumdem malefactorum, qui nuper in diversis partibus regni Anglie, contra fidem et ligeanciam suam domino nostro regi Anglie debitas, ac pacem ipsius domini regis, se una cum aliis malefactoribus levaverunt, et prodiciones, felonias, et alia malefacta plurima perpetrarunt. Et eadem nomina domino nostro regi, in parliamento suo apud Westm' in crastino animarum, anno regni sui Anglie quinto [3 November 1381] tento, tanquam nomina illarum personarum que de hujusmodi insurreccionibus, feloniis, et malefactis principales ductores, abettatores, procuratores, et inceptores notorie pro communitate regni Anglie rectati sunt, per eandem communitatem liberata fuerunt: ad effectum, ut ipse persone et earum quelibet ab omni gratia per ipsum dominum regem populo suo in eodem parliamento facta et concessa excipientur, et omnino excluderentur. Et quod processus versus easdem personas ad accusacionem ipsius communitatis in hac parte, ac si inde prius legitime indictati fuissent, fieret. Quod postmodum per dominum nostrum regem, de assensu procerum et magnatum sibi in parliamento suo assistencium concessum est; et ulterius ordinatum quod eadem nomina ex hac causa coram ipso rege in bancum regis mittantur, ibidem execucioni debite demandanda, juxta ordinacionem predictam.

send her council to the said manors, to learn from the people of the said town or of the said manors the truth concerning the title of which he died in seisin, but that the said Thomas had never advised the said lady to enter the said manors, as he called upon the said Lady Despenser and her council to witness. As for the seventh point, that the said Thomas Hungerford bargained for the manor of Heytesbury, to be held by him and his heirs by enfeoffment from the said Lady Despenser, as a result of which the said William and Margaret would have no right or claim in this matter, because of the maintenance of the said Thomas; the said Thomas put himself to God and on all his country, that he was not a maintainer, or embracer of suits, and that he had never had feoffment or title in the said manor in demesne or by deed in reversion: as he called upon the said lady and her council to witness. On the eighth point, that although the said Thomas had been nominated a justice of the peace in Wiltshire he had, before those who had arrived and gathered for the sessions, contrary to the wish of his companions, refused to have inquiry made on behalf of our lord the king touching the said sessions, but had informed the said people of the region that the Lady Despenser had a right to the said manors, and that the entry of the said lady was good and lawful: the response of the said Thomas was that at the sessions during which it was claimed that he had acted thus, the said Thomas and his companions were burdened with inquests on behalf of our lord the king concerning matters which had to be inquired into there, and other matters which were his duty; and he cited the good people of the region, and the rolls of the said sessions as record. And the declaration that he made for Lady Despenser against the interests of the said William and Margaret his wife were to exonerate himself from the wicked and injurious words on those matters publicly uttered by the said William and his kin in the full county court at Wilton, just before the said sessions, to the slander and undermining of the estate of the said Thomas. And he cited all the good people who had attended the said county court as record.

The names of those excluded from the grace in parliament.
63. Be it known that the names listed below are the names of certain malefactors, who lately rebelled with other malefactors in various parts of England, contrary to the faith and allegiance they owed to our lord the king of England, and the peace of the lord king, and perpetrated treasons, felonies, and many other misdeeds. And these same names were submitted to our lord the king by the commons in his parliament held at Westminster on the morrow of All Souls, in the fifth year of his reign [3 November 1381], together with the names of those persons who were publicly judged on behalf of the community of the kingdom of England to be the principal leaders, abettors, agents, and instigators of such insurrections, felonies, and misdeeds: with the intent that these persons and every one of them shall be excepted and wholly excluded from all grace granted and conceded by this lord king to his people in the same parliament. And that a process shall be begun against these same persons at the accusation of the community in the matter, and if they shall first have been lawfully indicted, let it be done. And later, by the lord our king, with the assent of the nobles and magnates assisting him in his parliament, it was conceded and also ordained that the same names for that reason should be sent before the king in the king's bench, for due action to be taken there, in accordance with the aforesaid ordinance.

---

[13]This list spans membranes six and five which form a separate leaf stitched to the foot of membrane seven and overlapping membrane five of the main body of the roll.

Norfolk.
John Wattes, of Scothowe.
Richard Filmond.
Thomas Gentilhomme, of Buxton.
Thomas Suffolk.
William Quynbergh', chaplain of Scothowe.
Henry Reyse, of Dilham.
John atte Chaumbre, of Heigham Potter.
John Spaigne, of Lynn, cordwainer.
Thomas Aslak, of Norwich, cordwainer.
John of Norwich, cook.
Robert Wodehewer, formerly dwelling in Norwich.
William Belhouse, of Aylsham.
John Creyk, of Wymondham.
Adam Pulter, of Heigham.
Thomas Thakstere, of Curson Carleton.
Walter Clerc of Filby, residing with the prior of Wymondham.
John Betes, of Wymondham.

Suffolk.
John Wrawe, chaplain.
John Talmage.
Geoffrey Denham.
John Clak, of Bury St Edmunds.
Robert Westbrom, of Bury St Edmunds.
John Cartere, otherwise known as Robert Warner.
Robert Sad, of Bury St Edmunds.
William Benington, of Bumpstead.
Geoffrey Parfay, vicar of the church of All Saints, Sudbury.
John Wrawe, late parson of the church of Ringsfield.
Edmund Barbour, of Beccles.
John Batisford, parson of the church of Bucklesham.
Thomas Sampson.
John le Dene, pedlar.
James Bedyngfeld.
Robert Prior, of Mendlesham.
Thomas Halsworth, of Bury St Edmunds.
Thomas Yoxford, of Bury St Edmunds.
Thomas Underwood, of Finchingfield.
. . . . Botemor.

Cambridge.
John Peper, of Linton.
Thomas Furbour, of Cambridge.
John Deye, of Willingham.
Walter Barbour, of Royston.

Essex.
Adam Michel.
Robert Cardemaker, of Bocking.
John Taillour, chaplain.

Johannes Smyth, clerc.
Henricus Ive.
Johannes Turnour, herde, boclerplaier de Stistede.
Johannes Wynterflode, de Cokeshale.
Richard Coventre, laborer.
Johannes Poyntol.
Johannes Adam, serviens Ricardi Wight de Branketre.
Gregorius Skynner, de Branketre.

Hertford'.
Willelmus Bliche, de Aldbery.
Johannes Coltman, de Claverynge.
Stephanus Treubody, de Codicote.
Willelmus de Stable, de Sancto Albano.

Page iii-112

Midd'.
Willielmus filius Nicholai Gardyner, de Sancystret.
Ricardus Taillour, de Harwe.
Johannes Litle de Eggeswere, brewer.
Thomas Bedford, de Holbourn'.
Thomas Ernesby.
Willelmus Shepherd, de Totehill.
Thomas Tayllour, de Charryngg.
Johannes Foke Meriell'.
Johannes Knot, de Chelchith'.
Johannes Pecche de Fulham, boteman.
Johannes in the Hale, de Rysshlep'.
Johannes Tornour, de Risshlep.
Petrus Walsh, de parochia de Chesewyk.
Johannes Martyn, de Heston'.
Ricardus Cully, de Twykenham.
Johannes de Aston', de hundredo de Istelworth'.
Thomas Grene, de hundredo de Istelworth'.
Johannes Gamelyn, nuper serviens prioris Sancti Johannis.
Johannes Carpenter, de Grenford.
Robertus Webbe, de Wyke.
Robertus Parys, de Houndeslowe, webbe.
Willelmus Walsh, de Houndeslowe.
Johannes Barcelot, junior, de Heston'.

London'.
Johannes atte Chaumbre.
Johannes Spryngald, carpenter, de Sutton' juxta Derteford'.
Thomas Rote, de Kent.
Johannes Millere, wyndrawer, de vinetria London'.
Thomas Graunt, wyndrawer, socius ejus.
Edmundus Silk, tilere.
[14]Johannes Horsman, boteman.
Willelmus Waleys.
Willelmus Dymbilby, grynder, serviens Johannis Ferrour.
Johannes Wade, wyndrawer..

John Smyth, clerk.
Henry Ive.
John Turnour, herder, buckle-maker of Stisted.
John Wynterflode, of Cocksalls.
Richard Coventre, labourer.
John Poyntol.
John Adam, servant of Richard White of Braintree.
Gregory Skinner, of Braintree.

Hertford.
William Bliche, of Aldbury.
John Coltman, of Clavering.
Stephen Treubody, of Codicote.
William Stable, of St Albans.

Middlesex.
William son of Nicholas Gardyner, of Sancystret.
Richard Taillour, of Harrow.
John Litle of Edgware, brewer.
Thomas Bedford, of Holborn.
Thomas Ernesby.
William Shepherd, of Tothill.
Thomas Tayllour, of Charing Cross.
John Foke Meriell'.
John Knot, of Chelsea.
John Pecche of Fulham, butler.
John in the Hale, of Ruislip.
John Tornour, of Ruislip.
Peter Walsh, of the parish of Chiswick.
John Martyn, of Heston.
Richard Cully, of Twickenham.
John Aston, of Isleworth hundred.
Thomas Grene, of Isleworth hundred.
John Gamelyn, late servant of the prior of St John's.
John Carpenter, of Greenford.
Robert Webbe, of Wick.
Robert Parys, of Hounslow, weaver.
William Walsh, of Hounslow.
John Barcelot, the younger, of Heston.

London.
John atte Chaumbre.
John Spryngald, carpenter, of Sutton by Dartford.
Thomas Rote, of Kent.
John Millere, vintner, of the London vintry.
Thomas Graunt, vintner, his partner.
Edmund Silk, tiler.
John Horsman, boatman.
William Waleys.
William Dymbilby, grinder, servant of John Ferrour.
John Wade, vintner.

---

[14] This is the beginning of a new column on m.6 and a contemporary heading reads 'Adhuc London''.

Willelmus Pouchemaker, cobeler	William Pouchemaker, cobbler.
Willelmus, serviens Johannis Durham, taillour.	William, servant of John Durham, tailor.
Thomas Carpenter, quondam apprenticius Roberti Hatfeld.	Thomas Carpenter, sometime apprentice of Robert Hatfield.
Thomas Kent, brewere, de comitatu Kanc'.	Thomas Kent, brewer, of Kent.
Ricardus Scot, hosier.	Richard Scot, hosier.
Stephanus Ryslep, alutarius.	Stephen Ryslep, tawyer.
Ricardus Rislep, taillour.	Richard Rislep, tailor.
Stephanus Coventre, allutarius.	Stephen Coventre, tawyer.
Walterus Taunton', sadeler.	Walter Taunton', saddler.
Willelmus Gibewyn', sporier.	William Gibewyn', spurrier.
Jacobus Breuersman.	Jacob Breuersman.
Willelmus Pycoys, webbe.	William Pycoys, weaver.
Ricardus Bone, webbe.	Richard Bone, weaver.
Johannes Noke, webbe.	John Noke, weaver.
Robertus Blaunchard de Hibernie, portour.	Robert Blaunchard of Ireland, porter.
Thomas Bunny, shether.	Thomas Bunny, sheather.
Hamo Cobeler, de parochia Sancti Leonardi.	Hamo Cobeler, of the parish of St Leonard.
Johannes Roo, laborer.	John Roo, labourer.
Thomas Raven, de Suthwerk.	Thomas Raven, of Southwark.
Johannes Bateman, webbe.	John Bateman, weaver.
Johannes Canterbury, capper.	John Canterbury, capper.
Johannes Bentele, fuller.	John Bentele, fuller.
Johannes Brond, webbe.	John Brond, weaver.
Ricardus Waterberer, del Stokkis.	Richard Waterberer, of the Stocks.
Robertus Enefeld, cobeler.	Robert Enefeld, cobbler.
Simon Gerard, fuller.	Simon Gerard, fuller.
Johannes Lucas, portour.	John Lucas, porter.
Henricus Blundell', de Kanc'.	Henry Blundell', of Kent.
Thomas Willes, carpenter, de Belyeterlane.	Thomas Willes, carpenter of Belwether Lane.
Ricardus Carpenter, de eadem.	Richard Carpenter, of the same.
Andreas, apprenticius Henricus Bitreden.	Andrew, apprentice of Henry Bitreden.
Johannes Leycestre, skynnere, juxta Crichirch', London'.	John Leicester, skinner, near Christchurch, London.
Johannes Sawyer, de parochia Sancte Katerine Colman, London'.	John Sawyer, of the parish of St Katherine Coleman, London.
Jacobus Bruer de Porjurie, London'.	Jacob Bruer of Poor Jewry, London.
Johannes Castell', ibidem.	John Castell', of the same.
Willelmus Bocher, portour, de Billyngesgate, London'.	William Bocher, porter of Billingsgate, London.
[Col. b] Johannes Horsham, juxta Crichirch, London'.	[Col. b] John Horsham, near Christchurch, London.
Ricardus Goldsmyth, extra Algate, London'.	Richard Goldsmyth, outside Aldgate, London.
Ricardus Carpenter, de parochia beate Marie atte Naxe, London'.	Richard Carpenter, of the parish of St Mary Axe, London.
Johannes Tynker, de Holbourn.	John Tynker, of Holborn.
Willelmus Brewer, pyper.	William Brewer, piper.
Johannes Yonge, de comitatu Hereford'.	John Yonge, of the county of Hereford.
Johannes Awedyn, de comitatu Essex'.	John Awedyn, of Essex.
Thomas Rote, de Kanc'.	Thomas Rote, of Kent.
Nicholaus Purser, de Milende.	Nicholas Purser, of Mile End.
Johannes Stotesfold, de comitatu Bed'.	John Stotesfold, of the county of Bedford.
Willelmus Hosteler, serviens Willelmi Rothewell.	William Hosteler, servant of William Rothwell.
Johannes Quyltemaker.	John Quiltmaker.
Johannes Stotesbury, childe-shomakere.	John Stotesbury, children's shoemaker.

Robertus Sandewych, serviens Roberti de York, alutarii.	Robert Sandwich, servant of Robert of York, tawyer.
Janyn, serviens ejusdem Roberti de York.	Janyn, servant of the same Robert of York.
Johannes Hostelere, nuper serviens Johannis Lawe, cook.	John Hostelere, late servant of John Law, cook.
Johannes Brewersman, manens apud le Tabbard, London'.	John Brewersman, staying at the Tabard, London.
Thomas Claypole, sherman.	Thomas Claypole, shearman.
Philippus Walssh', water-ledere.	Philip Walssh, water-bearer.
Johannes Cornewaille, daubere.	John Cornewaille, plasterer.
Ricardus Redyng, skynnere.	Richard Redyng, skinner.
Johannes Grantham, serviens atte castelle in Friday-Strete, London'.	John Grantham, servant at the Castle in Friday Street, London.
Johannes Bokeden, travelyngman.	John Bokeden, travelling-man.
Johannes, serviens Ricardi Cornewaill, de Fryday-Strete, London'.	John, servant of Richard Cornewaille, of Friday Street, London.
Johannes Sakkere, malemaker.	John Sacker, sack-maker.
Simon Cook, nuper serviens Roberti Harngeye.	Simon Cook, late servant of Robert Harngeye.
Willelmus Caus, fullere.	William Caus, fuller.
Henricus Potton', quernpekker.	Henry Potton, quern-picker.
Rogerus Glovere, serviens Abrahe Seintfeye.	Roger Glovere, servant of Abraham Seintfeye.
Robertus Panyere, de Paternosterrowe.	Robert Panyere, of Paternoster Row.
Quidam Ledes, capper.	One Ledes, capper.
Johannes Sutton', materas-maker.	John Sutton, mattress-maker.
Ricardus, frater ejus.	Richard, his brother.
Willelmus Inglond, boteman.	William Inglond, boatman.
Johannes Forest.	John Forest.
Thomas Crowe, fullere.	Thomas Crowe, fuller.
Thomas Wolf.	Thomas Wolf.
Nicholaus Cornemetre, de Quenhithe.	Nicholas Cornemetre, of Queenhythe.
Ricardus, vocatus 'Grete Richard', diere.	Richard, called 'Great Richard', dyer.
Ricardus Trent, dyere.	Richard Trent, dyer.
Willelmus Clere, cobeler, del Quenhithe.	William Clere, cobbler, of Queenhythe.
Willelmus Potkyn, webbe.	William Potkyn, weaver.
Johannes Thurgore.	John Thurgore.
Thomas Fauconer, juxta Wyndesore.	Thomas Fauconer, near Windsor.
Walterus Keye.	Walter Keye.
Johannes Mounford, dyeres-man.	John Mounford, dyer's man.
Laurentius Wythtegretelegg, sawyer.	Laurence Wythtegretelegg, sawyer.
Ricardus Tracy, sawyer.	Richard Tracy, sawyer.
Simon Tylere, manens extra Cripelgate.	Simon Tylere, dwelling outside Cripplegate.
Johannes Gamelyn.	John Gamelyn.
Willelmus Andrewe, de Clerkenwelstrete.	William Andrewe, of Clerkenwell Street.
Robertus Warrewyk, glovere.	Robert Warrewyk, glover.
Willelmus Hampermaker, de Wodestrete.	William Hampermaker, of Wood Street.
Thomas Mortymer, daubere.	Thomas Mortymer, plasterer.
Johannes Wykere.	John Wykere.
Membrane 5a Johannes, serviens Johannis Seman.	*Membrane 5a* John, servant of John Seman.
Willelmus Bate, cappere.	William Bate, capper.
Thomas Stoteman.	Thomas Stoteman.
Johannes March'.	John March.
Johannes Kyrton, alius dictus Ethard.	John Kyrton, otherwise called Ethard.
Johannes Thorn'.	John Thorn.
Ricardus Malmeshill, clerc.	Richard Malmeshill, clerk.
Johannes, brewere et hostelere.	John, brewer and inn-keeper.

Ricardus Taillour, de Harwe.	Richard Taillor, of Harrow.
Nicholaus Thurston, carpenter.	Nicholas Thurston, carpenter.
Johannes Ellesworth.	John Ellesworth.
Radulphus Pauly.	Ralph Pauly.
Johannes Marham.	John Marham.
Ricardus Ampton', taillour.	Richard Ampton, tailor.
Thomas filius Galfridi, daubere.	Thomas son of Geoffrey, plasterer.
Johannes Miles, flexman.	John Miles, flaxman.
[Col. a] Walterus de Dene, bocheresman.	[Col. a] Walter Dene, butcher's man.
Stephanus Sondaye.	Stephen Sondaye.
Johannes Cayse, de Storteford.	John Cayse, of Stortford.
Silvester Daubere.	Silvester Daubere.
Johannes Salman, taverner.	John Salman, taverner.
Thomas Beton, taillour.	Thomas Beton, tailor.
Willelmus Mareshall, de Stebenhith.	William Mareshall, of Stepney.
Johannes More, tynkere.	John More, tinker.
Johannes Essex, serviens Johannis Gauncely.	John Essex, servant of John Gauncely.
Willelmus Camys.	William Camys.
Johannes Naillere, goldsmythe.	John Naillere, goldsmith.
Johannes Nevyle, barbour.	John Nevyle, barber.
Willelmus Barston', sadelere.	William Barston, saddler.
Ricardus Flechere, serviens Ricardi Purdieu.	Richard Flechere, servant of Richard Purdieu.
Ricardus Vaucy, tylere.	Richard Vaucy, tiler.
Johannes Pope, tavernersman.	John Pope, taverner's man.
Willelmus, serviens Johannis Ferrour de vinetria London'.	William, servant of John Ferrour of the London vintry.
Edwardus Coteler, nuper serviens Johannis Twyford.	Edward Coteler, late servant of John Twyford.
Thomas, serviens Johannis \[Kent, shether.]/	Thomas, servant of John Kent, sheather.
Ricardus Forster, sadelere.	Richard Forster, saddler.
\[Willelmus]/ Hatfeld, boteler.	William Hatfeld, butler.
Johannes \[Lyghtbury,]/ brewere.	John Lyghtbury, brewer.
Willelmus Brampton, nuper custos porte de Cripilgate, London'.	William Brampton, formerly gate-keeper of Cripplegate, London.
Thomas, serviens Pauli Salesbury.	Thomas, servant of Paul Salesbury.
Nicholaus Cordewaner, manens apud le Herber.	Nicholas Cordewaner, staying at le Herber.
Johannes Mason', webbe.	John Mason, weaver.
Henricus Naffe, webbe.	Henry Naffe, weaver.
Willelmus Pypere, webbe.	William Pypere, weaver.
Willelmus Harwe, webbe.	William Harwe, weaver.
Johannes Wrawe, webbe.	John Wrawe, weaver.
Thomas Absolon', shereman.	Thomas Absolon, shearman.
Thomas Walsh', brewere.	Thomas Walsh, brewer.
Willelmus Polfote, serviens Ricardi Brendwode.	William Polfoot, servant of Richard Brentwood.
Thomas Cook de Kanc', nuper manens cum S. archiepiscopo Cantuar'.	Thomas Cook of Kent, formerly dwelling with Simon archbishop of Canterbury.
Wynton'.	Winchester.
Johannes Queynylde.	John Queynylde.
Thomas Fauconer.	Thomas Falconer.
Henricus Clerc.	Henry Clerk.

John Brusebon.
Peter Frenssch, servant of Philip Dunstaple.
Thomas Webbe, of Kingate Street.
William Morewe.
William Wygge.

Kent.
John Begyndenne, John Onewyne, of Cranbrook.
William Anne, Stephen, son of John Donet, of Small Hythe.
Thomas Castellayn, John Lethe, of Kenardington.
Philip Cheperegge, Ralph Oyn, of Tenterden.
Of the seven hundreds.
John Boucher, from Borden Wood.
Master John Ferrour, of Rochester.
John Brise, of Headcorn.
Thomas Berghamstede, of Gillingham.
John Goldbounde, of Rainham.
Forster, of Dartford.
John Modelegh.
John Man, of Burham.
Robert Senyng.
Robert Hemery, of Lenham.
Robert Cave, of Dartford.
John Atte Berche, the younger, of Frittenden.

Sussex.
Thomas Willot, of Burghhersch.
John Harry, of Northiam.
Stephen Holstok.
Robert Hodge.
John Jamyn, of Warbleton.
John Hunt, weaver, of Waldron.
Thomas Cutberd, of Wadhurst.
Nicholas Basset, of Hatfield.

Somerset.
Thomas Ingelby.
Richard Bercorn.
John Blake, scrivener.
John Kelly, hosier.
William Souter, servant of John Gondred.
Matthew Pottere.
William Fychet, waller.
John Stone, weaver.
John Canon, sheather.
John Notyngham.
John Say, soothsayer.
Richard Skynnere, the younger.
Thomas Barber, of Wells.

Canterbury.
John London.
Henry Waleys.

/Johannes Coggere, de Cantuar'.\
/Willelmus Sporiere.\
/Robertus Toneforde.\
/Henricus Twysdenn'.\
/Johannes Twysdenn'.\
/Henricus Aleyn, de parochia de Chertham, in comitatu Kantie.\

Membrane 5b

[15] Adjournement de parlement.

64. Et fait a remember qe puis apres quant cest parlement avoit longement endurez, et pur tant qe le feste de Nowell s'estoit proscheinement avenir, et auxint pur la venue de madame la roigne deinz le roialme fust bien pres; et avec ce, pur tant qe le mariage nostre seignour le roi et la corounement de la dite roigne si estoient moelt proscheinement venantz: et d'autre part, les greinours et plus chargeantz busoignes et pluis necessaires pur profit del roialme fi si remaignent encores nient esploitez en effect, a cause de les autres occupacions devant euz en mesme le parlement, si estoit cest parlement, le .xiij. jour de Decembre [1381], par nostre seignour le roi, de l'assent des prelatz, seignours, et communes illoeqes esteantz en mesme le parlement, soit adjourne tanqe al vendredy proschein devant la Conversion de Seint Poul lors procheinement ensuant [24 January 1382]; et ensi fust fait le dit .xiij. jour [14 December 1381]. Et voloit le roi et commandast qe les plees, causes, et autres matires touchez ore en \ce/ parlement nient terminez, et toutes autres choses avec lours dependences demoergent in statu quo nunc tanqe al vendredy dessusdit [24 January 1382]. Et comandast nostre dit seignour le roi qe touz les prelatz, seignours et communes, et autres q'avoient somonce de ce parlement q'ils alassent chescun en son marche, et retournassent al dit vendredy, toute excusacion ou dilacion cessante. Et comandast a touz illoeqes presentz, et lour chargeast estroitement qe sur toutes les matires touches devaunt en parlement, sibien c'estassavoir sur le bone governement del roialme, et maintenance de bone paix deinz le roialme toutes partes, come autrement sur les remedes a purvoier sur les marchandises, et sur les monoies, et maintenours et enhauceours des quereles en paiis, d'autres meschiefs dont devaunt ad este touchez, chescun s'advisast bien et profoundement par soi et de sa part de bone remede, encontre sa revenue al dit vendredy. Et einsi departist cest parlement a celle .xiij.jour.

Page iii-114

Revenue et reassemble de parlement.

65. A quel vendredy [24 January 1382], vindrent en parlement partie des prelatz et seignours del roialme; mais pur tant qe la greindre partie de eulx si failloist a celle foitz pur lour occupacion q'ils avoient euz devaunt entour la mariage et corounement de ma dame la roigne qe novellement estoient faitz, si fust cest parlement autrefoitz adjournez tanqe al lundy lors proschein ensuant [27 January 1382]. A quel lundy, les prelatz et seignours vindrent en parlement, et la commune y fist reherceaille sur les matires dont ils furent chargez de adviser a lour derrain departir: empriantz qe de celles feusse bone remede purvez.

Del profre le duc de Lanc'.

66. Et puis apres estoit grant disputison et altercacioun en dit parlement, del viage de monseignour d'Espaigne duc de Lancastre quel il profrist de faire en Portugal et en Espaigne, si le roialme voussist apprester .lx. mille*li*. pur les gages

[15] There is a change of hand at this point.

John Coggere, of Canterbury.
William Sporiere.
Robert Toneforde.
Henry Twysdenn.
John Twysdenn.
Henry Aleyn, of the parish of Chatham, in Kent.

Adjournment of parliament.

64. And be it remembered that later, when this parliament had continued for a long time, and because the feast of Christmas was fast approaching, and also because the arrival of our lady the queen in the kingdom was imminent; and also because the marriage of our lord the king and the coronation of the said queen were very near: and also, the more serious and weighty matters of business, most necessary for the benefit of the kingdom, still remained largely unsettled because of other concerns before them in the same parliament, it was decided by our lord the king, with the assent of the prelates, lords, and commons attending the same parliament, that on the 13 December this parliament should be adjourned until the Friday before the Conversion of St Paul next coming [24 January 1382]; and so it was done on the said thirteenth day. And the king willed and ordered that the pleas, causes, and other matters raised in this parliament yet not settled, and all other business together with its associated material should remain as they now are until the aforesaid Friday. And our said lord the king ordered that all the prelates, lords, and commons, and others who had been summoned to this parliament, should all depart, and return on the said Friday, all excuses or delays set aside. And he commanded all present there, and charged them strictly that all matters previously raised in parliament, that is to say as well the good government of the realm, and the maintenance of good peace throughout the kingdom, as the provisions to be made concerning merchandise, the coinage, maintainers and promoters of disputes in the land and of other troubles which have been discussed, they should each consider fully and deeply to find some good remedy, before their return on the said Friday. And so this parliament was adjourned on the thirteenth day.

The return and re-assembly of parliament.

65. On the which Friday [24 January 1382], some of the prelates and lords of the realm returned to parliament; but because the greater number of them failed to do so on this occasion because they had been preoccupied with the marriage and coronation of our lady the queen which had just occurred, so the parliament was again adjourned until the following Monday [27 January 1382]. On the which Monday, the prelates and lords came to parliament, and the commons there rehearsed the matters which they had been charged to discuss on their last departure: praying that they might be provided with effective remedy.

Concerning the duke of Lancaster's proposal.

66. And then, there was great argument and altercation in the said parliament, concerning the journey of our lord of Spain, duke of Lancaster, which he proposed to make to Portugal and Spain, if the kingdom would lend him £60,000 in wages

de .iim. hommes d'armes et .iim. archiers par un demy an, sibien pur salvacioun de noz gentz q'ore sont illoeqes, come autrement pur recovrer son droit q'il y ad, et pur la salve garde du meer et del roialme d'Engleterre; et, si Dieux plest, en grant destruccioun des enemys. Et profrist a nostre seignour le roy en parlement qe si Dieu lui donast la vie, et feusse franch de son corps hors de prisone, deinz trois ans il se vorroit obliger et ses terres en Engleterre de repaier au roi nostre seignour la dite somme, ou en deniers, ou autrement en service qe deust estre acceptable. Et sur celles profres et viage les seignours furent longement .... occupiez en dite altercacioun; aucuns disantz qe profitable chose serroit pur le roialme q'il y alast par manere q'il ad profrez, et meement \purtant qe ce/ tourneroit a salvacioun de noz gentz en Portugal, queux l'en tenoit pur destruitz s'ils n'aient de socours et aide. Et autres tienantz la contraire, c'estassavoir, qe s'il y alast, et esmesnast tiel poair avec lui come il ad demandez, le poair du roi et de son roialme serroit grantement empeirez et enfebliz; paront, si ryot, qe Dieux ne veulle, autrefoitz sourdast deinz le roialme, adonqes serroit moelt de plus a douter pur l'absence de mon dit seignour de Lancastre, et des nobles seignours, chivalers, esquiers, et autres q'il averoit avec luy.

Grant del subside des leynes, etc.

67. Item, les seignours et communes /del\ roialme d'Engleterre assemblez en ce parlement, le mardy en le .xxv. jour de Feverer l'an present [1382], entendantz /coment\ le grant del subside des leynes, peaulx lanutz, et quirs soi finist a la Chandeleure darrein passez [2 February 1382] parmy le grant ent darrein fait, et apparceivantz clerement les grantz efforcementz et multitude des enemys de nostre seignour le roi et de son roialme avauntdit, chescun part de mesme le roialme sibien par terre come par meer, et les grantz despenses qe necessairement l'en faut mettre sur la defens du dit roialme en resistence de tantz de enemys ove l'aide Nostre Seignour, mesmes les seignours et communes de leur liberale voluntee et /bone gree grantent\ a nostre seignour le roi, sibien pur eulx en ce parlement ore presentz en lours persones, come pur toute la dite commune d'Engleterre, autielles subsides des leines, peaulx lanutz, et quirs, oultre l'anciene custume ent due, come nostre dit seignour le roy ent preignoit ou purroit prendre parmy le darrein autre grant ent a lui fait en ce mesme parlement. A avoir et resceivre mesmes les subsides des leines, peaulx, et quirs del jour present tanqe a la Nativitee de Seint Johan le Baptistre proschein venant [24 June 1382], et de mesme la feste de Seint Johan par quatre ans entiers proscheinement ensuantz, a emploier \sur et/ en defens del dit roialme, et sur la resistence de la malice des enemys avantditz, soit il affaire par le viage q'ad este profrez d'estre fait par monsire de Lancastre in Espaigne, ou par autre manere quelconqe dont par l'advis de seignours mesme le roialme se purra mieultz estre defendez, al honour de Dieux, et salvacion d'icelle roialme. Faisantz nientmains lour protestacion expressement qe l'entention de la commune d'Engleterre n'est mye de leur obliger parmy aucunes

[Col. b] paroles devant ditz a la querele, conquest, ou la guerre del roialme d'Espaigne en especial par aucune voie, einz soulement en general, al defens du roialme d'Engleterre, et resistence des ditz enemys, par l'avis des seignours del dit roialme, \come/ mieultz \lour /semblera a ordenir.

---

for two thousand men-at-arms and two thousand archers for half a year, both for the security of our men who are now there, as well as to recover the right which he had there, and for the safekeeping of the sea and of the kingdom of England; and, if it please God, for the great destruction of our enemies. And he proposed to our lord the king in parliament that if God were to grant him his life, and preserve him from captivity, he himself and his lands in England would be bound to repay the king our lord the said sum within three years, either in money, or else in some acceptable service. And over those offers and that journey the lords were long occupied in the said argument; some saying that it would be beneficial for the kingdom that he should go in the manner which he proposed, and likewise because it would be the salvation of our people of Portugal, who would be destroyed if they did not receive succour and aid. And others argued to the contrary, that is to say, that if he were to go there, and take with him the the kind of force he had requested, the power of the king and his kingdom would be greatly impaired and weakened; so that, if a rebellion should once more arise within the kingdom, which God forbid, then there would be much more to fear from the absence of our said lord of Lancaster, and the noble lords, knights, squires, and others he would have with him.

The grant of the subsidy on wool, etc..

67. Also, the lords and commons of the kingdom of England assembled in this parliament, on Tuesday 25 February in the present year [1382], recognizing that the grant of the subsidy on wool, woolfells, and hides had ended last Candlemas [2 February] under the terms of the grant thereof made, and perceiving clearly the great strength and members of the enemies of our lord the king and his aforesaid kingdom, against every part of the realm both by land and sea, and the great expenses which would have to be invested in the defence of the said realm, with the aid of Our Lord, against such enemies, the same lords and commons of their own free accord and good grace granted to our lord the king, as well for themselves now present in person in this parliament, as for all the said commons of England, those subsidies on wool, woolfells, and hides, beyond the ancient customs thereon due, which our said lord the king took or could have taken from the last grant of those made to him in this same parliament, to have and receive the same subsidies on wool, fells, and hides, from the present day until the Nativity of St John the Baptist next [24 June 1382], and from the same feast of St John for the whole of the following four years, to be used for the defence of the said realm, and to oppose the malice of the aforesaid enemies, be it spent on the expedition which our lord of Lancaster has offered to undertake in Spain, or on anything else which, with the advice of the lords, will enable the same realm to be better defended, for the honour of God, and the security of the same kingdom. Protesting nevertheless that the intention of the commons of England was certainly not to commit themselves by any

[Col. b] words previously spoken concerning the dispute, conquest of, or war in the kingdom of Spain by any means, but only in general terms, with regard to the defence of the kingdom of England, and resistance to the said enemies, with the advice of the lords of the said kingdom, as it seemed best to them to ordain.

68. Et veullent mesmes les seignours et communes, et leur entencion est qe si pur viage affaire d'oultre la meer, ou pur autre chargeante cause, le roi nostre seignour eust busoigne de monoie, ou de faire chevance de monoie, qe en tiel cas le roi, par l'advis et discretion /de son bon et honurable\ conseil, face de sa grace ottroier licence et congie par ses lettres a ses creanceours et autres, ou mieultz luy semblera pur son profit, de passer leines, peaulx lanutz, et quirs aillours as parties de dela qe a Caleys, a durer pur un temps solonc lour bons advis et discrecions, et selonc la necessitee lors apparante; nientcontresteant estatut, chartre, .. ordenance, /ou proclamacion\ faitz au contraire.

69. Et prient les communes qe si paix ou trieves puisse estre fait avec les adversaires du roialme, q'adonqes cessantes les guerres les revenues et profitz du dit subside soient si discretement et salvement gardez qe quant y busoigne autrefoitz le roialme ent purra estre aidez, et la dite commune supportez.

70. Item, prient les dites communes a nostre dit seignour le roi et as seignours du parlement qe pur salvacioun et quiete de la terre, et en supportacion de leur charge \quiel ils/ ont treslongement portez et sustenuz, et a tiele guyse q'ils sont ore cheuz en moelt grant poverte, issint q'a peine ont de quoi eux mesmes sustenir; qe les charges des guerres et les autres oultrageouses despenses de long temps sustenuz par le roialme soient par temps de tout, ou en partie, oustez, et issint amesnusez qe la povre commune puisse vivre en paix et quiete, qe Dieux grante pur ses mercys.

Des obligacions, etc., faitz par duretee et compulsioun en le rumour estatut.

71. Et sur ce estoit assentuz en ce parlement qe toutes feffementz des terres et des rentes et \toutz/ obligacions et relesses et entrees en terres et tenementz, faitz par compulsioun et par constreinte de poair et multitude des gentz, ou par manace, en temps de ceste darreins rumour et ryot, encontre les loys de la terre et bone foi, soient de tout cassez, irritez, et tenuz pur voides; et ceulx qi ont fait faire /ou\ detiegnent tielx obligacions, relesses, ou autres faitz par duresce faitz, soient envoiez devant le roy et son conseil a certain jour, pur ent faire la deliverance /a ceulx qi les firent\ \encontre lour gree/). Et le roi defende qe nulluy face desore entree es terres ou tenementz sinoun en cas ou entree est donez par la loy; et en tieu cas nemye encores a forte main, ne a multitude des gentz, mais tantsoulement en lisible, aisee, et peisible manere, et selonc ce qe la loy de la terre demande. Et si nulluy face desore a contraire \et ent soit convict,/ soit puniz par emprisonement de son corps, et reint a la voluntee le roy.

Des muniementz arz et destruitz, etc., en dit rumour.

72. Item, est assentuz qe ceulx qi se sentent grevez par esloignement, arsure, ou autre destruccioun fait de lour chartres, relees, obligacions, estatutz-marchantz, courteroulles, ou d'autres lours evidences perduz en cest derrain rumour et ryot, q'ils viegnent parentre cy et la Nativitee de Seint Johan proschein [24 June 1382] a pluis oultre devant le conseill nostre seignour le roi, et illoeqes facent suffisante proeve d'iceulx lours munimentz issint perduz, arses, et destruitz, et de la forme et tenure d'icelles; et le roi, par l'advis de son conseil, lour ferra purvoier de remede, si avant come il le purra faire par la loy.[16]

Page iii-115

68. And the same lords and commons wish and intend that if for the expedition to be made overseas, or for any other important cause, the king our lord has need of money, or to borrow money, that then the king, with the advice and discretion of his good and honourable council, should of his grace cause licence and permission to be granted by his letters to his creditors and others, wheresover it seems most beneficial to him, to send wool, woolfells, and hides to places overseas other than Calais, and that to remain in force for a time in accordance with their good advice and discretion, and the state of need then apparent; notwithstanding any statute, charter, ordinance, or proclamation made to the contrary.

69. And the commons prayed that if peace or truces be made with the adversaries of the realm that then, the wars being ended, the revenues and profits from the said subsidy shall be so discreetly and carefully guarded that when there is need again, the kingdom may be aided by this and the said commons supported.

70. Also, the said commons pray of our said lord the king and the lords of parliament that for the security and tranquillity of the land, and in support of the charge which they have borne and sustained for a very long time, in such a way that they have now lapsed into great poverty so that they have scarcely anything on which to survive; that the burdens of wars and the other outrageous expenses so long sustained by the kingdom shall soon be abolished completely or in part, and so reduced that the poor commons may live in peace and tranquillity, may God grant this in his mercy.

A statute concerning obligations, etc., made under duress and by compulsion during the uprising.

71. And hereon it was agreed in this parliament that all feoffments of lands and rents, and all bonds, releases, and entries on to lands and tenements made by compulsion or constraint by the power and multitude of the people, or by menaces during the late uprising and riot, contrary to the laws of the land and good faith, should be altogether quashed, invalidated, and held void; and those who caused such bonds, releases, or other deeds to be made under duress, or who now retain them, shall be sent before the king and his council on a certain day, to deliver them up to those who granted them against their will. And the king forbids anyone, henceforth, to grant entry onto lands and tenements except where entry is granted by law; and then, not by force, nor by a multitude of people, but only in a lawful, free and peaceable manner, and in accordance with the law of the land. And if anyone, henceforth, acts to the contrary and is so convicted, he shall be punished with bodily imprisonment, and held at the king's will.

Concerning muniments burnt and destroyed, etc., in the said uprising.

72. Also, it is agreed that those who feel harmed by the removal, burning, or other destruction inflicted on their charters, releases, bonds, statutes-merchant, court-rolls, or other evidences lost in this last uprising and riot, shall come before the council of our lord the king between now and the Nativity of St John next [24 June 1382], and there shall provide sufficient proof of those their muniments lost, burned and destroyed, and of the form and tenor of the same; and the king, with the advice of his council, shall provide them with remedy, so far as he is able according to the law.

---

[16] The rest of this membrane has been left blank.

YCY ENSOUNT LES PETICIONS BAILLEES AVANT EN PARLEMENT PAR LA COMMUNE D'ENGLETERRE, AVEC LES RESPONCES FAITES EN MESME LE PARLEMENT A LES PETICIONS AVANTDITES.

I.

73. [Confirmation of the liberties of the church, and of the charters] En primes, supplient les communes qe seinte esglise eit toutes ses libertees et franchises entierment, et qe la grande chartre, et la chartre de la foreste, et touz les autres bones estatutz et ordinances avant ces heures faitz et ordenez, soient tenuz et gardez, et duement executz, selonc la forme et effect d'icelle.
Responsio.
Le roi le voet.

II.

74. [Restraint on royal grants] Item, prient les communes q'il plese au roi nostre seignour q'il puisse au present estre escrit en rolle de parlement, coment ordenez est par lui, noz autres seignours et toute la commune, qe desore en apres, nul doun de terre, de rente, de garde, ne de mariage, ne de nul manere eschete soit grantez a nulluy tanqe le roi nostre dit seignour soit hors de dette, et hors des tielx charges de guerre come y ad au present. Et si aucune persone demande aucun doun au contraire de ceste peticioun, perde les service et compaignie nostre dit seignour pur touz jours apres.
Responsio.
Il ne semble mye honeste, ne chose honurable au roi ne a sa dignitee q'il se lieroit a tielle guyse paront il ent fuist si oultrement constreint, mais plest au roi, et il voet, pur le bien de lui mesmes et de son roialme, soi restreindre et abstiner a doner ou granter a aucune persone terre, rente, garde, mariage, ou eschete, sanz l'assent et acord des seignours et autres de son counseil.

III.

75. [The royal household] Item, prient les communes qe les grantz officers del hostiel nostre dit seignour le roi soient \ore/ expressement jurez devant touz les seignours du parlement, a garder par eux et par les autres petitz officers du dit hostiel l'ordenance et governement du dit hostiel, come ore ad este ordenez et apoyntez par noz seignours a ce esluz; et ce sibien en quantitee de meignee, come autrement.

Responsio.
Les ditz officers ont este charges et jurez de ce faire et perfournir en presence du roi et les seignours en ce parlement.

IV.

76. [Purveyance] Item, prient les communes qe l'estatut de purveiours fait en temps nostre seignour le roi l'aielle soit ore renovellez et affermez en touz les pointz, et commissions ent faitz a chescun viscont, a proclamer par toute sa baillie le dit estatut, et qe punissement soit duement fait a les faisours de l'encontre sanz nule remissioun; et a tant des foiz come offense notable soit trovez en aucun purveiour dedeinz le roialme, soit il purveiour du roi ou d'autry, qi contre la fourme du dit estatut y face, eit il qe soit atteint le punissement compris en le dit estatut sanz pardon.

Responsio.
Le roi voet qe l'estatutz faitz des purveiours soient tenuz et gardez, et mises en due et bone execucioun.

HERE FOLLOW THE PETITIONS SUBMITTED TO PARLIAMENT BY THE COMMONS OF ENGLAND, TOGETHER WITH THE REPLIES GIVEN IN THE SAME PARLIAMENT TO THE AFORESAID PETITIONS.

I.

73. [Confirmation of the liberties of the church, and of the charters]. Firstly, the commons pray that holy church have all its liberties and franchises intact, and that the Great Charter, and the charter of the forest, and all other good statutes and ordinances made and ordained in the past, be upheld and preserved, and duly executed, in accordance with the form and effect of the same.
Answer.
The king wills it.

II.

74.[Restraint on royal grants]. Also, the commons pray that it may please our lord the king now to cause it to be written in the rolls of parliament that it is ordained by him, our other lords, and all the commons that henceforth no grant of land, rent, wardship, marriage, nor any kind of escheat shall be granted to anyone until the king our said lord be out of debt, and free from the present burdens of war. And if anyone demands such a gift contrary to this petition, let him lose the service and company of our said lord the king for ever.

Answer.
It does not indeed seem befitting nor honourable to the king nor to his dignity that he bind himself in such a way that he should be entirely thus constrained, but it pleases the king, and he wills, for the good of himself and his kingdom that he should be restrained and abstain from giving and granting to any person land, rent, wardship, marriage, or escheat, without the assent and agreement of the lords and others of his council.

III.

75. [The royal household]. Also, the commons pray that the great officers of the household of our said lord the king be now expressly sworn before all the lords of parliament to observe, and ensure that the other lesser officers of the said household observe, the ordinance and regimen of the said household now ordained and appointed by our lords elected for this purpose; and this both in the numbers of the household, as other features.
Answer.
The said officers have been charged and sworn, in the presence of the king and the lords in this parliament, so to do.

IV.

76. [Purveyance]. Also, the commons pray that the statute of purveyors made in the time of our lord the king the grandfather [Edward III] be now renewed and confirmed in all respects, and each sheriff commissioned to proclaim the said statute throughout his bailiwick, and that punishment be duly inflicted, without remission, on those who act to the contrary; and as often as a notable offence be found in any purveyor within the kingdom, be he a purveyor for the king or any other, which has been committed contrary to the form of the said statute, let him convicted receive the punishment contained in the said statute without pardon.
Answer.
The king wills that the statutes made on purveyors shall be upheld and observed, and duly and effectively executed.

V.

77. [Debts to the crown] Item, prient les communes qe declaracion soit faite en ce parlement qe les dettes dues au roi par la morte la roigne qe darrein morust, queux furont dues au dite roigne devant l'an quarantisme le roi Edward [III] l'aiel [1366-7], deivent currer deinz la pardon fait l'an cynquantisme de mesme le roi l'aiel, par quel, entre autres, sont pardonez touz dettes duez au /dit\ roi devant l'an de son

[Col. b] regne quarantisme, nientcontresteant qe la dite roigne murrust apres la dit an quarantisme.
Responsio.
Il ne semble mye reson qe si la dite roigne feusse unqores endettez as aucunes gentz du roialme, as queux pur defaute d'avoir n'ad mye peu estre satisfait, qe devant qe ses dettes soient perpaiez tiele pardoun feusse fait. Mes le roi voet qe proclamacioun soit faite parentre cy et la Seint Michel proschein [29 September 1382] venant qe si nully se vorra pleindre de dette a lui due par mesme la roigne, viegnent et mettent avant lour pleinte; et ce fait, selonc ce qe le pleinte se ferra au roi il entende de modifier sa grace en le cas.

VI.

78. [Respite of accounts due in Trinity term 1381] Item, prient les communes qe toutz les visconts, et autres persones q'avoient jour d'accompter, ou autres choses faire a l'escheqier, la terme de la Trinitee darrein passe [19 June-10 July 1381], et qe furent ou serroient mys a perde par cause de lour nounvenue a l'escheqier le dit terme, soient deschargez de chescuns tielx perdes; considerantz le perillouses levees des communes qe furent a cel temps.
Responsio.
Le roi de sa grace l'ad grantez.

VII.

79. [Pardon to collectors of lay subsidy] Item, prient les communes, d'ordener remede de ceux qi furent collectours et countrollours del darrein subside, et ont perduz grantz sommes des issues par cause de lour nounvenue a l'escheqier le terme de Seint Hiller l'an quart [23 January-12 February 1381]; q'ils puissent avoir pardoun en celle partie, considerantz qe s'ils eussent venuz mesme le terme ils ne purroient avoir fait gree par cause de brieftee du temps.
Responsio.
Le roi le voet.

VIII.

80. [Lay subsidies of 1332-3 and 1334-5] Item, prient les communes, d'ordener remede pur ceux qi sont heirs ou terretenantz a ceux qi fuerent collectours ou taxours del disme et quinzisme grantez par les layes au roi l'aiel, l'ans de son regne sisme [1332-3] et oeptisme [1334-5]; q'ils puissent estre chargez et contribucioun faire ove les villes ou lours dites terres sont a chescune tiel grant, desore quitz et deschargez des sommes qe furent assis sur les ditz collectours et taxours aucuns des ditz ans sisme ou oeptisme; ou autrement, q'ils soient chargiez desore a chescune tiel grant, selonc la quantitee de lours biens et chateux queux ils aueront sur lour dites terres et tenementz au temps des tieles grantz. Et ce par serement des collectours des ditz grantes affaires sur lour accompts devaunt les barons de l'escheqier.

Responsio.
Le roi voet et grante de sa grace qe les dites heirs et terre tenantz soient desore chargez a chescun tiel grant

V.

77. [Debts to the crown]. Also, the common pray that announcement be made in this parliament that the debts owed to the king as a result of the death of the queen who lately died [Philippa of Hainault], which were owed to the said queen before the fortieth year of King Edward [1366-7], the grandfather, shall be included in the pardon made in the fiftieth year of the same king the grandfather, in which, amongst other things, are pardoned all debts owed to the said king before the

[Col. b] fortieth year of his reign, notwithstanding that the said queen died after the said fortieth year.
Answer.
It would have seemed unreasonable, had the queen still been indebted to anyone in the realm who had not received any satisfaction owing to her lack of means, if such a pardon had been issued before her debts had been discharged, but the king wills that proclamation be made between now and Michaelmas next [29 September 1382] that if anyone wishes to complain of a debt owed him by the same queen, he shall appear and submit his plea; and that done, the king will moderate his grace in the matter according to the nature of the plea.

VI.

78. [Respite of accounts due in Trinity term 1381]. Also, the commons pray that all sheriffs and others who had a day for accounting or discharging other business at the exchequer in Trinity term last past [19 June-10 July 1381], and who have or will have suffered loss by their non-appearance at the exchequer in the said term, be discharged from all such losses; considering the dangerous risings amongst the commons which occurred then.
Answer.
The king of his grace has granted it.

VII.

79. [Pardon to collectors of the lay subsidy]. Also, the commons pray that remedy be ordained for those who were collectors or controllers of the last subsidy, and who lost great sums from issues because of their non-appearance at the exchequer in Hilary term in the fourth year [23 January-12 February 1381]; that they be pardoned on that behalf, considering that if they had appeared during the same term they could not have made an account for want of time.
Answer.
The king wills it.

VIII.

80. [Lay subsidies of 1332-3 and 1334-5]. Also, the commons pray that remedy be ordained for those who are heirs or tenants of those who were collectors or assessors of the tenth and fifteenth granted by the laity to the king the grandfather in the sixth [1332-3] and eighth [1334-5] years of his reign; that they be charged and contribute to each such grant with the towns in which their said lands lie, and therefore quit and discharged from the sums which were assessed on the said collectors and assessors in the said sixth and eighth years; or otherwise, that they shall be charged henceforth for each such grant, in accordance with the quantity of the goods and chattels which they had on their said lands and tenements at the time of such grants. And that on the oath of the collectors of the said grants to be made on their accounts before the barons of the exchequer.
Answer.
The king wills and grants of his grace that henceforth, the said heirs and tenants shall be charged only, for each such

soulement selonc la quantitee de lours biens et chateux queux ils averont sur lours ditz terres et tenementz au temps du tielx grantz; et ce par serement des collectours des ditz grantez affaires sur lours acomptes devant les barons de l'escheqier, sanz ent estre autrement chargez.

IX.

81. [Debts to the crown] Item, pur ce qe plusours gentz sont empeschez a l'escheqier pur aunciens dettes qe comencerent en temps le roi l'aiel long temps devant l'an de son regne quarantisme [1366-7]; et coment qe le dit aiel graciousement fist pardon generale as touz grantz ou petitz de son roialme *[Page iii-116]*
[Col. a] des touz tielx dettes a lui dues devant le dit an quarantisme, nientmeins, par cause d'une exepcioun contenue en le dite pardoun par paroles q'ensuent 'forspris dettes adjuggez par seisine de terre,' les dites gentz nul avantage n'ont, n'avoir purront, del generale pardoun susdite.

Dont plese a nostre dit seignour le roy granter en ce present parlement qe la dite pardoun se poet extendre as touz ses liges, et a chescun de eux, nient contresteant la dite excepcioun des touz dettes qi furent dues au dit aielle devant le dit an quarantisme, sibien deinz le roialme d'Engleterre, come dehors.

Responsio.
Le roi n'est mye advisez de present de soi ouster si generalment de toutes \terres/ seisiz en sa main par causes des dettes. Mais si ascun en especial se sente grevez, monstre le manere coment, et pur quel dette, et queux terres sont issint seisiz, et le roy nostre seignour ent purra faire sa grace hors de parlement, par l'advis de son conseille.

X.

82. [Prests in the exchequer] Item, prient les communes qe nule somme d'apprest desore soit mys sur aucune persone al receite de l'escheqier par paiement ou par assignement, si mesme la persone ne soit la present en sa propre persone, ou par son attourne de record.
Responsio.
Le roi le voet.

XI.

83. [Collectors of lay subsidies] Item, qe touz les collectours, assessours, et countrollours, sibien del derrain subside, come des touz autres subsides grantez a nostre seignour le roi par les laies, soient chargez sur lour acomptes par les rolles faitz parentre les collectours et lours ditz countrollours, sanz aucun autre charge mettre sur eux par cause d'aucunes novelles enquerres faites par aucunes gentz a ce assignez par commissiouns faites puis la date de les commissions faites as dites collectours de coiller les subsides avauntdites: salve des tieles sommes come purra estre trovez par serementz des collectours et lours countrollours q'ils ont receuz par vertu des tieles novelles enquerres; et processe cesse tout outrement vers touz ceux qi furent assignez par commissioun nostre seignour le roi de faire tieles novelles enquerres de queconqe subside grante en temps passe.
Responsio.
Le roi le voet; salvez qe si en temps avenir purra apparoir par la prove ou tesmoignance des conestables des villes qe les ditz coillours eient plus resceuz pur le dit subside qe mesmes les coillours n'aient paiez a l'escheqier, qe de ce \les/ coillours soient chargez.

XII.

84. [The forest] Item, prient les communes qe come les nobles rois Henry [III] et Edward [I], voz progenitours,

grant, an amount which is in proportion to the quantity of goods and chattels they had on their said lands and tenements at the time of such grants; and that on the oath of the collectors of the said grants to be made on their accounts before the barons of the exchequer, without being otherwise charged.

IX.

81. [Debts to the crown]. Also, whereas many are impeached at the exchequer for ancient debts, which began in the time of the king the grandfather long before the fortieth year of his reign [1366-7]; and although the said grandfather graciously granted his general pardon to all great and small in his kingdom *[Page iii-116]*
[Col. a] of all such debts owed him before the said fortieth year, nevertheless, because of an exception made in the said pardon, worded as follows, 'except debts adjudged by seisin of land,' the said people do not gain and cannot derive any benefit from the aforesaid general pardon.

Wherefore may it please our said lord the king to grant in this present parliament that the said pardon be extended to all his lieges, and to each one of them, notwithstanding the said exception of all debts owed to the said grandfather before the said fortieth year, both within the kingdom of England and without.

Answer.
The king is not advised at present to relinquish so widely all lands taken into his hands because of those debts. But if anyone feels particularly aggrieved, let him explain why and for what debt his lands were seised and which lands they are, and the king our lord may grant his grace hereon, outside parliament, by the advice of his council.

X.

82. [Prests in the exchequer]. Also, the commons pray that that no prest of any amount shall be imposed on anyone at the receipt of the exchequer by payment or by assignment, unless they are present in person, or represented by an attorney of record.
Answer.
The king wills it.

XI.

83. [Collectors of lay subsidies]. Also, that all collectors, assessors, and controllers of the last subsidy, as well as of other subsidies granted to our lord the king by the laity, be charged on their accounts by the rolls made between the collectors and their said controllers, without any other charge being imposed on them because of new inquiries made by anyone assigned thereto by commissions issued since the date of the commissions issued to the said collectors to collect the aforesaid subsidies: saving such sums which are found, on the oaths of the collectors and their controllers, to have been received by them by virtue of such new inquiries; and that process shall cease entirely against all those who were appointed by commission of our lord the king to carry out such new inquiries concerning any subsidy granted in the past.
Answer.
The king wills it; saving that if, in future, it emerges by the proof or testimony of the constables of the towns that the said collectors received more from the said subsidy than they paid into the exchequer, they shall be charged for it.

XII.

84. [The forest]. Also, the commons pray that whereas the noble kings Henry [III] and Edward [I], your progenitors,

granterent lours chartres de foreste as ditz communes, vous plese considerer \[les grantz tortz et]/ oppressions queux voz ministres du foreste parmy le roialme la ou foreste est, font de jour en autre a les enhabitantz hors du foreste, surmettantz q'il est foreste, et \[pur doute, et]/ .... \[de]/ vostre grant hautesse, les ditz enhabitantz se doubtent et n'osent mettre claym sur lour heritage et droit propre: et ensi remaynent disheritez de plus en plus, \[sans tourner]/ au profit de vous ou de vostre coroune, mais soulement en oppression de voz ditz communes.

Par quoy vous plese de confermer les dites chartres, et faire perambulation selonc la fourme d'icelles; considerez le grant fyn qe le poeple fist a celle temps pur la grant des chartres avauntdites.

Responsio.

Le roi voet qe les chartres de la foreste soient confermez, tenuz, et gardez, et qe perambulacion soit faite la ou il busoigne, selonc les boundes faitez et chivachez parmy le derraine ordenance ent faite, en temps le noble roi Edward [I], filz le roi Henry.

XIII

85. [17][Muniments destroyed during the revolt] Item, prient les communes qe come plusours chartres et munimentz queux sont enrollez en diverses places nostre dit seignour le roi de record, pur queux enrollementz les parties ont paiez les fees dues et acustumez;

[Col. b] et ore tarde, par les gentz levez en la grande rebellion, plusours de /tielx\ faitz et munimentz furent ars et destruitz.

Qe plese grantir qe chescun qi voudra pursuir en la chancellerie pur avoir tielx faitz et munimentz exemplifiez q'ils les puissent avori einsi exemplifiez de vostre tresexcellente grace sanz rien doner. Et qe par la ou en plusours courtes parmy le roialme, sibien en courtes de l'estaple come ailleurs, plusours recordes et processes sont ars et destruitz, a grant damage de tout le roialme, qe vous plese ent ordener remede. Et en toutes villes et burghes de franchise ou plees des assises estoient comencez devaunt le dit rebellion, et les processes d'icelles alors arses, q'adonqes toutz tielx plees soient et puissent au present resumer en mesme la nature qe les plees susdites estoient au temps qe les processes estoient arses.

Responsio.

Quant as exemplifications affaires des munimentz enroullez de record, et destruitz en darein rumour sanz see de seal, le roi le voet. Et quant a ce q'est demandez des recordz et processes arses et destruitz, ce ne poet mye estre en nul manere par la loy.

Membrane 3

XIV.

86. [Farms of the shires] Item, prient les communes qe come les viscounts des pluseures countees parmy le roialme soloient tenir certeines fermes du roi, les quelles en partie lour sont toluz par mandement nostre seignour le roi, et les visconts sur lour accomptz sont chargiez sibien de celles parcelles ensi toluz come de remenant.

Par quoy plese a vostre hautesse qe lour dit charge soit rebatuz, ou autrement q'ils soient rejointez a leur dite parcelle. Qar coment q'il soit q'aucune enquerree ent soit faite, et duement retourne, unqore ils ne purront nulle allouance avoir, a grande defesance et anientisment des plusours vaillantz du

---
[17] A change of hand occurs at this point.

granted their charters of the forest to the said commons, it please you to consider the great wrongs and oppressions which your ministers of the forest throughout the kingdom, wheresoever there is forest, commit from day to day against people living outside the forest, claiming that it is forest, and through fear and.....of your great highness, the said inhabitants are afraid and dare not claim their inheritance and proper right: and so they are more and more disinherited, without profit to you or you kingdom, but simply to the oppression of your said commons.

Wherefore may it please you to confirm the said charters, and carry out a perambulation in accordance with the form of the same; considering the great fine which the people paid at that time for the granting of the aforesaid charters.

Answer.

The king wills that the charters of the forest shall be confirmed, kept and upheld, and that the perambulation shall be carried out wheresoever it be needed, in accordance with the boundaries fixed and ridden under the last ordinance made thereon, in the time of the noble King Edward [I], son of King Henry [III].

XIII

85. [Muniments destroyed during the revolt]. Also, the commons pray that whereas many charters and muniments were enrolled in various places of our said lord the king as of record, for which enrolments the parties paid the due and customary fees;

[Col. b] yet lately, many such deeds and muniments were burned and destroyed by those who took part in the great rebellion.

May it please you to grant that anyone who wishes to request in the chancery to have such deeds and muniments copied, may have them thus copied with your most excellent grace without paying anything. And that, since in many courts throughout the kingdom, both in courts of the staple as well as elsewhere, numerous records and processes have been burned and destroyed, to the great injury of the entire realm, it may please you to ordain a remedy therefor. And in all towns and boroughs of franchise where pleas of assizes were begun before the said rebellion, and the processes of the same then burned, that then all such pleas shall and may now be resumed in the same state in which the aforesaid pleas were at the time when the processes were burned.

Answer.

As to the copies to be made of the muniments enrolled as of record, and destroyed in the last uprising without a seal affixed, the king wills it. And as to that which is requested concerning the records and processes burned and destroyed, that cannot not be done by any lawful means.

XIV.

86. [Farms of the shires]. Also, the commons pray that whereas the sheriffs of many shires throughout the kingdom used to hold certain farms of the king, of which they have now been deprived in part, by acts of our lord the king, yet the sheriffs on their accounts are charged as well for those parcels thus taken as for what remains to them.

Wherefore may it please your highness that their said charge be reduced, or otherwise that they have the said parcels restored. Since although a certain inquiry was made hereon, and duly returned, they have still had no allowance made, to the great injury and ruin of the more worthy men of the

kingdom. Wherefore may it please you to redress the matter in the present parliament.
Answer.

It pleases our lord the king that where farms and profits which customarily pertain to sheriffs have since been granted to lords and others of the kingdom at fee-farm, or for an annual rent to be paid to the exchequer, such rent and profit paid to the king shall be allowed henceforth to the sheriff of the place in his account, in compensation for such a sum lost from the farm of the shire.

XV.

87. [Tithes of woods]. Also, the commons pray that prohibition shall not be denied where tithes are demanded from woods which are over twenty years old, on pain of a grievous penalty.....regard that the bishops who have been chancellor have denied it notwithstanding the statute made thereon in the past.
Answer.

Let it be dealt with as it has customarily been in the past.

XVI.

88. Also, whereas by the Great Charter it was ordained and generally confirmed in all other parliaments, 'That the law shall not be denied nor sold to anyone', contrary to which charter it is customary in the chancery to take fines for the issuing of various writs, greatly injuring the estate of all the people and of the law.

May it please you to ordain in this present parliament that everyone who wishes to purchase a writ in the said chancery shall have the said writ without paying a fine.
Answer.

Our lord the king assuredly does not intend to deprive himself of so large a commodity, which has been levied continually in the said chancery, both before as well as after the making of the said charter, in the time of all his noble progenitors who since have been kings of England.

XVII.

89. [Kirkley Roads]. Also, the commons of Norfolk and Suffolk, and of all the other counties of England pray that whereas in the past it was ordained that every liege of the kingdom might buy and sell without hindrance in a city, borough, sea-port, and elsewhere throughout the entire kingdom; and if charters or letters patent had been granted to the contrary they were to be held at naught; the which statutes have as yet not been repealed. Nevertheless, our lord the king has granted to *[Page iii-117]*

[Col. a] the men of Yarmouth that no one may buy or sell within seven miles of their said town, and that a place called Kirkley Roads in Suffolk which is six miles from Yarmouth shall be annexed to the same town, which is in the county of Norfolk: and a charter on the said matter was repealed in full parliament, as appears on record, because the said charter was damaging and harmful to the commons of England, and contrary to the law; and because ships anchored in the said roadstead when the wind was against them could by no means enter the harbour of Yarmouth, but were compelled to thow all their herring into the sea, as the people of Yarmouth, because of that grant, will not suffer the said commons at any time of the year in any manner to buy or sell victuals or merchandise in the said area. And a bill was sued on the matter in the last parliament held at Northampton, to repeal the said charter for the aforesaid reasons; which bill was endorsed at the king's command that if the inquest lately certified in the chancery touching the said franchise seemed sufficient to

vieue suffisante a conseil le roi, soit faite commissioun as persones suffisantz et indifferentz d'enquerre de novel en due manere, come plus pleinement piert par l'endossement du dite bille. A cause de quel endosement, par avys de conseil une commissioun issist d'enquere des pointz suisdites, quele est retourne en la chancellerie. Par force de quele commissioun les pointz contenuz en la dite bille sue al Norhampton' sont trovez veritables, sur quoi les ditz communes supplient qe la dite chartre soit repellee as touz jours; et qe nule autre desormes soit grante au contraire.

Responsio.

Le roi voet qe la dite chartre soit repelle quant al \dit/ novel grant compris en ycelle, avec la novelle encrees de lour ferme faite et compris en leur chartre par cause del dit novel grant, tout dys salvez as burgeys illoeqes lours ancienes chartres, et bones custumes.

XVIII.

90. [Provisors] Item, prient les communes qe come devant ces heures diverses estatutz et ordenances ont este faitz encountre ceux qi purchacent abbacies et priories, par provisions en la \[court de Rome, nientmeins]/ tieles provisions plus habundent en le roialme a ore qe unqes ne furent avaunt ces heures, quelles s'ils soient issint sustenues serront \[apert]/ destruccion des \[franches elections,]/ .... \[des]/ droits qe les seignours et patrons ont en lour patronages, et desolacioun de la religioun de seinte esglise parmy le roialme; siqe les aliens, les \[mendivantz, les apostates, et autres persones nient]/ dignes \[occupieront]/ tielx benefices, sicome ils font en France et en Itaille, quele chose serroit aperte perdicion des droitz des seignours du roialme, et occasion des \[autres damages nient recovrables; asses]/ come ore tard l'en ad .... en ceste derrain riote, en quele meynte honurable persone fuist \[occise,]/ et pluseurs monstiers et abbeies en poigne d'estre arses \[et destruitz ovesqe les]/ enhabitantz.

Par quoi cestes grantz meschiefs et damages diligealment considerez, plese ore par advis et commune assent de vostre parlement adjouster a cestes estatutz qe les \[esluz des tieles]/ esglises par congie nostre seignour le roi puissent avoir liveree de leur temporaltees, en cas qe nul defaute ne demoert en eux, en sustenance de la religion de seinte esglise, \[et augmentacion de lour]/ devocioun, et auxint en maintenance des droitures et loies du roialme. Et oultre ce mander par briefs, ou lettres patentes, en diverses parties d'Engleterre, estroitement chargeantz qe nul \[soit si]/ hardiz de maintenir ou de parler overtement en maintenance des tielx provisours. Et si par cas, qe Dieux defende, q'aucun en soit empeschez et enditez, q'il face fin et rauncoun au roi pour le contempt, come reson et la loy demandent.

Responsio.

Les estatutz ent faitz suffisent, queux le roi voet qe soient gardez et tenuz, et mises en due execution.

XIX.

91. [Alien clergy] Item, prient les communes qe come plusours estatutz et ordenances aient este faitz avaunt ces heures des dignitees et autres benefices electives deinz mesme le roialme, queux sont donez as aliens, et aucunfoitz as aperts enemys nostre seigneur le roi et de son roialme, paront le tresor est tret hors du roialme, le conseil du roialme descovert, et autres pluseurs meschiefs ent aviegnent, come pluis pleinement appiert as ditz estatutz et ordenances. Et nientcontresteant celles estatutz, mesmes les aliens si preignent

the king's council, a commission would be directed to worthy and indifferent persons to make fresh inquiries in an appropriate manner, as appears more fully in the endorsement of the said bill [Parliament of November 1380, Item 39]. Because of which endorsement, by the advice of the council a commission was set up to inquire into the aforesaid points, which was returned to the chancery. By force of which commission the points contained in the said bill sued at Northampton were found to be true, whereupon the said commons request that the said charter be repealed forever; and that no other shall henceforth be granted to the contrary.
Answer.

The king wills that the said charter shall be repealed in respect of the said new grant contained in the same, together with the new increment of their farm made and contained in their charter because of the said new grant, saving always to the burgesses of the place their ancient charters and good customs.

XVIII.

90. [Provisors]. Also, the commons pray that whereas in the past divers statutes and ordinances have been made against those who purchase abbacies and priories by provisions in the court of Rome, and yet such provisions are now more abundant in the kingdom than ever before, which, if they are thus tolerated, will cause the open destruction of free elections..... of the rights which the lords and patrons have in their patronage, and the desolation of the religion of holy church throughout the kingdom; and thus aliens, mendicants, apostates, and other unworthy persons will occupy such benefices, as they do in France and Italy, which would clearly destroy the rights of the lords of the realm, and occasion other irreparable damage; bearing in mind that of late there has ..... in this last riot, in which many honourable people were slain, and many monasteries and abbeys on the point of being burnt and destroyed together with their occupants.

Wherefore, having diligently considered those great troubles and injuries, may it please you now by the advice and common assent of your parliament to add to those statutes, that the elect of such churches by permission of our lord the king shall have delivery of their temporalities, where there is no default in them, for the sustenance of the religion of holy church, the increase of their devotion, and for the maintenance of the rights and laws of the kingdom. Furthermore, to send by writs or letters patent, into various parts of England, strict injunction that no one should be so presumptuous as to maintain or speak openly in support of such provisors. And if by chance, which God forbid, anyone should be accused and indicted, he shall pay a fine and ransom to the king for this contempt, as reason and the law demand.
Answer.

The statutes made thereon are adequate and the king wills that they shall be kept and upheld, and duly executed.

XIX.

91. [Alien clergy]. Also, the commons pray that whereas many statutes and ordinances have been made in the past concerning dignities and other elective benefices within the kingdom, which are given to aliens, and sometimes to the open enemies of our lord the king and his kingdom, whereby wealth is withdrawn from the kingdom, the secrets of the kingdom disclosed, and many other mischiefs arise, as appears more fully in the said statutes and ordinances. Yet notwithstanding those statutes, the same aliens still take

possession of the said dignities from one day to the next, and occupy both the said dignities and elective benefices as well as other benefices in all parts of England; and they have there their proctors and farmers from foreign nations as well as from the kingdom itself, contrary to the ordinance recently made thereon in your parliament.

May it please you for the security of the rights of your crown, and for the aforesaid common benefit, to ordain and decree in this parliament that all the said statutes and ordinances shall be duly enforced, and similarly ordain that the free elections made and to be made within your kingdom may remain as they have in the past; and that no person of whatsoever degree, status, or condition he may be, alien or denizen, shall henceforth be proctor, farmer, or administrator of the said aliens in any way for their benefices within the said kingdom, on pain of forfeiting all that they can forfeit in body and in goods.

Answer.

Divers statutes have been made on the matter, which the king wills shall be upheld and put into proper and due execution.

XX.

92. [Mortmain]. Also, the commons pray that whereas it was ordained by a statute made in the time of the noble king Edward [I], son of King Henry [III], that no man of religion nor any other, should purchase land or tenement, nor appropriate them in mortmain, without the will and permission of the lords from whom such lands and tenements are held, on pain of a penalty contained in the same statute; yet nevertheless some men of religion, and others at their instigation and procurement, cause the king to purchase both lands and tenements and advowsons of churches, with intent to exclude the mesne lords, and take their feoffment of such lands and tenements and appropriations of churches thus into mortmain directly from the king; whereby the lords and many of the kingdom, from whom such lands and tenements and advowsons of churches are held, lose wardships, marriages, reliefs, escheats, and other profits from the lordship, and suffer the very mischief against which the said statute was ordained; which is plainly contrary to the tenor of the said statute: may it please you to ordain a remedy for this.

Answer.

The king would not indeed have inflicted such injury on the lords by such cunning if he had been duly informed; and he wills that if from now on lands, tenements, or advowsons be purchased on behalf of any persons of holy church, and then by such device the king is enfeoffed with them on misleading information, with the intention of excluding the mesne lords, and then the king enfeoffs those of holy church, from whom......were originally purchased, as it is said, without the assent of the mesne lords; then let entry be given to each of the mesne lords against the said persons of holy church..... manner comprised in the said statute De Religiosis. Saving always to our lord the king his prerogative, that he may freely purchase and give in mortmain to him.....in devotion, as he is accustomed to do.

XXI.

93. [Recovery of retainers' wages]. Also, the commons pray that whereas the knights and men-at-arms of your kingdom are retained whensoever it pleases your high lordship that they shall go on your wars, wheresoever you please, and for this they receive their wages in accordance with the terms of their indentures; and if it should happen that any of them are captured or slain, that neither *[Page iii-118]*

[Col. a] eux, ne lour heirs, ne leur executours, ne soient tenuz pur repaier pur les persones ensi prises ou mortz.
Responsio.

Soit usez come ad este usez.

XXII.

94. [Retainers' allowances] Item, come les ditz chivalers et gentz d'armes soient retenuz come dessuis, et aient lours lettres du roi pur estre au certein jour sur la \[meer proschein]/ \[monstrer]/qe de cel jour enavaunt leur gages lour soient allouez, et leur terme comencez.
Responsio.

Soit fait come devant ad este.

XXIII.

95. [Pardon to excepted towns] Item, \prient/ les communes qe come le roi nostre seignour de sa grace especiale ad fait grantes grace et pardoun a sa dite commune, forspris certeines villes a cause de lour malice et rebellioun.
Qe plese a vostre tresgraciouse seignourie granter voz ditz grace et pardoun as dites villes, ensi exceptz, en general ovesque vostre dite commune, salvant toutes voies les nouns de ceux queux sont excepts par especial.
Responsio.

Le roi de sa grace voet qe toutes les villes pardevant pur certaine cause exceptz hors de sa grace soient ore comprises en mesme sa grace, come autres villes sont parmy le roialme; horspris par expres la ville de Bury Seint Esmon, quele le roi ne voet mie, a cause de leur outrageouse et horrible mesfait de long temps continuez, ait par aucune voie part de la grace avauntdite, ne ne soit compris en ycelle. Excepte auxint par expres les persones en especial des quieux les nouns aient este livereez avaunt en parlement come chiefs et principalx comenceours, abettours, et procuratours, del outrageouse traison nadgairs fait deinz le roialme avauntdit.

XXIV.

96. [Inquiries into robberies] Suppliont les communes, pur les grantz robberies et larsyns faitz en diverses countees de roialme plus qe unqes ne soloient, qe les justices qe sont assignez pur punir les rebelx et les levours encountre le pees, eient poair pur proceder a deliverances, a touz foitz et quantz les ditz justices sembleront, si tielx soient pris par maynoevere sibien deinz franchise come dehors.
Responsio.

Eient les commissioners plein poair d'enquere, oier, et terminer, et d'aler a la deliverance de touz ceux persones qi sont pris et emprisonez pur cause del derrain rumour; et de touz ceux auxint \[qe sont]/.................... en apres serront pris enfaisantz homicides, roberies, ou autres larcins avec mainovre, a toutes les foitz qe par lours discrecions bon lour semblera: parissint qe y soient trois persones \[au meins des]/ commissioners presentz, dont un encores soit apris de la loy de la terre.
Membrane 2

XXV.

97. [Pleas of discharge in the exchequer] Item, prient les communes qe come y a plusours grantz defautes et malx usages en l'escheqier, al nosance de vostre poeple sanz aucun profit a vous.
Qe vous plese les faire amender, en aise et quiete de vostre poeple avauntdit. Primerement, porce qe les heirs, executours, occupiours des biens, et terre tenantz de diverses

[Col. a] they, nor their heirs or executors, should be obliged to repay those wages.
Answer.

Let that be done which has usually been done.

XXII.

94. [Retainers' allowances]. Also, whereas the said knights and men-at-arms are retained as above, and have letters from the king to be on the sea by a certain date .....to request that from that day onwards their wages should be allowed them, and their term of service begin.
Answer.

Let it be done as it has been done in the past.

XXIII.

95. [Pardons to excepted towns]. Also, the commons pray that whereas the king our lord by his special grace has granted grace and pardon to the said commons, excepting certain towns by reason of their malice and rebellion.
May it please your most gracious lordship to grant your said grace and pardon to the said towns thus excepted, in general together with your said commons, saving always the names of those who have been specifically excluded.
Answer.

The king, of his grace wills that all the towns previously excluded from his grace for a particular reason shall now be included in the same grace, like other towns throughout the kingdom; expressly excepting the town of Bury St Edmunds, which the king will not allow to enjoy any part of the aforesaid grace in any manner nor be included in the same by reason of its outrageous and horrible misdeeds for long continued, and excepting also those persons in particular whose names have been submitted to parliament as the leaders and principal instigators, abettors, and procurers in the outrageous treason recently committed within the kingdom aforesaid.

XXIV.

96. [Inquiries into robberies]. The commons beseech, for the great robberies and thefts perpetrated in divers counties of the kingdom and more than ever before, that the justices who are appointed to punish rebels and insurgents against the peace shall have the power to proceed to deliveries, whensoever and howsoever the justices see fit, if any such be taken in the act whether within franchise or without.
Answer.

Let the commissioners have full power to inquire, hear and determine, and proceed to the delivery of all those persons who were taken and imprisoned because of the last uprising; and also of all those who are..... subsequently taken in the act of committing homicides, robberies, or other thefts, whensoever it seems necessary according to their discretion: so that there be at least three commissioners present, one of whom shall always be learned in the law of the land.

XXV.

97. [Pleas of discharge in the exchequer]. Also, the commons pray that whereas great defects and evil practices are to be found in the exchequer, which vex your people without any profit to you.
May it please you to cause them to be amended, for the ease and tranquillity of your aforesaid people. Firstly, because heirs, executors, occupiers of goods, and the tenants

persones, et autres q'ont este empeschez en l'escheqier des dettes, accompts, ou autres demandes qe se ont /offertz\ illoqes a monster ou pleder lour descharges des tielx empeschementz, et n'ount mye este a ce receuz meint foiz devant ces heures; einz est este grandement delaie, et mis a grantz costages, a cause qe les barons de l'escheqier ont dit q'ils n'avoient mye poair d'oier les plees ne les responces des ditz empeschez, sanz brief \[ou lettres]/ de grant ou prive seal nostre seignour le roi comandant as tresorer et as barons del dit escheqier de faire droit as ditz empeschez; a grant meschief et diseaise des seignours et de communes, et a nul \[avantage du]/ roy. Dont vous plese ordeiner remede.

Responsio.

Le roi voet qe les barons de l'escheqier eient plein poair d'oier chescuny responce de queconqe demande a le dit escheqier: issint qe chescun persone qe soient empeschez [*Col. b*] ou empeschable de quelconqe cause al dit escheqier, pur lui mesmes ou pur autre persone, soit receu en le dit escheqier a pleder, suir, et avoir sa descharge resonable en celle part, sanz attendre ou suer brief de grant seal, lettres de prive seal nostre seignour le roi, ou autre mandement.

XXVI.

98. [Indentures of service to be of record in the exchequer] Item, purce qe grandes meschiefs ont eschuz devaunt ces heures as diverses persones qe furent retenuz ou assignez de servir nostre seignour le roi par endentures, ou sanz endentures, aucuns en ses guerres par terre ou par mier, aucuns en ses messages, et en diverses autres maneres: et par tieles causes /resceurent\ certeines summes des deniers al resceite de l'escheqier, ou aillours, par assignement, queux sommes furent mys sur eux \[illoeqes come]/ deniers receuz par voie d'apprest, et currerent en demande en l'escheqer come dette clere; et coment qe les dites persones ensi retenuz, lours heirs, executours, occupiours des biens, ou terre tenantz, \[apres lour mort]/ sovent ont demandez d'estre receivez en le dit escheqer d'accompter des tieles sommes ensi receuz, ils ne furent mye a ce receuz, einz furent mis a suer garant du prive seal ou de grant \[seal le roi,]/ directz as ditz tresorer et barons d'accompter ovesqe eux en tiele part: queux garantz lour ont deniez sovent foitz, par cause qe les ministres le roi queux firent tielx \[retenuz]/ furent \[mortz, ou]/ removez hors de lours offices devaunt qe tieles suites furent comencez, et autres estranges mys en lours lieuz, queux n'avoient conisance des tieles retenues, et en diverses \[autres maneres; et]/ aucunfoitz ont este grantez mais nemye \si/ pleinement come droit et reson vorroient, a cause qe aucun tiel garant voloit qe tiel accompt ne deust estre receu forsqe soulement \[de la somme ensi receu d'apprest,]/ la ou greindre somme fuist due de reson, as grantz meschiefs des diverses persones. Dont la dite commune vous prie auxint de remede.

\[*Responsio.*]/

Le roi voet qe de touz les gentz qi serront retenuz ou assignez desore enavaunt de servir a nostre dit seignour le roi, soient lours covenantz mys en escrit, \[et envoiez en l'escheqier, a y demurer de record; issint qe a quele heure qe la persone ensi retenuz, ses heirs,]/ ou ses executours, occupiours des biens ou terre tenantz, viegnent d'accompter \[de ce en l'escheqier, ils soient a ce receuz, et eiont due allouance en lour]/ accompte, \[solonc le contenu de leur covenant.]/ Et si aucun repelle soit faite de tiele retenue d'acune persone apres qe ses \[covenantz sibien mys en escript et envoiez a l'escheqier, come desuis est dit, soit]/ mesme le repelle mis en escript et envoiez al escheqer, issint qe par vieue de celle

of divers persons, and others who have been cited in the exchequer for debts, accounts, or other demands, and who have offered to answer there or plead for their discharge from such citations, have not indeed been allowed to do so on many occasions in the past; but have instead spent much time, and been put to great expense, because the barons of the exchequer have said that they do not have the power to hear the pleas or the answers of the said accused without a writ or letters under the great or privy seal of our lord the king ordering the treasurer and barons of the said exchequer to do justice to the said accused; to the great mischief and trouble of the lords and the commons, and of no advantage to the king. For which may it please you to ordain remedy.

Answer.

The king wills that the barons of the exchequer shall have full authority to hear any answer to any demand whatsoever at the said exchequer: so that anyone who is accused [*Col. b*] or accusable for any reason at the said exchequer, shall be received in the said exchequer either in person or by another, to plead, sue, and gain his just discharge in the matter, without waiting or suing for a writ of great seal, letters of privy seal of our lord the king, or other mandate.

XXVI.

98. [Indentures of service to be of record in the exchequer]. Also, whereas great trouble has in the past befallen divers persons who have been retained or appointed to serve our lord the king by indentures, or without indentures, some in his wars by land or sea, some as his messengers and in divers other ways: wherefore they received certain sums of money at the receipt of the exchequer, or elsewhere, by assignment, which sums were bestowed on them there as money received by way of a prest, and run in the exchequer on demand as a clear debt; and although the said persons thus retained, their heirs, executors, holders of goods, or tenants of lands have after their death often asked to be received in the said exchequer to account for such sums thus received, they have not been allowed to do so, but have been forced to sue a warrant of the king's privy or great seal directing the said treasurer and barons to account with them in the matter: which warrants have often been denied them, because the king's ministers who had made such retinues were dead, or removed from their posts before such suits began, and strangers appointed in their place who had no knowledge of such retinues, and for divers other reasons; and sometimes they have been granted but not as fully as right and reason would wish, because such a warrant requires that such accounts ought not to be received except only for the sum thus received as a prest, even though a larger sum was due in reason, to the great harm of many. For which the commons pray that you find remedy.

Answer.

The king wills that all men retained or appointed henceforth to serve our said lord the king shall have their covenants in writing, and send them to the exchequer, to remain there on record; so that when those thus retained, their heirs, or executors, holders of goods, or tenants of lands, come to account in the exchequer, they shall be received and have due allowance made on their account, in accordance with the terms of their covenant. And if any repeal be made of the retaining of anyone after their contracts have been placed in writing and sent to the exchequer, as said above, the same repeal shall be put in writing and sent to the exchequer, so that by reference to the repeal and the covenants sent before

repelle et des covenantz devant \[illoeqes envoiez, les barons du dit escheqer facent droit a la partie solonc ce qe la lei et]/ reson demande. Et si rien lour soit due par mesmes les accomptes, les tresorer et chamberleins \[lour facent paiement ou assignement de ce qe lour serra due par]/ mesmes les accomptes, par certificacion de mesme l'escheqer, sanz attendre ou suer autre garant ou mandement de \[grant seal ou prive seal.]/

99. [Exchequer accounts] Et auxint voet le roi qe les accomptes en l'escheqer \soient/ pluis briefment oiez, faitz, et engrossez q'ils ne soloient a \[devant, salve qe les parcelles de mesmes les accomptes]/............................
\[faitz auxi pleinement come]/ ils soloient en temps passe; et ce par ordeinance affaire par les barons de l'escheqer, a durer a record de tout temps avenir.

100. [Expenditure accounts in the exchequer] Et auxint, qe deux clercs soient assignez pur faire parcelles d'accomptes en mesme l'escheqier a ceux qe ce voillent demander, \[et soient jurrez q'ils ne ferront nul fauxine en lour office, et prendront]/ pur lour travaille de ceux as queux ils serveront resonablement, selonc l'ordenance des barons de dit escheqier.

Page iii-119

101. [Nil accounts to be discharged on oath] Et auxint \est assentuz,/ qe les accomptes de nichil en le dit escheqier soient de tout oustez, ou si aucuns tieles accompts deivent demurrer, soient \[les accomptantz maintenant apres lour serement fait en le dit]/ escheqier examinez par les barons, s'ils puissent ou deivent de rien respondre au roi en celle part. Et si trovez soit par lour serement \[qe noun, qe par mesme lour serement ils soient deschargez d'autre]/ accompt rendre devaunt aucun auditour, toutdys le droit le roi salvez.

102. [Discharged accounts to be registered in the exchequer] Et auxint, qe le clerc de pipe et les remembrancers de l'escheqier soient jurez qe de terme en terme eux mesmes verront, tant come le dit escheqier est \[overt, touz les briefs]/ de grant seal et lettres de prive seal nostre seignour le roi qe sont mandez al dit escheqier mesme le terme, pur final descharge d'aucune persone du roialme d'aucun demande currant al dit escheqir; et qe chescun de eux a qi il appartient ferra due execucioun du dit mandement.

Et auxint, soient les ditz deux remembrancers jurrez qe chescun terme ils ferront une cedule de toutes les persones qi sont deschargez en lours offices, par juggement ou en autre manere, \en/ mesmes les termes, d'aucunes demandes en le dit escheqer; contenant la manere de mesme le descharge: et face liverez cest cedule al clerc du pipe, mesme le terme, a fin qe le clerc de pipe face ent descharger les dites parties en le grant rolle. Et soit le dit clerc de pipe jurrez q'il demandera chescun terme les dites cedules, et mesmes les cedules par lui issint receuz il dischargera les dites parties en manere suisdit. Et en mesme le manere face le clerc del pipe as ditz remembrancers de touz tielx descharges qe serront faitz en son office, au fyn qe homme descharge en une place soit deschargez en touz autres places del dit escheqier.

XXVII.

103. [Exchequer suits to terminate on judgment of livery] Item, prient les communes qe la ou devaunt ces heures diverses persones ont euez livere de diverses terres et tenementz hors de mayn le roi, par juggement pur eux renduz en le bank le roi, et de ce ont portez le tenure del record de dit juggement par breve de mittimus en l'escheqier, pur eux descharger des accomptes demandez de mesme les tenementz

them there, the barons of the said exchequer may do justice to the party as the law and reason demand. And if anything be due to them through the same accounts, the treasurer and chamberlains shall make them a payment or assignment of that which shall be owed to them upon the same accounts, by the certification of the same exchequer, without waiting or suing for another warrant or mandate of the great or privy seal.

99. [Exchequer accounts]. The king also wills that the accounts in the exchequer shall be heard, drawn up, and engrossed more expeditiously than in the past, save that the details of the same accounts ..... made as fully as they were in the past; and that by ordinance to be made by the barons of the exchequer, to remain on record for all time to come.

100. [Expenditure accounts in the exchequer]. Moreover, that two clerks be appointed to draw up detailed accounts in the same exchequer for those who require them, and they shall be sworn to commit no fraud in their office, and they shall take reasonable payment for their work from those whom they serve, in accordance with the ordinance of the barons of the said exchequer.

101. [Nil accounts to be discharged on oath]. It is agreed also that accounts de nichil in the said exchequer shall be entirely abolished, or if any should remain, those accounting, immediately after taking their oath in the said exchequer shall be examined by the barons, as to whether they wish or ought to answer to the king for anything in the matter. And if the answer is found upon their oath to be no, that by their same oath they shall be discharged from rendering another account before any auditor, saving always the king's right.

102. [Discharged accounts to be registered in the exchequer]. Moreover, that the clerk of the pipe and the remembrancers of the exchequer shall be sworn from term to term that they themselves will inspect, as long as the said exchequer is open, all the writs of great seal and letters of privy seal of our lord the king which are sent to the said exchequer during that term, for the final discharge of any person of the realm from any demand pending at the said exchequer; and that each to whom this pertains shall duly put the said mandate into effect.

And in addition, the said two remembrancers shall swear that each term they shall draw up a schedule of all persons who are discharged in their offices, by judgment or in any other way, during the same terms, from any demand in the said exchequer; including the nature of the same discharge: and they shall cause this schedule to be delivered to the clerk of the pipe, during the same term, so that the clerk of the pipe can discharge the said parties in the great roll. And let the said clerk of the pipe be sworn to ask each term for the said schedules, and the same schedules having been received by him, he shall discharge the said parties in the aforesaid manner. And in the same way the clerk of the pipe shall inform the said remembrancer of all such discharges made in his office, so that a man discharged in one place may be discharged in all other places in the said exchequer.

XXVII.

103. [Exchequer suits to terminate on judgment of livery]. Also, the commons pray that whereas in the past divers persons have had livery of lands and tenements from the king's hands by a judgment rendered in their favour in the king's bench, and have taken the tenor of the record of the said judgment to the exchequer by writ de mittimus, to have themselves discharged from accounts demanded of the same

devant ces heures, ne furent deschargez en celle part devant qe le dit record fust de novelle entree en le dit escheqier par parole en parole, et novel proces, et novel juggement illoeqes fuist rendu; a grant damage et delai des dites gentz.
Responsio.

Le roi voet qe maintenant apres qe tiel record est venuz en l'escheqier \par\ \mandement,/ qe le remembrancer en qi office tieles accomptes sont demandez maintenant face cesser la suite en celle part, par paroles a entrers sur l'endossement de son brief; vouchant le tenour de recorde de dit juggement, sanz autre proces ou juggement faire en celle part.

104. Et voet le roi auxint qe ne soit desore donez pur une comission affaire en le dit escheqier qe deux soldz pur le fee de clerc qe le ferra, et pur le recorde d'un nisi prius ovesqe le brief deux soldz soulement, come soleit estre fait, sanz pluis prendre en temps avenir.

XXVIII.

105. [Officers of the exchequer] Item, prient les communes qe desore enavant ne soit fait baron de l'escheqer, clerc de pipe, remembrancer, opposour, comptrollour, clerc de plees, et clerc de forein somons, auditour, n'autre chief ministre en l'escheqer, sy ne soit homme bien apris de la commune loye, ou autrement bien apris de les loies, course, et usages de l'escheqer.
Responsio.

Le roi le voet.

XXIX.

106. [Charters of pardon] Item, est assavoir qe les communes prierent a nostre seignour le roi qe les chartres de pardoun par \[lui graciousement grantez en cest parlement soient, si lui plest, en partie amendez et enlargez;]/ c'estassavoir, celle chartre q'est grante pur les bones gentz qe ne se \[leverent mye, en quele sont exceptz ceux qi furent detenuz en prison pur felonie le xiij jour de Decembre,]/ l'an present [1381], par quele exception ceulx qi se sont voluntrifment renduz a la \[prisone pur ester a la lei sont de pire condicion sur ceste grace qe ceux qi soi esloignent,]/ et sont futifs et utlagez, quelle chose par reson ne doit estre faite ne soeffert.

\[Qe lui pleust par tant ouster celle excepcion, et autres excepcions]/ \[comprises,]/ pur queles les justices font grant difficultee de les \[allouer devant eux.]/
Responsio.

Le roi le voet de sa grace et ad ordene quant a ce, d'amender la dite grace quant as felonies, \[en]/ la forme qe s'ensuit:
Pardonavimus, A. de B. sectam pacis nostre que ad nos pertinet pro omnimodis feloniis per ipsum A. ante quartumdecimum diem Decembris ultimo preteritum [1381] perpetratis, unde indictatus, rectatus, vel occasionatus existit, prodicionibus, murdris, raptibus mulierum exceptis; ac eciam utlagarias si que, etc., et firmam pacem nostram, etc., dumtamen non videtur quod est communis latro sive communis homicida; et eciam quod non sit probator vel appellatus de latrocinio, et quod non sit appellatus de morte hominis, unde appellum pendet ad sectam partis; nec a prisona evaserit seu recesserit, et eandem prisonam se non reddiderit; et quod dicto quartodecimo die Decembris [1381] in prisona pro latrocinio tantum detentus non fuerit, etc.

XXX.

Item, \le roi,/ a la priere de la dite commune, ad fait amender et enlargir la dite autre sa grace faite en ceste parlement pur

tenements in the past, they have not been so discharged until the said record has been entered anew in the said exchequer word by word, and a new process, and new judgment rendered there; to the great injury and delay of the said people.
Answer.

The king wills that as soon as such a record comes into the exchequer by mandate, the remembrancer in whose office such accounts fall shall at once cause the suit in the matter to be ended, by words to be entered on the dorse of his writ; vouching for the tenor of the said judgment, without any other process or judgment made in the matter.

104. The king also wills that henceforth, for a commission made in the said exchequer in future, no more than two shillings shall be given as the fee for the clerk who makes it, and only two shillings for the record of a nisi prius together with the writ, as used to be done in such cases, without anything more being taken.

XXVIII.

105. [Officers of the exchequer]. Also, the commons pray that henceforth none shall be appointed baron of the exchequer, clerk of the pipe, remembrancer, examiner, controller, clerk of the pleas, clerk of foreign summons, auditor, nor other chief minister in the exchequer, unless he be fully learned in the common law, or otherwise well versed in the law, procedure, and usages of the exchequer.
Answer.

The king wills it.

XXIX.

106. [Charters of pardon]. Also, it is to be known that the commons prayed of our lord the king that the charters of pardon graciously granted by him in this parliament should, if it please him, be in part amended and enlarged; namely, that charter which was granted for the honest men who did not rebel, from which those were excluded who were detained in prison for felony on 13 December in this regnal year [1381], as a result of which exclusion those who voluntarily surrendered themselves for imprisonment in obedience to the law are in a worse position in respect of the grace than those who absconded and are fugitives and outlaws, which in reason should not happen, nor be suffered.

May it please him for that reason to waive the exclusion, and other exclusions..... contained, because the justices are most unwilling to accept such a plea.
Answer.

The king wills it of his grace, and has ordered that the said pardon be amended as to felonies, in the following way:
We have pardoned A. of B., for the suit of our peace which pertains to us, of all felonies perpetrated by the same A. before 14 December last past [1381], when he was indicted, judged, or prosecuted, excluding treasons, murders, and ravishment of women; and also of outlawries if, etc., and our firm peace, etc, in as much as it does not seem that he is a common thief or a common murderer; nor yet an approver or appealer of theft, and is not acused of homicide in which a suit is pending; neither has he escaped nor fled from prison, and not returned to the same prison; and on the said 14 December [1381] will not be detained in prison for some theft, etc..

XXX.

Also, the king, at the request of the said commons, has caused his other said grace granted in this parliament for the

les \[traitors qe se]/ leverent \[contre luy.]/ . . . .
C'estassavoir, qe par la ou en ycelle forme furent exceptz touz appelez des dites treisons, par quele excepcion \[touz les appellez en celle; partie sont forclos]/ del grace, combien qe le provour ou appellour soit descunsit, ou mort: qe tielx appellez dont l'appellour ou provour n'est \[mye en pleine vie soient]/ compris en ceste grace, et ne soient forsclos d'icelle.

Et le roi voet qe les chartres qe aient este faitz et enseallez sur sa dite grace devaunt ceste heure, soient eles de \[l'une forme ou de l'autre, soient]/ celes amendez, \et/ de novel escritez et enseallez, accordantz a cest grace, sanz novelle \[fee paier pur ycelles a l'oeps de roy suisdit.]/

Et n'est mye l'entencion du roi nostre seignour qe une soule persone enjoisse de \[l'une et l'autre sa dite grace d'avoir; c'estassavoir l'une et l'autre chartre. Et est determinez]/ en parlement qe ceux de Gales et de Cestreshire, /ou\ ceux de la franchise de Duresme, a cause de la \[franchise ne doivent rienz emporter a cestez gracez.]/

Membrane 1

Si l'en poet et voet soeffrir un resonable temps les articles apres \[escritz]/ estre executz, semblable \[est]/ le roialme relever de povertee selonc ce qe homme savera a present penser, considerant en quel estat le roialme en est au present. Pur queux articles monstrer \[et enformer par leur scient]/ estoient certains marchantz de touz les bones villes et burghes de le roialme chargez et commandez par leur serementz et lour liegeance, d'enformer a noz seignours et communes du roialme, coment le roialme d'Engleterre purroit alors mieultz estre relevez de povert par l'encrees des comodites crues en le roialme, et les marchandies einz venantz, a meliour marchee.

107. En primes, soit defenduz par *[tout le roialme sur peine de perdre la somme ent atteinte,]* qe nullui del roialme, n'autre persone qeconqe, apporte monoie du roialme, or, n'argent en monoie, en plate, n'en vessele, *[Page iii-120]*

[Col. a] overtement ne secretement, ne auxi par eschaunge faite en Engleterre, en *[nule parte, pur estre resceu]* par dela sur mesme la peyne avauntdite; forspris gages de Caleys et autres forteresses en noz mayns par dela, *[qar autrement]* la monoie *[s'en ira]* tout \[outrement apportez,]/ a confusioun de toute la terre, faisant estreit serche par touz les ports et passages dedeins le roialme, pur fermement garder qe nully face \[au contraire,]/ . . . . chescun qe savera notoirement affermer \[et prover or ou]/ argent apportez a contraire de l'ordinans suisdite, eit la quarte partie ensi atteinte. Et \[est]/especialment defenduz ceste dit article a touz pelerins \[et provisours passantz outre mier, sur mesme la]/ peyne avantdite; \[et qe null passage soit]/ suffert \[aillours qe a certeins portz]/ limitez, sur forfaiture du nief et des biens de lui qe les \[amenera autrement qe ordene soit. Et si]/ aucun sercheour soit ordene pur sercher le passage des gentz \[passantz hors du]/ roialme, soeffre par sa science aucune persone passer ove or ou argent, encontre \[l'ordinance]/ avauntdite, et de ce soit atteint, \[eyt]/ la peyne de \[forfaiture]/ de touz \[ses biens, et son corps]/ a prisone par un an, sanz redempcion.

\[*Responsio.*]/

Quant a ce q'est demandez qe or ou argent, en monoie, plate, vessele, n'en joialx, \[ne soit apportez n'envoiez]/ hors del roialme, overtement \[ne secretement, ne par]/ aucune manere des . . . . affaire par denszein ou forein marchant, \[n'autre, de quelconqe estat ou]/ condicion \[q'il soit, exceptez les]/ gages de Caleys et d'autres forteresses du roi depar dela; le roi le voet et grante en touz pointz, horspris

traitors who rose against him to be amended and enlarged. That is to say that in the original version there were excepted all those accused of the said treasons, as a consequence of which all the accused in the matter were barred from grace, even though the approver or accuser was unknown or dead: and now those whose accuser or approver is not known to be alive shall be included in this grace, and not barred from the same.

And the king wills that the charters which have been made and sealed in respect of the said grace in the past, be they of the one form or the other, shall be amended, and written and sealed anew in accordance with this grace, without further fee being paid for the same to the use of the king aforesaid.

And it is not indeed the intention of our lord the king that anyone shall have both said graces; namely the one charter and the other. And it has been decided in parliament that neither those of Wales and Cheshire, nor those of the franchise of Durham, because of their franchise, ought to benefit from these graces.

If a reasonable time and will can be found for the articles written below to be put into effect, it seems that the kingdom could be relieved of poverty, according to what is at present known and, considering the state of the kingdom. To expound which articles and explain them to the best of their knowledge, certain merchants from all the good towns and boroughs of the kingdom were charged and ordered on their oaths and the strength of their allegiance to inform our lords and commons of the realm, how the kingdom of England might best be relieved at that time from poverty by increasing commodities produced in the kingdom, and the merchandise brought in, to a better trade.

107. First, it should be forbidden throughout the entire realm on pain of loss of the sum specified, for anyone of the kingdom, or any other person whatsoever, to take money out of the kingdom, gold, or silver, in coin, plate, or vessel, *[Page iii-120]*

[Col. a] openly or secretly, nor by exchange made in England, to any other place to be received overseas, on pain of the aforesaid penalty; except as wages for Calais, and other fortresses in our hands overseas, for otherwise all our money will be carried away, to the confusion of all the land, conducting a strict search throughout all the ports and crossing places in the kingdom, to ensure that no one acts to the contrary. . . . . . anyone who can fully affirm and prove that gold or silver has been carried off contrary to the aforesaid ordinance, shall have a fourth part of what is confiscated. And this said article especially prohibits all pilgrims and provisors from passing beyond the sea, on pain of the same aforesaid penalty; and that no passage shall be allowed other than at certain specified ports, on pain of forfeiture of the ship and goods by him who travels contrary to what is ordained. And if any searcher be appointed to inspect the passage of those travelling out of the kingdom, and in full knowledge allows anyone to travel with gold or silver contrary to the aforesaid ordinance, and is so convicted, let him suffer the penalty of forfeiting all his goods, and being imprisoned for one year, without remission.

Answer.

As for what is asked, that neither gold nor silver, in money, plate, vessels, or jewels be taken or sent out of the kingdom, openly or secretly, or by any other means by denizen or foreign merchant, or any other, of whatsoever status or condition he be, excepting the wages of Calais and other forts of the king overseas; the king wills and grants it in all respects, excepting prelates, lords, and others who need to make

les prelatz, seignours, et autres as queux \[necessairement coviendra a la foitz]/ de faire paiementz depar dela qe de celles paiementz purront ils faire eschanges en Engleterre par bones et suffisantz marchantz; \[eue]/ sur ce primerement especial \[congie et licence de nostre seignour le roi et son]/ counseil, sibien pur le changeour come pur la persone qi ferra l'eschange, sur la peyne de forfaire la somme chaunge. Et voet le roi nostre seignour qe les marchantz \[qe ensi ferront les ditz eschaunges par]/ license, soient examinez diligeaument, et jurrez en lour propres persones, a tantz des foitz come ils averont la \[dite]/ licence, q'ils \[n'envoieront aucun manere d'or ne d'argent, en plate vessel]/ monoie n'autrement, depar dela, souz colour de mesme l'eschaunge. Et s'il soit atteint q'il avera fait \[envoier]/ or ou argent depar dela \[countre ceste ordenance, forface devers le roy la somme ou]/ la value d'ycelle. Et le roi defende oultrement passage a touz maneres des gentz, sibien clercz come \[autres,]/ en chescun port, et autre \[ville, et lieu sur la costee de meer, horspris tantsoulement]/ les seignours et autres grantz persones du roialme; et horspris verrois notables marchantz et les soldeours le roi; sur peyne de forfaiture de \[quanqe ils ont en terres et biens. Et si qelconqe persone,]/ autre qe dessuis sont exceptz, passe le roialme sanz especial congie et licence du roi, \[quele]/ licence ne serra fait sinoun \[tantsoulement en un des portz dessouz escritz,]/ c'estassavoir, Londres, Dovorr', Sandewiz, Suthampton, Plymuth', Dertemuth, Bristuyt, Jernemuth, Seint Bothulf, Hull et Neof-Chastell sur Teyne, \et en les portz vers Irlaund et autres isles appartenantz al roialme, forface devers le roy/ come dessuis est dit, \[et avec ce forface le mariner son vessell, si nulle persone amesne hors du roialme contre cest estatut.]/ Et celui qi espiera aucune persone q'avera mespris contre ceste ordenance en aucun point apres ce qe proclamacioun ent \[soit fait parmy le roialme, et a sa pursuite soit]/ convict, le roi voet q'il eit la moitee de la forfaiture pur son travaille. Et si nul \[sercheour,]/ ou gardein de port, scientment soeffre estre \[fait en aucun point le contraire de ceste]/ ordenance, encourge la peyne de forfaire \son office/ et ses biens, et son corps a la prisone pur un an entier, sanz redempcioun, etc.

Item, come voirs est, \[qe le sovereign]/entente de touz marchantz soit de \[repeirer]/ la ou mieulx il poet estre seure de lui mesmes et de ses biens, et amyablement estre tretez et governez a gayner, soit ordenez et proclamez
[Col. b] \[qe touz]/ maneres des marchantz de queconqe nacioun q'ils soient, et qe \[ne sont enemys au]/ roi ne al roialme, serront bien venuz al roialme, et receuz seurement, et amiablement tretez par loy-marchant en chescun lieu ou ville q'ils repeirent, et de lour marchandises \[franchement vendre a qi]/ qe lour plest, en grosse, sanz un estrange pur vendre a autre estraunge pur revendre, paiantz les custumes ent dues et establiz; et nullui lour destourber de la condicioun susdit. Par quele repeire des estranges amyablement tretez, come avaunt est dit, et par \[noz]/ gentz liges qe \[ameneront des marchandies]/ dedeins le roialme, semblable est qe toutes choses serront \[meillour]/ marchez qe ne ont este par avant, purveuz toutdys qe le article par amount soit fermement tenuz en touz lours \[pointz, sibien vers]/ denszeins come foreins, faisantz a chescune nacioun repeirante a nous sicome nous sumes receuz entre eux. Et soit proclamez par touz les portz et bones villes du roialme, \[qe null]/ lige a nostre seignour le roi face eskipper ses marchandises venantz vers \[cea nulle]/ parte, ne alantz par dela escun part, fors en niefs del alligeance, sur une dure peyne; entendantz \[qe si la navie]/ du roialme ne soit \[remountez]/ autrement qe n'est, semblable la \[soverein]/ cause par quoi le roialme serroit doutez ou serra perduz, qe

payments overseas, which payments they may make by exchanges in England through good and worthy merchants; having first received special permission and licence therefor from our lord the king and his council, both for the exchanger as well as for him making the exchange, on pain of forfeiting the sum changed. And the king our lord wills that the merchants who thus perform the said exchanges by licence shall be diligently examined and sworn in person, as often as they receive the said licence, that they will not send any manner of gold or silver, in plate, vessels, coin, or otherwise overseas, under cover of the same exchange. And if anyone be convicted of having sent gold or silver overseas contrary to this ordinance, he shall forfeit to the king the sum or the value of the same. And the king entirely forbids the passage of all manner of men, both clerks and others, in every port and other town and place on the coast of the sea, excepting only lords and other great persons of the realm; and excepting well known merchants, and the king's soldiers; on pain of forfeiting whatsoever they have in goods and lands. And if anyone, save those above excepted, travels outside the kingdom without the special permission and licence of the king, which licence will only be issued in one of the ports listed below, namely, London, Dover, Sandwich, Southampton, Plymouth, Dartmouth, Bristol, Yarmouth, Boston, Hull, and Newcastle upon Tyne, and in the ports towards Ireland, and other isles pertaining to the realm, let him forfeit to the king as is said above, and with the forfeit the mariner shall lose his vessel if he take anyone out of the kingdom contrary to this statute. And whosoever observes anyone acting against this ordinance in any way after proclamation has been made thereon throughout the kingdom, if at his suit that person is convicted, the king wills that he shall have half the forfeiture for his labour. And if any searcher or keeper of a port knowingly allows anything to be done in any way contrary to this ordinance, he shall incur the penalty of forfeiting his office and his goods, and being imprisoned for a whole year, without remission, etc.

Also, as it is true that the chief aim of all merchants is to go wheresoever they and their goods will be safest, and where they are amicably treated and able to make profit, let it be ordained and proclaimed
[Col. b] that all manner of merchants, from whatsoever land they come, who are not enemies of the king or the kingdom, shall be welcomed to the kingdom, safely received and amicably treated under law-merchant in every place or town they visit, and their merchandise freely sold to whomsoever they choose, in gross, without one foreigner selling it to another for resale, paying the customs due and established; and none shall disturb them in the aforesaid business. By which visits of foreigners who have been amicably treated, as said above, and by our liege men who bring merchandise into the kingdom, it is likely that trade will go better than ever before, provided always that the article above be strictly upheld in all respects, as well by denizens as by foreigners, so that all those who come amongst us are treated as well as we are treated by them. And let it be proclaimed throughout all the ports and good towns of the kingdom that no liege of our lord the king shall cause his merchandise to be shipped anywhere on this side of the sea, nor anywhere overseas, except in ships of our allegiance, on pain of a severe penalty; bearing in mind that if the kingdom's fleet be not restored to a better condition than it now is in, that will be the chief reason for the kingdom being emperilled or lost, which God forbid. Requesting of the king our lord and of our other lords

Dieux ne veulle. Requerantz au roi nostre seignour \[et a noz autres]/ seignours, qe lour plese modyfier la forfaiture des niefs et vesselle auxibien par meer come par eawe doulce forfaitz par paroles des deodandz; la quele chose usez en manere come ad este usez \[monstre grant]/ cause a retrehere la \[corage]/ de toutes gentz affaire aucun vesselle novell, et s'il endure, a la destruccioun de la navie a touz jours.
Responsio.

Quant al \[second article qe]/ touz estraunges marchantz del amistee nostre seignour le roi venantz ou repeirantz deinz le roialme avec lours marchandises serront amiablement tretez et governez .... roialme \[deins franchise et dehors;]/le roi le voet, et grante en touz pointz. Et ad ordene et establi, del assent de les prelats, \[seignours, et]/ autres en ce parlement, \[qe mesme les marchantz estranges venantz ou]/ repeirantz, \[demurrantz, conversantz,]/ et retournantz avec lour niefs, mariners, biens, marchandises, et lours autres hernois et possessions \[qelconqes]/ .. \[souz la protection et salve garde nostre seignour,]/ .... \[et souz mesme la proteccion]/ y purront et demurront franchement demurrer si longement come bon lour semblera; et illoeqes \[vendre et achater]/ .... \[par manere q'est demande, sanz]/ empeschement ou desturbance \de nully./ Et par especial le roi defende estroitement a touz ses \[foialx lieges, et toutes autres maneres de gentz venantz ou repairantz deinz]/ ..... poair, sibien grantz come petitz, deinz franchise et dehors, sur paine de \[quant ils purront]/ .... as ditz \[marchantz]/ estrangers, venantz, repairantz, demurantz, et retournantz, \[ne a lours servantz et familiers issint esteantz souz le salve garde le roy; ne facent ne ne procurent]/ ..... corporel \[damage par]/ quelconqe voie, \[n'autre]/ moleste ou \[impediment contre la loy.]/

Et quant \[a ce q'est demande qe]/ nul liege le roi face eskipper ses marchandises, en alantz hors \[ou venantz dedeinz le roialme d'Engleterre aucun part, forsqe soulement es niefs de la ligeance]/ nostre seignour \[le roy, le roy le voet]/ .... . Et quelconqe persone apres qe proclamacioun \[en soit fait a contraire,]/ forface devers le \[roi ses]/ marchandises \[en autres niefs qe de la dite lige]/ .... \[en quelconqe places]/ ycelles marchandises \[soient]/ apres trovez. Et le roi voet qe celluy qe \[l'espiera, et vorra suer pur]/ le roi en celle partie, et \[proevera ou fera proever]/ .... \[paront forfaiture]/ escherra par vertu de \[ceste]/ ordenance, eit la tierce partie pur son travaille del demy \[le roy.]/ Et tendra lieu ceste ordenance des niefs \[a la Pask prochein venant [6 April 1382]. Et quant as deodands]/ en le meer, illoeqes ne deivent deodandz estre demandez pur aventure \[illoeqes eschuz,]/ come de mort de persone. Et quant as deodandz \[en ewe doulce, le roy n'entende mye]/ de soi ouster de sa jouste possession, *[Page iii-121]*

[Col. a] quele les rois d'Engleterre ont \[euz d'aunciente,]/ et continuez tanqe en cea.

Et \[si ley voet ordener]/ aucun remede pur aucun marchandise en especial, come pur vins, ou autres choses delitables q'ad este a haut \[pris]/ devaunt ces heures, sibien par defaute des \[achatours come de les vendours, l'ein]/ poet ordener pur vin en manere q'ensuit, en essay pur savoir a quel esploit homme poet venir. C'estassavoir, q'environ la Pentecost [25 May 1382] soit defenduz qe nul Engleis ... \[hors du roialme nul part]/ pur vin achater, s'il ne poet soeffrer a vendre ycy al afferant de galoun a .vi. d. sur peine d'ensi arter a vendre a lour retournir. Et si l'en voet \[soeffrer un an ou deux a plus, il est]/ semblable d'estre bone marchee par tut nostre temps apres, si grande fortune ne soit au contraire. Tutdys purveuz qe le primer article soit bien et fermement tenuz, \[qar]/ .... \[aviendra qe draps,]/ et

that it may please them to modify the forfeiture of ships and vessels on the sea and in fresh water by way of deodands; which practice, carried out as it has always been, contributes greatly to the reluctance of men to build new vessels, and if it endure it will destroy the fleet forever.

Answer.

With reference to the second article that all foreign merchants having friendly relations with our lord the king and visiting or travelling in the kingdom with their merchandise, shall be amicably treated and governed..... kingdom within franchise or without; the king wills it, and grants it in all respects. And he has ordained and decreed, with the assent of the prelates, lords, and others in this parliament that the same foreign merchants coming, repairing, dwelling, trading, and returning with their ships, mariners, goods, merchandise, and their other belongings and possessions whatsoever....... under the protection and safeguard of our lord....... and under the same protection they may remain there freely as they see fit; and there sell and buy...... in the manner which is requested, without being prosecuted or harassed by anyone. In particular, the king strictly forbids all his faithful lieges, and all manner of persons coming or travelling within...... power, both great and small, within franchise or without, on pain of whatsoever they have..... to the said foreign merchants, coming, repairing, dwelling, and returning, nor to their servants and familiars thus being under the safeguard of the king; nor shall they do nor procure..... bodily injury by any means, or otherwise harass or impede contrary to the law.

And as for the demand that none of the king's lieges shall ship his merchandise going overseas or coming anywhere within the kingdom of England, except only in ships of allegiance to our lord the king, the king wills...... . And any person who acts to the contrary after this proclamation has been made, shall forfeit to the king his merchandise carried in other ships than those of the said allegiance..... wheresoever that merchandise may later be found. And the king wills that anyone who observes and wishes to sue on the king's behalf in this matter, and proves or causes to be proven....... and as a result thereof a forfeit is made under this ordinance, shall have a third of the king's half for his labours. And this ordinance concerning ships shall take effect at Easter next [6 April 1382]. As for deodands, they ought not to be demanded for accidents happening at sea, such as the death of a person. As for deodands in fresh water, the king certainly does not intend to be ousted from his just possession, *[Page iii-121]*

[Col. a] which the kings of England have had since antiquity, and have still today.

And if the law will ordain remedy for any merchandise in particular, like wines, or other luxuries which have been at a high price in the past, as well by the fault of the sellers as the buyers, it could be ordained for wine in the following manner to try what can be done. Namely, around Whitsun [25 May 1382] it should be forbidden that any Englishman........ anywhere outside the kingdom to buy wine, if he does not allow it to be sold here at 6 d a gallon, on pain of then being forced to sell it thus on his return. And if that is borne for one year or two at the most, it is likely to prove cheaper for us all in the future, if fortune smile upon us. Provided always that the first article be well and firmly upheld, since..... it should happen that cloth, and other commodities of the kingdom go to seek wine and other things which we shall need.

263

Provided always that no trouble shall arise through this ordinance for the town of Bordeaux, nor for our other lieges and places. Provided also, for the best, that in future no sweet nor yellow wine be sold anywhere in the kingdom, considering that many evils and deceits have occurred through such retail sales thereof.

Also, for the third article, touching wine and the dearness of the same, the king wills and forbids any type of sweet or yellow wine to be sold by retail in any part of the kingdom henceforth, on pain of forfeiting the same. And this ordinance shall begin to take effect from the Nativity of St John next [24 June 1382]. And concerning other wines, such as wines from Gascony, wines from La Rochelle, Rhenish wines, and wines of Alsace and Spain, if any Englishman henceforth wishes to cross the sea, seek them out, and bring them back to the same kingdom, he will not be able to sell them within the same kingdom, on pain of forfeiting them, for more than the prices specified below; namely, a cask of the best wine from Gascony, Alsace, or Spain, at one hundred shillings, and

[Col. b] other casks of common wine from the same countries for a lower price according to their value, for example for seven marks, six and a half marks, and six marks; and a cask of the best wine from La Rochelle for six marks, and a cask of other such wine at a lesser price, according to its value, for example five and a half marks, five marks, four and a half marks and four marks. And pipes of those wines and other vessels of smaller size shall be sold by the tun, taking into account the abundance of supply. And as for the sale of the said wines of Gascony, Alsace, and Spain thus imported, not a gallon of the best such wine shall be sold in the kingdom, on pain of the same penalty of forfeiture of all the wine, for more than six pence or less, according to its value; and a gallon of the best wine from La Rochelle at four pence or less, according to its value. And as for Rhenish wine, because neither the vessels nor the measures of Rhenish wines guarantee a precise quantity, it is agreed that a gallon of the best Rhenish wine shall not be sold in any part of the aforesaid kingdom either in gross or by retail by the said Englishmen for more than six pence, on pain of the same penalty. And it is thus agreed that if any Englishman refuses nor will not put his wines on sale for the prices appointed above, but wishes to keep them solely for the purpose of selling them at a higher price, by fraud and contrary to the form of this ordinance, after the buyer has, in accordance with this ordinance, once or twice offered the seller a reasonable sum for the same wine, let him and the mayor, bailiffs, and other governors of the city, borough, town, or other place within whose authority and jurisdiction the said wine shall be found, be it within franchise or without, have power by this ordinance to have delivery of the said wines, being bargained for by the said buyer, and they shall deliver them immediately, without delay, as they are required to do, for the price ordained above. And if any said mayor, bailiffs, or other governors after they have been duly asked, refuse and do not make the said delivery, and it be proven, let them forfeit to our lord the king the value of the said .....
And the king wills that . . . .
. .

Appendix

3 November 1381

Westminster

1. Petition to the king and council from the officers of the Mint in the Tower of London complaining of the lack of money being coined at the Mint because of the scarcity of foreign bullion being imported and the prevalence of clipping, and claiming that if the situation is not soon remedied most of the gold and silver coin of England will be exported from the realm.
Endorsed: The warden, master and other officers of the Mint are ordered to appear before the lords in parliament to give their advice on this matter. [See (2) below].
Source: Printed in full in *RP*, III.126.

2. Petition to the king, lords and commons from the officers of the Mint in the Tower of London repeating the warnings given in (1) above, followed by the advice given by five named moneyers as to the root of the problem of scarcity of bullion and their suggested remedies: Richard Leicester, 'Lincoln goldsmith', 'Crantren', John Hoo and Richard Aylesbury.
Source: Printed in full in *RP*, III.126-7.

3. Petition to the king and council from Michael de la Pole requesting payment of an annuity of 400 marks from the ancient custom in the port of Hull which Edward III granted to his father William.
Endorsed:: It is agreed in parliament that he shall have writs enabling him to be paid.
Source: Printed in full in *RP*, III.127.

4. Petition to the king and council from Margaret, daughter of Thomas de Brotherton former earl of Norfolk and marshal of England, claiming that her husband had been promised 10,000 marks a year in lands and rents by King Edward II, of which he never received more than 7000 marks, and asking that she be granted the remainder.
No endorsement
Source: Printed in full in *RP*, III.127-8.

5. Petition to the king from the commons of the county of Essex complaining that oysters are being taken on the Essex coast during the breeding season, whereby the stock is being diminished, and asking that no-one be permitted to take oysters between 1 May and 30 September.
No endorsement
Source: Printed in full in *RP*, III.128.

6. Petition to the king and lords of parliament from Roger Sapurton, warden of the Fleet prison, complaining of the forcible rescue from his prison of John Hayward, vicar of St Pulcres without Newgate, by Sir John Wiltshire and John Chester on 22 November last [?1381], and praying remedy for this.
No endorsement
Source: Printed in full in *RP*, III.128.

7. Petition to the king and parliament from William Wells, esquire, whom the king has made warden of Bedlam Hospital without Bishopsgate, claiming that he is not accepted as warden by the people of the city because they say that the hospital ought to be in the charge of a knight, and asking the king to confirm and enforce his appointment.
Endorsed: This bill is to be sent to the chancery, where the parties will be summoned to appear and right will be done.
Source: Printed in full in *RP*, III.128.

8. Petition to the king and his parliament from the collectors of the subsidy granted to the king by the clergy in the parliament at Northampton [November 1380], claiming that they have been unable to collect all the subsidy and asking that they be allowed to account and be acquitted for no more than what they have received.
Endorsed: This is to be done, of the king's grace.
Source: Printed in full in *RP*, III.128.

9. Petition to the king and council from the master and scholars of Corpus Christi College, Cambridge, asking the king to compel the mayor and bailiffs of Cambridge to make good the damage which they did to the college during the recent insurrection.
No endorsement
Source: Printed in full in *RP*, III.128-9.

10. Petition to the king and lords of parliament from the abbey of St Albans asking that any charters concerning franchises and liberties which they were compelled to deliver to the rebels during the insurrection last June [1381] be declared null and void.
No endorsement
Source: Printed in full in *RP*, III.129.

11. Petition to the king and council in parliament from the abbess and convent of Shaftesbury claiming that the abbey has been greatly impoverished by plague, murrain and other afflictions in recent years and asking that the king's escheator, sheriff and other ministers be prohibited from interfering in the affairs of the convent apart from the taking of an appropriate sum during each vacancy.
Endorsed: This petition is granted, on the advice of the council.
Source: Printed in full in *RP*, III.129.

12. Petition to the king and council from Ralph, baron of Greystock, keeper of the castle of Roxburgh, who has been captured by the earl of the March of Scotland and put to ransom for [blank] thousand marks, because William, baron of Hilton, and various men of Northumberland seized a number of Scottish merchant ships; he asks that Hilton be obliged to compensate him for his ransom.
Endorsed: A commission is to be established to enquire into this matter.
Source: Printed in full in *RP*, III.129.

13. Petition to the king and council in parliament from Richard Filongley, king's esquire, concerning a grant to him of the office of tronage and pesage of wools and wool-fells in London.
Endorsed: Let a commission be set up according to the form of the statute.
Source: Printed in full in *RP*, III.129-30. See also *CPR 1381-85*, 82 (Appointment of the commission, dated 6 February 1382).

14. Petition to the king and council from Sir William de Windsor asking to be put in possession of various lands [forfeited by his wife, Alice Perrers] which he had been promised in return for leading an expedition to France and Brittany at his own expense, which he has now done. He also asks that the manor of Wendover [Buckinghamshire], for which Alice paid five hundred pounds, be granted to him.
Attached schedule mentioning the manor of East Hanney and a tenement in Bermondsey.
Endorsed: 'Before the king himself and his council'.
Source: Printed in full in *RP*, III.130.

15. Petition to the king, lords and good commons of parliament from William Skele of Kent concerning certain lands and tenements in Sevenoaks [Kent] of which he has been forcibly deprived by one James de Peckham, for which he prays remedy.
No endorsement.
Source: Printed in full in *RP*, III.130.

16. Petition to the king and council in parliament from Thomas de Morley asking to be granted the office of marshal of Ireland, seized into the king's hands during the time of his father William de Morley, and that he be allowed to exercise this office by deputy.
Endorsed: Enquiry is to be made by the lieutenant or governor of Ireland as to why this office was taken into the king's hands.
Source: Printed in full in *RP*, III.130.

17. Petition to the king and council from Cecily Deumarcz, widow of Southwark, asking for payment of a rent of ten marks which she held in a tenement held by Alice Perrers in the parish of All Saints in London, in which tenement the earl of Cambridge lived for a year and a half without paying any rent apart from forty shillings, so that she is owed twelve marks.
Endorsed: Let her sue at common law.
Source: Printed in full in *RP*, III.130.

18. Petition to the king and council from Alice Fesant asking for remedy against one John Goding, by whom she has been deprived of her rightful inheritance in the lordship of the Hospital of St John in Hackney.
Endorsed: Let her sue at common law.
Source: Printed in full in *RP*, III.131.

19. Petition to the king from Sir John Clifton, who claims the right of acting as butler at the king's coronation because he holds the manors of Rockingham and Wymundham, which office was usurped by the earl of Arundel at Richard II's coronation.
No endorsement.
Source: Printed in full in *RP*, III.131.

20. Order to the sheriffs throughout England, by counsel and assent of the prelates, nobles and lords in the last parliament, to make proclamation of the Statute of Winchester and to ensure that it is kept. By king and council in parliament. Dated 24 March 1382.
Source: *CCR 1381-85*, 120.

21. Writs of *supersedeas omnino* to the 'guardians of the justices of the peace' in various towns, following a petition to the council in parliament, for the revocation of powers formerly granted to the mayor and bailiffs of those towns. By petition in parliament. Dated 9 December 1381.
Source: *CCR 1381-85*, 104.

22. Order to the treasurer and barons of the exchequer, following the presentation of a petition to this parliament by Joan, widow of Sir Thomas Felton, to examine certain muniments of hers concerning the manors of Fordham, Wilby, Banham, Greys in Banham and Barrow (Norfolk and Suffolk). Dated 20 December 1381.
Source: *CCR 1381-85*, 30, 33.

23. Pardon to Thomas de Farringdon for offences during the recent insurrection of London of which he is indicted, with the assent of divers prelates, earls and lords of parliament. Dated 25 February 1382.
Source: *CPR 1381-85*, 103.

24. Protection to the following, upon petition to the king and council in parliament, in their proceedings in parliament against certain evildoers concerning the recent insurrection at Beverley (Yorkshire): Thomas de Beverlay, Adam Coppendale, John de Erghum, John Wellyng, Nicholas de Ryse, William Dudhill and John Gerveis, merchant. Dated 20 December 1381
Source: *CPR 1381-85*, 66. (See also *CCR 1381-85*, 38, 87).

1382 May

Westminster

7 - 22 May 1382

(C 65/38. *RP*, III.122-125. *SR*, II.23-26)

C 65/38 is a roll of two membranes, each approximately 320mm in width, sewn together in chancery style and numbered in a later hand. The text, written in the official chancery script of several scribes, occupies the rectos of the membranes only. The dorses are blank apart from a contemporary heading at the foot of membrane 1, and a later heading on membrane 2 which reads 'Rot. Parliamt' R. secundi anno V^o'. The condition of the roll is generally good, though the foot of membrane 1 is stained with gallic acid, making the text illegible in places. The Arabic numerals are of a later date. The roll appears to be complete.

The parliament of November 1381, which had eventually been dissolved on 25 February 1382, had refused to make a grant of direct taxation, but had renewed the wool subsidy for the substantial period of four and a half years (until June 1386). This was in order to provide a secure form of collateral against which the government could raise loans to prosecute the war, and thus as soon as the parliament was over the government summoned a council to Windsor and began negotiating with the mercantile community in the hope that they could be persuaded to make a loan to the crown. Unfortunately the merchants refused to do so; as a result, the bankruptcy of the treasury meant that there was really no option but to summon another parliament, and on 24 March writs were issued for an assembly to meet on 7 May.[1] The list of spiritual peers who were summoned included the new archbishop of Canterbury, William Courtenay, and the new bishop of Durham, John Fordham, but excluded the bishop of Bath and Wells, the bishop of Coventry and Lichfield, and the abbot of Eynsham. The most significant omission from the list of lords temporal compared with the previous parliament was the earl of Suffolk, William Ufford, who had collapsed and died on 15 February, during the previous parliament, on the steps of St Stephen's chapel at Westminster, having just (according to the chronicler Thomas Walsingham) made a speech to the lords.[2] As a result of his death without any surviving issue, the earldom of Suffolk reverted to the crown - shortly to be granted, controversially, to Michael de la Pole.

The reason for holding another parliament so soon was explained by the chancellor, Richard le Scrope, in his opening speech, which was delivered to the lords and commons in the painted chamber of Westminster palace on Thursday 8 May, following the customary day's delay for late arrivals. He explained what had happened at the council at Windsor, and told the assembly that King Richard (who was now fifteen) had agreed to lead an expedition to France in person. He did not ask for taxation: parliament had been summoned, he declared, to determine what security should be offered to the merchants were they to give the government a loan, to make arrangements for the government of the realm during the king's anticipated absence, and 'for no other reason' (Items 2-4).[3] The commons considered this overnight, and on the Friday came before the king and lords again to ask how much the government thought would be needed for the king's expedition: the absolute minimum, they were told, was sixty thousand pounds (Item 9). After a further day's consideration, they announced on the Saturday that they thought the merchants should be responsible for arranging the loan (Item 10). The merchants, however, were wary of becoming involved in such a scheme, citing the unhappy fates - both personal and financial - suffered by great merchants such as William de la Pole and Walter Chiriton, who had brokered large mercantile loans for Edward III in the 1340s and 1350s; they were not willing to make a loan unless the lords and knights did likewise (Item 11). In the end, then, no loan was forthcoming, and the only way the government could think of to try to raise cash speedily was to offer inducements, in the form of a rebate of half a mark per sack and the freedom to export their wool whithersoever they wished, to any merchants prepared to pay their export duties in cash at the exchequer in advance - that is, to pay their customs duties for the year to September 1383 before 19 July 1382. Not surprisingly, very few seem to have taken advantage of this offer.[4]

These exchanges all seem to have taken place during the first four days of the assembly, for the resulting ordinance was proclaimed on 11 May (a Sunday, it is worth noting). Apart from the grant of tunnage and poundage, which was to be used for the defence of the seas (Item 15), the only other business recorded on the roll were a general

---

[1] *CCR 1381-5*, 121-2.
[2] *St Albans Chronicle 1376-1394*, 578; *Westminster Chronicle 1381-1394*, 22.
[3] G. Dodd, 'The lords, taxation and the community of parliament in the 1370s and early 1380s', *Parliamentary History*, 20 (2001), 287-310.
[4] Lloyd, *The English Wool Trade*, 228-9.

admonition to all those summoned to make the effort to attend parliaments (Item 16), and the well-known statute ordering commissions to be given to sheriffs to arrest unlicensed preachers of 'heresies and notorious errors' and other slanders (Item 17). The importance of this act was that it marked the first significant step towards giving the lay authorities the right to search out and arrest heretics.[5] It was, in part, a by-product of the 1381 revolt (for some believed that the rebels had been incited by heretical preachers), but more immediately it was in response to a recommendation from the church council which met simultaneously with the parliament under the leadership of Archbishop Courtenay. This so-called 'Earthquake Council' met on 17 May at Blackfriars in London, but was brought to a premature end by the earthquake which struck parts of southern England on 21 May (whether the earthquake also precipitated the dissolution of parliament is not clear, but it certainly ended the next day, when the writs *de expensis* were issued).[6] If the St Albans chronicler Thomas Walsingham is to be believed, the decision to act against heretics may also have been prompted by an attempt by John Wyclif to convince the assembled lords and magnates of certain of his 'evil doctrines'. Walsingham also noted that John Wrawe, one of the leaders of the Suffolk rebels during the 1381 revolt, was, at the petition of the knights of the shire, condemned to be drawn and hanged during this parliament.[7] Apart from Walsingham, however, the chroniclers barely noticed the parliament of 1382, which is not really surprising: judged against the reasons for which it had been summoned, its achievements were virtually negligible.

---

[5] H. G. Richardson 'Heresy and the lay power under Richard II', *EHR*, 51 (1936).
[6] *CCR 1381-5*, 133-4.
[7] *St Albans Chronicle 1376-1394*, 582-4, 608; for Wrawe, cf. Dobson, *The Peasants' Revolt*, 249.

Text and Translation

Text

Page iii-122, Membrane 1

\[ROTULUS]/PARLIAMENTI TENTI APUD WESTM' IN CRASTINO SANCTI JOHANNIS ANTE PORTAM LATINAM ANNO REGNI REGIS RICARDI SECUNDI QUINTO.

Membrane 2

ANNO QUINTO RICARDI SECUNDI.

1. Fait a remembrer qe au parlement tenuz a Westm' lendemain de Johan Portlatyn, qe fuist meskardy, et le .vij.^{me} jour de Maii, l'an du regne nostre seignour le roi dessuisdit quint, nostre dit seignour le roi estoit venuz en sa persone a dit parlement, et plusours prelatz, seignours et autres q'avoient la somonce de parlement. Mais pur tant qe aucuns des viscontz des countees de roialme n'avoient mye retourniz lours briefs de parlement, et auxint grant partie des prelats et seignours q'avoient mesme la somonce n'estoient mye encores venuz, si ne fuist mye la cause del somonce de ce parlement monstrez a celle meskardy, einz fust mesme le parlement, del commandement le roi, estoit adjournez tanqe al joefdy proschein ensuant; et de ce proclamacioun faite en la sale de Westm', comandant a ycelle proclamacioun a touz q'avoient la dite somonce, qe sur le peril q'appent ils y fussent le dit joefdy par temps, pur oier les causes dessuisdites.

2. A quiel lendemain, si revint en parlement sibien nostre seignour le roi come les prelatz, ducs^8 contes, barons et autres q'avoient la dite somonce, et illoeqes en la chambre depeinte, appellez la einz primerement par lours nouns les chivalers des countees, citezeins des citees et burgeys de burghes, retournez pur cest parlement, monsire Richard le Scrope, chivaler, chanceller d'Engleterre, del comandement le roi avoit les paroles depar le roi, pur exposer et monstrer illoeqes les causes de la somonce de cest parlement, et dist, Sires et seignours, il n'est mye desconue chose a la greindre partie de vous, coment al derrain parlement estoit grantez a nostre seignour le roi le subside des leynes, etc., a durer par quatre ans et demy, al entente qe pur aucun grant viage affaire en defens du roialme, selonc l'ordinance et bon advis de nostre dit seignour le roi et des seignours, homme purroit de ce \subside/ faire chevance suffisante de monoie, come feust promis d'estre fait si l'enbusoigneroit.^{9}

3. Et feust par tant suffert les leynes aler a large, et surce, tantost apres le dit parlement finiz, nostre dit seignour le roi fist reassembler un grant conseil a Wyndesore, a quiel grant partie des prelatz et seignours du roialme y furent presentz, et illoeqes nostre dit seignour, par lours advis, /et\ l'advis et deliberacion d'autres de son conseil, prist son ferm purpos d'aler en sa persone propre vers les parties de France avec son host roial; et les ditz seignours apperceivantz le scarcetee qe l'en ad ore de monoie deinz le roiaume, et d'autrepart le grant bien et profit qe purront avenir del dit viage, si Dieux plest, de lour liberaltee et grant corage profrirent illoeqes a nostre dit seignour, de lui servir en dit host par un an entier chescun de eux, c'estassaver, a certain grant nombre de gentz d'armes et archiers, pur sengles gaiges et sengles regardz de

[Col. b] guerre acustumez prendre en dit viage, tantsoulement. Et sur celle profre fait a nostre dit seignour le roi fist assembler a diverses foitz certains marchantz, sibien

Translation

THE ROLL OF THE PARLIAMENT HELD AT WESTMINSTER ON THE MORROW OF THE FEAST OF ST JOHN BEFORE THE LATIN GATE IN THE FIFTH YEAR OF THE REIGN OF KING RICHARD THE SECOND.

THE FIFTH YEAR OF RICHARD THE SECOND.

1. Be it remembered that at the parliament held at Westminster on the morrow of the feast of St John before the Latin Gate, which was Wednesday 7 May, in the fifth year of the reign of our aforesaid lord the king [1382], our said lord the king had come in person, with many prelates, lords and others who had been summoned to the parliament. But because some sheriffs of the counties of the kingdom had not yet returned their writs of parliament, and also because a large number of the prelates and lords who had received the same summons, had not yet arrived, the reason for the summoning of this parliament was not expounded on that Wednesday, but instead, the same parliament, by order of the king, was adjourned until the Thursday next following [8 May 1382]; and that was proclaimed in the hall of Westminster, and in the same proclamation orders were given to all who had received the said summons that on pain of the penalty declared they should appear early on the said Thursday, to hear the aforesaid reasons.

2. On the next day, our lord the king returned to parliament, together with the prelates, dukes, earls, barons and others who had received the said summons, and there, in the Painted Chamber, the knights of the shires, citizens of the cities, and burgesses of the boroughs who had been returned to this parliament having first been called within by name, Sir Richard le Scrope, knight, chancellor of England, who was to speak on the king's orders for the king, setting out and explaining there the reasons for summoning the parliament, said, Sirs and lords, it is certainly not unknown to most of you that at the last parliament, the subsidy of wool, etc., was granted to our lord the king for four and a half years, with the intention that, for any great expedition to be made in defence of the kingdom, in accordance with the ordinance and good advice of our said lord the king, and the lords, an adequate loan of money would be made from this subsidy, as it was promised would be done if the need arose.

3. And for that reason wool was allowed to be traded freely, and thereupon, immediately after the said parliament had ended, our said lord the king caused a great council to be assembled at Windsor, which a great number of the prelates and lords of the kingdom attended, and there our said lord, by their advice, and the advice and recommendation of others of his council, firmly undertook to go in person to France together with his royal host; and the said lords, observing on the one hand the scarcity of money in the kingdom, and on the other that great good and benefit might come from the said expedition, if it pleased God, of their own free will and great courage offered to serve our said lord the king in the said host, each one of them for a whole year, namely, with a certain great number of men-at-arms and archers, for simple wages, and simple rewards of

[Col. b] war customarily taken on such an expedition, and those alone. And that offer made, our said lord the king assembled certain merchants at various times, both foreigners

---

^{8}*Original* duc,
^{9}Parliament of 1381, item 67.

as well as denizens; firstly, those of London on their own, and later two or three of the more wealthy merchants from every city, borough and worthy town within the kingdom, to provide the said loan. Yet, in the assembly of the said merchants it seemed for many reasons put forward that if the said loan were to be made, no adequate surety could be ordained without parliament for the repayment of the great sum of money to be loaned for such an expedition. And so for that reason, and to provide for the governance of the kingdom in the absence of the king our lord if the said expedition should take place, as mentioned above, was this parliament summoned, and for no other reason. And this appears plainly enough in the writs issued for this parliament, which make express mention thereof and for nothing else.

4. And the king our lord most earnestly requests of you that you tenderly undertake this your charge, and keep it as close to your heart as you desire his honour and the common benefit of all the kingdom and of yourselves. But chiefly and in particular that you consider the nature of the said loan, and the surety to be given to the lenders, as has been said, and that you consider the rest later. And for another thing, the king wishes you to know that he has caused to be appointed certain clerks for receiving, and certain prelates, lords and justices, for trying and determining the petitions to be submitted in this parliament, as has customarily been done in other parliaments; the names of whom and the order in which they have been listed and shall be read to you by the clerk of parliament, here follow:

5. Receivers of petitions from England, Ireland, Wales and Scotland:

Sir John Waltham

Sir Richard Ravenser

Sir Thomas Newenham

Sir John Freton.

6. Receivers of petitions from Gascony, and from other lands and countries overseas, and from the Channel Islands:

Sir Michael Ravendale

Sir Piers Barton

Sir John Bowland

Sir Thomas Thelwall.

And those who wish to submit bills should submit them between now and next Monday inclusive [12 May 1382].

7. The following are assigned to be triers of petitions from England, Ireland, Wales and Scotland:

The king of Castile and of Leon, the duke of Lancaster

The archbishop of Canterbury

The bishop of London

The bishop of Winchester

The bishop of Ely

The bishop of Lincoln

The bishop of Salisbury

The abbot of Westminster

The abbot of Waltham

The earl of Kent, marshal of England

The earl of Arundel

The earl of Salisbury

Lord Neville

Sir John Cobham

Monsire Guy de Bryen

Monsire Robert Tresilian

Monsire Robert Bealknapp'

Monsire William Skipwith'

- touz ensemble, ou .vi. des prelatz et seignours avantditz au meins, appellez a eux chanceller, tresorer, seneschal et chamberlein, et auxint les sergeantz nostre seignour le roi, quant il busoignera. Et tendront lour place en la chambre de chamberlein, pres de la chambre depeinte.

8. Et sont assignez triours des peticions de Gascoigne, et d'autres \[terres]/ et paiis dela la meer, et des Isles:

L'evesqe de Duresm

L'evesqe de Hereford

L'evesqe de Excestr'

L'abbe de Abyndon'

L'abbe de Evesham

Le cont de Bukyngham', conestable d'Engleterre

Le cont de Staff'

Le seignour Fitz Wautier

Le seignour de Wilughby

Monsire Roger de Fulthorp'

Monsire Henry de Asty

- touz ensemble, ou quatre des prelatz et seignours avauntditz; appellez a eux chanceller, tresorer, seneschal, chamberlein et les sergeantz le roi, quant il busoinegra. Et tendront lour place en la chambre marcolf.

9. Item, le vendredy proschein venant, le communes demanderent declaracioun de la somme de deniers qe l'en coviendroit a fyne force avoir par voie de chevance al dit viage. Et lour feust responduz qe meinz qe .lx. mille*li*. ne purroit suffire a si grant viage, qe serroit le primer viage qe unqes nostre seignour lige fist sur ses enemys. Et par tant, et auxint pur son apparaille qe coustera moelt grantement, meindre somme ne purra bien suffire a ce qe semble /de\ certein; qar meinz qe a .iij.mille hommes d'armes et .iij. mille archiers, gaigez pur un demy an, ne osereit homme conseiller lour dit seignour lige de passer en dit viage. Et pur ce lour feust dit q'ils s'advisassent diligeaument de la manere de la dite chevance affaire; qar depuis qe y n'ad ore suffisantie de monoie en tresorie, expedient est et profitable pur tout le roialme de faire mesme la chevance combien qe le roi soit par ycelle chevance perdant en une manere. Mais, si Dieux plest, celle perde tournera a double gain d'autre part, et salvacioun et defens de tout le roialme d'Engleterre, qe Dieux grante, pur ses mercys. Et le roy voet qe auxi bone et suffissante seuretee soit faite as creanceours de la dite somme pur lour repaiement, come par lour advis et l'advis des seignours et autres sages en \cest/ parlement /purra\ resonablement estre accordez et assentuz.

[10]10. Item, le samedy proschein ensuant, quant les communes s'avoient un poy advisez sur lour dit charge, /les\ chivalers des contees par eux mesmes prierent as seignours de parlement, desicome notoire chose est a toutes gentz, qe a tielle chevance faire, et pur deviser estre fait, le principal confort et aide si convient a fine
[Col. b] force esteer par les marchantz, qe les marchants ore presentz en cest parlement ent eussent le charge en especial; qar il scievent pluis de tielle affaire, et mieltz ent sachent

---

[10] A change of hand occurs at this point.

Sir Guy Bryan

Sir Robert Tresilian

Sir Robert Bealknapp

Sir William Skipwith

- to act all together, or at least six of the aforesaid prelates and lords, consulting with the chancellor, treasurer, steward and chamberlain, and also the serjeants of our lord the king, when necessary. And they will hold their session in the chamberlain's room, near the Painted Chamber.

8. The following are assigned to be triers of petitions from Gascony, and from other lands and countries overseas, and from the Channel Islands:

The bishop of Durham

The bishop of Hereford

The bishop of Exeter

The abbot of Abingdon

The abbot of Evesham

The earl of Buckingham, constable of England

The earl of Stafford

Lord FitzWalter

Lord Willoughby

Sir Roger Fulthorpe

Sir Henry Asty

- to act all together, or at least four of the aforesaid prelates and lords; consulting with the chancellor, treasurer, steward, chamberlain and the king's serjeants, when necessary. And they will hold their session in the Marcolf Chamber.

9. Also, the following Friday [9 May 1382], the commons requested a declaration of the sum of money which out of sheer necessity would be required by way of a loan for the said expedition. And it was answered that any sum less than £60,000 would not suffice for so great an expedition, which would be the first expedition our lord the king had ever made against his enemies. And for that reason, and also because of his equipment which would be very costly, a lesser sum would be inadequate, or so it certainly seemed; since no one would dare advise their said lord to embark on the said expedition with fewer than three thousand men-at-arms and three thousand archers, with wages for half a year. And therefore they were told to discuss thoroughly amongst themselves the manner in which the said loan was to be made; since because there was not at present enough money in the treasury, it would be expedient and beneficial for the entire realm if a loan were to be made which equalled the amount which the king might lose by the expedition. But, if it pleased God, this loss could, on the other hand, turn into a double gain, and be the safeguard and defence of the whole kingdom of England, which God grant in his mercy. And the king wishes that as good and adequate a surety of repayment shall be given to the lenders of the said sum, as can be reasonably agreed and assented to by their advice and the advice of the lords and other wise men in this parliament.

10. Also, on the following Saturday [10 May 1382], when the commons had consulted briefly amongst themselves upon their said charge, the knights of the shires, of their own accord, informed the lords of parliament of a matter well known to all, namely that in the making of such a loan, and arranging it, the chief source of reassurance and assistance [Col. b] was necessarily in the merchants, and that the merchants now present in this parliament had been especially entrusted with this; since they knew about it, and knew

treter qe nul autre degree del roiaume. Et sur ce les prelatz et seignours du dit parlement firent nommer certains marchantz en especial, pur treter et communer de lour part, et par eux mesmes, sur la matire. Queux furent chargez illoeqes sur lour ligeance de faire lour diligence sur la matire, aufin qe bone conclusion soi ent feist, et par tant cest parlement feust en haste mys a bon et gracious fyn, qe Dieux grante. Des queux marchantz issint nommez et esluz les nouns s'ensuent:

Monsire Johan Philipot

Monsire Nicholas Brembre

Johan Haddeleye

Thomas Beaupyne

Hugh Fastolf

Johan Pulmond

Robert de Sutton

Johan Organ

William Grevell'

William Spaigne

Estiephne Heym

Johan de Gysburn

William More, vynter

et William Venour.

Et semblablement y furent adonqes les chivalers des contees, et le remenant des citezeins et burgeys, chargez de entreter et communer de lour part en le meen temps.

Membrane 1

11. Item, quant les communes lour avoient longement advisez et tretez de lour charge a eux donee, les chivalers des contees firent relacioun as seignours de parlement, q'ils ne savoient coment homme purroit chevir la somme demande, n'autre grant somme, sinoun par les marchantz, et les marchantz se doutent de chevir a lour seignour lige, ou de faire /rienz\ en celle partie, paront homme poaist autre foitz lour surmettre q'ils, ou nul de eux, avoient enginez ou desceuz lour dit seignour, sicome autre foitz ad este fait devant ceste heure en cas semblable; come de monsire William de la Pole, Johan Wesenham, Johan Malewayn, Wauter Chiryton' et des plusours autres grantz marchantz, les queux pur tieles chevances faites au roi en sa grant necessitee pur un poy de gain ont este depuis empeschez par celles causes, et par autres collaterales voies, et au drain \aucuns de eulx/ destruitz oultrement. Par quoy les marchantz q'ore sont en ce parlement se doutent de /semblable\ empeschement s'ils feissent la dite chevance, et nel voillent par tant faire /en\ aucune /manere\ par voie de chevance, mais aucuns marchantz diont qe si les prelatz et seignours temporelx, ... et autres chivalers, esquiers et clercs du roiaume, veullent de lour part appester au roi franchement sanz gain reprendre aucune notable somme, l'en trovera des marchantz queux ferront semblablement pur suretee suffisante; mais en autre manere ne vorront ne ne osont riens apprester.[11]

[12.] Item, puis apres quant le roi estoit apris qe les marchantz ne /lui\ voloient chevir /la\ somme demandez, n'autre notable somme \et/ suffisante pur la dit viage, n'autrement qe par chevance homme ne savoit /coment\ avenir a tielle somme, si furent faites en ce parlement certeines ordinances de la passage des leynes, esperantz par tant d'avenir le pluis bien et le pluis en haste grant quantitee de monoie. Par quelle et par aucune autre petit aide homme

better how to negotiate it than any other estate in the kingdom. Whereupon, the prelates and lords of the said parliament nominated particular merchants to consider and discuss the matter amongst themselves. They were charged thereon the strength of their allegiance, to do their utmost in the matter, to reach a useful conclusion, and so that parliament might soon be brought to a good and gracious ending, God willing. The names of the merchants thus named and elected are as follows:

Sir John Philpot

Sir Nicholas Brembre

John Hadley

Thomas Beaupyne

Hugh Fastolf

John Pulmond

Robert Sutton

John Organ

William Grevell

William Spain

Stephen Heym

John Gysburn

William More, vintner

and William Hunter.

In the meantime, the knights of the shires, and the rest of the citizens and the burgesses, were likewise charged to discuss and consider the matter.

11. Also, when the commons had deliberated and considered at length the charge given them, the knights of the shires reported to the lords of parliament that they did not know how the sum demanded, or any other large sum, could be lent, unless by the merchants, yet the merchants were fearful of lending to their liege lord, or of doing anything in this matter which could result at a later time in them being accused of beguiling or deceiving their said lord, as had happened on a similar occasion in the past; for example, when Sir William de la Pole, John Wesenham, John Malwayn, Walter Chiryton and many other great merchants had made such loans to the king in his great need for a small gain, and had later been prosecuted for those reasons, and for other related matters, and at last, some of them had been entirely ruined. Because of which, the merchants now attending this parliament feared a similar prosecution if they were to make the said loan, and therefore they did not wish to grant anything by way of a loan, but some of the merchants said that if the prelates and lords temporal and other knights, squires and clerks of the realm would for their part freely lend the king a considerable sum without gain, the merchants would do likewise in exchange for an adequate surety; but they did not wish and would not dare lend anything under any other circumstances.

[12.] Also, subsequently, when the king had learnt that the merchants did not wish to loan him the sum demanded, or any other considerable sum sufficing for the said voyage, and that no one knew how such a sum could be arrived at except through loans, certain ordinances on the passage of wool were made in this parliament, in the hope that as a result, a large amount of money might be well and swiftly raised. With which sum and with another small amount of

---

[11] A section of parchment, approximately twenty-five lines in length, is left blank here.

pensoit de bien faire, si Dieux plerroit. Et autres ordinances auxint y furent faites, les quelles cy apres s'ensuent.

[13.] Pur commune profit du roialme d'Engleterre, aient este faites par nostre seignour le roi, les prelatz, seignours et communes du dit roialme esteantz en ceste parlement tenuz a Westm', lendemain de Seint Johan Portlatyn, l'an du regne nostre seignour le roi Richard quint, certaines ordinances et establissementz en la forme qe s'ensuit: primerement est assentuz et accordez en parlement qe toutes maneres d'estraunges marchantz de quelconqe nacion ou paiis q'ils soient, esteantz del amistee nostre seignour le roi et de son roialme, soient bien venuz et franchement venir purront deinz le roialme d'Engleterre, et aillours *[Page iii-124]*

[Col. a] en la poair nostre dit seignour, sibien deinz franchise come dehors, et illoeqes converser, marchander, et demurrer si longement come bon lour semblera; come ceux les queux trestouz nostre seignour le roi, par le tenour d'ycestes, prent en sa proteccioun et salve garde, avec lours biens, merchandies et familiers quelconqes. Et par tant voet le roi et comande q'ils et chescun de eux soit et soient bien amiablement et marchandeablement tretez et demesnez toutes partz deinz les ditz roialme et poair, avec lours marchandies et biens quelconqes, et soeffertz d'aler, venir, et en lours propres paiis peisiblement retournir, sanz destourbance ou empeschement de nully.

14. Item, est assentuz et accordez en parlement qe le passage des leines, quirs et peaux lanutz, soit overt a toutz maneres de marchantz et autres, sibien foreins come denszeins, qe les vorront achater, et prestement paier pur ycelles les custumes, subsides et devoirs de Caleys, duz decy tanqe a la Seint Michel proschein venant en un an, en tiele manere, qe en le moien temps ils les purront faire eskipper et cokettier es portz deinz le roialme acustumez, et d'illoeqes le faire carier et amesner vers quelconqes parties ils vorront eslire ou choiser depar dela, sanz impediment ou empeschement quelconqe, horspris le roialme de France. Et enoultre, de l'assent avantdit, le roi voet et grante a touz yceux marchantz et autres, qi parentre cy et la quinszeine de Seint Martyn proschein venant paieront devaunt la main les ditz subsides, custumes et devoirs pur les leynes, quirs et peaux lanutz queux ils vorront passer et faire amesner depar dela, parentre le primer jour de Septembre proschein venant, et la dite feste de Seint Michel proschein venant en un an, relees et pardoun de demy marc a chescun saak de leyne, et de demy marc a chescun deux centz et quarante peaux lanutz, et einsi de lours quirs, selonc l'afferant, sur lours ditz paiementz ensi affaires devant la main, come dit est. Et avec ce, averont ils et chescun de eux franchement le passage d'yceulx lours leynes, quirs et peaux lanutz a large ou et quant ils vorront, come dessuis est dit, devant la feste de Seint Michel avauntdit, sanz empeschement ou impediment quelconqe. Mais l'entencioun du roi autrement n'est mye, qe ceux qi ne paieront les subsides de lours leynes, quirs et peaux lanutz devaunt la dite quinszeine, ils paieront entierment les custumes, subsides et devoirs de lours leines, quirs et peaux lanutz a passiers depar dela, sanz remission avoir del dite demy marc par aucune voie. Et le roi promette, et assentuz est et accordez par toutes les estatz de parlement, qe encontre cestes grant et ordinance, n'encontre celles persones qi paieront ensi devant la main et devant la dite quinszeine lours subsides, custumes et devoirs, et averont par tant le dit passage de lours leynes, quirs et peaux lanutz, et relees del dite demy marc, come dit est, ne serra fait repelle, revocacion, contremandement, impediment, n'autre rienz quelconqe, par nostre seignour le roi, son conseil, ses ministres, ne nul autre qe purra tournir ou soner en destourbance de lour convenant ou passage avauntdit, par voie del monde quelconqe. Et le roi voet et grante

help one could plan to do good, if it pleased God. And further ordinances were made which follow below.

[13.] For the general benefit of the kingdom of England, certain ordinances and decrees were issued of the following nature by our lord the king, the prelates, lords and commons of the said kingdom attending this parliament held at Westminster, the morrow of St John before the Latin Gate, in the fifth year of the reign of our lord the king Richard [7 May 1382]: firstly, it is agreed in parliament that all kinds of foreign merchants of whatever nation they might be, friendly towards our lord the king and his kingdom, shall be able to come and go freely within the kingdom of England, and elsewhere *[Page iii-124]*

[Col. a] under the authority of our said lord, as well within franchises as without, and to live, trade and dwell there as seems good to them; as people whom our lord the king, by the tenor of these, has taken under his protection and safeguard, together with their goods, merchandise and servants whatsoever. And for that reason, the king wills and commands that they and each one of them shall be treated and dealt with wholly amicably and in the fashion of merchants in all parts of the said kingdom and domain, together with their merchandise and goods of any sort, and shall be allowed to come and go and return to their own countries, without disturbance or hindrance by any.

14. Also, it is agreed and assented in parliament that the passage of wool, hides and woolfells should be open to all kinds of merchants and others, both foreign as well as denizen, who wish to buy them, and promptly pay the customs, subsidies and duties for the same at Calais, from now until Michaelmas in a year's time [29 September 1383], in such a way that in the meantime they may cause them to be shipped and cocketed in the usual ports of the kingdom, and cause them to be carried thence and transported to whatsoever parts they wish to choose or select overseas, without impediment or prosecution of any kind, except the kingdom of France. And further, with the aforesaid assent, the king wills and grants to all those merchants and others, who between now and the quinzaine of Saint Martin next [19 July 1382] shall pay the said subsidies, customs and duties in cash, for the wool, hides and woolfells which they wish to send and transport overseas, between 1 September next, and the said Michaelmas in a year's time [29 September 1383], release and pardon of half a mark on every sack of wool, and half a mark on every two hundred and forty woolfells, and a similar amount on their hides, proportionately, their said payments to be thus made in cash, as has been said. Moreover, they and every one of them shall have a free passage for their wool, hides and woolfells where and whensoever they wish, as mentioned above, before the aforesaid Michaelmas, without prosecution or impediment of any kind. But the firm intention of the king is that those who do not pay the subsidies on their wool, hides, and woolfells before the said quinzaine, shall pay the full amount of the customs, subsidies and duties on their wool, hides, and woolfells to be sent overseas, without receiving the remission of half a mark in any way. And the king promises, and it is agreed and assented by all the estates of parliament that neither contrary to this grant and ordinance, nor against those people who shall thus pay in cash and before the said quinzaine their subsidies, customary dues and duties, and shall have for this reason the said passage of their wool, hides, and woolfells, and release of the said half a mark, as said, shall there be any repeal, revocation, countermand, impediment or anything else, by our lord the king, his council, ministers or any other which might result in or threaten the disruption of their covenant or aforesaid passage, by any worldly means. And the king wills

a la requeste de sa commune qe les deniers provenantz del subside des dites leynes, quirs et peaux lanutz, grantez au derrain parlement,[12] soient entierment appliez sur le defens du roialme d'Engleterre, et la garde et governance de ses villes et forteresces depar dela, selonc le bone advis des seignours du roialme et les autres sages du conseil nostre seignour le roi.[13]

15. Item, sur le profre q'ad este fait en parlement par les mariners del west, pur faire une armee sur la meer a durer decy tanqe a le Seint Michel proschein venant en deux ans, les seignours et communes esteantz en cest parlement ont grantez a nostre seignour le roi un subside de deux soldz, a prendre de chescun tonel de vin, et de meindre

[Col. b] vesselle solonc l'afferant, amesnez deinz le roialme d'Engleterre. Et auxint .vi. d. al livre, a prendre et resceivoir de toutes maneres d'autres marchandies a amesners hors et venantz deinz le roialme avantdit; sibien c'estassavoir de toutes maneres de draps de leyne come d'autres marchandies quelconqes; horspris leynes, quirs et peaux lanutz, oultre les custumes et subsides ent duz pardevant cest grant, del .xxi. jour de Maii l'an present tanqe al feste de Seint Michel proschein venant; et de mesme la feste de Seint Michel par deux ans entiers proscheinement ensuantz. Issint toutes voies qe les deniers ent provenantz soient entierment appliez sur la salve garde de la meer, et nulle part aillours. Et a la requeste de la commune le roi voet qe monsire Johan Philipot chivaler, soit resceivour et gardein de les deniers sourdantz del dit subside, de la ville de Southampton' vers le northe, et Johan Polymond et Thomas Beaupyne, soient resceivours et gardeins del dit subside en la dite ville de Southampton', et d'illoeqes vers le west, par patentes du roi ent affaires as dites persones en due fourme. Et serront auxint assignez certaines suffisantes persones depar le roi d'estre contrerollours ou coillours avauntditz. Et aueront les dites gentz esteantz en dit armee entierment toutes lours gaignes et profitz, a departir entre eux durante l'arme dessuisdite. Et serront les admiralx et autres esteantz en dite armee assurez de salver les amys et allies du roi nostre seignour, sanz dampnage faire a eux ou a nul de eux par ascune voie. Et s'ils facent, et ceo soit duement provez, ils se obligeront sur grief peine de ent faire duement les amendes.

16. Item, le roi voet et comande et est assentuz en parlement par les prelats, seignours et communes qe toutes singulers persones et comminaltees q'aueront desore la sommonce de parlement, viegnent desenavant as parlementz par manere come ils sont tenuz de faire, et ad este acustumez deinz le roialme d'Engleterre d'auncientee. Et \[si]/ quelconqe persone de mesme le roialme qe auera desore la dite somonce, \[soit]/ il arcevesqe, evesqe, abbe, priour, duc, cont, baron, banerett, chivaler de countee, citezein de citee, burgeys de burghe, ou autre singulere persone ou comminaltee quelconqe, soi absente ou ne viegne mye a la dite somonce, s'il ne su purra resonablement et honestement ent excuser devers le roi nostre seignour, soit amerciez et autrement puniz selonc ce qe auncienement a este usez deinz le roialme avantdit en dit cas. Et si ascun viscount du roialme soit desore negligent en faisant ses retournes des briefs du parlement, ou q'il face entrelesser hors des ditz retornes aucunes citees ou burghs queux sont tenuz et d'auncien \temps/ soloient

and grants at the request of his commons that the money arising from the subsidy on the said wool, hides and woolfells granted at the last parliament shall be devoted entirely to the defence of the kingdom of England, and the guarding and governance of his towns and fortresses overseas, in accordance with the good advice of the lords of the realm and the other wise men in the council of our lord the king.

15. Also, following the offer which had been made in parliament by the mariners of the west, to place a fighting force on the sea from now until Michaelmas two years hence [29 September 1384], the lords and commons attending this parliament granted our lord the king a subsidy of two shillings, to be taken on each cask of wine, and a proportionate amount on smaller

[Col. b] vessels to be imported into the kingdom of England. And also 6 d. in the pound, to be taken and received on all other kinds of merchandise to be exported from and imported into the aforesaid kingdom; namely from all kinds of woollen cloth as well as all other types of merchandise; except wool, hides and woolfells, over and above the customs and subsidies due therefrom before this grant, from 21 May in the present year [1382] until Michaelmas next [29 September 1382]; and from the same Michaelmas for the whole of the following two years [29 September 1384]. Ensuring in every way that the money arising shall be spent solely on the safeguard of the sea, and on nothing else.. And at the request of the commons, the king wills that Sir John Philpot, knight, shall be the receiver and keeper of the money produced by the said subsidy north of the town of Southampton, and John Polymond and Thomas Beaupyne, shall be receivers and keepers of the said subsidy for the said town of Southampton, and for the region to the west, by letters patent of the king thereon to be issued to the said persons in due form. Moreover, certain worthy persons shall be appointed by the king to be the aforesaid controllers and collectors. And the said men of the said fighting force shall receive their wages and profits in their entirety, to be shared out amongst them for the duration of the aforesaid force. And let the admirals and others belonging to the said force swear to protect the friends and allies of the king our lord, without harming them or any one of them in any way. And if they are guilty thereof, and it be duly proved, they shall be obliged to make proper amends on pain of a grievous penalty.

16. Also, the king wills and commands, and it is agreed in parliament by the prelates, lords and commons, that all individuals and communities who henceforth receive a summons to parliament shall appear at future parliaments, as they are obliged to do, and as has been customary in the kingdom of England since bygone times. And if any person of the same kingdom who shall henceforth receive the said summons, be he archbishop, bishop, abbot, prior, duke, earl, baron, banneret, knight of the shire, citizen of a city, burgess of a borough or any other individual or community whatsoever, is absent or does not come in response to the said summons, he shall be fined and otherwise punished in accordance with the established practice of the aforesaid kingdom of England in such cases, unless he can offer an honest and reasonable excuse to the king our lord. And if any sheriff of the kingdom is negligent from now on in making his returns of writs of parliament, or if he omits from the said returns any cities or boroughs which are bound to and have customarily been represented in parliament since bygone times, let him

---

[12] Parliament of 1381, item 40.
[13] 5 Ric.2 stat.2 c.2.

venir au parlement, soit puniz en manere q'estoit acustumez d'estre fait en le cas d'aunciente.[14]

17. Item, \[purce qe notoire chose]/ est, coment y a plusours malurees persones deinz le dit roialme, alantz de countee en countee, et de ville a ville, en certains habitz souz \[dissimulacion de grant saintee,]/ et sanz licence du seint pere \[le pape, ou]/ des ordinairs des lieux, ou autre auctoritee suffisant, \[prechent]/ de jour en autre nemye soulement es esglises, et cimitoirs, einz es marches, feires et autres lieux publiques ou greindre congregacioun des poeple y est, diverses \[predications conteignantz]/ heresyes et errours notoirs, a grant emblemissement de la foy et destructioun des loys et de l'estat de seinte \[esglise, a grant peril des almes du poeplee et de tout le roialme]/ d'Engleterre; come pluis pleinement \[est trovez et]/ suffisauntement provez devant le reverent pere en Dieux l'ercevesqe de Canterbirs, et les \[evesques et autres prelats, et maistres]/ de divinitee, et doctours de canoun et \[civile,]/ et grante partie del clergie del dit roialme, especialment pur *[Page iii-125]*

[Col. a] celle cause assemblez. \[Et queles persones prechent]/ auxint diverses matires d'esclaundre pur discord et dissencioun faire entre diverses estatz du dit roialme, sibien temporelx come \[espiritelx, en commocion du poeplee, et a]/ grant peril de tout le roialme. Les queles prechantz \[citez ou]/ somonez devaunt les ordinairs des lieux pur y \[respondre dont ils sont]/ empeschez, \[ne veullient]/ obeire a lours somonce et mandementz, ne lours monicions, ne les censures de seinte esglise chargent \[point, einz les despisent]/ expressement. Et enoultre, par lours subtiles paroles attreent et engynent le poeple d'oier lours sarmons, et de les maintenir en lours errours par forte

[Col. b] main, \[et par grantz routes; ordene est en]/ cest parlement, qe commissions du roi soient directz as visconts et autres ministres du roi, ou as autres suffisantz persones, apres et selonc les certificacions des prelatz ent affaires en la chancellerie, du temps en temps d'arester touz tieux precheours et lours fautours, maintenours et abbettours, et de les tenir en arest et forte \[prisone tanqe]/ ils se veullent justifier selonc reson et la loy de seinte esglise. Et le roi voet et commande qe le chanceller face tielles commissions a toutes \[les fois q'il serra]/ . . . .
par les prelatz ou ascun de eux certifie, et ent requis, come dessuis est dit.

17. Also, whereas it is well known that there are many wicked persons within the said kingdom, journeying from county to county, and from town to town, dressed in certain habits and adopting the guise of great sanctity, without licence from our holy father the pope, or from the ordinaries of those places, or any other sufficient authority; who from one day to the next preach not only in churches and churchyards, but in markets, fairs and other public places where there are great gatherings of people, various sermons containing heresies and notorious errors, to the great emblemishment of the faith and destruction of the laws and the estate of holy church, and the great peril of the souls of the people of the whole realm of England; as was fully discovered and sufficiently proven before the reverend father in God the archbishop of Canterbury, and the bishops and other prelates, and masters of divinity, and doctors of canon and civil law, and a great part of the majority of the clergy of the said kingdom, specially *[Page iii-125]*

[Col. a] assembled for that reason. And those people also preach various slanderous matters to sow discord and dissension between the various estates of the said kingdom, both temporal as well as spiritual, to the perturbation of the the people and the great peril of all the kingdom. Which preachers, being cited or summoned to appear before the ordinaries of those places to answer to the accusations made against them, will not obey either their summons and mandates, nor their admonishments, nor yet the censures of holy church, which they openly despise. And further, by their crafty words they attract and beguile people into hearing their sermons, and maintain their belief in these errors by force

[Col. b] and in great companies; it is ordained in this parliament that commissions from the king shall be directed to sheriffs and other king's ministers, or to other sufficient persons, after and in accordance with the certifications of the prelates to be made thereon in the chancery from time to time, to arrest all such preachers, along with their supporters, maintainers and abettors, and to keep them under arrest and strict confinement until they be willing to justify themselves in accordance with reason and the law of holy church. And the king wills and commands that the chancellor shall make such commissions at all times it shall be . . . . certified and required by the prelates or any one of them, as mentioned above.

---
[14] 5 Ric.2 stat.2 c.4.

Appendix

7 May 1382

Westminster

1. Order to various sheriffs to make proclamation of the grant of two shillings on every tun of wine imported and six pence in every pound made in the last parliament, to be paid for 21 May 1382 until 29 September 1384, all of which money is to be used for the safeguard of the seas. Dated 27 June 1382.
    Source: *CCR 1381-5*, 204-5.

1382 October

Westminster

6 - 24 October 1382

(C 65/39. *RP*, III.132-143. *SR*, II.26-30)

C 65/39 is a roll of eight membranes, each approximately 340mm in width, sewn together in chancery style and numbered in a later hand. The text, written in the official chancery script of several scribes, occupies the rectos of the membranes only. The dorses are blank apart from two later headings: 'Parliamentum de anno sexto Ricardi secundi. Pars prima' on membrane 1, and 'R^o Parl' Ric' secundi' on membrane 8. The condition of the roll is good, though there are natural holes in membranes 8, 5 and 3. The lower halves of membranes 7, 6 and 5 are blank. The Arabic numerals are of a later date, while the Roman numerals alongside the common petitions are contemporary. The roll appears to be complete.

The parliament of May 1382 having failed to make any serious headway on the financial question, it was inevitable that it would only be a matter of months before a new assembly was required, and on 9 August, just eleven weeks after the dissolution of its predecessor, writs were duly issued for parliament to meet on 6 October at Westminster.[1] One of the new spiritual peers summoned was Robert Braybrooke, who had replaced Archbishop Courtenay as bishop of London and who also, just two weeks before parliament met, replaced Richard le Scrope as chancellor following the latter's dispute with the king over a question concerning the misuse of royal patronage.[2] Missing from the list of heads of religious houses were the abbots of St Mary's York and - for the fourth parliament in succession - of Bury St Edmunds. The only newcomer of significance among the lords temporal was John Charlton of Powys, whose ancestors had been summoned since 1313 but whose father had died in 1374, at which time John had been just twelve years old.

Following the customary day's delay for non-arrivals, the formal opening of the session took place on Tuesday 7 October, when Bishop Braybrooke delivered a rather anodyne speech listing the various theatres of war in which England was involved, which, as well as the usual Scotland, Ireland and Gascony, also included Portugal and Flanders. Two days later, this theme was taken up in a more arresting speech given by John Gilbert, bishop of Hereford, a clerk with strong links to the government. The kingdom, he declared, was in great danger, from which two 'ways' presented themselves as potential routes to salvation: the 'way of Flanders' and the 'way of Portugal'. The first consisted of a proposal by Henry Despenser, bishop of Norwich, to lead a 'crusade' - for which he had already obtained papal sanction - to crush the pro-French schismatics in Flanders and 'restore' the county to the allegiance of both Rome and England. The second, which Bishop Gilbert made it clear that he favoured, involved finding the sum of £43,000 to send an army to Iberia under the command of John of Gaunt, partly in order to bring relief to the Portuguese in their struggle against the Castilians, and partly to enable Gaunt to press home his claim to the throne of Castile, following which he would be in a position to deliver a blow against the French. In fact, the Portuguese were not in quite such mortal danger, since they had recently (in August) concluded a truce with the Castilians,[3] but if news of this had reached Bishop Gilbert he omitted to mention it. How many of the commons had confidence in Gaunt's declaration that he only required the £43,000 as a loan, and that he would repay it in two years, must also remain an open question (Items 9-13).

Gaunt had already moderated his plan for a campaign to Iberia considerably since he had first put it to parliament in January, at which time he had requested a loan of £60,000 for the wages of the same number of men.[4] He had also managed to persuade at least some of the lords to support him, for when the 'prelates, earls, barons and noblemen' were asked whether they thought that 'the way of Portugal' would prove profitable to England, they answered in the affirmative, although some doubt was expressed as to whether 4000 men would suffice to conquer a kingdom (Item 23). The commons, however, remained opposed to the venture. According to the St Albans chronicler, Thomas Walsingham, Bishop Despenser had the papal bulls for his crusade read out in parliament, and publicised them widely. Walsingham also states that a delegation from the Flemings came to the parliament offering to submit themselves to the English allegiance in return for help in the war which they were currently waging against the king of France, although since they were not regarded as sufficiently representative they were promptly sent home with a request to send 'men of

---

[1] *CCR 1381-5*, 210-11.
[2] *St Albans Chronicle 1376-1394*, 620-24.
[3] Goodman, *John of Gaunt*, 93-4.
[4] Parliament of November 1381, Item 66.

greater prestige and reputation' from the Flemish towns.[5] Despite this, the commons clearly preferred the idea of a campaign to Flanders, largely it seems because of the importance of the mercantile contacts between England and the Flemish towns. They submitted a petition asking the king to support it (Item 46), and their request for the wool staple to be moved from Calais (Item 22) was also probably a move designed to succour the Flemings, for - although this is not stated on the roll - the probability is that they hoped to have it moved to Bruges in an attempt to cement an alliance with Ghent.[6] Moreover, they did agree to grant a fifteenth and tenth, the first grant of direct taxation for nearly two years (although only after 'a great deal of wrangling', according to the Westminster chronicler),and although they did not specify the purpose to which it was to be put, it was in fact later earmarked for Bishop Despenser's crusade.[7] John of Gaunt had been humiliated. This would not, of course, mark the end of his attempts to win support for a campaign to Iberia, but for the moment he was forced to put his plans on hold.[8]

Apart from 'the way of Flanders' and 'the way of Portugal', parliament also dealt with a number of items which in one way or another still represented the aftershocks of the 1381 revolt. York, Scarborough and Beverley, the three Yorkshire towns involved in the revolt, all purchased comprehensive charters of pardon from the king, though only in return for substantial fines (Items 18-21). The mayor and aldermen of London presented a petition against the fishmongers of the city, at the root of which seems to have lain not just the customary rivalry between guilds but the belief (or at least the allegation) that certain members of the victualling guilds had lent support to the rebels who sacked London in 1381. Although modern research has shown that these allegations were almost certainly groundless, the result was a series of ordinances restricting the trading and political privileges of the fishmongers - ordinances of which Walsingham for one did not approve, and which in fact were overturned a few months later in the next parliament (Items 43, 55-65).[9] Finally, it is interesting to note that the statute against unlicensed preachers which had been enacted in the parliament of May 1382 was annulled: according to the commons, they had never agreed to it in the first place - which may well be true, since it clearly originated with the prelates at the so-called 'Earthquake Council' - and they therefore asked that it be rescinded, 'since it was certainly not their intention that they or their successors be controlled by nor obliged to the prelates more than their ancestors had been in the past'. The king agreed without demur (Item 53).[10]

On 24 October, after just two and a half weeks, Richard dissolved parliament.[11] By the time that the next one met, in February 1383, he would have turned sixteen; the hallmark of the next few years, clearly reflected in the parliamentary debates of the mid and late 1380s, was the increasing personal role of the king, and the effect that this had on the politics of the time.

---

[5] *St Albans Chronicle 1376-1394*, 624-6.
[6] Lloyd, *The English Wool Trade*, 229.
[7] *Westminster Chronicle*, 28.
[8] Goodman, *John of Gaunt*, 94; Palmer, *England, France and Christendom*, 10.
[9] *St Albans Chronicle 1376-1394*, 626; Dobson, *Peasants' Revolt*, 212-26.
[10] Parliament of May 1382, Introduction.
[11] *CCR 1381-5*, 227-8.

Text and Translation

Text

Page iii-132, Membrane 1
\PARLIAMENTUM DE ANNO SEXTO RICARDI SECUNDI. PARS PRIMA./
Membrane 8
1. Fait a remembrer qe le lundy en les oetaves de Seint Michel qe fuist le primer jour de ceste parlement donez par la dite somonce d'icelle, si vindrent a Westm' aucuns des grantz prelatz et seignours du roialme. Et yceulx assemblez illoeqes en la chambre arraiez pur parlement avec les grantz officers du roi nostre seignour, et longement attendue par eux la venue d'autres seignours et communes q'avoient mesme la somonce et nient comparantz, au drain, mesme le jour pur tant qe y estoit dit pur voir qe plusours des viscontz n'avoient encores fait retourner lours briefs de parlement, et qe le greindre partie des seignours et autres q'avoient la somonce n'estoient venuz a la ville, si feust cest parlement adjournez a la voluntee et commandement nostre seignour le roi tanqe a mesqardy proschein ensuant. Et puis apres de mesme l'adjournement overte proclamacione faite en la sale de Westm', ou estoit comandez depar le roi qe toutz les prelatz, seignours, chivalers, citezeins et burgeys et autres q'avoient la dite somonce, retournassent bien matin le dit mesqardy, pur y oier en presence de nostre seignour le roi les causes pur queles ce present parlement estoit especialment somonez. Et qe toutz les viscontz qe encores n'avoient fait retourner les briefs de parlement les retornassent sanz delay, sur peril q'appent.
2. A quiel mesqardy, si vint en parlement q'estoit deinz en la chambre depeintee, sibien nostre seignour le roi en sa persone, avec la greindre partie des prelatz, ducs[12] conts, barons et autres seignours du roiaume, et appellez la einz singulerement par les nouns les chivalers des countees, citezeins des citees et burgeis des burghs, l'evesqe de Londres, chanceller d'Engleterre, q'avoit les paroles depar le roi, et par commandement le roi a lui donez, dist, Seignours et sires, sachez qe combien qe je sui moelt insufficient par plusours encheisons de dire ou counter chose qe porte charge en presence de si nobles, sages et discretz seignours et autres persones de cest roialme come vous estez ycy presentz, toutes voies il me faut ore a fine force par le comandement de nostre seignour lige cy present, qi Dieux salve.
3. Et devrez savoir qe les causes de la somonce de cest parlement si est fait especialment pur trois causes; l'une est qe nostre dit seignour le roi desire moelt entierment et principalment qe, al honur de Dieux et de seinte esglise, la franchise et libertees de seinte esglise deinz son roialme d'Engleterre soient entierment sanz emblemisseure gardez, et auxi avaunt come aient este mieultz gardez en temps de nul de ses nobles progenitours rois d'Engleterre: et si rienz y soit fait au contraire, qe ce soit ore redressez et duement amendez.
[Col. b] La secounde cause est qe les bones loys, usages et custumes de son roialme avauntdit soient tenuz et gardez en touz lours pointz, et si rienz ait este fait ou usez au contraire, qe demande amendement ou correccione, qe ce soit ore fait par l'advis de vous toutz. La tierce cause est touchant la governail de mesme le roialme sibien dedeinz come dehors, et la salve garde d'ycelle dedeinz; c'estassaver qe purvoiance soit fait et bone ordinance encontre le riotours et autres malfaisours, queux encores en chescun paiis de mesme le roialme sont mieultz propis et apparaillez s'ils

---
[12] *Original* duc,

Translation

THE PARLIAMENT OF THE SIXTH YEAR OF RICHARD THE SECOND. PART ONE.

1. Be it remembered that on the Monday [6 October 1382] on the octave of Michaelmas, which was the first day of this parliament as specified in the summons, there came to Westminster some of the great men, prelates and lords of the realm, and they, having assembled in the chamber prepared for the parliament, together with the great officers of the king our lord, long awaited the arrival of the others lords and commons who had received the same summons and had not yet appeared. At length, on the same day, because it emerged that many of the sheriffs had still not returned their writs of parliament, and the greater part of the lords and others who had received summons had not come to town, so the parliament was adjourned at the will and command of our lord the king until the following Tuesday [7 October 1382]. And after that same adjournment a public announcement was made in the hall at Westminster, where it was ordered on the king's behalf that all the prelates, lords, knights, citizens and burgesses, as well as others who had had the said summons, return early on the said Tuesday, to hear in the presence of our lord the king the reasons why this parliament had been especially summoned. And that all the sheriffs who had still not returned their writs of parliament, return them without delay, on pain of the appointed penalty.
2. On which Tuesday, our lord the king in person, together with a large number of the prelates, dukes, earls, barons and other lords of the realm arrived in parliament, which was held in the Painted Chamber, and the knights of the counties, citizens of the cities and burgesses of the boroughs having been called individually by name, the bishop of London, chancellor of England, who was to speak on the king's behalf, and at his command, said, Lords and sirs, you know that although I am most unworthy for many reasons to say or report anything of great importance before such noble, wise and discreet lords and other persons of this realm as yourselves here present, nevertheless, sheer necessity compels me now to do so, at the command of our lord the king here present, whom God preserve.
3. And you ought to know that the particular reasons for the summoning of this parliament are threefold; one is that our said lord the king chiefly and most earnestly desires that, in honour of God and holy church, the franchise and liberties of holy church within his kingdom of England be fully preserved without impairment, and as they were best kept in the time of any of his noble progenitors, the kings of England: and if anything be done to the contrary that it be redressed and duly amended.

[Col. b] The second reason is that the good laws, usages and customs of his aforesaid kingdom should be kept and upheld on all counts, and if anything be done or practised to the contrary which demands amendment or correction, that that now be done by the advice of you all. The third reason concerns the governance of the same kingdom, both within and without, and the safeguard of the same within; namely, that provision and an effective ordinance be made against rioters and other malefactors, who in each county of the same kingdom are still well prepared and equipped, if they see an

veissent temps covenable et lieu, et recomencer leurs malfaitz et riotz, qe Dieux ne veulle: et par dehors sibien de purvoiance faire pur salve garde de la meer et de la navie, et socours de les nobles gentz esteantz en Portugal, illoeqes esteantz en grant peril; come pur les frountiers et bastiles del dit roialme par dela la meere qe sont ores en moelt grant peril et de mal arraie. Et de la marche d'Escoce est a douter en certain q'ils ne vorront avoir paix, ne sanz grant prejudice du roi et del roialme assenter qe les treves devant prises /soient proloignez oultre la feste de\ la Chaundeleure proschein venant en un an; a quiel temps toutes les trieves devant prises avec les ditz Escotz doivent finir et faillir. Et conuz chose doit estre a vous trestouz qe si Dieu veullie, amendement et remede soient purveuz encontre les meschiefs q'ore sont apparantz toutes partz par terre et par meer, come bien le sachez, et dessus est dit: avec ce qe l'en faut a fyne force mettre sur le salvacione d'Irlande et de Gascoigne, queux sont auxint en moeltz grantz perils pur defaute d'aide et de socours; ce ne purra mye encores estre fait sanz grant avoir de quoy home le poaist faire. Et pur tant nostre seignour le roi vous prie moelt entierment qe en salvacione de lui, de son roialme, et de vous touz, veulliez vous bien aviser sur cestes matires: c'estassavoir, vous les prelats et seignours temporelx de vostre part, et vous la commune de vostre part, et sur ce lui conseiller le mieultz qe vous ent semblera; toutes voiez considerez les grantz perils apparantz, et par tant avoir consideracion et bon pensee coment home avendra al avoir, de quoy purvoiance et resistence purra estre fait encontre tantz des enemys et lours efforcementz, et par especial, de quoi et coment les communes del paiis de Flandres, q'ore sont en bone volontee pur estre de nostre accord et partie, a ce q'ome pense, serront par nous socourez et aidez si l'accord parentre nous se preigne; et auxint noz gentz en Portugal. Et le roi voet qe si nul de ses liges voille mettre avaunt en parlement peticion de grief a lui fait, en especial ou en commune, qe demande redresse ou amendement de parlement, qe ce soit fait et baillez a un des clercz dessouz escritz, pur ce especialment assignez. Et auxint, certains prelats, seignours et justices sont assignez de trier les peticions a baillers en ce parlement par la forme et manere q'ensuent:

Page iii-133
4. Resceivours des peticions d'Engleterre, Irlande, Gales et Escoce:

Sire Johan de Waltham

Sire Richard Ravenser

Sire Thomas de Newenham

Sire Johan de Freton'.

5. Resceivours des peticions de Gascoigne, et d'autres terres et paiis depar dela, et des Isles:
Sire Michel Ravendale

Sire Piers de Barton'

Sire Johan Bouland'

Sire Johan Scarle.

Et ceux qi veullient bailler lours \billes/ les baillent avant parentre cy et dymenge proschein, le dit dymenge accomptez.

6. Et sont assignez triours des peticions d'Engleterre, Irlande, Gales et Escoce:

Le roi de Castill' et de Leon, duc de Lancastre

L'ercevesqe de Cantirbirs

L'evesqe de Wyncestr'

opportune time and place, to resume their misdeeds and riots, which God forbid: and outside the kingdom, provision be made for the keeping of the sea and the fleet, and to assist the noble people of Portugal, who are in great danger; as well as for the frontiers and fortresses of the said kingdom overseas which are now in great danger and poorly equipped. And as for the march of Scotland, it is indeed to be feared that they do not wish to have peace, and will not agree, without considerable disadvantages for the king and the kingdom, to extending the truce previously concluded beyond the feast of Candlemas next in a year's time [2 February 1384]; at which point in time all the truces formerly concluded with the said Scots ought to end and cease. And you should know that, if God will it, correction and remedy shall be provided for the troubles which now appear everywhere on land as well as at sea, as well you know, and as was said above: and in addition, necessity demands investment in the security of Ireland and Gascony, which are also at very great risk through lack of aid and support; which cannot be done without a grant with which to do it. And therefore, our lord the king most sincerely prays of you that, for his security as well as that of his kingdom, and of you yourselves, you thoroughly consider these matters: namely, you, the prelates and lords temporal for your part, and you, the commons for your part, and advise him of what seems best to you; forever bearing in mind the great perils which have arisen, and for that reason, giving consideration and as deep thought as you can to the ways in which provision and resistance can be made against such enemies and their forces, and in particular to consider how the country of Flanders, which is now favourably inclined toward an agreement with us and our cause, according to popular opinion, might be supported and assisted by us so that the agreement between us shall be preserved; and also our people in Portugal. And the king wills that if any of his lieges wishes to submit a petition to parliament concerning injury done him, individually or in common, which requires redress or amendment by parliament, that it shall be made and delivered to one of the clerks named below, especially appointed for this. Moreover, certain prelates, lords and justices have been appointed to try petitions to be submitted in this parliament, in the following manner:

4. Receivers of petitions from England, Ireland, Wales and Scotland:
Sir John Waltham

Sir Richard Ravenser

Sir Thomas Newenham

Sir John Freton.

5. Receivers of petitions from Gascony, and from other lands and countries overseas, and from the Channel Islands:
Sir Michael Ravendale

Sir Piers Barton

Sir John Bowland

Sir John Scarle.

And let those who wish to submit their bills deliver them between now and next Sunday, including that day [12 October 1382].

6. The following are assigned to be triers of petitions from England, Ireland, Wales and Scotland:
The king of Castile and Leon, the duke of Lancaster

The archbishop of Canterbury

The bishop of Winchester

L'evesqe de Ely	The bishop of Ely
L'evesqe de Nichole	The bishop of Lincoln
L'evesqe de Salesbirs	The bishop of Salisbury
L'abbe de Seint Austin de Cantirbirs	The abbot of St Augustine's, Canterbury
L'abbe de Waltham	The abbot of Waltham
Le cont de Kent, mareschal d'Engleterre	The earl of Kent, marshal of England
Le cont d'Arundell	The earl of Arundel
Le cont de Salesbirs	The earl of Salisbury
Le seignour de Nevill'	Lord Neville
Monsire Johan Cobham	Sir John Cobham
Monsire Guy de Bryene	Sir Guy Bryan
Monsire Robert Tresilian	Sir Robert Tresilian
Monsire Robert Bealknap'	Sir Robert Bealknap
Monsire William Skipwith	Sir William Skipwith

- touz ensemble, ou .vi. des prelatz et seignours avauntditz au meins; appellez a eux chanceller, tresorer, seneschal et chamberlein, et auxint les sergeantz nostre seignour le roi, quant il busoignera. Et tendront lour place en la chambre du chamberlein, pres de la chambre depeintee.

7. Et sont assignez triours des peticions et de Gascoigne, et d'autres terres et paiis dela la meere, et des Isles:

L'evesqe de Duresm	The bishop of Durham
L'evesqe de Norwiz	The bishop of Norwich
L'evesqe d'Excestr'	The bishop of Exeter
L'evesqe de Hereford'	The bishop of Hereford
L'abbe de Glastyngbirs	The abbot of Glastonbury
L'abbe de Selby	The abbot of Selby
Le cont de Buk', conestable d'Engleterre	The earl of Buckingham, constable of England
Le cont de Staff'	The earl of Stafford
Le seignour Fitz-Wauter	Lord FitzWalter
Le seignour de Wylughby	Lord Willoughby
Monsire Roger Fulthorp	Sir Roger Fulthorp
Monsire Henry de Asty	Sir Henry Asty

- touz ensemble, ou .iiij. des prelatz et seignours avauntditz; appellez a eux chanceller, tresorer, seneschal, chamberlein et les sergeantz le roi, quant il busoignera. Et tendront lour place en la chambre marcolf.

8. /Et le roi vous comande qe vous retornez\ demain par temps pur avoir declaracione en pluis especial manere sur les causes de la somonce avauntdite. Et enoultre, le roi comande a touz q'avoient la dite somonce q'ils viegnent de jour en autre au dit parlement, et q'ils ne se absentent mye ou departent d'ycelle, sanz especial coungie de lui, sur peril q'appent.

9. Item, le joefdy proschein, les prelatz, seignours et communes, touz assemblez en la chambre blanke, et illoeqes

[Col. b] l'evesqe de Hereford avoit les paroles depar le roi, et dist, Seignours et sires, del comandement de mes seignours cy presentz me covient parler, et de vous dire depar eux ce q'ore dirra. Et devrez savoir qe quatre choses principalment font chescun armee de overer et labourer sur la chose q'il desire: des queux quatre choses, les deux quelles n'appartiegnent mye a nostre purpos quant au present lerrai, et dirrai les autres deux qe sont; c'estassavoir doute, et esperance. Qar doute de mal apparant, ou qe legerement semble a venir, ou d'autre part pur esperance d'atteindre a honeur, estat, fame, ou autre profit temporel ou espiritel, ce

- to act all together, or at least six of the aforesaid prelates and lords; consulting with the chancellor, treasurer, steward and chamberlain, and also the serjeants of our lord the king, when necessary. And they shall hold their sessions in the chamberlain's room, near the Painted Chamber.

7. The following are assigned to be triers of petitions from Gascony, and from the other countries and lands overseas, and from the Channel Islands:

- to act all together, or at least four of the aforesaid prelates and lords; consulting with the chancellor, treasurer, steward, chamberlain and the king's serjeants when necessary. And they shall hold their session in the Marcolf Chamber.

8. Furthermore, the king orders that you return early tomorrow to hear a special announcement of the reasons for the aforesaid summons. In addition, the king orders all who have received the said summons, to attend the said parliament each day, without absenting themselves or departing from the same without his special permission, on pain of the appointed penalty.

9. Also, on the following Thursday [9 October 1382], the prelates, lords and commons, assembled in the White Chamber, and there

[Col. b] the bishop of Hereford spoke on the king's behalf, saying, Lords and sirs, at the command of my lords here present it befits me to tell and inform you on their behalf, of that which I shall now say. And you should know that four chief things spur all armies to work and labour for what they desire: of which four things, two are not relevant to our purpose and I shall omit them for the moment, and speak of the other two which are fear and hope. Since fear stems from evil, or seems to arise readily from it, whereas on the other hand, in hope of attaining honour, status, good repute,

fait homme, /combien\ q'il soit bien necgligent, de soi moever et laborer.

10. Et ores est il einsi qe si homme regarde discretement toutes partz, cest roialme n'estoit unqes en greindre peril q'ore n'est, dedeinz le roialme mesme come dehors, sicome apparisante chose est a touz qe resoun ont ou discrecione: en tant qe si Dieux n'y mette sa main de grace, et les enhabitantes se peinent pur leur defendre, ceste roiaume est sur le point d'estre conquiz, qe Dieu ne veullie, et mys en subjeccione de ses enemys; et par tant la lange et nacione Engleys estre outrement destruit: issint qe maintenant autrement n'est mye qe eslire un de deux, de nous rendre, ou \nous/ defendre.

11. Et d'autre part, combien qe semble clerement qe le terme deinz quiel cel meschief deust avenir, toutes voies encores Dieu nous ad overt deux nobles chymyns par queles de resoun, et par sa grace, homme eschapera toutz les ditz perils, et avendra a grant honur. L'une chemyn est de ceulx de Flandres, queux se vorront offrer al service nostre seignour le roi, et a toute bone alliance avoir avec lui et son roialme, \a ce q'est dit:/ et celle chemyn si est moelt noble et large de grever les enemys pluis qe grant piece ne furent, si homme eust de quoy de tenir celle chemyn overt, et maintenir les ditz Flamenz encontre lours enemys et les noz, si l'alliance se preigne, qe Dieu grante. L'autre chemyn est en Portugal': qar de certain il n'a mye place en monde si semblable de faire fin, et venir a bon et brief purpos de les guerres, come celle place n'est de present.

12. Qar si monsire d'Espaigne y voise ore avec un suffisant poair, et y viegne en salvetee a l'aide Nostre Seignour, et illoeqes avec les seignours et poair qe y sont a devant viegne es champes, il serra roi d'Espaigne, ou avera la bataille deinz un demy an proschein apres la venue illoeqes. Et si Dieu lui doigne prosperitee illoeqes, le remenant de noz guerres tost serra mys au fin. Et pur tant l'esperance d'avoir bon et hastive fin de noz guerres par celle autre chemyn nous devroit de resoun \[venier]/ de mettre travail, diligence et coustages en tiel guyse, qe par tant, si Dieux plest, en apres homme fuist mys a repos et quiete pur touz jours. Et sur le profre qe monsire le duc ad fait d'avoir .ij. mille hommes d'armes et .ij. mille archers, et gages et rewardz pur eux pur demy \an/ tantsoulement, quelles gages et rewardz par le dit demy an amontent a .xliij. mille livres - pur la quelle somme il se profre de lier al roy nostre seignour et a son roialme de faire repaiement, ou en monoie, ou en service, al election de nostre seignour le roi, deinz trois ans proschein ensuantz apres le departir du dit duc hors du roialme, si einsi soit qe Dieu lui doigne la vie si longement, et il soit frank en le moien temps de son corps hors de prisone, et q'il viegne en salvetee avec son host a terre d'oultre la meere - semble pur voir qe chescun homme se doit prendre ore moelt pres d'aider a cest foitz en resous del roialme, et de lui mesme. Et pur tant en briefs paroles, nostre seignour le roi vous prie entierment, et chescun vrai lige et bienveulliant au roialme deust avancer la busoigne, par les causes dessuisdites, en tiel manere *[Page iii-134]*

[Col. a] qe vous vous vorrez, c'estassavoir bien adviser sur ceste matire, et ent communer parfoundement et diligeaument entre vous et chescun de sa part.

13. Et especialment sur le point, coment \en la pluis aisee manere,/ a meindre grief et nuisance du poeple, l'en purra venir a la somme de monoie dont homme purra mettre les deux purpos et viages, /de\ Espaigne et Flandres, a bon fin, ou a meins l'un d'ycelle; c'estassavoir celle d'Espaigne, aiant nientmeins reward covenable vers Flandres, si l'accord se preigne. Et si einsi soit fait, et qe homme y vorra ore mettre sa paine, n'est pas a douter qe Dieu ne nous \mettra/

or other temporal or spiritual benefit, even the most slothful man is inspired to rouse himself and labour.

10. And it happens that if all things are well taken into account, this kingdom has never been in as much danger as it is in now, both within and without, as will be apparent to all who possess either reason or judgment: so that if God does not bestow his grace on the land and the inhabitants do not strive to defend themselves, this kingdom will be on the verge of being conquered, which God forbid, and made subject to its enemies; and as a consequence, the language and nation of England will be completely destroyed: so that now, we are faced with only two choices, to surrender or to defend ourselves.

11. For another thing, although it seems clear that this trouble is inevitable, nevertheless God has shown us two noble ways, along which, by reason, and with his grace, we may escape all the said perils and arrive at great honour. One such way is that of the people of Flanders, who wish to offer their service to our lord the king, and to enjoy a friendly alliance with him and his kingdom, as it is said: and that path is most noble and broad enough to cause the enemy more trouble than they have known for a long while, if we have the means to keep that path open, and maintain the hostility of the said Flemings towards their enemy and ours, and preserve that alliance, which may God grant. The other way is by Portugal: for there is no place on earth so likely to bring an end to the wars, swiftly and effectively concluding them, as is that place at present.

12. For if our lord of Spain should now go there with an adequate force, and arrive there safely with the aid of Our Lord, and meet with the lords and force which have taken the field, he shall be king of Spain, or do battle within six months of his arrival there. And if God grant him good fortune there, the remainder of our wars shall soon be concluded. And in such hope of putting an effective and speedy end to our wars by this other way, we ought with reason to invest labour, effort and money therein, so that, if it please God, we may subsequently enjoy peace and repose forever. And as for the offer which our lord the duke has made to provide two thousand men-at-arms and two thousand archers, and wages and rewards for them for half a year only, which wages and rewards for the said six months will amount to £43,000 - for which sum he offers to bind himself to the king our lord and his kingdom to make repayment, either in money, or in service, according to the choice of our lord the king, within three years of his departure from the kingdom, if it should be that God grants him life so long, and if he shall remain free and out of prison in the meantime, and arrive safely in this land from overseas with his host - it seems that every man should now take it upon himself to assist more closely in the rescue of the realm, and of himself. And therefore, in brief, our lord the king earnestly prays you, and each true liege and well-wisher of the kingdom, that you further this matter for the aforesaid reasons, as you *[Page iii-134]*

[Col. a] will, namely by fully considering it, and holding deep and thorough consultation amongst yourselves, each contributing his own share.

13. And particularly on the issue of how, with the least trouble and inconvenience to the people, it might be easiest to arrive at the sum of money which would achieve the two plans and expeditions, that is to say to Spain and to Flanders, or one of them at least; namely that of Spain, but nevertheless leaving a suitable sum for Flanders, if agreement be reached, which if it be done, and trouble taken over it, we need not fear that God will fail to improve our plight

en bon plit devant les treis[13] ans dessuisditz finiz. Et si doit homme moelt le pluis avoir bone volentee /ore\ de bien faire qe unqes devant, par cause de les deux croiseryes qe nostre seint pere le pape ad fait, grantez et envoiez ore devers le roialme d'Engleterre, l'un a monsire d'Espaigne fait en especial encontre son adversaire d'Espaigne, et l'autre croiserye general fait a l'evesqe de Norwiz encontre l'antipape et touz ses adherentz, complices, fautours et maintenours, /en\ quelconqe parties il les purra trover: en queux viages homme avera autiele remissione et pardoun en toutes choses come auroit en viage fait en la terre seinte. Et pur ce, seignours et sires, pur Dieux, tendrement vorrez vous adviser, et penser del salvacion de cest roialme et de vous mesmes, au fin qe l'en purra veoir qe les doutes et l'esperances devantdites, quelles vous sont ore monstrez, noun pas de cause feinee, einz de droite veritee, q'est conue a vous toutz, vous purront exciter de bien faire, qe Dieu grant pur ses mercies.

Membrane 7

14. Item, fait a remembrer qe entendue par la commune lour dite charge ils se departirent d'illoeqes vers lours place en l'abbeye de Westm', pur entrecommuner et treter pluis avant de lour charge avantdite. Mais devant q'ils \ent/ firent rienz en effect, pur tant qe lour dite charge touchast moelt haute et chargeante matire, a ce qe lour sembloit, ils firent requere as seignours de parlement, d'avoir assignez a eux en especial certains prelatz et autres seignours del roiaume, dont les nouns s'ensuent, pur communer avec eux de les charges dessuisditz, c'estassavoir, l'evesqe de Wyncestre, l'evesqe de Norwiz et l'evesqe d'Excestre, le duc de Lancastre, les conts d'Arondell', de Stafford et de Salesbirs, le seignour de Nevill', monsire Guy de Bryan, monsire Richard le Scrop'. Et celle requeste lour estoit grantez.
[14]

15. Item, les seignours et communes du roialme d'Engleterre assemblez en cest parlement apperceivantz clerement, sibien par les enchesons alleggez en la pronunciacion des causes de la somonce de cest parlement, come autrement par diligente examinacione sur ce faite, et en partie par grante experience, l'outrageouse multitude des enemys du roi nostre seignour et de son roialme avauntdit, chescune part de mesme le roialme sibien par terre come par meere, et lours grantz efforcementz de guerre qe cressent de jour en autre pluis et pluis: et d'autre part les grantz despenses qe necessairement l'en faut mettre sur le defens et salvacion de mesme le roiaume, en resistence de tantz des enemys ove l'aide \[Nostre]/ Seignour, mesmes les seignours et communes de lour liberale voluntee, combien qe ce soit ore moelt grevous charge pur eux a porter toutes choses considerez, grantent a nostre seignour le roi, sibien pur eux en cest parlement ore present, come pur tout la comminaltee, sibien c'estassavoir, et auxi avant et entierment de touz ducs, conts, barons, banerettz, chivalers et esquiers, et de toutz autres seculers seignours des manoirs, villes et autres lieux parmy le roiaume, deinz franchise et dehors, pur la quantitee et afferant de toutz lours bledz et bestaille, ou l'afferant et quantitee des profitz de

[Col. b] toutes lours demesnes terres en chescune ville et autre lieu parmy le roiaume dessuisdit, si par cas autry terres en aucunes dites villes et lieux a ce ore soient assis, come d'aucuns autres liges le roi en chescune des villes et lieux avauntdites; et en mesme le manere des profitz de toutes les terres et tenementz approprietz a mort main depuis l'an .xxme le roi Edward fitz au roi Henry parentre cy et la feste de la Purification Nostre Dame proschein venant, ou en

before the three aforesaid years are up. And we ought to be the more inclined now to act well than ever before, because of the two crusades which our holy father the pope has now declared, granted and sent for the kingdom of England, one to our lord of Spain issued in particular against his adversary of Spain, and the other crusade appointed for the bishop of Norwich against the anti-pope and all his adherents, accomplices, supporters and maintainers, wherever they be found: for which journeys people shall receive the same remission and pardon of all things as they would for a journey to the Holy Land. For this reason, lords and sirs, for love of God, may you carefully consider and ponder the security of this kingdom and yourselves, to the end that if it prove that the aforesaid fears and hopes, which have now been explained to you, are the real truth rather than of false imagination, as you all know them to be, you will be moved to do good, which God grant his mercy.

14. Also, be it remembered that the commons, having understood their said charge, departed for their session in the abbey of Westminster, to consider further and discuss their aforesaid charge. But before they did anything therein, because their said charge concerned so important and serious a matter, as it seemed to them, they requested of the lords of parliament that they might have especially assigned to them certain prelates and other lords of the kingdom to consult with them over the aforesaid charges, that is to say, the bishop of Winchester, the bishop of Norwich, the bishop of Exeter, the duke of Lancaster, the earls of Arundel, Stafford and Salisbury, Lord Neville, Sir Guy Bryan and Sir Richard le Scrope. And that request was granted them.

15. Also, the lords and commons of the kingdom of England assembled in this parliament, fully perceiving from the reasons presented for the summoning of this parliament, as well as from diligent investigation thereof, and in part from their own experience, the awful multitude of enemies of the king our lord and his aforesaid kingdom, threatening every part of the same kingdom by land and by sea, with their military strength growing greater by the day: and realizing for another thing the large amount of money which would need to be spent in the defence and security of the same kingdom, and in resisting such enemies with the aid of Our Lord, the same lords and commons, of their own free will, although it would now be a most grievous burden for them to bear, all things being considered, granted to our lord the king, on behalf of themselves now attending this parliament, as well as on behalf of all the commons, and also all the dukes, earls, barons, bannerets, knights and esquires, and all other secular lords of the manors, towns and other places throughout the kingdom, within franchises and without, according to the quantity and number of their corn and cattle, or the scale and size of their profits from

[Col. b] all their demesne lands in each town and other place throughout the aforesaid kingdom, or of such other lands and other said towns and places as shall now be assessed for this, as of other lieges of the king in each of the aforesaid towns and places; and in the same way from the profits on all the lands and tenements appropriated to mortmain since the twentieth year of King Edward, son of King Henry [1291-2], between now and the feast of the Purification of Our Lady

---

[13] *Original* deux

[14] Approximately a third of a membrane has been left blank at the end of item 14.

mesme la feste a pluis \tarde./Issint toutes voies qe autielle somme soit ore demandez, resceuz et levez, pur les dites disme et quinszime en chescune des dites villes et lieux come au derrain grant d'une disme et quinszime estoit demandez et resceue, et nemy greindre ou meindre somme, par colour de la dite taxacione issint affaire des biens des ditz seignours, a quoy ils se sont ore expressement consentuz, et l'ont voluz et grantez pur ceste foitz tantsoulement, al reverence del Dieux, et en supportacione, aide et relevement de la povre commune, laquelle lour semble est ore pluis feoble et pluis povre qe grant piece ne fuist pardevant: mais qe quanqe serra des ditz seignours levez par la dite taxacion de lours dites terres et biens tourne soulement en eide et socour a la dite commune en mesme lour charge come dite est; a avoir les dites quinszime et disme de lour doun pur emploier soulement et mettre entierment sur le defens du roialme d'Engleterre avauntdit, par quelconqe manere qe mieultz semblera a nostre seignour le roi par advis de son conseil et des autres seignours de son roiaume, toutes perils considerez, soit affaire en le cas. Et prient humblement les dites communes a nostre dit seignour le roi qe cest lour grant voille bonement prendre a gree, et lour avoir pur excusez de ce qe pluis ne lour poent charger quant au present pur lour grant povertee, et pur les autres causes dessuis alleggez.

Et est assentuz en parlement qe la grant quelle les ditz ducs, conts et barons, et autres seignours temporelx ont ore par les dites causes fait en pluis especial fourme et manere q'ils ne l'firent devant sur le grant de au tielles dismes et quinszimes es autres parlementz, ne tourne en prejudice des ditz seignours, ou soit trait en consequencie devers eux en aucun temps avenir, pur lour ent charger autrement q'ils ne soleient ou devroient de resoun.

16. Et fait a remembrer qe par certains seignours du roialme esteantz en ce parlement si furent deliverez en ce parlement les nouns de Thomas Farndon', Richard Mory, et Richard Dell, pur estre exceptz de toute grace a faire par nostre seignour le roi a ses liges de dit roiaume, come de celles persones les quelles furent principalx comenceours, abettours et procurours, de le grant et horrible rumour et insurreccione nadgairs treiterousement faitz deinz le roiaume, encontre la paix, la coroune et le dignitee nostre dit seignour le roi: et especialment principalx del arsure et destruccione del maisoun et manoirs de l'ordre Seint Johan \Jerusalem/ en Engleterre. Et est assentuz qe par tant ils soient forclos de toute grace et pardoun, et qe au tiel proces soit fait envers eux et chescun de eux come ordenez est d'estre fait envers les autres traitours qi sont semblablement exceptz de grace pur la dite cause, en parlement tenuz a Westm' lendemain des almes, l'an du regne nostre seignour le roi dessuisdit quint.[15] Et qe par celle cause lours nouns soient liverez ou envoiez par brief en bank le roi.

17. Item, Johan Hende de Londres, Johan Bataill' et Thomas Bataill', avec monsire Nicholas Dagworth', chivaler, viendrent en ce parlement, et illoeqes se submistrent haut et baas en la grace et ordinance de nostre seignour le roi et de son sage conseil, touchant la suite q'ad este faite par eux et autres de long temps del manoir de Bradwell en Essex, dont le plee est pendant nient *[Page iii-135]*

[Col. a] discus en bank le roi. Confessantz expressement illoeqes qe s'ils eussent scieuz al comencement de lour dite suite, come ils sachent de present, n'ent eussent unqes lour medlez tant avant, ny fait tiel pursuite come il ont fait. Et oultre diont q'ils sont bien contentz de faire et resceiver en

next [2 February 1383], or on the same feast at the latest. So that as much be now demanded, received and levied, for the said tenth and fifteenth in each of the said towns and places as was demanded and received at the last grant of a tenth and fifteenth, and no greater or lesser sum, by colour of the said taxation thus to be made of the goods of the said lords, to which they have now expressly consented, and which they have willed and granted for this occasion only, out of reverence for God, and in support, aid and relief of the poor commons, who seem to them at the present time to be weaker and more impoverished than ever before: although whatsoever shall be levied from the said lords by the same taxation from their said lands and goods shall be directed solely towards the aid and succour of the said commons in their same charge as has been said; to have the said fifteenth and tenth by their gift to use only and invest completely in the defence of the aforesaid kingdom of England, in whatsoever way shall seem best to our lord the king with the advice of his council and the other lords of his kingdom, all dangers considered. And the said commons humbly pray of our said lord the king that he will graciously accept this their grant and excuse them that they cannot grant him more at present because of their great poverty, and for the other reasons explained above.

And it was agreed in parliament that the grant which the said dukes, earls and barons, and other lords temporal had now made in special form and nature for the said reasons which had not been granted with the grant of these tenths and fifteenths in other parliaments, should not turn to the disadvantage of the said lords, or hold against them in time to come, as they ought not to be, and had not customarily been so charged.

16. And be it remembered that the names of Thomas Farndon, Richard Mory, and Richard Dell were submitted in this parliament by certain lords of the realm present in this parliament, to be excluded from all grace to be granted by our lord the king and his lieges of the said kingdom, as the people who were the chief instigators, abettors and procurers of the great and terrible rising and insurrection lately treacherously committed within the kingdom, contrary to the peace, crown and dignity of our said lord the king: and especially the leaders of the firing and destruction of the house and manors of the order of St John of Jerusalem in England. And it was agreed therefore that they should be barred from all grace and pardon, and that such process be brought against them and each one of them as was ordained for other such traitors who were similarly excluded from grace for the said reason, in the parliament held at Westminster on the day after All Souls, in the fifth year of the reign of our aforesaid lord the king. And that for that reason their names should be delivered or sent by writ to the King's Bench.

17. Also, John Hende of London, John Battle and Thomas Battle, together with Sir Nicholas Dagworth, knight, came to this parliament, and there they submitted themselves high and low to the grace and ordinance of our lord the king and his wise council, concerning the suit which had been brought by them and others for a long while over the manor of Bradwell in Essex, for which the plea is pending, unexamined *[Page iii-135]*

[Col. a] in the King's Bench. Openly confessing there that if they had known at the beginning of their suit, what they knew now, they would never have involved themselves as much as they did, nor have brought such a suit as they did. Furthermore, they said that they were fully content to do and

---

[15] Parliament of 1381, item 63.

celle partie quanqe nostre dit seignour le roi, par l'advis de son noble conseil, en vorra ordiner.

18. Et est assavoir qe de l'assent des prelatz, seignours et autres de conseil le roi esteantz en ce parlement, nostre seignour le roi de sa grace especial, et par fin de mille marcz, ad grantez et fait sa chartre de pardoun as citezeins d'Everwik general, de toutes maneres de treisons, felonies, trespasses et autres mesprisions par manere come pluis pleinement appiert en la dite chartre /q'est\ enrollez en cest parlement.[16]

19. Item, semblablement ad grantez une autre chartre general a les burgeys et commune de Scardeburgh', horspris Robert Acclom et Robert de Rillyngton', par fyn de .ix.^{c} marz; dont la commune doit paier .iiij.^{c} marz par eux mesmes, /et\ .xl. persones des mieultz vanez burgeys de mesme la ville, dont les nouns sont expressez en lour dite chartre, q'est auxint enrolle en mesme cest parlement, doivent paier par soi mesmes les residuez cynk centz marz. Et auxint le roi ad grantez a chescun des ditz Robert Acclom' et Robert de Rillyngton, par severals fyns par eux affaires a nostre seignour le roi, chartres de pardoun.

Item, le roi ad grantez, de l'assent avauntdit, as burgeis et la comminaltee de Beverley, horspris Thomas de Beverlee, Richard son fitz, /Richard\ de Botston, Johan Treylle, Johan Materesmaker, de Beverley, Thomas de Ireland, Roger Coupere, Thomas Fynell', Johan de Holyme \et/ Thomas Gue, de Beverley, /autrement\ appellez Thomas Greue, par fin de .xl.^{c} marz, une autre chartre general de la forme des autres chartres d'Everwik' et de Scardeburgh', mutatis mutandis. Item, par fin de .x. marz le roi, de sa grace et del assent avauntdit, ad grante a Adam Perkyn de Housom chartre de pardoun pur la mort William Clerc de Wynstowe, tuez le dymenge en la feste de l'Exaltacion le Seinte Crois derrain passe.

Item, a William, fitz Johan Pert, chivaler, par fin de .x.$li.$ chartre de pardon general, c'estassavoir, pur toutes maneres de treisons, murdres, felonies, trespasses et mesprisions, par lui faites, etc.

Item, a Rauf, fitz Johan de Aston, par un autre fin, chartre de pardon pur la mort Anneys nadgairs sa femme, tuez le lundy proschein devaunt la feste de Seint Pere ad Vincula derrain passe, en Aghton wode. Et fait a remembrer qe les seignours de cest parlement s'accorderent et voilloient, qe combien qe nostre dit seignour le roi, de lour dit assent, par les ditz fins ad ore fait les dites pardons, pur certeins enchesons especialment lui moevantz, toutes voies ne soit ce jamais tret en ensample ou consequencie.

Membrane 6

20. Rex omnibus ballivis etc, salutem. Sciatis quod de gracia nostra speciali, ac de assensu magnatum et procerum nobis in presenti parliamento nostro assistentium, pardonavimus civibus civitatis nostre Ebor', et eorum cuilibet, sectam pacis nostre et quicquid ad nos pertinet, pro omnimodis insurrectionibus, proditionibus, seditionibus, obsidionibus, mulierum raptibus, homicidiis, murdris, feloniis, roberiis, latrociniis, incendiis, transgressionibus, mesprisionibus, contemptibus, rebellionibus, inobedientiis, extorsionibus, duriciis, oppressionibus, confederationibus,

[Col. b] conspiracionibus, cambipartiis, ambidextriis, forstallariis, regratariis, falsitatibus, decepcionibus, congregacionibus illicitis, alligantiis, conventiculis, manutenenciis et quibuscumque aliis malefactis, dampnis, graviaminibus et excessibus, nobis aut progenitoribus nostris, seu quibuscumque ligeis nostris vel progenitorum nostrorum per prefatos cives, seu eorum aliquem, tam infra civitatem

---
[16] See below, item 20.

receive in this matter whatever our said lord the king, by the advice of his noble council, would wish to ordain.

18. Be it known that, with the assent of the prelates, lords and others of the king's counsel attending this parliament, our lord the king, of his special grace, and for a fine of a thousand marks, granted and issued a charter of pardon to the citizens of York in general, of all manner of treasons, felonies, trespasses and other offences as appears more fully in the said charter itself, which is enrolled in this parliament.

19. Also, he granted similarly another general charter to the burgesses and commons of Scarborough, excepting Robert Acclom and Robert Rillington, for a fine of nine hundred marks; of which the commons were to pay four hundred marks themselves, and forty of the most prosperous burgesses of the same town, whose names are recorded in the said charter, which is enrolled in this same parliament, were to pay the remaining five hundred marks themselves. In addition, the king granted charters of pardon to both the said Robert Acclom and Robert Rillington, for several fines paid by them to our lord the king.

Also, the king granted, with the aforesaid consent, to the burgesses and community of Beverley, excepting Thomas Beverley, Richard his son, Richard Botston, John Treylle, John Matressmaker, of Beverley, Thomas of Ireland, Roger Cooper, Thomas Fynelle, John Holyme and Thomas Gue, of Beverley, otherwise known as Thomas Greue, for a fine of 4,000 marks, another general charter in the form of the other charters of York and Scarborough, mutatis mutandis. Also, for a fine of ten marks the king, of his grace and with the aforesaid consent, granted to Adam Perkin of Howsham a charter of pardon of the death of William Clerk of Wistow, killed on the Sunday of the feast of the Exaltation of the Holy Cross last past [14 September 1382].

Also, to William, son of John Pert, knight, for a fine of £10, a general charter of pardon, namely of all kinds of treason, murders, felonies, trespasses and offences committed by him, etc.

Also, to Ralph son of John Aston, for another fine, a charter of pardon of the death of Anneys late his wife, killed on the Monday before the feast of St Peter ad vincula last past [28 July 1382], in Aughton wood. And be it remembered that the lords of this parliament agreed and wished that although our said lord the king, with their said assent, had granted the said pardons for the said fines and for particular reasons influencing him, it should in no way be treated as an example or precedent.

20. The king to all bailiffs etc, greeting. Know that, of our special grace, and with the assent of our magnates and nobles attending our present parliament, we have pardoned the citizens of our city of York, and every one of them, the suit of our peace and whatsoever pertains to us, for all insurrections, treasons, seditions, sieges, rapes of women, homicides, murders, felonies, robberies, thefts, fires, trespasses, misdeeds, contempts, rebellions, disobedience, extortion, harshness, duress, confederacies,

[Col. b] conspiracies, collusions, ambidexterities, forestallings, regratings, frauds, deceptions, unlawful assemblies, oaths, conventicles, maintenance and whatsoever other offences, injuries, damages and excesses, committed, inflicted or otherwise perpetrated against us or our progenitors, or upon any of our lieges and their progenitors by the aforesaid citizens, or any one of them, both within our aforesaid

nostram predictam quam extra ubicumque, ante festum Exaltacionis Sancte Crucis proxime preteritum factis, illatis, aut quomodolibet perpetratis, aut etiam pro omnibus et singulis articulis unde coram justiciariis nostris vel heredum nostrorum itinerantibus inquisicio fieri debeat vel possit in futuro, unde indictati, rectati, vel appellati, vel alias qualitercumque impetiti, seu occasionati existunt, sive molestari aut occasionari poterunt in futuro: ac etiam utlagariis, si que in ipsos seu eorum aliquem hiis occasionibus fuerint promulgate, et firmam pacem nostram eis et eorum cuilibet inde concedimus, ita quod stent recto in curia nostra si qui versus eos seu eorum aliquem loqui voluerint de premissis, seu aliquo premissorum. Pardonavimus etiam eisdem omnibus et eorum cuilibet omnimodas forisfacturas que erga nos occasionibus premissis qualitercumque post dictum festum Exaltacionis Sancte Crucis incurrebant, seu quovis modo erga nos vel heredes nostros incurrere poterunt in futuro. Pardonavimus eisdem civibus et eorum cuilibet omnimodas traducciones lanarum, corriorum, pellium lanutarum ac aliarum rerum et mercandisarum quarumcumque ad quascumque partes transmarinas, seu ad partes Scocie, absque custuma seu subsidio inde solutis, seu contra prohibicionem et defensionem nostram seu progenitorum nostrorum, ac quascumque traductiones et asportaciones cujuscumque monete auri et argenti, ac plate, vel masse, sive jocalium ad /predictas partes\ transmarinas, vel Scocie, necnon quascumque ductiones seu portaciones cujuscumque monete de Scocia in regnum nostrum Anglie, contra hujusmodi prohibicionem \et defensionem,/ ante festum Exaltacionis Sancte Crucis predictum factas, et quascumque forisfacturas quas erga nos occasionibus predictis post festum illud incurrebant, vel nobis seu heredibus nostris inde pertinere poterunt in futuro. Pardonavimus insuper eisdem civibus et eorum cuilibet quoscumque fines, redempciones et amerciamenta coram carissimo avunculo nostro Johanne, rege Castelle et Legion' duce Lancastr', et sociis suis justiciariis nostris ad insurrecciones, prodiciones, sediciones, obsidiones, felonias, transgressiones et alia malefacta in comitatu Eborum, tam infra libertates quam extra, audiendum et terminandum assignandis, quibuscumque de causis, post idem festum Exaltacionis Sancte Crucis facta. Ac eciam quoscumque exitus coram eisdem justiciariis hiis occasionibus post idem festum forisfactos seu adjudicatos, vel exnunc forisfiendos vel adjudicandos. Et insuper, cum diversi majores, et alii cives dite civitatis, et eorum antecessores seu predecessores, in diversis pecuniarum summis per eorum diversas recogniciones, tam in cancellarum nostra quam in cancellarum progenitorum nostrorum, et alibi coram justiciariis et judicibus nostris et progenitorum nostrorum, tam pro seipsis quam pro aliis diversis personis, sub certis condicionibus tam de pace gerenda quam aliis pluribus et diversis condicionibus inde limitatis, nobis et progenitoribus nostris ante hec tempora obligati fuerint, pardonavimus et remisimus eisdem civibus, et eorum cuilibet, omnes et singulas hujusmodi summas per ipsos majores et cives, seu eorum aliquem, antecessores vel predecessores suos, nobis, vel progenitoribus nostris, ante vicesimum septimum diem Februarii proxime preteritum qualitercumque recognitas, et execuciones earundem recognicionum, sive recogniciones ille sub condicionibus, sive simpliciter facte fuerint, ac eciam /quascumque\ condiciones, manucapciones et assumpciones, quas ipsi vel eorum aliquis super recognicionibus illis, et racione earundem recognicionum, debebant vel tenebantur, seu debent vel tenentur, et ipsos cives et eorum quemlibet, ac eorum heredes, executores et terre tenentes, de omnibus et singulis summis simpliciter vel condicionaliter ante dictum

city as well as anywhere without, before the feast of the Exaltation of the Holy Cross last past [14 September 1382], and also for each and every article upon which inquest ought to or could be held in the future in the presence of our itinerant justices or our heirs, whereof they stand indicted, adjudged or accused, or otherwise charged, or molested, or may, in future, be vexed or troubled: and also outlawries if such were proclaimed against them on any one of them on those grounds, and we have granted our firm peace to them and each one of them, provided that they stand trial in our court if any wish to plead against them or one of them concerning the aforesaid or any of the aforesaid. Also, we have pardoned each and every one of them all manner of forfeitures which they may have incurred towards us on the aforesaid grounds in any way, after the said feast of the Exaltation of the Holy Cross [14 September 1382], or might in any way incur towards us or our heirs in future. We have pardoned the same citizens and each one of them for all kinds of exports of wool, hides, woolfells, and other items and merchandise whatsoever overseas, or into the parts of Scotland, without customs or the subsidy paid on them, or contrary to our prohibition or proscription or that of our progenitors, and for all exports and imports of any gold or silver money and plate, or bullion, or jewels to the aforesaid parts overseas, or Scotland, and also for any bringing or carrying of Scottish money into our kingdom of England, contrary to such prohibition and proscription, done before the aforesaid feast of the Exaltation of the Holy Cross [14 September 1382], and of any forfeitures which they incurred towards us on the aforesaid grounds after that feast, or which might pertain to us and our heirs in the future. We have also pardoned those citizens and every one of them any fines, redemptions and amercements adjudged before our beloved uncle John, king of Castile and Leon, duke of Lancaster, and his companions our justices assigned to hear and determine insurrections, treasons, seditions, sieges, felonies, trespasses and other offences committed in the county of York, within liberties as without, for whatever reasons, after that same feast of the Exaltation of the Holy Cross [14 September 1382]. And also any issues forfeited or adjudged before the same justices on these grounds after the same feast, or yet to be forfeited or adjudged. And further, since various great men and other citizens of the said city, and their ancestors and predecessors, were bound to us and our progenitors before this time for various sums of money through their recognizances, both in our chancery and in the chanceries of our progenitors, and elsewhere before our justices and judges and those of our progenitors, both on their own account as well as for various other persons, upon certain conditions both for the keeping of peace as well as numerous other conditions specified, we have pardoned and remitted these citizens, and every one of them, each and every one of the sums nominated in any way by those great men and citizens, or any of them, or of their ancestors or predecessors, to us, or our progenitors, before 27 February last [1382], and executions of the same recognizances, whether of recognizances made on certain conditions, or simple, and also any conditions, mainprises or undertakings, which they or any one of them owed or were bound by concerning those recognizances, and by reason of the same, or might be so obliged, and by the tenor of these presents we acquit and exonerate in perpetuity each and every one of these citizens, and their heirs, executors and assigns, from all sums simply or conditionally recognized before the said 27 February, and from all manner of

vicesimum septimum diem Februarii sic recognitis, ac quibuscumque condicionibus, manucapcionibus et assumpcionibus super hiis qualitercumque habitis vel limitatis erga nos *[Page iii-136]*

[Col. a] et heredes nostros, tenore presencium acquietamus et exoneramus imperpetuum. Ipsas insuper recogniciones ante eundem vicesimum septimum diem Februarii factas, ut predictum est, et earum quamlibet, ubicumque repperte vel contra dictos cives seu eorum aliquem in futuro allegate fuerint in judicio sive extra, nullius de cetero decernimus esse vigoris seu virtutis. Ac insuper, pro ipsorum civium et eorum cujuslibet majori securitate et quiete, volumus et concedimus pro nobis et heredibus nostris, quod predicti cives, seu eorum aliquis, ratione seu colore vel occasione aliquarum hujusmodi insurreccionum, proditionum, sedicionum, obsidionum, mulierum raptuum, homicidiorum, murdrorum, feloniarum, roberiarum, latrociniorum, incendiorum, transgressionum, mesprisionum, contemptuum, rebellionum, inobedienciarum, extorsionum, duriciarum, oppressionum, confederacionum, conspiracionum, cambipartiarum, ambidextriarum, forstalliarum, regratariarum, falsitatum, decepcionum, congregacionum, alliganciarum, conventiculorum, manutenenciarum, seu quorumcumque aliorum malefactorum, dampnorum, gravaminum vel excessuum, nobis seu progenitoribus aut ligeis nostris, vel progenitorum nostrorum qualitercumque ante predictum festum, tam infra civitatem nostram predictam quam extra, ubicumque factorum vel perpetratorum, seu aliquarum forisfacturarum predictarum, seu aliquorum articulorum coram justiciariis nostris vel heredum nostrorum /itinerantibus\ Inquirendorum, aut occasione aliquarum traduccionum lanarum, coriorum, seu pellium lanutarum, aut aliarum rerum vel mercandisarum, sive monete, plate vel masse auri vel argenti, seu jocalium, ad aliquas partes transmarinas, seu ad partes Scotie, aut duccionis vel portacionis monete de Scocia in regnum nostrum Anglie, aut etiam occasione finium, redempcionum, amerciamentorum, seu exituum predictorum, vel eciam occasione aliquarum recognicionum de aliquibus pecuniarum summis, per ipsos cives seu eorum aliquem, seu eorum antecessores seu predecessores, aut aliquos majores vel cives ejusdem civitatis vivos seu defunctos ante dictum vicesimum septimum diem Februarii factarum, seu aliquarum condicionum, manucapcionum, seu assumpcionum, licet hujusmodi condiciones, manucapciones vel assumpciones complete fuerint sive non; aut heredes vel executores sive terre tenentes ipsorum civium defunctorum sive superstitum vel eorum alicujus, per nos vel heredes nostros nullatenus impetantur, occasionentur, molestentur in aliquo, seu graventur, nec inde trahantur in responsum aut judicium in curia nostra, coram nobis, seu cancellario nostro vel heredum nostrorum, aut coram aliquibus justiciariis, seu aliis judicibus, vel ministris nostris, seu heredum nostrorum in futuro, set omnino inde sint quieti et exonerati, et quilibet eorum inde sit quietus et exoneratus imperpetuum per presentes. Et ut omnibus et singulis ligeis et fidelibus nostris quorum interest de premissis omnibus et singulis plenarie patefiat, et ut singuli cives ejusdem civitatis, et quelibet persona eorundem, per se presenti pardonatione nostra gaudeant et gaudeat secure atque clare, de gracia nostra speciali, et ex concensu et assensu et voluntate magnatum et procerum predictorum, volumus et concedimus pro nobis et heredibus nostris quod presens pardonatio nostra generalis de omnibus et singulis in presentibus literis nostris contentis talis et tanti vigoris, virtutis et valoris existat, et tantum proficiat et valeat omnibus et singulis civibus nostris predictis,

conditions, mainprises and undertakings held or specified therein towards us *[Page iii-136]*

[Col. a] and our heirs. Moreover, those recognizances, made before the same 27 February, as said above, and every one of them, wheresoever they shall be found or alleged against the said citizens or any one of them in the future, in judgment or otherwise, we henceforth shall not hold to be of any force or validity. Furthermore, for the greater peace and security of those citizens and every one of them, we will and grant for us and our heirs that neither the aforesaid citizens, nor any of them, by reason, colour or occasion of any such insurrections, treasons, seditions, sieges, rapes of women, homicides, murders, felonies, robberies, thefts, fires, trespasses, misdeeds, contempts, rebellions, disobedience, extortion, duress, oppressions, confederacies, conspiracies, collusions, ambidexterities, forestallings, regratings, frauds, deceptions, gatherings, oaths, conventicles, maintenance, or any other misdeeds, injuries, damages or excesses, wheresoever committed or perpetrated against us or our progenitors or our lieges or their progenitors in whatever way before the aforesaid feast, both within our aforesaid city and outside, or of other aforesaid forfeitures, or of other articles to be investigated before our itinerant justices and those of our heirs, or upon the occasion of any exports of wool, hides or woolfells, or other items or merchandise, whether money, plate, gold or silver bullion, or jewels, to any parts overseas or to Scotland, or the bringing or carrying of Scottish money into our kingdom of England, or moreover, on the occasion of the aforesaid fines, redemptions, amercements, or issues, or also on the grounds of any recognizances of any sums of money made by these citizens or any one of them, or their ancestors or predecessors, or other great men or citizens of the same city, alive or dead before the said 27 February, or any conditions, mainprises or undertakings, whether such conditions, mainprises or undertakings shall have been completed or not; nor shall the heirs, executors or assigns of such dead or living citizens or any one of them be attached, harassed or molested in any way on account of anything by us or our heirs, nor grieved, nor brought to answer or judgment in our court, before us, or the chancellor of us or our heirs, or before any of our justices, judges, or ministers, or those of our heirs in future, but shall be entirely quit and exonerated, and every one of them shall be quit and exonerated thereof in perpetuity by these presents. And that each and every one of our lieges and faithful men whom this concerns shall be fully apprised of all the aforesaid matters, and that all citizens of this city and every person amongst them, shall openly rejoice on account of our present pardon, by our special grace, and with the consent, assent and wish of the aforesaid magnates and lord, we will and concede for us and our heirs that our present general pardon of each and every one contained in our present letters shall be of such force, validity and value, that it shall benefit and hold for each and every one of our aforesaid citizens, and particular individuals amongst the same, and if any individual from amongst the aforesaid citizens wishes, he shall have and obtain particular, separate letters from us of our present pardon. Nevertheless we do not wish and neither is it our intention that anyone who was especially excluded by name in our parliaments of the fifth and sixth years of our reign, nor any such, shall be included in the present pardon, nor regain our grace by colour of these

et cuilibet speciali et singulari persone eorundem per se, ac si quelibet persona specialis vel singularis predictorum civium per se speciales et separales literas nostras de presenti pardonacione nostra penes se haberet vel optineret. Nolumus tamen nec intencionis nostre existit quod persone quarum nomina in parliamentis nostris annis regni nostri quinto et sexto in speciali excepta fuerunt, nec ipsarum personarum aliqua, in presenti pardonacione nostra comprehendantur, nec gratiam inde colore presentium reportent quovis modo. In cujus, etc. Teste rege apud Westm' .xviij. die Octobris. Per ipsum regem et consilium in parliamento, et per finem mille marcarum in quibus major et communitas dicte civitatis per scriptum suum sub

[Col. b] communi sigillo suo obligantur, unde quingentas marcas solverunt, et quingentas marcas in festo Pasche proximo futuro solvent.

21. Rex omnibus ballivis etc, salutem. Sciatis quod de gracia nostra speciali, ac de assensu magnatum et procerum nobis in presenti parliamento nostro assistencium, pardonavimus burgensibus et communitati ville nostre de Scardeburgh' in comitatu Ebor', et eorum cuilibet, exceptis specialiter Henr' de Ruston', seniori, Johanne de Rillyngton', Johanne de /Wawyn,\ Willelmo de Shropham, Roberto Paa, Johanne de Stokwith', Johanne de Brun', Willelmo Sage, Johanne de Barton', Johanne de Morsham, seniori, Willelmo Carter, Alano Waldyff', Johanne de Acclom, Henr' de Ruston', juniori, Willelmo Scot, Ricardo de Shropham, Willelmo Percy, Johanne Coroner, Ricardo Colman, Thoma del Lane, Petro Wistowe, Johanne de Seterington', Johanne Coke, Ricardo Couper, Reginaldo Gerrard, Thoma Sergeant, Thoma Peke, Adam Clerc, Adam Seterington', Johanne de Scalby, Thoma de Brun, Johanne Page, Willelmo de Novo Castro, Hugone de Barton', Willelmo Manby, Ricardo del Kechin, Henr' Wresill', Roberto Erll', Rogero Baxster, Thoma Maldson de Whallesgrave, Roberto Acclom' et Roberto Rillyngton, de dicta villa de Scardeburgh', sectam pacis nostre, et quicquid ad nos pertinet, pro omnimodis insurrectionibus, etc., ut supra usque hic, - exnunc forisfaciendos vel adjudicandos, - mutatis mutandis; et tunc sic,- Ac insuper pro ipsorum burgensium, et communitatis, et eorum cujuslibet, exceptis semper preexceptis, majori securitate et quiete volumus, etc.,-ut supra, usque hic,- seu exituum predictorum et tunc sic,- aut heredes, vel executores, sive terre tenentes ipsorum burgensium et communitatis defunctorum sive superstitum, etc., ut supra mutatis mutandis, usque hic,-imperpetuum per presentes - et tunc sic,-Volentes insuper eisdem burgensibus et communitati /gratiam\ In hac parte facere ampliorem, concessimus eisdem, et eorum cuilibet, exceptis prexceptis, omnia bona et catalla sua que nobis racione cujuscumque prodicionis, felonie, transgressionis, vel alterius mesprisionis, per ipsos vel eorum aliquem in insurrectione seu rumore ibidem anno regni nostri suborte, ut dicitur, facte seu quomodolibet perpetrate, dici poterunt forisfacta; ac bona et catalla, illa eciam, si ipsi vel eorum aliquis ex hac causa fugam fecerint, integre restituimus, et restitui volumus eisdem. Et ut omnibus et singulis ligeis et fidelibus nostris quorum interest, etc., ut supra. In cujus, etc. Teste ut supra.[17]

18

Membrane 5

22. Item, coment q'autre foitz estoit ordenez en parlement qe l'estaple des leins, quirs et peaulx lanutz serroit tenuz a Caleys, et nul part aillours hors du roialme,[19] nientmeins pur

presents in any way. In testimony of which, etc. Witnessed by the king at Westminster 18 October [1382].

By the king and council in parliament, and for a fine of one thousand marks to which the mayor and community of the said town bound themselves in a document under

[Col. b] their common seal, of which they have paid five hundred marks, and shall pay five hundred marks at Easter next [22 March 1383].

21. The king to all bailiffs, etc., greeting. Know that, of our special grace, and with the assent of our magnates and nobles attending our present parliament, we have pardoned the burgesses and community of our town of Scarborough in the county of York, and every one of them, with the particular exceptions of Henry Ruston, the elder, John Rillington, John Wawyn, William Shropham, Robert Paa, John Stokwith, John Brown, William Sage, John Barton, John Morsham, the elder, William Carter, Alan Waldiff, John Acclom, Henry Ruston, the younger, William Scot, Richard Shropham, William Percy, John Coroner, Richard Colman, Thomas Lane, Peter Wistowe, John Seterington, John Coke, Richard Cooper, Reginald Gerrard, Thomas Sergeant, Thomas Peek, Adam Clerk, Adam Seterington, John Scalby, Thomas Brown, John Page, William Newcastle, Hugh Barton, William Manby, Richard Kechin, Henry Wresill, Robert Earl, Roger Baxter, Thomas Maldson of Whallesgrave, Robert Acclom and Robert Rillington, of the said town of Scarborough, of the suit of our peace, and whatsoever pertains to us, for all kinds of insurrections, etc., as above, thus far - yet to be forfeited or adjudged - mutatis mutandis; and then thus, - and also for those burgesses and community, and every one of them, excepting always those excepted above, for greater security and peace we will, etc., - as above, thus far, - or the issues of the aforesaid, and then thus, - or the heirs, or executors, or assigns of those burgesses and community, whether dead or living, etc., as above, mutatis mutandis, thus far, - in perpetuity through these present letters, thus - and then thus, - wishing further to grant more ample grace in the matter to the same burgesses and community, we have conceded to the same and every one of them, excepting those previously excepted, all goods and chattels forfeited to us by reason of whatsoever treason, felony, transgression or other offences, committed or in any way perpetrated by them or any one of them during the insurrection or uprising which occurred in the same year of our reign, as it was said; and moreover we have fully restored and shall have restored such goods and chattels, if they or any of them fled for that reason. And that each and every one of our lieges and faithful men whom this concerns, etc., as above. In testimony of which, etc. Witnessed as above [18 October 1382].

22. Also, although on another occasion it was ordained in parliament that the staple of wool, hides and woolfells should be held at Calais and nowhere else outside the realm,

---

[17] *CPR 1381-5*, 209.
[18] The rest of m.6 has been left blank.
[19] 36 Edw.3 stat.1 c. 7.

le grant bien et profit qe, si Dieux plest, aviendra a nostre seignour le roi et a tout son roialme d'Engleterre, parmye le traitee q'en partie a este comenciez, et qe proscheinement serra tenuz parentre nostre seignour le roi et les Flamentz sur certains articles touchez pur commune profit de l'un et de l'autre paiis, est assentuz et accordez en ce parlement qe par cause de mesme le traitee homme puisse remeuer la dite estaple hors de mesme la ville de Caleys, et le faire metter en autre ville et /lieu\ covenable: et enoultre par celle cause faire tielles ordinances des leins et autres marchandises de l'estaple come mieultz semblera a nostre seignour le roi et son conseil de faire en le cas, pur commune profit del dit roialme, et salvacione des marchandises avauntdites, nient contreesteant aucune ordinance ou grant faite au contraire devant ceste heure.

23. Item, sur le profre qe a diverses foitz a este fait es parlementz par monsire d'Espaigne, duc de Lancastre, et ore par le dit duc rehercez en ce parlement devant les prelats et seignours, c'estassavoir, d'aler en *[Page iii-137]*

[Col. a] Espaigne avec deux mille hommes d'armes, et atantz des archers, as gaiges le roi nostre seignour pur demy an, et dubble reward, dont la somme totale \oultre lour eskippesoun/ amonteret bien entour .xliij. mille livres d'esterlings; de la quelle somme, ou en monoie ou en servise, le dit duc vorroit faire repaiement deinz trois ans proschein apres son alee, si einsi feust qe Dieux lui donast si longement la vie, et feust si longement a large de son corps hors de prisone, et arrivast a salvatee de lui et de ses gentz depar dela. Et enoultre, sur ceste profre demande et questione fait as prelatz, conts, barons et banerettz, esteantz en ce parlement, sibien en general come severalment, c'estassavoir, si lour semblast celle viage ore affaire en Espaigne par le dit duc avec le nombre des gentz avauntdites, feust profitable pur nostre

[Col. b] seignour le roi et son roialme d'Engleterre, ou nemye. Mesmes les prelatz, contz, barons et bacheliers respondirent qe si plest a nostre seignour le roi, lour semblast tout a certain qe aiant regard sibien al socours et rescous des nobles seignours et autres gentz Engleys q'ores sont en celles marches, come autrement a ce qe homme pense al aide nostre seignour de mettre celle guerre a hastive et bon fin, /et\ par consequens le pluis tost et le pluis aisement les autres; qe celle viage d'Espaigne si feust profitable et honurable au roi et a son roialme avantdit, par manere come le dit profre purporte. Purveuz toutes voies qe le dit duc y voise assez fort des gentz et d'autres apparaillementz de guerre; qar lour semble qe la nombre des gentz demande si est assez petit pur faire guerre a si forte roialme.

Membrane 4

YCY S'ENSUENT LES PETICIONS BAILLEZ AVANT EN CEST PARLEMENT PAR LA COMMUNE D'ENGLETERRE, AVEC LES RESPONSES DONEZ ET FAITES ILLOEQES PAR NOSTRE SEIGNOUR LE ROY, DE L'ADVIS DES PRELATZ, SEIGNOURS ET AUTRES DE SON CONSEILLE, ESTEANTZ EN DIT PARLEMENT.

24. A nostre trespuissant et tresredoute seignour nostre seignour le roi, et a son tresnoble conseil, prelatz et autres seignours en cest present parlement tenuz a Westm' le lundy en les oetaves de Seint Michel, l'an du regne nostre dit seignour le roy sisme, supplient voz humbles communes pur les peticions dessouz escriptz:

---

nevertheless, for the great good and profit which, if it please God, shall befall our lord the king and all his kingdom of England, through the treaty which is begun in part, and which shall shortly be made between our lord the king and the Flemings over certain articles touching the mutual benefit of both countries, it is assented and agreed in this parliament that by reason of the same treaty, the said staple may be transferred out of the same town of Calais, and put in another suitable town and place: and further, for that reason, to make such ordinances concerning wool and other merchandise of the staple as shall seem best to our lord the king and his council in those circumstances, for the common profit of the said kingdom, and the preservation of the aforesaid merchandise, notwithstanding any ordinance or grant made to the contrary in the past.

23. Also, concerning the offer which has been made on various occasions in parliaments by monsire of Spain, the duke of Lancaster, and now offered by word of mouth by the said duke in this parliament before the prelates and lords, namely to go to *[Page iii-137]*

[Col. a] Spain with two thousand men-at-arms, and as many archers, at the wages of the king our lord for half a year, and double reward, the sum total of which, over and above their transportation, amounts to almost £43,000 pounds sterling; which sum, the said duke would repay within three years of his going, either in money or in service, if God thus grants him a life so long, and if he remains free from imprisonment for so long a time, and returns safely with his men from overseas. Furthermore, the prelates, earls, barons and bannerets attending this parliament were asked and questioned, both together and individually, whether it seemed to them that the expedition now to be made to Spain by the said duke with the aforesaid number of men, would prove profitable to our

[Col. b] lord the king and his kingdom of England, or not. The same prelates, earls, barons and noblemen answered that if it pleased our lord the king, it seemed certain to them that bearing in mind both the succour and rescue of the noble lords and other English people who are now in those marches, and as an aid to our lord by bringing that war to a swift and hasty conclusion, and in consequence more swiftly and readily concluding the others; that the expedition to Spain would be profitable and honourable to the king and his aforesaid kingdom, in the manner outlined in the said proposal. Provided always that the said duke was well enough prepared with men and other equipment of war; since it seems to them that the number of men requested was too small to wage war against so strong a kingdom.

HERE FOLLOW THE PETITIONS SUBMITTED TO THIS PARLIAMENT BY THE COMMONS OF ENGLAND, TOGETHER WITH THE ANSWERS GIVEN AND MADE THERE BY OUR LORD THE KING, WITH THE ADVICE OF THE PRELATES, LORDS AND OTHERS OF HIS COUNCIL ATTENDING THE SAID PARLIAMENT.

24. To our most exalted and redoubtable lord our lord the king, and his most noble council, the prelates, and other lords in this present parliament held at Westminster on Monday the octave of Michaelmas, in the sixth year of the reign of our said lord the king [6 October 1382], your humble commons request your favour for the petitions written below:

I. [Confirmation of liberties, charters, and statutes.]

En primes supplient voz ditz communes qe seinte esglise eit et enjoise toutes ses libertees et franchises, et qe la grande chartre, la chartre de la foreste, l'estatut des purveours et les autres bons estatutz et ordinances avant ces heures faitz, soient tenuz et gardez, et duement executz selonc l'effect d'icelles.

Responsio.

Le roi le voet.[20]

II. [Actions of debt, etc., to be pleaded in the county where the contract was made.]

25. Item, prient les communes: qe si homme porte sur autre brief d'appele \de/ felonie, de trespas, de dette, ou de queconqe cause, en un forein countee ou le fait n'estoit fait, ne le defendour n'est demurrant, n'ad possession des terres, tenementz, rents, ne chateaux, par queux il poet estre garniz ne destreint, qe le dit proces poet estre adnulle, et le pursuour et les conspiratours puissent porter mesme la peyne qe le defendour deust porter en cas q'il feust pursuy a l'exigende, ou al utlagarie, par la dite suite. Et soit trie par enqueste, la moitee del un countee et l'autre moitee de l'autre countee ou le fait fuist fait, et sur ce donez juggement. Et soit grante auxibien pur les plees pendantz, come pur les plees avenirs.

Responsio.

/Le roi voet qe si desore homme port brief de dette, d'accompte, de detenue ou d'autres tieles actions, et en plee pledant face son countee de contract fait en autre countee\ qe le brief n'est porte, qe maintenant brief s'abate.[21]

III. [Actions on writ of nuisance viscontel to be heard at the election of the plaintiff.]

26. Item, prient les communes: qe come juggement soit done en courte le roi pur le pleintif en briefs d'anusance viscontels, come des mures, ou mesons, et autres semblables levez en anusance d'aucuny, et l'execucione faite par le viscont, les tenantz ou defendantz lendemain apres l'execucione faite relevent ou font tielx anusances

[Col. b] en mesmes les villes, et autre remede n'est done sinoun de recomencer novel brief, et sic infinitum: quel est grant meschief et delaye pur le pleintif, qar tieux juggementz en courte le roi preignent nul effect.

Si plest a nostre dit seignour le roi, en les dites cas d'anusance, et lour semblables, grantir assises d'anusance, terminables pardevant justices d'assises ou autres justices come autres assises d'anusance et reddisseisine auxi, si meister y soit.

Responsio.

Il plest au roi qe toutes tielx briefs soient al eleccione du pleintif faites et prises en nature d'assises devant les justices del un bank ou del autre, ou devant les justices d'assises.[22]

IIII. [Where no English ships are available, ships of other friendly powers may be used.]

27. Item, prient les communes: qe come en le derrain parlement estoit fait estatut qe nul lige nostre seignour le roi deusse eskipper nule marchandise as parties de dela, ne d'illoeqes en Engleterre, sinoun es vesselx des liges nostre dit seignour; a comencer mesme l'ordinance a la feste de

I. [Confirmation of liberties, charters, and statutes.]

First, your said commons pray that holy church may have and enjoy all its liberties and franchises, and that the Great Charter, the Charter of the Forest, the Statute of Purveyors, and the other good statutes and ordinances made in the past, be upheld and preserved, and duly enforced in accordance with the tenor of the same.

Answer.

The king wills it.

II. [Actions of debt, etc., to be pleaded in the county where the contract was made.]

25. Also, the commons pray: that if a man brings a writ of appeal against another for felony, trespass, debt, or any other cause, in a county where the deed was not done, or where the defendant is not dwelling, and has no lands, tenements, rents or chattels, with which he can be summoned or distrained, that the said process be annulled, and the suitor and his abettors suffer the same penalty which the defendant would have suffered in a cause in which he had been taken to exigent or outlawry, by the said suit. And let it be tried by inquest, half by one county and half by the other where the deed was done, and judgment delivered thereon. And let it be granted as well for pending pleas, as for pleas to come.

Answer.

The king wills that if, henceforth, anyone brings a writ of debt, account, detinue or other such actions, and in pleading the plea gives an account of a contract made in another county where the writ was not brought, that the writ shall be immediately annulled.

III. [Actions on writ of nuisance viscontel to be heard at the election of the plaintiff.]

26. Also, the commons pray: whereas judgment is given in the king's court in favour of the plaintiff in sheriffs' writs of nuisance, as of walls, houses or the like built to the annoyance of any, and execution is made by the sheriff, the day after such execution, the tenants or defendants rebuild or cause similar nuisances

[Col. b] in the same towns, and no other remedy is provided than reissuing the writ, and thus it never ends: which causes great trouble and delay to the plaintiff, since such judgments in the king's court take no effect.

May it please our said lord the king, in the said cases of nuisance, and the like, to grant assizes of nuisance, determinable before justices of assizes, or other justices as well as other assizes of nuisance and redisseisin, if need be.

Answer.

It is pleasing to the king that all such writs, at the decision of the plaintiff, be issued and held in the nature of assizes before the justices of the one Bench or the other, or before the justices of the assizes.

IIII. [Where no English ships are available, ships of other friendly powers may be used.]

27. Also, the commons pray: whereas in the last parliament a statute was made that no liege of our lord the king should ship any merchandise to places overseas, nor thence to England, except in vessels belonging to lieges of our said lord; the same ordinance to begin at Easter next [22 March 1383]:

---

[20] 6 Ric.2 stat.1 c.1. The statutes of this parliament are printed in *SR*, II, 26-30.
[21] 6 Ric.2 stat.1 c.2.
[22] 6 Ric.2 stat.1 c.3.

Pasqe proschein:[23] quel estatut semble as ditz communes trope damageous, sanz remede d'amendement d'icel.
Qe plese amender le dit estatut qe entant come aucuns niefs des liges soient trovez sibien en Engleterre come dela, ou marchantz liges sont repairantz ovesqe lours marchandises, q'ils frettent mesmes les niefs devant autres, tancome les ditz niefs soient ables et suffisantz.

Responsio.

Le roi le voet.[24]

V. [Voidance of fraudulent annuities.]
28. Item, prient les communes: qe la ou gentz sont enheritez de leur heritage, ou de purchace, aucunes par leur subtilitees se forgent et monstrent annuetees long temps apres la morte de les auncestres de cellui a qi tielx terres sont decenduz, ou de celluy a qi tielle terre est purchace, et viegnent dys ans, ou vynt ans, ou grant temps apres et pursuent lours annuetees; qe nul tiel annuetee preigne effect, mais soit jugge come nul, si ensi /ne\ soit q'il ad este seisi et paie overtement et effectuelment de la summe contenue en l'annuetee, et ce par conisance du paiis.

Responsio.

Le roi s'advisera.

Page iii-138

VI. [Bounds of the admiralties.]
29. Item, prient les communes: qe les admiraltees del west et del north soient departiz come ils ont este en temps de voz nobles progenitours, et ne soit chaunge en autre condicion n'en autre manere. Qar l'entente et la supplicacione des communes estoit au derrain parlement qe l'admiral del north qe lors feust ordene dusse avoir eue la garde del mier jesqes al entree del port de Hampton': mais n'estoit my leur entent qe la jurisdiccione de l'admiraltee del west feust en rien amenusez, mais qe l'admiral del north eust soulement la garde du meer, de bouche del eawe de Thamise devers le north.

Responsio.

Soient les ditz admiraltees tenues et gardez en lours boundes et droitures, come d'ancien temps ont este.

VII. [Keeping the sea.]
30. Item, prient les communes: qe come pur defaut de bone governance sur la meere pluseurs vesselx du roialme sont prises par noz enemys, et les gentz de mesmes les vesselx, et les ditz vesselx raunceonez as grandes summes, et aucuns des dites gentz amesnez es parties de France, et illoeqes avec noz enemys detenuz pur descoverer les privitees du roialme, et amesner les ditz enemys en les pluis secretz et privez portz du roiaume en bone defense ne poet estre fait sanz grantz coustages, a l'annientissement et destruccione du dit roialme, et la navie d'icelle, si remede n'y soit mys.
Qe plese avoir consideracione a les meschiefs avauntditz, eiantz regarde qe .vi. *d.* de la livre des marchandises sont grantez pur bone governance de la miere, dont nul est ordene, et en affiance d'icelle governance pluseurs vesselx sont perduz, et les gentz d'iceux raunceonez as summes importables.

Responsio.

Le roi, par advis de son conseil, ent ordeignera de remede.

which statute seems to the said commons to be most damaging unless amendment be made.
May it please you to amend the said statute, to the effect that as long as ships of lieges are available in England and overseas where liege merchants are present with their merchandise, they shall transport their goods on those ships in preference to others, if the said ships are seaworthy and suitable.

Answer.

The king wills it.

V. [Voidance of fraudulent annuities.]
28. Also, the commons pray: whereas people have right of inheritance by heredity, or by purchase, some craftily forge and claim annuities long after the death of the ancestors from whom the lands have descended, or from whom they were purchased, and ten or twenty years later, or longer, they come and claim their annuities; that no such annuity have effect, but shall be considered invalid, unless the sum contained in the annuity has been seised and paid openly and effectually, and this through the witness of the county.

Answer.

The king will consider this further.

VI. [Bounds of the admiralties.]
29. Also, the commons pray: that the admiralties of the west and north be divided as they were in the time of your noble progenitors, and not changed in any respect, for the intention and request of the commons at the last parliament was that the admiral of the north, who was then appointed, ought to have the keeping of the sea as far as the entrance to the port of Southampton: and it was certainly not their intention that the jurisdiction of the admiralty of the west should be reduced in any way, but that the admiral of the north should have sole keeping of the sea from the mouth of the River Thames northwards.

Answer.

Let the boundaries and rights pertaining to the said admirals hold and be kept in accordance with ancient practice.

VII. [Keeping the sea.]
30. Also, the commons pray: whereas through a lack of good governance on the sea many vessels of the kingdom are taken by our enemies, and the men on the same vessels and the vessels themselves ransomed for great sums, and some of the said men taken to the parts of France and there they are kept by our enemies to discover the secrets of the kingdom, and to lead the said enemies to the most secret and private ports of the kingdom which cannot be well defended without great expense, to the ruin and destruction of the said kingdom, and the fleet of the same, unless remedy be supplied.
May it please you to consider the aforesaid troubles, bearing in mind that 6 *d.* in the pound on merchandise have been granted for the safe keeping of the sea, which has not been ordained, and because of the lack of such governance many vessels are lost, and the people of the same ransomed for intolerable sums.

Answer.

The king, by the advice of his council, will ordain remedy for this.

---

[23] 5 Ric.2 c.3.
[24] 6 Ric.2 stat.1 c.8.

VIII. [No aliens to hold benefices.]

31. Item, prient les communes: qe come pluseurs estatutz et ordinances aient este faitz avaunt ces heures des dignitees et autres benefices electives deinz mesmes le roialme, queux sont donez as aliens, et aucun foitz as apertz enemys nostre seignour le roi et de son roialme, paront le tresor est tret hors du roialme, le conseil du roialme descovert, et plusours autres meschiefs ent aviegnent, come pluis pleinement appiert es ditz estatutz et ordinances. Et nient contresteant celles estatutz, mesmes les aliens \si/ preignent possessione des dignitees de jour en autre, et sibien les dites dignitees et benefices electives come autres benefices en chescune partie d'Engleterre occupient, et y ont lours procuratours et fermers d'estranges nacions, come du roialme mesmes, contre l'ordinance ent nadgairs faite en vostre parlement.

Qe plese, en sauvacion du droit de vostre coroune, et pur commune profit avauntdit, faire ordener et establer en ce parlement qe toutz les ditz estatutz et ordinances soient mises en due execucione; et tielment ordener qe les franches eleccions faites et affaires deinz vostre roialme purront esteer come ils soloient en temps passe, et nule persone de quecunqe degree, estat ou condition q'il soit, alien ou denszein, soit desore procuratour, fermer ou administrour des ditz aliens de nul manere de lours benefices deinz le dit roiaume, sur peyne de quant q'ils purront forfaire en corps et en biens.

Responsio.
Estoisent les estatutz faitz en le cas.[25]

IX. [Prices of sweet wines.]

32. Item, prient les communes: qe come il feust ordene au derrain parlement par estatut qe nully venderoit vins douces a retaille mais tanqe al feste de Seint Johan proschein ensuant, et apres ycel feste soulement en groos,[26] qe le dit estatut soit enlargie, ensi qe chescun purra vendre vin douce a retaille a mesme le pris come vin de Ryn, ou vin de Gascoigne est venduz, et nemy pluis haut, sur peyne contenue deinz l'estatut avauntdit.

Responsio.
Le roi le voet, issint qe mesmes les vins douces ne soient venduz a pluis haut pris qe les autres vins ne sont ou serront, sur peyne de forfaiture d'ycelle.[27]

X. [Security against the Scots.]

33. Item, prient les communes: pur les tresgrantz perils qe purront avenir par les Escotz, purce qe commune fame est qe certein est q'ils sont en purpos pur avoir guerre sur nous, et ce serroit le pluis fort et le pluis malveis guerre qe nous purroit avenir.

Q'il plese a nostre dit seignour le roi qe l'ercevesqe d'Everwyk, l'evesqe de Duresme, le counte de Northumbr', le seignour de Nevill' et le seignour de Clifford', demoergent en lour paiis pur garder les frounters, et pur le tresgrant peril qe purra avenir au roi et au roialme: et q'il plese au roi et a nostre dame la roigne q'ils se treient vers Everwyk tanq'il soit ensure de pluis longe trieve, ou q'il sache finalment le purpos de les Escotz suisditz.

Responsio.
Quant as seignours avauntditz, y plest au roi, si ensi soit q'ils n'eient excusacion resonable au contrarie. Et quant au roi mesmes et ma dame la roigne, le roi, par advis des seignours

VIII. [No aliens to hold benefices.]

31. Also, the commons pray: whereas many statutes and ordinances have been made in the past concerning dignities and other elective benefices within the same kingdom, which have been given to aliens, and sometimes to open enemies of our lord the king and his kingdom, as a result of which treasure is withdrawn from the kingdom, the king's counsel disclosed, and many other troubles ensue, as appears more plainly in the said statutes and ordinances. Yet, notwithstanding these statutes, such aliens still take possession of dignities from one day to the next, and occupy the said dignities and elective benefices as well as other benefices in all parts of England, and there they install their proctors and farmers from foreign lands, as well as from the kingdom itself, contrary to the ordinance recently made thereon in your parliament.

May it please you, to save the right of your crown, and for the aforesaid common profit, to cause it to be ordained and decreed in this parliament that all the said statutes and ordinances be put into proper practice; and ordained in such a way that the free elections made and to be made within your kingdom may remain as they have done in the past, and that no person of whatever degree, status or condition he be, alien or denizen, shall henceforth be a proctor, farmer or administrator for the said aliens in any way of their benefices within the said kingdom, on pain of forfeiting whatsoever they can of their bodies and their goods.

Answer.
Let the statutes made thereon remain in force.

IX. [Prices of sweet wines.]

32. Also, the commons pray: whereas it was ordained at the last parliament by statute that no one should sell sweet wine by retail after the feast of St John following [24 June 1382], and after that feast only in gross, that the said statute may be extended, so that anyone may sell sweet wine by retail at the same price at which Rhenish or Gascon wine is sold, and for no more, on pain of the penalty contained in the aforesaid statute.

Answer.
The king wills it, so that the same sweet wines be not sold at a higher price than that at which the other wines are or shall be sold, on pain of forfeiture of the same.

X. [Security against the Scots.]

33. Also, the commons pray: for the very great dangers which may arise on account of the Scots, that whereas rumour has it that they do indeed intend to wage war on us, and it may be the most fierce and bitter war we have ever experienced.

May it please our said lord the king to decree that the archbishop of York, the bishop of Durham, the earl of Northumberland, Lord Neville and Lord Clifford shall remain in their counties to guard the marches, because of the very great peril which might arise for the king and his kingdom: and may it please the king and our lady the queen to repair to York until a longer truce is ensured, or the intention of the aforesaid Scots is finally learnt.

Answer.
As for the aforesaid lords, it pleases the king, if they have no reasonable excuse for acting to the contrary. As regards the king himself and our lady the queen, the king, by the advice

---

[25] 3 Ric.2 c.3.
[26] Parliament of 1381, item 107; 5 Ric.2 c.5.
[27] 6 Ric.2 stat.1 c.7.

autres de son conseil, en ferra ce qe mieultz lui semblera affaire.

XI. [Records burned in the revolt.]
34. Item, prient les communes: qe come au derrain parlement tenuz a Westm' estoit grantez qe toutz les faitz et munimentz enroullez, qi furent debrusez en pleusers lieux par les gentz q'ore tarde traiterousement leverent encontre leur ligeance, serroient exempliez et qe homme averoit la exemplificacion sanz rien paier pur le fee, entant qe home avoit paiez pur les enrollementz des ditz faitz devant.[28]
Q'il plese ratifier et conferner la dite grante; et outre ordener en ce present parlement qe chescune tiele exemplificacione soit de mesme le force et effect come les ditz faitz furent; et qe ceste peticione soit mys en estatut perpetuelment a durere.
Responsio.
Le roi le voet.[29]

XII. [No eyres or commissions of trailbaston.]
35. Item, prient les communes: qe eiantz regarde a le grant meschief des paiis, et le grant povert des communes, q'il plese a nostre seignour le roi grantir qe le justice d'eire, ne trail-bastoun, ne courge parmy le roialme durantz les guerres.
Responsio.
Le roi de sa grace voet et grant q'il se abstinera de faire tenir les eyres par ces deux ans proschein avenirs: et de tenir aucun trailbastoun pur l'an proschein avenir.

XIII. [Trade with alien merchants in amity.]
36. Item, prient les communes et les marchantz Lumbards en Engleterre: qe come en le derrain parlement estoit ordenez qe nul eschange serroit fait parentre marchant et marchant ne autres, lequel lour semble grant prejudice et damage au roi et a son roialme, par cause qe leynes et plusours autres marchandises d'Engleterre ne sont my venduz sibien come ils soloient, ne ne poent sanz eschange entre marchant et marchant, come usez est en toutes bones citees et villes du monde.
Par quoy plese ent ordener due remede, sibien pur profit du roi et de son roiaume come pur ease des marchantz avauntditz.
Responsio.
Demandent conge del chanceller, et si le demande soit resonable il /le\ purra granter.[30]

XIIII. [The admiral to the north.]
37. Item, prient les communes: qe plese ordener en ce present parlement un suffisant admiral pur le north, qi poet par bone ordinance prendre la charge pur salvacione du couste et des biens passantz sur la miere, au fyn qe les enemys ne facent tiel destruccione a voz ditz liges come ils ont faitz ces trois ans passez, et meement en cest an derrain; deinz quel an ils ont destruitz et pris en le north coste .lx. niefs et craiers, outre autres meindres des queux ils ont pris grant fuysoun.
Responsio.
Il plest au roi, et ce /soit\ fait.
Page iii-139

XV. [No justice of assize, etc., to sit in his own county.]
38. Item, prient les communes: qe nul justice de loy soit assigne justice as assises, deliverances, n'en autres

of the other lords and his council, will do whatever he thinks should be done for the best.

XI. [Records burned in the revolt.]
34. Also, the commons pray: whereas at the last parliament held at Westminster it was granted that all the enrolled deeds and muniments, burnt in many places by those who recently rebelled treacherously and contrary to their allegiance, be copied; and that copies be had without payment of a fee, given that payment had been made for the enrolments of the said deeds in the first place.
May it please you to ratify and confirm the said grant; and also to ordain in this present parliament that each such copy shall be of the same force and validity as the said deeds; and that this petition be made into a statute to last forever.
Answer.
The king wills it.

XII. [No eyres or commissions of trailbaston.]
35. Also the commons pray: that bearing in mind the great troubles of the land, and the great poverty of the commons, it might please our lord the king to grant that neither the justices of eyre nor trailbaston shall operate throughout the kingdom for the duration of the wars.
Answer.
The king of his grace wills and grants that he will abstain from causing eyres to be held for two years to come: and from holding any trailbaston for one year to come.

XIII. [Trade with alien merchants in amity.]
36. Also, the commons and the Lombard merchants in England pray: whereas in the last parliament it was ordained that no exchange should be made between merchant and merchant or any others, this seems to them greatly to prejudice and injure the king and his kingdom, because wool and many other merchandises of England do not sell as well as they used, nor will they without exchange between merchant and merchant, which is the practice in all good cities and towns of the world.
On account of which may it please you to ordain a remedy, as well for the benefit of the king and his kingdom, as for the ease of the aforesaid merchants.
Answer.
Let them ask permission from the chancellor, and if the request is reasonable he may grant it.

XIIII. [The admiral to the north.]
37. Also, the commons pray: that it may please him to ordain in this present parliament a worthy admiral for the north, who is able through good ordinance to take responsibility for defending the coast, and goods crossing the sea, so that the enemy shall not inflict such ruin on your said lieges as they have inflicted in the last three years, and especially in this last year; during which they have destroyed and captured on the north coast sixty ships and crayers, not to mention other smaller vessels of which they have captured a great number.
Answer.
It pleases the king, and shall be done.

XV. [No justice of assize, etc., to sit in his own county.]
38. Also, the commons pray: that no justice of the law shall be appointed a justice of assize, delivery or any other

---
[28] Parliament of 1381, item 85; 5 Ric 2 c.9.
[29] 6 Ric.2 stat.1 c.4.
[30] 6 Ric.2 stat.1 c.10.

enquerres en paiis ou ils sont conversantz, par cause des grantz alliances envers seignours et les grantz du paiis, come par diverses douns; issint qe les povres communes ne purront ent avoir droit.
Responsio.
Le roi s'advisera.

XVI. [Sessions in northern counties.]
39. Item, /prient\ les communes qe les justices qi font lours sessions en le countee d'Everwyk, si purront faire lours sessions es countes de Northumbr', Cumbr' et Westmerl', deux foitz par an, a grant ease de celles parties, sur peine de forfaiture de ce q'ils purront forfaire devers le roi, qar en deux ans nule session est faite par les ditz justices, a grant damage de ditz communes.
Responsio.
Le roi voet qe les justices tiegnent lours sessions selonc la forme de l'ordinance ent faite, sinoun q'ils eient resonables causes par quelles ils ne le purront faire.
Membrane 3

XVII. [Assize towns.]
40. Item, prient les communes: qe come plusours justices d'assises et deliverances sovent foitz tiegnent leur sessions en les pluis loyntismes lieux des countees, a grant disease de les enhabitantz es dites countees, et des autres qi ont affaire as dites sessions.
Par quoy plese ordeiner en ce present parlement qe desore toutes assises et deliverances soient tenuz en les principalx villes des countees et nul part aillours, a grant ease des communes suisditz.
Responsio.
Le roi le voet q'ils tiegnent leur sessions en les principalx et chiefs villes ou les countees sont tenuz.[31]

XVIII. [Enrolments of process.]
41. Item, prient les communes: qe come par l'estatut soit ordene qe les justices nostre seignour le roi averont clercs d'enroller touz les recordz devant eux attamez ou pledez, et auxint d'ensealer billes de ce q'ils ne veullent mettre en record; et aucuns des ditz justices ne veullent perfournir la dite ordinance, mais les concelent et detiegnent, encountre l'effect du dit estatut, /en\ oppressione et disheritance des pleusurs gentz.
Qe plese ordener qe le dit estatut soit duement execut par eux deinz un quarter d'un an apres les records enrollez, et les billes issint ensealez, ou q'ils respondrent as parties de ce q'ils serront endamagez en lour defaut par celle enchesoun.
Responsio.
L'estatut fait en le cas suffist, le quel le roi voet qe soit tenuz et gardez.[32]

XIX. [Costs of the royal household.]
42. Item, prient les communes: q'il plese au roi nostre seignour, considerez la grande destabiltee de ses communes, par avis de son tressage conseil et des seignours a ore esteantz en parlement, ordener, pur quiete et tranquillitee des dites communes, aufin qe par la grace de Dieu vostre roiaume, et voz liges puissent viver en quiete et amour, et qe droit et justice soient faitz des toutz partz: et enoultre, considerez la grant povert et disease de voz ditz communes, sibien par pestilence de gentz, moryne des bestes, et les fruytes de la terre pur la greindre partie faillez et suroundez,

---
[31] 6 Ric.2 stat.1 c.5.
[32] 9 Edw.3 c.5.

inquests in the county where he lives, because of close alliances with the lords and great men of the county, as well as various gifts; as a result of which the poor commons cannot obtain justice.
Answer.
The king will consider it further.

XVI. [Sessions in northern counties.]
39. Also, the commons pray: that the justices who hold their sessions in the county of York, also hold their sessions in the counties of Northumberland, Cumberland and Westmorland, twice a year, for the greater convenience of those parts, on pain of forfeiting whatsoever they can to the king, as no session has been held by the said justices for the last two years, to the great injury of the said commons.
Answer.
The king wills that the justices shall hold their sessions in accordance with the ordinance made thereon, unless they have good reasons for not being able to do so.

XVII. [Assize towns.]
40. Also, the commons pray: whereas many justices of assize and delivery often hold their sessions in the most distant places in the counties, to the inconvenience of the inhabitants of the said counties, and others who have business to conduct at the said sessions.
May it please you to ordain in this present parliament that, henceforth, all assizes and deliveries be held in the principal towns of the counties, and nowhere else, for the greater convenience of the aforesaid commons.
Answer.
The king wills that they hold their sessions in the chief and principal towns where the county courts are held.

XVIII. [Enrolments of process.]
41. Also, the commons pray: whereas it was ordained by statute that the justices of our lord the king should have clerks to enrol all records brought or pleaded before them, and also to seal bills of matters which they did not wish to place on record; yet some of the said justices will not observe the said ordinance, but conceal and detain records, contrary to the purpose of the said statute, to the oppression and disinheritance of many people.
May it please you to ordain that the said statute be duly observed by them within one quarter of a year of the records being enrolled, and the bills thus sealed, or that they answer to the parties injured through their failing in that matter.
Answer.
The statute made on this matter is adequate and the king wills that it be kept and upheld.

XIX. [Costs of the royal household.]
42. Also, the commons pray: that it may please the king our lord, considering the great restlessness of his commons, by the advice of his most wise council and the lords now attending parliament, to ordain, for the peace and tranquillity of the said commons, that through the grace of God, your realm and your lieges may live in love and peace, and that right and justice may be done to all parties: and further, considering the great poverty and discomfort of your said commons, on account of human pestilence, murrain of cattle, and the fruits of the soil having for the most part been flooded and

come autrement, ordeigner qe bone governail soit mys entour vostre honurable persone, siqe vous purrez honestement et roialment viver deinz les revenues de vostre roialme, et qe toutes maneres des gardes, mariages, reliefs, eschets, forfaitures et toutes autres commoditees puissent estre gardez pur voz guerres, et en defens de vostre roialme, et nul part ailleurs donez; en supportacion et eyde de voz povres communes, et grant honour et profit a vous.

Responsio.

Le roi est de bone volentee, et le desire moelt entierment, de faire et ordener en ce cas par l'avis des seignours de son roialme ce qe lui semblera mieultz affaire pur son honur et profit.

XX. [Pardons for rebels.]

43. Item, prient les communes: qe come au parlement tenuz a Westm' l'an quint, de vostre grace especiale une pardoun feust grante as touz yceux qi vorroient purchacer leur chartres de pardoun de tresoun, et de felonie,[33] forspris certains articles, et certeines persones qi furent forsprises au dit parlement, parissint q'ils purchassent leur chartres parentre le dit parlement et le Penticost proschein ensuant. Et porce grant nombre des gentz qi sont enditez de tresoun par cause de le rumour sont laborers, et tielx qi riens n'ont, et ne furent pas de poair de purchacer lours chartres, issint q'ils sont hors de mesme la pardoun: et a cause q'ils se doutent d'estre mys en exigende et utlagarie, et en cas q'ils soient prises d'estre myses a mort, s'enfuent ensemble as boys et autres lieux, et auxint grant nombre des autres qi ne sont pas enditez se doutent d'estre en mesme le cas, dont purra sourdre grant meschief.

Par quoy plese granter une pardoun general de tresoun de le rumour suisdit, forspris ceux qi furent forsprises, sanz chartre avoir, forspris murdre et felonie.

Responsio.

Le roi voet q'ils ent eient pardon de toutes traisons et /felonies\ faites en le dit rumour, c'estassavoir parentre le primer jour de May l'an quart et la feste de la Nativitee Seint Johan lors proschein ensuant; exceptes toutes les persones en especial, des queux les nouns aient este deliverez es /parlementz des ans del regne nostre dit seignour le roi quint et sisme, pur estre exemptz de toute grace du roi faite en les ditz parlementz; come celles persones qe sont arettez principalx comenceours et abbettours\ du dit rumour. Et horspris toutz ceaulx de la ville de Bury; et horspris Johan Horn', Adam Karlill' et Wauter Sibill', de Londres, acusez en cest parlement de certains horribles pointz; et excepts toutz autres esteantz pleinement en le cas de ditz Johan, Adam et Wauter, ou nul de eux.[34]
[35]

XXI. [Depredations of Cheshire men.]

44. Item, prient les communes: qe come plusours countees d'Engleterre sont outrement oppressez et destruitz par y ce qe les gentz del countee de Cestre viegnent quant il lour plest, forciblement armes encontre la paix, es ditz countees, et ravisent lours femmes et leur files countre lour gree, et les amesnent el countee de Cestre et illoeqes extorcionousement les detiegnent: et outre ce, a lour volentee font diverses quereles, et en diverses maneres, encontre les gentz des ditz countees; et tout soit il qe les ditz quereles soient feynes et nient verroies, si les dites gentz ne veullent faire gree a lour

destroyed, as well as other things, to ordain that good governance be set in place around your honourable person so that you may live honestly and regally within the revenues of your kingdom, and that all kinds of wardships, marriages, reliefs, escheats, forfeitures and all other resources be kept for your wars, and for the defence of your kingdom, and not used elsewhere; to support and assist your poor commons, and to your great honour and benefit.

Answer.

The king is willing, and desires most earnestly to do and ordain in this instance, by the advice of the lords of his kingdom, whatsoever shall seem best to him in terms of his honour and benefit.

XX. [Pardons for rebels.]

43. Also, the commons pray: whereas at the parliament held at Westminster in the fifth year, by your special grace a pardon was granted to all those who wished to purchase their charters of pardon of treason, and for felony, excepting certain articles, and certain people who were excluded at the said parliament, that they might purchase their charters between the said parliament and the Whitsun following [25 May 1382]. Yet a large number of the people who were indicted for treason because of the said uprising are labourers and the like who have nothing, and are not in a position to purchase their charters, so that they remain without the same pardon: and because they fear that they will be placed in exigent or outlawry, or seized and put to death, they flee into woods and other places, and what is more, a large number of others who have not been indicted fear the same plight, from which great trouble may ensue.

On account of which may it please you to grant a general pardon of treason in the aforesaid uprising, excepting those who were excluded, without a charter being necessary, except for murder and felony.

Answer.

The king wills that they shall receive a pardon of all treasons and felonies committed in the said uprising, namely between 1 May in the fourth year [1381] and the feast of the Nativity of St John following [24 June 1381]; excepting all those in particular whose names were submitted to the parliaments held in the fifth and sixth years of the reign of our said lord to be exempted from the king's grace granted in the said parliaments, as people held to be the chief instigators and abettors of the said uprising. And excepting all those of the town of Bury; and excepting John Horn, Adam Karlile and Walter Sibil, of London, accused in this parliament of certain horrible matters; and excepting all others clearly involved in the matter of the said John, Adam and Walter, or any one of them.

XXI. [Depredations of Cheshire men.]

44. Also, the commons pray: whereas many counties of England are entirely ruined and oppressed because men from Cheshire appear in the said counties as they please, well armed against the peace, and ravish their women and daughters without mercy, and carry them off into Cheshire and there tortiously detain them. And further, they pursue various disputes at will and in various ways against the people of the said counties; and even though the said complaints are feigned and untrue, if the said people do not wish to compensate them of their own free will, they at once rise with

---

[33] Parliament of 1381, item 32.
[34] 6 Ric.2 stat.1 c.13.
[35] The section from 'esteantz' to 'nul de eux' has been added later in a contemporary hand.

volentee, meintenant ils se levent ove grant nombre des gentz armez, et entrent es ditz countees, et les ditz parties par tiele mestrie batent, naunfrent, maheyment, ardent et destruent, et les raunceonent torceonousement.

Par quoy plese ent ordener remede, ou autrement les dites communes ne le purront pluis endurere.

Responsio.

Le roi, par advis de son conseil, ent purvoera remede au mieultz qe purra, sauvant la franchise del countee de Cestre.

XXII. [Ravishers and consentient victims to lose title to settled estates.]

45. Item, prient les communes: qe come diverses mesfesours de jour en autre ravisent femmes, dames, damoiseles et files des gentils du roialme, a grant deshonur et desease des plusours du roialme, dont punissement de vie et de membre n'est pas donez par la loy pur nule partie, en cas qe les dites femmes se agreent et assentent apres.

Par quoy plese ordeiner qe desormes la ou femmes, dames, damoiseles ou files en temps avenir soient ravisez, et apres ce assentuz, qe les ravisours et les ravises soient desablez de lour dowere, joynture, ou heritage avoir apres la mort lour barons et auncestres: et qe le pluis proschein de sank a qi l'eritage, jointure ou dowere devroit descendre, revertir, ou avenir apres la mort le ravisour ou la ravisee, *[Page iii-140]*

[Col. a] eit title inmediate d'entrer sur le ravisour ou la ravisee, lours heirs ou lours assignez, et qe les barons de tieles femmes en cas q'ils soient mariez, ou lours pieres ou proscheins de sank en cas q'ils n'eient barons en pleyne vie, eient suite a pursuir les ditz mesfesours, et les atteindre de vie et de membre, tout soient les dites femmes apres le ravisement assentuz. Et qe nul defendant soit receu de /gager\ batail en tiel cas, einz soit la veritee trie par enqueste, considerez les grantz meschiefs et perils en celle partie.

Responsio.

Le roi le voet, sauvant au roi et as seignours lours eschetes del ravisour, en cas q'il ent soit atteint.[36]

XXIII. [Bishop Despenser's crusade.]

46. Item, prie la commune: qe come conuz soit a touz, coment le reverent pier en Dieux l'evesqe de Norwiz ad une croicerie encontre le antipape, et touz ses adherentz; entre queux vostre adversaire de France et les gentz Franceis sont principalx, come bien appiert de fait, et les queux sont pluis grevouses a vous et a vostre roialme qe nuls autres; la quelle croicerie y semble a voz ditz communes q'il deust estre pluis grant allegeance des coustages de voz dites guerres, et le greindre esploit et hastif fyn de voz guerres et conquest de vostre heritage, par diverses causes, come leur semble. C'estassavoir, en primes q'il poet aler as meindres coustages de vous et de vostre roialme par l'eide du dite croicerie, au quele le poeple ad grant devocion, en salvacion de seinte esglise et de lours almes, et le pluis ardantement pur le recoeverer del droit de vostre heritage. Item, y semble a voz ditz communes q'il est le pluis grant eide et esploit a perfournir l'alliance entre vous et Flandres, qe trope est necessaire a vous et a vostre roialme, dont est a douter impediment par tretys des Franceys, s'il ne soit hastivement succurez de poair. Item, il lour semble qe s'il soit mis hastifment en esploit q'il serra le pluis grant rescous pur Gascoigne et voz

a great number of men-at-arms, and enter the said counties in great force, and beat, kill, maim, burn and destroy the said parties, and wrongfully ransom them.

In consequence of which may it please you to ordain a remedy, for otherwise the said commons will not be able much longer to endure it.

Answer.

The king, by the advice of his council, will provide a remedy as best he can, saving the franchise of Cheshire.

XXII. [Ravishers and consentient victims to lose title to settled estates.]

45. Also, the commons pray: whereas various malefactors daily ravish the wives, ladies, damsels and daughters of the nobles of the realm, to the great dishonour and injury of many in the said kingdom, for which punishment of life and limb is never granted by law against any party, lest the said women subsequently give their assent and agreement.

May it please you to ordain that henceforth, when wives, ladies, damsels or daughters are ravished in time to come, and later assent, that the ravishers and the ravished shall be prevented from receiving their dowry, jointure or inheritance after the death of their husbands and ancestors: and that the closest blood relation to whom the inheritance, jointure or dowry ought to descend, revert or come after the death of the ravisher or the ravished, *[Page iii-140]*

[Col. a] shall be immediately entitled to enter upon the lands of the ravisher or the ravished, their heirs or their assignees, and that the husbands of such women, if they be married, or their fathers or closest blood relations if they do not have husbands still living, shall bring legal action against the said malefactors, and convict them with loss of life and limb, even where the women have later assented after the ravishment. And that no defendant be allowed to do battle in such a case, but let the truth be established by inquest, considering the great troubles and perils in this matter.

Answer.

The king wills it, saving to the king and the lords their escheats from the ravisher, if he be so convicted.

XXIII. [Bishop Despenser's crusade.]

46. Also the commons pray: whereas it is well known to all that the reverend father in God, the bishop of Norwich, has a crusade against the anti-pope, and all his adherents; the chief of whom are your enemy of France and the French people, as is indeed apparent, and who inflict more injury on you and your kingdom than any others; which crusade, it seems to your said commons, might greatly alleviate the expense of your said wars, and enable greater exploits and a speedy conclusion of your wars and the conquest of your inheritance, for various reasons, as it seems to them. That is, firstly because it could proceed with least cost to you and your kingdom with the aid of the said crusade, to which the people are greatly devoted, for the salvation of holy church and their souls, and the more ardently for the recovery of your rightful inheritance. Also it seems to your said commons that it would be of great use and help in cementing the alliance between you and Flanders, which is most necessary for you and your kingdom, since an obstacle in the shape of a treaty with France is to be feared, if Flanders is not assisted by reinforcement soon. Also, it seems to them that if this be quickly performed, it will result in the more effective rescue

---

[36] 6 Ric.2 stat.1 c.6.

autres frounters de part dela, qar y ferra vostre adversaire de France retreer son poair hors de Gascoigne, et de voz autres frounters avaunditz devers Pikardye d'encontrer le dit evesqe. Item, il destourbera les Frounceys q'ore sont en France, et le duc d'Angoie ove son poair s'il retournast pur aler en Spaigne encountre vostre honorable uncle le roi d'Espaigne, paront mesme vostre uncle vendra pluis hastifment al esploit del conquest de son roialme d'Espaigne.

Par quoy, eiantz consideracione a les causes avantdites, et a meindre coustages de l'eskippesoun, et le pluis grant ease a vous, et a touz voz liges qi veullent passer a lours propres ou d'autry coustages en le dit viage par le court mier, pur passer a Caleys q'ailleurs; et auxi, a ce qe touz maneres des aliens obeissantz al droit pape puissent venir sauvement al marche de Caleys et de Pikardie, pur affeccione et aide del dit croicerie, sanz daunger du mier ou des enemys, et al le pluis pres a vostre adversaire ore en l'absence le duc d'Aungoie et de son grant poair, si vous prient treshumblement voz ditz communes, pur final esploit de cestes necessaires et profitables busoignes a vous et a vostre roialme, d'ottroier au dit evesqe le frounter de Caleys pur un temps, ovesqe une covenable summe pur comencer le viage, et coiller ses gentz en eide del dit frounter, et refresshement de Flandres, ou le dit evesqe serra prest d'aler si busoigne soit.

Responsio.

Le roi ad chargez son conseil de treter ove le dit evesqe sur la matire.

XXIV. [Escheats.]

47. Item, prient les communes: qe la ou estoit ordeine par estatut l'an du regne le roi Edward aiel nostre seignour le roi q'orest .xxxiiij. eit nul homme qi mette chalange ou cleym as terres seisiz par enqueste d'office prise devant l'eschetour, qe l'eschetour mande l'enqueste en la chancellerie deinz le moys apres les terres issint seisiz, et qe brief lui soit livere de certifier la cause de sa seisine en la chancellerie, et illoeqes soit oye sanz delaye a traverser l'office ou autrement monstrer son droit, et d'illoeqes mande devaunt le roi a faire final discussion,

[Col. b] sanz attendre autre mandement. Et en cas qe aucun viegne devaunt le chanceller et monstre son droit, par quelle demonstrance par bone evidence de son auncien droit et bone title, qe le chanceller par sa bone discretion et avis de conseil, si le semble qe lui busoigne d'avoir conseil, q'il lesse et baille les terres issint en debate au tenant, rendant ent au roi la value, si au roi appartient, en manere come il et les autres chancellers devant lui ont faitz devant ces heures de leur bone discrecion; issint q'il face seuretee q'il ne ferra wast ne destruccione tanqe il soit ajugge, come pleinement appiert en le dit estatut. Et qe mesmes les terres issint seisiz ne soient lessez par patente nostre seignour le roi a nully pendant le plee des dites terres nient discusse, forsqe al tenant de mesmes les terres. Et s'ils soient aucuns patentes grantez devaunt ces heures par nostre dit seignour le roi, ou autre son officer, des tieles terres issint seisiz et cleymez par les tenantz de mesmes les terres, et le plee d'icelles terres pendant nient discusse, qe mesmes les patentes soient repellez tanqe les plees pendantz entre nostre seignour le roi et les tenantz des terres issint seisiz soient terminez et discussez.

Responsio.

Y ad estatut fait en le cas, quel le roi voet q'il soit tenuz.[37]

of Gascony and your other territories overseas, for your enemy, France, will have to withdraw its troops from Gascony and your other aforesaid lands towards Picardy to counter the said bishop. Also, it would divert the French now in France, and the duke of Anjou with his force so that he would abandon going to Spain to oppose your most honourable uncle the king of Spain, as a result of which your same uncle would effect the conquest of his kingdom of Spain more swiftly.

In view of which, bearing in mind the aforesaid reasons, and the minimal costs of transportation, and the greater ease of you and all your lieges who wish to cross the sea on the said expedition at their own expense or some other expense, to travel to Calais rather than elsewhere; and also, in so far as all kinds of aliens, showing obedience to the true pope might come safely to the march of Calais and Picardy, to support and assist the said crusade, without the danger of the sea of or of enemies, and get all the closer to your said adversary now in the absence of the duke of Anjou and his great force, so your said commons humbly pray, for the final settlement of these urgent and profitable concerns of you and your kingdom, that you grant to the said bishop the territories of Calais for a time, together with an adequate sum to launch the said expedition, and collecting his men for the aid of the said frontier, and the relief of Flanders, where the said bishop shall be ready to go if need be.

Answer.

The king has charged his council to discuss the matter with the said bishop.

XXIV. [Escheats.]

47. Also, the commons pray: whereas it was ordained by statute in the thirty-fourth year of the reign of King Edward, grandfather of our lord the present king,, that if any man should challenge or claim lands taken by inquest of office held before the escheator, that the escheator would send the inquest to the chancery within a month of the lands having been thus seized, and that a writ would be sent instructing him to certify in the chancery the cause of the seisin, and let him be heard there without delay to disavow his office or else demonstrate his claim, and from there let it be sent before the king for a final discussion,

[Col. b] without awaiting further order. And if any should come before the chancellor and prove his claim, and by good evidence demonstrate genuine entitlement, that the chancellor at his good discretion and with the advice of counsel, if he feels the need to have counsel, shall release and deliver the lands thus in question to the tenant, paying the value of them to the king, if it pertain to the king, as other chancellors before him have done in the past at their good discretion; so that he shall guarantee not to make waste or destruction until it be adjudged, as appears fully in the said statute. And that the same lands thus seised shall not be leased by patent of our lord the king to anyone pending the plea of the said lands not yet settled, except to the tenant of the same lands. And if other patents have been granted before this time by our said lord the king, or other of his officers, of such lands thus seised and claimed by the tenants of the same lands, and the plea of the same lands is pending and remains unsettled, that the same patents be repealed until the pleas pending between our lord the king and the tenants of the lands thus taken shall have been determined and settled.

Answer.

A statute has been made thereon, which the king wishes be upheld.

---

[37] 36 Edw.3 stat.1 c.13. This is the ruling statute, not 34 Edw.3 as invoked in the text.

XXV. [Justices to review bonds made under constraint.]
48. Also, the commons pray: whereas certain lieges of our lord the king, like felons and traitors contrary to their allegiance, rebel against our said lord the king, and commit various treasons and felonies; and the same traitors force many good people to accompany them against their will to various parts where the said traitors carry out various felonies, and there are various maintainers, like jurors, bailiffs and others, plotting to grieve many good people for no reason, some of whom against their will have been captured and led off by the said traitors, and others who are not with the said traitors, alleging against them that they have helped and advised them. As a result of which many good people have been thus threatened with indictment and ruin by the said maintainers, and fear of such threats has enabled the said maintainers to seize and extort various great sums from the said commons, some more, some less, and many of the said commons have made numerous bonds containing various great sums to the said maintainers, to be paid on certain days. On account of which the said commons, for those reasons and because of the unbearable charges and extortion placed on them by the said maintainers, are on the point of being utterly ruined and destroyed, and unable to aid their liege lord in his state of great need because of such oppressions inflicted on them, unless remedy be given them.
May it please you, for the relief of the said poor commons, to grant commissions of oyer and terminer on the said matters, as well at the suit of the king as the individual, and the most worthy of each county who shall be named in the present parliament by the knights and burgesses now in parliament: and that the said obligations made for this reason through fear, as said above, be cancelled and annulled, and that the same commissioners have the power to ordain such officers to execute their mandates as seem best to them; because there is no bailiff in the said counties who has not extorted various sums from many good people, as said above.

Answer.

The king will consider this further.

XXVI. [Pardons for minor offences.]
49. Also, the commons pray that it may please the king our lord to grant and make a statute on the general pardon of all that can be pardoned, except treason, murder, robbery, and the rape of women; and that no justice of eyre or trailbaston shall be sent upon the commons for offences committed before this time.

Answer.

The king wills that they shall have the said pardon for all kinds of trespass; except trespass touching lands and tenements; and trespasses made by the *[Page iii-141]* *[Col. a]* officers of the king and of great lords; and except jurors and maintainers of quarrels.

XXVII. [Shrievalties of Essex and Hertfordshire.]
50. Also, the poor commons of the counties of Essex and Hertford pray: whereas very great trouble has arisen in the said counties amongst the said commons over the office of sheriff, because every year some one in the said counties is ruined and destroyed, so that the worthy persons of the said counties decline to live there. Concerning which, our said lord the king, at his parliament lately held at Gloucester,

especiale al viscont des ditz countees allouance et pardoun de .c. marz par an durantz trois ans;[40] et puis de sa grace de an en an tanqe en cea l'ad continue, en relevement de les tresgrantz meschiefs et damages supportez du dit viscont, come piert par lour peticione de record en le rolle del parlement de Glouc' suisdit.

Qe plese a vostre tresgraciouse seignourie grantir a ses ditz povres communes, oultre continuance de allouance et pardoun de .c. marz dessuisditz par trois ans proschein avenir, pur Dieu, et en oevre de charitee, entendant autrement ne demurra gentilhomme de value par un an en le paiis suisditz, pur doute de le meschief avauntdit.
Responsio.

Le roi voet qe apres le terme fini par le quiel ils avoient derrainement pardoun de .c. marz par an, ils aient semblable pardoun et remissioun de .c. marz par an, de especiale grace du roi, a durer par trois ans deslors proscheinement ensuantz.

XXVIII. [First fruits.]
51[41] Item, supplie le dite commune: qe come d'auncien temps nulles primers fruitz soloient estre paiez a nostre seint pere le pape, sinoun pur benefices qe voideront en la courte, et pur confirmacions eues en mesme la courte; la les collectours del dit seint pier ore de novelle demandent fruitz des benefices grantez par commune grace, et par especiale expectacioun, qe amont a grant summe, et grant empoverissement del roialme. Et oultre ce, des benefices qe voideront /en\ la courte dusze ans, ou quatorse, et outre passez, les queux fruitz furent paiez par les incumbentz adonqes esteantz, qi sont a Dieu comandez, issint qe les incumbentz a ore ne purront monstrer les aquitances: et issint levont les ditz fruitz deux foitz, ou trois, a lour voluntee, a cause qe les parties n'osent contreester pur lours horribles censures.

Qe plese ordeiner qe nulles primers fruitz soient levez, sinoun come il soleit estre fait en aucun temps. Et ce qe doit estre leve soit leve deinz les trois ans proschein ensuantz apres qe collacion soit fait, ou qe la leve des ditz primers fruitz pur celle voidance cesse pur touz jours.
Responsio.

Si riens de novel issint soit \[attemptez,]/ soient prohibitions faitz tielx come suffisent en le cas.

XXIX. [Discharges in the exchequer without writ.]
52[42]. Item, prie le commune: qe come en vostre derrain parlement tenuz a Westm' estoit ordene par estatut qe les barons de l'escheqer eient plein poair d'oier chescun respounse de queconqe demande a le dit escheqer, issint qe chescune persone qe soit empesche ou empeschable de quecunqe cause al dit escheqier, pur lui mesmes, ou par autres persones, soit receu en le dit escheqer a pleder, suir et avoir sa descharge resonable en celle partie, sanz attendre ou suir brief de grant seal, lettres de prive seal nostre seignour le roi, ou autre comandement, come dessuis.[43] Et nientcontresteant cest estatut et ordeinance, les ditz barons ne voillent resceivre ceux qi sont empeschez, et se offeront a lours descharges monstrer en le dit escheqer.

granted of his special grace to the sheriff of the said counties allowance and pardon of one hundred marks a year for three years; and then of his grace he continued it from one year to the next until now, for the relief of the great troubles and expense borne by the said sheriff, as appears in their petition recorded on the roll of the aforesaid parliament of Gloucester.

May it please your most gracious lordship to grant to his said poor commons, a continuance of the allowance and pardon of the aforementioned hundred marks for a further three years, for God and by way of charity, bearing in mind that otherwise no gentleman of worth will dwell for a year in the aforesaid counties, through fear of the aforesaid burden.
Answer.

The king wills that after the end of the term for which they last received pardon of a hundred marks a year, they shall have a similar pardon and remission of a hundred marks a year, of the king's special grace, to last for three years to follow.

XXVIII. [First fruits.]
51. Also, the said commons request that whereas since ancient times no first fruits have been customarily paid to our holy father the pope, unless for benefices which became vacant in the curia, and for confirmations made in the same curia; now the collectors of the holy father newly demand the fruits of benefices granted by the common grace, and by special expectation, which amount to a great sum, and greatly impoverish the kingdom. Furthermore, from benefices which became vacant in the curia twelve or fourteen years ago, or more, the fruits of which had been paid by the then incumbents, who are called to God, so that the present incumbents cannot show the acquittances: and so they levy the said fruits twice, or three times, at their will, because the parties dare not resist them because of their terrible censures.

May it please you to ordain that no first fruits shall be levied, unless they have customarily been levied in the past. And that that which ought to be levied shall be levied within three years of the collation being made, or that the levy of the said first fruits for this vacancy cease forever.
Answer.

If anything novel is thus attempted, let such prohibitions be made as shall suffice in the matter.

XXIX. [Discharges in the exchequer without writ.]
52. Also, the commons pray: whereas in your last parliament held at Westminster it was ordained by statute that the barons of the exchequer should have full power to hear the answers of all those called to the said exchequer, so that anyone impeached or impeachable for whatsoever cause at the said exchequer, either himself or by other persons, be received in the said exchequer to plead, sue and have his reasonable discharge in the matter, without waiting or suing for a writ of great seal, letters of privy seal from our lord the king, or any other order, as said above. Yet, notwithstanding that statute and ordinance, the said barons will not receive those who are accused, and offer to defend themselves in the said exchequer.

---

[40] Parliament of 1378, item 59.
[41] *Original* 50.
[42] *Original* 51.
[43] Parliament of 1381, item 97.

Par quoi plese a vostre hautesse, de confermer le dit estatut et ordenance en cest present parlement, et qe le dit estatut soit tenuz sur grant peyne.

Responsio.
Le roi le voet.[44]

XXX. [Preachers of heresy.]
53.[45] Item, supplient les communes: qe come un estatut fuist fait en derrain parlement en ces paroles,
[Col. b] Ordenez est en cest parlement qe commissions du roi soient directes as viscounts et autres ministres du roi, ou as autres suffisantz persones, apres et solonc les certificacions des prelatz ent affaires en la chancellerie du temps en temps, d'arester touz tieux precheours et lours fautours, mayntenours, et abettours, et de les tenir en arest et forte prisone tanqe ils se veullent justifier selonc reson et la loy de seinte esglise: et le roi voet et comande qe le chanceller face tieles commissions a touz les foitz qe serra par les prelatz ou aucun de eux certifie et ent requis, come dessuis est dit. La quiel ne fuist unqes assentu ne grante par les communes, mes ce qe fuist parle de ce, fuist sanz assent de lour; qe celui estatut soit annienti, qar il n'estoit mie lour entent d'estre justifiez, ne obliger lour ne lour successours as prelatz pluis qe lours auncestres n'ont este en temps passez.

Responsio.
Y plest au roi.

XXXI. [Exports of grain.]
54.[46] Item, compleignent les communes des countees d'Everwik et Nicole, ove toutes les citees et burghes qe lours blees sont, par diverses patentes grantez, a si grant fuison cariez hors du roialme, et par celle cause tiele escharestee et chiertee est avenuz en la paiis, q'il y est au present grant damage, et pluis grant apparant si remedie n'y soit mys. Pur quoy supplient ses lieges suisditz qe lui plese abstiner de granter tielx patentes, repellant ceux qe sont grantez, et ordeinant en cest parlement qe nully desore amesne nief charge ove blees pur vendre, ou descharger hors du roialme, sinoun a Caleys, ou a Berwyk sur Twede, ou a Burdeux. Et qe les meistres, come lours niefs serront chargez, viegnent a proschein bone ville ou port est, et paient lour custume, et preignent un certein signe devers les villes avauntdites, et remaigne un autre signe la ou ils paeront lour custume: issint qe poet estre conuz ou ils serront deliverez et chargez, et ce par grevouse peine a mettre par avis du parlement.

Responsio.
Le roi voet qe pur la cause suisdite defens general se face parmy le roialme, issint qe nul blee ne passe aucune part hors du roialme, horspris a Caleys, Gascoigne, Brest, Chirburghe et la ville de Berewyk, sur paine de forfaiture d'ycelle et des vesselx qi l'amesneront. Et qe nule licence soit grantez au contraire sanz l'advis de son conseil, et resonable cause, et qe ceux encore q'averont /tielle licence et congie,\ troefent seuretee suffisante de reporter lettres testimoniales de lour descharge /faite\ es lieux vers quelles ils en averont celles congies.

Because of this may it please your highness to confirm the said statute and ordinance in the present parliament, and ordain that the said statute be enforced on pain of a severe penalty.

Answer.
The king wills it.

XXX. [Preachers of heresy.]
53. Also, the commons request: whereas a statute was made in the last parliament in the following words,
[Col. b] It is ordained in this parliament that the king's commissions shall be directed to sheriffs and other ministers of the king, or to other worthy persons, after and according to the certifications of the prelates to be made in the chancery from time to time, to arrest all such preachers, and their supporters, maintainers and abettors, and to keep them under arrest and securely imprisoned until they be willing to justify themselves in accordance with reason and the law of holy church: and the king wills and commands that the chancellor grant such commissions as often as he be notified and required to do this by the prelates or any one of them, as is said above. Which was never agreed or granted by the commons, and although it was spoken of, it lacked their assent; that this statute be annulled, since it was certainly not their intention that they or their successors be controlled by nor obliged to the prelates more than their ancestors had been in the past.

Answer.
It pleases the king.

XXXI. [Exports of grain.]
54. Also, the commons of the counties of York and Lincoln, together with all the cities and boroughs complain: that their grain, by various patents granted, is carried in great quantities out of the kingdom, and for that reason such a scarcity and dearth has arisen in the country that it is greatly damaging, and much harm will result if remedy is not provided. In view of which the aforesaid lieges request that it may please him to abstain from granting such patents, repealing those which have been granted, and ordaining in this parliament that none shall henceforth take a ship laden with corn to sell or discharge outside the kingdom, unless at Calais, Berwick upon Tweed, or Bordeaux. And that the masters, when their ships are laden, shall go to the next good town where there is a port, and pay their custom, and take a certain certificate to the aforesaid towns, and leave another certificate where they pay their custom: so that it may be known where they shall be delivered and laden, and that on pain of a grievous penalty to be prescribed by the advice of parliament.

Answer.
The king wills that for the aforesaid cause a general prohibition be promulgated throughout the kingdom that no corn shall pass outside the realm to anywhere except Calais, Gascony, Brest, Cherbourg, and the town of Berwick, on pain of forfeiture of the same and of the vessels which carry it. And that no permission be given to the contrary without the advice of his council, and reasonable cause, and that those who continue to have such licence and permission give sufficient surety to bring back letters testimonial of their discharge made in the places for which they have such licence.

---

[44] 5 Ric.2 stat.1 c.10.
[45] *Original* 52.
[46] *Original* 53.

[The retail fish trade in London.]

55[47] Item, supplient humblement ses liges, mair, aldermans et la commune de vostre citee de Londres, pur commune profit sibien de vous lour seignour, come de touz autres seignours, et toute la commune de vostre roialme; qe come par long temps einz ces heures ad este soeffert en vostre dite citee un grevous errour, encontre tout manere de droit et resoun; et ce par maintenance et torcenouse outremesner des fisshemangers noz concitizeins, c'estassavoir, qe quant aucun estranger ou forein de la terre ou d'aillours amenast ou fesoit amesner aucun pesson freshe ou salee par terre ou par eawe a la citee, pur vendre illoeqes, meintenant les fisshemongeres ont seisi mesme le pessoun encontre le gree de celui qe le devoit, et sanz bargaigner ovesqe lui, ou aucun pris demander, le ount mys a vente come lour propre, a trope greindre chieretee q'ele ne duist avoir este vendu, si les propres possessours d'icelle poissent avoir vendu mesme le pessoun en lour due manere, come use est, et touzjours ad estee parmy toute la terre et tout le mounde fors soulement en Londres. Et apres qe ycelle pessoun ad issint este vendu par les fisshmangeres, les possessours d'ycelle ont este leez de resceivre pur ycelle si poy come les fisshmongeres *[Page iii-142]*

[Col. a] les veullient paier, et plusours foitz meins q'il cousta a les ditz possessours. Et nientmeins ils n'osoient pluis demander, ne soi pleindre, pur doute de prendre greindre damage en lours corps, ou autre manere, la ou nostre seignour le roi ne soeffre ses purveours, n'achatours propres, oppresser son poeple en si dure manere. Et auxint mesmes les fisshemongeres ont affermez qe toutes maneres briges et controversies touchantz lour mistier serront attamez et terminez en lours courtes propres, quiels ils ont tenuz entre eux mesmes de lour auctoritee propre, et nemy aillours. Et auxint ils ont usez par plusours ans lour panyers quieles ils appellent dorsers, de meindre mesure q'ils ne dussent estre par veile ordinance, les unes a la moitee, et aucuns meindres, en deceit des seignours et de touz autres qe sont acustumez d'achatre mesmes les dorsers entiers: des quiels oppressions et contemptz y semble q'ils deussent respoundre au roi en especial.

Sur quoi, trespuissant seignour, nous voz subgitz, mair et aldermans, come voz ministres de la dite citee, ov l'avys de les communes, apperceivantz le grief, meschief et grant commune damage a vous, nostre seignour, et tout vostre roialme ad trop longement encurru par les errours suisditz, veulliantz de nostre part, en quanqe en nous atteint, restreindre les tortz et errours avauntditz, toutdys par amendement de vous noz seignour, et vostre tressage conseil, avons surveux et rehercez plusours veiles et profitables ordenances faitz en temps de noz sages et renomez predecessours sur mesme la matire. Queux ordeinances par commune avis en partie correctz avons pur commune profit renovellez, et faitz publier et proclamer parmy vostre dite citee: par vertu de quiele proclamacioun plusours estrangeres et foreins ont puis amesnez pesson a la citee, et le ont vendu illoeqes a moelt meindre pris qe ne soleit estre vendu devant par les mains de fisshemongeres. Et avons auxint arssez les faux dorsers, et forfait le pessoun amesne en ycelle, come nous trovons avant fait en temps de noz ditz predecessours. Quiele chose par les ditz fisshmongeres apperceu, et supposantz qe lours veiles prives affaires serroient overtement conuz et descoveritz, et auxint qe lours extorsions et errours avauntditz serroient par ycelle destruitz, confederent et comettent par toutes voies q'ils savont ou poont de contreester mesmes les ordinances et proclamacions, si par vous nostre tresredoute seignour, et

---

[47] *Original* 54.

[The retail fish trade in London.]

55. Also, his lieges the mayor, aldermen and the commons of your city of London humbly request, for the common profit as well of you their lord, as of all other lords, and all the commons of your kingdom: whereas a grievous error has long been endured in your said city, against all manner of right and reason; and that by the maintenance and wrongful excess of the fishmongers, our fellow citizens, namely, that when any stranger or foreigner of the land or from elsewhere brings or causes to be brought any fresh or salted fish by land or by water to the city, to sell there, the fishmongers immediately seize the same fish against the will of those who own it, and without bargaining with them, or paying anything for it, they place it on sale as their own, at a far higher price than it would have fetched if the true owners of the same had sold the same fish in their usual way, as is customary, and as has always been the case throughout the land and all the world, except in London alone. And after the same fish has been sold by the fishmongers, the owners of the same are left to receive for it as little as the fishmongers *[Page iii-142]*

[Col. a] wish to pay them, and often less than it cost the said owners. Nevertheless, they dare not ask for more, nor complain, through fear of suffering great bodily harm, or harm of some other kind, even though our lord the king does not allow his purveyors, nor his own buyers, to oppress his people in so harsh a manner. Moreover, the same fishmongers have affirmed that all kinds of brawls and disputes touching their mistery shall be discussed and determined in their own courts, which they hold amongst themselves on their own authority, and nowhere else. Furthermore, for many years they have used baskets which they calls 'dorsers', which provide a smaller measure than they ought, according to the old ordinance, some just a half, and other less, to the deceit of the lords and all others who are accustomed to buying full dorsers: for which oppressions and contempts it seems that they ought to answer to the king in particular.

In consequence whereof, most potent lord, we your subjects, the mayor and aldermen, as your ministers of the same city, with the advice of the commons, perceiving that injury, mischief and great harm to you, our lord, and all your realm has continued too long because of the aforesaid errors, wishing for our part, as far as it lies in us, to resist the aforesaid wrongs and errors, by the correction of you our lord, and your most wise council, have surveyed and rehearsed many old and beneficial ordinances made in the time of our wise and renowned predecessors on the same matter. Which ordinances, corrected in part by common advice, we have renewed for the common good, and caused them to be published and proclaimed throughout your said city: by virtue of which proclamations many strangers and aliens have since brought fish to the said city, and have sold it there at a much lower price than previously it was sold for by the fishmongers. And we have also burned the false dorsers, and confiscated the fish contained therein, as we find was done in the time of our said predecessors. The fishmongers, perceiving that, and supposing that their old, secret methods of business will be openly known and disclosed, and also that their aforesaid extortion and errors will be destroyed by the same, will band together and strive in all the ways they can devise to oppose the same ordinances and proclamations, unless

vostre tressage conseil ne soit le pluis hastive remedie sur ycelle ordenez et establiz.

Qe plese a vostre treshaute puissance, pur Dieux, et pur maintenir commune profit parmy tout vostre roialme, et auxint pur pluis sure pees et bon governail avoir en vostre citee, avoir regard as errours et meschiefs avauntditz, et \a/ les grevouses oppressions qe vostre people ont soeffertz long temps par ycelle; et ordener sur ycelle tiel remede come mieultz semblera a vous, tresredoute seignour, et a vostre conseil. Entendantz, tresredoute seignour, qe moelt est grant ennoy et pesantie as coers de touz voz autres communes, de eux soeffrer en lours si torcinouses affaire, et outremesners q'ils ont si longement usez, et come lour semble de jour en autre unqore comettent de perseverer par lours subtiles compassementz et covyne de lours maintenours, encontre touz maners de droit et resons, et commune profit, dount ils suppliont, pur Dieux, et en oevre de charitee, et pur commune profit, hastive remedie: nomement, entre autres remedies qe nul fisshmongere de Londres, n'autre vitailler qeconqe, porte desore enavaunt aucun estat judicial en la citee. Et auxint qe touz les foreins enmesnantz pessoun fresshe de la miere a la citee pur vendre, le puissent tailler et vendre en mesnuz peces sibien come en grosse, et q'ils soient en especial proteccioun du roi en venantz et retornantz, sibien lour pessoun et lour voiture, come lours corps. Et oultre ce qe touz les hostes en touz paiis de la terre soient defenduz sur grief peine, de vendre, ou bargaigner, aucun manere de pessoun fresshe du miere, ou aucun fisshmongere, ou autre frank de la citee de Londres. Auxint qe nul fisshmongere, n'autre frank de la citee,

[Col. b] achate desore enavaunt, loins ne pres, aucun manere de pessoun fresshe du miere, ne de eawe douce, pur revendre en mesme la citee; forspris pikes, anguilles fresshes, queux sont en commune d'achatre et vendre sibien as denszeins come foreins. Issint toutfoitz qe les denszeins ne destourbent les foreins de franchement vendre tiel manere de pessoun, as touz temps, q'ils amesnent ycelle a la citee pur vendre illoeqes, et qe toutes les ordinances faites en la citee en remedie des tortz et errours avauntditz, et auxint en remedie de usure, usurers et brocours d'icelle, soient ratifiez et confermez en cest present parlement. Et pur pluis seure continuance d'ycestes, soit ajouste desore enavaunt a la charge qe chescun mair devera prendre en l'escheqer, q'il tiegne les ordinances suisditz faitz sur les fisshemongeres et usureres, en manere \[suisdite,]/ sanz flescher d'un part ou d'autre par acception de persone. Salvant toutfoitz as prelatz les libertees de seinte esglise.

Responsio.

56[48] Quant au primer demande, touchant l'estat judiciel en dite citee, est assentuz qe nul manere de vitailler ait ou port desoreenavant aucun estat judiciel en mesme la citee, n'en aucun autre citee, ville, port du mier, parmy le roialme, horspris en les villes ou n'y a autre persone suffisant de porter tiel estat: adonqes en ce cas qe tiel juge cesse oultrement pur le temps q'il serra officer de soi medler de vendre vitailles, par lui ou par autre, sur payne de forfaiture d'icelle vitailles.[49]

56[50] Item, quant al secounde demande, touchant retaille des vitailles, est assentuz qe touz foreins de quelconqes paiis q'ils soient, esteante del amistee nostre seignour le roi, venantz deinz la dite citee, et as autres citees et villes deinz le roialme avauntdit avec lour pessoun et autres vitailles quelconqes, illoeqes demurrantz, et en lour paiis

remedy is most swiftly ordained and decreed most swiftly by you our most redoubtable lord, and your most wise council. May it please your most exalted might, for God, and to maintain the common good throughout your entire realm, and also for the greater certainty of peace and good governance in your city, to consider the aforesaid errors and troubles, and the grievous oppressions which your people have long suffered through the same; and to ordain such remedy as seems best to you, most redoubtable lord, and to your council. Considering, most redoubtable lord, how great is the vexation and displeasure in the hearts of all your other commons, that they should be allowed to commit the wrongs and excesses which they have long practised, and continue from one day to the next by their subtle plots and the craft of their maintainers, contrary to right and reason, and the common good, for which they seek a swift remedy, for God and by way of charity, and for the common good: namely, amongst other remedies, that no fishmonger of London, or any other victualler, shall henceforth hold any judicial post in the city. And also that all strangers bringing fresh fish from the sea to the city to sell, may weigh and sell it as well in small portions as in gross, and that they shall enjoy the special protection of the king in coming and returning, for their fish and their transport, as well as their persons. And further, that all hosts in all regions of the land shall be forbidden on pain of grievous penalty, to sell or bargain in any way for fresh fish from the sea, with any fishmonger, of other freeman of the city of London. Also, that no fishmonger, or other freeman of the city,

[Col. b] shall henceforth buy, far or near, any kind of fresh fish from the sea, or from fresh water, to resell in the same city; except pike and fresh eels, which are to be bought and sold as well by denizens as aliens. Provided always that denizens shall not prevent aliens from selling freely at all times whatsoever fish they bring to the city to sell there, and that all the ordinances made in the city to remedy the aforesaid wrongs and errors, and also to counter usury, usurers and brokers of the same, shall be ratified and confirmed in the present parliament. And for the more certain continuance of those things, it should be added to the charge which each mayor must accept in the exchequer, that he shall enforce the aforesaid ordinances made uoon the fishmongers and usurers, in the aforesaid manner, without yielding in any detail, or making exception for anyone. Saving always to the prelates the liberties of holy church.

Answer.

56. As for the first request, touching the judicial post in the said city, it is agreed that no kind of victualler shall henceforth enjoy or occupy any judicial post in the same city, nor in any other city, town or seaport throughout the kingdom, except in towns where there is no other person fit to occupy such a post: and in that case, that such a judge, for the time he is officer, shall cease entirely to concern himself with the sale of victuals, in person or through another, on pain of forfeiting the same victuals.

57. Also, as for the second request, touching the retail of victuals, it is agreed that all aliens from whatever country they may be, bearing friendship towards our lord the king, entering the said city, and other cities and towns within the aforesaid kingdom with their fish, and other kinds of victuals, residing there, and returning to their countries, shall

---

[48] *Original* 54.
[49] 6 Ric.2 stat.1 c.9.
[50] *Original* 55.

retornantz, soient souz la proteccioun especiale et salve garde nostre seignour le roi, et illoeqes les dites pessoun et autres vitailles puissent desore franchement et sanz contredit de nully trencher, tailler et vendre en groos, ou par parcelles, a lour voluntee, nientcontreesteant privilege,
Membrane 1 ordinance, usage, n'autre rienz fait au contraire.

57[51] Item, quant a ce q'est demandez des ditz peschours ou pessoners, q'ils soient defenduz, est assentuz qe toutes tieux hostes en chescun port, ville et autre lieu sur les coustiers du miere, et aillours parmye le roialme, sibien a \Londres,/ Jernemuth', Scardeburgh', Wynchelsee et Rye, come aillours parmy le roialme, deinz franchise et dehors, soient de tout oustez de lour nuisant et maluree affaire et forstallerie, et lour est oultrement defenduz, sur peine q'appent, q'ils ne lour medlent desore d'embracer harang, n'autre pessoun, ou vitaille quelconqe, n'autre destourbance facent en prive ... n'en appert, paront aucun persone, denszein ou estrange, esteant del amistee del roialme d'Engleterre, soit aucunement empeschez; einz qe toutes maneres des peschours et vitaillers soient frankes et a large de vendre lour pessoun et autres vitailles, ou et quant, et a quelconqe persone lour plerra deinz le roiaume avauntdit, nientcontreesteant custume, usage, privilege n'autre rienz faitz ou usez devaunt ces heures a contraire par les ditz hostes, ou autre persone del monde quelconqe. Et par especial est defenduz qe nul tiel hoste se medle desore de vendre ou bargainer aucun manere de pessoun fresshe du miere, al oeps d'aucun fisshemongere ou autre frank de la dite citee. Et semblablement est defenduz qe nul fisshemongere, n'autre frank de mesme la citee, achate desore enavaunt, loins ne pres de mesme la citee, aucune manere de pessoun fresshe, du miere, ne de eawe doulce, pur revendre en mesme la citee, horspris anguilles fresshes, beketes ou pikes, queux soient en commune d'achatre et vendre, sibien as denszeins come as foreins. *[Page iii-143]*
[Col. a] Issint toutes foitz qe les denszeins ne destourbent les foreins de franchement vendre tiel manere de pessoun en mesme la citee, en quelconqe temps ils les amesnent pur vendre illoeqes.

59[52] Item, /quant a\ce q'est demande de /usure,\ usurers et progours d'ycelle comprises en dite bille, le roi voet qe seinte esglise eit sa jurisdiccione come ele soloit avoir d'ancientee; a la quele le roi n'entende mye de faire prejudice en aucun manere. Et si damage ou grief soit fait a aucuny en la dite citee; c'estassavoir, par voie d'accompte nient renduz, trespas, extorsione, oppressione, fauxetee, deceite, ou en aultre /manere\ quelconqe, encontre la loy de la terre, /semble qe la\ commune loy, avec les bones usages et custumes de la dite citee doivent assez suffire de faire redresse, punissement et amendement de les grevances et damages avauntditz en due manere.

60[53] Item, qant a ce q'est demandez qe chescun mair eit desore especialment en son charge a l'escheqier, et qe soit annexe en soun serement illoeqes a faire, q'il tiegne et face garder la dite ordinance de vitaillers sanz flescher a nulle partie; le roi le voet. Et semblablement eient en lour charge touz autres mairs, baillifs et autres governours des citees, burghs et villes, et vitaillers parmye /le\ roiaume, sur lours serementz affaires al entree en lours offices et novelle creacione.[54]

enjoy the special protection and safeguard of our lord the king, and that there the said fish and other victuals may henceforth be cut up, weighed and sold freely and without impediment, in gross, or in portions, at their will, notwithstanding privilege,
Membrane 1 ordinance, usage or anything else to the contrary.

58. Also, as to what is demanded concerning the said fishermen or fishmongers, 'that they be forbidden', it is agreed that all such hosts in every port, town and other place on the coasts of the sea, and elsewhere throughout the realm, as well at London, Yarmouth, Scarborough, Winchelsea and Rye, as elsewhere throughout the realm, within franchise and without, be entirely ousted from their wicked and evil trading and forestalling, and they are utterly forbidden, on pain of the appointed penalty, to deal henceforth in herring, or any other fish, or victuals of any kind, or cause any other disturbance whether in private or openly, by means of which any person, denizen or alien, friendly to the kingdom of England, is in any way hindered; but that all kinds of fishermen and victuallers be free and at liberty to sell their fish and other victuals, where and whenever and to whomsoever they choose within the aforesaid kingdom, notwithstanding custom, usage, privilege, or anything else done or practised to the contrary before this time by the said hosts, or anyone else in the world. And in particular, it is forbidden that any such host involve himself henceforth in selling or bargaining for any kind of fresh fish of the sea, for the benefit of any fishmonger or other freeman of the said city. Similarly, it is forbidden to any fishmonger, or other freeman of the same city, to buy henceforth, whether far from or near the same city, any kind of fresh fish, from the sea, or from fresh water, to resell in the same city, except fresh eels, bream and pike, which are to be bought and sold generally, as well by denizens as aliens. *[Page iii-143]*

[Col. a] Provided always that denizens shall not prevent strangers from selling freely any kind of fish in the same city, whensoever they bring it there to sell.

59. Also, as to that which is sought on usury, usurers and hoarders contained in the said bill, the king wills that holy church shall have its jurisdiction as it used to have of old; which the king does not intend to prejudice in any way. And if injury or harm is done on anyone in the said city; namely, by means of account unpaid, trespass, extortion, oppression, falsehood, deceit, or in any other way whatsoever, contrary to the law of the land, it seems that the common law, together with the good usages and customs of the said city ought to suffice to redress, punish and correct the aforesaid injuries and damages in due course.

60. Also, with regard to the request that every mayor, henceforth, shall have especially included in his charge at the exchequer, and added to his oath to be made there, that he shall enforce and protect the said ordinance of victuallers without yielding to any party; the king wills it. And it similarly shall be included in the charge of all other mayors, bailiffs and other governors of the cities, boroughs and towns, and victuallers throughout the realm, on their oaths made on entry into office and new investiture.

---

[51] *Original* 56.
[52] *Original* 57.
[53] *Original* 58.
[54] 6 Ric.2 stat.1 c.12.

[The fishmongers' company.]

61. Also, on the bill submitted in parliament by the mayor, aldermen and commons of London against the fishmongers of London; both the said mayor, aldermen and a large number of the said commons, as well as a great number of the said fishmongers having appeared there, and the said bill having been read in parliament, Nicholas Exton, who was to speak on behalf of the fishmongers, prayed of our lord the king and the lords of parliament on behalf of himself and all the other fishmongers of London, that it might please the king to take them into his protection and safeguard, so that bodily harm might not come to them because of this affair, since he said that there was considerable tumult in the city, which they greatly feared, and the more greatly because this suit had been brought not for the common profit of the realm, as was supposed, but out of hatred, rancour and envy alone. To which the mayor replied that what had been done there by him or any of his men had been done for the common profit of the lords and the entire realm; and events would show that plainly proven, with the aid of Our Lord. And as for the fishmongers fearing tumult and bodily injury to be inflicted upon them in the said city, the mayor replied that in all his life the commons had never shown greater unity, love and concord, except only towards the fishmongers, who strove to oppress the people and extort from them. And the said mayor undertook at all costs that good peace would be preserved within his bailiwick, unless the same fishmongers were to commence riot and madness; for which, it was said, they were preparing themselves each day.

62. Whereupon, orders were given on the king's behalf to both parties that on pain of them and each and every one of them

[Col. b] forfeiting all he could forfeit to our lord the king in body and goods, they and every of them should strictly preserve and show peace towards one another. And to avoid bodily harm which might easily arise, it was said that the king our lord would take all the fishmongers and every one of them into his special protection. It was further said to those fishmongers that although it seemed to the lords of parliament that the said bill against them, and the requests contained in the same were most reasonable and beneficial to the entire kingdom, nevertheless the king willed that if they wished to complain of any harm or injury done them in particular, they should make their bill or plea thereon in particular, and right would be done them.

63. And then, later, Walter Sibil, present amongst the said fishmongers, prayed of the lords, for love of God, that it might please them to hear him for a short while, and said, My lords, it is not indeed unknown to you all how before this time, some of the persons here present, who were instrumental in the suit against us, were by order of the king who is dead, whom God absolve, taken and imprisoned for certain offences alleged against them, at which time the chief ministers of the city who carried out the orders of the king belonged to our mistery and livery of fishmongers. And for this reason alone, and the ancient hatred and rancour conceived against us, they now bring their suit to destroy us, and take away our franchise and liberty granted to us of old, and confirmed by the noble kings of England of the time; because of which we have greater need for good security of the peace from them and their supporters.

64[58] A quoy Johan More, mercer, respondist illoeqes et dist, Wauter Sybille, les bones gentz de ceste citee sont assez fortz de maintenir la paix encontre vous touz, sinon qe einsi soit qe vous facez amesner autre foitz deinz ceste citee les communes de Kent et de Essex, come nadgairs feistes en le treitereuse rumour.

65[59] Et le dit Wauter priast as seignours de parlement qe le dit Johan More feust comandez de rehercer illoeqes celles paroles q'il avoit dit, a fin qe ce qe touchast si hautement son estat feust clerement entenduz. Et adonqes le dit Johan More dist, Messeignours, fist il je ne die mye expressement qe einsi est, mais je die qe commune fame et parlance est en nostre citee, qe Johan Horn, fisshemonger, et Adam Karlill' de Londres, estoient en dit rumour les primers et principalx conseillours, confortours, abettours et excitours, qe les communes de Kent et de Essex nadgairs treiterousement levez et assemblez encontre le roi et son roialme approcheassent leur citee, et entrassent en ycelle: et qe le dit Wauter fuist le primer et principal destourbour a William de Walleworth' lors mair, et a diverses autres persones foialx nostre seignour le roi q'ils ne poaient a celle foitz clore les portz de la citee, ne lever le pount, ou defendre mesme la citee, encontre les ditz treitours, combien qe le dit William de Walleworth' et les autres a ce lour afforcerent moelt grantement. Et priast le dit Johan qe de ce fuist enquerre fait par bones gentz de la citee, et il pensast qe ce q'il ad dit serra trovez pur voir.

Et ce estoit grantez illoeqes.

64. To which John More, mercer, there replied, saying, Walter Sibil, the good people of this city are strong enough to keep the peace against you all, unless you lead the commons of Kent and Essex once more into the said city, as you recently did during the treacherous uprising.

65. And the said Walter prayed of the lords in parliament that the said John More be ordered to repeat the words he had spoken, so that what bore so seriously upon his honour might be plainly understood. And then the said John More said, My lords I do not say that it is definitely so, but I say that common rumour and parlance in our city has it that John Horn, fishmonger, and Adam Karlile of London, were, in the said uprising, the prime and principal advisers, supporters, abettors and instigators of the idea that the commons of Kent and Essex, who had recently rebelled and gathered to oppose the king and his kingdom, should approach the city, and enter the same: and that the said Walter was the prime and principal harasser of William Walworth, then mayor, and various other persons faithful to our lord the king, so that they were unable on that occasion to close the gates of the city, or raise the bridge, or defend the same city against the said traitors, even though the said William Walworth and the others strove hard to do so. And the said John prayed that inquiry into this might be made by the good people of the city, and he believed that what he had said would be found to be true.

And that was granted there.

---

[58] *Original* 62.
[59] *Original* 63.

Appendix

6 October 1382

Westminster

1. John de Falvesle and his wife Elizabeth, daughter of William Lord Say, have petitioned the parliament for livery of the lands held before his death by John de Say, Elizabeth's brother, which by advice of the council have been granted to them despite the fact that they did not obtain the king's licence to marry. Dated 5 December 1382.
Source: *CCR 1381-5*, 234-5.

2. Order to various sheriffs not to allow corn or malt to be exported to anywhere except Gascony, Bayonne, Calais, Brest, Cherbourg or Berwick-upon-Tweed without the king's licence. By king and council, Dated 22 October 1382.
Source: *CCR 1381-5*, 236.

3. Order to the chancellor and proctors of the University of Oxford to allow the prior of St Frideswide's to hold a fair at Oxford, until such time as the dispute between the prior and the university can be decided by the king and council. By the council in parliament. Dated 19 October 1382.
Source: *CCR 1381-5*, 162.

4. Pardons to the following, 'by the king of his grace in parliament', and for certain sums paid in the hanaper:
Adam Perkyn of Howsham (Yorkshire) for the death of William Clerk of Westow at Mennethorpe (Yorkshire). Dated 18 October 1382.
Ralph son of John Aston for the death of his wife Agnes in Aughton Wood (Yorkshire). Dated 30 October 1382.
William son of John Pert, knight, for all felonies, treasons, murders, etc. committed before 14 September 1382. Dated 17 October 1382.
Source: *CPR 1381-5*, 181-2.

5. Pardon to John of Norfolk, late keeper of the gaol of Warwick, for all escapes of felons before 4 November 1380. By king and council in parliament. Dated 12 November 1382.
Source: *CPR 1381-5*, 183.

1383 February

Westminster

23 February - 10 March 1383

(C 65/40. *RP*, III.144-148. *SR*, II.30-31)

C 65/40 is a roll of four membranes, each approximately 323mm in width, sewn together in chancery style and numbered in a later hand. The text, written in the official chancery script of several scribes, occupies the rectos of the membranes only. The dorses are blank apart from two later headings: 'Parliamentum de anno sexto Ricardi secundi' on membrane 1, and 'Rott' Parliamt' Ric' secundi anno vi ^{o}' on membrane 4. The condition of the roll is generally good, though membranes 2 and 1 are stained with gallic acid, making the text illegible in places. Stitched to the foot of membrane 1 is a piece of parchment on which a later hand has written, 'Rotulus parliamenti Ricardi secundi anno sexto apud Westm' die lune in septimana tertia quadragesime'. The Arabic numerals are of a later date, while the Roman numerals alongside the common petitions are contemporary. The roll appears to be complete.

In the parliament of October 1382, the commons had made it clear that they favoured an expedition to Flanders rather than one to Iberia, despite the fact that John of Gaunt and many of the lords were equally clear that they preferred the latter. Yet, while the commons had granted a fifteenth and tenth for the war, nothing had as yet been decided as to exactly how this money should be spent, and during the winter of 1382-3 both the advocates of the 'way of Flanders' and those who favoured some other form of military action, be it in France or in Iberia, continued to try to win support for their policies. The defeat of the Flemish rebels at Roosebeke on 27 November made the case for aiding Ghent more urgent, and on 6 December Bishop Despenser was given permission to start recruiting for his Flemish 'crusade'.[1] Gaunt was still vehemently opposed to the bishop's plans, however, and at a council meeting in early January it was proposed that the king himself, now sixteen, might instead lead the campaign in person. This, in fact, was precisely what was advocated in the writs of summons sent out from the council on 7 January: the king of France had overrun most of Flanders, they declared, and was 'hastening to besiege Calais'; Richard planned to go abroad in person to raise the siege, succour his allies, and recover the crown of France.[2] This was the plan that the February 1383 parliament was invited to sanction.

The writs of summons to the spiritual peers were the same as for the parliament of October 1382, except that the see of Llandaff was vacant (the king's unpopular confessor, Thomas Rushook, was in fact provided to it just a week after the writs were issued), and the abbot of St Mary's York was reinstated after being omitted for the previous assembly. The list of temporal lords included the king's uncle, the earl of Cambridge, by now returned from his futile expedition to Portugal, along with the newcomers John de Beaumont, John le Strange of Knockin and Richard de Poynings, all of whose ancestors had previously been summoned.

Following a day's postponement for late arrivals, Robert Braybrooke, bishop of London and chancellor, made the opening speech to the assembled lords and commons on Tuesday 24 February. Should the king go to France in person?, he asked them. If not, what should be done instead, 'bearing in mind the amount of money granted' (Items 2-3)? He was referring, of course, to the fifteenth and tenth granted in the parliament of October 1382; there was no new request for taxation in this parliament.[3] Having considered this question for a day or two, the commons asked to be allowed to discuss it with a committee of lords, to which the king agreed (Item 8). Following a further day or two of 'intercommuning', the commons once again came before the king and lords and, through the person of their Speaker, James Pickering, MP for Yorkshire, declared - as tactfully as possible - that they were in favour of accepting Bishop Despenser's offer to lead the expedition to Flanders. The danger from the Scots on the northern border was too immediate, they said, to make it sensible for either the king or his uncles to quit the realm for the time being (Item 10). In order to clarify matters, Despenser's offer was then once again spelt out in detail: if he were to be granted the fifteenth and tenth, plus the proceeds of tunnage and poundage for the time being, he would undertake to lead 3000 men-at-arms and 3000 archers to France, with 1000 of them (500 of each) going immediately to the relief of Ghent. All the other costs of the campaign, including shipping, he would meet himself - that is, they would be covered by the sums that he would raise under the guise of crusading taxes (Item 11).

---

[1] For these events see Saul, *Richard II*, 102-3; Goodman, *John of Gaunt*, 94-5.
[2] *CCR 1381-5*, 246-7.
[3] Dodd, 'The Lords, Taxation and the Community of Parliament', 297.

The roll is, as usual, relatively taciturn about the process by which the decision to support Despenser's offer was arrived at, but the chroniclers made it clear that the debate was both protracted and bitter. Walsingham declared that it was only on the final Saturday of the session (7 March), 'after many arguments... and a great deal of disputation', that general agreement was reached to support the bishop's plans (although he later implied that 'almost all the magnates of the realm' continued to oppose the crusade). The author of the *Vita Ricardi Secundi* said that there was a 'great controversy' in the parliament, with the lords wanting Gaunt to lead the expedition, even if it was to Flanders; 'eventually', however, 'the commons prevailed against the lords... although to the great indignation of the lords'. The Westminster chronicler stated that Despenser 'met with prolonged opposition from the ill-will of the lords', ostensibly on the grounds that a campaign fought under the papal banner might encourage the pope to try to usurp the rights of the English king in France - although in fact, he declared, they opposed it 'from motives of base jealousy'. The commons stood fast, however, with the two sons of the earl of Devon, Sir Peter and Sir Philip Courtenay, especially vociferous on Despenser's behalf. John of Gaunt was so angered by this that, after uttering certain threats which, when repeated, 'set the commons in a ferment', he promptly walked out and left the parliament to its own devices.[4] Some of the mutual hostility of the lords and commons on this issue may be reflected in the decision, apparently taken at the very end of the parliament, to reduce the bishop's force from 6000 to 5000 men and not to grant him the proceeds of tunnage and poundage. He was also at this stage asked to name the men who would act as commanders of his army, which he seems to have been very reluctant to do in open parliament, although he did in the end write down four names on a schedule which he handed to the king (Items 20-21).[5] It is also possible that the request from the commons that the king should make it clear to the lords that nobody ought to depart from parliament until the commons' petitions had been fully dealt with should be seen as a (thinly) veiled criticism of Gaunt for walking out (Item 19). Relations between the duke and the commons had certainly reached a new low.

The remaining petitions of the commons focused for the most part either on the military situation (Items 13 and 14, the defence of the seas and the Scottish March respectively) or the royal household and administration. These latter were clearly causing some concern: one of the commons' requests was that the king should choose the wisest and noblest persons to fill high offices in the government, and that he should announce their names in parliament (Item 16). This may have been intended as a criticism of the chancellor, Robert Braybrooke (whose advice the commons had now twice failed to heed), who resigned on the last day of the session, to be replaced three days later by Michael de la Pole.[6] Another petition encouraged the king to surround himself with worthy persons and to restrict the expenses of his household, so that resources could be spared for the war effort (Item 18). Such requests clearly irritated Richard: his reply in each case was that he would appoint or choose such men as seemed best to him.[7] A further petition requested the full restoration of London's liberties and franchises, including those of the victuallers, who (the fishmongers especially) had had severe restrictions placed on their political and mercantile activities in the previous parliament. The king agreed to this, although he stipulated that the victuallers were not to try to evade the control of the mayor of the city (Item 19).[8] All these matters were, however, subordinate to the great debate over foreign policy, which clearly dominated this parliament, and once the decision to support Despenser's crusade had been taken, however reluctantly in some quarters, the parliament rapidly came to an end, being dissolved on 10 March.[9] Just over two months later, on 16 May, the bishop's army crossed to Calais and set off on its way. Unfortunately, the 'Flemish crusade' turned out to be a military fiasco, which meant that foreign policy would dominate the next parliament, that of October 1383, to almost the same extent as it had this one.

---

[4] *St Albans Chronicle 1376-1394*, 662-6; *Vita Ricardi Secundi*, 76; *Westminster Chronicle*, 34-6; Philip Courtenay was knight of the shire for Devon, but it is not clear why his brother was present in this parliament.

[5] Walsingham names his commanders as Sir Hugh Calveley, Sir William Farringdon, Sir William Elmham and Sir Thomas Trivet: *St Albans Chronicle 1376-1394*, 664-6.

[6] *HBC*, 87.

[7] Cf. Tuck, *Richard II and the English Nobility*, 89-90.

[8] *St Albans Chronicle 1376-1394*, 666-8.

[9] *CCR 1381-5*, 290-1.

Text and Translation

Text

Page iii-144, Membrane 1
\PARLIAMENTUM DE ANNO SEXTO RICARDO SECUNDI./
Membrane 4

1. Fait a remembrer qe le lundy en la tierce semaigne de Quaresme, qe feust le primer jour de ce parlement et le .xxiij. jour del moys de Feverer, l'an du regne nostre seignour le roi Richard, qi Dieux salve, \sisme,/ si vindrent aucuns des prelats et seignours du roialme en le palays du roi a Westm' ou cest parlement estoit sommonez depar le roi. Et quant ils avoient longement /demurrez\ illoeqes avec le chanceller, tresorier et les autres grantz officers du roi en la chambre acustumee, et a ce apparaillez, purtant qe lour estoit reportez qe les viscounts des contees n'avoient mye toutz fait retournir lours briefs de parlement, et auxi, pur ce qe la greindre partie des prelatz et seignours q'avoient la dite somonce n'estoient encores venuz, si estoit cest parlement adjournez depar le roi nostre seignour et de son comandement tanqe al lendemain lors proschein venant: et de mesme l'adjournement proclamacion publique estoit fait en la sale de Westm', donant en comandement par la dite proclamation a touz q'avoient ycelle somonce, q'ils y retournassent le dit lendemain par temps, pur y oier les causes de la somonce de ce parlement.

2. Item, le dit lendemain qe feust mardy, si vient en parlement sibien nostre seignour mesmes en sa persone, come monsire d'Espaigne duc de Lancastre, l'ercevesqe de Cantirbirs et les autres prelatz, seignours et communes q'avoient la dite somonce pur la greindre partie, et illoeqes maistre Robert Braybrok, evesqe de Londres et chanceller d'Engleterre, del commandement du roi nostre seignour, avoit les paroles, et dist, Seignours et sires, nostre seignour le roi cy present, qi Dieux salve, m'ad commandez de vous exposer et monstrer depar lui les causes de la somonce de cest son parlement, qe sont tielles: primerement, al honour de Dieux et de seinte esglise, nostre dit seignour desire sovereinement qe la franchise de seinte esglise et les bones loys de sa terre, et la paix d'ycelle, soient bien gardez et maintenuz, auxi avant come aient este gardez en temps de nul de ses progenitours rois d'Engleterre; et qe ses bons et vrois subgitz sibien depar decea come depar dela soient maintenuz en tout droit et quiete. Et si riens en celle \partie/ busoigne d'amendement, qe ce soit ore amendez a mieltz q'ome purra, par l'advis de chescun degree de ce parlement.

3. Item, vous savez coment au drain parlement nostre dit seignour le roi avoit pris purpos d'aler, ove l'aide de Dieux, en sa persone as parties de France, pur le recovrir de son droit heritage; paront la commune de son roialme par soi lui ad grantez une .xvme et la clergie par soi une .xme a lever as termes limitez, en defens du roialme, et aide a nostre seignour le roy dessuisdit. Et doivez entendre qe maintenant apres le dit parlement finiz si
[Col. b] vindrent tielles novelles depar dela qe furent moelt grantement desplesantes au roi nostre seignour dessuisdit, de ce qe l'adversaire de France ove son ost roial avoit este armez en la countee \et terre/ de Flandres, qi furent noz bien veullantz et amys, et \y\ avoit euz bataille d'arest et desconfit noz ditz amys, et conquis le paiis entier a sa main propre, horspris la ville de Gaunt qi se tient encores. Par quoy tantost le roi nostre seignour, ceste novelle oiez, fist somoner un grant conseil cy a Westm' tost apres la Epiphanie derrain passez; en quiel conseil si estoit grant partie des seignours du roialme esperitelx et temporelx, et grant nombre des pluis suffisantz bachilers du roialme: et celle

Translation

THE PARLIAMENT OF THE SIXTH YEAR OF RICHARD II.

1. Be it remembered that on the Monday of the third week in Lent, the first day of this parliament and 23 February in the sixth year of the reign of our lord the king [1383], whom God preserve, some of the prelates and lords of the kingdom appeared in the king's palace at Westminster where the parliament had been summoned on the king's behalf. And when they had remained there a long while with the chancellor, treasurer and other great officers of the king in the chamber customarily appointed and arrayed for that purpose, because it was reported that not all the sheriffs of the counties had yet returned their writs of parliament, and also, because a large number of the prelates and lords who had received the said summons had still not arrived, the parliament was adjourned by order of our lord the king until the following day: and a public announcement of the same adjournment was made in Westminster Hall, orders being given in the said announcement that all who had received the same summons return early the following day [24 February 1383], to hear there the reasons for summoning this parliament.

2. Also, on the said following day, which was a Tuesday [24 February 1383], our lord the king appeared in parliament in person, along with my lord of Spain, duke of Lancaster, the archbishop of Canterbury, and most of the other prelates, lords and commons who had received the said summons, and there Mr Robert Braybrook, bishop of London and chancellor of England, who spoke at the command of the king our lord, said, Lords and sirs, our lord the king here present, whom God preserve, has ordered me to explain and show you on his behalf the reasons for summoning this his parliament, which are these: first, to the honour of God and holy church, our said lord the king chiefly desires that the franchises of holy church, the good laws of his land, and the peace of the same be kept and maintained, as ever they were in the time of any of his predecessors the kings of England; and that his good and true subjects on both sides of the sea enjoy justice and tranquillity. And if anything requires amendment in that respect, that it be amended as well as possible, by the advice of every degree in this parliament.

3. Also, you know how, at the last parliament, our said lord the king stated his intention of journeying in person, with the aid of God, to the parts of France, to recover his rightful inheritance; for which the commons of his realm for their part granted him a fifteenth and the clergy for their part a tenth to be levied at specified terms, in defence of the realm, and to aid our aforesaid lord the king. And it must be understood that as soon as the said parliament had ended
[Col. b] there arrived news from overseas greatly displeasing to the king our aforesaid lord, inasmuch as the enemy of France with its royal host had taken up arms in the county and land of Flanders, which is our well-wisher and friend, and battle had been waged resulting in the capture and defeat of our said friends and the conquest of the entire land by the enemy, except the town of Ghent which still holds out. On account of which, as soon as the king our lord heard the news, he caused a great council to be convened at Westminster immediately after Epiphany last; which was attended by a large number of the lords of the realm, spiritual and temporal, and many of the more worthy gentlemen of the realm:

novelle illoeqes declarree, avec la bone volentee qe la dite ville de Gaunt porte toutdys en loialtee a nostre dit seignour le roy et a son roialme, estoit finalment par plusours resons l'advis de toutz qe pur le rescous de Gaunt, et recovrir du paiis de Flandres, qe nostre dit seignour le roi passast en sa persone avec son ost roial, si ce il poiast faire son honur salvez. Qar y feust dit, et apparissant chose est qe chescun loial lige homme du roi vorroit \pluis tost et de pluis ardant desir/ travailler en la presence de son seignour lige, q'ad le droit et verroi title a la coroune de France, qe avec nule autre persone du monde, et as meindres coustages. Mais pur tant qe la busoigne estoit et est si chargeante, sibien touchant le governaille du roialme en absence du dit nostre seignour s'il y passat, come autrement sur son dit aler, qe homme ne voloit ne n'osast, pur perils apparissantz, finalment assentir al un ne a l'autre sanz parlement. Et pur ce le roi nostre seignour vous charge et prie moelt entierment qe vous veulliez diligeaument aviser vous les seignours, c'estassavoir par vous mesmes, et vous la commune par vous mesmes, de ceste matire; et par especial si vous semble qe nostre seignour le roy devra et purra en sa persone passer, come dit est, ou nemye. Et si vous semblera qe, salvez son honur, il ne purra passer, adonqes vorrez vous adviser diligealment quiel armee ou viage serra et purra estre fait, et par qi, et en quelle manere; eiant regard as coustages affaires, et al haste qe le viage demande pur le rescous de Gaunt: \et auxint eiant regard/ a la quantitee de monoie grantez. Et voz advis ent prises, \les/ vorrez en haste monstrer avant a nostre dit seignour le roi et a son conseille: qar le roi nostre seignour est prest et apparaillez de faire et parfournir en ce cas quanqe vous lui vorrez conseiller pur le mieultz. Et si vous avez pleintes ou peticions affaires en ce parlement de chose qe ne purra estre remediez sinoun en parlement, les mettez avant en parlement, qar le roi nostre seignour ad fait assigner certains clercz de resceivre, et certains prelatz, seignours et justices de oier et trier voz dites quereles et peticions, par manere le clerc de parlement vous les lirra. Et sont lours nouns tielx come s'ensuent:

Page iii-145

4. Resceivours des peticions d'Engleterre, Irlande, Gales et Escoce:

Sire Johan de Waltham

Sire Richard Ravenser

Sire Thomas de Newenham

Sire Johan de Freton'.

5. Resceivours des peticions de Gascoigne, et d'autres terres et paiis depar dela:

Sire Piers de Barton'

Sire Johan Bouland'

Sire Robert de Faryngton'

Sire Robert de Muskham.

Et ceux qi veullent bailler lours billes les baillent avaunt parentre cy et samady proschein, le dit samady accomptez.

6. Et sont assignez triours des peticions d'Engleterre, Irlande, Gales et Escoce:

Le roi de Castille et de Leon, duc de Lancastre

L'ercevesqe de Canterbirs

L'evesqe de Wyncestre

L'evesqe de Ely

L'evesqe de Salesbirs

L'abbe de Seint Austin de Cantirbirs

and that news having been announced there, together with the good will which the said town of Ghent loyally bore towards our said lord the king and his kingdom, it was at last the advice of all, for many reasons, that for the rescue of Ghent and the recovery of the land of Flanders, our said king should journey there in person together with his royal host, if he could, saving his honour. For it was said, and is plainly so, that every loyal liegeman of the king would more eagerly and ardently desire to labour beside his liege lord, who has the right and true title to the crown of France, than beside any other person in the world, and for less money. But because the matter was and is so weighty, touching both the governance of the kingdom in the absence of our said lord if he should go, as well as his said journey itself, no one either wished or dared, because of the evident dangers, to agree to the one or the other without parliament. Therefore, the king our lord charges you and prays most earnestly that you, the lords, diligently consult amongst yourselves, and you, the commons, amongst yourselves, upon the matter; and especially whether it seems to you that our lord the king should and could go in person, as said, or not. And if it seems to you that, saving his honour, he cannot go, then will you diligently suggest which army or expedition shall and could be sent, and by whom, and in what way; bearing in mind the costs to be incurred and the haste required for the expedition to rescue Ghent: bearing in mind also the amount of money granted. And having consulted amongst yourselves, you shall immediately apprise our said lord the king and his council of your conclusions: since the king our lord is ready and equipped to do and perform herein whatsoever you wish to advise him for the best. And if you have complaints or petitions to make in this parliament concerning anything which cannot be remedied except in parliament, lay them before parliament, for the king our lord has appointed certain clerks to receive, and certain prelates, lords and justices to hear and try, your said complaints and petitions, whose names the clerk of parliament will read to you. And their names are as follows:

4. Receivers of petitions from England, Ireland, Wales and Scotland:

Sir John Waltham

Sir Richard Ravenser

Sir Thomas Newenham

Sir John Freton.

5. Receivers of petitions from Gascony and from other lands and countries overseas:

Sir Piers Barton

Sir John Bowland

Sir Robert Farington

Sir Robert Muskham.

And those who wish to submit their bills should deliver them between now and Saturday next, including the said Saturday [28 February 1383].

6. The following are assigned to be triers of petitions from England, Ireland, Wales and Scotland:

The king of Castile, duke of Lancaster

The archbishop of Canterbury

The bishop of Winchester

The bishop of Ely

The bishop of Salisbury

The abbot of St Augustine's, Canterbury

L'abbe de Waltham	The abbot of Waltham
Le cont de Kent, mareschal d'Engleterre	The earl of Kent, marshal of England
Le cont d'Arundell'	The earl of Arundel
Le cont de Stafford'	The earl of Stafford
Le seignour de Nevill'	Lord Neville
Monsire Guy de Bryene	Sir Guy Bryan
Monsire Robert Tresilian	Sir Robert Tresilian

-touz ensemble, ou .vi. des prelats et seignours avauntditz au meins; appellez a eux chanceller, tresorer, seneschal et chamberlein, et auxint les sergeantz nostre seignour le roi quant il busoignera. Et tendront lour place en la chambre de chamberlein, pres de la chambre depeintee.

7. Et sont assignez triours des peticions de Gascoigne, et d'autres terres et paiis dela la meer, et des Isles:

- to act all together, or at least six of the aforesaid prelates and lords; consulting with the chancellor, treasurer, steward and chamberlain, and also the king's serjeants, when necessary. And they shall hold their session in the chamberlain's room, near the Painted Chamber.

7. The following are assigned to be triers of petitions from Gascony and from other lands and countries overseas, and from the Channel Islands:

L'evesqe de Norwiz	The bishop of Norwich
L'evesqe d'Excestr'	The bishop of Exeter
L'evesqe de Herford'	The bishop of Hereford
L'abbe de Westm'	The abbot of Westminster
L'abbe de Selby	The abbot of Selby
Le cont de Cantebr'	The earl of Cambridge
Le cont de Buk, constable d'Engelterre	The earl of Buckingham, constable of England
Le cont de Salesbirs	The earl of Salisbury
Le seignour fitz Wauter	Lord FitzWalter
Monsire Richard le Scrop	Sir Richard le Scrope
Monsire Johan de Cobham de Kent	Sir John Cobham of Kent
Monsire Robert Bealknapp'	Sir Robert Bealknap

- touz ensemble, ou .iiij. des prelats et seignours avauntditz; appellez a eux chanceller, tresorer, seneschal, chamberlein et les sergeantz le roi quant il busoignera. Et tendront lour place en la chambre marcolf.

8. Et sur ce, quant la dite commune s'avoient bien advisez deux jours ou trois sur lour dit charge, ils prierent a nostre seignour le roi qe pur tant qe lour dit charge a eux donez touchast si hautement et si pres l'estat de lour seignour lige, leur pleust a eulx granter certeins prelatz, contes et barons de roialme par eux a ce nomiers pur entrecommuner avec eux de lour dit charge: issint qe par lour bon conseil et entrecommunement ils purroient le pluis tost venir a bone conclusioun et certain purpos de

[Col. b] lour charge avauntdite. Et firent illoeqes les dites communes a ce nommer l'ercevesqe de Canterbirs, les evesqes de Ely et de Herford, les contes de Cantebr', Staff' et Northumbr', le seignour de Nevill', le seignour fitz Wauter, le seignour de Cobham. Et ceux mesmes prelats, contes \et seignours/ par la commune issint nomez, ... nostre dit seignour le roi lour grantast pur l'entrecommunement avauntdit, combien qe feust, est, et doit estre de droit en l'election de nostre dit seignour le roi /d'assigner a ce les ditz\ prelatz et seignours issint nommez, ou autres a sa propre denominacioun.

9. Item, quant mesme la commune s'avoient longement deliberez et entrecommunez avec les prelatz et seignours dessuisditz de lour charge avantdite, ils vindrent en parlement en presence de nostre seignour le roi et des seignours de parlement; et illoeqes monsire James de Pikeryng, chivaler, q'avoit les paroles pur la commune, dist, en faisant sa protestacion qe s'il deist rienz par ignorance ou autrement depar la commune qe ne feust par eulx devaunt accordez, qe celle defaute purroit estre amendez par la commune avauntdite; le quele, il dist, feust de si bone volentee envers lour

- to act all together, or at least four of the aforesaid prelates and lords; consulting with the chancellor, treasurer, chamberlain and the kings serjeants when necessary. And they shall hold their session in the Marcolf Chamber.

8. Whereupon, when the said commons had fully discussed their said charge for two or three days, they prayed of our lord the king that because the charge given them bore so strongly and closely upon the estate of their liege lord, it might please him to grant them certain prelates, earls and barons of the realm to be nominated by them, to confer with them upon their said charge: so that by their good advice and consultation they might sooner arrive at an effective conclusion and sure purpose in

[Col. b] their aforesaid charge. And the said commons nominated the archbishop of Canterbury, the bishops of Ely and Hereford, the earls of Cambridge, Stafford and Northumberland, Lord Neville, Lord FitzWalter and Lord Cobham. And those same prelates, earls and lords, thus nominated by the commons, our said lord the king granted for the aforesaid consultation, even though it was, is and ought rightfully to be the prerogative of our said lord the king to appoint the said lords and prelates thus nominated, or others of his own choosing.

9. Also, when the same commons had long deliberated and communed with the aforesaid prelates and lords on the aforesaid charge, they appeared in parliament before our lord the king and the lords of parliament; and there Sir James Pickering, knight, who was to speak on behalf of the commons, said, in making his protestation, that if he should say anything through ignorance or else on the commons' behalf which had not received their prior assent, that that fault might be rectified by the aforesaid commons; who he said, felt more good will towards their liege lord than any other

seignour lige come nulle commune mieultz purroit estre. Et oultre y dist qe combien qe ceste leur charge de le passage nostre seignour le roy, ne l'ordinance de son viage, ou de nul autre grant viage affaire, soleit /ne doit appertenir\ a la commune einz au roy mesmes et as seignours du roialme, come lour semble; toutes voies, depuis qe en especial ils ent sont chargez depar le roi nostre seignour, leur semble, qe si ce purroit estre fait bonement, et feust prest en main de quoy ce purroit estre fait en la persone du roi, q'ad le verroi droit a la coroune de France, serroit tiel viage mieultz emploiez qe en nule autre persone del monde. Mais depuis qe ce ne purra estre parfourniz, come ad este declarrez \entre eulx/ par moeltz des bones resons, lour advis est qe aiant consideration a la quantitee de monoie q'est grantez a nostre seignour le roi pur le defens du roialme, et as grantz et nobles profres qe l'evesqe de Norwiz fait a nostre seignour le roi, pur servir Dieux et seinte esglise en la croiserie a lui grantee par nostre seint pere le pape Urban, et avec ce pur servir a nostre seignour le roi dessuisdit en sa guerre de France, et rescous et confort de Gaunt;[10] qe mesme le profre \serroit/ bonement et efectuelment acceptez: par le quiel profre, \si/ ce soit parfourniz, semble \qe/moelt grant bien et profit ent doit avenir, sibien a nostre seignour le roi, come a son roiaume avantdit.

10. Et oultre y dist le dit James qe entenduz \le troboil q'est encores toutes partz deinz le roialme mesmes, et/ les novelles quelles viegnent de jour en autre de la marche d'Escoce; et \par especial,/ coment proscheinement, si accord ou pluis longe trieve ne soient faites parentre les roialmes d'Engleterre et d'Escoce a ceste fest de la Nativitee Seint Johan, est a douter grantement qe la guerre serra overte parentre les ditz roialmes, qe serroit le pluis perileuse et pluis nusante guerre qe nous purroiens avoir. Et pur tant qe commune fame est qe le Scotz sont ore si fortz et orgoillouses q'ils n'assenteront legierment a nule paix ou trieve, si ce ne soit bien damageouse et prejudicele au roi nostre seignour et a son roialme, s'il ne soient a ce chacez pluis par doute et force de vous nostre seignour lige, et de voz honorez uncles et autres seignours du roialme, qe en autre manere par beles tretees et parlances, semble \a/ la commune avauntdite qe /vous\\ nostre seignour lige, ne nul/ de voz trois uncles, de Lancastre, de Cantebr' et de Bukyngham, purra quant au present estre desportez hors de vostre roialme, ne ne purra /par\ quelconqe voie, tanqe vous nostre seignour lige aiez, si Dieux plest, mis \vostre roialme et/ la dite marche en une manere ou en autre a repos et quiete. Et ce est l'advis de vostre commune d'Engleterre sur lour dite charge a eulx donee depar vostre roial majeste. Mais ils nel diont mye, ce dit le dit monsire James, par voie de conseil ent doner a vous, einz soulement vous ent monstrent lour plein advis sur lour dite charge. A quoy feust /dit\ de [Page iii-146]

[Col. a] par le roi illoeqes tantost, q'ome ne purroit legierment mettre grant difference en celle partie; /c'estassavoir, entre les ditz paroles,\ conseil, et advis.[11]

11. Item, quant le profre del dit evesqe fait devant le roi nostre seignour et les seignours du roialme en parlement sur le comencement d'icelle \parlement/ feust tielle; c'estassavoir, qe si nostre dit seignour le roi lui voussist granter les .xvme et disme entiers ore derrain grantez a nostre seignour le roi par les lays gentz et par le clergie, et avec \ce/ les .vi. d. au libre et .ij. s. au tonelle de vin nadgairs grantez pur la salve garde de la meer, il se ferra fort d'avoir el roiaume de France procheinement en temps et seison covenables .iij.

commons. Furthermore, he said that although this their charge concerning the journey of our lord the king, or the ordinance of his expedition, or any other great expedition to be made, did not normally, and ought not, pertain to the commons, but to the king himself and the lords of the realm, as it seemed to them; nevertheless, since they had been especially charged therewith by the king our lord, it seemed to them that if it could be done well - and it was already in hands capable of doing so, in the person of the king, who had a true right to the crown of France - the expedition would be better conducted by him than by any other person in the world. But since that could not be done, for many reasons voiced amongst them, their advice was that, considering the amount of money granted to our lord the king for the defence of the kingdom and the great and noble proposal made by the bishop of Norwich to our lord the king, to serve God and holy church on a crusade granted to him by our holy father the pope Urban, and in the process serving our lord the aforesaid king in his war in France, and in the rescue and relief of Ghent, that the same proposal should be warmly and readily accepted; from the execution of which proposal it seems that great good and benefit might ensue, both for our lord the king and for his aforesaid kingdom.

10. Moreover, the said James said that given the trouble still befalling all parts of the kingdom, and the news daily arriving from the marches of Scotland; and in particular, that if a settlement or a longer truce was not made between the kingdoms of England and Scotland by the coming feast of the Nativity of St John [24 June 1383], it is greatly to be feared that there would be open war between the said kingdoms, which would be the most dangerous and harmful war that we could have; and inasmuch as it is common knowledge that the Scots are now so strong and haughty that they would not agree easily to any peace or truce unless it was wholly damaging and prejudicial to the king our lord and his kingdom, so that they no longer felt compelled to agree through fear of the strength of our liege lord and his honoured uncles and the other lords of the realm, or in any other way by fair treaties and speeches, it seems to the aforesaid commons that neither our liege lord nor any of his three uncles of Lancaster, Cambridge and Buckingham should at present be taken from his kingdom by any means, until our liege lord, if it please God, has placed his kingdom and the said march in a state of peaceful repose, by one means or another. And that was the advice of the commons of England on their said charge given them by his royal majesty. But the said James said that they certainly did not intend their words to be taken as counsel to be given to the king, but simply as their fullest advice upon their said charge. To which the immediate reply on [Page iii-146]

[Col. a] the king's behalf was that the difference between the said words 'counsel' and 'advice' was not easily discernible.

11. Also, the proposal which the said bishop made before the king our lord and the lords of the realm in parliament at the beginning of this same parliament was thus; namely, that if our lord the king would grant him the full fifteenth and tenth lately granted to our lord the king by the laity and clergy, together with the 6d. in the pound and 2s. per tun of wine lately granted for the safeguard of the sea, he would guarantee to take to the kingdom of France, at a suitable time and season, three thousand men-at-arms and three thousand

---

[10] Parliament of October 1382, items 11-13.

[11] The phrase 'C'estassavoir, entre les ditz paroles' has been added later in a contemporary hand.

mille hommes d'armes et .iij. mille archers, bien mountez et arraiez, dont .d. hommes d'armes et .d. archers [Col. b] serront a la meer prestz pur passer en rescous et confort de Gaunt, deinz les .xx. jours proschein apres q'il serra paiez de la primer paiement. Et avec \ce,/ il paiera les coustages de l'eskippesoun de son dit ost, et ent sustendra touz autres charges necessaires; issint qe le roi nostre seignour ne serra chargez de pluis paier al dit evesqe qe dessus n'est dit, forsqe de lui ottroier commissions et lettres necessaires, \et/ qe les officers du roi soient attendantz au dit evesqe en celle partie. Et sanz ce \encores/ le dit evesqe, s'il purra avoir l'attendance de west-admirall, trovera sur la meer, pur la salve garde d'icelle parentre cy et la Seint Michel proschein venant, .x. grosses niefs et .x. bones barges armez; en les queux, sanz les mariners necessairs, il trovera au meins .d. combatantz par le dit terme.[12]

Membrane 3

SEQUNTUR PETICIONES PER COMMUNITATEM REGNI DOMINO REGI IN PRESENTI PARLIAMENTO PORRECTE, CUM RESPONSIONIBUS EARUMDEM.

/A nostre\ tresgracious et tresredoute seignour nostre seignour le roi supplient les communes pur les peticions dessouzescrites:

I. [Affirmation of the liberties of the church, and of the charters.]
12. Enprimes, qe seinte esglise eit et enjoise entierment toutes ses libertees et franchises; et qe la grande chartre et la chartre de la foreste soient tenuz et gardez, et duement executz, selonc l'effect d'icelles.
Responsio
Le roy le voet.

II. [Keeping the sea.]
13. Item, prient les communes q'il plese a vostre hautesse hastifment ordeigner suffisante garde sur la meer, sanz quele voz liges ne poent avoir seuretee de lours biens, ne en haut meer, ne dedeinz voz portz, come y ad este provez, sur toutes les coustes de la terre, et meement sur le northcost, qar voz subgitz et autres voz amys depar dela ont tant perduz, sur l'espoire q'ils ont eues qe la meer deust avoir este gardez par les .vi. d. al livre et .ij. s. al tonel de vin, queux furent nadgairs grantez pur la garde du dit meer, qe plusours de eux sont bien pres anientiz, et eux ne autres de voz amys n'osent pluis aventurer, en venant n'en alant.
Responsio.
Le roi voet qe ses chanceller, tresorer et gardein du prive seal, avec les evesqes de Wyncestre et Hereford', les contes de Staff' et de Salesbirs, et monsire Guy de Bryen, et monsire Johan de Cobham, appellez a eux certaine nombre des chivalers et marchantz ore esteantz en ce parlement, ent facent tielle et si bone et hastive ordinance come mieltz lour semblera affaire /qe\ soit portable, aiant consideracion a la quantitee de tout l'avoir q'est grantez al oeps del dit salve garde, ou qe purroit a ce estre appliez del avoir nostre dit seignour le roi, apres les autres grantz et necessaires busoignes del roialme et /des terres\ et seignouries nostre seignour le roi depar dela parforniz.

III. [Security of the marches of Scotland.]
14. Item, prient les communes, pur salvacion de la marche d'Escoce et de toute la terre apres: qe come les Escotz ont

archers, fully mounted and equipped, five hundred of these men-at-arms and five hundred of these archers [Col. b] being by the sea and ready to cross for the rescue and relief of Ghent within twenty days of his receiving the first payment. And with that, he would pay the costs of transporting his said host, and sustain all other necessary charges; so that the king our lord would not be obliged to pay the said bishop more than was stated above, except for granting him the necessary commissions and letters, and that the king's officers would be attendant upon the said bishop in the matter. Not to mention the fact that if the said bishop could have the assistance of the admiral to the west, he would place on the sea, for the safeguard of the same between now and next Michaelmas [29 September 1383], ten large ships and ten well-armed barges; in which he would place at least five hundred fighting men for the said term, excluding the necessary mariners.

HERE FOLLOW THE PETITIONS SUBMITTED BY THE COMMONS OF THE KINGDOM TO THE LORD KING IN THIS PRESENT PARLIAMENT, ALONG WITH THE ANSWERS TO THE SAME.
To our most gracious and redoubtable lord, our lord the king, the commons make the petitions written below:

I. [Affirmation of the liberties of the church, and of the charters.]
12. Firstly, that holy church shall have and fully enjoy all its liberties and franchises; and that the Great Charter and the Charter of the Forest shall be upheld and protected, and duly executed according to the tenor of the same.
Answer.
The king wills it.

II. [Keeping the sea.]
13. Item, the commons pray that it may please your highness swiftly to ordain sufficient keeping of the sea - without which your lieges lack security for their goods on the seas and in your ports, as has been proven - on all the coasts of the land, and especially on the north coast, for your subjects and your other friends overseas have lost so much, in the hope they had that the sea would be secured by the 6d. in the pound and 2s. per tun of wine which were recently granted for the keeping of the same, that many of them are well nigh ruined, and they and other friends of yours dare not venture more in coming or going.
Answer.
The king wills that his chancellor, treasurer and keeper of the privy seal, with the bishops of Winchester and Hereford, the earls of Stafford and of Salisbury, and Sir Guy Bryan and Sir John Cobham, calling to them a certain number of knights and merchants attending this parliament, shall make as good and speedy ordinance as they see fit and would be sustainable, bearing in mind the amount of revenue which has been granted to the king's use for the said keeping, or which might be applied to it from the revenue of our said lord the king, after the other important and necessary business of the kingdom and the lands and lordships of our lord the king overseas has been discharged.

III. [Security of the marches of Scotland.]
Item, the commons pray, for the security of the marches of Scotland and all the land behind it: whereas the Scots

---
[12] The phrase 'par le dit terme' has been added later in a contemporary hand.

have wasted a great area of your land in many of their raids, may it please your most exalted lordship tenderly to ensure that should a truce or peace be concluded with your aforesaid enemies of Scotland, it should be so firmly established that your lieges may enjoy [Col. b] as secure a peace in your land as the said enemy enjoy in their own. And in particular, that your towns of Berwick and Carlisle, the chief towns of your march there, be inspected and provisioned to prevent greater loss here or further within your land: for otherwise your enemies will push the frontier much further into your kingdom than they have ever done before. Furthermore, lord, that the wardens of the march be charged to do reasonable right by your lieges in Teviotdale, so that they have no cause to rebel or support your aforesaid enemies of Scotland. And that all the lords and others who have castles or fortalices in the said march of Scotland, and elsewhere in marches and coasts throughout the kingdom, shall provision them and install in them men who reside continually in the same before Whitsun next [10 May 1383], on pain of a certain penalty to be ordained by you.

Answer.

The king has ordained that his most dear uncle of Spain together with certain other lords of his realm be sent soon to the said march, with sufficient power and mandate to negotiate with the Scots, and according to the nature of the agreement to be concluded, if it please God, make as secure an ordinance thereon as can be devised. And as for those of Teviotdale and the towns of Berwick and Carlisle and the other fortresses, the king will ordain thereon as best he can for the security and effective protection of the same.

IV. [Purveyors.]

15. Item, the commons pray: that the statute of purveyors be fully kept and enforced in its original form, so that no purveyor of our lord the king takes, for the use of him or of our most noble lady the queen, any kind of victuals, without paying a price which has been amicably agreed between the parties; or at least on the valuation of the constables of each town where they make their prise. And that no lord of the land nor other person shall make such prises, except our said lord the king and our most noble lady the queen alone, but let them make their prise and full payment to the vendors without the intervention of the constables and other ministers.

Answer.

The king wills that the statute be upheld and duly executed.

V. [Appointment of the officers of state.]

16. Item, the commons pray: whereas after our lord the king, the whole land is and desires to be governed chiefly by the superior officers of our said lord the king; yet it commonly happens that many virtuous and wise men who are skilled in certain requisite matters of business are not skilled in others.

May it please our most redoubtable lord the king, with the advice of the nobles and other great lords summoned to this present parliament, inasmuch as they have full knowledge of the conditions of the most wise and discreet men in the land, to elect those endowed with the greatest loyalty and knowledge of the governance of his people on the king's behalf to exercise office without favour or partiality for any person, and that the names of those thus elected be openly declared in this present parliament; and if it pleases the king

seignour qe les ditz officers ne soient remouez sanz cause resonable.

Responsio.

Le roi nostre seignour, par l'advis des seignours de son roialme, ferra ses principalx officers des tieux suffisantes persones come mieultz lui semblera affaire pur le bon governement de ses roialme et subgitz; les queux officers il n'entende mye remuer devant le proschein parlement, sinoun par cause resonable.

VI. [Pardons for the revolt.]

17. Item, supplient les communes: qe la pardoun grantez au derrain parlement a ceux qi leverent encontre nostre seignour le roi et sa pees soit enlargiz, entant qe nule persone soit excepte del dite pardoun, forspris ceux qi furent exceptz par noun en le proschein parlement apres la insurreccioun avantdite.[14] Et si aucune ou aucunes persones soit ou soient ou apres cest temps serra ou serront empeschez, enditez, rettez, appellez ou utlagez par cause de celle insurreccioun, queux ne furent exceptz en le parlement suisdit proschein apres la insurreccioun avantdite, soient entierment quitz et relessez d'icelle par ceste present pardoun, si avaunt come chescun de eux eust sur ycelle chartre especiale. Et qe celui qi voet suir devers aucune persone pur aucune trespas faite en la dite insurreccioun, q'il comence sa suite devant la quinzeine Seint Johan proschein avenir. Et en cas qe aucune suite soit prise devers aucune tielle persone pur aucune tiele trespas, et il se voet ent acquiter, q'il ne y unqes vient, ne damage fist, mais parmy ce q'il feust constreint de ce faire, q'il adonqes viegne ove trois ou quatre bones gentz et suffisantes, et nient suspectz, devant les juges ou tiel plee serra pendant: et sur ce par tesmoignance des dites bones gentz soit oultrement ent acquitz.

Responsio.

Le roi voet et grante de sa grace la dite pardoun par manere q'est demandez; excepte par especial, qe ceux de Bury troefsent seuretee suffisante de lour bon port en temps avenir sibien a nostre seignour le roi come al abbeye de Bury, par manere q'ad este ordenez par le conseil nostre seignour le roi devant ceste heure.[15]

VII. [Management of the king's household.]

18. Item, prient les communes, pur honor et profit de vous, tresredoute seignour, et quiete et confort de voz ditz communes qe de vostre grant grace vous plese comander qe certains seignours soient assignez de mettre entour vostre honurable persone, par l'advis de vous, tres redoute seignour, de les pluis sages, honestes et discretz persones de vostre roialme, pur vous conseiller. Et oultre si vous plese, tresredoute seignour, ordener, par advis des seignours, qe vostre hostiel puisse estre einsi amesnez, q'il vous plerroit de vivre deinz les revenues de vostre roialme. Et qe le subside des leines, gardes, mariages, eschetes et autres commoditees, soient entierment gardez en eide de voz guerres, en supportacion et ease de voz ditz povres communes: considerez q'ils sont a ore grandement anientiz par pestilence, moryne des bestes et les grantz deluvies q'ore tarde ont este, et auxint les grandes taillages, et autres diseases q'ils ont suffertz, siqe voz ditz povres communes puissent estre desportez pur un temps, en oevre de charitee.

Responsio.

Le roi prendra entour sa persone des tielles suffisantes persones, seignours et autres, come mieultz lui semblera pur son honur et profit. Et quant a la reule et governance de son

our lord, that the said officers not be removed without reasonable cause.

Answer.

The king our lord, with the advice of the lords of his kingdom, will appoint his principal officers from such worthy persons as he thinks it best to do for the good government of his kingdom and subjects; which officers he certainly does not intend to remove before the next parliament, unless on reasonable grounds.

VI. [Pardons for the revolt.]

17. Item, the common request: that the pardon granted at the last parliament to those who rebelled against our lord the king and his peace be extended, so that no one be excepted from the said pardon except those who were excluded by name in the parliament which followed the aforesaid insurrection. And if anyone or any persons be now or in the future impeached, indicted, blamed, appealed or outlawed because of the insurrection, who were not excluded in the parliament next after the aforesaid insurrection, let them be wholly quit and released from the same by this present pardon, as if each one of them had received a special charter thereon. And let him who wishes to sue anyone for an offence committed in the said insurrection begin the suit before the quinzaine of St John next [8 July 1383]. And if a suit is brought against such a person for any such offence, and he wishes to acquit himself of participating or inflicting damage except in so far as he was forced to do so, then let him come with three or four good and worthy men, not themselves suspected, before the judges where the plea be pending: and thereupon, by the testimony of the said good men he shall be completely acquitted of this.

Answer.

The king wills and grants the said pardon of his grace as requested; with the particular exception that those of Bury find sufficient surety for their future good bearing towards our lord the king as well as towards the abbey of Bury, as was ordained by the council of our lord the king before this time.

VII. [Management of the king's household.]

18. Item, the commons pray, for the honour and profit of you, most redoubtable lord, and the peace and solace of your said commons, that of your great grace, it might please you to command that certain lords be appointed on your advice, most redoubtable lord, to choose the most wise, honest and discreet persons of your realm to remain about your honourable person and advise you. And further, if it please you, most redoubtable lord, that you ordain, by the advice of the lords, that your household be so managed that it would please you to live within the revenues of your kingdom. And that the subsidy on wool, wardships, marriages, escheats and other resources be entirely devoted to your wars, to the support and relief of your said poor commons: considering that they are now greatly weakened by the pestilence, murrain of cattle and the great floods which have recently occurred, and also the great taxes and other troubles which they have suffered, so that your said poor commons might be spared for a while, by way of charity.

Answer.

The king shall take lords and others about his person from amongst such worthy people as he deems best for his honour and profit. And as to the rule and governance of his

---

[14] Parliament of 1381, item 63.
[15] 6 Ric 2 st.2 c.1.

household, the king, by the advice of the lords and others of his council, shall make as good an ordinance as he sees fit, saving his honour.

VIII. [Franchises and liberties of London.]

19. Item, the commons request, for the greater harmony and nurture of peace between his lieges, that the city of London be wholly restored to its franchise and free usages, by confirmation of you, our lord, in this present parliament, which it possessed in the time of your noble progenitors, and which were graciously confirmed by you, most exalted lord, with the clause 'de licet'; and notwithstanding any judgments rendered, or statutes, ordinances, or other charters made or granted to the contrary before this time; since denial of the same has in many ways weakened and damaged their estate, and contributed nothing to the common good of the realm.

The king wills that they should have their franchises and liberties as entirely and fully as they had them in the time of his noble grandfather, whom God absolve, and as they were granted and confirmed in the time of our lord the present king, saving always that the intention of the king is certainly not that, by colour of this grant, merchants from foreign lands who have their franchises within the kingdom by the grant of the progenitors of our lord the king, and by confirmation of our said lord the king, should be excluded from their franchises and liberties in any way: nor that the victuallers of London should have or enjoy any special or general charters or liberties by themselves; but that the said victuallers shall be generally included in this grace with the other citizens of London, except that those victuallers, and every one of them, together with their victuals, shall henceforth be under the governance and rule of the mayor of London at the time.

IX. [Attendance at parliament.]

Item, the commons pray: that it might please our lord, of his great regality, to charge the lords and his other lieges not to leave parliament until the aforesaid petitions have been determined and duly put into effect, and that those charged with the said business be made known to your said commons before their departure, that they may make their report to their neighbours in all parts, to the great comfort of your aforesaid commons.

20. Item, be it known that after the said bishop of Norwich, who made the said proposal included above, had reflected on matters a short while, he appeared before the king and the lords of the realm in parliament and made another proposal of the following nature. That is to say, that if it should please our lord the king to give and grant him the whole fifteenth lately granted to our same lord the king by the laity of his said kingdom, he would serve the king for a whole year in his wars within the kingdom of France together with two thousand five hundred men-at-arms and two thousand five hundred archers, all well equipped and mounted; of which number one thousand men-at-arms and one thousand archers would be, if it pleased God, by the sea, ready and equipped to cross to the rescue and aid of the town of Ghent and the land of Flanders, within twenty days of his having received the first payment of the same fifteenth; bearing himself the costs of transporting them and other charges, as is said above; and that he would perform, with the aid of Our Lord. Yet although it seemed to our lord the king and his council and to the lords of the realm that the same proposal would be most loyal and splendid if it could be performed, nevertheless, it

qe le roy feust aidez des persones qi serroient doustres, chiefteins et governours del dit ost. *[Page iii-148]*

[Col. a] Qar conue chose est a touz qe sanz governement des plusours \[grantz et nobles persones, seignours,]/ et autres, ne purroit gairs si grant ost longement endurer en prosperitee. Et par tant feust dit depar le roi al dit evesqe, \[q'il fist aider nostre seignour le roi et son]/ conseil del nombre et des nouns des chiefteins et doustres q'il pensoit avoir \avec lui/ el dit viage. A quoy feust responduz depar le dit evesqe qe si plest au roy nostre seignour d'accepter son dit profre, et de lui ottroier le dit viage par manere q'est demandez, il se face fort \[d'aver]/ avec luy des meillours chieftains du roialme d'Engleterre apres la persone nostre dit seignour le roy et les \autres/ roialx. Mais il dit q'il ne \voloit/ monstrer lours nouns en especial devant q'il feust \[sure]/ qe le dit viage lui feust grantez. Et surce estoit demandez del dit evesqe quiel seignour du roialme il desiroit d'avoir avec lui pur estre lieutenant du roi nostre seignour en dit ost, desicome un lieutenant depar le roy y feust moelt grantement necessaire en si haute et chargeante busoigne, q'averoit poair de conoistre en cryme, et de faire autres choses necessaires: quiel office n'ad mie este avant ces heures employez en la persone de prelat, \ne/ d'autre homme de seinte esglise. A quoy le dit evesqe respondist q'il mettroit en escrit les nouns des certeins seignours, et les baillerent a nostre seignour le roi; empriant a nostre dit seignour qe de ceux mesmes persones lui pleust eslire quiel persone mieltz lui plerroit a tielle affaire, et celle mesme persone creer en son dit lieutenant, le quel *[feust]* chargez d'estre obeissant al dit evesqe en toutes \[choses q'apperteignoient]/ a la croiserie: et le dit evesqe pur sa partie s'accorda, \[q'il serroit obeissant al dit]/ lieutenant en toutes \[choses q'appartiendroient]/ al lieutenancie. Et promist oultre le dit evesqe qe si deinz le \[dit an avenoit qe le roiaume]/ de France se \[voroit convertir al foi del verroi pape Urban,]/ mesme l'evesqe serroit \[tenuz]/ deslors de \[compliquer et ouster tantost la banere de la croiserie, et deslors]/ servir \[a nostre dit seignour le roi en dite guerre avec]/ sa propre banere, et par \[le nombre des gentz dessus limitez, tanqe al fin de l'an dessusdit.]/

21. \[Et ceste profre]/ issint \[fait rehercez en plein parlement devant le roi mesmes et tout la commune, sembloit a touz estre moelt bon et grantement profitable a tout]/ le roialme, si ce soit \[bien parfourniz, qe Dieux la grante: et par tant si estoit mesme le profre acceptez par nostre seignour le roi. Et enoultre illoeqes escrit]/ ....
\[par le dit nostre seignour]/ le roi grantez a qelconqes \[ses subgitz qi voloient passer avec le dit evesqe en dit viage, licence de passer sanz contredit ou destourbance de]/ nully, horspris \[la retenue du roi nostre seignour, et les retenues]/ des autres grantz seignours, as queux \[le roi defende q'ils ne passent sanz le congie de lours seignours]/ en aucune manere. \[Et puis apres quant le dit]/ evesqe avoit \[livere a]/ nostre seignour le roi les \[nouns de quatre persones du roiaume, desqueux nostre dit seignour]/ le roy esliroit \[son lieutenant, nostre seignour le roy desirant la commune profit de son roialme, et ne voloit q'ome auroit matire d'arretter as seignours du]/ roialme, qe tiel viage, \[qe par le dit profre sembloit si profitable, serroit par eulx sans]/ bone et jouste cause \[voluntrisment destourbez ou entrelessez,]/ desicome la \[commune du roiaume ent ont dit leur plein advis, fust]/ grantez par nostre seignour le roi, et rehercez en plein parlement, qe si le \[dit evesqe ne]/ purroit accorder avec \[nul des seignours par lui nomez, ne avec autre]/ suffisante persone qe feust dignez de \[porter]/ si grant estat

was most necessary that the king be aided by persons who were leaders, captains and governors of the said host. *[Page iii-148]*

[Col. a] For it is well known to all that without the direction of many great and noble persons, lords and others, so large a host cannot enjoy prosperity for long. And for that reason the bishop was told, on the king's behalf, that he would assist our lord the king and his council if he were to supply the number and names of the captains and leaders he expected to accompany him on his said expedition. To which the said bishop replied that if it pleased the king our lord to accept his said proposal, and grant him the said expedition as requested, he would guarantee to have with him the best captains of the kingdom of England after the person of our said lord the king and the royal princes. But he said that would not wish to declare their names before he was sure that the said expedition would be granted to him. Thereupon the said bishop was asked which lord of the realm he would wish to have with him as the lieutenant of the king our lord in the said host, since a lieutenant acting on the king's behalf was most necessary in so high and weighty a business, for he would have the power of judging crimes, and the power to do other necessary things: which office had never been invested in a prelate before this time, or in any other man of holy church. To which the said bishop replied that he would place the names of certain lords in writing and deliver them to our lord the king, praying of our said lord that from those same persons it might please him to choose whomsoever it best pleased him, and to appoint the same person as his said lieutenant, charging him with obedience to the said bishop in all things which pertained to the crusade: and the said bishop for his part agreed that he would be obedient to the said lieutenant in all matters pertaining to the lieutenancy. And the said bishop promised further that if, within the said year, it should happen that the kingdom of France wished to change to the faith of the true pope Urban, he would be obliged thereupon to lay down and abandon the banner of the crusade and serve our said lord the king in the said war under his own banner, and with the number of men specified above, until the end of the aforesaid year.

21. And that proposal having been rehearsed in full parliament before the king himself and all the commons, it seemed to them all that it would be good and greatly profitable to *[Col. b]* all the realm if it were well performed, which God grant: and for that reason the same proposal was accepted by our lord the king. Furthermore, it was written there ..... on behalf of the said lord the king, licence was granted to any of his subjects who wished to go with the said bishop on the said expedition to travel without obstacle or hindrance from anyone; apart from those of the retinue of the king our lord and the retinues of the other great lords, whom the king forbade to go without the permission of their lords in any way. Later, when the said bishop had given our lord the king the names of four persons of the kingdom from whom our said lord the king would elect his lieutenant, our lord the king, desiring the common profit of his kingdom, and not wishing that anyone should have grounds to accuse the lords of the realm of disrupting and abandoning such an expedition without good reason - which expedition seemed from the said proposal so beneficial, as the commons had made clear in their advice on this - it was granted by our lord the king and rehearsed in full parliament that if the said bishop could not agree with any of the lords named by him, nor with any other person who was worthy of holding so exalted a position as lieutenant, over the manner of their retaining in

[Peace with Castile.]

22. Item, the commons pray of our lord the king: that he give hearing and audience to the lord of Lesparre, who recently arrived from the kingdom of Spain, which lord said and swore that, with the aid of our lord the king, if you our liege lord would incline thereto your grace, he would show you various good and honourable ways in which peace might honourably be made with the said kingdom of Spain; which peace, if you our liege lord might have it, saving your honour, you would accept and make, for love of God, to the great profit of you and your kingdom and the tranquillity of your subjects.

Answer.

To which it was answered on the king's behalf and at his command that the king would consider the matter with the lords of his realm, and do whatever seemed appropriate therein by their advice, saving his honour.

---

[16] Stitched to the last membrane is a piece of parchment on which a later hand has written, Rotulus parliamenti Ricardi secundi anno sexto apud Westm' die lune in septimana tertia quadragesim [23 February 1383.]

Appendix

23 February 1383

Westminster

1. Note that it was decided in this parliament that a Hanseatic ship called the 'Fredeland' from Eastland should not be held for deodand, despite the fact that its masters had inadvertently been the cause of death of a number of men at Great Yarmouth.
   Source: *CCR 1381-5*, 286.

1383 October

Westminster

26 October - 26 November 1383

(C 65/41. *RP*, III.149-165. *SR*, II.32-36)

C 65/41 is a roll of ten membranes, each approximately 335mm in width, sewn together in chancery style, and numbered in a later hand. The text, written in the official chancery script of several scribes, occupies the rectos of the membranes only. The dorses are blank apart from a later heading, 'Rotulus parliamenti de anno 7 R. 2^{di} pars prima', and later notes where the membranes are joined, 'Parl' 7 R. 2 proxima apud Westm'. The condition of the roll is good, though membrane 4 is stained with gallic acid, and there is a natural hole in membrane 10. The lower half of membrane 6 is blank. The marginal notes are contemporary. The Arabic numerals are of a later date. The roll appears to be complete.

The principal item of business in the parliament of February 1383 had been the decision to sanction and finance the 'Flemish crusade' of Bishop Henry Despenser of Norwich, a decision clearly taken against the advice of several of the lords, and a bitter disappointment in particular to John of Gaunt, duke of Lancaster, who had hoped to persuade the commons to back his own proposed expedition to Iberia. Despenser duly crossed to the continent on 16 May, but his campaign was a fiasco, and by the time the last stragglers from his army had made their way back to England in early October it must have been all too apparent to him that his opponents were busy sharpening their knives for revenge. On 20 August, when writs had been issued summoning this second parliament of the year, this had not yet become apparent, for the fate of Despenser's crusade still hung in the balance, and the ostensible reason for the summons was the need to consider peace terms with the Scots.[1] As it turned out, however, Scottish affairs played only a walk-on part in the parliament of October 1383; its main business was the impeachment of the unfortunate bishop and the consideration of a series of charges against his captains.

The list of spiritual peers summoned showed only minor changes from that of the February parliament (the abbot of Cirencester was omitted, while the abbot of Bury was summoned for the first time since January 1380), although it is worth noting that the summons to Bishop Despenser included the words 'or his proctor' - it clearly being uncertain as to whether he would have returned from the continent in time. The newcomers among the lords temporal included Thomas Mowbray, who had inherited the earldom of Nottingham following the death of his brother John; Robert de Vere, who had come of age to inherit the earldom of Oxford; Hugh Burnell, and Thomas Nevill of Halumshire. A further two names were added to the end of the list of lords temporal, those of John de Falvesle and Thomas Camoys. These two were clearly an afterthought, for they were added in the nominative rather than the usual (and grammatically correct) dative case, and in the case of Thomas Camoys the reason for this is fairly clear. Camoys had in fact been elected as knight of the shire for Surrey, but on 8 October the king wrote to the sheriff of Surrey ordering him to discharge Camoys, since he was 'a banneret as were most of his ancestors', and 'bannerets used not to be elected knights of the shire'. In fact, there may have been a more political motive behind Camoys' discharge: Thomas Morwelle, chamberlain of Princess Joan's household, and James Berners, a knight of the king's chamber, were similarly discharged from taking their seats as knights of the shire in this parliament, suggesting that there may have been a move to exclude from the commons certain persons with known connections to the royal court - or alternatively, perhaps, that there were suspicions that their elections had been marred by some kind of irregularity.[2]

Following the customary adjournment for a day to await late arrivals, parliament assembled on Tuesday 27 October to hear a somewhat apologetic opening speech from the new chancellor, Michael de la Pole. Having excused himself on the grounds that, despite being a mere layman, he was nevertheless obliged to do what all previous chancellors had done, he went on to set out the chief matters to be dealt with. The first of these was Scotland (Item 3). It may have been at the behest of John of Gaunt, who had been much involved with Anglo-Scottish relations over the previous few years, that de la Pole chose to emphasise the Scottish question, and according to the Westminster chronicler there was a Scottish raid on Northumberland while the parliament was in session. Thomas Walsingham, the St Albans chronicler, also noted the inclusion of Scottish affairs in the discussions, claiming that the northern lords demanded a portion of the taxes granted in order to defend the northern border, but that Bishop Wykeham of Winchester opposed this, saying that they already had sufficient resources. Walsingham also said that certain Scottish lords came to the parliament - as

---

[1] *CCR 1381-5*, 390-1.
[2] *CCR 1381-5*, 398; Given-Wilson, *Royal Household and King's Affinity*, 247.

had apparently been agreed between the two sides - in order to try to avert an English invasion, but were sent home in disgrace because they were not regarded as trustworthy.[3]

The roll, however, says little of Scottish affairs, concentrating rather on events in Flanders. This was the second point in de la Pole's speech. As a result of its occupation by a French royal army - the same army which had sent Despenser's forces hastening back across the Channel - the Flemings could no longer be regarded as allies. England, he declared, had been forced on to the defensive - but, he went on (urging the commons to grant a tax), the best form of defence was attack, and this was what the government planned to do (Items 4-5). This was the prelude to Despenser's impeachment, with which much of the main body of the roll is concerned (Items 15-25). The trial of the bishop and his captains has been discussed at length, and only the barest outline of events will be given here.[4] Despenser was accused on four main counts: of failing to take to Flanders the full number of men specified in his contract; of failing to maintain his army in Flanders for the full year for which he had contracted; of refusing to inform the king as to who would be the captains of his army; and of refusing to accept a secular lieutenant of the king to lead his army, as a result of which he had remained in sole control of his forces, with the consequent losses to both king and kingdom. De la Pole, as chancellor, presented the charges, and there is no doubt (as both the roll and the Westminster chronicler made clear) that he pursued Despenser with both zeal and personal animosity. Despite being given two opportunities to defend himself (cf. Item 22), the bishop's answers were deemed inadequate, and he was duly sentenced to loss of his temporalities, although according to the Westminster chronicler the king comforted him and reassured him that, whatever parliament might think, 'he himself remained well disposed' towards him.[5] The charges against his captains, which turned mainly on the question of whether they had surrendered castles and provisions to the French in return for gold, were also for the most part regarded as proven, and they were sentenced to imprisonment and payment of fines at the king's mercy (Items 16-17, 24-5), although Walsingham noted correctly that in fact they were soon released.[6]

Despenser's impeachment apart, the principal item of interest in the records of the parliament of October 1383 is the evidence of increasingly strained relations between the king and certain of the magnates. Of this, the roll has little to say, but the Westminster chronicler stated that 'in the course of this parliament a serious quarrel arose between the king and the lords temporal, because, as it seemed to them, he clung to unsound policies and for this reason excluded wholesome guidance from his entourage; they therefore strove to take the full burden of control upon themselves'. This was the most personal attack of the reign thus far upon the king's choice of counsellors, and Richard did not take kindly to it, rebuking the lords for their 'effrontery' and responding that he would continue to be guided by counsellors of his own choosing; it was, however, a complaint which would grow increasingly insistent over the next few years.[7]

Eventually, albeit reluctantly, the commons were persuaded to grant a fifteenth and tenth, half of which was to be raised immediately and the other half only if no peace had been agreed by Easter 1384. There were, apparently, genuine prospects of peace with France, for, according to a deleted passage in the Westminster chronicle, King Charles VI wrote to Richard II during the parliament suggesting a meeting of high-ranking ambassadors at Calais to discuss peace terms, to which Richard responded promptly, appointing a delegation, headed by Gaunt, which set off around 10 November, two weeks before the parliament was dissolved.[8] Nothing was being taken for granted, however, and as a condition of their grant the commons also insisted that the clergy be constrained to grant a tenth, and that the money - both English and French - still in the keeping of Bishop Despenser's captains be recovered from them and used towards the war (Items 12-13).

One further consequence of the failure of Despenser's Flemish campaign manifested itself in a petition concerning the staple (Item 31). Merchants from Flanders were finding it increasingly difficult to reach English-held Calais, and as a result English wool exports were being severely curtailed. Pending negotiations with the French, no decision was taken about this for the moment, but on 24 January 1384 it was decided to establish a compulsory staple at Middelburg in Zeeland.[9] The rumbling disputes between London's merchant guilds also surfaced once more. On 13 October 1383, the grocer Nicholas Brembre had replaced the draper John of Northampton as mayor of the city, and with the victuallers once more in the ascendant a petition was submitted asking that full liberties be restored to the citizens of London, including the fishmongers, who had so recently been deprived of their privileges in parliament (Item 37). The order to the sheriffs and mayors to proclaim the revocation of the legislation against the fishmongers was sent out on 27 November, the day after the parliament was dissolved.[10] There were many, including the king perhaps, who must have been relieved at the dissolution, for it had been another fractious parliament. In a sense, however, it also marked a watershed in the parliamentary history of Richard's reign; the disagreements of the last few parliaments had mainly been over foreign policy; from now onwards, domestic policy would take centre stage, and particularly the question of the king and his counsellors.

---

[3] Goodman, *John of Gaunt*, 97-8; *Westminster Chronicle*, 48-54; *St Albans Chronicle 1376-1394*, 712-4.
[4] Margaret Aston, 'The impeachment of Bishop Despenser', *BIHR*, 38 (1965), 127-48.
[5] *Westminster Chronicle*, 52-4.
[6] *St Albans Chronicle 1376-1394*, 714; Saul, *Richard II*, 106.
[7] *Westminster Chronicle*, 54; Tuck, *Richard II and the English Nobility*, 90-91.
[8] *Westminster Chronicle*, 524; Goodman, *John of Gaunt*, 98.
[9] Lloyd, *English Wool Trade*, 230.
[10] *CPR 1381-5*, 338; *CCR 1381-5*, 414-6.

Text and Translation

Page iii-149, Membrane 10

ROTULUS PARLIAMENTI TENTI APUD WESTM', DIE LUNE PROXIMO ANTE FESTUM OMNIUM SANCTORUM, ANNO REGNI REGIS RICARDI SECUNDI POST CONQUESTUM SEPTIMO.

Adjournement.

1. Fait assavoir qe le lundy proschein devaunt la feste de Tousseintz, l'an du regne nostre seignour le roi Richard secound apres le conquest septisme, qe fuist le .xxvi. jour d'Octobre, et le primer jour de cest present parlement, si come par la somonce d'icelle appiert pluis au plein, aucuns des prelatz, seignours et autres del roialme q'avoient la dite somonce, vindrent en ce parlement tenuz a Westm', et illoeqes attenderent longement la venue des autres prelatz et seignours, et au drain, pur tant qe fuist recordez illoeqes devant les ditz prelatz et seignours, et auxint les grantz officers du roialme, qe aucuns viscontz n'avoient mie encores fait retournir lours briefs de parlement, et auxint qe plusours des prelatz et autres seignours du roiaume q'avoient mesme la somonce ne estoient encores venuz a lours hostelx, si estoit cest parlement par la volentee et comandement nostre seignour le roi adjournez tanqe a lendemain proschein ensuant. Et de celle adjournement overte proclamacione faite de par le roi en la sale de Westm', et comande y feust par le dit cry a touz ceux q'avoient mesme la somonce qe sur le paril qe appent ils fuissent lendemain devant le roi en parlement par temps, pur oier les causes de la dite somonce: et auxint fuist proclamez et criez qe les viscontz retournassent tantost et distinctement les briefs du parlement sur mesme le paril.

Pronunciacio parliamenti.

2. A quiel lendemain, qe fuist mardy, vindrent en parlement sibien les prelatz, seignours temporelx, come les justices, et autres du conseil nostre dit seignour le roi, en la chambre depeintee a Westm', en presence du roi mesmes; appellez la einz les chivalers des countees, les barons des cynk portz, citezeins des citees et burgeys de burghes, par lours nouns sicome les viscontz lour avoient fait retourner. Monsire Michel de la Pole, chivaler, chancellor d'Engleterre, par comandement nostre seignour le roi avoit les paroles de la pronunciacion des causes de la somonce de cest present parlement, y dist, Vous, messires, prelatz et seignours temporelx, et vous mes compaignons les chivalers et autres de la noble commune d'Engleterre cy presentz, deivez entendre qe combien qe je ne soie dignes, mes insufficient /de sen et de\\ tout/ autre bien, toutes voies pleust a nostre seignour le roi nadgairs de moy creer en son chanceller, et sur ce ore moy ad comandez q'ore en voz honurables presences je vous doie depar luy exposer les causes de la somonce de son present parlement. Et par tant purra clerement apparoir qe si haute busoigne come ce est de parler si chargeante matire devaunt tantes et tielles si nobles et sages persones qe vous estez, je ne ferroie mye par presumpcione ou sur quiderie de moy mesmes, einz soulement par deux enchesons resonables. L'une est qe

[Col. b] longement et communement ad este accustumee deinz mesme le roialme, qe les chancellers d'Engleterre devant moy si ont faitz chescun en son temps pronunciation depar le roy de semblables parlementz devaunt ore tenuz; \et/ ne vorroie, si pleust a Dieu, qe en mon temps defaute

Translation

THE ROLL OF THE PARLIAMENT HELD AT WESTMINSTER, ON THE MONDAY BEFORE THE FEAST OF ALL SAINTS IN THE SEVENTH YEAR OF THE REIGN OF KING RICHARD, THE SECOND SINCE THE CONQUEST.

Adjournment.

1. Be it known that on the Monday before the feast of All Saints, in the seventh year of the reign of our lord King Richard, the second since the conquest, which was 26 October [1383], and the first day of the present parliament, as plainly appears from the summons of the same, some of the prelates, lords and others of the kingdom who had received the said summons came to the parliament held at Westminster, and there waited a long while for the arrival of the other prelates and lords, until at length, because it was reported before the said prelates and lords and also the great officers of the realm that some sheriffs had not yet returned their writs of parliament, and also that many of the prelates and other lords of the realm who had received the same summons had not yet reached their lodgings, the parliament was adjourned until the following day [27 October 1383] at the will and command of our lord the king. And a public announcement was made of this adjournment on the king's behalf in Westminster Hall, and the said announcement instructed all those who had received the same summons to appear early the next day before the king in parliament on pain of the appointed penalty, to hear the reasons for the said summons: and it was also proclaimed and announced that the sheriffs should immediately and duly return their writs of parliament, on pain of the same penalty.

The opening of parliament.

2. On the following day, which was Tuesday [27 October 1383], the prelates and lords temporal as well as the justices and others of the council of our said lord the king appeared in parliament in the Painted Chamber at Westminster, before the king himself; the knights of the shires, barons of the Cinque Ports, citizens of the cities, and burgesses of the boroughs having been called by name as they were returned by the sheriffs. Sir Michael de la Pole, knight, chancellor of England, explained the reasons for the summoning of this parliament on the king's orders, and said there, You, my lords, prelates and lords temporal, and you my companions the knights and others of the noble commons of England here present, should understand that although I be not worthy, and lack adequate knowledge and all other merit, nevertheless it has pleased our lord the king lately to make me his chancellor, and so he has now ordered me to explain on his behalf in your honourable presence the reasons for summoning this present parliament. And so, it should be plainly apparent that I would not undertake so serious a business as informing such nobles and wise persons as you are of so important a matter, either by presumption or folly, but for two reasons alone. One is that

[Col. b] it has long been an established tradition in the realm that previous chancellors of England in their own times have made the announcement on the king's behalf concerning parliaments held in the past; and I would not wish, if it pleased God, that in my time fault should be found in my person, or

y fuist trovez en ma persone, ne arriressement de l'estat de mon dit office, si avaunt come je le purroie meintenir en tout bien et honour. La seconde cause est, pur quoy je assume de present si grant charge sur moy devant touz les autres sages cy presentz, qar le roi nostre seignour lige ycy present m'ad comandez del faire, a qi me faut a fyn force en ce et en touz autres ses comandementz qe purroient tournir au profit de luy et de son roialme obeire: et issint ne ferroie ceste chargeante busoigne en aucun manere, sinoun constreint par reson de mon office, et comandement de monseignour lige, come dit est.

3. Et seignours et sires, la principale et primere cause pur quoy nostre dit seignour le roy ad fait somondre son present parlement, qe touche le roialme d'Escoce, si est expressee et contenue en les briefs a vous faites de mesme la somonce, la quele est tiele. Nostre seignour le roy apparceivant coment les grantz trieves jadys prises parentre les roiaumes d'Engleterre et d'Escoce si doivent par la forme d'ycelles fynir et faillir a ceste proschein feste de la Purification Nostre Dame proschein venant, et pur tant qe homme ny feust desgarniz en celle partie al dit fin des trieves, pleust a nostre dit seignour le roy d'envoier a la marche d'Escoce lui puissant et noble seignour son treschere uncle d'Espaigne, duc de Lancastre, cy present, avec autres seignours et sages du conseil le roi, pur assaier et taster si l'en purroit honurablement avoir la paix ovesqe les Escotes, ou autrement prorogacion d'icelles trieves pur un temps notable. Et si furent ils en dite marche d'Escoce, et ent avoient parlance et tretee avec mesmes les Escotz, et finalment ent ont reportez a nostre dit seignour le roy relacion et lettres del adversaire d'Escoce, contenantes, q'il envoieroit suffisantes persones de son roialme avec poair et auctoritee suffisante depar lui a /Londres, pur y treter\ de mesme la matire. Et celle report fait a nostre dit seignour le roy pur ce qe voirs est qe plusours de vous estez enheritez des plusours terres et seignouries deinz le roialme d'Engleterre, appertenantz a les Escotz d'ancientee, \[et aussi aiez]/ en chalange plusours terres et tenementz deinz le roialme \[d'Escoce,]/ dont les Escotz sont auxint de present enheritez. Et si paix se ferroit parentre les roialmes, \[avendront]/ ensi par cas, qe plusours translacions \[des droitz a]/ ycelles terres et seignouries d'ambes partz serroient faitz, ou par cas mesmes les droitz serroient \[surrenduz]/ decea et dela: et par celle cause et autres matires plusours \[incidentz qe ne]/ viegnent ore a memoire; mais par especial pur tant qe le roiaume *[Page iii-150]*

[Col. a] d'Escoce \[si est tielment]/ annexe \[d'auncientee a la coroune]/ d'Engleterre lui quiel de temps Bruyt primer enhabitour d'icelles roialmes, le roialme d'Escoce avauntdit, et le roy d'icelle pur le temps esteant, aient este continuelment subjugatz et attendantz au roi et al roialme d'Engleterre, ou en possession, ou en chalange, sembloit de verite qe homme ne poait sur tielle haute et chargeante matire finalment treter ou accorder aillours qe en parlement, ou si paix ou trieves ne se y purroient prendre encores, le remede pur defendre faut estre purveu en parlement. \[Et einsi]/\ si/ nule autre matire eussez d'avoir parlement, si est ce qe j'ai dit une grant cause.

4. Une autre cause y ad, purquoy le roi nostre seignour ad fait sommondre cest son parlement, est tiele, si einsi avenist qe paiis ou trieves ne se preignent point en Escoce, adonqes la pluis perileuse guerre qe nous purroions avoir si est tantost . . . . dont est moult grandement a douter, et par tant faire par temps bone purvoiance encontre lour grant orgoille, fauxine et force, aiant consideracion coment ils purront chescun jour entrer nostre roialme a terre seek, sanz impediment de la meer ou de eaue fresshe. Mes

injury done to the estate of my said office, when I might keep it in all goodness and honour. The second reason for which I undertake so great a charge before all the other wise men here present is that, since the king our liege lord here present has ordered me to do it, I am compelled to obey him in this and in all his other orders which might make for the profit of himself or of his kingdom: and so I do not undertake so serious a matter for any other reason than the constraints inherent in my office, and the order given by my liege lord, as has been said.

3. And lords and sirs, the chief and first reason why our said lord the king caused his present parliament to be summoned concerns the kingdom of Scotland, as is expressed and contained in the writs of summons issued to you, and is this. Our lord the king, perceiving that the great truce once made between the kingdoms of England and Scotland would, according to the form of the same, end and expire at the feast of the Purification of Our Lady next to come [2 February 1384], and because there would be no warning of the matter at the said end of the truce, it pleased our said lord the king to send to the march of Scotland the most exalted and noble lord, his most beloved uncle of Spain, duke of Lancaster, here present, with other lords and wise men of the king's council, to see and to try whether peace could honourably be had with the Scots, or else a prorogation of the same truce for a significant length of time. And so they were in the said march of Scotland, and discussed and negotiated with the same Scots, and finally they brought to our said lord the king a report and letters from the Scottish enemy, stating that they would send some worthy persons of their realm to London, with adequate power and authority on their behalf to discuss the same matter. And this report was made to our said lord the king because it is true that many of you have right of inheritance to lands and lordships within the kingdom of England which anciently pertained to the Scots, and you have also disputed claims to many lands and tenements in the kingdom of Scotland, which the Scots also, at present, hold by inheritance. And if peace were to be made between the kingdoms, it would result in the transfer of many such rights to lands and lordships on either side, or perhaps the rights might be surrendered on one side or the other: and for that reason as well as for many others which cannot at present be called to mind; but especially because the kingdom *[Page iii-150]*

[Col. a] of Scotland has been so annexed from antiquity to the crown of England, which aforesaid kingdom of Scotland and the successive kings of the same, since the time of Brutus, first inhabitant of these kingdoms, have been continually subject to and attendant upon the king and kingdom of England, whether in possession or challenged, it seems true that one could not ultimately discuss or settle such an important and burdensome matter anywhere other than in parliament, and if peace and truce could no longer be had, some defensive remedy must be provided in parliament. And so, if there were no other reason for the holding of a parliament, that of which I have spoken is reason enough.

4. Yet there is another reason for which the king our lord caused his parliament to be summoned, and that is that if a peace or truce be not reached in Scotland, then the most perilous war we could experience will be imminent, which is greatly to be feared, and for that reason early provision must be made against their great pride, deceit, and strength, bearing in mind that they can enter our kingdom at any time on dry land, without impediment of sea or fresh water. And yet it is not simply against the said Scots that provision must

encores non pas soulement de faire purveiance encontre les ditz Escotes, einz d'autres partz, \et/ envers troiz de plus grandes roialmes et paiis de Cristianetee, c'estadire, France, Espaigne, et ore de novelle acreue le paiis de Flandres, avek toutz leurs adherantz et allies, qi sont /come innumerables,\ mortelx enemys a cest petit roialme d'Engleterre, qe Dieu salve, toutz partz environez par terre et par meer; envers queux si Dieu de sa grace n'y mette remede, et homme de sa part /ne\ face ceo qe en lui est de purveiance en resistence de lour malice, vraisemblable est qe le greindre meschief est hastivement a avenir, qe Dieu ne veulle, a cest petit roialme, qe unqes mes n'y avenist.

5. Et purceo qe meschief semble par les /ditz\ causes si dure et si prochein, si est droit qe homme se haste le plus tost pur ordeiner de bone et effectuel remedy. Q'est principalemement, apres la grace de Dieu, d'avoir de quoy homme purra venir a les despences qe l'en y faut mettre, qe covient a fyn force venir de la commune, qar commune defens demande commune charge. Et voirs est et certein qe troys des pluis riches roys Cristiens ne purroient endurer les charges de tantz et tielles guerres sanz l'eide de lour commune, et pur tant l'en faut ordiner coment defendre, et de quoy l'en avera despences necessaries. Et quant a defens faire en celle partie, salvez meillour advis, il doit apparoir a chescun sage qe nostre defens si est d'assailler les enemys par dehors nostre roialme. Qar tiel assaut si semble estre resonable, profitable et honurable. Primerement, si est nostre assaut resonable, par enchesoun qe nous sumes actours, demandours et chalangeours, ou appellours; et reson voet qe le demandant et chalangeour assaille le defendour, et noun pas e converso. Secoundement, nostre assaut est profitable, qar si nous attendismes leur assaut deinz nostre roialme, l'assemble et chivachee de nostre host envers lour host ferroit a nostre roialme, l'un et l'autre ost esteant en ycelle, a tant de damage come ferroit l'ost des enemys, horspris prise de prisoners, et arsuree des villes et mesons, sicome vous messeignours et sires avez mesmes veuz estre fait es parties depar dela. Et mieltz est et plus profitable qe nostre ost soit sustenuz par les vitailles et biens des enemys qe de nos biens propres. Tiercement, il est plus honorable d'assailer qe defendre; qar communement les cowardz n'assaillent mye. Et pur eschuir les meschifs de lour assaut d'un part, et la vilenie qe nous auroions si nous, qi sumes demandours et chalangeours come dit est, pur defaute del pursuyte de nostre droit qe nous avons comencuz devaunt ore, feussons appellez meyntenant, ou tenuz d'autres noz veisins, qe Dieu ne veulle, pur cowardz, si avant come

[Col. b] nous purrons eschuir l'occacion, pur quoy tielle noun enporteroions? Qar il nous faut faire un des deux choses, ou de pursuir nostre droit par fort main et assaut, ou de lesser hounteusement. Et, seignours et sires, toutes voies vous ne durez mye aretter sur la persone du roy nostre seignour, qe cestes importables charges de les guerres avanditz soient par lui introductz, ou par singuleritee de lui comencies, einz furent comences devant son temps, come bien sachez. Et auxi avant come la honurable coroune d'Engleterre lui est descenduz par successione de droit heritage, auxi avant lui sont eschuiz avec l'onour et profit de la coroune les chargeantz guerres et querelles d'ycelles devant son temps commencez, come dit est.

6. Item, un autre cause de la sommonce de cest parlement est tielle; c'estassavoir, d'ordeigner qe salve garde de la paix deinz le roialme, /et\ l'obbeisance due a nostre seignour le roy de toutz ses subgitz, soit mieltz fait et gardez qe ce n'ad estee fait devant cest heure. Qar le disobeissance et rebellion q'omme ad fait devant ore, \et qe/ sont continues de jour en autre envers les petitz ministres du roy, come viscontz,

be made, but against other peoples, and in particular against three of the greatest kingdoms and lands of Christendom, that is to say, France, Spain, and now the recently gained land of Flanders, with all their adherents and allies, who seem innumerable, mortal enemies of this small kingdom of England, which God preserve, surrounded on all sides by land and sea; from whom, unless God of his grace provide remedy, and man for his part does whatsoever he can to resist their malice, greater trouble than ever before shall soon beset this tiny kingdom, which God forbid.

5. And because misfortune seems for these said reasons to be so severe and so imminent, it is proper that one should hasten to ordain at once a good and effective remedy. Which is chiefly, with the grace of God, to arrange the means of raising the money it would be necessary to invest, which task necessarily falls to the commons, since common defence demands a common charge. And it is certainly true that the three richest Christian kings could not endure the charges of such wars without the aid of their commons, and for that reason an ordinance must be made for our defence and to meet the necessary costs. And as to the mode of defence to be adopted, in the absence of better advice it must be apparent to all wise men that our best defence is to attack the enemies outside our realm. For such an attack seems reasonable, profitable and honourable. Firstly, our attack is reasonable because we are plaintiffs, demandants, and claimants, or appellants; and reason dictates that the demandant and claimant attack the defendant, and not the other way around. Secondly, an assault is advantageous, for if we await an attack in our own kingdom, the assembly and expedition of our host against their host will be borne by our kingdom, both hosts being in the same, and the enemy host will inflict great damage, not to mention the capturing of prisoners and the burning of towns and houses, as you my lords and sirs have seen overseas. And it is better and more advantageous that our host be sustained by the victuals and goods of the enemy than by our own. Thirdly, it is more honourable to attack than defend; for cowards do not ordinarily attack. And to avoid the misfortune of their attack on the one hand, and the opprobrium we should suffer if we, who are the demandants and claimants as has been said, through failure to pursue our right previously sought, were now labelled, or considered by our other neighbours to be cowards, which God forbid; as

[Col. b] we can avoid the occasion, why should we have to bear it? For we must do one of two things, either pursue our right by force and assault, or shamefully abandon it. And lords and sirs, you would be wrong to accuse the person of the king our lord of introducing or initiating these unbearable charges for the aforesaid wars, since they were begun before his time, as you well know. And just as the honourable crown of England has descended to him by the succession of rightful inheritance, so there have fallen to his lot, along with the honour and profit of the crown, the burdensome wars and complaints of the same begun before his time, as has been said.

6. Also, another reason for summoning this parliament is, namely, to ordain that the keeping of peace within the realm and the obedience owed to our lord the king by all his subjects should be better performed and maintained than ever before. For the disobedience and rebellion occurring in the past, and daily persisting against the lesser ministers of the king, such as sheriffs, escheators, other

escheteours et les coillours de les subsides, et autres tielx, estoient sours et cause principale del traitureus insurreccion nadgairs fait par la commune d'Engleterre deins mesme le roialme. La quel primerement estoit rebelle as ditz petitz ministres, et puis as grantes officers del roialme, et al drain au roi mesmes, combien le savez. Et si avant come rebellion si estoit et est le sours et comencement de meschief et truboille deinz le roialme, si est areremain verroi obeissance au roi et ses ministres foundement de tut paix et quietee en mesme le roialme, \sicome clerement apparoit /par l'obeissance qe les gentils firent au roi en dit insurreccion.\/ Et pur cestes causes devanditz, et pur purveiances des remedies bosoignables en celle partie, et auxint pur ordinance faire pur le salve gard des terres et seignouries nostre dit seignour le roy, sibien decea come dela, et pur remedie fair et purvoier a toutz les liges le roy en ceo parlement, s'ils, ou ascuns de eux, lour vorront compleindre de chose qe ne poet estre remediez forsqe en parlement, ad nostre dit seignour le roy fait somondre ce present parlement; . . . . et si ad il auxint ordeignez certeins prelates, seignours et justices triours, et certeins clercs de sa chauncellerye resceivours des peticions q'omme vorra bailler avant en ce parlement, par manere come vous orrez lire par le clerk de parlement en escript, qe s'ensuit de /mot a\ mot:'

7. Resceivours des peticions d'Engleterre, Irlande, Gales et Escoce:

Sire Johan de Waltham

Sire Richard Ravenser

Sire Thomas Newenham

Sire Johan de Freton'

Sire Robert Faryngton'.

8. Resceivours des peticions de Gascoigne, et d'autres terres et paiis depar dela:

Sire Piers de Barton'

Sire Johan Bouland'

Sire Robert Muskham

Sire Johan Scarle.

Et ceux qi veullent bailler lours billes les baillent avant parentre cy et la feste de Tousseintz proschein venant, ycelle mesme jour accompte.

Page iii-151

9. Et sont assignez triours des peticions d'Engleterre, Irlande, Gales et Escoce:

Le roi de Castille et de Leon', duc de Lancastre

L'ercevesqe de Cantirbirs

L'evesqe de Londres

L'evesqe de Wyncestre

L'evesqe de Ely

L'evesqe de Salesbirs

L'abbe de Seint Austyn, de Canterbirs

L'abbe de Waltham

Le cont de Kent, mareschal d'Engleterre

Le cont d'Arrundell

Le cont de Warr'

Le cont de Northumbr'

Le seignour de Nevill'

Monsire Richard le Scrop'

Monsire Guy de Bryen

Monsire Robert Tresilian

Monsire Robert Bealknap'

collectors of the subsidies and the like, were the source and principal cause of the treacherous insurrection lately made by the commons of England in the same kingdom, which first took the form of a rebellion against the said lesser ministers, and then against the great officers of the kingdom, and at last against the king himself, as you well know. And just as rebellion was and is the source and instigator of trouble and misfortune in the kingdom, so, conversely, true obedience to the king and his ministers is the foundation of all peace and tranquillity in the same, as appears plainly from the obedience which the nobles showed the king in the said insurrection. And for the aforesaid reasons, and to provide the remedies necessary in this matter, and also to make an ordinance for the safeguard of the lands and lordships of our said lord the king on this side of the sea and overseas, and to supply and provide remedy for all the king's lieges in this parliament, if they, or any of them, wish to complain of anything which cannot be remedied without parliament, our lord the king has caused this present parliament to be summoned; and has also appointed certain prelates, lords, and justices as triers, and certain clerks of his chancery as receivers, of the petitions which people may wish to submit in this parliament, whose names you will hear read out by the clerk of parliament from the written text, which is as follows:

7. Receivers of petitions from England, Ireland, Wales, and Scotland:

Sir John Waltham

Sir Richard Ravenser

Sir Thomas Newenham

Sir John Freton

Sir Robert Farrington.

8. Receivers of petitions from Gascony, and from other lands and countries overseas:

Sir Piers Barton

Sir John Bowland

Sir Robert Muskham

Sir John Scarle.

And those who wish to submit their bills should hand them in between now and the feast of All Saints next, the day allotted to them [1 November 1383].

9. The following are assigned to be triers of petitions from England, Ireland, Wales and Scotland:

The king of Castile and Leon, duke of Lancaster

The archbishop of Canterbury

The bishop of London

The bishop of Winchester

The bishop of Ely

The bishop of Salisbury

The abbot of St Augustine's, Canterbury

The abbot of Waltham

The earl of Kent, marshal of England

The earl of Arundel

The earl of Warwick

The earl of Northumberland

Lord Neville

Sir Richard le Scrope

Sir Guy Bryan

Sir Robert Tresilian

Sir Robert Bealknap

- toutz ensemble, ou .vi. des prelats et seignours avauntditz au meins, appellez a eux chanceller, tresorer, senescal et chamberleyn; et auxint les sergeantz nostre seignour le roi quant il busoignera. Et tendront lour place en la chambre de chamberlein, pres de la chambre depeinte.

10. Et sont assignez triours des peticions de Gascoigne, et d'autres terres et paiis dela la meer, et de les Isles:

L'evesqe de Nichole

L'evesqe de Norwiz

L'evesqe de Seint Davy

L'evesqe d'Excestre

L'evesqe de Herford'

L'abbe de Westm'

L'abbe de Glastyngbirs

Le cont de Cantebrug'

Le cont de Buk', conestable d'Engleterre

Le cont de Staff'

Le cont de Salesbirs

Le seignour Fitz Wauter

Le priour de Seint Johan Jerusalem en Engleterre

Monsire Johan de Cobham, de Kent

Monsire William Skipwith'

Monsire Roger Fulthorp'

Monsire Davyd Hannemer

- touz ensemble, ou .iiij. des prelatz et seignours avantditz, appellez a eux chanceller, tresorer, seneschal, chamberlein et les sergeantz le roy quant il busoignera. Et tendront lour place en la chambre marcolf.

11. Et la dite cedule lue en dit parlement, mesme le chanceller parlast autrefoitz, et dit, 'Seignours et sires trestouz cy presentz, q'avez la somonce de cest parlement, le roy vous comande sur la peine q'appent qe aiantz due consideracione a les necessaires matires a vous ore monstrez, et a les importables meschiefs apparantz, et auxint a la grant necessitee qe le roi ad ore de tresor et d'avoir pur remedier ycelles meschiefs, queux sanz grant fuyson d'avoir ne poent jammays estre remediez; vous, messires les prelatz et seignours temporelx, par vous mesmes, et vous, seignours de la commune, par vous mesmes veulliez communer diligeaument sur cestes matires, et des remedes busoignables, a toute le haste qe vous purrez, oustant de tout le communement d'autre matire collaterale quelconqe en le moien temps: et voz advis ent pris reporter de temps en temps au roi nostre seignour, au fin qe les matires necessaires touchez, et a toucheres, soient a bone deliberacion examinez, tretez et esploitez, et toute autre impertinent matire mys a derire pur le temps, et le parlement par tant mys a graciouse et bone fyn, qe Dieu grante. Et le roy vous comande trestouz qe vous retournez de jour en autre pur treter et faire ce pur quoy vous estes venuz dont vous avez maintenant vostre charge, sanz departir de cest parlement par voie qelconqe, si einsi

[Col. b] ne soit qe vous ent averez especiale congie de dit seignour le roy, sur le peril avauntdit.'[11]

12. Item, fait a remembrer qe les seignours et communes en cest parlement assemblez, considerez les oultrageouses charges qe nostre seignour le roy porte parmy les guerres overtes de toutes partz et autrement, granterent a nostre dit seignour le roy une quinszisme, a avoir et resceivoir de eux par les forme et condicions \en/ toutz pointz comprises en

- to act all together, or at least six of the aforesaid prelates and lords, consulting with the chancellor, treasurer, steward and chamberlain; and also the serjeants of our lord the king when necessary. And they shall hold their session in the chamberlain's room near the Painted Chamber.

10. The following are assigned to be triers of petitions from Gascony and from other lands and territories overseas, and from the Channel Islands:

The bishop of Lincoln

The bishop of Norwich

The bishop of St Davids

The bishop of Exeter

The bishop of Hereford

The abbot of Westminster

The abbot of Glastonbury

The earl of Cambridge

The earl of Buckingham, constable of England

The earl of Stafford

The earl of Salisbury

Lord FitzWalter

The prior of St John of Jerusalem in England

Sir John Cobham of Kent

Sir William Skipwith

Sir Roger Fulthorp

Sir David Hanmer

- to act all together, or at least four of the aforesaid prelates and lords, consulting with the chancellor, treasurer, steward, chamberlain and the king's serjeants when necessary. And they shall hold their session in the Marcolf Chamber.

11. The said schedule having been read in the said parliament, the same chancellor spoke again, and said, Lords and sirs here present, who have received summons to this parliament, the king orders you on pain of the penalty decreed that, giving due consideration to the urgent matters now explained to you, and to the unbearable troubles appearing, and also to the great need which the king now has for treasure and for a remedy for these misfortunes, which can never be remedied without great means; you, my lords the prelates and lords temporal, amongst yourselves, and you, lords of the commonalty, amongst yourselves, shall diligently discuss these matters and their necessary remedies with all the haste you can, abandoning all discussion of other peripheral matters in the meantime: and that you will from time to time report your conclusions to the king our lord, so that the urgent matters touched upon, and to be touched upon, can be well examined, discussed and accomplished, and all irrelevant matters set aside for the time being, and the parliament thus brought to a good and gracious ending, which God grant. And the king orders you all to return each day to do and discuss that for which you have come and which you now have in your charge, without departing from this parliament by any means, unless

[Col. b] you have the special permission of the said lord the king, on pain of the aforesaid penalty.

12. Also, be it remembered that the lords and commons assembled in this parliament, considering the outrageous charges which our lord the king bears because of the open wars on every side and for other reasons, have granted to our said lord the king one fifteenth, to have and receive from them in the form and on the conditions set out in detail in

---

[11] A lengthy section of the roll has been left blank after this item.

une cedule sur ce faite, endentee et liveree avaunt en parlement par mesmes les communes, et nemye en autre manere par voie quelconqe. Et pria la dite communqe par especial a nostre dit seignour le roy qe la dite cedule quelle ils ont fait, come celle qe pleinement contient la manere de lour grant, dont mesme la commune y fist pleine declaracion par bouche devaunt nostre dit seignour le roy en plein parlement, si feust entree en roulle de parlement de mot a mot, et en nulle autre manere par aucune voie; quele request lour estoit ottroiez. De quele cedule issint liveree le tenure s'ensuit de mot a mot:

Grant del .xv.^{e}.

13. Les communes d'Engleterre assemblez en ce present parlement, ovesqe l'assent des seignours, pur diverses perils considerez avenir a la roialme sibien par terre come par mier, si bone ordinance et defense ne soit ordeignez pur ycelle, grauntent a nostre seignour le roi, en defense du roialme, et pur eschuir les perils semblables avenir des toutz partz tant par terre come par mier, sur condicions q'ensuent, la moitee d'un quinzisme q'est acustumez entre les laies d'estre levez quant un tiel grant est grantez, pur estre paiez et mys en execucion la ou pluis y bosoigne, et selonc qe le temps demande, ore a les oetaves de Seynt Hiller prochein avenir. Et auxi grantent les ditz communes, par assent des seignours, en pleisance du roy leur seignour suisdit, et pur sa prier moevez par bouche de chaunceller, en eidant par especial al sauf garde du mier, le subside de .vi. *d*. par livere, et .ij. *s*. del tonel de vin, nadgairs grauntez, a durer tanq'a le Seint Michel proschein avenir, pur la dit mier garder en troys parties, come ensuyt; c'estassavoir de Mont de Seint Michel tanq'a Hastinges, pur estre despenduz tout ceo q'entre les ditz boundes ent purra estre levez; et de Hastinges tanq'a Kirkele Rode, pur estre despenduz come prochein devant; et par mesme la manere parentre Kirkele Rode et l'eawe de Twede: purveuz qe toutz les deniers qe purront sourdre du dit subside soient duement levez, et loialment controllez sanz estre lessez a ferme, mes entierment liverez a les admiralx ore nomez, en cas q'ils veullent en ce present parlement emprendre pur la saufe garde du mier suisdit. Et si cas aveigne, come Dieux ne veulle, qe paix final, ne trieve sufficiente pur une resonable temps se preigne n'acorde parentre le roy nostre seignour suisdit et son adversarie de France parentre cy et Pasqe prochein, adonqes la dit commune, considerant le bone corage et volentee du roy nostre seignour, et la necessite pur defense du dit roialme, grauntent une autre moite d'un quinzisme tiel come paramont est dit, pur estre levez des toutz les laies al fest de Pentecost prochein venant, toutz voiez entendant qe si ascun paix ou trieve se preigne, come dessuis est dit, parentre cy et la Pentecost, q'alors nul denier de la darrein moitee du quinzisme soit levez, ne brief issez pur la lever, par cest protestacione escripte et endentee. Protestant outre qe l'un moitee ne l'autre n'est nostre entent a graunter sanz les condicions ensuantz: primerement qe l'estat de clergie emportent et grauntent a leur afferant sibien pur la salvacion de eux come de nous, as mesmes les jours et termes come devant est dit. Auxint, qe toutz maners des gentz layes d'estat d'avoir, de quielconqe degree qe ceo soit, en soient contributoires ovesqe les povers sanz nully esparnir.

Requeste de la commune econtre l'evesqe de Norwiz, et autres.[12]

Et auxint, qe tut le service due par l'evesqe de Norwitz, et toutz les capitains et autres qi furent en sa compaignie, nient deserviz *[Page iii-152]*

---

[12]This note is in a different yet contemporary hand.

a schedule made thereon, indented and placed before parliament by the same commons, and in no other way nor by any other means. And the said commons pray particularly of our said lord the king that the said schedule which they have made, as plainly setting out the manner of their grant, which the same commons fully declared by word of mouth before our said lord the king in full parliament, be entered on the roll of parliament word for word, and in no other manner nor by any other means; which request was granted them. Which schedule thus delivered follows word for word:

The grant of the fifteenth.

13. The commons of England assembled in this present parliament, with the assent of the lords, because of various perils threatening the kingdom both by land and sea unless good ordinance and defence be arranged for the same, grant to our lord the king, in defence of the kingdom, and to avoid similar dangers occurring on all sides by land and sea, on the conditions which follow, half of one fifteenth which is customarily levied amongst the laity when such a grant is made, to be spent and used wheresover it be most needed, and as the moment requires, from now until the octave of St Hilary next [20 January 1384]. And the said commons also grant, by the assent of the lords, to please the king their aforesaid lord, and in response to his request made through the chancellor, to assist in particular the keeping of the seas, the subsidy of 6*d*. in the pound and 2*s*. per tun of wine formerly granted, to last until Michaelmas next [29 September 1384], to keep the said seas in three areas, as follows; namely, from Mont St Michel to Hastings, everything being spent there which can be levied between the said boundaries; and from Hastings to Kirkley Roads, to be spent as before; and in the same way, between Kirkley Roads and the water of the Tweed: provided that all the money which may arise from the said subsidy be duly levied and faithfully managed, without being leased to farm, but wholly delivered to the admirals here named, if they are willing in this present parliament to undertake the keeping of the sea aforesaid. And if it happen, which God forbid, that neither a firm peace nor an adequate truce is reached or agreed within a reasonable space of time between the king our aforesaid lord and his enemy of France between now and Easter next [10 April 1384], then the said commons, considering the good heart and will of the king our lord and the need to defend the said realm, will grant another half-fifteenth like the one above, to be levied on all the laity at Whitsun next [29 May 1384], on the understanding however that if any peace or truce be reached, as mentioned above, between now and Whitsun, no penny of the last half-fifteenth shall be levied, nor any writ issued to levy it, by this written and indented protestation. Protesting further that it is not our intention to grant either the one half or the other except on the following conditions: first, that the estate of the clergy shall grant and contribute according to their means for the salvation of themselves as well as of us, and on the same terms as mentioned above. And also, that all kinds of laymen of landed estate, of whatever degree they be, shall contribute alongside the poor with none being spared.

The request of the commons against the bishop of Norwich and others.

And also that all the service owed by the bishop of Norwich, and by all the captains and others who were in his company, which was not performed *[Page iii-152]*

[Col. a] for the time agreed by them, together with all the gold improperly received by them from the enemies of the king our lord overseas or on this side of the sea; together with the service owed to our aforesaid lord the king for the silver received towards Guyenne, or towards Brittany, and still not performed, be loyally used for the profit of the king our said lord in support and relief of his poor people. Praying also of the king our lord, and of all the officers, that an ordinance soon be made for the march of Scotland, such that, the country about it and all the kingdom of England behind it be not destroyed by a lack of good and swift remedy and succour for the same.

14. And be it known that the substance of this schedule having been rehearsed in parliament, as is said, the commons prayed that whatsoever they requested in the said schedule be well performed, and put into good and proper effect. Whereupon the earl of Northumberland, there present, replied and expressly stated as well for himself as admiral towards the north appointed by our lord the king as on behalf of his companion the earl of Devonshire, who was similarly appointed admiral towards the west; that they would certainly not perform such an undertaking for the keeping of the sea in any other way, but that whatever they received for the same, and yet more, would be loyally spent on the same. He further promised that in good faith he would invest diligence, labour and money in the same keeping as well as he could; taking into consideration the amount of the sum he would receive for the purpose: but he expressly stated that he would not undertake the aforesaid keeping in any other way.

The bishop of Norwich, Fulmer and Bowet.

15. Also, be it remembered that upon the request of the commons made in this parliament on various occasions, asking that in relief of the aforesaid commons the service of the bishop of Norwich, and of all the captains and others who were recently in his company overseas and who had not performed the service which they had agreed and promised the lord our king that they would do in his wars, together with the gold which had been taken and received from the enemies of the king our lord on this side of the sea or overseas by the same persons in an improper manner, which amounted to eighteen thousand or more francs of gold, as it is said, be used and devoted entirely to the service of the king in the marches of Scotland, or wherever there be great need of it, to the end that the same commons might now be charged with less towards the king, and so supported in the charge which they must now bear, the said bishop of Norwich prayed of our lord the king that for love of God it might please him to of his benignity and grace to lend him audience, ear, time and opportunity, that he might excuse himself in this parliament of the gold of which the commons spoke and of all other things which people might seek to allege against him. And if it would please the king so to do, he thought, so he said, that with the aid of Our Lord, to make such a declaration of his actions and of his innocence in the matter that every reasonable man would hold him fully excused. And further, he stated expressly that he had never received anything from any enemy of the king our lord neither on this side of the sea nor overseas, whether gold or silver, in money, plate or jewels, nor any other gift by any means in the world: and if anyone could ever prove the contrary, he would willingly bear such blame and defamation as he deserved. Whereupon Mr Henry Bowet, clerk of the said bishop, having been examined and charged there on his allegiance in parliament to say whether he knew any gold to have been received or

ou depuis lour revenue deinz le roialme, dist et confessast illoeqes qe voirs estoit qe sur certeins covenances taillez par endenture parentre le dit evesqe, \et les capitains Engleys/ et les Franceys sur la voidance du paiis du Flandres et de la ville de Gravenynge,

[Col. b] dont monsire William de Elmham et monsire William de Faryndon' et autres estoient entremettours, si feust certeine somme des franks d'or resceuz en manere qe s'ensuit, a ce q'il ad oeiz, mais autrement nel sciet il mye, a cause q'il n'estoit present sur la fesance des dites endentures. Primerement, quant la dite endenture feust monstrez a mesme l'evesqe, qe contenoit entre autres choses q'il auroit certeine somme des franks d'or, bien entour .x. mille pur ses coustages faitz entour la fortificacione de mesme la ville de Gravenynge, et pur ses vitailles en ycelle, mesme l'evesqe fist raser mesme l'endenture, et ouster la cause, fesant mencion de la receite del dit or a son oeps; et jurast illoeqes q'il ne prendroit unqes riens d'icelle. Et sur /ce,\ lendemain proschein ensuant, si vindrent certeins persones depar les ditz Franceoys, et porterent ovesqe eux cynk mille franks d'or de la somme de .x. mille franks avantditz, et les lesseront en la chambre du dit maistre Henry a Gravenynge. Et ce fait, le dit maistre Henry fist assavoir tantost al dit evesqe, coment le dit or lui estoit envoiez.

A quoi le dit evesqe en respoignant comandast qe tantost ce feust rebaillez as portours d'icelle, et qe monsire William de Faryndon', chivaler, alast au duc de Bretaigne, ou il estoit alors bien pres en l'ost de France, avec les ditz portours del or, et veist qe mesme l'or fuist entierment rebaillez a celluy qi l'envoiast. Qar il dist q'il n'averoit \[ja]/ aise a coer tanqe il scieust en certain qe celle or feust fait retournir entierment: .... allegeant cause en especial q'il ne vorroit autre foitz ent porter reproche ou vilenie en presence de son seignour lige en Engleterre, n'autrement, pur tout l'or qe l'adversaire de France purroit arramer. Et surce, les ditz portours se retournerent, et le dit monsire William \de Farndon'/ avec eux, lessantz derere eulx en la dite chambre les ditz cynk mille franks. Et quant le dit Maistre Henry retournast en son dit chambre, et vist l'or avauntdit lessez illoeqes, et qe ceux qe einsi le deussent avoir reportez furent passez, il prist a lui Sire Robert de Fulmere, clerc et tresorier le dit evesqe, lui monstrant le dit or, et la manere coment le dit evesqe ent avoit comandez, et coment encontre son dit comandement si feust mesme l'or lessez illoeqes. Et surce, le dit Maistre Henry dist al dit seignour /Robert\ de Fulmere, 'Preignez garde a ceste or, qe ce soit seurement gardez en cas \qe/ demande ent pluis aviegne \en/ avant.' Et ce dit, /le\ dit maistre Henry departi d'illoeqes vers Gaunt en les busoignes de mesmes l'evesqe, ou il estoit grant piece apres, et ne vist plus le dit evesqe, ne le dit sire Robert, ne riens pluis savoit ou celle or estoit devenuz tanqe il venist en Engleterre, ou l'en lui ad contez pluis au plein de la matire. Et einsi, il dit, est il innocent de celle receite, et des covenances ent taillez, si nulles soient, come cellui qi ne se ent medlast unqes pluis avaunt en aucune manere q'il n'ad ore dit, ne pluis n'ent sciet dire ou conter pur veritee, forsqe ce voet il dire et prover par manere tiele qe homme de soun degree doit faire, qe le dit evesqe son seignour ne fuist unqes conissant qe le dit or estoit issint lessez avec son dit tresorier.

Et puis apres le dit sire Robert Foulmere examinez sur sa ligeance de dire \ce/ q'il savoit de veritee sur mesme la matire, confessast qe quanqe /le\ dit maistre Henry ent avoit dit et countez si contenoit pleine veritee. Et dist oultre qe monsire William de Elmham, monsire Thomas Tryvet,

agreed for the use of the said bishop from the said enemies on the last expedition to Flanders, or since their return to the kingdom, said and confessed there that it was true that on certain covenants having been drawn up by indenture between the said bishop and the English and French captains on leaving the land of Flanders and the town of Gravelines, [Col. b] in which Sir William Elmham and Sir William Faringdon and others were participants, so was a certain sum of gold francs to be received in the following manner, or so he had heard, but other than that he knew nothing, because he had not been present at the making of the said indentures. Firstly, when the same bishop had been shown the said indenture, which stated amongst other things that he should have a certain number of gold francs, amounting to almost ten thousand, for the expenses he had incurred in fortifying the same town of Gravelines and for victualling the same, he caused the said indenture to be erased, removing the clause which mentioned the receipt of the said gold for his use; and swore there that he would not take anything else for the same. Whereupon, the following day, certain persons appeared on behalf of the said French and brought with them five thousand gold francs of the aforesaid sum of ten thousand francs, and left them in the chamber of the said Master Henry at Gravelines. And thereupon, the said Master Henry immediately notified the said bishop that the said gold had been sent to him.

Whereupon, the said bishop ordered that it be returned at once to the bearers of the same, and that Sir William Faringdon, knight, go to the duke of Brittany, who was then nearby in the French host, with the said bearers of the gold, and see that the same gold was returned in full to him who sent it. For he said that he would not have peace of mind until he knew for certain that the gold had been returned in full: saying especially that he would not wish to incur the reproach or wrath of his liege lord in England, nor anything else, for all the gold which the French enemy could offer. Whereupon the said bearers returned, and the said Sir William Faringdon with them, leaving the said five thousand francs behind them in the said chamber. And when the said Master Henry returned to his said chamber and saw that the aforesaid gold had been left there, and that those who ought to have taken it back had left, he took Sir Robert Fulmer, clerk and treasurer of the said bishop, to one side and showed him the said gold, explaining what the said bishop had ordered, and how the gold had been left there contrary to that command. Whereupon, the said Master Henry told the said Sir Robert Fulmer, Take care of this gold and let it be securely kept in case there should be any question about it in future. And this said, the same Master Henry left for Ghent on the bishop's business, where he remained for a long while after, and he saw the said bishop no more, nor the said Sir Robert, nor did he learn what had become of the gold until he came to England, where someone told him the whole story. And so, he said, he was innocent of the receipt, and of the covenants drawn up thereon, if there were any, as someone whose involvement had been no greater than he had described, nor did he know anything else to tell or recount in truth, except that he wished to state and prove in a manner appropriate to a man of his degree that the said bishop his lord had never known that the said gold had been thus left with his said treasurer.

Then, the said Sir Robert, having been examined on his allegiance to speak the truth in the matter, confirmed that everything the said Master Henry had said and recounted thereon had been the whole truth. He said also that Sir William Elmham, Sir Thomas Trivet, Sir Henry Ferrers, Sir John

monsire Henry de Ferriers, monsire /Johan de Drayton,\ monsire William de Faryndon', et autres qi furent /presentz\ al dit tretee, sachent dire qe le dit evesqe ne savoit unqes tanqe ore qe mesme la monoie feust demurrez devers le dit seignour Robert Foulmere, einz quidast le dit evesqe toutdys qe cel or eust este entierement par son dit comandement rebaillez as Frauncoeys. Et puis apres, le dit Robert chargez illoeqes de dire la cause pur quoy il fist einsi detenir en si secree manere la \dite/ monoie, encontre le comandement son dit seignour ent fait, dist et confessast expressement qe la cause est tiele, c'estassavoir, q'il mesmes pensast coment son dit seignour l'evesqe avoit grant busoigne de monoie pur paiement *[Page iii-153]*

[Col. a] faire a Caleys, et aillours, pur achatz des vitailles, et pur eskippesoun de lui et des soens vers Engleterre: et qe a yceux paiementz faire il n'avoit rienz sinoun par chevance, ne pur gaiges paier /a\ ses souldeours: les quieles s'ils eussent sciue de celle monoie pur veritee, il ose dire l'eussent tolluz de lui par force. Et auxint, pur ce qe semblast a lui qe mieltz feust de getter tout celle or en /la\ meer qe de le reenvoier ensi as ditz enemys a lour refreschement, finalment son purpoys ent y prist, del faire issint garder salvement /et\ privement, pur doute de les ditz souldeours, et pur doute qe soun dit seignour /l'evesqe n'ent scieust rienz, et tanqe il\ serroit venuz deinz le roialme: a quiel temps celle or purroit estre appliez al profit du roi .... ou de son dit seignour, \mieltz/ qe d'estre re-envoiez as enemys avauntdiz. Et issint, il dist, est mesme la monoye prest, et en salvetee horspris une certeine quantitee d'icelles franks, quelles il ad dispenduz sur l'eskippesone son dit seignour, et de ses gentz, et sur paiementz de lours vitailles a Caleys, sanz la science son dit seignour l'evesqe, a qi il ad toutdis fait entendre qe pur mesmes les paiementz faire il avoit fait chevance et purvoiance des marchantz a Caleys. Et issint lui semble q'il y ad bien fait, et nounpas malfait; et s'il ad rienz en celle partie offenduz son seignour lige, il se ent mette en sa bone grace.

/Et le dit chanceller repliast, et dist depar le roi qe mieltz feust qe les enemys eussent lour or propre, qe aucun lige du roi le prendroit de eux en tiel guise. Qar autrement, chescun treitour qe desore dorroit ou vendroit les chastelx et autres forteresces du\ roi a tieux enemys, pur or, ou autre avoir, se purroit excuser del treisone en mesme le manere; et enoultre le dit chanceller \dist/ depar le roi /au dit\ seignour Robert, 'Pur ce qe les resons queux \vous/ avez donez pur excusacione de vostre persone de la receite et detenue de mesme la monoie ne semblent mie, ne ne sont, assetz suffisantz pur vostre excusacione, est agardez qe vostre corps demoerge en prisone tanqe vous aiez fait plein paiement de quanqe vous avez einsi resceuz des enemys avauntditz, et autrement soit ordenez pur vostre deliverance.'

Proclamacion en parlement.[13]

16. Item, a la dite priere de la commune, et auxint pur tant qe le roi nostre seignour estoit enformiz qe plusours chivalers, esquiers, et autres q'estoient en dit derrain viage en compaignie l'evesqe de Norwiz en Flaundres, si avoient receuz plusours grandes et diverses sommes de monoie, et autres choses, des enemys nostre seignour le roi par tretiz faitz avec les ditz enemys, et en autre noun due manere, sanz comandement, licence, et la volentee du roi nostre seignour, ou de son lieu tenant, au profit d'yceux enemys, et damage a nostre seignour le roy, fust chargez depar le roy en parlement publiquement, et ordenez \en// ycelle\ parlement, le .xvi. jour de Novembre qe touz ceux q'avoient riens receuz des

Drayton, Sir William Faringdon and others who had been present at the said treaty could confirm that the said bishop had never known until now that the same money had remained with the said Sir Robert Fulmer, but that he had always supposed the gold to have been returned in full to the said French on his orders. Then the said Robert, charged there to explain why he had kept the said money in so secretive a fashion, contrary to the orders given by his said lord, stated and plainly confessed that the reason was such, namely, that he himself thought that his said lord the bishop had great need of the money to make payments *[Page iii-153]*

[Col. a] at Calais and elsewhere, to buy victuals, and for the passage of him and his men to England: and that he had nothing except by loan to make those payments, and nothing with which to pay his soldiers, who, if they had known of this money, in truth would have seized it from him by force, he dared to say. And also, because it seemed to him better to throw all the gold into the sea than to send it back to the said enemies for their reinforcement, he finally decided to keep it safely and secretly, through fear of the said soldiers, and so that the said lord bishop should learn nothing of it, and until he should arrive in the kingdom: at which time this gold might be used for the profit of the king or of his said lord rather than being sent back to the aforesaid enemies. And so, he said, the same money had been kept intact and in safety, with the exception of a certain number of francs which he had spent on transporting his said lord and his men, and on their victuals at Calais, without the knowledge of his said lord the bishop, whom he had always led to believe that the same payments were enabled by a loan and purveyance from the merchants of Calais. And so it seemed to him that he had acted well and not at all badly; and if he had offended his liege lord in any way, he submitted to his good grace.

And the said chancellor replied on the king's behalf that it would have been better for the enemies to have their own gold than that any liege of the king should have taken it from them under such a guise. Since otherwise, every traitor who should henceforth hand over or sell the castles and other fortresses of the king to such enemies, for gold or anything else, might excuse himself of treason in the same manner; furthermore the said chancellor said on the king's behalf to the same Sir Robert, Because the excuses you have made for receiving and keeping the same money do not seem, nor yet are, sufficient for your pardon, it has been decided that you shall remain in prison until you have fully repaid whatever you thus received from the aforesaid enemies, or your deliverance be otherwise ordained.

A proclamation in parliament.

16. Also, at the said prayer of the commons, and also because the king our lord had been informed that many knights, squires and others who had accompanied the bishop of Norwich on the said last expedition to Flanders had received various large sums of money and other things from the enemies of our lord the king by agreements made with the said enemies, and in other improper ways, without the order, permission or will of the king our lord or his lieutenant, to the advantage of those enemies and the injury of our lord the king, it was charged and ordained on the king's behalf in open parliament, on 16 November, that all those who had received anything from the said enemies on this expedition

---

[13] This heading is written in a different yet contemporary hand.

ditz enemys en ycelle viage, par tretiz, ou en autre manere quelconqe qe ce feust, horspris tantsoulement expresse duetee de guerre, qe yceux, et chescun de eux, sur peril d'estre tenuz pur treitours du roi et de son roialme, ils venissent lendemain prochein ensuant en presence du dit chanceller d'Engleterre, et a mesme le chanceller conoissent et confessasent entierment et clerement les choses rescouz par eux et chescun de eux d'yceux enemys, ou d'autres en lours nouns; avec la manere et cause d'ycelle lour resceite de mesme la /chose.\

Cressyngham et Spykesworth.

17. Item, sur la pleinte q'estoit fait au roi de Pierres de Cressyngham et Johan de Spykesworth', esquiers, de ce qe la ou ils estoient faitz en dit viage capitains et gardeins du chastelle de Drinkham en Flandres, q'estoit gaignez des enemys, et puis apres bien et suffisantement estuffez des vitailles et autres necessaires, et assez fort de tenir encontre les enemys; ils

[Col. b] lesserent et rendirent mesme le chastelle as ditz enemys, repreignant devers eux pur celle liveree et susrendre par tretiz faitz avec les enemys une somme d'or, et par covenant fait avec mesmes les enemys, sanz la volentee et comandement de mesme nostre seignour le roi ou de soun lieu tenant: paront les ditz esquiers si furent mys en arest par comandement du roi, et puis mys a lour responce en parlement. Et le dit Johan Spykesworth' soi excusast devant le roy en parlement en tiele manere q'il n'avoit unqes garde de mesme le chastell, ne riens a faire d'ycelle, sinoun soulement q'il estoit chivacheant en la paiis bien pres . le dit chastelle de Drinkham pur son profit faire sur les enemys, ou par force des ditz enemys il estoit chacez a mesme le chastelle adonqes esteant en la garde del dit Pierres de Cressyngham. Et puis apres il dist qe sur l'assaut fait al barbican illoeqes par les enemys, il estoit malement naufrez, et un de ses valletz tuez en la garnison \pres de lui,/ ou il demurra toutdys tanqe le dit Pierres le rendist: et autrement n'avoit il unqes illoeqes riens affaire, ne come souldeour d'ycelle, n'en autre manere qelconqe. Empriant qe par tant pleust a nostre seignour le roi, pur Dieu, lui ent tenir pur excusez.

A quoy feust responduz depar le roi qe si homme ne scieust pluis dire devers /le\ dit Johan a contraire de sa dite responce ore faite qe le roi lui tenoit pur excusez, et voloit q'il feust disarestuz, et suffert d'aler a large. Et le dit Pierres de Cressyngham, en conissant q'il avoit la garde du dit chastelle, dist qe si tost come les enemys furent venuz devant Burburgh', en quele le seignour de Beaumond, monsire William de Elmham, monsire Thomas Tryvet et monsire William Faryndon', \et plusours autres Engleys/ furent, et les ville et chastelle de Burburghe estoient renduz as enemys, de touz les souldeours q'il avoit avec lui a Drinkham nul voloit illoeqes avec lui demurrer sur la salve garde d'ycelle chastelle de Drinkham, forsqe tantsoulement cynk persones en tout; paront grant necessitee lui chaceast de faire tretee avec les enemys, en salvacione de sa persone et de ses gentz, pur deliverer le dit fort; et einsi fist il, et nemye pur autre cause n'en autre manere, forsqe soulement par constreinte del poair des ditz enemys, come dit est. Et oultre il dist q'il ne receust unqes rienz des ditz enemys par doun ne en autre manere: paront il pense qe homme ne doit aretter /en sa persone\ nulle manere de blasme ne de reproche. Mais si semble q'il ent ad malfait en aucun manere, il se ent mette haut et baas en la grace de son seignour lige. Et pur ce qe celle excusacion /ne sembloit\\mye estre/ assez suffisante, il estoit agardez a la prisone, pur y demurrer tanqe le roy nostre seignour ait autrement de lui dit sa volentee.

by treaty, or in any other way, excepting only the express dues of war, that they and each one of them, upon peril of being considered traitors of the king and his kingdom, should appear on the following day [17 November 1383] before the said chancellor of England, to acknowledge and confess to the same chancellor fully and explicitly the things received by them and each one of them from those enemies, or by any others in their name; together with the manner and reason for their receipt of the same.

Cressingham and Spikesworth.

17. Also, upon the complaint which was made to the king about Peter Cressingham and John Spikesworth, squires, that although, on the said expedition, they had been appointed captains and keepers of the castle of Drincham in Flanders, which had been captured from the enemies, and subsequently well and adequately provisioned with victuals and other necessaries, strong enough to be held against the enemies, they

[Col. b] had surrendered and returned the same castle to the said enemies, receiving a sum of gold in return for this delivery and surrender by treaty and covenant made with the enemies, and without the will and command of our same lord the king or his lieutenant: as a result of which the said squires were placed under arrest by order of the king, and then brought to answer in parliament. And the said John Spikesworth excused himself before the king in parliament by saying that he had never had the keeping of the same castle, nor anything to do with it, except insofar as he had been raiding in the area very close to the said castle of Drincham to take booty from the said enemies when he was driven by the enemy forces into the same castle, which was then in the keeping of the said Peter Cressingham. Then later he said that during the assault made on the barbican by the enemies he was badly wounded, and one of his men killed in the garrison close by him, and there he remained until the said Peter surrendered it: and otherwise he had had no other involvement there, neither as a member of the garrison, nor in any other way whatsoever. And he prayed for that reason that it might please our lord the king, for love of God, to hold him excused thereof.

To which it was replied on the king's behalf that if no one had anything else to add concerning the said John which contradicted the answer he had given, the king would consider him excused, and order that he be released and allowed to go free. And the said Peter Cressingham, acknowledging that he had had the keeping of the said castle, said that as soon as the enemy came before Bourburg, in which Lord Beaumont, Sir William Elmham, Sir Thomas Trivet, Sir William Faringdon and many other Englishmen were stationed, and the town and castle of Bourburg had been surrendered to the enemies, none of the soldiers he had with him at Drincham would remain there to safeguard it, except just five in all; in consequence of which, sheer necessity forced him to negotiate with the enemy, for the salvation of himself and his men, to surrender the said fort; and he did so for no other reason, nor otherwise than under the constraint of enemy force, as has been said. He also said that he had never received anything from the said enemies by way of gift or anything else: in view of which he felt that no manner of blame or reproach ought to be levelled at him. But if it seemed that he had offended in some way, he would submit completely to the grace of his liege lord. And because this excuse seemed inadequate, he was sent to prison to remain there until the king our lord should declare his will concerning him.

La primer empeschement et responce de l'evesqe de Norwiz.

18. Item, Henry evesqe de Norwiz estoit empeschez en ce parlement de plusours choses, mais especialment de quatre articles a lui monstrez par le chanceller d'Engleterre, en presence du roi mesmes et de monsire de Lancastre en plein parlement. Lequiel chanceller einsi dist, 'Monsire l'evesqe de Norwiz, je sui comandez de vous dire ce qe je dirra ore depar le roy. Voirs est, combien qe par endenture et covenances taillez parentre le roi et vous, si estez vous obligez et avez emprys de servir au roy nostre seignour en ses guerres de France avec deux mille et cynk centz hommes d'armes, et atantz des archers, bien armez, arraiez, et mountez, dont vous ferroiez vostre monstre covenablement a la ville de Caleys par un an entier, toutes voies einsi est il ore qe vous n'avez mye issint serviz au roi par un an, \ne/ encores par un demy an. Einz devaunt le demy an estez vous retournez, et vostre ost despareilez encontre la fourme de mesme l'endenture: paront moult grant vilenie, perde, et damage sont avenuz au roi nostre seignour, et a tout son roialme. Et par tant quant a ce si estez vous en moelt grant defaute. Item, quant a la dite nombre des gentz pur quele vous vous aveistez obligez par mesme l'endenture, *[Page iii-154]*

[Col. a] et de faire le dit monstre auxint a Caleys, vous avez failliz de l'un l'autre. Et en ce autre grant defaute a vous. Item, qe par la ou al derrain parlement estoit assentuz qe monsire d'Espaigne, ou aucun des autres uncles nostre seignour le roy auroit le viage vers France, al honur du roiaume, vous feistes induire le roi nostre seignour le roy,[14] par grant promesses par vous faitz, et par especial pur tant qe vous empristes primerement a la commune assemblez en dit derrain parlement, et puis au roy mesmes en ycelle parlement, qe si pleust au roi de vous granter le viage avauntdit, vous auroiez en vostre compaignie en mesme le viage le nombre dessuis limitez, et avec eux des meillours capitans du roiaulme d'Engleterre apres les roiaulx. A quiel temps le roi vous demandast de lui certefier \en especial/ des nouns des capitans, et doustres qi vous auroiez en vostre compaignie, en cas qe le viage vous feust grantez. Et vous lui respondistes qe /pur certaines enchesons ne monstroiez\\ lours/ nouns tanqe vous feustes surs qe le viage vous feust finalment ottroiez. Mais vous vous feistes assez fort, et promistes surement qe si pleust au roi de vous granter mesme le viage, si auroiez /avec\ vous des meillours et pluis suffisantz capitans du roialme apres les roialx, come dit est. Paront, et par autres voz promesses par vous faitz, dont vous avez depuis tout failliz, /sicome vous mesmes le sachez, le roi nostre seignour ent estoit grantement desceuz, et ensi\ le dit viage vous estoit grantez, et le eustes en fait sicome vous mesmes l'aveistes desirez, et les ditz seignours les uncles au roy ent oultrement /par tielles desceites\ oustez, a grant damage et vilenie du roi nostre seignour, et de son roialme avauntdit. Item, sur le grant et ottroi a vous fait de mesme le viage, come dit est, le roy vous fist profrer en dit parlement, pur le bone governance et salvetee del dit ost, de faire et creer un suffisant seignour temporel du roiaume d'Engleterre en son lieutenant, qi serroit obeissant a vous durant celle ost, en quanqe touchast la croiserie, et vous a lui en quanqe touchast le lieutenancie. Quiel profre a vous fait einsi par le roi nostre seignour /ne vous\ pleust mye, einz de fait le refusastes; /et qe pir\ est, par mesmes voz \beaux/ promesses et autres le roi feust tiellement desceuz, et einsi mesnez en dit parlement par voz autres affaires, vous aveistes le dit viage, et la governance d'ycelle /soul.\ Et par tout, et notoire chose

The first impeachment and answer of the bishop of Norwich.

18. Also, Henry bishop of Norwich was accused in this parliament of many things, but of four articles in particular, put to him by the chancellor of England, in the presence of the king himself and my lord of Lancaster in full parliament. Which chancellor said: My lord bishop of Norwich, I am ordered to inform you of that which I shall say on the king's behalf. It is true that, although by indenture and covenants made between the king and yourself you bound yourself and undertook to serve the king our lord in his wars in France with two thousand five hundred men-at-arms and as many archers, well armed, equipped and mounted, from which you would produce a suitable muster at Calais for a whole year, and now you have not, in fact, served the king for a whole year, nor even for half a year. But before the half year was up, you returned and disbanded your host, contrary to the form of the same indenture: resulting in great discredit, loss and damage to the king our lord and all his kingdom. And therefore, you are greatly at fault. Also, as for the said number of men to which you bound yourself by the same indenture, *[Page iii-154]*

[Col. a] and raising the said muster at Calais, you have failed in both. And there too, you are greatly at fault. Also, although at the last parliament it was agreed that my lord of Spain or another uncle of our lord the king would lead the expedition to France, to the honour of the kingdom, you induced our lord the king to grant it to you by the great promises you made, and especially because first you promised the commons assembled in the said last parliament, and then the king himself in the same parliament, that if it would please the king to grant you the aforesaid expedition, you would have in your company on the same expedition the number specified above, together with the best captains of the kingdom of England after the royal princes. At which time the king asked you to especially notify him of the names of the captains and commanders you would have in your company, if the expedition were granted to you. And you answered that for certain reasons you would not reveal their names until you were sure that the expedition had been finally granted to you. But you made great promise and assurance that if it pleased the king to grant you the same expedition, you would be accompanied by the best and most worthy captains of the kingdom after the royal princes, as has been said. As a result of which, and because of the other promises you made, in which you have since utterly failed, as you yourself know, the king our lord was greatly deceived, and so the said expedition was granted to you, and you received it on the terms for which you asked, and the said lords the king's uncles were entirely excluded by such deceits, to the great injury and harm of the king our lord and all his aforesaid realm. Also, as for the grant and levy made to you for the same expedition, as was said, the king proposed in the said parliament, for the good governance and security of the said host, to appoint and create a worthy lord temporal of the kingdom of England as his lieutenant, who would be obedient to you during this expedition in whatever touched the crusade, and you to him in whatever touched the lieutenancy. Which proposal thus made to you by the lord our king did not please you, and in fact you refused it; and what is worse, by your same handsome promises and others the king was greatly deceived, and being thus distracted in the said parliament by your other business, you gained both the

---

[14] le roy, *repeated*

est a touz qe pur defaute de lieutenant, et des bones capitaines et governours, si sont les grantz vilenies et damages /importables avenuz,\ soulement en vostre defaute, al dit ost, et par consequens au roi et a son dit roiaume q'ore sont avenuz. Par quoi vous estez auxint quant a ce en un autre moelt grant defaute: desquelles choses a vous ore surmises depar le roi vous purrez dire ce qe vous semble mieltz affaire en le cas.'

19. A quoi le dit evesqe respondist et dist qe combien qe /de\ droit par la licence son seignour lige il devroit avoir conseil, et y doner ses responces par son conseil en le cas: toutes voies, faisant sa protestacion qe si en sa responce q'il durra il forsvoie de sa matire, ou die chose par necgligence ou ignorance en si haute place, ou q'il die meinz ou pluis q'il ne doit dire, q'il se ent puisse amender et corriger autre foitz, et si tost come lui semblera mieltz affaire, il mesmes en sa propre persone qi mieltz est conissant en le cas qe nul autre, par licence de son seignour lige ent durra sa responce, empriant humblement a son dit lige seignour, de luy doner audience et ascoult. Et dist primerement, quant a ce qe lui est ore surmis, q'il n'ad mye serviz au roi par le terme q'il avoit promis, ne par le moitee d'ycelle, il dit qe par les dites covenances taillez il estoit tenuz, et auxint avoit en charge de son seignour lige, qe principalment, et devant autres choses, avec ses gentz il se mist al rescous de la ville de Gaunt. Et par vertu de celle charge, si

[Col. b] tost come il fuist arrivez depar dela il prist soun chimyn avec ses gentz vers la dite ville de Gaunt; et en son dit chimyn, si come pleust a Dieu, si avoit il affaire avec les enemys, sibien a Gravenynge come a Donkirke, et aillours. Et al drain, quant les gentz de Gaunt lui avoient encontrez, et ils eussent entrecommunez et conseillez qe serroit deslors mieltz affaire, sibien a lour aide, come al esploit del viage comencez, si feust le purpos final de ceux de Gaunt tiel, c'estassavoir, qe homme mettroit siege a la ville de Ipre; affermantz par lours paroles qe Ipre n'estoit /mye\ estuffez des gentz ne de vitailles pur endurer gairs encontre les poairs d'Engleterre et de Gaunt. Et oultre y disoient qe si la ville de Ipre, en quele les ciefs de tout Flandres estoient, feusse gaignez, si serroit le remenant tantost gaignez. Et issint, par excitation et confort de ceux de Gaunt, et par assent des touz les capitans Engleys qi furent en dit viage, si estoit le siege mys illoeqes; en le quele plusours de ses gentz escheierent en diverses grantz maladies et plusours y furent naufrez et mortz, et grant nombre des malveys gentz qi furent rebelx et desobeissantz a mesme l'evesqe si furent retournez avec lour pilage en Engleterre.

Membrane 7 Et par tant, et auxint purce qe sur le departement de ceux de Gaunt de mesme le siege, les capitans del ost Engleys apperceivantz qe apres le departement de ceulx de Gaunt si estoit l'ost Engleys moelt grantement amenusez, et entant appetizez par les dites causes qe encontre tiele poair come les Fraunceoys avoient assemblez les Engleys ne voloient, ne ne poaient, tenir les champs en aucune manere. Et issint aiantz due consideracione a celles causes par luy alleggiez, et a les journes qe le dit evesqe avec ses gentz ad euz en dit viage, al honor et profit de nostre seignour lige et de son roiaume; et especialment, a ce qe par le dit viage trieves sont prises et profres du tretee de paix faitz par l'adversaire de France, \qe/ si Dieu plest serra introduccione a final paix; et ce q'est einsi avenuz ne doit mye par reson estre surmys en son defaute, meement come \ce/ est avenuz pluis par l'aventure de Dieux qe en autre manere, lui semble qe quant a celle article il doit estre tenuz pur excusez en toutes choses.

said expedition and the sole command of the same. And it is common knowledge everywhere that it was for want of a lieutenant and good captains and governors that there arose the great injuries and intolerable harm suffered by the said host, the king and his said kingdom, which were entirely your fault. Wherefore you are again grievously at fault: to which matters alleged against you by the king, you may now answer as you see fit.

19. To which the said bishop replied that although by right, with the permission of his liege lord, he should have counsel, and make answer through his counsel in the matter: nevertheless, protesting that if in the answer he gave he should wander from the matter, or say anything through negligence or ignorance in so exalted a place, or if he should say less or more than he ought, he might be amended and corrected hereafter; and as soon as it seemed best, he himself, who knew more of the matter than anyone else, would, with the permission of his liege lord, give his answer thereon, requesting humbly of his said liege lord that he give him an audience and a hearing. And first of all he said to the present allegation that he had not in fact served the king for the promised term, nor even for half of the same, which by the said covenants drawn up he had been bound and charged by his liege lord, first and foremost, to rescue the town of Ghent with his men. And by virtue of that charge, as

[Col. b] soon as he had arrived overseas he set off with his men towards the said town of Ghent; and on the way, as it pleased God, he came upon his enemies both at Gravelines and at Dunkirk and elsewhere. And at length, when the people of Ghent had met him and they had talked together and discussed the best course of action for themselves and for the accomplishment of the expedition which he had begun, the people of Ghent finally decided that the town of Ypres should be besieged; asserting that Ypres was not well enough provisioned with either men or victuals to stand against the power of England and Ghent. And further, they said that if the town of Ypres, in which the chief men of Flanders were, were to be won, so would the rest be won. And thus, with the encouragement and support of the people of Ghent, and with the assent of all the English captains on the said expedition, the siege was begun there; during which many of his men fell victim to various great maladies, and many were wounded and killed there, and a large number of wicked persons, disobeying and rebelling against the same bishop, returned with their booty to England.

Membrane 7 And therefore, and because of the departure of the people of Ghent from the same siege, the captains of the English host, realizing then that the English host was greatly reduced as a result, and that it was so much diminished for the said reasons, that the English neither would nor could hold the field in any way against an army of the size assembled by the French; and therefore, considering also the reasons given by the said bishop, and the days spent by him and his men on the said expedition, to the honour and profit of our liege lord and his kingdom; and especially that through the said expedition truces were arranged and proposals for peace treaties made by the French enemy, so that if it should please God a lasting peace might be achieved; and that that which happened ought not to be attributed to fault on his part, but rather to God's providence than to anything else, it seemed to him that as to this article he ought to be considered excused in all respects.

Item, quant a ce qe lui est surmis q'il ne fist mie sa monstre a Caleys, il dit qe pur haster ses gentz de venir al dit viage en rescous de Gaunt, par manere come il l'avoit promys, il passa a Caleys devant /ses autres\ capitains, avec tielx persones en petite nombre come il poiait amasser, et ne demurra apres son rivaille a Caleys qe deux jours ou trois, einz tantost prist son chimyn vers Gravenynge, et le prist par l'aide Nostre Seignour. Et puis quant il estoit venuz devant Ipre, combien q'il ne fist mye sa dite monstre a Caleys par la dite cause, toutes voies il avoit devaunt Ipre son entier nombre des gentz en chescun degree, et encores pluis, a mesme la ville de Ipre. Et ce est il prest de prover par bones et suffisantz tesmoignes, ou par autre resonable manere quele le roy lui vorra assigner: et issint, quant a ce n'est il mye, a ce qe lui semble, a blasmer. Et quant a ce \q'est dit,/ q'il n'avoit mie avec lui des meillours chiefteins du roialme apres les roialx, lui semble q'il avoit des bons chiefteins, et suffisantz. Mes des meillours eust il avec lui, si homme les vousist avoir ottroiez licence et congie, come le seignour de Nevill' qi profra en presence du roi d'avoir alez en dit viage, si pleust au roy de lui doner congie, qe lui estoit deniez; et issint lui semble qe quant a ce il n'est mye a blasmer. Et quant a ce qe lui est surmys q'il deust avoir refusez d'avoir un lieutenant, il dit qe voirs est qe nostre seignour le roi envoiast la luy ses lettres et message en Flandres, ou il estoit avec son ost, touchant ceste matire d'avoir un lieutenant. As quelles lettres et message le dit evesqe par ses lettres fist sa responce, rendant graces et mercies a son seignour lige en tant come il poaist, de ce qe pleust a lui de soveigner de lui, et d'estre tendre de lui [Page iii-155]

[Col. a] et de son estat. La quelle sa lettre fist mencione expresse, /qe\ quanqe nostre dit seignour le roy et son conseil vousissent ordener de tiel lieutenaunt, ce pleust tresbien a lui. Et issint il ne refusast mye d'avoir le lieutenant avauntdit, einz se tenoit pur bien paiez de quanqe le roi ent ordeinast. Et issint lui semble auxint qe quant a ce ne deust il mye estre blasmez par aucune voie, einz pluis tost par la dite cause, et par les autres causes dessus allegiez pur sa partie et pur autre son service q'il ad fait au roi nostre seignour et son roialme devant ore, et encores volenters vorra faire a son petite poair, si pense il q'il ent eust deserviz guerdone et bone gree, et nemye mal gree, tiele come l'en lui vorroit ore susmettre. Empriant a nostre seignour le roy qe lui plese accepter cestes ses excusacions veritablement par lui donez a les quatre articles a luy surmises, et lui estre gracious seignour, se semble a sa hautesce qe en celle partie rienz il ad mespris.

20. A quoy le dit chanceller repliast et dist, 'Qe voirs est qe quant vous estoiez issint en Flandres, apres qe vous y avoiez un poy de terme demurrez, et novelx certeins vindrent a nostre seignour le roy et son conseil en Engleterre, plusours foitz, par lettres et en autre manere envoiees a lui hors de Flandres par les capitains de vostre ost, continantes qe mesme l'ost si estoit en moelt grant peril, et de jour en autre pur defaute de lieutenant et bon governement d'icelle empirast, si fist le roi nostre seignour treter avec le conte d'Arundell' de la matire, et finalment avec mesme le conte estoit accordez q'il serroit lieutenant du roi en mesme l'ost, et vendroit a vous en haste avec une suffisante nombre des bones gentz d'armes et archers, en aide et socours de vous, et de mesme l'ost, si a ce voussissez assentir. Qar sanz vostre assent le roi ne voloit rienz faire accomplir en le cas; et par tant il vous envoiast ses lettres et message en Flandres, pur ent avoir vostre advis. A quoy vous respondistes par voz lettres, quelles encores sont prestes a monstrer, en tiele guise qe par la forme d'ycelles voz lettres, quelles sont faites de double entendement, et par autres paroles de vous autre part

Also, as for the allegation that he did not raise his muster at Calais, he said that in order to hasten his men on the said expedition to rescue Ghent, as he had promised, he crossed to Calais before his other captains, with the small number of persons he could amass, and he stayed at Calais for no more than two or three days after his arrival, setting off at once for Gravelines, and capturing it by the aid of Our Lord. And then, when he arrived at Ypres, although he had not in fact produced his said muster at Calais for that reason, nevertheless he had his full quota of men of every degree, and more, before the same town of Ypres. And this he was ready to prove by good and worthy testimony, or in any other reasonable manner which the king might wish to appoint: and so he was not in fact, in his opinion, to be blamed for that. And as for the claim that he did not have with him the best leaders of the realm after those royal princes, it seemed to him that he had good and worthy leaders. But he would have had the best if they had been granted permission and leave, as for example, Lord Neville, who offered in the king's presence to go on the said expedition, if it pleased the king to grant him leave, yet it was denied him; and so it seemed to him that he was not to blame in that respect. And as for the allegation that he had refused to have a lieutenant, he said that it was true that our lord the king sent him letters and word in Flanders, where he was with his said host, concerning the appointment of a lieutenant. To which letters and message the said bishop replied expressing as much gratitude and appreciation for his liege lord as he could, that it had pleased him to be mindful of him and concerned for him [Page iii-155]

[Col. a] and his estate. In which reply it was said particularly that whenever our said lord the king and his council wished to ordain such a lieutenant, it would be greatly pleasing to him. And so he had indeed not refused to have the aforesaid lieutenant, but had been well pleased with what the king had ordained thereon. And so it again seemed to him that in this he could not be blamed by any means, but rather, for the said reason, and for the other reasons given above in his defence and for the other service he had rendered the king our lord and his kingdom before now, and would still willingly render to the best of his meagre ability, he thought that he deserved reward and good favour, rather than the ill-will to which he was now subjected. Praying of our lord the king that it might please him to accept these his excuses, honestly made in response to the four articles alleged against him, and to be a gracious lord to him, if it seemed to his highness that he had done no wrong in this matter.

20. To which the said chancellor answered and said, It is true that when you were in Flanders, after you had been there a short while, and certain news reached our lord the king and his council in England on several occasions, by letters and other means sent him from Flanders by the captains of your host, saying that the same host was in very great danger, and weakening from one day to the next through lack of a lieutenant and good government, the king our lord discussed the matter with the earl of Arundel, and finally agreed with the same earl that he should be the king's lieutenant in the same host, and should hasten to you with an adequate number of good men-at-arms and archers to help and assist you and the same host, if you would agree to that. For the king would not wish to act without your assent in the matter; and so he sent you his letters and a message to Flanders, to seek your advice. To which you replied in your letters, which are still here to be shown, in such a way that from the tone of them, which was full of double meaning, and from your other words reported, it could evidently appear that you did not wish to have a lieutenant. And although you have now

reportez, evidentement poet apparoir qe vous ne voloistes avoir lieutenant. Et combien qe vous avez ore alleggez ceste derraine matire comprise en voz dites lettres pur excusacion, come ce n'est \mye/ suffisant, mesme vostre lettre bien entendue; toutes voies celle allegeance n'est mye a purpos de ce qe vous est surmis pardevaunt: c'estassavoir, qe vous refusastes d'avoir un lieutenant oultrement /en\ fait devant vostre departement hors del roialme, solonc le primer ofre a vous ent fait, come dit est, \et depuis auxint. Paront, et auxi pur defaute des bones chiefteins et governours tout le meschef y est avenuz a vostre ost./ Et issint, quant a ce vous n'avez mye, ne ne purrez aucunement en veritee vous excuser.

Et est assavoir, qe ceste matire oiez et entendue en parlement, le dit chanceller, par commandement du roy mesmes illoeqes present, dist a mesme l'evesqe, Monsire evesqe de Norwiz, le roi nostre seignour ad bien entenduz ce qe vous avez einsi dit et alleggiez en excusacione de les articles et mesprisions a vous surmises, et ent ad euz bone deliberacione avec les seignours temporelx et autres sages de son conseil cy presentz. Et semble a nostre seignour le roy et as seignours temporelx avaunditz qe les responces quelles vous avez einsi donez pur excusacione de vous ne sont riens en effect al purpos de la matire a vous surmise, ne ne suffisent mye de vous excuser des /vilenies,\ ... importables damages, /perdes,\ et autres mesprisions qe sont faitz au roy et son roiaume par vous, et vostre procurement, come dit est. Par quoy /semble auxint qe vous pur defaute de suffisante responce serroiez convict de les mesprisions comprises en les quatre articles a vous surmises; et par tant feussez auxint mis au fin et raunceone a volentee du roi pur vostre mesfait. Et semble ensement qe a ce faire le roi vous devroit constreindre par la seisine des temporaltees de vostre eveschee de Norwiz, quant lui plerra.\

Ordinance des vacatz et veint.
21./Item, parmy la dite requeste faite par la commune d'Engleterre\ ....
en ce parlement, le samady en le /.xiij.ᵉ jour\ de Novembre,[15] faisant mencione coment le dit evesqe de Norwiz emprist a parfournir le dit derrain viage deinz le roialme de France avec une certeine nombre des gentz, par un an entier, pur la .xv.ᵐᵉ grantee au roi nostre seignour par la dite commune, et pur autres biens du roialme d'Engleterre, queux il resceust principalment pur celle cause et pur celle emprise /a moelt\ grant somme, estoit chargez en parlement depar le roi, de certifier mesme nostre seignour le roy et son conseil, distinctement et par escrit, de les nouns, estatz et degrees de touz ceux qi furent retenuz avec luy en dit viage, et queux n'ont mye encores parfourniz lours services et covenances faites; et par especial \de/ la manere de lour retenue, et le terme par quiel \ils/ sont tenuz encores de servir au roi par forme des covenances ent taillez, au fin qe celle lour service encores due puisse estre emploiez et parfourniz en le service du roi, et defens du roialme d'Engleterre avantdit, en lieu ou greindre busoigne est apparant, en descharge par tant de mesme la commune, la quele estoit moelt grantement chargez pur cause d'ycelle viage.

A quoy le dit evesqe respondist, et dist qe voirs est qe plusours de sa retenue n'ont mye perfourniz lour service solonc lour retenue fait /avec eux.\ Et par tant, si pleust au roi nostre seignour granter qe seignour Robert de Foulmere, \son/ clerc et tresorier en dit viage, q'ad en garde toutes les endentures, et autres evidences et remembrances touchantz sa

cited the contents of your said letters by way of exoneration, it is not enough, even if the letter is taken positively, for it is useless in the face of the previous accusation against you: namely, that you refused to have a lieutenant before you left the kingdom, according to the first offer made to you, as already said, and also later. In consequence of which, and because of an absence of good leaders and governors, all that misfortune befell your host. And so, by what you have said, you have not exonerated yourself, and cannot truthfully do so in any way.

And thereupon, the matter having been heard and considered in parliament, the said chancellor, by order of the king himself there present, said to the bishop, My lord bishop of Norwich, the king our lord has well understood what you have said and claimed by way of excuse for the articles and offences alleged against you, and has thoroughly deliberated thereon with the lords temporal and other wise men of his council here present. And it seems to our lord the king and to the aforesaid lords temporal that the answers which you have thus given by way of excuse in no way support your claims in the matter alleged against you, nor do they serve to excuse you of the villainies, intolerable damage, losses, and other misdeeds which have been inflicted on the king and his kingdom by you and your machinations, as has been said. Accordingly, it seems that you, for want of sufficient answer, should be convicted of the misdeeds contained in the four articles alleged against you; and for that reason you shall also be put to fine and ransom at the king's will for your offence. And it seems also that [Col. b] to do that the king should constrain you by seizing the temporalities of your bishopric of Norwich, when it shall please him.

Ordinance concerning the absent and the faint-hearted.
21. Also, among the said requests made by the commons of England ....
in this parliament, on Saturday 13 November, making mention that the said bishop of Norwich undertook to perform the said last expedition in the kingdom of France with a certain number of men for a whole year, in return for the fifteenth granted to the king our lord by the said commons and for other goods of the kingdom of England which he had received principally for that purpose and undertaking to a very great sum; and he was charged in parliament, on the king's behalf, to certify our same lord the king and his council, plainly and in writing, of the names, estate and degrees of all those had been retained by him on the said expedition, and who had not yet discharged their services and covenants made; and in particular of the manner of their retaining, and the term for which they are still bound to serve the king according to the form of the covenants prepared thereon, so that their service still owing may be put to use in the king's service and for the defence of the aforesaid kingdom of England, wheresoever there be greatest need, thereby discharging the same commons, who have been greatly burdened because of that expedition.

To which the said bishop replied and said that it was true that many of his retinue had not indeed performed their service according to the terms of their contract. And for that reason, if it should please the king our lord to grant that Sir Robert Fulmer, his clerk and treasurer on the aforesaid expedition, who had in his keeping all the indentures and other

---
[15] 13 November 1383 was a Friday.

retenue de mesme le viage, soit mis a large hors de prisone ou il est detenuz par comandement \du roi,/ et sur ce luy doner terme et espace covenable, a cause qe la chose demande moelt grant occupation, volenters si ferroit il sa diligence de perfournir le dite charge a lui donee par son seignour lige. Par quoy le dit seignour Robert Foulmere estoit deliverez de prisone pur un terme covenable, par meinprise trovez en le cas. Et comandez y fuist depar le roy al dit evesqe qe celle certificacione il feist par manere come dessuis est dit, mesqardy proschein ensuant apres la dite charge donee a pluis tard. Lui quiel evesqe respondist autrefoitz, et dist qe volenters la ferroit il a tout le haste qe bonement purroit. Et puis apres, a la requeste del dit evesqe, le terme a lui limitez de faire la dite certificacione, come dit est, si estoit prorogez par .viij. jours proschein ensuantz.

La secounde arrenement, et la responce l'evesqe de Norwiz.

22. Item, autrefoitz le dit evesqe alleggeant en presence du roi qe pur tant q'il estoit en moelt des maneres destourbez et interrupt en donant ses responces a les articles dont il estoit empeschez, tant par paroles capciouses a lui faites, come en autre manere, paront il avoit enterlessez et mys en ublie grant partie de la matire quele il ent avoit a dire pur sa excusacion, il priast au roi nostre seignour qe, pur Dieu, lui pleust doner \a lui/ un autre jour, et audience covenables, sanz interrupcion en cest parlement, et adonqes, dist il q'a l'aide Nostre Seignour, il se excuseroit en dit parlement si clerement de quanqe l'en lui avoit surmis qe par resoun devroit suffire. Et celle requeste lui estoit grantez, et autre jour donez, c'estassavoir le .xxiiij.^{e} jour de Novembre.

A quele jour, le dit evesqe reherceant les quatre articles a lui surmises pardevaunt en parlement, et en presence du roy mesmes, et y donast ses responces tielles /bien pres\ come devant, de toutes les choses avauntdites. Adjustant a ycelles qe au temps q'il avoit novelles qe l'avant garde de l'ost de France s'estoit entreez *[Page iii-156]* *[Col. a]* le paiis de Flandres, et sur ce le dit siege de Ipre s'estoit issint revenuz, il prist purpos d'avoir encontrez mesme l'avaunt garde, pur avoir combatuz avec eux. Le quiel son purpos il ne poait parfournir, pur tant qe les chiefteins de son ost ne voloient a ce assentir; einz yceulz capitains, et autres de son ost, luy ent contrarierent en tant qe a fine force, \et/ pur doute des enemys, lour /covenoit\ eux departir, et /lour recepter\ \en/ lours forteresces. Et par tant le dit evesqe retournast a la dite ville de Gravenynge, et la vousist il avoir tenuz assez bien encontre touz gentz, et les tenist tanqe les autres capitains avoient renduz lours fortz as Franceoys; et encores tant avaunt qe aucuns Engleys venoient a lui, en contantz, coment y avoit bien entour .vi. ou .vij. mille des Engleys gisantz sur les sablons pres de Caleys, qi furent faitz veuder hors des ditz fortz renduz, \a grant meschief et mesaise, a cause q'ils/ n'avoient dont vivre, ne ne poaient avoir entree en la ville de Caleys. Et partant qe les trieves prises pardevaunt devroient cesser deinz deux ou trois jours proschein lors ensuantz, ... les Franceys avoient en purpos de lour coure suis et \les/ occire trestouz, si tost come les dites treves feussent finiz, quele occisione, si ce feusse fait, tournereit al dit evesqe principalment, et puis a les autres capitains, al pluis grant vilenie et meschief qe nule autre chose ferroit. En requerantz par tant, et chargeantz depar le roi nostre seignour mesme l'evesqe q'il rendist la ville as enemys, ou l'abatist tantost, et alast son chemyn al socour des ditz gentz, et d'illoeqes vers Engleterre, en salvacione de lui mesmes, et des autres de son ost. Qar ils disoient qe

documents and memoranda touching his retinue on the same expedition, be set free from prison, where he was detained by order of the king, and thereupon given adequate time and opportunity, because the matter demanded great work, he would willingly strive to perform the said charge given him by his liege lord. As a result of which the said Sir Robert Fulmer was released from prison for a suitable length of time on bail. And the said bishop was ordered on the king's behalf to make that notification in the manner specified above, on the Wednesday following the giving of the said charge at the latest. To which the bishop once more replied and said that he would willingly do so as soon as he well could. And later, at the request of the said bishop, the term fixed for him to make his said notification, as said, was extended for another eight days.

The second arraignment, and the bishop of Norwich's answer.

22. Also, the said bishop further claimed in the king's presence that because he had been disturbed and interrupted in various ways whilst giving his answers to the articles of which he was accused, both by carping comments aimed at him as well as in other ways, so that he had omitted and forgotten most of what he had wished to say in his excuse, he prayed of the king our lord, for love of God, that it might please him to fix another day and a suitable hearing for him, without interruption, in this parliament, and then, he said, with the help of Our Lord he would excuse himself in the said parliament of what was alleged against him as clearly as reason demanded. And that request was granted to him, and another day appointed, namely 24 November.

On which day the said bishop, rehearsing the four articles previously alleged against him in parliament, and in the presence of the king himself, gave almost exactly the same answers as before to all the aforesaid things. Adding to the same that at the time he had received news that the vanguard of the French host had entered *[Page iii-156]* *[Col. a]* the land of Flanders, whereupon the said siege of Ypres had been thus raised, he decided to confront the same vanguard in battle. Which plan he could not carry out, because the leaders of his host would not agree to it; but those captains, and others of his host, opposed him so strongly that out of sheer necessity and through fear of the enemy they had to depart and take refuge in their fortresses. And therefore the said bishop returned to the said town of Gravelines, and held it well enough against all men, and continued until the other captains had surrendered their forts to the French; and before long some Englishmen came to him, saying that there were some six or seven thousand Englishmen encamped on the beaches near Calais, who had been expelled from their said fortresses which had been surrendered, to their great injury and misfortune, because they had no means by which to live, nor could they enter the town of Calais. And because the truces previously made were due to end within the following two or three days, the French intended to overrun them and kill them all, as soon as the said treaties had ended, which slaughter, if it were carried out, would be blamed on the said bishop first of all, and then on the other captains, causing greater trouble and harm than could anything else. And for that reason they requested and charged the same bishop on behalf of our same lord the king that he surrender the town to the enemy, or raze it at once, and go to the help of the said men, and thence go to England, for the salvation of himself and the others of his host. For they said that if anything other than good should befall the said men

si riens autre qe bien avenist as ditz gentz gisantz sur les sablons, ils ent vorroient accouper mesme l'evesqe devant le roi mesmes.

Par quoy luy covenist, ce dist le dit evesqe, de abatre et voider la ville de Gravenynge, come bien lui list de faire come la sue propre conquiz des enemys. Et par tant, et par les autres resons par lui devaunt ore alleggiez; et auxint pur ce qe lettre du roi nostre seignour lui venoit devaunt, en comandant qe s'il eust grant defaute de vitaille en la dite ville, come de veritee il avoit; adonqes, en salvacione de lui et de ses dites gentz, il voidast la ville, \et et[16] fist socourer les ditz gentz, et puis/ retournast en Engleterre: lui semble q'il doit estre bien excusez de quanqe lui est surmis.

23. A quoy le dit chanceller repliast, et dist, 'Monsire evesqe, quant a ceste vostre derrain reson, voirs est qe vous aveistes de vitaille suffisant quant celle lettre vous vient, et sanz ce le roy vous envoiast d'autre vitaille, /grant pleintee: \et/ auxint, avec ce, autres bones lettres contenantes,\ coment il avoit ordeinez son uncle d'Espaigne de venir hastivement a vous en vostre aide et socours. Et tout ce nonobstant vous departistes d'illoeqes, lessant mesme la ville as enemys, encontre la forme de vostre endenture, par la quele le roi vous avoit donez et grantez quanqe vous purroiez conquere, noun pas a rendre, vendre, ou lesser as enemys, einz a tenir et possider. /Et auxint, quant a ce qe vous avez dit en vostre primere responce qe parmy vostre dite viage trieves aient este prises parentre les roialmes, et bealx ofres de paix faitz par l'adversaire de France, qe serroit, vous dites, introduccione de bon paix et final, qe Dieu grante, ce ne contient mie veritee. Qar voirs est qe la novelle espandue en l'ost de France de la venue nostre seignour le roi, et de monsire de Lancastre, q'estoit a la meer prest a passer en vostre socour, fuist la cause principale des trieves et profres avauntditz, et de la tretee ja comencee. Qar il n'est mye vraisemblable chose, n'accordante de rienz a reson qe vous q'estoiez avec voz gentz par force des enemys chacez hors des champs, et puis ensegez par eux deinz vos forteresces, feussez cause de mesme le tretee par aucune voie. Et issint, quant a ce, ne auxint parmy les autres resons devant alleggiez, ne pur rebellione de voz capitains ou d'autres de vostre retenue, ne pur quelconqes autres defautes qe vous avez ou purrez a eux surmettre, considerez qe vous les aveistes trestouz de vostre propre choisement et eleccione, et noun pas a la denominacione de nostre seignour le roi ou de son conseil, vous ne purrez ne ne doivez mie estre excusez de les damages, desceites, vilenies, contemps et les autres perdes et mesprisions a vous surmises: ne par especial del tretiz fait avec les enemys sur la deliverance des ditz forteresces, dont y a certeins endentures faites et tailles parentre vous et voz capitains d'une part et les enemys du roi d'autre part, seales de vostre seal et les sealx des autres capitains, sanz auctorite ou la volentee de mesme nostre seignour le roi, come dessus est dit.' Et enoultre il dist le dit chanceller depar le roy, 'Seignour evesqe, combien qe le roi nostre seignour vous ent purroit clerement mesner et jugger come persone temporele de son roiaume, a cause qe vous vous avez et portez come persone temporele: qar par expres vous vous liez au roi nostre seignour par voz endentures d'estre soldeour le roi, a guerroier le poeple Christien apres le terme de vostre croiserie finiz, et vous usez communement d'avoir vostre espeie portez devant vous. Et plousurs autres choses semblables faites vous chescun jour come seignour temporel, publiquement, encontre la commune custume de l'estat du prelat d'Engleterre. Nientmeins, par resoun de vostre estat le roi nostre seignour de sa grace soi abstiner quant a present

---
[16] et *repeated*

encamped on the beaches, they would accuse the same bishop before the king himself.

On account of which he decided, said the same bishop, to raze and vacate the town of Gravelines, as was permissible in the face of certain conquest by the enemy. And for that reason and others previously alleged by him; and also because a letter of our lord the king came to him ordering that if he was suffering a great shortage of victuals in the said town, as indeed he was, then, for the salvation of himself and his men, he should vacate the town and aid the said men and then return to England: it seemed to him that he ought to be fully excused of whatever was alleged against him.

23. To which the said chancellor replied and said, My lord bishop, as to this your last reason, the truth is that you had sufficient victuals when this letter reached you, and in addition to this the king sent you further victuals in plentiful supply: and also, together with that, other good letters saying that he had ordered his uncle of Spain to come swiftly to your help and aid. Notwithstanding that, you left, abandoning the same town to the enemy, contrary to the form of your indenture, in which the king gave and granted you all that you could require, not so as to surrender, sell or abandon it to the enemy, but to hold and keep it. And also, as for what you said in your first answer, that as a result of your said expedition truces were arranged between the kingdoms and handsome offers of peace made by the enemy of France, which you said, would be the prelude to a good and final peace, which God grant, this contains no element of the truth. For the truth is that the spreading of the news amongst the French host of the arrival of our lord the king and of my lord of Lancaster, who was at the coast and ready to cross to your succour, was the principal reason for the aforesaid truces and proposals, and the treaty already begun. For it is most unlikely and does not accord with reason that you, who were chased from the field with your men by the might of the enemy and then besieged by them in your fortresses, should have been the cause of the same treaty in any way. And so, neither for this, nor for the other reasons previously given, nor for the rebellion of your captains or of others in your retinue, nor for *[Col. b]* any of the other faults you have or could attribute to them - considering that you yourself chose and selected them all, and they were not nominated by our lord the king or his council - you cannot nor ought to be excused of the damage, deceits, villainies, contempts and other injuries and offences alleged against you: nor especially of the treaty made with the enemy for the deliverance of the said fortresses, for which certain indentures were made and cut between you and your captains on the one hand and the king's enemies on the other, sealed with your seal and the seals of the other captains, without the authority or wish of our same lord the king, as is said above. The chancellor also said on the king's behalf, My lord bishop, the king our lord could clearly deal with you and judge you as a layman of his realm, because you have acted and borne yourself as a layman: since you expressly bound yourself to the king our lord by your indentures to be a soldier of the king, to wage war for Christian people according to the terms of your crusade, and you habitually have your sword carried before you. And in many other such ways you bear yourself every day like a temporal lord, in public, contrary to the common custom of a bishop's status in England. Nevertheless, by reason of your estate, the king our lord, of his grace, will abstain at present from laying hands upon you, but because he has been informed that you have complained to many lords of the

de mettre la main a vostre corps, mais pur tant q'il est enformez qe vous vous avez compleint as plusours seignours du roialme qe tort vous ent estoit nadgairs fait al derrain jour, affermant par voz paroles qe ce qe estoit fait adonqes ne passast mye par assent ou del science de voz peres du roialme, si est grantement a merveiller de vous et d'icelles voz paroles, desicome la busoigne ne touche rienz vostre peraltee, einz soulement certeines mesprisions queles vous come soldeour le roi, encontre la forme de voz endentures et covenances ent taillez avec le roi nostre seignour, avez fait et perpetrez, a grant damage du roi come dessus est \[dit,]/\ dont la conissance et punissement de commune droit, et anciene custume du roialme d'Engleterre, soul et par tout appertient au roi nostre seignour et a nul autre. Et voirs est qe vous n'avez mye ore par ceste vostre derrain responce riens amendez vostre matire en excusacione de vous sur les choses a vous surmises, einz pluis grantement, a ce qe semble, avez empeirez. Par quoy, del assent des conts, barons, et autres seignours temporelx presentz en ce parlement, est assentuz et accordez qe vous soiez en la mercy le roi, et mis au fin et raunceon pur vostre malfait solonc la quantitee et qualitee d'icelle: et a ce faire vous soiez compuls et constreint par la seisine de voz temporaltees del eveschee de Norwiz. Et le roi vous comande qe de cy enavaunt vous ne facez ne ne soeffrez estre fait l'espeie estre portez devant vous, come ad este fait, sur le peril q'appent. Et est agardez expressement en ce parlement qe quanqe ad este despenduz en vostre oeps des ditz franks d'or, vous facez plein paiement en la tresorie nostre seignour le roi, sanz delaye ou difficultee.

Membrane 6

Encontre Elmham, Tryvet, Farndon', Ferriers et Fitz Rauf.
24. Item, monsire William de Elmham, monsire Thomas Tryvet, monsire Henry de Ferriers, et monsire William de Farndon', chivalers, et Robert Fitz-Rauf, esquier, les queux parmy la dite charge doneez en parlement pardevant avoient este avec le chanceller, et a lui conuz et confessez, coment ils avoient /resceuz\ certeines sommes des franks d'or des Franceys, en lisible et due manere et nemye autrement, a ce q'ils disoient: primerement, c'estassavoir, les ditz messires William de Elmham, Thomas /Tryvet,\ et William Farndon en une parcelle trois mille franks d'or. Item, en une autre parcell les ditz monsire William de Elmham, /monsire William\ Farndon, monsire Henry de Ferriers, monsire Johan de Drayton, et Robert Fitz Rauf deux mille franks. Item, en une autre parcelle le dit monsire William de *[Page iii-157]*
[Col. a] Elmham resceust des Fraunceoys pur le chastelle de Burburghe, dont monsire William de Hoo lors estoit capitain, et pur les vitailles del dit monsire William de Hoo esteantz en dit chastel de Burburghe, deux mille franks, dont le dit monsire William de Elmham paiast tantost, a ce q'il dist, mille franks au dit monsire William de Hoo, et les autre mille franks il promtast pur un terme de mesme cellui monsire William de Hoo. Item, en une autre parcelle monsire Henry de Ferriers resceust del doun des ditz Franceys mille franks. Si furent puis apres aresounz en plein parlement, en presence du roi mesmes, et de son comandement, par le dit chanceller, a la requeste de la commune, alleggeante en especial qe fuist grantement a merveiller, coment les ditz chivalers et esquier, qi moelt grantement \estoient/ diffamez de celles receites d'or, et d'autres lours mesprisions faitz en le dit ost, serroient issint desportez q'ome ne purroit avoir appart conissance de lour arreinement, auxi avant come l'en avoit pardevant del arenement l'evesqe de Norwiz, q'est pere du roialme, et par tant doit mieltz estre desportez qe les autres dessusditz: et lour dist einsi le dit chanceller, 'Sires, vous deivez entendre

realm that wrong was lately done you on that last day, affirming by your words that what was then done did not have the assent or knowledge of your peers of the realm, you and your words are greatly to be wondered at, since the matter had no bearing at all on your status as a peer, but simply on certain offences which you, as a soldier of the king, committed and perpetrated contrary to the form of your indentures and agreements drawn up with the king our lord, to the great injury of the king as said above; cognizance and punishment of which pertain, by common right and the ancient custom of the kingdom of England, to the king our lord alone and no other. And the truth is that you have not improved your position at all by your last answer to the things alleged against you, but have further and the more weakened it. Accordingly, with the assent of the earls, barons and other lords temporal present in this parliament, it is agreed and assented that you shall be at the king's mercy, and put to fine and ransom for your offence in accordance with the size and nature of the same: and to that end you shall be compelled and constrained by the seizure of your temporalities of the bishopric of Norwich. And the king orders that from now on you shall not have your sword carried before you nor allow it to be done, as in the past, on pain of the penalty decreed. And it was judged explicitly in this parliament that whatever was taken for your use from the said gold francs should be fully reimbursed in the treasury of our lord the king, without delay or hindrance.

Against Elmham, Trivet, Faringdon, Ferrers and FitzRalph.
24. Also, Sir William Elmham, Sir Thomas Trivet, Sir Henry Ferrers and Sir William Faringdon, knights, and Robert FitzRalph, esquire, who through the said charge previously given in parliament appeared with the chancellor, had acknowledged and confessed that they had received certain sums in gold francs from the French, in a proper and lawful manner and in no other way, according to them: first, namely, the said sirs William Elmham, Thomas Trivet and William Faringdon had received a consignment of three thousand gold francs. Also, in another consignment, the said Sir William Elmham, Sir William Faringdon, Sir Henry Ferrers, Sir John Drayton and Robert FitzRalph received two thousand francs. Also, in another consignment the said Sir William *[Page iii-157]*
[Col. a] Elmham received from the French, for the castle of Bourbourg, of which Sir William Hoo was then captain, and for the provisions of the said Sir William Hoo found in the said castle of Bourbourg, two thousand francs, of which the said Sir William Elmham immediately paid, as he said, one thousand francs to the said William Hoo, and the other thousand francs he borrowed for a time from the same William Hoo. Also, in another consignment Sir Henry Ferrers received a thousand francs by gift of the said French. Therefore they were later questioned in full parliament, in the presence of the king himself, and at his command by the said chancellor, at the request of the commons, who emphasized in particular that it was great wonder that the said knights and esquire, who had been so greatly denounced for those receipts of gold and other offences committed by them in the said host, should have supposed that none would have cognizance of their arraignment, as it was also with the arraignment of the bishop of Norwich, who was a peer of the realm, and was therefore even better known than the others aforementioned: and so the said chancellor told them, Sirs,

coment il n'est mye lisible chose, einz moelt grant mesprisione en la persone de chescun lige homme du roi, de faire treitie avec aucun enemy du roi sanz la volentee et expresse auctorite du roi mesmes, ou de son lieutenant. Item, une autre grant mesprisione est il qe aucun lige du roi rendroit ou durroit as ditz enemys chastel, forteresce, vitaille, armure, ou autre refreschement, sanz commandement et auctorite del roy especial, ou de mesme son lieutenant. Mais encores pir est, de vendre et aliener a mesmes les enemys aucun fort, vitaille, armure, ou autre refreschement, par repreignant d'iceulx enemys monoie ou autres biens, sanz auctorite du roy, ou de mesme son lieutenant. Et, sires, vous savez bien, et nel purrez dedire, coment par certeines covenances taillees parentre les enemis Franceoys et vous messires William de Elmham, Thomas Tryvet, Henry de Ferriers, et William de Farndon, \et autres,// dont y a certeines endentures faites\\ et ensealees de voz sealx,/ vous feistes nadgairs tretee avec les ditz enemys sanz la volentee et auctorite del roy ou de son lieutenant; et parmy cell trettee et la vostre vente d'icelles fortz, vitailles, et armures, vous resceustes les dites sommes d'or. Et issint par ce, et par autres vos affaires et rebellions faitz a vostre chieftein, le dit ost feust desparpullez et destruit, al grevouse damage, vilenie, et contempt du roi nostre seignour, et moelt grant profit et confort as ditz enemys, dont vous estez dignes d'emporter reproche et grevouse punissement. Qar vous, monsire de[17] William de Elmham, resceustes des ditz enemys les dites deux mille franks pur la vente et suisrendre del dit chastelle de Burburgh', et des vitailles, armures, et autres biens en ycelle lors esteantz, a grant nombre et value, sanz la volentee et auctorite du roi nostre seignour, et le bon gree du dit monsire William de Hoo, capitain d'icelle, combien qe mesme le chastel estoit assez fort del avoir tenuz pur un grant terme encontre toutz gentz. Et vous auxint, les ditz messires William de Elmham, Thomas Tryvet, et William de Farndon', resceustes a vostre oeps propre en commune les ditz trois mille franks del doun d'iceulx enemys, pur voz consentement et aide al dit tretiz fait /sur\ le voydance des Engleys hors du paiis, et la deliverance de la ville de Gravenynge, et /des\ autres forteresces occupiez adonqes en celles parties. Et vous auxint, les ditz monsire William de Elmham, William de Farndon', Henry de Ferriers, et Robert Fitz Rauf, avec monsire Johan de Drayton', chivaler, resceutes en semblable manere autre foitz d'yceulx enemys deux mille franks clerement de lour doun, a ce qe vous dites, dont est a merveiller qe les Fraunceys qi sont tenuz pur sages gentz vousissent doner si grant somme a vous, si \ce/ ne fuist pur aucun grant profit, \damageous au roi nostre seignour,/ fait a eulx par vous d'autrepart. Et vous, monsire Henry de Ferriers, devant et depuis qe vostre seignour

[Col. b] l'evesqe de Norwiz estoit venuz en Engleterre, feistes grant pursuite devers mesmes les enemys, et aveistes grant tretee avec eux pur les residues cynk mille franks, quelles le dit evesqe deust avoir resceuz de eux s'il eust voluz, et les resceustes d'yceux enemys, et de fait les portastes deinz le roialme, avec autres mille franks d'or \queux/ vous resceustes auxint de lour doun, sanz comandement et auctorite du roi nostre seignour, ou de son lieutenant, et la volentee ou science de mesme l'evesqe vostre seignour. Dont est semblablement a merveiller, pur quoy \les/ ditz Franceys, qi sont assez sages, vous durroient tielle somme, si ne feust a lour grant avauntage, et damage du roi nostre seignour. Et vous, monsire Thomas Tryvet, avez de vostre auctorite propre, sanz auctorite du roy nostre seignour ou de son lieutenant avantdit, acrochez poair roial a vous, en

---

[17] de *superfluous*

you should understand that it is indeed not lawful, rather it is a great offence against the person of every liege man of the king, to negotiate with any of the king's enemies without the wish and express authority of the king himself or his lieutenant. Also, it is also a grave offence for any liege of the king to surrender or hand over to the said enemies a castle, fortress, victuals, weaponry, or other reinforcement, without the special command and authority of the king or his same lieutenant. But it is yet worse to sell and transfer to the same enemies any fort, victuals, weaponry, or other reinforcement in return for money or other goods from the same enemies, without the king's authority or that of his same lieutenant. And sirs, you know well and cannot deny that by certain covenants drawn up between the French enemy and you, messires William Elmham, Thomas Trivet, Henry Ferrers, William Faringdon and others, for which there exist certain indentures drawn up and sealed with your seals, you recently made a treaty with the said enemy without the will and authority of the king or his lieutenant; and by that treaty and your sale of the same forts, victuals and weaponry, you received the said sums of gold. And so as a result of that, and your other deeds and rebellions carried out against your leader, the said host was scattered and destroyed, to the grievous injury, defamation and contempt of the king our lord, and the very great profit and advantage of the said enemy, for which you deserve condemnation and grievous punishment. Since you, Sir William Elmham, received from the said enemy the said two thousand francs for the sale and surrender of the said castle of Bourburg and the victuals, weaponry, and other goods found therein, of great quantity and value, without the wish and authority of the king our lord, and the good will of the said Sir William Hoo, captain of the same, even though the same castle was strong enough to withstand all attack for a long time. Moreover, you, the said messires William Elmham, Thomas Trivet and William Faringdon, jointly received for your own use the said three thousand francs by gift of the same enemy for your consent and assistance with the said treaty made on the withdrawal of the English from the land, and the surrender of the town of Gravelines and of other fortresses then occupied in those parts. And also you, the said Sir William Elmham, William Faringdon, Henry Ferrers and Robert FitzRalph, along with Sir John Drayton, knight, similarly received on another occasion from the enemy two thousand francs, ostensibly by way of gift, yet it seems incredible that the French, who are considered clever people, should give you so great a sum of money unless it was for their own great profit and injurious to the king our lord. And you Sir Henry Ferrers, before and after your lord

[Col. b] the bishop of Norwich arrived in England, you made great overtures towards the same enemies, and agreed an important treaty with them for the remaining five thousand francs, which the said bishop ought to have received from them if he had wished, and the receipts of those enemies, and indeed you brought them into the kingdom, together with the other thousand gold francs which you also received by their gift, without the command and authority of the king our lord or his lieutenant, and the wish and knowledge of the same bishop your lord. Concerning which it is similarly to be wondered why the said French, who are clever enough, would give you such a sum, unless it was to their great gain and to the injury of the king our lord. And you, Sir Thomas Trivet, have, by your own authority, without that of the king our lord or his aforesaid lieutenant, accroached the royal power,

in issuing to the king's enemies, on various occasions and in great number, many letters sealed under your seal of safe conduct and protection, to come, go and remain in the said host, and from there return to their own land and homes: you receiving in return for those your letters various great sums of money; whence great trouble came to the said host, and injury to the king and his kingdom. And you, the said Sir William Faringdon, are also greatly at fault, because you would not return to the said enemy the said five thousand francs left by you at Gravelines, contrary to the wish and command of the said bishop your leader.

To which all the said persons answered individually, except Sir John Drayton, who, because it was proved that he had had the permission of the king himself to receive whatever he received there, was not impeached in this parliament; namely, the said Robert FitzRalph said that for his part he had received only four hundred francs by gift of the duke of Brittany, without making a treaty or any other covenant with the enemy in any way, except only that he was charged by the said companions, partners in the receipt of the said two thousand francs, to say nothing of the same receipt. And the said Sir William Elmham said that whatsoever he had thus received from the aforesaid sums had been for the victuals, prisoners and other goods which he had had in the fortress of Bourburg and elsewhere in those parts, and which together with the same fortress he had surrendered by the same treaty, as he had been constrained to do by necessity, to save himself and his people; for otherwise the town of Bourburg, where Lord Beaumont, Sir Thomas Trivet, Sir William Elmham and a large number of their host were being besieged and attacked by the enemy in great number, and which was all at once being set alight, would have been captured by them by force, and all those within taken or killed. And for that reason he thought that in acting thus he had done no wrong. But nevertheless, if it seemed to the king our lord that he had done wrong in any way, he would submit himself to his noble grace. And the said Sir Thomas Trivet replied and said that he had not granted or given safe-conduct to any enemy of the king, except only to certain poor men, countrymen there, who brought them victuals and other essentials; and for the rest he had received nothing from those enemies except for victuals and his other things lost and taken from him by enemy force at Bourburg, in the manner recently described by Sir William Elmham. In truth of which, if he had also offended in any way, he would wholly submit himself to the grace of our lord the king. And the said Sir William Faringdon replied and said that certain persons of France had paid him a certain sum of gold which they should have paid him by rights, and for which he was fully reimbursed by them: and for that reason, and for another honest cause, he gave to the same French the near equivalent value in good horses, and otherwise he received nothing from those enemies except for a small sum which the duke of Brittany freely gave him. And as to the allegation that he would not return to the enemy the said *[Page iii-158]* five thousand francs, he said that it seemed to him better that all the gold were thrown into the sea than that it be repaid to them even though it were a most considerable sum. And so he believed, as he said, that he had done no wrong; yet if he had, he would throw himself on the mercy of the king our lord. And the said Sir Henry confessed receipt of five thousand francs from the enemy, together with another thousand gold francs which the French freely gave him, he said, in return for his labours. In which if he had offended in any way, he would also submit to the good grace of his liege lord.

25. And the said chancellor in replying to the said Sir William Faringdon, Henry and Robert, said that it was greatly to be wondered at, and incompatible with reason that so shrewd a people as the French should have given such sums to their enemies in such a way, unless they were certain of receiving something in return, or of profiting from their same enemies in one way or another. And assuredly, as regards the statement which you, Sir William Faringdon, made, that it would have been better to throw it in the sea than send it back to the said enemies, that is certainly not true, since it would have been better had the enemies had their own gold, than that any traitor of

[Col. b] the king our lord, who would henceforth sell the king's fortresses to the enemy for gold, or their other goods, should excuse himself in the way in which you now would excuse yourself. And then, after the statements made by the same persons by way of excuse had been heard, and had been considered and adjudged inadequate as excuses in this matter, the said chancellor said on the king's behalf, It has been decided in parliament that, you messires William Elmham, Thomas Trivet, Henry Ferrers, William Faringdon and Robert FitzRalph shall compensate and fully reimburse our lord the king with whatsoever you and each one of you have thus received and taken from the aforesaid enemy. In addition, that you all, the said Sir William Elmham, Thomas, Henry and Robert, shall be sent to prison and ransomed thence at the king's will for your misdeeds; taking into consideration the nature and extent of the offence committed by each of you: and you, Sir William Faringdon, because you have expressly acknowledged before the king himself receipt of various sums of gold from the said enemy, and presenting them with horses, to their great reinforcement, for which you did not have the king's permission or that of his lieutenant, you shall be at the king's mercy, in your body and possessions, for him to do with you as he pleases.

HERE FOLLOW THE PETITIONS DELIVERED TO OUR LORD KING IN THE PRESENT PARLIAMENT BY THE COMMUNITY OF THE KINGDOM OF ENGLAND, TOGETHER WITH THE ANSWERS GIVEN TO THE SAME PETITIONS BY THE SAID LORD KING AND HIS COUNCIL IN THE SAME PARLIAMENT.

To our most gracious, most potent and most redoubtable lord, our lord the king, your humble commons, now assembled in this present parliament held at Westminster on the Monday before the feast of All Saints in the seventh year of your reign, pray favour for the petitions written below:

[Confirmation of the liberties and franchises of the church, and of the charters and all statutes in force.]

26. First, that holy church have and enjoy all its liberties and franchises, and that the Great Charter, and the Charter of the Forest, and all other good statutes and ordinances made and ordained before this time, be upheld, strictly kept, and duly executed in accordance with the tenor of the same.

Answer.

The king wills it.

[Judges to be sworn in parliament.]

27. Also, the commons pray that it may please the king our lord to cause all justices of one Bench or the other, and of the exchequer, to swear now in the presence of you all and of the commons that henceforth they will lawfully uphold the laws and good ordinances made and to be made for all

---
[18] The rest of m.6 has been left blank.
[19] 7 Ric.2 cc.1,2. The statutes of this parliament are printed in *SR*, II.32-36

egalement, eantz consederacione en lour juggementz a nulle persone grande ne petite, mais selonc la commune loy ordenez et establiz, sur peine de forfaire l'estat de lour office par la contraire trovez, nient contresteant lettre de grant seal ne de petit seal quelconqe a eux mandez au contraire.

\[Responsio.]/
Ils sont jurez devant ceste heure de faire droit a chescuny, et s'il embusoigne, le roy lour vorra faire autre foitz duement charger et serementer.

[Justices to examine vagrants.]
28. Item, prient les communes: ordeigner briefs directes as justices du paix assignez \vers/ chescun countee, pur diligentement faire examiner et enquerre qe toutz vagrants et faytours par la paix currantz, soient compellez de trover seuretee de lour bone port, tiele come soit destreignable si aucun defaute fuisse trovez en eux en apres; et s'ils ne poent tiele seuretee trover, soient mandez al proscheine gaole tanq'al venue des justices assignez pur deliverance, queux en tiel cas \ent/ ordeneront de remede pur quiete de la commune.
\[Responsio.]/
Le roi le voet.[20]

[Proclamation of the statute of Winchester.]
29. Item, prient les communes: qe briefs soient mandez a chescun viscont de la terre, sur grevouse peyne, q'il face proclamacione overtement de l'estatut de Wyncestr' sur larons et robbours illoeqes establiz, en chescun hundred par leur mesmes, et en chescune ville marchee par lour southbaillifs, sibien deinz franchise come dehors, et ce par quatre foitz l'an sanz aucun negligence. Proclamant oultre ce qe par estatut a ore en ce present parlement establir, si aucune persone robbez ou pilez en chemyn, ou en ville ou en village, monstre notoirement la robberie fait en lieu nient desconuz, et saunz engyn, q'il avera son recoverir en quelconqe lieu qe ce soit dedeinz le roialme, sanz contredit, selonc l'estatut de Wynchestre suisditz.
\[Responsio.]/
Le roy le voet[21]

[Purveyors.]
30. Item, prient les communes: qe l'estatut de purveiours soit fermement gardez, et de novel proclamez [Page iii-159] [Col. a] par toute la terre, en confort de poeple, qi lour ont en diverses paiis compleignez de grant damage a eux estre fait par les purveours nostre seignour le roi, et par autres qi s'appellent purveours as autres seignours, fesantz ore tarde as certeins countees a contraire de l'estatut suisdit, a grant esclandre del hostiel nostre dit seignour le roy, et damage au povre commune: et qe les justices de la pees en chescun countee parmy le roialme aient poair d'enquerre de toutes tielx grevances et oppressions ensi faitz par les ditz purveours, et de les punir, et faire execucione sur eux selonc l'effect du dit estatut.

\[Responsio.]/
Le roi voet qe les estatutz ent faitz qe sont assez fortz soient tenuz et gardez en touz pointz, et duement mys en execution. Et oultre ce assentuz est qe si les servantz d'autres seignours riens issint preignent desore en paiis autrement q'ils ne purront accorder avec les vendours, ou devant q'ils

---
[20] 7 Ric.2 c.5.
[21] 7 Ric.2 c.6.

persons equally, showing favour in their judgment to no one, great or small, but according to the common law ordained and decreed, on pain of forfeiting the estate of their office if they are found to do the contrary, notwithstanding any letter of great nor small seal sent to them instructing them to the contrary.
Answer.
They have sworn in the past to do right to all, and if need be, the king will cause them to be duly charged and sworn again.

[Justices to examine vagrants.]
28. Also, the commons pray: that writs be directed to the justices of the peace appointed for each county, instructing them diligently to examine and ensure that all vagrants and tricksters wandering the land, be compelled to find surety for their good behaviour, such as is distrainable if any fault is found with them later; and if they cannot find such surety, let them be sent to the nearest prison until the arrival of the justices appointed for delivery, who in such cases shall ordain remedy thereon for the common peace.
Answer.
The king wills it

[Proclamation of the statute of Winchester.]
29. Also, the commons pray: that writs be sent to every sheriff of the land, on pain of a grievous penalty, that they make a public proclamation of the statute on thieves and robbers decreed at Winchester, and that it be done by themselves in each hundred, and by their deputy officers in each market town, both within franchise and without, four times a year without fail. Proclaiming moreover, that by the statute now to be decreed in this parliament, if any person robbed or mugged on a highway, or in a town or village, can show that the robbery occurred in a known place, and was planned, he shall have his recovery in whatsoever place that may be in the kingdom without impediment, according to the aforesaid statute of Winchester.
Answer.
The king wills it

[Purveyors.]
30. Also, the commons pray: that the statute of purveyors be strictly enforced, and newly proclaimed [Page iii-159] [Col. a] throughout the land, for the comfort of the people, who in various places have complained of great injury done them by the purveyors of our lord the king, and by others who call themselves purveyors of other lords, acting of late in certain counties contrary to the aforesaid statute, to the great disrepute of the household of our said lord the king and the injury of the poor commons: and that the justices of the peace in each county throughout the realm shall have the power to inquire into all such injuries and oppressions thus committed by the said purveyors, and punish them, and carry out execution on the same according to the tenor of the said statute.
Answer.
The king wills that the statutes made thereon, which are strong enough, be upheld and enforced in all respects, and duly executed. Furthermore, it is agreed that if the servants of other lords henceforth take anything in the land for which they do not have the assent of the sellers, or before they have

ent facent paiement en poigne si sur ce autrement ne purront accorder avec mesmes \les/ vendours; qe mesmes celles servantz encourgent la peine comprise es ditz estatutz des purveiours. Et nientmeins, eit la partie endamagee sa suite /a\ la commune loy s'il vorra.[22]

[The staple.]

31. Item, prient les communes, pur honor et profit du roi nostre seignour, et en relevation de toute la terre: q'ore par sage deliberacion en ce present parlement soit ordenez aucun bon remede pur deliverance des commoditees du roiaume, come des leines, pealx lanutz et autres commodites touchantz l'estaple, queux ont este deux ou trois ans pardevant malement deliverez, a damage du roy et du poeple, et plus assez est semblable pur ent venir, si remede n'y soit ore ordenez. \[Responsio.]/

Si paix soit, ou trieves generalx se preignent parentre les roialmes d'Engleterre et de France par terre et par meer trois ans ou oultre, soit l'estaple tenuz a Caleys. Et si tielles paix ou trieves ne se preignent mye illoeqes, adonqes soit l'estaple tenuz deinz le roialme d'Engleterre, en lieu ou es lieux, et par manere, come serra accordez par nostre seignour le roy et son conseil et autres sages du roialme pur celle cause /a\ appellers, si mestier soit. Salvant toutdys qe bien lise as merchantz Janeveys, Veniciens, et autres, de carier leynes, et pealx lanutz vers le west, come ils soloient faire devant ceste heure, solonc l'ordinance sur ce faite et grante.

[Dimensions of cloth.]

32. Item, prient les communes, pur ease et commune profit du poeple: qe l'estatut ordenez pur la laeure et longure des draps soit renovellez et establiz, et fermement desore executz, qar grant deceyt en y ad sibien es draps de colour come des rayes, a commune damage; et rienz n'ad este execut pur le remede. Ordeignantz qe ceux qi vendont aucuns draps /faitz\ deinz le roialme ou dehors, et ne soient de laeure et longure come droit en est, soient tielx draps taillez en trois pieces, et reliverez al vendour les pieces, et l'argent al achatour. \[Responsio.]/

Soient l'estatutz ent faitz tenuz et duement executz; adjoustez a ycelles qe celluy qi espiera et provera desore tiel defaute es draps apres qe tiels draps soient mys a vente, eit la tierce partie de chescun tiel drap pur son travaille, par la liveree des viscontz s'ils soient presentz, ou les seignours des feires et marchees et autres lieux ou tielx draps defectives serront trovez, ou de lours baillifs, ou conestables des villes. Pur la quele tierce partie q'appartient au roi nostre seignour, parmy les ordinances devant ore faitz, l'auneours nostre seignour le roi et le coillour del subside des draps assignez el countee, as queux par mesmes les ordinances appartient expressement de auneer toutes draps vendables, et surveoir diligeaument l'assise des draps en longure et laeure d'icelles, et puis celles draps sils tiegnent l'assise ensealler du seal, a ce ordenez, facent nientmeins gree au roy, sibien del value de celle tierce partie come del remenant des ditz [Col. b] draps, \et ent/respoignont a nostre seignour le roy entierment a son escheqer. Et enoultre encourgent la peine devaunt ordeignez par estatut pur lour negligence et concelement.

paid for it in ready money if no other arrangement has been made with the same sellers; that the same servants shall incur the penalty contained in the said statutes of purveyors. And nevertheless, let the injured party have his suit at the common law if he will.

[The staple.]

31. Also, the commons pray, for the honour and profit of the king our lord, and the relief of all the land: that there now be ordained by wise deliberation in this present parliament a good remedy for the trade in commodities of the realm like wool, woolfells and other commodities associated with the staple, which have previously been ill-managed two or three times a year, to the injury of the king and the people, and that is likely to occur again if remedy is not ordained.
Answer.

If there be peace, or a general truce is agreed between the kingdoms of England and France by land and by sea for three years or more, let the staple be held at Calais. And if such a peace or truce are not arranged, then let the staple be held in the kingdom of England, in a place or in places and in a manner to be agreed upon by our lord the king, his council and other wise men of the realm to be called upon for that purpose, if need be. Saving always that it be wholly lawful for Genoese, Venetian and other merchants to transport wool and woolfells to the west, as they have been accustomed to do in the past, in accordance with the ordinance thereon made and granted.

[Dimensions of cloth.]

32. Also, the commons pray, for the ease and common profit of the people: that the statute ordained for the width and length of cloth be renewed, promulgated and henceforth strictly enforced, for deceitful practice abounds in coloured and striped cloth, to the injury of all, and nothing has been done by way of remedy. And let it be ordained that if anyone sells cloth within the kingdom or outside it which is not of the rightful length and width, that that cloth shall be cut in three pieces, and the pieces sent back to the vendor, and the money returned to the buyer.
Answer.

Let the statutes made hereon be upheld and duly enforced; adding to the same that anyone who in future notices and proves there to be such a fault in cloths which have been put on sale, shall have a third of each such cloth for his efforts, at the hands of the sheriffs if they be present, or the lords of the fairs, markets and other places where such defective cloth shall be found, or by their bailiffs, or the constables of towns. For which third part pertaining to the king our lord, by ordinances made in the past, the alnagers of our lord the king and the collector of the subsidy on cloths assigned to the county - to whom, by the same ordinances, it clearly falls to inspect all saleable cloths and thoroughly gauge the size of cloths in terms of the length and width of the same, and then if they meet the required size, to stamp them with a seal devized for this - shall compensate the king, as well for the value of the third part as for the remainder of the said [Col. b] cloths, and they shall answer our lord the king fully at his exchequer. Furthermore, they shall incur the penalty previously ordained by statute for their negligence and concealment.

---

[22] 7 Ric.2 c.8.

[Those leaving the realm with the king's licence to have power to appoint general attorneys.]

33. Also, the commons pray: that it be ordained in this parliament that those who are summoned by writ of premunire facias, at the suit of the king as well of a party, may appear by their attorneys, or an attorney of record if they be overseas, to answer the said writs, as if they were present in person: bearing in mind that people have often been in danger of being placed outside the protection of our said lord the king without just cause, when often they have been overseas with the king's permission and have known nothing of any such suit.

Answer.

It is agreed and assented, firstly concerning those who are overseas at present, and are of good repute, and have appointed their attorneys general by patent of our lord the king, that the chancellor, by the advice of the justices, can grant that they may appear and answer before any of the king's judges through their attorneys in the said plea of premunire facias. And as for those who are still to cross, if they ask to appoint their general attorneys by patent of the king before their departure from the realm, and in particular in a case such as premunire facias, that the said chancellor, by the advice of the said justices, may grant it. Provided nevertheless that concerning this grant express mention be made of premunire facias in letters patent of the king to be made thereon in future. And after they have received such special patents, those attorneys may and should answer for their masters in the said writs of premunire facias, notwithstanding the statute thereon made to the contrary.

[Term of office of sheriffs, under sheriffs, and escheators.]

34. Also, the commons pray: whereas it is decreed by statute that no sheriff, deputy sheriff nor escheator remain in office longer than a year, may it please the king our lord that the said statute be firmly upheld from now on, without contravention, for the great ease and tranquillity of all the realm. And if any commission be made to the contrary, that it be repealed.

Answer.

The king wills that the statute made thereon be upheld and enforced: and if a patent or commission be granted to the contrary, that it be repealed; saving always to the king our lord his prerogative and regality in the matter, as in all others.

[Additional charges levied on wool.]

35. Also, the commons show that whereas the ordinances and proclamations recently made that every merchant may travel freely wherever he chooses with wool and woolfells, paying only the customs and subsidies owed to our lord the king; namely, each denizen 50*s*. and each alien 53*s*., 4*d*. and no more: against those ordinances and proclamations they complain, because they are constrained by the king's customs officers to find surety of 19*d*. per sack, which seems to them a novel and wrongful charge, because no charge which has not previously been ordained by statute ought to be imposed without the assent of parliament. From which surety and payment they ask to be discharged in the present parliament, according to the tenor of the aforesaid ordinances and proclamations, and that those who have paid be recompensed.

It seems reasonable to the lords, if it please the king, that on all wool which is not henceforth sold at Calais, the said 19*d*.

---

[23] See PRO SC8/162/8068.
[24] 7 Ric.2 c.14.
[25] 28 Edw.3 c.7.

~~ne serront demandez, einz qe les marchantz et possessours de celles leynes ent soient deschargez, nientcontresteant l'ordinances nadgairs fait au contraire.~~
*Vacat, quia sic non placuit domino regi pro tunc illud concedere. Et ideo cancellatur et dampnatur.*²⁶
Mais puis apres le roi grantast et voloit qe les denszeins serroient desore quitz des ditz .xix. *d.* al saak de lours leins propres, qe ne serront deschargez a Calays tantseulement.
Membrane 4, Page iii-160

[Keeping the seas.]
36. Item, prient les communes: qe come nadgairs en voz parlementz estoit grantez qe les marchantz de vostre roialme deussent paier de chescun .xx. *s.* de marchandise .vi. *d.* et .ij. *s.* de chescun tonelle de vyn, pur peril et damage qe purroit avenir a eux et lour marchandise en la meer pur defaut de sauf garde de passer et revenir, quele chose estoit grantez a greindre seuretee de eux et salvacione de lours corps, marchandies et de lour estat, de quel grant riens n'avient au profit, sauf-conduyt, ne defense de eux, mais oultre ce, de lours deniers propres ils font lours coustages, pur salvement garder eux, leur marchandise et leur estat; issint q'ils emportent double charge.
Par quoy plese a vostre roiale magestee grantir q'ils puissent estre et soient deschargez del grant et charge avauntditz issint grantez.
\[*Responsio.*]/
Le roy, par l'advis de son conseil et de ses admiralx, ordenera pur la sauve-garde de la meer et des marchandises venantz et passantz a mieltz q'il purra. Et voet nostre seignour le roi qe sur celle sauve garde le dit subside soit entierment emploiez, et nule part ailours.

[Victuallers in London.]
37. Item, prient les communes: pur greindre quiete et nurture de paix parentre voz lieges, et pur commune profit, qe voz citeins de vostre citee de Londres soient entierment en ce present parlement restitutz a lour franchises et franks usages; et q'il plese a vous, tresredoute seignour, de vostre grace especiale, granter et confermer as voz ditz citeins et a lours successours par voz lettres patentes toutes lours libertees et franks usages, auxi entierment et pleinement come ils, ou lours predecessours, les avoient en temps d'aucuns des voz tresnobles progenitours, ove clause de licet usi non fuerint, vel abusi fuerint; ensemblement ove les franchises q'ils ont en especial de vostre tresgraciouse grant ou confermement: nient contresteantz aucuns estatutz, juggementz renduz, ordinances, ou chartres faites ou grantez einz ces heures a contraire, sibien en temps d'aucuns de voz ditz progenitours come en le vostre, issint come le restreinte de lour libertees et franks usages ad en plusours maneres avaunt ces heures empirez et arreriz l'estat de eux, et riens valu a commune profit du roialme. Et qe touz les vineters²⁷ et vitaillers, sibien pessoners come autres, ove lours vitailles venantz a vostre dite citee, soient desore enavaunt desouz le governail et reule del mair et aldermannes de la citee avauntdite pur le temps esteantz, come auncienement soloient estre. Et oultre granter qe nul mair de la dite citee desore enavaunt ne face, ne soit constreint de faire, en vostre escheqer, tresredoute seignour, n'ailleurs, autre serement mais soulement l'auncien serement use en temps le roi Edward vostre tresnoble aiel, qi Dieux assoille, aucun estatut ou ordinance au contraire ent faitz noun obstantz.

~~should not be demanded, but that merchants and owners of that wool shall be discharged thereof, notwithstanding the ordinances made to the contrary.~~
Cancelled, because it did not please the lord king to concede it at that time. And therefore it was cancelled and annulled.
But later the king granted and willed that denizens should henceforth be quit of the said 19*d.* only on sacks of their own wool which would not be sent to Calais.

[Keeping the seas.]
36. Also, the commons pray: whereas it was formerly granted in your parliaments that the merchants of your kingdom should pay 6*d.* for every 20*s.* worth of merchandise and 2*s.* per tun of wine, because of the danger and injury which could happen to them or their merchandise on the sea for want of security in crossing and returning, which was granted for their greater security, and for the salvation of themselves, their merchandise and their estate, and from which grant they have gained no benefit, safe-conduct nor protection for themselves, and what is more, they use their own money to protect themselves, their merchandise and their estate; so that they are paying a double charge.
Wherefore, may it please your royal majesty to grant that they may and shall be relieved of the aforesaid grant and charge thus made.
Answer.
The king, by the advice of his council and his admirals, will ordain for the safe guard of the sea and of merchandise coming and going as best he can. And our lord the king wills that the said subsidy shall be entirely spent on that safe guard, and on nothing else.

[Victuallers in London.]
37. Also, the commons pray: for the greater tranquillity and nurture of peace amongst your lieges, and for the common good, that the citizens of your city of London be fully restored to their franchises and free customs in this parliament; and that it may please you, most redoubtable lord, of your special grace, to grant and confirm to your said citizens and their successors by your letters patent all their liberties and free customs, as wholly and fully as they or their predecessors had them in the time of any of your most noble progenitors, with the clause licet usi non fuerint, vel abusi fuerint; together with the franchises which they have in particular of your most gracious grant or confirmation: notwithstanding any statutes, judgements rendered, ordinances, or charters made or granted before this time to the contrary, both in the time of any of your said progenitors as well as in your own time, since the restraint on their liberties and free usages in the past has in many ways weakened and injured their estate, and been of no benefit to the kingdom as a whole. And that all vintners and victuallers, both fishmongers and others, together with their victuals coming to your said city, shall henceforth be under the governance and rule of the mayor and aldermen of the aforesaid city at the time, as was customary of old. And also to grant that no mayor of the said city henceforth shall take, or be forced to take, either in your exchequer, most feared lord, or elsewhere, any oath save the ancient oath used in the time of King Edward [III], your most noble grandfather, whom God absolve, notwithstanding any statute or ordinance made to the contrary.

---

²⁶This note occurs in the margin alongside the section below.
²⁷*Original* vins,

\[Responsio.]/
Le roi le voet.[28]

[Against suits prolonged to the cost of jurors.]
38. Item, prient les communes pur les gentz queux sont demurrantz es loigntismes parties du roialme: qe la ou une enqueste est joynte en aucun des voz courts, les jurrours sont destreintz de terme en terme, issint q'aucuns perdent par an pluis qe la value de lours terres, par cause qe la dite enqueste n'est pursuez au fyn par ceux qi sont parties; en grant empoverissement et destruccione des lieges suisditz.

Qe plese a vous, tresredoute seignour, granter qe apres ce qe les nouns de les jurrours soient retournez en aucune des dites courtes, et la cause touche le roy, q'il envoie ascun des soens en la paiis dont les jurrours sont, deinz un demy an apres l'enqueste joynte, pur terminer la cause susdite: ou autrement ordeigner qe les ditz jurrours ne soient perdantz. Et si la dite enqueste touche autres persones q'ils la pursuent en mesme la manere, ou autrement q'ils perdent leur cause, ou soient convictz d'icelle, issint
[Col. b] qe les ditz jurrours ne soient mys au tiel meschief et destruccione.

\[Responsio.]/
Accordez est qe desore en toutes maneres des plees en queux brief de nisi prius est grantable d'office, apres la grande destresse trois foitz serviz et retournez devaunt les justices vers la \juree,/ et surce les parties demandez, si nul des dites parties veulle pursure, ou qeles parties refusent d'avoir brief de nisi prius en le cas, adonqes, a la pursuite d'aucun d'iceux jurrours qi soit present, soit brief de nisi prius fait et grante: et ce auxibien en l'escheqer come aillours, et sur ce la loy parfourniz en chescun tiele cas, et la querele sanz delays mys a fyn, solonc /ce\ qe la loy demande.[29]

[Those convicted of fraud to be barred from their posts.]
39. Item, prient les communes qe par estatut soit ordenez qe desormes nul homme ou officer atteint ou convict d'aucune fauxine ou deceite faite, et par tiele \cause/ remuez en aucun de les courtes nostre seignour le roy, jammais, pur nul favour ne brocage, soit restitut a son office ou autre estat es dites courtes.
\[Responsio.]/
Le roy le voet, si einsi ne soit qe tielle persone ent eit sa grace especiale au contraire.

[Cheminage wrongfully levied.]
40. Item, prie la commune qe come il soit ordenez par l'estatut de foreste qe nul chimynage soit pris deinz foreste de nully cariant boys, carbons, fuail ou autre chose pur son oeps demesne, sinoun de ceux qi careont tiels choses pur les vendre et marchandier; la les ministres du foreste parmy le roialme preignent chimynage deinz foreste de touz maneres des gentz du pais, et autres, cariantz boys, carbones ou autre fuail a lour oeps propre a despendre en lour meisons; a tresgrant damage de poeple, et encontre la fourme de l'estatut avantdit.
Qe pleise a vostre tresgracious seignourie ent ordeigner remede.
\[Responsio.]/
Le roy voet qe l'estatut de la foreste, et les autres estatutz ent faitz estoisent en lour force et vertu; et si ascun se vorra pleindre en manere pluis especiale, monstre sa greivance, et droit lui ent serra fait.

---

[28] 7 Ric.2 c.11.
[29] 7 Ric.2 c.7.

Answer.
The king wills it.

[Against suits prolonged to the cost of jurors.]
38. Also, the commons pray for the people who live in distant parts of the realm: whereas when an inquest is held in one of your courts, the jurors are distrained from time to time, so that some lose, each year, more than the value of their lands, because the said inquest is not pursued to the end by the parties involved, to the great impoverishment and destruction of the aforesaid lieges.

May it please you, most redoubtable lord, to grant that after the names of the jurors are returned in any of the said courts, in the matter concerning the king, that he shall send one of his men to the county where the jurors are to be found, within half a year of the inquest being joined, to determine the said case: or otherwise to ordain that the said jurors shall not lose thereby. And if the said inquest concerns other persons, that they shall pursue it in the same way, or otherwise let them lose their case, or be convicted of the same, so
[Col. b] that the said jurors shall not be so troubled and ruined.
Answer.
It is agreed that henceforth, in all kinds of pleas in which a writ of nisi prius is grantable by office, after the great distress three times served and returned before the justices towards the jury, and thereupon the parties demanded, if none of the said parties wish to pursue, or if the parties refuse to have a writ of nisi prius in the case, then, at the suit of any of those jurors who are present, let a writ of nisi prius be made and granted: and that in the exchequer as elsewhere, and thereupon the law applied in each such case, and the complaint settled without delay, as the law demands.

[Those convicted of fraud to be barred from their posts.]
39. Also, the commons pray: that it be ordained by statute that henceforth no man or officer attainted or convicted of any fraud or deceit, and for that reason removed from office in any of the courts of our lord the king, be ever restored to his office or other estate in the said courts through favour or brokage.
Answer.
The king wills it, unless it be that such a person has his special grace to the contrary.

[Cheminage wrongfully levied.]
40. Also, the commons pray: whereas it was ordained by the Statute of the Forest that no cheminage should be taken in the forest from anyone carrying wood, coal, fuel, or anything else for his own use, excepting those who carried such items to sell or trade; yet the ministers of the forest throughout the kingdom take cheminage in the forest from all manner of local people and others carrying wool, coals or other fuel for their own use in their houses, to the very great injury of the people, and contrary to the aforesaid statute.

May it please your most gracious lordship to ordain a remedy for this.
Answer.
The king wills that the Statute of the Forest and the other statutes made thereon remain in force; and if anyone wishes to complain in some particular, let him explain his grievance and right shall be done him.

[Appeals against escheats.]

41.]/ Item, prie la commune qe la ou il estoit ordeignez par estatut en temps le roy Edward aiel nostre seignour le roy q'ore est, qe s'il /eit\ nul homme qe mette challenge ou cleym as terres seisez par enqueste d'office prise devant l'eschetour, qe l'eschetour mande l'enqueste en la chauncellerie deinz le moys apres les terres issint seisiz, et qe brief lui soit levere de certefier la cause de la seisine en la chauncellerie, et illoeqes soit oiez saunz delay a traverser l'office, ou autrement monstrer son droit; et d'illoeqes mandez devant le roy affaire final discucion sanz attendre autre mandement. Et en cas q'aucun viegne devant le chaunceller et monstre son droit, par quele demonstrance et bone evidence de son auncien droit et bone title, qe le chaunceller par sa bone discrecion, et avys du conseil s'il lui semble qe lui busoigne d'avoir conseil, q'il lesse et baille les terres issint en debat a tenant, rendant au roy la value, si au roy appartient, en manere come il et les autres chaunccellers devaunt lui ont fait devant ces hures de leur bone discrecion, issint qe il face seurete q'il ne ferra wast ne destruction tanqe il soit adjuggez, come pleinement appiert en le dit estatut. \[Nepurqant,]/ il est usez communement qe terres et tenementz seisez par tieles enquestes sont grantez par patentes de la chancellerie, as diverses gentz aucun foitz pursuantz tieles enquestes par malice pur lour profit demesne, ou as autres de lour covyne, devant ce qe ceux qe sont oustez par tieles enquestes poent venir a la courte pur les traverser. Paront, coment q'ils se offrent de traverser tieles enquestes il les covient suir brief de scire facias vers ceux qe les ont einsi par patentes, en quele suyte ils sont grandement delaiez par eide prier du roi, et en autre manere, devant qe le dit travers poet estre trie. Et en le mesne temps les *[Page iii-161]*

[Col. a] occupiours par les dites patentes parnont les profitz, et degastent les tenementz, a grande desheritance des pluseurs. Et coment qe trovez soit au derrain pur les compleignantz, et adjuggez soit q'ils eient restitucione ove les issues, ils ne sont restorez de rien sinoun de les terres et tenementz ensi degastez, a grant et importable damage des ditz compleignantz.

Qe plese a nostre seignour le roi de sa grace especiale grantir a sa dite commune qe nul ne soit ouste par cause de nule enqueste prise par office par brief ou par commission, tanqe mesmes les enquestes soient returnes en la chauncellerie, et les occupiours garniz par scire facias de respondre a certein jour. A quel jour s'ils viegnent et veullent traverser les dites enquestes, et trover seuretee de sauver les tenementz saunz wast, et de respondre au roy des issues, si trovez soit par le roy q'ils soient a ce receuz. Et si aucune patente soit grantez, ou autre riens fait a contraire, qe le chaunceller a plustost qe le chose soit a lui monstre face repeller la dite patente, et restorer le compleynant a sa possession, sanz garnir celuy a qi tiele patente soit grantez, ou autre occupiour par tiele cause, sibien du temps passe come de temps avenir.

\[*Responsio.*]/

~~Le roy voet et comande, sur grief paine, qe les eschetours facent desore duement retourner toutes les enquestes par eux prises deinz le terme, et sur la peine devant ces heures ordenez par estatut. Et enoultre est accordez par les seignours du roialme, si plest au roy, qe devant qe tielles enquestes soient returnez en la chauncellerie du roy nostre seignour, ou autrement, q'il soit certifiez de record en mesme sa chancellerie de la cause del seisine des tieux terres et tenementz, il ne ferra faire desore aucune patente des tielles terres et tenementz en debat a nully. Et encores, au fyn qe la partie ne soit desore en tiele manere mis en delay par tiele~~

[Appeals against escheats.]

[41.] Also, the commons pray: whereas it was ordained by a statute in the time of King Edward [III], grandfather of our lord the present king, that if any man disputed or claimed lands taken by inquest of office held before the escheator, that the escheator should send the inquest to the chancery within a month of the lands having been thus seized, and that a writ should be delivered to him certifying the reason for the seisin in the chancery, and there he should be heard without delay to renounce the office or otherwise prove his right; and from there it be sent before the king for final discussion to be held without awaiting any other mandate. And if any should come before the chancellor and demonstrate his claim, giving good evidence of his ancient claim and good title, that the chancellor at his good discretion, and the advice of his council if he consider counsel necessary, should release and deliver the lands thus in dispute to the tenant, who should pay the king their worth, if it pertain to the king, as he and other chancellors before him have done in the past at their good discretion, so that he will give surety not to waste or destroy them until it be adjudged, as plainly appears in the said statute. Nevertheless, it is common practice for lands and tenements seized upon such inquests to be granted by patents of the chancery to various people sometimes pursuing such inquests through malice for their own profit, or to others conspiring with them, before those who have been ousted by such inquests can come to the court to traverse them. As a result of which, although they offer to traverse such inquests, they have to sue a writ of scire facias against those who hold them thus by patent, in which suit they are greatly delayed by prayer in aid from the king, and in other ways, before the said traverse can be tried. And in the meantime the *[Page iii-161]*

[Col. a] occupiers of the said patents take the profits and waste the tenements, to the great disinheritance of many. And even if it be found and adjudged at last that the plaintiffs should have restitution with the issues, they regain nothing except the lands and tenements thus wasted, to the great and unbearable injury of the said plaintiffs.

May it please our lord the king of his special grace to grant to his said commons that none be ousted because of any inquest held by office, writ or commission, until the same inquests be returned in the chancery and the occupiers warned by scire facias to answer on a certain day. On which day, if they appear and wish to traverse the said inquests, and guarantee to tend rather than waste the lands, and to answer to the king for the issues, so let it be found by the king that they shall be received thereto. And if any patent be granted, or anything else issued to the contrary, that the chancellor, as soon as the matter be put to him, shall repeal the said patent and restore the plaintiff to his possession, without warning the person to whom such a patent was granted or any other occupier on similar terms, both of time past and time to come.

Answer.

~~The king wills and commands, on pain of grievous penalty, that the escheators shall henceforth duly return the inquests taken by them during the term, and on pain of the penalty previously ordained by statute. Furthermore, it is agreed by the lords of the realm, if it please the king, that before such inquests are returned to the chancery of our lord the king, or otherwise, that the reason for the seisin of such lands and tenements be placed on record in his same chancery, so that from now on no patent will be granted to anyone for such lands and tenements in dispute. In addition, to the end that the party shall not in future be delayed in such a~~

suite de scire facias, le roy de sa pluis habundante grace ad grantez q'il attendra, et se vorra de tout abstiner, par un moys proschein ensuant apres les ditz retournes et certificacion affaires desore en tieu cas en sa dite chancellerie, de faire tielles patentes: deinz quiel terme la partie purra venir et traverser l'office si lui semble affaire, et y resceivre qe la loy doune. Ne ne ferra faire auxint nostre seignour le roy aucune tiele patente, de tieulx terres et tenementz esteantz en debat, a aucuny estrange persone pendant ent tiel travers et plee nient discus, n'autrement ferra contre la fourme de l'estatutz faitz en ce cas devant ceste heure. Et si desore aucune patente soit faite au contraire de ceste grante et ordinance, qe ce soit tenuz pur nulle et de nule value. Mais quant a ce q'est demandez des patentes faites devant ceste heure, se vorra adviser.[30]

Vacat, quia dominus rex noluit istam responsionem affirmare, set verius illam negavit pro majori parte, dicens, Soit usez come devant en temps de ses nobles progenitours rois d'Engleterre ent ad este \usez;/ et ideo cancellatur et dampnatur.[31]

way by a suit of scire facias, the king of his most abundant grace has granted that he will desist and entirely abstain from granting such patents for a month after the said returns and certification to be made henceforth in such causes in his said chancery: during which time the party may come and traverse the office if appropriate, and receive there whatever the law grants. Neither also will our lord the king cause any such patents to be issued concerning such lands and tenements in dispute to any third party during such a traverse or unsettled plea, nor will he do so in any other way contrary to the form of the statutes made thereon in the past. And if in future any patent be issued contrary to this grant and ordinance, it shall be held at naught and invalid. But as for that which is requested concerning patents issued in the past, he will consider it further.

Cancelled, because the lord king does not wish to affirm this answer, but indeed refuses it for the most part, saying, Let it be done as it was done before in the time of his noble progenitors the kings of England; and therefore it is cancelled and annulled.

[Actions of novel disseisin to recover rent.]

42[32] Item, prie la commune qe purce q'en cas qe tenementz esteantz es diverses countees soient chargiez a aucuny de aucun rente qe soit a derer, n'y ad autre recoverer a l'entent des pluseurs, forsqe a destreindre pur mesme le rente: a quel recoverer sont plusours foitz grantz delays et perils, come rescous ou replevyne; ou si tieles tenementz gisassent fresches, et nulle destresse feust trove, homme serroit de leger sanz recoverer.

Par quoy, pur remede en certein et amendement faire sur tieles delaies, perils et doutes, plese a nostre seignour le roi en cest present parlement ordener par estatut qe le disseisi de tiel rent en tiel cas puisse avoir son recoverer s'il veulle par assise de novelle disseisine, a tenir en la confinye des countees deinz queux les tenementz sont ou serront issint chargez, pur estre triez par gentz de mesmes les countees, semblablement come la loy est de commune en un contee appendant as tenementz en autre countee. Et qe cest estatut tiegne lieu sibien des disseisines faites devant ore come des disseisines affaires en tout temps avenir. Et qe briefs originales et patentes en tiel cas en la chancellerie soient surce faitz

[*Col. b*] selonc l'advis des justices, issint q'ils puissent covenablement vadler sur tiele matire.

\[*Responsio.*]/

Il plest au roy.[33]

Membrane 3

[Actions of novel disseisin to recover rent.]

[42.] Also, the commons pray: whereas in cases where tenements being in various counties are charged to someone for a rent which is in arrears, and many have no other recovery except to distrain for the same rent: in recovering which there are often great delays and risks involved, such as rescue and replevin; or if such tenements lie fallow, and no distress can be taken, one can easily fail to recover them.

Accordingly, for a certain remedy and particular redress of such delays, may it please our lord the king in this present parliament to ordain by statute that the disseised of such rent in such a cause may have his recovery if he will by assize of novel disseisin, to be held within the confines of the county in which the tenements are or shall be thus charged, to be tried by men of the same counties, as the law is concerning common in one county appendant to tenements in another county. And that this statute shall hold for disseisins made before now as well as disseisins to be made in all time to come. And that original writs and patents in such a case in the chancery shall be made thereon

[*Col. b*] in accordance with the advice of the justices, so that they might be suitable and valid in this matter.

Answer.

It pleases the king.

[Garrisons of castles in the marches.]

43[34] Item, prie la commune q'il pleise a nostre seignour le roy ordeigner qe touz ceux q'ont chastelx ou forteresses pres les marches d'Escoce, qe ceux qi preignent les profitz et revenues d'icelles soient tenuz de les garder suffisantement, et les estuffer des gentz et vitails, solonc la quantitee d'iceux, sur peril d'aucun certeintee ent a ordeigner par nostre seignour le roy: issint qe ses lieges, le roy, et le paiis ne soient endamagez ne destrutz a cause d'icelle. Et qe gentz estranges qi serront ordeignez pur le lieutenant du roy celles parties puissent estre entour son corps, et pur garde des chastelx et villes du roy es marches susditz tantsoulement.

[Garrisons of castles in the marches.]

[43.] Also, the commons pray: that it may please our lord the king to ordain that all those who have castles and fortresses near the marches of Scotland, and those who take profits and revenue from the same, shall be obliged to guard them adequately and provision them with men and victuals, according to the quantity thereof, on pain of a penalty to be ordained hereon by our lord the king: so that his lieges, the king, and the country shall not be endangered nor destroyed thereby. And that strangers who are appointed as the king's lieutenants in these parts shall be there in person, and guard the king's castles and towns in the aforesaid marches only.

---

[30] This whole passage has been crossed out.
[31] This note occurs in the margin alongside the section below.
[32] *Original* 41.
[33] 7 Ric.2 c.10.
[34] *Original* 42.

\[Responsio.]/
Le roy le voet et l'ad grantez.

[Curbs on commissions of oyer et terminer.]
44[35] Item, prie la commune qe come oiers et terminers sont grantez trope legerement, et devant qe les pursuantz aient fait serement qe leur querele est loiale, la quele chose ne solet estre faite par tiele manere, qar devant ces hures y n'avoit nules grantz s'il ne feust de orrible trespas, et par creable proeve qe la seute feust verroie. Et sont meint foit pursuiz encontre executours pur choses qe deussent avoir este faites par lour testatour et en temps de son vivant coment q'ils ne sont pas nomez executours en le brief; dont grant damage en purra venir, qar nul se osera entremettre a prendre la charge d'executrie, si remede n'y soit mys.

Qe pleise a vostre tresgraciouse seignourie, desore enavant nules grantir, s'il n'est par bone deliberacion de vostre noble conseil, et par bone et loial proeve come de droit appartient. Et si aucuns soient grantez a contraire q'ils soient repellez.

\[Responsio.]/
Y a estatutz faitz en le cas, les queux le roy voet qe soient tenuz et gardez, salvant nientmains au roy nostre seignour toutdys sa regalie et prerogatif entierment.

[Allowances on farms of counties.]
45[36] Item, prient les communes: qe come diverses hundredes, et autres commoditees appurtenantz al plusours countees en Engleterre, sont donez sibien par vos nobles progenitours come par vous, tresredoute seignour, as diverses seignours et autres gentz; et nient contresteantz tielx douns, les viscontz de tielx countees qi pur le temps sont acomptent et paient l'entierte pur les ditz countees si avant come ils paierent au temps qe les ditz hundredes et les autres commodites furent entierment annexes as ditz countes, a grant damage, empoverisement et defesance de ditz viscontz.

Par quoi pleise a vostre tresgraciouse seignourie ordeigner en ceo present parlement qe desormes due allowance se face as ditz viscontz qi pur le temps serront sur leur acompt pur les ditz hundredes et les autres commoditees ensi donez; ou autrement qe les ditz hundredes et les autres commoditees puissent estre rejoyntz as ditz countes, come ils furent /d'auncien\ temps.

\[Responsio.]/
Ceux qi se sentent grevez en especial monstrent as chanceller et tresorer lour grevance, et par especial les causes pur quelles ils serroient mys einsi a perde. Et le roi voet qe les ditz chanceller et tresorer de temps en temps facent tielle descharge ou allouance as ditz compleignantz sur lours accomptes en celle partie, qe par lour discrecione et bon advis semblera estre resonable, et doit suffire en le cas.

[Sales of wine and of fish in London.]
46[37] Item, prient les communes qe les estatutz faitz les ans de vostre regne quint et sisme sur la vente de vyns, et pessoners de Londres,[38] soient repellez et adnullez en toutes pointz par proclamacione ent affaire par toute la roialme, sibien au profit et ease des seignours come de toute la commune.

Answer.
The king wills it and has granted it.

[Curbs on commissions of oyer et terminer.]
[44.] Also, the commons pray: whereas oyer and terminers are granted too lightly, and before the suitors have sworn an oath that their complaint is genuine, which used never to happen in such a fashion, for before this time none was granted unless it were for a terrible offence, and unless it had been credibly proved that the suit was genuine. And suits are often brought against executors for things which ought to have been dealt with by their testator in his lifetime even though they were not named executors in the writ; as a result of which great trouble may arise, since none will dare involve himself in undertaking the charge of execution unless a remedy be set in place.

May it please your most gracious lordship, to grant none from now on, except by the good deliberation of your noble council, and by such good and trustworthy proof as pertains to right. And if any be granted to the contrary, that they be repealed.

Answer.
Statutes have been made thereon, which the king wills to be upheld and enforced, nevertheless saving always to our lord the king his regality and prerogative intact.

[Allowances on farms of counties.]
[45.] Also, the commons pray: whereas various hundreds and other liberties pertaining to various counties in England have been granted by your noble progenitors as well as by you, most redoubtable lord, to various lords and other men; and notwithstanding such gifts, the sheriffs of such counties at the time account and pay the whole sum for the said counties just as they paid it at the time when the said hundreds and other liberties were wholly attached to the said counties, to the great injury, impoverishment and ruin of the said sheriffs.

On account of which may it please your most gracious lordship to ordain in this present parliament that, henceforth, due allowance be made to the said sheriffs who shall be in office for the said hundreds and the other liberties thus granted; or otherwise that the said hundreds and other liberties be re-united with the said counties, as they were of old.

Answer.

Let those who feel themselves especially injured explain their grievance to the chancellor and treasurer, and in particular the reasons for which they will suffer loss. And the king wills that the said chancellor and treasurer from time to time shall grant such relief or allowance in this matter to the said plaintiffs on their accounts as may seem reasonable and sufficient to them in the circumstances by their discretion and good advice.

[Sales of wine and of fish in London.]
[46.] Also, the commons pray: that the statutes made in the fifth and sixth years of your reign, on the sale of wine and the fishmongers of London, be repealed and annulled in all respects by proclamation thereon to be made throughout the realm, both for the profit and ease of the lords, and for the commons.

---

[35] *Original* 43.
[36] *Original* 44.
[37] *Original* 45.
[38] 5 Ric.2 c.4; 6 Ric. 2 st.1 c.11.

Page iii-162
\[Responsio.]/

Le roy de sa grace voet qe les ordinances de pessoners et des vyns derrainement faitz soient de tout oustez et repellez; esteant nientmains l'estatut des vins fait l'an .xxxvij.^{me} du noble roi Edward aielle nostre seignour le q'orest entierment en sa force et vertu,[39] salvez nientmeins a nostre seignour le roy toutz les forfaitures a luy appartenir par vertu del derrain /ordenance\ des vins, quant al temps passez.[40]

[Defence of Scarborough.]

47[41] Item, prient les communes pur les povres burgeises et gentz de vostre ville de Scardeburgh': qe come la dite ville est assise tout overt sur la meer, et de jour en autre est assaille par barges et pleusours autres niefs sibien d'Escoce come de France, Flemmynges, et autres enemys nostre seignour le roy, parensi qe plusours gentz mariners du dite ville et costes illoeqes aient perduz lours niefs a la value de deux mille*li.* q'ont este pris ore tarde par les ditz enemys; issint qe la dite ville, et les coustees la environe sont en point d'estre anientiz et destruitz si hastive remede n'ent soit fait. Sur quoy aucuns des ditz povres burgeys ont achatez une barge et une balynger pur la defense encontre les ditz enemys, les queux vesseaux les ditz burgeys ne poent sanz eide avoir sustenir, ne mayutenir ovesqe gentz defensables encontre les ditz enemys.

Qe plese a nostre tresredoute seignour le roy et son bon conseil, considerer les meschiefs suisditz, et les perils qe purront avenir au dite ville, et les coustes la environe, grantir commissione directe al counte de Northumbr', q'est lour surveour par patent nostre seignour le roy, et as baillifs et autres gentz de mesme la ville, et q'ils poent prendre gentz defensables pur l'estuffure du dite barge et balynger as toutesfoitz qe mestier serra, sibien par les coustes suisditz come par la dite ville, pur la defense suisdite: et q'ils poent lever, pur la sustenance des dites gentz, barge et balynger, pur la defense suisdite, c'estassaver de chescun last de harang illoeqes venant .xij. *d.* et de chescun cent de grant pessone a tant, et de chescun manere de marchandise .vi. *d.* Et qe ce poet estre levable sibien des foreins come des denszeins, issint par les coustees la environe, parentre la ville de Hertilpole et l'eawe de Hunbre.

\[Responsio.]/

Le roy, par l'advis de son conseil et de ses admiralx, ent ordeignera de remede tielle come mieutz lui semblera affaire.

[Liberties of Scarborough.]

48[42] Item, prient les communes pur les burgeises et gentz de vostre ville de Scardeburghe: qe come ils avoient certeines franchises par chartres des progenitours nostre dit seignour le roy, sibien devaunt temps de memoire come puis; queles franchises en grande partie, aucunes par estatutz, et aucunes par grantz faites as autres persones, leur sont toluz, en perpetuel anientissement des dites ville et burgeis, paront ils ne poent demandes n'autres charges nostre dit seignour le roy supporter, come leurs ancestres et lours predecessours soloient, si gracious remede ne leur soit mys.

Qe plese a nostre dit seignour le roy, considerez les grantz et sovent charges et perdes queux les ditz burgeises et tenantz ont sovent suffertz, sibien en grandes perdes par enemys sur la meer, come en autre manere, grantir as ditz burgeises q'ils,

Answer.

The king of his grace wills that the ordinances on fishmongers and wine lately made be completely ousted and repealed; nevertheless, the statute on wine made in the thirty-seventh year of the noble king Edward, grandfather of our lord the present king, shall remain fully in force and valid, and saving, nevertheless, to our lord the king all forfeitures pertaining to him by virtue of the last ordinance on wine, from time past.

[Defence of Scarborough.]

[47.] Also, the commons pray for the poor burgesses and people of your town of Scarborough: whereas the said town stands open to the sea, and from one day to the next is attacked by barges and various other ships from Scotland and from France, and by Flemings and other enemies of our lord the king, so that many mariners of the said town and coasts there have lost ships which have been lately captured by the said enemies, to the value of £2,000; so that the said town, and the coasts surrounding it are on the point of being ruined and destroyed unless swift remedy is found. In view of which, some of the said poor burgesses have bought a barge and a balinger for their defence against the said enemies, the upkeep of which vessels the said burgesses cannot bear without help, nor equip them with fighting men against the said enemies.

May it please our most redoubtable lord the king and his good council to consider the aforesaid troubles and the dangers which threaten the said town and the surrounding coasts, and grant a commission addressed to the earl of Northumberland, who is their supervisor by patent of our lord the king, and to the bailiffs and other people of the same town, to raise fighting men to crew the said barge and balinger, as often as need be, as well from the aforesaid coasts as the said town, for the aforesaid defence: and levy a sum for the support of the said men, barge and balinger involved in the aforesaid defence, namely, 12*d.* on each last of herrings coming there and as much on each hundred large fish, and 6*d.* on every kind of merchandise. And that it shall be raised from strangers as well as denizens on the neighbouring coasts, between the town of Hartlepool and the mouth of the Humber.

Answer.

The king, with the advice of his council and his admirals, will ordain such a remedy as seems best to him.

[Liberties of Scarborough.]

[48.] Also, the commons pray for the burgesses and people of your town of Scarborough: whereas they have certain franchises by charters of the progenitors of our said lord the king, both from time immemorial and since; which franchises have been taken from them for the most part, some by statute, and some by grants made to other persons, to the lasting ruin of the said town and burgesses, as a result of which they cannot meet the demands or other charges of our said lord the king as their ancestors and predecessors used to, unless gracious remedy be given them.

May it please our said lord the king, considering the great and frequent burdens and losses which the said burgesses and tenants have often suffered, both in great losses inflicted by enemies on the sea, as well as in other ways, to grant

---

[39] 27 Edw.3 st.1 cc.6-8.
[40] 7 Ric.2 c.11.
[41] *Original* 46.
[42] *Original* 47.

lours heirs, et successours, aient et enjoient toutz lours franchises, usages et libertees, si entierment come lours ancestres et predecessours les avoient en temps passe, par vertu de lours chartres avauntdites.

\[*Responsio.*]/

Eient ils lours franchises, usages et libertes avantditz par manere q'eles sont demandez, nient contresteant estatut, grant ou ordinance fait au contraire. Et sur cest grace le roy voet q'ils aient lettres patentes, tielles come soient busoignables.

[Mainpernors to meet liabilities of defaulting defendants.]

49[43] Item, prient les communes: qe come il est usez en le roialme, quant un homme ad pursuiz devers un autre par brief de dette, de trespas ou d'acompt, si

[Col. b] avant qe le defendant soit arestuz par son corps par brief de capias, et amesnez devant les justices, et les parties ont pleidez et jour de triement donez, a quel jour la partie defendant ove touz ses biens et chateux se retreit hors du paiis, et les maynparnours soulement facent fyn a nostre seignour le roy.

Pleise a nostre seignour le roy en ce present parlement ensi ordeigner en tiel cas: primes, qe les maynparnours soient suffisantz selonc la quantitee du chose demande: et s'ils ne rendent le corps devant les justices au jour assigne q'ils soient chargez de respondre devers les parties a tant qe le defendant, s'il feust la en propre persone.

\[*Responsio.*]/

Assentuz est qe es ditz cas /et\ touz autres ou menprise est trovez, et brief de supersedeas est grantable, si les persones meinprises ne viegnent point devant ses justices al jour compris en dit meinprise, et par tant le pleintif soit mys en delay; \en/ tielx cas soient les ditz meinparnours respoignables au pleintif d'une certeine somme, a limiter par la discrecion et advys des justices; eiant joust consideracion al quantitee des damages et perdes de mesme le pleintif, et au qualitee de la chose q'est demande. Et durera ceste ordinance en assay tanqe al prochein parlement tantsoulement.[44]

[Aliens not to hold benefices.]

50[45] Item, prient les communes: qe come pluseurs estatutz et ordinances aient este faitz avant ces hures des dignitees et autres benifices electives deinz mesme le roialme, queux sont donez as aliens, et aucun foitz as apertz enemiz nostre seignour le roy et de son roialme, paront le tresor est tret hors du roialme, le conseil du roialme descovert et pluseurs autres meschiefs ent aviegnent, come plus pleinement appiert es ditz estatutz et ordinances.[46] Et nient contresteantz celles estatutz, mesmes les aliens si preignent possession des dignitees de jour en autre, et sibien les ditz dignitees et benefices electives come autres benefices en chescune partie d'Engleterre occupient, et y ont lours procuratours et fermers sibien d'estranges nacions come du roialme mesmes, contre l'ordinance ent nadgairs faite en vostre parlement.

Qe plese, en salvacione de droit de vostre coroune, et pur commune profit avauntdit, faire ordener et establir en ce parlement qe toutz les ditz estatutz et ordinances soient mises en due execucione; et tielment ordener qe les franches elections faites et affaires deinz vostre roialme purront esteer come ils soloient en temps passe; et nule persone de quelconqe degree, estat ou condicione q'il soit, alien ou denszein, soit desore procuratour, fermer ou administrour des ditz aliens

to the said burgesses that they, their heirs and successors, may have and enjoy all their franchises, usages and liberties as fully as their ancestors and predecessors had them in the past, by virtue of their aforesaid charters.

Answer.

Let them have their aforesaid franchises, usages and liberties as they request, notwithstanding any statute, grant or ordinance made to the contrary. And concerning this grace, the king wills that they have such letters patent as may be needed.

[Mainpernors to meet liabilities of defaulting defendants.]

[49.] Also, the commons pray: whereas it is the practice in the kingdom that when a man has sued another by writ of debt, trespass or account, in such

[Col. b] a way that the defendant person is attached by writ of capias and led before the justices, and the parties having pleaded and been given a date of trial, on that day the defending party with all his goods and chattels leaves the county, and only the mainpernors answer to our lord the king.

May it please our lord the king in this present parliament thus to ordain in such case: first, that the mainpernors have the means to bear the cost of any judgment: and that if they do not appear before the justices on their appointed day, they be charged to answer towards the parties for the defendant, as if he were there in person.

Answer.

It is agreed that in this particular case and in all others where mainprise is involved and a writ of supersedeas is grantable, if the persons bailed do not appear at all before the justices on the day specified in the said mainprise, and thus the plaintiff is delayed; then let the said mainpernors be answerable to the plaintiff for a certain sum, to be determined at the discretion and advice of the justices; giving just consideration to the sum of the damage and loss suffered by the plaintiff, and the nature of the thing demanded. And this ordinance shall remain on trial only until the next parliament.

[Aliens not to hold benefices.]

[50.] Also, the commons pray: whereas many statutes and ordinances have been made in the past on dignities and other elective benefices within the same realm, which are given to aliens, and sometimes to open enemies of our lord the king and his kingdom, whereby treasure is withdrawn from the kingdom, the counsels of the realm disclosed, and many other troubles arise, as more plainly appears in the said statutes and ordinances. Yet notwithstanding those statutes the same aliens still take possession of dignities from one day to the next, and occupy both the said dignities and elective benefices as well as other benefices in all parts of England, and there they have their proctors and farmers from foreign lands as well as from the kingdom itself, contrary to the ordinance recently made thereon in your parliament.

May it please you, to preserve the right of your crown, and, for the aforesaid common profit, to ordain and decree in this parliament that all the said statutes and ordinances be duly enforced; and so ordain that free elections conducted and to be conducted in your kingdom may continue as they have in the past; and that no person of whatsoever degree, estate or condition he may be, alien or denizen, shall henceforth be

---

[43] *Original* 48.
[44] 7 Ric.2 c.17.
[45] *Original* 49.
[46] 3 Ric.2 c.4.

de nul manere de leur benefices deinz le dit roialme, sur peine de forfaiture de quant q'ils purront forfaire en corps et en biens.
\[*Responsio.*]/

L'estatut fait devant ceste heure estoise en sa force, et soit mys en bone et due execucione, adjoustant a ycelle qe toutz aliens purchaceantz tielx benefices en Engleterre, et en lours propres persones preignantz possessione d'iceulx benefices, ou les ditz benefices occupiantz de fait deinz le roiaume avauntdit, soit il a lour oeps propre ou al oeps d'autry, sanz especial congie du roi, soient desore compris en dit estatut; et enoultre eient et encourgent en toutz pointz tielx peines et forfaitures come sont ordenez par un autre estatut fait en l'an del regne du noble roy Edward aielle nostre seignour le roy .xxv.^{e} contre ceulx qi purchacent provisions des abbeyes et priories.[47]

[Commissions issued without due process; petitions in parliament.]
51[48] Item, prient les communes: qe desormes nule comissione soit directe hors de la chancellerie, ne lettre de prive seal, pur destourber la possessione d'aucun liege le roy, sanz due proces et respons du partie, et especialment quant la partie est prest de faire ce qe la loy demande: et qe toutes tieles commissions faites devaunt ces heures, et directes encontre la loy de la terre, soient en ce parlement repellez. Et q'en ce present parlement, et chescun qe serra, soient toutes les
[Page iii-163]
[Col. a] billes respunduz et endossez des toutes les liges qe ne poent avoir autre remede qe par peticione, eiantz consideration de les grantz diseases et damages qe les lieges q'ont longement pursuiz avoient et ont de jour en autre tanqe /due\ remede ent soit ordenez.
\[*Responsio.*]/

Ceux qi se sentent grevez monstrent lour grevance en especial a chanceller, /qi\ lour purvoiera de remede. Et quant as ditz peticions et billes, le roy voet qe celles qe ne purront estre esploitez sanz parlement soient esploitez en parlement, et celles qe purront estre esploitez par le conseil du roy soient mis devaunt le conseil, et celles billes qe sont de grace soient baillez au roy mesmes.
Membrane 2

[Accounts for indentured service.]
52[49] Item, prient les communes: qe come les seignours de vostre roialme, et autres voz lieges travaillantz outre la mier en diverses viages en voz guerres, quant ils ont receuz vos gages pur eux et leur retenue, et sur ceo receuz par voz officers a leur monstre, et vous servy bien et loialment ovesqe leur dit retenue leur terme durant ou pluis. Et ceo nient contresteant mandementz issent hors de vostre escheqer sur toutes leur terres, pur vous rendre arere l'argent q'ils ont ensi receuz come ils vous n'eussent nul service fait, ou come le dit argent leur feust apprestez a rendre arere a un certein jour: et s'ils viegnent en vostre dit escheqer, monstrant qe eux et leur dit retenue vous ont serviz leur covenant pur le dit argent q'ensi leur est demandez, et sur ceo offrer leur accompt, ils serront taryez, par cause q'ils senteront qe le roy leur devera, ou par defaute q'ils ne poent avoir garrant resonable un an ou deux; as grantz costages et destruccion de eux. Et si ascun de eux moerge avant q'il avera acomptez, toutz ses terres et biens serront seisez et pris en vos maynes par la dite cause,

proctor, farmer or administrator of the said aliens in any way for their benefices in the said kingdom, on pain of forfeiting whatever they can forfeit in body and goods.
Answer.

Let the statute made before this time remain in force and be duly executed, adding to the same that all aliens purchasing such benefices in England, and taking possession of those benefices in person, or occupying the said benefices in the aforesaid realm, whether for their own personal use or the use of another, without special permission of the king, shall henceforth be included in the said statute; and further they shall suffer and incur in all respects such penalties and forfeitures as are ordained by another statute made in the twenty-fifth year of the reign of the noble king Edward, grandfather of our lord the king [1351], against those who purchase provisions of abbeys and priories.

[Commissions issued without due process; petitions in parliament.]
[51.] Also, the commons pray that henceforth no commission be directed out of the chancery, nor letter of privy seal, to interfere with the possession of any king's liege, without due process and answer from the party, and especially when the party is ready to do that which the law demands: and that all such commissions made before this time and directed contrary to the law of the land be repealed in this parliament. And that in this parliament, and all those to come, all the
[Page iii-163]
[Col. a] bills which cannot gain remedy except by petition shall be answered and endorsed for all lieges, bearing in mind the great misfortunes and injuries which the lieges, who have sued at length, have endured and endure from one day to the next until due remedy be ordained.
Answer.

Let those who feel aggrieved explain their particular grievance to the chancellor, who will provide them with a remedy. And as for the said petitions and bills, the king wills that those which cannot be dealt with outside parliament be considered in parliament, and those which can be settled by the king's council be placed before the council, and those bills which concern grace be submitted to the king himself.

[Accounts for indentured service.]
[52.] Also, the commons pray: whereas when the lords of your kingdom and your other lieges employed overseas on various expeditions in your wars have received wages for themselves and their retinue from your officers at their muster, and have served you well and loyally with their said retinue for the duration of their term or longer. Yet notwithstanding that, mandates are issued from your exchequer on all their lands, ordering them to return to you the money they have thus received as if they had done you no service, or as if the said money had been lent them to be repaid on a certain day: and if they come to your said exchequer showing that they and their said retinue have served you according to their covenant for the said money which is demanded of them, and offer to account for that, they are delayed, because they believe that the king owes them their due, or by default they lack a reasonable warrant for one or two years, to their great expense and ruin. And if any of them should die before they have accounted, all his lands and goods are seized and taken into your hands for the said reason, without any return.

---
[47] 25 Edw.3 st.4; 7 Ric 2 c.12.
[48] *Original* 50.
[49] *Original* 51.

sanz nul retourn. Et par celle voie sont pluseurs de voz ditz lieges destruitz et desheritez, encontre resoun et bone foye. Qe pleise a vostre haute magestee et gratiouse seignourie, pur Dieu, et en oevere de charitee, ordeigner par estatut en ce present parlement qe desore enavant nules tieux mandementz plus ne issent hors de vostre courte par tiele cause, mais a leur retourne en paiis a leur requeste franchement prendre leur acompt par leur endentures, sanz les tarier ou attendre autre garant. Et s'ils soient duement trovez en vostre dette qe le dit dette soit pris de eux, si grace ne poent avoir. Et si duement soit trovez qe vous leur deivez q'ils soient bien paiez, ou prestement bien assignez. Et qe toutz les prestez q'ensi issent hors de vostre escheker sur les terres de vos lieges pur tieles causes du temps de vostre noble aiel, qe Dieux assoille, soient desore dampnez et adnullez, sanz pluis les mettre en demande, qar quant ils ont serviz leur covenant ce ne serroit my droit de prendre de eux l'argent arere. Entendant, tresredoute seignour q'en ceo fesant vous ferrez charitee et grant almoigne.

\[Responsio.]/
Celui qi se sente grevez en especial sue au conseil le roy, et droit lui serra fait.

[Presentations to benefices during the voidance of temporalities.]
53^{50} Item, prient les communes: qe come le roy Edward vostre aiel, qi Dieux assoille, l'an de son regne cynquantisme, entre autres remissiones et graces q'il fist a ses liegees deinz sa regalie, graunta q'il ne ferroit collacione, presentement, ne doneson a nul benefice de seint esglise par cause des voidancez des temporaltees des ercheveschies, eveschies, abbeies, priories, et autres maisons de religion en sa mayne esteantz deinz sa regalie suisdite, devant le .xvme jour de Feverer l'an de son regne .l.^{me}; mais toutz collacions, presentementz et donesons des tielx benefices, des queux ne furent adeptez corporele possessione devant le dit .xvme jour de Feverer, de sa grace especiale revoca, cassa et adnulla, come plus pleynement piert par la dite grante: et vos ligees d'Irland sont reulez et governez par les loyes, estatutz et ordinances faitez en Engleterre auxi avant
[Col. b] come ceux d'Engleterre.
Qe pleise de vostre grace especiale fair plener declarisement del grante suisdite, issint q'il puisse estre effectuele et de force en toutz poyntz, sibien deinz vostre dite terre d'Irland come il soit en Engleterre, et ceo de tout temps limite en la grante avandite faite par nostre dit seignour le roy, qi Dieux assoille.

\[Responsio.]/
Le roy s'advisera.

[Citations to distant ecclesiastical courts.]
54^{51} Item, prient les communes: qe come ils sont souvent grevez et destrutz par outrageouse costages, a cause q'en loy de seynt esglise ils sont souvent summonez et garniz en diverses causes d'apparoir en estranges paiis devant les ordinaires par long chemyne de leur demoere, sibien a la suyte de courte come a suyte de partie a la foiz, plus pur les grever qe pur ascune cause droiturele, et pur singuler profit des gentz de seinte esglise, et universel damage as ditz communes.
Qe pleise ordeigner qe tiels causes soyent terminez en paiis ou les parties sont demurantz, pur eschuir costages et perillouses chemyns pur greindre ease de lour simple estate; eantz regard q'ils sont souvent tailliez as subsides nostre seignour le roy.

And by those means, many of your said lieges are ruined and disinherited, contrary to reason and good faith.
May it please your high majesty and gracious lordship, for the love of God and by way of charity, to ordain a statute in this present parliament that henceforth no more such mandates shall issue from your court for such a reason, but that on the return of your lieges to the country, at their request their account on their indentures shall be freely taken, without them being delayed or having to await another warrant. And if it be duly found in your debt, that the said debt should be taken from them, unless they have grace. And if it is duly found that you owe them their due, that they shall be fully paid, or at once well assigned. And that all the prests thus issued from your exchequer on the lands of your lieges for such reasons from the time of your noble grandfather, whom God absolve, be henceforth cancelled and annulled without further demands, for once they have served their covenant it would not be right to take the money back; on the understanding, most redoubtable lord, that in so doing, you will be bestowing charity and great alms.

Answer.
Let anyone who feels particularly aggrieved sue to the king's council, and right shall be done him.

[Presentations to benefices during the voidance of temporalities.]
[53.] Also, the commons pray: whereas the king Edward, your grandfather, whom God absolve, in the fiftieth year of his reign, amongst other remissions and graces which he granted to his lieges in his regality, granted that he would not exercise collation, presentation, nor gift of any benefice of holy church occasioned by vacancies of the temporalities of archbishoprics, bishoprics, abbeys, priories and other religious houses being in his hands within his aforesaid regality, before 15 February in the fiftieth year of his reign [1376]; but all collations, presentations and gifts of such benefices which were not in corporal possession before the said 15 February, he revoked, cancelled and annulled of his special grace, as appears more fully in the said grant; and your lieges of Ireland are ruled and governed by the laws, statutes and ordinances made in England as are
[Col. b] those of England.
May it please you of your special grace to make a fuller declaration of the aforesaid grant, so that it may be effective and valid in all respects within your said land of Ireland as it is in England, and that for the time appointed in the aforesaid grant made by our said lord the king, whom God absolve.

Answer.
The king will consider it further.

[Citations to distant ecclesiastical courts.]
[54.] Also, the commons pray: whereas they are often grieved and ruined by outrageous expense, because by the law of holy church they are often summoned and warned in various causes to appear before the ordinaries far from where they live, at the suit of the court as well as at suit of a party on occasion, rather to grieve them than for any rightful purpose, and to the singular profit of the men of holy church, and the general injury of the said commons.
May it please you to ordain that such cases be determined in the county or parts where they dwell, to avoid the expense and perilous travel for the greater ease of their simple estate; bearing in mind that they are often taxed for the subsidies of our lord the king.

---
^{50}Original 52.
^{51}Original 53.

\[Responsio.]/

Le roy parlera as prelatz, pur fair owele droit as toutz lours subgitz en le pluis esee manere q'ils purront.

[Licences for beneficed aliens.]

55[52] Item, prient les communes: q'il pleise a nostre tresredoute seignour le roi considerer les grandes resons monstrez as diverses parlementz en son temps, a l'effect qe nul aliene ne serroit beneficez dedeinz son roialme, et les bones ordinances sur ce faitez, si ne fuist celle excepcione q'estoit faite de licencie especial a doner par nostre dit seignour le roy as ceux aliens; parmy quelle excepcione diverses persones de son roialme ont pursuiz pur tiel licence, pur leur singuler profit, au plesir de cardinalx, et autrement: paront les benefices sont occupiez par aliens a grant fuysoun, et pluseurs unquore vacantz de fait, dont tielx aliens ont ferme esperance de leur purchacer licence de nostre dit seignour le roy par tielx meens come dit est. Et coment par cause de la guerre ore apparante des Escots serroit bien mestier, qe toutz les benefices par decea fuissent occupiez par gentz de mesme la roialme, et en ycelles demurantz; come par la demoere personele des tielx persones et de leur familiers, et par les deniers surdantz des ditz beneficez a y despendre, le roialme purroit estre efforcez tresgrandement.

Et qe sur ceo pleise a nostre dit seignour le roy, pur le grant bien, profit et efforcement de lui et de son dit roialme, et a tresgrant confort et ease des coers de ses ditz communes, affermer et approver les ditz bones ordinances, oustee la dite exceptione, et graunter expressement en ce present parlement en parol roial qe desormes, durantez les guerres, vostre roial magestee s'abstiendra finalment et de tout d'aooune tiele licencee donor a nully, par nul colour ou cause. Et qe si ascun de vos lieges, de quel estat q'il soit, pursue desore enavant a vostre hautesse pur ascune tiele licence, q'il encourge tiele peyne par vous, tresredoute seignour, et vostre conseil a limiter, qe doit suffire pur example as autres de lour abstenir d'aucune tiele suyte faire.

Cest responce, escrit de mot en mot en une cedule, estoit baillee au clerc de parlement par le roi mesmes, /qi comandast\ qe ce einsi feust entree.
53

Le roy voet qe ses liegees lour abstiegnent de lui prier d'aucunes tielles licences doner; et /se\ voet auxint le roy abstiner de douner ascune tielle licence durantes les guerrers, horspris au cardinalle de Naples, ou autre especiale persone, a qi le roy soit pur especiale cause tenuz.

[Non-resident incumbents.]

56[54] Item, prient les communes q'en eide et defens du roialme soit fait tiel estatut des clercs q'ont beneficez dedeinz le roialme d'Engleterre, et noun pas demurrancz personelement en mesme le roialme, come [Page iii-164] [Col. a] estoit fait nadgairs touchant les clercs beneficez en Irland; et ce sibien des aliens qi sont de present avancez dedeinz mesme le roialme d'Engleterre, de quel estat ou dignitee q'ils soient, come des Engleis ou q'ils soient hors du dit roialme, si ce ne soit effectuelement en le service du roy.

\[Responsio.]/

Le roy s'advisera.

Answer.

The king will speak to the prelates, that they do impartial justice to all their subjects in the most convenient way they can.

[Licences for beneficed aliens.]

[55.] Also, the commons pray that it may please our most redoubtable lord the king to consider the important reasons shown to various parliaments in his time why no alien should be beneficed in his kingdom, and to consider the good ordinances made thereon, if it were not for the exception which was made by special licence to be given by our said lord the king to such aliens; because of which exception various people of his kingdom have sought such a licence, for their singular benefit, to please the cardinals or for other reasons: so that the benefices are occupied by aliens in great number, and many more are still vacant of which such aliens have the farm in the hope of buying themselves a licence from our said lord the king by such means, as it is said. And because war with the Scots is now imminent it is most necessary that all benefices on this side of the sea be occupied by men of the same kingdom and dwelling in the same; since through the personal residence of such people and their households, and by the money arising from the said benefices to be spent there, the kingdom may be greatly strengthened.

And that therefore, it may please our said lord the king, for the great good, profit and strengthening of himself and his said kingdom, and for the great comfort and peace of mind of his said commons, to affirm and approve the said good ordinances, having removed the said exception, and to grant expressly in this present parliament by royal word that henceforth, during the wars, your royal majesty will finally and altogether refrain from granting such licence to anyone on any ground or pretext. And that if one of your lieges, of whatsoever estate he be, seeks any such licence from your highness, he shall incur a penalty to be determined by you, most redoubtable lord, and your council, which should serve as an example to others to abstain from making any such suit.

This answer, written word for word in a schedule, was delivered to the clerk of parliament by the king himself, who ordered that it be entered thus.

The king wills that his lieges abstain from asking him to grant any such licences; and the king himself will refrain from granting any such licences during the wars, except to the cardinal of Naples or any other special person, to whom the king is especially obliged.

[Non-resident incumbents.]

[56.] Also, the commons pray that for the aid and defence of the realm a statute be made concerning clerics who are beneficed within the kingdom of England and do not personally reside in the same kingdom, as [Page iii-164] [Col. a] was recently made touching clerics beneficed in Ireland; and that including aliens who are at present promoted in the same kingdom of England, of whatsoever estate or dignity they be, as well as the English where they are outside the said kingdom, if it be not on urgent business of the king.

Answer.

The king will consider it further.

---

[52] Original 54.
[53] This note is written in the margin alongside the section below.
[54] Original 55.

[No man to ride armed.]

57. Item, prient les communes, pur paix et quiete du roialme: q'il soit ordeigniez en ceo present parlement, et proclamacione fait en chescun countee parmy le roialme qe desormes nul homme chivache armez, ne ove lancegay, mes qe les lancegays de tout soient outrement oustez et abatuz, sur peyne de forfaire leur armure, et leur autres herneys, et qe l'estatut de Norhampton' soit de novel proclamez et duement execut solonc l'effect d'icell.

\[Responsio.]/
Le roi le voet, sinoun q'il eit doune sa licence en especial au contraire. Et outre \il voet./ qe l'estatut de Norhampton' avandit soit duement gardez, et estoise en sa force en toutz poyntz.

[Unauthorised erasure of an entry in common pleas.]

58. Item, prient les communes: qe come nostre seignour le roy sue un brief de quare impedit devant les justices de commune bank, vers Elizabethe qe feust la femme Edward nadgairs seignour de Despenser pur l'esglise de Avene en Glomorgan en Gales; a quel brief la dite Elizabethe pleida un certein plee, quel plee fuist entre en rolle en manere come il fuist pleidez, et al fyn du terme de la Trinitee darrein passe le dit rolle fuist raisee, et la force du plee la dit Elizabethe fauxement ent emble, a grande desheriteson la dite Elizabethe: de quelle chose si amendement ne soit fait, grant meschief et desheriteson purroit estre en temps avenir a plusours gentz du roialme, sibien as grantes come as petitz.

Qe pleise a nostre seignour le roy et les seignours en parlement ordeigner qe le dit rolle puisse resonablement estre amendez; nient contresteant qe le dit terme est passe en quel le plee fuist pleidez. Et qe resonable chastisement soit fait a celui qi fist la dite rasure, en ensample des autres mesfaisantz.

\[Responsio.]/
Tiel plee come les justices voillent recorder, q'ent estoit pledez, soit de novel entree en le lieu de la rasure, nient contresteant qe le terme en quel le dit plee estoit pledez soit ja passez. Et le roy voet qe cellui qi fist issint la rasure soit puniz pur son malfait.

[Abuse of protections.]

59. Item, prient les communes: qe come diverses gentz de la terre sont souvent delaiez et oustez de leur droit par proteccions grantez as certeinz gentz, pluis par leur pursuite pur delaier et restreindre leur creditours et autres gentz en lour droiturele pursuyte, qe pur les services nostre seignour le roy.

Qe pleise au present ordeigner qe desore en apres ceux q'ont proteccions puissent respondre par lour attornes, si avant come la partie mesmes, de gayner ou perdre selonc ce qe la loy voet.

\[Responsio.]/
Si aucun se sent grevez en especial, pleigne a chanceller, et il lui ferra droit en le cas, sicome lui semblera affaire de bone foy et resoun.

[A ban on exports to Scotland.]

60. Item, prient les communes: q'il soit defenduz et proclamacione faite parmy le roialme qe desormes nulles blees,

---

[No man to ride armed.]

[57.] Also, the commons pray, for the peace and tranquillity of the realm, that it be ordained in this present parliament, and proclamation be made in every county throughout the kingdom, that henceforth no man ride armed, nor with a javelin, but that javelins be completely ousted and banned, on pain of forfeiture of their weaponry and their other equipment, and that the statute of Northampton be newly proclaimed and duly enforced according to the tenor of the same.

Answer.
The king wills it, unless he has granted special licence to the contrary. And he also wills that the aforesaid statute of Northampton be duly kept, and remain in force in all respects.

[Unauthorised erasure of an entry in common pleas.]

[58.] Also, the commons pray: whereas our lord the king sued a writ of quare impedit before the justices of the Common Bench against Elizabeth wife of Edward, late Lord Despenser, for the church of Afan in Glamorgan in Wales; to which writ the said Elizabeth pleaded a certain plea, which plea was entered on the roll in the manner in which it was pleaded, and at the end of Trinity term last the said roll was erased, and the force of the said Elizabeth's plea thereon was fraudulently destroyed, to the great disinheritance of the said Elizabeth: concerning which matter, if it be not amended, great trouble and disinheritance may arise in time to come for many in the kingdom, both great and small.

May it please our lord the king and the lords in parliament to ordain that the said roll be reasonably amended; notwithstanding that the said term in which the plea was pleaded is past. And that reasonable punishment be inflicted on whoever made the erasure, as an example to other malefactors.

Answer.
Let such a plea as the justices wish to record, and which was pleaded hereon, be newly entered at the point of the erasure, notwithstanding that the term in which the said plea was pleaded be already past. And the king wills that whoever thus made the erasure be punished for his misdeed.

[Abuse of protections.]

[59.] Also, the commons pray: whereas various men of the land are often delayed and ousted from their right by protections granted to certain persons, rather because of their quest to delay and hinder their creditors and others in pursuit of their right than for the service of our lord the king.

May it please you now to ordain that from now on those who have protections may answer through their attorneys as completely as the parties themselves, to gain or lose according to the king's law.

Answer.
If anyone feels particularly aggrieved, let him complain to the chancellor, and right shall be done him in the matter, in accordance with good faith and reason.

[A ban on exports to Scotland.]

[60.] Also, the commons pray that it be forbidden henceforth to take corn, victuals, weaponry, or other reinforcements of

---

[55] Original 56.
[56] 2 Edw.3 c.3.
[57] 7 Ric.2 c.13.
[58] Original 57.
[59] Original 58.
[60] Original 59.

vitailles, armures, n'autre refresement qeconqes, soient cariez en Escoce, par eawe ou par terre. Et si aucun face a contraire qe le roi eit la moitee des ditz blees, vitailles, armures et autre refresement qeconqes, et son corps rent a la volentee du roy; et celui qi lui einsi trovera eit l'autre moitee pur son travaille. Et si aucune commissione soit grantez au contraire q'il soit repellez.

\[Responsio.]/
Le roy le voet, sinoun q'il eut doune si licence especiale au contraire.[61]

[Pleas of the forest.]
61[62] Item, prient les communes: qe come plusours grevances, oppressions, extorsions et emprisonementz, sont faitz a vostre poeple pluis qe unqes ne fuist veue ou oiez par plusours de voz ministres de forest.

Par quoy vous plese q'ils soit ordenez par cest present parlement qe nul ministre de forest preigne enqueste de trespas de forest, de vert ou de venesone, s'il ne soit par serement des verders eslieux en plein countee, queux sont faitz par brief du roy, et regardours. Et s'ils soient autres sinoun tieux eslieuz, qe l'enqueste soit pur nulle, et qe nul enqueste soit compellee par voie de manace, ne par ajournement de lieu en lieu, pur dire lour verdit de tielx ministres encontre lour gree: mes dient lour verditz en mesme le lieu ou ils sont chargez, come en temps voz nobles progenitours ad este fait. Et qe nul homme ne soit pris ne enprisonez sanz due enditement, ou mainoevre ou trove trespassant en la forest, ne destreintz de faire obligacione ou redempcione a nul ministre de forest. Et si aucun ministre face encontre l'assise de forest, et encontre ceste ordinance, soit sa baillie forfait au roi sanz restitucione a lui ou ses heires en apres.

\[Responsio.]/
Les estatutz de la foreste et les autres estatutz ent faitz, estoisent en lour force /et\ vertu. Et le roy defende, /qe\ nul manere de jurree soit artez desore par nully de ses ministres, n'autre quelconqe, a travailler issint de lieu en lieu par malice contre lour bone gree, ou autrement par manace ou duretee constreint de dire lour verdit autrement qe lour conscience ne lour vorra clerement enformer. Et le roy defende auxint qe nul homme soit pris n'emprisonez contre l'assise de foreste, ne compuls issint de faire obligacione, n'autre lien, encontre son bone gree. Et si aucun face encontre ceste ordinance, et de ce soit atteint, paie les doubles damages as parties par tant grevez, et nientmeins face fin et raunceone au roy pur son malfait.[63]

[Queen-gold not to be levied in wardship or marriage.]
62[64] Item, prient les les[65] communes: qe come autre foitz il estoit ordenez en parlement qe nule somme qe l'empelle quene-gold serroit leve de nulle q'ad garde ou mariage du grant noster seignour le roy.

Qe plese a nostre dit seignour le roi comander ses officers de l'escheqier, /qe\ nul brief, ne nul autre precept ne isse hors de le dit escheqier pur le lever, encontre l'ordinance suisdite.

Membrane 1
Soit usez desore enavant come ent ad este usez, sibien en temps de dame Phelippe nadgairs roigne d'Engleterre, come en temps d'autres roignes d'Engleterre d'ancientee.

any kind to Scotland by water or land, and that proclamation be made thereon throughout the kingdom. And that if anyone acts to the contrary, the king shall have half of the said corn, victuals, weaponry and other reinforcements, and his person shall be restrained at the king's will; and let whosoever thus discovered him have the other half for his labours. And if any commission be granted to the contrary, that it be repealed.

Answer.
The king wills it, unless he has granted his special permission to the contrary.

[Pleas of the forest.]
[61.] Also the commons pray: whereas many grievances, oppressions, extortions and imprisonment are inflicted on your people more often than has ever been seen or heard of before by many of your ministers of the forest.

May it please you to ordain in this present parliament that no minister of the forest hold inquest of trespass of forest, or vert or venison, if he be not elected in full county court by the oaths of the verderers, who are appointed by the king's writ, and regarders. And if they be other than those elected, that the inquest be invalidated, and that no inquest be forced by means of threat, nor by adjournment from place to place, to give their verdict for such ministers against their will: but they shall speak their verdict in the same place in which they are charged, as was done in the time of your nobles progenitors. And that no man be seized or imprisoned without due indictment, or unless caught in the act of trespassing in the forest, nor distrained to make a bond or redemption to any minister of the forest. And if any minister act contrary to the assize of the forest, and contrary to this ordinance, let his office be forfeit to the king without restitution later made to him nor his heirs.

Answer.
Let the statutes of the forest and the other statutes made thereon remain valid and in force. And the king forbids that any manner of jury be forced from now on by any of his ministers, or anyone else, to thus travel from place to place through malice against their good will, or be otherwise constrained through threat or duress to give a verdict which their conscience would not plainly advise. And the king also forbids that any man be taken or imprisoned contrary to the assize of the forest, or forced thus to make an obligation or any other bond against his will. And if anyone acts contrary to this ordinance, and be attainted thereof, let him pay double damages to the parties thus injured, and also make fine and ransom to the king for his misdeed.

[Queen-gold not to be levied in wardship or marriage.]
[62.] Also, the commons pray: whereas it was once ordained in parliament that no sum under the name of 'Queen's gold' should be levied on anyone who had a wardship or marriage by grant of our lord the king.

May it please our said lord the king to order his officers of the exchequer that no writ nor any other precept be issued from the said exchequer to levy it, contrary to the aforesaid ordinance.

[Answer]: Let the practice henceforth be as it was in the past, both in the time of the Lady Philippa late queen of England, as well as anciently in the time of other queens of England.

---

[61] 7 Ric.2 c.16.
[62] *Original* 60.
[63] 7 Ric.2 cc.3, 4.
[64] *Original* 61.
[65] les *repeated*

[Destruction of records at Guildford.]

63 Item, prie la commune pur la ville de Guldeford: qe come en la derrain rumour de certeines voz liges toutes les chartres et munimentz des ditz voz tenantz par voz nobles progenitours a eux grantez furent arsez et destruitz.

Qe plese a vostre tresgraciouse seignourie grantir qe mesmes les chartres purrent estre renovellez par voz roulles, enpaiantz le petit fee, c'estassavoir, de .xxij. s., .iiij. d.

\[Responsio.]/

Le roy, a la requeste de la commune en parlement, ad grantez ceste bille.

[Confirmation of pardon to Sir Robert Pleasington.]

64 A nostre tresgracious seignour, nostre seignour le roi, supplie humblement vostre povre servant Robert de Plesyngton': qe come nadgairs y vous pleust de vostre grace lui ottroier pardoun generale, come en voz lettres patentes ent faites est contenuz pluis au plein.

Qe plese de vostre grace faire ratifier et conferment les dites lettres patentes par assent du parlement ja present, pur Dieu, et en oevre de charitee.

Page iii-165

\[Responsio.]/

Et ceste bille pur monsire Robert de Plesyngton' qe feust livereee en parlement le quart jour de Novembre l'an present, lue en dit parlement devaunt le roy mesmes, en presence des plusours prelats, seignours temporelx, et autres sages du conseil le roy, mesme nostre seignour le roy respondist et dist illoeqes par sa bouche propre qe depuis qe le dit monsire Robert avoit chartre de pardon de soun grant devaunt celle heure, sicome la bille purporte, il pleist bien au roi, et il voet qe le dit monsire Robert enjoisse entierment la grace q'il lui ad fait par ycelle: et /le roi voet bien qe si le\\ dit Robert le vorra demander/ q'il ait mesme sa chartre renovellee de la date present. Et le roy de sa grace voet et grante, de l'assent de son conseil, qe celle chartre il ne ferra mye repeller ou revoquer \sanz grant cause./ Mais le roy ne voet mye qe de celle chartre, ne d'aucune autre chose qe clerement touche sa propre /grace et\ regalie, confirmacione soit fait en parlement, ou auctorizez par autre qe par lui mesmes; n'autre chose fait en privee n'en appart par quoy derogacione purra estre faite a sa droite regalie et dignitee par aucune voie.

[Destruction of records at Guildford.]

[63.] Also, the commons pray for the town of Guildford that, whereas during the last uprising of certain of your lieges, all the charters and muniments of your said tenants, granted them by your noble progenitors, were burned and destroyed. May it please your most gracious lordship to grant that the same charters be renewed by your rolls, on payment of a small fee, namely, 22*s*., 4*d*.

Answer.

The king, at the request of the commons in parliament, has granted this bill.

[Confirmation of pardon to Sir Robert Plesington.]

[64.] To our most gracious lord, our lord the king, your poor servant Robert Plesington humbly requests that whereas it pleased you formerly, of your grace, to grant him a general pardon, as is contained more fully in your letters patent issued thereon.

May it please your grace to cause the said letters patent to be ratified and confirmed with the assent of the parliament now sitting, for God and by way of charity.

Answer.

And this bill for Sir Robert Plesington, submitted in parliament on 4 November in the present year [1383], having been read in the said parliament before the king himself, in the presence of many prelates, lords temporal, and other wise men of the king's council, our same lord the king replied and said there by word of mouth that since the said Sir Robert had had a charter of pardon of his own grant before this time, as the bill claimed, it well pleased the king, and he willed that the said Sir Robert should fully enjoy the grace he had granted him by the same: and the king earnestly willed that if the said Robert *[Col. b]* would ask it, he might have the same charter renewed with the present date. And the king of his grace willed and granted, with the assent of his council, that he would not cause this charter to be repealed or revoked without good reason. But the king willed also that neither concerning this charter nor any other matter which touched his own grace and regality, should confirmation be made in parliament, or authorised by anyone other than himself; nor anything else done in private or in public which might in any way derogate from his true regality and dignity.

---

[66] *Original* 62.
[67] See *CPR 1422-9*, 158.
[68] *Original* 63.

Appendix

26 October 1383

Westminster

1. Writ of supersedeas to the treasurer and barons of the exchequer ordering them to cease their process against Hugelin Gerard, servant of Peter de Matmano merchant of Bologna, who was accused of not paying the custom and subsidy on various precious stones and other items which he had imported to England; since Hugelin has presented a petition to parliament, and the case has been adjourned to be heard by the chancellor in chancery. Dated 16 December 1383.

Source: *CCR 1381-5*, 419.

1384 April

Salisbury

29 April - 27 May 1384

(C 65/42. *RP*, III.166-174)

C 65/42 is a roll of six membranes, each approximately 310mm in width, sewn together in chancery style, and numbered in a later hand. The text, written in the official chancery script of several scribes, occupies the rectos of the membranes only. The dorses are blank apart from a later heading, 'Parliamentum de anno 7 R. 2^{di} pars prima', and later notes where the membranes are joined, 'Parl' 7 R. 2 apud Novum Sar'. The condition of the roll is good, though membranes 6 and 4 are stained with gallic acid, making the text illegible in places, and there is a natural hole in membrane 4. The marginal notes are contemporary. The Arabic numerals are of a later date, while the Roman numerals alongside the common petitions are contemporary. The roll appears to be complete, although there is no Statute Roll for this parliament with which it might be compared

With the abandonment of the 'way of Flanders' following the collapse of Bishop Despenser's 'Flemish crusade' in the autumn of 1383, attention turned to the possibility of securing a lasting peace with France. Even before the parliament of October 1383 had ended, John of Gaunt, duke of Lancaster, had set off for Leulinghen (between Calais and Boulogne) to open negotiations with his French counterparts, and on 26 January 1384 a truce was concluded until 1 October. At the same time, articles for a 'final peace' between England and France were also drafted, although naturally it was recognised that these would have to be referred back to the respective kings and their councils for ratification. In fact, consideration of the draft peace terms was probably the main reason (apart from the perennial need for money) why writs were issued on 3 March summoning another parliament to meet on 29 April, although the fall of Lochmaben castle to the Scots in early February also served as a sharp reminder of the need to make provision for the defence of a number of different fronts.[1]

The list of spiritual and temporal peers summoned was almost exactly the same as for the previous parliament, the only significant addition being Richard Talbot of Blakmere. It is not clear why the parliament was summoned to meet at Salisbury rather than the customary Westminster: perhaps there was a desire to avoid the factional rivalries of London, which were more than usually intense at this time. At any rate, it was in the great hall of the bishop of Salisbury's palace that the plenary sessions of the parliament were held, although it suffered a number of false starts. On Friday 29 April, the day for which it had been summoned, it was postponed until the following Tuesday to allow Gaunt and the other lords who had been leading a retaliatory raid against the Scots to arrive, but on the Tuesday it was again postponed until the Thursday. Despite the fact that Gaunt and several of the other lords had still not arrived, it was decided that further delay was not practicable, and it was on Thursday 5 May, therefore, that the parliament eventually got under way in the great hall with an opening address from chancellor Michael de la Pole (Items 1-2).

The chief item on de la Pole's agenda was, naturally, the draft Anglo-French treaty. A 'certain form for the final peace' had been agreed between the envoys of England and France, he declared, which had also been scrutinised, and apparently approved, by the royal councils of each kingdom. The king did not wish to ratify the treaty unless it met with approval from parliament, however, so the lords and commons were now being asked to give an opinion on it. There was, of course, a sting in the tail: whether or not peace was agreed with France, there were all sorts of reasons why the government needed money. If a treaty were to be ratified, the meeting between the kings would inevitably be a splendid affair, and the English king must not be outshone by his French counterpart; if, on the other hand, peace were not agreed, it was equally inevitable that money would be needed to continue the war - as indeed it was in any case, for the government's commitments were numerous (Items 3-4).

Discussion of the peace treaty was prolonged and probably divisive. On 9 May, the commons asked for an intercommuning committee of lords to help them to debate the issues. This was granted to them, and when Gaunt and his brothers, the earls of Cambridge and Buckingham, eventually arrived at Salisbury (presumably a day or two after this), they were added to the committee (Item 9). For the most part, however, lords and commons seem to have deliberated separately, although in the end neither was willing to endorse the treaty with any enthusiasm. When asked for an answer, the commons initially said that it was not up to them to decide such lofty matters (Item 16). When pressed, they declared themselves unhappy with certain articles of the peace, such as the fact that Calais and certain lands in Gascony

---

[1] *CCR 1381-5*, 437-8; Tuck, *Richard II and the English Nobility*, 92-4; Saul, *Richard II*, 130-2; Goodman, *John of Gaunt*, 98-9.

would now be under French sovereignty (Item 17). When told that this was the inescapable price of peace, they said that if the lords had been unwilling to endorse such terms, they wished to agree with the lords (Item 18). In the end, it is clear that the draft peace - the full terms of which have not been preserved - did not command sufficient support. On 27 May, the last day of the parliament, Gaunt and Buckingham were commissioned to re-open negotiations with the French: the search for an acceptable peace would have to go on.[2]

The extent to which disagreements over foreign policy were responsible for the rift which clearly opened up between, on the one hand, the king and de la Pole (the architect of the French peace policy) and, on the other hand, certain of the magnates, is difficult to gauge, but this was clearly a more than usually fractious parliament. The Westminster chronicler claimed that 'churchmen and temporal lords alike, by their astonishing squabbles among themselves, almost nullified the effect of the parliament'. The earl of Arundel in particular had a blazing row with the king: the country lacked 'prudent government', he asserted, and was 'at present almost in a state of decay'. Richard's response was furious: 'white with passion', he rounded bitterly on Arundel, telling him that if his words were intended as a personal criticism, 'You lie in your teeth. You can go to the devil!'. 'A complete hush followed as these words were heard', said the chronicler, until at length Gaunt rose from his seat and managed to calm both men down.[3] Arundel showed himself throughout the reign to be an advocate of a hawkish line against France, and it may be that it was the prospect of a 'shameful' peace which really angered him, although it may also be that this was symptomatic of the fact that he was increasingly excluded from the inner councils of the king, and that the latter was the underlying cause of his resentment.[4]

There was worse to come, however. Sensational as was the row between the king and Arundel, what really gripped the attention of the chroniclers during this parliament was the notorious affair of the Carmelite friar, John Latimer, who, after celebrating mass one day in the king's presence, in the apartment of the earl of Oxford, suddenly set up a diatribe against Gaunt, insisting to the king that his uncle was plotting to have him killed and to seize the throne. According to the Westminster chronicler, Richard immediately ordered Gaunt to be put to death, although other chroniclers do not support this, and in any case the king seems to have been rapidly dissuaded from such an intemperate course of action. When Gaunt heard what had happened, he demanded an audience with the king to exculpate himself, as a result of which the friar was led away for interrogation, during which he was tortured so horrifically that he died of his injuries. The question remained, however, as to whether he had been incited by others to make his accusations against Gaunt, or whether he was simply, as some believed, insane. Chief among those whom he was said to have implicated was Lord William la Zouche of Harringworth, who, despite being seriously ill, was brought to Salisbury on a litter to prove his innocence, which he succeeded in doing. Perhaps a more likely candidate as the friar's inciter, however, was Robert de Vere, the young earl of Oxford, who was rapidly establishing himself as one of the king's foremost confidants, and who clearly had no love for Gaunt. Yet if the 'affair of the Carmelite friar' more or less ended with Latimer's death, it had served to highlight both the impetuosity of the young king and the developing hostility between him and his eldest uncle - which, over the next year or so, would deepen to a chasm.[5]

Among the other items of business in this parliament, two in particular are worth noting, one of which is mentioned on the roll while the other is not. The first of these was the dispute between the chancellor, Michael de la Pole, and a London fishmonger, John Cavendish, which according to the roll was heard in parliament on 24 May. Cavendish's complaint amounted, in effect, to an accusation that de la Pole had accepted bribes (or at least sweeteners) from him in a case involving stolen merchandise, but had then failed to do him justice when the case should have been heard in the chancery (Items 11-14). When de la Pole denied the charges, Cavendish hastily shifted his ground, claiming that the real culprit in the affair was not the chancellor himself but his clerk, John Otter. De la Pole was determined to clear his name, however, and the lords decided to refer the case to the King's Bench, where, three weeks after the parliament ended, Cavendish was duly found guilty of defaming the chancellor and was ordered to pay de la Pole damages of 1000 marks. The record of this judgment was included on the roll (Item 15).

The second matter concerned the issue of law and order, and is recorded in the Westminster chronicle. According to this chronicler, the commons 'complained bitterly' about the lords' habit of distributing livery badges, as a result of which 'certain locally powerful persons' were able to set up petty tyrannies in their localities and generally disregard the law. Their request for a statute to be passed prohibiting this came up against stiff opposition from the lords, however, and especially from John of Gaunt, who took the occasion to issue his famous retort that 'the complaint was expressed in too general terms... since every lord was competent and well able to correct and punish his own dependants for such outrages'. At this, the commons were apparently 'reduced to silence', and agreed to drop the matter - but only for the moment. The issue of livery badges would surface again in the parliament of September 1388, and would remain a contentious issue throughout the last decade of Richard II's reign and well into Henry IV's.[6]

---

[2] Goodman, *John of Gaunt*, 101; for the likely terms of the draft treaty, see Saul, *Richard II*, 136-7; Palmer, *England, France and Christendom*, 33.

[3] *Westminster Chronicle*, 66-8.

[4] Palmer, *England, France and Christendom*, 50-51, 81; Saul, *Richard II*, 131.

[5] Several chroniclers include lengthy accounts of the Latimer affair, although there are important differences between the stories they tell: see *Westminster Chronicle*, 68-80; *St Albans Chronicle 1376-1394*, 722-6; *Vita Ricardi Secundi*, 81-2; the incident must have occurred close to the end of the Parliament, for on the last day of the session, 27 May, a writ was issued for Latimer to be delivered from Salisbury gaol: *CPR 1381-5*, 478.

[6] *Westminster Chronicle*, 80-82; N. Saul, 'The commons and the abolition of badges', *Parliamentary History*, 9 (1990), 302-315.

Having failed to give their backing to the draft Anglo-French treaty, the commons probably felt obliged to make a grant of taxation, although according to the Westminster chronicler it took much persuasion, and even the threat from the king to institute trailbaston proceedings against 'usurpers of the royal prerogative', in order to secure it. Even then, it was not a large grant: the second half-fifteenth and tenth granted at the October 1383 parliament was confirmed, and a further half-fifteenth and tenth granted, though the latter was not to be levied if peace were made, and even if it were not it was not to be collected until March 1385. In addition, the commons insisted that their grant should be conditional upon the clergy also granting a half-tenth, which they duly did on 31 May (Item 10).[7] Writs for the expenses of the knights and burgesses were issued on 27 May,[8] and within a month Gaunt and Buckingham were back at the negotiating table in France. They found that the attitude of the French had hardened, however, and despite spending most of the summer in France, the royal uncles were able to secure no more than an extension of the truce until 1 May 1385. Thus when parliament met again in November, it would face much the same problems as the Salisbury assembly; more ominously, though, relations between Richard and John of Gaunt deteriorated markedly during the summer, to the point where, during the winter of 1384-5, the tension between them began seriously to threaten the stability of the realm.[9]

---

[7] *Westminster Chronicle*, 82.
[8] *CCR 1381-5*, 452-4.
[9] Goodman, *John of Gaunt*, 101-2.

Text and Translation

Text
Page iii-166, Membrane 6
ROTULUS PARLIAMENTI TENTI APUD NOVAM SARUM, DIE VENERIS PROXIMO POST FESTUM SANCTI MARCI EWANGELISTE, ANNO REGNI REGIS RICARDI SECUNDI POST CONQUESTUM SEPTIMO.

Pars II.
\Adjournement./
1. Le vendredy proschein apres la feste de Seint Marc Ewangelist, qe fuist le .xxix. jour del moys d'Averille, l'an du regne le roi Richard secound \apres le conquest/ septisme, qe fuist le primer jour de ce parlement tenuz a Novel Salesbirs, pur tant qe les seignours q'estoient nadgairs en la marche d'Escoce, et autres seignours auxint, n'estoient mye encores venuz: et auxint pur tant qe aucuns des viscontz n'avoient mye fait retourner lours briefs de parlement, si n'estoit[10] mye cest parlement pronunciez: einz de la volentee et comandement nostre seignour le roi si feust ce continuez tanqe al mesqardy lors proschein, au fin qe monsire d'Espaigne, et les autres seignours q'estoient tard en Escoce, et ore a ce q'est dit en venantz sur lour chemyn, /puissent oier la pronunciacion.\ Et enoultre est comandez depar le roy, et proclamez publiquement, qe touz yceux q'avoient la somonce de \cest/ parlement en chescune degree y fuissent le dit mesqardy par temps, pur oier la volentee le roi noster seignour, et les causes pur qe il ad fait sommoner \cest/ son parlement. Et comandez fuist a les communes qe en le moien temps il tretassent de la persone qi auroit les paroles en cest parlement pur la commune, au fin qe pur l'eleccioun de tielle persone le parlement ny fuist tariez come ad este devant ore.
2. Et puis apres, al dit mesqardy, si fuist encores autre foitz mesme cest parlement continuez tanqe le joefdy lors proschein ensuant.

Pronunciacion de parlement.
3. Item, de dit joefdy, si vindrent en parlement sibien nostre seignour le roi en sa persone, come les prelatz, seignours, conseillers et communes q'avoient la dite somonce; horspris les seignours q'estoient avec monsire de Lancastre en Escoce les queux ne furent mye encores venuz hors de celles marches, et exceptes auxint ceux prelatz et seignours as queux pur diverses causes s'avoient ent fait excuser devers nostre dit seignour le roi. Assemblez en la grant sale del palays l'evesqe de Salesbirs, en Salesbirs, arraiez honurablement pur le parlement tenir en ycelle, monsire Michel de la Pole, chivaler, chanceller d'Engleterre, avoit les paroles del comandement le roi, en manere qe s'ensuit, et dist, 'Messires et sires cy presentz, nostre seignour le roi cy present, qe Dieu salve, moy ad commandez, a cause qe je sui son officer, de vous dire depar luy les causes pur quelles il ad fait somondre cest son parlement, qe sont tielles: primerement, al reverence de Dieu et pur le bone governement de son roialme le quiel il desire grantement, et sur tute autre rienz il voet qe les franchises et libertees de seint esglise soient tenuz et gardez en tout bien et honur auxi avant come elles ont este en temps d'aucun de ses nobles progenitours roys
[Col. b] d'Engleterre devant luy; et auxint qe les bones loys et usages, et la paix de son roialme soient auxint fermement tenuz et gardez en touz pointz. Et si rienz soit fait a l'encontre qe demande amendement en parlement, qe ce

[10] *Original* n'estoient

Translation

THE ROLL OF THE PARLIAMENT HELD AT SALISBURY, ON THE FRIDAY FOLLOWING THE FEAST OF SAINT MARK THE EVANGELIST, IN THE SEVENTH YEAR OF THE REIGN OF KING RICHARD, THE SECOND SINCE THE CONQUEST.

Part two.
Adjournment.
1. On the Friday after the feast of St Mark the Evangelist, which was 29 April, in the seventh year of the reign of King Richard, the second since the conquest [1384], which was the first day of this parliament held at Salisbury, because the lords who were lately in the marches of Scotland, and other lords as well, had still not arrived, and also because some of the sheriffs had not returned their writs of parliament, the parliament was not declared in session: but at the will and command of our lord the king, it was adjourned until the following Tuesday [3 May 1384], so that our lord of Spain and the other lords who had lately been in Scotland, and were now said to be on their way, might hear the opening announcement. Furthermore, it was ordered on the king's behalf and publicly proclaimed that all those of every degree who had received the summons of this parliament should be there early on the said Tuesday, to hear the will of the king our lord and the reasons for which he had caused this his parliament to be summoned. And it was ordered that the commons, in the meantime, should consider who would speak on their behalf in this parliament, so that the parliament would not be delayed by the election of such a person, as it had been in the past.
2. Later, on the said Tuesday, the same parliament was once again adjourned until the following Thursday [5 May 1384].

Opening of parliament.
3. Also, on the said Thursday [5 May 1384], there came to parliament our lord the king in person, as well as the prelates, lords, counsellors, and commons who had received the said summons; except the lords who were with our lord of Lancaster in Scotland and who had still not left those marches, and except also those prelates and lords who had excused themselves on various grounds before our said lord the king. When they had assembled in the great hall of the bishop of Salisbury's palace, in Salisbury, which was honourably furnished for the holding of a parliament, Sir Michael de la Pole, knight, chancellor of England, spoke at the king's command in the following manner: My lords and sirs here present, our lord the king here present, whom God preserve, has ordered me, because I am his officer, to inform you on his behalf of the reasons for which he has caused this his parliament to be summoned, which are these: first, out of reverence for God, and for the good government of his kingdom which he greatly desires, he wills above all else that the franchises and liberties of holy church be upheld and kept in all good and honour as they were in the time of any of his progenitors, the kings
[Col. b] of England before him; and also that the good laws and usages and the peace of his kingdom be firmly upheld and kept in all respects. And if anything should be done to the contrary which requires amendment in parliament, that

soit ore par voz sages discrecions covenablement amendez. Item, sur la tretee de la paix qe longement ad durez et continue parentre nostre dit seignour le roi et son adversaire de France, les messages d'ambes partz en dit tretee se sont ore assentuz sur certeine forme de paix final prendre parentre les roialmes, sur l'advis des rois et de lour conseilx d'ambes partz, dont y a certeins articles faitz prestz de vous monstrer en temps et lieu covenables. Et pur tant qe nostre seignour le roi vous ent voet monstrer naturesce \et/ perfit amour; et considerant voz grevouses charges quelles vous avez longement sustenuz parmy celle guerre, si ne voet mye nostre seignour le roi finalment accorder en le cas sanz vostre assent et science, combien q'il le purroit bien faire, come chose quele a ce qe homme pense n'appartient mye en rienz au droit ne a la coroune d'Engleterre d'ancientee. Et le roi vous prie et charge moelt entierment qe les ditz articles veues et entenduz, avec le manere d'icelle tretee, ent luy veullez doner vostre conseil tiel come vous semblera qe mieltz soit affaire pur son honour, et profit a lui et son dit roialme.

4. Item, si la paix se prendra, qe Dieux grante, encores il est voirs qe ycelle paix ne purra ja estre perfaite ne perfourniz sanz la presence des deux rois avaunditz: et n'y a point de doute qe si son adversaire y vendra, si serra il de moelt grant et honurable apparail. Et grant hounte serroit a nostre seignour le roy et a tout son roialme, si mesme noster seignour le roi n'y feust d'auxi honurable apparail et ordinance. Et pur tant, et auxint pur ce qe sibien sur la marche d'Escoce come en les marches de Caleys, Chirburgh, et Brest, et pur salvetee de ses foialx liges en Guyenne et Irlande, si ad nostre seignour le roi despenduz moelt grantement, et encores convient a despendre, et rienz n'est /ore\ remys de ses revenues, ne de ce qe lui ad este grantez par sa commune dont \despendre ou/ paier, sinoun qe a \grant/ peine pur les despenses de sa maisoun, sicome l'en vous purra clerement monstrer en temps et lieu covenables. Par quoi, \sibien/ en salvacione del dit roialme, et de vous mesmes, et chescun de vous, come pur salver \le/ honeur et l'estat nostre dit seignour le roi, le roi vous charge de conseiller et communer coment a meindre charge et desaise de vous le roi nostre seignour purra avenir a la monoie qe necessairement luy ent faut mettre: et auxint, coment et de quoi il defendra le dit roialme et la navye d'icelle encontre les Espaignardz et Flemynges: et auxint, pur despendre *[Page iii-167]*
[Col. a] sur le defens del dit roialme encontre les Franceys et Escotz, si paix n'y se pregne mye: et auxint, de vous adviser de les autres charges ore a vous donez depar lui. Et celle advis pris, d'ent certifier le roi et soun conseil a pluis en haste qe vous purrez, a fin qe cest parlement soit hastivement esploitez. Et le roi vous comande et charge sur vostre ligeance qe sur cestes voz charges vous vous veullez de jour en autre adviser, et diligeaument entrecommuner, au bien et profit de tout le roialme, entrelessantz de tout chescune autre \foreine/ matire en le moien temps. Qar par foreins matires, quelles n'ont de riens profitez au bien de commune, ont delaiez les parlementz devaunt ceste heure \moelt oultrageousement./ Et ce est la cause pur quoi le roi vous charge qe vous n'attamez nule matire forsqe tiele qe soit necessaire et profitable a nostre dit seignour le roy et son dit roialme, et de quoy avez de luy ore vostre charge. Et si vous vorrez de rienz pleindre en ce parlement, il a certeins seignours assignez d'estre triours et certeins clercs d'estre resceivours de voz peticions en le cas, par manere qe s'ensuit:

it should now be suitably amended by your wise discretion. Also, concerning the treaty of peace which has long endured and continued between our said lord the king and his adversary of France, the envoys on either side in the said treaty are now agreed on a certain form for the final peace to be made between the kingdoms, upon the advice of the kings and their councils on either sides, for which particular articles are ready to be shown to you at a suitable time and place. And because our lord the king wishes to show you all kindliness and perfect love, and considering the grievous charges which you have long sustained about this war, he does not wish finally to agree in this matter without your assent and knowledge (even though he could well do so), treating it as a matter which, so one might think, did not belong in any way to the right or the crown of England since antiquity. And the king prays of you and charges you most earnestly that having seen and understood the said articles, together with the nature of the same treaty, you will give him your advice as to what you think best for his honour and the benefit of him and of his said realm.

4. Also, if peace were to be attained, which God grant, it is still true that that same peace could not be made and concluded without the presence of the two kings aforesaid: and there is not the smallest degree of doubt that if his adversary were to appear there, he would be most splendidly and honourably arrayed. And great shame would befall our lord the king and all his kingdom if our same lord the king should not be as honourably arrayed and prepared. Therefore, and also because, in the march of Scotland as well as in the marches of Calais, Cherbourg and Brest, and for the security of his faithful lieges in Guyenne and Ireland, our lord the king has spent a great deal, and still more needs to be spent even though nothing remains of his revenues nor of that granted by his commons with which to meet those expenses, unless it should be at the considerable expense of his household, as he can plainly demonstrate to you at a suitable time and place. In view of which, both for the security of the said realm and yourselves, and each one of you, as well as to save the honour and estate of our said lord the king, the king charges you to discuss and consider how, with the least burden and injury to yourselves, the king our lord might have the money which he must necessarily spend: and also how and by what means he might defend the said kingdom and the navy of the same against the Spaniards and Flemings: and also, to spend *[Page iii-167]*
[Col. a] on the defence of the said kingdom against the French and the Scots, if peace be not concluded: and also, to discuss amongst yourselves the other charges now given you on his behalf; and, all that considered, to inform the king and his council of the results as soon as you can, so that this parliament may be swiftly concluded. And the king orders and charges you on your allegiance that you consult amongst yourselves on these your charges, and diligently discuss them, to the good and profit of all the kingdom, putting aside all extraneous concerns in the meantime. Since by extraneous matters, which have been of no benefit to the common good, previous parliaments have been most seriously delayed. And that is why the king now charges you to attend to no matter except that which is necessary and profitable to our said lord the king and his said kingdom, and with which you have now been charged by him. And if you wish to complain of anything in this parliament, there are certain lords appointed as triers, and certain clerks as receivers of your petitions, in the following manner:

Membrane 5

5. Resceivours des peticions d'Engleterre, Irlande, Gales et Escoce:

Sire Johan de Waltham

Sire Richard Ravenser

Sire Thomas Newenham

Sire Johan de Freton.

6. Resceivours des peticions de Gascoigne, et d'autres terres et paiis depar dela la meer, et des Isles:

Sire Piers de Barton'

Sire Robert de Faryngton'

Sire Johan Bouland'

Sire Johan Scarle.

Et ceux qi veullent bailler lours billes les baillent avaunt par-entre cy et samedy proschein venant. Et apres le dit samedy ne soit aucune partiale peticion resceuz.

7. Et sont assignez triours des peticions d'Engleterre, Irlande, Gales et Escoce:

L'evesqe de Wyncestr'

L'evesqe de Excestr'

L'abbe de Glastyngbirs

L'abbe de Saint Austin, de Cantirbirs

Le cont d'Arondell'

Le cont de Staff'

Le seignour le Zouche

Le seignour de Nevill'

Monsire Guy Bryen'

Monsire Robert Tresilian

Monsire Robert Bealknap'

- appellez a eux chanceller, tresorer, seneschal, chamberleyn, et les sergeantz le roi, quant il busoignera. Et tendront lour place en la chambre du chamberlein.

8. Et sont assignez triours des peticions de Gascoigne, et d'autres terres et paiis dela la meer, et des Isles:

L'evesqe de Nichole

L'evesqe de Hereford'

L'abbe de Hide

Le priour de Saint Johan Jerusalem in Engleterre

Le cont de Oxenford'

Le cont de Salesbirs

Le seignour de Cobham

Monsire William de Skipwith

Monsire Davy Hanmere

- appellez a eux chanceller, tresorier, seneschal, chamberleyn, et les sergeantz le roy, quant il busoignera. Et tendront lour place en la chambre du chauntour pres de la porte de la sale.

Et surce le dit chanceller chargeast illoeqes depar le roi touz les prelats, conts, barons, chivalers, citeins, burgeys et autres q'avoient la somonce de ce parlement, q'ils retournassent lendemayn par temps pur communer sur la charge a eux ore donee depar le roy, et einsi de jour en jour, a tielle bone diligence qe ce parlement soit en haste mys a bon fin, qe Dieu grante. Et le roi defende a touz qe nul se depart de se parlement sanz especial congie de lui devant le fin de mesme le parlement, sur peril q'appent.

5. Receivers of petitions from England, Ireland, Wales, and Scotland:

Sir John Waltham

Sir Richard Ravenser

Sir Thomas Newenham

Sir John Freton.

6. Receivers of petitions from Gascony and from other lands and countries overseas, and from the Channel Islands:

Sir Peter Barton

Sir Robert Farington

Sir John Bowland

Sir John Scarle.

And those who wish to submit bills should deliver them between now and Saturday next [7 May 1384]. And after the said Saturday no individual petition should be received.

7. The following are appointed triers of petitions for England, Ireland, Wales, and Scotland:

The bishop of Winchester

The bishop of Exeter

The abbot of Glastonbury

The abbot of St Augustine's, Canterbury

The earl of Arundel

The earl of Stafford

Lord le Zouche

Lord Neville

Sir Guy Bryan

Sir Robert Tresilian

Sir Robert Bealknap

- consulting with the chancellor, treasurer, steward, chamberlain, and the king's serjeants, when necessary. And they shall hold their session in the chamberlain's room.

8. The following are appointed triers of petitions from Gascony and from other lands and countries overseas, and the Channel Islands:

The bishop of Lincoln

The bishop of Hereford

The abbot of Hyde

The prior of St John of Jerusalem in England

The earl of Oxford

The earl of Salisbury

Lord Cobham

Sir William Skipwith

Sir David Hanmer

- consulting with the chancellor, treasurer, steward, chamberlain, and the king's serjeants when necessary. And they shall hold their session in the precentor's chamber near the door of the hall.

Whereupon the said chancellor, on the king's behalf, there charged all the bishops, earls, barons, knights, citizens, burgesses and others who had received summons to this parliament to return early the next day to discuss the charge given to them by the king, and so on from day to day, with such good diligence that this parliament might swiftly be brought to a good conclusion, which God grant. And the king forbids anyone to depart without his special permission from this parliament before the end of the same, on danger of the appointed penalty.

Seignours assignez a la commune.

9. Item, le lundy en le .ixme jour de May, les communes assemblez en ce parlement prierent a nostre seignour le roi qe lui pleust granter a eux qe les prelatz, contes et barons dessouz escritz, en especial purroient estre avec mesme la commune de temps en temps, et atant des foitz q'ils le requeissent, pur entrecommuner et conseiller avec mesme la commune sur lour charge a eux donee, a fyn qe le pluis en haste, al aide de Nostre Seignour, l'en purra venir a bone et graciouse conclusion sur les matires comprises deinz lour dite charge; quelles demandent de moelt grant conseil et bone deliberacioun des pluis sages de tout le roialme d'Engleterre. Et celle requeste estoit grantez a la dite commune en dite parlement. Et est assavoir qe ceux sont les nouns des prelatz et seignours a ce demandez; c'estassaver, les evesqes de Wyncestr', Ely et d'Excestr'; les conts de Kent, d'Arondell' et de Salesbirs; et des banerettz, messeignours Guy de Bryan, Johan Lovell et Johan Devrose.

Item, puis apres, quant monseignour de Lancastre et les autres grantz seignours del roialme q'estoient osteiantz de guerre en le roialme d'Escoce estoient venuz hors d'Escoce a ycest parlement, la commune d'Engleterre avantdite priast autre foitz a nostre dit seignour le roi et as seignours du parlement, d'avoir sibien mon dit seignour de Lancastre, come monseignour de Cantebrigge et monseignour de Bukyngham, avec les autres sages seignours du roiaume venuz ore novellement, en lour compaignie, pur entrecommuner et conseiller avec eulx sur lour dite charge auxi avaunt come les autres prelats et seignours devant ore demandez, come dessuis est dit. Et ce lour estoit semblablement ottroiez et grantez.

Grant d'une moite de la .xv.^{e}.

10. Item, puis apres, quant la dit commune s'avoit longement advisez sur lours dites charges a eux donez depar le roy al comencement de cest parlement, et apperceivantz clerement les grantz charges porte et soeffre a poy continuelment, sibien dedeinz son roialme d'Engleterre pur maintenir son honurable estat et honour, qe Dieu salve, come autrement sur les outrageouses charges de la grant multitude des guerres qe le roi nostre seignour porte toutes partz de mesme son roialme par terre et par meer, granterent a mesme nostre seignour le roy la moitee d'une disme et quinszime, a lever et resceiver de lays gentz de son roialme al terme de Seint Michel proschein venant, par fourme et manere come en une cedule sur ce faite par mesme la commune et endentee et liveree avant en parlement par mesme la commune pluis au plein est contenuz; de quele cedule le verroie tenour s'ensuit yci de mot a mot:

Les seignours et communes d'Engleterre considerantz les universeles guerres sibien par terre come par meer, et les perils semblables avenir de touz partz si remede ne soit mys, et ce par temps, grantent a nostre seignour le roi pur les causes suisdites, en defense du roialme, la moitee d'une .xvme quele fuist grantez au derrain parlement, et quele deust avoir este levez a cest fest de Pentecost, sur certein condicion comprise en mesme le grante; a avoir et lever de les laies en manere et fourme come la quinszime ad este usez d'estre levee devant ces heures, a la feste de Seint Michel proschein *[Page iii-168]*

[Col. a] avenir, nientcontreesteant la condicion avauntnomee; pur estre mys et emploiez la ou pluis y busoigne, par advys de nostre seignour le roy et de son conseil. Et si cas aveigne, come Dieu ne veulle, qe paix ne preigne parentre nostre dit seignour le roy et son adversaire de France, et les guerres se continuent celle parte, ou si les guerres d'Escoce

Lords assigned to the commons.

9. Also, on Monday 9 May [1384], the commons assembled in this parliament prayed of our lord the king that it might please him to grant them that the bishops, earls, and barons listed below might be especially assigned to the same commons from time to time, and as often as they asked it, to join with and consult with the same commons on the charge given them, so that they might reach a good and gracious conclusion on the matters contained in their said charge the more speedily, with the aid of Our Lord; which matters demand grave discussion and thorough deliberation amongst the most wise of all the kingdom of England. And that request was granted to the said commons in the said parliament. And be it known that these are the names of the prelates and lords sought therefor; namely, the bishops of Winchester, Ely and Exeter; the earls of Kent, Arundel and Salisbury; and from amongst the bannerets, messires Guy Bryan, John Lovell, and John Devereux.

Also, later, when messire of Lancaster and the other great lords of the realm who had been waging war in the kingdom of Scotland had come to this parliament from Scotland, the aforesaid commons of England prayed once more of our said lord the king and the lords of parliament that they might have both my said lord of Lancaster and my lords of Cambridge and Buckingham, together with other wise lords of the realm newly arrived, in their company, to discuss and consult with them upon their said charge together with the other prelates and lords previously requested, as is said above. And that likewise was agreed and granted them.

Grant of a half-fifteenth.

10. Also, later, when the said commons had long discussed the said charges assigned to them on the king's behalf at the beginning of this parliament, plainly recognizing the great burdens to be borne and suffered almost continually within the kingdom of England to maintain his honourable estate and honour, which God preserve, and in other ways, and also the exorbitant expenses of the great multitude of wars which the king our lord bears in all parts of the same realm, by land and sea, they granted our same lord the king a half-tenth and half-fifteenth, to be levied and received from the laity of his kingdom in Michaelmas term next [29 September 1384], in the form and manner laid out more fully in a schedule made thereon by the same commons and indented and delivered in the same parliament by the same commons; the true tenor of which schedule here follows word for word:

The lords and commons of England, considering the universal wars both by land and by sea, and the similar perils likely to arise in all parts unless remedy is soon provided, grant to our lord the king for the aforesaid causes, in defence of the realm, the half-fifteenth which was granted at the last parliament, and which ought to have been levied at this Whitsun under certain conditions set out in the same grant; to be had and levied from the laity in the manner and form in which the fifteenth has been raised before this time, at Michaelmas next [29 September 1384], *[Page iii-168]*

[Col. a] notwithstanding the aforementioned condition; to be used and employed wherever the need be greatest, upon the advice of our lord the king and his council. And if it should happen, which God forbid, that peace be not made between our said lord the king and his adversary of France, and the wars continue in those parts, or if the wars of

se continuent overtement, adonqes les ditz seignours et communes considerantz la grande necessitee alors semblable d'estre, grantent a nostre dit seignour le roi, en defense du dit roialme ou pluis y busoignera d'estre despenduz, une autre moitee d'une quinszime tiele come paramont est dit, d'estre levez et paiez al feste de l'Anunciacione Nostre Dame proschein avenir. Et en cas qe paix final, ou trieves, se preignent parentre nostre dit seignour le roi et ses ditz adversaires de France et d'Escoce, q'adonqes nul levee se face du dite derrain moitee du quinszime, ne nule commissione isse hors pur la lever d'ycelle en nule manere, par ceste protestacione escrite et endentee. Protestantz outre, qe l'une moitee ne l'autre ne soit en nule manere levable, ne levee, sanz la condicion ensuante, c'estassavoir, qe l'estat de clergie emporte et grante selonc lour afferant a l'une moitee et l'autre du dite quinszime, a les termes et jours suisditz, sibien en salvacion de eux come des ditz seignours et communes.

Membrane 4

Pole. Cavendissh'.

11. Item, fait assavoir qe le .xxiiij. jour de May, l'an present, un Johan Cavendissh' de Londres, pessoner, soi pleignast en ce parlement, primerement devant la commune d'Engleterre en lour assemble, en presence d'aucuns prelatz et seignours temporelx illoeqes lors esteantz, et puis apres devant touz les prelatz et seignours esteantz en ce parlement, au comencement de quiel sa pleinte il priast as ditz seignours, qe pur Dieu ils lui feisent surte et hastive purvoiance pur salvetee de sa vie, et q'il eust suffisante seuretee de paix de ceux des queux il serroit sa pleinte. Et par especial il demandast suretee de la paix de monsire Michel de la Pole, chanceller d'Engleterre; et celle requeste a lui fuist grantez. Et sur ce, par comandement des seignours avauntditz, le dit monsire Michel illoeqes present y trovast meinprise pur lui et pur toutes les soens de bone paix porter envers le dit Johan: c'estassavoir, le count de Stafford et le count de Salesbirs.

12. Et ce fait le dit Johan reherceast, coment au derrain parlement, il avoit fait pursuite par une sa bille envers Gyboun Manfeld, Robert de Parys, Johan Hankyn' et [William] Horsman, pur avoir restitucione de certains biens et marchandises de grant value perduz sur la meer, en defaute des ditz Giboun, Robert, Johan et William, \[du temps quant ils]/ avoient empris la salve garde de la meer et des marchandises passantz et venantz en le moien temps, encontre touz enemys horspris poair roial, quelle sa bille estoit endossez en dit parlement, il dist, et comys a la chancellerie pur discuter et terminer la matire y comprise solonc loy et resoun. Et dist oultre le dit Johan qe de \sa/ dite busoigne il avoit parlance et tretee avec un clerc et familier de dit chanceller, q'ad a noun Johan Otere: et par especial de ce, coment sembloit au dit Johan Otere qe le dit pessoner purroit mieltz avenir d'avoir bone seignourie et aide en son cas de mesme le chanceller, en qi mains l'esploit de sa dite busoigne gisoit haut et baas. Luy quiel clerc demandast copies de ses billes et de mesme la busoigne entier; les quelles il lui delivrast, et celles veues et entendues il lui promist, qe pur .xl.*li.* al oeps de son dit seignour, et quatre livres a son oeps propre, ent serroit il bien et graciousement aidez de soun dit seignour et de lui sanz nulle difficultee. Et sur celle promesse le dit Johan Cavendissh' s'accordast bien, et grantast de lui paier les dites .xliiij.*li.* en manere q'il les demandast. Mais

[Col. b] pur tant, il dist q'il n'avoit mye \alors/ la somme prest en main de paier, il se obligeroit volentiers par ses lettres al paiement faire bien et loialment a certein jour, et einsi fuist fait. Et puis apres le dit pessoner, ce dit il, baillast au dit clerc certaine quantitee de harang, sturgeon, et d'autre pesson, de la value de .ix. ou de .x. marz, al hostel et oeps

Pole. Cavendish.

11. Also, be it known that on 24 May in the present year [1384], one John Cavendish of London, fishmonger, complained in this parliament, first before the commons of England there assembled, in the presence of some of the bishops and lords temporal there present, and later before all the bishops and lords attending this parliament, at the beginning of which plaint he prayed of the said lords that for God they might make him surety and swift provision for the safety of his life, and that he might have sufficient surety of peace from those of whom he would complain. And in particular he demanded surety of the peace from Sir Michael de la Pole, chancellor of England; and this request was granted him. Whereupon, by order of the aforesaid lords, the said Sir Michael there present found mainprise on behalf of himself and all his men to bear good peace towards the said John: namely, the earl of Stafford, and the earl of Salisbury.

12. And that done, the said John described how, at the last parliament, he had pursued a bill against Gibon Manfield, Robert Paris, John Hankin and William Horsman to gain restitution of certain goods and merchandise of great value lost at sea through the fault of the said Gibon, Robert, John and William, from the time when they had undertaken the safekeeping of the sea and of the merchandise coming and going in the meantime, against all enemies except royal power; which bill was endorsed in the said parliament, he said, and committed to the chancery for the matter contained therein to be considered and settled in accordance with law and reason. And the said John also said that he had talked about and discussed his said business with a clerk and servant of the said chancellor, named John Otter: and particularly how it seemed to the said John Otter that the said fishmonger might best obtain good lordship and aid in his case from the same chancellor, in whose hands the conduct of his said business entirely lay. Which clerk asked for copies of his bills and of all the said business, which he delivered to him; and having seen and understood them, he promised that for £40 for the use of his said lord, and £4 for his own use, he would be well and graciously aided by his said lord and himself without any difficulty. And with that same promise the said John Cavendish fully agreed, and undertook to pay him the said £44 in the required manner. But

[Col. b] because, he said, he did not then have the money to hand with which to pay, he would willingly bind himself by his letters to make the payment well and loyally on a certain day, and thus it was done. And later, the said fishmonger, as he said, delivered to the said clerk a certain quantity of herring, sturgeon and other fish, to a value of nine or

de chancheller avauntdit, en partie de paiement des les .xl.*li.* avantdites: et trois verges de drape de scarlett qe luy cousta entour .xxxij. *s.* il deliverast al dit clerc en pris de deux marz, en partie de paiement de les quatre livres a lui promises. Et dist oultre le dit Cavendissh' qe combien q'il avoit tant fait et promys al oeps de l'une persone et del autre, toutes voies il ne trovast gairs longement aide, favour ne socour en effect, en la persone del dit chanceller en sa dite querele: einz il fuist par le dit chanceller delaiez, et encores est, et justice ne ent /purroit il avoir\ devant luy, combien qe as grantz travailx et coustages il ent avoit fait sa pursuite devers lui continuelment de jour en autre, et de terme en terme. Affermant oultre par ses paroles q'il ent avoit \la/ greindre suspicion del mal, et pur quoi einsi fust fait, pur tant qe le dit Johan Otere lui avoit countez a diverses foitz, q'il poiast avoir resceuz greindre somme de mesmes ses adversaires, pur avoir este avec eux encontre le dit Johan Cavendissh', q'il n'avoit d'ycelle Johan. Et auxint pur tant il dist qe bien pres as toutes les foitz q'il venoit a l'hostel del dit chanceller, pur parler avec lui de sa matire, il trovast illoeqes ses adversairs devant luy, ou il les encontrast en venantz de mesme le chanceller. Mais si le dit chanceller doit estre reputez pur conissant de cest affaire, entenduz quanqe il ad ore contez, il dit, ou nemye, Dieu le sciet, mais les jugez, vous messeignours. Mais il dist qe voirs est qe a certain jour passez le dit chanceller lui fist faire paier pur son dit pessoun, et avec ce fist debriser la dite obligacion: mais si ce fist il pur loialtee et conscience, ou autrement pur eschuir esclandre et reproche en le cas, il ne sciet ore dire, mais \le/ juggez, vous messeignours. Et il dist oultre pur certein qe pur les trois alnes de scarlet ne fuist il mye encores paiez.

Response du chanceller.

13. Et sur ce le dit chanceller, primerement devant les prelatz et seignours en parlement, et secondement devant les seignours et communes respondist, et dist qe de ceste affaire et de toute ceste matire il est innocent en chescun degree. Et primerement, quant a ce qe lui est surmys par l'accusacion ore dite, qe le dit pessoner ad este toutdys delaiez, et encores est, par le dit chanceller, et qe droit et justice ne lui est fait en sa dite querele, ce ne contient veritee. Et ce vouche le dit chanceller a record toutz les justices et sergeantz del roialme, q'ont este presentz en la chancellerie moelt sovent quant la matire ad este pledez parentre les parties; en quelle querelle est pledez tanqe a l'issue, dont partie gist en juggement, et partie remeint en travers, issint qe rienz ne remeint affaire ore forsqe le juggement rendre de ce qe remeint en juggement, et trier ce q'est traversez. Les queux juggement et travers ont este mys aucunement en delay pur difficultee, et pur nule autre cause; paront il n'est mye veritee, ce dit le chanceller, qe le pessoner /ad\ ore dit q'il n'ent poet avoir justice, et q'il est malement delaiez. Et quant al remenant de l'accusacion ore faite, le dit chanceller jurast par le sacrement de Jhesu Crist, q'il est oultrement innocent et sanz coulpe, et pluis n'ent vient unqes a sa conisance, forsqe en manere q'il dirra, q'est tiel.

Il dist qe novellement il avoit parlance avec les officers de sa maisoun pur savoir l'estat d'icelle, et pur ordener paiement as ceulx as queux pur les despenses de son dit hostel il estoit dettour. Et alors primerement, et nounpas devant, aucuns d'yceulx officers lui conterent la manere, coment une tielle quantitee de harang et sturgeon q'estoit portez a sa dite maison, nounpas par voie *[Page iii-169]*

ten marks, for the household and use of the aforesaid chancellor, in part payment of the aforesaid £40: and he delivered to the said clerk three yards of scarlet cloth, which cost him around 32*s.*, valued at two marks, in part payment of the four pounds promised to him. And the said Cavendish said further that although he had given as much as he had promised for the use of the one and the other, nevertheless, he had received neither aid, favour nor indeed support for a very long time from the person of the said chancellor in his said quarrel: but he had been delayed by the said chancellor, and still is, and he cannot have justice thereon before him, even though, at great trouble and expense, he has sued before him continually from one day to the next and from term to term. Affirming further, by his words, that he greatly suspected malpractice, and that because the said John Otter had told him on various occasions that he could have received a larger sum from his same adversaries to side with them against the said John Cavendish than he had had from the same John. And he said also that almost every time he had gone to the said chancellor's household to discuss the matter with him, he had found there his adversaries before him, or he had met them when leaving the chancellor. But whether the said chancellor should be supposed to have been aware of the matter, God knows, but it is up to the judges, you my lords, to decide, having heard what he has now recounted. But he said that it was true that on a certain day past the said chancellor had paid him for his said fish, and therewith had caused the said obligation to be cancelled: but whether he did that out of loyalty and conscience, or else to avoid slander and reproach in the matter, he could not now say; but you, my lords, may judge for yourselves. And he said further for certain that he had still not been paid for the three ells of scarlet.

The chancellor's response.

13. Whereupon the said chancellor, first before the prelates and lords in parliament, and second before the lords and commons, replied and said that he was wholly innocent in the matter. And first, as to that which was alleged against him in the accusation now made that the said fishmonger had been constantly delayed, and still was, by the said chancellor, and that right and justice had not been done him in the said case, there was no truth in it. And the said chancellor called to witness therein all the justices and serjeants of the kingdom, who had often been present in the chancery when the matter had been pleaded between the parties; in which dispute it was pleaded as to the issue, whereof one part lay in judgment, and the other part remained in traverse, so that nothing now remained to be done except a judgment to be rendered on what remained to be judged, and to try that which was traversed. Which judgment and traverse had been somewhat delayed through difficulty and for no other reason; and so, said the chancellor, the fishmonger's present claim that he could not gain justice and was wickedly delayed was quite untrue. And as to the rest of the accusation now made, the said chancellor swore by the sacrament of Jesus Christ that he was wholly innocent and without blame, and that nothing more had come to his knowledge than he would recount, as follows:

He said that he had recently spoken with the officers of his household to learn about the state thereof, and to ordain payment to those to whom he was indebted for the expenses of his said household. And then for the first time, and not before, some of those officers had told him of the manner in which such a quantity of herring and sturgeon which had been brought to his said household, not by means *[Page iii-169]*

[Col. a] d'achat ne de purvoiance, einz en une autre manere, estoit despenduz en mesme sa maisoun: dont il se merveillast, pur cause q'il n'avoit conisance del dit pessoner. Et avec ce alors luy conterent mesmes les officers, coment une tielle obligacione estoit auxint faite par le dit pessoner, q'avoit une querelle pendant devant lui, et tantost celle matire a luy desclose et par luy entendue, il estoit moelt grevousement ennoiez et corucez, et jurast a ses ditz officers q'il ne mangeroit ne ne beveroit deinz mesme son hostel tanqe le dit pessoner feust apaiez de quanqe il avoit fait envoier ou liverer deinz son hostel avantdit, et tanqe mesme l'obligacion feusse derompuz oultrement et defait. Et sur ce si estoit tantost le dit pessoner de son commandement fait venir en presence del dit chancellor en la chapelle deinz son hostel, ou il demoert au present quant il est a Londres; en la quelle chapelle, ou le corps Nostre Seignour Jhesu Crist sacrez remeint continuelment, il jurast par mesme le sacrement, en presence de son dit clerc, et del dit pessoner, combien q'il \[n'estoit mye tenuz]/ del faire, qe son dit clerc \[n'avoit]/ unqes touches a lui de la matire devant contez, n'autrement en avoit il conisance en prive ne en appert, sinoun qe par la relacion de ses autres officers, en manere avauntdite: et q'il n'estoit \[unqes]/ parcener al dit covenant en fait n'en parlance en aucun manere. \[Et sur ce il fist tantost]/ le dit clerc debriser mesme l'obligacion, et fist auxint le dit pessoner estre paiez pur son pesson avauntdit. Et /le dit chancellor y jurast devant les\ seignours par le sacrement de Jhesu Crist, \qe sa excusacion ore donee si contient pleine veritee, et encores/ il est prest de l' prover en quelconqe manere qe plest a nostre seignour le roi et as nobles seignours du roialme cy presentz de faire ordener. Et priast le dit chancellor as seignours avauntditz qe aiant due consideracion al estat q'il porte deinz le roialme parmy son dit office de chanceller qe lour pleust de lui ordener de due remede et justice de mesme le pessoner, sur le diffame et grevouse esclaundre q'il ad ore fait si fauxement et si horriblement de sa persone en parlement, q'est le pluis haute courte del roialme. A quoi le dit pessoner tantost illoeqes respondist et dist q'il, n'y avoit par sa dite pleinte de rienz fait accuser mesme le chancellor, einz soulement son clerc dessuisdit.

14. Et pur tant qe le dit pessoner desavouast en partie sa dite accusacione, et issint le deniast par sa bouche q'il nel avoit mye fait de la persone del dit chancellor, einz de son dit clerc, et auxint, parmy ce qe sibien le dit clerc, come le dit pessoner, sur ce examinez conustrent, qe l'obligacione avauntdite si estoit fait al dit clerc soulement, et en son noun, sanz nommer la persone del dit chancellor en ycelle, et qe mesme le clerc sur son serement fait en le cas \si/ fesoit toutdys oultrement excuser son dit seignour le chancellor, q'il n'estoit unqes conisant d'icelle obligacion, ne del covenant avauntdit, autrement qe dessuis n'est dit; et pur tant auxint, qe les ditz Giboun, Robert, Johan et William, esteantz personelment en ce parlement, et examinez sur lours ligeances a dire veritee de lour part en le cas, deposerent expressement, q'ils ne donerent unqes rienz, ne ne promistrent doun ne reward au dit chancellor, en prive ne en appert, par eux ne par autre persone del monde, les seignours avauntditz tenoient la persone del dit chancellor pur excusez de quanqe estoit compris en l'accusacion avauntdite. Et sur ce le dit chancellor priast dereschief as seignours illoeqes qe /combien\ qe le dit pessoner lui avoit issint par sa dite desavouerie en \partie/ excusez, toutes voies, purtant qe purroit apparoir clerement a chescune discrete persone qi oiast la dite accusacion, qe l'entente des paroles quelles le dit pessoner avoit dit sonerent expressement en moelt horrible esclaundre de sa persone,

[Col. a] of purchase or purveyance, but in another manner, had been used in the same household: at which he had marvelled, because he had no knowledge of the said fishmonger. And furthermore, the same officers had then informed him that such an obligation had also been made by the said fishmonger, who had an action pending before him, and as soon as this matter had been revealed to him and understood by him, he had been most grievously vexed and angered, and had sworn to the said officers that he would neither eat nor drink in his same household until the said fishmonger had been paid for whatever he had caused to be sent or delivered to his aforesaid household, and until the same bond had been entirely torn up and destroyed. And thereupon, on his orders, the said fishmonger was immediately brought before the said chancellor in the chapel within his hospice where he at present dwells when he is in London; in which chapel, where the body of Our Lord Jesus Christ continually remains, he swore by the same sacrament, in the presence of his said clerk and the said fishmonger, even though he was not obliged to do so, that his said clerk had never informed him of the matter previously related, neither had he gained knowledge of it in secret or in public by other means, except by what he had been told by his other officers in the aforesaid manner: and that he had never been party to the said covenant in word or deed in any way. Whereupon he immediately caused the said clerk to destroy the same obligation, and he also caused the said fishmonger to be paid for his aforesaid fish. And the said chancellor swore there before the lords by the sacrament of Jesus Christ that his excuse now given contained the whole truth, and that even so he was ready to prove it in any way it might please our lord the king and the noble lords of the realm here present to ordain. And the said chancellor prayed of the aforesaid lords that, duly considering his status in the realm by virtue of his said office of chancellor, it might please them to ordain for him due remedy and justice against the same fishmonger for the defamation and grievous slander of his person which the fishmonger had now perpetrated so fraudulently and horribly in parliament, which is the highest court of the realm. To which the said fishmonger at once replied and said there that he had not accused the same chancellor of anything in his said complaint, but only his aforesaid clerk.

14. And because the said fishmonger disavowed his said accusation in part, and thus denied by his own words that he had alleged anything against the person of the said chancellor, but only against his said clerk, and also because both the said clerk and the said fishmonger, on being questioned, admitted that the aforesaid obligation had been made to the said clerk alone, and in his name, without the person of the said chancellor being named in the same, and that the same clerk on his oath made in the case caused his said lord the chancellor to be forever and completely excused, as he had never had knowledge of the same obligation, nor of the aforesaid covenant, other than that mentioned above; and also because the said Gibon, Robert, John and William, attending this parliament in person, and being asked on pain of their allegiance to speak the truth of their part in the matter, expressly denied that they had given anything, nor promised any gift or reward to the said chancellor, in private nor in public, either themselves or through any other person in the world; the aforesaid lords considered the person of the said chancellor excused of whatever had been contained in the aforesaid accusation. Whereupon, the said chancellor prayed again of the lords there that although the said fishmonger had thus excused himself by his partial disavowal, nevertheless, because it should be plainly apparent to every discreet person who had heard the said accusation that the tone of

qe mesme le pessoner feusse mis en arest, tanqe il auroit trovez suffisante meinprise d'attendre ce qe serra juggez sur

[Col. b] ceste matire; et especialment sur le faux esclaundre avantdite. La quele requeste estoit ottroiez, et avec ce comandez par les seignours, qe sibien le dit pessoner come le dit clerc feussent mys en arest. Et einsi fuist fait; et puis apres si estoient ils lessez aler a large; c'estassavoir, le dit pessoner par la mainprise de Thomas Spicer et Esteven Skynner, qi estoient obligez corps pur corps d'avoir le dit pessoner de jour en autre devant les seignours avauntditz, ou devant quelconqes autres juges qi a ce serront assignez. Et puis apres, pur tant qe le parlement si feust a celle foitz bien pres sur le fyn, et les seignours furent auxint grantement occupiez illoeqes entour les autres grosses busoignes del roialme, si estoit en ce parlement la dite querelle, avec toutes choses dependentes et incidentes, commys as justices nostre seignour le roi, pur oier et terminer ycelle finalment, sibien pur le roi nostre seignour come pur les parties, selonc la loy, auxi avant come les seignours de parlement eusset peu fair si la querelle eust este tretez pluis avant en lour presence, et en mesme parlement.

Recordum factum apud Westm' per justiciarios etc.
15. Et postea die martis proxime post octabas sancte trinitatis, videlicet .xiiij. die Junii, anno regni domini regis Ricardi secundi post conquestum .vij.° Robertus Tresilian, capitalis justiciarius in banco ipsius regis, Robertus Bealknap, capitalis justiciarius in communi banco, et Rogerus de Fulthorp, unus justiciariorum in communi banco, vigore commissionis eis in parliamento dicti domini regis apud Novam Sarum ultimo tento facte, unde in rotulo parliamenti predicti mencio facta est specialis, contra quendam Johannem Cavendish de London, fishmonger, qui in parliamento predicto, videlicet coram communitate regni Anglie congregata, et postmodum alia vice coram magnatibus ejusdem regni in eodem parliamento, de Michaele de la Pole, milite, cancellario domini regis, et Johanne Otere, clerico ipsius cancellarii, de diversis meinprisionibus sibi per eosdem factis, et asseruit, graviter querelavit, et ipsum cancellarium per hoc multipliciter et minus vere accusavit, et alias enormiter diffamavit, processerunt in hunc modum; inprimis, videlicet ipsum Johannem Cavendish coram eisdem justiciariis apud Westm' dicto .xiiij. die Junii - assidentibus sibi tunc ibidem Hugone Segrave, milite, thesaurario Anglie, magistro Waltero de Skirlawe, custode privati sigilli, Johanne de Waltham, custode rotulorum cancellarie, necnon Waltero Clopton, Willelmo Rikhill, et Johanne de Lokton, servientibus ipsius regis, - venire fecerunt; qui ibidem comparens, et de accusacione sua, ut predictum est, facta, et in rotulo parliamenti predicti plenius irrotulata, cujus materia, una cum responsionibus per dictum cancellarium in eodem parliamento ad hoc in excusacionem suam datis, prout continetur in rotulo predicto, pro majori parte recitata coram ipso Johanne Cavendish, tunc ibidem allocutus fuit per justiciarios predictos, et super hoc quesitum fuit ab eodem, si quid haberet pro se vel ulterius dicere sciret quare penam in statuto contra hujusmodi diffamatores edito subire non debeat; maxime cum idem cancellarius se inde in parliamento illo excusavit, et omni alio modo possibili se inde excusare est paratus? Qui quidem Johannes ad hoc respondebat, et dixit, Quod ipse nunquam personam dicti cancellarii in parliamento illo diffamavit, nec aliquid sinistrum sive inhonestum de persona ipsius cancellarii clam vel palam in parliamento illo dixit, vel alias affirmavit quovis modo. Set dicit,

fishmonger's words clearly resounded with the most horrible slander of his person, the same fishmonger might be placed under arrest, until he should have found sufficient mainprise to await that which would be judged in
[Col. b] the matter; and especially on the aforesaid false slander. Which request was granted, and thereupon the lords ordered that both the said fishmonger and the said clerk be placed under arrest. And so it was done. And later they were set free, namely, the said fishmonger by the mainprise of Thomas Spicer and Stephen Skinner, who were obliged body for body to have the said prisoner before the aforesaid lords from one day to the next, or before any other judges who should be assigned thereto. Later, because the parliament was drawing to a close and the lords were also greatly concerned with other important matters of the realm, so, in this parliament, the said action with all its dependent and incidental matters was delegated to the justices of our lord the king, who were to hear and also determine it both for the king our lord and for the parties, in accordance with the law, just as the lords of parliament would have done if the cause had been taken further in their presence and in the same parliament.

The record made at Westminster by the justices etc.
15. And later on the Tuesday next after the octave of Holy Trinity, namely 14 June in the seventh year of the reign of the lord King Richard the second after the Conquest [1384], Robert Tresilian, chief justice of the King's Bench, Robert Bealknap, chief justice of the Common Bench, and Roger de Fulthorp, one of the justices of the Common Bench, on the strength of a commission made to them in the last parliament of the said lord king held at Salisbury - of which specific mention is made on the roll of the aforesaid parliament, against a certain John Cavendish of London, fishmonger, who, in the aforesaid parliament, that is before the assembled commons of the kingdom of England, and later on another occasion before the great men of the same realm in the same parliament, gravely complained and protested of Michael de la Pole, knight, the lord king's chancellor, and John Otter, clerk of the same chancellor, concerning certain mainprises issued for him by the same, and thereby accused in many and false ways and otherwise outrageously defamed the same chancellor - proceeded in this manner; first, that is, they caused the same John Cavendish to appear before the same justices at Westminster on the said 14 June, with Hugh Segrave, knight, treasurer of England, Master Walter de Skirlaw, keeper of the privy seal, John de Waltham, keeper of the rolls of chancery, and also Walter Clopton, William Rikhill, and John de Lokton, serjeants of the same king, then assisting them there; who, coming there, and with his complaint having been made, as is said above, and more fully enrolled on the roll of the aforesaid parliament - the substance of which, together with the answers given thereupon by the said chancellor in the same parliament in his defence, as is contained on the aforesaid roll, with the majority having been read out in the presence of John Cavendish himself - was then addressed there by the aforesaid justices, and thereupon he was asked by the same if he had anything to say for himself, or moreover why he ought not to incur the penalty in the statute published against such defamers, especially since the same chancellor had absolved himself thereupon in that parliament, and is prepared to absolve himself thereupon by all other possible means? Which John replied to this and said that he never defamed the person of the said chancellor in that parliament, nor said anything adverse or

quod quicquid per eum in hac parte tunc dictum fuerat, hoc solum de prefato Johanne Otere, clerico ipsius cancellarii, dixit et asseruit, et sic non intendit quod de diffamacione ipsius cancellarii aliquis posset ipsum impetere quovis modo. Et super hoc racionibus ipsius Johannis Cavendish in dicto parliamento in ista materia factis, et sentencia verborum suorum, ac modo et forma eorumdem, necnon responsionibus et excusacionibus ipsius cancellarii et aliorum ex parte sua hinc inde factis et datis, ibidem debite ponderatis et intellectis; et ulterius *[Page iii-170]*

[Col. a] habendo respectum ad hoc, quod ubi prefatus Johannes Cavendish dixit quod justiciam coram dicto cancellario in causa sua habere non potuit, contrarium expresse habetur de recordo in cancellaria predicta, prout alias prefatus cancellarius allegavit in eodem parliamento, clare constare debet cuicunque discreto et intelligenti quod idem Johannes Cavendish per accusacionem suam predictam ipsum cancellarium in eodem parliamento false et maliciose diffamavit. Per quod consideratum est, quod prefatus Johannes Cavendish super diffamacione ista convincatur, et idem cancellarius recuperet versus eum dampna sua, que ad mille marcas de avisamento justiciariorum et aliorum predictorum sunt taxata. Et quod Johannes Cavendish predictus committatur prisone domini regis, ibidem moraturus quousque tam prefato cancellario de dampnis suis predictis, quam dicto domino regi pro fine competenti sibi inde debito plenarie satisfecerit.

De la paix.

16. Item, la dite commune touchant la charge a eux donez en ce parlement de la paix qe se ferra, si Dieux plest, \parentre nostre seignour le roi et/ son adversaire de France - de quoi certeins articles, ent faites et appointez novellement au tretee de mesme la paix q'ad este en la marche de Caleys parentre les ambassatours d'ambes partz, estoient liverez a mesme la commune, pur leur meillour informacion del tretee avauntdit, et del effect d'ycelle - mesme la commune ont fait lour responce a nostre seignour le roi en parlement par la manere qe s'ensuit: en disantz qe pur les outrageouses perils q'ils y veiont clerement chescune part, ils ne poent ne ne osent par aucune manere ent conseiller lour seignour lige expressement ne a l'une ne a l'autre, combien qe la dite paix, si pleust a Dieu del ottroier tielle qe feust honurable et profitable a lour dit seignour lige et son roialme, si lour serroit .... la pluis noble et graciouse aide et confort qe homme purroit en monde deviser. Et lour semble qe nostre dit seignour le roi poet et doit faire en celle partie sicome a sa noble seignourie mieltz semblera affaire, come de chose q'est son propre heritage, q'est par droit lignage roiale descenduz a sa noble persone, et nounpas appartenant al roialme ne a la coroune d'Engleterre. Enpriantz humblement a mesme lour seignour lige qe pur Dieu il ent veulle faire sicome par l'advis de son conseil mieltz luy ent semblera affaire, al honour et profit de lui, et confort et aide de son roialme avauntdit, et qe pur les perils et meschiefs importables qe purroient avenir, qe Dieu defende, la poevre commune feusse deschargez de doner autre responce en ce cas quant au present.

17. Et sur \ce,/ la commune \[estoient]/chargez depar le roi a dire illoeqes lour volentee de deux choses, c'estassavoir, ou ils desirent la paix, ou la guerre, avec lours enemys Franceys:

dishonourable in secret or in public concerning the person of the chancellor himself in that parliament, or spoke out in any way at another time. But he says that whatever had then been said by him in that regard he had said and claimed this only of the aforesaid John Otter, the same chancellor's clerk, and thus he did not intend that the chancellor himself be accused of the defamation in any way. And thereupon, with the claims of the same John Cavendish on this matter having been made in the said parliament, and the judgment of his words, and the manner and form of the same, and also with the answers and excuses of the same chancellor and other persons thus made and given on his behalf, having been duly considered and understood there; and moreover, *[Page iii-170]*

[Col. a] having consideration for this, that when the aforesaid John Cavendish had said that he was unable to have justice in his plea in the presence of the said chancellor, expressly the opposite is held on record in the aforesaid chancery, as the aforesaid chancellor has claimed on another occasion in the same parliament, it ought to be clearly evident to any wise and intelligent person that the same John Cavendish falsely and maliciously defamed the aforesaid chancellor by his aforesaid complaint in the same parliament. Whereby it is adjudged that the aforesaid John Cavendish be convicted of this defamation, and the same chancellor shall recover his damages against him, which are assessed at 1,000 marks by the advice of the aforesaid justices and other persons. And that the aforesaid John Cavendish be committed to the lord king's prison, to remain there until he has fully satisfied both the aforesaid chancellor of his aforesaid damages and the said lord king with a suitable fine due to him thereupon.

Of peace.

16. Also, the said commons, touching the charge given them in this parliament concerning the peace which might be made, if it please God, between our lord the king and his adversary of France - concerning which, certain articles, newly made and appointed thereon at the treaty of the same peace which was reached in the march of Calais between the ambassadors of either side, having been delivered to the same commons, the better to inform them of the aforesaid treaty and the effect of the same - made their reply to our lord the king in parliament in the following manner: saying that because of the awful dangers they clearly saw on every part, they could not nor dare not in any way advise their liege lord on the one or the other, even though the said peace, if it pleased God to grant one that would be honourable and profitable to their said liege lord and his kingdom, would be to them the most noble and gracious aid and comfort one could devise. And it seemed to them that our said lord the king could and ought to do in this matter whatever seemed best to his noble lordship, as something which is his own inheritance, descended to his noble person by true royal lineage, and not pertaining to the kingdom nor the crown of England. Requesting humbly of our same liege lord that for love of God he would do whatsoever he thought best, with the advice of his council, to his own honour and profit and the comfort and aid of his aforesaid kingdom; and that because of the unbearable perils and troubles which might arise, God forbid, the poor commons should be discharged from giving another answer in this matter at present.

17. Thereupon, the commons were charged on the king's behalf to state their preference in two matters: namely, whether they desired peace or war with their French enemies: since

qar y n'ad autre moiene voie, a cause qe as trieves qe serroient bones ou profitables au roi et son roialme ne veullient les Franceys ore assentir. Et sur ce la dite commune respondist et dist qe moelt \grantment/ desiront ils qe bone paix et honurable au roi nostre seignour et son roialme si feust faite, qe Dieu grante, mais par les articles a eux ent liverez, des queux pur plusours termes de loy civil y comprises ils n'ont mye cler entendement, et auxint par la relation a eux ent fait d'autrepart, ils entendont qe aucunes seignouries et terres qe mesme lour seignour lige auroit ore par cest accord en Guyenne si serroient tenuz del roi Franceys par homage et service, mais ne pensont mye qe lour dit seignour lige vorroit assentir trop legierment de tenir d'iceux Franceys par tielle service la ville de Caleys, et autres terres conquises des Franceys par l'espeye, ne ne vorroit la commune qe einsi feust fait, si autrement l'en y purroit bien faire, ou eschapir sanz damage.

18. A quoy fuist dit a la commune qe autrement qe de les tenir del roy Franceys, homme n'avendra mye avec eux a la paix pur rienz qe homme ad peu apperceivoir en dite tretee devant ceste heure. Et sur ce la commune autre foit requis de dire a lour seignour lige coment ils vorroient ore faire quant a la prise de ceste paix, si ensi feust qe la dite commune feusse roi del roialme, ou en estat qe lour roy est, considerez la multitude des guerres chescune part overtz toutz a un foitz encontre cest petit roialme; et coment les enemys si sont confederez trestouz ensemble qe nul prendra trieves ne paix legierment sanz autre; et le grant force et richesce des enemys, et le feoblesce et povertee de nostre roialme. A quoy la commune respondist et dist q'ils ont entenduz qe les prelatz et seignours temporelx ent ont auxint este chargez devaunt ceste heure en semblable manere; c'estassavoir, de doner lour conseil et advis a nostre seignour le roi en le cas. Et mesmes les prelatz et seignours avantditz ont fait lour responce nounpas come pur lour conseil ou advis doner en celle partie, ne a la paix, c'estassaver, ne a la guerre: einz soulement, come lour est fait a entendre, mesmes les prelatz et seignours ont dit qe toutes choses et meschiefs apparantz considerez, s'ils feussent en l'estat du roi, ils s'accorderoient a la paix pluis tost qe a la guerre. Et issint la dite commune, par protestacione q'ils ne soient desore chargez come conseillers en le cas, ne par tant ent portent charge de conseiller a l'une ou a l'autre, ils s'accordent en lour responce sur ceste lour charge en toutes choses as prelatz et seignours avauntditz; et tiele responce, et nulle autre qe les ditz prelatz et seignours ent ont donez ils donent ore a lour seignour lige, sur lour charge dessuisdite.

Membrane 3

Bury.

19. Item, l'abbe et convent de Bury myst avant en parlement une lour peticion en la fourme qe s'ensuit:

A nostre tresredoute seignour le roi et a tout son tressage conseil en cest parlement supplient treshumblement voz devoutz oratours, abbe et convent de Bury Seint Esmon: qe come les gentz de la ville de Bury, apres lours horribles mesprisions par eux attemptez en la derrain riote des communes rebeulx encontre vostre roiale majestee et voz ditz oratours, et lour esglise q'est de vostre patronage, en salvacion de lours vies se submistrient en haut et baas a la noble grace et ordinance de vous nostre seignour le roi suisdit, come piert de record, et depuis ce il ad este tressovent ordinee, grantee et establi par gracious consent de vous nostre seignour et de autres seignours de vostre roialme, sibien en parlement tenuz a Westm' le lundy en la tierce semaigne de Quaresme l'an de

there was no middle way, because the French would not now agree to a truce which would be good and profitable for the king and his kingdom. And thereupon the said commons replied and said that they most greatly desired that good and honourable peace be made for the king our lord and his kingdom, which God grant, but from the articles submitted to them, of which they had no clear understanding because of the many terms of civil law contained therein, and also because they had had another account of it, they understood that some of the lordships and lands in Guyenne which their same liege lord would now hold by this agreement would be held of the French king for homage and service, but they did not think that their said liege lord would agree lightly to holding the town of Calais and other lands conquered from the French by the sword from the French by such service, and neither would the commons wish that to be done, if it could be done otherwise or avoided without injury.

18. It was said to the commons that other than holding them of the French king, there could be no peace with them on any other grounds than had been considered in the said negotiations. And thereupon the commons were once more asked to tell their liege lord what they would now do to achieve the said peace, if it were they who were king of the realm, or placed as the king now is, considering the multitude of open wars on every side and waged together against this small kingdom; and considering that the enemies are all agreed together to make no truce lightly without the other; and the great strength and wealth of the enemies, and the weakness and poverty of our own kingdom. To which the commons replied and said that they understood that the bishops and lords temporal had also been charged before this time in a like manner; namely, to give their counsel and advice to our lord the king in the matter, and the same aforesaid bishops and lords had replied not by giving their counsel or advice thereon, namely on the peace or war, but had simply said that, as they had been given to understand it, considering all the apparent issues and troubles, if they were in the king's position, they would more readily agree to peace than war. And so the said commons, with the protestation that they should not be charged henceforth as counsellors in that matter, nor that as a result they bear the charge of counselling the one or the other, agreed in all respects with the aforesaid prelates and lords in their reply to this their charge; and they now made that reply to their liege lord, and none other than that which had been given by the said prelates and lords thereon.

Bury.

19. Also, the abbot and convent of Bury laid before parliament a petition in the following form:

To our most redoubtable lord the king and all his most wise council in this parliament, your devout orators the abbot and convent of Bury St Edmunds most humbly pray: whereas the men of the town of Bury, after the terrible misdeeds attempted by them in the last riot of the common rebels against your royal majesty and your said orators and their church, which is of your patronage, for the saving of their lives surrendered themselves high and low to the noble grace and ordinance of you, our aforesaid lord the king, as appears on record, and since then it has been frequently ordained, granted and decreed by the gracious consent of you, our lord, and the other lords of your realm, both in the parliament held at Westminster on the Monday in the third week of Lent in

vostre regne sisme,[11] come en plusours autres voz nobles conseils, qe les ditz gentz de Bury, a cause de lours mesfaitz et custumables rebellions encontre vostre corone et la dite esglise, deussent faire auxi suffisante seuretee de lour bon port envers vous et la dite esglise en tout temps avenir come mieltz purroit estre devisee, et a ce estre obligez sibien a vous nostre seignour, come a voz oratours, abbe et convent dessuisditz severalment, pur seuretee du pees perpetuele, devant q'ils eussent aucune chartre de pardoun, grace ou remission par voie queconqe.

Plese a vostre tresgracious seignourie, considerantz lours ditz submissions a vostre roiale majestee einsi faitz, et coment les ditz gentz ne ont voluz tanqe en cea faire la dite seuretee en aucun manere, combien qe par force de lour dit submissione ce ad este ordene tressovent, et la manere d'icelle seuretee qe serroit une reconisance affaire en vostre chancellerie lour ad este monstrez et profri en escrit, ore faire bone ordinance en cest parlement, et comander estroitement qe les dites seuretees sanz pluis longe proloignement soient faitz et perfournis par toutz les gentz et enhabitantz de mesme la ville de Bury, et chescune singuler persone d'icelle, en manere et par fourme come y fuist declarre en especial par vostre grant conseil tenuz a Westm' a comencement de Quaresme *[Page iii-171]*

[Col. a] proschein passee. La manere et fourme de quelle seuretee ordene en vostre derrain grant conseil est contenuz en une cedule annexe a ceste bille; faisantz nientmeins expresse protestacione de adder ou ouster de mesme la cedule, selonc ce qe semblera resonable en cest parlement a vostre tresgraciouse seignourie suisdite. Outre ce, voz ditz oratours, abbe et convent, priont treshumblement, pur tant qe plusours des ditz gentz ore par tres sutil engyn, et par voie de fraude, ont alienez lours terres et tenementz a foreins gentz et autres persones qe ne sont mye de la ville de Bury suisdite, al entente, qe lour tenementz ne serroient mye chargez par les reconisances affaires; qe lours dites reconisances unqore affaires par ordinances et establissementz ent affaires en cest present parlement, emportent plenere vertu de lien et de obligacion par reconisance soi extendantz sibien a touz les terres et tenementz queux les ditz gentz avoient et tenoient come lours propres, et furent seisiz en ycelles; ou autrement autres gentz a lour profit, le dit lundy en la tierce semaigne de Quaresme avantdit, come autres lours tenementz en la ville de Bury queconqes, auxi avant come mesmes les reconisances ferroient si celles eussent este faitz duement en la chancellerie par mesmes les gentz de Bury a lundy desuisdit. Et ce par cause qe en celle vostre parlement especiale mencion fuist faite de lours dites seuretes a trovers; come il appiert overtement par expresses paroles en le roule du dit parlement; et auxint par une especiale bille en mesme le parlement endossee, desicome fraude et deceyte ne deivent doner a eide a nulluy par voie de resoun.

Item, ils prient qe .vi. persones, c'estassavoir Richard White, Thomas Lakforthe, Johan Osbern, Johan Tollere, Roger Rose et Richard de Rougham, qi sont de les pluis suffisantz persones du dite ville de Bury, et ore sont personelment en ceste ville de Novell' Salesbury, facent les dites reconisances en manere et par fourme avauntditz, devaunt q'ils departent hors de ceste ville de Salesbury suisdite. Item, qe cynquant autres persones de la dite ville de Bury, par nominacion de voz ditz oratours, abbe et convent, soient appellez, et par vostre roiale majestee compellez, pur venir et faire les dites reconissances, en la chancellerie suisdite a la quinszeine de la Trinitee proschein avenir, ou autre jour covenable et brief par voz oratours avauntditz a vostre noble conseil si vous

---
[11] Parliament of February 1383.

the sixth year of your reign, and in many other noble councils of yours, that the said people of Bury, because of their misdeeds and frequent rebellions against your crown and the said church, ought to provide as sufficient a guarantee of their good bearing towards you and the said church for all time to come as can best be devised, and moreover be bound both to you, our lord, as well as to your orators, the abbot and convent aforesaid, individually, for a surety of perpetual peace, before they receive any charter or pardon, grace or remission whatsoever.

May it please your most gracious lordship - considering their said submissions thus made to your royal majesty, and that the said people have not wished until now to give the said surety in any way, although by force of their said submission this has often been ordered; and the manner of the same surety, which would be a recognizance to be made in your chancery, has been shown and offered to them in writing - to make now a good ordinance in this parliament, and order strictly that the said sureties be made and performed without further delay by all the men and inhabitants of the same town of Bury and every single one of the same, in the manner and according to the form specified by your great council held at Westminster at the beginning of Lent last *[Page iii-171]*

[Col. a] past [24 February 1384]; the manner and form of which surety ordained in your last great council are contained in a schedule annexed to this bill. Making nevertheless the express protestation that you may add or remove things from the same schedule in accordance with whatever shall seem reasonable in this parliament to your most gracious lordship. Moreover your said orators, the abbot and convent, most humbly pray: whereas many of the said people now, by subtle contrivance, have alienated their lands and tenements to outsiders and others who are not of the aforesaid town of Bury, to the intent that their tenements should not be charged by the recognizances to be made; that their said recognizances yet to be made by ordinances and decrees to be made thereon in this parliament may carry the full charge of bond and obligation by recognizance extending to all the lands and tenements which the said people had and held as their own, and were seised of the same, or otherwise by other people to their profit, on the said Monday in the third week of the aforesaid Lent [14 March 1384], as well as any of their other tenements in the town of Bury, just as the same recognizances would have been made had they been duly made in the chancery by the same people of Bury on the aforesaid Monday. And this because in your parliament special mention was made of their said sureties to be found, as is plainly stated in the roll of the said parliament, and also by a special bill endorsed in the same parliament, inasmuch as, by way of reason, neither fraud nor deceit ought to be used to help anyone.

Also, they pray that six persons, namely Richard White, Thomas Lakeforth, John Osbern, John Toller, Roger Rose and Richard Rougham, who are amongst the most substantial persons of the said town of Bury, and are now in this town of Salisbury in person, make the said recognizances in the aforesaid manner and form before they leave the aforesaid town of Salisbury. Also, that fifty other persons of the said town of Bury, on the nomination of your said orators, the abbot and convent, be summoned, and by your royal majesty constrained, to come and make the said recognizances in the aforesaid chancery on the quindene of Trinity next coming [19 June 1384], or another suitable date close by to be fixed and appointed by your aforesaid orators at your noble

plest a limiter et nomer. Et quant a toutz les autres persones enhabitantz en la dite ville, vous plese granter suffisante poair et commissione a ascune suffisantz persones, qe vendront a certein brief terme personelment a la dite ville de Bury, as coustages de voz ditz oratours, pur prendre les dites reconissances en fourme et \en/ manere suisditz, de toutz autres et de chescune singuler persone enhabitantz ou enhabitante mesme la ville de Bury. Item, voz ditz oratours prioent treshumblement qe due remedie soit ordene en cest present parlement, pur chastier et arter suffisantement les persones rebeulx des ditz gentz, en cas qe aucuns de eux ne veullient obeier ne faire les dites reconissances en manere et fourme ordenez et establiz, come ils deivent et sont tenuz de faire par force de lour submissione et l'ordinance avauntditz, sibien c'estassavoir par emprisonement de lours corps sanz meynprise en le cas, come autrement par seisine de lours terres, biens et chateux.

Et plese a vostre tresgraciouse seignourie granter et ordener qe toutes cestes seuretees avantdites soient trovez et executz sanz proloignement faire, et si hastiement come ils poent bonement: qar le proloignement qe unqore est et qe ad este tanqe en cea, est et ad este trop perillíouse a voz oratours, abbe et convent desuisditz. Et si tost come les dites seuretees soient plenerement trovez par les dites gentz, en manere et fourme come par vostre noble et graciouse dignitee est ordenez, voz ditz oratours, abbe et convent resceivantz des dites gents .d. marcz, qe lour sont ordenez par vous et vostre [Col. b] conseil pur lours grantz perdes et damages, sont et serront delors et tantost prestz de faire tielle acquitance ad dites gentz en le cas, come vous nostre seignour par advis de vostre conseil lour avez promys sur la faisance de lour fin de .ij. mille marcz q'est de record.

La teneur de la cedule dont ceste bille fait mencion s'ensuit de parole en parole:

A. B. et C. de villa Sancti Edmundi de Bury recognoverunt, se et heredes suos, et quemlibet eorum, et heredes cujuslibet eorum, insolidum debere domino regi /decem\ mille librarum, solvendarum ei in festo Sancti Michaelis proximo futuro: et nisi fecerint, concedunt quod predicta pecunia levetur de terris et catallis suis in villa de Bury Sancti Edmundi in comitatu Suff'. Et memorandum quod ista recognitio facta est sub tali condicione, videlicet, quod si prefati A. B. et C. seu eorum heredes, aut terrarum /et\ tenementorum suorum in villa de Sancto Edmundo tenentes, aut aliqui eorum, seu aliqui alii ex eorum seu alicujus eorundem procuracione, assensu, abbetto, manutenencia, auxilio vel precepto, versus abbatem et conventum de Sancto Edmundo, seu eorum successores, aut abbaciam predictam, seu aliquem vel aliquos qui sunt vel pro tempore erunt de abbacia illa, armata vel violenta potencia in conventiculis vel congregacionibus illicitis, seu alias quovis modo, contra pacem et legem Anglie futuris temporibus non[12] insurrexerint, vel[13] aliquam transgressionem que per consilium domini regis, seu heredum suorum, vel per justiciarios suos qui pro tempore fuerint, sive per legem terre adjudicata seu considerata fuerit horribilis, predictis abbati et conventui, seu successoribus suis, aut alicui vel aliquibus qui sunt vel pro tempore erunt de abbacia predicta aliquibus temporibus futuris, fecerint vel intulerint, tunc predicta recognicio nullius sit roboris vel virtutis. Et si predicti A. B. et C. aut eorum heredes, seu terrarum et tenementorum suorum in villa de Sancto Edmundo de Bury tenentes, vel eorum aliqui, seu aliqui alii ex eorum seu alicujus eorundem procuracione, assensu, abbetto, manutenencia, auxilio, vel precepto, contra predictos

---

[12] non *superfluous*
[13] *Original* nec

---

council if it please you. And as to all the other people inhabiting the said town, may it please you to grant sufficient power and commission to some sufficient persons to come within a short space of time to the said town of Bury in person, at the expense of your said orators, to take the said recognizances in the aforesaid form and manner from each and every other person dwelling in the same town of Bury. Also, your said orators most humbly pray that due remedy be ordained in this present parliament adequately to punish and restrain the rebellious persons amongst the said people, lest any of them should not obey or make the said recognizances in the manner and form ordained and decreed, as they ought and are bound to do by the force of their submission and the aforesaid ordinance, namely by imprisonment of their body without bail in such cases, or else by seizure of their lands, goods and chattels.

And may it please your most gracious lordship to ordain that all these aforesaid sureties be found and executed without delay as soon as they well may: since the procrastination there still is and has been until now is and has been most perilous for your orators, the aforesaid abbot and convent. And as soon as the said sureties be fully found by the said men in the manner and form ordained by your noble and gracious dignity, your said orators, the abbot and convent, when they have received the five hundred marks from the said people which was ordained by you and your [Col. b] council for their great losses and damages, are and shall be from then on ready at once to grant such acquittance to the said men in this case, as you, our lord, by the advice of your council, promised them on the payment of their fine of two thousand marks which is on record.

The tenor of the schedule of which this bill makes mention follows word for word:

A. B. and C. of the town of Bury St Edmunds acknowledge themselves and their heirs, and every one of them, and every one of their heirs, to be together indebted to our lord the king for ten thousand pounds, to be paid him at Michaelmas next [29 September]: and unless they do so, they concede that the aforesaid money shall be levied from their lands and chattels in the town of Bury St Edmunds in Suffolk. And be it remembered that this recognizance is made on a certain condition, namely, that if the aforementioned A. B. and C. or their heirs, or the tenants of their lands and tenements in the town of St Edmund, or any one of them, and any others from amongst them or anyone by their procurement, assent, abetting, maintenance, help or upon their orders, shall rebel against the abbot and convent of St Edmund, or their successors, or the aforesaid abbey, or any person or persons who are or shall be connected with that abbey, having gathered an armed and violent force in unlawful conventicles and assemblies, or in any other way, contrary to the peace and law of England in the future, or commit or attempt any other transgression which by the council of the lord king, or of his heirs, or by his justices of the time, or by the law of the land shall be adjudged and considered to be horrible, against the aforesaid abbot and convent or their successors, or any person or persons who are or shall be connected with the aforesaid abbey at any future date, then the aforesaid recognizance shall be of no force or virtue. And if the aforesaid A. B. and C. or their heirs, or the tenants of their lands and tenements in the town of Bury St Edmunds, or any of them, or any others amongst them or anyone by their procurement, assent, abetting, maintenance, help, or upon their orders, shall

abbatem et conventum, vel successores suos, aut abbaciam predictam, seu aliquem vel aliquos qui sunt vel pro tempore erunt de abbacia illa aliquibus temporibus futuris, armata vel violenta potencia in conventiculis vel congregacionibus illicitis, vel alias quovis modo, contra pacem et leges predictas exnunc, quod absit, insurrexerint, vel transgressionem horribilem, ut predictum est, fecerint vel intulerint, tunc predicta recognicio contra omnes illos per quorum actum, procuracionem, assensum, abbettum, manutenenciam, auxilium, vel preceptum hujusmodi insurreccionem vel transgressionem horribilem fieri vel foveri, ut premittitur, adjudicari contigerit, super catallis et terris hujusmodi delinquencium et cujuslibet eorundem, et non contra alios non delinquentes, in suo robore et virtute permaneat, ac execucioni debite demandetur. Que quidem adjudicacio per consilium domini regis et heredum suorum, vel per justiciarios suos qui pro tempore fuerint, sive per legem terre, ut predictum est, dumtaxat fieri debet. A. B. et C. de villa Sancti Edmundi de Bury recognoverunt, se et heredes suos, et quemlibet eorum et heredes cujuslibet eorum insolidum debere abbati et conventui de Sancto Edmundo decem milia librarum solvend' eis in festo Sancti Michaelis proximo futuro. Et nisi, etc., concedunt quod dicta pecunia levetur de terris et catallis eorum in villa Sancti Edmundi de Bury in comitatu Suff'. Et memorandum quod ista recognicio facta est sub condicione precedenti; quam quidem condicionem abbas de Sancto Edmundo in cancellario domini regis, tali die et anno, personaliter constitutus, cognovit et expresse fatebatur.[14]

Responce.

Est assavoir qe la dite cedule lue en parlement, et illoeqes amende en partie et corrigee par manere come mesme la cedule purporte, estoit accordez illoqes qe chescun singuler persone de la ville de Bury ferroit la seuretee par reconisance a faire en la chancellerie, si [Page iii-172] [Col. a] bien au roi nostre seignour come a l'abbe et convent avaunditz, par fourme et manere en toutes choses, et par les condicions comprises en mesme la cedule; les quelles condicions l'abbe de Bury grantera et conoistra de record pur sa partie.

Item, la dite bille est grantez et assentuz en ceste mesme parlement en touz pointz; et especialment pur obvier la malice conceuz parmy l'alianacion de lours \[terres et tenementz]/ en Bury puis le dit parlement tenuz l'an sisme: et assentuz et accordez qe toutes les reconisances quelles sont encores affaires et \a/ resceivoires de ceulx de Bury par celle cause, et chescune d'icelle, tiegne et tiegnent tielle force et vertu de reconisances en touz pointz, et lient eux et lours terres en Bury auxi avaunt del dit lundy quant le dit parlement l'an sisme estoit tenuz q'est ja passez, come elles ferroient si mesmes les reconisances qe sont issint affaires eussent este faites par mesmes les gentz de Bury al lundy avantdit. Et enoultre est assentuz qe touz les rebeulx en le cas, si nulles y soient, soient compuls par emprisonement de lours corps sanz mainprise, et s'il embusoigne par seisine de lours tenementz, biens et chateux en Bury, de faire la dite seuretee, par manere qe par la dite bille est demande, nientcontreesteant qe la commune cours du loy de la terre \si/ est encontre ceste grant et ordinance, les queux sont ore faitz tant soulement pur le bien de pees maintenir desore en dit lieu, et salvetee de l'abbeye de Bury avauntdite, qe a diverses foitz devant ceste heure ad este mys a grant meschief et destruction par les gentz de Bury, qi sont lours propres tenantz trestoutz, et pur nulle autre cause.

rise, which God forbid, against the aforesaid abbot and convent or their successors, or the aforesaid abbey, or against any person or persons who are or may be of the abbey in time to come, having gathered an armed and violent force in conventicles or assemblies, or in any other way, contrary to the aforesaid peace and laws in the future, or commit or attempt any horrible trespass, as aforesaid; then the said recognizance, against all those by whose deeds, procurement, assent, abetting, maintenance, help or order such insurrection or horrible trespass shall be adjudged to have been done or attempted, as mentioned above, on the chattels and lands of such delinquents and every one of them, and not against others not offending, shall remain valid and in force, and due execution demanded. Which adjudication shall be made by the council of the lord king and of his heirs, or by his justices for the time being, or by the law of the land, as said above. And A. B. and C. of the town of St Edmund of Bury acknowledge themselves and their heirs, and every one of them and their heirs, to be together indebted to the abbot and convent of St Edmund for ten thousand pounds, to be paid them at Michaelmas next [29 September]. And unless, etc., they concede that the said money shall be levied on their lands and chattels in the town of St Edmund of Bury in Suffolk. And be it remembered that this recognizance is made on the preceding condition; which condition the abbot of St Edmund, being personally present in the chancery of the lord king, on such a day and in such a year, acknowledged and expressly accepted.

Answer.

Be it known that, the said schedule having been read in parliament, and there amended in part and corrected in the manner shown in the same schedule, it was agreed there that every single person of the town of Bury should find surety by recognizance to be made in the chancery, both [Page iii-172] [Col. a] to the king our lord and to the aforesaid abbot and convent, according to that form and manner in all respects, and on the conditions contained in the same schedule; which conditions the abbot of Bury will grant and acknowledge on record for his part.

Also, the said bill was granted and agreed to in this same parliament in all respects; and especially to counteract the malice conceived by the alienation of their lands and tenements in Bury since the said parliament held in the sixth year [23 February 1383]: and it was assented and agreed that all the recognizances which are still to be made and received from those of Bury for this reason, and each one of the same, shall have the force and validity of recognizances in all respects, and bind them and their lands in Bury from the said Monday on which the said parliament of the sixth year was held [23 February 1383], which is already passed, as they would if the same recognizances which are thus to be made had been made by the same people of Bury on the aforesaid Monday. And it is further agreed that all the rebels in this instance, if there be any, be constrained under threat of imprisonment of their persons, without bail, and if necessary by seizure of their tenements, goods and chattels in Bury, to find the said surety in the manner required by the said bill, notwithstanding that the common course of the law of the land runs contrary to this grant and ordinance, which are now made solely for the good keeping of the peace in future in the said place, and for the security of the aforesaid abbey of Bury, which has been greatly troubled and injured on many occasions in the past by the people of Bury, who are altogether its tenants, and for no other reason.

---

[14] PRO SC8/255/9577.

Seymour. Mountagu.

20. Item, le priour et convent de Mountagu firent mettre avant en parlement une lour bille, en la fourme qe s'ensuit: 'A nostre seignour le roy et seignours en cest present parlement, monstrent ses humbles chapelleins, priour et convent de Mountagu: qe come monsire Richard Seymour autrefoitz porta un brief de scire facias vers le dit priour, retourne en bank le roy al quinszeine de Pasqe, l'an nostre seignour le roi q'ore /est\ sisme, d'avoir execucion del manoir de Tyntenhull' ove les appurtenantz, par cause d'un fyn qe fuist levee en la court le roi Edward jadys roy d'Engleterre, besaiel nostre seignour le roy q'ore \est,/ entre un Richard Lovell' et autres certeins persones, quiel manoir est grant partie de la substance del dite priorie, et dount le dit prior et ses predecessours ont este seisiz del temps Henry [I] jadys roi d'Engleterre, fitz a William Conquerrour, tanqe al recoverer ore: quele priorie, ove toutes les possessions d'icelle, fuist seisi en main le roy Edward aiel nostre seignour le roy q'orest, a cause de la guerre de France, pur ce qe la dite priorie fuist de poair de France. Et le dit Edward aiel commist la gard del dite priorie, ove les possessions appurtenantz a icelle, par ses lettres patentes au dit priour, a tenir tanqe come il estoit a demurer en sa mayn par la cause suisdite, salvant au roi fees et avowesons expressement en la dite patente, a quele l'avoweson de l'esglise del manoir suisdit est appendant, et en mayn du roy encore par celle cause esteant.

A quiel brief de scire facias le dit priour apparust en court, et allegea, coment le dit Richard Seymour, lendemayn de Seint Martyn, l'an sisme le roi q'oreest, porta un brief de droit vers le dit priour del dit manoir, a quiel brief il apparust; le quiel brief de scire facias fuist purchace pendant le brief de droit; et demandast juggement du brief de scire facias purchacez pendant le brief de droit. Et nientcontreestant ceste excepcion le brief de scire facias fuist agarde bon, et le priour agarde de respondre par juggement; quiel agarde n'est pas entre en roulle. Et auxint le dit priour apres le dit agarde monstra la matire devaunt, ensemblement ove la dite patente du roi, provant le dit grant la reservacion au roi de fees

[Col. b] et avowesons, et par celle cause pria eide du roi: de quiel eide prier le dit priour fuist ouste par juggement, quel agarde n'est pas entre en roulle. Et oultre ce, apres la dit agard fait, le dit priour mist avaunt la chartre le roy Henry [I], fitz a Conquerrour, provant qe mesme le roi dona mesme le manoir ove les appurtenantz a l'esglise de Mountagu et a les moignes illoeqes Dieu servantz, en pure et perpetuele almoigne: et alleggea, coment il et ses predecessours avoient continue la possessione a cause del dit doun, et par diverses confirmacions des rois puis tanqe en cea; et sur ce prie aide du roy. Et nientmeins les ditz justices alerent avaunt en le plee, et apres le dit priour pleda al action, la ou par les dites patentes et confermementz droit fuist prove au roy.

Sur quoy suppliont les ditz priour et convent qe plese a voz tresgraciouses seignouries, pur Dieux, et en oevre de charitee, d'appeller devant vous les ditz justices, et de les examiner del matire suisdite, et de les charger qe les dites agardes puissent estre entreez come ils fuissent pledez, solonc la fourme d'une autre bille \q'est annexe a cestes,/ faite en pluis especial manere sur la matire, contenant par expresses paroles, coment les ditz enroullementz et record deussent estre corrigez et amendez; la quelle bille estoit fait et liveree devaunt ore as justices del dit bank. Qar autrement,

Seymour. Montacute.

20. Also, the prior and convent of Montacute submitted a bill in parliament, in the following form:
To our lord the king and the lords in this present parliament, his humble chaplains, the prior and convent of Montacute show: whereas Sir Richard Seymour on another occasion brought a writ of scire facias against the said prior, returned in the King's Bench on the quindene of Easter in the sixth year of our lord the present king [6 April 1383], to have execution of the manor of Tintinhull with appurtenances, by reason of a fine which was levied in the court of King Edward [III], late king of England, grandfather of our lord the present king, between one Richard Lovell and certain other persons; which manor represents much of the said priory's wealth, and the said prior and his predecessors have had possession of it since the time of Henry [I], late king of England, son of William the Conqueror, until the present recovery: which priory, with all its possessions, was taken into the hands of King Edward, grandfather of our lord the present king, because of the war with France, because the said priory was under the power of France. And the said Edward, the grandfather, committed the keeping of the said priory, with the possessions pertaining to the same, by his letters patent to the said prior, to be held for as long as it was to remain in his hands for the aforesaid reason, saving to the king in the said patent fees and advowsons in particular, to which the advowson of the church of the aforesaid manor is attached, and still in the hands of the king for that reason.
To which writ of scire facias the said prior appeared in court, and claimed that the said Richard Seymour, on the morrow of Martinmas, in the sixth year of the present king [12 November 1382], brought a writ of right against the said prior over the said manor, to which writ he appeared; which writ of scire facias had been purchased pending a writ of right; and he demanded judgment of the writ of scire facias purchased pending the writ of right. And notwithstanding that exception the writ of scire facias was held good and the prior was held to answer by judgment; which decision is not entered on the roll. Furthermore, the said prior, after the said decision, presented the aforesaid matter, together with the said king's patent, proving the said grant of the reservation to the king of the fees

[Col. b] and advowsons, and for that reason he sought aid of the king: from which aid thus requested the said prior was ousted by judgement, which award is not entered on the roll. Moreover, after the said award was made, the said prior presented the charter of King Henry [I], son of the Conqueror, proving that the same king gave the same manor with appurtenances to the church of Montacute and to the monks serving God there in pure and perpetual alms: and he claimed that he and his predecessors had continued in possession until now because of the said gift, and by various confirmations of the kings since; and thereupon he prayed aid of the king. Yet nevertheless the said justices continued in the plea, and after the said prior pleaded to the action, because right was proved to lie with the king by the said patents and confirmations.

Whereupon the said prior and convent request that it might please your most gracious lordship, for God and by way of charity, to call before you the said justices, and to question them on the aforesaid matter, and to charge them that the same awards shall be entered as they were pleaded, in accordance with the form of another bill which is annexed to those directed more especially to the matter, stating expressly that the said enrolments and record should be corrected and amended; which bill was made and submitted before now to the justices of the said Bench. For

treshonurez seignours, sanz vostre tresgracious aide la dite priorie est destruit et annintiz pur touz jours. Et, treshonurez seignours, le dit priour ad pursuiz del comencement del plee plede tanqe en cea as ditz justices d'entrer les ditz plees en manere come ils furent pledez, quele chose les ditz justices lui outrement ount denyez.'

Item, les ditz priour et convent mistrent avant en parlement une cedule dont la dite bille fait mention, en la fourme qe s'ensuit:

Cedule.
'Memorandum quod ubi in recordo et processu habitis inter Ricardum Seymour et priorem de Monte Acuto, \modo/ sic continetur, videlicet: et quia per tenores brevis et recordi predicti hic missos non constabat curia quod predictus Ricardus Seymour ad breve predictum aliquando comparuit, nec quod breve predictum aliquando comparuit, nec quod breve predictum adtunc pendebat, quesitum fuit a prefato priore si quid, etc.. Predictus prior petit quod predictum recordum emendetur sub hac forma, videlicet quod ubi est 'Quesitum fuit', etc., in eodem recordo corrigatur sic et fiat, quia videtur curie quod predictum breve de scire facias manuteneri posset racionibus et allegationibus predictis non obstantibus, dictum est prefato priori quod ulterius respondeat, etc.. Item, prior petit quod ex quo petiit auxilium de domino rege, etc., unde in dicto recordo jam sic scribitur, videlicet, 'Quia videtur curie quod auxilium predictum prefato priori in hoc casu non est concedendum,' quesitum fuit a prefato priore, si quid, etc., predictus prior petit recordum illud emendari sub hac forma, scilicet, quod ubi scribitur 'Quesitum', etc., corrigatur irrotulamentum, et fiat, ibi dictum est per curia prefato priori quod ulterius respondeat, etc., sive auxilio predicto, etc..'

Membrane 2
Quelles bille et cedule luez en parlement en presence des seignours, justices del bank le roi, monsire Robert Bealknap chief justice, del commune bank, seignour Johan de Waltham gardein des roulles, monsire Robert de Plesyngton' chief baron del escheqier, Wauter de Clopton' et William Rikyll', sergeantz le roi, et d'autres sages illoeqes presentz; et avec ce les record et proces dont les dites bille et cedule font mencion, queux par comandement des seignours furent portez en parlement, et illoeqes \devant/ les seignours du roialme, justices et les autres dessuisditz, venes et examinez; et sur ce la matire comprise es dites bille et cedule diligeaument debatue et examine, finalment par l'advis des justices et les autres sages dessuisditz est agardez et comandez en parlement qe l'enroullement einsi fait en dit plee soit amendez et corrigez accordantement en toutes choses, a *[Page iii-173]*

[Col. a] ce qe par les dites bille et cedule est ore demandez, et ce encores par la forme et manere qe s'ensuit. C'estassavoir, qe les roulles en quelles les dites defautes sont pretenduz estre compris soient horstretz de la bundell en quiel celles roulles sont de present contenuz, et autres roulles de novell faitz escritz, et tantost myses et affilez en lieu des ditz autres roulles en la bundell dessuisdit, compernantz mesme la nombre des roulles, et avec ce compernantz la matire en toutes choses qe les ditz autres primers roulles y firent comprehendre; horspris en especial, qe celles novelles roulles, et cell novell entre ent a faires s'accordent oultrement a ce qe par les dites bille et cedule est demandez. Et celles novelles roulles issint faitz et affilez, soient /ycelle\ novelles roulles deslors de record, et les autres

otherwise, most honoured lords, without your most gracious aid, the said priory will be ruined and destroyed forever. And, most honoured lords, the said prior has requested the justices, from the beginning when the plea was pleaded until now, to enter the said pleas in the manner in which they were pleaded, which the said justices have utterly denied him.

Also, the said prior and convent laid before parliament the schedule of which the said bill made mention, in the following form:

Schedule.
Be it remembered that where in the record and process had between Richard Seymour and the prior of Montacute it is contained thus, namely - and because by the tenor of the aforesaid writ and record thus submitted, the court did not know that the aforesaid Richard Seymour had once appeared at the aforesaid writ, nor that he had ever appeared at the aforesaid writ, nor that the aforesaid writ was still pending, it was asked of the aforesaid prior whether, etc. - the aforesaid prior asked that the aforesaid record be amended in this way: namely that where it said 'It was asked', etc., in the same record it should be thus corrected - because it seemed to the court that the aforesaid writ of scire facias could be kept notwithstanding the aforesaid reasons and allegations, it was said to the aforementioned prior that he should also answer, etc.. Also, the prior asked that since he had sought the aid of the lord king, etc., whence it shall now be written thus in the said record, namely: - Because it seems to the court that the aforesaid aid ought not to be conceded in this case to the aforementioned prior,' it was asked of the aforementioned prior, if, etc. - the aforesaid prior requested this record to be amended in this manner, namely, that where it shall be written 'It was asked',etc., the enrolment should be corrected - and let it be done, there it was said by the court to the aforementioned prior that he also answer, etc., or the aforesaid aid, etc..

Which bill and schedule having been read in parliament in the presence of the lords, the justices of the King's Bench, Sir Robert Bealknap, chief justice of the Common Bench, Sir John Waltham, master of the rolls, Sir Robert Plessington, chief baron of the exchequer, Walter Clopton and William Rikhill, king's serjeants, and other wise men there present; and therupon with the record and process of which the said bill and schedule made mention, which at the order of the lords were brought to parliament, and there inspected and examined before the lords of the realm, justices and others aforementioned; and the matter contained in the said bill and schedule diligently debated and examined; finally, upon the advice of the justices and other aforesaid wise men it was decided and ordered in parliament that the enrolment thus made in the said plea should be amended and corrected, according in all respects, with *[Page iii-173]*

[Col. a] the requests in the said bill and schedule, and that still in the form and manner which follow. Namely, that the rolls in which the said faults were allegedly contained be removed from the bundle in which those rolls were then contained, and other rolls newly written, and immediately put and filed in place of the said other rolls in the aforesaid bundle, comprising the same number of rolls, and also matching the matter in all respects which the said other rolls there contained; except in particular, that the new rolls and the new entry to be made should agree entirely with what the said bill and schedule required. And the new rolls thus made and

primers roulles dessuisditz tenuz pur voides et nulles a touz jours.

21. Item, puis apres quant l'enroullement des ditz record et proces estoit par vertu del dit agard en parlement amendez en la forme suisdite, si estoit une autre bille mys avant en parlement depar le priour et convent dessuisditz, en la forme qe s'ensuit:

A nostre tresredoute seignour le roy et a ses nobles seignours en cest present parlement, monstre le priour de Mountagu, come Richard Seymor, cousyn et heir Richard Lovel, suit un brief de scire facias /devers\ le dit priour en bank nostre dit seignour le roi, retournable a la quinszeine de Pasqe, l'an sisme nostre dit seignour le roy q'orest, d'avoir execucioun del manoir de Tyntenhull' ove les appertenantz hors d'un fyn qe se leva en la courte le roy Edward, besaiel nostre dit seignour le roy q'orest, a les oeptaves de Seint Michel, l'an du regne le roi Edward unszime devant monsire William de Bereford et ses compaignons adonqes justices de commune bank, entre le dit Richard Lovel et Muriele sa femme pleignantz, et meistre Richard de Clare et meistre Richard de Blokesworth' deforceantz, de dit manoir, et autres maneres proces, tant suy sur le dit brief qe execucione de dit manoir de Tyntenhulle ove les appertenantz est agarde a dit Richard countre le dit priour, come en le record ent fait en le dit bank demurrant pleinement appiert.

[Col. b] En quiel record diverses errours y sont, come le dit priour serra prest d'assigner.

Par quoi supplie le dit priour qe ordene soit en ceste present parlement qe certeins gentz de conseil nostre dit seignour le roi soient assignez, devant queux le dit record soit envoie, et qe eux eient plein poair et auctoritee par force de mesme l'ordenance d'oier l'assignement des errours avauntditz; et de faire garnir le dit Richard Seymor d'estre devant eux a certein jour par eux a assigner, d'oier l'assignement dez ditz errours, et qe eux poent corriger et redresser mesmes les errours, et droiturel juggement ent rendre: et qe nul proteccione soit alowe pur le dit Richard Seymor en la dit suite, eiant regard a la defaute q'est ore trove en parlement, et al delay qe le dit priour ad euz, pur defaute de bone entree del plee; et eiant regard qe nostre seignour le roy ad grant interesse qe celle chose soit redresse en hast, a cause qe pur l'ouster de l'eide, et le recoverir del manoir, le roi est ouste de les fees et avowesons autrefoitz expressement reservez par sa patente; et qe l'esglise de Mountagu ad este seisi de dit manoir de Tyntenhulle de temps le roi Henry [I] fitz au roi William primer, come par chartres des roys appiert overtement, tanqe al temps de dit juggement, pur Dieu, et en oevre de charitee.

Et celle bille auxint lue en parlement, estoit agardez par assent du parlement qe le priour de Mountagu dessuisdit eit brief de scire facias, fait et founduz en son cas, retournable en proschein parlement, de faire garnir le dit monsire Richard .... Seymor d'estre a mesme le proschein parlement, en quelqe \lieu qe ce/ soit tenuz deinz le roialme d'Engleterre, pur y oier les errours quelles ore sont ou serront monstrez ou alleggez par le dit priour estre contenuz en les record et proces avauntditz; et enoultre de faire et resceivoir ce qe par la loy de la terre serra juggez en celle partie. Et est comandez qe mesmes les record et proces, ove toutes choses celles record et proces touchantz, soient en dit proschein parlement par celle cause. Et est grantez et assentuz pluis avant illoeqes qe nulle proteccione quelle est ou serra purchacez pur le dit monsire Richard par feinte cause, soit allouez en ceste querelle par aucune voie.

filed were to be be new rolls of record, and the other original rolls aforesaid to be considered null and void forever.

21. Also, later when the enrolment of the said record and process had been amended in the aforesaid form by virtue of the said award in parliament, another bill was submitted in parliament by the aforesaid prior and convent, in the form which follows:

To our most redoubted lord the king and to the noble lords in this present parliament, the prior of Montacute shows that Richard Seymour, cousin and heir of Richard Lovell, sued a writ of scire facias against the said prior in the Bench of our said lord the king, returnable at the quindene of Easter in the sixth year of our said lord the present king [6 April 1383], to have execution of the manor of Tintinhull with appurtenances from a fine which was levied in the court of King Edward [II], great-grandfather of our said lord the present king, on the octave of Michaelmas in the eleventh year of King Edward, before Sir William Bereford and his companions, then justices in the Common Bench, between the said Richard Lovell and Muriel, his wife, plaintiffs, and Master Richard Clare and Master Richard Bloxworth, defendants, concerning the said manor [7 October 1317], and other process, it was sued upon that execution of the said manor of Tintinhull with its appurtenances was awarded to the said Richard against the said prior, as more plainly appears in the record made thereon, remaining in the King's Bench.

[Col. b] In which record various errors are to be found, which the said prior is ready to show.

On account of which the said prior requests that it be ordained in this present parliament that certain men of the council of our said lord the king be appointed, before whom the said record be sent, and that they shall have full power and authority by force of the same ordinance to hear the account of the aforesaid errors; and to warn the said Richard Seymour to appear before them on a certain day appointed by them to hear the account of the said errors, and that they might correct and redress the same errors, and pass true judgment thereon: and that no protection be allowed to the said Richard Seymour in the said suit, having regard for the fault which is now found in parliament and the delay which the said prior has suffered because of the lack of an accurate entry of the plea; and bearing in mind that our lord the king has a great interest in this matter being speedily redressed, because in the ouster and aid and the recovery of the manor, the king is ousted from the fees and advowsons once expressly reserved by his patent; and that the church of Montacute has been seised of the said manor of Tintinhull from the time of King Henry [I], son of King William I, as the kings' charters clearly show, until the time of the said judgment; for love of God and by way of charity.

And the bill having also been read in parliament, it was decided by the assent of parliament that the aforesaid prior of Montacute should have a writ of scire facias made and based on his case, returnable in the next parliament, to warn the said Sir Richard Seymour to be at the same next parliament, wheresover it might be held in the kingdom of England, to hear there the errors which were now or would be shown or alleged by the said prior to be contained in the aforesaid record and process; and also to do and submit to what the law of the land may judge in this matter. And it is ordered that the same record and process, together with all things touching such record and process, be available in the said next parliament for that purpose. And it is granted and agreed there moreover, that no protection which is or shall be purchased for the said Sir Richard by fraudulent means be allowed in this dispute in any way.

SECUNTUR PETICIONES LIBERATE PER COMMUNITATEM REGNI ANGLIE IN PARLIAMENTO, ANNO ET DIE SUPRADICTIS, APUD NOVAM SARUM TENTO.

Membrane 1
A nostre tresgracious, trespuissant et tresredoute seignour, nostre seignour le roi, supplient les communes d'Engleterre pur les peticions dessouthescritz:

I. [Affirmation of the liberties of the church, the charters, and the statutes.]
22. En primes, qe seinte esglise eit toutes ses libertees et franchises, et qe la grande chartre et la chartre de la foreste, l'estatut des purveours, et toutes les autres bones estatutz et ordinances avant ces heures faitz, soient tenuz et gardez, et duement et joustement executz /selonc l'effect d'ycelles.\
Responsio.
Le roi le voet.

II. [Term of office of sheriffs, under-sheriffs, and escheators.]
23. Item, prient les communes: qe come ordenez soit par estatutqe nul viscont, south-viscont n'eschetour, demoerge en son office oultre un an.[15]
Qe plese au roi nostre seignour qe le dit estatut soit fermement tenuz
[Col. b] desore enapres, sanz estre fait au contraire, pur grant ease et quiete de tout le roialme. Et si aucune commissione soit faite au contraire, q'il soit repellez.
Responsio.
Diverses estatutz sont faitz en la cas devant ceste heure, les queux le roi voet qe soient tenuz et gardez.

III. [Election of London aldermen.]
24. Item, prient les communes, pur paix et tranquillitee mayntenir en la citee de Londres en temps avenir, a cause qe touz les aldermans, electives de mesme la citee de an en an en la feste de Seint Gregoir le pape, ore tard ont este remoeuez, et nul de eux reeslu pur l'an ensuant, mais autres mys en lour lieu tout de novel, a grant annyntesment de la governail du dite citee, come ore est pleinement approvez.
Qe plese a nostre dit seignour le roi grantir as mair et communes du dite citee et leurs successours, en ce present parlement, qe les aldermans electives soient d'an en an al dit fest de Seint *[Page iii-174]*
[Col. a] Gregoir franchement esluz, de les pluis suffisantes persones, et de bone fame, sibien de ceux q'ont este en mesme l'an come des autres, par les gardes de la dite citee; nientcontreesteantz aucunes ordinances ou chartre faitz au contraire, sauvant toutesfoitz a chescune garde leur franche eleccion en manere suisdit.
Responsio.
Le roi le voet et grante a durer tantcome bone governement soit en la dite citee par celle cause.

IV. [Losses to the farm of shires.]
25. Item, prient les communes: qe come diverses hundredes, chastelx et autres commodites appurtenantz as plusours countees d'Engleterre, sont donez sibien par voz nobles progenitours come par vous, tresredoute seignour, as diverses seignours et autres gentz; et nientcontreesteantz tielx douns, les viscontz des tielx countees qi pur le temps accomptent et paient l'entiertee pur les ditz countees, si avaunt come ils paierent au temps qe les ditz hundredes, chastelx et les autres commodites furent entierment annexez as

HERE FOLLOW THE PETITIONS SUBMITTED BY THE COMMONS OF THE KINGDOM OF ENGLAND IN THE PARLIAMENT HELD AT SALISBURY IN THE AFORESAID YEAR AND ON THE AFORESAID DAY.

To our most gracious, most exalted, and redoubtable lord, our lord the king, the commons of England pray for the petitions written below:

I. [Affirmation of the liberties of the church, the charters and the statutes.]
22. First, that holy church have all its liberties and franchises, and that the Great Charter and the Charter of the Forest, the statute of purveyors, and all the other good statutes and ordinances made in the past, be upheld, kept and justly executed, according to the tenor thereof.
Answer.
The king wills it.

II. [Term of office of sheriffs, under-sheriffs, and escheators.]
23. Also the commons pray: whereas it is ordained by statute that no sheriff, deputy sheriff, nor escheator, shall remain in office longer than a year.
May it please the king our lord that the said statute be firmly kept
[Col. b] henceforth, without contravention, for the great ease and quiet of all the realm. And if any commission be made to the contrary, that it be repealed.
Answer.
Various statutes have been made on this matter in the past, which the king wills to be upheld and protected.

III. [Election of London aldermen.]
24. Also, the commons pray, for the keeping of peace and tranquillity in the city of London in time to come: whereas all aldermen elected by the same city from year to year on the feast of St Gregory the pope have lately been removed, and none of them re-elected for the following year, but others newly set in their place, to the great injury of the governance of the said city, as is now plainly evident.
May it please our said lord the king to grant to the mayor and commons of the said city and their successors, in this present parliament, that the elective aldermen be freely elected from year to year on the said feast of St *[Page iii-174]*
[Col. a] Gregory from the persons most worthy and of good repute, both those who have been in office in the same year and others, by the wards of the said city, notwithstanding any ordinances or charter made to the contrary; saving at all times to each ward their free election in the aforesaid manner.
Answer.
The king wills it, and grants that it endure as long as there be good governance of the said city by that means.

IV. [Losses to the farm of shires.]
25. Also, the commons pray: whereas various hundreds, castles and other benefices pertaining to many counties of England have been given both by your noble progenitors and by you, most redoubtable lord, to various lords and other men; and notwithstanding such gifts, the sheriffs of such counties then in office account and pay the entire sum for the said counties, just as they paid in the time when the said hundreds, castles and other benefices were wholly annexed to

---
[15] 28 Edw.3 c.7.

dites countees, a grant damage et empoverissement de ditz viscontz.

Par quoy les ditz communes en le derrain parlement suerent a vostre tresgraciouse seignourie, d'ordeigner qe due allouance purroit estre faite as ditz viscontz qi pur le temps furent, sur lours accompts, pur les ditz hundredes, chastelx et autres commoditees ensi donez; ou autrement qe les ditz hundredes, chastelx et autres commoditees puissent estre rejointz as ditz countees, come ils furent d'auncien temps. Sur quoi il estoit grantez en le \dit/ derrain parlement qe ceux qi leur senterent grevez monstrerent as chancellor et tresorier, qi pur le temps furent, leurs grevances en especial, et leurs causes pur quelles ils furent ensi mys a perde et les ditz chancellor et tresorier du temps en temps ferroient tieux descharges et allouances as compleignantz sur lours accompts en celle partie, come par lour descrecion et bon advis lour sembleroit resonablement affaire. Et ore ensi est qe pluseurs gentz grevez en celle partie ont pursuez as ditz chancellor et tresorer, pur avoir allouance de lour perde en temps q'ils furent viscontz, selonc le dite grante; et les ditz chancellor et tresorer ne veullent prendre sur eux de le faire.

Vous plese, en oevre de charitee, ordener en ce present parlement qe due allouance et descharge soient faitz as ditz viscontz qi pur le temps serront, sibien pur l'an passe come en temps avenir, sur lours accompts pur les ditz chastelx, hundredes et autres commoditees ensi donez; ou qe mesmes les hundredes, chastelx et commoditees puissent estre rejointz as ditz countees come ils furent devaunt,

[Col. b] sicome il purra bien estre provez de record, ou autrement pluseurs viscontz serront destruitz et empoverissez pur touz jours, et les communes des dites countees grantement endamagez et oppressez par les ditz viscontz, en abreggement de lour perde en celle partie.

Responsio.

Quant al temps passez, le roi voet qe les ditz chancellor et tresorier facent due allouance as compleignantz des toutes choses qe de resoun leur deivent estre allouez en le cas. Et quant al temps avenir, le roi a son proschein parlement, par advis de son conseil, ent ordeignera de remede pluis au plein en especial.

V. [Actions against ravishers and consentients.]

26. Item, prient les communes: qe come ordenez fust au parlement tenuz a Westm' l'an du regne nostre \[dit seignour le roi sisme,[16] q'en quel lieu, et a]/ quele heure aucunes femmes feussent ravisez, et apres tiel rape eussent assentuz as tielx ravissours, qe sibien les ravissours come les femmes \[ravyes, et chescun de eux,]/ feusse desable et et pur nounable tenuz a chalenger ou avoir aucun manere d'eritage, dower ou jointfeoffement, apres la deces lours barons, et de lours auncestres;[17] \[et qe meintenant en cel cas le proschein]/ de sank de les avauntditz ravisours ou ravys, a qi heritage, dower, ou jointefeoffement devroit descendre, revertir, remendre ou approcher, \[apres la mort de]/ tielx ravissours ou ravys, eit title, meintenant apres cel rape, d'entrer sur les ravisours ou ravissez, et leur assignez, et terre tenantz en mesme l'eritage, dower, \[ou jointefeoffement, et]/ ce enheritablement tenir. Et qe les barons de celles femmes, ou s'ils n'eient pas barons en vie q'adonqes leurs piers, ou autres proscheins de leur sank, \[puissent suir, et]/ eussent la pursuite devers tielx malfeisours et ravissours, a ceux atteindre de vie et de membre, tout \[soit]/ qe les ditz femmes apres cel ravissement as tielx ravissours eussent assentuz; et oultre feust ordenez qe le defendant en ce cas ne

---
[16] Parliament of May 1382, item 45.
[17] 6 Ric.2 st.1 c.6.

the said counties, to the great injury and impoverishment of the said sheriffs.

Because of which the said commons in the last parliament sued to your most gracious lordship to order due allowance to be given to the said sheriffs for the time being on their accounts for the said hundreds, castles and other benefices thus granted; or else that the said hundreds, castles and other benefices might be reunited with the said counties, as they were of old. Whereupon it was granted in the said last parliament that those who felt aggrieved should show their particular grievances to the chancellor and treasurer for the time being, together with the reasons why they had thus been set at a loss, and the said chancellor and treasurer from time to time would grant such discharges and allowances to the plaintiffs on their accounts in the matter as would seem reasonable to them, upon their discretion and good advice. Yet now it happens that many persons aggrieved in that way have sought from the said chancellor and treasurer allowance for their losses in the time when they were sheriffs, in accordance with the said grant, but the said chancellor and treasurer will not take it upon themselves to do that.

May it please you, by way of charity, to order in this present parliament that due allowance and relief be given to the said sheriffs for the time being, both for the past year and in time to come, on their accounts for the said castles, hundreds and other benefices thus granted; or that the same hundreds, castles and benefices be reunited with the said counties as they were before,

[Col. b] as is well proven on record; for otherwise, many sheriffs will be destroyed and impoverished forever, and the commons of the said counties greatly harmed and oppressed by the said sheriffs attempting to reduce their loss in the matter.

Answer.

As for time past, the king wills that the said chancellor and treasurer make due allowance to the plaintiffs for all things which ought by reason to be allowed them in such cases. And as for time to come, the king at his next parliament, with the advice of his council, will ordain a more thorough remedy in detail.

V. [Actions against ravishers and consentients.]

26. Also, the commons pray: whereas it was ordained at the parliament held at Westminster in the sixth year of the reign of our said lord the king that wheresoever and whensoever women were ravished, and after such rape have acquiesced to such ravishers, that both the ravishers and the ravished women, and each of them, should be held disabled and wholly incapable of claiming or holding any manner of inheritance, dower or joint feoffment after the death of their husbands and their ancestors; and that then in such cases the closest in blood of the aforesaid ravishers or ravished to whom the inheritance, dower or joint enfeoffment ought to descend, revert or fall after the death of such ravishers or ravished shall be entitled, immediately after such a rape, to enter upon the ravishers or ravished, and their assignees and tenants in the same inheritance, dower or joint feoffment, and hold it by hereditary right. And that the husbands of those women, or their fathers if they have not husbands living, or others near them in blood, may sue and bring a suit against such malefactors and ravishers to attaint them of loss of life and limb, albeit that the said women have acquiesced to such ravishers after such a ravishment; further it was ordained that

serroit pas receuz de gagier le batail, mais qe la veritee de ce serroit triee par enqueste.

Qe plese a nostre dit seignour le roy, considerant qe la dite ordinance est faite a trop dure et redde loy as liges nostre dit seignour le roy, ordener qe la dite ordinance soit en ce present parlement adnullee et annientie, et tenuz pur nul, sibien de tout temps passe come du temps avenir; et qe l'auncien estatut fait de rape des femmes estoise en sa force. *Responsio.*

Le roi voet qe l'estatut dessuisdit tiegne sa force: salvant nientmeins a lui et as autres seignours du roialme pleinement lours forfaitures dues en le cas, sicome ils les eurent devant mesme l'estatut fait.

the defendant in such cases should not be allowed to wage battle, but that the truth of the matter be tried by inquest.

May it please our said lord the king, considering that the said ordinance has resulted in too harsh and strict a law for the lieges of our said lord the king, to ordain that the said ordinance be annulled and cancelled in this present parliament, and held invalid for time past as well as time to come; and that the ancient statute on rape of women remain in force. *Answer.*

The king wills that the aforesaid statute remain in force: saving nevertheless to him and the other lords of the realm all their forfeitures due in such cases which they would have had before the same statute was made.

Appendix

29 April 1384

Salisbury

1. Appointment of the earl of Devon and others to investigate a complaint concerning disturbers of the peace who have pursued and threatened various of the bishop of Exeter's servants at both Crediton (Devon) and Exeter. Dated 8 May 1384. By the council in parliament.
Source: *CPR 1381-5*, 427.

1384 November

Westminster

12 November - 14 December 1384

(C 65/43. *RP*, III.184-202. *SR*, II.36-7)

C 65/43 is a roll of seven membranes, each approximately 315mm in width, sewn together in chancery style and numbered in a later hand. The original numbering of the membranes is confused; they have thus been renumbered as follows, with the original number shown in brackets: 7 (10), 6 (1), 5 (8), 4 (7), 3 (8), 2 (6), 1 (no number). The text, written in the official chancery script of several scribes, occupies the rectos of the membranes only. The dorses are blank apart from a later heading, 'Parliamentum de anno 8° R. 2^{di}', and later notes where the membranes are joined, 'Parl' 8 R. 2 pars unica', or 'Parliamentum anno 8° R. 2'. The condition of the roll is good, though membranes 7, 2 and 1 are stained with gallic acid. The marginal notes are contemporary. The Arabic numerals are of a later date. The writs and returns mentioned in item no. 15 are also recorded on two pieces of parchment stitched to membrane 6 as follows: the first, as far as 'per Johannem Fauconer et Robertum Coker', is recorded on the lower piece, which measures approximately 315mm in width and 50mm in length; the second, as far as 'prout istud breve requirit', is recorded on the top piece, which measures approximately 300mm in width and 45mm in length. In addition, the Crown Pleas on membrane 3 continue on four separate membranes (numbered i-iv) stitched together exchequer style to the foot of the dorse of membrane 6. These membranes measure approximately 235mm in width. The text occupies the rectos and dorses of membranes i-iii, while membrane iv has only five lines of text at its head.

Once the Salisbury parliament of April 1384 had failed to ratify the draft Anglo-French treaty, there was little choice but to return to the negotiating table, yet, despite the fact that John of Gaunt, duke of Lancaster, and his brother the earl of Buckingham spent much of the summer on the continent trying to work out a peace formula acceptable to both sides, the best that they could achieve was an extension of the truce until 1 May 1385. This was agreed in early September, and on 28 September writs were issued summoning parliament to meet on 12 November.[1] This was the third year in a row, and the fourth in the past five, that parliament had met twice in a year, a relatively uncommon occurrence over the fourteenth century as a whole. The writs of summons to the spiritual peers included the abbot of Bury but were otherwise identical to those issued for the April parliament. Among the lords temporal there were two newcomers, Ralph Lumley and John Devereux. Lumley's great-grandfather, Marmaduke Thweng, had been summoned to parliament in the early fourteenth century, but none of his three sons had ever been summoned. Devereux was a banneret and former royal councillor, but none of his ancestors had ever been summoned to parliament. On the other hand, he must have attended the April parliament, for he was one of the bannerets chosen to advise the commons on the question of taxation. Presumably he had attended in some official capacity, despite being a banneret.[2]

Since 12 November was a Saturday, the opening of parliament was postponed to the Monday, and then again, on the king's orders, to Tuesday 15th. The opening speech was delivered, as was customary, by the chancellor, Michael de la Pole. Despite the fact that de la Pole was probably the foremost advocate of a policy of peace with France, even he, as he made clear, saw little prospect that peace would be achieved in the near future.[3] England was imperilled on all sides, he declared: from the French, who had conducted themselves deceitfully in the negotiations, from the Spanish and Flemish with their galleys, and from the Scots. England did, however, have a young king - Richard II was now approaching his eighteenth birthday - who was keen to go to war in person, and nothing was more likely to inspire a supreme effort on the part of English knighthood. De la Pole encouraged the commons to be suitably generous, as well as suitably brief (Items 3-5).

The commons were indeed reasonably generous, but their generosity came with strings attached. They granted two fifteenths and tenths, the first to be collected by 25 March 1385, the second by 24 June 1385. In return, however, they requested that the second half fifteenth and tenth granted in April be cancelled, and - in a move which smacked of calling the king's and chancellor's bluff - they insisted that if Richard did not lead the projected military campaign in person, the grant of the second fifteenth and tenth should also be cancelled. Here then was a challenge which could hardly be ignored, and it doubtless goes at least part of the way towards explaining why Richard did indeed lead his first military expedition in the summer of 1385, although not to France (Item 10).

---

[1] *CCR 1381-5*, 586-7.
[2] Powell and Wallis, *House of Lords in the Middle Ages*, 394.
[3] Saul, *Richard II*, 137-8.

Despite the length of the roll, the parliament of November 1384 was not a particularly eventful assembly. Approximately three-quarters of the roll is taken up with the inordinately protracted and repetitive recital of the legal records relating to a dispute between Richard Seymour (or Saint Maur), lord of Castle Cary and a peer of parliament, and the prior of Montacute, over the ownership of the manor of Tintinhull (Somerset). The eventual decision of the parliament, by which the manor was awarded to the prior, involved the reversal of a previous decision, which may explain why it was felt necessary to set out the proceedings at such length (Item 15). A contemporary memorandum on the close roll records that all the records relating to the case were removed and taken into parliament, 'and so they remain among other records of that parliament, because the judgment here recorded is reversed, and nought here remains of record concerning that cause'.[4]

A number of other judicial items of some interest were also dealt with. For the second parliament in succession, a member of the London merchant class was arraigned for defaming a peer of the realm. In the April parliament the fishmonger John Cavendish had accused Michael de la Pole of denying him justice; in this parliament Walter Sibill, also a fishmonger, was brought in to answer for having accused Robert de Vere, earl of Oxford and the king's chamberlain, of maintenance (Item 12; it is also worth noting that maintenance and its effect on the judicial system was the subject of two petitions from the commons, Items 17 and 18). De Vere and de la Pole were both members of the king's inner circle of advisers, and these accusations probably reflect the growing unpopularity of the royal court as well as its entanglement with the factional rivalries which rent the city. John of Northampton, the draper and controversial former mayor, had been hauled before a meeting of the royal council just two months before this parliament met and convicted of treason (although his death sentence was commuted to life imprisonment), while his successor, the grocer Nicholas Brembre, would also be convicted of treason in the parliament of February 1388 - and for him there would be no relaxation of the ultimate penalty. In the circumstances, Sibill could probably count himself lucky to get away with a fine of fifty marks for damages.[5] Also fortunate in this parliament was Alice Perrers, the former mistress of Edward III, whose petition for the repeal of the sentence of banishment passed against her in 1377 was upheld, even if the terms of the repeal did not offer her any great hope of recovering the lands which she had forfeited at the time (Item 13).

None of this greatly excited the interest of the chroniclers. Thomas Walsingham, the St Albans chronicler, remarked that 'nothing worth recording took place' during the parliament, while the Westminster chronicler said that the quarrels of the lords meant that nothing was achieved. Both chroniclers did, however, mention two other events which occurred during the parliament. The first was the arrival of news of the capture by the Scots of Berwick-upon-Tweed. Gaunt seized the opportunity to subject the earl of Northumberland, who had the keeping of Berwick, to public humiliation; after apparently undergoing some form of public censure, Northumberland marched hastily north and soon re-took the town. The second incident, which was mentioned in several of the chronicles, was the duel between an English esquire, John Walsh of Grimsby, and a Navarrese esquire called Martlet de Villeneuve who had accused Walsh of treason. Walsh won the duel, which was fought on 30 November, and Martlet was duly drawn, hanged and beheaded, the penalty for failing to prove an accusation of treason.[6]

The parliament was dissolved on 14 December.[7] According to the Westminster chronicler it broke up in dissension, and certainly dissension continued to mar relationships between the leading political players in the kingdom during the following year. At a meeting of the great council held at Waltham in early February 1385, Gaunt tried to persuade the king to undertake his proposed expedition to France; when he failed to do so, he walked out in disgust. A few days later, he was warned of a plot by a group of Richard's confidants to have him assassinated, and although a reconciliation between Richard and his uncle was brokered by the king's mother, Princess Joan, early in March, there is no doubt that the royal court had become a dangerous place by the mid-1380s.[8] Richard did, in the end, take the field as a military commander in the summer of 1385, leading an expedition to Scotland, but disagreements over strategy led him to quarrel yet again with Gaunt, and by the time the next parliament met in October the political tension at Westminster was strained almost to breaking point.

---

[4] *CCR 1381-5*, 498-9, 612.
[5] His trial probably took place on 28 November; he had been arrested three days previously: *CCR 1381-5*, 494.
[6] *St Albans Chronicle 1376-1394*, 732-4; *Westminster Chronicle*, 102-4; *Vita Ricardi Secundi*, 84-5; *Knighton's Chronicle*, 334.
[7] *CCR 1381-5*, 599-600.
[8] Saul, *Richard II*, 133-4.

Text and Translation

Text

Page iii-184, Membrane 7[9]

ROTULUS PARLIAMENTI TENTI APUD WESTM' IN CRASTINO SANCTI MARTINI, ANNO REGNI REGIS RICARDI SECUNDI POST CONQUESTUM OCTAVO.

1. Memorandum quod presens parliamentum summonitum apud Westm' in crastino Sancti Martini, anno regni regis Ricardi secundi post conquestum octavo, quod \[quidem crastinum die sabbati]/ contingebat, de precepto regis adjornatum fuit certis de causis usque diem lune tunc proximum sequentem.

2. Et dicto die lune, iterum de precepto regis adjornatum \[fuit ex causis predictis]/ usque in crastinum, scilicet diem martis; quo die, sedente rege in parliamento, et circumsedentibus prelatis et proceribus, ac militibus comitatuum, et civibus et burgensibus \[civitatum et burgorum, nominatim]/ invocatis prout moris est, circumstantibus, dominus Michael de la Pole, cancellarius Anglie, premissis quibusdam verbis de benivolentia regis, et \[ejus affeccione multiplici]/ erga ecclesiam Anglicanam et libertates et privilegia ecclesiastica inviolabiliter conservanda, ac tactis periculis regno iminentibus, enumeratisque regis et \[regni precipuis inimicis,]/ videlicet Gallicis qui populi multitudine, Hispanis qui Galeis, et Flandrensibus qui grossis navibus vehementer abundant, ac Scotis qui regnum Anglie \[intrare poterunt cito]/ pede, dixit principalem causam summonicionis et convocacionis istius parliamenti existere ad ordinandum et providendum pro salvacione et defensione dicti regni, tot \[inimicis mortiferis]/ ad invicem confederatis undique circumsepti; et unde custus et expense necessarii in hac parte melius et celerius ad minorem pauperis populi oneracionem levari poterunt et haberi, cum sit verisimile dictum regnum infra breve absque ordinacione et auxilio hujusmodi variis tribulacionibus et angustiis affici et gravari.

3. Et quod \[dictus dominus rex, qui]/ se subditis et ligeis suis ejusdem regni semper hactenus in diversis pardonacionibus et concessionibus ac alias multipliciter munificum exhibuit et graciosum, \[in bona et promptissima jam existit voluntate]/ se in propria persona sua laboribus et inquietacionibus pro defensione regni et ligeorum suorum predictorum contra pericula hujusmodi exponere, et ad \[quascunque partes ea occasione]/ per avisamentum consilii sui, habito prius prout regiam decet excellenciam auxilio sufficienti, personaliter se transferre. Et ideo quilibet de eodem regno \[animum tenetur]/ assumere ferventiorem eidem domino regi in tanta regni et reipublice necessitate, cum corpore et bonis libentius adjuvare, ~~eum~~ meliorem sibi nequeat \[impendere responsuram. Et quod id quod]/ in auxilium defensionis regni necessario concedi oportebit, levetur de quolibet, tam magno quam parvo, tam divite quam paupere, \[fideliter juxta ratam. Et sic summa major, et]/ collectio levior, ac successus inde melior et prosperior indubie subsequentur.

4. Tetigit etiam dictus cancellarius de infidelitate et versutie dictorum Gallicorum, qui in \[ultimo]/ pacis tractatu inter dominum regem et adversarium suum Francie apud Cales' habito, videntes nuncios et ambassatores dicti domini regis ad omnem viam pacis rationabilem et honestam, prout rex

Translation

THE ROLL OF THE PARLIAMENT HELD AT WESTMINSTER ON THE MORROW OF MARTINMAS, IN THE EIGHTH YEAR OF THE REIGN OF KING RICHARD, THE SECOND SINCE THE CONQUEST [12 November 1384].

Be it remembered that the present parliament, summoned to Westminster on the morrow of Martinmas in the eighth year of the reign of King Richard, the second since the conquest, which fell on a Saturday [12 November 1384], was adjourned on the king's orders for certain reasons until the following Monday [14 November 1384].

2. And on the said Monday [14 November 1384], it was again adjourned on the king's orders for the aforesaid reasons until the next day, namely Tuesday [15 November 1384]; on which day, the king being seated in parliament, and the prelates and nobles being seated about him, and the knights of the shires and citizens and burgesses of the cities and boroughs who had been severally summoned, as is customary, standing there, Sir Michael de la Pole, chancellor of England, beginning with some words on the king's kindness and his deep devotion to the English church and the inviolable conservation of ecclesiastical liberties and privileges, and touching upon the dangers threatening the kingdom and the notable enemies of the king and kingdom, namely the French who abound greatly in number, the Spanish who abound greatly in galleys, the Flemish who with their many great ships, and the Scots who can readily enter the kingdom of England on foot, said that the chief reason for the summoning and convocation of this parliament was to ordain and provide for the safe-keeping and defence of the said kingdom, entirely surrounded as it was by deadly enemies all in league with one another; and to decide how the costs and expenses necessarily incurred in the matter might best and most swiftly be raised and levied with the least burden upon the poor people, since in all likelihood, without ordinance or help of this kind, the said kingdom would soon be afflicted and grieved by various trials and tribulations.

3. And that the said lord king, who had always shown himself to be most kind and gracious to his subjects and lieges of the same kingdom until now with various pardons and concessions and in other ways, was now wholly and most readily desirous of involving himself in labours and troubles for the defence of the kingdom and his aforesaid lieges against such dangers, and of himself journeying to certain parts for this purpose by the advice of his council, having first obtained sufficient help as befitted royal majesty. And so everyone of the same kingdom was morally bound to assume a spirit of greater fervour in freely assisting the lord king with matters necessary for the kingdom and public weal, in body and in goods, since no better response could be given him. And that whatever it would be necessary to concede for the defence of the kingdom would be levied from everyone, great and small, rich and poor, faithfully according to their means. And thus a larger sum, an easier collection, and a greater and happier success would undoubtedly ensue.

4. The said chancellor also mentioned the ill faith and treachery of the said French, who in the last peace reached between the lord king and his adversary of France at Calais, seeing that the messengers and ambassadors of the said lord king were inclined towards every reasonable and honest road

---

[9] The membranes are numbered as follows on the MS: 10, 1, 8, 7, 8, 6, with the last membrane unnumbered.

eis injunxerat, inclinatos, ad locum medium inter Cales' et Bolon' \[inter ipsos et]/ ambassatores \[regios supradictos]/ prius pro tractatu pacis hujusmodi concordatum et promissum venire, seu de plurimis pacis articulis quibus antea consenserant \[quomodolibet tractare sive loqui]/ penitus recusabant, et \[ob hoc jus]/ ipsius domini regis in hac parte multum roboratum et impugnatum existere, et dictam nichilominus \[ipsorum Gallicorum infidelitatem]/ causam fore sufficientem, \[etsi alias]/ non haberent, eos tanquam pacis contradictores et inimicos audacius debellandi.

5. Adjecit \[insuper dictus cancellarius quod per]/ quatuor posset parliamentum multum abbreviari, et breviter expediri; videlicet quolibet die mane venire, omnem materiam \[melancolie et invidie penitus omittere, ad]/ efficacissimam materiam incipere, et eam sine admixtione alterius terminare. Et quod manutenentia per totum fere regnum diffusa \[tollatur et penitus destruatur. Et quod hii qui de]/ manutenentia hujusmodi, seu \[de aliqua]/ re alia ubi non sufficit lex communis, conqueri voluerint, peticiones suas certis clericis de cancellarum ad hoc assignatis, quorum nomina per clericum parliamenti legerentur, liberarent et exhiberent, oportunum inde remedium, opitulante domino, habituri.

6. Receivours des peticions d'Engleterre, Irland, Gales et Escoce:
Sire Johan de Waltham
Sire Richard Ravenser
Sire Thomas Newenham
Sire Johan Searle, clerc del parlement.
Et ceux qi veullent liverer lour billes les baillent avaunt parentre cy et Samady proschein venant au soir.

7. Receivours des peticions de Gascoigne, et d'autres terres et paiis de par dela la meer, et des Isles:
Sire Piers de Barton'
Sire Johan Bouland'
Sire Robert Faryngton'
Sire Robert Muskham.

Page iii-185
8. Et sont assignez triours des peticions d'Engleterre, Irlande, Gales et Escoce:
Le roy de Castill' et de Leon, duk de Lancastre
L'ercevesqe de Canterbirs
L'evesque de Londres
L'evesqe de Wyncestr'
L'evesqe de Ely
L'evesqe de Salesbirs
L'abbe de Seint Austyn de Canterbirs
L'abbe de Waltham
Le count de Kent, mareschall d'Engleterre
Le count d'Arundell
Le count de Warr'
Le count de Northumbr'
Le seignour de Nevill'
Monsire Richard le Scrop'
Monsire Guy de Brien
Monsire Robert Tresilian
Monsire Robert Bealknap
Monsire Johan Holt

to peace, as the king had enjoined them, entirely refused to come to a place midway between Calais and Boulogne to arrange peace by such accord and engagement between themselves and the ambassadors of the aforesaid kings first of all or to consider or discuss in any way the many articles of peace previously agreed by them, and for that reason the right of the same lord king in this matter is greatly strengthened and unassailable, and the said bad faith of the French is reason enough, even if no there were no other reason, for fighting those contravenors and enemies of the peace all the more boldly.

5. The same chancellor said further that there were four ways in which this parliament could be greatly shortened and sooner concluded; namely, by arriving early each day, by avoiding all occasions of spite and envy, by embarking on the most useful business, and by settling it without any further digression. And that maintenance, diffused almost throughout the entire kingdom, be crushed and entirely destroyed. And that those who wished to complain of such maintenance, or of any other matter in which the common law did not suffice, should submit and show their petitions to certain chancery clerks assigned thereto, whose names were to be read out by the clerk of parliament, that they might thereby find a suitable remedy, God willing.

6. Receivers of petitions from England, Ireland, Wales and Scotland:
Sir John Waltham
Sir Richard Ravenser
Sir Thomas Newenham
Sir John Searle, clerk of parliament.
And those who wish to submit their petitions should hand them in between now and Saturday next, in the evening [19 November 1384].

7. Receivers of petitions from Gascony and from other lands and countries overseas, and from the Channel Islands:
Sir Piers Barton
Sir John Bowland
Sir Robert Farington
Sir Robert Muskham.

8. The following are assigned to be triers of petitions from England, Ireland, Wales and Scotland:
The king of Castile and Leon, duke of Lancaster
The archbishop of Canterbury
The bishop of London
The bishop of Winchester
The bishop of Ely
The bishop of Salisbury
The abbot of St Augustine's, Canterbury
The abbot of Waltham
The earl of Kent, marshal of England
The earl of Arundel
The earl of Warwick
The earl of Northumberland
Lord Neville
Sir Richard le Scrope
Sir Guy Bryan
Sir Robert Tresilian
Sir Robert Bealknap
Sir John Holt

- touz ensemble, ou .vi. des prelatz et seignours avantditz au meyns; appellez a eux chanceller, tresorer, seneschall et chamberleyn, et auxint les sergeantz nostre seignour le roy quant il busoignera. Et tendront lour place en la chambre de chamberleyn, pres de la chambre depeint.

9. Et sont assignez triours des peticions de Gascoigne, et d'autres terres et paiis de dela la meer, et les Isles:

L'evesqe de Nichole

L'evesqe de Norwicz

L'evesqe de Seint Davy

L'evesqe d'Excestre

L'evesqe de Hereford

L'abbe de Westm'

L'abbe de Glastyngbirs

Le count de Cantbrugg

Le count de Bukyngham, conestable d'Engleterre

Le count de Staff'

Le count de Salesbirs

Le seignour Fitz Wauter

Le priour del hospital Seint Johan Jerusalem en Engleterre

Monsire Johan de Cobham de Kent

Monsire William Skipwith

Monsire Roger Fulthorp'

Monsire Davyd Hannemere

Monsire William Burgh'

- touz ensemble, ou .vi. des prelatz et seignours avauntditz; appellez a eux chanceller, tresorer, seneschal, chamberleyn et les sergeantz le roy quant il busoignera. Et tendront lour place en la chambre marcolf.

10. Item, domini et communitates regni Anglie in presenti parliamento congregati, considerantes qualiter dominus rex, per avisamentum consilii sui, laborare intendit super inimicos suos in propria persona sua, prout superius declaratur, et quod hoc esset primum viagium ipsius domini regis, concesserunt eidem domino regi in eodem parliamento, pro defensione regni, et salva custodia maris et marchiarum Scotie, duas quintasdecimas, levandas et colligendas inter laicos dicti regni, unam videlicet quintamdecimam ad festum Annunciationis Beate Marie Virginis proximo futuro, et alteram /quintamdecimam ad festum Nativitatis\ Sancti Johannis Baptiste tunc proximum sequens, per modum et formam ac condiciones in quadam cedula indentata per dictas communitates in eodem parliamento liberata contentos, cujus quidem cedule tenor sequitur, in hec verba:

Les seignours et communes assemblez a ce present parlement, considerez coment nostre seignour le roi est purposez,

[Col. b] par avys et conseil des seignours, de travailler en propre persone sur ses enemys, come declarez feust par le chanceller al pronunciation de parlement, en presence du roi mesmes et des ditz seignours et communes, et puis declarez plus en especial par mesme le chanceller as ditz communes en la maison du chapitre a Westm'; et porce qe ce serroit ore le primer viage nostre /dit seignour le roy,\ al honour de Dieu et de nostre seignour le roi grantent a mesme nostre seignour le roi, pur defense du roialme, et pur la saufe garde du meer, et de les marches d'Escoce, deux quinszismes, d'estre levez et paiez entre les layes; c'estassavoir l'une quinszisme al fest de l'Anunciation Nostre Dame proschein avenir; et l'autre quinszisme al fest de la Nativite Seint

- to act all together, or at least six of the aforesaid prelates and lords; consulting with the chancellor, treasurer, steward and chamberlain, and also the serjeants of our lord the king when necessary. And they shall hold their session in the chamberlain's room, near the Painted Chamber.

9. The following are assigned to be triers of petitions from Gascony and from the other lands and countries overseas, and from the Channel Islands:

The bishop of Lincoln

The bishop of Norwich

The bishop of St David's

The bishop of Exeter

The bishop of Hereford

The abbot of Westminster

The abbot of Glastonbury

The earl of Cambridge

The earl of Buckingham, constable of England

The earl of Stafford

The earl of Salisbury

Lord FitzWalter

The prior of the hospital of St John of Jerusalem in England

Sir John Cobham of Kent

Sir William Skipwith

Sir Roger Fulthorp

Sir David Hanmer

Sir William Burgh

- to act all together, or at least six of the aforesaid prelates and lords; consulting with the chancellor, treasurer, steward, chamberlain, and the king's serjeants when necessary. And they shall hold their session in the Marcolf Chamber.

10. Also, the lords and commons of the kingdom of England assembled in the present parliament, considering that the lord king, with the advice of his council, planned to strive against his enemies in person, as mentioned above, and how that would be the first expedition of the same lord king, granted to that same lord king in this parliament, for the defence of the kingdom and the safe-keeping of the sea and marches of Scotland, two fifteenths, to be levied and collected from the laity of the said kingdom, that is to say one fifteenth at the feast of the Annunciation of the Blessed Virgin Mary next [25 March 1385], and the other fifteenth at the feast of the Nativity of St John the Baptist then next following [24 June 1385], according to the manner, form and conditions contained in a certain indented schedule delivered by the said commons in this parliament, the tenor of which schedule follows in these words:

The lords and commons assembled in this present parliament, considering how our lord the king proposes,

[Col. b] with the advice and counsel of the lords, to strive in person against his enemies, as was declared by the chancellor at the opening of parliament, in the presence of the king himself and the said lords and commons, and was later declared more particularly by the same chancellor to the said commons in the chapter house at Westminster; and because it would be the first expedition of our said lord the king, to the honour of God and of our lord the king they grant to our same lord the king, for the defence of the kingdom and for keeping the sea and the marches of Scotland, two fifteenths, to be levied from and paid by the laity; that is to say one fifteenth at the feast of the Annunciation of Our Lady next [25 March 1385]; and the other fifteenth at the feast of the

Johan alors proschein ensuant: sur les condicions q'ensuent, c'estassavoir qe la moite du darreine quinzisme grante a Salesbirs sur certeines conditions soit finalement adnullye et tenuz pur nulle. Et en cas qe nostre seignour le roi ne travaille en propre persone sur les ditz enemys, come declarez est par dessuis, ou si paix ou trieve se preigne en le meen temps, q'adonqes la dite darreine quinzisme qe se deust estre levez al dit fest de la Nativite Seynt Johan, cesse tout outrement, et qe nulle commission isse pur la levee d'icelle. Et qe nulle autre charge n'emposicion soit mys de novel sur le poeple outre les grantes dessuisdites.

11. Item, cum quedam lites et discordie nuper inter cancellarium et scolares universitatis Cantebr' et majorem et ballivos ejusdem ville super deputacione et deliberacione quarumdam mensurarum, videlicet busselli, dimidii busselli et peck, ac quorumdam proficuorum inde proveniencium, videlicet quatuor denariorum de bussello, et de dimidio bussello et peck secundum ratam, pro eo quod mensure et proficua predicta in carta et concessione domini regis eisdem cancellario et scolaribus nuper inde factis clare non exprassabantur, suborte fuissent, dictus dominus rex volens lites et discordias hujusmodi pacificare et sedare, de avisamento prelatorum, procerum et magnatum sibi in presenti parliamento assistencium, intencionem suam in hac parte ex certa scientia sua sic declaravit; videlicet quod deputacio et deliberacio busselli, dimidii busselli et peck, tam in feriis et mercatis quam in portu et omnibus aliis locis infra villam predictam et suburbia ejusdem, ac eciam quatuor denarii de bussello hujusmodi, et de dimidio bussello et peck secundum ratam percepti et percipiendi; qui quidem quatuor denarii per ipsum majorem per nomen custume sive prestacionis indebite vendicabantur; necnon omnia alia proficua de mensuris illis proveniencia, ad ipsum cancellarium et successores suos, vigore et virtute carte et concessionis ipsius domini regis predictarum a tempore confeccionis earumdem, pertinent et pertinere debent, quodque major et communitas dicte ville nullum jus sive titulum ad mensuras hujusmodi ibidem a tempore concessionis predicte deputandas et deliberandas, seu dictos quatuor denarios de bussello, et de dimidio bussello et peck secundum ratam, a tempore predicto percipiendos ullatenus habuerunt. Et insuper, cum in dicta carta domini regis expressa non fit mencio per quem processum dictus cancellarius, et successores sui, vel eorum vicesgerentes, homines dicte ville coram se /venire\ facere possent, ad inquisiciones de forstallatoribus et regratariis, ac de defectibus victualium faciendas, dictus dominus rex de avisamento predicto sic declaravit; videlicet quod cancellarius sive presidens dicte universitatis pro tempore existens, vel eorum vicesgerentes, summonere possint per ministros suos proprios homines dicte ville Cantebr' et suburbiorum ejusdem, per quos rei veritas melius sciri poterit, ad veniendum et comparendum coram eis, et ad presentandum per eorum sacramentum tam de forstallatoribus et regratariis, ac carnibus et piscibus putridis, viciosis et alias incompetentibus, quam de aliis victualibus; et eos qui coram ipsis per summonicionem hujusmodi venire recusaverint punire per amerciamenta, per ministros suos proprios levanda, vel sicut cancellarius et scolares [Page iii-186]

[Col. a] universitatis Oxon' hactenus fecerunt et faciunt in presenti.

12. Item, dominus rex, ad prosecutionem Roberti de Veer comitis Oxon', suggerentis eidem domino regi Walterum Sibille de London' ipsum comitem de manutenencia graviter diffamasse, precepit arestare prefatum Walterum in presenti parliamento, inde responsurum; qui quidem Walterus de precepto domini regis sic arestatus, et in parliamento ductus, allocutus fuit coram dicto domino rege, prelatis et dominis

Nativity of St John then following [24 June 1385]: on the following conditions, namely that half of the last fifteenth granted at Salisbury on certain conditions be finally annulled and invalidated. And if it should happen that our lord the king does not strive in person against the said enemies, as described, or if a peace or truce be reached in the meantime, then the said last fifteenth which ought to be levied at the said feast of the Nativity of St John [24 June 1385], shall cease entirely, and no commission issued for levying the same. And that no other charge nor imposition be imposed anew on the people over and above the aforesaid grants.

11. Also, whereas certain disputes and disagreements have arisen recently between the chancellor and scholars of the university of Cambridge and the mayor and bailiffs of the same town concerning the estimation and reckoning of certain measures, namely bushels, half-bushels and pecks, and of certain revenues arising from them, namely four pence from the bushel and proportionate amounts from the half-bushel and peck, because the aforesaid measures and revenues were not clearly set out in the charter and grant of the lord king lately made to the same chancellor and scholars, the said lord king wishing to pacify and calm such disputes and disagreements, with the advice of the prelates, nobles and magnates attending the present parliament, thus declared his intention in the matter out of his certain knowledge: namely that the estimation and reckoning of bushels, half-bushels and pecks, both in fairs and markets, and at the gates and all other places within the aforesaid town and its suburbs, and also the four pence from each bushel, and from each half-bushel and peck proportionately, taken or to be taken; which four pence were unduly claimed by that mayor in the name of custom or prest; and also all other profits arising from those measures; pertain and ought to pertain to the chancellor and his successors, by force and virtue of the aforesaid charter and concession of this lord king from the time when the same was made, and that the mayor and commons of the said town had no right or title whatsoever to the estimation or reckoning of such measures in that place from the time of the aforesaid concession, nor to receive the said four pence from the bushel, or from the half-bushel and peck proportionately, from the aforesaid time. And further, since in the said charter of the lord king no express mention was made of the process by which the said chancellor and his successors, or their deputies, could cause the men of the said town to appear before them at inquests to be held into forestallings and regratings and defective victuals, the said lord king with the aforesaid advice declared thus; namely that the chancellor or president of the said university at the time, or their deputies, could summon through their own officers men of the said town of Cambridge and its suburbs, through whom the truth could best be known, to come and appear before them, and to present upon oath not only forestallings and regratings but also putrid meat and flesh unwholesome and otherwise unsuitable and other victuals; and to punish those who should refuse to appear before them in response to such summons by fines levied by their own officers, or as the chancellor and scholars [Page iii-186]

[Col. a] of the university of Oxford have done in the past and do now.

12. Also, the lord king, at the suit of Robert de Vere earl of Oxford, who had suggested to the same lord king that Walter Sibille of London had gravely defamed that earl of maintenance, ordered the aforementioned Walter to be arrested in the present parliament to answer to this; which Walter, having been arrested on the king's orders and brought to parliament, spoke before the said lord king, bishops and lords

in eodem parliamento, de eo quod ipse prefatum comitem, parem regni, et camerarium regis, de manutenencia, ut premittitur, diffamaverat; referendo Johanni regi Castell' et Legionis, duci Lancastr', et avunculo regis, ac excellenciori et digniori persone regni post regem, quod idem comes quandam querelam habitam inter ipsum Walterum /et Nicholaum Twyford, chivaler, et Willelmum Coggeshale, chivaler, contra ipsum Walterum in tantum\manutenuerat, quod idem Walterus justiciam in hac parte propter manutenenciam ipsius comitis consequi non poterat. Et prefatus Walterus premissa protestacione corrigendi et emendandi si quid ipsum in tam excellenti curia improvide vel indecenter loqui contingeret, dixit quod dedicere non potuit quin dicto domino duci de dicta materia tetigisset, et quod materiam illam voluit /cum\ protestacione predicta manifestius declarare. Unde dixit quod propter quasdam graves dissensiones et debatas inter ipsum et prefatos Nicholaum et Willelmum exortas ambe partes coram consilio domini regis fuerunt personaliter evocate; et auditis /ibidem\ hinc inde earum racionibus et querelis, ac tacto inter cetera de quodam brevi de audiendo et terminando prefato Waltero, et de quadam speciali assisa prefatis Nicholao et Willelmo concedendis, tandem per dictum consilium dictum fuit utrique partium predictarum, /quod\ ad communem legem prosequerentur, si sibi viderent expedire. Et nichilominus /uterque predictorum Nicholai et Willelmi habuit\ postmodum quandam specialem assisam de materia supradicta, per quas \quidem speciales assisas/ idem Walterus pro re valorem annuum octo solidorum non excedente in octingentis /libris\ extitit condempnatus, ac quamplura bona et catalla sua asportata, et alia dampna et gravamina sibi per prefatos Nicholaum et Willelmum illata fuerunt; et hoc per manutenenciam ipsius comitis, prout supponebat. Et predictus comes tunc ibidem presens asseruit se de dicta manutenencia sic sibi per prefatum Walterum maliciose imposita innocentem fore penitus et immunem, et se inde omnibus viis et modis quibus curia considerare vellet optulit excusare; petendo quod idem Walterus haberet penam statuti contra diffamatores hujusmodi editi et provisi. Super quo, prefatus Walterus custodie commissus, et post triduum in parliamentum reductus gratie domini regis humiliter se submisit, asserendo pariter et affirmando quod non credebat, nec intendebat, dictum comitem in hac parte adeo offendisse: et supplicando dominis parliamenti, ut ad hujusmodi gratiam dicti domini regis, et benivolenciam dicti comitis captandas, manus vellent apponere adjutrices. Et super hoc quesitum est a prefato Waltero, si vellet accusacionem suam hujusmodi de dicto comite sic factam prosequi et probare. Et dixit quod non. Per quod consideratum est quod predictus Walterus super diffamacione predicta convincatur: et quod idem comes recuperet versus eum dampna sua, que ad quingentas marcas de avisamento dominorum sunt taxata. Et quod predictus Walterus committatur prisone domini regis, ibidem moraturus quousque tam eidem comiti de dampnis suis predictis, quam domino regi de fine et redempcione competentibus plenarie satisfecerit.

13. Memorandum insuper quod Alicia que fuit uxor Willelmi de Wyndesore, chivaler, exhibuit quandam peticionem suam in presenti parliamento, in hec verba:
A tresexcellent et tresredoute seignour nostre seignour le roi, et as seignours del parlement, supplie humblement Alice qe fuist la femme William de Wyndesore, chivaler, qe plese a vostre hautesse, de vostre grace rial, qe l'estatut et ordinance queux furent faitz ou ordenez a Westm' en temps de vostre tresnoble aiel, sur la dite Alice par noun de Alice Perrers, et puis en vostre parlement tenuz a Westm' al quinseyne

in the same parliament, of the maintenance of which he had accused the aforesaid earl, a peer of the realm and king's chamberlain; referring to John king of Castile and Leon, duke of Lancaster, and the king's uncle, and the most excellent and worthy person of the kingdom after the king, that the same earl maintained a certain cause moved between that Walter and Nicholas Twyford, knight, and William Coggeshale, knight, against Walter, so that he could not obtain justice in the matter because of the maintenance of the earl. And the aforementioned Walter correcting and amending the aforesaid protestation lest anything unintended or improper should happen to be uttered in so distinguished a court, said that he could not deny that the matter touched the said lord duke, and that he wished to explain it more fully with the aforesaid protestation. Whereupon he said that, because of certain grave dissensions and disputes arising between himself and the aforesaid Nicholas and William, both parties had been summoned in person before the council of the lord king; and the arguments and complaints on both sides having been heard there, and a certain writ of oyer and terminer granted to the aforementioned Walter, and a certain special assize granted to the aforementioned Nicholas and William having been touched on, amongst other things, at length the said council informed both parties thereon that they should proceed at common law, if it seemed good to them. And nevertheless both the aforesaid Nicholas and William later obtained a certain special assize on the aforesaid matter, by which special assizes the same William was fined eight hundred pounds for something worth no more than eight shillings a year, and many of his possessions and chattels were carried off, and other losses and injuries suffered through the said Nicholas and William; and this was by the maintenance of the said earl, as he supposed. And the aforesaid earl then present in the same place declared himself completely innocent and blameless of the said maintenance wickedly alleged against him by the said Walter, and said that he would exonerate himself thereof by any ways or means the court willed; requesting that the same Walter suffer the penalty included in and provided by the statute against defamers. Whereupon the aforementioned Walter having been committed to prison, and having been led back to parliament after three days, humbly threw himself on the king's grace, asserting and equally affirming that he did not believe nor think that the said earl had thus offended in the matter, and begging the lords of parliament, in order to gain the grace of the said lord king and the goodwill of the said earl, to lend him their support. And thereupon it was asked of the said Walter if he wished to pursue or prove his accusation thus made against the said earl. And he said that he did not. As a result of which it was concluded that the aforesaid Walter should be convicted of the aforesaid defamation, and that the same earl should recover damages from him, which were assessed at fifty marks on the advice of the lords. And that the aforesaid Walter should be thrown into the lord king's prison, to remain there until the same earl had been fully compensated for his aforesaid damages, and the lord king satisfied with a suitable fine and ransom.

13. Be it remembered moreover that Alice who was the wife of William Windsor, knight, exhibited a certain petition in this present parliament, in these words:
To the most excellent and most redoubtable lord, our lord the king, and to the lords of parliament, Alice who was wife of William Windsor, knight, humbly requests: that it may please your highness, of your royal grace, that the statute and ordinance made or ordained at Westminster in the time of your most noble grandfather concerning the said Alice, by the name of Alice Perrers, and later declared in your

de Seynt Michel, l'an de vostre regne primer, les ditz estatut et ordinance furont declarez, et execucion ent en vostre temps agarde sur la dite Alice, et sur autres queux furont feoffes al oeps du dite Alice,[10] en cest present parlement soient voidez /en\ tout, et pur voidez declarez, et tenuz pur nulle, et la dite Alice et les autres feoffez queux furont oustez a cause suisdite soient restituitz a lour possessions dont eux furont oustez, et restorez enterement a lour primer estat en qe mayns q'ils soient, noun obstantz l'estatut, ordinance, declaracion ou execucion suisditz, pur Dieu, et en oevre de charite.

Tenor vero responsionis et indorsamenti ejusdem peticionis sequitur, in hec verba:

Nostre seignour le roi, eu bone deliberacion sur la requeste compris deinz ceste peticion, voet et grant, par avys et assent des prelatz, seignours et communes en plein parlement, a la suppliante, qe l'ordinance et estatut par queux la dite suppliante estoit bannyz hors du roialme, et ses terres, chateux, tenementz et possessions, sibien en demeigne come en reversion, forfaitz a nostre seignour le roi, soient repellez, et la dite suppliante hablee et restitut a la paix et commune loi de la terre; issint toutes voies qe cest repelle, habilitacion, et restitucion, portent force et tiegnent lieu tant soulement desore enavant, et qe l'ordinance et estatutz suisditz estoisent entierment en lour effect et virtue, tanq'al temps de ceste repelle: et qe toutes maneres feffementz, douns et grantz, alienations et estatz des terres, tenemenz, rentes, reversions, possessions et chateux, et toutes autres choses faitz devant le temps de cest repelle, par force et virtue del ordinance et estatut suisditz, estoisent toutdys et demorgent avant en lour force et virtue, sanz estre empeschez, defaitz, anientiz ou emblemys en nulle manere, par cause ou colour del repelle, habilitacion ou restitution avantditz. Et accorde est et assentuz en parlement qe les ditz repelle, habilitacion et restitucion, ove les declaracions ensuantz, soient tenuz pur estatut.

Et sciendum est quod concordatum fuit in parliamento quod revocacio, habilitacio et restitucio predicte, una cum declaracionibus sequentibus, teneantur pro statuto, sicut predictum est.

14[11] Memorandum etiam quod in parliamento tento apud Novam Sarum, die veneris proximo ante festum Sancti Marci Evangeliste, anno regni regis Ricardi secundi post conqestum septimo, prior de Monte Acuto exhibuit quandam peticionem suam in eodem parliamento, in hec verba:[12]

A nostre tresredoute seignour le roy, et a ses nobles seignours en cest present parlement, monstre le priour de Montagu, come Richard Seymor, cousyn et heir Richard Lovel, suit un brief de scire facias devers le dit priour en bank nostre dit seignour le roy, retornable a la quinszeine de Pasqe l'an sisme nostre \dit/ seignour le roi q'orest, d'avoir execucion del manoir de Tyntenhull' ove les appurtenantz hors d'un fyn qe se leva en la court le roi Edward besaiel nostre dit seignour le roy q'orest, a les oeptaves de Seint Michel l'an du regne le roi Edward unszime, devant monsire William de Bereford et ses compaignons adonqes justices de commune bank, entre le dit Richard Lovell' et Muriele sa femme pleignantz, et meistre Richard *[Page iii-187]*

[Col. a] de Clare et meistre Roger de Blokesworth' deforceantz, de dit manoir, et autres maneres proces tant suy sur le dit brief, qe execucion de dit manoir de Tyntenhull

---
[10] Parliament of 1377, item 43.
[11] *Original* 15.
[12] Parliament of April 1384, item 21.

parliament held at Westminster on the quinzaine of Michaelmas in the first year of your reign, execution of which was ordered thereon in your time upon the said Alice and others who were feoffees to the use of the said Alice, be completely annulled in this parliament and declared invalid and held at naught, and the said Alice and the other feoffees who were ousted for the aforesaid reason be restored to the possessions from which they were ousted and fully restored to their former condition, in whosoever's hands they be, notwithstanding the aforesaid statute, ordinance, declaration or execution, for God and by way of charity.

The true tenor of the answer and endorsement to the same petition follows in these words:

Our lord the king, having thoroughly considered the request contained in this petition, wills and grants, by the advice and assent of the prelates, lords and commons in full parliament, to the supplicant, that the ordinance and statute by which the said supplicant was banished from the realm and her lands, chattels, tenements and possessions, both in demesne and in reversion, forfeited to our lord the king, be repealed, and the said supplicant enabled and restored to the peace and common law of the land; provided always that this repeal, rehabilitation and restitution have force and take effect only from this time onwards, and that the aforesaid ordinance and statutes have entirely kept their force and effect until the time of this repeal: and that all manner of enfeoffments, gifts and grants, alienations and estates of lands, tenements, rents, reversions, possessions and chattels, and all other things made before the time of this repeal by force and virtue of the aforesaid ordinance and statutes do stay and remain forever in force and virtue, without being obstructed, undone, annulled or impaired in any way by cause or colour of the aforesaid repeal, rehabilitation or restitution. And it is agreed and assented in parliament that the said repeal, rehabilitation and restitution, together with the following declarations, be taken as statute.

And be it known that it was agreed in parliament that the aforesaid revocation, rehabilitation and restitution, together with the following declarations, were to be held as statute, as is said above.

14. Be it remembered moreover that in the parliament held at Salisbury on the Friday next after the feast of St Mark the Evangelist in the seventh year of the reign of King Richard, the second since the conquest [29 April 1384], the prior of Montacute showed a certain petition in the same parliament in these words:

To our most redoubtable lord the king and his noble lords in this parliament, the prior of Montacute shows that whereas Richard Seymour, kinsman and heir of Richard Lovell, sued a writ of scire facias against the said prior in the bench of our said lord the king, returnable on the quinzaine of Easter in the sixth year of the said lord the present king [6 April 1383], to have execution of the manor of Tintinhull together with appurtenances, out of a fine which was levied in the court of King Edward, great-grandfather of our said lord the present king, on the octave of Michaelmas in the eleventh year of the reign of King Edward [7 October 1317], before Sir William Bereford and his colleagues then justices of the Common Bench, between the said Richard Lovell and Muriel his wife, plaintiffs, and master Richard *[Page iii-187]*

[Col. a] de Clare and master Roger Bloxworth, deforciants, of the said manor, and other manner of process thus sued on the said writ, that execution of the said manor of

ove les appurtenances est agarde a dit Richard countre le dit priour, come en le record ent fait en le dit bank demurant pleinement appiert; en quiel record diverses errours y sont, come le dit priour serra prest d'assigner.

Par qoy supplie le dit priour qe ordene soit en cest present parlement qe certeins gentz de conseil nostre dit seignour le roi soient assignez, devant queux le dit record soit envoie, et qe eux eient plein poair et auctorite par force de mesme l'ordenance d'oier l'assignement des errours avauntditz, et de faire garnir le dit Richard Seymor d'estre devaunt eux a certein jour par eux a assigner, d'oier l'assignement des ditz /errours,\ et qe eux poent corriger et redresser mesmes les errours, et droiturel juggement ent rendre, et qe nul proteccion soit alowe pur le dit Richard Seymor en la dite suite; eiant regard a le defaute q'est ore trove en parlement, et al delay qe le dit priour ad euz pur defaute de bone entree del plee; et eiant regard qe nostre seignour le roi ad grant interesse qe celle chose soit redresse en hast, a cause qe pur l'ouster de l'eide et le recoverir del manoir, le roi est ouste de les fees et avowesons autre foitz expressement reservez par sa patente, et qe l'esglise de Mountagu ad este seisi de dit manoir de Tyntenhull' de temps le roy Henry [I], fitz au roy William primer, come par chartres des roys appiert overtement tanqe al temps de dit juggement, pur Dieu, et en oevre de charite.[13]

Et dicta peticione in eodem parliamento lecta, de assensu parliamenti consideratum fuit quod predictus prior haberet breve de scire facias factum et fundatum in suo casu, retornabile in proximo parliamento, ad scire faciendum prefato Ricardo Seymor essendi ad dictum proximum parliamentum in quocumque loco infra regnum Anglie tentum foret, ad audiendum errores quos per prefatum priorem in recordo et processu predictis fore ostendi sive allegari contingeret, et ad faciendum ulterius et recipiendum quod per legem terre adjudicari contingeret in hac parte. Et quod recordum et processus predicta cum omnibus ea tangentibus essent in dicto proximo parliamento ex causa supradicta quodque nulla proteccio que per dictum Ricardum tunc fuit, aut extunc foret, per fictam causam impetrata allocaretur in illa querela ullo modo. Subsequentique summonito parliamento tenendo apud Westm' in crastino Sancti Martini tunc proximo futuro, prefatus prior prosecutus fuit, et habuit dictum breve de scire facias super materia predicta directum vicecomiti Somers' retornabile in eodem parliamento sic tenendo apud Westm' ad predictum crastinum Sancti Martini. Et modo in isto eodem parliamento tento apud Westm' in crastino predicto Johannes Strech vicecomes Somers' retornavit breve predictum, cujus quidem brevis tenor sequitur, in hec verba[14]:

[15.]/ Ricardus, Dei gratia, rex Anglie et Francie, et dominus Hibernie, vicecomiti Somers', salutem. Quia in recordo et processu, ac eciam in redicione judicii loquele que fuit coram nobis, per breve nostrum scire facias inter Ricardum Seymor, consanguineum et heredem Ricardi Lovell', et priorem de Monte Acuto, de manerio de Tyntenhulle cum pertinentiis error intervenit manifestus, ad grave dampnum ipsius prioris sicut ex querela sua accepimus, nos errorem, si quis fuerit, modo debito corrigi, et partibus predictis plenam et celerem justiciam fieri volentes in hac parte, tibi precipimus quod scire facias prefato Ricardo quod sit coram nobis in parliamento nostro apud Westm' in crastino Sancti Martini proximo futuro, ad audiendum ibidem recordum et

Tintinhull with the appurtenances was awarded to the said Richard against the said prior, as fully appears in the record made thereon remaining in the said bench; in which record there are various errors, as the said prior will be ready to show.

For which reason the said prior requests that it be ordered in this parliament that certain men of the council of our said lord the king be appointed, before whom the said record be sent, and that they have full power and authority by force of the same ordinance to hear the attribution of the aforesaid errors, and to warn the said Richard Seymour to appear before them on a certain day to be appointed by them, to hear the attribution of the said errors, and that they be able to correct and redress the same errors and pass a rightful judgment, and that no protection be allowed for the said Richard Seymour in the said suit; bearing in mind the default now found in parliament and the delay which the said prior has suffered for want of a proper entry of the plea; and bearing in mind that our lord the king has a great interest in this matter being swiftly redressed, because by the ousting from the aid and the recovery of the manor, the king is ousted from the fees and advowsons once expressly reserved by his patent, and that the church of Montacute has been seised of the said manor of Tintinhull from the time of King Henry [I], son of William I, until the time of the said judgment, as fully appears in the king's charters; for God and as a work of charity. And the said petition having been read in the same parliament, it was decided with the assent of parliament that the aforesaid prior should have a writ of scire facias made and founded upon his case, returnable at the next parliament, to instruct the aforementioned Richard Seymour to be at the said next parliament wheresoever that should be held in the kingdom of England to hear the errors which would be shown or alleged by the said prior in the aforesaid record and process, and also to do and receive whatsoever should be adjudged in this matter by the law of the land. And that the aforesaid record and process with all other things relating to them be available in the said next parliament for the aforesaid reason, and that no protection obtained by the said Richard or yet to be obtained by pretence be allowed in this case in any way. And subsequently, a parliament being summoned to be held at Westminster on the morrow of Martinmas next following, the aforesaid prior sued and had the said writ of scire facias on the aforesaid matter sent to the sheriff of Somerset, returnable in the same parliament thus to be held at Westminster on the morrow of Martinmas [12 November 1384]. And now in the same parliament thus held at Westminster on the aforesaid morrow, John Stretch, sheriff of Somerset returned the aforesaid writ, the tenor of which follows in these words:

15. Richard, by the grace of God, king of England and France and lord of Ireland, to the sheriff of Somerset, greeting. Whereas in the record and process, and also in the rendering of judgment in the case which was before us, by our writ of scire facias between Richard Seymour, kinsman and heir of Richard Lovell, and the prior of Montacute, concerning the manor of Tintinhull with appurtenances, there is manifest error, to the grievous injury of this prior, of which we have received his complaint, and we, wishing duly to correct the error, if any there be, and to do full and speedy justice to the aforesaid parties in the matter, order you to instruct the aforementioned Richard to appear before us in our parliament at Westminster on the morrow of Martinmas

---

[13] PRO C49/9/19.

[14] The following writ and return as far as 'per Johannem Fauconer et Robertum Coker' are also transcribed on the second slip of parchment stitched to m.6. The versions are identical except that on the slip 'per peticionem de parliamento' is added at the end of the writ.

processum predicta si sibi viderit expedire, necnon errores quos per prefatum priorem in recordo et processu predictis fore allegari contigerit, et ad faciendum ulterius et recipiendum quod curia nostra consideraverit in hac parte. Et habeas ibi nomina illorum per quos
[Col. b] ei scire feceris, et hoc breve. Teste meipso apud Westm', .xv. die Octobris, anno regni nostri octavo.

Tenor returni et indorsamenti brevis illius sequitur, in hec verba:
Ego Johannes Strecch' vicecomes scire feci Ricardo Seymor, consanguineo et heredi Ricardi Lovell', quod sit coram domino rege in parliamento suo apud Westm' in crastino Sancti Martini proximo futuro ad audiendum recordum et processum prout istud breve requirit, necnon errores quos per priorem de Monte Acuto in recordo et processu predictis fore allegari contigerit, et ad faciendum ulterius et recipiendum quod curia domini regis consideraverit in hac parte, per Johannem Fauconer et Robertum Coker.
[15]

Ricardus, Dei gratia, rex Anglie et Francie, et dominus Hibernie, dilecto sibi in Christo abbati de Muchelneye, salutem. Sciatis quod dedimus vobis potestatem recipiendi attornatos prioris de Monte Acuto, quos coram vobis loco suo attornare voluerit ad prosequendum coram nobis in parliamento nostro apud Westm' in crastino Sancti Martini proximo futuro errores quos in recordo et processu, ac etiam in reddicione judicii loquele que fuit coram nobis per breve nostrum scire facias inter Ricardum Seymor, consanguineum et heredem Ricardi Lovell', et prefatum priorem, de manerio de Tyntenhull cum pertinentiis idem prior intervenisse asserit, sicut ex querela sua accepimus. Et ideo vobis mandamus quod cum attornatos illos receperitis, nobis de nominibus eorundem attornatorum in parliamento nostro predicto sub sigillo vestro distincte et aperte constare feceritis, remittentes nobis hoc breve. Teste meipso apud Westm', .xvi.die Octobris, anno regni nostri octavo.

Holm'.
Ego Willelmus abbas de Muchelnye vobis significo quod prior de Monte Acuto venit coram me, et attornavit loco suo Radulphum priorem de Barnestaple, vel Willelmum Crich' commonachum ejusdem prioratis de Monte Acuto, vel Johannem Fitelton, vel Johannem Janet, ad lucrandum vel perdendum versus Ricardum Seymor, consanguineum et heredem Ricardi Lovell', de placito terre, unde scire facias, prout istud breve requirit.
Et super hoc, prefato priore per Johannem de Fitelton', attornatum suum, et predicto Ricardo Seymor in propria persona sua, per premunicionem hujusmodi virtute dicti brevis de scire facias sibi factam, in eodem parliamento ad dictum crastinum comparentibus, preceptum fuit per dominum regem et dominos in eodem parliamento, ad peticionem predicti prioris, Roberto Tresilian, /capitali justiciario ipsius\ domini regis, quod recordum et processum predicta, cum omnibus ea tangentibus, in custodia sua existentia, in dictum parliamentum deferret ex causa supradicta. Qui quidem Robertus detulit in eodem parliamento recordum et processum predicta, cum omnibus ea tangentibus. Quod quidem recordum sequitur, in hec verba:

Somers'.
Placita coram domino rege apud Westm' de termino Sancti Michaelis, anno regni regis Ricardi secundi septimo, rotulo .xxxij. Alias scilicet termino Sancte Trinitatis, anno regni

next, there to hear the aforesaid record and process if it seems expedient, and also the errors to be alleged by the said prior in the aforesaid record and process, and further to do and receive whatsoever our court decides in the matter. And you shall have there the names of those by whom
[Col. b] you caused him to be notified, together with this writ. Witnessed myself at Westminster, 15 October, in the eighth year of our reign [1384].
The tenor of the return and endorsement of the writ follows, in these words:
I John Stretch, sheriff, made known to Richard Seymour, kinsman and heir of Richard Lovell, that he should be before the lord king in his parliament at Westminster on the morrow of Martinmas next [12 November 1384] to hear the record and process as this writ requires, and also the errors which would be alleged by the prior of Montacute to be in the aforesaid record and process, and also to do and receive whatsoever the court of the lord king would decide in the matter, by John Fauconer and Robert Coker.

Richard, by grace of God, king of England and France and lord of Ireland, to his beloved in Christ, the abbot of Muchelney, greeting. Know that we have given you power to receive the attorneys of the prior of Montacute, whom he wishes to represent him before you to pursue before us in our parliament at Westminster on the morrow of Martinmas next [12 November 1384] the errors which the same prior claims to be present in the record and process and also in the judgment rendered in the cause which came before us by our writ of scire facias between Richard Seymour, kinsman and heir of Richard Lovell, and the aforementioned prior, concerning the manor of Tintinhull with appurtenances, according to his plea which we have received. And therefore we order you that when you have received those attorneys you shall clearly and distinctly notify us of the names of the same attorneys in our aforesaid parliament under your seal, returning this writ to us. Witnessed myself at Westminster, 16 October, in the eighth year of our reign [1384].
Holme.
I, William, abbot of Muchelney, inform you that the prior of Montacute appeared before me and appointed as his attorneys Ralph, prior of Barnstaple, or William Creech monk of the said priory of Montacute, or John Fitelton, or John Janet, to win or lose against Richard Seymour, kinsman and heir of Richard Lovell, in the plea of land, whereof the scire facias, as that writ requires.

And thereupon the said prior, by John Fitelton, his attorney, and the aforesaid Richard Seymour in his own person, appearing in the same parliament on the said morrow by virtue of the summons made in the said writ of scire facias, the lord king and lords in the same parliament, at the petition of the aforesaid prior, ordered Robert Tresilian, chief justice of the lord king, to bring to the said parliament for the aforesaid purpose the record and process and all relevant matter in his keeping. Which Robert brought to that parliament the aforesaid record and process, together with all other relevant matters. Which record follows in these words:

Somerset.
Pleas before the lord king at Westminster in Michaelmas term in the seventh year of the reign of King Richard II [9 October - 29 November 1383], in roll 23. Otherwise,

---
[15] The following writ and return as far as 'prout istud breve requirit' are to be found on the first slip of parchment stitched to m.6.

regis Ricardi secundi quinto. Dominus rex mandavit dilecto et fideli suo Roberto Tresilian, capitali justiciario, etc., breve suum clausum, in hec verba:

Ricardus, Dei gratia, rex Anglie et Francie, et dominus Hibernie, dilecto et fideli suo Roberto Tresilian, capitali justiciario, salutem. Tenorem pedis cujusdam finis levati in curia domini Edwardi filii regis Edwardi nuper regis Anglie, progenitoris nostri, anno regni ejusdem Edwardi filii regis Edwardi undecimo, coram Willelmo de Bereford et sociis suis tunc justiciariis ejusdem Edwardi filii regis Edwardi de banco, per breve *[Page iii-188]*

[Col. a] ejusdem Edwardi filii regis Edwardi inter Ricardum Lovell' et Muriellam' uxorem ejus, querentes, et magistrum Ricardum de Clare et magistrum Rogerum de Blokerworth, deforciantes, de maneriis de Blakeford', Southbarewe, Northbarewe, Cherleton' Makerell', Tyntenhull' et Prestelee, cum pertinentiis, vobis mittimus sub pede sigilli nostri, mandantes, ut inspecto tenore pedis finis predicti, ulterius, ad prosecucionem Ricardi Seymor consanguinei et heredis predicti Ricardi Lovell', inde fieri facias quod de jure et secundum legem et consuetudinem regni nostri Anglie fuerit faciendum. Teste meipso apud Westm', .xx. die Junii, anno regni nostri quinto. 'Tenor pedis finis de quo in brevi predicto fit mencio sequitur, in hec verba:

Hec est finalis concordia facta in curia domini regis apud Westm', in octabis Sancti Michaelis, anno regni regis Edwardi filii regis Edwardi undecimo, coram Willelmo de Bereford, Gilberto de Roubury, Johanne de Benstede, Johanne Bacun et Johanne de Mutford, justiciariis, et aliis domini regis fidelibus tunc ibi presentibus, inter Ricardum Lovell' et Muriellam uxorem ejus, querentes, per Thomam de Croukern positum loco ipsius Murielle ad lucrandum vel perdendum, et magistrum Ricardum de Clare et magistrum Rogerum de Blokerworth, deforciantes, de maneriis de Blakeford, Southbarewe, Northbarewe, Cherleton' Makerell et Tyntenhull' et Prestele, cum pertinentiis, unde placitum convencionis summonitum fuit inter eos in eadem curia; scilicet quod predictus Ricardus Lovell' recognovit predicta maneria cum pertinentiis esse jus ipsorum magistri Ricardi de Clare et magistri Rogeri, ut illa que iidem magister Ricardus et magister Rogerus habent de dono predicti Ricardi Lovell'. Et pro hac recognicione, fine et concordia, iidem magister Ricardus et magister Rogerus concesserunt predictis Ricardo Lovell' et Murielle predicta maneria cum pertinentiis; et illa eis reddiderunt in eadem curia; habenda et tenenda eisdem Ricardo Lovell' et Murielle, et heredibus ipsius Ricardi, scilicet predicta maneria de Southbarewe, et Northbarewe, et Tyntenhull', cum pertinentiis, de domino rege et heredibus suis, et predicta maneria de Blakeford, Cherleton' Makerell' et Prestele, cum pertinentiis, de capitalibus dominis feodi illius, per servitia que ad predicta maneria pertinent imperpetuum. Et hec concordia quo ad predicta maneria de Southbarewe, Northbarewe et Tyntenhull', cum pertinentiis, facta fuit per preceptum ipsius \domini/ regis.[16]
Somers'.

Postea ad sectam Ricardi Seymor, asserentis se fore consanguineum et heredem predicti Ricardi Lovell, videlicet filius Murielle, filie Jacobi filii predicti Ricardi Lovell' et quod predicti Ricardus Lovell' et Muriella mortui sunt, et quod ipse execucionem de predicto manerio de Tyntenhull'

namely from Trinity term in the fifth year of the reign of King Richard II [19 June - 10 July 1381]. The lord king directed to his beloved and faithful Robert Tresilian, chief justice, etc., his writ close, in these words:

Richard, by grace of God, king of England and France and lord of Ireland, to his beloved and faithful Robert Tresilian, chief justice, greeting. The tenor of a certain foot of fine levied in the court of the lord Edward [II], son of Edward [I] late king of England, our progenitor, in the eleventh year of the reign of the same Edward son of King Edward, in the presence of William Bereford and his colleagues, then justices of the Bench of the same Edward, son of King Edward, by writ *[Page iii-188]*

[Col. a] of the same Edward son of King Edward, between Richard Lovell and Muriel his wife, plaintiffs, and master Richard de Clare and master Roger Bloxworth, deforciants, concerning the manors of Blackford, South Barrow, North Barrow, Charlton Mackrell, Tintinhull and Prestley, with appurtenances, we send you under our half-seal, ordering that having inspected the tenor of the aforesaid foot of fine, at the suit of Richard Seymour, kinsman and heir of the aforesaid Richard Lovell, you shall do therein that which ought to be done by right and according to the law and custom of our kingdom of England. Witnessed myself at Westminster, 20 June, in the fifth year of our reign [1382]. The tenor of the foot of fine of which mention is made in the aforesaid writ follows in these words:

This is the final concord made in the court of the lord king at Westminster, on the octave of Michaelmas in the eleventh year of the reign of King Edward son of King Edward, in the presence of William Bereford, Gilbert Rothbury, John Benstead, John Bacon and John Mutford, justices, and other faithful men of the lord king there present, between Richard Lovell and Muriel his wife, plaintiffs, with Thomas Crewkerne representing that Muriel to win or lose, and master Richard de Clare and master Roger Bloxworth, deforciants, concerning the manors of Blackford, South Barrow, North Barrow, Charlton Mackrell, Tintinhull and Prestley, with appurtenances, whence a plea of contract was summoned between them in the same court; namely that the aforesaid Richard Lovell acknowledged the aforesaid manors with appurtenances to be the right of this master Richard de Clare and master Roger, as those which the same master Richard and master Roger had by gift of the aforesaid Richard Lovell. And for this acknowledgement, fine and agreement, the same master Richard and master Roger granted to the aforesaid Richard Lovell and Muriel the aforesaid manors with appurtenances, and rendered them to them in the same court; to have and to hold by the same Richard Lovell and Muriel and the heirs of Richard, namely the aforesaid manors of South Barrow, North Barrow, and Tintinhull, with appurtenances, of the lord king and his heirs, and the aforesaid manors of Blackford, Charlton Mackrell and Prestley, with appurtenances, of the chief lord of that fee, by the service pertaining to the aforesaid manors in perpetuity. And this concord relating to the aforesaid manors of South Barrow, North Barrow and Tintinhull, with appurtenances, was made by order of the lord king himself.
Somerset.

Later, at the suit of Richard Seymour, claiming to be the kinsman and heir of the aforesaid Richard Lovell, namely the son of Muriel daughter of James son of the aforesaid Richard Lovell, and that the aforesaid Richard Lovell and Muriel were dead, and he had not yet had execution of the

---

[16] Somerset, 11 Edward II, Michaelmas term, 34: *Feet of fines for Somerset, 1 Edward II - 20 Edward III*, ed. E. Green (Somerset Record Society, 12, 1898).

nondum est assecutus, et quod prior de Monte Acuto predictum manerium de Tyntenhull', cum pertinentiis, post mortem predictorum Ricardi Lovell' et Murielle ingressus fuit, et illud tunc tenuit et occupavit contra formam finis predicti: et petit execucionem de \predicto/ manerio de Tyntenhull' juxta formam finis predicti, etc. Per quod preceptum fuit vicecomiti Somers' quod per probos, etc., scire faceret prefato priori quod esset coram domino rege a die Pasche ultimo preterito in .xv. dies ubicumque, etc., ad ostendum si quid pro se haberet, vel dicere sciret, quare predictus Ricardus Seymor, consanguineus et heres predicti Ricardi Lovell' in forma predicta execucionem de predicto manerio de Tyntenhull' cum pertinentiis versus eum habere non deberet. Et ulterius, etc. Idem dies datus fuit predicto Ricardo Seymor. Ad quem diem coram domino rege venit predictus Ricardus Seymor per Johannem de Hulton' attornatum suum. Et vicecomes retornavit quod scire fecit prefato priori quod esset coram domino rege ad prefatum terminum ad ostendum secundum formam brevis predicti, et ulterius facturum et recepturum quod curia domini regis consideraverit in hac parte, per Willelmum Atte More et Ricardum Grene: qui quidem prior sic premunitus in propria persona sua venit. Et predictus Ricardus Seymor, ut supra, petiit execucionem de predicto manerio de Tyntenhull', cum pertinentiis, etc. Et predictus prior dixit quod predictus Ricardus Seymor, per nomen Ricardi de Sancto Mauro, chivaler, tulit quoddam

[Col. b] breve de recto versus predictum priorem, per nomen Francisci prioris de Monte Acuto, de predicto manerio de Tyntenhull', retornabile coram justiciariis domini regis de banco in crastino Sancti Martini, anno regni domini regis nunc sexto. Ad quod breve idem Ricardus Seymor ad tunc comparuit, et idem prior essoniatus fuit, et habuit diem per essonium suum usque a die Pasche in tres septimanas tunc proximo sequento. Et quod predictum breve de scire facias perquisitum fuit pendente predicto brevi de recto, quod fuit de altiori natura, etc., et peciit judicium de brevi de scire facias, etc. Et protulit tunc in curia regis coram rege tenorem dicti brevis de recto, simul cum tenore irrotulamenti de essonia predicta inde habiti per cancellarium domini regis per manus Johannis de Waltham custodis rotulorum in /cancellaria,\ etc., in eadem curia missi, que premissa testantur, etc., quorum brevis, recordi et processus tenores sequntur inferius. Tenor videlicet brevis, in hec verba:

Ricardus, Dei gracia, rex Anglie et Francie et dominus Hibernie, vicecomiti Somers', salutem. Precipe Francisco priori de Monte Acuto quod juste et sine dilacione reddat Ricardo de Sancto Mauro, chivaler, manerium de Tyntenhull' cum pertinentiis, quod clamat esse jus et hereditatem suam, et tenere de nobis in capite: et unde queritur quod predictus /prior\ ei injuste deforciavit. Et nisi fecerit, et predictus Ricardus fecerit te securum de clameo suo prosequendo, tunc summoneas per bonos summonitores predictum priorem quod sit coram justiciariis nostris apud Westm' in crastino Sancti Martini ostensurus quare non fecerit. Et habeas ibi summonitores, et hoc breve. Teste meipso apud Westm' .xiiij. die Octobris, anno regni nostri sexto.

Et tenor recordi et processus inde, in hec verba:

Somers'. Non summonitus per precipe in capite.
Essonia capta apud Westm', coram Roberto Bealknap' et sociis suis, justiciariis domini regis de banco, /de\

aforesaid manor of Tintinhull, and that the prior of Montacute had entered the aforesaid manor of Tintinhull, with appurtenances, after the death of the aforesaid Richard Lovell and Muriel, and then held and occupied it contrary to the form of the aforesaid fine: and he sought execution of the aforesaid manor of Tintinhull according to the form of the aforesaid fine. As a result of which the sheriff of Somerset was ordered that through good men, etc., he instruct the aforementioned prior to appear before the lord king within fifteen days of the day of Easter last [6 April 1383], wheresoever, etc., to show whether he had anything to say as to why the aforesaid Richard Seymour, kinsman and heir of Richard Lovell, ought not to have the execution of the aforesaid manor of Tintinhull with appurtenances against him in the aforesaid form. And further, etc. And the same day was given to the aforesaid Richard Seymour. On which day the aforesaid Richard Seymour appeared before the lord king through John Hulton, his attorney. And the sheriff returned that he had notified the aforementioned prior to appear before the lord king at the said time to show according to the form of the aforesaid writ, and also to do and receive whatsoever the court of the lord king decided in the matter, by William Atte More and Richard Green: which prior thus summoned appeared in person. And the aforesaid Richard Seymour, as mentioned above, sought execution of the aforesaid manor of Tintinhull with appurtenances, etc. And the said prior said that the said Richard Seymour, by the name of Richard de Sancto Mauro, knight, brought a certain

[Col. b] writ of right against the said prior, by the name of Francis, prior of Montacute, for the aforesaid manor of Tintinhull, returnable before the lord king's justices of the Bench on the morrow of Martinmas in the sixth year of the reign of the present lord king [12 November 1382]. To which writ the same Richard Seymour then appeared, and the same prior was essoined, and had a day for his essoin until three weeks from Easter [12 April 1383] and that the aforesaid writ of scire facias was sought pending the aforesaid writ of right, which was of a higher nature, etc., and he sought judgment concerning the writ of scire facias, etc. And he then proffered in the king's court before the king the tenor of the said writ of right, together with the tenor of the enrolment of the aforesaid essoin had thereon from the lord king's chancellor by the hand of John Waltham keeper of the rolls in the chancery, etc., submitted in the same court, as witnessed by the foregoing, etc., the tenors of which writ, record, and process follow below. The tenor of the writ is, namely, in these words:

Richard, by grace of God, king of England and France and lord of Ireland, to the sheriff of Somerset, greeting. Order Francis, prior of Montacute, that justly and without delay he return to Richard de Sancto Mauro, knight, the manor of Tintinhull with appurtenances, which he claims to be his right and inheritance, and to hold of us in chief: and from which he complains the aforesaid prior unjustly ejected him. And unless he does so, and the aforesaid Richard gives surety of his claim pursued, then you shall summon by good summoners the aforesaid prior to appear before our justices on the morrow of Martinmas [12 November 1382] to explain why he has not done so. And you shall have there the summoners and this writ. Witnessed by myself at Westminster, 14 October, in the sixth year of our reign [1382].

And the tenor of the record and process follow in these words:

Somerset. Not summoned by writ of precipe in capite.
Essoins received at Westminster in the presence of Robert Bealknap and his colleagues, justices of the King's Bench,

crastino Sancti Martini, anno regnorum Ricardi regis Anglie et Francie sexto, rotulo secundo. Franciscus prior de Monte Acuto versus Ricardum de Sancto Mauro, chivaler, de placito terre per Johannem Davy, a die Pasche in tres septimanas afforciando, unde ut prius petiit judicium de predicto brevi de scire facias, etc. Et predictus Ricardus Seymor protestando, dixit quod ipse non cognovit quod ipse tulit aliquod tale breve de recto versus predictum priorem de manerio predicto: et ulterius dixit quod per tenores brevis, recordi et processus predictorum non constat quod idem Ricardus Seymor ad breve predictum aliquando comparuit, nec quod breve predictum adtunc pendebat, unde peciit judicium et execucionem, etc. Et quia per tenores brevis et recordi predictorum hic missos non constabat curia quod predictus Ricardus Seymor ad /breve\ predictum aliquando comparuit, nec quod breve predictum adtunc pendebat, quia videtur curie quod predictum breve de scire facias manuteneri potest, racionibus et allegacionibus predictis non obstantibus, dictum est prefato priori quod ulterius respondeat, etc. Qui quidem prior dixit quod dominus Edwardus nuper rex Anglie, avus domini regis nunc, de avisamento parliamenti sui, nuper seisire fecit in manus suas omnes possessiones prioratuum alienigenarum in Anglie de potestate Francie existentium, tenendas in manu sua quamdiu guerra inter ipsum tunc regem et adversarios suos de Francie durare contigerit; et, inter alia, prioratus de Monte Acuto una cum omnibus possessionibus suis seisitus fuit in manus ipsius Edwardi nuper regis, etc., ex causa predicta; qui quidem Edwardus rex, etc., postea per litteras suas patentes, quas idem prior protulit hic in curia que sequuntur, in hec verba:

Edwardus, Dei gratia, rex Anglie et Francie et dominus Hibernie, omnibus ad quos presentes littere pervenerint, salutem. Sciatis quod commisimus dilecto nobis in Christo fratri Francisco, priori prioratus de Monte Acuto alienigene, custodiam prioratus predicti, et omnium possessionum eidem prioratui spectancium, quem jam pace inter nos et Gallicos adversarios nostros apud Cales' inita, et per ipsos Gallicos dissoluta, inter alios prioratus et domos religiosorum alienigenarum, de dominio et potestate Francie *[Page iii-189]*

[Col. a] existencium in regno nostro Anglie et alibi infra dominium et potestatem nostra, de assensu parliamenti nostri capi fecimus in manum nostram, habendum a festo Sancti Michaelis proximo preterito quamdiu prioratum, terras et possessiones predictos in manu nostra ex causis predictis contigerit remanere. Reddendo inde nobis annuatim ad scaccarium nostrum, vel alibi ad mandatum nostrum, ad festa Pasche et Sancti Michaelis, per equales porciones, centum et viginti libras: salvis nobis feodis militum, et advocacionibus ecclesiarum, ad dictum prioratum spectantibus sive pertinentibus. Pro quo quidem priore Johannes Fytelton' et Johannes Halle de comitatu Somers', in cancellaria nostra personaliter constituti, manuceperunt quod ipse super prioratu et possessionibus predictis moram continuam faciet, et numerum clericorum et servientium ab antiquo ordinatorum in eisdem prioratu et possessionibus, et cantarias et alia divina servicia, ac elemosinas, pia opera et cetera onera eisdem prioratui et possessionibus incumbencia integre de exitibus et proficuis et emolumentis eorundem manutenebit et inveniet, et edificia prioratus et possessionum illorum in adeo bono statu quo nunc sunt reparabit et dimittet. Et quod dictus prior, seu clerici et servientes sui extra regnum nostrum Anglie /se\ non transferent nec divertent: nec statum,

on the morrow of Martinmas in the sixth year of the reign of Richard king of England and France [12 November 1382], in the second roll. Francis, prior of Montacute, against Richard de Sancto Mauro, knight, in the plea of land by John Davy, to be afforced within three weeks of Easter [12 April 1383], wherein as above he sought judgment upon the aforesaid writ of scire facias, etc. And the said Richard Seymour, protesting, said that he was not aware that he had brought any such writ of right against the aforesaid prior concerning the aforesaid manor: and further he said that from the tenors of the said writ, record and process it did not seem that the same Richard Seymour had at any time appeared in answer to the aforesaid writ, nor that the said writ was yet pending, for which reason he sought judgment and execution, etc. And because by the tenor of the aforesaid writ and record submitted here it did not seem to the court that the aforesaid Richard Seymour had ever appeared in answer to the aforesaid writ, nor that the aforesaid writ was yet pending, because it appeared to the court that the said writ of scire facias could be maintained, notwithstanding the aforesaid reasons and allegations, it was said to the aforementioned prior that he should answer further, etc. Which prior said that lord Edward [III], late king of England, grandfather of the present lord king, with the advice of his parliament, formerly caused to be taken into his hands all the possessions of alien priories in England being in the power of France, to be held in his hand for as long as the war between him then king and his adversaries of France should last; and amongst other things, the priory of Montacute together with all its possessions was taken into the hands of Edward, lately king, etc., for the aforesaid reason; which King Edward, etc., afterwards by his letters patent, which the same prior produced here in court, which follow, in these words:

Edward, by grace of God, king of England and France and lord of Ireland, to all those to whom the present letters come, greeting. Know that we have committed to our beloved brother in Christ Francis, prior of the alien priory of Montacute, custody of the aforesaid priory and of all the possessions pertaining to the same priory, which along with other alien priories and religious houses, being under the lordship and power of France *[Page iii-189]*

[Col. a] in our kingdom of England and elsewhere within our dominion and power, following the dissolution by the French of the peace initiated between us and our French enemies at Calais, with the assent of our parliament, we caused to be taken into our hands, to have from Michaelmas last [29 September 1371] for as long as the aforesaid priories, lands and possessions should happen to remain in our hands for the aforesaid reasons. Paying to us each year at our exchequer, or elsewhere at our mandate, at Easter and Michaelmas [29 September] in equal portions, one hundred and twenty pounds: saving to us the knights' fees and advowsons of churches belonging or pertaining to the said priory. For which prior, John Fitelton and John Hall of Somerset, appointed in person in our chancery, have undertaken that he shall continually dwell in the aforesaid priory and possessions, and maintain and provide for the number of clerics and servants ordained of old in the same priory and possessions, and the chantries and other divine services, and alms, pious works and other duties incumbent upon the same priory and possessions, wholly from the issues, profits and emoluments of the same, and that he shall repair and leave the buildings of the priory and its possessions in as good a state as they are in now. And that neither the said prior nor his clerics or

negotia aut secreta dicti regni nostri Anglie alicui persone extranee, quocumque colore vel ingenio, dicent vel revelabunt; nec aurum vel argentum in massa vel moneta, aut jocalia, vel armaturas, seu quicquam aliud quod in nostri vel populi nostri prejudicium aliqualiter cedere poterit, per litteras, vel per verba, vel alio modo, ad partes exteras transmittent. Et quod idem prior dictam firmam centum et viginti librarum ad terminos predictos bene et fideliter solvet; et de arreragiis ejusdem, sique fuerint de firma prioratus et possessionum predictorum de tempore quo ultimo fuerunt in manibus nostris, respondebit; et bona et catalla, /aut\ alias res ad prioratum et possessiones illos spectancia jam ibidem existencia, a dictis prioratu et possessionibus aut /locis ad\ eosdem spectantibus non alienabit seu elongabit; nec vastum seu destruccionem faciet.

Volumus eciam et de gracia nostra speciali concedimus quod idem prior de decimis et quintisdecimis, lanis et omnibus aliis quotis nobis per clerum et communitate regni nostri Anglie a tempore ultime capcionis eorundem prioratus et possessionum in manum nostram concessis, vel extunc concedendis, seu eidem clero per dominum summum pontificem impositis vel imponendis: ac etiam de custodia terre maritime, et de prestacionibus lanarum, et aliis oneribus quibuscumque ad eosdem prioratum et possessiones spectantibus, contingentibus, erga nos quietus sit et exoneratus, quamdiu iidem prioratus et possessiones in manu nostra, et in custodia prefati prioris extiterint ex causa supradicta, ita quod idem prior de eisdem prioratu et possessionibus disponere, et commodum suum ... facere possit, prout melius et ad majorem utilitatem suam sibi viderit expedire. In cujus rei testimonium has litteras nostras fieri fecimus patentes. Teste meipso apud Westm' .x. die Novembris, anno regni nostri Anglie quadragesimo quinto, regni vero nostri Francie tricesimo secundo.

Commisit prefato priori, per nomen fratris Francisci prioris prioratus de Monte Acuto, alienigene, custodiam prioratus predicti, et omnium possessionum eidem prioratui spectancium, habendas a festo Sancti Michaelis tunc proximo preterito quamdiu prioratum, terras et possessiones predictas in manu regis ex causis predictis contigerit remanere. Reddendo inde eidem regi annuatim ad scaccarium suum, vel alibi ad mandatum ipsius regis, ad festa Pasche et Sancti Michaelis, per equales portiones, centum et viginti libras: salvis eidem regi feodis militum, et advocacionibus ecclesiarum, ad dictum prioratum spectantibus sive pertinentibus. Et sic dicit idem prior quod ipse sine domino rege nunc non potest inde respondere; et petiit auxilium /de\ domino rege, etc. Et predictus Ricardus Seymor dixit quod predictus prior per aliqua

[Col. b] preallegata auxilium de domino rege habere non deberet. Dixit enim quod predictus Edwardus, nuper rex avus, etc., nuper fuit seisitus de advocacione prioratus predicti in dominico suo ut de feodo, et eandem advocationem, diu ante concessionem predictam dicto priori de custodia predicta factam, per litteras suas patentes dedit et concessit Willelmo de Monte Acuto, nuper comiti Sarum et marescallo Anglie, advocacionem prioratus de Monte Acuto,[17] habendam et tenendam sibi et heredibus suis de ipso rege et heredibus suis imperpetuum. Volensque idem rex ipsum comitem hac parte ampliorum gracie prosequi ubertate, concessit pro se et heredibus suis prefato comiti quod ipsi et heredes sui imperpetuum haberent custodiam prioratus predicti, tam temporibus quibus idem prioratus occasione guerrarum inter ipsum regem et heredes suos et illos de Francie seu inter regna

---

[17] advocacionem prioratus de Monte Acuto, *repeated*

servants shall leave or remove themselves from our kingdom of England: nor speak of nor reveal the condition, affairs nor secrets of our said kingdom of England to any foreigner, by any trick or device; nor send to foreign parts by letter or by word nor in any other way gold or silver in bullion or coin, nor jewels, weaponry, nor anything else which could prove detrimental in any way to us or our people. And that the same prior shall fully and faithfully pay the said farm of one hundred and twenty pounds at the aforesaid terms, and shall answer for the arrears of the same, if there be any, from the farm of the aforesaid priory and possessions since the time when they were last in our hands; and that he shall not alienate nor withdraw goods and chattels, nor other things pertaining to that priory and those possessions and now being there, from the said priory and possessions or places attached to them; nor carry out waste nor destruction.

We will moreover and of our special grace we have granted that the same prior be quit and exonerated towards us and free of tenths and fifteenths, wool and all other quotas granted to us by the clergy and commons of our kingdom of England since the last time that the same priory and possessions were taken into our hands, or yet to be granted, or imposed or to be imposed on the same clergy by the lord supreme pontiff: and also from custody of maritime land, and from levies of wool, and other burdens of any sort pertaining to the same priory and possessions, for as long as the same priory and possessions shall be in our hands, and in the custody of the aforementioned prior for the aforesaid reasons, so that the same prior may dispose of the same priory and possessions as it shall seem to him best and most useful for him to do. In testimony whereof we have caused these our letters to be made patent. Witnessed myself at Westminster, 10 November in the forty-fifth year of our reign over England and the thirty-second of our reign over France [1371].

He committed to the aforementioned prior, by the name of brother Francis, prior of the alien priory of Montacute, custody of the aforesaid priory and all the possessions pertaining to the same priory, to have from Michaelmas then last past [29 September 1371], for as long as the aforesaid priory, lands and possessions should remain in the king's hands for the aforesaid reason. Paying to the king annually at his exchequer, or elsewhere at the king's mandate, at Easter and Michaelmas [29 September] in equal portions, a hundred and twenty pounds: saving to the same king the knights' fees and advowsons of churches attached or pertaining to the said priory. And thus he said to the same prior that he could not now answer without the lord king; and sought the help of the lord king, etc. And the aforesaid Richard Seymour said that the aforesaid prior by other matters

[Col. b] alleged before ought not to have the king's help. For he said that the aforesaid Edward, late king and grandfather, etc., was lately seised of the advowson of the aforesaid priory in his demesne as of fee, and long before the said grant made of the said custody to the said prior, he gave and granted the same advowson by his letters patent to William Montagu, late earl of Salisbury and marshal of England, to have and to hold to him and his heirs from this king and his heirs in perpetuity. And the same king, wishing to bestow even greater grace on the earl in the matter, granted on behalf of himself and his heirs to the aforementioned earl that he and his heirs should have custody of the aforesaid priory in perpetuity, as well during the time when the same priory, because of war waged between this king and his heirs and those of France or between the same kingdoms, or for some

eadem motarum, aut quacumque alia de causa, inter alios prioratus, domos et possessiones religiosorum alienigenarum infra regnum Anglie, capta fuit in manum regis, seu eorundem heredum suorum, quam temporibus quibus prioratum illum vacare contingeret, sive per mortem, deposicionem vel resignacionem, prioris loci illius qui pro tempore fuerit, sive alio quovis modo, cum omnibus ad custodiam illam spectantibus. Et quod idem comes, et heredes sui \inde/ disponere et ordinare possent, prout melius pro commodo suo proprio et utilitate prioratus predicti viderent expedire. Exitusque et proficua inde proveniencia ad opus suum, tam guerrarum hujusmodi, quam ipsius prioratus vacacionum temporibus, perciperent et haberent, adeo plene et integre sicut ille rex et heredes sui ea haberent, si prioratum illum seu custodiam in manibus suis propriis retinuisset, absque eo quod ille rex aut ministri sui quicumque de prioratu aut custodia hujusmodi temporibus predictis in aliquo intromitteret. Quodque prefato comiti de firma, quam custodes sive monachi prioratus predicti occasione guerre inter illum regem et alios de Francie mote in manibus \suis/ tunc existentibus ipsi regi pro custodia ejusdem annuatim reddere tenebantur, una cum arreragiis ejusdem firme si que forent, responderetur; et quod custodes ejusdem prioratus de firma et arreragiis illis erga dictum regem omnino exonerarentur.

Ac postmodum Willelmus de Monte Acuto, nunc comes Sarum, filius et heres predicti nuper comitis, ipsi regi supplicavit, ut cum prioratus predictus, pace tunc inter dictum avum et Gallicos adversarios suos apud Cales' inita per ipsos Gallicos dissoluta, capta fuit in manum dicti domini Edwardi avi, etc., vellet ei custodiam dicti prioratus, una cum exitibus et proficuis inde a tempore capcionis ejusdem prioratus in manus ipsius regis perceptis, juxta concessionem dicto patri suo et heredibus suis per ipsum regem sic factam, liberare jubere; idem rex avus, etc., considerans quod licet ad tempus quod in parliamento suo consideratum extitit quod prioratus, domus et possessiones religiosorum hujusmodi, in auxilium guerre sue, caperentur in manum suam concordatum fuisset, et ordinatum in eodem parliamento quod priores et alii presidentes locorum eorundem, seu eorum procuratores, tam pro bono regimine locorum predictorum quam pro divinis officiis ibidem faciendis et sustentandis, ceteris prefererentur de custodia hujusmodi prioratum, domorum et possessionum habenda, reddendo inde ipsi regi prout inter ipsum regem et illos poterit concordari, affectans tamen idem rex concessionem suam prefato nuper comiti et heredibus suis de custodia prioratus predicti prius factam, quatenus fieri potuit absque offensione concordie supra dicte debitum sortiri effectum, voluit idem rex quod in auxilium guerre predicte, ut idem comes se in guerris suis melius manutenere possit, idem

Membrane 4 comes haberet et reciperet durante guerra supradicta de priore loci predicti tantam firmam quantam regi pro custodia ejusdem prioratus, antequam concessio predicta prefato nuper comiti sic facta fuit, *[Page iii-190]*

[Col. a] solvi consuevit, et prout prior loci predicti regi solvere deberet si custodia ejusdem prioratus /eidem priori per regem\ commissa fuisset. Idemque rex avus, etc., per breve suum mandavit tunc thesaurario et baronibus suis de scaccario quod prefato nunc comiti dictam firmam, una cum arreragiis ejusdem firme a tempore capcionis ejusdem prioratus in manum ipsius regis perceptis, liberari et habere, et ipsum priorem inde ad idem scaccarium exonerari et quietum esse facerent.

other reason, along with other priories, houses and possessions of alien religious in the kingdom of England, had been taken into the king's hands or those of his heirs, as at times when the priory should happen to be vacant, whether by the death, deposition or resignation of the prior of that place for the time being, or in any other way, together with all things pertaining to such keeping. And that the same earl and his heirs might dispose and order it as seemed to them best suited to their own purpose and the benefit of the aforesaid priory. And that they should receive and have the issues and profits arising from this for their use, as well in time of war as well as during vacancies of this priory, as fully and wholly as this king and his heirs would have had them if they had retained that priory or custody in their own hands, without that king or his ministers intromitting upon the priory or custody in any way during the aforesaid times. And that the keepers or monks of the aforesaid priory should answer to the aforesaid earl for the farm which they were bound to pay the king annually for the custody of the same, being in their hands on the occasion of war between that king and others of France, together with arrears of the same farm if there were to be any; and that the custodians of the same priory would be exonerated from that farm and those arrears towards the said king.

Later, William Montagu, now earl of Salisbury, son and heir of the aforesaid late earl, petitioned the king that since the aforesaid priory had been taken into the hands of the said lord Edward [III] the grandfather, etc., the peace then initiated between the said grandfather and his French adversaries at Calais having been dissolved by the French, he might order the delivery to him of the custody of the said priory, together with the issues and profits received from it from the time when the same priory was taken into the king's hands, according to the concession made to his said father and heirs by that king; the same king the grandfather, etc. - considering that although at the time when in his parliament it was decided that the priory, house and possessions of those religious, to help his war, were to be taken into his hands, it was agreed and ordained in the same parliament that the priors and other heads of the same places, or their proxies, both for the good government of the aforesaid places and for the performing and sustaining of divine offices there, should be preferred over others for the custody of the same priory, houses and possessions, paying to the king whatever was to be agreed between that king and themselves - the king, nevertheless, disposed towards bringing into due effect his grant previously made to the aforesaid late earl and his heirs of the custody of the aforesaid priory, without contravening the aforesaid agreement, and to help the aforesaid war, so that the same earl could the better maintain himself in his wars, willed the same

Membrane 4 earl to have and receive during the aforesaid war from the prior of the aforesaid place such a farm as the latter had been accustomed to pay to the king for the custody of the same priory before the aforesaid concession was thus made to the aforesaid late earl, *[Page iii-190]*

[Col. a] and as the prior of the place ought to have paid to the aforesaid king if the custody of the same priory had been assigned to the same prior by the king. And the same king the grandfather, etc., by his writ then ordered his treasurer and barons of his exchequer that the said farm, together with the arrears of the same farm received since the time when the same priory was taken into the king's hands, be delivered to and held by the then aforesaid earl, and that they should hold the same prior exonerated and quit of them at the exchequer.

Mandavit eciam idem rex avus, etc., aliud breve suum prefato priori quod de firma predicta \eidem/ nunc comiti esset intendens et respondens, quorum brevium transcripta premissa testificantur. Dominus rex nunc mandavit justiciarios suis hic sub pede sigilli, et quorum brevium data sunt secundo die Decembris, anno regni regis Edwardi avi, etc., quadragesimo quinto. Et sic dixit idem Ricardus Seymor quod predictus Edwardus avus, etc., de advocacione, firma et quicquid sibi de prioratu illo occasione aliqua pertinere potuit, taliter se dimisit, et prefato nunc comiti filio et heredi prefati nuper comitis plenarie restitucionem inde, juxta vim et effectum concessionis predicto patri sui nuper facte, fieri fecit: per quod quicquam de prioratu illo, aut de possessionibus ejusdem, in persona ipsius regis avi, etc., reservari non potuit, sic nec in persona domini regis nunc residere potest. Unde non intendit quod idem nunc prior auxilium de domino rege in hoc casu versus eum habere deberet, etc. Et predictus prior dixit quod in litteris predictis domini regis avi, etc., patentibus eidem priori de custodia prioratus predicti factis, continetur quod dictus rex avus, etc., reservavit sibi feoda militum, et advocaciones ecclesiarum; et in brevibus predictis per predictum Ricardum Seymor in curia hic prolatis continetur quod idem nunc comes de custodia seu regimine domus predicte in aliquo se non intromitteret. Et in eisdem brevibus non continetur quod in restitucione predicta predicto nunc comiti facta aliqua specialis mencio facta fuit feodis militum, et advocacionibus ecclesiarum. Et ulterius dixit quod dominus rex nunc post restitucionem predictam presentavit ad ecclesiam de Tyntenhull' quendam clericum suum Johannem de Stone occasione reservacionis predicte per predictum avum suum de feodis militum et advocacionibus ecclesiarum prioratus predicti facte, unde ex /causis\ predictis peciit auxilium de domino rege, etc. Et predictus Ricardus Seymor dixit quod per restitucionem predictam advocacio prioratus predicti, simul cum custodia ejusdem, et omnibus aliis ad dictum prioratum spectantibus sive quovis modo pertinentibus, in personam ipsius nunc comitis de jure transierunt; unde non intendit quod predictus prior auxilium suum predictum habere deberet, \etc./ Et super hoc dies datus fuit partibus predictis coram domino rege usque in octabis Sancte Trinitatis /tunc proximo sequento\ ubicumque, etc., in statu quo tunc; salvis partibus racionibus et responsibus suis, etc.

Ad quem diem coram domino rege apud Westm' venerunt tam predictus Ricardus Seymor per attornatum suum predictum, quam predictus prior per Stephanum del Fall' attornatum suum. Et continuato inde inter partes predictas processu coram domino rege de die in diem usque in crastinum Sancti Johannis Baptiste tunc proximo sequenti ubicumque, etc. Ad quem crastinum, coram domino rege apud Cantebr' venerunt tam predictus Ricardus Seymor quam predictus prior per attornatos suos predictos, etc. Et quia videtur curie quod auxilium predictum predicto priori in hoc casu non est concedendum, dictum est per curiam prefato priori quod ulterius respondeat, etc., sine auxilio predicto, etc. Et predictus prior dixit quod predictus Ricardus Seymor execucionem /virtute\ finis predicti versus eum habere non deberet, quia dixit quod dominus Henricus [I] filius Willelmi conquestoris quondam rex Anglie nuper fuit seisitus de manerio predicto in dominico suo ut de feodo, et idem manerium cum suis pertinentiis per cartam suam, quam idem nunc prior profert hic in curia que sine est data, dedit et concessit in liberam, puram et perpetuam elemosinam Deo et sanctis apostolis ejus

Petro et Paulo de Monte Acuto, et monachis Clunasensibus ibidem Deo servientibus, habendum et tenendum sibi et successoribus suis imperpetuum.

[Col. b] Quas quidem donacionem et concessionem dominus rex nunc, et quamplures progenitores sui reges Anglie, per cartas suas ratificaverunt et confirmaverunt. Virtute eujus concessionis tunc prior et monachi supradicti seisiti fuerunt de manerio predicto ut de jure ecclesie sue sanctorum apostolorum Petri et Pauli de Monte Acuto, et seisinam suam inde pacifice continuaverunt usque ad diem veneris proximum ante festum Assumpcionis \Beate/ Marie Virginis, anno regni domini Edwardi [II] filii regis Edwardi [I] proavi domini regis nunc nuper regis Anglie decimo, qui quidem Edwardus, etc., antea per litteras suas patentes concessit cuidam Stephano tunc priori loci predicti quod quandocumque prioratum illum per mortem vel cessionem ipsius Stephani vacare contigeret quod supprior et conventus loci illius haberent custodiam dicti prioratus tempore vacationis predicte per duos menses, si prioratum illum per tantum tempus vacare contigeret. Pro qua quidem concessione prefatus Stephanus dedit prefato nuper regi, etc., quadraginta marcas. Ac postmodum prioratus ille per cessionem /ejusdem\ Stephani vacavit, et prioratu illo in possessione ejusdem supprioris et monachorum loci predicti virtute concessionis regis predicti existente, quidam Ricardus Lovell' antecessor predicti Ricardi Seymor, cujus heres ipse est, in manerium predictum cum maxima multitudine hominum armata potencia, predicto die Veneris, se intrusit, et manerium illud \sic/ occupavit, quo tempore finis ille de manerio illo levatus fuit.

Ac postmodum predictus Edwardus nuper rex, etc., pro eo quod querimoniam tunc prioris loci illius per inquisicionem coram dilectis et fidelibus ipsius regis Willelmo Martyn, Hugone de Courtenay et Michaele[18] de Meldon', de mandato suo captam, intrusio illa comperta fuit in forma predicta, manerium illud cum suis pertinentiis prefato tunc priori plenarie restituit. Et protulit tunc /in curia\ tenorem recordi et processus restitucionis predicte in hec verba:

Dominus rex mandavit Willelmo Martyn, Hugoni de Curteneye et Michaeli de Meldon', breve suum in hec verba:
Edwardus Dei gracia, rex Anglie, dominus Hibernie, et dux Aquitanie dilectis et fidelibus suis Willelmo Martyn, Hugoni de Courteneye et Michaeli de Meldon', salutem. Cum tertiodecimo die Julii, anno regni nostri decimo, per finem quadraginta marcarum quem Stephanus tunc prior de Monte Acuto fecit nobiscum, concesserimus per litteras nostras patentes quod quandocumque \[prioratum illum]/ per mortem, resignacionem aut cessionem ejusdem Stephani vacare contigeret, supprior et conventus ejusdem loci haberent custodiam dicti prioratus, et omnium temporalium ad illum spectancium, per duos menses a tempore mortis, resignationis aut cessionis, dicti Stephani numerandos: salvis nobis feodis militum, et advocacionibus ecclesiarum ejusdem prioratus. Et si prioratus ille ultra duos menses vacaret, tunc idem prioratus et ejus temporalia in manum nostram resumerentur, et extunc in manu nostra remanerent durante ulterius vacacione prioratus predicti, prout in litteris nostris predictis plenius continetur. Et postmodum, duodecimo die Octobris, anno predicto, ceperimus fidelitatem dilecti nobis in Christo fratris Johannis Caprarii, quem abbas Clunacen' in priorem dicte domus de Monte Acuto prefecerat, et ei temporalia prioratus illius, prout moris est, mandaverimus liberari, sicut per inspeccionem rotulorum cancellarie nostre nobis constat: ac

[18] *Original* Machaele

and his holy apostles Peter and Paul of Montacute and to the monks of Cluny serving God there, to be had and held by them and their successors in perpetuity.

[Col. b] Which gift and grant the present lord king and several of his progenitors the kings of England ratified and confirmed by their charters, by virtue of which grant the then said prior and monks gained possession of the said manor by right of their church of the holy apostles Peter and Paul of Montacute, and continued peacefully in their possession until the Friday next before the feast of the Assumption of the Blessed Virgin Mary in the tenth year of the reign of the lord Edward [II], son of King Edward [I] [13 August 1316], great-grandfather of the present lord king and late king of England. Which Edward, etc., had earlier by his letters patent granted to a certain Stephen then prior of the aforesaid place, that whensoever that priory should happen to fall vacant by the death or resignation of Stephen, the subprior and convent of that place would have custody of the said priory during the period of the aforesaid vacancy for two months, if the priory should happen to be vacant for that length of time. In return for which concession the aforementioned Stephen gave to the said late king, etc., forty marks. And later, the priory fell vacant through the resignation of the same Stephen, and the priory being in the possession of the same subprior and monks of the aforesaid place by virtue of the grant of the said king, a certain Richard Lovell, ancestor of the aforesaid Richard Seymour, whose heir he is, entered upon the aforesaid manor with a great force of men-at-arms on the aforesaid Friday, and thus seized the manor, at which time the fine concerning the same manor was made.

And later the aforesaid Edward late king, etc. - because, as a result of a complaint of the then prior of the place, through an inquest taken on his orders before that king's beloved and faithful men, William Martin, Hugh Courtenay and Michael Meldon, that intrusion was discovered in the aforesaid form - fully restored that manor with its appurtenances to the then aforementioned prior. And he then presented in court the tenor of the aforesaid record and process of the restitution in these words:

The lord king ordered William Martin, Hugh Courtenay and Michael Meldon by his writ worded as follows:
Edward by grace of God, king of England, lord of Ireland, and duke of Aquitaine to his beloved and faithful William Martin, Hugh Courtenay and Michael Meldon, greeting. Whereas on 13 July, in the tenth year of our reign [1316], for a fine of forty marks which Stephen then prior of Montacute paid to us, we granted by our letters patent that whensoever the priory should happen to fall vacant through the death, resignation or decease of the same Stephen, the subprior and convent of that place would have custody of the said priory and all temporalities pertaining to it, for two months counting from the time of the death, resignation, or demise of the said Stephen: saving to us the knights' fees, and the advowsons of the churches of that priory. And if that priory should be vacant for more than two months, then the same priory and its temporalities would be restored into our hands, and would then remain in our hands for the rest of the vacancy of the aforesaid priory, as is more fully set out in our aforesaid letters.

And later, on 12 October in the said year [1316], we took the fealty of our beloved brother in Christ John Cheverer, whom the abbot of Cluny had appointed prior of the said house of Montacute, and we ordered the temporalities of that priory to be delivered to him, as is customary, as may be established from an inspection of the rolls of our chancery: and now,

jam, ex gravi querela dicti Johannis nunc prioris dicte domus acceperimus quod licet prefatus Stephanus predecessor suus die quo cessit regimini prioratus predicti seisitus fuisset de maneriis de Tyntenhull' et Estchynnok, et de hundredis de Tyntenhull' et Hundesbergh', cum pertinentiis, in comitatu Somers', ut de jure ecclesie sue de Monte Acuto: ac predecessores ejusdem Stephani, quondam priores loci illius, maneria et hundreda illa cum pertinentiis successive a tempore cujus contrarii memoria non existit tenuissent, quidam tamen malefactores et pacis nostre perturbatores, dicto prioratu per cessionem dicti fratris Stephani vacante, et in custodia dictorum /supprioris\ et conventus per commissionem nostram ut predictum est existente, dicta maneria et hundreda armata potencia ingressi fuerunt, et ipsos *[Page iii-191]*

[Col. a] suppriorem et conventum inde expulere, carucas, blada et alia bona et catalla ejusdem domus, in eisdem maneriis inventa occupando, et explecias hundredorum predictorum capiendo, et suis usibus applicando; et maneria et hundreda illa adhuc detinent taliter occupata, in nostri contemptum et grave prejudicium, et prioratus predicti depressionem et exheredacionem manifestam. Nos igitur, qui secundum tenorem magne carte de libertatibus Anglie prefato priori temporalia prioratus predicti adeo plene et integre sicut ad manus nostras devenere, ac totam terram ejusdem instauratam, ut de carucis et omnibus aliis rebus ad minus sicut eam cepimus, liberare et restituere tenemur; nolentes premissa sub dissimulacione preterire, ac de vestra fidelitate et industria plenam fiduciam optinentes, assignavimus vos et duos vestrum, quos vos prefate Michael alterum esse volumus, ad inquirendum per sacramentum tam militum quam aliorum proborum et legalium hominum de comitatu predicto, tam infra libertates quam extra, per quos rei veritas melius sciri poterit, utrum predictus Stephanus fuit seisitus die quo cessit regimini dicti prioratus de maneriis et hundrediis predictis, ut de jure ecclesie sue, nec ne. Et si sic, tunc utrum maneria et hundreda illa, dicto prioratu in custodia dictorum supprioris et conventus ex commissione nostra ut predictum est existente, occupata fuerunt, per quos, et quo tempore, et qualiter, et quo modo, et que bona et catalla in eisdem maneriis, et que explecie de dictis hundredis tunc capta fuerunt, et per quos, et ad quorum manus devenerunt: et ad maneria illa et hundreda cum pertinentiis, si ea per inquisicionem hujusmodi inveneritis, vacante prioratu predicto et in custodia dictorum supprioris et conventus ex commissione nostra existente, fuisse taliter occupata, in manum nostram resumenda, et prefato priori liberanda ut jus ecclesie sue, salvo jure cujuslibet. Et ideo vobis mandamus quod ad certos dies et loca, quos vos vel duo vestrum, quorum vos prefate Michael alterum esse volumus ad hoc provideritis, premissa omnia et singula faciatis et expleatis in forma predicta. Et nos de tenore inquisicionis illius, et de toto facto vestro in hac parte sub sigillis vestris distincte et aperte reddatis certiores. Mandavimus enim vicecomiti nostro comitatus predicti quod ad certos dies et loca quos vos vel duo vestrum, quorum vos prefate Michael alterum esse volumus, ei sciri faciatis venire faciendo coram vobis vel duobus vestrum, quorum vos prefate Michael alterum esse volumus, tot et tales tam milites quam alios probos et legales homines de comitatu predicto, tam infra libertates quam extra, per quos rei veritas in premissis melius sciri poterit et inquiri; et quod vobis in premissis pareat et intendat. In cujus rei testimonium has litteras nostras fieri fecimus patentes. Teste

from the grave complaint of the said John the present prior of the said house, we understand that although the aforementioned Stephen his predecessor, on the day on which he ceased to rule the aforesaid priory, was in possession of the manors of Tintinhull and East Chinnock, and the hundreds of Tintinhull and Houndsborough, with appurtenances in Somerset, as by right of his church of Montacute: and the predecessors of the same Stephen, once priors of that place, had in succession held those manors and hundreds since time immemorial; nevertheless, certain malefactors and disturbers of our peace, after the said priory fell vacant by the death of the said brother Stephen, and was in the custody of the said subprior and convent by our commission as aforesaid, entered upon the said manors and hundreds with armed might, and *[Page iii-191]*

[Col. a] expelled the subprior and convent, seizing ploughs, corn and the other goods and chattels of the same house found on the same manors, and taking the profits of the aforesaid hundreds, and using them for their own purposes; and they still retain those manors and hundreds thus occupied, in contempt of us and to our grave injury, and the evident oppression and disinheritance of the aforesaid priory. We, therefore, who are bound according to the tenor of the Great Charter of the liberties of England to deliver and restore to the aforementioned prior the temporalities of the aforesaid priory as fully and wholly as they came into our hands, as well as all the stocked land of the same, such as ploughs and all other things, at least as we received them; not wishing to neglect the aforesaid things by dissembling, and placing complete trust in your loyalty and assiduity, we have assigned you and two of you, of whom we will the aforementioned Michael to be one, to inquire by the oath both of knights and other good and law-worthy men of the aforesaid shire, within liberties and without, through whom the truth of the matter might best be learnt, whether the aforesaid Stephen, on the day on which he ceased to rule the said priory, was in possession of the aforesaid manors and hundreds by right of his church or not. And whether both the manors and hundreds, the said priory being in the custody of the said subprior and convent by our commission as said above, were seized, and by whom, and when, and how, and in what way, and what goods and chattels on the same manors and what profits of the said hundreds were then taken, and by whom, and into whose hands they came: and if you discover by that inquest that on the said priory falling vacant and being in the custody of the said subprior and convent by our commission, those manors and hundreds with appurtenances were thus seized, you shall take them back into our hands and deliver them to the aforementioned prior as the right of his church, saving the right of whomsoever. And thus we order you that at certain times and places, which you or two of you, of whom we wish the aforementioned Michael to be one, shall appoint thereto, you do and fulfil each and every one of the aforesaid things in the said form. And that you clearly and openly inform us under your seal of the outcome of the inquest and of all your actions in the matter. For we ordered our sheriff of the aforesaid county that at certain times and places which you or the two of you, one of whom we wish to be the aforementioned Michael, would make known to him, he was to cause to appear before you or two of you, one of whom we wish to be the aforementioned Michael, as many and such knights and other good and law-worthy men of the aforesaid county, within liberties and without, from whom the truth of the aforesaid matter might best be learnt and inquired; and that he obey and assist you in the aforesaid. In testimony of which matter we have caused these our

meipso apud Eboracum, .xiij. die Novembris, anno regni nostri duodecimo.

Pretextu cujus brevis, iidem Willemus, Hugo et Michael, mandavere vicecomitem Somers' quod venire faceret coram eis apud Ivele, die Lune proximo post festum Epiphanie domini, viginti quatuor, tam milites quam alios probos et legales homines de visneto de Tyntenhull' et Estchynnok, et etiam de visneto hundredorum de Tyntenhull' et Hundesbergh', per quos rei veritas melius inde sciri poterit et inquiri, secundum tenorem predicti brevis domini regis predictis Willelmo, Hugoni et Michaeli inde prius directi. Ad quem diem, idem vicecomes Somers' retornavit breve domini regis sibi inde directum, et eciam breve ipsorum Willelmi, Hugonis et Michaelis, et similiter nomina juratorum, etc., secundum quod ei preceptum fuit, et per sufficientem manucaptorem, qui non venerunt. Ideo preceptum \[est]/ vicecomes quod distringat predictos juratores per omnes terras et catalla sua, etc. Et quod domino regi respondeat de exitibus, etc. Et quod habeat corpora eorum coram prefatis Willelmo, Hugone et Michaele, vel \coram//duobus eorum, quorum, etc., apud\ Ivele, die mercurii proximo ante festum Sancti Hillarii proximo venturo. Et preter illos venire faciant coram eis, ad eundem diem, tot et tales tam milites quam alios, etc. Ita quod negocium predictum pro defectu juratorum non remaneat infectum.

Inquisitio capta apud Ievele, die mercurii proximo ante festum Sancti Hillarii, anno regni regis Edwardi filii regis Edwardi duodecimo, per sacramentum Radulphi de Gorges, Johannis Mautravers senioris, Johannis de Erlegh', Johannis de Meriet, Henrici de Glaston', Petri de Evercy, Edwardi Everard', Willelmi de Wygehere, Johannis de Clyvedon', militum, Johannis Peytevyn, Johannis Musket et Henrici de Estfeld, ad hoc electorum, etc., qui dicunt super sacramentum suum quod Stephanus quondam prior de Monte Acuto, predecessor Johannis Caprarii nunc prioris ejusdem domus, fuit seisitus ut de jure ecclesie sue de Monte Acuto, de maneriis de Tyntenhull' et Estchynnok, et de hundredis de Tyntenhull' et Hundesbergh', tempore et die quo cessit regimini dicti prioratus, videlicet tertiodecimo die Julii, anno regni regis Edwardi [II] filii regis Edwardi [I] decimo, et quod ipse et predecessores sui predicti prioratus, a tempore cujus contrarii memoria non existit, semper hactenus seisiti fuerunt pacifice de predictis maneriis et hundredis ut de jure ecclesie sue de Monte Acuto, cum omnibus suis pertinentiis. Et dicunt quod tempore vacacionis predicti prioratus, videlicet die veneris proximo ante festum Assumpcionis Beate Marie Virginis anno predicto quando predicta maneria et hundreda fuerunt in manus supprioris et conventus ejusdem prioratus, vacantis per commissionem ipsius domini regis per duos menses, exceptis feodis militum et advocacionibus ecclesiarum prioratus predicti de temporalibus rebus, quod quidam Ricardus Lovell', Henricus de Pupelpenne, magister Hugo Cocus, Mauricius Mareschall', Walterus de Welham, et Margeria uxor ejus, et Thomas filius ejusdem Walteri, magister Willelmus de Modeford, Eva que fuit uxor Ricardi Sumpte, et Thomas Revenyng, armata potencia predicta maneria et hundreda cum pertinentiis sunt ingressi, et predicta maneria et hundreda occupaverunt, et suis usibus applicaverunt, et bona et catalla in eisdem maneriis inventa, videlicet blada, boves, carucas et carectas, currus, equos et oves, ac alia bona et catalla ad valenciam mille librarum ceperunt, abduxerunt et asportaverunt, in contemptum domini regis, et grave prejudicium ipsius prioris, et oppressionem et depauperacionem manifestam: et sic occupata predicta maneria et hundreda cum pertinentiis per duos annos et viginti

letters to be made patent. Witnessed by myself at York, 13 November, in the twelfth year of our reign [1318].

On the authority of which writ, the same William, Hugh and Michael ordered the sheriff of Somerset that he cause to appear before them at Yeovil, on the Monday next after the feast of the Lord's Epiphany [8 January 1319], twenty-four men, as well knights and other good and law-worthy men of the neighbourhood of Tintinhull and East Chinnock as of the neighbourhood of the hundreds of Tintinhull and Houndesborough, by whom the truth of the matter might best be learnt and inquired, according to the tenor of the aforesaid writ of the lord king previously sent to William, Hugh and Michael. On which day, the sheriff of Somerset returned the writ of the lord king sent to him thereon, and also the writ of the same William, Hugh and Michael, and likewise the names of the jurors, etc., as he had summoned, and had not appeared by sufficient mainpernor. Therefore, the sheriff was ordered to distrain the aforesaid jurors by all their lands and chattels, etc. And that he answer to the lord king for the issues, etc. And that he have the aforesaid persons before the aforementioned William, Hugh and Michael, or before the two of them, of whom, etc., at Yeovil, on the Wednesday before the feast of St Hilary next following [10 January 1319]. And that besides them, he cause to appear before them on the same day as many and such knights and others, etc. So that the aforesaid business would not be left undone through a lack of jurors.

The inquest held at Yeovil on the Wednesday next before the feast of St Hilary, in the twelfth year of the reign of King Edward [II], son of King Edward [I] [10 January 1319], by the oath of Ralph Gorges, John Mautravers the elder, John Erlegh, John Merriot, Henry Glastonbury, Peter Evercy, Edward Everard, William Wighorough, John Clevedon, knights, John Peytevyn, John Musket and Henry Eastfield, elected thereto, etc., who say on oath that Stephen sometime prior of Montacute, predecessor of John Caprary now prior of the same house, was seised by right of his church of Montacute of the manors of Tintinhull and East Chinnock, and of the hundreds of Tintinhull and Houndsborough, at the time and on the day when he ceased to rule the said priory, namely 13 July in the tenth year of the reign of King Edward II, son of King Edward I [1316], and that he and his predecessors of the aforesaid priory, from time immemorial, had peacefully possessed the aforesaid manors and hundreds until now as by right of their church of Montacute, together with all their appurtenances. And they say that at the time when the aforesaid priory fell vacant, namely on the Friday before the feast of the Assumption of the Blessed Virgin Mary in the aforesaid year [20 August 1316] when the aforesaid manors and hundreds were in the hands of the subprior and convent of the same priory, vacant by commission of this lord king for two months, excluding knights' fees and the advowsons of the churches of the aforesaid priory from temporal things, that a certain Richard Lovell, Henry Pupelpenne, master Hugh Cook, Maurice Marshal, Walter Welham and Margaret his wife, and Thomas, son of the same Walter, master William Mudford, Eva who was wife of Richard Sumpte and Thomas Revenyng, with armed might entered upon the aforesaid manors and hundreds with appurtenances, and occupied the aforesaid manors and hundreds, and put them to their own use, and seized, took and carried off goods and chattels found on the same manors, namely corn, oxen, ploughs and carts, wagons, horses and sheep, and other goods and chattels to the value of a thousand pounds, in contempt of the lord king and to the grave injury of the prior, and manifest oppression and impoverishment: and so occupied the said manors and hundreds with

septimanas tenuerunt, et de expleciis predictorum hundredorum ignoratur. Ideo prefati justiciarii predicta maneria de Tyntenhull' et Estchynnok, et hundreda de Tyntenhull' et Hundesbergh', ceperunt in manum domini regis, juxta tenorem commissionis predicte, et predicto priori liberarunt, tenenda ut jure ecclesie sue de Monte Acuto, salvo jure cujuslibet, sicut predecessores sui priores ejusdem domus ea tenere et habere consueverunt a tempore cujus contrarii memoria non existit. Et preceptum est vicecomes quod premissa exequatur, etc.

Ac postmodum manerio illo in possessione ejusdem prioris existente, predictus Ricardus Lovell' per factum suum, quod idem nunc prior protulit tunc in curia, concessit, remisit et omnino pro se et heredibus suis imperpetuum quietum clamavit, priori et conventui de Monte Acuto, et successoribus suis, totum jus suum et clameum quod habuit vel aliquo modo habere potuit in predicto manerio de Tyntenhull' cum suis pertinentiis, et ulterius recognovit per dictum scriptum suum dictum manerium cum pertinentiis esse jus ipsius prioris et conventus et successorum suorum imperpetuum: ita quod nec ipse Ricardus Lovell', nec heredes sui, in manerio predicto cum suis pertinentiis, nec in aliqua parte ejusdem, aliquid juris vel clamei exigere vel vendicare poterint in futuro. Et ulterius concessit predictus Ricardus Lovell' per idem scriptum suum quod si aliquis finis de predicto manerio cum pertinentiis suis, aut in aliqua parte ejusdem, in curia domini regis fuerit levatus inter ipsum Ricardum Lovell' et Muriellam uxorem ejus querentes, et magistrum Ricardum de Clare et magistrum Rogerum de Blokerworth deforciantes, virtute cujus finis aliquid juris vel clamei sibi vel heredibus suis quoquomodo accrescere potuit, voluit et concessit idem Ricardus Lovell' pro se et heredibus suis quod finis ille ipso jure foret nullus, et pro nullo imperpetuum *[Page iii-192]*

[Col. a] haberetur. Et protulit tunc in curia scriptum concessionis et remissionis predicti Ricardi Lovell' premissa testificans, quod sequitur in hec verba:

"Omnibus Christi fidelibus ad quos presens scriptum pervenerit, Ricardus Lovell' dominus de Carycastell, salutem in Domino. Noveritis, me concessisse, remisisse et omnino de me et heredibus meis imperpetuum quietum clamasse, priori et conventui de Monte Acuto et eorum successoribus totum jus meum et clameum quod habui vel aliquo modo habere potero in maneriis de Tyntenhull' et Estchynnok cum pertinentiis in comitatu Somers', et in advocacionibus ecclesiarum earundem villarum de Tyntenhull' et Estchynnok, et eciam in hundredis de Tyntenhull' et Estchynnok, et etiam in hundredis de Tyntenhull et Hundesbergh', cum omnibus suis pertinentiis, feriis et mercatis de Tyntenhull', et eciam in omnibus aliis rebus ad maneria, advocaciones, hundreda, ferias et mercata predicta qualitercumque spectantur. Et per presentes recognosco omnia tenementa predicta cum advocacionibus, hundredis, feriis et mercatis

Membrane 3 predictis esse jus ipsius prioris et conventus et successorum suorum imperpetuum. Ita quod nec ego dictus Ricardus Lovell', nec heredes mei, nec aliquis per nos, seu nomine nostro, in maneriis, advocacionibus, hundredis, feriis vel mercatis predictis cum omnibus suis pertinentiis seu aliqua parte eorundem, de cetero aliquid juris vel clamei exigere vel vendicare poterimus in futuro, set ab omni accione cujuscumque juris aliquid petenti maneriorum de Tyntenhull' et Estchynnok cum advocacionibus ecclesiarum earundem villarum, et hundredis de Tyntenhull' et Hundesbergh', feriis et mercatis de Tyntenhull', et omnibus aliis pertinentiis dictorum maneriorum, advocacionum ecclesiarum predictarum, hundredorum, feriarum, et

appurtenances for two years and twenty weeks, and nothing is known of the profits of the aforesaid hundreds. Therefore the aforementioned justices took the aforesaid manors of Tintinhull and East Chinnock and the hundreds of Tintinhull and Houndsborough into the hands of the lord king, according to the tenor of the aforesaid commission, and delivered them to the aforesaid prior, to hold by right of his church of Montacute, saving the rights of any, as his predecessors, priors of the same house, had been accustomed to hold and have them since time immemorial. And the sheriff was ordered that he carry out the aforesaid, etc.

And afterwards, that manor being in the possession of the same prior, the aforesaid Richard Lovell, by his deed, which the same present prior then presented in court, granted, remitted and entirely quit-claimed on behalf of himself and his heirs in perpetuity, to the prior of Montacute and their successors, the whole right and claim which he had or could in any way have in the aforesaid manor of Tintinhull with its appurtenances, and he also acknowledged by his said writing that the said manor with appurtenances was the right of that prior and convent and their successors in perpetuity: so that neither Richard Lovell nor his heirs could in future demand or assert any right or claim in the aforesaid manor with its appurtenances, nor in another part of them. And further, the aforesaid Richard Lovell granted by his same writing that if any fine should be levied upon the aforesaid manor with its appurtenances, or in any other part of the same, in the court of the lord king between that Richard Lovell and Muriel his wife, plaintiffs, and master Richard de Clare and master Roger Bloxworth, deforciants, by virtue of which fine any right or claim should accrue to him or his heirs in any way, the same Richard Lovell willed and granted, for him and his heirs, that that fine should have no bearing upon his right and be forever held at naught. *[Page iii-192]*

[Col. a] And he then presented in court the written grant and remission of the aforesaid Richard Lovell testifying to the aforesaid, which follows in these words:

To all faithful in Christ to whom this present writing shall come, Richard Lovell lord of Castle Cary, greeting in the Lord. Know that I have granted, remitted and entirely quit-claimed on behalf of myself and my heirs in perpetuity, to the prior and convent of Montacute and their successors all the right and claim which I had or could in any way have in the manors of Tintinhull and East Chinnock with appurtenances in Somerset, and in the advowsons of the churches of the same towns of Tintinhull and East Chinnock, and also in the hundreds of Tintinhull and East Chinnock, and also in the hundreds of Tintinhull and Houndsborough, with all their appurtenances, the fairs and markets of Tintinhull, and also in all other things in any way pertaining to the aforesaid manors, advowsons, hundreds, fairs and markets. And by these presents I acknowledge all the aforesaid tenements with the advowsons, hundreds, fairs and markets

Membrane 3 to be the right of the prior and convent and their successors in perpetuity, so that neither I, Richard Lovell, nor my heirs, nor any of us, nor anyone acting in our name, will be able henceforth to demand or assert any right or claim in the aforesaid manors, advowsons, hundreds, fairs or markets with all their appurtenances or in any part of the same, but by these presents we shall be forever excluded from all actions of any kind seeking any right in the manors of Tintinhull and East Chinnock, with the advowsons of the churches of the same towns, and the hundreds of Tintinhull and Houndsborough, the fairs and markets of Tintinhull, and all other appurtenances of the said manors, advowsons of the aforesaid churches, hundreds, fairs and markets of the

mercatorum predictorum, seu aliqua parte eorundem, in dominico vel in servicio, per presentes imperpetuum simus. exclusi. Et si aliquis finis de predictis tenementis vel hundredis, vel aliqua parte eorundem, in curia domini regis fuerit levatus inter me et Muriellam uxorem meam querentes, et magistrum Ricardum de Clare et magistrum Rogerum de Blakesworth' deforciantes, virtute cujus finis aliquid juris vel clameum michi vel heredibus meis quoquomodo accrescere potuit, volo et concedo pro me et heredibus meis quod ipso jure sit nullus, et pro nullo imperpetuum habeatur. In cujus rei testimonium huic presenti scripto sigillum meum apposui. Hiis testibus, nobili viro domino Thoma comite Lancastrie, domino Johanne comite Richemond', domino Roberto de Holand', domino Willelmo \le Latymer,/ domino Fulcone Lestraunge, domino Nicholae de Segrave, domino Johanne de Claveryng, domino Fulcone filio Waryni, domino Geraldo Salveyn, domino Willelmo Tuchet, domino Johanne Beek, domino Willelmo Trussell', domino Johanne de Kynerdesey, domino Michaele de Melden', Rogero Boker, Johanne de Lancastr' et aliis multis. Datum apud Eboracum die jovis in octabis Ascensionis Domini, anno regni regis Edwardi [II] filii regis Edwardi [I] duodecimo, tempore parliamenti ibidem tenti. Hanc vero quietam clamantiam ego Ricardus Lovell' antedictus recognovi, et eam irrotulari procuravi tam in cancellaria domini regis quam coram Henrico de Scrop et sociis suis justiciarum domini regis tunc ibidem presentibus, die, loco et anno predictis. Unde idem nunc prior petiit judicium si predictus Ricardus Seymor contra factum predictum predicti antecessoris sui, cujus heres ipse est, execucionem de manerio predicto versus eum habere deberet, \etc./

Et predictus Ricardus Seymor dixit, non cognoscendo aliqua per predictum priorem superius allegata, quod placitum ejusdem prioris est duplex vel triplex, unde non intendit quod idem prior ad tale placitum duplex \de jure/ admitti deberet, etc. Unde petiit judicium et execucionem, etc. Et predictus prior dixit quod ipse placitavit solomodo predictum scriptum ut factum antecessoris ipsius Ricardi Seymor, in barram execucionis sue predicte, et pro principali et finali exitu placiti sui prediti, et residuum cepit tantum per viam protestacionis et conduccionis totius materie sue ad exitum illum. Et dixit ut prius quod predictus Ricardus Lovell', antecessor, etc., per scriptum suum predictum concessit et remisit, et omnino pro se et heredibus suis imperpetuum

[Col. b] quietum clamavit, priori et conventui de Monte Acuto qui tunc fuerat, et successoribus suis, totum jus suum, et clameum quod habuit vel aliquo modo habere potuit, in manerio predicto de Tyntenhull' cum suis pertinentiis, dum idem nuper prior fuit in possessione ejusdem manerii. Et ulterius recognovit, etc. Ita quod nec ipse Ricardus Lovell' nec heredes sui, etc. Et ulterius concessit quod si aliquis finis, etc. Unde petit judicium, si predictus Ricardus Seymor contra factum predictum predicti antecessoris sui, cujus heres ipse est, execucionem de manerio predicto versus eum habere deberet, etc. Et predictus Ricardus Seymor dixit, non cognoscendo aliqua per predictum priorem superius preallegata, quod quidam Hugo Lovell', consanguineus predicti Ricardi Seymor, cujus heres ipse est, fuit seisitus de dicto manerio de Tyntenhull' in dominico suo ut de feodo, et diu ante levacionem finis predicti concessit predictum manerium cuidam priori de Monte Acuto, predecessori nunc prioris; tenendum ad voluntatem[19] ipsius Hugonis, in auxilium operis ecclesie ibidem, dum eidem Hugoni placeret, absque hoc quod idem prior vel successores sui aliquem alium

---
[19] *Original* voluntem

aforesaid, or in any part of the same, in demesne or in service. And if any fine upon the aforesaid tenements or hundreds, or any part of the same, be levied in the court of the lord king between me and my wife Muriel, as plaintiffs, and master Richard de Clare and master Roger Bloxworth, as deforciants, by virtue of which agreement any right or claim might accrue in any way to me or my heirs, I will and grant, for myself and my heirs, that that shall be null, and be forever held at naught. In testimony whereof I have affixed my seal to this present writing. Witnessed by that noble man Sir Thomas, earl of Lancaster, Sir John, earl of Richmond, Sir Robert Holland, Sir William Latimer, Sir Fulk Lestraunge, Sir Nicholas Segrave, Sir John Clavering, Sir Fulk FitzWarin, Sir Gerald Salveyn, Sir William Tuchet, Sir John Beek, Sir William Trussell, Sir John Kynerdesey, Sir Michael Melden, Roger Boker, John Lancaster and many others. Given at York on Thursday on the octave of the Ascension of the Lord, in the twelfth year of the reign of King Edward [II], son of King Edward [I], at the time of the parliament held there. Which quit-claim, I, the aforesaid Richard Lovell, acknowledged, and caused to be enrolled both in the chancery of the lord king as well as in the presence of Henry Scrope and his colleagues, justices of the lord king then present, on the aforesaid day and in the aforesaid place and year. Whereupon the present prior requested judgment on whether the aforesaid Richard Seymour ought to have execution of the aforesaid manor against him, contrary to the said deed of his aforesaid ancestor, whose heir he was, etc.

And the aforesaid Richard Seymour, not acknowledging anything alleged by the said prior above, said that the plea of the same prior was double and triple, and hence he did not think that the same prior ought to be allowed such a double plea, etc. Whereupon he sought judgment and execution, etc. And the aforesaid prior said that he pleaded the aforesaid writing only as the deed of an ancestor of Richard Seymour, in barring his aforesaid execution, and for the chief and last issue of his aforesaid plea, and the rest he took by way of protestation and conduct of all his material to that issue. And he said as before that the aforesaid Richard Lovell, ancestor, etc., by his aforesaid writing conceded and resigned and entirely quit-claimed on behalf of himself and his heirs in perpetuity

[Col. b] to the prior and convent of Montacute at the time, and his successors, all the right and claim he had or could in any way have in the aforesaid manor of Tintinhull with its appurtenances, while the same late prior was in possession of the same manors. And he also acknowledged, etc. So that neither this Richard Lovell nor his heirs, etc. And he also granted that if any agreement, etc. Whereupon he sought judgment as to whether the aforesaid Richard Seymour, contrary to the aforesaid deed of his said ancestor whose heir he was, ought to have execution of the said manor against him, etc. And the aforesaid Richard Seymour, not acknowledging anything alleged above by the aforesaid prior, said that a certain Hugh Lovell, kinsman of the aforesaid Richard Seymour, whose heir he was, was in possession of the said manor of Tintinhull in his demesne as of fee, and long before the levy of the said fine he had granted the aforesaid manor to a certain prior of Montacute, a predecessor of the present prior, to be held at the will of Hugh, to help the work of the church there, so long as it pleased the same Hugh, without the same prior or his successors ever having any other estate

statum in eodem manerio ante levacionem finis predicti unquam habuerunt, etc. Colore cujus concessionis, prefatus prior, et successores sui occupaverunt predictum manerium in jure ipsius Hugonis et heredum suorum, etc., quousque Ricardus Lovell', consanguineus et heres predicti Hugonis, manerium predictum in manus suas proprias seisivit et resumpsit, et seisinam suam in eodem manerio continuavit, quousque idem Ricardus Lovell' de dicto manerio simul cum aliis maneriis predictis feoffavit magistrum Ricardum de Clare, magistrum Rogerum de Blokerworth', in feodo simplici. Qui quidem magister Ricardus et magister Rogerus, virtute feoffamenti illius inde seisiti fuerunt tempore confeccionis scripti predicti, absque hoc, quod prior qui tunc fuerat aliquid habuit in eodem manerio tempore confecionis ejusdem scripti; et hoc paratus est verificare, etc. Qui quidem magister Ricardus et magister Rogerus, predictum manerium cum aliis maneriis predictis prefato Ricardo Lovell' et Murielle, in fine predicto nominatis, habenda sibi et heredibus ipsius Ricardi Lovell', concesserunt et reddiderunt. De quo quidem manerio de Tyntenhull', virtute finis predicti, predictus Ricardus Seymor, consanguineus et heres predicti Ricardi Lovell', modo petit executionem, etc. Et dicit quod nec Henricus [I] rex, filius conquestoris, nec aliquis regum Anglie, de manerio predicto unquam seisiti fuerunt ante levacionem finis predicti. Unde petit judicium et execucionem, etc.

Et predictus prior non cognoscendo aliqua per ipsum Ricardum Seymor superius allegata, dixit quod placitum predicti Ricardi fuit duplex; unde non intendit quod ipse ad tale placitum duplex de jure necesse habet respondere. Et quia videtur curie quod placitum predicti Ricardi Seymor fuit duplex, dictum fuit eidem Ricardo per curiam, quod ipse responderet ad predictum scriptum quod predictus prior asserit fore factum antecessoris sui, et quod idem prior placitavit versus eum in barram execucionis finis predicti, etc., si, etc. Et predictus Ricardus Seymor habito visu scripti predicti, dixit quod ipse non cognovit scriptum illud fore factum tempore quo per datum ejusdem supponitur fieri. Et dixit ulterius quod prior de Monte Acuto qui tunc fuerat, non fuit seisitus de manerio de Tyntenhull, nec de aliqua parcella ejusdem manerii, tempore confeccionis scripti predicti, set predicti magister Ricardus de Clare et magister Rogerus de Blokerworth, qui idem manerium reddiderunt per finem predictum, adtunc inde seisiti fuerunt; et hoc paratus est verificare, etc. Et dixit quod ipse residuum omnium materiarum suarum per ipsum superius propositarum cepti per viam protestacionis et conductionis tocius placiti sui ad exitum illum.

Unde peciit judicium, si ipse ab execucione sua predicta virtute scripti predicti excludi deberet, etc. Et peciit execucionem, etc. Et predictus prior dixit quod tempore confeccionis scripti predicti prior de Monte Acuto qui tunc fuerat, fuit seisitus de dicto manerio de Tyntenhull' cum pertinentiis; et hoc paratus /fuit\ verificare per *[Page iii-193]*

[Col. a] patriam, etc. Et predictus Ricardus Seymor dixit quod tempore confeccionis scripti predicti prior de Monte Acuto qui tunc fuerat non fuit seisitus de predicto manerio de Tyntenhull' cum pertinentiis, nec de aliqua parcella ejusdem: et hoc paratus est verificare per patriam, etc. Et predictus prior similiter, \etc./ Ideo preceptum fuit /vicecomes Somers'\ quod venire faceret coram domino\ rege ad hunc diem, scilicet a die Sancti Michaelis in .xv. dies ubicumque etc., .xxiiij. tam milites, etc., de visneto de Tyntenhull, per quos, etc. Et qui nec, etc., ad recognicionem, etc. Quia tam, etc. Idem dies datus fuit partibus predictis, etc.

in the same manor before the levying of the fine, etc. By colour of which grant, the aforementioned prior and his successors occupied the aforesaid manor which by right belonged to this Hugh and his heirs, etc., until Richard Lovell, kinsman and heir of the aforesaid Hugh, took and reclaimed the aforesaid manor into his own hands, and continued his seisin in the same manor until the same Richard Lovell enfeoffed master Richard de Clare and master Roger Bloxworth with the said manor together with the other aforesaid manors in fee simple. Which master Richard and master Roger, by virtue of that enfeoffment, were thus seised at the time of the making of the aforesaid document, without the prior at that time holding anything in the same manor at the time of the making of the same document; and this he was ready to prove, etc. Which master Richard and master Roger granted and returned the aforesaid manor with the other aforesaid manors to the aforementioned Richard Lovell and Muriel, named in the aforesaid fine, to have to them and the heirs of the said Richard. Of which manor of Tintinhull, by virtue of the aforesaid settlement, the aforesaid Richard Seymour, kinsman and heir of the aforesaid Richard Lovell, sought execution etc. And he said that neither King Henry [I], son of the Conqueror, nor any other king of England had ever been seised of the said manor before the making of the said fine. Hence he sought judgment and execution, etc.

And the aforesaid prior, not acknowledging anything alleged above by Richard Seymour, said that the plea of the aforesaid Richard was double; therefore he did not think that he had necessarily to answer to a such a double plea by right. And because it seemed to the court that the plea of the aforesaid Richard Seymour was double, the same Richard was told by the court that he should answer the aforesaid document which the said prior claimed had been made by his ancestor, and which the same prior pleaded against him to bar execution of the aforesaid settlement, etc., if, etc. And the said Richard Seymour, having perused the said document, said that he did not accept that the document had been made when it was supposed to have been made according to its date. And he further said that the prior of Montacute at that time had not been in possession of the manor of Tintinhull, nor any part of the same manor, when the same document was made, but that the aforesaid Richard Clare and master Roger Bloxworth, who returned the same manor by the said fine, had then been seised; and this he was ready to prove, etc. And he said that he took all the rest of his matter proposed above by way of protest and conduct of his plea to that end.

Whereupon he sought judgment whether he should be excluded from his aforesaid execution by virtue of the aforesaid document, etc. And he sought execution, etc. And the aforesaid prior said that at the time when the aforesaid document was made the prior of Montacute of the time was seised of the said manor of Tintinhull with its appurtenances; and this he was ready to prove by *[Page iii-193]*

[Col. a] his country, etc. And the said Richard Seymour said that at the time when the said document was written the then prior of Montacute had not been seised of the aforesaid manor of Tintinhull with appurtenances, nor any parcel of the same: and this he was ready to prove by his country, etc. And the said prior likewise, etc. So the sheriff of Somerset was ordered to cause to appear before the lord king on this day, namely on the day of Michaelmas in fifteen days wheresoever etc. [13 October 1383], twenty-four knights, etc., of the neighbourhood of Tintinhull, by whom, etc. And who neither, etc., to acknowledge, etc. Because both, etc. The same day was given to the aforesaid parties, etc.

Ad quem diem, coram domino rege apud Westm' venerunt tam predictus Ricardus Seymor, quam predictus prior, per attornatos suos predictos. Et vicecomes retornavit nomina predictorum .xxiiij., etc., quorum nullus venit. Ideo vicecomes habeat corpora eorum coram domino rege in octabis Sancti Martini ubicumque, etc., ad faciendam jurationem predictam, etc. Idem dies datus est partibus predictis, etc. Et continuato inde processu inter partes predictas per juratio positus in respectum usque a die Sancti Hillar' in .xv. dies tunc proximo sequente ubicumque, etc. Ad quem diem coram domino rege apud Westm' venit predictus Ricardus Seymor per attornatum suum predictum, et predictus prior per attornatum suum predictum similiter venit. Et juratores similiter venerunt, qui ad hoc electi, triati et jurati, dicunt super sacramentum suum quod ipse qui fuerat prior de Monte Acuto tempore confectionis scripti predicti quod predictus nunc prior placitavit versus predictum Ricardum Seymor in barram execucionis sue finis predicti de predicto manerio de Tyntenhull' cum suis pertinentiis, non fuit seisitus de predicto manerio de Tyntenhull' cum pertinentiis, nec de aliqua parcella ejusdem, tempore confeccionis ejusdem scripti, sicut predictus Ricardus Seymor placitando allegavit, etc. Ideo consideratum est quod predictus Ricardus Seymor habeat execucionem versus predictum nunc priorem de manerio predicto de Tyntenhull', cum pertinentiis, etc.

Et lectis et auditis in isto eodem parliamento recordo et processu predictis, prefatus Ricardus petit quod predictus /prior\ assignet et declaret errores si qui fuerint in recordo et processu predictis. Super quo, predictus prior per dictum attornatum suum dicit quod erratum fuit in recordo et processu predictis, in primis, videlicet, ubi dictus prior allegavit quod predictus Ricardus Seymor, per nomen Ricardi de Sancto Mauro, chivaler, tulit quoddam breve de recto, cujus data est quartodecimo die Octobris, anno regni regis nunc sexto, versus dictum priorem, per nomen Francisci, prioris de Monte Acuto, de predicto manerio de Tyntenhull', retornabile coram justiciarii domini regis de banco in crastino Sancti Martini, dicto anno sexto, ad quod breve idem Ricardus Seymor tunc comparuit, et dictus prior essonatus fuit, et habuit diem per essonium suum a die Pasche in tres septimanas tunc proxime sequenti, prout per tenores dicti brevis de recto, et irrotulamenti /essonii predicti,\ coram rege de mandato suo missos, et in recordo predicto irrotulatos, plene liquet, et quod dictum breve de scire facias perquisitum fuit pendente dicto brevi de recto, quod fuit de altiori natura quam fuit predictum breve de scire facias, et petiit judicium de dicto brevi de scire facias: et in hoc quod consideratum fuit quod predictus prior ad dictum breve de scire facias ulterius responderet, non obstante excepcione predicta, ubi si recte et modo legitimo adjudicatum fuisset, idem breve de scire facias cassari debuisset, erratum fuit. Et etiam, ubi dictus prior allegavit quod dominus Edwardus [III], nuper rex Anglie, avus domini regis nunc, nuper de avisamento parliamenti sui, occasione guerre inter ipsum et Gallicos mote, seisire fecerat in manus suas omnes possessiones prioratuum alienigenarum in Anglie de potestate Francie existencium, quamdiu dicta guerra duraret; et inter alia prioratus de Monte Acuto, cum omnibus possessionibus ad prioratum illum spectantibus, seisitus fuit in manus dicti regis Edwardi, ex causa supradicta, qui quidem Edwardus rex postea per litteras suas patentes, quarum data est apud Westm' decimo die Novembris, anno regni sui quadragesimo quinto, quas idem prior protulit in eadem

On which day, the said Richard Seymour and the aforesaid prior came before the lord king at Westminster, represented by their attorneys aforesaid. And the sheriff returned the names of the aforesaid twenty-four, etc., of whom none appeared. Therefore the sheriff was to have their persons before the lord king on the octave of Martinmas [18 November 1383], wheresoever, etc., to make the aforesaid testimony, etc. The same day was given to the aforesaid parties, etc. And the process between the aforesaid parties was adjourned, the jury being put in respite until fifteen days after the day of St Hilary [27 January 1384], wheresoever, etc. On which day the said Richard Seymour, represented by his said attorney, appeared before the lord king at Westminster, and the aforesaid prior came likewise by his attorney. And the jurors similarly came, who had been elected, tried and sworn thereto, and they said on oath that he who was prior of Montacute at the time of the making of the aforesaid document, which the aforesaid prior pleaded against the aforesaid Richard Seymour in barring his execution of the aforesaid settlement concerning the aforesaid manor of Tintinhull with its appurtenances, was not in possession of the aforesaid manor of Tintinhull with appurtenances, nor any parcel of the same, at the time when the same document was made, as the aforesaid Richard Seymour in pleading had claimed, etc. Therefore it was considered that the said Richard Seymour should have execution against the said present prior concerning the aforesaid manor of Tintinhull, with appurtenances, etc.

And the aforesaid record and process having been read in the same parliament, the aforementioned Richard asked that the aforesaid prior indicate and declare errors in the aforesaid record and process if there were any. Whereupon, the aforesaid prior said through his said attorney that error was to be found in the aforesaid record and process, that is to say, first where the said prior alleged that the said Richard Seymour, by name of Richard de Sancto Mauro, knight, brought a certain writ of right, dated 14 October in the sixth year of the reign of the present king [1382], against the said prior, by the name of Francis, prior of Montagu, concerning the aforesaid manor of Tintinhull, returnable before the justices of the King's Bench on the morrow of Martinmas in the said sixth year [12 November 1382], to which writ the same Richard Seymour then appeared, and the said prior was essoined, and had a day for his essoin three weeks after Easter next [12 April 1383], as appears fully from the tenors of the said writ of right and enrolments of the aforesaid essoins sent before the lord king on his orders and enrolled in the aforesaid record, and that the said writ of scire facias requested was pending the said writ of right, which was of a higher nature that the aforesaid writ of scire facias, and he requested judgment upon the said writ of scire facias: and there was error therein, in so far as it was decided that the aforesaid prior should also answer the said writ of scire facias, notwithstanding the aforesaid exception, whereas if it had been correctly and legitimately adjudged, the same writ of scire facias ought to have been annulled. Moreover, the said prior alleged that Lord Edward [III], late king of England, grandfather of the present lord king, lately with the advice of his parliament on the occasion of war between him and the French, caused all the possessions of the alien priories in England being under French power to be taken into his hands for as long as the said war should last; and among others, the priory of Montacute with all the possessions pertaining to it was taken into the hands of the said king Edward for that reason, which Edward later by his letters patent, dated at Westminster 10 November in the forty-fifth year of his reign [1371], which the prior brought to the same

[Col. b] curiam, et que in recordo predicto inseruntur, commisit prefato priori, per nomen fratris Francisci /prioris\ prioratus de Monte Acuto alienigene, custodiam prioratus predicti, et omnium possessionum eidem prioratui spectantium, habendum a festo Sancti Michaelis tunc proxime preterito quamdiu prioratum, terras et possessiones predictas in manu ipsius regis ex causa supradicta contingeret remanere, reddendo inde eidem domino regi \annuatim/ ad scaccarium suum, vel alibi ad mandatum suum, ad festa Pasche et Sancti Michaelis, per equales porciones, centum et viginti libras, salvis expresse in eisdem litteris eidem regi feodis militum, et advocacionibus ecclesiarum ad dictum prioratum spectantibus sive pertinentibus; et quod dictus dominus rex nunc, occasione reservacionis predicte de dictis feodis militum et advocacionibus ecclesiarum dicti prioratus, presentavit ad ecclesiam de Tyntenhull' quendam clericum suum Johannem Stone. Et sic dixit idem prior quod ipse sine domino rege nunc non potuit inde respondere, et peciit auxilium de dicto domino rege nunc: et in hoc quod consideratum fuit quod predictus prior ulterius responderet sine hujusmodi auxilio habendo, erratum fuit.

Et insuper, ubi placitum super dicto brevi de scire facias recordatum fuit, et pro recordo irrotulatur termino Sancti Michaelis, anno dicti domini regis nunc septimo et non antea, et breve ejusdem domini regis mandatum fuit vicecomes Somers' de venire faciendo juratores essendi coram /ipso domino\ rege in quindena Sancti Michaelis eodem anno septimo ubicumque tunc foret in Anglie, ad faciendam juratam inter partes predictas super exitu placiti predicti, cujus quidem brevis data est undecimo die Julii dicto anno septimo, quod est diu ante predictum terminum Sancti Michaelis, \et/ quod quidem breve de venire faciendo est breve judiciale et de recordo irrotulato ante exitum brevis hujusmodi de jure et per legem terre warantizari debuisset, set per /dictum recordum\ irrotulatum dicto termino Sancti Michaelis warantizari non potuit. Immo exiit sine waranto, et tamen retornatum fuit per dictum vicecomitem cum nominibus juratorum ad quindenam supra dictam, continuatoque inde processu quosque per juratam in hac parte captam, et per judicium super hoc redditum predictus prior amisit manerium suum predictum. Unde ex hoc quod predicta jurata capta fuit per returnum predictum virtute dicti brevis de venire faciendo, quod per dictum recordum, ut premittitur, warantizari non potuit; et in hoc quod consideratum fuit quod predictus Ricardus haberet execucionem de dicto manerio, super hujusmodi processu erratum fuit, eo quod si /rite\ et modo legitimo adjudicatum fuisset, considerari debuisset quod totus processus super predicto brevi de scire facias discontinuari debuisset, vel aliter quod partes predicte ad placitandum de novo per legem terre compelli debuissent. Unde propter errores illos, et alios in predictis recordo et processu contentos, petit dictus prior per dictum attornatum suum quod judicium predictum tanquam erroneum revocetur et adnulletur, et quod ipse ad possessionem suam manerii predicti, una cum exitibus inde medio tempore perceptis restituatur.

Et predictus Ricardus Seymor in propria persona sua, quoad predictos tres articulos pro errore assignatos, dicit quod non habetur error in articulis supradictis: quia, ubi primo assignatum est pro errore, quod dictum breve de scire facias impetratum fuit pendente dicto brevi de recto, et quod dictus Ricardus Seymor ad dictum breve de recto comparuit, dicit quod non habetur aliquod verbum in recordo probans ipsum

[Col. b] court, and which are included in the aforesaid record, assigned to the aforementioned prior by the name of brother Francis prior of the alien priory of Montacute, custody of the aforesaid priory, and all possessions attached to the same, to have from Michaelmas last past [29 September 1371] for so long as the aforesaid priory, lands and possessions should happen to remain in the king's hands for the aforesaid reason, paying to the same lord king annually at his exchequer, or elsewhere at his order, at Easter and Michaelmas [29 September] in equal portions, one hundred and twenty pounds, expressly excepting in the letters of the same king the knights' fees and advowsons of churches attached or pertaining to the said priory; and that the said present lord king, on the said occasion of the reservation of the said knights' fees and advowsons of the churches of the said priory, presented to the church of Tintinhull a certain cleric of his named John Stone. And thus the same prior said that he could not now answer to this without the lord king, and he requested the aid of the said present lord king: and there was error in so far as it was decided that the aforesaid prior should again answer without such aid.

And further, there was error in so far as the plea on the said writ of scire facias was recorded and enrolled as a record in the term of Michaelmas in the seventh year of the said present lord king [9 October - 28 November 1383] and not before, and by a writ of the same lord king the sheriff of Somerset was ordered to cause the jurors to appear before the lord king on the quinzaine of Michaelmas in the same seventh year [8 October 1383], wheresoever he should then be in England, to determine right between the aforesaid parties upon the issue of the aforesaid plea, the writ of which is dated 11 July in the said seventh year [1383], which was long before the aforesaid term of Michaelmas [9 October - 28 November 1383], and which same writ of venire faciendo was a judicial writ and of record enrolled, which ought by right and by the law of the land to have been warranted before the issue of a writ of that kind, but it could not be warranted by the said record enrolled in the said term of Michaelmas [9 October - 28 November 1383]. Indeed it issued without warrant, and was nevertheless returned by the said sheriff with the names of the jurors on the aforesaid quinzaine, the process having been held by the jury being adjourned, and through the judgment rendered thereon the aforesaid prior lost his aforesaid manor. Hence there was error in the manner of procedure in as far as the aforesaid trial was held through the aforesaid return by virtue of the said writ of venire faciendo, which by the said record, as said above, could not be warranted; and in so far as it was decided that the aforesaid Richard should have execution of the said manor, whereas, if it had been corrected and legitimately adjudged, it ought to have been decided that the entire process regarding the aforesaid writ of scire facias should be discontinued, or otherwise that the aforesaid parties be compelled to plead anew by the law of the land. Therefore, on account of those errors and others contained in the aforesaid record and process, the said prior requested through his said attorney that the aforesaid judgment, erroneous as it was, be revoked and annulled, and that he be restored to his possession of the aforesaid manor, together with the profits received in the meantime.

And the aforesaid Richard Seymour in his own person says in response to the aforesaid three articles assigning error that no error was to be found in the aforesaid articles: because, concerning the first error claiming that the said writ of scire facias was obtained pending the said writ of right, and that the said Richard Seymour appeared upon the said writ of right, he said that there was not a single word on record

Ricardum ad dictum breve de recto unquam apparuisse; et dictum breve de scire facias fuit breve judiciale ad habendum execucionem cujusdam finis qui quidem finis est judicium finale in sua natura executorium infra annum, absque responsione partis, et post annum per breve de scire facias: in quo casu, apparencia sive impetracio brevis pendente alio brevi non debet cassare tale breve executorium; et sic in illo articulo non est error.

Item, ubi secundo allegatum est pro errore quod dominus Edwardus [III] nuper rex Anglie avus domini regis *[Page iii-194]*

[Col. a] nunc, prioratum de Monte Acuto in manibus suis occasione guerre inter ipsum et adversarios suos Francie \seisitum/ prefato priori pro certa firma inde annuatim reddenda commisserat, reservatis eidem regi Edwardo feodis militum, et advocacionibus ecclesiarum; et quod idem prior eo pretextu sine auxilio domini regis nunc respondere non potuit; et tamen consideratum fuit quod idem prior sine auxilio predicto habendo responderet; dicit quod manifeste probatum est per recordum quod predictus rex Edwardus [III] dedit et concessit patronatum dicti prioratus, et eciam custodiam et firmam ejusdem prioratus, tempore pacis et guerre, Willelmo nuper comiti Sarum et heredibus suis imperpetuum; quodque Willelmus de Monte Acuto nunc comes Sarum filius et heres predicti nuper comitis prosequebatur in cancellaria dicti regis Edwardi et habuit liberacionem custodie et firme dicti prioratus absque aliquo inde eidem regi solvendo virtute donacionis et concessionis predictarum, que quidem liberacio est plena revocacio dictarum litterarum patencium eidem priori ut premittitur factarum: et quod brevia inde thesaurario et baronibus de scaccario de exonerando dictum priorem de dicta firma, et alia brevia eidem priori de intendendo prefato nunc comiti et non regi de custodia et firma predictis facta fuerunt, et ita sine causa \[non]/ deberet auxilium concedi in illo casu. Et insuper dicit quod dictum recordum non facit mencionem in aliquo loco quod dictum manerium de Tyntenhull' est parcella dicti prioratus, et sic dictus prior nichil amisit, nec amittere potuit, pretextu amocionis auxilii predicti, quod esset quoddam dilatorium et non ad materiam: set per placitum ad jus et ad accionem dictus prior per exitum patrie dictum manerium amisit, unde error non assignatur nec allegatur; et sic in articulo illo non habetur error.

Et quo ad tercium articulum, ubi assignatur pro errore, quod dictum breve de venire faciendo perquisitum fuit ante exitum junctum, dicit quod aperte probatur per recordum quod partes predicte placitaverunt ad exitum patrie in crastino Sancti Johannis Baptiste, quod /fuit\ in mense Junii, et breve predictum portat datam de mense Julii tunc proximo sequento, et ita contrarium apparet de recordo; et sic in articulo illo aut in aliquo alio articulo recordi et processus predictorum non habetur error, et petit quod judicium in hac parte pro ipso redditum affirmetur.

Et super hoc, auditis hinc inde partium rationibus, allegacionibus et responsionibus \in hac parte,/ ac visis et examinatis recordo et processu predictis, et aliis omnibus dicta recordum et processum tangentibus et concernentibus, pro eo quod dictum breve de scire facias impetratum fuit pendente dicto brevi de recto, et dictum breve de recto pendebat post diem quo dictum breve de scire facias fuit retornabile et retornatum, ad quod breve de recto idem Ricardus comparuit prout per tenorem recordi placiti super predicto brevi de recto coram justiciariis de banco nuper habitum, et coram prefatis justiciariis de banco regis missum, liquet manifeste, in quo casu dictum breve de scire facias per legem terre

proving that the same Richard had ever appeared upon the said writ of right; and the said writ of scire facias was a judicial writ for the execution of a certain fine, which fine was a final judgment of its nature to be performed within a year, without the response of party, and after a year by writ of scire facias: in which case, the appearance or obtaining of a writ pending another writ ought not to be annulled by such a writ of execution; and so no error lay in the article.

Also, as for the second error claimed - that Lord Edward [III], late king of England, grandfather of the present lord king *[Page iii-194]*

[Col. a] committed the priory of Montacute, taken into his hands on the occasion of the war between him and his adversaries of France, to the aforementioned prior for the annual payment of a certain farm, reserving to the same King Edward knights' fees and advowsons of churches; and that the same prior could not, on those grounds, answer now without the help of the lord king; and nevertheless it was decided that the same prior should answer without having the aforesaid help - he says that it was clearly proven by record that the aforesaid king Edward gave and granted patronage of the said priory, and also the custody and farm of the same priory, in times of peace and war, to William late earl of Salisbury and his heirs in perpetuity; and that William of Montagu now earl of Salisbury, son and heir of the aforesaid late earl, sued in the chancery of the said King Edward and had delivery of the custody and farm of the said priory without paying anything to the same king in exchange for the aforesaid gift and concession, which delivery was an entire revocation of the said letters patent made, as said above, for the same prior: and that writs to the treasurer and barons of the exchequer exonerating the said prior of the said farm, and other writs de intendendo were made to the same prior notifying him that the custody and farm now lay with the aforementioned present earl and not with the king, and so help ought not be given without reason in this case. And he further says that the said record made no mention anywhere that the said manor of Tintinhull was a part of the said priory, and thus the said prior had not lost nor could lose anything, on the pretext of the withdrawal of the aforesaid help, that would be a matter of delay and of substance: but by the plea of right and action the said prior by the outcome of the trial lost the said manor, wherein error is not to be assigned or alleged; and so no error was to be found in that article.

As regards the third article - where it was claimed as error that the said writ de venire faciendo was sought before the issue was joined - he said that it was clearly proven on record that the aforesaid parties pleaded for a verdict from the jury on the morrow of St John the Baptist [25 June 1383], which was in the month of June, and the aforesaid writ bore the date of the month of July then following [1383], and so the record suggests the contrary; and thus error is not to be found in that article or in any other article of the aforesaid record and process, and he asked that the judgment rendered in this matter in his favour be affirmed.

And thereupon, the arguments, claims and answers of both parties having been heard in the matter, and the aforesaid record and process having been seen and examined, as well as all other things touching and concerning the said record and process, because the said writ of scire facias was obtained pending the said writ of right, and the said writ of right was pending after the day on which the said writ of scire facias was returnable and returned, to which writ of right the same Richard appeared as is manifestly clear from the tenor of the record of the plea on the aforesaid writ of right lately held before the justices of the bench, and before the aforementioned justices sent from the King's Bench, in

cassari debuisset, et in hoc quod justiciarii consideraverunt dictum breve de scire facias fore bonum, ac dictum priorem ulterius respondere, videtur curie in parliamento quod erraverunt.

[20] Et insuper, ubi predictus prior in placito predicto peciit auxilium de dicto domino rege nunc causa in recordo et processu predictis preallegata: et in hoc quod dicti justiciarii consideraverunt quod prefatus prior sine auxilio predicto habendo ulterius responderet, videtur etiam dicte curie in parliamento quod erraverunt. Ideo ob errores illos consideratum est quod judicium predictum tanquam erroneum revocetur, cassetur et penitus adnulletur; et quod predictus prior plenariam habeat restitutionem manerii predicti cum pertinentiis una cum exitibus ejusdem manerii a tempore reddicionis dicti judicii pro predicto Ricardo sic erronice redditi inde perceptis. Et preceptum est vicecomes Somers' quod eidem priori plenam restitucionem et seisinam manerii predicti cum pertinentiis habere faceret juxta consideracionem supradictam. Et quod inquirat de exitibus ejusdem manerii medio tempore inde perceptis, et inde certificet in

[Col. b] cancellaria. Et facta certificacione hujusmodi habeat dictus prior breve vicecomitis Somers' de exitibus hujusmodi levandis, et sibi restituendis. Et preceptum est cancellarius domini regis in pleno parliamento quod tam de seisina et restitucione prefato priori de manerio predicto habendis, quam de exitibus manerii illius, a tempore predicti judicii erronici pro predicto Ricardo redditi quovis modo perceptis, ad opus ejusdem prioris levandis et fieri faciendis ac de premissis omnibus et singulis in predicto parliamento consideratis, secundum legem et consuetudinem regni Anglie plenam execucionem fieri faciat et demandet. Intentionis tamen \dicti/ domini regis non existit, quin predictus Ricardus Seymor per breve de recto vel per /breve\ de scire facias de novo prosequi possit in hac parte, si sibi viderit expedire.

Membrane i[21]

PLACITA CORAM DOMINO REGE APUD WESTMON' DE TERMINO SANCTI MICHAELIS, ANNO REGNI REGNI RICARDI SECUNDI SEPTIMO.

Adhuc de termino Sancti Michaelis. Robertus Tresilian. *Somers'.*

Alias, scilicet termino Sancte Trinitatis, anno regni regis Ricardi secundi quinto, dominus rex mandavit dilecto et fideli suo Roberto Tresilian, capitali justiciario, etc., breve suum clausum, in hec verba:

Ricardus, Dei gratia, rex Anglie et Francie, et dominus Hibernie, dilecto et fideli suo Roberto Tresilian, capitali justiciario suo, salutem. Tenorem pedis cujusdam finis levati in curia domini Edwardi filii regis Edwardi nuper regis Anglie progenitoris nostri, anno regni ejusdem Edwardi filii regis Edwardi undecimo, coram Willelmo de Bereford et sociis suis tunc justiciariis ejusdem Edwardi filii regis Edwardi de banco, per breve ejusdem Edwardi filii regis Edwardi inter Ricardum Lovel et Muriellam uxorem ejus querentes, et magistrum Ricardum de Clare et magistrum Rogerum de Blokerworth deforciantes, de maneriis de Blakeford, Southbarewe, Northbarewe, Cherleton' Makerell, Tyntenhull' et

this case the said writ of scire facias ought to be annulled by the law of the land, and in so far as the justices had decided that the said writ of scire facias was good, and that the said prior should again answer, it seemed to the court in parliament that they had erred.

And furthermore, in so far as the aforesaid prior had sought help in the aforesaid plea from the said present lord king for the reasons claimed above in the aforesaid record and process, and in so far as the said justices had decided that the aforementioned prior should again answer without having the aforesaid help, it also seemed to the said court in parliament that they erred. Thus on account of those errors it was decided that the aforesaid judgment, being erroneous, should be revoked, cancelled and entirely annulled; and that the said prior should have full restitution of the aforesaid manor with appurtenances together with the profits received from the same manor from the time of the said judgment erroneously made in favour of the aforesaid Richard. And the sheriff of Somerset was ordered to cause the same prior to have full restitution and seisin of the aforesaid manor with appurtenances according to the aforesaid decision. And that he should inquire into the revenues from the same manor received in the meantime and certify them in

[Col. b] chancery. And, notification having been made, the said prior should have a writ from the sheriff of Somerset of the revenues levied in this way and to be restored to him. And the chancellor of the lord king was ordered in full parliament to cause and demand full execution to be made, according to the law and custom of the kingdom of England, of the seisin and restitution to the aforementioned prior of the aforesaid manor, as well as of the revenues of that manor received in any way since the time of the aforesaid erroneous judgment made in favour of the aforesaid Richard, to be levied and set aside for the use of the same prior, and of each and every one of the aforesaid things decided in the said parliament. Nevertheless, it was not of the intention of the said lord king that the aforesaid Richard Seymour should be prevented from further pursuing this matter by writ of right or by writ of scire facias, if it seemed expedient to him.

PLEAS IN THE PRESENCE OF THE LORD KING AT WESTMINSTER IN MICHAELMAS TERM, IN THE SEVENTH YEAR OF THE REIGN OF KING RICHARD II [9 October - 28 November 1383].

Thus far in Michaelmas term. Robert Tresilian. *Somerset.*

At another time, namely from Trinity term in the fifth year of the reign of King Richard II [11 June - 2 July 1382], the lord king sent to his beloved and faithful Robert Tresilian, chief justice, etc., his writ close, in these words:

Richard, by grace of God, king of England and France and lord of Ireland, to his beloved and faithful Robert Tresilian, his chief justice, greeting. The tenor of a certain foot of fine levied in the court of the lord Edward [II], son of King Edward [I] late king of England, our progenitor, in the eleventh year of the reign of the same Edward son of King Edward [1317], before William Bereford and his colleagues then justices of the bench of the same Edward son of King Edward, by a writ of the same Edward son of King Edward, between Richard Lovell and Muriel his wife, plaintiffs, and master Richard de Clare and master Roger Bloxworth, deforciants, concerning the manors of Blackford, South Barrow, North

---
[20] 15 added later in the margin in error.
[21] The following pleas continue over four separate membranes (numbered i-iv) stitched together exchequer style to the foot of the dorse of membrane 6.

Prestelee, cum pertinentiis, vobis mittimus sub pede sigilli nostri, mandantes, ut inspecto tenore pedis finis predicti, ulterius, ad prosecucionem Ricardi Seymor consanguinei et heredis predicti Ricardi Lovel, inde fieri facias quod de jure et secundum legem et consuetudinem regni nostri Anglie fuerit faciendum. Teste meipso apud Westm', .xx. die Junii, anno regni nostri quinto.

Tenor pedis finis de quo in brevi predicto fit mentio sequitur, in hec verba:
Hec est finalis concordia facta in curia domini regis, apud Westm' in octabis Sancti Michaelis, anno regni regis Edwardi filii regis Edwardi undecimo, coram Willelmo de Bereford, Gilberto de Roubury, Johanne de Benstede, Johanne Bacun et Johanne de Mutford, justiciariis, et aliis domini regis fidelibus, tunc ibi presentibus, inter Ricardum Lovel et Muriellam uxorem ejus querentes, per Thomam de Croukern positum loco ipsius Murielle ad lucrandum vel perdendum, et magistrum Ricardum de Clare et magistrum Rogerum de Blokerworth deforciantes, de maneriis de Blakeford, Southbarewe, Northbarewe, Cherleton' Makerel, Tyntenhull' et Prestele, cum pertinentiis, unde placitum conventionis summonitum fuit inter eos in eadem curia, scilicet quod predictus Ricardus Lovel recognovit predicta maneria cum pertinentiis esse jus ipsorum magistri Ricardi de Clare et magistri Rogeri, ut illa que iidem magister Ricardus et magister Rogerus habent de dono predicti Ricardi Lovel. Et pro hac recognicione, fine et concordia iidem \magister/ Ricardus et magister Rogerus concesserunt predictis Ricardo Lovel et Murielle, predicta maneria cum pertinentiis. Et illa eis reddiderunt in eadem curia, habenda et tenenda eisdem Ricardo Lovel, et Murielle, et heredibus ipsius Ricardi, scilicet predicta maneria de Southbarewe, et Northbarewe et Tyntenhull, cum pertinentiis, de domino rege et heredibus suis; et predicta maneria *[Page iii-195]*

[Col. a] de Blakeford, /Cherleton\ Makerel et Prestele, cum pertinentiis, de capitali dominis feodi illius, per servitia que ad predicta maneria pertinent imperpetuum.
Et hec concordia quo ad predicta maneria de Suthbarewe, Northbarewe et Tyntenhull' cum pertinentiis, facta fuit per preceptum ipsius domini regis.
Somers'.

Postea ad sectam Ricardi Seymor, asserentis se fore consanguineum et heredem predicti Ricardi Lovel, videlicet filius Murielle, filie Jacobi filii predicti Ricardi Lovel; et quod predicti Ricardus Lovel et Muriella mortui sunt; et quod ipse execucionem de predicto manerio de Tyntenhull' nondum est assecutus; et quod prior de Monte Acuto predictum manerium de Tyntenhull' cum pertinentiis post mortem predictorum Ricardi Lovel et Murielle ingressus fuit, et illud tunc tenuit et occupavit, contra formam finis predicti, et petiit executionem de predicto manerio de Tyntenhull', juxta formam finis predicti, etc. Per quod preceptum fuit vicecomes Somers' quod per probos, etc., scire faceret prefato priori quod esset coram domino rege, a die Pasche ultimo preterito in .xv. dies ubicumque, etc., ad ostendendum si quid pro se haberet vel dicere sciret, quare predictus Ricardus Seymor, consanguineus et heres predicti Ricardi Lovel, in forma predicta execucionem de predicto manerio de Tentenhull' cum pertinentiis versus eum habere non deberet. Et ulterius, etc. Idem dies datus /fuit\ predicto Ricardo Seymor.

Ad quem diem, coram domino rege venit predictus Ricardus Seymor per Johannem de Hulton', attornatum suum. Et

Barrow, Charlton Mackrell, Tintinhull and Prestley, with appurtenances, we send you under our half-seal, ordering that, having inspected the tenor of the aforesaid foot of fine, you then proceed with the suit of Richard Seymour, kinsman and heir of the aforesaid Richard Lovell, and therein to do what ought to be done by right and in accordance with the law and custom of our kingdom of England. Witnessed by myself at Westminster, 20 June in the fifth year of our reign [1382].
The tenor of the foot of fine of which the writ made mention follows in these words:
This is the final concord made in the court of the lord king at Westminster on the octave of Michaelmas in the eleventh year of the reign of King Edward, son of King Edward [7 October 1317], in the presence of William Bereford, Gilbert Rothbury, John Benstead, John Bacon and John Mutford, justices, and other faithful men of the lord king, then present there, between Richard Lovell and Muriel his wife, plaintiffs, with Thomas Crewkerne representing Muriel to win or to lose, and master Richard de Clare and master Roger Bloxworth, deforciants, concerning the manors of Blackford, South Barrow, North Barrow, Charlton Mackrell, Tintinhull and Prestley, with appurtenances, for which a plea of contract was summoned between them in the same court, namely that the said Richard Lovell acknowledged the aforesaid manors with appurtenances to be the right of master Richard de Clare and master Roger, as those which the same master Richard and master Roger had by gift of the aforesaid Richard Lovell. And for that acknowledgement, settlement and agreement the same master Richard and master Roger granted the aforesaid manors with appurtenances to the aforesaid Richard Lovell and Muriel. And they returned them to them in the same court, to have and to hold to them, the same Richard Lovell and Muriel, and the heirs of Richard, namely the aforesaid manors of South Barrow, North Barrow and Tintinhull, with appurtenances, of the king and his heirs; and the aforesaid manors *[Page iii-195]* *[Col. a]* of Blackford, Charlton Mackrell and Prestley, with appurtenances, of the chief lord of that fee, for the services which pertain in perpetuity to the aforesaid manors.
And this agreement relating to the aforesaid manors of South Barrow, North Barrow and Tintinhull with appurtenances, was made by order of the lord king.
Somerset.

Later, at the suit of Richard Seymour, claiming that he was a kinsman and heir of the aforesaid Richard Lovell, namely son of Muriel, daughter of James, son of the aforesaid Richard Lovell; and that the aforesaid Richard Lovell and Muriel were dead; and that the execution of the aforesaid manor of Tintinhull was not yet conveyed; and that the prior of Montacute had entered upon the aforesaid manor of Tintinhull with appurtenances after the death of the aforesaid Richard Lovell and Muriel and then held and occupied it, contrary to the form of the aforesaid settlement, and asked for execution of the aforesaid manor of Tintinhull according to the form of the aforesaid settlement, etc. On account of which the sheriff of Somerset was ordered that by good men, etc., he instruct the aforementioned prior to appear before the lord king within fifteen days of Easter [20 April 1382], wheresoever, etc., to show whether he had anything to say or knew why the aforesaid Richard Seymour, kinsman and heir of the aforesaid Richard Lovell, ought not to have execution of the said manor of Tintinhull with appurtenances in the aforesaid form against him. And also, etc. The same day was given to the aforesaid Richard Seymour.
On which day, the aforesaid Richard Seymour appeared before the lord king by John Hulton, his attorney. And the

vicecomes retornavit quod scire fecit prefato priori quod esset coram domino rege ad prefatum terminum ad ostendendum secundum formam brevis predicti, et ulterius facturus et recepturus quod curia domini regis consideraverit in hac parte, per Willelmum atte More et Ricardum Grene. Qui quidem prior sic premunitus in propria persona sua venit. Et predictus Ricardus Seymor, ut supra petiit execucionem de predicto manerio de Tyntenhull', cum pertinentiis, etc. Et predictus prior dixit quod predictus Ricardus Seymor, per nomen Ricardi de Sancto Mauro, chivaler, tulit quoddam breve de recto versus predictum priorem, per nomen Francisci prioris de Monte Acuto, de predicto manerio de Tyntenhull', retornabile coram justiciariis domini regis de banco in crastino Sancti Martini, anno regni domini regis nunc sexto. Ad quod breve idem Ricardus Seymor adtunc comparuit, et idem prior essonatus fuit, et habuit diem per essonium suum usque a die Pasche in tres septimanas tunc proximo sequenti. Et quod predictum breve de scire facias perquisitum fuit pendente predicto brevi de recto, quod fuit de altiori natura, etc. Et peciit judicium de brevi de scire facias, etc. Et protulit tunc in curia regis coram rege tenorem dicti brevis de recto, simul cum tenore irrotulamenti de essonio predicto inde habiti per cancellarium domini regis per manus Johannis de Waltham, custodis rotulorum in cancellaria, etc. in eadem curia missi, que premissa testantur, etc. Quorum brevis, recordi et processus tenores sequntur inferius; tenor videlicet brevis, in hec verba:

'Ricardus, Dei gracia, rex Anglie, et Francie et dominus Hibernie, vicecomiti Somers', salutem. Precipe Francisco priori de Monte Acuto quod juste et sine dilacione reddat Ricardo de Sancto Mauro, chivaler, manerium de Tyntenhull' cum pertinentiis, quod clamat esse jus et hereditatem suam, et tenere de nobis in capite. Et unde queritur quod predictus prior ei injuste deforciavit. Et nisi fecerit, et predictus /Ricardus\ fecerit te securum de clameo suo prosecuto, tunc summoneas per bonos summunitores predictum priorem quod sit coram justiciariis nostris apud Westm' in crastino Sancti Martini, ostensurus quare non fecerit. Et habeas ibi summonitores et hoc breve. Teste meipso apud Westm' .xiiij. die Octobris, anno regni nostri sexto.

Et tenor recordi et processus inde, in hec verba:
'Essonia capta apud Westm', coram Roberto Bealknapp' et sociis suis, justiciariis domini regis de banco, de crastino Sancti Martini, anno regnorum Ricardi regis Anglie et Francie sexto.
Rotulo secundo.
Somers'. Non summonitus per precipe in capite.

Franciscus prior de Monte Acuto versus Ricardum de Sancto Mauro, chivaler, de placito terre per Johannem Davy, die Pasche in tres septimanas, afforciando. Unde ut prius peciit judicium de predicto brevi de scire facias, etc. Et predictus Ricardus Seymor protestando dixit quod ipse non cognovit quod ipse tulit aliquod tale breve de recto versus predictum priorem de manerio predicto. Et ulterius dixit quod per tenores brevis, recordi et processus predictorum, non constat quod idem Ricardus Seymor ad breve predictum aliquando comparuit, nec quod breve predictum adtunc pendebat. Unde peciit judicium et execucionem, etc. Et quia per tenores brevis et recordi predictorum hic missos, non constabat curie, quod predictus Ricardus Seymor ad breve predictum aliquando comparuit, nec quod breve predictum adtunc pendebat: \quia videtur curie, quod predictum breve

sheriff returned that he had instructed the aforementioned prior to come before the lord king at the aforementioned time to show according to the form of the aforesaid writ, and further to do and receive whatever the court of the lord king decided in the matter, by William atte More and Richard Green. The which prior, thus forewarned, appeared in person. And the aforesaid Richard Seymour, as mentioned above, sought execution of the aforesaid manor of Tintinhull with appurtenances, etc. And the aforesaid prior said that the aforesaid Richard Seymour, by the name of Richard de Sancto Mauro, knight, brought a certain writ of right against the aforesaid prior, by the name of Francis prior of Montacute, concerning the aforesaid manor of Tintinhull, returnable before the justices of the King's Bench on the morrow of Martinmas in the sixth year of the reign of the present lord king [12 November 1382]. To which writ the same Richard Seymour then appeared, and the prior was essoined and had a day for his essoin three weeks after Easter next [12 April 1383]. And that the aforesaid writ of scire facias was sought pending the aforesaid writ of right, which was of a higher nature, etc. And he requested judgment concerning the writ of scire facias, etc. And he then presented in the king's court and in the king's presence the tenor of the said writ of right, along with the tenor of the enrolment of the aforesaid essoin had from the lord king's chancellor by the hand of John Waltham, keeper of the rolls in chancery, etc., sent to the same court, which testified to the aforesaid. The tenors of which writ, record and process follow below; namely the tenor of the writ in these words:

Richard, by grace of God, king of England and France and lord of Ireland, to the sheriff of Somerset, greeting. Order Francis prior of Montacute that he justly and without delay return to Richard de Sancto Mauro, knight, the manor of Tintinhull with appurtenances, which he claims to be his right and inheritance, and to hold of us in chief. And of which he complained that the aforesaid prior had unjustly deprived him. And if he does not do so, and the aforesaid Richard provides you with proof of his claim thus pursued, then you shall summon the aforesaid prior through good summoners to appear before our justices at Westminster on the morrow of Martinmas to explain why he has not done so. And you shall have with you the summoners and this writ. Witnessed myself at Westminster on 14 October, in the sixth year of our reign [1382].

And the tenor of the record and process thereon is as follows:
Essoins taken at Westminster in the presence of Robert Bealnap and his colleagues, justices of King's Bench, on the morrow of Martinmas in the sixth year of the reign of Richard king of England and France [12 November 1382].
In the second roll.
Somerset. Not summoned by writ of precipe in capite.

Francis prior of Montacute against Richard de Sancto Mauro, knight, concerning the plea of land, by John Davy, three weeks after Easter [12 April 1383], to be afforced. Wherefore he requested judgment on the aforesaid writ of scire facias, etc. And the aforesaid Richard Seymour, protesting, said that he did not acknowledge that he had brought any writ of right against the aforesaid prior concerning the aforesaid manor. And he also said that from the tenors of the aforesaid writ, record and process, it did not seem that the same Richard Seymour had ever appeared upon the said writ, nor that the aforesaid writ was yet pending. Wherefore he requested judgment and execution, etc. And because from the tenors of the aforesaid writ and record submitted there it did not seem to the court that the aforesaid Richard Seymour had ever appeared upon the aforesaid

de scire facias manuteneri potest, rationibus et allegationibus predictis non obstantibus,/ dictum est prefato priori quod ulterius respondeat, etc. Qui quidem prior dixit quod dominus Edwardus [III] nuper rex Anglie, avus domini regis nunc, de avisamento parliamenti sui, nuper seisire fecit in manus suas omnes possessiones prioratuum alieniginarum in Anglie de potestate Francie existentium, tenendas in manu sua quamdiu guerra inter ipsum /tunc\ regem et adversarios suos de Francia durare contigeret; et inter alia prioratus de Monte Acuto, una cum omnibus possessionibus suis, seisitus fuit in manus ipsius Edwardi nuper regis, etc., ex causa predicta. Qui quidem Edwardus rex, etc. Postea per litteras suas patentes, quas idem prior protulit hic in curia, que sequntur, in hec verba:

'Edwardus, Dei gracia, rex Anglie et Francie et dominus Hibernie, omnibus ad quos presentes littere pervenerint, salutem. Sciatis quod commisimus dilecto nobis in Christo fratri Francisco priori prioratus de Monte Acuto, alienigene, custodiam[22] prioratus predicti, et omnium possessionum eidem prioratui spectantium, quem jam pace inter nos et Gallicos adversarios nostros apud Cales' inita, et per ipsos Gallicos dissoluta, inter alios prioratus et domos religiosorum alienigenarum de dominio et potestate Francie existencium in regno nostro Anglie et alibi infra /dominium\ et potestatem nostra, de /assensu parliamenti\ nostri capi fecimus in manum nostram; habendum a festo Sancti Michaelis proximo preterito quamdiu prioratum, terras et possessiones predictos, in manu nostra ex causis predictis contigerit remanere. Reddendo inde nobis annuatim ad scaccarium nostrum, vel alibi ad mandatum nostrum, ad festa Pasche et Sancti Michaelis,

Membrane i, dorse per equales portiones, centum et viginti libras. Salvis nobis feodis militum, et advocationibus ecclesiarum ad dictum prioratum spectantibus sive pertinentibus, pro quo quidem priore Johannes Fitelton et Johannes Halle, de comitatu Somers', in cancellaria nostra personaliter constituti, manuceperunt quod ipse super prioratu et possessionibus predictis moram continuam faciet, et numerum clericorum et servientium ab antiquo ordinatorum in eisdem prioratu et possessionibus, et cantarias et alia divina servicia, ac elemosinas, pia opera et cetera onera eisdem prioratui et possessionibus incumbencia, integre de exitibus, et proficuis, et emolumentis eorundem, manutenebit et inveniet; et edificia prioratus et possessionum illorum in adeo bono statu quo nunc sunt reparabit et dimittet. Et quod dictus prior, seu clerici et servientes sui, extra regnum nostrum Anglie se non transferent nec divertent, nec statum, negocia, aut secreta, dicti regni nostri Anglie alicui persone extranee, quocumque colore vel ingenio, dicent vel revelabunt; nec aurum vel argentum in massa vel moneta, aut jocalia, vel armaturas, seu quicquam aliud quod in nostri vel populi nostri prejudicium aliqualiter cedere poterit, per litteras, vel per verba, vel alio modo, ad partes exteras transmittent. Et quod idem prior dictam firmam centum et viginti librarum ad terminos predictos bene et fideliter solvet, et de arreragiis, si que fuerint, de firma prioratus et possessionum predictorum de tempore quo ultimo fuerunt in manibus nostris respondebit, et bona et catalla, aut alias res ad prioratum *[Page iii-196] [Col. a]* et possessiones illos spectancia, jam ibidem existencia, a dictis prioratu et possessionibus, aut locis ad

eosdem spectantibus, non alienabit seu elongabit, nec vastum seu destructionem faciet.

writ, nor that the aforesaid writ was still pending: because it seemed to the court that the aforesaid writ of scire facias could be maintained notwithstanding the aforesaid claims and allegations, it was said to the aforementioned prior that he should reply further, etc. Which prior said that Lord Edward [III], late king of England, grandfather of the present lord king, with the advice of his parliament, formerly caused to be taken into his hands all the possessions of alien priories in England being under French power, to hold in his hands for as long as the war between him then king and his adversaries of France should last; and amongst others the priory of Montacute and its possessions were taken into the hands of that Edward late king, etc., for the said reason. Which King Edward, etc. Afterwards, by his letters patent, which the same prior presented here in court, which follow in these words:

Edward, by grace of God, king of England and France and lord of Ireland, to all to whom the present letters shall come, greeting. Know that we committed to our beloved brother in Christ Francis, prior of the alien priory of Montacute, custody of the aforesaid priory, and all of the possessions pertaining to the same priory, which, when the peace initiated between us and our French enemies at Calais had been broken by the same French, we took into our hands with the assent of parliament along with other alien priories and religious houses under the dominion or power of France in our kingdom of England and elsewhere within our dominion and power; to have from Michaelmas last [29 September 1371], for as long as the aforesaid priories, lands and possessions should happen to remain in our hands for the aforesaid reasons. Paying us each year at our exchequer, or elsewhere upon our mandate, at Easter and Michaelmas [29 September]

Membrane i, dorse in equal portions, one hundred and twenty pounds. Saving to us the knights' fees and advowsons of churches attached or pertaining to the said priory, concerning which a certain prior John Fitelton and John Hall of Somerset, personally appointed in our chancery, guaranteed that he would continue to dwell in the aforesaid priory and possessions, appointing and maintaining the number of clerics and servants ordained of old in the same priory and possessions, and chantries and other divine services, and alms, pious works, and other duties incumbent upon the same priory and possessions, wholly from the issues, profits and emoluments of the same; and that he would repair and leave the buildings of the priory and their possessions in as good a state as they were in now. And that neither the said prior nor his clerics or servants would leave or depart from our kingdom of England, nor betray nor reveal the state, affairs or secrets of our said kingdom of England to any foreigner, by any scheme or device; nor withdraw to foreign parts by letters, or by words, or in any other way, gold nor silver in bullion or money, nor jewels, weapons, nor anything else which could in any way result in harm to us or our people. And that the same prior would fully and faithfully pay the said farm of one hundred and twenty pounds at the aforesaid terms and answer for the arrears, if there were any, from the farm of the aforesaid priory and possessions from the time when they were last in our hands, and that he would not alienate or remove from the said priory and possessions or places attached to those the goods, chattels and other things pertaining to the priory and its possessions, *[Page iii-196] [Col. a]* located there now, nor carry out waste and destruction.

---

[22] *Original* custodi

Volumus etiam, et de gratia nostra speciali concedimus quod idem prior de decimis et quintisdecimis, lanis et omnibus aliis quotis, nobis per clerum et communitatem regni nostri Anglie, a tempore ultime capcionis eorundem prioratus et possessionum in manum nostram concessis, vel extunc concedendis, seu eidem clero per dominum summum pontificem impositis vel imponendis, ac eciam de custodia terre maritime, et de prestacionibus lanarum, et aliis oneribus quibuscumque ad eosdem prioratum et possessionibus spectantibus, contingentibus, erga nos quietus sit et exoneratus, quamdiu iidem prioratus et possessiones in manu nostra et in custodia prefati prioris extiterint ex causa supradicta; ita quod \idem/ prior de eisdem prioratu et possessionibus disponere, et comodum suum facere possit, prout melius et ad majorem utilitatem suam sibi viderit expedire. In cujus rei testimonium has litteras nostras fieri fecimus patentes. Teste meipso apud Westm' .x. die Novembris, anno regni nostri Anglie quadragesimo quinto, regni vero nostri Francie tricesimo secundo.

Commisit prefato priori, per nomen fratris Francisci prioris prioratus de Monte Acuto, alienigene, custodiam prioratus predicti, et omnium possessionum eidem prioratui spectancium: habendam a festo Sancti Michaelis tunc proximo preterito, quamdiu prioratum, terras et possessiones predictas in manu regis ex causis predictis contigerit remanere. Reddendo inde eidem regi annuatim ad scaccarium suum, vel alibi ad mandatum ipsius regis, ad festa Pasche et Sancti Michaelis, per equales porciones, centum et viginti libras, salvis eidem regi feodis militum, et advocacionibus ecclesiarum, ad dictum prioratum spectantibus sive pertinentibus. Et sic dicit idem prior quod ipse sine domino rege nunc non potest inde respondere. Et preciit auxilium de domino rege, etc. Et predictus Ricardus Seymor dixit quod predictus prior per aliqua preallegata auxilium de domino rege habere non deberet. Dixit enim quod predictus Edwardus [III], nuper rex, avus, etc., nuper fuit seisitus de advocacione prioratus predicti in dominico suo ut de feodo, et eandem advocacionem, diu ante concessionem predictam dicto priori de custodia predicta factam, per litteras suas patentes dedit et concessit Willelmo de Monte Acuto, nuper comiti Sarum et marescallo Anglie, advocacionem prioratus de Monte Acuto[23]: habendam et tenendam sibi et heredibus suis de ipso rege et heredibus suis imperpetuum. Volensque idem rex ipsum comitem in hac parte amplioris gracie prosequi ubertate, concessit pro se et heredibus suis prefato comiti quod ipse et heredes sui imperpetuum haberent custodiam prioratus predicti, tam temporibus quibus idem prioratus, occasione guerrarum inter ipsum regem et heredes suos et illos de Francie seu inter regna eadem motarum, aut quacumque alia de causa, inter alios prioratus, domos et possessiones religiosorum alienigenarum infra regnum Anglie, captus fuit in manum regis, seu eorundem heredum suorum, quam temporibus quibus prioratum illum vacare contigeret, sive per mortem, deposicionem, vel resignacionem prioris loci illius qui pro tempore fuerit, sive alio quovis modo, cum omnibus ad custodiam illam spectantibus. Et quod idem comes et heredes sui inde disponere et ordinare possent, prout melius pro commodo suo proprio et utilitate prioratus predicti viderent expedire; exitusque et proficua inde proveniencia ad opus suum, tam guerrarum hujusmodi quam ipsius prioratus vacacionum temporibus, perciperent et haberent, adeo plene et integre sicut ille rex et heredes sui ea haberent, si prioratum illum, seu custodiam, in manibus suis propriis retinuisset, absque eo quod ille rex aut ministri sui quicumque de prioratu aut custodia hujusmodi temporibus predictis in aliquo

---

[23] advocacionem prioratus de Monte Acuto *repeated*

Moreover we willed and of our special grace conceded that the same prior should be quit towards us and exonerated of tenths and fifteenths, wool and all other quotas granted to us by the clergy and commons of our kingdom of England since the last time when the priory and possessions were taken into our hands, or yet to be conceded, or imposed or to be imposed on the same clergy by the lord pope, and also from the custody of the coasts of the sea, and from prestations on wool, and all other burdens of any sort that fall to the same priory and possessions, for as long as the same priory and possessions should be in our hands and in the custody of the aforementioned prior for the aforesaid reason; so that the same prior may arrange the same priory and possessions, and be able to do as seems best to him for his greater benefit as it seems to him. In testimony of which we have caused these our letters to be made patent. Witnessed myself at Westminster, 10 November in the forty-fifth year of our reign over England, the thirty-second of our reign over France [1371].

He committed to the aforementioned prior, by the name of brother Francis, prior of the alien priory of Montacute, custody of the aforesaid priory and of all the possessions pertaining to the same priory: to have from Michaelmas then last past [29 September 1371], for as long as the aforesaid priory, lands, and possessions should happen to remain in the king's hands for the aforesaid reasons. Paying to the same king each year at his exchequer, or elsewhere at the king's mandate, at Easter and Michaelmas [29 September] in equal portions, one hundred and twenty pounds, saving to the same king the knights' fees and advowsons of churches attached or pertaining to the said priory. And thus the same prior said that he could not answer herein without the present lord king. And he prayed the aid of the lord king, etc. And the said Richard Seymour said that the aforesaid prior ought not to have the aid of the lord king for certain reasons given above. For he said that the aforesaid Edward [III], late king, the grandfather, etc., was lately seised of the advowson of the aforesaid priory in demesne and as of fee, and long before the said grant of the said custody made to the said priory he granted and conceded the same advowson by his letters patent to William Montagu, late earl of Salisbury and marshal of England, to have and to hold to him and his heirs of the same king and his heirs in perpetuity. And the same king, wishing to bestow even greater grace on the earl in this matter, granted on behalf of himself and his heirs to the aforementioned earl and his heirs custody of the aforesaid priory in perpetuity during the time when the same priory, because of war waged between this king and his heirs and those of France or between the same kingdoms, or for some other reason, together with other priories, houses and possessions of alien religious in the kingdom of England, had been taken into the king's hands or those of his heirs, as well as during the time when that priory should happen to be vacant, whether through the death, deposition or resignation of the prior of that place at the time, or for any other reason, together with everything pertaining to that custody. And that the same earl and his heirs might dispose and order it as seemed best suited to their own purpose and to the benefit of the said priory. And that they should receive and have the issues and profits arising from this for their use, both in times of such wars and during vacancies of the priory, as fully and wholly as this king and his heirs would have had them if they had kept the priory or custody in their own hands, without the king or any of his ministers intruding in any way upon the priory or custody during the said times.

intromitteret. Quodque prefato comiti de firma quam custodes sive monachi prioratus predicti occasione guerre inter illum regem et illos de

[Col. b] Francia mote in manibus suis tunc existentibus ipsi regi pro custodia ejusdem annuatim reddere tenebantur, una cum arreragiis ejusdem firme sique forent, responderetur; et quod custodes ejusdem prioratus de firma et arreragiis illis erga dictum regem omnino exonerarentur.

Ac postmodum Willelmus de Monte Acuto, nunc comes Sarum, filius et heres predicti nuper comitis, ipsi regi supplicavit, ut cum prioratus predictus, pace tunc inter dictum avum et Gallicos adversarios suos apud Cales' inita per ipsos Gallicos dissoluta, captus fuerit in manum dicti domini Edwardi avi, etc., vellet ei custodiam dicti prioratus, una cum exitibus et proficuis inde a tempore capcionis ejusdem prioratus in manus ipsius regis perceptis, juxta concessionem dicto patri suo et heredibus suis per ipsum regem sic factam, liberari[24] jubere: idem rex avus, etc., considerans quod licet ad tempus quod in parliamento suo consideratum extitit, quod prioratus, domus et possessiones religiosorum hujusmodi in auxilium guerre sue caperentur in manum suam, concordatum fuisset et ordinatum in eodem parliamento quod priores et alii presidentes locorum eorundem, seu eorum procuratores, tam pro bono regimine locorum predictorum, quam pro divinis officiis ibidem faciendis et sustentandis, ceteris prefererentur de custodia hujusmodi prioratuum, domorum et possessionum habendum; reddendo inde ipsi regi prout inter ipsum regem et illos poterit concordari; affectans tamen idem rex concessionem suam prefato nuper comiti et heredibus suis de custodia prioratus predicti prius factam, quatenus fieri potuit absque offencione concordie supradicte, debitum sortiri effectum, voluit idem rex quod in auxilium guerre predicte, ut idem comes se in guerris suis melius manutenere possit, idem comes haberet et reciperet durante guerra supra dicta de priore loci predicti tantam firmam quantam regi pro custodia ejusdem prioratus, antequam concessio predicta prefato nuper comiti sic facta fuit, solvi consuevit, et prout prior loci predicti regi solvere deberet si custodia ejusdem prioratus eidem priori per regem commissa fuisset. Idemque rex avus, etc., per breve suum mandavit tunc thesaurario et baronibus suis de scaccario quod prefato nunc comiti dictam firmam, una cum arreragiis ejusdem firme a tempore capcionis ejusdem prioratus in manum ipsius regis perceptis, liberari et habere, et ipsum priorem inde ad dictum scaccarium exonerari et quietum esse facerent. Mandavit eciam idem rex avus, etc., aliud breve suum prefato priori quod de firma predicta eidem nunc comiti esset intendens et respondens, quorum brevium \transcripta,/ premissa testificancia, dominus rex nunc mandavit justiciariis suis hic sub pede sigilli sui, et quorum brevium datum sunt secundo die Decembris, anno regni regis Edwardi [III] avi, etc., quadragesimo quinto. Et sic dixit idem Ricardus Seymor quod predictus Edwardus avus [III], etc., de advocacione, firma, et quicquid sibi de prioratu illo occasione aliqua pertinere potuit, taliter se dimisit, et prefato nunc comiti, filio et heredi prefati nuper comitis, plenarie restitucionem inde, juxta vim et effectum concessionis [25]

And that the keepers or monks of the aforesaid priory should answer to the aforesaid earl for the farm which they were obliged to pay the king annually for the custody of the same, being in their hands on the occasion of war between that king and those

[Col. b] of France, together with arrears of the same farm if there should be any; and that the keepers of the same priory would be entirely exonerated of that farm and those arrears towards the said king.

And later, William Montagu, now earl of Salisbury, son and heir of the aforesaid late earl petitioned that whereas the aforesaid priory, on the dissolution by the French of the peace initiated between the said grandfather and his French adversaries, had been taken into the hands of the said Lord Edward the grandfather, etc., the king might order the custody of the said priory, together with the issues and profits received from it since the time when the same priory was taken into the king's hands, delivered to him in accordance with the grant to his said father and heirs thus made by the same king: the same king, the grandfather, etc., considering that although at the time when it was decided in his parliament that the priory, house and possessions of the religious of this kind should be taken into his hands to help the war, it had been agreed and ordained in the same parliament that the priors and other heads of the same places, or their proctors, as well for the good governance of the aforesaid places as for the performing and sustaining of divine offices there, should be preferred over others for the holding of the custody of these priories, houses and possessions, paying for this to the same king whatsoever could be agreed between this king and themselves; nevertheless, the same king, disposed to give due effect to his grant of the custody of the aforesaid priory previously made to the aforesaid late earl and his heirs without contravening the aforesaid agreement, in order to support the aforesaid war, so that the same earl could the better maintain himself in his wars, the earl should have and receive during the aforesaid war from the prior of the aforesaid place such a farm as the latter had been accustomed to pay to the king for the custody of the same priory before the aforesaid concession was thus made to the aforesaid late earl, and which the prior of the place ought to have paid to the aforesaid king if the custody of the same priory had been assigned to the same prior by the king. And the same king, the grandfather, etc., by his writ then ordered his treasurer and barons of his exchequer that the said farm, together with the arrears of the same farm received since the time when the same priory was taken into the king's hands, be delivered to and held by the said then earl, and that they should cause the same prior to be exonerated and quit thereof at the exchequer. Moreover, the same king the grandfather, etc., sent another writ to the aforementioned prior saying that he should now be accountable and answerable to the same present earl for the aforesaid farm; transcripts of which writs testifying to the above the lord king then sent to his justices under his half-seal, these writs being dated 2 December in the forty-fifth year of the reign of King Edward [III] the grandfather [1371]. And thus the same Richard Seymour said that the aforesaid Edward [III], the grandfather, etc., so disposed of the advowson, farm and whatsoever else could have pertained to him from the aforesaid priory on that occasion; and to the aforementioned then earl, son and heir of the aforementioned late earl, he caused restitution thereof to be fully made according to the force and effect of the grant

---

[24] *Original* liberare

[25] A contemporary note at the foot of this membrane reads 'plus in rotulo sequenti de eodem'.

Membrane ii predicto patri suo nuper facte, fieri fecit, per quod quicquam de prioratu illo aut de possessionibus ejusdem in persona ipsius regis avi, etc., reservari non potuit, sic nec in persona domini regis nunc residere potest. Unde non intendit quod idem nunc prior auxilium de domino rege in hoc casu versus eum habere deberet, etc.

Et predictus prior dixit quod in litteris predictis domini regis avi, etc., patentibus eidem priori de custodia prioratus predicti factis continetur, quod dictus rex avus, etc., reservavit sibi feodis militum et advocaciones ecclesiarum; et in brevibus predictis per predictum Ricardum Seymor in curia prolatis continetur, quod idem nunc comes de custodia seu regimine domus predicte in aliquo se non intromitteret; et in eisdem brevibus non continetur quod in restitucione predicta predicto nunc comiti facta aliqua specialis mencio facta fuit de feodis militum et advocationibus ecclesiarum. Et ulterius dixit quod dominus rex nunc, post restitucionem predictam presentavit ad ecclesiam de Tyntenhull' quendam *[Page iii-197]*

[Col. a] clericum suum Johannem de Stone occasione reservacionis predicte per predictum avum suum de feodis militum et advocationibus ecclesiarum prioratus predicti facte. Unde ex causis predictis petiit auxilium de domino rege, etc.

Et predictus Ricardus Seymor dixit quod per /restitucionem\ predictam advocatio prioratus predicti, simul cum custodia ejusdem et omnibus aliis ad dictum prioratum spectantibus seu quovismodo pertinentibus, in personam ipsius nunc comitis de jure transierunt. Unde non intendit quod predictus prior auxilium suum predictum habere \deberet,/ etc. Et super hoc dies datus fuit partibus predictis coram domino rege usque in octabis Sancte Trinitatis tunc proximis sequentibus ubicumque, etc. in statu quo tunc, salvis partibus racionibus et responsionibus suis, etc. Ad quem diem, coram domino rege apud Westm' venit tam predictus Ricardus Seymor per attornatum suum predictum quod predictus prior per /Stephanum del\ Fall attornatum suum: et continuato inde inter partes predictas processu coram domino rege de die in diem usque in crastinum Sancti Johannis Baptiste tunc proximo sequenti ubicumque; ad quem /crastinum,\ coram domino rege apud Cantebr' venerunt tam predictus Ricardus Seymor quam predictus prior per attornatos suos predictos, etc. Et quia videtur curie quod auxilium predictum predicto priori in hoc casu non est concedendum, dictum est \per curiam/ prefato priori quod ulterius respondeat, etc. \sine auxilio predicto, etc./

Et predictus prior dixit quod predictus Ricardus Seymor execucionem virtute finis predicti versus eum habere non deberet: quia dixit quod \dominus/ Henricus [I] filius Willelmi conquestoris, quondam rex Anglie, nuper fuit seisitus de manerio predicto in dominico suo ut de feodo, et idem manerium cum suis pertinentiis, per cartam suam quam idem nunc prior profert hic in curia, que \sine/ datum est, dedit et concessit in liberam, puram et perpetuam elemosinam Deo et sanctis apostolis ejus Petro et Paulo de Monte Acuto et monachis Clunacensibus ibidem Deo servientibus; habendum et tenendum sibi et successoribus suis imperpetuum. Quas quidem donacionem et concessionem dominus rex nunc, et quamplures progenitores sui reges Anglie, per cartas suas ratificaverunt et confirmaverunt. Virtute cujus concessionis, tunc prior et monachi supradicti seisiti fuerunt de manerio predicto ut de jure ecclesie sue sanctorum apostolorum Petri et Pauli de Monte Acuto, et seisinam suam inde pacifice continuaverunt usque ad diem veneris proximum ante festum Assumptionis Beate Marie Virginis, anno regni domini Edwardi [II] filii regis Edwardi proavi

Membrane ii to his aforesaid father, as a result of which nothing from that priory, nor from the possessions of the same, could be set aside for the person of that king the grandfather, and thus they could not now reside in the person of the king. And so he did not think that the same present prior ought to have the aid of the lord king in a case against him, etc.

And the aforesaid prior said that in the aforesaid letters patent of the lord king the grandfather, etc., granted to the same prior concerning the custody of the aforesaid priory, it was stated that the said king the grandfather, etc. reserved for himself knights' fees and advowsons of churches; and in the aforesaid writs presented in court by the aforesaid Richard Seymour it was stated that the same present earl should not intrude himself on the custody or governance of the aforesaid house in any way; and in the same writs it was not said that in the aforesaid restitution made to the aforesaid present earl any special mention was made of the knights' fees and advowsons of churches. And he also said that the present lord king, after the aforesaid restitution, presented to the church of Tintinhull a certain *[Page iii-197]*

[Col. a] clerk of his named John Stone on the grounds of the aforesaid reservation made by his said grandfather of the knights' fees and advowsons of the churches of the aforesaid priory. And so for these reasons he requested the aid of the lord king, etc.

And the said Richard Seymour said that through the aforesaid restitution the advowson of the aforesaid priory, together with the custody of the same and all other things attached or in any way pertaining to the said priory, passed by right to the person of this present earl. Therefore he did not consider that the said prior should have his aforesaid aid, etc. And thereupon a day was given to the aforesaid parties before the lord king on the octave of Holy Trinity next [7 June 1383] wheresoever, etc., in its present state, saving to the parties their arguments and answers, etc. On which day, before the lord king at Westminster there came both the aforesaid Richard Seymour by his aforesaid attorney, and the said prior by Stephen Fall, his attorney: and the process between the two parties was adjourned from one day to the next before the lord king until the morrow of St John the Baptist next [25 June 1383], wheresoever; on which morrow, both the aforesaid Richard Seymour and the aforesaid prior appeared before the lord king at Cambridge by their aforesaid attorneys, etc. And because it seemed to the court that the said aid ought not to be granted to the aforesaid prior in the case, the court told the aforementioned prior to answer again, etc. without the aforesaid aid, etc.

And the said prior said that the said Richard Seymour ought not to have execution by virtue of the said settlement against him: for he said that Lord Henry [I], son of William the Conqueror, sometime king of England, was formerly seised of the aforesaid manor in demesne as of fee, and the same manor with its appurtenances, by his charter which the same present prior presented here in court and which was undated, gave and granted in free, pure and perpetual alms to God and his holy apostles Peter and Paul of Montacute and the monks of Cluny serving God there, to be had and held by him and his successors forever. Which gift and grant the present lord king, and several of his progenitors, kings of England, ratified and confirmed by their charters. By virtue of which grant the aforesaid prior and monks were then in possession of the aforesaid manor as of the right of their church of the holy apostles Peter and Paul of Montacute, and they continued peacefully in their seisin until the Friday before the feast of the Assumption of the Blessed Virgin Mary in the tenth year of the reign of the Lord Edward [II] son of King Edward, great-grandfather of the present lord king and late

domini regis nunc nuper regis Anglie, decimo. Qui quidem Edwardus, etc., antea per litteras suas patentes concessit cuidam Stephano tunc priori loci predicti quod quandocumque prioratum illum per mortem vel cessionem ipsius Stephani vacare contigeret, quod supprior et conventus loci illius haberent custodiam dicti prioratus, tempore vacacionis predicte, per duos menses si prioratum illum per tantum tempus vacare contigeret; pro qua quidem concessione prefatus Stephanus dedit prefato nuper regi, etc., quadraginta marcas.

Ac postmodum prioratus ille per cessionem ejusdem Stephani vacavit, et prioratu illo in possessione ejusdem supprioris et monachorum loci predicti virtute concessionis regis predicti existente, quidam Ricardus Lovell', antecessor predicti Ricardi Seymor, cujus heres ipse est, in manerium predictum cum maxima multitudine hominum, armata potentia, predicto die veneris se intrusit, et manerium illud sic occupavit, quo tempore finis ille de manerio illo levatus fuit. Ac postmodum predictus Edwardus nuper rex, etc., pro eo quod querimoniam tunc prioris loci illius, per inquisicionem coram dilectis et fidelibus ipsius regis Willelmo Martyn, Hugone de Courtenay et Michaele de Meldon de mandato suo captum, intrusio illa comperta fuit in forma predicta, manerium illud cum suis pertinentiis prefato tunc priori plenarie restituit. Et protulit tunc in curia tenorem recordi et processus restitucionis predicte in hec verba:

'Dominus rex mandavit Willelmo Martyn, Hugoni de Courteneye et Michaeli de Meldone, breve suum in
[Col. b] hec verba:
'Edwardus, Dei gratia, rex Anglie, /dominus Hibernie et Dux Aquitanie,\ dilectis et fidelibus suis Willelmo Martyn, Hugoni de Courteneye et Michaeli de Meldon, salutem Cum tertiodecimo die Julii, anno regni nostri decimo, per finem quadraginta marcarum quem Stephanus tunc prior de Monte Acuto fecit nobiscum, concesserimus per litteras nostras patentes quod quandocumque \[prioratum illum]/ per mortem, resignacionem, aut cessionem ejusdem Stephani, vacare contigeret, supprior et conventus ejusdem loci haberent custodiam dicti prioratus, et omnium temporalium ad illum spectancium, per duos menses, a tempore mortis, resignacionis, aut cessionis dicti Stephani numerandos, salvis nobis feodis militum, et advocacionibus ecclesiarum ejusdem prioratus; et si prioratus ille ultra duos menses vacaret, tunc idem prioratus et ejus temporalia in manum nostram resumerentur, et extunc in manu nostra remanerent durante ulterius vacacione prioratus predicti, prout in litteris nostris predictis plenius continetur.
Et postmodum, duodecimo die Octobris, anno predicto, ceperimus fidelitatem dilecti nobis in Christo fratris Johannis Caprarii, quem abbas Clunacen' in priorem dicte domus de Monte Acuto prefecerat, et ei temporalia prioratus illius, prout moris est, mandaverimus liberari, sicut per inspectionem rotulorum cancellarie nostre nobis constat; ac jam ex gravi querela dicti Johannis nunc prioris dicte domus acceperimus quod licet prefatus Stephanus, predecessor suus, die quo cessit regimini prioratus predicti seisitus fuisset de maneriis de Tyntenhull', et Estchynnok, et de hundredis de Tyntenhull' et Hundesbergh', cum pertinentiis, in comitatu Somers', ut de jure ecclesie sue de Monte Acuto, ac predecessores ejusdem Stephani, quondam priores loci illius, maneria et hundreda illa cum pertinentiis successive, a tempore cujus contrarii memoria non existit, tenuissent, quidam tamen malefactores, et pacis nostre perturbatores, dicto prioratu per cessionem dicti fratris Stephani vacante, et in custodia dictorum supprioris et conventus per commissionem

king of England [13 August 1316]. The which Edward, etc., previously by his letters patent granted to a certain Stephen, then prior of the aforesaid place, that whensoever that priory should happen to fall vacant by the death or resignation of this Stephen, the subprior and convent of that place would have custody of the said priory for the time of the aforesaid vacancy, for two months if the priory should happen to be vacant for so long; in return for which concession the aforementioned Stephen gave the aforementioned late king, etc., forty marks.
And later that priory through the resignation of the same Stephen fell vacant, and the priory being in the possession of the subprior and the monks of the aforesaid place by virtue of the grant of the aforesaid king, a certain Richard Lovell, ancestor of the aforesaid Richard Seymour, whose heir he is, entered upon the aforesaid manor on the said Friday [13 August 1316] with a great multitude of men in an armed force, and thus occupied that manor, at a time when the fine concerning that manor was made. And later the aforesaid Edward late king, etc., because in consequence of a complaint by the then prior of the place, by an inquest held on his orders before the king's beloved and faithful men, William Martin, Hugh Courtenay and Michael Meldon, that intrusion was discovered in the aforesaid form, he fully restored that manor with its appurtenances to the then aforementioned earl. And he then produced in court the tenor of the aforesaid record and process of the restitution in these words:
The lord king sent his writ to William Martin, Hugh Courteney and Michael Meldon,
[Col. b] in these words:
Edward, by the grace of God, king of England, lord of Ireland and duke of Aquitaine, to his beloved and faithful William Martin, Hugh Courteney and Michael Meldon, greeting. Whereas on 13 July in the tenth year of our reign [1316], for a fine of forty marks which Stephen then prior of Montacute paid us, we granted by our letters patent that whensoever by the death, resignation or demise of the same Stephen that priory should fall vacant, the subprior and convent of the same place would have custody of the said priory and all the temporalities pertaining to it for two months, counting from the time of the death, resignation or demise of the said Stephen, saving the knights' fees and advowsons of the churches of the same priory; and if the priory should be vacant beyond two months, then the same priory and its temporalities would be resumed into our hands and then remain in our hands for the duration of the vacancy of the aforesaid priory, as is more fully set out in our aforesaid letters.

And later, on 12 October in the aforesaid year [1316], we took the fealty of our beloved brother in Christ John Caprary, whom the abbot of Cluny appointed prior of the said house of Montacute, and we ordered the temporalities of that priory to be delivered to him, as is the custom, and as is clear to us from an inspection of the rolls of our chancery; and then, as the result of a grave complaint of the said John then prior of the said house, we learnt that although the aforementioned Stephen, his predecessor, on the day on which he ceased to rule the aforesaid priory, was seised of the manors of Tintinhull and East Chinnock, and the hundreds of Tintinhull and Houndsborough, with appurtenances, in Somerset, as the right of his church of Montacute, and the predecessors of the same Stephen, once priors of that place, had successively held those manors and hundreds with appurtenances from time immemorial, nevertheless certain malefactors and disturbers of our peace, the said priory having fallen vacant on the demise of the said brother Stephen and being in the

nostram ut predictum est existente, dicta maneria et hundreda, armata potentia, ingressi fuerunt, et

Membrane ii, dorse ipsos suppriorem et conventum inde expulerunt, carucas, blada et alia bona et catalla ejusdem domus in eisdem maneriis inventa, occupando et explecias hundredorum predictorum capiendo, et suis usibus applicando, et maneria et hundreda illa adhuc detinent taliter occupata; in nostri contemptum et grave prejudicium, et prioratus predicti depressionem et exheredationem manifestam. Nos igitur, qui secundum tenorem magne carte de libertatibus Anglie, prefato priori temporalia prioratus predicti adeo plene et integre sicut ad manus nostras devenerunt, ac totam terram ejusdem instauratam ut de carucis, et omnibus aliis rebus ad minus sicut eam cepimus, liberare et restituere tenemur, nolentes premissa sub dissimulacione preterire, ac de vestra fidelitate et industria plenam fiduciam optinentes, assignamus vos et duos vestrum, quorum vos prefate Michael alterum esse volumus, ad inquirendum per sacramentum tam militum quam aliorum proborum et legalium hominum de comitatu predicto, tam infra libertates quam extra, per quos rei veritas melius sciri poterit, utrum predictus Stephanus fuit seisitus, die quo cessit regimini dicti prioratus, de maneriis et hundredis predictis ut de jure ecclesie sue, necne; et si sic, tunc utrum manerium et hundreda illa, dicto prioratu in custodia dictorum supprioris et conventus ex commissione nostra ut predictum est existente, occupata fuerunt, per quos, et quo tempore, et qualiter, et quo modo, et que bona et catalla in eisdem maneriis, et que explecie de dictis hundredis tunc capta fuerunt, et per quos, et ad quorum manus devenerunt. Et ad maneria illa et hundreda cum pertinentiis, si ea per inquisicionem hujusmodi inveneritis vacante prioratu predicto et in custodia dictorum supprioris et conventus ex commissione nostra existente fuisse taliter occupata, in manum nostram resumenda, et prefato priori liberanda; tenendum ut jus ecclesie sue, *[Page iii-198]*

[Col. a] salvo jure cujuslibet.
Et ideo vobis mandamus quod ad certos dies et loca, quos vos vel duo vestrum, quorum vos prefate Michael alterum esse volumus, ad hoc provideritis, premissa omnia et singula faciatis et expleatis in forma predicta: et nos de tenore inquisicionis illius, et de toto facto vestro in hac parte sub sigillis vestris distincte et aperte reddatis certiores. Mandavimus enim vicecomiti nostro comitatus predicti quod ad certos dies et loca, quos vos vel duo vestrum, quorum vos prefate Michael alterum esse volumus, ei scire feceritis, venire faciendo coram vobis vel duobus vestrum, quorum vos prefate Michael alterum esse volumus, tot et tales, tam milites, quam alios probos et legales homines de comitatu predicto, tam infra libertates quam extra, per quos rei veritas in premissis melius sciri poterit et inquiri; et quod vobis in premissis pareat et intendat. In cujus rei testimonium has litteras nostras fieri fecimus patentes. Teste meipso apud Eboracum, .xiij. die Novembris, anno regni nostri duodecimo.

Pretextu cujus brevis iidem Willelmus, Hugo et Michael mandaverunt vicecomiti Somers' quod venire faceret coram eis apud Ivele, die lune proximo post festum Epiphanie Domini, viginti quatuor tam milites quam alios probos et legales homines, de visneto de Tyntenhull' et Estchynnok, et etiam de visneto hundredorum de Tyntenhull' et Hundesbergh', per quos rei veritas melius inde scire poterit et inquiri,

custody of the said subprior and convent by our commission as aforesaid, had invaded the manors and hundreds with armed might and

Membrane ii, dorse expelled the subprior and convent, seizing ploughs, corn and the other goods and chattels of the same house found on the same manors and taking the profits of the aforesaid hundreds and applying them to their own use, and they still retain those manors and hundreds thus occupied, in contempt of us and to our great detriment, and the clear impoverishment and disinheritance of the aforesaid priory. We therefore, who are bound according to the tenor of the Great Charter of the liberties of England to deliver and restore to the aforementioned prior the temporalities of the aforesaid priory as fully and entirely as they fell into our hands, and all the land-stock of the same such as ploughs and all other things at least as we received them, not wishing to omit the aforesaid by any device, and placing full trust in your fidelity and industry, we assign to you and two of you, of whom we wish one to be the aforementioned Michael, to inquire by the oath of knights as well as other good and law-worthy men of the said county, both within liberties and without, by whom the truth of the matter might best be learned, whether the aforesaid Stephen was in possession, on the day on which he ceased to rule the said priory, of the said manors and hundreds as the right of his church, or not; and if so, whether those manors and hundreds, the said priory being in the custody of the said subprior and convent by our commission as aforesaid, were taken, by whom, and at what time, and how, and by what means, and what goods and chattels on the same manors, and what profits from the said hundreds were then taken, and by whom, and into whose hands they came. And if you find by such an inquest that the aforesaid priory, being vacant and in the custody of the said subprior and convent by our commission, and those manors and hundreds with appurtenances were thus seized, you shall take them into our hands and deliver them to the aforementioned prior, to be held as by right of his church, *[Page iii-198]*

[Col. a] saving the right of any.
And therefore I order you that on certain days and at certain times and places, you or the two of you, of whom I wish one to be the aforementioned Michael, do provide for this, and perform and fulfil each and every one of the aforesaid matters in the said manner: and that you inform us clearly and distinctly of the tenor of this inquest and of all your actions in this matter under your seal. For we have ordered our sheriff of the aforesaid county that at certain times and places, you or two of you, of whom I wish one to be the aforementioned Michael, should instruct him to bring before you or the two of you, of whom I wish one to be the aforementioned Michael, as many and such men, as well knights as good and law-worthy men of the aforesaid county, within liberties and without, through whom the truth of the aforesaid matter might best be known and learned; and that he obey and assist you in the aforesaid. In testimony of which we caused these our letters to be made patent. Witnessed by myself at York, 13 November in the twelfth year of our reign [1318].

On the authority of which writ the same William, Hugh and Michael ordered the sheriff of Somerset to cause to appear before them at Yeovil on the Monday following the feast of the Lord's Epiphany [8 January 1319] twenty-four men, as well knights as other good and worthy men, from the neighbourhood of Tintinhull and East Chinnock, and also from the neighbourhood of the hundreds of Tintinhull and Houndsborough, through whom the truth of the matter might best be known and learned, according to the tenor of the aforesaid

secundum tenorem predicti brevis domini regis predictis Willelmo, Hugoni et Michaeli, inde prius directi.

Ad quem diem, idem vicecomes Somers' retornavit breve domini regis sibi inde directum, et eciam breve ipsorum Willelmi, Hugonis et Michaelis, et similiter nomina juratorum, etc., secundum quod ei preceptum fuit, et per sufficientem manucapcionem, qui non venerunt. Ideo preceptum est vicecomes quod distringat predictos juratores per omnes terras et catalla sua, etc., et quod domino regi respondeat de exitibus, etc. Et quod habeat corpora eorum coram prefatis Willelmo, Hugone et Michaele, vel coram duobus eorum quorum, etc., apud Juvele, die mercurii proximo ante festum Sancti Hillar' proximum venturum. Et preter illos venire faciant coram eis ad eundem diem tot et tales tam milites quam alios, etc., ita quod negocium predictum pro defectu juratorum non remaneat infectum. Inquisicio capta apud Jevele, die mercurii proximo ante festum Sancti Hillar', anno regni regis Edwardi filii regis Edwardi duodecimo, per sacramentum Radulphi de Gorges, Johannis Mautravers senioris, Johannis de Erlegh, Johannis de Meriet, Henrici de Glaston', Petri de Evercy, Edmundi de Everard, Willelmi de Wygebere, Johannis de Clyvedon', militum, Johannis Peytevyn, Johannis Musket et Henrici de Estfeld, ad hoc electorum, etc., qui dicunt super sacramentum suum quod Stephanus quondam prior de Monte Acuto, predecessor Johannis Caprarii nunc prioris ejusdem domus, fuit seisitus, ut de jure ecclesie sue de Monte Acuto, de maneriis de Tyntenhull' et Estchynnnok, et de hundredis de Tyntenhull' et Hundesbergh', tempore et die quo cessit regimini dicti prioratus, videlicet tertiodecimo die Julii, anno regni regis Edwardi filii regis Edwardi decimo; et quod ipse et predecessores sui predicti prioratus, [26]

Membrane iii a tempore cujus contrarii memoria non existit, semper hactenus seisiti fuerunt pacifice de predictis maneriis et hundredis, ut de jure ecclesie sue de Monte Acuto, cum omnibus suis pertinentiis. Et dicunt quod tempore vacacionis predicti prioratus, videlicet die veneris proximo ante festum Assumpcionis Beate Marie Virginis anno predicto, quando predicta maneria et hundreda fuerunt in manu supprioris et conventus ejusdem prioratus vacantis per commissionem ipsius domini regis per duos menses, exceptis feodis militum et advocacionibus ecclesiarum prioratus predicti de temporalibus rebus, quod quidem Ricardus Lovell', Henricus de Pupelpenne, magister Hugo Cocus, Mauricius Marescall', Walterus de Welham et Margeria uxor ejus, et Thomas filius ejusdem Walteri, magister Willelmus de Modeford, Eva que fuit uxor Ricardi Suncte et Thomas Revenyng, armata potencia predicta

[Col. b] maneria et hundreda cum pertinentiis sunt ingressi, et predicta maneria et hundreda occupaverunt, et suis usibus applicaverunt, et bona et catalla /in\ eisdem maneriis inventa, videlicet blada, boves, carucas et carectas, currus, equos et oves et alia bona et catalla ad valenciam mille librarum ceperunt, abduxerunt, et asportaverunt, in contemptum domini Ricardi, et grave prejudicium ipsius prioris et oppressionem et depauperacionem manifestam; et sic occupata predicta maneria et hundreda cum pertinentiis per duos annos et viginti septimanas tenuerunt, et de expleciis predictorum hundredorum ignoratur.

Ideo prefati justiciarii predicta maneria de Tyntenhull' et Estchynnok, et hundreda de Tyntenhull' et Hundesbergh', ceperunt in manum domini regis, juxta tenorem commissionis predicte, et predicto priori liberarunt: tenenda ut de jure ecclesie sue de Monte Acuto, salvo jure cujuslibet, sicut

writ of the lord king already sent to the aforesaid William, Hugh and Michael.

On which day, the same sheriff of Somerset returned the writ of the lord king addressed to him and also the writ of William, Hugh and Michael, and likewise the names of the jurors, etc., as he had been ordered, and by sufficient bail, none of whom appeared. Therefore the sheriff was ordered to distrain the aforesaid jurors by all their lands and chattels, etc. And that he should answer to the lord king for the issues, etc., and that he should have their persons before the aforementioned William, Hugh and Michael, or before two of them, of whom, etc., at Yeovil, on the Wednesday before the feast of St Hilary next following [10 January 1319]. And further, that he cause to appear before them on the same day as many and such knights as well as others, etc., so that the aforesaid matter should not remain incomplete for want of jurors. At the inquest held at Yeovil, on the Wednesday before the feast of St Hilary in the twelfth year of the reign of King Edward [II] son of King Edward [10 January 1319], Ralph Gorges, John Mautravers the elder, John Erlegh, John Meriet, Henry Glastonbury, Peter Evercy, Edmund Everard, William Wigborough, John Clevedon, knights, John Peytevyn, John Musket, and Henry Eastfield, elected thereto, etc., said on their oath that Stephen sometime prior of Montacute, predecessor of John Caprary now prior of the same house, was seised as of the right of his church of Montacute of the manors of Tintinhull and Estchynnnok and the hundreds of Tintinhull and Houndsborough at the time and on the day when he ceased to rule the said priory, namely 13 July in the tenth year of the reign of King Edward [II], son of King Edward [1316]; and that he and his predecessors of the aforesaid priory,

Membrane iii since time immemorial, had always until now been peacefully seised of the aforesaid manors and hundreds as of the right of their church of Montacute, together with all their appurtenances. And they said that at the time when the aforesaid priory fell vacant, namely on the Friday before the feast of the Assumption of the Blessed Virgin Mary in the aforesaid year [13 August 1316], when the aforesaid manors and hundreds were in the hands of the subprior and convent of the same vacant priory by commission of the same lord king for two months, excluding knights' fees and advowsons of the churches of the aforesaid priory from temporal things, that a certain Richard Lovell, Henry Pupelpenne, master Hugh Cook, Maurice Marshal, Walter Welham and Marjory his wife, and Thomas son of the same Walter, master William Mudford, Eva who was wife of Richard Suncte and Thomas Revenyng, with armed might entered upon the aforesaid

[Col. b] manors and hundreds with appurtenances, and occupied the aforesaid manors and hundreds, and turned them to their own uses, taking, removing and carrying off the goods and chattels found on the same manors, namely corn, oxen, ploughs and carts and wagons, horses, sheep and other goods and chattels to the value of a thousand pounds, in contempt of Sir Richard, and to the grave injury and manifest impoverishment and disinheritance of that prior; and thus they held the aforesaid seized manors with appurtenances for two years and twenty weeks; and nothing is known of the profits of the aforesaid hundreds.

Therefore the aforementioned justices took the aforesaid manors of Tintinhull and East Chinnock and the hundreds of Tintinhull and Houndsborough into the hands of the lord king, according to the tenor of the aforesaid commission, and delivered them to the aforesaid prior, to be held as of the

---

[26] A contemporary note at the foot of this membrane reads 'Plus in rotulo sequenti de eodem'.

predecessores sui priores ejusdem domus ea tenere et habere consueverunt, a tempore cujus contrarii \memoria/ non existit. Et preceptum est vicecomes quod premissa exequatur, etc. Ac postmodum manerio illo in possessione ejusdem prioris existente, predictus Ricardus Lovel, per factum suum quod idem nunc prior /protulit\ tunc in curia, concessit, remisit, et omnino pro se et heredibus suis imperpetuum quietum clamavit, priori et conventui de Monte Acuto et successoribus suis, totum jus suum et clameum quod habuit, vel aliquo modo habere potuit, in predicto manerio de Tyntenhull' cum suis pertinentiis; et ulterius recognovit per dictum scriptum suum dictum manerium cum pertinentiis esse jus ipsius prioris et conventus et successorum suorum imperpetuum. Ita quod nec ipse Ricardus Lovel nec heredes sui in manerio predicto cum suis pertinentiis, nec in aliqua parte ejusdem, aliquid juris vel clamei exigere vel vendicare poterint in futuro. Et ulterius concessit predictus Ricardus Lovel per idem scriptum suum quod si aliquis finis de predicto manerio cum suis pertinentiis, aut in aliqua parte ejusdem, in curia domini regis fuerit levatus, inter ipsum Ricardum Lovell' et Muriellam uxorem ejus querentes, et magistrum Ricardum de Clare et magistrum Rogerum de Blokerworth' deforciantes, virtute cujus finis aliquid juris vel clamei sibi vel heredibus suis quoquomodo accressere potuit, voluit et concessit idem Ricardus Lovell' pro se et heredibus suis quod finis ille ipso jure foret nullus, et pro nullo imperpetuum haberetur. Et protulit tunc in curia scriptum concessionis et remissionis predicti Ricardi Lovell' premissa testificans quod sequitur in hec verba:

Omnibus Christi fidelibus ad quod presens scriptum pervenerit, Ricardus Lovel, dominus de Carycastel, salutem in Domino. Noveritis, me concessisse, remisisse et omnino de me et heredibus meis imperpetuum quietum clamasse, priori et conventui de Monte Acuto, et eorum successoribus, totum jus meum et clameum quod habui vel aliquo modo habere potero in maneriis de Tyntenhull' et Estchynnok, cum pertinentiis, in comitatu Somers', et in advocacionibus ecclesiarum earundem villarum de Tyntenhull' et Estchynnok, et eciam in hundredis de Tyntenhull' et Hundesbergh', cum omnibus suis pertinentiis, feriis et mercatis de Tyntenhull', et eciam in omnibus aliis rebus ad maneria, advocaciones, hundreda, ferias et mercata predicta qualitercumque spectantibus. Et per presentes recognosco, omnia tenementa predicta cum advocacionibus, hundredis, feriis et mercatis predictis, esse jus ipsius prioris et conventus, et successorum suorum imperpetuum, ita quod nec ego Ricardus Lovel, nec heredes mei, nec aliquis per nos seu nomine nostro, in maneriis, advocacionibus, hundredis, feriis vel mercatis predictis, cum omnibus suis pertinentiis, seu aliqua parte eorundem, de cetero aliquid juris vel clamei exigere vel vendicare poterimus in futuro; set ab omni actione cujuscumque juris aliquid petendi maneriorum de Tyntenhull' et Estchynnok, cum advocacionibus ecclesiarum earundem villarum, et hundredorum de Tyntenhull' et Hundesbergh', feriis et mercatis de Tyntenhull, et omnibus aliis pertinentiis dictorum maneriorum, *[Page iii-199]*

[Col. a] advocacionum ecclesiarum predictarum hundredorum, feriarum, et mercatorum predictorum, seu aliqua parte eorundem, in dominico vel in servitio, per presentes imperpetuum simus exclusi. Et si aliquis finis de predictis tenementis, vel hundredis, vel aliqua parte eorundem, in curia domini regis fuerit levatus inter me et Muriellam uxorem meam querentes, et magistrum Ricardum de Clare et magistrum Rogerum de Blokesworth deforciantes, virtute cujus finis aliquid juris vel clamei michi vel heredibus meis quoquo \modo/ accressere potuit, volo et concedo pro me et heredibus meis quod ipse jure sit nullus, et pro nullo

right of his church of Montacute, saving the right of any, as his predecessors, priors of the same house, had been accustomed to hold and have them from time immemorial. And the sheriff was ordered to perform the aforesaid things, etc. And later, that manor being in the possession of the same priory, the aforesaid Richard Lovell, by his deed which the same present prior then presented in court, granted, remitted and entirely quit-claimed on behalf of himsef and his heirs in perpetuity, to the prior and convent of Montacute and their successors, all the right and claim which he had or could in any way have in the aforesaid manor of Tintinhull with its appurtenances; and he further acknowledged in his said document the said manor with appurtenances to be the right of the prior and convent and their successors in perpetuity. So that neither Richard Lovell nor his heirs could demand or assert any right or claim to the aforesaid manor with its appurtenances nor to any part of the same in future. And the aforesaid Richard Lovell also granted in the same document that if any fine concerning the aforesaid manor with its appurtenances, or any part of the same, should be levied in the court of the lord king, between that Richard Lovell and Muriel his wife, plaintiffs, and master Richard Clare and master Roger Bloxworth, deforciants, by virtue of which fine any right or claim could accrue to him or to his heirs, the same Richard Lovell willed and granted on behalf of himself and his heirs that the fine would be as nothing to his right, and be forever held at naught. And he then presented in court the writing of the grant and remission of the aforesaid Richard Lovell testifying to the aforesaid, which follows in these words:

To all Christ's faithful to whom this present document shall come, Richard Lovell, lord of Castle Cary, greeting in the Lord. Know that I have granted, remitted and entirely quit-claimed forever on behalf of myself and my heirs to the prior and convent of Montacute and their successors all my right and claim which I had or in any way could have in the manors of Tintinhull and East Chinnock, with appurtenances, in Somerset, and in the advowsons of the churches of the same towns of Tintinhull and East Chinnock, and also in the hundreds of Tintinhull and Houndsborough, with all their appurtenances, fairs and markets of Tintinhull, and also in all other things pertaining in any way to the aforesaid manors, advowsons, hundreds, fairs and market. And by these presents I acknowledge all the aforesaid tenements with the advowsons, hundreds, fairs and markets to be the right of that prior and convent and their successors in perpetuity, so that neither I, Richard Lovell, nor my heirs, nor anyone through us or in our name shall be able to demand or assert any right or claim in the aforesaid manors, advowsons, hundreds, fairs or markets, with all their appurtenances, or any part of the same, in future; but by these presents we shall be forever excluded from all actions of any kind seeking any right in the manors of Tintinhull and East Chinnock, with the advowsons of the churches of the same towns, the hundreds of Tintinhull and Houndsborough, the fairs and markets of Tintinhull, and all other appurtenances of the said manors, *[Page iii-199]*

[Col. a] advowsons of the aforesaid churches of the aforesaid hundreds, fairs and markets, or any part of the same, in demesne or in service. And if any fine concerning the aforesaid tenements or hundreds, or any part of the same, be levied in the court of the lord king between myself and Muriel my wife, plaintiffs, and master Richard Clare and master Roger Bloxworth, deforciants, by virtue of which fine any right or claim could accrue to me or to my heirs in any way, I will and grant on behalf of myself and my heirs that that right shall carry no weight and be forever held at naught. In testimony of which I have affixed my seal to

imperpetuum habeatur. In cujus rei testimonium /huic presenti scripto\ sigillum meum apposui. Hiis testibus, nobili viro domino Thoma comite Lancastr', domino Johanne comite Richemond', domino Roberto de Holand', domino Willelmo le Latymer, domino Fulcone Lestrange, domino Nicholao de Segrave, domino Johanne de Claveryng, domino Fulcone filio Warini, domino Geraldo Salveyn, domino Willelmo Tuchet, domino Johanne Beek, domino Willelmo Trussel, domino Johanne de Kynardeseye, domino Michaele de Meldon', Rogero Beler, Johanne de Lancastre et aliis multis. Datum apud Eborum, die jovis in octabis Assensionis Domini, anno regni regis Edwardi filii regis Edwardi duodecimo, tempore parliamenti ibidem tenti. Hanc vero quietam clamanciam ego Ricardus Lovel ante dictus recognovi, et eam irrotulari procuravi tam in cancellaria domini regis quam coram Henrico de Scrop et sociis suis, justiciariis domini regis tunc ibidem presentibus, die, loco et anno predictis.

Unde idem nunc prior petiit judicium si predictus Ricardus Seymor, contra factum predictum predicti antecessoris sui cujus heres ipse est, execucionem de manerio predicto versus eum habere deberet, etc.

Et predictus Ricardus Seymor dixit, non cognoscendo aliqua per predictum priorem superius preallegata, quod placitum ejusdem prioris est duplex vel triplex, unde non intendit quod idem prior ad tale placitum duplex de jure admitti deberet, etc. Unde petit judicium et execucionem, etc.

Membrane iii, dorse Et predictus prior dixit quod ipse placitavit solomodo predictum scriptum ut factum antecessoris ipsius Ricardi Seymor in barram execucionis sue predicte, et pro principali et finali exitu placiti sui predicti; et residuum cepit tantum per viam protestacionis et conduccionis totius materie sue ad exitum illum. Et dixit ut prius quod predictus Ricardus Lovel, antecessor, etc., per scriptum suum predictum concessit et remisit, et omnino pro se et heredibus suis imperpetuum quietum clamavit priori et conventui de Monte Acuto qui tunc fuerat, et successoribus suis, totum jus suum et clameum quod habuit vel aliquo modo habere potuit in predicto manerio de Tyntenhull' cum suis pertinentiis, dum idem nuper prior fuit in possessione ejusdem manerii. Et ulterius recognovit, etc. Ita quod nec ipse Ricardus Lovel, nec heredes sui, etc. Et ulterius concessit quod si aliquis finis, etc. Unde petit judicium, si predictus Ricardus Seymor contra factum predictum predicti antecessoris sui, cujus heres ipse est, execucionem de manerio predicto versus eum habere deberet, etc.

Et predictus Ricardus Seymor dixit, non cognoscendo aliqua per predictum priorem superius preallegata, quod quidam Hugo Lovel, consanguineus predicti Ricardi Seymor, cujus heres ipse est, fuit seisitus de dicto manerio de Tyntenhull', in dominico suo ut de feodo, et diu ante levationem finis predicti concessit predictum manerium cuidam priori de Monte Acuto, predecessori nunc prioris, tenendum ad voluntatem ipsius Hugonis, in auxilium operis ecclesie ibidem, dum eidem Hugoni placeret, absque hoc quod idem prior vel successores sui aliquem alium statum in eodem manerio ante levacionem finis predicti unquam habuerunt, etc. Colore cujus concessionis, prefatus prior et successores sui occupaverunt predictum manerium in jure prefati Hugonis et heredum suorum, etc., quousque Ricardus Lovel, consanguineus et heres predicti Hugonis, manerium predictum in manus suas proprias seisivit et resumpsit, et seisinam suam in eodem manerio continuavit, quousque

[Col. b] idem Ricardus Lovel de dicto manerio, simul cum aliis maneriis predictis feoffavit magistrum Ricardum de Clare, magistrum Rogerum de Blokerworth, in feodo

the present writing. Witnessed by the noble man Sir Thomas earl of Lancaster, Sir John earl of Richmond, Sir Robert Holland, Sir William Latimer, Sir Fulk Lestrange, Sir Nicholas Segrave, Sir John Clavering, Sir Fulk FitzWarin, Sir Gerald Salveyn, Sir William Tuchet, Sir John Beek, Sir William Trussel, Sir John Kynardeseye, Sir Michael Meldon, Roger Beler, John Lancaster, and many others. Given at York, on Thursday on the octave of the Lord's Ascension in the twelfth year of the reign of King Edward [II] son of King Edward [24 May 1319], at the time of the parliament held there. And truly this quit-claim I, the aforesaid Richard Lovell, have acknowledged and caused to be enrolled both in the chancery of the lord king as well as before Henry Scrope and his colleagues, justices of the lord king then present there, on the aforesaid day, at the aforesaid place and in the aforesaid year.

Whereupon the same present prior requests judgment as to whether the aforesaid Richard Seymour ought to have execution of the aforesaid manor against him, contrary to the aforesaid deed of his aforesaid ancestor whose heir he is, etc. And the aforesaid Richard Seymour, not acknowledging anything alleged above by the aforesaid prior, said that the plea of the same prior was double or triple, and therefore he did not think that the same prior should be allowed such a double plea by right, etc. Whereupon he sought judgment and execution, etc.

Membrane iii, dorse And the aforesaid prior said that he only pleaded the aforesaid document as the deed of the ancestor of Richard Seymour in barring his aforesaid execution, and as the first and last issue of his aforesaid plea; and the rest he took by way of protestation and conducing of all his matter to that issue. And he said as before that the aforesaid Richard Lovell, the ancestor, etc., by his aforesaid document granted, remitted and entirely quit-claimed on behalf of himself and his heirs in perpetuity to the prior and convent of Montacute of that time and their successors all his right and claim which he had or in any way could have in the aforesaid manor of Tintinhull with his appurtenances, while the same late prior was in possession of the same manor. And he also acknowledged, etc. So that neither this Richard Lovell, nor his heirs, etc. And he also granted that if any settlement, etc. Whereupon he requested judgment as to whether the aforesaid Richard Seymour ought to have execution of the aforesaid manor against him contrary to the said deed of his said ancestor, whose heir he is, etc.

And the aforesaid Richard Seymour said, not acknowledging anything alleged above by the aforesaid prior, that a certain Hugh Lovell, kinsman of the aforesaid Richard Seymour whose heir he is, was in possession of the said manor of Tintinhull, in his demesne as of fee, and long before the levying of that fine he granted the aforesaid manor to a certain prior of Montacute, a predecessor of the present prior, to be held at the will of Hugh, in support of the work of the church there, as it should please the same Hugh, without the same prior or his successors ever having had any other estate in the same manor before the levying of the said fine, etc. By colour of which grant, the said prior and his successors occupied the aforesaid manor which in the aforementioned Hugh and his heirs, etc., until Richard Lovell, kinsman and heir of the aforesaid Hugh, seised and resumed the aforesaid manor into his own hands and continued in seisin of the same manor until

[Col. b] the same Richard Lovell enfeoffed master Richard Clare and Roger Bloxworth in fee simple of the said manor, together with the other aforesaid manors; which master

simplici; qui quidem magister Ricardus et magister Rogerus, virtute feoffamenti illius inde seisiti fuerunt tempore confectionis scripti predicti, absque hoc quod prior qui tunc fuerat aliquid habuit in eodem manerio tempore confectionis ejusdem scripti: et hoc paratus est verificare, etc. Qui quidem magister Ricardus et magister Rogerus dictum manerium cum aliis maneriis predictis prefato Ricardo Lovel et Murielle, in fine predicto nominatis, habendum sibi et heredibus ipsius Ricardi Lovel, concesserunt et reddiderunt. De quo quidem manerio de Tyntenhull' virtute finis predicti predictus Ricardus Seymor, consanguineus et heres predicti Ricardi Lovel, modo petit execucionem, etc. Et dicit quod nec Henricus [I] rex, filius conquestoris, nec aliquis regum Anglie, de manerio predicto unquam seisiti fuerunt ante levacionem finis predicti. Unde petit judicium et execucionem, etc.

Et predictus prior non cognoscendo aliqua per ipsum Ricardum Seymor superius allegata, dixit quod placitum predicti Ricardi fuit duplex, unde non intendit quod ipse ad tale placitum duplex de jure necesse habet respondere. Et quia videtur curie quod placitum predicti Ricardi Seymor fuit duplex, dictum fuit eidem Ricardo per curiam, quod ipse responderet ad predictum scriptum quod predictus prior asserit fore factum antecessoris sui, et quod idem prior placitavit versus eum in barram executionis finis predicti, etc., si, etc. Et predictus Ricardus Seymor habito visu scripti predicti, dixit quod ipse non cognovit scriptum illud fore factum tempore quo per datam ejusdem supponitur fieri. Et dixit ulterius quod prior de Monte Acuto qui tunc fuerat non fuit seisitus de manerio de Tyntenhull', nec de aliqua parcella ejusdem manerii, tempore confeccionis scripti predicti: set predicti magister Ricardus de Clare et magister Rogerus de Blokerworth', qui idem manerium reddiderunt per finem predictum, ad tunc inde seisiti fuerunt. Et hoc paratus est verificare, etc. Et dixit quod ipse residuum omnium materiarum suarum per ipsum superius propositarum cepit per viam protestationis et conductionis totius placiti sui ad exitum illum. Unde peciit judicium, si ipse ab execucione sua predicta virtute scripti predicti excludi deberet, etc. Et petiit execucionem, etc.

Et predictus prior dixit quod tempore confectionis scripti predicti prior de Monte Acuto qui tunc fuerat fuit seisitus de dicto manerio de Tyntenhull' cum pertinentiis. Et hoc paratus fuit verificare per patriam, etc. Et predictus Ricardus Seymor dixit quod tempore confeccionis scripti predicti prior de Monte Acuto qui tunc fuerat non fuit seisitus de predicto manerio de Tyntenhull' cum pertinentiis, nec de aliqua parcella ejusdem. Et hoc paratus fuit verificare per patriam, etc. Et predictus prior similiter, etc. Ideo preceptum fuit vicecomes Somers' quod venire faceret coram domino rege ad hunc diem, scilicet a die Sancti Michaelis in .xv. dies ubicumque, etc., .xxiiij. tam milites, etc., de visneto de Tyntenhull', per quos, etc. Et qui nec, etc. ad recognicionem, etc. Quia tam, etc. Idem dies datus fuit partibus predictis, etc.

Ad quem diem, coram domino rege apud Westm' venerunt tam predictus Ricardus Seymor quam predictus prior per attornatos suos predictos. Et vicecomes retornavit nomina predictorum .xxiiij., etc., quorum nullus venit. Ideo vicecomes habeat corpora eorum coram domino rege in octabis Sancti Martini ubicumque, etc., ad faciendam juratam predictam, etc. Idem dies datus est partibus predictis, etc. Et continuato inde processu inter partes predictas per juratos positos in respectu usque a die Sancti Hillar' in .xv. dies tunc proximo sequenti ubicumque, etc. Ad quem diem, coram domino

Richard and master Roger by virtue of that enfeoffment were seised thereof at the time when the aforesaid writing was made, without the prior of the time having anything in the same manor at the time when that writing was made: and this he was ready to verify, etc. Which master Richard and master Roger granted and rendered the said manor with all the aforesaid manors to the aforementioned Richard Lovell and Muriel, named in the aforesaid settlement, to be held by them and the heirs of the same Richard Lovell. Of which manor of Tintinhull, by virtue of the aforesaid fine, the aforesaid Richard Seymor, kinsman and heir of the aforesaid Richard Lovell, now sought exeution, etc. And he said that neither King Henry [I], son of the Conqueror, nor any other king of England was ever seised of the aforesaid manor before the levying of the aforesaid fine. For which reason he requested judgment and execution, etc.

And the aforesaid prior, not acknowledging anything alleged above by this Richard Seymour, said that the plea of the aforesaid Richard was double, and so he did not think that he need by rights answer such a double plea. And because it seemed to the court that the plea of the aforesaid Richard Seymour was double, the same Richard was informed by the court that he should answer the aforesaid document, which the said prior claimed to be the deed of his ancestor, and which the same prior pleaded against him in barring execution of the aforesaid settlement, etc., if, etc. And the aforesaid Richard Seymour, having seen the aforesaid document, said that he did not accept that the document had been made at the time suggested by the date on the same. And he also said that the prior of Montacute at the time was not seised of the manor of Tintinhull, nor any parcel of the same manor, at the time when the aforesaid document was made: but the aforesaid master Richard Clare and master Roger Bloxworth, who returned the same manor by the aforesaid fine, had then been in possession. And that he was ready to verify, etc. And he said that he took the rest of his matter proposed above by way of protest and conducing to all his plea at that issue. And so he sought judgment as to whether he ought to be excluded from his aforesaid execution by virtue of the aforesaid document, etc. And he requested execution, etc.

And the aforesaid prior said that at the time when the aforesaid document was made the prior of Montacute of the time was seised of the said manor of Tintinhull with appurtenances. And that he was ready to verify by his country, etc. And the aforesaid Richard Seymour said that at the time when the aforesaid document was made the prior of Montacute at the time was not seised of the aforesaid manor of Tintinhull with appurtenances, nor any parcel of the same. And that he was ready to prove by his country, etc. And the aforesaid prior likewise, etc. Therefore, the sheriff of Somerset was ordered to bring before the lord king on that day, namely fifteen days from the day of Michaelmas [8 October 1383], wheresoever, etc., twenty-four men as well knights, etc., from the neighbourhood of Tintinhull, by whom, etc. And who neither, etc., for the acknowledgement, etc. Since both, etc. The same day was given to the aforesaid parties, etc.

On which day, the aforesaid Richard Seymour and the aforesaid prior appeared by their said attorneys before the lord king at Westminster. And the sheriff returned the names of the aforesaid twenty-four, etc., of whom none came. Therefore let the sheriff have their persons before the lord king on the octave of Martinmas [18 November 1383], wheresoever, etc., to make up the aforesaid jury, etc. The same day was given to the aforesaid parties, etc. And the process between the aforesaid parties was adjourned, the jury being put in respite until fifteen days after the day of St

rege apud Westm' venit predictus Ricardus Seymor per attornatum suum predictum, et predictus prior per attornatum suum predictum similiter venit. Et juratores similiter venerunt, qui ad hoc electi, triati et jurati dicunt super sacramentum suum, quod ipse qui fuerat prior de Monte Acuto tempore confectionis scripti predicti, quod predictus nunc prior placitavit versus predictum Ricardum Seymor, in barram *[Page iii-200]*

[Col. a] execucionis sue finis predicti de predicto manerio de [27]
Membrane iv Tyntenhull cum suis pertinentiis, non fuit seisitus de predicto manerio de Tyntenhull' cum pertinentiis, nec de aliqua parcella ejusdem, tempore confectionis ejusdem scripti, sicut predictus
[Col. b] Ricardus Seymor placitando allegavit, etc. Ideo consideratum est quod predictus Ricardus Seymor habeat executionem versus predictum nunc priorem de manerio predicto de Tyntenhull cum pertinentiis, etc.[28]
[29]

SECUNTUR PETICIONES LIBERATE PER COMMUNITATEM REGNI ANGLIE IN PRESENTI PARLIAMENTO, UNA CUM RESPONSIONIBUS EISDEM PETICIONIBUS IN EODEM PARLIAMENTO FACTIS.

A lour tresexcellent, tresgracious et tresredoute seignour nostre seignour le roy supplient ses lieges communes du roialme d'Engleterre pur les peticions dessouzescriptz:

[Confirmation of the liberties of the church, and of the charters.]
16. En primes, qe seinte esglise eit et enjoise toutes ses libertes et franchises, et qe la grande chartre, la chartre de la foreste, les estatutz des purveours et laborers, et touz les autres bones estatutz et ordinances faitz avant ces heures soient tenuz et gardez, et duement executz solonc les forme et effect d'icelles.
\[*Responsio.*]/
Le roy le voet.[30]

[None to be justice of assize in his own county.]
17. Item, prient les communes: qe par la ou justices des assises sont en lour propre paiis, qi sont as fees et robes des pleusours seignours en mesmes les paiis, et ont grandes alliances et autres affinitees illoeqes, dont grantz malx et grevances aviegnent diversement au poeple, desqueux n'est my honest de parler en especial: einz entre autres ils lour covient de faire, et font, trop grant favour as unes, et reddour as autres.
Qe plese a nostre seignour le roi en ce present parlement ordeigner par estatut qe nul homme de loi desore enavant soit justice des assises en son propre pais, pur grant ease et relevement de sa dite commune; ne qe le chief justice de l'un bank ne de l'autre ne soit my justice des nulles assises, a cause qe s'ils font errour ce serroit redresse devant eux mesmes; et entendable chose est, q'ils serroient trop favorables en lour juggementz demesne.
Responsio.
Quant al primer point de ceste peticion, le roy le voet. Et quant al seconde poynt tochant le chief justice de commune bank, le roi voet q'il soit assigne justice d'assises entre

Hilary [27 January 1384], wheresoever, etc. On which day, the aforesaid Richard Seymour through his aforesaid attorney appeared before the lord king at Westminster, and the aforesaid prior similarly appeared through his attorney. And the jurors similarly appeared, who had been elected, tried and sworn thereto, and they say on oath that he who had been prior of Montacute at the time when the aforesaid document was made - which the aforesaid present prior pleaded against the aforesaid Richard Seymour in barring *[Page iii-200]*
[Col. a] his execution of the aforesaid settlement concerning the aforesaid manor of
Membrane iv Tintinhull with its appurtenances - was not in possession of the aforesaid manor of Tintinhull with appurtenances, nor of any parcel of the same, at the time when the same document was made, as the aforesaid
[Col. b] Richard Seymour in pleading claimed, etc. Therefore it was decided that the aforesaid Richard Seymour should have execution against the aforesaid present prior of the said manor of Tintinhull with appurtenances, etc.

HERE FOLLOW THE PETITIONS SUBMITTED BY THE COMMUNITY OF THE KINGDOM OF ENGLAND IN THE PRESENT PARLIAMENT, TOGETHER WITH THE ANSWERS TO THE SAME PETITIONS GIVEN IN THE SAME PARLIAMENT.

To their most excellent, most gracious and most redoubtable lord our lord the king, his liege commons of the kingdom of England request the granting of the petitions written below:

[Confirmation of the liberties of the church, and of the charters.]
16. Firstly, that holy church shall have and enjoy all its liberties and franchises, and that the Great Charter, the Charter of the Forest, the statutes of purveyors and labourers, and all the other good statutes and ordinances made in the past be upheld and preserved and duly executed in accordance with the form and effect of the same.
Answer.
The king wills it.

[None to be justice of assize in his own county.]
17. Also, the commons pray: whereas justices of assizes when they are in their own country take fees and robes from many lords in the same country, and have great alliances and other affinities there, from which serious troubles and grievances arise in different ways for the people, of which it would not be honourable to speak in detail: but amongst other things they desire to do, and indeed do, very great favours for some, and injury to others.
May it please our lord the king in this present parliament to ordain by statute that no man of the law shall henceforth be justice of assize in his own country, to the great ease and relief of his said commons; nor that the chief justice of either bench be made justice of any assizes, since if they were to commit an error it would be redressed before themselves, and understandably they would be too favourable in their judgment of themselves.
Answer.
As to the first point of this petition, the king wills it. And as to the second point touching the chief justice of the Common Bench, the king wills that he be appointed justice of assize

---

[27] A contemporary note at the foot of this membrane reads 'plus in rotulo sequento de eodem'.
[28] A contemporary note in the margin reads 'Judicium'.
[29] The common petitions, unlike the pleas, are in the main body of the roll.
[30] Stat. 8 Ric.2 c.1. The statutes of this parliament are printed in *SR*, II.36-7.

autres. Mes quant al chief justice de bank le roy, le roy voet q'il soit fait come ad este fait et use pur la greindre partie de centz ans darrein passez.[31]

[No justice to accept fee or reward except from the king.]
18. Item, prient les communes: qe la ou y ad grant rumour et pleinte qe la commune ley n'ad my son cours come avoir devoit, a cause qe les justices de l'un bank et de l'autre, et barons de l'escheqer, sont de retenue et as fees des seignours et autres, et come dit est parnent grantz dons des parties eantz affaire devant eux, sibien en lour places, come aillours ou ils sont appellez au conseil, sibien parentre le roi et partie, come parentre partie et partie.

Qe plese a nostre seignour le roy ordeigner par estatut en ce present parlement qe nul des justices ne des barons suisditz, par lui mesmes ne par autre, en prive n'en apert, preigne robe, fee, n'empension,
[Col. b] doun, ne regard, de nully, fors soulement du roi, s'il ne soit mangier ou boire, et ce de petite value, sur tielle grevouse peyne a limyter en cest parlement, qe chacun de lour estat eit doubt de faire ou venir a l'encontre en temps avenir.
\[Responsio.]/
Le roy le voet, sur peine de perdre lour office, et outre de faire fyn et ranceon au roi: et soit ce fait par estatut.[32]

[No distress for debt to the king without judgment.]
19. Item, prient les communes: qe terres, tenemenz, biens ne chateux de nully, en sa vie ne apres son deces, soient seisez en la mayn nostre seignour le roi, par suggestion de nully par cause d'ascun dette due a nostre seignour le roi, si cestuy de qi terres, tenemenz, biens, ou chateux sont ensi seisez, ne soit trovez /dettour\ a nostre dit seignour le roi par chose de record, ou par autre due proces de loi. Et si ascune seisine soit fait a contraire, soit outrement tenuz par nul. Et outre ce, si ascun ministre ensi face, q'il soit puniz grevousement, sibien a seute du roi come de partie.
\[Responsio.]/
Soit use come ad este en temps passe.

[Security of the Scottish marches.]
20. Item, prient les communes qe come en la parlement tenuz a Westm' l'an du regne nostre seignour le roi q'or est sisme, il estoit ordeigne qe touz ceux q'ont chastelx, ou forteresses pres les marches d'Escoce, qe touz qi preignent les profitz et revenues d'icelles soient tenuz de les garder suffisantement, et les estuffer des gentz et vitailles selonc la quantite d'iceux; sur peril d'ascun certeintee ent a ordeiner par nostre seignour le roi, et les paiis ne soient endamagez ne destruitz a cause d'icelle. Et qe les gentz estranges qi serront ordeignez pur le lieutenant du roi celles parties, puissent estre entour son corps, et pur garde des chastelx et villes du roi es /marches\ suisditz tantsoulement; en quele ordinance /n'estoit nulle\ peine establie as contrevenantz d'icelle.

Qe plese ordeigner en cest cas covenable peine; adjustant a cella qe touz ceux q'ont ascune ferme, annuite ou quelconqe autre annuel profit a prendre des tielx chastelx ou forteresses, q'ils soient chargez de la garde, defense et vitaille, en la fourme avauntdite: c'estassavoir, pur ferme, annuel profit, provenant al verroie value annuel des tielx chastelx

---
[31] Stat. 8 Ric.2 c.2.
[32] Stat. 8 Ric.2 c.3.

among others. But as to the chief justice of the King's Bench, the king wills that he be appointed according to the practice and usage in existence for the best part of a hundred years past.

[No justice to accept fee or reward except from the king.]
18. Also, the commons pray: whereas there is great murmur and complaint that the common law has not run its course as it ought to have done, because the justices of both benches and the barons of the exchequer are of the retinue of, and receive fees from, lords and others, and so it is said accept large gifts from parties having business before them, both in their sessions and elsewhere where they are summoned to counsel, as well between the king and party as between party and party.
May it please our lord the king to ordain by statute in this present parliament that none of the aforesaid justices or barons, neither himself nor through another, in private nor in public, shall take robes, fees or pension,
[Col. b] gift or reward, from anyone, except only from the king, unless it be to eat or drink, and be of small value; on pain of such a grievous penalty to be specified in this parliament that each of their estate shall be afraid to act against or contravene this in future.
Answer.
The king wills it, on pain of their losing their office, and also paying a fine and ransom to the king: and let it be done by statute.

[No distress for debt to the king without judgment.]
19. Also, the commons pray: that the lands, tenements, goods and chattels of anyone, in life or death, shall not be taken into the hands of our lord the king on the accusation of anyone by reason of any debt owed to our lord the king, if he from whom the lands, tenements, goods or chattels are thus seized is not found to be a debtor of our said lord the king by record, or by other appropriate process of law. And if any seisin be made to the contrary, let it be completely invalid. And moreover, if any minister act thus, that he be punished severely, both at the suit of the king and of the party.
Answer.
Let it be done as it has been done in the past.

[Security of the Scottish marches.]
20. Also, the commons pray: whereas in the parliament held at Westminster in the sixth year of the reign of our lord the present king [1382-3], it was ordained that all those who held castles or fortresses near the marches of Scotland and who took the profits and revenues of the same should be obliged to guard them adequately, and provision them with men and supplies in accordance with their size, on pain of a certain penalty to be ordained by our lord the king, so that the land should neither be damaged nor destroyed because of the same. And that strangers who were to be appointed as king's lieutenant in those parts should be about their person and guard only the castles and towns of the king in the aforesaid marches; in which ordinance no punishment was decreed for contravenors of the same.
May it please you to ordain a suitable punishment in such cases; adding to this that all those who have any farm, annuity or any other profit to take from such castles or fortresses be charged with the guard, defence and supply of the same, in the aforesaid manner: namely, for a farm or annual profit amounting to the true annual value of such

ou forteresses, de la garde et charge entier; et de meindre quantite, solonc l'afferant. Sur la peine avandite a ordeigner en ce present parlement; c'estassavoir, de forfaire a nostre seignour le roy la verroie value des profitz a prendres des tielx chastelx ou forteresses par trois ans, de celuy de qi ascune tiel notable serra trovez.

\[Responsio.]/

Le roi chargera les seignours de garder lours chastelx en manere come ils soleient devant ces heures en temps de guerre.

Page iii-201

[Tithes of woodland.]

21. Item, prient les communes: qe come il soit ordeine par estatut, /q'une generale\ prohibicion serra grante en la chancellerie, par la ou gentz avancez as benefices de seinte esglise demandent dismes en courte cristiene de grosse boys q'est passez l'age de vint, trent ou quarrant ans, quant le dit bois est coupez et venduz. Et a cause qe nulle probicion est grante par le dit estatut en especial, les ditz gentz de seinte esglise pursuent en court christiene pur les dismes suisdites, nient contresteant la dite prohibicion[33] generale a eux directe, a grant damage et meschief de ceux qi vendent lour bois en la forme suisdite.

Qe plese a nostre seignour le roi grante une prohibicion, ove les attachementz sur mesme la prohibition en especial vers les ordinairs, et ceux qi pursuent contre l'estatut, come desuis est dit.

\[Responsio.]/

Soit fait come autrefoitz fuist ordeine par estatut fait a Westm' l'an .xlv. l'aiel, qe Dieux assoille.[34]

[Depredations by Cheshire men.]

22. Item, prient les communes des countes de Salop', Staff', Wircestre, Glouc', Hereford', Lanc', Notyngh', Derb', Warr', Leyc' et Everwyk: qe come plusours gentz del counte de Cestre de jour en autre, et a la foitz de noet, viegnent et chivachent en les countes suisdites, ove grantz routes des gentz armez et arraiez a faire de guerre, et illoeqes plusoures felonies, trespasses et extorsions facent; c'estassaver tuent gentz, ardent maisons, ravissent dames et damoisels, et autres gentz maheyment, batent et malement naufront, et lour boefs de lour charettes et autres chateux maheyment, et tuent, en grande destruction et oppression des communes suisdites, dont nul punisement, ne forfaiture est ordeigne de lour biens ne chateux q'ils ont deinz le counte de Cestre suisdite, a cause de lour franchise.

Qe plese ordeiner owele forfaiture de lour terres et chateux q'ils ont deins le counte de Cestre, sibien pur trespasses et felonies faites hors de le dit counte deinz le roialme, come pur felonies et trespasses faites deinz le dit counte; nient contresteantz les franchises del countee suisdit. Ou qe vous plese ordeigner autre remede sufficeante en ce cas; et qe mesme l'ordinance se purra tenir deinz l'eveschie de Duresme, et autres tieles franchises, et aillours parmy le roialme.

\[Responsio.]/

Le roy, par avys de son conseil, ordeinera tiel remede qe serra plesant au poeple, si Dieu plest.

[Overfishing of rivers.]

23. Item, prient les communes: qe come y ad en la ryvere de Thamise, Medewey et autres grantz ryvers deinz le roialme,

castles or fortresses, the whole guard and charge; and for a lesser amount in accordance with their means. On pain of the aforesaid penalty to be ordained in this present parliament; namely, of forfeiting to our lord the king the true value of the profits to be taken from such castles or fortresses for three years, from anyone in whom anything significant is found.

Answer.

The king will charge the lords to guard their castles in the manner in which they have been accustomed to do in the past during times of war.

[Tithes of woodland.]

21. Also, the commons pray: whereas it was ordained by statute that a general prohibition would be granted in the chancery, nevertheless people promoted to benefices of holy church demand tithes in the court Christian on great woods more than twenty, thirty or forty years old, when the said wood is cut and sold. And because no specific prohibition was granted by the said statute, the said people of holy church request the aforesaid tithes in the court Christian, notwithstanding the said general prohibition directed at them, to the great injury and harm of those who sell their wood in the aforesaid manner.

May it please our lord the king to grant a prohibition, with the attachments on the same prohibition in particular against the ordinaries and those who sue contrary to the statute as is said above.

Answer.

Let it be done as was once ordained in a statute made at Westminster in the forty-fifth year of the grandfather [Edward III], whom God absolve.

[Depredations by Cheshire men.]

22. Also, the commons of the counties of Shropshire, Stafford, Worcester, Gloucester, Hereford, Lancashire, Nottingham, Derby, Warwick, Leicester and York pray: whereas many people from Cheshire from one day to the next, and sometimes at night, come and ride in the aforesaid counties, in great bands of armed men arrayed for war, and there commit many felonies, trespasses and extortion; that is to say, they kill men, burn houses, ravish ladies and damsels, and maim, beat and sometimes wound others, and injure and kill the oxen from their carts and other cattle, to the great destruction and oppression of the aforesaid commons; for which no punishment nor forfeiture has been ordained for the goods or chattels which they have in Cheshire aforesaid, because of their franchise.

May it please you to ordain equal forfeiture of their lands and chattels which they have in Cheshire, both for trespasses and felonies committed outside the said county within the realm, as well as for felonies and trespasses committed within the said county; notwithstanding the franchises of the aforesaid county. Or that it may please you to provide another sufficient remedy in the case; and that the same ordinance may be upheld within the bishopric of Durham and other such franchises, and elsewhere throughout the realm.

Answer.

The king, by the advice of his council, will ordain such a remedy as will please the people, God willing.

[Overfishing of rivers.]

23. Also, the commons pray: whereas there is in the rivers of Thames, Medway and other great rivers of the kingdom a

---

[33] Original probicion
[34] Stat. 45 Edw.3 c.3.

grant fuyson de fry de pesson, c'estassavoir des troutes, samons, pykes, roches, barbils et d'autre pesson, le quel fry s'il feust gardez et cherriz il serroit grant profit a les seignours et communes de la terre, et ore est use communement qe diverses persones demurantz pres tieles ryvers preignent la dite fry ovesqe lour subtils reetz et autres subtils instrumentz, et vendent la dite fry pur sustenance des porcs le bussell pur .l. d., et ascun foitz le busselle pur .vi. oefs, a grande destruccion du dit pesson, et grant damage de tout le poeple entour tiels ryveres.

Qe plese a nostre seignour le roi ordeiner qe nully preigne en les ditz ryveres nul tiel fry, ne ne pesche ove nul manere de reetz, sinoun qe le masche d'icelle soit si large come ordeignez est par estatut en fait devant ces heures.

\[Responsio.]/

Soient les estatutz devant ces heures en faitz tenuz et gardez, et mys en due execution.

[Security of Rye and Winchelsea.]
24. Item, prient les communes: qe come les villes de la Rie et Wynchelse, et les enhabitantz en ycelles, soient a pein tout outrement par souventz arsons et invasions
[Col. b] des enemys destruitz, issint q'ils ne poent bien ne suffisantment resister les enemys si ascun poair lour surviegne.

Qe vous plese considerer queux forteresses les dites villes serroient as enemys s'ils les puissent gayner; et auxi les grantz perils et damages emynantz avenirs au roialme pur defaut de bone /garde\ des dites villes, et ordeigner pur icelles tiel manere remede qu'eles puissent le plus seurement resister et contresteer la malice de lour enemys. Entendantz qe si les dites villes furent prises, qe Dieu defende, tout le paiis serroit destruit par ycelles.

\[Responsio.]/

Le roy ent ordenera come mueltz luy semble, par advys de son conseil.

[Term of office of sheriffs and others.]
25. Item, prient les communes: qe come y soit ordeignez par estatutz devant ces heures faitz,[35] qe viscontz, southvisconts, n'eschetours qi sont en ycelles offices en un counte par un an, ne serroient my apres en les ditz offices deinz mesme le counte par trois ans proschein ensuantz; et ore es diverses countees d'Engleterre pluseurs sont esluz as ditz offices deinz les trois ans, la ou y sont autres suffisantz deinz mesme le counte, a grant disease et oppression des communes, et encontre les estatutz ent faitz.

Qe plese qe les ditz estatutz soient tenuz, issint qe viscontz, southvisconts et eschetours qi sont ore esluz a contraire des ditz estatutz, soient removez et oustez, et autres suffisantz esluz, et qe grevouse peine poet estre mys et ordenez, sibien pur eux qi eslisent a contraire des estatutz les ditz officers, come sur les officers, par cause de quele peine tielles elections poient estre eschuiz.

\[Responsio.]/

Le chanceller respondra par bouche.[36]

Et le responce du chanceller fuist tielle, q'il serroit trop prejudiciel au roi et a sa corone d'estre ensi restreint, qe quant un viscont s'ad bien et loialment porte en son office au roi et au poeple par un an, qe le roi par avys de son conseille ne purroit reeslir et faire tielle bon officer viscont pur l'an

great abundance of fishspawn, namely of trout, salmon, pike, roach, barbel and other fish, which fry, if it were protected and valued, would bring great profit to the lords and commons of the land, yet now it is common practice for various people dwelling near such rivers to catch the fry with special nets and other ingenious instruments, and sell the said fry as pig food at 50 d. a bushel, and sometimes six eggs for a bushel, to the great destruction of the said fish and the great injury of all the people around such rivers.

May it please our lord the king to ordain that none shall take any such fry from the said rivers, nor fish with any kind of net, unless the mesh of the same be of the size ordained by the statute made thereon before this time.

Answer.

Let the statutes made thereon in the past be upheld and kept, and duly executed.

[Security of Rye and Winchelsea.]
24. Also, the commons pray: whereas the towns of Rye and Winchelsea and the inhabitants of the same are almost entirely destroyed by the frequent burning and invasions *[Col. b]* of the enemy, such that they could resist the enemy neither well nor adequately if any power were to descend upon them.

May it please you to consider what strong places the said towns would be to the enemy if they could win them; and also the great and eminent dangers and injuries which would occur in the kingdom through the absence of adequate keeping of the said towns, and to ordain for the same such a remedy that they may the more confidently resist and oppose the malice of their enemies. Bearing in mind that if the said towns were captured, which God forbid, the whole land will be ruined as a result.

Answer.

The king will ordain thereon as seems best to him, by the advice of his council.

[Term of office of sheriffs and others.]
25. Also, the commons pray: whereas it was ordained by statutes made in the past that sheriffs, deputy sheriffs and escheators who had occupied the same office in one county for a year should not be re-appointed to the said office in the same county within the space of three years; yet now, in various counties of England many people are elected to the said offices within three years, even though there are others worthy in the same county, to the great injury and oppression of the commons, and contrary to the statutes made thereon.

May it please you to ordain that the said statutes be upheld, so that sheriffs and escheators now elected contrary to the said statutes be removed and ousted, and other worthy men elected, and that a grievous penalty be imposed and ordained, both for those who elect the said officers contrary to the statutes, and for the officers, as a consequence whereof such elections might be discouraged.

Answer.

The chancellor answered by word of mouth.

And the answer of the chancellor was that it would be extremely prejudicial to the king and his crown to be restrained in such a way that when a sheriff had performed his office loyally and well for the king and people for one year, the king could not by the advice of his council re-elect and re-appoint such a good officer for the following year. And

---

[35] Stat. 1 Ric.2 c.11.
[36] This answer has been added later in a different hand.

ensuant. Et purce le roi voet faire en tielle cas come meultz semblera pur profit de lui et de son poeple.

[None to be compelled to serve outside his own county.]
26. Item, prient les communes: qe come entre autres estatutz faitz en temps le roi Edward aiel nostre seignour le roi q'ore est, soit ordeignez qe nulle homme d'armes, archer, ne hobiler, soit arcez d'aler armez en service le roi hors des countees ou ils sont receantz, a lour costages /demesne,\ ne as coustages des countees, encontre lour volunte et bone gree. Et ore de novel diverses commissions furent myses hors de la chancellerie as diverses gentz des diverses countees d'Engleterre, par qoi pluseurs gentz furent chacez d'aler en Escoce, ascuns a lour coustages demesne, et ascuns as coustages des countees, a grant empoverisement de eux, et encontre l'estatut avantdit, nient contresteant q'ils paient lour dismes et quinzismes come ils soleient faire.

Qe plese a nostre dit seignour le roi ordeigner /qe\ desormes ne soient tieles commissions faites, et qe ceux commissions queux sont issint envoiez soient repellez.
\[Responsio.]/
Soit l'estatut ent fait l'an primer l'aiel nostre seignour le roi tenuz et gardez.[37]

[False entries in plea rolls.]
27. Item, prient les communes: pur la grande desheritison q'ad este fait, et se purra faire au poeple en temps avenir par fauxes entrees des plees, rasure des rolles et changement des verediz, par quoi desheritison d'une des parties ensuyte, ou se purra ensuire: qe si ascun juge ou clerc soit de ce ateint, q'il forface al volente du roi, et qe ceux ou lour heirs qi de soi sentent grevez soient restituez a lour enheritement

Page iii-202
\[Responsio.]/
Y plest au roi qe si ascun soit sufficeantment atteint devant le roi et son conseil de tielle defaut, deinz deux ans apres le defaut fait si le pleintif soit de pleine age, et s'il soit deinz age adonqes deinz deux ans proscheins apres q'il vendra a son pleine age, q'il soit puniz par fyn et ranceon a la volunte le roi, et face gree au partie. Et quant al restitucion d'enheritement, sue la partie par brief d'errour, ou autrement come la lei voet.[38]

[Production of plea rolls in court.]
28. Item, prient les communes: qe come les clercz q'ont en garde les rolles del commune bank et del bank le roi deveroient de droit sanz riens prendre apporter les ditz rolles en les dites places, a toutes le foitz qe les attornees de mesmes les places enbosoignent de les avoir en courte, pur diverses plees queux ils gardent des seignours, prelats et communes d'Engleterre: et ore est use qe les ditz clercs ne voillent apporter les ditz rolles en les dites places s'ils n'eient louer de le faire, a grant damage et disease a touz ceux qi y ont affaire.

Qe plese ordeigner en ce present parlement qe chescun an al fyn del terme de Seint Hiller, et al fyn del terme de la Trinite, le chanceller le roi face enquere par les ditz attornes par lour seremenz des tielx defautes, et des autres en lour places, et si ascune persone soit atteinte de tiele defautz, q'il eit emprisonement par un an entier, et face fyn et ranceon au volunte le roi, et perde son office.

therefore the king wished to act in a way which seemed of most benefit to himself and his people.

[None to be compelled to serve outside his own county.]
26. Also, the commons pray: whereas among other statutes made in the time of King Edward [III], grandfather of our lord the present king, it was ordained that no man-at-arms, archer nor hobelar be forced to travel armed in the king's service outside the counties where they were resident, either at their own expense or at the expense of the counties, against their will and consent. Yet now various commissions have been sent out from the chancery to various men from several counties of England, in consequence of which many men have been forced to go to Scotland, some at their own expense, and some at the expense of the counties, to their great impoverishment, and contrary to the aforesaid statute, notwithstanding that they pay their tenths and fifteenths as they are accustomed to do.
May it please our said lord the king to ordain that from now on no such commissions shall be made, and that those commissions which have thus been sent out be repealed.
Answer.
Let the statute made in the first year of the grandfather of our lord the king be upheld and kept.

[False entries in plea rolls.]
27. Also, the commons pray, because of the great disinheritance which has occurred, and could occur for the people in future by false entries of pleas, erasure of rolls and alteration of the records of verdicts, as a result of which disinheritance of one of the parties follows, or could follow: that if any judge or clerk be convicted thereof, that he forfeit at the king's will, and that those or their heirs who feel aggrieved be restored to their inheritance.

Answer.
It pleases the king that if anyone be sufficiently convicted before the king and his council of such a fault, within two years of the fault being made if the plaintiff be of age, and within two years of his coming of age if he is under age, he be punished by fine and ransom at the king's will and compensate the party. And as to the restitution of the inheritance, let the party sue by writ of error, or otherwise as the law will have it.

[Production of plea rolls in court.]
28. Also, the commons pray: whereas the clerks who have the rolls of the Common Bench and King's Bench in their keeping ought by right to take the said rolls to the said session without receiving anything, as often as the attorneys of those places require to have them in court, for various pleas which they settle from the lords, prelates and commons of England: yet now the practice is that the said clerks will not bring the said rolls to the said places unless they are paid to do so, to the great injury and harm of all those who have business there.
May it please you to ordain in this present parliament that each year at the end of St Hilary term and at the end of Trinity term, the king's chancellor shall inquire through the said attorneys by their oaths into such faults, and of others in their courts, and if anyone be convicted of such faults, he be imprisoned for one whole year, and pay a fine and ransom at the king's will, and lose his office.

---

[37] Stat. 1 Edw.3 st.2 c.5.
[38] Stat. 8 Ric.2 c.4.

\[Responsio.]/

Celuy qe se sente greve se pleigne a chanceller qe lui ferra droit et reson.

[Pardons under statute for debt.]

29. Item, prient les communes: qe come le roi Edward, aiel nostre seignour le roi q'orest, granta a son poeple diverses graces et pardons l'an de son regne .xxxvi. et .l.,[39] come par les pardons ent faites piert plus au plein, qe nul de ses liges soit grevez ne molestez, s'ils alleggent mesme la pardon devant quelconque justice, tresorer et barons de l'escheqer, de nul article compris deinz mesme la grace, q'il ne serroit ent hastifment allouez devant eux. Et ore les dites communes q'ont affaire devant les tresorer et barons de l'escheqer ne purront estre allouez de lour cleyme de les grace et pardon avauntdites, sanz grantz coustages et damage du poeple; et outre ce sont delaiez par mesmes ceux tanq'ils soient mys en grant povert et meschief.

Qe plese a nostre seignour le roi ordeigner sur ce covenable remede en ce present parlement, siqe desormes la commune poeple ne soit ensi grevez en la manere suisdit.

\[Responsio.]/

Celuy qe se sente greve se pleigne a conseille, et droit lour serra fait.[40]

[Pardon for escapes of felons, and other charges.]

30. Item, prient les communes qe considerez lour grant poverte au present, et les grantz charges queux ils portent a ore, et ont portez devaunt ces heures, sibien parmy les guerres come autrement, vous plese faire grace, pardoun et relees, a eux, et a chescun de eux, des toutz eschapes des felons et chateux des felons et des futifs, trespasses, negligences, mesprisions et ignorances, et toutes autres choses eschuz ou advenuz deinz vostre roialme d'Engleterre, dont le punisement cherroit en fyn, ou en ranceon, ou en autres peynes pecunieres, ou en emprisonment des corps, ou en amerciement des communes des villes, ou des singulers persones; ou en charge de franc tenement de ceux q'unqes ne trespasserent, come heirs ou terretenantz des eschetours, viscontes et coroners; et touz maneres des douns, alienacions et purchacez faitz par eux, ou par ascun de eux, des terres et tenementz tenuz de vous en chief saunz licence de vous; et toutz maners des entrees, si ascuns aient faitz, en lour heritages apres la mort lour auncestres, sanz les pursuire hors des maynes de voz progenitours et de les voz par due proces; et touz fyns et amerciementz, et toutz autres articles d'eyre, forspris tresons, murdres, roberies, rapes et felonies, pur queux homme emportera penance de vie et de membre; et forspris eschetes et terres et tenementz amortisez saunz licence. Et auxint vous plese pardoner et relesser as voz ditz communes, et a chescun de eux, toutes maneres de trespasses, mesprisions et negligences, et autres choses faites deinz forestes et chaces, et toutes autres choses pur les queux homme emporteroit amerciement, ou autre corporele penance.

\[Responsio.]/

Le roy s'avisera.

[Jurisdiction of the constable and the marshal.]

31. Item, prient les communes: qe come plusours plees qe touchent la commune loi de la terre sont traiez devant les conestable et mareschalle, a grant damage et disease des ditz communes, qe desormes les plees qi touchent la commune

---

[39] Stat. 36 Edw.3 st.2; st. 50 Edw.3.

[40] A change of hand occurs at this point.

Answer.

Let whosoever feels aggrieved complain to the chancellor, so that right and justice may be done him.

[Pardons under statute for debt.]

29. Also, the commons pray: whereas King Edward [III], grandfather of our lord the present king, granted to his people various graces and pardons in the thirty-sixth and fiftieth years of his reign, as is plainly apparent from the pardons made thereon, that none of his lieges should be grieved or molested, if they cited the same pardon before any justice, treasurer and barons of the exchequer, of any article contained in the same grace, if it were not swiftly allowed before them. Yet now the said commons who have business before the treasurer and barons of the exchequer are not allowed to claim the aforesaid grace and pardon without great expense and injury to the people; and further they are delayed by the same people until they suffer great poverty and mischief.

May it please our lord the king to ordain a suitable remedy thereon in this present parliament, so that henceforth the common people are not grieved in the aforesaid manner.

Answer.

Let whosoever feels aggrieved complain to the council, and right shall be done him.

[Pardon for escapes of felons, and other charges.]

30. Also, the commons pray: that considering their great poverty at present, and the great charges which they now bear and have borne in the past, as well through the wars as other things, it may please you to grant grace, pardon and relief to them and to every one of them of all escapes of felons and chattels of felons and of fugitives, trespasses, negligences, misdeeds and ignorances, and all other things which have arisen or occurred in your kingdom of England, for which the punishment would be in fine, or in ransom, or in other pecuniary penalties, or in bodily imprisonment, or in amercement of the commons of the towns, or of individuals; or in charge of free tenement of those who have never offended, as heirs or land-tenants of escheators, sheriffs and coroners; and all kinds of gifts, alienations and purchases made by them, or by any one of them, of lands and tenements held of you in chief without your licence; and all manner of entries, if any have been made, into their inheritances after the death of their ancestors, without pursuing them out of the hands of your progenitors and your own hands by due process; and all fines and amercements, and all other articles of eyre, except treasons, murders, robberies, rapes and felonies, which carry the penalty of life and limb; and except escheats, and lands and tenements amortised without licence. Moreover, may it please you to pardon and release to your said commons and to every one of them all kinds of trespasses, misdeeds and negligences, and other offences within forests and chases, and all other things for which one might suffer amercement or other corporal penalty.

Answer.

The king will consider it further.

[Jurisdiction of the constable and the marshal.]

31. Also, the commons pray: that because many pleas touching the common law of the land are brought before the constable and marshal, to the great harm and injury of the said commons, that henceforth the pleas which touch the

loi de la terre ne soient traiez devant les ditz conestable et mareschalle; mais qe celle courte ait ce q'a lui attient, et qe la commune loy soit usez come a luy attient, et come il ad este usez en temps de voz nobles progenitours.

\[Responsio.]/
Le roy le voet desore enavant.[41]

common law of the land shall not be brought before the said constable and marshal; but that the court shall have that which pertains to it, and that the common law shall be used as intended, and as it has been used in the time of your noble progenitors.
Answer.
The king wills it henceforth.

---

[41] Stat. 8 Ric.2 c.5.

Appendix

12 November 1384

Westminster

1. Order to the treasurer, various sheriffs and other royal officials, following a petition from Walter Skirlaw, keeper of the privy seal, and several other persons, mostly from York, to compensate the petitioners with money seized from the king's enemies from France and now in the treasurer's, sheriffs' or other officials' hands; for the petitioners have sued at the parliaments held at Salisbury (April 1384) and Westminster (November 1384), as well as at the Anglo-French negotiations held at Calais, for restoration of their ships and goods to the value of £5000 seized by the French during time of truce, but without success. By the council. Dated 14 March 1385.

Source: *CCR 1381-5*, 536.

2. Exemption of the burgesses and community of Kingston-upon-Hull (Yorkshire) from sending any members to this parliament, as they are undertaking the fortification of the town at great expense. Dated 22 October 1384.

Source: *CPR 1381-5*, 475.

Lightning Source UK Ltd.
Milton Keynes UK
UKHW030408211020
371868UK00003B/60